Houghton
Mifflin
Harcourt

Modern Chemistry

Sarquis • Sarquis

AUTHORS

Mickey Sarquis
CEO, Terrific Science
Professor Emerita
Department of Chemistry
 and Biochemistry
Miami University (Ohio)

Jerry L. Sarquis, Ph.D.
Professor Emeritus
Department of Chemistry
 and Biochemistry
Miami University
Oxford, Ohio

ISBN 978-0-544-81784-5

10 11 12 13   0868   25 24 23 22 21 20 19

4500757860   B C D E F G

ACKNOWLEDGMENTS

Inclusion Specialists

Joan Altobelli
Special Education Director
Austin Independent School District
Austin, Texas

John A. Solorio
Multiple Technologies Lab Facilitator
Austin Independent School District
Austin, Texas

Reviewers

Eric V. Anslyn, Ph.D.
Professor
Department of Chemistry
and Biochemistry
University of Texas at Austin
Austin, Texas

George F. Atkinson, Ph.D.
Professor of Chemistry
Department of Chemistry
University of Waterloo
Waterloo, Ontario, Canada

Sonal S. D. Blumenthal, Ph.D.
Life Science Consultant
Austin, Texas

G. Lynn Carlson, Ph.D.
Senior Lecturer Emeritus
Department of Chemistry
University of Wisconsin—Parkside
Kenosha, Wisconsin

Scott A. Darveau, Ph.D.
Associate Professor
Department of Chemistry
University of Nebraska at Kearney
Kearney, Nebraska

Deirdre L. Davenport, M.Ed.
*Chemistry Instructor, Medical Magnet
Liaison, Instructional Coach*
Central Medical Magnet High School
Beaumont, Texas

Brandy L. Dean
Chemistry Teacher
Clifton J. Ozen Media Technology &
Fine Arts Magnet High School
Beaumont, Texas

Cassandra T. Eagle, Ph.D.
Professor of Chemistry
Department of Chemistry
Appalachian State University
Boone, North Carolina

Diana Gano, M.Ed., M.ChE.
Science Department Chair
Glenda Dawson High School
Pearland, Texas

Linda Gaul, Ph.D., M.P.H.
Epidemiologist
Infectious Disease Epidemiology
and Surveillance
Department of State Health Services
Austin, Texas

Pamela Gollhofer
Science Teacher
Princeton High School
Cincinnati, Ohio

Hima Joshi, Ph.D.
Department of Chemistry
University of San Diego
San Diego, California

Doris Ingram Lewis, Ph.D.
Professor of Chemistry
Suffolk University
Boston, Massachusetts

Renee Martnez, M.S. C&I
Chemistry Teacher
Tegeler Career Center
Pasadena, Texas

Gary E. Mueller, Ph.D.
Associate Professor
Department of Nuclear Engineering
University of Missouri
Rolla Rolla, Missouri

Daniel B. Murphy, Ph.D.
Professor Emeritus of Chemistry
Department of Chemistry
Herbert H. Lehman College
City University of New York
Bronx, New York

R. Thomas Myers, Ph.D.
Professor Emeritus of Chemistry
Kent State University
Kent, Ohio

Keith B. Oldham, Ph.D.
Professor of Chemistry
Trent University
Peterborough, Ontario, Canada

Brian L. Pagenkopf, Ph.D.
Assistant Professor
Department of Chemistry
and Biochemistry
University of Texas at Austin
Austin, Texas

Stanford Peppenhorst, Ed.D.
Chemistry Teacher
Germantown High School
Germantown, Tennessee

Charles Scaife, Ph.D.
Professor of Chemistry, Emeritus
Union College
Schenectady, New York

Peter Sheridan, Ph.D.
Professor
Department of Chemistry
and Biochemistry
Colgate University
Hamilton, New York

Larry Stookey, P.E.
Physics and Chemistry Teacher
Antigo High School
Antigo, Wisconsin

David C. Taylor, Ph.D.
Professor of Chemistry
Department of Chemistry
Slippery Rock University
Slippery Rock, Pennsylvania

ACKNOWLEDGMENTS, continued

Richard S. Treptow, Ph.D.
Professor of Chemistry
Department of Chemistry and Physics
Chicago State University
Chicago, Illinois

Barry Tucker
Chemistry Teacher
Colerain High School
Cincinnati, Ohio

Martin Van Dyke, Ph.D.
Chemistry Professor, Emeritus
Front Range Community College
Westminster, Colorado

Joseph E. Vitt, Ph.D.
Associate Professor
Chemistry Department
University of South Dakota
Vermillion, South Dakota

Verne Weidler, Ph.D.
Professor of Chemistry, Retired
Science and Engineering
Black Hawk College
Kewanee, Illinois

Dale Wheeler, Ph.D.
Associate Professor of Chemistry
A. R. Smith Department of Chemistry
Appalachian State University
Boone, North Carolina

David Wilson, Ph.D.
Professor Emeritus
Chemistry Department
Vanderbilt University
Nashville, Tennessee

Candace Woodside
Science Teacher
Winton Woods High School
Forest Park, Ohio

Charles M. Wynn, Sr., Ph.D.
Professor of Chemistry
Department of Physical Sciences
Eastern Connecticut State University
Willimantic, Connecticut

HMH MODERN CHEMISTRY

Yes, it's educational.
No, it's not boring.

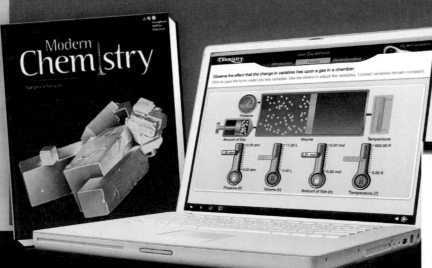

Student Edition

Explore the world around you with pages of colorful photos, helpful illustrations, and activities using everyday materials. This book is built to help you succeed in chemistry, with content chunked into Main Ideas, relevant and motivating features, and in-depth skills support.

Interactive Online Edition

The new Interactive Online Edition provides 24/7 point-of-use access to all program resources. In addition to a complete eBook version of your textbook, the Online Edition includes alternative explanations and experiences through a wealth of multimedia activities, including videos, interactive simulations, virtual labs, and exciting review games.

New Focus on Engineering

Added resources help you concentrate on STEM (Science, Technology, Engineering, and Math) skills—and introduce you to the 21st-century careers that use those skills.

ONLINE Chemistry
HMHScience.com

v

↗ HMH Interactive

GO ONLINE  **Animated Chemistry**
HMHScience.com

Bring chemistry concepts and principles to life with animations and simulations.

NEW

Google Expeditions

Take virtual-reality field trips into the unknown with Google Expeditions!

GO ONLINE  **SOLUTION TUTOR**
HMHScience.com

Get hints and personalized feedback as the Solution Tutor walks you through key problems step by step.

GO ONLINE

↗ **Learn It!** Videos
HMHScience.com

↗ **Solve It!** Cards
HMHScience.com

Strengthen your problem-solving skills with these tools:
• Videos with tips
• Printable skills cards

GO ONLINE

↗ **Interactive** Review
HMHScience.com

Review Games
Concept Maps

Online Edition

HMHScience.com

GO ONLINE

Why It Matters Videos
HMHScience.com

Explore engaging application-focused videos.

JESSI COMBS

GO ONLINE

WebLinks
HMHScience.com

Extend and enrich each chapter's content with hand-selected resource links.

Labs Online

Standard Labs
Focus on experimental skills and the application of chapter concepts through the use of scientific methods.

QuickLabs
Encounter key concepts in your classroom with QuickLabs. They're right in your book!

Core Skill Labs
Practice hands-on skills and techniques.

Open Inquiry Labs
Drive the lab activity—you make decisions about what to research and how to do it.

STEM Labs
Explore the engineering design process through hands-on inquiry projects.

Probeware Labs
Integrate data-collection technology into your labs.

Forensics Labs
Investigate practical applications of chemistry, such as crime-scene analysis.

Virtual Labs
Conduct meaningful experiments with tools, instruments, and techniques that take you beyond your classroom.

VIRTUAL Lab

CONTENTS

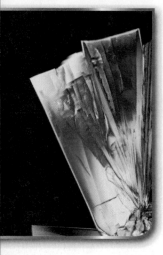

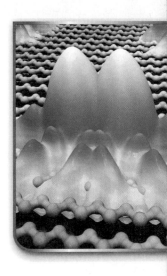

(br) ©Silvestre Machado/SuperStock; (tr) ©Drs. Ali Yazdani & Daniel J. Hornbaker/Photo Researchers, Inc.

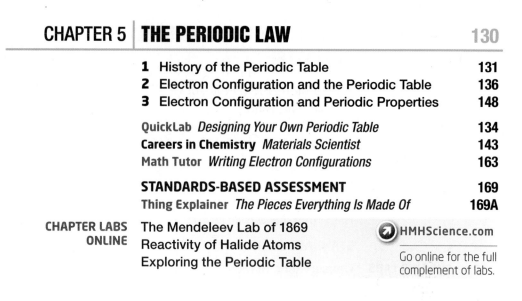

HMHScience.com

Go online for the full complement of labs.

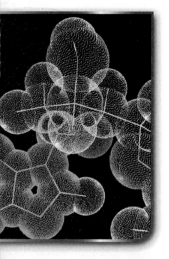

HMHScience.com

Go online for the full complement of labs.

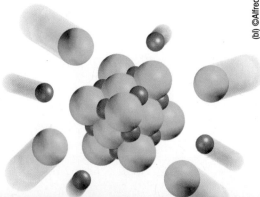

Contents   **xi**

HMHScience.com

Go online for the full complement of labs.

HMHScience.com

Go online for the full complement of labs.

HMHScience.com

Go online for the full
complement of labs.

HMHScience.com

Go online for the full
complement of labs.

(bl) ©Jean-Paul Chassenet/Photo Researchers, Inc.; (tl) ©Pictor International/ImageState/Alamy

(tl) ©Exactostock-1672/Superstock; (cl) ©Royalty Free/Corbis; (bl) ©Steffen Hauser/botanikfoto/Alamy Images

(tr) ©Charles D. Winters; (cr) ©Steven Puetzer/Photographer's Choice/Getty Images; (br) ©Altrendo Travel/Getty Images

Contents **xv**

HMHScience.com

Go online for the full
complement of labs.

HMHScience.com

Go online for the full
complement of labs.

HMHScience.com

Go online for the full
complement of labs.

HMHScience.com

Go online for the full
complement of labs.

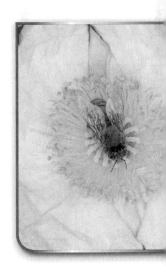

HMHScience.com

Go online for the full
complement of labs.

SAMPLE PROBLEMS AND MATH TUTORS

FEATURE ARTICLES

REFERENCE

(bc) ©Dirk Wiersma/Science Source

STRATEGIES FOR ENGLISH LANGUAGE LEARNERS

Are you learning English? You can learn science and English at the same time. You already know a lot about science from the world around you. You can also learn English from the world around you. Your teacher will help you. Other students will be happy to help. But there are things you can do too.

Below are some ideas that will help you get ready to learn English. Other ideas will help you learn better in class and while you read. There are also some ideas to help you remember and use what you learn.

GET READY TO LEARN

You can do these things before you go to science class.

GET READY TO LEARN STRATEGIES	
Visit Your Classroom and Teacher	Go with other students if you can. Look carefully around the room. What things are there? • Ask your teacher to tell you the names of things you do not know. You can ask, "What is this?" or "Will we use this in class?" or "What does it do?" • Learn how to say and read the names of things you will use to learn science. • Are there signs on the wall? What do they say? If you do not know, ask your teacher or other students, "What does this sign say? What does it mean?" • Remember the words on signs. Signs in many places can have the same words.
Learn Some Science Words	You will learn a lot of new words in your science class. It is easier to learn them if you already know a few science words. • Ask your teacher to say and write some words you need to know. • Ask what the words mean. Then learn the words very well. • Learn how to say and read the words. Learn what they mean.
Ask Your Teacher for Help with Reading	Your teacher can help you read your science book. He or she can help you learn new words that you need to know before you read. • Your teacher might give you a list of the important words or ideas you will read or a list of questions to answer when you read. • He or she might give you a graphic organizer to help you understand what you read. A graphic organizer is a drawing that helps you learn and remember.
Read Before Class	Your teacher tells you what he or she will talk about tomorrow. If part of your book tells about the same thing, read the book today. When you are done reading, you already know some of what the teacher will say. Then it is easier for you to understand when the teacher talks.

GET READY TO LEARN STRATEGIES	
Look at Pictures Before You Read	You need to read some pages in your science book. • What should you do first? Look at the pictures. Use what you already know. • If there are words with the pictures, read the words. Try to figure out what the pictures show. • It will be easier to read the pages if you already know a little bit from looking at the pictures.
Get Ready to Ask Questions	You might have a question about what you read before class. • First, write down your question. If you are worried about how to say the question, practice it. • Bring your question to class. Listen carefully when the teacher talks about the same thing as your question. Maybe the teacher will answer the question. • If you still do not have an answer, raise your hand. Ask the question you wrote and practiced. • Listen carefully to the answer.
Start Taking Notes Before Class	Taking notes means writing something to help you remember what you read or hear. • You do not write all the words you read or hear. Write just a few important words or make drawings. • It can be hard to take notes when you listen. It is easier if you start your notes before class, when you read your book. Write down important words that you read. Write your own words or draw something to help you remember important ideas. Leave lots of space on your paper. • Then, take your notes to class. Use the same paper to take notes when you listen in class. Write more notes in the space you left.
Get Ready to Answer Questions	Science teachers ask a lot of questions. Learn these question words: *what*, *where*, *when*, *who*, *why*, *how much*, *is it*, *will it*. Learn how to answer questions that use each word. • *What:* Tell the name of a thing. • *What will happen, what happened, what happens when we:* Tell how something changes or stays the same. • *Where:* Tell a place. • *When:* Tell a time (you can also say before or after something). • *Who:* Tell a person. Your teacher might ask, "Who can tell me . . .?" That means, "Do you know the answer?" If you do, raise your hand. • *How much:* Tell an amount. • *Why:* Tell what made something happen or explain a reason. • *Is it or Will it:* Answer yes or no. You can also give a reason for your answer.

WHILE YOU LEARN

You can do these things in your science class.

WHILE YOU LEARN STRATEGIES	
Use What You Know	When you hear or read about something new, think about what you already know.
	If a new word sounds like a word you already know, maybe the two words mean close to the same thing. Maybe you already know something about a new idea.
	Use what you know to help you understand the new word or idea.
Get Help If You Do Not Understand	If you don't understand something, get help.
	• Ask your teacher or another student. Raise your hand and ask in class or wait until the teacher is done talking.
	• If you do not understand a word, try to say the word. Then ask, "What does that word mean?"
	• If you do not know how to do something, you can ask, "How do I do this?"
	• If you do not understand an idea or picture, tell what you do know. Then ask about the part you do not understand.
Understand Instructions	Instructions tell you how to do something. They are sometimes called directions.
	You need to follow instructions many times in science class. Sometimes your teacher says the instructions. Sometimes you need to read the instructions.
	Most instructions have many parts, called steps. Sometimes the teacher or book will use numbers (1, 2, 3 . . .) to tell you when to do each step.
	Other times, instructions use words. Learn the words that tell you when to do things:
	• *first*
	• *then*
	• *next*
	• *before*
	• *after*
	• *while*
	• *last*
	Listen and look for these words in instructions. Use them to help you know when to do things.
	You can also use these words to give other people instructions. You can use them when you write or tell about something you did.

WHILE YOU LEARN STRATEGIES	
Answer Questions	When your teacher asks you a question, you need to answer. Here are some things that can help you: • Listen carefully to the question. If you do not understand the words, you can ask, "Could you repeat the question?" or "Can you say that more slowly?" • Listen for the question word. It tells you what kind of answer to give. • Look to see if the teacher is pointing at something. The question is probably about that thing. You can talk about that thing in your answer. • Remember what the teacher said before the question. The question might be about what the teacher said. Maybe you can use some of the teacher's words in your answer. • If you do not know an answer, tell the teacher you do not know. You can say, "I don't know" or "I did not understand that very well" or "I don't remember that."
Talk in Groups	In science class, you often work with other students. You need to understand what your group should do. • Read instructions if you have them. You can ask, "Can I have some more time to read?" • If you do not understand the instructions, you can ask, "Do you understand Step 4?" or "Can you help me understand this step?" • Talk about the instructions after you read. You can ask, "Who should . . .?" or "What should we do first?" • Tell what you can do. Ask the other students what they will do. • As you work, you can ask your partner for help. You can say, "Can you hold this?" or "What do we do next?" • Be sure to help your partner. You can say, "Do you need me to pour that?" • If you have an idea, you can say, "I think we should do this" or "What if we do it this way?" or "I have an idea."

REMEMBER AND USE WHAT YOU LEARN

You can do these things to help you learn important science words and ideas. Do them before class, in class, or after class.

REMEMBER AND USE WHAT YOU LEARN STRATEGIES	
Say It Again (and Again and Again)	One way to learn new words is to repeat them, or say them many times. • First, make sure that you can say the word correctly. • Be sure you know what it means too. Ask a friend or your teacher. Have the person tell you if you need to say the word differently or if you do not have the right meaning. • When you can say the word correctly and know what it means, say the word several times. This is more fun with a partner. Take turns saying the word and telling each other the meaning. • You will remember better if you say the meaning in your own words. You will remember even better if you say your own sentence that uses the word. Try to say a different sentence each time you repeat.
Use Flash Cards	Flash cards help you learn new words. • To make flash cards, use some pieces of paper that are all the same size. Get the words you need to learn. • Write one word on a piece of paper. Turn the paper over. Write the meaning of the word. • Use your own words or draw pictures to help you remember. • Write the other words on other pieces of paper. Write the meaning of each word on the back of the paper. To use flash cards, look at a word. Say what you think it means. Check the back of the paper. • If you got the meaning right, do not look at that card again. Do this with all your words. • If you get some wrong, look at them again and again. You can use flash cards alone or with a partner.
Tell Somebody	Ask a friend or a person in your family to help you learn. Have the person ask you a question. If you need to learn some science words, have him or her ask you what the words mean. If you need to remember how something in science works, have the person ask you. Then use your own words to tell what you know from your book or class. Tell the person what the words mean or how something works. Answer all the person's questions. Helping that person understand helps you understand and remember too.

REMEMBER AND USE WHAT YOU LEARN STRATEGIES	
Make a Picture	Sometimes a picture can help you remember better than words can.
	You can draw pictures when you take notes. Draw your own picture or use a graphic organizer.
	A graphic organizer is a drawing that helps you learn and remember. There are many different graphic organizers.

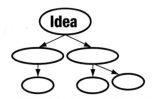

A concept map shows how information is connected. Write one word or idea in the large circle. Write and draw lines to other words to show how they explain or are like the thing in the large circle.

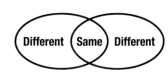

Use a Venn diagram to show how two things are the same and how they are different. Write how they are different in the two circles. Write how they are the same where the two circles come together.

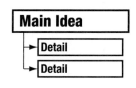

Use a drawing like this to show a main idea and some important details to remember about the idea.

Summarize

When you use your own words to tell the most important parts of something, you summarize it.

- You can summarize what your teacher says in class.
- You can summarize what you read.

Write or say in your own words what you learned in class or from your reading. Do not tell everything. Tell only the most important parts.

Summarizing can help you understand and remember better.

SAFETY IN THE CHEMISTRY LABORATORY

Any chemical can be dangerous if it is misused. Always follow the instructions for the experiment. Pay close attention to the safety notes. Do not do anything differently unless told to do so by your teacher.

Chemicals, even water, can cause harm. The challenge is to know how to use chemicals correctly. To make sure you are using chemicals correctly, follow the rules stated below, pay attention to your teacher's directions, and obey the cautions on chemical labels and in an experiment's procedure.

Specific experiments will use a system of Safety Symbols to highlight specific types of precautions. No matter what Safety Symbols an experiment may contain, the following safety rules apply any time you are in the lab.

BEFORE YOU BEGIN

1. **Read the entire activity before entering the lab.** Be familiar with the instructions before beginning an activity. Do not start an activity until you have asked your teacher to explain any parts of the activity that you do not understand.

2. **Student-designed procedures or inquiry activities must be approved by your teacher before you attempt the procedures or activities.**

3. **Wear the right clothing for lab work.** Before beginning work, roll up loose sleeves, and put on any required personal protective equipment as directed by your teacher. If your hair is longer than where the bottom of a shirt collar would be, tie your hair back. Avoid loose clothing or any kind of jewelry that could knock things over, catch on fire, get caught in moving parts, contact electrical connections, or absorb chemical solutions. In addition, chemical fumes may react with and ruin some jewelry, such as pearl jewelry. Wear pants rather than shorts or skirts. Nylon and polyester fabrics burn and melt more readily than cotton does. Protect your feet from chemical spills and falling objects. Do not wear open-toed shoes, sandals, or canvas shoes in the lab. Do not apply cosmetics in the lab. Some hair-care products and nail polish are highly flammable.

4. **Do not wear contact lenses in the lab.** Even though you will be wearing safety goggles, chemicals could get between contact lenses and your eyes and could cause irreparable eye damage. If your doctor requires that you wear contact lenses instead of glasses, then you should wear eye-cup safety goggles—similar to goggles worn for underwater swimming—in the lab. Ask your doctor or your teacher how to use eye-cup safety goggles to protect your eyes.

5. **Know the location and usage of all safety and emergency equipment used in the lab.** Know proper fire-drill procedures and the location of all fire exits. Ask your teacher where the nearest eyewash stations, safety blankets, safety shower, fire extinguisher, first-aid kit, and chemical spill kit are located. Be sure that you know how to operate the equipment safely.

WHILE YOU ARE WORKING

6. **Always wear a lab apron and safety goggles.** Wear these items even if you are not working on an activity. Labs contain chemicals that can damage your clothing, skin, and eyes. Keep the strings of your lab apron tied. If your safety goggles cloud up or are uncomfortable, ask your teacher for help. Lengthening the strap slightly or washing the goggles with soap and warm water may relieve the problem.

7. **NEVER work alone in the lab.** Work in the lab only when supervised by your teacher. Do not leave assembled equipment unattended.

8. **Perform only activities specifically assigned by your teacher and no others.** Use only materials and equipment listed in the activity or authorized by your teacher. Steps in a procedure should be performed only as described in the activity or as approved by your teacher.

9. **Keep your work area neat and uncluttered.** Have only books and other materials that are needed to conduct the activity in the lab. Keep backpacks, purses, and other items in your desk, locker, or other designated storage areas.

10. **Always heed safety symbols and cautions listed in activities, listed on handouts, posted in the room, provided on chemical labels, and given verbally by your teacher.** Be aware of the potential hazards of the required materials and procedures, and follow all precautions indicated.

11. **Be alert, and walk with care in the lab.** Be aware of others near you and your equipment.

12. **Do not take food, drinks, chewing gum, or tobacco products into the lab.**

13. **Use extreme caution when working with hot plates and other heating devices.** Keep your head, hands, hair, and clothing away from the flame or heating area. Remember that metal surfaces connected to the heated area will become hot by conduction. Use tongs when heating containers and never hold or touch them. Gas burners should be lit only with a spark lighter, not with matches. Make sure that all heating devices and gas valves are turned off before you leave the lab. Never leave a heating device unattended when it is in use. Metal, ceramic, and glass items may not look hot when they are. Allow all items to cool before storing.

14. **Remember that glass breaks easily and can cause serious cuts.** Check the condition of any glassware before and after using it. Inform your teacher of any broken, chipped, or cracked glassware because it should not be used. Handle all glassware with care. To protect your hands, wear heavy cloth gloves or wrap toweling around the glass and the tubing, stopper, or cork, and gently push the glass. Do not pick up broken glass with your bare hands. Dispose of broken glass appropriately.

15. **Exercise caution when working with electrical equipment.** Do not use electrical equipment with frayed or twisted wires. Be sure that your hands are dry before using electrical equipment. Do not let electrical cords dangle from work stations. Dangling cords can cause you to trip and can cause an electrical shock. The area under and around electrical equipment should be dry; cords should not lie in puddles of spilled liquid. In drier weather, be careful of static electrical discharges that may occur when you touch metal objects. Not only can these hurt, but sometimes they can short out electrical circuits.

16. **Do not fool around in the lab.** Take your lab work seriously, and behave appropriately in the lab. Lab equipment and apparatus are not toys; never use lab time or equipment for anything other than the intended purpose. Be aware of the safety of your classmates as well as your safety at all times.

WORKING WITH CHEMICALS

17. **NEVER taste chemicals or allow them to contact your skin.** Keep your hands away from your face and mouth, even if you are wearing gloves.

18. **Do not inhale fumes directly.** When instructed to smell a substance, use your hand to wave the fumes toward your nose, and inhale gently.

19. **Read chemical labels.** Follow the instructions and safety precautions stated on the labels.

20. **If you are working with flammable liquids, use only small amounts.** Be sure no one else is using a lit Bunsen burner or is planning to use one when you are working with flammable liquids, because the fumes can ignite.

21. For all chemicals, take only what you need. However, if you do happen to take too much and have some left over, DO NOT put it back in the bottle. If somebody accidentally puts a chemical into the wrong bottle, the next person to use it will have a contaminated sample. Ask your teacher what to do with any leftover chemicals.

22. NEVER take any chemicals out of the lab. (This is another one that you should already know. You probably know the remaining rules also, but read them anyway.)

EMERGENCY PROCEDURES

23. Follow standard fire-safety procedures. If your clothing catches on fire, do not run. STOP— DROP—AND ROLL. If another student's clothes catch on fire, keep the person from running and wrap him or her in the fire blanket provided in your lab to smother the flames. While doing so, call to your teacher. In case of fire, alert your teacher and leave the lab according to instructions.

24. Report any accident, incident, or hazard— no matter how trivial—to your teacher immediately. Any incident involving bleeding, burns, fainting, nausea, dizziness, chemical exposure, or ingestion should also be reported immediately to the school nurse or to a physician. If you have a close call, tell your teacher so that you and your teacher can find a way to prevent it from happening again.

25. Report all spills to your teacher immediately. Call your teacher rather than trying to clean a spill yourself. Your teacher will tell you whether it is safe for you to clean up the spill; if it is not safe, your teacher will know how to clean up the spill.

26. If you spill a chemical on your skin, wash the chemical off in the sink and call your teacher. If you spill a solid chemical onto your clothing, brush it off carefully without scattering it onto somebody else, and call your teacher. If you get liquid on your clothing, wash it off right away by using the faucet at the sink, and call your teacher. Rinse your skin for 10–15 minutes. If the spill is on your pants or something else that will not fit under the sink faucet, use the safety shower. Remove the pants or other affected clothing while you are under the shower, and call your teacher. (It may be temporarily embarrassing to remove pants or other clothing in front of your classmates, but failure to flush the chemical off your skin could cause permanent damage.)

27. If you get a chemical in your eyes, walk immediately to the eyewash station, turn it on, and lower your head so your eyes are in the running water. Hold your eyelids open with your thumbs and fingers, and roll your eyeballs around. You have to flush your eyes continuously for at least 15 minutes. Have a classmate call your teacher while you are doing this.

WHEN YOU ARE FINISHED

28. Clean your work area at the conclusion of each lab period as directed by your teacher. Broken glass, chemicals, and other waste products should be disposed of in separate, special containers. Dispose of waste materials as directed by your teacher. Put away all material and equipment according to your teacher's instructions. Report any damaged or missing equipment or materials to your teacher.

29. Wash your hands with soap and hot water after each lab period. To avoid contamination, wash your hands at the conclusion of each lab period and before you leave the lab.

A FINAL REMINDER

30. Whether or not the lab instructions remind you, ALL OF THESE RULES APPLY ALL OF THE TIME!

SAFETY SYMBOLS

To highlight specific types of precautions, the following symbols are used throughout the lab program. Remember that no matter what safety symbols you see in the textbook, all 30 of the lab safety rules previously described should be followed at all times.

EYE PROTECTION

- Wear safety goggles in the lab at all times.

- Know how to use the eyewash station. If chemicals get into your eyes, flush your eyes (including under the eyelids) with running water at the eyewash station for at least 15 minutes. Use your thumb and fingers to hold your eyelids open and roll your eyeball around. While doing so, ask another student to notify your teacher.

CLOTHING PROTECTION

- Wear an apron or lab coat at all times in the lab.

- Tie back long hair, secure loose clothing, and remove loose jewelry so that they do not knock over equipment or come into contact with hazardous materials.

HAND SAFETY

- Wear protective gloves when working with chemicals.

- Use a hot mitt or tongs to handle equipment that may be hot.

GLASSWARE SAFETY

- Inspect glassware before use; do not use chipped or cracked glassware.

- Never place glassware, containers of chemicals, or anything else near the edges of a lab bench or table.

CHEMICAL SAFETY

- Never return unused chemicals to the original container. Take only what you need.

- Label the beakers and test tubes you use with the chemicals they contain.

- Never transfer substances by sucking on a pipette or straw; use a suction device.

- Do not mix any chemicals unless specifically instructed to do so by your teacher.

- If a chemical spills on the floor or lab bench, tell your teacher and wait for instructions before cleaning it up yourself.

CAUSTIC SUBSTANCE SAFETY

- Do not pour water into a strong acid or base. The mixture can produce heat and can splatter.

HEATING SAFETY

- Avoid using open flames. If possible, work only with hot plates having an on/off switch and an indicator light.

- When heating a chemical in a test tube, point the open end of the test tube away from yourself and others.

HYGIENE CARE

- Keep your hands away from your face and mouth while you work in the lab.

- Do not eat or drink any food from laboratory containers.

- Wash your hands thoroughly before you leave the lab.

WASTE DISPOSAL

- Help protect our environment by following the instructions for proper disposal.

SAFETY USING MSDS

Do you help with the housekeeping at home? Do you clean your bathtub? Do you use a commercial product intended just for that purpose? Or do you use bleach or powdered cleanser? It is important to know that you should never mix bleach and powdered cleanser together—doing so results in a chemical reaction that releases poisonous chlorine gas. The vapor from the reaction could do very serious damage to your lungs.

One important thing that you can take away from chemistry class is how to use the many chemicals in the world around you safely. Most of us don't think much about chemical safety when we're in our own homes or in a place that we think of as "safe," such as a school. However, hazardous chemicals are sometimes found in the most ordinary places.

WHAT IS AN MSDS?

Because there are dangerous chemicals all around us, chemical manufacturers are required to provide an *MSDS* for all their products sold in the United States. MSDS stands for Material Safety Data Sheet. Such sheets are lists of safety information and procedures for handling chemicals. These can range from household products, such as vinegar, soap, and baking soda, to some extremely powerful and dangerous chemicals. They are based on guidelines from the U.S. Department of Labor's Occupational Safety and Health Administration (OSHA). A hypothetical example of an MSDS is provided on the next page. It's for a compound you probably know well.

WHAT KINDS OF INFORMATION DOES AN MSDS GIVE?

There are many different types of information on an MSDS. Some of the information is meant for emergency responders, such as firefighters and emergency medical professionals. There are, however, many things in an MSDS that you need to know to be successful with your chemistry laboratory experiments. These sheets should be kept handy at all times when using chemicals. It's also important to read your lab experiment in advance and look up the MSDS for any chemicals to be used. Study the hypothetical example of an MSDS on the following page. Does this seem like a dangerous chemical? Do you recognize the chemical?

WHAT DO THE COLORED LOGOS ON AN MSDS MEAN?

OSHA requires all chemical manufacturers to label hazardous substances with specific types of information. Many companies use either the National Fire Prevention Association (NFPA) format or the Hazardous Materials Information Systems (HMIS) format. An example of each logo is shown below. The logos use the same color and number designations but slightly different ways of presenting them. A zero indicates that no hazard exists, while a 4 indicates an extreme hazard. Always look for hazard labels on bottles of chemicals before you use the chemicals.

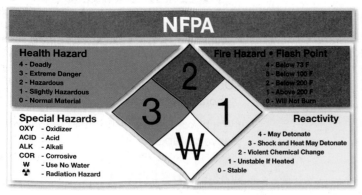

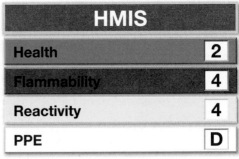

SECTION 9 | Handling and Storage

...metal containers for prolonged periods.
...ed container that is not pressure-sealed.
...ntainer for prolonged periods, as compound
...when freezing.
...d.
...any soluble compounds will result in complete dissolution.

SECTION 10 | Stability and Reactivity

...ions contributing to instability: Generally stable except when ...osed to high temperatures or electrical current.
...ncompatibility: Rapid temperature increase can occur when added to strong acids or bases. Reaction with sodium metal can result in fire or explosion.
Hazardous decomposition products: Hydrogen—Highly flammable and explosive gas.
Oxygen—Supports rapid combustion.
Conditions contributing to hazardous polymerization: None
Forms solutions readily.

SECTION 11 | Toxicological Information

Acute effects: Harmful liquid if inhaled or skin contact in excess of 100 °C
Chronic effects: Oxidation of metals
Target organs: Respiratory system
Commonly found in tumor cells.
Accumulates in vesicles formed from contact with compound at temperatures exceeding 100 °C.

SECTION 12 | Ecological Information

Organism exposure to either extreme amounts of compound or prolonged evaporation of compound may result in injury or death.

SECTION 13 | Transportation Information

Shipping name: Dihydrogen monoxide; Liquid
Hazard class: Not regulated

SECTION 14 | Disposal Information

May be safely disposed of down sink or drain.
Disposal of excessive amounts may be subject to local, state, or federal regulations.

SECTION 15 | Regulatory Information

Not regulated

SECTION 16 | Other

This Material Safety Data Sheet (MSDS) is provided as a guideline only. MegaChem Corp., Inc., does not accept or assume any responsibility or liability for use, handling, storage, transportation, or disposal of this product, as these are beyond the control of MegaChem Corp., Inc. FOR THESE REASONS MEGACHEM CORPORATION, INC., EXPRESSLY DISAVOWS ALL KNOWLEDGE OR LIABILITY FOR LOSS, DAMAGE, OR EXPENSES RESULTING FROM THIS PRODUCT.

...burns to exposed body areas.
...gital vasoconstriction.
...ance to hypothermia.

...sures

...tment following first aid.
...effective, apply artificial respiration

...death.
...se immersion immediately;
...to dry affected areas.

...Fighting and ...plosion Measures

...licable
...ature: Not applicable
...r (% by Vol.): Not applicable
...not use water to extinguish; this will

...dures: Not applicable
...Hazard: Explosive vaporization can occur in ...increasing temperature.

...tal Spill or Release Measures

...rom area.
...and soak up spill.

...otection and ...asures

...r clothing, particularly at

...l-resistant apron when working

...g exposure to solid or
...below 0 °C, respectively.

(d) ©Sinclair Stammers/Photo Researchers, Inc; (b) ©corbis

...ideo

Matter and Change

BIG IDEA
Chemistry is the study of the properties and structure of matter, how matter changes, and how both affect our lives.

(➔) **ONLINE** Chemistry
HMHScience.com

ONLINE LABS
- Mixture Separation
- S.T.E.M. Living in a Thirsty World

GO ONLINE

(➔) **Why It Matters** V
HMHScience.com

Chemistry Matters

Chemistry Is a Physical Science

Key Terms
science   chemistry   chemical

SECTION 1

Main Ideas

▶ Chemistry is the study of matter and its processes.

▶ There are several branches of chemistry.

▶ Chemistry helps us understand our world.

▶ Chemistry helps us change and improve our world.

What is science? Science is many things. It is the study of the natural world and the living things in it. If you've ever observed birds as they built a nest, you've done science. Science is also a systematic way of thinking, of solving problems, of coming to conclusions. In a way, you're using scientific thinking each time you look through a window and draw conclusions about the weather outside by observing how the sky appears. We might define **science as the knowledge obtained by observing natural events and conditions in order to discover facts and formulate laws or principles that can be verified or tested.**

▶ MAIN IDEA

Chemistry is the study of matter and its processes.

Chemistry is the study of the composition, structure, and properties of matter, the processes that matter undergoes, and the energy changes that accompany these processes. Chemistry deals with questions such as: What is a material's makeup? and How do different materials react with one another? Many topics in chemistry are of interest to the other natural sciences, such as physics and biology.

Chemists use instruments such as those shown in **Figure 1.1** to extend their ability to observe and make measurements. For example, a balance helps chemists make accurate measurements of a material's mass. The scanning tunneling microscope makes it possible to look at objects that are smaller than the wavelength of visible light allows our eyes to see.

FIGURE 1.1

Scientific Observations

(a) A balance is an instrument used to measure the mass of materials.

(b) A sample of DNA can be placed in a scanning tunneling microscope to produce an image showing the contours of the DNA's surface.

Chemists also use x-rays to determine microstructures of materials. They analyze the patterns made by the x-rays to determine the arrangement of atoms, molecules, or other particles that make up the material. By learning about microstructures, chemists can explain the behavior of macrostructures—the visible things all around you.

▶ MAIN IDEA

There are several branches of chemistry.

Chemistry includes many different branches of study and research. The following are six main areas of study. But like the biological and physical sciences, these branches often overlap.

1. *Organic chemistry*—the study of most carbon-containing compounds

2. *Inorganic chemistry*—the study of non-organic substances, many of which have organic fragments bonded to metals (organometallics)

3. *Physical chemistry*—the study of the properties and changes of matter and their relation to energy

4. *Analytical chemistry*—the identification of the components and composition of materials

5. *Biochemistry*—the study of substances and processes in living things

6. *Theoretical chemistry*—the use of mathematics and computers to understand the principles behind observed chemical behavior and to design and predict the properties of new compounds

In all areas of chemistry, scientists work with chemicals. **A chemical is any substance that has a definite composition.** Chemicals can be produced in a lab, but most chemicals are natural. For example, consider the material called sucrose, or cane sugar, shown in **Figure 1.2**. It has a definite composition in terms of the atoms that compose it. It is produced by certain plants in the chemical process of photosynthesis. Sucrose is a chemical. You come into contact with countless other chemicals daily.

Knowing the properties of chemicals allows chemists to find suitable uses for them. For example, researchers have synthesized new substances, such as artificial sweeteners and synthetic fibers. The reactions used to make these chemicals can often be carried out on a large scale to make new consumer products such as flavor enhancers and fabrics.

FIGURE 1.2

Sucrose For centuries, people have harvested sucrose, or table sugar, from various sources, such as plants from the genus *Saccharum*, commonly known as sugar cane. Organic chemists study the structures of sucrose and similar molecules.

sucrose

©funkyfood London - Paul Williams/Alamy Images

Basic Research

Basic research is carried out for the sake of increasing knowledge, such as how and why a specific reaction occurs and what the properties of a substance are. Chance discoveries can be the result of basic research. The properties of Teflon®, for example, were first discovered by accident. A researcher named Roy Plunkett was puzzled by the fact that a gas cylinder used for an experiment appeared to be empty even though the measured mass of the cylinder clearly indicated there was something inside. Plunkett cut the cylinder open and found a white solid. Through basic research, Plunkett's research team determined the nonstick properties, molecular structure, and chemical composition of the new material.

Applied Research

Applied research is generally carried out to solve a problem. For example, when certain refrigerants escape into the upper atmosphere, they damage the ozone layer. The ozone layer helps block harmful ultraviolet rays from reaching the surface of Earth. In response to concerns that this atmospheric damage could pose health problems, chemists have developed new refrigerants. In applied research, researchers are driven not by curiosity or a desire to know but by a desire to solve a specific problem.

Technological Development

Technological development typically involves the production and use of products that improve our quality of life. Examples include computers, catalytic converters for cars, and biodegradable materials.

Technological applications often lag far behind the discoveries that are eventually used in technologies. For example, nonstick cookware, a technological application, was developed well after the accidental discovery of Teflon. When it was later discovered that the Teflon coating on cookware often peeled off, a new challenge arose. Using applied research, scientists were then able to improve the bond between the Teflon and the metal surface of the cookware so that it did not peel.

Basic research, applied research, and technological development often overlap. Discoveries made in basic research may lead to applications that can result in new technologies. For example, knowledge of crystals and light that was gained from basic research was used to develop lasers. It was then discovered that pulses of light from lasers can be sent through optical fibers, like the ones shown in **Figure 1.3**. Today, Internet data and cable television signals are carried quickly over long distances using fiber optics.

☑ **CHECK FOR UNDERSTANDING**

Apply Would testing a new drug to find if it is an effective treatment for a disease be considered basic research or applied research? Explain your answer.

FIGURE 1.3

Applying Research The chemical structure of the material in an optical fiber gives it the property of total internal reflection. This property, which allows these fibers to carry light, was discovered through basic and applied research. The use of this property to build networks by sending data on light pulses is the technological development of fiber optics.

► MAIN IDEA
Chemistry helps us understand our world.

Chemistry is not something confined to the laboratory. It is also a tool you can use to help you understand the world around you. Each day, you are bombarded with suggestions urging you to buy something or take some action in the name of science. News reports, magazine articles, and product marketing materials offer what may seem to be persuasive arguments simply because they claim to be scientific. Knowing some chemistry can help you make better-informed, more-logical judgments when attempting to assess these claims.

Current Events: Radon Gas

You already may have heard of the health risks posed by radioactive radon gas seeping into homes. It is a concern that all homeowners should take seriously. So if you were to hear the warning that "granite counter-tops contain radon gas," you might naturally be concerned. However, before you decide to avoid contact with granite altogether, stop for a moment to consider if you've fully understood the claim. Do you know what it means for a substance to be radioactive? Do you know what radon gas is or whether granite rock can have gases trapped in it?

To say that a substance is "radioactive" means that the atoms that make up that substance literally break apart, or decay. When they do, they emit radiation in the form of subatomic particles and energy. This radiation can cause damage to living tissues by interfering with cellular functions. You will learn more about radioactivity later on in this book. Understand, however, that radioactivity is a natural phenomenon. There is radioactivity all around you. It usually is not at a level that could cause harm.

Radioactive radon gas indeed is a hazard in many homes. It seeps into basements through cracks and other openings in a home's foundation. The radon gas then rises upward. It decays into other radioactive substances, which then can become attached to dust particles. These particles, if inhaled, can pose a serious health risk to those living in the home. **Figure 1.4** shows the ways radon gas can enter a home. The best way to eliminate the risk from radon gas is to seal off the home so it can't penetrate the living space or ventilate so the gas gets quickly removed.

So should granite countertops be of concern? Granite can indeed have radioactive materials in it. Most all rocks do. However, the Environmental Protection Agency has stated that the amount of radioactive material in most granite is not enough to be of much concern. Any granite in the home also is usually in well-ventilated areas. Therefore, if it did contain radon, the gas would ventilate quickly. Check that any warnings you hear come from reliable sources.

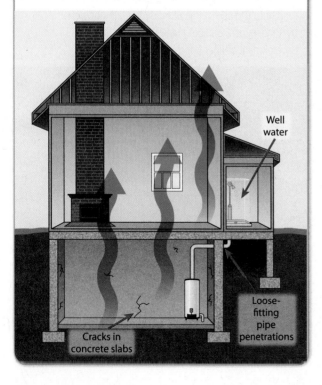

FIGURE 1.4

Radon Gas Radon gas is a problem for many homeowners. As this simple diagram illustrates, radon enters homes primarily through ground sources and then travels upwards. Sealing off these sources and installing ventilation eliminates most dangers posed by radon gas.

Well water

Loose-fitting pipe penetrations

Cracks in concrete slabs

Products and Services

Products and services often use science as a selling point. A label may claim a product has been "laboratory tested" or that it has a "special formula" not found in similar products. As a smart consumer, you should consider that the goal of promotional material is to make products sell.

For many consumers, an appeal to science can be a strong selling point. For instance, the choice of shampoos can seem almost limitless, with each one claiming to do something better than the others. **Figure 1.5** gives an example of what one of the choices might look like. While this is not a real product, the claims may sound familiar and seem pretty reasonable. Ask yourself, however, what they really mean. While a "no tear formula" is an obvious selling point, what exactly does it mean to be "scientifically proven to rejuvenate hair"? Hair is essentially dead cells and so would seem past any hope of "rejuvenation." Also, simply because a shampoo has "Improved Foaming Agents," does that mean it washes hair more effectively? The chemicals listed at the bottom also appear impressive, but what exactly do they do? For example, methylparaben has little to do with cleaning hair. It is a preservative placed in many shampoos to prevent the growth of bacteria or fungus. Methylcellulose is a thickener to make the shampoo pour better. To be sure, both these chemicals have a purpose in a shampoo. But do they contribute to its ability to get hair clean? Do they make one brand more effective than another brand? Studying chemistry can make you better able to answer such questions.

FIGURE 1.5

Product Labels Hair shampoos make many claims and may even list chemicals to influence the consumer.

QuickLAB — READING PROMOTIONAL MATERIALS AND PRODUCT LABELS

QUESTION
What can you learn from promotional materials and labels for products or services?

PROCEDURE
1. Collect labels advertising products or services from around your home, from the Internet, or provided by your teacher. Try to find information on several products and at least one service. Any product or service will do, but you should be able to find the ingredients in it and claims made regarding it.

2. Construct a chart of what you feel to be the more interesting scientific claims made about these products or services. Include in that chart any ingredients about which you would like to know more.

DISCUSSION
1. What types of scientific claims do these products or services make? Do they sound believable? Which appear the most difficult to believe? What additional questions would you want to ask the manufacturer? Write your questions in your chart.

2. Research one of the ingredients in a product. Do you understand what purpose it serves? Is it used in similar or even dissimilar products? Do you think the ingredient only sounds impressive but does not serve any real purpose?

MATERIALS
- product labels
- Internet

Chemistry helps us change and improve our world.

Few aspects of our lives are unaffected by chemistry. Whether it be the clothes we wear, the foods we eat, the medications we take, or the money we use to pay for all these things, chemistry has played some role in their manufacture. Today's chemists work in many diverse industries, in both indoor and outdoor settings. Chemists can be educators, consultants, or entrepreneurs. They can work in the legal field or in the government helping to form public policy. Chemists today and chemists throughout recorded history all studied the substances around them and the changes that those substances undergo.

Chemists of the Past

Chemistry is said to have come from an ancient field of study known as alchemy. The word *chemistry* is in fact derived from the word *alchemy*. The study of alchemy was more a philosophical tradition than a science. Alchemists believed that by studying changes in matter, they were unlocking fundamental secrets about the world that they could then use to gain great wealth or eternal youth. One quest of the alchemists was to find the philosopher's stone, a substance that could turn base metals, such as lead, into precious metals, such as gold or silver. While the goals of the alchemists may seem more fantasy than science, one aspect of their work that links them to chemists of today is the tradition of experimentation. Alchemists heated, mixed, crushed, and burned all kinds of substances in their search to unravel the mysteries they believed were hidden inside of them.

Alchemists throughout history achieved advances in chemical knowledge that had profound impacts on society. Their discoveries contributed to our present-day understanding of the nature of material substances, and the advances in chemical knowledge gave us inks, purified metals, and gunpowder. By observing the reactions of materials, people learned how to produce higher-quality crops and how to improve the sanitary conditions in towns and cities.

Yet we shouldn't view chemistry as a study only concerned with some sort of practical end. The same body of chemical knowledge that brought us medications and cleansers, food preservatives and pottery glazes, also gave us cosmetics and dyes whose primary applications were purely ornamental. And while gunpowder is often used for destructive purposes, it has been and still remains a central focus for many celebrations. For centuries, people have gathered to watch the dizzying array of sparks and colors in a fireworks display, as shown in the two scenes depicted in **Figure 1.6**. These displays may be separated by hundreds of years, but both images show that the work of those who investigated matter often took center stage in the lives of the people around them. Regardless of how much ordinary people may have known about the interactions of matter, it was true centuries ago, and is still true today, that the study of chemistry had a profound effect on their lives.

FIGURE 1.6

Fireworks For centuries, people have enjoyed the public spectacle of fireworks.

(a) Past fireworks This painting depicts a fireworks display from a previous century.

(b) Modern times Today's fireworks appear much like those of the past.

Chemistry Today

Today, researchers in the chemical sciences are doing some exciting work. **Figure 1.7** shows examples of a few of today's more popular fields of study in chemistry.

In the field of pharmaceuticals, chemists are using highly advanced computer-modeling techniques to build molecules with desirable and predictable properties. With the aid of the computer visualization, chemists can rotate a molecular model to view it in any orientation. They even can simulate how the molecule might react under different conditions. Chemists are relying more on computer models, such as the one in **Figure 1.7a,** as they are learning how to make more-complex molecules whose behaviors are not easily predicted.

Forensic chemistry also is a growing field of study. You probably have seen scenes from movies of forensic chemists analyzing evidence, such as hair samples, blood stains, fingerprints, and paint chips, from crime scenes. Forensic chemists, however, also work in the field of crime prevention. For example, they help combat counterfeiting by designing dyes for money that are extremely difficult to reproduce. In the last twenty years, most denominations of U.S. currency, such as the $20 bill shown in **Figure 1.7b,** received a complete overhaul, with forensic chemists being responsible for many aspects of the new designs. Many chemists find the field interesting because they are able to employ knowledge from other sciences, such as biology, mineralogy, and genetics. One important, but perhaps not readily obvious, skill forensic chemists must have is the ability to speak accurately and clearly about their work. They are often called upon to be expert witnesses in court and must give objective, yet unambiguous, conclusions.

Green chemistry is a field of study that is concerned with more than just recycling. It is a set of principles for thinking about products and processes that minimize the production of substances harmful to society. Green chemists operate on the principle that it's better to prevent waste than to clean it up. To that end, they endeavor to design processes that minimize harmful byproducts. They also strive to make products, such as the cup shown in **Figure 1.7c,** that break down after their intended use and so leave fewer waste materials. In short, green chemistry is a call for chemists to work in environmentally smarter ways and can have applications in all other areas of chemistry and other sciences.

(tr) ©Houghton Mifflin Harcourt; (cr) ©Bob Daemmrich/Corbis (br) ©GIPhotoStock X/Alamy

FIGURE 1.7

Areas of Research in Chemistry Today

(a) Computer Modeling Computer model of a heart medication.

(b) Forensic Chemistry The new U.S. currency owes much to forensic chemistry.

(c) Green Chemistry This cup is made from 100% recycled material.

✔ SECTION 1 FORMATIVE ASSESSMENT

▶ Reviewing Main Ideas

1. What is science? What is chemistry?

2. How can chemistry help you make wiser decisions and be a better consumer?

3. What are some currently popular areas of study in chemistry?

✔ Critical Thinking

4. **INFERRING RELATIONSHIPS** Scientific and technological advances are constantly changing how people live and work. Discuss a change you have observed in your lifetime that has made life easier or more enjoyable for you.

Matter and Its Properties

Key Terms

mass	physical change	chemical reaction
matter	change of state	reactant
atom	solid	product
element	liquid	mixture
compound	gas	homogeneous
extensive property	plasma	solution
intensive property	chemical property	heterogeneous
physical property	chemical change	pure substance

All things are made up of matter, but exactly what is matter? What characteristics, or properties, make matter what it is? In this section, you will learn the answers to these questions.

Explaining what matter is involves finding properties that all matter has in common. That may seem difficult, given that matter takes so many different forms. For the moment, just consider one example of matter—a rock. The first thing you might notice is that the rock takes up space. In other words, it has *volume*. Volume is the amount of three-dimensional space an object occupies. All matter has volume. All matter also has a property called mass. **Mass is a measure of the amount of matter.** Mass is the measurement you make using a balance. **Matter can thus be defined as anything that has mass and takes up space.** These two properties are the general properties of all matter.

▶ **MAIN IDEA**

Atoms are the building blocks of matter.

Matter comes in many forms. The fundamental building blocks of matter are atoms and molecules. These particles make up elements and compounds. **An atom is the smallest unit of an element that maintains the chemical identity of that element. An element is a pure substance that cannot be broken down into simpler, stable substances and is made of one type of atom.** Carbon is an element and contains one kind of atom. The model of diamond in **Figure 2.1a** consists of carbon atoms.

FIGURE 2.1

Atoms as Building Blocks Both elements and compounds are made of atoms, as shown in these models of diamond and table sugar.

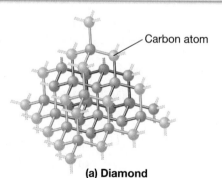

Carbon atom

(a) Diamond

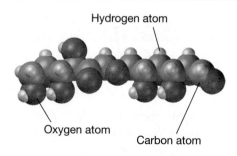

Hydrogen atom

Oxygen atom

Carbon atom

(b) Sucrose (table sugar)

A **compound** is a substance that can be broken down into simple stable substances. Each compound is made from the atoms of two or more elements that are chemically bonded. Sucrose, in **Figure 2.1b,** is an example of a compound. It is made of three elements: carbon, hydrogen, and oxygen. The atoms are chemically bonded to form a molecule. You will learn more about the particles that make up compounds when you study chemical bonding. For now, you can think of a *molecule* as the smallest unit of an element or compound that retains all of the properties of that element or compound.

▶ MAIN IDEA
All substances have characteristic properties.

Every substance, whether it is an element or a compound, has characteristic properties. Chemists use properties to distinguish between substances and to separate them. Most chemical investigations are related to or depend on the properties of substances.

A property may be a characteristic that defines an entire group of substances. That property can be used to classify an unknown substance as a member of that group. For example, many elements are classified as metals. The distinguishing property of metals is that they conduct electricity well. Therefore, if an unknown element is tested and found to conduct electricity well, it is a metal.

Properties can help reveal the identity of an unknown substance. However, conclusive identification usually cannot be made based on only one property. Comparisons of several properties can be used together to establish the identity of an unknown. Properties are either intensive or extensive. **Extensive properties** depend on the amount of matter that is present. Such properties include volume, mass, and the amount of energy in a substance. In contrast, **intensive properties** do not depend on the amount of matter present. Such properties include the melting point, boiling point, density, and ability to conduct electricity and to transfer energy as heat. Intensive properties are the same for a given substance regardless of how much of the substance is present. For example, iron melts at 1538°C regardless of whether or not you have 20 g or 20 kg of it. Properties can also be grouped into two general types: physical properties and chemical properties.

Physical Properties and Physical Changes

A **physical property** is a characteristic that can be observed or measured without changing the identity of the substance. We commonly use physical properties to describe a substance. Examples of physical properties are melting point and boiling point. For example, water melts from ice to liquid at 0°C (273 K or 32°F). Liquid water, as shown in **Figure 2.2,** boils to vapor at 100°C (373 K or 212°F). Density is also another physical property. Water's density at 4°C (277 K or 39°F) is about 1000 kg/m³. Unlike most substances, the density of water decreases when it freezes to become ice. As a result, a pond or lake that freezes in the winter does so from the top down, enabling some fish to survive in the water at the bottom.

FIGURE 2.2

Physical Properties Water boils at 100°C. This is an example of a physical property.

✔ **CRITICAL THINKING**

Classify Is the boiling point of water an extensive or an intensive property? Explain.

A change in a substance that does not involve a change in the identity of the substance is called a **physical change.** Examples of physical changes include grinding, cutting, melting, and boiling a material. These types of changes do not change the identity of the substance present.

States of Matter

Melting and boiling are part of an important class of physical changes called changes of state. As the name suggests, a **change of state** is a physical change of a substance from one state to another. The three common states of matter are solid, liquid, and gas. **Figure 2.3** shows the differences between the three states of matter at the molecular level.

Matter in the **solid** state has definite volume and definite shape. For example, a piece of quartz or coal keeps its size and its shape, regardless of the container it is in. Solids have this characteristic because the particles in them are packed together in relatively fixed positions. The particles are held close together by the strong attractive forces between them and only vibrate about fixed points. The amount of attraction varies with different solids. This accounts for some solids being more easily compressible.

Modeling States of Matter

Models for water in three states. The molecules are close together in the solid and liquid states but far apart in the gas state. The molecules in the solid state are relatively fixed in position, but those in the liquid and gas states can flow around each other.

Solid

Gas

Liquid

Matter in the **liquid** state has a definite volume but an indefinite shape. A liquid assumes the shape of its container. For example, a given quantity of liquid water takes up a definite amount of space, but the water takes the shape of its container. Liquids have this characteristic because the particles in them are close together but can move past one another. The particles in a liquid move more rapidly than those in a solid. This causes them to overcome the strong attractive forces between them and flow.

Matter in the **gas** state has neither definite volume nor definite shape. For example, a given quantity of helium expands to fill any size container and takes the shape of the container. All gases have this characteristic because they are composed of particles that move very rapidly and are at great distances from one another compared with the particles of liquids and solids. At these great distances, the attractive forces between gas particles have a lesser effect than they do at the small distances between particles of liquids and solids.

An important fourth state of matter is plasma. **Plasma is a physical state of matter in which atoms lose most of their electrons (the negatively charged particles that move about the atomic nucleus).**

Melting, the change from solid to liquid, is an example of a change of state. Boiling is a change of state from liquid to gas. Freezing, the opposite of melting, is the change from a liquid to a solid. A change of state does not affect the identity of the substance. For example, when ice melts to liquid water or when liquid water boils to form water vapor, the same substance, water, is still present. The water has simply changed state, but it has not turned into a different compound. Only the distances and interactions between the particles that make up water have changed.

Chemical Properties and Chemical Changes

Physical properties can be observed without changing the identity of the substance, but properties of the second type—chemical properties— cannot. **A chemical property relates to a substance's ability to undergo changes that transform it into different substances.** Chemical properties are easiest to see when substances react to form new substances. For example, the ability of charcoal (carbon) to burn in air is a chemical property. When charcoal burns, it combines with oxygen in air to become carbon dioxide gas. After the chemical change, the amounts of the original substances, carbon and oxygen, are not less than before. They simply have recombined to form different substances with different properties. **Figure 2.4** shows how a chemical property of a substance known as Benedict's solution is used to test for sugars in urine.

A change in which one or more substances are converted into different substances is called a **chemical change** or **chemical reaction.** The substances that react in a chemical change are called the **reactants.** The substances that are formed by the chemical change are called the **products.** In the case of burning charcoal, carbon and oxygen are reactants, and carbon dioxide and water vapor are products. "Ashes" consist of minor components of the wood that don't react and that remain solid.

FIGURE 2.4

Chemical Properties Because Benedict's solution possesses certain chemical properties, a test strip containing it is used to test for the presence of sugar in urine. The test strip is dipped into the sample. The test strip is then matched to a color scale to determine the sugar level in the urine.

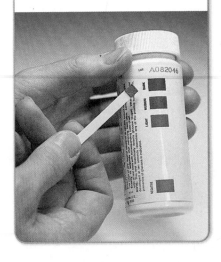

FIGURE 2.5

Chemical Changes When mercury(II) oxide is heated, it decomposes to form oxygen gas and mercury (which can be seen on the side of the test tube). Decomposition is a chemical change that can be observed by comparing the properties of mercury(II) oxide, mercury, and oxygen.

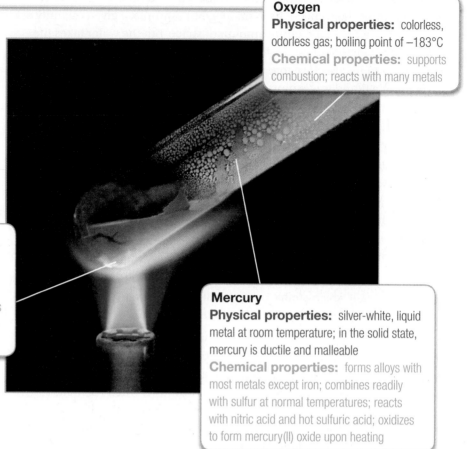

Oxygen
Physical properties: colorless, odorless gas; boiling point of −183°C
Chemical properties: supports combustion; reacts with many metals

Mercury(II) oxide
Physical properties: bright red or orange-red; odorless crystalline solid; almost insoluble in water
Chemical properties: decomposes when exposed to light or at 500ºC to form mercury and oxygen gas

Mercury
Physical properties: silver-white, liquid metal at room temperature; in the solid state, mercury is ductile and malleable
Chemical properties: forms alloys with most metals except iron; combines readily with sulfur at normal temperatures; reacts with nitric acid and hot sulfuric acid; oxidizes to form mercury(II) oxide upon heating

Chemical reactions are normally written with arrows and plus signs. These stand for the words *yields* and *plus,* respectively. For example, to describe the decomposition of the mercury compound shown in **Figure 2.5,** we'd write it as follows:

$$\text{mercury(II) oxide} \longrightarrow \text{mercury} + \text{oxygen}$$

In other words, mercury(II) oxide *yields* mercury *plus* oxygen.

Although chemical reactions form products whose properties can differ greatly from those of the reactants, they do not affect the total amount of matter present before and after a reaction. The law of conservation of mass is always followed in chemical reactions.

Energy and Changes in Matter

When physical or chemical changes occur, energy is always involved. The energy can take several different forms, such as heat or light. Sometimes heat provides enough energy to cause a physical change, as in the melting of ice, and sometimes heat provides enough energy to cause a chemical change, as in the decomposition of water vapor to form oxygen gas and hydrogen gas. But the boundary between physical and chemical changes isn't always so clear. For example, although most chemists would consider the dissolving of sucrose in water to be a physical change, many chemists would consider the dissolving of table salt in water to be a chemical change. The boundaries can sometimes be confusing.

 CHECK FOR UNDERSTANDING
Explain An antacid tablet is dropped into a glass of water and dissolves. The tablet fizzes, and bubbles of gas rise to the surface. Is this a physical change or a chemical change? Explain your answer.

©Charles D. Winters

Accounting for all the energy present before and after a change is not a simple process. But it is a fundamental law of science that the total amount of energy remains the same. Although energy can be absorbed or released in a change, it is not destroyed or created. It simply assumes a different form. This is the law of conservation of energy.

▶ MAIN IDEA

Matter can be a pure substance or a mixture.

Matter exists in an enormous variety of forms. Any sample of matter, however, can be classified either as a pure substance or as a mixture. The composition of a pure substance is the same throughout and does not vary from sample to sample. A pure substance can be an element or a compound. Mixtures, in contrast, contain more than one substance. They can vary in composition and properties from sample to sample and sometimes from one part of a sample to another part of the same sample. All matter, whether it is a pure substance or a mixture, can be classified in terms of uniformity of composition and properties of a given sample. **Figure 2.6** illustrates the overall classification of matter into elements, compounds, and mixtures.

Mixtures

You deal with mixtures every day. Nearly every object around you, including most things you eat and drink and even the air you breathe, is a mixture. Mixtures can be very simple or very complex, and they can have some unique properties.

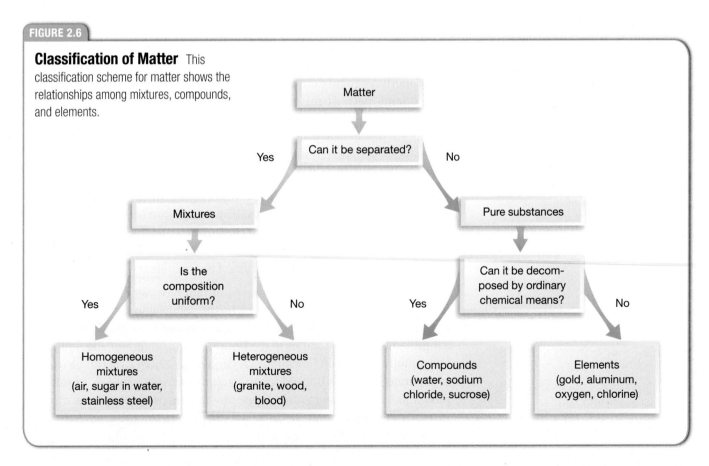

FIGURE 2.6

Classification of Matter This classification scheme for matter shows the relationships among mixtures, compounds, and elements.

Matter

Can it be separated?
Yes   No

Mixtures   Pure substances

Is the composition uniform?
Yes   No

Can it be decomposed by ordinary chemical means?
Yes   No

Homogeneous mixtures (air, sugar in water, stainless steel)

Heterogeneous mixtures (granite, wood, blood)

Compounds (water, sodium chloride, sucrose)

Elements (gold, aluminum, oxygen, chlorine)

FIGURE 2.7

Separating Mixtures

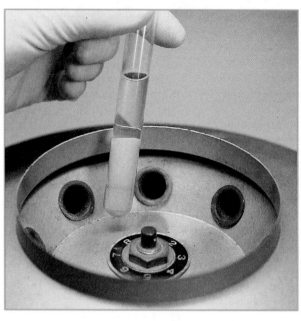

✓ **CRITICAL THINKING**

Classify Would the mixtures shown in the photos be defined as homogeneous or heterogeneous? Explain.

(a) Filtration Barium chromate can be separated from the solution in the beaker using filtration.

(b) Using a Centrifuge A centrifuge can be used to separate certain solid components. The centrifuge spins rapidly, which causes the solids to settle to the bottom of the test tube.

(c) Chromatography The components of food coloring can be separated using paper chromatography.

A **mixture** is a blend of two or more kinds of matter, each of which retains its own identity and properties. The parts, or components, of a mixture are simply mixed together physically and can usually be separated. As a result, the properties of a mixture are a combination of the properties of its components. Because mixtures can contain various amounts of different substances, a mixture's composition must be specified. This is often done in terms of percentage by mass or by volume. For example, a mixture might be 5% sodium chloride and 95% water by mass.

Mixtures that are uniform in composition are said to be **homogeneous.** They have the same proportion of components throughout. Homogeneous mixtures are also called **solutions.** A saltwater solution is an example of such a mixture. Mixtures that are not uniform throughout are said to be **heterogeneous.** For example, in a mixture of clay and water, heavier clay particles concentrate near the bottom of the container.

Some mixtures can be separated by filtration or vaporized to separate the different components. In **Figure 2.7a,** the yellow barium compound is trapped by the filter paper, but the solution passes through. If the solid in a liquid-solid mixture settles to the bottom of the container, the liquid can be carefully poured off (decanted). A centrifuge **(Figure 2.7b)** can be used to separate some solid-liquid mixtures, such as those in blood. Another technique, called paper chromatography, can be used to separate mixtures of dyes or pigments, because the different substances move at different rates on the paper **(Figure 2.7c).**

Pure Substances

A **pure substance** has a fixed composition. Pure substances are always homogeneous. They differ from mixtures in the following ways:

1. *Every sample of a given pure substance has exactly the same characteristic properties.* All samples of a pure substance have the same characteristic physical and chemical properties. These properties are so specific that they can be used to identify the substance. In contrast, the properties of a mixture depend on the relative amounts of the mixture's components.

2. *Every sample of a pure substance has exactly the same composition.* All samples of a pure substance have the same makeup. For example, pure water is always 11.2% hydrogen and 88.8% oxygen by mass.

Pure substances are either compounds or elements. A compound can be decomposed, or broken down, into two or more simpler compounds or elements by a chemical change. Water is made of hydrogen and oxygen chemically bonded to form a single substance. Water can be broken down into hydrogen and oxygen through electrolysis, as shown in **Figure 2.8a**.

Sucrose is made of carbon, hydrogen, and oxygen. Sucrose breaks down under intense heating to produce carbon and water (**Figure 2.8b**).

FIGURE 2.8

Decomposition of Compounds

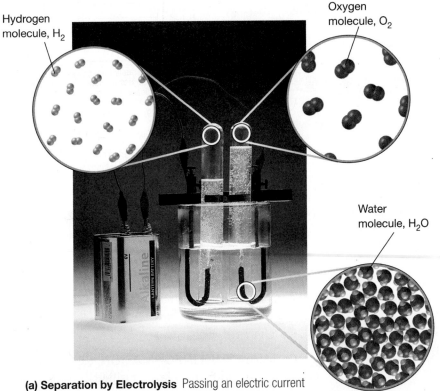

Hydrogen molecule, H_2

Oxygen molecule, O_2

Water molecule, H_2O

(a) **Separation by Electrolysis** Passing an electric current through water causes the compound to break down into the elements hydrogen and oxygen, which differ in composition from water.

(b) **Decomposition by Heating** Sucrose breaks down when heated into compounds responsible for the caramel color and taste.

FIGURE 2.9

SOME GRADES OF CHEMICAL PURITY

↑ Increasing purity

| Primary standard reagents |
| ACS (American Chemical Society–specified reagents) |
| USP (United States Pharmacopoeia) |
| CP (chemically pure; purer than technical grade) |
| NF (National Formulary specifications) |
| FCC (Food Chemicals Codex specifications) |
| Technical (industrial chemicals) |

Laboratory Chemicals and Purity

The chemicals in laboratories are generally treated as if they are pure. However, all chemicals have some impurities. The purity ranking of the grades can vary with different agencies, as seen in **Figure 2.9**. For most chemicals, the USP grade generally specifies higher purity than the CP grade. The primary standard reagent grade is always purer than the technical grade for the same chemical.

Chemists need to be aware of the kinds of impurities in a reagent, because these impurities could affect the results of a reaction. The chemical manufacturer must ensure that the standards set for that reagent by the American Chemical Society (ACS) are met. Reading and understanding the labels placed on chemicals, such as those shown in **Figure 2.10**, is a crucial skill for chemists.

FIGURE 2.10

Chemical Purity The labeling on this bottle lists the grade of the reagent **(a)** and the percentages of impurities for that grade **(b)**. What grade is this chemical?

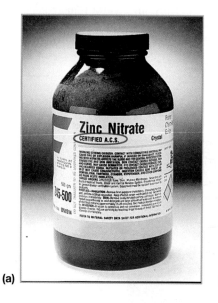

(a)

$Zn(NO_3)_2 \bullet 6H_2O$ F.W. 297.47

Certificate of Actual Lot Analysis

Acidity (as HNO_3)	0.008%
Alkalies and Earths	0.02%
Chloride (Cl)	0.005%
Insoluble Matter	0.001%
Iron (Fe)	0.0002%
Lead (Pb)	0.001%
Phosphate (PO_4)	0.0002%
Sulfate (SO_4)	0.002%

Store separately from and avoid contact with combustible materials. Keep container closed and in a cool, dry place. Avoid contact with skin, eyes and clothing.

LOT NO. 917356

FL-02-0588   CAS 10196-18-6

(b)

✓ SECTION 2 FORMATIVE ASSESSMENT

▶ Reviewing Main Ideas

1. a. What is the main difference between physical properties and chemical properties?

  b. Give an example of each.

2. Classify each of the following as either a physical change or a chemical change.

  a. tearing a sheet of paper

  b. melting a piece of wax

  c. burning a log

3. How do you decide whether a sample of matter is a solid, a liquid, or a gas?

4. Contrast mixtures with pure substances.

✓ Critical Thinking

5. ANALYZING INFORMATION Compare the composition of sucrose purified from sugar cane with the composition of sucrose purified from sugar beets. Explain your answer.

Secrets of the Cremona Violins

What are the most beautiful-sounding of all violins? Most professionals will pick the instruments created in Cremona, Italy, between the 16th and 18th centuries. At that time, Antonio Stradivari, members of the Guarneri family, and other designers created instruments of extraordinary sound. The craftsmen were notoriously secretive about their techniques, but based on almost 30 years of research, Dr. Joseph Nagyvary, an emeritus professor of biochemistry at Texas A&M University, thinks he has discovered the key to the violins' sound hidden in the chemistry of their materials.

According to Dr. Nagyvary, instruments made by Stradivari are nearly free of the shrill, high-pitched noises produced by modern violins. Generally, violin makers attribute this to the design of the instrument, but Dr. Nagyvary traces it to a different source. In Stradivari's day, wood for the violins was transported by floating it down a river from the mountains to Venice, where it was stored in seawater. Dr. Nagyvary first theorized that the soaking process could have removed ingredients from the wood that made it inherently noisy. Images taken with a scanning electron microscope showed the remains of a slimy fungus that grew the wood. Dr. Nagyvary's experiments revealed that the fungus released enzymes that destroyed a structural material in the plants, called hemicellulose. In later work, he proved that the wood also suffered other damages, possibly from chemicals and heat. Attempting to reproduce the effects of seawater, Dr. Nagyvary soaks all his wood in a "secret" solution. One of his favorite ingredients is a cherry-and-plum puree, which contains an enzyme called pectinase. The pectinase softens the wood, making it resonate more freely. It also contains boron, fluorine, and aluminum, which Dr. Nagyvary also found to be present in the instrument made in Cremona.

"The other key factor in a violin's sound," says Dr. Nagyvary, "is the finish, which is the filler and the varnish covering the instrument. Most modern finishes are made from rubbery materials, which limit the vibrations of the wood." Modern analysis has revealed that the Cremona finish was different: it was a brittle mineral microcomposite that included substances which are not present in natural woods, such as borax, fluorides, chromium, and iron salts.

Dr. Joseph Nagyvary

Many new violins made from the treated wood and replicated finish have been made, and their sound has been analyzed by modern signal analyzers. These violins have been favorably compared with authentic Stradivari violins.

Dr. Claudia Fritz, a physicist at a French research institute, claims that new violins, if carefully made, can sound as good as those made by the masters of Cremona. In one of her experiments, 21 blindfolded violinists in a hotel room were asked to play both old and new violins, including Cremona examples. Surprisingly, the violinists tended to prefer the newer violins. A follow-up experiment in a concert hall gave much the same results. Dr. Nagyvary believes it is unacceptable to use unidentified, possibly inferior Stradivari violins in comparisons with the best modern violins. Many of these instruments are in a worn-down condition, and those in museums are far from the ones with the best sound. Only the violins used in concerts by the best 20 artists are by far the best of these instruments in existence.

Questions

1. According to Dr. Nagyvary, what are two factors that are believed to have created the unique sound of the Stradivari violins?

2. What technology did Dr. Nagyvary use in his experiments to recreate the violins?

3. Design an experiment that would either prove or disprove Dr. Nagyvary's claim that Dr. Fritz's experiments didn't fairly compare modern and Cremona violins.

SECTION 3

Main Ideas

- The periodic table organizes elements by their chemical properties.
- Some elements are metals.
- Some elements are nonmetals or metalloids.

Elements

Key Terms

group	period	nonmetal
family	metal	metalloid

As you have read, elements are pure substances that cannot be decomposed by chemical changes. The elements serve as the building blocks of matter. Each element has characteristic properties. The elements are organized into groups based on similar chemical properties. This organization of elements is the *periodic table*, which is shown in **Figure 3.2** on the next page.

MAIN IDEA

The periodic table organizes elements by their chemical properties.

Each small square of the periodic table shows the symbol for an element and its atomic number. For example, the first square, at the upper left, represents element 1, hydrogen, which has the symbol H. As you look through the table, you will see many familiar elements, including iron, sodium, neon, silver, copper, aluminum, sulfur, and lead. You can often relate an element's symbol to its English name. Some symbols come from the element's older name, which was often in Latin. Still others come from German. For example, the symbol W for tungsten comes from its German name, wolfram. **Figure 3.1** lists some elements and their older names.

FIGURE 3.1

ELEMENTS WITH SYMBOLS BASED ON OLDER NAMES

Modern name	Symbol	Older name
antimony	Sb	stibium
copper	Cu	cuprum
gold	Au	aurum
iron	Fe	ferrum
lead	Pb	plumbum
mercury	Hg	hydrargyrum
potassium	K	kalium
silver	Ag	argentum
sodium	Na	natrium
tin	Sn	stannum
tungsten	W	wolfram

FIGURE 3.2

The Periodic Table The names of the elements can be found in the larger periodic table inside the back cover of your book.

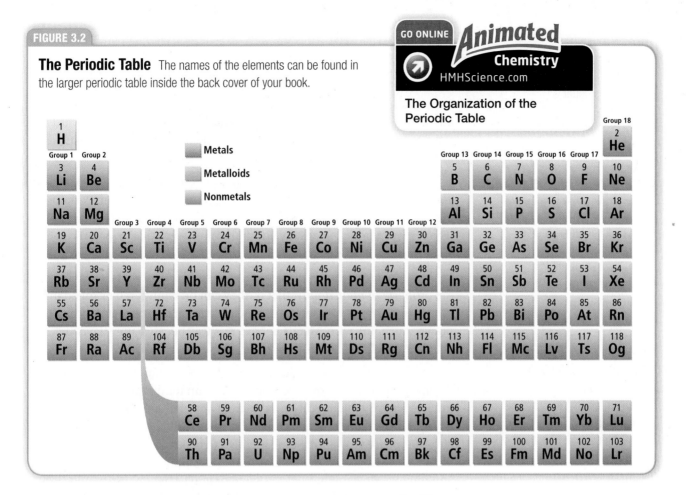

The vertical columns of the periodic table are called **groups, or families.** Notice that they are numbered from 1 to 18 from left to right. Each group contains elements with similar chemical properties. For example, the elements in Group 2 are beryllium, magnesium, calcium, strontium, barium, and radium. All of these elements are reactive metals with similar abilities to bond to other kinds of atoms. The two major categories of elements are metals and nonmetals. Metalloids have properties intermediate between those of metals and nonmetals.

The horizontal rows of elements in the periodic table are called **periods.** Physical and chemical properties change somewhat regularly across a period. Elements that are close to each other in the same period tend to be more similar than elements that are farther apart. For example, in Period 2, the elements lithium and beryllium, in Groups 1 and 2, respectively, are somewhat similar in properties. However, their properties are very different from the properties of fluorine.

The two sets of elements placed below the periodic table make up what are called the lanthanide series and the actinide series. These metallic elements fit into the table just after elements 57 and 89. They are placed below the table to keep the table from being too wide.

There is a section in the back of this book called the *Elements Handbook* (Appendix A), which covers some elements in greater detail. You will use information from the handbook to complete the questions in the *Using the Handbook* sections in the chapter reviews.

▶ **MAIN IDEA**

Some elements are metals.

The periodic table is broadly divided into two main sections: metals and nonmetals. As you can see in **Figure 3.2** on the previous page, the metals are at the left and in the center of the table. The nonmetals are toward the right. Some elements, such as boron and silicon, show characteristics of both metals and nonmetals.

Some of the properties of metals may be familiar to you. For example, you can recognize metals by their shininess, or metallic luster. Perhaps the most important characteristic property of metals is the ease with which they conduct electricity and transfer energy. **Thus, a metal is an element that is a good electrical conductor and a good heat conductor.**

At room temperature, most metals are solids. Most metals also have the property of *malleability*; that is, they can be hammered or rolled into thin sheets. Metals also tend to be *ductile*, which means that they can be drawn into a fine wire. Metals behave this way because they have high *tensile strength*, the ability to resist breaking when pulled.

Although all metals conduct electricity well, metals also have very diverse properties. Mercury is a liquid at room temperature, whereas tungsten has the highest melting point of any element. The metals in Group 1 are so soft that they can be cut with a knife, yet others, such as chromium, are very hard. Some metals, such as manganese and bismuth, are very brittle, yet others, such as iron and copper, are very malleable and ductile. Most metals have a silvery or grayish white *luster*. Two exceptions are gold and copper, which are yellow and reddish brown, respectively. **Figure 3.3** shows three examples of metals: gold, copper, and aluminum.

FIGURE 3.3

Characteristic Properties of Metals

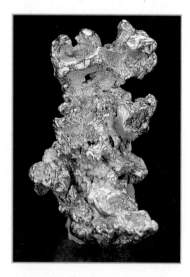

(a) Gold has a low reactivity, which is why it may be found in nature in relatively pure form.

(b) Copper is used in wiring because it is ductile and conducts electrical energy.

(c) Aluminum is malleable. It can be rolled into foil that is used for wrapping food.

(bc) ©Ron Elmy/First Light/Alamy

Copper, shown in **Figure 3.3b,** has a characteristic reddish color and a metallic luster. It is found naturally in minerals such as chalcopyrite and malachite. Pure copper melts at 1083°C and boils at 2567°C. It can be readily drawn into fine wire, pressed into thin sheets, and formed into tubing. Copper conducts electricity with little loss of energy. Copper remains unchanged in pure, dry air at room temperature. When heated, it reacts with oxygen in air. It also reacts with sulfur and the elements in Group 17 of the periodic table. The green coating on a piece of weathered copper comes from the reaction of copper with oxygen, carbon dioxide, and sulfur compounds. Copper is also an essential mineral in the human diet.

✓ **CHECK FOR UNDERSTANDING**
Mercury is a metal that is liquid at room temperature. Using the *Elements Handbook* (Appendix A) as a reference, are there any nonmetals that are liquids at room temperature?

▶ **MAIN IDEA**
Some elements are nonmetals or metalloids.

Many nonmetals are gases at room temperature. These include nitrogen, oxygen, fluorine, and chlorine. One nonmetal, bromine, is a liquid. The solid nonmetals include carbon, phosphorus, selenium, sulfur, and iodine. These solids tend to be brittle rather than malleable and ductile. Some nonmetals are illustrated in **Figure 3.4.**

Low conductivity can be used to define nonmetals. **A nonmetal is an element that is a poor conductor of heat and electricity.** If you look at the periodic table, you will see that there are fewer nonmetals than metals.

Phosphorus, shown in **Figure 3.4c,** is one of five solid nonmetals. Pure phosphorus is known in two common forms. Red phosphorus is a dark red powder that melts at 597°C. White phosphorus is a waxy solid that melts at 44°C. Because it ignites in air at room temperature, white phosphorus is stored under water. Phosphorus is too reactive to exist in pure form in nature. It is present in huge quantities in phosphate rock, where it is combined with oxygen and calcium. All living things contain phosphorus.

FIGURE 3.4

Nonmetallic Elements

(a) Carbon   (b) Sulfur   (c) Phosphorus   (d) Iodine

FIGURE 3.5

Noble Gases Some noble gases are used to make lighted signs of various colors.

The elements in Group 18 of the periodic table are the noble gases. These elements are generally unreactive, although some can be made to form compounds, such as xenon hexafluoroplatinate. Low reactivity makes the noble gases very different from the other families of elements. Group 18 elements are gases at room temperature. Neon, argon, krypton, and xenon are all used to make lighted signs, like the one in **Figure 3.5**.

As you look from left to right on the periodic table, you can see that the metalloids are found between the metals and the nonmetals. **A metalloid is an element that has some characteristics of metals and some characteristics of nonmetals.** All metalloids are solids at room temperature. They tend to be less malleable than metals but not as brittle as nonmetals. Some metalloids, such as antimony, have a somewhat metallic luster.

Metalloids tend to be semiconductors of electricity. That is, their ability to conduct electricity is intermediate between that of metals and that of nonmetals. Metalloids are used in the solid-state circuitry found in desktop computers, digital watches, televisions, and radios.

✔ SECTION 3 **FORMATIVE ASSESSMENT**

▶ **Reviewing Main Ideas**

1. Use the periodic table to write the names for the following elements: O, S, Cu, Ag.

2. Use the periodic table to write the symbols for the following elements: iron, nitrogen, calcium, mercury.

3. Which elements are most likely to undergo the same kinds of reactions, those in a group or those in a period?

4. Describe the main differences between metals, nonmetals, and metalloids.

✔ **Critical Thinking**

5. **INFERRING CONCLUSIONS** If you find an element in nature in its pure elemental state, what can you infer about the element's chemical reactivity? How can you tell whether that element is a metal or a nonmetal?

Math Tutor | Converting SI Units

SI units of measurement are based on multiples of 10, making them much easier to work with mathematically than the unrelated units of the U.S. standard measurements, such as ounces, pounds, feet, and gallons. Most calculations with SI units can be converted from one unit to another simply by moving the decimal point.

For example, look at the illustration below.

10^3 m	10^2 m	10^1 m	10^0 m	10^{-1} m	10^{-2} m	10^{-3} m
kilo	hecto	deka	**Base Unit**	deci	centi	milli
king	harry	drools	ugly	dark	chocolate	milk

To convert the SI base unit for distance, meters, to centimeters, the decimal point is simply moved 2 spaces to the right. One meter is equal to 100 centimeters.

Problem-Solving TIPS

- Make note of the unit that is given at the beginning of the problem, and check to see if the answer you are seeking is given in the same or a different unit.
- Is the unit given at the beginning an SI base unit?
- If you are converting from a smaller unit to a larger unit, the decimal point will move to the left.
- If you are converting from a larger unit to a smaller unit, the decimal point will move to the right.
- The number of places you move the decimal point is equal to the power of 10 that is indicated by the prefix.
- If you are converting from a unit with a prefix back to a base unit, start with the prefix unit. Make note of the power of 10 of that prefix in the table in your text.
- Check your final unit to see if it makes sense in terms of the answer sought. For example, if you are measuring the length of a tabletop, an answer in tens of kilometers would not be appropriate.

Sample

How many liters are there in 9.844 mL?

The prefix *milli* has a power of 10 of −3. It is therefore smaller than the base unit of liters. Because you are converting from a smaller unit (mL) to a larger unit (L), move the decimal point 3 places to the left:
9.844 mL = 0.009844 L

Convert 0.35543 km into meters.

The power of 10 for the prefix *kilo* is 3. It is therefore a larger value than the base unit of meters. To convert from a larger unit (km) to a smaller unit (m), move the decimal point 3 places to the right:
0.35543 km = 355.43 m

Summary

SECTION 1 Chemistry Is a Physical Science

KEY TERMS

- Science is the knowledge obtained by observing natural events and conditions in order to discover facts and formulate laws or principles that can be verified or tested.
- Chemistry is the study of the composition, structure, and properties of matter and the changes that matter undergoes.
- A chemical is any substance that has a definite composition or is used or produced in a chemical process.
- Basic research is carried out simply to increase knowledge. Applied research is carried out to solve practical problems.
- A knowledge of chemistry can help you make wiser decisions.

science
chemistry
chemical

SECTION 2 Matter and Its Properties

KEY TERMS

- All matter has mass and takes up space. Mass is one measure of the amount of matter.
- Chemical properties refer to a substance's ability to undergo changes that alter its composition and identity.
- An element is composed of one kind of atom. Compounds are made from two or more elements in fixed proportions.
- All substances have characteristic properties that chemists use to distinguish and separate them.
- Physical changes do not change the identity of a substance.
- The three major states of matter are solid, liquid, and gas. Changes of state are physical changes.
- In a chemical change—or a chemical reaction—the identity of the substance changes.
- Energy changes accompany physical and chemical changes. Energy may be released or absorbed, but it is neither created nor destroyed.
- Matter can be classified into mixtures and pure substances.

mass
matter
atom
element
compound
extensive property
intensive property
physical property
physical change
change of state
solid
liquid

gas
plasma
chemical property
chemical change
chemical reaction
reactant
product
mixture
homogeneous
solution
heterogeneous
pure substance

SECTION 3 Elements

KEY TERMS

- Each element has a unique symbol. The periodic table shows the elements organized by their chemical properties. Columns on the table represent groups or families of elements that have similar chemical properties. Properties vary across periods.
- The elements can be classified as metals, nonmetals, and metalloids. These classes occupy different areas of the periodic table. Metals tend to be shiny, malleable, and ductile and tend to be good conductors. Nonmetals tend to be brittle and tend to be poor conductors.
- Metalloids are intermediate in properties between metals and nonmetals. The noble gases are generally unreactive.

group
family
period
metal
nonmetal
metalloid

CHAPTER 1 **Review**

GO ONLINE
 Interactive Review
HMHScience.com

Review Games
Concept Maps

SECTION 1
Chemistry Is a Physical Science

 REVIEWING MAIN IDEAS

1. What is the definition of science?

2. What branch of chemistry is most concerned with the study of carbon compounds?

3. Identify each of the following as an example of either basic research, applied research, or technological development:
   a. A new type of refrigerant that is less damaging to the environment is developed.
   b. A new element is synthesized in a particle accelerator.
   c. A computer chip is redesigned to increase the speed of the computer.

4. What is said to be the origin of chemistry?

5. Should you believe any "scientific claim" you hear? Why?

SECTION 2
Matter and Its Properties

 REVIEWING MAIN IDEAS

6. a. What is mass?
   b. What is volume?

7. How does the composition of a pure compound differ from that of a mixture?

8. a. Define *property*.
   b. How are properties useful in classifying materials?

9. What is the difference between extensive properties and intensive properties?

10. a. Define *chemical property*.
    b. List two examples of chemical properties.

11. Distinguish between a physical change and a chemical change.

12. a. How does a solid differ from a liquid?
    b. How does a liquid differ from a gas?
    c. How is a liquid similar to a gas?
    d. What is a plasma?

13. What is meant by a change in state?

14. Identify the reactants and products in the following reaction:

    potassium + water $\longrightarrow$

    potassium hydroxide + hydrogen

15. Suppose different parts of a sample material have different compositions. What can you conclude about the material?

SECTION 3
Elements

REVIEWING MAIN IDEAS

16. What is the significance of the vertical columns of the periodic table? What is the significance of the horizontal rows?

17. Compare the physical properties of metals, nonmetals, metalloids, and noble gases, and describe where in the periodic table each of these kinds of elements is located.

18. Suppose element X is a poor conductor of electricity and breaks when hit with a hammer. Element Z is a good conductor of electricity and heat. In what area of the periodic table does each element most likely belong?

19. Use the periodic table to write the names of the elements that have the following symbols, and identify each as a metal, nonmetal, metalloid, or noble gas.
    a. K
    b. Ag
    c. Si
    d. Na
    e. Hg
    f. He

20. An unknown element is shiny and is found to be a good conductor of electricity. What other properties would you predict for it?

21. Use the periodic table to identify the group numbers and period numbers of the following elements:
a. carbon, C
b. argon, Ar
c. chromium, Cr
d. barium, Ba

Mixed Review

▶ REVIEWING MAIN IDEAS

22. a. Define *physical property*.
b. List two examples of physical properties.

23. How can you tell the difference between an element and a compound?

24. Identify each of the following as either a physical change or a chemical change. Explain your answers.
a. A piece of wood is sawed in half.
b. Milk turns sour.
c. Melted butter solidifies in the refrigerator.

25. Write a paragraph that shows that you understand the following terms and the relationships between them: *atom, molecule, compound,* and *element.*

26. Pick an object you can see right now. List three of the object's physical properties that you can observe. Can you also observe a chemical property of the object? Explain your answer.

CRITICAL THINKING

27. Interpreting Concepts One way to make lemonade is to start by combining lemon juice and water, then adding sugar to suit your specific desire for sweetness. Is this combination classified as a compound or a mixture? Explain your answer.

28. Analyzing Results A pure white, solid material that looks like table salt releases gas when heated under certain conditions. There is no change in the appearance of the solid, but the reactivity of the material changes.
a. Did a chemical or physical change occur? How do you know?
b. Was the original material an element or a compound?

29. Interpreting Concepts
a. Is breaking an egg an example of a physical or chemical change? Explain your answer.
b. Is cooking an egg an example of a physical or chemical change? Explain your answer.

USING THE HANDBOOK

30. Review the information on trace elements in the *Elements Handbook* (Appendix A).
a. What are the functions of trace elements in the body?
b. What transition metal plays an important role in oxygen transport throughout the body?
c. What two Group 1 elements are part of the electrolyte balance in the body?

RESEARCH AND WRITING

31. Research any current technological product of your choosing. Find out about its manufacture and uses. Also find out about the basic research and applied research that made its development possible.

32. Investigate current and proposed technological applications of superconductors. Find out which of these applications have been successfully tested or are already in use.

ALTERNATIVE ASSESSMENT

33. During a 1 h period, make a list of all the changes that you see around you and that involve matter. Note whether each change seems to be a physical change or a chemical change. Give reasons for your answers.

34. Make a concept map using at least 15 terms from the vocabulary lists. An introduction to concept mapping is found in the *Study Skills Handbook* of this book.

Standards-Based Assessment

Record your answers on a separate piece of paper.

MULTIPLE CHOICE

1 A student investigates how adding a solvent to water affects the water's freezing point. Her data are shown below.

Amount of solute	Freezing point
9 g	−8.7°C
12 g	−11.4°C
15 g	−21.1°C
18 g	−21.2°C

What scientific explanation can the student logically draw from the data she collected?

A As solute is added, the freezing point decreases.

B As solute is added, the freezing point increases.

C The freezing point of the water solution is always −21.1°C.

D Water is saturated if 15 grams of solute are added.

2 You find an unknown substance that cannot be separated by filtration, evaporation, or distillation. Would the explanation that this substance is an element be scientifically valid?

A Yes, because elements cannot be separated by ordinary chemical means.

B Yes, because elements are pure substances made of one type of atom.

C No, because the substance could be a homogeneous mixture.

D No, because the substance could be a compound, which also cannot be separated by physical means.

3 We know that air is a mixture and not a compound because —

A it can be heated to a higher temperature

B it can be compressed to a smaller volume

C its components are chemically combined

D its composition can vary

4 The label on a tube of toothpaste tells you it contains "the most whitening power of any toothpaste on the market." What would be the best way for you to start to evaluate this claim?

A See if it's repeated anywhere else on the packaging.

B Compare the color of the toothpaste with the colors of others on the market.

C Research what ingredients actually whiten teeth, and see if the toothpaste contains one of those ingredients.

D See if there's a similar brand of toothpaste that claims to have the "second-most whitening power of any toothpaste on the market."

GRIDDED RESPONSE

5 A student collects the following data about a particular substance.

Substance's Properties	
temperature	25°C
state of matter	solid
mass	89.5 grams
length	2.5 cm
width	2 cm
volume	10.0 cm^3
conductivity	excellent

Based on these data, calculate one intensive property, represented with the unit g/cm^3, for this substance.

Test Tip
Remember that if you can eliminate two of the four answer choices, your chances of choosing the correct answer choice will double.

CHAPTER 2
Measurements and Calculations

BIG IDEA
Scientists use observations and measurements to formulate hypotheses and theories about the world.

ONLINE Chemistry
HMHScience.com

SECTION 1
Scientific Method

SECTION 2
Units of Measurement

SECTION 3
Using Scientific Measurements

ONLINE LABS
- Laboratory Procedures
- Hit and Run
- The Parking Lot Collision
- Percentage of Water in Popcorn
- Accuracy and Precision in Measurements
- Specific Heat
- S.T.E.M. Measure for Measure

GO ONLINE

 Why It Matters Video
HMHScience.com

Measurements and Calculations

(c) ©National Institute of Standards & Technology/Photo Researchers, Inc; ©Corbis

Scientific Method

Key Terms

scientific method   model
system   theory
hypothesis

Sometimes progress in science comes about through accidental discoveries. Most scientific advances, however, result from carefully planned investigations. The process researchers use to carry out their investigations is often called the scientific method. **The scientific method is a logical approach to solving problems by observing and collecting data, formulating hypotheses, testing hypotheses, and formulating theories that are supported by data.**

▶ MAIN IDEA

Observation includes making measurements and collecting data.

Observing is the use of the senses to obtain information. Observation often involves making measurements and collecting data. The data may be descriptive (qualitative) or numerical (quantitative) in nature. Numerical information, such as the fact that a sample of copper ore has a mass of 25.7 grams, is *quantitative*. Non-numerical information, such as the fact that the sky is blue, is *qualitative*.

Experimenting involves carrying out a procedure under controlled conditions to make observations and collect data. To learn more about matter, chemists study systems. The students in **Figure 1.1** are doing an experiment to test the effects absorbed water has on popcorn. **A system is a specific portion of matter in a given region of space that has been selected for study during an experiment or observation.** When you observe a reaction in a test tube, the test tube is the system.

FIGURE 1.1

Observation in an Experiment Students observe whether the volume of popped corn is greater when the kernels have been soaked in water prior to popping or when they have not.

FIGURE 1.2

Formulating Hypotheses A graph of data can show relationships between variables. In this case, the graph shows data collected during an experiment to determine the effect of phosphorus fertilizer compounds on plant growth.

✓ **CRITICAL THINKING**

Predict Outcomes How would you finish this hypothesis:
  If phosphorus stimulates corn-plant growth, *then* . . . ?

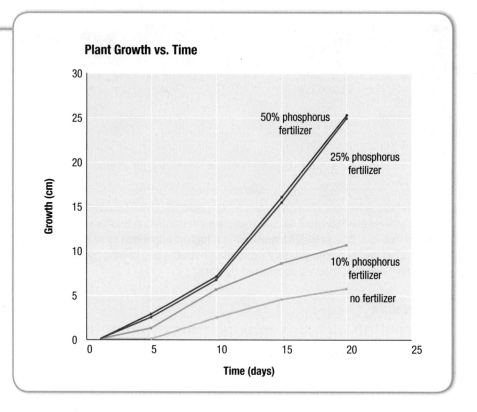

Plant Growth vs. Time

50% phosphorus fertilizer

25% phosphorus fertilizer

10% phosphorus fertilizer

no fertilizer

Growth (cm)

Time (days)

▶ **MAIN IDEA**

Hypotheses are testable statements.

As scientists examine and compare the data from their experiments, they attempt to find relationships and patterns—in other words, they make generalizations based on the data. Generalizations are statements that apply to a range of information. To make generalizations, data are sometimes organized in tables and analyzed using statistics or other mathematical techniques, often with the aid of graphs and a computer.

Scientists use generalizations about the data to formulate a **hypothesis,** or **testable statement.** The hypothesis serves as a basis for making predictions and for carrying out further experiments. **Figure 1.2** shows data collected to test a hypothesis about the effects of phosphorus fertilizer on plant growth. A good hypothesis, however, doesn't just predict what is expected to happen. A good hypothesis gives a possible explanation for the reason something occurs. It's not enough to say, "If we add phosphorus to the soil, plant growth will increase." A good hypothesis would say, "If we add phosphorus to the soil, plant growth will increase because phosphorus is essential for growth processes such as energy transfer and photosynthesis."

Hypotheses often are referred to as tentative statements. However, before a scientist would publicly support a particular hypothesis, the hypothesis would need to be tested over a wide variety of conditions to ensure its validity. It's not uncommon, especially in newer fields of study, to have several competing hypotheses for a phenomenon, each one having its own supporters and detractors.

Controls and Variables

Have you ever opened a package you've received in the mail to find a packet of what appears to be small beads or crystals? Most likely, this is a package of silica gel (**Figure 1.3**), which is a desiccant. Desiccants are materials that remove moisture from the air. In packaging, they help insure that the contents of the package aren't exposed to excessive amounts of moisture that could damage them. While the sender can't control the weather conditions the package will pass through on its way to its recipient, the desiccant can help ensure the moisture inside the package doesn't vary greatly. The silica gel helps control a variable.

Testing a hypothesis also requires the control of variables. During testing, scientists attempt to control all external conditions that possibly could have an effect on the outcome of an experiment. Any conditions they cannot control or allow to change are known as *variables*. Any change observed, therefore, has a greater likelihood of being due to the effects of the variable being tested. If testing reveals that the predictions were not correct, the hypothesis on which the predictions were based must be discarded or modified.

Repetition and Replication

Just one prediction, or even several correct predictions, does not make a hypothesis strong. It's also important that the same experiments continue to get the same results and that what one scientist claims his or her experiments show can be verified by others. These considerations are known as repetition and replication.

Repetition is the expectation that an experiment will give the same results when it is performed under the same conditions. Sometimes an experiment can give inaccurate or unusual results. This could happen for many unknown and unforeseeable reasons. It does not necessarily mean the scientist has not done the experiment well. However, repeating the experiment provides a check on its accuracy and prevents scientists from jumping to unwarranted conclusions. Results from multiple trials ensure that the scientist is using the most accurate and complete data.

Replication is the idea that experiments should be reproducible by other scientists. Any scientist in the world should be able to perform the same experiment and get similar results. Replication is a major reason that scientists publish detailed notes on how they performed their trials.

Recipes exist for much the same purpose (**Figure 1.4**). Providing exact amounts of ingredients and specific mixing and heating instructions greatly increases the chances that a cake made today tastes like one made last week. The chance that a cake made by one baker will taste similar to one made by another also is increased.

FIGURE 1.3

Controlling Variables Silica gel packets are placed in packages in order to absorb excess moisture that could harm the contents of the package.

FIGURE 1.4

Replication Exact measurements and instructions allow recipes to be replicated many times.

● MAIN IDEA

Scientific theories are well-established and highly reliable explanations.

A hypothesis is an explanation for why a certain outcome should be expected. Hypotheses can be supported by evidence, but they cannot be proven to be true. They can only be disproved when they fail to account for what is observed. Remember that it is possible that several hypotheses could account for the same observation equally well.

However, when a hypothesis or group of related hypotheses has survived repeated testing over a reasonable period of time, it can form the basis for a scientific theory. **A theory is a broad generalization that explains a body of facts or phenomena.** Theories also encompass a wider area, explaining a greater number of observations in more-general terms.

Theories in Chemistry

Only about a hundred years ago, there was still some confusion over how to explain the kinetics of some chemical reactions, especially those occurring at low pressures. Some scientists believed these only could be caused by background radiation that "energized" the molecules. This "radiation hypothesis" had a relatively short life in the history of chemistry. It was quickly abandoned for the collision theory, which states that reactions occur when reacting atoms and molecules collide in the right orientation and with sufficient energy.

FIGURE 1.5

The Collision Theory For centuries, the mortar and pestle have been used to grind up substances to encourage a faster reaction, even before chemists had formulated the collision theory.

The collision theory explains a great deal about chemical reactions. For example, it explains why substances that have been ground up, as in **Figure 1.5**, react more vigorously than those that haven't been. The greater surface area means more of the reactant molecules can come into contact (collide) with one another, providing a greater opportunity for them to react. Heating also increases a reaction's rate because the increased energy results in faster-moving molecules. Faster-moving molecules produce increased collisions with greater energy and so a greater chance for reaction.

As theories change, discarded theories can still provide insight into scientific phenomena. For example, there is some evidence that suggests that radiation causes some reactions at low pressures, where collisions between molecules are not so frequent. However, experiments have yet to provide conclusive evidence that radiation plays a role in reactions, so this idea is not currently widely accepted.

Even widely accepted theories do not necessarily account for all observations. Theories represent merely the best, most-consistent explanations scientists have found to explain a variety of observations.

©Charlie Winters/Houghton Mifflin Harcourt

FIGURE 1.6

The Scientific Method The scientific method is not a single, fixed process. Scientists may repeat steps many times before there is sufficient evidence to formulate a theory. You can see that each stage represents a number of different activities.

STAGES IN THE SCIENTIFIC METHOD

OBSERVING
• collecting data
• measuring
• experimenting
• communicating

FORMULATING HYPOTHESES
• analyzing data
• classifying
• inferring
• predicting

TESTING
• predicting
• experimenting
• communicating
• collecting data
• measuring

THEORIZING
• constructing models
• predicting
• communicating

PUBLISH RESULTS
• communicating

Not supported—revise or reject hypothesis

Results confirmed by other scientists—validate theory

Theories and Models

After formulating what they feel to be strong theories or even hypotheses, scientists typically try to explain the phenomena they are studying by constructing a model. A **model** in science is more than a physical object; it is often an explanation of how phenomena occur and how data or events are related. Models may be visual, verbal, or mathematical. One important model in chemistry is the atomic model of matter, which states that matter is composed of tiny particles called atoms.

Figure 1.6 attempts to summarize the steps of the scientific method from observing phenomena to hypothesizing to theorizing. Don't be fooled by what's depicted as a very linear process. Most scientists will agree that their actual work is rarely this simple. Hypotheses are formed and rejected, and scientists can spend months, even years, following a hypothesis that eventually is proven false. The important thing to take away from the above is the constant questioning. Scientists are always asking questions, always testing, and always attempting to gather more support for their ideas, regardless of how strong they may seem.

✓ SECTION 1 FORMATIVE ASSESSMENT

▶ Reviewing Main Ideas

1. What is the scientific method?

2. How do hypotheses and theories differ?

3. Once scientists have agreed upon a theory, will that theory ever change? Are all scientific theories perfect?

4. How are models related to theories and hypotheses?

✓ Critical Thinking

5. **INTERPRETING CONCEPTS** Suppose you had to test how well two types of soap work. Describe your experiment by using the terms *control, variable, reproducible,* and *repetition.*

Models in Chemistry

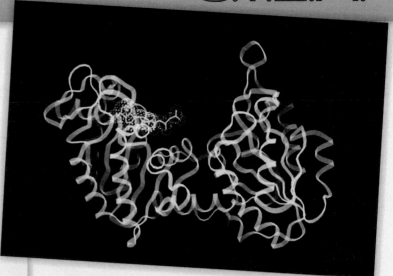

Seeing is believing, but much of science deals with objects and events that cannot be seen. Models help explain the unseen, from the structures of far-off galaxies to the probable look and feel of subatomic particles. Models, however, must be based on observations. And how exactly do you model something as small as atoms or molecules?

Scientists developed the atomic theory to account for the behavior of matter they could not see directly. At first, atoms were modeled as tiny billiard balls. Then, the models became increasingly complex, until they included nuclei and electron clouds. These models give an idea of what atoms and molecules look like and can help predict their reactions.

Today, however, supercomputers are creating very detailed atomic models that are unsurpassed in their ability to help scientists make predictions about molecular behavior in chemical reactions. Scientists feed information about the chemical behavior of a molecule into the supercomputer, which produces the model. The scientists can then manipulate the model's orientation and the conditions under which it exists. They can even highlight certain parts of the model at different times to study different aspects of the molecule. Then they can test hypotheses about matter and how it behaves in a way they can see and discuss.

Computer modeling can be especially useful for studying the complex molecules, such as enzymes, found in living organisms. Enzymes are proteins that catalyze cellular reactions. Scientists use X-ray crystallography, NMR spectroscopy, and amino acid sequencing to study the structure of proteins outside cells. However, enzymes carry out their functions inside cells, where the environment is crowded with organelles and ongoing, nearly instantaneous reactions. Computer models can be used to simulate this dynamic intracellular environment. For example, in 2010, two scientists at the University of Houston used computers to build a three-dimensional model of an enzyme linked to both Alzheimer's disease and cancer.

The enzyme is known as phosphoglycerate kinase, or PGK. Scientists thought that to perform its metabolic function, a PGK molecule opened and closed like a door hinge. The researchers used their supercomputer model to look at PGK's structure and to simulate changes to its cellular environment to study how PGK functioned. The model showed that, instead of a hinge structure, PGK has two lobes with a narrow connecting region between them, like a partly-sliced sandwich roll. The model also let scientists simulate what happens when PGK catalyzes the formation of ATP during cellular glycolysis. The models showed that PGK binds to the substrates it needs. Then the lobes close, correctly positioning the substrates for the rest of the reaction—a process that could not be observed directly. Scientists also discovered that PGK was much more active in cell conditions than in a diluted test tube environment. The computer modeling led the researchers to change their ideas about the structure of PGK and how it functions in a cellular environment.

Although new modeling techniques promise models that include more detail, one thing is worth remembering. All models are still only our best guess of the unknown using empirical evidence—that is, evidence we can see. While the atomic model of tiny billiard balls was too limiting, thinking of models as "right" or "wrong" misses the point of building and using them. Good models are not always the "right" ones. Good models are any models that help explain what we observe and help us make predictions.

Questions

1. How have you used models in science classes?

2. How did these models help you understand concepts?

©Laboratory of Molecular Biophysics, University of Oxford/Photo Researchers, Inc

Units of Measurement

Key Terms

quantity	derived unit	conversion factor
SI	volume	dimensional analysis
weight	density	

Main Ideas

▶ Scientists worldwide use SI measurements.

▶ Prefixes added to SI base units indicate larger or smaller quantities.

▶ SI base units combine to form derived units.

▶ Conversion factors change one unit to another.

Measurements are quantitative information. A measurement is more than just a number, even in everyday life. Suppose a chef wrote a recipe, listing quantities such as 1 salt, 3 sugar, and 2 flour. Cooks could not use the recipe without more information. They would need to know whether the numbers 1, 3, and 2 represented teaspoons, tablespoons, cups, ounces, grams, or some other unit for salt, sugar, and flour, respectively.

Measurements *represent* quantities. **A quantity is something that has magnitude, size, or amount.** A quantity is not the same as a measurement. For example, the quantity represented by a teaspoon is volume. The teaspoon is a unit of measurement, while volume is a quantity. A teaspoon is a measurement standard in this country. Units of measurement compare what is to be measured with a previously defined size. Nearly every measurement is a number plus a unit. The choice of unit depends on the quantity being measured.

Many centuries ago, people sometimes marked off distances in the number of foot lengths it took to cover the distance. But this system was unsatisfactory because the number of foot lengths used to express a distance varied with the size of the measurer's foot. Once there was agreement on a standard for foot length, confusion as to the actual length was eliminated. It no longer mattered who made the measurement, as long as the standard measuring unit was correctly applied.

▶ **MAIN IDEA**

Scientists worldwide use SI measurements.

Scientists all over the world have agreed on a single measurement system called Le Système International d'Unités, abbreviated SI. This system was adopted in 1960 by the General Conference on Weights and Measures. SI now has seven base units, and most other units are derived from these seven. Some non-SI units are still commonly used by chemists and are also used in this book.

SI units are defined in terms of standards of measurement. The standards are objects or natural phenomena that are of constant value, easy to preserve and reproduce, and practical in size. International organizations monitor the defining process. In the United States, the National Institute of Standards and Technology (NIST) plays the main role in maintaining standards and setting style conventions. For example, numbers are written in a form that is agreed upon internationally. The number seventy-five thousand is written 75 000, not 75,000, because the comma is used in other countries to represent a decimal point.

▶ MAIN IDEA

Prefixes added to SI base units indicate larger or smaller quantities.

The seven SI base units and their standard abbreviated symbols are listed in **Figure 2.1**. All the other SI units can be derived from these seven fundamental units.

Prefixes added to the names of SI base units are used to represent quantities that are larger or smaller than the base units. **Figure 2.2** lists SI prefixes using units of length as examples. For example, the prefix *centi-*, abbreviated *c*, represents an exponential factor of 10^{-2}, which equals 1/100. Thus, 1 centimeter, 1 cm, equals 0.01 m, or 1/100 of a meter.

Mass

As you learned in the chapter "Matter and Change," mass is a measure of the quantity of matter. The SI standard unit for mass is the kilogram. The standard for mass defined in **Figure 2.1** is used to calibrate balances all over the world. A kilogram is about 2.2 pounds on the surface of Earth.

FIGURE 2.1

SI BASE UNITS				
Quantity	Quantity symbol	Unit name	Unit abbreviation	Defined standard
length	l	meter	m	the length of the path traveled by light in a vacuum during a time interval of 1/299 792 458 of a second
mass	m	kilogram	kg	the unit of mass equal to the mass of the international prototype of the kilogram
time	t	second	s	the duration of 9 192 631 770 periods of the radiation corresponding to the transition between the two hyperfine levels of the ground state of the cesium-133 atom
temperature	T	kelvin	K	the fraction 1/273.16 of the thermodynamic temperature of the triple point of water
amount of substance	n	mole	mol	the amount of substance of a system that contains as many elementary entities as there are atoms in 0.012 kilogram of carbon-12
electric current	I	ampere	A	the constant current that, if maintained in two straight parallel conductors of infinite length, of negligible circular cross section, and placed 1 meter apart in vacuum, would produce between these conductors a force equal to 2×10^{-7} newton per meter of length
luminous intensity	I_v	candela	cd	the luminous intensity, in a given direction, of a source that emits monochromatic radiation of frequency 540×10^{12} hertz and that has a radiant intensity in that direction of 1/683 watt per steradian

The gram, g, which is 1/1000 of a kilogram, is more useful for measuring masses of small objects, such as flasks and beakers. One gram is about the mass of a paper clip. For even smaller objects, such as tiny quantities of chemicals, the milligram, mg, is often used. One milligram is 1/1000 of a gram, or 1/1 000 000 of a kilogram.

Mass versus Weight

Mass is often confused with weight. Remember that mass is a measure of the amount of matter. **Weight is a measure of the gravitational pull on matter.** Mass is determined by comparing the mass of an object with a set of standard masses on two sides of a balance. When the masses on each are the same, the sides balance. Unlike weight, mass does not depend on gravity. Thus, weight changes as gravitational force changes, while mass does not change.

Mass is measured on instruments such as a balance, and weight is typically measured on a spring scale. Taking weight measurements involves reading the amount that an object pulls down on a spring. As the force of Earth's gravity on an object increases, the object's weight increases. The weight of an object on the moon is about one-sixth of its weight on Earth.

 **CHECK FOR UNDERSTANDING**

Apply The gravity on the moon is 1/6 of Earth's gravity. What would your weight be on the moon? Would your mass on the moon be different from your mass on Earth? Explain.

FIGURE 2.2

SI PREFIXES

Prefix	Unit abbreviation	Exponential factor	Meaning	Example
tera	T	10^{12}	1 000 000 000 000	1 terameter (Tm) = 1×10^{12} m
giga	G	10^{9}	1 000 000 000	1 gigameter (Gm) = 1×10^{9} m
mega	M	10^{6}	1 000 000	1 megameter (Mm) = 1×10^{6} m
kilo	k	10^{3}	1000	1 kilometer (km) = 1000 m
hecto	h	10^{2}	100	1 hectometer (hm) = 100 m
deka	da	10^{1}	10	1 dekameter (dam) = 10 m
		10^{0}	1	**1 meter (m)**
deci	d	10^{-1}	1/10	1 decimeter (dm) = 0.1 m
centi	c	10^{-2}	1/100	1 centimeter (cm) = 0.01 m
milli	m	10^{-3}	1/1000	1 millimeter (mm) = 0.001 m
micro	μ	10^{-6}	1/1 000 000	1 micrometer (μm) = 1×10^{-6} m
nano	n	10^{-9}	1/1 000 000 000	1 nanometer (nm) = 1×10^{-9} m
pico	p	10^{-12}	1/1 000 000 000 000	1 picometer (pm) = 1×10^{-12} m
femto	f	10^{-15}	1/1 000 000 000 000 000	1 femtometer (fm) = 1×10^{-15} m
atto	a	10^{-18}	1/1 000 000 000 000 000 000	1 attometer (am) = 1×10^{-18} m

FIGURE 2.3

Metric Length The meter is the SI unit of length, but the centimeter is often used to measure smaller distances. What is the length in cm of the rectangular piece of aluminum foil shown?

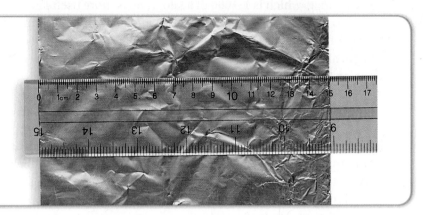

Length

The SI standard unit for length is the meter. A distance of 1 m is about the width of an average doorway. To express longer distances, the kilometer, km, is used. One kilometer equals 1000 m. To express shorter distances, the centimeter, as shown **Figure 2.3**, is often used. The centimeter is about the width of a paper clip. From **Figure 2.2,** on the previous page, you can see that one centimeter equals 1/100 of a meter.

▶ MAIN IDEA
SI base units combine to form derived units.

Many SI units are combinations of the quantities shown in **Figure 2.1**. **Combinations of SI base units form derived units.** Derived units are produced by multiplying or dividing standard units. For example, area, a derived unit, is length times width. If both length and width are expressed in meters, the area unit equals meters times meters, or square meters, abbreviated m^2. Some derived units are shown in **Figure 2.4**. The last column of **Figure 2.4** shows the combination of SI units used to obtain derived units. **Figure 2.5,** on the next page, shows a speedometer measuring speed, another example of a derived unit.

FIGURE 2.4

DERIVED SI UNITS

Quantity	Quantity symbol	Unit	Unit abbreviation	Derivation
area	A	square meter	m^2	length × width
volume	V	cubic meter	m^3	length × width × height
density	D	kilograms per cubic meter	$\dfrac{kg}{m^3}$	$\dfrac{mass}{volume}$
molar mass	M	grams per mole	$\dfrac{g}{mol}$	$\dfrac{mass}{amount\ of\ substance}$
molar volume	V_m	cubic meters per mole	$\dfrac{m^3}{mol}$	$\dfrac{volume}{amount\ of\ substance}$
energy	E	joule (J)	$\dfrac{kg}{m^2/s^2}$	force × distance

Some combination units are given their own names. For example, pressure expressed in base units is the following:

$$\text{kg/m} \cdot \text{s}^2$$

The name *pascal*, Pa, is given to this combination. You will learn more about pressure in the chapter "Gases." Prefixes can also be added to express derived units. For example, area can be expressed in cm^2, square centimeters, or mm^2, square millimeters.

Volume

Volume is the amount of space occupied by an object. The derived SI unit of volume is cubic meters, m^3. One cubic meter is equal to the volume of a cube whose edges are 1 m long. Such a large unit is inconvenient for expressing the volume of materials in a chemistry laboratory. Instead, a smaller unit, the cubic centimeter, cm^3, is often used. There are 100 centimeters in a meter, so a cubic meter contains 1 000 000 cm^3.

$$1 \text{ m}^3 \times \frac{100 \text{ cm}}{1 \text{ m}} \times \frac{100 \text{ cm}}{1 \text{ m}} \times \frac{100 \text{ cm}}{1 \text{ m}} = 1\,000\,000 \text{ cm}^3$$

When chemists measure the volumes of liquids and gases, they often use a non-SI unit called the liter. The liter is equivalent to one cubic decimeter. Thus, a liter, L, is also equivalent to 1000 cm^3. Another non-SI unit, the milliliter, mL, is used for smaller volumes. There are 1000 mL in 1 L. Because there are also 1000 cm^3 in a liter, the two units—milliliter and cubic centimeter—are interchangeable. **Figure 2.6** shows some of these different volume measurements.

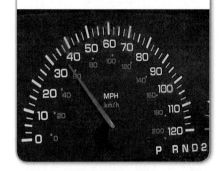

FIGURE 2.6

Comparing Liquid Volumes One liter contains 1000 mL of liquid, and 1 mL is equivalent to 1 cm^3. A small perfume bottle contains about 15 mL of liquid. There are about 5 mL in 1 teaspoon. The volumetric flask (far left) and graduated cylinder (far right) are used for measuring liquid volumes in the lab.

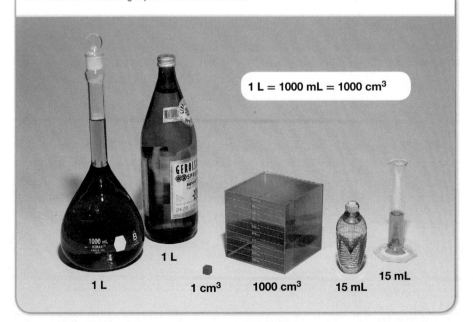

$$1 \text{ L} = 1000 \text{ mL} = 1000 \text{ cm}^3$$

1 L   1 L   1 cm^3 1000 cm^3 15 mL   15 mL

FIGURE 2.7

Relative Densities Density is the ratio of mass to volume. Both water and copper shot float on mercury because they are less dense than mercury.

✓ **CRITICAL THINKING**

Explain Using **Figure 2.8**, explain where a diamond would be in the layers in the graduated cylinder in **Figure 2.7**.

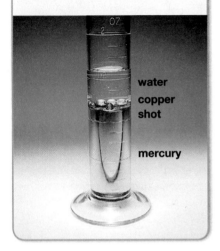

water
copper shot

mercury

Density

A piece of cork is lighter than a piece of lead of the same size. Liquid mercury, as shown in **Figure 2.7**, is heavier than the same volume of water. In other words, different substances contain different masses per volume. This property is called density. **Density is the ratio of mass to volume, or mass divided by volume.** Density is expressed by the equation

Density	$\text{density} = \dfrac{\text{mass}}{\text{volume}}$ or $D = \dfrac{m}{V}$

The quantity m is mass, V is volume, and D is density.

The SI unit for density is derived from the units for mass and volume—the kilogram and the cubic meter, respectively—and can be expressed as kilograms per cubic meter, kg/m^3. This unit is inconveniently large for the density measurements you will make in the laboratory. You will often see density expressed in grams per cubic centimeter, g/cm^3, or grams per milliliter, g/mL. The densities of gases are generally reported either in kilograms per cubic meter, kg/m^3, or in grams per liter, g/L.

Density is an intensive physical property of a substance. It does not depend on the size of a sample, because as the mass of a sample increases, its volume increases proportionately. The ratio of mass to volume is constant. Therefore, density is one property that can help to identify a substance. **Figure 2.8** shows the densities of some common materials. As you can see, cork has a density of only $0.24\ g/cm^3$, which is less than the density of liquid water. Because cork is less dense than water, it floats on water. Lead, on the other hand, has a density of $11.35\ g/cm^3$. The density of lead is greater than that of water, so lead sinks in water.

Note that **Figure 2.8** specifies the temperatures at which the densities were measured. That is because density varies with temperature. Most objects expand as temperature increases, thereby increasing in volume. Because density is mass divided by volume, density usually decreases with increasing temperature.

FIGURE 2.8

DENSITIES OF SOME FAMILIAR MATERIALS			
Solids	**Density at 20°C (g/cm³)**	**Liquids**	**Density at 20°C (g/mL)**
cork	0.24*	gasoline	0.67*
butter	0.86	ethyl alcohol	0.791
ice	0.92†	kerosene	0.82
sucrose	1.59	turpentine	0.87
bone	1.85*	water	0.998
diamond	3.26*	seawater	1.025**
copper	8.92	milk	1.031*
lead	11.35	mercury	13.6
† measured at 0°C		** measured at 15°C	
* typical density			

PROCEDURE

1. Using the balance, determine the mass of the 40 pennies minted prior to 1982. Repeat this measurement two more times. Average the results of the three trials to determine the average mass of the pennies.

2. Repeat step 1 with the 40 pennies minted after 1982.

3. Pour about 50 mL of water into the 100 mL graduated cylinder. Record the exact volume of the water. Add the 40 pennies minted before 1982. CAUTION: Add the pennies carefully so that no water is splashed out of the cylinder. Record the exact volume of the water and pennies. Repeat this process two more times. Determine the volume of the pennies for each trial. Average the results of those trials to determine the average volume of the pennies.

4. Repeat step 3 with the 40 pennies minted after 1982.

5. Review your data for any large differences between trials that could increase the error of your results. Repeat those measurements.

6. Use the average volume and average mass to calculate the average density for each group of pennies.

7. Compare the calculated average densities with the density of copper, listed in **Figure 2.8.**

DISCUSSION

1. Why is it best to use the results of three trials rather than a single trial for determining the density?

2. How did the densities of the two groups of pennies compare? How do you account for any difference?

3. Use the results of this investigation to formulate a hypothesis about the composition of the two groups of pennies. How could you test your hypothesis?

MATERIALS
- balance
- 100 mL graduated cylinder
- 40 pennies dated before 1982
- 40 pennies dated after 1982
- water

SAFETY

Wear safety goggles and an apron.

Density

Sample Problem A In an experiment to identify an unknown gas, it is found that 1.82 L of the gas has a mass of 5.430 g. What is the density of the gas in g/L?

1 ANALYZE

Given: mass $(m_{gas}) = 5.430$ g
volume $(V_{gas}) = 1.82$ L
least number of significant figures = 3 (in 1.82 L)

Unknown: density $(D_{gas}) = ?$ g/L numerical result
density $(D_{gas}) = ?$ g/L rounded result

2 PLAN

$$\text{density} = \frac{\text{mass}}{\text{volume}}$$

3 SOLVE

$$\text{density} = \frac{5.430 \text{ g}}{1.82 \text{ L}} = 2.983516484 = 2.98 \text{ g/L}$$

Density (continued)

Density is given in units of mass per unit volume. The mass had three significant figures, so the answer was rounded to three significant figures. The units are correct for density.

Practice   Answers in Appendix E

1. Calculate the density of a block of metal with a volume of 12.5 cm³ and mass of 126.0 g.
2. Copper has a density of 8.96 g/cm³. What is the mass of a piece of copper with a volume of 2.62 cm³?
3. What is the volume of a sample of liquid mercury that has a mass of 76.2 g, given that the density of mercury is 13.6 g/mL?

▶ **MAIN IDEA**

Conversion factors change one unit to another.

A **conversion factor** is a ratio derived from the equality between two different units that can be used to convert from one unit to the other. For example, suppose you want to know how many quarters there are in a certain number of dollars. To figure out the answer, you need to know how quarters and dollars are related. There are four quarters per dollar and one dollar for every four quarters. Those facts can be expressed as ratios in four conversion factors.

$$\frac{4 \text{ quarters}}{1 \text{ dollar}} = 1 \quad \frac{1 \text{ dollar}}{4 \text{ quarters}} = 1 \quad \frac{0.25 \text{ dollar}}{1 \text{ quarter}} = 1 \quad \frac{1 \text{ quarter}}{0.25 \text{ dollar}} = 1$$

Notice that each conversion factor equals 1. That is because the two quantities divided in any conversion factor are equivalent to each other— as in this case, where 4 quarters equal 1 dollar. Because conversion factors are equal to 1, they can be multiplied by other factors in equations without changing the validity of the equations. You can use conversion factors to solve problems through dimensional analysis. **Dimensional analysis** is a mathematical technique that allows you to use units to solve problems involving measurements. When you want to use a conversion factor to change a unit in a problem, you can set up the problem in the following way.

quantity sought = quantity given × conversion factor

For example, to determine the number of quarters in 12 dollars, you would carry out the unit conversion that allows you to change from dollars to quarters.

number of quarters = 12 dollars × conversion factor

Next, you need to decide which conversion factor gives you an answer in the desired unit. In this case, you have dollars, and you want quarters. To eliminate dollars, you must divide the quantity by dollars. Therefore, the conversion factor in this case must have dollars in the denominator and quarters in the numerator: 4 quarters/1 dollar.

Thus, you would set up the calculation as follows:

$$? \text{ quarters} = 12 \text{ dollars} \times \text{conversion factor}$$

$$= 12 \cancel{\text{ dollars}} \times \frac{4 \text{ quarters}}{1 \cancel{\text{ dollar}}} = 48 \text{ quarters}$$

Notice that the dollars have divided out, leaving an answer in the desired unit—quarters.

Suppose you had guessed wrong and used 1 dollar/4 quarters when choosing which of the two conversion factors to use. You would have an answer with entirely inappropriate units.

$$? \text{ quarters} = 12 \text{ dollars} \times \frac{1 \text{ dollar}}{4 \text{ quarters}} = \frac{3 \text{ dollars}^2}{\text{quarter}}$$

It is always best to begin with an idea of the units you will need in your final answer. When working through the Sample Problems, keep track of the units needed for the unknown quantity. Check your final answer against what you've written as the unknown quantity.

Deriving Conversion Factors

You can derive conversion factors if you know the relationship between the unit you have and the unit you want. For example, from the fact that *deci-* means "1/10," you know that there is 1/10 of a meter per decimeter and that each meter must have 10 decimeters. Thus, from the equality 1 m = 10 dm, you can write the following conversion factors relating meters and decimeters.

$$\frac{1 \text{ m}}{10 \text{ dm}} \quad \text{and} \quad \frac{0.1 \text{ m}}{1 \text{ dm}} \quad \text{and} \quad \frac{10 \text{ dm}}{1 \text{ m}}$$

The following sample problem illustrates an example of deriving conversion factors to make a unit conversion. When there is no digit shown in the denominator, you usually can assume the value is 1.

GO ONLINE

SolveIt! Cards
HMHScience.com

Learn It! Video
HMHScience.com

Conversion Factors

Sample Problem B Express a mass of 5.712 grams in milligrams and in kilograms.

1 ANALYZE

Given: 5.712 g

Unknown: mass in mg and mass in kg

The equality that relates grams to milligrams is
1 g = 1000 mg

2 PLAN

The possible conversion factors that can be written from this equality are
$$\frac{1000 \text{ mg}}{1 \text{ g}} \quad \text{and} \quad \frac{1 \text{ g}}{1000 \text{ mg}}$$

Continued ▶

Measurements and Calculations   **45**

③ SOLVE

To derive an answer in mg, you'll need to multiply 5.712 g by 1000 mg/g.

$$5.712 \text{ g} \times \frac{1000 \text{ mg}}{1 \text{ g}} = 5712 \text{ mg}$$

The kilogram problem is solved similarly.

$$1 \text{ kg} = 1000 \text{ g}$$

Conversion factors representing this equality are

$$\frac{1 \text{ kg}}{1000 \text{ g}} \quad \text{and} \quad \frac{1000 \text{ g}}{1 \text{ kg}}$$

To derive an answer in kg, you'll need to multiply 5.712 g by 1 kg/1000 g.

$$5.712 \text{ g} \times \frac{1 \text{ kg}}{1000 \text{ g}} = 0.005712 \text{ kg}$$

④ CHECK YOUR WORK

The first answer makes sense because milligrams is a smaller unit than grams and therefore there should be more milligrams. The second answer makes sense because kilograms is a larger unit than grams and therefore there should be fewer kilograms.

Practice   Answers in Appendix E

1. Express a length of 16.45 m in centimeters and in kilometers.
2. Express a mass of 0.014 mg in grams.

✔ SECTION 2 FORMATIVE ASSESSMENT

▶ Reviewing Main Ideas

1. Why are standards needed for measured quantities?

2. Label each of the following measurements by the quantity each represents. For instance, a measurement of 10.6 kg/m^3 represents density.
   a. 5.0 g/mL   f. 325 ms
   b. 37 s   g. 500 m^2
   c. 47 J   h. 30.23 mL
   d. 39.56 g   i. 2.7 mg
   e. 25.3 cm^3 j. 0.005 L

3. Complete the following conversions.
   a. 10.5 g = _____ kg
   b. 1.57 km = _____ m
   c. 3.54 μg = _____ g
   d. 3.5 mol = _____ μmol
   e. 1.2 L = _____ mL
   f. 358 cm^3 = _____ m^3
   g. 548.6 mL = _____ cm^3

4. Write conversion factors for each equality.
   a. 1 m^3 = 1 000 000 cm^3
   b. 1 in. = 2.54 cm
   c. 1 μg = 0.000 001 g
   d. 1 Mm = 1 000 000 m

5. a. What is the density of an 84.7 g sample of an unknown substance if the sample occupies 49.6 cm^3?
   b. What volume would be occupied by 7.75 g of this same substance?

✔ Critical Thinking

6. **INFERRING CONCLUSIONS** A student converts grams to milligrams by multiplying by the conversion factor $\frac{1 \text{ g}}{1000 \text{ mg}}$. Is the student performing this calculation correctly?

Classical Ideas About Matter

The Greeks were among the many ancient peoples who sought to understand the nature of matter. One group of Greek philosophers, called the *atomists*, believed that matter could be broken down into pieces of a minute size. These pieces, called *atoms* or *atomos,* which means "indivisible," possessed intrinsic, unchanging qualities. Another group of Greeks believed that matter could be divided an infinite number of times and could be changed from one type of matter into another.

Between 500 and 300 BCE, the Greek philosophers Leucippus and Democritus formulated the ideas that the atomists held. Leucippus and Democritus believed that all atoms were essentially the same but that the properties of all substances arose from the unique characteristics of their atoms. For example, solids, such as most metals, were thought to have uneven, jagged atoms. Because the atoms were rough, they could stick together and form solids. Similarly, water was thought to have atoms with smooth surfaces, which would allow the atoms to flow past one another. Though atomists did not have the same ideas about matter that we have today, they did believe that atoms were constantly in motion, even in objects that appeared to be solid.

Some Greek philosophers who studied matter between 700 and 300 BCE described matter in a way that differed from the way atomists described it. They attempted to identify and describe a fundamental substance from which all other matter was formed. Thales of Miletus (640–546 BCE) was among the first to suggest the existence of a basic element. He chose water, which exists as liquid, ice, and steam. He interpreted water's changeability to mean that water could transform into any other substance. Other philosophers suggested that the basic element was air or fire. Empedocles (ca. 490–ca. 430 BCE) focused on four elements: earth, air, fire, and water. He thought that these elements combined in various proportions to make all known matter.

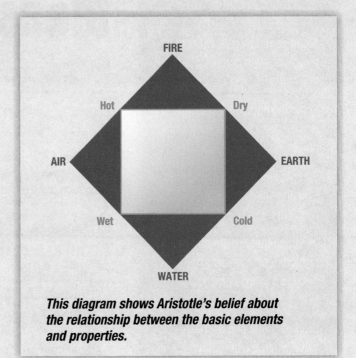

This diagram shows Aristotle's belief about the relationship between the basic elements and properties.

Aristotle (384–322 BCE), a student of Plato, elaborated on the earlier ideas about elements. He argued that in addition to the four elements that make up all matter, there were four basic properties: hot, cold, wet, and dry. In Aristotle's view, the four elements could each have two of the basic properties. For example, water was wet and cold, while air was wet and hot. He thought that one element could change into another element if its properties were changed.

For more than 2,000 years, Aristotle's classical ideas dominated scientific thought. It was not until the 1700s that the existence of atoms was shown experimentally and that the incredible intuition of the atomists was realized.

Questions

1. In Aristotle's system of elements, fire opposes water. Why do you think Aristotle chose this relationship?

2. Use the ideas of the atomists to describe the atoms of the physical phases of matter—solid, liquid, and gas.

▶ Accuracy is different from precision.

▶ Significant figures are those measured with certainty, plus one estimated digit.

▶ Scientific notation is used to express very large or very small numbers.

▶ Sample problems are guides to solving similar types of problems.

▶ Variables that are directly proportional increase or decrease by the same factor.

▶ Quantities are inversely proportional if one decreases in value when the other increases.

Using Scientific Measurements

Key Terms

accuracy   significant figures   inversely proportional
precision   scientific notation
percentage error   directly proportional

If you have ever measured something several times, you know that the results can vary. In science, for a reported measurement to be useful, there must be some indication of its reliability or uncertainty.

▶ **MAIN IDEA**
Accuracy is different from precision.

The terms *accuracy* and *precision* mean the same thing to most people. However, in science, their meanings are quite distinct. **Accuracy refers to the closeness of measurements to the correct or accepted value of the quantity measured. Precision refers to the closeness of a set of measurements of the same quantity made in the same way.** Thus, measured values that are accurate are close to the accepted value. Measured values that are precise are close to one another but not necessarily close to the accepted value.

Figure 3.1 on the facing page can help you visualize the difference between precision and accuracy. Several darts thrown separately at a dartboard may land in various positions, relative to the bull's-eye and to one another. The closer the darts land to the bull's-eye, the more accurately they were thrown. The closer they land to one another, the more precisely they were thrown. Thus, the set of results shown in **Figure 3.1a** is both accurate and precise: the darts are close to the bull's-eye and close to each other. In **Figure 3.1b**, the set of results is inaccurate but precise: the darts are far from the bull's-eye but close to each other. In **Figure 3.1c**, the set of results is both inaccurate and imprecise: the darts are far from the bull's-eye and far from each other. Notice also that the darts are not evenly distributed around the bull's-eye, so the set, even considered on average, is inaccurate. In **Figure 3.1d**, the set on average is accurate compared with the third case, but it is imprecise. That is because the darts are distributed evenly around the bull's-eye but are far from each other.

Percentage Error

The accuracy of an individual value or of an average experimental value can be compared quantitatively with the correct or accepted value by calculating the percentage error. **Percentage error is calculated by subtracting the accepted value from the experimental value, dividing the difference by the accepted value, and then multiplying by 100.**

FIGURE 3.1

Comparing Precision and Accuracy

(a) Darts within small area
= High precision

Area centered on bull's-eye
= High accuracy

(b) Darts within small area
= High precision

Area far from bull's-eye
= Low accuracy

(c) Darts within large area
= Low precision

Area far from bull's-eye
= Low accuracy

(d) Darts within large area
= Low precision

Area centered around bull's-eye
= High accuracy (on average)

Percentage Error

$$\text{Percentage error} = \frac{\text{Value}_{\text{experimental}} - \text{Value}_{\text{accepted}}}{\text{Value}_{\text{accepted}}} \times 100$$

Percentage error has a negative value if the accepted value is greater than the experimental value. It has a positive value if the accepted value is less than the experimental value. The following sample problem illustrates the concept of percentage error.

GO ONLINE

Learn It! Video
HMHScience.com

Percentage Error

Sample Problem C A student measures the mass and volume of a substance and calculates its density as 1.40 g/mL. The correct, or accepted, value of the density is 1.30 g/mL. What is the percentage error of the student's measurement?

● **SOLVE**

$$\text{Percentage error} = \frac{\text{Value}_{\text{experimental}} - \text{Value}_{\text{accepted}}}{\text{Value}_{\text{accepted}}} \times 100$$

$$= \frac{1.40 \text{ g/mL} - 1.30 \text{ g/mL}}{1.30 \text{ g/mL}} \times 100 = 7.7\%$$

Practice   Answers in Appendix E

1. What is the percentage error for a mass measurement of 17.7 g, given that the correct value is 21.2 g?
2. A volume is measured experimentally as 4.26 mL. What is the percentage error, given that the correct value is 4.15 mL?

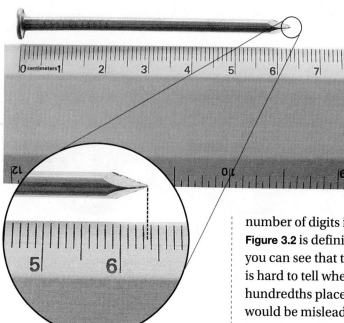

Significant Figures The length of this nail is between 6.3 cm and 6.4 cm.

✓ **CRITICAL THINKING**

Apply Suppose you record the nail's length as 6.36 cm. Which part of this measurement is uncertain?

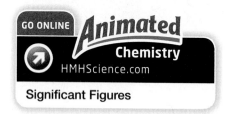

GO ONLINE
Animated
Chemistry
HMHScience.com

Significant Figures

Error in Measurement

Some error or uncertainty always exists in any measurement. The skill of the measurer places limits on the reliability of results. The conditions of measurement also affect the outcome. The measuring instruments themselves place limitations on precision. Some balances can be read more precisely than others. The same is true of rulers, graduated cylinders, and other measuring devices.

When you use a properly calibrated measuring device, you can be almost certain of a particular number of digits in a reading. For example, you can tell that the nail in **Figure 3.2** is definitely between 6.3 and 6.4 cm long. Looking more closely, you can see that the value is halfway between 6.3 and 6.4 cm. However, it is hard to tell whether the value should be read as 6.35 cm or 6.36 cm. The hundredths place is thus somewhat uncertain. Simply leaving it out would be misleading, because you do have *some* indication of the value's likely range. Therefore, you would estimate the value to the final questionable digit, perhaps reporting the length of the nail as 6.36 cm. You might include a plus-or-minus value to express the range, for example, 6.36 cm ± 0.01 cm.

▶ **MAIN IDEA**

Significant figures are those measured with certainty, plus one estimated digit.

In science, measured values are reported in terms of significant figures. **Significant figures in a measurement consist of all the digits known with certainty plus one final digit, which is somewhat uncertain or is estimated.** For example, in the reported nail length of 6.36 cm discussed above, the last digit, 6, is uncertain. All the digits, including the uncertain one, are significant, however. All contain information and are included in the reported value. Thus, the term *significant* does not mean *certain*. In any correctly reported measured value, the final digit is significant but not certain. Insignificant digits are never reported. As a chemistry student, you will need to use and recognize significant figures when you work with measured quantities and report your results and when you evaluate measurements reported by others.

Determining the Number of Significant Figures

When you look at a measured quantity, you need to determine which digits are significant. That process is very easy if the number has no zeros, because all the digits shown are significant. For example, in a number reported as 3.95, all three digits are significant. The significance of zeros in a number depends on their location, however. You need to learn and follow several rules involving zeros. After you have studied the rules in **Figure 3.3**, use them to express the answers in the sample problem that follows.

FIGURE 3.3

RULES FOR DETERMINING SIGNIFICANT ZEROS

Rule	Examples
1. Zeros appearing between nonzero digits are significant.	a. 40.7 L has three significant figures. b. 87 009 km has five significant figures.
2. Zeros appearing in front of all nonzero digits are not significant.	a. 0.095 897 m has five significant figures. b. 0.0009 kg has one significant figure.
3. Zeros at the end of a number and to the right of a decimal point are significant.	a. 85.00 g has four significant figures. b. 9.000 000 000 mm has 10 significant figures.
4. Zeros at the end of a number but to the left of a decimal point may or may not be significant. If a zero has not been measured or estimated but is just a placeholder, it is not significant. A decimal point placed after zeros indicates that they are significant.	a. 2000 m may contain from one to four significant figures, depending on how many zeros are placeholders. **For measurements given in this text, assume that 2000 m has one significant figure.** b. 2000. m contains four significant figures, indicated by the presence of the decimal point.

Significant Figures

GO ONLINE

SolveIt! Cards
HMHScience.com

Sample Problem D Determine the number of significant figures in the following measurements:

- **a.** 30 040 g
- **b.** 0.663 kg
- **c.** 20.05 mL
- **d.** 1500. mg
- **e.** 0.0008 m

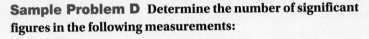 **SOLVE**

Determine the number of significant figures in each measurement using the rules listed in **Figure 3.3.**

- **a.** 30 040 g
  By rule 1, the zeros between 3 and 4 are significant, but the final zero is not, so there are 4 significant figures.
- **b.** 0.663 kg
  The zero to the left of the decimal point is not significant, so there are 3 significant figures.
- **c.** 20.05 mL
  By rule 1, the zeros between 2 and 5 are significant. so there are 4 significant figures.
- **d.** 1500. mg
  By rule 4, the zeros are significant because they are immediately followed by a decimal point, so there are 4 significant figures.
- **e.** 0.0008 m
  By rule 2, the zeros are not significant, so there is 1 significant figure.

 Continued

Significant Figures (continued)

1. Determine the number of significant figures in each of the following.
   a. 640 cm³
   b. 200.0 mL
   c. 0.5200 g
   d. 1.005 kg
   e. 10 000 L
   f. 20.900 cm

2. Suppose the value "seven thousand centimeters" is reported to you. How should the number be expressed if it is intended to contain the following?
   a. 1 significant figure
   b. 4 significant figures
   c. 6 significant figures

Rounding

When you perform calculations involving measurements, you need to know how to handle significant figures. This is especially true when you are using a calculator to carry out mathematical operations. The answers given on a calculator can be derived results with more digits than are justified by the measurements.

Suppose you used a calculator to divide a measured value of 154 g by a measured value of 327 mL. Each of these values has three significant figures. The calculator would show a numerical answer of 0.470948012. The answer contains digits not justified by the measurements used to calculate it. Such an answer has to be rounded off to make its degree of certainty match that in the original measurements. The answer should be 0.471 g/mL.

The rules for rounding are shown in **Figure 3.4**. The extent of rounding required in a given case depends on whether the numbers are being added, subtracted, multiplied, or divided.

FIGURE 3.4

RULES FOR ROUNDING NUMBERS		
If the digit following the last digit to be retained is:	then the last digit should:	Example (rounded to three significant figures)
greater than 5	be increased by 1	42.68 g ⟶ 42.7 g
less than 5	stay the same	17.32 m ⟶ 17.3 m
5, followed by nonzero digit(s)	be increased by 1	2.7851 cm ⟶ 2.79 cm
5, not followed by nonzero digit(s), and preceded by an odd digit	be increased by 1	4.635 kg ⟶ 4.64 kg (because 3 is odd)
5, not followed by nonzero digit(s), and the preceding significant digit is even	stay the same	78.65 mL ⟶ 78.6 mL (because 6 is even)

Addition or Subtraction with Significant Figures

Consider two mass measurements, 25.1 g and 2.03 g. The first measurement, 25.1 g, has one digit to the right of the decimal point, in the tenths place. There is no information on possible values for the hundredths place. That place is simply blank and cannot be assumed to be zero. The other measurement, 2.03 g, has two digits to the right of the decimal point. It provides information up to and including the hundredths place.

Suppose you were asked to add the two measurements. Simply carrying out the addition would result in an answer of 25.1 g + 2.03 g = 27.13 g. That answer suggests there is certainty all the way to the hundredths place. However, that result is not justified, because the hundredths place in 25.1 g is completely unknown. The answer must be adjusted to reflect the uncertainty in the numbers added.

When adding or subtracting decimals, the answer must have the same number of digits to the right of the decimal point as there are in the measurement having the fewest digits to the right of the decimal point. When you compare the two values 25.1 g and 2.03 g, the measurement with the fewest digits to the right of the decimal point is 25.1 g. It has only one such digit. Following the rule, the answer must be rounded so that it has no more than one digit to the right of the decimal point. The answer should therefore be rounded to 27.1 g.

When working with whole numbers, the answer should be rounded so that the final significant digit is in the same place as the leftmost uncertain digit. For example, 5400 + 365 = 5800, having 2 significant figures.

✔ **CHECK FOR UNDERSTANDING**

Analyze Suppose you measure the classroom once using a piece of rope you know to be 10 m long and again with a measuring tape marked in m, cm, and mm. You then take the average of the two measurements. Which would determine the number of significant figures in your answer? Explain your answer.

Multiplication and Division with Significant Figures

Suppose you calculated the density of an object that has a mass of 3.05 g and a volume of 8.47 mL. The following division on a calculator will give a value of 0.360094451.

$$\text{density} = \frac{\text{mass}}{\text{volume}} = \frac{3.05\ \text{g}}{8.47\ \text{mL}} = 0.360094451\ \text{g/mL}$$

The answer must be rounded to the correct number of significant figures. The values of mass and volume used to obtain the answer have only three significant figures each. The degree of certainty in the calculated result is not justified. *For multiplication or division, the answer can have no more significant figures than are in the measurement with the fewest number of significant figures.* In the calculation just described, the answer, 0.360094451 g/mL, would be rounded to three significant figures to match the significant figures in 8.47 mL and 3.05 g. The answer would thus be 0.360 g/mL.

Sample Problem E Carry out the following calculations. Express each answer to the correct number of significant figures.

  a. 9.66 cm − 4.5204 cm
  b. 1.6 g/L × 7.68 L

 SOLVE

Carry out each mathematical operation. Follow the rules in **Figures 3.3** and **3.4** for determining significant figures and for rounding.

a. The answer is rounded to 5.14 cm, because for subtraction there should be two digits to the right of the decimal point, to match 9.66 cm.

b. The answer is rounded to 12 g, because for multiplication there should be two significant figures in the answer, to match 1.6 g/L.

Practice

1. What is the sum of 1.0566 μm and 0.09425 μm?
2. Calculate the quantity 47.6 mL − 1.733 mL.
3. Calculate the area of a rectangular crystal surface that measures 1.34 μm by 0.7488 μm. (Hint: Recall that area = length × width and is measured in square units.)
4. Polycarbonate plastic has a density of 1.2 g/cm^3. A photo frame is constructed from two 3.0 mm sheets of polycarbonate. Each sheet measures 28 cm by 22 cm. What is the mass of the photo frame?

Conversion Factors and Significant Figures

Earlier in this chapter, you learned how conversion factors are used to change one unit to another. Such conversion factors are typically exact. That is, there is no uncertainty in them. For example, there are exactly 100 cm in a meter. If you were to use the conversion factor 100 cm/m to change meters to centimeters, the 100 would not limit the degree of certainty in the answer. Thus, 4.608 m could be converted to centimeters as follows.

$$4.608 \text{ m} \times \frac{100 \text{ cm}}{\text{m}} = 460.8 \text{ cm}$$

The answer still has four significant figures. Because the conversion factor is considered exact, the answer would not be rounded. Most exact conversion factors are defined, rather than measured, quantities.

Counted numbers also produce conversion factors of unlimited precision. For example, if you counted that there are 10 test tubes for every student, that would produce an exact conversion factor of 10 test tubes/student. There is no uncertainty in that factor.

▶ MAIN IDEA
Scientific notation is used to express very large or very small numbers.

In **scientific notation,** numbers are written in the form $M \times 10^n$, where the factor M is a number greater than or equal to 1 but less than 10, and n is a whole number. For example, to put the quantity 65 000 km in scientific notation and show the first two digits as significant, you would write:

$$6.5 \times 10^4 \text{ km}$$

Writing the M factor as 6.5 shows that there are exactly two significant figures. If, instead, you intended the first three digits in 65 000 to be significant, you would write 6.50×10^4 km. When numbers are written in scientific notation, only the significant figures are shown.

Suppose you are expressing a very small quantity, such as the length of a flu virus. In ordinary notation, this length could be 0.000 12 mm. That length can be expressed in scientific notation as follows.

$$0.000\ 12 \text{ mm} = 1.2 \times 10^{-4} \text{ mm}$$

Move the decimal point four places to the right, and multiply the number by 10^{-4}.

1. Determine M by moving the decimal point in the original number to the left or the right so that only one nonzero digit remains to the left of the decimal point.

2. Determine n by counting the number of places that you moved the decimal point. If you moved it to the left, n is positive. If you moved it to the right, n is negative.

Mathematical Operations Using Scientific Notation

1. *Addition and subtraction* These operations can be performed only if the values have the same exponent (n factor). If they do not, adjustments must be made to the values so that the exponents are equal. Once the exponents are equal, the M factors can be added or subtracted. The exponent of the answer can remain the same, or it may then require adjustment if the M factor of the answer has more than one digit to the left of the decimal point. Consider the example of the addition of 4.2×10^4 kg and 7.9×10^3 kg. We can make both exponents either 3 or 4. The following solutions are possible.

$$
\begin{aligned}
4.2\ \ &\times 10^4 \text{ kg} \\
+0.79 &\times 10^4 \text{ kg} \\
\hline
4.99 &\times 10^4 \text{ kg rounded to } 5.0 \times 10^4 \text{ kg}
\end{aligned}
$$

or

$$
\begin{aligned}
42\ \ &\times 10^3 \text{ kg} \\
+7.9\ &\times 10^3 \text{ kg} \\
\hline
49.9 &\times 10^3 \text{ kg} = 4.99 \times 10^4 \text{ kg rounded to } 5.0 \times 10^4 \text{ kg}
\end{aligned}
$$

Note that the units remain kg throughout.

FIGURE 3.5

Significant Figures and Calculators When you use a scientific calculator to work problems in scientific notation, don't forget to express the value on the display to the correct number of significant figures and show the units when you write the final answer.

5.44 [EE] 7 [÷] 8.1 [EE] 4 [ENTER]
671.6049383
rounded to 6.7×10^2 g/mol

5.44 [EXP] 7 [÷] 8.1 [EXP] 4 [=]
671.6049383
rounded to 6.7×10^2 g/mol

2. *Multiplication* The M factors are multiplied, and the exponents are added algebraically.

   Consider the multiplication of 5.23×10^6 μm by 7.1×10^{-2} μm.

   $(5.23 \times 10^6 \, \text{μm})(7.1 \times 10^{-2} \, \text{μm}) = (5.23 \times 7.1)(10^6 \times 10^{-2})$

   $= 37.133 \times 10^4 \, \text{μm}^2$ (adjust to two significant digits)

   $= 3.7 \times 10^5 \, \text{μm}^2$

   Note that when length measurements are multiplied, the result is area. The unit is now μm^2.

3. *Division* The M factors are divided, and the exponent of the denominator is subtracted from that of the numerator. The calculator keystrokes for this problem are shown in **Figure 3.5**.

   $$\frac{5.44 \times 10^7 \, \text{g}}{8.1 \times 10^4 \, \text{mol}} = \frac{5.44}{8.1} \times 10^{7-4} \, \text{g/mol}$$

   $= 0.6716049383 \times 10^3$ (adjust to two significant digits)

   $= 6.7 \times 10^2 \, \text{g/mol}$

   Note that the unit for the answer is the ratio of grams to moles.

▶ **MAIN IDEA**

Sample problems are guides to solving similar types of problems.

Learning to analyze and solve such problems requires practice and a logical approach. In this section, you will review a process that can help you analyze problems effectively. Most sample problems in this book are organized by four basic steps to guide your thinking in how to work out the solution to a problem.

Step 1. Analyze

The first step in solving a quantitative word problem is to read the problem carefully at least twice and to analyze the information in it. Note any important descriptive terms that clarify or add meaning to the problem. Identify and list the data given in the problem. Also identify the unknown—the quantity you are asked to find.

Step 2. Plan

The second step is to develop a plan for solving the problem. The plan should show how the information given is to be used to find the unknown. In the process, reread the problem to make sure you have gathered all the necessary information. It is often helpful to draw a picture that represents the problem. For example, if you were asked to determine the volume of a crystal given its dimensions, you could draw a representation of the crystal and label the dimensions. This drawing would help you visualize the problem.

Decide which conversion factors, mathematical formulas, or chemical principles you will need to solve the problem. Your plan might suggest a single calculation or a series of them involving different conversion factors. Once you understand how you need to proceed, you may wish to sketch out the route you will take, using arrows to point the way from one stage of the solution to the next. Sometimes you will need data that are not actually part of the problem statement. For instance, you'll often use data from the periodic table.

Step 3. Solve

The third step involves substituting the data and necessary conversion factors into the plan you have developed. At this stage, you calculate the answer, cancel units, and round the result to the correct number of significant figures. It is very important to have a plan worked out in step 2 before you start using the calculator. All too often, students start multiplying or dividing values given in the problem before they really understand what they need to do to get an answer.

Step 4. Check Your Work

Examine your answer to determine whether it is reasonable. Use the following methods, when appropriate, to carry out the evaluation.

1. Check to see that the units are correct. If they are not, look over the setup. Are the conversion factors correct?

2. Make an estimate of the expected answer. Use simpler, rounded numbers to do so. Compare the estimate with your actual result. The two should be similar.

3. Check the order of magnitude in your answer. Does it seem reasonable compared with the values given in the problem? If you calculated the density of vegetable oil and got a value of 54.9 g/mL, you should know that something is wrong. Oil floats on water.

Therefore, its density is less than the density of water. So the value obtained should be less than 1.0 g/mL.

4. Be sure that the answer given for any problem is expressed using the correct number of significant figures.

Look over the following quantitative Sample Problem. Notice how the four-step approach is used, and then apply the approach yourself in solving the practice problems that follow.

Solving Problems Using the Four-Step Approach

GO ONLINE

Learn It! Video
HMHScience.com

Solve It! Cards
HMHScience.com

Sample Problem F Calculate the volume of a sample of aluminum that has a mass of 3.057 kg. The density of aluminum is 2.70 g/cm³.

① ANALYZE

Given: mass = 3.057 kg, density = 2.70 g/cm³

Unknown: volume of aluminum

② PLAN

The density unit in the problem is g/cm³, and the mass given in the problem is expressed in kg. Therefore, in addition to using the density equation, you will need a conversion factor representing the relationship between grams and kilograms.

$$1000 \text{ g} = 1 \text{ kg}$$

Also, rearrange the density equation to solve for volume.

$$\text{density} = \frac{\text{mass}}{\text{volume}} \quad \text{or} \quad D = \frac{m}{V}$$

$$V = \frac{m}{D}$$

③ SOLVE

$$V = \frac{3.057 \text{ kg}}{2.70 \text{ g/cm}^3} \times \frac{1000 \text{ g}}{\text{kg}} = 1132.222\ldots \text{ cm}^3 \text{ (calculator answer)}$$

The answer should be rounded to three significant figures.

$$V = 1.13 \times 10^3 \text{ cm}^3$$

④ CHECK YOUR WORK

The unit of volume, cm³, is correct. An order-of-magnitude estimate would put the answer at over 1000 cm³.

$$\frac{3}{2} \times 1000$$

The correct number of significant figures is three, which matches that in 2.70 g/cm³.

Practice   Answers in Appendix E

1. What is the volume, in milliliters, of a sample of helium that has a mass of 1.73×10^{-3} g, given that the density is 0.178 47 g/L?
2. What is the density of a piece of metal that has a mass of 6.25×10^5 g and is 92.5 cm × 47.3 cm × 85.4 cm?
3. How many millimeters are there in 5.12×10^5 kilometers?
4. A clock gains 0.020 second per minute. How many seconds will the clock gain in exactly six months, assuming exactly 30 days per month?

► MAIN IDEA

Variables that are directly proportional increase or decrease by the same factor.

Two quantities are **directly proportional** to each other if dividing one by the other gives a constant value. For example, if the masses and volumes of different samples of aluminum are measured, the masses and volumes will be directly proportional to each other. As the masses of the samples increase, their volumes increase by the same factor, as you can see from the data. Doubling the mass doubles the volume. Halving the mass halves the volume.

When two variables, x and y, are directly proportional to each other, the relationship can be expressed as $y \propto x$, which is read as "y is *proportional* to x." The general equation for a directly proportional relationship between the two variables can also be written as follows.

$$\frac{y}{x} = k$$

The value of k is a constant called the proportionality constant. Written in this form, the equation expresses an important fact about direct proportion: the ratio between the variables remains constant. Note that using the mass and volume values in **Figure 3.6** gives a mass-volume ratio that is constant (neglecting measurement error). The equation can be rearranged into the following form.

$$y = kx$$

The equation $y = kx$ may look familiar to you. It is the equation for a special case of a straight line. If two variables related in this way are graphed versus one another, a straight line, or linear plot, that passes through the origin results. The data for aluminum from **Figure 3.6** are graphed in **Figure 3.7**. The mass and volume of a pure substance are directly proportional to each other. Consider mass to be y and volume to be x. The constant ratio, k, for the two variables is density. The slope of the line reflects the constant density, or mass-volume ratio.

FIGURE 3.7

Mass versus Volume The graph of mass versus volume shows a relationship of direct proportion. Notice that the line is extrapolated to pass through the origin.

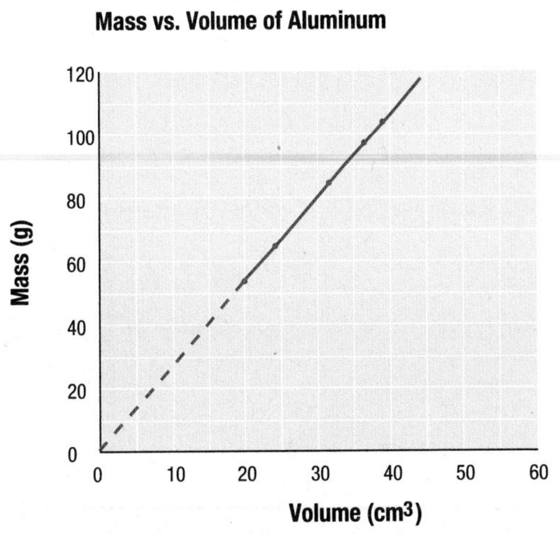

Mass vs. Volume of Aluminum

FIGURE 3.6

MASS-VOLUME DATA FOR ALUMINUM AT 20°C

Mass (g)	Volume (cm³)	$\frac{m}{V}$ (g/cm³)
54.7	20.1	2.72
65.7	24.4	2.69
83.5	30.9	2.70
96.3	35.8	2.69
105.7	39.1	2.70

For aluminum, this value is 2.70 g/cm³ at 20°C. Notice also that the plotted line passes through the origin (0,0). All directly proportional relationships produce linear graphs that pass through the origin.

▶ **MAIN IDEA**
Quantities are inversely proportional if one decreases in value when the other increases.

Two quantities are **inversely proportional** to each other if their product is constant. An example of an inversely proportional relationship is that between speed of travel and the time required to cover a fixed distance. The greater the speed, the less time that is needed to go a certain fixed distance. Doubling the speed cuts the required time in half. Halving the speed doubles the required time.

When two variables, x and y, are inversely proportional to each other, the relationship can be expressed as follows.

$$y \propto \frac{1}{x}$$

This is read "y is *proportional* to 1 divided by x." The general equation for an inversely proportional relationship between the two variables can be written in the following form.

$$xy = k$$

In the equation, k is the proportionality constant. If x increases, y must decrease by the same factor to keep the product constant.

When the temperature of a sample of nitrogen is kept constant, the volume (V) of the gas sample decreases as the pressure (P) increases, as shown in **Figure 3.8**. Note that $P \times V$ gives a reasonably constant value. Thus, P and V are inversely proportional to each other. The graph of this data is shown in **Figure 3.9**. A graph of variables that are inversely proportional produces a curve called a *hyperbola*.

FIGURE 3.8

PRESSURE-VOLUME DATA FOR NITROGEN AT CONSTANT TEMPERATURE		
Pressure (kPa)	Volume (cm³)	$P \times V$
100	500	50 000
150	333	49 950
200	250	50 000
250	200	50 000
300	166	49 800
350	143	50 050
400	125	50 000
450	110	49 500

FIGURE 3.9

Volume versus Pressure The graph of volume versus pressure shows an inversely proportional relationship. The curve is called a hyperbola. Note the difference between the shape of this graph and that of the graph in **Figure 3.7.**

✓ **CRITICAL THINKING**

Apply For this graph, if $V \propto 1/x$, what does x represent?

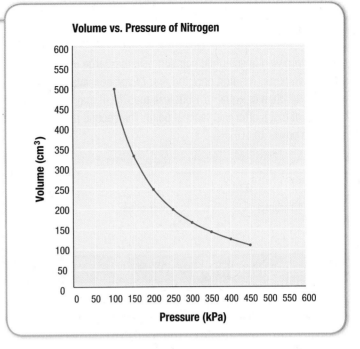

Volume vs. Pressure of Nitrogen

✓ SECTION 3 **FORMATIVE ASSESSMENT**

▶ **Reviewing Main Ideas**

1. The density of copper is listed as 8.94 g/cm³. Two students each make three density determinations of samples of the substance. Student A's results are 7.3 g/mL, 9.4 g/mL, and 8.3 g/mL. Student B's results are 8.4 g/cm³, 8.8 g/cm³, and 8.0 g/cm³. Compare the two sets of results in terms of precision and accuracy.

2. Determine the number of significant figures.

   a. 6.002 cm   **d.** 7000 kg

   b. 0.0020 m   **e.** 7000. kg

   c. 10.0500 g

3. Round 2.6765 to two significant figures.

4. Carry out the following calculations.

   a. 52.13 g + 1.7502 g

   b. 12 m × 6.41 m

   c. $\dfrac{16.25 \text{ g}}{5.1442 \text{ mL}}$

5. Perform the following operations. Express each answer in scientific notation.

   a. $(1.54 \times 10^{-2} \text{ g}) + (2.86 \times 10^{-1} \text{ g})$

   b. $(7.023 \times 10^{9} \text{ g}) - (6.62 \times 10^{7} \text{ g})$

   c. $(8.99 \times 10^{-4} \text{ m}) \times (3.57 \times 10^{4} \text{ m})$

   d. $\dfrac{2.17 \times 10^{-3} \text{ g}}{5.002 \times 10^{4} \text{ mL}}$

6. Write the following numbers in scientific notation.

   a. 560 000

   b. 33 400

   c. 0.000 4120

7. A student measures the mass of a beaker filled with corn oil. The mass reading averages 215.6 g. The mass of the beaker is 110.4 g.

   a. What is the mass of the corn oil?

   b. What is the density of the corn oil if its volume is 114 cm³?

8. Calculate the mass of gold that occupies 5.0×10^{-3} cm³. The density of gold is 19.3 g/cm³.

9. What is the difference between a graph representing data that are directly proportional and a graph of data that are inversely proportional?

✓ **Critical Thinking**

10. **APPLYING CONCEPTS** The mass of a liquid is 11.50 g, and its volume is 9.03 mL. How many significant figures should its density value have? Explain the reason for your answer.

Any value expressed in scientific notation, whether large or small, has two parts. The first part, the *first factor*, consists of a number greater than or equal to 1 but less than 10. It may have any number of digits after the decimal point. The second part consists of a power of 10.

To write the first part, move the decimal point to the right or the left so that there is only one nonzero digit to the left of the decimal point. The second part is written as an exponent, which is determined by counting the number of places the decimal point must be moved. If it is moved to the right, the exponent is negative. If it is moved to the left, the exponent is positive.

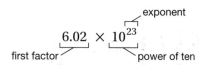

first factor — 6.02×10^{23} — exponent, power of ten

Problem-Solving TIPS

- In addition and subtraction, all values must first be converted to numbers that have the same exponent of 10. The result is the sum or the difference of the first factors, multiplied by the same exponent of 10. Finally, the result should be rounded to the correct number of significant figures and expressed in scientific notation.
- In multiplication, the first factors are multiplied, and the exponents of 10 are added.
- In division, the first factors of the numbers are divided, and the exponent of 10 in the denominator is subtracted from the exponent of 10 in the numerator.

Sample Problems

Write 299 800 000 m/s in scientific notation.

The decimal must move to the left 8 places, which indicates a positive exponent.

299 800 000. m/s

8 7 6 5 4 3 2 1

The value in scientific notation is 2.998×10^8 m/s.

Solve the following equation, and write the answer in scientific notation.

$(3.1 \times 10^3)(5.21 \times 10^4)$

Multiply the first factors, and then add the exponents of 10.

$(3.1 \times 5.21) \times 10^{(3+4)} = 16.151 \times 10^7 = 16 \times 10^7 = 1.6 \times 10^8$

Practice

1. Rewrite the following numbers in scientific notation.
   a. 0.0000745 g
   b. 5 984 102 nm

2. Solve the following equations, and write the answers in scientific notation.
   a. $1.017 \times 10^3 - 1.013 \times 10^4$
   b. $\dfrac{9.27 \times 10^4}{11.24 \times 10^5}$

CHAPTER 2 **Summary**

BIG IDEA Scientists use observations and measurements to formulate hypotheses and theories about the world.

SECTION 1 Scientific Method

- The scientific method is a logical approach to solving problems that lend themselves to investigation.
- A hypothesis is a testable statement that serves as the basis for predictions and further experiments, and a theory is a broad generalization that explains a body of known facts or phenomena.
- A theory has a lot of evidence to support it, but it still can change over time.

KEY TERMS

scientific method
system
hypothesis
model
theory

SECTION 2 Units of Measurement

- The result of nearly every measurement is a number and a unit.
- The SI system of measurement is used in science. It has seven base units: the meter (length), kilogram (mass), second (time), kelvin (temperature), mole (amount of substance), ampere (electric current), and candela (luminous intensity).
- Weight is a measure of the gravitational pull on matter.
- Derived SI units include the square meter (area) and the cubic meter (volume).
- Density is the ratio of mass to volume.
- Conversion factors are used to convert from one unit to another.

KEY TERMS

quantity
SI
weight
derived unit
volume
density
conversion factor
dimensional analysis

SECTION 3 Using Scientific Measurements

- Accuracy refers to the closeness of a measurement to the correct or accepted value. Precision refers to the closeness of values for a set of measurements.
- Percentage error is the difference between the experimental and the accepted value that is divided by the accepted value and then multiplied by 100.
- The significant figures in a number consist of all digits known with certainty plus one final digit, which is uncertain.
- After addition or subtraction, the answer should be rounded so that it has no more digits to the right of the decimal point than there are in the measurement that has the smallest number of digits to the right of the decimal point. After multiplication or division, the answer should be rounded so that it has no more significant figures than there are in the measurement that has the fewest number of significant figures.
- Exact conversion factors are completely certain and do not limit the number of digits in a calculation.
- A number written in scientific notation is of the form $M \times 10^n$, in which M is greater than or equal to 1 but less than 10 and n is an integer.
- Two quantities are directly proportional to each other if dividing one by the other yields a constant value. Two quantities are inversely proportional to each other if their product has a constant value.

KEY TERMS

accuracy
precision
percentage error
significant figures
scientific notation
directly proportional
inversely proportional

GO ONLINE

Interactive Review
HMHScience.com

Review Games
Concept Maps

SECTION 1
Scientific Method

▶ **REVIEWING MAIN IDEAS**

1. How does quantitative information differ from qualitative information?

2. What is a hypothesis? How does it differ from a theory?

3. **a.** What is a model in the scientific sense?
   b. How does a model differ from a theory?

SECTION 2
Units of Measurement

▶ **REVIEWING MAIN IDEAS**

4. Why is it important for a measurement system to have an international standard?

5. How does a quantity differ from a unit? Use two examples to explain the difference.

6. List the seven SI base units and the quantities they represent.

7. What is the numerical equivalent of each of the following SI prefixes?
   a. kilo-   **d.** micro-
   b. centi-   **e.** milli-
   c. mega-

8. Identify the SI unit that would be most appropriate for expressing the length of the following.
   a. width of a gymnasium
   b. length of a finger
   c. distance between your town and the closest border of the next state
   d. length of a bacterial cell

9. Identify the SI unit that would be most appropriate for measuring the mass of each of the following objects.
   a. table
   b. coin
   c. a 250 mL beaker

10. Explain why the second is not defined by the length of the day.

11. **a.** What is a derived unit?
    b. What is the SI derived unit for area?

12. **a.** List two SI derived units for volume.
    b. List two non-SI units for volume, and explain how they relate to the cubic centimeter.

13. **a.** Why are the units that are used to express the densities of gases different from those used to express the densities of solids or liquids?
    b. Name two units for density.
    c. Why is the temperature at which density is measured usually specified?

14. **a.** Which of the solids listed in **Figure 2.8** will float on water?
    b. Which of the liquids will sink in milk?

15. **a.** Define *conversion factor*.
    b. Explain how conversion factors are used.

PRACTICE PROBLEMS

16. What is the volume, in cubic meters, of a rectangular solid that is 0.25 m long, 6.1 m wide, and 4.9 m high?

17. Find the density of a material, given that a 5.03 g sample occupies 3.24 mL. (Hint: See Sample Problem A.)

18. What is the mass of a sample of material that has a volume of 55.1 cm^3 and a density of 6.72 g/cm^3?

19. A sample of a substance that has a density of 0.824 g/mL has a mass of 0.451 g. Calculate the volume of the sample.

20. How many grams are in 882 μg? (Hint: See Sample Problem B.)

21. Calculate the number of milliliters in 0.603 L.

22. The density of gold is 19.3 g/cm^3.
    a. What is the volume, in cubic centimeters, of a sample of gold that has a mass of 0.715 kg?
    b. If this sample of gold is a cube, what is the length of each edge in centimeters?

23. **a.** Find the number of kilometers in 92.25 m.
    b. Convert the answer in kilometers to centimeters.

SECTION 3

Using Scientific Measurements

 REVIEWING MAIN IDEAS

24. Compare accuracy and precision.

25. a. Write the equation that is used to calculate percentage error.
b. Under what condition will percentage error be negative?

26. How is the average for a set of values calculated?

27. What is meant by a mass measurement expressed in this form: $4.6 \text{ g} \pm 0.2 \text{ g}$?

28. Suppose a graduated cylinder were not correctly calibrated. How would this affect the results of a measurement? How would it affect the results of a calculation using this measurement?

29. Round each of the following measurements to the number of significant figures indicated.
a. 67.029 g to three significant figures
b. 0.15 L to one significant figure
c. 52.8005 mg to five significant figures
d. 3.174 97 mol to three significant figures

30. State the rules governing the number of significant figures that result from each of the following operations.
a. addition and subtraction
b. multiplication and division

31. What is the general form for writing numbers in scientific notation?

32. a. By using x and y, state the general equation for quantities that are directly proportional.
b. For two directly proportional quantities, what happens to one variable when the other variable increases?

33. a. State the general equation for quantities, x and y, that are inversely proportional.
b. For two inversely proportional quantities, what happens to one variable when the other increases?

34. Arrange in the correct order the following four basic steps for finding the solution to a problem: check your work, analyze, solve, and plan.

PRACTICE PROBLEMS

35. A student measures the mass of a sample as 9.67 g. Calculate the percentage error, given that the correct mass is 9.82 g. (Hint: See Sample Problem C.)

36. A handbook gives the density of calcium as 1.54 g/cm^3. Based on lab measurements, what is the percentage error of a density calculation of 1.25 g/cm^3?

37. What is the percentage error of a length measurement of 0.229 cm if the correct value is 0.225 cm?

38. How many significant figures are in each of the following measurements? (Hint: See Sample Problem D.)
a. 0.4004 mL
b. 6000 g
c. 1.000 30 km
d. 400. mm

39. Calculate the sum of 6.078 g and 0.3329 g.

40. Subtract 7.11 cm from 8.2 cm. (Hint: See Sample Problem E.)

41. What is the product of 0.8102 m and 3.44 m?

42. Divide 94.20 g by 3.167 22 mL.

43. Write the following numbers in scientific notation.
a. 0.000 673 0
b. 50 000.0
c. 0.000 003 010

44. The following numbers are in scientific notation. Write them in standard notation.
a. $7.050 \times 10^3 \text{ g}$
b. $4.000 \, 05 \times 10^7 \text{ mg}$
c. $2.350 \, 0 \times 10^4 \text{ mL}$

45. Perform the following operation. Express the answer in scientific notation and with the correct number of significant figures.
$0.002115 \text{ m} \times 0.0000405 \text{ m}$

46. A sample of a certain material has a mass of $2.03 \times 10^{-3} \text{ g}$. Calculate the volume of the sample, given that the density is $9.133 \times 10^{-1} \text{ g/cm}^3$. Use the four-step method to solve the problem. (Hint: See Sample Problem F.)

Mixed Review

47. A man finds that he has a mass of 100.6 kg. He goes on a diet, and several months later, he finds that he has a mass of 96.4 kg. Express each number in scientific notation, and calculate the number of kilograms the man has lost by dieting.

48. A large office building is 1.07×10^2 m long, 31 m wide, and 4.25×10^2 m high. What is its volume?

49. An object has a mass of 57.6 g. Find the object's density, given that its volume is 40.25 cm³.

50. A lab worker measures the mass of some sucrose as 0.947 mg. Convert that quantity to grams and to kilograms.

51. A student calculates the density of iron as 6.80 g/cm³ by using lab data for mass and volume. A handbook reveals that the correct value is 7.86 g/cm³. What is the percentage error?

USING THE HANDBOOK

52. Find the table of properties for Group 1 elements in the *Elements Handbook* (Appendix A). Calculate the volume of a single atom of each element listed in the table by using the equation for the volume of a sphere.

$$\frac{4}{3}\pi \cdot r^3$$

53. Use the radius of a sodium atom from the *Elements Handbook* (Appendix A) to calculate the number of sodium atoms in a row 5.00 cm long. Assume that each sodium atom touches the ones next to it.

54. a. A block of sodium that has the measurements 3.00 cm × 5.00 cm × 5.00 cm has a mass of 75.5 g. Calculate the density of sodium.
b. Compare your calculated density with the value in the properties table for Group 1 elements. Calculate the percentage error for your density determination.

RESEARCH AND WRITING

55. How does the metric system, which was once a standard for measurement, differ from SI? Why was it necessary for the United States to change to SI?

56. What are ISO 9000 standards? How do they affect industry on an international level?

ALTERNATIVE ASSESSMENT

57. Performance Obtain three metal samples from your teacher. Determine the mass and volume of each sample. Calculate the density of each metal from your measurement data. (Hint: Consider using the water-displacement technique to measure the volume of your samples.)

58. Use the data from the Nutrition Facts label below to answer the following questions:
a. Use the data given on the label for grams of fat and calories from fat to construct a conversion factor that has the units calories per gram.
b. Calculate the mass in kilograms for 20 servings of the food.
c. Calculate the mass of protein in micrograms for one serving of the food.
d. What is the correct number of significant figures for the answer in item a? Why?

Nutrition Facts
Serving Size ¾ cup (30g)
Servings Per Container About 14

Amount Per Serving	Corn Crunch	with ½ cup skim milk
Calories	120	160
Calories from Fat	15	20

	% Daily Value**	
Total Fat 2g*	3%	3%
Saturated Fat 0g	0%	0%
Cholesterol 0mg	0%	1%
Sodium 160mg	7%	9%
Potassium 65mg	2%	8%
Total Carbohydrate 25g	8%	10%
Dietary Fiber 3g		
Sugars 3g		
Other Carbohydrate 11g		
Protein 2g		

*Amount in Cereal. A serving of cereal plus skim milk provides 2g fat, less 5mg cholesterol, 220mg sodium, 270mg potassium, 31g carbohydrate (19g sugars) and 6g protein.

**Percent Daily Values are based on a 2,000 calorie diet. Your daily values may be higher or lower depending on your calorie needs:

	Calories	2,000	2,500
Total Fat	Less than	65g	80g
Sat Fat	Less than	20g	25g
Cholesterol	Less than	300mg	300mg
Sodium	Less than	2,400mg	2,400mg
Potassium		3,500mg	3,500mg
Total Carbohydrate		300g	375g
Dietary Fiber		25g	30g

Standards-Based Assessment

Record your answers on a separate piece of paper.

MULTIPLE CHOICE

1 There are 6.02×10^{23} atoms in one mole of carbon. Using scientific notation, how many atoms are there in 2.06 moles of carbon?

A 1.24×10^{22}
B 1.24×10^{23}
C 1.24×10^{24}
D 1.24×10^{25}

2 A typical aspirin dosage is described in milligrams. Using scientific notation, about how many milligrams of aspirin are in 0.000 325 kilograms?

A 3.25×10^{-4} mg
B 3.25×10^{-7} mg
C 3.25×10^{2} mg
D 3.35×10^{3} mg

3 A student calculates that the volume of his textbook is 990.880 cm^3. Which of the following is the volume written with 3 significant figures?

A 991 cm^3
B 990.9 cm^3
C 990.90 cm^3
D 991.000 cm^3

4 The accuracy of a measurement —

A is how close it is to the true value
B does not depend on the instrument used to measure the object
C indicates that the measurement is also precise
D is how close the measurements in a set are to one another

5 A metal sample has a mass of 45.65 g. The volume of the sample is 16.9 cm^3. What is the density of the sample?

A 2.7 g/cm^3
B 2.70 g/cm^3
C 0.370 g/cm^3
D 0.37 g/cm^3

6 In 400 BCE, the Greek philosopher Democritus first proposed the idea that all matter was composed of atoms. Since that time, scientists have learned that, far from resembling tiny marbles, atoms actually have very complex structures. Since it has been changed so many times, why is it referred to as the atomic *theory* rather than the atomic *hypothesis*?

A It was proposed by two different scientists.
B Hypotheses are testable, and theories are not.
C Even though the details have been modified, the idea that matter contains tiny particles called atoms explains a lot of observations.
D Atoms cannot be seen with the naked eye, and hypotheses must be observable.

7 A student is investigating factors that might influence solubility. In one experiment, she places one sugar cube each into two different glasses of water at room temperature. She also places a third sugar cube into a third glass of water at a higher temperature. She notices that the cube in the water at the higher temperature dissolves more quickly. Which of the following statements was ***most likely*** the hypothesis she was testing?

A Stirring a solution increases the rate at which a substance will dissolve.
B Sugar cubes dissolve more quickly in smaller volumes of water than larger ones.
C Increasing temperature will increase the rate at which a substance dissolves, because the particles have more energy.
D Stirring a solution increases the rate at which a solute dissolves more than heating a solution.

GRIDDED RESPONSE

8 A student accurately determines that the distance between two points on a football field is 105.0 feet. If there are about 3.28 feet in one meter, about how many meters is the distance? Express the answer using the correct number of significant figures.

Test Tip

Choose an answer to a question based on both information that you already know and information that is presented in the question.

A BOOK EXPLAINING
COMPLEX IDEAS USING
ONLY THE 1,000 MOST
COMMON WORDS

RANDALL MUNROE
XKCD.COM

HOW TO COUNT THINGS

A counting system to help people agree with each other

You've learned that scientists all over the world have agreed on a single measurement system called SI. Here's a look at how we use SI to measure the length, velocity, temperature, and mass of things in our world.

THE STORY OF COUNTING HOW LONG, WARM, FAST, AND HEAVY

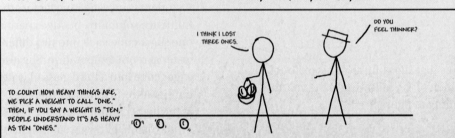

TO COUNT HOW HEAVY THINGS ARE, WE PICK A WEIGHT TO CALL "ONE." THEN, IF YOU SAY A WEIGHT IS "TEN," PEOPLE UNDERSTAND IT'S AS HEAVY AS TEN "ONES."

WE DO THE SAME FOR COUNTING OTHER THINGS, LIKE HOW FAST OR HOT THINGS ARE.

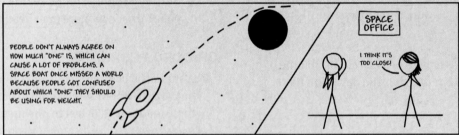

PEOPLE DON'T ALWAYS AGREE ON HOW MUCH "ONE" IS, WHICH CAN CAUSE A LOT OF PROBLEMS. A SPACE BOAT ONCE MISSED A WORLD BECAUSE PEOPLE GOT CONFUSED ABOUT WHICH "ONE" THEY SHOULD BE USING FOR WEIGHT.

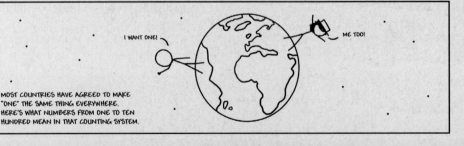

MOST COUNTRIES HAVE AGREED TO MAKE "ONE" THE SAME THING EVERYWHERE. HERE'S WHAT NUMBERS FROM ONE TO TEN HUNDRED MEAN IN THAT COUNTING SYSTEM.

HOW LONG THINGS ARE

In this system, "one" is about half as tall as a tall person.

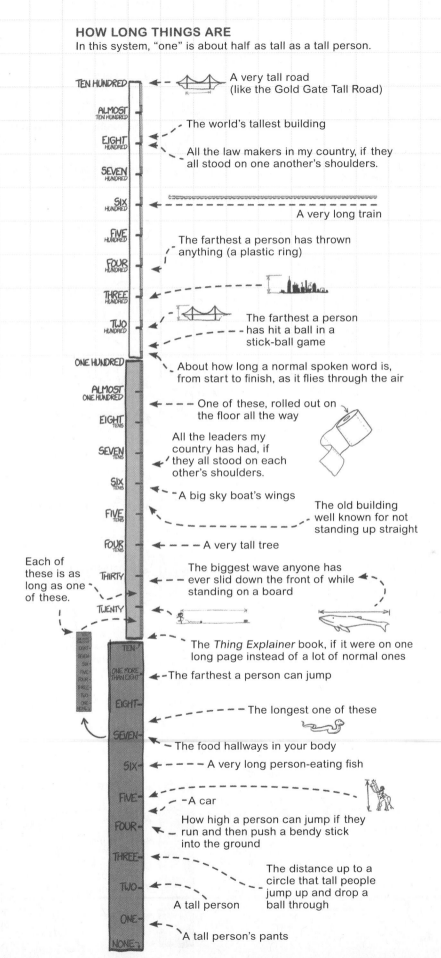

TEN HUNDRED — A very tall road
(like the Gold Gate Tall Road)

ALMOST TEN HUNDRED

EIGHT HUNDRED — The world's tallest building

— All the law makers in my country, if they all stood on one another's shoulders.

SEVEN HUNDRED

SIX HUNDRED — A very long train

FIVE HUNDRED

FOUR HUNDRED — The farthest a person has thrown anything (a plastic ring)

THREE HUNDRED

TWO HUNDRED — The farthest a person has hit a ball in a stick-ball game

ONE HUNDRED — About how long a normal spoken word is, from start to finish, as it flies through the air

ALMOST ONE HUNDRED — One of these, rolled out on the floor all the way

EIGHT TENS

SEVEN TENS — All the leaders my country has had, if they all stood on each other's shoulders.

SIX TENS — A big sky boat's wings

FIVE TENS — The old building well known for not standing up straight

FOUR TENS — A very tall tree

THIRTY — The biggest wave anyone has ever slid down the front of while standing on a board

TWENTY

TEN — The *Thing Explainer* book, if it were on one long page instead of a lot of normal ones

Each of these is as long as one of these.

ONE MORE THAN EIGHT — The farthest a person can jump

EIGHT — The longest one of these

SEVEN — The food hallways in your body

SIX — A very long person-eating fish

FIVE — A car

FOUR — How high a person can jump if they run and then push a bendy stick into the ground

THREE — The distance up to a circle that tall people jump up and drop a ball through

TWO — A tall person

ONE — A tall person's pants

NONE

HOW HEAVY THINGS ARE

In this system, "one" means the weight of a large bottle of water. (In other systems, "one" is the weight of a normal bottle of water.)

HOW FAST THINGS ARE

In this system, "one" means going one distance number every second. (Cars don't use this system, so you don't see it as much, but people who use numbers to learn how things work like it.)

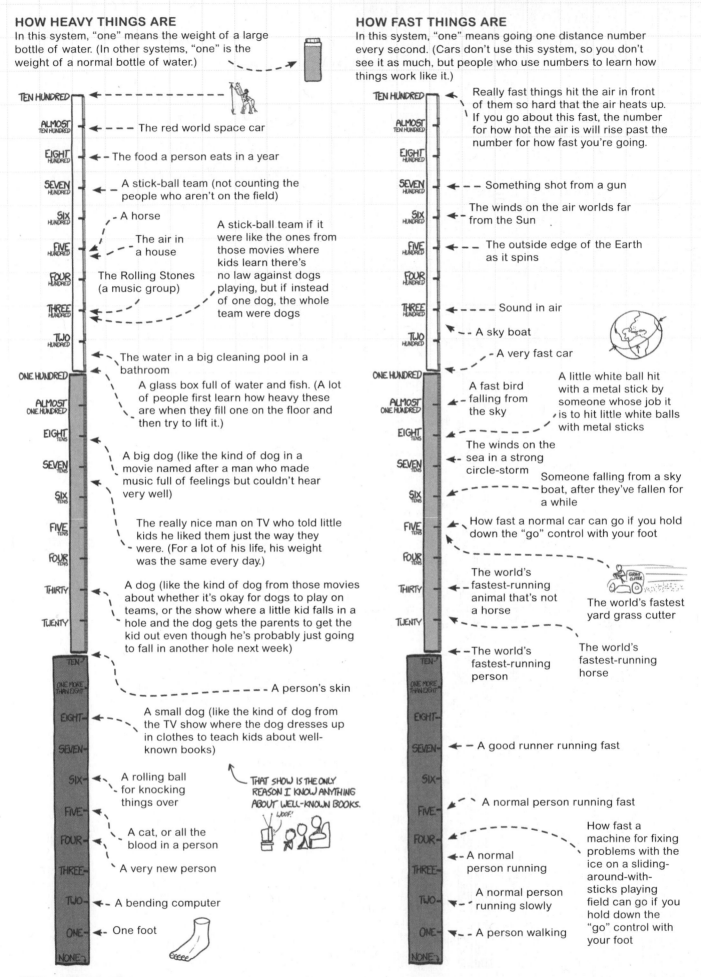

TEN HUNDRED

ALMOST TEN HUNDRED ← The red world space car

EIGHT HUNDRED ← The food a person eats in a year

SEVEN HUNDRED ← A stick-ball team (not counting the people who aren't on the field)

SIX HUNDRED ← A horse

FIVE HUNDRED — The air in a house

The Rolling Stones (a music group)

A stick-ball team if it were like the ones from those movies where kids learn there's no law against dogs playing, but if instead of one dog, the whole team were dogs

FOUR HUNDRED

THREE HUNDRED

TWO HUNDRED

← The water in a big cleaning pool in a bathroom

ONE HUNDRED ← A glass box full of water and fish. (A lot of people first learn how heavy these are when they fill one on the floor and then try to lift it.)

ALMOST ONE HUNDRED

EIGHT TENS ←

A big dog (like the kind of dog in a movie named after a man who made music full of feelings but couldn't hear very well)

SEVEN TENS

SIX TENS

FIVE TENS

The really nice man on TV who told little kids he liked them just the way they were. (For a lot of his life, his weight was the same every day.)

FOUR TENS

THIRTY ← A dog (like the kind of dog from those movies about whether it's okay for dogs to play on teams, or the show where a little kid falls in a hole and the dog gets the parents to get the kid out even though he's probably just going to fall in another hole next week)

TWENTY

TEN

ONE MORE THAN EIGHT - - - - A person's skin

EIGHT ← A small dog (like the kind of dog from the TV show where the dog dresses up in clothes to teach kids about well-known books)

SEVEN

SIX ← A rolling ball for knocking things over

THAT SHOW IS THE ONLY REASON I KNOW ANYTHING ABOUT WELL-KNOWN BOOKS.
WOOF!

FIVE

FOUR ← A cat, or all the blood in a person

THREE ← A very new person

TWO ← A bending computer

ONE ← One foot

NONE

TEN HUNDRED

Really fast things hit the air in front of them so hard that the air heats up. If you go about this fast, the number for how hot the air is will rise past the number for how fast you're going.

ALMOST TEN HUNDRED

EIGHT HUNDRED

SEVEN HUNDRED ← Something shot from a gun

SIX HUNDRED ← The winds on the air worlds far from the Sun

FIVE HUNDRED ← The outside edge of the Earth as it spins

FOUR HUNDRED

THREE HUNDRED ← Sound in air

TWO HUNDRED ← A sky boat

← A very fast car

ONE HUNDRED

A little white ball hit with a metal stick by someone whose job it is to hit little white balls with metal sticks

ALMOST ONE HUNDRED ← A fast bird falling from the sky

EIGHT TENS

The winds on the sea in a strong circle-storm

SEVEN TENS ←

Someone falling from a sky boat, after they've fallen for a while

SIX TENS

How fast a normal car can go if you hold down the "go" control with your foot

FIVE TENS

FOUR TENS

THIRTY ← The world's fastest-running animal that's not a horse

The world's fastest yard grass cutter

TWENTY

TEN ← The world's fastest-running person

The world's fastest-running horse

EIGHT

SEVEN ← A good runner running fast

SIX

FIVE ← A normal person running fast

How fast a machine for fixing problems with the ice on a sliding-around-with-sticks playing field can go if you hold down the "go" control with your foot

FOUR

THREE ← A normal person running

TWO ← A normal person running slowly

ONE ← A person walking

NONE

HOW WARM THINGS ARE

In this system, "none" means how cold water has to be to turn to ice, and "one hundred" means how hot it has to be to turn to air.

TEN HUNDRED — ← Hot rocks coming out of the ground

ALMOST TEN HUNDRED — ← If your kitchen table somehow got this hot, the silver eating sticks would turn to water and run off onto the floor.

EIGHT HUNDRED — ← A wood fire

SEVEN HUNDRED — ← If glass gets this hot, you can pour it like water.

SIX HUNDRED — ← Anything that gets this hot will start making red light

FIVE HUNDRED —

FOUR HUNDRED — ← The air at the surface of the hot sky world near Earth

THREE HUNDRED — ← If food gets this hot, it will turn black and start smoking, and the box on your ceiling that yells when it gets too hot will start yelling.

TWO HUNDRED — ← The inside of a food-heating box

ONE HUNDRED — ← Water that's hot enough to turn to air

ALMOST ONE HUNDRED — ← Hot tea

← If you're heating food made from animals, getting the inside hotter than this will make the food bad (not everyone agrees about this).

EIGHT TENS —

SEVEN TENS — ← The wet air in those hot cloud rooms where people sit without any clothes and don't do anything

SIX TENS — ← The air in the world's hottest places

FIVE TENS — ← The inside of your body if it's having a very, very bad problem

FOUR TENS — ← The inside of your body

THIRTY — ← A warm pool people play in

TWENTY — ← How warm the air in a house should be. (Not everyone agrees about this.)

← Cold enough that your parents will tell you that you need a coat

TEN —

ONE MORE THAN EIGHT — ← Cold enough that you actually do need a coat

EIGHT —

SEVEN —

SIX — ← The cold box in your kitchen shouldn't get this warm. If food gets warmer than this, things can grow in it and make you sick.

FIVE —

FOUR —

THREE — ← Water deep in the sea

TWO —

ONE — ← Ice

NONE — ←

©Barry Blackburn/Shutterstock

Heat numbers are a little confusing to work with, since the idea of "none" and "one" aren't as simple with heat as with distance or weight, and there are a few systems for counting it.

The system shown here is the one used in most of the world, but there are two other systems used in a lot of places. One is a system that's like this one, but "none" is the coldest anything can get. In that system, the air where most people live is around three hundred. The other is a system where the air where most people live doesn't get much hotter than one hundred or colder than none.

CHAPTER 3
Atoms: The Building Blocks of Matter

BIG IDEA
Atoms are the smallest particles of elements. The atoms of one element differ from the atoms of another by the number of protons they contain.

ONLINE Chemistry
HMHScience.com

ONLINE LABS
- Conservation of Mass
- Studying What You Can't See

GO ONLINE

Why It Matters Video
HMHScience.com

Atoms

The Atom: From Philosophical Idea to Scientific Theory

SECTION 1

Main Ideas

▶ Three basic laws describe how matter behaves in chemical reactions.

▶ Compounds contain atoms in whole-number ratios.

▶ Atoms can be subdivided into smaller particles.

Key Terms

law of conservation of mass
law of definite proportions
law of multiple proportions

When you crush a lump of sugar, you can see that it is made up of many smaller particles of sugar. You may grind these particles into a very fine powder, but each tiny piece is still sugar. Now suppose you dissolve the sugar in water. The tiny particles seem to disappear completely. Even if you look at the sugar-water solution through a powerful microscope, you cannot see any sugar particles. Yet if you were to taste the solution, you'd know that the sugar is still there. Observations like these led early philosophers to ponder the fundamental nature of matter. Is it continuous and infinitely divisible, or is it divisible only until a basic, invisible particle that cannot be divided further is reached?

The particle theory of matter was supported as early as 400 BCE by certain Greek thinkers, such as Democritus. He called nature's basic particle an *atom*, based on the Greek word meaning "indivisible." Aristotle was part of the generation that succeeded Democritus. His ideas had a lasting impact on Western civilization, and he did not believe in atoms. He thought that all matter was continuous, and his opinion was accepted for nearly 2000 years. Neither the view of Aristotle nor that of Democritus was supported by experimental evidence, so each remained under speculation until the eighteenth century. Then scientists began to gather evidence favoring the atomic theory of matter.

▶ **MAIN IDEA**

Three basic laws describe how matter behaves in chemical reactions.

Virtually all chemists in the late 1700s accepted the modern definition of an element as a substance that cannot be further broken down by ordinary chemical means. They also assumed that these elements combined to form compounds that have different physical and chemical properties than those of the elements that make them. What troubled them, however, was the understanding of just exactly how the different substances could combine with one another to form new ones, what we know as *chemical reactions*. Most historians date the foundation of modern chemistry to this time when scientists finally began to ascribe rules to how matter interacts.

FIGURE 1.1

Table Salt Crystals Each of the salt crystals shown here contains exactly 39.34% sodium and 60.66% chlorine by mass.

In the 1790s, the study of matter was revolutionized by a new emphasis on the quantitative analysis of chemical reactions. Aided by improved balances, investigators began to accurately measure the masses of the elements and compounds they were studying. This led to the discovery of several basic laws. One of these laws was the **law of conservation of mass,** which states that mass is neither created nor destroyed during ordinary chemical reactions or physical changes. This discovery was soon followed by the assertion that, regardless of where or how a pure chemical compound is prepared, it is composed of a fixed proportion of elements. For example, sodium chloride, also known as ordinary table salt, as shown in **Figure 1.1**, *always* consists of 39.34% by mass of the element sodium, Na, and 60.66% by mass of the element chlorine, Cl. The fact that a chemical compound contains the same elements in exactly the same proportions by mass regardless of the size of the sample or source of the compound is known as the **law of definite proportions.**

It was also known that two elements sometimes combine to form more than one compound. For example, the elements carbon and oxygen form two compounds, carbon dioxide and carbon monoxide. Consider samples of each of these compounds, each containing 1.00 g of carbon. In carbon dioxide, 2.66 g of oxygen combine with 1.00 g of carbon. In carbon monoxide, 1.33 g of oxygen combine with 1.00 g of carbon. The ratio of the masses of oxygen in these two compounds is 2.66 to 1.33, or 2 to 1. This illustrates the **law of multiple proportions:** If two or more different compounds are composed of the same two elements, then the ratio of the masses of the second element combined with a certain mass of the first element is always a ratio of small whole numbers.

▶ **MAIN IDEA**

Compounds contain atoms in whole-number ratios.

In 1808, an English schoolteacher named John Dalton proposed an explanation that encompassed all these laws. He reasoned that elements were composed of atoms and that only whole numbers of atoms can combine to form compounds. His theory can be summed up by the following statements.

1. All matter is composed of extremely small particles called atoms.

2. Atoms of an element are identical in size, mass, and other properties; atoms of different elements differ in size, mass, and other properties.

3. Atoms cannot be subdivided, created, or destroyed.

4. Atoms of different elements combine in simple whole-number ratios to form chemical compounds.

5. In chemical reactions, atoms are combined, separated, or rearranged.

Dalton's atomic theory explains the law of conservation of mass through the concept that chemical reactions involve merely the combination, separation, or rearrangement of atoms and that during reactions atoms are not subdivided, created, or destroyed. **Figure 1.2,** on the next page, illustrates this idea for the formation of carbon monoxide from carbon and oxygen.

FIGURE 1.2

Atoms and the Law of Conservation of Mass

Carbon, C
Mass x

Oxygen, O
Mass y

Carbon monoxide, CO
Mass x + Mass y

(a) An atom of carbon, C, and an atom of oxygen, O, can combine chemically to form a molecule of carbon monoxide, CO. The mass of the CO molecule is equal to the mass of the C atom plus the mass of the O atom.

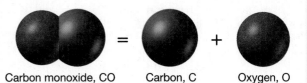

Carbon monoxide, CO
Mass x + Mass y

Carbon, C
Mass x

Oxygen, O
Mass y

(b) The reverse holds true in a reaction in which a CO molecule is broken down into its elements.

FIGURE 1.3

Law of Multiple Proportions

Carbon, C   Oxygen, O   Carbon monoxide, CO

(a) CO molecules are always composed of one C atom and one O atom.

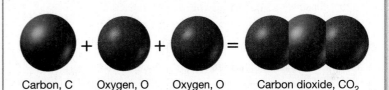

Carbon, C   Oxygen, O   Oxygen, O   Carbon dioxide, CO_2

(b) CO_2 molecules are always composed of one C atom and two O atoms. Note that a molecule of carbon dioxide contains twice as many oxygen atoms as does a molecule of carbon monoxide.

Figure 1.3 illustrates how Dalton's atomic theory explained the other laws. The law of definite proportions results from the fact that a given chemical compound always contains the same combinations of atoms. As for the law of multiple proportions, in the case of the carbon oxides, the 2-to-1 ratio of oxygen masses results because carbon dioxide always contains twice as many atoms of oxygen (per atom of carbon) as does carbon monoxide.

▶ MAIN IDEA

Atoms can be subdivided into smaller particles.

By relating atoms to the measurable property of mass, Dalton turned Democritus's *idea* into a *scientific theory* that could be tested by experiment. But not all aspects of Dalton's atomic theory have proven to be correct. For example, today we know that atoms are divisible into even smaller particles (although the law of conservation of mass still holds true for chemical reactions). And as you will see in Section 3, we know that a given element can have atoms with different masses. Atomic theory has not been discarded—only modified! The important concepts that (1) all matter is composed of atoms and that (2) atoms of any one element differ in properties from atoms of another element remain unchanged.

NANOTECHNOLOGIST

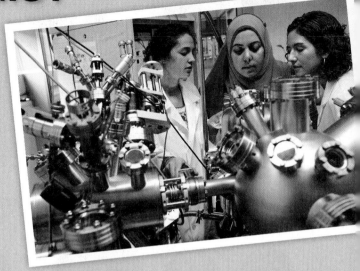

Nanotechnologists at work

To appreciate the world of nanotechnology, we must think small—very, *very* small. The basic endeavor in this field is the manipulation of matter at the atomic scale. The nanotechnologist builds molecules and molecular scale structures atom by atom.

The term *nanotechnology* is derived from the metric unit of length called a nanometer, nm. A nanometer is one billionth of a meter, that is, $1 \text{ nm} = 1 \times 10^{-9}$ m. It is hard to picture things at the nanometer scale. The figure helps you compare these very small things with visible objects. For example, a large molecule measures about 1 nm, and the smallest visible objects are about 100,000 nm in diameter.

In 1959, Nobel laureate Richard Feynman discussed the possibility of manipulating individual atoms to form molecules. His talk was titled "Plenty of Room at the Bottom." Thirty years after Feynman made his suggestion, someone succeeded at synthesizing molecules from individual atoms. The essential tool needed to make this breakthrough was the scanning tunneling microscope (STM), which was developed in 1981. Here's how it works: A voltage difference is created between the sample being examined and a conducting tip that has been sharpened to a single atom. This causes electrons to "tunnel" from the tip to the sample. By varying the voltage and the position of the tip, scientists can create an image that reveals individual atoms. Atoms may then be manipulated to form new substances.

One of the first successes in nanotechnology was the discovery and then construction of "buckyballs," also called fullerene. Fullerene is a form of carbon with the formula C_{60} and a symmetrical, nearly spherical shape. It is named after Buckminster Fuller, an architect who designed buildings with a similar shape.

Cryo-electron microscopy is a recent advance in electron microscopy that has been useful in studying very small organic structures such as viruses and organelles of cells. This instrument operates at very low temperatures and uses lower energy radiation, which is less likely to damage the specimens.

Part of a nanotechnologist's job is to operate and maintain sophisticated instruments such as those described above. It is also necessary to have good computer skills, which are needed to analyze the results of experiments. Nanotechnologists are employed by companies and research groups whose goals vary widely. In addition to working in the fields of biotechnology and medicine, these specialists work in energy production and storage, electronics, and food science.

Nanotechnology has a number of applications in medicine. Nanoparticles have been used to deliver drugs directly to the cells that need them. This reduces the side effects caused by the reaction to drugs by cells that don't need them. Nanorobotics may lead to other medical applications in the future. It is believed that nano-scale, self-sufficient robots could be introduced into the body that would be capable of repairing damaged or diseased tissue. Because of their exceptional strength, nanotubes have a wide variety of uses. Nanotechnologists are part of the effort to create artificial photosynthesis, which would provide a renewable, nonpolluting energy source. Perhaps the only thing all nanotechnologists have in common is that they work with devices and materials that are very, *very* small.

Questions

1. About how many times greater is the thickness of hair than the diameter of a molecule?

2. What part of an atom is detected by an STM?

QuickLAB — CONSTRUCTING A MODEL

QUESTION

How can you construct a model of an unknown object by (1) making inferences about an object that is in a closed container and (2) touching the object without seeing it?

PROCEDURE

Record all of your results in a data table.

1. Your teacher will provide you with a can that is covered by a sock sealed with tape. Without unsealing the container, try to determine the number of objects inside the can as well as the mass, shape, size, composition, and texture of each object. To do this, you may carefully tilt or shake the can. Record your observations in a data table.

2. Remove the tape from the top of the sock. Do *not* look inside the can. Put one hand through the opening, and make the same observations as in step 1 by handling the objects. To make more-accurate estimations, practice estimating the sizes

and masses of some known objects outside the can. Then compare your estimates of these objects with actual measurements using a metric ruler and a balance.

DISCUSSION

1. Scientists often use more than one method to gather data. How was this illustrated in the investigation?

2. Of the observations you made, which were qualitative, and which were quantitative?

3. Using the data you gathered, draw a model of the unknown object(s) and write a brief summary of your conclusions.

MATERIALS

- can covered by a sock sealed with tape
- one or more objects that fit in the container
- metric ruler
- balance

SAFETY

  Wear safety goggles and an apron.

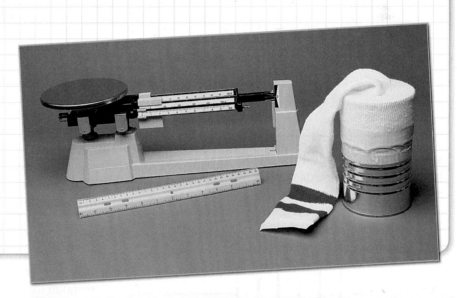

✓ SECTION 1 FORMATIVE ASSESSMENT

◉ Reviewing Main Ideas

1. List the five main points of Dalton's atomic theory.

2. What chemical laws can be explained by Dalton's theory?

✔ Critical Thinking

3. **ANALYZING INFORMATION** Three compounds containing potassium and oxygen are compared. Analysis shows that for each 1.00 g of O, the compounds have 1.22 g, 2.44 g, and 4.89 g of K, respectively. Show how these data support the law of multiple proportions.

SECTION 2

Main Ideas

▶ Atoms contain positive and negative particles.

▶ Atoms have small, dense, positively charged nuclei.

▶ A nucleus contains protons and neutrons.

▶ The radii of atoms are expressed in picometers.

The Structure of the Atom

Key Terms

atom
nuclear force

Although John Dalton thought atoms were indivisible, investigators in the late 1800s proved otherwise. As scientific advances allowed a deeper exploration of matter, it became clear that atoms are actually composed of smaller particles and that the number and arrangement of these particles within an atom determine that atom's chemical properties. **Therefore, today we define an atom as the smallest particle of an element that retains the chemical properties of that element.**

All atoms consist of two regions. The *nucleus* is a very small region located at the center of an atom. In every atom, the nucleus is made up of at least one positively charged particle called a *proton* and usually one or more neutral particles called *neutrons*. Surrounding the nucleus is a region occupied by negatively charged particles called *electrons*. This region is very large compared with the size of the nucleus. Protons, neutrons, and electrons are referred to as *subatomic particles*.

▶ MAIN IDEA

Atoms contain positive and negative particles.

The first discovery of a subatomic particle came in the late 1800s. At that time, many experiments were performed in which electric current was passed through various gases at low pressures. (Gases at atmospheric pressure don't conduct electricity well.) These experiments were carried out in glass tubes, like the one shown in **Figure 2.1**, that had been hooked up to a vacuum pump. Such tubes are known as *cathode-ray tubes*.

Cathode Rays and Electrons

Investigators noticed that when current was passed through the tube, the surface of the tube directly opposite the cathode glowed. They hypothesized that the glow was caused by a stream of particles, which they called a cathode ray. The ray traveled from the cathode to the anode when current was passed through the tube. Experiments devised to test this hypothesis revealed the following observations:

1. Cathode rays were deflected by a magnetic field in the same manner as a wire carrying electric current, which was known to have a negative charge (see **Figure 2.2** on the next page).

2. The rays were deflected away from a negatively charged object.

FIGURE 2.1

Structure of a Cathode-Ray Tube Particles pass through the tube from the *cathode*, the metal disk connected to the negative terminal of the voltage source, to the *anode*, the metal disk connected to the positive terminal.

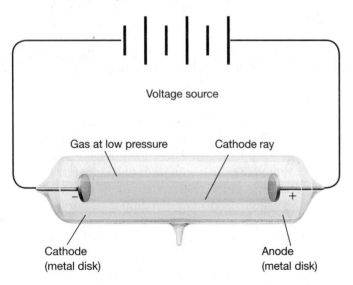

Voltage source

Gas at low pressure   Cathode ray

Cathode
(metal disk)

Anode
(metal disk)

These observations led to the hypothesis that the particles that compose cathode rays are negatively charged. This hypothesis was strongly supported by a series of experiments carried out in 1897 by the English physicist Joseph John Thomson. In one investigation, he was able to measure the ratio of the charge of cathode-ray particles to their mass. He found that this ratio was always the same, regardless of the metal used to make the cathode or the nature of the gas inside the cathode-ray tube. Thomson concluded that all cathode rays must be composed of identical negatively charged particles, which were named electrons.

FIGURE 2.2

Finding Negative Particles Holding a magnet near a cathode-ray tube (attached to a vacuum pump) causes negatively charged particles in the beam to be deflected.

Cathode   Anode

Charge and Mass of the Electron

Cathode rays have identical properties regardless of the element used to produce them. Therefore, it was concluded that electrons are present in atoms of all elements. Thus, cathode-ray experiments provided evidence that atoms are divisible and that one of the atom's basic constituents is the negatively charged electron. Thomson's experiment also revealed that the electron has a very large charge-to-mass ratio. In 1909, experiments conducted by the American physicist Robert A. Millikan measured the charge of the electron. Scientists used this information and the charge-to-mass ratio of the electron to determine that the mass of the electron is about one two-thousandth the mass of the simplest type of hydrogen atom, which is the smallest atom known. More-accurate experiments conducted since then indicate that the electron has a mass of 9.109×10^{-31} kg, or 1/1837 the mass of the simplest type of hydrogen atom.

Based on what was learned about electrons, two other inferences were made about atomic structure.

1. Because atoms are electrically neutral, they must contain a positive charge to balance the negative electrons.

2. Because electrons have so much less mass than atoms, atoms must contain other particles that account for most of their mass.

Thomson proposed a model for the atom that is called the *plum pudding model* (after the English dessert). He believed that the negative electrons were spread evenly throughout the positive charge of the rest of the atom. This arrangement is like seeds in a watermelon: the seeds are spread throughout the fruit but do not contribute much to the overall mass. However, shortly thereafter, new experiments disproved this model. Still, the plum pudding model was an important step forward in our modern understanding of the atom, as it represents the first time scientists tried to incorporate the then-revolutionary idea that atoms were not, strictly speaking, indivisible.

✔ **CHECK FOR UNDERSTANDING**

Analyze Why is it necessary to use experiments such as those of J. J. Thomson and Robert A. Millikan to infer information about electrons?

Atoms have small, dense, positively charged nuclei.

More detail of the atom's structure was provided in 1911 by New Zealander Ernest Rutherford and his associates Hans Geiger and Ernest Marsden. The scientists bombarded a thin piece of gold foil with fast-moving *alpha particles,* which are positively charged particles with about four times the mass of a hydrogen atom. Geiger and Marsden assumed that mass and charge were uniformly distributed throughout the atoms of the gold foil, as one would expect from the plum pudding model. They expected the alpha particles to pass through with only a slight deflection, and for the vast majority of the particles, this was the case. However, when the scientists checked for the possibility of wide-angle deflections, they were shocked to find that roughly 1 in 8000 of the alpha particles had actually been deflected back toward the source (see **Figure 2.3**). As Rutherford later exclaimed, it was "as if you had fired a 15-inch [artillery] shell at a piece of tissue paper and it came back and hit you."

After thinking about the startling result for a few months, Rutherford finally came up with an explanation. He reasoned that the deflected alpha particles must have experienced some powerful force within the atom. And he figured that the source of this force must occupy a very small amount of space because so few of the total number of alpha particles had been affected by it. He concluded that the force must be caused by a very densely packed bundle of matter with a positive electric charge. Rutherford called this positive bundle of matter the nucleus (see **Figure 2.4** on the next page).

Rutherford had discovered that the volume of a nucleus was very small compared with the total volume of an atom. In fact, if the nucleus were the size of a marble, then the size of the atom would be about the size of a football field. But where were the electrons? This question was not answered until Rutherford's student, Niels Bohr, proposed a model in which electrons surrounded the positively charged nucleus as the planets surround the sun. Bohr's model is discussed in a later chapter.

FIGURE 2.3

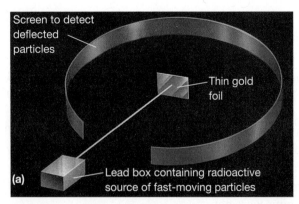

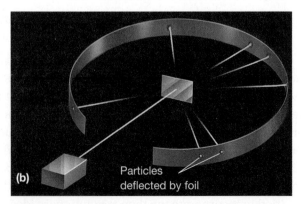

a) Geiger and Marsden bombarded a thin piece of gold foil with a narrow beam of alpha particles.

b) Some of the particles were deflected by the gold foil back toward their source.

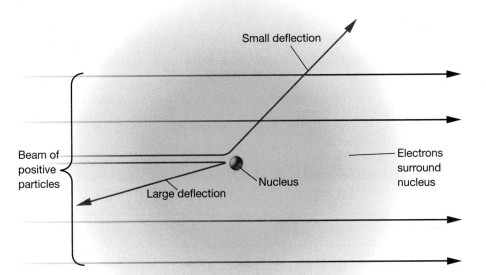

Small deflection

Beam of positive particles

Large deflection

Nucleus

Electrons surround nucleus

FIGURE 2.4

Finding the Nucleus Rutherford reasoned that each atom in the gold foil contained a small, dense, positively charged nucleus surrounded by electrons. A small number of the alpha particles directed toward the foil were deflected by the tiny nucleus (red arrows). Most of the particles passed through undisturbed (black arrows).

▶ **MAIN IDEA**

A nucleus contains protons and neutrons.

Except for the nucleus of the simplest type of hydrogen atom, all atomic nuclei are made of two kinds of particles, protons and neutrons. A proton has a positive charge equal in magnitude to the negative charge of an electron. Atoms are electrically neutral because they contain equal numbers of protons and electrons. A neutron is electrically neutral.

The simplest hydrogen atom consists of a single-proton nucleus with a single electron moving about it. A proton has a mass of 1.673×10^{-27} kg, which is 1836 times greater than the mass of an electron and 1836/1837, or virtually all, of the mass of the simplest hydrogen atom. All atoms besides the simplest hydrogen atom also have neutrons. The mass of a neutron is 1.675×10^{-27} kg—slightly larger than that of a proton.

The nuclei of atoms of different elements differ in their number of protons and, therefore, in the amount of positive charge they possess. Thus, the number of protons determines that atom's identity. Physicists have identified other subatomic particles, but particles other than electrons, protons, and neutrons have little effect on the chemical properties of matter. **Figure 2.5** on the next page summarizes the properties of electrons, protons, and neutrons.

Forces in the Nucleus

Generally, particles that have the same electric charge repel one another. Therefore, we would expect a nucleus with more than one proton to be unstable. However, when two protons are extremely close to each other, there is a strong attraction between them. In fact, as many as 83 protons can exist close together to help form a stable nucleus. A similar attraction exists when neutrons are very close to each other or when protons and neutrons are very close together. **These short-range proton-neutron, proton-proton, and neutron-neutron forces hold the nuclear particles together and are referred to as nuclear forces.**

FIGURE 2.5

PROPERTIES OF SUBATOMIC PARTICLES

Particle	Symbols	Relative electric charge	Mass number	Relative mass (u*)	Actual mass (kg)
Electron	e^-, $_{-1}^{0}e$	−1	0	0.000 5486	9.109×10^{-31}
Proton	p^+, $_1^1H$	+1	1	1.007 276	1.673×10^{-27}
Neutron	$n°$, $_0^1n$	0	1	1.008 665	1.675×10^{-27}

*1 u (unified atomic mass unit) = $1.660\ 5402 \times 10^{-27}$ kg

▶ **MAIN IDEA**

The radii of atoms are expressed in picometers.

It is convenient to think of the region occupied by the electrons as an electron cloud—a cloud of negative charge. The radius of an atom is the distance from the center of the nucleus to the outer portion of this electron cloud. Because atomic radii are so small, they are expressed using a unit that is more convenient for the sizes of atoms. This unit is the picometer. The abbreviation for the picometer is *pm* (1 pm = 10^{-12} m = 10^{-10} cm). To get an idea of how small a picometer is, consider that 1 cm is the same fractional part of 10^3 km (about 600 mi) as 100 pm is of 1 cm. Atomic radii range from about 40 to 270 pm. By contrast, the nuclei of atoms have much smaller radii, about 0.001 pm. Nuclei also have incredibly high densities, about 2×10^8 metric tons/cm^3.

✓) SECTION 2 FORMATIVE ASSESSMENT

▶ **Reviewing Main Ideas**

1. Define each of the following:
   a. atom
   b. electron
   c. nucleus
   d. proton
   e. neutron

2. Describe one conclusion made by each of the following scientists that led to the development of the current atomic theory:
   a. Thomson
   b. Millikan
   c. Rutherford

3. Compare the three subatomic particles in terms of location in the atom, mass, and relative charge.

4. Why are cathode-ray tubes, like the one in **Figure 2.1**, connected to a vacuum pump?

 Critical Thinking

5. **EVALUATING IDEAS** Nuclear forces are said to hold protons and neutrons together. What is it about the composition of the nucleus that requires the concept of nuclear forces?

Counting Atoms

Key Terms

atomic number

isotope

mass number

nuclide

unified atomic mass unit

average atomic mass

mole

Avogadro's number

molar mass

SECTION 3

Main Ideas

All atoms of an element must have the same number of protons but not neutrons.

Atomic mass is a relative measure.

Average atomic mass is a weighted value.

A relative mass scale makes counting atoms possible.

Consider neon, Ne, the gas used in many illuminated signs. Neon is a minor component of the atmosphere. In fact, dry air contains only about 0.002% neon. And yet there are about 5×10^{17} atoms of neon present in each breath you inhale. In most experiments, atoms are much too small to be measured individually. Chemists can analyze atoms quantitatively, however, by knowing fundamental properties of the atoms of each element. In this section, you will be introduced to some of the basic properties of atoms. You will then discover how to use this information to count the number of atoms of an element in a sample with a known mass. You will also become familiar with the *mole*, a special unit used by chemists to express numbers of particles, such as atoms and molecules.

▶ MAIN IDEA

All atoms of an element must have the same number of protons but not neutrons.

All atoms contain the same particles. Yet all atoms are not the same. Atoms of different elements have different numbers of protons. Atoms of the same element all have the same number of protons. **The atomic number (Z) of an element is the number of protons in each atom of that element.**

Look at a periodic table. In most, an element's atomic number is indicated above its symbol, and the elements are placed in order of increasing atomic number. Hydrogen, H, is at the upper left of the table and has an atomic number of 1. All atoms of the element hydrogen have one proton. Next in order is helium, He, which has two protons. Lithium, Li, has three protons (see **Figure 3.1**); beryllium, Be, has four protons; and so on. The atomic number identifies an element. If the number of protons in the nucleus of an atom were to change, that atom would become a different element.

Isotopes

But just because all hydrogen atoms, for example, have only a single proton, it doesn't mean they all have the same number of neutrons, or even any neutrons at all. In fact, three types of hydrogen atoms are known. The most common type of hydrogen is sometimes called *protium*. It accounts for 99.9885% of the hydrogen atoms found on Earth, and its nucleus consists of only a single proton. Another type of hydrogen, *deuterium*, accounts for 0.0115% of Earth's hydrogen atoms; its nucleus has one proton and one neutron. The third form of hydrogen, *tritium*, has one proton and two neutrons in its nucleus. Tritium is radioactive, so it is not very common at all on Earth. However, it is still hydrogen.

FIGURE 3.1

Atomic Numbers The atomic number in this periodic table entry indicates that an atom of lithium has three protons in its nucleus.

3
Li
Lithium
6.94
[He]2s^1

FIGURE 3.2

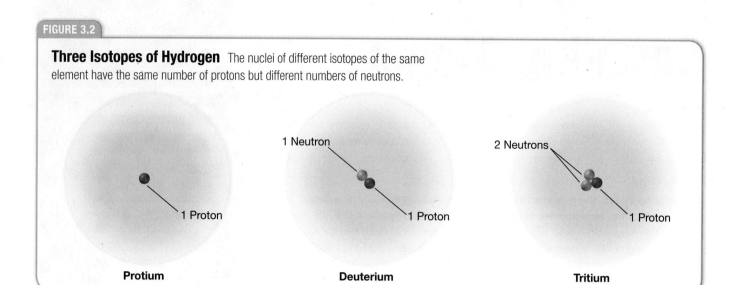

Three Isotopes of Hydrogen The nuclei of different isotopes of the same element have the same number of protons but different numbers of neutrons.

Protium, deuterium, and tritium are isotopes of hydrogen. **Isotopes are atoms of the same element that have different masses.** The isotopes of a particular element all have the same number of protons and electrons but different numbers of neutrons. In all three isotopes of hydrogen, shown in **Figure 3.2,** the positive charge of the single proton is balanced by the negative charge of the electron. Most of the elements consist of mixtures of isotopes. Tin has 10 stable isotopes, for example—the most of any element.

The atoms in any sample of an element you may find most likely will be a mixture of several isotopes in various proportions. The detection of these isotopes and determination of their relative proportions have become extremely precise—so precise that scientists can determine where some elements come from by measuring the percentages of different isotopes in a sample.

Mass Number

Identifying an isotope requires knowing both the name or atomic number of the element and the mass of the isotope. **The mass number is the total number of protons and neutrons that make up the nucleus of an isotope.** The three isotopes of hydrogen described earlier have mass numbers 1, 2, and 3, as shown in **Figure 3.3.**

FIGURE 3.3

MASS NUMBERS OF HYDROGEN ISOTOPES			
	Atomic number (number of protons)	Number of neutrons	Mass number (protons + neutrons)
Protium	1	0	$1 + 0 = 1$
Deuterium	1	1	$1 + 1 = 2$
Tritium	1	2	$1 + 2 = 3$

Identifying Isotopes

There are two methods for specifying isotopes. In the first, the mass number appears with a hyphen after the name of the element. Tritium, for example, is written as hydrogen-3. We call this method *hyphen notation.* The uranium isotope with mass number 235, commonly used as fuel for nuclear power plants, is known as uranium-235. The second method shows the composition of a nucleus using the isotope's *nuclear symbol.* So uranium-235 is shown as $^{235}_{92}U$. The superscript indicates the mass number (protons + neutrons). The subscript indicates the atomic number (number of protons). The number of neutrons is found by subtracting the atomic number from the mass number.

$$\text{mass number} - \text{atomic number} = \text{number of neutrons}$$
$$235 \text{ (protons + neutrons)} - 92 \text{ protons} = 143 \text{ neutrons}$$

Figure 3.4 gives the names, symbols, and compositions of the isotopes of hydrogen and helium. **Nuclide** is a general term for a specific isotope of an element.

FIGURE 3.4

ISOTOPES OF HYDROGEN AND HELIUM

Isotope	Nuclear symbol	Number of protons	Number of electrons	Number of neutrons
Hydrogen-1 (protium)	^1_1H	1	1	0
Hydrogen-2 (deuterium)	^2_1H	1	1	1
Hydrogen-3 (tritium)	^3_1H	1	1	2
Helium-3	^3_2He	2	2	1
Helium-4	^4_2He	2	2	2

Subatomic Particles

Sample Problem A How many protons, electrons, and neutrons are there in an atom of iron-57?

❶ ANALYZE

Given: name and mass number of iron-57

Unknown: numbers of protons, electrons, and neutrons

❷ PLAN

atomic number = number of protons = number of electrons
mass number = number of neutrons + number of protons

Continued

3 **SOLVE**

The mass number of iron-57 is 57. Consulting the periodic table reveals that iron's atomic number is 26. Therefore, we know that

atomic number = number of protons = number of electrons =
26 protons and 26 electrons

number of neutrons = mass number − atomic number =
57 − 26 = 31 neutrons

An atom of iron-57 is made up of 26 electrons, 26 protons, and 31 neutrons.

4 **CHECK YOUR WORK**

The number of protons in a neutral atom equals the number of electrons. The sum of the protons and neutrons equals the given mass number (26 + 31 = 57).

Practice   Answers in Appendix E

1. How many protons, electrons, and neutrons make up an atom of bromine-80?
2. Write the nuclear symbol for chromium-50.
3. Write the hyphen notation for an isotope with 28 electrons and 32 neutrons.

▶ **MAIN IDEA**

Atomic mass is a relative measure.

Masses of atoms expressed in grams are very small. As we shall see, an atom of oxygen-16, for example, has a mass of 2.656×10^{-23} g. For most chemical calculations, it is more convenient to use *relative* atomic masses. As you learned when you studied scientific measurement, scientists use standards of measurement that are constant and the same everywhere. In order to set up a relative scale of atomic mass, one atom has been arbitrarily chosen as the standard and assigned a mass value. The masses of all other atoms are expressed in relation to this standard.

The standard used by scientists to compare units of atomic mass is the carbon-12 atom, which has been arbitrarily assigned a mass of exactly 12 unified atomic mass units, or 12 u. **One unified atomic mass unit, or 1 u, is exactly 1/12 the mass of a carbon-12 atom.** The atomic mass of any other atom is determined by comparing it with the mass of the carbon-12 atom. The hydrogen-1 atom has an atomic mass of *about* 1/12 that of the carbon-12 atom, or about 1 u. The precise value of the atomic mass of a hydrogen-1 atom is 1.007 825 u. An oxygen-16 atom has about 16/12 (or 4/3) the mass of a carbon-12 atom. Careful measurements show the atomic mass of oxygen-16 to be 15.994 915 u. The mass of a magnesium-24 atom is found to be slightly less than twice that of a carbon-12 atom. Its atomic mass is 23.985 042 u.

Some additional examples of the atomic masses of the naturally occurring isotopes of several elements are given in **Figure 3.5** on the next page. Isotopes of an element may occur naturally, or they may be made in the laboratory (*artificial isotopes*). *Although isotopes have different masses, they do not differ significantly in their chemical behavior.*

The masses of subatomic particles can also be expressed on the atomic mass scale (see **Figure 2.5**). The mass of the electron is 0.000 548 6 u, that of the proton is 1.007 276 u, and that of the neutron is 1.008 665 u. Note that the proton and neutron masses are close, but not equal, to 1 u. You have learned that the mass number is the total number of protons and neutrons that make up the nucleus of an atom. You can now see that the mass number and relative atomic mass of a given nuclide are quite close to each other. They are not identical, because the proton and neutron masses deviate slightly from 1 u and the atomic masses include electrons. Also, as you will read in a later chapter, a small amount of mass is changed to energy in the creation of a nucleus from its protons and neutrons.

Chemistry EXPLORERS

Discovery of Element 43

The discovery of element 43, technetium, is credited to Carlo Perrier and Emilio Segrè, who artificially produced it in 1937. However, scientists have found minute traces of technetium in Earth's crust that result from the fission of uranium. Astronomers have also discovered technetium in S-type stars.

▶ **MAIN IDEA**

Average atomic mass is a weighted value.

Most elements occur naturally as mixtures of isotopes, as indicated in **Figure 3.5** (see next page). Scientists determine the average mass of a sample of an element's isotopes by determining the percentages of each of the isotopes and then giving the proper weight to each value. **Average atomic mass** is the weighted average of the atomic masses of the naturally occurring isotopes of an element. Unlike atomic number, average atomic mass is a statistical calculation. Different samples of the same element can differ in their relative abundance of isotopes.

The following is an example of how to calculate a *weighted average*. Suppose you have a box containing two sizes of marbles. If 25% of the marbles have masses of 2.00 g each and 75% have masses of 3.00 g each, how is the weighted average calculated? You could count the number of each type of marble, calculate the total mass of the mixture, and divide by the total number of marbles. If you had 100 marbles, the calculations would be as follows:

$$25 \text{ marbles} \times 2.00 \text{ g} = 50 \text{ g}$$
$$75 \text{ marbles} \times 3.00 \text{ g} = 225 \text{ g}$$

Adding these masses gives the total mass of the marbles.

$$50 \text{ g} + 225 \text{ g} = 275 \text{ g}$$

Dividing the total mass by 100 gives an average marble mass of 2.75 g.

A simpler method is to multiply the mass of each marble by the decimal fraction representing its percentage in the mixture. Then add the products.

$$25\% = 0.25 \qquad 75\% = 0.75$$
$$(2.00 \text{ g} \times 0.25) + (3.00 \text{ g} \times 0.75) = 2.75 \text{ g}$$

FIGURE 3.5

ATOMIC MASSES AND ABUNDANCES OF SEVERAL NATURALLY OCCURRING ISOTOPES

Isotope	Mass number	Percentage natural abundance	Atomic mass (u)	Average atomic mass of element (u)
Hydrogen-1	1	99.9885	1.007 825	1.007 94
Hydrogen-2	2	0.0115	2.014 102	
Carbon-12	12	98.93	12 (by definition)	
Carbon-13	13	1.07	13.003 355	12.0107
Oxygen-16	16	99.757	15.994 915	15.9994
Oxygen-17	17	0.038	16.999 132	
Oxygen-18	18	0.205	17.999 160	
Copper-63	63	69.15	62.929 601	63.546
Copper-65	65	30.85	64.927 794	
Cesium-133	133	100	132.905 447	132.905
Uranium-234	234	0.0054	234.040 945	
Uranium-235	235	0.7204	235.043 922	238.029
Uranium-238	238	99.2742	238.050 784	

Calculating Average Atomic Mass

The average atomic mass of an element depends on both the mass and the relative abundance of each of the element's isotopes. For example, naturally occurring copper consists of 69.15% copper-63, which has an atomic mass of 62.929 601 u, and 30.85% copper-65, which has an atomic mass of 64.927 794 u. The average atomic mass of copper can be calculated by multiplying the atomic mass of each isotope by its relative abundance (expressed in decimal form) and adding the results.

$$0.6915 \times 62.929\ 601\ u + 0.3085 \times 64.927\ 794\ u = 63.55\ u$$

The calculated average atomic mass of naturally occurring copper is 63.55 u.

The average atomic mass is included for the elements listed in **Figure 3.5**. As illustrated in the table, most atomic masses are known to four or more significant figures. *In this book, an element's atomic mass is usually rounded to two decimal places before it is used in a calculation.*

▶ MAIN IDEA

A relative mass scale makes counting atoms possible.

The relative atomic mass scale makes it possible to know how many atoms of an element are present in a sample of the element with a measurable mass. Three very important concepts—the mole, Avogadro's number, and molar mass—provide the basis for relating masses in grams to numbers of atoms.

GO ONLINE

Animated Chemistry

HMHScience.com

Avogadro's Number

The Mole

The mole is the SI unit for amount of substance. **A mole (abbreviated mol) is the amount of a substance that contains as many particles as there are atoms in exactly 12 g of carbon-12.** The mole is a counting unit, just like a dozen is. We don't usually buy 12 or 24 ears of corn; we order one dozen or two dozen. Similarly, a chemist may want 1 mol of carbon, or 2 mol of iron, or 2.567 mol of calcium. In the sections that follow, you will see how the mole relates to masses of atoms and compounds.

Avogadro's Number

The number of particles in a mole has been experimentally determined in a number of ways. The best modern value is $6.022\ 141\ 79 \times 10^{23}$. This means that exactly 12 g of carbon-12 contains $6.022\ 141\ 79 \times 10^{23}$ carbon-12 atoms.

The number of particles in a mole is known as Avogadro's number, named for the nineteenth-century Italian scientist Amedeo Avogadro, whose ideas were crucial in explaining the relationship between mass and numbers of atoms. **Avogadro's number—$6.022\ 141\ 79 \times 10^{23}$—is the number of particles in exactly one mole of a pure substance.** For most purposes, Avogadro's number is rounded to 6.022×10^{23}.

To get a sense of how large Avogadro's number is, consider the following: If every person living on Earth (about 7.0 billion people) worked to count the atoms in one mole of an element, and if each person counted continuously at a rate of one atom per second, it would take about 3 million years for all the atoms to be counted.

Molar Mass

An alternative definition of *mole* is the amount of a substance that contains Avogadro's number of particles. Can you calculate the approximate mass of one mole of helium atoms? You know that a mole of carbon-12 atoms has a mass of exactly 12 g and that a carbon-12 atom has an atomic mass of 12 u. The atomic mass of a helium atom is 4.00 u, which is about one-third the mass of a carbon-12 atom. It follows that a mole of helium atoms will have about one-third the mass of a mole of carbon-12 atoms. Thus, one mole of helium has a mass of about 4.00 g.

The mass of one mole of a pure substance is called the molar mass of that substance. Molar mass is usually written in units of g/mol. The molar mass of an element is numerically equal to the atomic mass of the element in unified atomic mass units (which can be found in the periodic table). For example, the molar mass of lithium, Li, is 6.94 g/mol, while the molar mass of mercury, Hg, is 200.59 g/mol (rounding each value to two decimal places). The molar mass of an element contains one mole of atoms. For example, 4.00 g of helium, 6.94 g of lithium, and 200.59 g of mercury all contain a mole of atoms. **Figure 3.6** shows one-mole masses of three common elements.

FIGURE 3.6

Molar Mass Shown is approximately one mole of each of three elements.

(a) carbon (graphite)

(b) iron (nails)

(c) copper (wire)

FIGURE 3.7

Relating Mass to the Number of Atoms
The diagram shows the relationship between mass in grams, amount in moles, and number of atoms of an element in a sample.

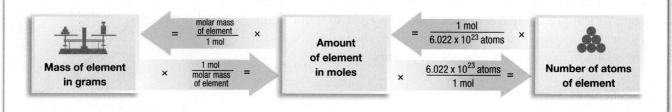

Gram/Mole Conversions

Chemists use molar mass as a conversion factor in chemical calculations. For example, the molar mass of helium is 4.00 g He/mol He. To find how many grams of helium there are in two moles of helium, multiply by the molar mass.

$$2.00 \text{ mol He} \times \frac{4.00_g \text{ He}}{1 \text{ mol He}} = 8.00 \text{ g He}$$

Figure 3.7 shows how to use molar mass, moles, and Avogadro's number to relate mass in grams, amount in moles, and number of atoms of an element.

GO ONLINE

Learn It! Video
HMHScience.com

Gram/Mole Conversions

Sample Problem B What is the mass in grams of 3.50 mol of the element copper, Cu?

① ANALYZE

Given: 3.50 mol Cu

Unknown: mass of Cu in grams

② PLAN

amount of Cu in moles ⟶ mass of Cu in grams

According to **Figure 3.7**, the mass of an element in grams can be calculated by multiplying the amount of the element in moles by the element's molar mass.

$$\text{moles Cu} \times \frac{\text{grams Cu}}{\text{moles Cu}} = \text{grams Cu}$$

③ SOLVE

The molar mass of copper from the periodic table is rounded to 63.55 g/mol.

$$3.50 \text{ mol Cu} \times \frac{63.55 \text{ g Cu}}{1 \text{ mol Cu}} = 222 \text{ g Cu}$$

④ CHECK YOUR WORK

Because the amount of copper in moles was given to three significant figures, the answer was rounded to three significant figures. The size of the answer is reasonable because it is somewhat more than 3.5 times 60.

Continued

Gram/Mole Conversions (continued)

Practice   Answers in Appendix E

1. What is the mass in grams of 2.25 mol of the element iron, Fe?
2. What is the mass in grams of 0.375 mol of the element potassium, K?
3. What is the mass in grams of 0.0135 mol of the element sodium, Na?
4. What is the mass in grams of 16.3 mol of the element nickel, Ni?

Gram/Mole Conversions

GO ONLINE

Learn It! Video
HMHScience.com

Solve It! Cards
HMHScience.com

Sample Problem C A chemist produced 11.9 g of aluminum, Al. How many moles of aluminum were produced?

❶ ANALYZE

Given: 11.9 g Al

Unknown: amount of Al in moles

❷ PLAN

mass of Al in grams $\longrightarrow$ amount of Al in moles

As shown in **Figure 3.7,** amount in moles can be obtained by *dividing* mass in grams by molar mass, which is mathematically the same as *multiplying* mass in grams by the *reciprocal* of molar mass.

$$\text{grams Al} \times \frac{\text{moles Al}}{\text{grams Al}} = \text{moles Al}$$

❸ SOLVE

The molar mass of aluminum from the periodic table is rounded to 26.98 g/mol.

$$11.9 \text{ g Al} \times \frac{1 \text{ mol Al}}{26.98 \text{ g Al}} = 0.441 \text{ mol Al}$$

❹ CHECK YOUR WORK

The answer is correctly given to three significant figures. The answer is reasonable because 11.9 g is somewhat less than half of 26.98 g.

Practice   Answers in Appendix E

1. How many moles of calcium, Ca, are in 5.00 g of calcium?
2. How many moles of gold, Au, are in 3.60×10^{-5} g of gold?
3. How many moles of zinc, Zn, are in 0.535 g of zinc?

Avogadro's number can be used to find the number of atoms of an element from the amount in moles or to find the amount of an element in moles from the number of atoms. While these types of problems are less common in chemistry than converting between amount in moles and mass in grams, they are useful in demonstrating the meaning of Avogadro's number. Note that in these calculations, Avogadro's number is expressed in units of atoms per mole.

GO ONLINE

Solve It! Cards
HMHScience.com

Conversions with Avogadro's Number

Sample Problem D How many moles of silver, Ag, are in 3.01×10^{23} atoms of silver?

❶ ANALYZE

Given: 3.01×10^{23} atoms of Ag

Unknown: amount of Ag in moles

❷ PLAN

number of atoms of Ag $\longrightarrow$ amount of Ag in moles

From **Figure 3.7,** we know that number of atoms is converted to amount in moles by dividing by Avogadro's number. This is equivalent to multiplying numbers of atoms by the reciprocal of Avogadro's number.

$$\text{Ag atoms} \times \frac{\text{moles Ag}}{\text{Avogadro's number of Ag atoms}} = \text{moles Ag}$$

❸ SOLVE

$$3.01 \times 10^{23} \text{ Ag atoms} \times \frac{1 \text{ mol Ag}}{6.022 \times 10^{23} \text{ Ag atoms}} = 0.500 \text{ mol Ag}$$

❹ CHECK YOUR WORK

The answer is correct—units cancel correctly and the number of atoms is one-half of Avogadro's number.

Practice   Answers in Appendix E

1. How many moles of lead, Pb, are in 1.50×10^{12} atoms of lead?
2. How many moles of tin, Sn, are in 2500 atoms of tin?
3. How many atoms of aluminum, Al, are in 2.75 mol of aluminum?

Conversions with Avogadro's Number

Sample Problem E What is the mass in grams of 3.01×10^{21} atoms of cobalt, Co?

❶ ANALYZE

Given: 3.01×10^{21} atoms of Co

Unknown: mass of Co in grams

Continued

Conversions with Avogadro's Number (continued)

② PLAN

number of atoms of Co ⟶ amount of Co in moles ⟶ mass of Co in grams

As indicated in **Figure 3.7,** the given number of atoms must first be converted to amount in moles by dividing by Avogadro's number. Amount in moles is then multiplied by molar mass to yield mass in grams.

$$\text{Co atoms} \times \frac{\text{moles Co}}{\text{Avogadro's number of Co atoms}} \times \frac{\text{grams Co}}{\text{moles Co}} = \text{grams Co}$$

③ SOLVE

The molar mass of cobalt from the periodic table is rounded to 58.93 g/mol.

$$3.01 \times 10^{21} \text{ Co atoms} \times \frac{1 \text{ mol Co}}{6.022 \times 10^{23} \text{ Co atoms}} \times \frac{58.93 \text{ g Co}}{1 \text{ mol Co}} = 295 \times 10^{-2} \text{ g Co}$$

④ CHECK YOUR WORK

Units cancel correctly to give the answer in grams. The size of the answer is reasonable—10^{21} has been divided by about 10^{24} and divided by about 10^{2}.

Practice

1. What is the mass in grams of 7.5×10^{15} atoms of nickel, Ni?
2. How many atoms of cadmium, Cd, are in 3.00 g of cadmium?
3. What mass of gold, Au, contains the same number of atoms as 9.0 g of aluminum, Al?

✓ SECTION 3 FORMATIVE ASSESSMENT

▶ Reviewing Main Ideas

1. Explain each of the following:
   a. atomic number
   b. mass number
   c. relative atomic mass
   d. average atomic mass
   e. mole
   f. Avogadro's number
   g. molar mass
   h. isotope

2. Determine the number of protons, electrons, and neutrons in each of the following isotopes:
   a. sodium-23
   b. calcium-40
   c. $^{64}_{29}\text{Cu}$
   d. $^{108}_{47}\text{Ag}$

3. Write the nuclear symbol and hyphen notation for each of the following isotopes:
   a. mass number of 28 and atomic number of 14
   b. 26 protons and 30 neutrons

4. To two decimal places, what is the relative atomic mass and the molar mass of the element potassium, K?

5. Determine the mass in grams of the following:
   a. 2.00 mol N
   b. 3.01×10^{23} atoms Cl

6. Determine the amount in moles of the following:
   a. 12.15 g Mg
   b. 1.50×10^{23} atoms F

✓ Critical Thinking

7. **ANALYZING DATA** Beaker A contains 2.06 mol of copper, and Beaker B contains 222 grams of silver. Which beaker contains the larger mass? Which beaker has the larger number of atoms?

Most calculations in chemistry require that all measurements of the same quantity (mass, length, volume, temperature, and so on) be expressed in the same unit. To change the units of a quantity, you can multiply the quantity by a conversion factor. With SI units, such conversions are easy because units of the same quantity are related by powers of 10, 100, 1000, or 1 million. Suppose you want to convert a given amount in milliliters to liters. You can use the relationship 1 L = 1000 mL. From this relationship, you can derive the following conversion factors.

$$\frac{1000 \text{ mL}}{1 \text{ L}} \text{ and } \frac{1 \text{ L}}{1000 \text{ mL}}$$

The correct strategy is to multiply the given amount (in mL) by the conversion factor that allows milliliter units to cancel out and liter units to remain. Using the second conversion factor will give you the units you want.

These conversion factors are based on an exact definition (1000 mL = 1 L exactly), so significant figures do not apply to these factors. The number of significant figures in a converted measurement depends on the certainty of the measurement you start with.

Sample Problem

A sample of aluminum has a mass of 0.087 g. What is the sample's mass in milligrams?

Based on SI prefixes, you know that 1 g = 1000 mg. Therefore, the possible conversion factors are

$$\frac{1000 \text{ mg}}{1 \text{ g}} \text{ and } \frac{1 \text{ g}}{1000 \text{ mg}}$$

The first conversion factor cancels grams, leaving milligrams.

$$0.087 \text{ g} \times \frac{1000 \text{ mg}}{1 \text{ g}} = 87 \text{ mg}$$

Notice that the values 0.087 g and 87 mg each have two significant figures.

A sample of a mineral has 4.08×10^{-5} mol of vanadium per kilogram of mass. How many micromoles of vanadium per kilogram does the mineral contain?

The prefix *micro-* specifies $\frac{1}{1\,000\,000}$, or 1×10^{-6}, of the base unit. So, 1 µmol = 1×10^{-6} mol. The possible conversion factors are

$$\frac{1 \text{ µmol}}{1 \times 10^{-6} \text{ mol}} \text{ and } \frac{1 \times 10^{-6} \text{ mol}}{1 \text{ µmol}}$$

The first conversion factor will allow moles to cancel and micromoles to remain.

$$4.08 \times 10^{-5} \text{ mol} \times \frac{1 \text{ µmol}}{1 \times 10^{-6} \text{ mol}} = 40.8 \text{ µmol}$$

Notice that the values 4.08×10^{-5} mol and 40.8 µmol each have three significant figures.

Practice

1. Express each of the following measurements in the units indicated.
   a. 2250 mg in grams
   b. 59.3 kL in liters
2. Use scientific notation to express each of the following measurements in the units indicated.
   a. 0.000 072 g in micrograms
   b. 3.98×10^6 m in kilometers

CHAPTER 3 Summary

BIG IDEA Atoms are the smallest particles of elements. The atoms of one element differ from the atoms of another by the number of protons they contain.

SECTION 1 The Atom: From Philosophical Idea to Scientific Theory

KEY TERMS

- The idea of atoms has been around since the time of the ancient Greeks. In the nineteenth century, John Dalton proposed a scientific theory of atoms that can still be used to explain properties of most chemicals today.

- Matter and its mass cannot be created or destroyed in chemical reactions.

- The mass ratios of the elements that make up a given compound are always the same, regardless of how much of the compound there is or how it was formed.

- If two or more different compounds are composed of the same two elements, then the ratio of the masses of the second element combined with a certain mass of the first element can be expressed as a ratio of small whole numbers.

law of conservation of mass
law of definite proportions
law of multiple proportions

SECTION 2 The Structure of the Atom

KEY TERMS

- Cathode-ray tubes supplied evidence of the existence of electrons, which are negatively charged subatomic particles that have relatively little mass.

- Rutherford found evidence for the existence of the atomic nucleus by bombarding gold foil with a beam of positively charged particles.

- Atomic nuclei are composed of protons, which have an electric charge of +1, and (in all but one case) neutrons, which have no electric charge.

- Atomic nuclei have radii of about 0.001 pm (pm = picometers; 1 pm = 10^{-12} m), and atoms have radii of about 40–270 pm.

atom
nuclear forces

SECTION 3 Counting Atoms

KEY TERMS

- The atomic number of an element is equal to the number of protons of an atom of that element.

- The mass number is equal to the total number of protons and neutrons that make up the nucleus of an atom of that element.

- The unified atomic mass unit (u) is based on the carbon-12 atom and is a convenient unit for measuring the mass of atoms. It equals $1.660\ 540 \times 10^{-24}$ g.

- The average atomic mass of an element is found by calculating the weighted average of the atomic masses of the naturally occurring isotopes of the element.

- Avogadro's number is equal to approximately 6.022×10^{23}. A sample that contains a number of particles equal to Avogadro's number contains a mole of those particles.

atomic number
isotope
mass number
nuclide
unified atomic mass unit
average atomic mass
mole
Avogadro's number
molar mass

CHAPTER 3 **Review**

GO ONLINE
Interactive Review
HMHScience.com
Review Games
Concept Maps

SECTION 1
The Atom: From Philosophical Idea to Scientific Theory

 REVIEWING MAIN IDEAS

1. Explain each of the following in terms of Dalton's atomic theory:
   a. the law of conservation of mass
   b. the law of definite proportions
   c. the law of multiple proportions

2. According to the law of conservation of mass, if element A has an atomic mass of 2 mass units and element B has an atomic mass of 3 mass units, what mass would be expected for compound AB? for compound A_2B_3?

SECTION 2
The Structure of the Atom

 REVIEWING MAIN IDEAS

3. a. What is an atom?
   b. What two regions make up all atoms?

4. Describe at least four properties of electrons that were determined based on the experiments of Thomson and Millikan.

5. Summarize Rutherford's model of the atom, and explain how he developed this model based on the results of his famous gold-foil experiment.

6. What number uniquely identifies an element?

SECTION 3
Counting Atoms

 REVIEWING MAIN IDEAS

7. a. What are isotopes?
   b. How are the isotopes of a particular element alike?
   c. How are they different?

8. Copy and complete the following table concerning the three isotopes of silicon, Si. (Hint: See Sample Problem A.)

Isotope	Number of protons	Number of electrons	Number of neutrons
Si-28			
Si-29			
Si-30			

9. a. What is the atomic number of an element?
   b. What is the mass number of an isotope?
   c. In the nuclear symbol for deuterium, ^2_1H, identify the atomic number and the mass number.

10. What is a nuclide?

11. Use the periodic table and the information that follows to write the hyphen notation for each isotope described.
    a. atomic number = 2, mass number = 4
    b. atomic number = 8, mass number = 16
    c. atomic number = 19, mass number = 39

12. a. What nuclide is used as the standard in the relative scale for atomic masses?
    b. What is its assigned atomic mass?

13. What is the atomic mass of an atom if its mass is approximately equal to the following?
    a. $\frac{1}{3}$ that of carbon-12
    b. 4.5 times as much as carbon-12

14. a. What is the definition of a *mole*?
    b. What is the abbreviation for *mole*?
    c. How many particles are in one mole?
    d. What name is given to the number of particles in a mole?

15. a. What is the molar mass of an element?
    b. To two decimal places, write the molar masses of carbon, neon, iron, and uranium.

16. Suppose you have a sample of an element.
    a. How is the mass in grams of the element converted to amount in moles?
    b. How is the mass in grams of the element converted to number of atoms?

PRACTICE PROBLEMS

17. What is the mass in grams of each of the following? (Hint: See Sample Problems B and E.)
   a. 1.00 mol Li
   b. 1.00 mol Al
   c. 1.00 molar mass Ca
   d. 1.00 molar mass Fe
   e. 6.022×10^{23} atoms C
   f. 6.022×10^{23} atoms Ag

18. How many moles of atoms are there in each of the following? (Hint: See Sample Problems C and D.)
   a. 6.022×10^{23} atoms Ne
   b. 3.011×10^{23} atoms Mg
   c. 3.25×10^5 g Pb
   d. 4.50×10^{-12} g O

19. Three isotopes of argon occur in nature—$^{36}_{18}\text{Ar}$, $^{38}_{18}\text{Ar}$, and $^{40}_{18}\text{Ar}$. Calculate the average atomic mass of argon to two decimal places, given the following relative atomic masses and abundances of each of the isotopes: argon-36 (35.97 u; 0.337%), argon-38 (37.96 u; 0.063%), and argon-40 (39.96 u; 99.600%).

20. Naturally occurring boron is 80.20% boron-11 (atomic mass = 11.01 u) and 19.80% of some other isotopic form of boron. What must the atomic mass of this second isotope be in order to account for the 10.81 u average atomic mass of boron? (Write the answer to two decimal places.)

21. How many atoms are there in each of the following?
   a. 1.50 mol Na
   b. 6.755 mol Pb
   c. 7.02 g Si

22. What is the mass in grams of each of the following?
   a. 3.011×10^{23} atoms F
   b. 1.50×10^{23} atoms Mg
   c. 4.50×10^{12} atoms Cl
   d. 8.42×10^{18} atoms Br
   e. 25 atoms W
   f. 1 atom Au

23. Determine the number of atoms in each of the following:
   a. 5.40 g B
   b. 0.250 mol S
   c. 0.0384 mol K
   d. 0.025 50 g Pt
   e. 1.00×10^{-10} g Au

Mixed Review

▶ **REVIEWING MAIN IDEAS**

24. Determine the mass in grams of each of the following:
   a. 3.00 mol Al
   b. 2.56×10^{24} atoms Li
   c. 1.38 mol N
   d. 4.86×10^{24} atoms Au
   e. 6.50 mol Cu
   f. 2.57×10^8 mol S
   g. 1.05×10^{18} atoms Hg

25. Copy and complete the following table concerning the properties of subatomic particles.

Particle	Symbol	Mass number	Actual mass	Relative charge
Electron				
Proton				
Neutron				

26. a. How is a unified atomic mass unit (u) related to the mass of one carbon-12 atom?
   b. What is the relative atomic mass of an atom?

27. a. What is the nucleus of an atom?
   b. Who is credited with the discovery of the atomic nucleus?
   c. Identify the two kinds of particles that make up the nucleus.

28. How many moles of atoms are there in each of the following?
   a. 40.1 g Ca
   b. 11.5 g Na
   c. 5.87 g Ni
   d. 150 g S
   e. 2.65 g Fe
   f. 0.007 50 g Ag
   g. 2.25×10^{25} atoms Zn
   h. 50 atoms Ba

29. State the law of multiple proportions, and give an example of two compounds that illustrate the law.

30. What is the approximate atomic mass of an atom if its mass is
   a. 12 times that of carbon-12?
   b. $\frac{1}{2}$ that of carbon-12?

31. What is an electron?

CRITICAL THINKING

32. Organizing Ideas Using two chemical compounds as an example, describe the difference between the law of definite proportions and the law of multiple proportions.

33. Constructing Models As described in Section 2, the structure of the atom was determined from observations made in painstaking experimental research. Suppose a series of experiments revealed that when an electric current is passed through gas at low pressure, the surface of the cathode-ray tube opposite the anode glows. In addition, a paddle wheel placed in the tube rolls from the anode toward the cathode when the current is on.
  a. In which direction do particles pass through the gas?
  b. What charge do the particles possess?

34. Analyzing Data Osmium is the element with the greatest density, 22.58 g/cm^3. How does the density of osmium compare to the density of a typical nucleus of 2×10^8 metric tons/cm^3? (1 metric ton = 1000 kg)

USING THE HANDBOOK

35. Group 14 of the *Elements Handbook* (Appendix A) describes the reactions that produce CO and CO_2. Review this section to answer the following:
  a. When a fuel burns, what determines whether CO or CO_2 will be produced?
  b. What happens in the body if hemoglobin picks up CO?
  c. Why is CO poisoning most likely to occur in homes that are well sealed during cold winter months?

RESEARCH AND WRITING

36. Prepare a report on the series of experiments conducted by Sir James Chadwick that led to the discovery of the neutron. In your report, evaluate the impact of this research on scientific thought about the structure of the atom.

37. Write a report on the contributions of Amedeo Avogadro that led to the determination of the value of Avogadro's number.

38. Trace the development of the electron microscope, and cite some of its many uses.

39. The study of atomic structure and the nucleus produced a new field of medicine called *nuclear medicine*. Describe the use of radioactive tracers to detect and treat diseases.

ALTERNATIVE ASSESSMENT

40. Observe a cathode-ray tube in operation, and write a description of your observations.

41. Performance Assessment Using colored clay, build a model of the nucleus of each of carbon's three naturally occurring isotopes: carbon-12, carbon-13, and carbon-14. Specify the number of electrons that would surround each nucleus.

Standards-Based Assessment

Record your answers on a separate piece of paper.

MULTIPLE CHOICE

1 Which of the following states an important result of Rutherford's gold-foil experiment?

  A Atoms have mass.

  B Electrons have a negative charge.

  C Neutrons are uncharged particles.

  D The atom is mostly empty space.

2 Identify the true statement regarding the mole as it relates to methane, CH_4.

  A A mole of methane has a mass of 18.02 grams.

  B A mole of methane has 6.02×10^{23} atoms of carbon and $4(6.02 \times 10^{23})$ atoms of hydrogen.

  C A mole of methane has $5(6.02 \times 10^{23})$ molecules of methane.

  D A liter of methane gas has more moles of methane than a liter of liquid methane.

3 A 2.33 mole sample of a substance weighs about 137 g. What is the substance?

  A copper

  B cobalt

  C xenon

  D carbon

4 A student collected a total of 36.04 g of water from a reaction. What number of moles of water does this represent?

  A 0.05 mol

  B 1.00 mol

  C 1.50 mol

  D 2.00 mol

5 Which of these is correct regarding Thomson's cathode-ray observations?

  A The experiments helped Thomson discover the proton.

  B The experiments helped Thomson discover the nucleus.

  C Negative charge deflects positive charge.

  D Cathode rays had identical properties regardless of the element used to produce them.

6 Experiments by J. J. Thomson and others led to the discovery of protons, electrons, and neutrons. Which part of Dalton's atomic theory did these discoveries cause scientists to modify?

  A Atoms of an element are identical in size, mass, and other properties.

  B Atoms cannot be subdivided.

  C Atoms of different elements combine in simple whole-number ratios to form chemical compounds.

  D All matter is composed of extremely small particles called atoms.

7 Dalton supported his atomic theory with experimental evidence. What experiment would have supported the postulate that in chemical reactions, atoms are combined, separated, or rearranged?

  A Dalton observes the properties of pure water.

  B Dalton passes an electric current through chlorine gas at low pressure.

  C Dalton compares the masses of helium and hydrogen atoms.

  D Dalton observes combustion in a closed chamber, noting that the mass is the same before and after the reaction, although the products looked quite different.

GRIDDED RESPONSE

8 What is the mass in grams of 1.20×10^{23} atoms of phosphorus?

Test Tip

Choose the best possible answer for each question, even if you think there is another possible answer that is not given.

CHAPTER 4

Arrangement of Electrons in Atoms

BIG IDEA
An atom's nucleus is surrounded by electrons that have both a wave and a particle-like behavior.

 ONLINE Chemistry
HMHScience.com

ONLINE LABS
- Flame Tests
- S.T.E.M. Lab Balloon Orbitals

SECTION 1
The Development of a New Atomic Model

SECTION 2
The Quantum Model of the Atom

SECTION 3
Electron Configurations

GO ONLINE

 Why It Matters Video
HMHScience.com

Atoms

(c) ©Silvestre Machado/SuperStock; (b) DOE

The Development of a New Atomic Model

SECTION 1

Main Ideas

▶ Light has characteristics of both particles and waves.

▶ When certain frequencies of light strike a metal, electrons are emitted.

▶ Electrons exist only in very specific energy states for atoms of each element.

▶ Bohr's model of the hydrogen atom explained electron transition states.

Key Terms

electromagnetic radiation
electromagnetic spectrum
wavelength
frequency

photoelectric effect
quantum
photon
ground state

excited state
line-emission spectrum
continuous spectrum

The Rutherford model of the atom was an improvement over previous models, but it was incomplete. It did not explain how the atom's negatively charged electrons are distributed in the space surrounding its positively charged nucleus. After all, it was well known that oppositely charged particles attract each other. So what prevented the negative electrons from being drawn into the positive nucleus?

In the early twentieth century, a new atomic model evolved as a result of investigations into the absorption and emission of light by matter. The studies revealed a relationship between light and an atom's electrons. This new understanding led directly to a revolutionary view of the nature of energy, matter, and atomic structure.

▶ **MAIN IDEA**

Light has characteristics of both particles and waves.

Before 1900, scientists thought light behaved solely as a wave. This belief changed when it was later discovered that light also has particle-like characteristics. Still, many of light's properties can be described in terms of waves. A quick review of these wavelike properties will help you understand the basic theory of light as it existed at the beginning of the twentieth century.

The Wave Description of Light

Visible light is a kind of **electromagnetic radiation,** which is a form of energy that exhibits wavelike behavior as it travels through space. Other kinds of electromagnetic radiation include x-rays, ultraviolet and infrared light, microwaves, and radio waves. Together, all the forms of electromagnetic radiation form the **electromagnetic spectrum.** The electromagnetic spectrum is represented in **Figure 1.1** on the next page. All forms of electromagnetic radiation move at a constant speed of 3.00×10^8 meters per second (m/s) through a vacuum and at slightly slower speeds through matter. Because air is mostly empty space, the value of 3.00×10^8 m/s is also light's approximate speed through air.

The significant feature of wave motion is its repetitive nature, which can be characterized by the measurable properties of wavelength and frequency. **Wavelength (λ) is the distance between corresponding points on adjacent waves.** The unit for wavelength is a distance unit.

FIGURE 1.1

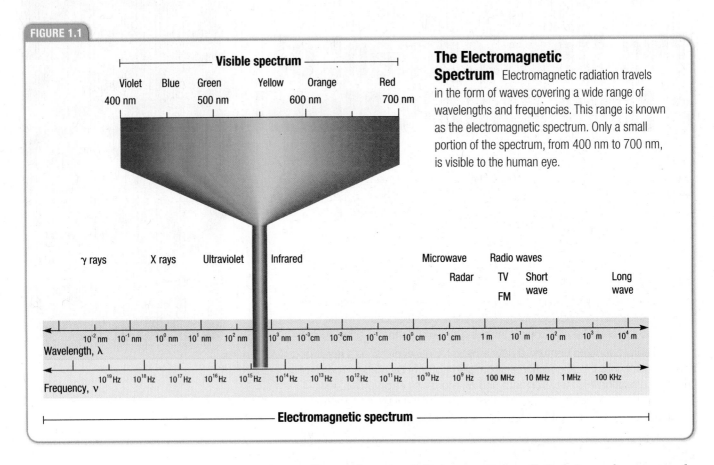

Visible spectrum

Violet Blue Green Yellow Orange Red
400 nm 500 nm 600 nm 700 nm

The Electromagnetic Spectrum Electromagnetic radiation travels in the form of waves covering a wide range of wavelengths and frequencies. This range is known as the electromagnetic spectrum. Only a small portion of the spectrum, from 400 nm to 700 nm, is visible to the human eye.

γ rays   X rays   Ultraviolet   Infrared   Microwave   Radio waves

Radar   TV   Short   Long
FM   wave   wave

Wavelength, λ
10^{-2} nm 10^{-1} nm 10^{0} nm 10^{1} nm 10^{2} nm 10^{3} nm 10^{-3} cm 10^{-2} cm 10^{-1} cm 10^{0} cm 10^{1} cm 1 m 10^{1} m 10^{2} m 10^{3} m 10^{4} m

Frequency, ν
10^{19} Hz 10^{18} Hz 10^{17} Hz 10^{16} Hz 10^{15} Hz 10^{14} Hz 10^{13} Hz 10^{12} Hz 10^{11} Hz 10^{10} Hz 10^{9} Hz 100 MHz 10 MHz 1 MHz 100 KHz

Electromagnetic spectrum

Depending on the type of electromagnetic radiation, it may be expressed in meters, centimeters, or nanometers, as shown in **Figure 1.1.**

Frequency (ν) is defined as the number of waves that pass a given point in a specific time, usually one second. Frequency is expressed in waves/second. One wave/second is called a hertz (Hz), named for Heinrich Hertz, who was a pioneer in the study of electromagnetic radiation. **Figure 1.2** illustrates the properties of wavelength and frequency for a familiar kind of wave, a wave on the surface of water. Frequency and wavelength are mathematically related to each other.

FIGURE 1.2

Wavelength and Frequency

The distance between two corresponding points on one of these water waves, such as from crest to crest, is the wave's wavelength, λ. We can measure the wave's frequency, ν, by observing how often the water level rises and falls at a given point, such as at the post.

✓ **CRITICAL THINKING**

Analyze Which waves have a greater wavelength, those in (a) or those in (b)? Which have the greater frequency? Explain each answer.

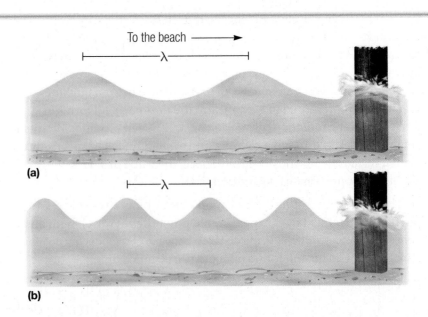

To the beach ⟶

(a)

(b)

For electromagnetic radiation, the mathematical relationship between frequency and wavelength is written as follows:

$$c = \lambda \nu$$

In the equation, c is the speed of light (in m/s), λ is the wavelength of the electromagnetic wave (in m), and ν is the frequency of the electromagnetic wave (in s^{-1}). Because c is the same for all electromagnetic radiation, the product $\lambda \nu$ is a constant.

● **MAIN IDEA**

When certain frequencies of light strike a metal, electrons are emitted.

In the early 1900s, scientists conducted two experiments involving interactions of light and matter that could not be explained by the wave theory of light. One experiment involved a phenomenon known as the photoelectric effect. **The photoelectric effect refers to the emission of electrons from a metal when light shines on the metal,** as illustrated in **Figure 1.3.**

The mystery of the photoelectric effect involved the frequency of the light striking the metal. For a given metal, no electrons were emitted if the light's frequency was below a certain minimum—regardless of the light's intensity. Light was known to be a form of energy, capable of knocking loose an electron from a metal. But the wave theory of light predicted that light of any frequency could supply enough energy to eject an electron. Scientists couldn't explain why the light had to be of a minimum frequency in order for the photoelectric effect to occur.

The Particle Description of Light

The explanation of the photoelectric effect dates back to 1900, when German physicist Max Planck was studying the emission of light by hot objects. He proposed that a hot object does not emit electromagnetic energy continuously, as would be expected if the energy emitted were in the form of waves. Instead, Planck suggested that the object emits energy in small, specific packets called quanta. **A quantum of energy is the minimum quantity of energy that can be lost or gained by an atom.** Planck proposed the following relationship.

> **Quantum of Energy** $\quad E = h\nu$

In the equation, E is the energy, in joules, of a quantum of radiation, ν is the frequency, in s^{-1}, of the radiation emitted, and h is a fundamental physical constant now known as Planck's constant; $h = 6.626 \times 10^{-34}$ J • s.

We can relate a quantum of energy to the speed of light as follows. Because $c = \lambda \nu$, we know that $\nu = c/\lambda$. Substituting this value for ν into the equation for a quantum of energy gives the following: $E = h\nu$, and $\nu = c/\lambda$, so $E = hc/\lambda$.

For example, for light of wavelength $\lambda = 500.0$ nm,

$$E = \frac{hc}{\lambda} = \frac{(6.626 \times 10^{-34} \text{ J} \bullet \text{s})(3.00 \times 10^{8} \text{ m/s})}{5.000 \times 10^{-7} \text{ m}} = 3.98 \times 10^{-19} \text{ J.}$$

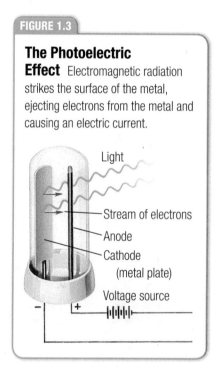

FIGURE 1.3

The Photoelectric Effect Electromagnetic radiation strikes the surface of the metal, ejecting electrons from the metal and causing an electric current.

Light
Stream of electrons
Anode
Cathode (metal plate)
Voltage source

In 1905, Albert Einstein expanded on Planck's theory by introducing the radical idea that electromagnetic radiation has a dual wave-particle nature. Light exhibits many wavelike properties, but it can also be thought of as a stream of particles. Each particle carries a quantum of energy. Einstein called these particles photons. **A photon is a particle of electromagnetic radiation having zero mass and carrying a quantum of energy.** The energy of a photon depends on the frequency of the radiation, or $E_{photon} = h\nu$.

Einstein explained the photoelectric effect by proposing that electromagnetic radiation is absorbed by matter only in whole numbers of photons. For an electron to be ejected from a metal surface, the electron must be struck by a single photon possessing at least the minimum energy required, which corresponds to a minimum frequency. Electrons in different metals are bound more or less tightly, so different metals require different minimum frequencies to exhibit the photoelectric effect.

▶ **MAIN IDEA**

Electrons exist only in very specific energy states for atoms of each element.

When current is passed through a gas at low pressure, the potential energy of the gas atoms increases. **The lowest energy state of an atom is its ground state. A state in which an atom has a higher potential energy than it has in its ground state is an excited state.** There are many possible excited states, each with a unique energy, but only one ground-state energy for atoms of a given element. When an excited atom returns to its ground state or a lower-energy excited state, it gives off the energy it gained in the form of electromagnetic radiation. The production of colored light in neon signs, as shown in **Figure 1.4**, is a familiar example of this process.

FIGURE 1.4

Light Emission Excited neon atoms emit light when electrons in higher energy levels fall back to the ground state or to a lower-energy excited state.

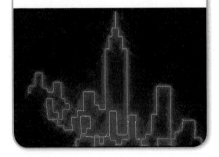

FIGURE 1.5

Emission-Line Spectra Excited hydrogen atoms emit a pinkish glow, as is shown in this diagram. When the visible portion of the emitted light is passed through a prism, it is separated into specific wavelengths that are part of hydrogen's emission-line spectrum. The line at 397 nm is in the ultraviolet and is not visible to the human eye.

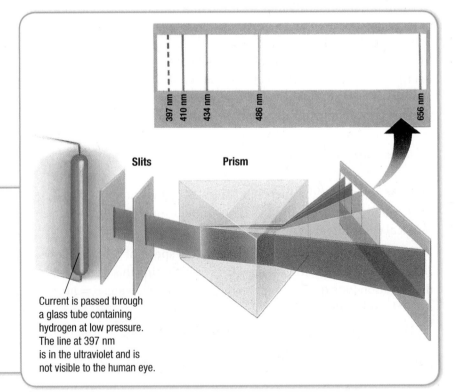

397 nm
410 nm
434 nm
486 nm
656 nm

Slits

Prism

Current is passed through a glass tube containing hydrogen at low pressure. The line at 397 nm is in the ultraviolet and is not visible to the human eye.

(cl) ©SuperStock

FIGURE 1.6

Explaining Energy-Levels A series of specific wavelengths of emitted light makes up hydrogen's emission-line spectrum. The letters below the lines label hydrogen's various energy-level transitions. Niels Bohr's model of the hydrogen atom provided an explanation for these transitions.

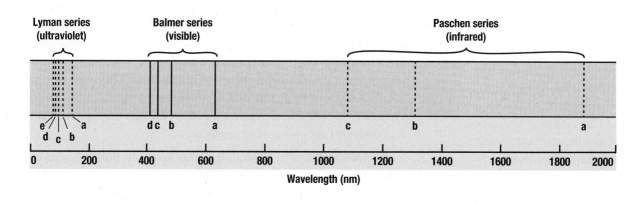

When investigators passed electric current through a vacuum tube containing hydrogen gas at low pressure, they observed the emission of a characteristic pinkish glow. **When a narrow beam of the emitted light was passed through a prism, it was separated into four specific colors of the visible spectrum. The four bands of light were part of what is known as hydrogen's emission-line spectrum.** The production of hydrogen's emission-line spectrum is illustrated in **Figure 1.5** (on the previous page). Additional series of lines were discovered in the ultraviolet and infrared regions of hydrogen's emission-line spectrum. The wavelengths of some of the spectral series are shown in **Figure 1.6**. They are known as the Lyman, Balmer, and Paschen series, after their discoverers.

Classical theory predicted that the hydrogen atoms would be excited by whatever amount of energy was added to them. **Scientists had thus expected to observe the emission of a continuous range of frequencies of electromagnetic radiation, that is, a continuous spectrum.** Why had the hydrogen atoms given off only specific frequencies of light? Attempts to explain this observation led to an entirely new atomic theory called *quantum theory.*

Whenever an excited hydrogen atom falls to its ground state or to a lower-energy excited state, it emits a photon of radiation. The energy of this photon ($E_{photon} = h\nu$) is equal to the difference in energy between the atom's initial state and its final state, as illustrated in **Figure 1.7**. The fact that hydrogen atoms emit only specific frequencies of light indicated that the energy differences between the atoms' energy states were fixed. This suggested that the electron of a hydrogen atom exists only in very specific energy states.

In the late nineteenth century, a mathematical formula that related the various wavelengths of hydrogen's emission-line spectrum was discovered. The challenge facing scientists was to provide a model of the hydrogen atom that accounted for this relationship.

FIGURE 1.7

Mathematical Model of Energy States When an excited atom with energy E_2 falls back to energy E_1, it releases a photon that has energy $E_2 - E_1 = E_{photon} = h\nu.$

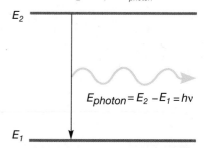

Bohr's model of the hydrogen atom explained electron transition states.

The puzzle of the hydrogen-atom spectrum was solved in 1913 by the Danish physicist Niels Bohr. He proposed a hydrogen-atom model that linked the atom's electron to photon emission. According to the model, the electron can circle the nucleus only in allowed paths, or *orbits*. When the electron is in one of these orbits, the atom has a definite, fixed energy. The electron—and therefore the hydrogen atom—is in its lowest energy state when it is in the orbit closest to the nucleus. This orbit is separated from the nucleus by a large empty space where the electron cannot exist. The energy of the electron is higher when the electron is in orbits that are successively farther from the nucleus.

The electron orbits, or atomic energy levels, in Bohr's model can be compared to the rungs of a ladder. When you are standing on a ladder, your feet are on one rung or another. The amount of potential energy that you possess corresponds to standing on the first rung, the second rung, and so forth. Your energy cannot correspond to standing between two rungs because you cannot stand in midair. In the same way, an electron can be in one orbit or another, but not in between.

How does Bohr's model of the hydrogen atom explain the observed spectral lines? While in a given orbit, the electron is neither gaining nor losing energy. It can, however, move to a higher-energy orbit by gaining an amount of energy equal to the difference in energy between the higher-energy orbit and the initial lower-energy orbit. When a hydrogen atom is in an excited state, its electron is in one of the higher-energy orbits. When the electron falls to a lower energy level, a photon is emitted, and the process is called *emission*. The photon's energy is equal to the energy difference between the initial higher energy level and the final lower energy level. Energy must be added to an atom in order to move an electron from a lower energy level to a higher energy level. This process is called *absorption*. Absorption and emission of radiation in Bohr's model of the hydrogen atom are illustrated in **Figure 1.8**. The energy of each absorbed or emitted photon corresponds to a particular frequency of emitted radiation, $E_{photon} = h\nu$.

Based on the different wavelengths of the hydrogen emission-line spectrum, Bohr calculated the allowed energy levels for the hydrogen atom. He then related the possible energy-level changes to the lines in the hydrogen emission-line spectrum. The five lines in the Lyman series, for example, were shown to be the result of electrons dropping from energy levels E_6, E_5, E_4, E_3, and E_2 to the ground-state energy level E_1.

FIGURE 1.8

Absorption and Emission   **(a)** Absorption and **(b)** emission of a photon by a hydrogen atom according to Bohr's model. The frequencies of light that can be absorbed and emitted are restricted because the electron can only be in orbits corresponding to the energies E_1, E_2, E_3, and so forth.

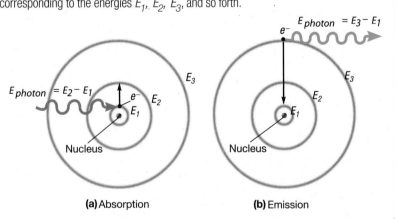

(a) Absorption   **(b)** Emission

FIGURE 1.9

Electron Energy Transitions This energy-state diagram for a hydrogen atom shows some of the energy transitions for the Lyman, Balmer, and Paschen spectral series. Bohr's model of the atom accounted mathematically for the energy of each of the transitions shown.

✔ **CRITICAL THINKING**

Explain Why might spectra of atoms with more than one electron be difficult to explain using Bohr's model?

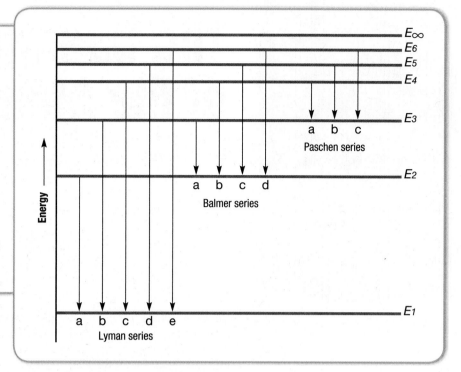

Bohr's calculated values agreed with the experimentally observed values for the lines in each series. The origins of three of the series of lines in hydrogen's emission-line spectrum are shown in **Figure 1.9.**

Bohr's model of the hydrogen atom explained observed spectral lines so well that many scientists concluded that the model could be applied to all atoms. It was soon recognized, however, that Bohr's approach did not explain the spectra of atoms with more than one electron. Nor did Bohr's theory explain the chemical behavior of atoms.

✔ SECTION 1 FORMATIVE ASSESSMENT

▶ Reviewing Main Ideas

1. What was the major shortcoming of Rutherford's model of the atom?

2. Write and label the equation that relates the speed, wavelength, and frequency of electromagnetic radiation.

3. Define the following:
  a. electromagnetic radiation
  b. wavelength
  c. frequency
  d. quantum
  e. photon

4. What is meant by the dual wave-particle nature of light?

5. Describe Bohr's model of the hydrogen atom.

✔ Critical Thinking

6. INTERPRETING GRAPHICS Use the diagram in **Figure 1.9** to answer the following:

  a. Characterize each of the following as absorption or emission: an electron moves from E_2 to E_1; an electron moves from E_1 to E_3; and an electron moves from E_6 to E_3.

  b. Which energy-level change above emits or absorbs the highest energy? the lowest energy?

⟩ Electrons have wavelike properties.

⟩ The velocity and position of an electron cannot be measured simultaneously.

⟩ Orbitals indicate probable electron locations.

⟩ Quantum numbers describe atomic orbitals.

The Quantum Model of the Atom

Key Terms

Heisenberg uncertainty principle	quantum number	magnetic quantum number
quantum theory	principal quantum number	spin quantum number
orbital	angular momentum quantum number	

To the scientists of the early twentieth century, Bohr's model of the hydrogen atom contradicted common sense. Why did hydrogen's electron exist around the nucleus only in certain allowed orbits with definite energies? Why couldn't the electron exist in a limitless number of orbits with slightly different energies? To explain why atomic energy states are quantized, scientists had to change the way they viewed the nature of the electron.

⟩ MAIN IDEA
Electrons have wavelike properties.

The investigations into the photoelectric effect and hydrogen's emission-line spectrum revealed that light could behave as both a wave and a particle. Could electrons have a dual wave-particle nature as well? In 1924, the French scientist Louis de Broglie asked himself this very question. And the answer that he proposed led to a revolution in our basic understanding of matter.

De Broglie pointed out that in many ways the behavior of electrons in Bohr's quantized orbits was similar to the known behavior of waves. For example, scientists at the time knew that any wave confined to a space can have only certain frequencies. De Broglie suggested that electrons be considered waves confined to the space around an atomic nucleus. It followed that the electron waves could exist only at specific frequencies. And according to the relationship $E = h\nu$, these frequencies corresponded to specific energies—the quantized energies of Bohr's orbits.

Other aspects of de Broglie's hypothesis that electrons have wave-like properties were soon confirmed by experiments. Investigators demonstrated that electrons, like light waves, can be bent, or diffracted. *Diffraction* refers to the bending of a wave as it passes by the edge of an object or through a small opening. Diffraction experiments and other investigations also showed that electron beams, like waves, can interfere with each other. *Interference* occurs when waves overlap (see the Quick Lab in this section). This overlapping results in a reduction of energy in some areas and an increase of energy in others. The effects of diffraction and interference can be seen in **Figure 2.1,** on the next page.

FIGURE 2.1

Interference Patterns Bright areas correspond to areas of increased energy, while dark areas indicate areas of decreased energy.

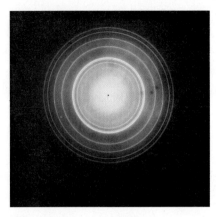

(a) Diffraction pattern produced by a beam of electrons passed through a substance.

(b) Diffraction pattern for a beam of visible light passed through a tiny aperture.

 **CRITICAL THINKING**

Apply How did evidence of diffraction and interference indicate that electrons behave like waves of light?

▶ **MAIN IDEA**

The velocity and position of an electron cannot be measured simultaneously.

The idea of electrons having a dual wave-particle nature troubled scientists. If electrons are both particles and waves, then where are they in the atom? To answer this question, we must consider a proposal first made in 1927 by the German theoretical physicist Werner Heisenberg.

Heisenberg's idea involved the detection of electrons. Electrons are detected by their interaction with photons. Because photons have about the same energy as electrons, any attempt to locate a specific electron with a photon knocks the electron off its course. As a result, there is always a basic uncertainty in trying to locate an electron (or any other particle). The **Heisenberg uncertainty principle** states that it is impossible to determine simultaneously both the position and velocity of an electron or any other particle. This was a difficult idea for scientists to accept at the time, but it is now fundamental to our understanding of light and matter.

▶ **MAIN IDEA**

Orbitals indicate probable electron locations.

In 1926, the Austrian physicist Erwin Schrödinger used the hypothesis that electrons have a dual wave-particle nature to develop an equation that treated electrons in atoms as waves. Unlike Bohr's theory, which assumed quantization as a fact, quantization of electron energies was a natural outcome of Schrödinger's equation. Only waves of specific energies, and therefore frequencies, provided solutions to the equation. Along with the uncertainty principle, the Schrödinger wave equation laid the foundation for modern quantum theory. **Quantum theory** describes mathematically the wave properties of electrons and other very small particles.

QuickLAB | THE WAVE NATURE OF LIGHT: INTERFERENCE

QUESTION

Does light show the wave property of interference when a beam of light is projected through a pinhole onto a screen?

PROCEDURE

Record all your observations.

1. To make the pinhole screen, cut a 20 cm × 20 cm square from a manila folder. In the center of the square, cut a 2 cm square hole. Cut a 7 cm × 7 cm square of aluminum foil. Using a thumbtack, make a pinhole in the center of the foil square. Tape the aluminum foil over the 2 cm square hole, making sure the pinhole is centered as shown in the diagram.

2. Use white poster board to make a projection screen 35 cm × 35 cm.

3. In a dark room, center the light beam from a flashlight on the pinhole. Hold the flashlight about 1 cm from the pinhole. The pinhole screen should be about 50 cm from the projection screen, as shown in the diagram. Adjust the distance to form a sharp image on the projection screen.

DISCUSSION

1. Did you observe interference patterns on the screen?

2. As a result of your observations, what do you conclude about the nature of light?

MATERIALS

- scissors
- manila folders
- thumbtack
- masking tape
- aluminum foil
- white poster board or cardboard
- flashlight

SAFETY

Wear safety goggles and an apron.

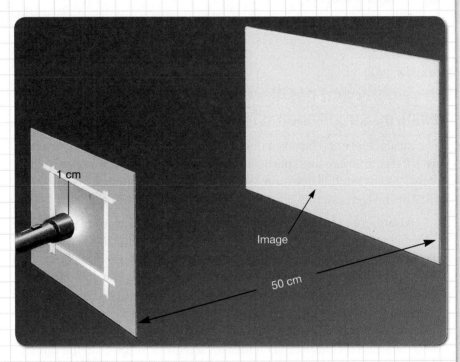

Solutions to the Schrödinger wave equation are known as wave functions. Based on the Heisenberg uncertainty principle, the early developers of quantum theory determined that wave functions give only the *probability* of finding an electron at a given place around the nucleus. Thus, electrons do not travel around the nucleus in neat orbits, as Bohr had postulated. Instead, they exist in certain regions called orbitals. **An orbital is a three-dimensional region around the nucleus that indicates the probable location of an electron. Figure 2.2**, on the next page, illustrates two ways of picturing one type of atomic orbital. As you will see later in this section, atomic orbitals have different shapes and sizes.

FIGURE 2.2

Atomic Orbitals Two ways of showing a simple atomic orbital are presented.

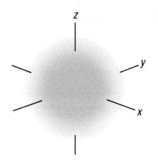

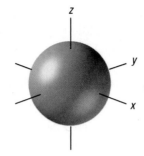

(a) In this atomic orbital model, the probability of finding the electron is proportional to the density of the cloud.

(b) An orbital can also be depicted as a surface within which the electron can be found a certain percentage of the time, conventionally 90%.

▶ **MAIN IDEA**

Quantum numbers describe atomic orbitals.

According to the Schrödinger equation, electrons in atomic orbitals also have quantized energies. Unlike in the Bohr atomic model, therefore, an electron's energy level is not the only characteristic of an orbital.

To describe orbitals accurately, scientists use quantum numbers. **Quantum numbers specify the properties of atomic orbitals and the properties of electrons in orbitals.** The first three quantum numbers result from solutions to the Schrödinger equation. They indicate the main energy level, the shape, and the orientation of an orbital. The fourth, the spin quantum number, describes a fundamental state of the electron that occupies the orbital.

Principal Quantum Number

The principal quantum number, symbolized by n, indicates the main energy level occupied by the electron. Values of n are positive integers only—1, 2, 3, and so on. As n increases, the electron's energy and its average distance from the nucleus increase, as shown in **Figure 2.3**. For example, an electron for which $n = 1$ occupies the first, or lowest, main energy level and is located closest to the nucleus. An electron for which $n = 2$ occupies the second energy level and is farther from the nucleus.

More than one electron can have the same n value. These electrons are said to be in the same electron *shell*. The total number of orbitals in a given shell, or main energy level, is equal to n^2.

FIGURE 2.3

The Principle Quantum Number The main energy levels of an atom are represented by the principal quantum number, n.

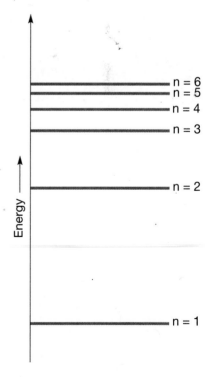

FIGURE 2.4

ORBITAL LETTER DESIGNATIONS

ℓ	Letter
0	s
1	p
2	d
3	f

Angular Momentum Quantum Number

Except at the first main energy level, orbitals of different shapes exist for a given value of *n*. These are known as *sublevels*. **The angular momentum quantum number, symbolized by ℓ, indicates the shape of the orbital.** For a specific main energy level, the number of orbital shapes possible is equal to *n*. The values of ℓ allowed are zero and all positive integers less than or equal to $n - 1$. For example, orbitals for which $n = 2$ can have one of two shapes corresponding to $\ell = 0$ and $\ell = 1$. Depending on its value of ℓ, an orbital is assigned a letter, such as *s, p,* and *d.* Orbital letter designations for values of ℓ are given in **Figure 2.4.**

As shown in **Figure 2.5a** on the next page, *s* orbitals are spherical, *p* orbitals have dumbbell shapes, and *d* orbitals are more complex. (The *f* orbital shapes are even more complex.) In the first energy level, $n = 1$, there is only one sublevel possible—an *s* orbital. As mentioned, the second energy level, $n = 2$, has two sublevels—the *s* and *p* orbitals. The third energy level, $n = 3$, has three sublevels—the *s, p,* and *d* orbitals. The fourth energy level, $n = 4$, has four sublevels—the *s, p, d,* and *f* orbitals. In an *n*th main energy level, there are *n* sublevels.

Each atomic orbital is designated by the principal quantum number followed by the letter of the sublevel. For example, the 1*s* sublevel is the *s* orbital in the first main energy level, while the 2*p* sublevel is the set of three *p* orbitals in the second main energy level. On the other hand, a 4*d* orbital is part of the *d* sublevel in the fourth main energy level. How would you designate the *p* sublevel in the third main energy level? How many other sublevels are in the third main energy level with this one?

GO ONLINE

Animated Chemistry

HMHScience.com

Energy Levels of an Atom

Magnetic Quantum Number

Atomic orbitals can have the same shape but different orientations around the nucleus. **The magnetic quantum number, symbolized by *m*, indicates the orientation of an orbital around the nucleus.** Values of *m* are intergers, including zero, from $-\ell$ to $+\ell$. Because an *s* orbital is spherical and is centered around the nucleus, it has only one possible orientation. This orientation corresponds to a magnetic quantum number of $m = 0$. There is therefore only one *s* orbital in each *s* sublevel.

As shown in **Figure 2.5b** on the next page, the lobes of a *p* orbital extend along the *x*-, *y*-, or *z*-axis of a three-dimensional coordinate system. There are therefore three *p* orbitals in each *p* sublevel, designated as p_x, p_y, and p_z orbitals. The three *p* orbitals occupy different regions of space, and those regions are related to values of $m = -1$, $m = 0$, and $m = +1$.

There are five different *d* orbitals in each *d* sublevel, as shown in **Figure 2.5c** on the next page. For the *d* orbital, the five different orientations, including one with a different shape, correspond to values of $m = -2$, $m = -1$, $m = 0$, $m = +1$, and $m = +2$. There are seven different *f* orbitals in each *f* sublevel. (The *f* orbitals are not shown in **Figure 2.5.**)

FIGURE 2.5

a. Orbital Shapes

The orbitals *s*, *p*, and *d* have different shapes. Each of the orbitals shown occupies a different region of space around the nucleus.

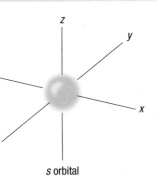

s orbital

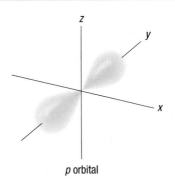

p orbital

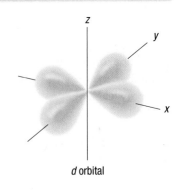

d orbital

b. Three Orientations of *p* Orbitals

The subscripts *x*, *y*, and *z* indicate the three orientations of *p* orbitals. The intersection of the *x*-, *y*-, and *z*-axes indicates the location of the center of the nucleus.

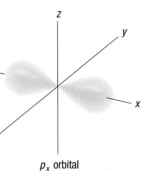

p_x orbital

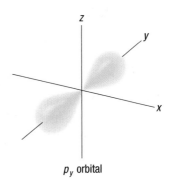

p_y orbital

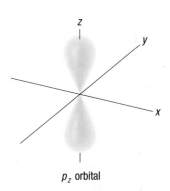

p_z orbital

c. Five Orientations of *d* Orbitals

Four of the *d* orbitals have the same shape but different orientations. The fifth has a different shape and a different orientation. Each orbital occupies a different region of space.

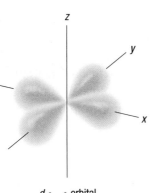
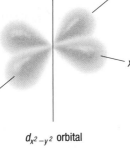

$d_{x^2-y^2}$ orbital

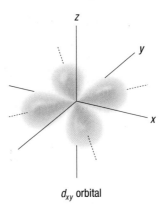

d_{xy} orbital

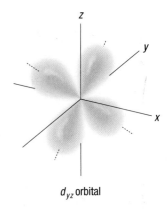

d_{yz} orbital

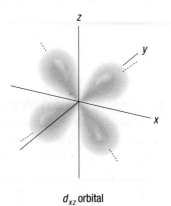

d_{xz} orbital

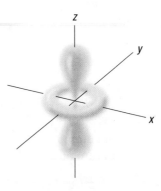

d_{z^2} orbital

FIGURE 2.6

QUANTUM NUMBER RELATIONSHIPS IN ATOMIC STRUCTURE

Principal quantum number: main energy level (n)	Sublevel in main energy level (n sublevels)	Number of orbitals per sublevel	Number of orbitals per main energy level (n^2)	Number of electrons per sublevel	Number of electrons per main energy level ($2n^2$)
1	s	1	1	2	2
2	s	1	4	2	8
	p	3		6	
3	s	1	9	2	18
	p	3		6	
	d	5		10	
4	s	1	16	2	32
	p	3		6	
	d	5		10	
	f	7		14	

As you can see in **Figure 2.6**, the total number of orbitals in a main energy level increases with the value of n. In fact, the number of orbitals at each main energy level equals the square of the principal quantum number, n^2.

Spin Quantum Number

An electron in an orbital behaves in some ways like Earth spinning on an axis. The electron exists in one of two possible spin states, which creates a magnetic field. To account for the magnetic properties of the electron, theoreticians of the early twentieth century created the spin quantum number. **The spin quantum number has only two possible values—(+1/2, −1/2)—which indicate the two fundamental spin states of an electron in an orbital.** A single orbital can hold a maximum of two electrons, but the two electrons must have opposite spin states.

CHECK FOR UNDERSTANDING

Analyze Why are quantum numbers used to describe electrons in atoms?

SECTION 2 FORMATIVE ASSESSMENT

▶ **Reviewing Main Ideas**

1. Define the following:
   a. main energy levels
   b. quantum numbers

2. a. List the four quantum numbers.
   b. What general information about atomic orbitals is provided by the quantum numbers?

3. Describe briefly what specific information is given by each of the four quantum numbers.

✔ **Critical Thinking**

4. INFERRING RELATIONSHIPS What are the possible values of the magnetic quantum number m for f orbitals? What is the maximum number of electrons that can exist in 4f orbitals?

Electron Configurations

SECTION 3

Main Ideas

▶ Electrons fill in the lowest-energy orbitals first.

▶ There are three ways to indicate electron configuration.

▶ No electrons can occupy a higher-energy sublevel until the sublevel below it is filled.

Key Terms

electron configuration
Aufbau principle

Pauli exclusion principle
Hund's rule

noble gas
noble-gas configuration

The quantum model of the atom improves on the Bohr model because it describes the arrangements of electrons in atoms other than hydrogen. **The arrangement of electrons in an atom is known as the atom's electron configuration.** Because atoms of different elements have different numbers of electrons, a unique electron configuration exists for the atoms of each element. Like all systems in nature, electrons in atoms tend to assume arrangements that have the lowest possible energies. The lowest-energy arrangement of the electrons for each element is called the element's *ground-state electron configuration*. A few simple rules, combined with the quantum number relationships discussed in Section 2, allow us to determine these ground-state electron configurations.

▶ MAIN IDEA

Electrons fill in the lowest-energy orbitals first.

To build up electron configurations for the ground state of any particular atom, first the energy levels of the orbitals are determined. Then electrons are added to the orbitals, one by one, according to three basic rules. (Remember that real atoms are not built up by adding protons and electrons one at a time.)

The first rule shows the order in which electrons occupy orbitals. **According to the Aufbau principle, an electron occupies the lowest-energy orbital that can receive it. Figure 3.1** shows the atomic orbitals in order of increasing energy. The orbital with the lowest energy is the 1s orbital. In a ground-state hydrogen atom, the electron is in this orbital. The 2s orbital is the next highest in energy, then the 2p orbitals. Beginning with the third main energy level, $n = 3$, the energies of the sublevels in different main energy levels begin to overlap.

Note in the figure, for example, that the 4s sublevel is lower in energy than the 3d sublevel. Therefore, the 4s orbital is filled before any electrons enter the 3d orbitals. (Less energy is required for two electrons to pair up in the 4s orbital than for those two electrons to occupy a 3d orbital.) Once the 3d orbitals are fully occupied, which sublevel will be occupied next?

FIGURE 3.1

Atomic Sublevels The order of increasing energy for atomic sublevels is shown on the vertical axis. Each individual box represents an orbital.

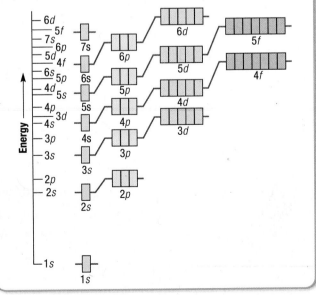

Arrangement of Electrons in Atoms   **111**

FIGURE 3.2

Pauli Exclusion Principle

According to the Pauli exclusion principle, an orbital can hold two electrons of opposite spin states. In this electron configuration of a helium atom, each arrow represents one of the atom's two electrons. The direction of the arrow indicates the electron's spin state.

↑↓

1s orbital

The second rule reflects the importance of the spin quantum number. **According to the Pauli exclusion principle, no two electrons in the same atom can have the same set of four quantum numbers.** The principal, angular momentum, and magnetic quantum numbers specify the energy, shape, and orientation of an orbital. The two values of the spin quantum number reflect the fact that for two electrons to occupy the same orbital, they must have opposite spin states (see **Figure 3.2**).

The third rule requires placing as many unpaired electrons as possible in separate orbitals in the same sublevel. In this way, electron-electron repulsion is minimized so that the electron arrangements have the lowest energy possible. **According to Hund's rule, orbitals of equal energy are each occupied by one electron before any orbital is occupied by a second electron, and all electrons in singly occupied orbitals must have the same spin state.** Applying this rule shows, for example, that one electron will enter each of the three *p* orbitals in a main energy level before a second electron enters any of them. This is illustrated in **Figure 3.3**. What is the maximum number of unpaired electrons in a *d* sublevel?

FIGURE 3.3

Hund's Rule The figure shows how **(a)** two, **(b)** three, and **(c)** four electrons fill the *p* sublevel of a given main energy level according to Hund's rule.

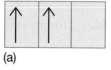

(a)

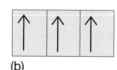

(b)

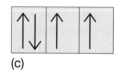

(c)

▶ MAIN IDEA

There are three ways to indicate electron configuration.

Three methods, or notations, are used to indicate electron configurations. Two of these notations will be discussed for the first-period elements, hydrogen and helium, on the following page. The third notation is used mostly with elements of the third period and higher and will be discussed later in this section.

In a ground-state hydrogen atom, the single electron is in the lowest-energy orbital, the 1s orbital. The electron can be in either one of its two spin states. Helium has two electrons, which are paired in the 1s orbital.

Orbital Notation

In orbital notation, an unoccupied orbital is represented by a line, ___ , with the orbital's name written underneath the line. An orbital containing one electron is represented as $\underline{\uparrow}$. An orbital containing two electrons is represented as $\underline{\uparrow\downarrow}$, showing the electrons paired and with opposite spin states. The lines are labeled with the principal quantum number and sublevel letter. For example, the orbital notations for hydrogen and helium are written as follows:

$$\text{H}\,\frac{\uparrow}{1s} \qquad \text{He}\,\frac{\uparrow\downarrow}{1s}$$

Electron-Configuration Notation

Electron-configuration notation eliminates the lines and arrows of orbital notation. Instead, the number of electrons in a sublevel is shown by adding a superscript to the sublevel designation. The hydrogen configuration is represented by $1s^1$. The superscript indicates that one electron is present in hydrogen's $1s$ orbital. The helium configuration is represented by $1s^2$. Here the superscript indicates that there are two electrons in helium's $1s$ orbital.

GO ONLINE

Learn It! Video
HMHScience.com

Electron Configurations

Sample Problem A The electron configuration of boron is $1s^2 2s^2 2p^1$. How many electrons are present in an atom of boron? What is the atomic number for boron? Write the orbital notation for boron.

● SOLVE

The number of electrons in a boron atom is equal to the sum of the superscripts in its electron-configuration notation: $2 + 2 + 1 = 5$ electrons. The number of protons equals the number of electrons in a neutral atom. So we know that boron has 5 protons and thus has an atomic number of 5. To write the orbital notation, first draw the lines representing orbitals.

$$\overline{\ \ }\ \overline{\ \ }\ \ \overline{\ \ }\ \overline{\ \ }\ \overline{\ \ }$$
$$1s\ \ 2s\ \ \ \ \ 2p$$

Next, add arrows showing the electron locations. The first two electrons occupy $n = 1$ energy level and fill the $1s$ orbital.

$$\frac{\uparrow\downarrow}{1s}\ \ \overline{\ \ }\ \ \ \overline{\ \ }\ \overline{\ \ }\ \overline{\ \ }$$
$$\quad\ 2s\ \ \ \ \ 2p$$

The next three electrons occupy the $n = 2$ main energy level. Two of these occupy the lower-energy $2s$ orbital. The third occupies a higher-energy p orbital.

$$\frac{\uparrow\downarrow}{1s}\ \frac{\uparrow\downarrow}{2s}\ \ \frac{\uparrow}{\ }\ \overline{\ \ }\ \overline{\ \ }$$
$$\qquad\qquad\quad 2p$$

Practice Answers in Appendix E

1. The electron configuration of nitrogen is $1s^2 2s^2 2p^3$. How many electrons are in a nitrogen atom? What is the atomic number of nitrogen? Write the orbital notation for nitrogen.
2. The electron configuration of fluorine is $1s^2 2s^2 2p^5$. What is the atomic number of fluorine? How many of its p orbitals are filled?

Arrangement of Electrons in Atoms   **113**

The Noble Decade

By the late nineteenth century, the science of chemistry had begun to be organized. In 1860, the First International Congress of Chemistry established the field's first standards. And Dmitri Mendeleev's periodic table of elements gave chemists across the globe a systematic understanding of matter's building blocks. But many important findings—including the discovery of a family of rare, unreactive gases that were unlike any substances known at the time—were yet to come.

Cross-Disciplinary Correspondence

In 1888, the British physicist Lord Rayleigh encountered a small but significant discrepancy in the results of one of his experiments. In an effort to redetermine the atomic mass of nitrogen, he measured the densities of several samples of nitrogen gas. Each sample had been prepared by a different method. All samples that had been isolated from chemical reactions exhibited similar densities. But the densities were about one-tenth of a percent less dense than the nitrogen isolated from air, which at the time was believed to be a mixture of nitrogen, oxygen, water vapor, and carbon dioxide.

Rayleigh was at a loss to explain his discovery. Finally, in 1892, he published a letter in *Nature* magazine to appeal to his colleagues for an explanation. A month later, he received a reply from a Scottish chemist named William Ramsay. Ramsay related that he too had been stumped by the density difference between chemical and atmospheric nitrogen. Rayleigh decided to report his findings to the Royal Society.

A Chemist's Approach

With Rayleigh's permission, Ramsay attempted to remove all known components from a sample of air and to analyze what, if anything, remained. Having removed water vapor, carbon dioxide, and oxygen from the air, Ramsay repeatedly passed the sample over hot magnesium. The nitrogen reacted with the magnesium to form solid magnesium nitride. As a result, all of the then-known components of air were removed. What remained was a minuscule portion of a mysterious gas.

Ramsay tried to cause the gas to react with chemically active substances, such as hydrogen, sodium, and caustic soda, but the gas remained unaltered. He decided to name this new atmospheric component *argon* (Greek for "inert" or "idle").

Periodic Problems

Rayleigh and Ramsay were sure that they had discovered a new element, which created a problem. Their calculations indicated that argon had an atomic mass of about 40. However, as it appeared in 1894, the periodic table had no space for such an element. The elements with atomic masses closest to that of argon were chlorine and potassium. Unfortunately, the chemical properties of the families of each of these elements were completely dissimilar to those of the strange gas.

SEPTEMBER 29, 1892   *NATURE*

LETTERS TO THE EDITOR.

[*The Editor does not hold himself responsible for opinions expressed by his correspondents. Neither can he undertake to return, or to correspond with the writers of, rejected manuscripts intended for this or any other part of* NATURE. *No notice is taken of anonymous communications.*]

Density of Nitrogen.

I AM much puzzled by some recent results as to the density of *nitrogen*, and shall be obliged if any of your chemical readers can offer suggestions as to the cause. According to two methods of preparation I obtain quite distinct values. The relative difference, amounting to about $\frac{1}{1000}$ part, is small in itself; but it lies entirely outside the errors of experiment, and can only be attributed to a variation in the character of the gas...

Is it possible that the difference is independent of impurity, the nitrogen itself being to some extent in a different (dissociated) state ?...

RAYLEIGH.

Terling Place, Witham, September 24.

This excerpt from Lord Rayleigh's letter was originally published in Nature *magazine in 1892.*

In 1893, Scottish chemist William Ramsay isolated a previously unknown component of the atmosphere.

Groups	III	IV	V	VI	VII	VIII	I	II	III	IV	V	VI	VII	0	I	II
Periods	b	b	b	b	b	b	b	b	a	a	a	a	a		a	a
1															H	He
2															Li	Be
3									B	C	N	O	F	Ne	Na	Mg
4									Al	Si	P	S	Cl	Ar	K	Ca
5	Sc	Ti	V	Cr	Mn	Fe Co Ni	Cu	Zn	Ga	Ge	As	Se	Br	Kr	Rb	Sr
6	Y	Zr	Nb	Mo	Tc	Ru Rh Pd	Ag	Cd	In	Sn	Sb	Te	I	Xe	Cs	Ba
7	La	Hf	Ta	W	Re	Os Ir Pt	Au	Hg	Tl	Pb	Bi	Po	At	Rn	Fr	Ra
8	Ac															

Transition elements · Main-group elements

This version of the periodic table shows how it looked after the discovery of the noble gases. The placement of the Group 1 and 2 elements at the far right of the table clearly illustrates how the noble gases fit in between the chlorine family and the potassium family of elements. The 0 above the noble-gas family indicates the zero valency of the gases.

Ramsay contemplated argon's lack of reactivity. He knew that Mendeleev had created the periodic table on the basis of valence, or the number of atomic partners an element bonds with in forming a compound. Because Ramsay could not cause argon to form any compounds, he assigned it a valence of zero. And because the valence of the elements in the families of both chlorine and potassium was one, perhaps argon fit in between them.

Ramsay's insight that argon merited a new spot between the halogen family and the alkali metal family on the periodic table was correct. And as Ramsay would soon confirm, his newly discovered gas was indeed one of a previously unknown family of elements.

New Neighbors

In 1895, Ramsay isolated a light, inert gas from a mineral called *cleveite*. Physical analysis revealed that the gas was the same as one that had been identified in the sun in 1868—helium. Helium was the second zero-valent element found on Earth, and its discovery made chemists aware that the periodic table had been missing an entire column of elements.

Over the next three years, Ramsay and his assistant, Morris Travers, identified three more inert gases present in the atmosphere: neon (Greek for "new"), krypton ("hidden"), and xenon ("stranger"). Finally in 1900, German chemist Friedrich Ernst Dorn discovered radon, the last of the new family of elements known today as the *noble gases*. For his discovery, Ramsay received the Nobel Prize in 1904.

Questions

1. What evidence led Ramsay to report that the mysterious gas was inert?

2. What property of argon caused Ramsay to propose a new column in the periodic table?

MAIN IDEA

No electrons can occupy a higher-energy sublevel until the sublevel below it is filled.

In the first-period elements, hydrogen and helium, electrons occupy the orbital of the first main energy level. **Figure 3.4** provides a pattern to help you remember the order in which orbitals are filled according to the Aufbau principle. The ground-state configurations in **Figure 3.5** illustrate how the Aufbau principle, the Pauli exclusion principle, and Hund's rule are applied to atoms of elements in the second period.

According to the Aufbau principle, after the 1*s* orbital is filled, the next electron occupies the *s* sublevel in the second main energy level. Thus, lithium, Li, has a configuration of $1s^2 2s^1$. The electron occupying the 2*s* level of a lithium atom is in the atom's highest, or outermost, occupied level. The *highest-occupied energy level* is the electron-containing main energy level with the highest principal quantum number. The two electrons in the 1*s* sublevel of lithium are no longer in the outermost main energy level. They have become *inner-shell electrons*, which are electrons that are not in the highest-occupied energy level.

The fourth electron in an atom of beryllium, Be, must complete the pair in the 2*s* sublevel because this sublevel is of lower energy than the 2*p* sublevel. With the 2*s* sublevel filled, the 2*p* sublevel, which has three vacant orbitals of equal energy, can be occupied. One of the three *p* orbitals is occupied by a single electron in an atom of boron, B. Two of the three *p* orbitals are occupied by unpaired electrons in an atom of carbon, C. And all three *p* orbitals are occupied by unpaired electrons in an atom of nitrogen, N. Hund's rule applies here, as is shown in the orbital notations in **Figure 3.5**.

According to the Aufbau principle, the next electron must pair with another electron in one of the 2*p* orbitals rather than enter the third main energy level. The Pauli exclusion principle allows the electron to pair with one of the electrons occupying the 2*p* orbitals as long as the spins of the paired electrons are opposite. Thus, atoms of oxygen, O, have the configuration $1s^2 2s^2 2p^4$. Oxygen's orbital notation is shown in **Figure 3.5**.

Two 2*p* orbitals are filled in fluorine, F, and all three are filled in neon, Ne. Atoms such as those of neon, which have the *s* and *p* sublevels of their highest occupied level filled with eight electrons, are said to have an *octet* of electrons. Examine the periodic table inside the back cover of the text. Notice that neon is the last element in the second period.

FIGURE 3.4

The Aufbau Principle Follow the diagonal arrows from the bottom of one column to the top of the next to get the order in which atomic orbitals are filled according to the Aufbau principle.

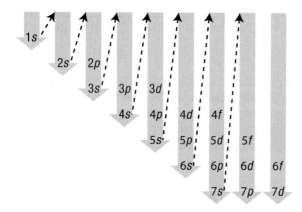

✔ **CRITICAL THINKING**

Interpret Review the statement of the Aufbau principle given at the beginning of this section, and then study Figure 3.4 carefully. Based on your understanding of the two, explain in your own words why electrons fill atomic orbitals in this seemingly unusual order.

FIGURE 3.5

ELECTRON CONFIGURATIONS OF ATOMS OF SECOND-PERIOD ELEMENTS SHOWING TWO NOTATIONS

Name	Symbol	Orbital notation					Electron-configuration notation
		1s	2s	2p			
Lithium	Li	↑↓	↑	—	—	—	$1s^2 2s^1$
Beryllium	Be	↑↓	↑↓	—	—	—	$1s^2 2s^2$
Boron	B	↑↓	↑↓	↑	—	—	$1s^2 2s^2 2p^1$
Carbon	C	↑↓	↑↓	↑	↑	—	$1s^2 2s^2 2p^2$
Nitrogen	N	↑↓	↑↓	↑	↑	↑	$1s^2 2s^2 2p^3$
Oxygen	O	↑↓	↑↓	↑↓	↑	↑	$1s^2 2s^2 2p^4$
Fluorine	F	↑↓	↑↓	↑↓	↑↓	↑	$1s^2 2s^2 2p^5$
Neon	Ne	↑↓	↑↓	↑↓	↑↓	↑↓	$1s^2 2s^2 2p^6$

Elements of the Third Period

After the outer octet is filled in neon, the next electron enters the s sublevel in the $n = 3$ main energy level. Thus, atoms of sodium, Na, have the configuration $1s^2 2s^2 2p^6 3s^1$. Compare the configuration of a sodium atom with that of an atom of neon in **Figure 3.5.** Notice that the first 10 electrons in a sodium atom have the same configuration as a neon atom, $1s^2 2s^2 2p^6$. In fact, the first 10 electrons in an atom of each of the third-period elements have the same configuration as neon. This similarity allows us to use a shorthand notation for the electron configurations of the third-period elements.

Noble-Gas Notation

Neon is a member of the Group 18 elements. **The Group 18 elements (helium, neon, argon, krypton, xenon, and radon) are called the noble gases.** To simplify sodium's notation, the symbol for neon, enclosed in square brackets, is used to represent the complete neon configuration: $[Ne] = 1s^2 2s^2 2p^6$. This allows us to write sodium's electron configuration as $[Ne]3s^1$, which is called sodium's *noble-gas notation.* **Figure 3.6,** on the next page, shows the electron configuration of each of the third-period elements using noble-gas notation.

The last element in the third period is argon, Ar, which is a noble gas. As in neon, the highest-occupied energy level of argon has an octet of electrons, $[Ne]3s^2 3p^6$. In fact, each noble gas other than He has an electron octet in its highest energy level. **A noble-gas configuration** refers **to an outer main energy level occupied, in most cases, by eight electrons.**

FIGURE 3.6

ELECTRON CONFIGURATIONS OF ATOMS OF THIRD-PERIOD ELEMENTS

Name	Symbol	Atomic number	Number of electrons in sublevels					Noble-gas notation
			1s	2s	2p	3s	3p	
Sodium	Na	11	2	2	6	1		*[Ne]3s^1
Magnesium	Mg	12	2	2	6	2		[Ne]3s^2
Aluminum	Al	13	2	2	6	2	1	[Ne]3s^{2}3p^1
Silicon	Si	14	2	2	6	2	2	[Ne]3s^{2}3p^2
Phosphorus	P	15	2	2	6	2	3	[Ne]3s^{2}3p^3
Sulfur	S	16	2	2	6	2	4	[Ne]3s^{2}3p^4
Chlorine	Cl	17	2	2	6	2	5	[Ne]3s^{2}3p^5
Argon	Ar	18	2	2	6	2	6	[Ne]3s^{2}3p^6

*[Ne] = $1s^2 2s^2 2p^6$

Elements of the Fourth Period

The electron configurations of atoms in the fourth-period elements are shown in **Figure 3.7** (on the next page). The period begins by filling the 4s orbital, the empty orbital of lowest energy. The first element in the fourth period is potassium, K, which has the electron configuration [Ar]4s^1. The next element is calcium, Ca, which has the electron configuration [Ar]4s^2.

With the 4s sublevel filled, the 4p and 3d sublevels are the next available vacant orbitals. **Figure 3.1** (on the first page of this section) shows that the 3d sublevel is lower in energy than the 4p sublevel. Therefore, the five 3d orbitals are next to be filled. A total of 10 electrons can occupy the 3d orbitals. These are filled successively in the 10 elements from scandium (atomic number 21) to zinc (atomic number 30).

Scandium, Sc, has the electron configuration [Ar]3d^{1}4s^2. Titanium, Ti, has the configuration [Ar]3d^{2}4s^2. And vanadium, V, has the configuration [Ar]3d^{3}4s^2. Up to this point, three electrons with the same spin have been added to three separate d orbitals, as required by Hund's rule.

Surprisingly, chromium, Cr, has the electron configuration [Ar]3d^{5}4s^1. Not only did the added electron go into the fourth 3d orbital, but an electron also moved from the 4s orbital into the fifth 3d orbital, leaving the 4s orbital with a single electron. Chromium's electron configuration is contrary to what is expected according to the Aufbau principle. However, in reality the [Ar]3d^{5}4s^1 configuration is of lower energy than a [Ar]3d^{4}4s^2 configuration. For chromium, having six orbitals with unpaired electrons is a more stable arrangement than having four unpaired electrons in the 3d orbitals and forcing two electrons to pair up in the 4s orbital. On the other hand, for tungsten, W, which is in the same group as chromium, having four electrons in the 5d orbitals and two electrons paired in the 6s orbital is the most stable arrangement. There is no simple explanation for such deviations from the expected order given in **Figure 3.4**.

Manganese, Mn, has the electron configuration $[Ar]3d^54s^2$. The added electron goes to the 4s orbital, completely filling this orbital while leaving the 3d orbitals still half-filled. Beginning with the next element, electrons continue to pair in the d orbitals. Thus, iron, Fe, has the configuration $[Ar]3d^64s^2$; cobalt, Co, has the configuration $[Ar]3d^74s^2$; and nickel, Ni, has the configuration $[Ar]3d^84s^2$. Next is copper, Cu, in which an electron moves from the 4s orbital to pair with the electron in the fifth 3d orbital. The result is an electron configuration of $[Ar]3d^{10}4s^1$—the lowest-energy configuration for Cu. As with Cr, there is no simple explanation for this deviation from the expected order.

In atoms of zinc, Zn, the 4s sublevel is filled to give the electron configuration $[Ar]3d^{10}4s^2$. In atoms of the next six elements, electrons add one by one to the three 4p orbitals. According to Hund's rule, one electron is added to each of the three 4p orbitals before electrons are paired in any 4p orbital.

FIGURE 3.7

ELECTRON CONFIGURATION OF ATOMS OF ELEMENTS IN THE FOURTH PERIOD

Name	Symbol	Atomic number	Number of electrons in sublevels above 2p					Noble-gas notation
			3s	3p	3d	4s	4p	
Potassium	K	19	2	6		1		*$[Ar]4s^1$
Calcium	Ca	20	2	6		2		$[Ar]4s^2$
Scandium	Sc	21	2	6	1	2		$[Ar]3d^14s^2$
Titanium	Ti	22	2	6	2	2		$[Ar]3d^24s^2$
Vanadium	V	23	2	6	3	2		$[Ar]3d^34s^2$
Chromium	Cr	24	2	6	5	1		$[Ar]3d^54s^1$
Manganese	Mn	25	2	6	5	2		$[Ar]3d^54s^2$
Iron	Fe	26	2	6	6	2		$[Ar]3d^64s^2$
Cobalt	Co	27	2	6	7	2		$[Ar]3d^74s^2$
Nickel	Ni	28	2	6	8	2		$[Ar]3d^84s^2$
Copper	Cu	29	2	6	10	1		$[Ar]3d^{10}4s^1$
Zinc	Zn	30	2	6	10	2		$[Ar]3d^{10}4s^2$
Gallium	Ga	31	2	6	10	2	1	$[Ar]3d^{10}4s^24p^1$
Germanium	Ge	32	2	6	10	2	2	$[Ar]3d^{10}4s^24p^2$
Arsenic	As	33	2	6	10	2	3	$[Ar]3d^{10}4s^24p^3$
Selenium	Se	34	2	6	10	2	4	$[Ar]3d^{10}4s^24p^4$
Bromine	Br	35	2	6	10	2	5	$[Ar]3d^{10}4s^24p^5$
Krypton	Kr	36	2	6	10	2	6	$[Ar]3d^{10}4s^24p^6$

*$[Ar] = 1s^22s^22p^63s^23p^6$

Elements of the Fifth Period

In the 18 elements of the fifth period, sublevels fill in a similar manner as in elements of the fourth period. However, they start at the 5s orbital instead of at the 4s orbital. Successive electrons are added first to the 5s orbital, then to the 4d orbitals, and finally to the 5p orbitals. This can be seen in **Figure 3.8.** There are occasional deviations from the predicted configurations here also. The deviations differ from those for fourth-period elements, but in each case the preferred configuration has the lowest possible energy.

FIGURE 3.8

ELECTRON CONFIGURATIONS OF ATOMS OF ELEMENTS IN THE FIFTH PERIOD

Name	Symbol	Atomic number	Number of electrons in sublevels above 3d					Noble-gas notation
			4s	4p	4d	5s	5p	
Rubidium	Rb	37	2	6		1		*[Kr]$5s^1$
Strontium	Sr	38	2	6		2		[Kr]$5s^2$
Yttrium	Y	39	2	6	1	2		[Kr]$4d^15s^2$
Zirconium	Zr	40	2	6	2	2		[Kr]$4d^25s^2$
Niobium	Nb	41	2	6	4	1		[Kr]$4d^45s^1$
Molybdenum	Mo	42	2	6	5	1		[Kr]$4d^55s^1$
Technetium	Tc	43	2	6	6	1		[Kr]$4d^65s^1$
Ruthenium	Ru	44	2	6	7	1		[Kr]$4d^75s^1$
Rhodium	Rh	45	2	6	8	1		[Kr]$4d^85s^1$
Palladium	Pd	46	2	6	10			[Kr]$4d^{10}$
Silver	Ag	47	2	6	10	1		[Kr]$4d^{10}5s^1$
Cadmium	Cd	48	2	6	10	2		[Kr]$4d^{10}5s^2$
Indium	In	49	2	6	10	2	1	[Kr]$4d^{10}5s^25p^1$
Tin	Sn	50	2	6	10	2	2	[Kr]$4d^{10}5s^25p^2$
Antimony	Sb	51	2	6	10	2	3	[Kr]$4d^{10}5s^25p^3$
Tellurium	Te	52	2	6	10	2	4	[Kr]$4d^{10}5s^25p^4$
Iodine	I	53	2	6	10	2	5	[Kr]$4d^{10}5s^25p^5$
Xenon	Xe	54	2	6	10	2	6	[Kr]$4d^{10}5s^25p^6$

*[Kr] = $1s^22s^22p^63s^23p^63d^{10}4s^24p^6$

Electron Configurations

Sample Problem B

a. Write both the complete electron-configuration notation and the noble-gas notation for iron, Fe.

b. How many electron-containing orbitals are in an atom of iron? How many of these orbitals are completely filled? How many unpaired electrons are there in an atom of iron? In which sublevel are the unpaired electrons located?

● SOLVE

a. The complete electron-configuration notation of iron is $1s^2 2s^2 2p^6 3s^2 3p^6 3d^6 4s^2$. The periodic table inside the back cover of the text reveals that $1s^2 2s^2 2p^6 3s^2 3p^6$ is the electron configuration of the noble gas argon, Ar. Therefore, as shown in **Figure 3.7**, iron's noble-gas notation is $[\text{Ar}]3d^6 4s^2$.

b. An iron atom has 15 orbitals that contain electrons. They consist of one 1s orbital, one 2s orbital, three 2p orbitals, one 3s orbital, three 3p orbitals, five 3d orbitals, and one 4s orbital. Eleven of these orbitals are filled, and there are four unpaired electrons. They are located in the 3d sublevel. The notation $3d^6$ represents:

$$3d \ \underline{\uparrow\downarrow} \ \underline{\uparrow} \ \underline{\uparrow} \ \underline{\uparrow} \ \underline{\uparrow}$$

Practice   Answers in Appendix E

1. a. Write both the complete electron-configuration notation and the noble-gas notation for iodine, I. How many inner-shell electrons does an iodine atom contain?
   b. How many electron-containing orbitals are in an atom of iodine? How many of these orbitals are filled? How many unpaired electrons are there in an atom of iodine?
2. a. Write the noble-gas notation for tin, Sn. How many unpaired electrons are there in an atom of tin?
   b. How many electron-containing d orbitals are there in an atom of tin? Name the element in the fourth period whose atoms have the same number of electrons in their highest energy levels that tin's atoms do.
3. a. Write the complete electron configuration for the element with atomic number 25. You may use the diagram shown in **Figure 3.2**.
   b. Identify the element described in item 3a.
4. a. How many orbitals are completely filled in an atom of the element with atomic number 18? Write the complete electron configuration for this element.
   b. Identify the element described in item 4a.

Elements of the Sixth Period

The sixth period consists of 32 elements. It is much longer than the periods that precede it in the periodic table. To build up electron configurations for elements of this period, electrons are added first to the 6s orbital in cesium, Cs, and barium, Ba. Then, in lanthanum, La, an electron is added to the 5d orbital.

Arrangement of Electrons in Atoms   **121**

With the next element, cerium, Ce, the $4f$ orbitals begin to fill, giving cerium atoms a configuration of $[Xe]4f^1 5d^1 6s^2$. In the next 13 elements, the $4f$ orbitals are filled. Next the $5d$ orbitals are filled, and the period is completed by filling the $6p$ orbitals. Because the $4f$ and the $5d$ orbitals are very close in energy, numerous deviations from the simple rules occur as these orbitals are filled. The electron configurations of the sixth-period elements can be found in the periodic table inside the back cover of the text. The seventh period is incomplete and consists largely of synthetic elements.

GO ONLINE

Solve It! Cards
HMHScience.com

Electron Configurations

Sample Problem C

a. Write both the complete electron-configuration notation and the noble-gas notation for a iridium atom.

b. Identify the elements in the second, third, and fourth periods that have the same number of highest-energy-level electrons as iridium.

● **SOLUTION**

a. $1s^2 2s^2 p^6 3s^2 p^6 d^{10} 4s^2 p^6 d^{10} f^{14} 5s^2 p^6 d^7 6s^2$; $[Xe]4f^{14}5d^7 6s^2$

b. Iridium has two electrons in its highest energy level (6). Elements with the same outermost configuration in their highest level are, in the second period, carbon; in the third period, silicon; in the fourth period, calcium, Ca; scandium, Sc; titanium, Ti; vanadium, Va; manganese, Mn; iron, Fe; cobalt, Co; nickel, Ni; zinc, Zn; germanium, Ge.

Practice   Answers in Appendix E

1. **a.** Write both the complete electron-configuration notation and the noble-gas notation for a barium atom.
   b. Identify the elements in the second, third, fourth, and fifth periods that have the same number of highest-energy-level electrons as barium.
2. **a.** Write the noble-gas notation for an antimony atom.
   b. Identify the elements in the sixth period that have an unpaired $5p$ electron.

✓ SECTION 3 FORMATIVE ASSESSMENT

▶ Reviewing Main Ideas

1. **a.** What is an atom's electron configuration?
   b. What three principles guide the electron configuration of an atom?

2. What three methods are used to represent the arrangement of electrons in atoms?

3. What is an octet of electrons? Which elements contain an octet of electrons?

4. Write the complete electron-configuration notation, the noble-gas notation, and the orbital notation for the following elements:
   a. carbon   **b.** neon   **c.** sulfur

5. Identify the elements having the following electron configurations:
   a. $1s^2 2s^2 2p^6 3s^2 3p^3$
   b. $[Ar]4s^1$
   c. contains just four electrons in its 3p orbitals
   d. contains one set of paired and three unpaired electrons in its fourth and outer main energy level

✓ Critical Thinking

6. **RELATING IDEAS** Write the electron configuration for the third-period elements Al, Si, P, S, and Cl. Is there a relationship between an element's group number and number of electrons in the outermost energy level?

You have learned that the mass of a proton is about 1 u and that a neutron is only slightly heavier. Because atomic nuclei consist of whole numbers of protons and neutrons, you might expect that the atomic mass of an element would be very near a whole number. However, if you look at the periodic table, you will see that the atomic masses of many elements lie somewhere between whole numbers. In fact, the atomic masses listed on the table are *average* atomic masses. The atomic masses are averages because most elements occur in nature as a specific mixture of isotopes. For example, 75.76% of chlorine atoms have a mass of 34.969 u, and 24.24% have a mass of 36.966 u. If the isotopes were in a 1:1 ratio, you could simply add the masses of the two isotopes together and divide by 2. However, to account for the differing abundance of the isotopes, you must calculate a *weighted average*. For chlorine, the weighted average is 35.45 u. The following two examples demonstrate how weighted averages are calculated.

Sample Problem

A sample of naturally occurring silver consists of 51.839% Ag-107 (atomic mass 106.905 093 u) and 48.161% Ag-109 (atomic mass 108.904 756 u). What is the average atomic mass of silver?

To find average atomic mass, convert each percentage to a decimal equivalent and multiply by the atomic mass of the isotope.

$$0.518\ 39 \times 106.905\ 093\ u = 55.419\ u$$
$$\underline{0.481\ 61 \times 108.904\ 756\ u = 52.450\ u}$$
$$107.869\ u$$

Adding the masses contributed by each isotope gives an average atomic mass of 107.869 u. Note that this value for the average atomic mass of silver is very near the one given in the periodic table.

A sample of naturally occurring magnesium consists of 78.99% Mg-24 (atomic mass 23.985 042 u), 10.00% Mg-25 (atomic mass 24.985 837 u), and 11.01% Mg-26 (atomic mass 25.982 593 u). What is the average atomic mass of magnesium?

Again, convert each percentage to a decimal and multiply by the atomic mass of the isotope to get the mass contributed by each isotope.

$$0.7899 \times 23.985\ 042\ u = 18.95\ u$$
$$0.1000 \times 24.985\ 837\ u = 2.499\ u$$
$$\underline{0.1101 \times 25.982\ 593\ u = 2.861\ u}$$
$$24.31\ u$$

Adding the masses contributed by each isotope gives an average atomic mass of 24.31 u.

Practice

1. Rubidium occurs naturally as a mixture of two isotopes, 72.17% Rb-85 (atomic mass 84.911 792 u) and 27.83% Rb-87 (atomic mass 86.909 186 u). What is the average atomic mass of rubidium?

2. The element silicon occurs as a mixture of three isotopes: 92.22% Si-28, 4.69% Si-29, and 3.09% Si-30. The atomic masses of these three isotopes are as follows: Si-28 = 27.976 926 u, Si-29 = 28.976 495 u, and Si-30 = 29.973 770 u.

   Find the average atomic mass of silicon.

Summary

SECTION 1 The Development of a New Atomic Model

KEY TERMS

- In the early twentieth century, light was determined to have a dual wave-particle nature.
- Quantum theory was developed to explain observations such as the photoelectric effect and the line-emission spectrum of hydrogen.
- Quantum theory states that electrons can exist only at specific atomic energy levels.
- When an electron moves from one main energy level to a main energy level of lower energy, a photon is emitted. The photon's energy equals the energy difference between the two levels.
- An electron in an atom can move from one main energy level to a higher main energy level only by absorbing an amount of energy exactly equal to the difference between the two levels.

electromagnetic radiation
electromagnetic spectrum
wavelength
frequency
photoelectric effect
quantum
photon
ground state
excited state
line-emission spectrum
continuous spectrum

SECTION 2 The Quantum Model of the Atom

KEY TERMS

- In the early twentieth century, electrons were determined to have a dual wave-particle nature.
- The Heisenberg uncertainty principle states that it is impossible to determine simultaneously the position and velocity of an electron or any other particle.
- Quantization of electron energies is a natural outcome of the Schrödinger wave equation, which describes the properties of an atom's electrons.
- An orbital, a three-dimensional region around the nucleus, shows the region in space where an electron is most likely to be found.
- The four quantum numbers that describe the properties of electrons in atomic orbitals are the principal quantum number, the angular momentum quantum number, the magnetic quantum number, and the spin quantum number.

Heisenberg uncertainty principle
quantum theory
orbital
quantum number
principal quantum number
angular momentum quantum number
magnetic quantum number
spin quantum number

SECTION 3 Electron Configurations

KEY TERMS

- The ground-state electron configuration of an atom can be written by using the Aufbau principle, Hund's rule, and the Pauli exclusion principle.
- Electron configurations can be depicted by using different types of notation. In this book, three types of notation are used: orbital notation, electron-configuration notation, and noble-gas notation.
- Electron configurations of some atoms, such as chromium, deviate from the predictions of the Aufbau principle, but the ground-state configuration that results is the configuration with the minimum possible energy.

electron configuration
Aufbau principle
Pauli exclusion principle
Hund's rule
noble gas
noble-gas configuration

CHAPTER 4   **Review**

GO ONLINE

Interactive Review
HMHScience.com

Review Games
Concept Maps

SECTION 1

The Development of a New Atomic Model

▶ **REVIEWING MAIN IDEAS**

1. **a.** List five examples of electromagnetic radiation.
   b. What is the speed of all forms of electromagnetic radiation in a vacuum?

2. Prepare a two-column table. List the properties of light that can best be explained by the wave theory in one column. List those best explained by the particle theory in the second column. You may want to consult a physics textbook for reference.

3. What are the frequency and wavelength ranges of visible light?

4. List the colors of light in the visible spectrum in order of increasing frequency.

5. In the early twentieth century, what two experiments involving light and matter could not be explained by the wave theory of light?

6. **a.** How are the wavelength and frequency of electromagnetic radiation related?
   b. How are the energy and frequency of electromagnetic radiation related?
   c. How are the energy and wavelength of electromagnetic radiation related?

7. Which theory of light—the wave or particle theory—best explains the following phenomena?
   a. the interference of light
   b. the photoelectric effect
   c. the emission of electromagnetic radiation by an excited atom

8. Distinguish between the ground state and an excited state of an atom.

9. According to Bohr's model, how is hydrogen's emission spectrum produced?

PRACTICE PROBLEMS

10. Determine the frequency of light whose wavelength is 4.257×10^{-7} cm.

11. Determine the energy in joules of a photon whose frequency is 3.55×10^{17} Hz.

12. Using the two equations $E = h\nu$ and $c = \lambda\nu$, derive an equation expressing E in terms of h, c, and λ.

13. How long would it take a radio wave whose frequency is 7.25×10^5 Hz to travel from Mars to Earth if the distance between the two planets is approximately 8.00×10^7 km?

14. Cobalt-60 is an artificial radioisotope that is produced in a nuclear reactor and is used as a gamma-ray source in the treatment of certain types of cancer. If the wavelength of the gamma radiation from a cobalt-60 source is 1.00×10^{-3} nm, calculate the energy of a photon of this radiation.

SECTION 2

The Quantum Model of the Atom

▶ **REVIEWING MAIN IDEAS**

15. Describe two major shortcomings of Bohr's model of the atom.

16. **a.** What is the principal quantum number?
    b. How is it symbolized?
    c. What are shells?
    d. How does n relate to the number of electrons allowed per main energy level?

17. **a.** What information is given by the angular momentum quantum number?
    b. What are sublevels, or subshells?

18. For each of the following values of n, indicate the numbers and types of sublevels possible for that main energy level. (Hint: See **Figure 2.6**.)
    a. $n = 1$
    b. $n = 2$
    c. $n = 3$
    d. $n = 4$
    e. $n = 7$ (number only)

19. **a.** What information is given by the magnetic quantum number?
    b. How many orbital orientations are possible in each of the s, p, d, and f sublevels?
    c. Explain and illustrate the notation for distinguishing between the different p orbitals in a sublevel.

20. a. What is the relationship between n and the total number of orbitals in a main energy level?

b. How many total orbitals are contained in the third main energy level? in the fifth?

21. a. What information is given by the spin quantum number?

b. What are the possible values for this quantum number?

22. How many electrons could be contained in the following main energy levels with n equal to the number provided?

a. 1

b. 3

c. 4

d. 6

e. 7

PRACTICE PROBLEMS

23. Sketch the shape of an s orbital and a p orbital.

24. How does a $2s$ orbital differ from a $1s$ orbital?

25. How do a $2p_x$ and a $2p_y$ orbital differ?

SECTION 3

Electron Configurations

▶ REVIEWING MAIN IDEAS

26. a. In your own words, state the Aufbau principle.

b. Explain the meaning of this principle in terms of an atom with many electrons.

27. a. In your own words, state Hund's rule.

b. What is the basis for this rule?

28. a. In your own words, state the Pauli exclusion principle.

b. What is the significance of the spin quantum number?

29. a. What is meant by the highest occupied energy level in an atom?

b. What are inner-shell electrons?

30. Determine the highest occupied energy level in the following elements:

a. He

b. Be

c. Al

d. Ca

e. Sn

31. Write the orbital notation for the following elements. (Hint: See Sample Problem A.)

a. P

b. B

c. Na

d. O

32. Write the electron-configuration notation for the element whose atoms contain the following number of electrons:

a. 3

b. 6

c. 8

d. 13

33. Given that the electron configuration for oxygen is $1s^2 2s^2 2p^4$, answer the following questions:

a. How many electrons are in each oxygen atom?

b. What is the atomic number of this element?

c. Write the orbital notation for oxygen's electron configuration.

d. How many unpaired electrons does oxygen have?

e. What is the highest occupied energy level?

f. How many inner-shell electrons does the atom contain?

g. In which orbital(s) are these inner-shell electrons located?

34. a. What are the noble gases?

b. What is a noble-gas configuration?

c. How does noble-gas notation simplify writing an atom's electron configuration?

35. Write the noble-gas notation for the electron configuration of each of the elements below. (Hint: See Sample Problem B.)

a. Cl

b. Ca

c. Se

36. a. What information is given by the noble-gas notation $[Ne]3s^2$?

b. What element does this represent?

37. Write both the complete electron-configuration notation and the noble-gas notation for each of the elements below. (Hint: See Sample Problem C.)

a. Na

b. Sr

c. P

38. Identify each of the following atoms on the basis of its electron configuration:
   a. $1s^2 2s^2 2p^1$
   b. $1s^2 2s^2 2p^5$
   c. $[Ne]3s^2$
   d. $[Ne]3s^2 3p^2$
   e. $[Ne]3s^2 3p^5$
   f. $[Ar]4s^1$
   g. $[Ar]3d^6 4s^2$

PRACTICE PROBLEMS

39. List the order in which orbitals generally fill, from the $1s$ to the $7p$ orbital.

40. Write the noble-gas notation for the electron configurations of each of the following elements:
   a. As   **e.** Sn
   b. Pb   **f.** Xe
   c. Lr   **g.** La
   d. Hg

41. How do the electron configurations of chromium and copper contradict the Aufbau principle?

Mixed Review

▶ REVIEWING MAIN IDEAS

42. a. Which has a longer wavelength: green light or yellow light?
   b. Which has a higher frequency: an x-ray or a microwave?
   c. Which travels at a greater speed: ultraviolet light or infrared light?

43. Write both the complete electron-configuration and noble-gas notation for each of the following:
   a. Ar   **b.** Br   **c.** Al

44. Given the speed of light as 3.00×10^8 m/s, calculate the wavelength of the electromagnetic radiation whose frequency is 7.500×10^{12} Hz.

45. a. What is the electromagnetic spectrum?
   b. What units can be used to express wavelength?
   c. What unit is used to express frequencies of electromagnetic waves?

46. Given that the electron configuration for phosphorus is $1s^2 2s^2 2p^6 3s^2 3p^3$, answer the following questions:
   a. How many electrons are in each atom?
   b. What is the atomic number of this element?
   c. Write the orbital notation for this element.
   d. How many unpaired electrons does an atom of phosphorus have?
   e. What is its highest occupied energy level?
   f. How many inner-shell electrons does the atom contain?
   g. In which orbital(s) are these inner-shell electrons located?

47. What is the frequency of a radio wave whose energy is 1.55×10^{-24} J per photon?

48. Write the noble-gas notation for the electron configurations of each of the following elements:
   a. Hf   **d.** At
   b. Sc   **e.** Ac
   c. Fe   **f.** Zn

49. Describe the major similarities and differences between Schrödinger's model of the atom and the model proposed by Bohr.

50. When sodium is heated, a yellow spectral line whose energy is 3.37×10^{-19} J per photon is produced.
   a. What is the frequency of this light?
   b. What is the wavelength of this light?

51. a. What is an orbital?
   b. Describe an orbital in terms of an electron cloud.

CRITICAL THINKING

52. Inferring Relationships In the emission spectrum of hydrogen shown in **Figure 1.5**, each colored line is produced by the emission of photons with specific energies. Substances also produce absorption spectra when electromagnetic radiation passes through them. Certain wavelengths are absorbed. Using the diagram below, predict what the wavelengths of the absorption lines will be when white light (all of the colors of the visible spectrum) is passed through hydrogen gas.

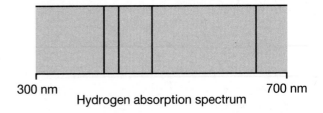

Hydrogen absorption spectrum

53. Applying Models In discussions of the photoelectric effect, the minimum energy needed to remove an electron from the metal is called the *threshold energy* and is a characteristic of the metal. For example, chromium, Cr, will emit electrons when the wavelength of the radiation is 284 nm or less. Calculate the threshold energy for chromium. (Hint: You will need to use the two equations that describe the relationships between wavelength, frequency, speed of light, and Planck's constant.)

54. Analyzing Information Four electrons in an atom have the four sets of quantum numbers given below. Which electrons are in the same orbital? Explain your answer.

a. 1, 0, 0, $-1/2$
b. 1, 0, 0, $+1/2$
c. 2, 1, 1, $+1/2$
d. 2, 1, 0, $+1/2$

55. Relating Ideas Which of the sets of quantum numbers below are possible? Which are impossible? Explain your choices.

a. 2, 2, 1, $+1/2$
b. 2, 0, 0, $-1/2$
c. 2, 0, 1, $-1/2$

USING THE HANDBOOK

56. Sections 1 and 2 of the *Elements Handbook* (Appendix A) contain information on an analytical test and a technological application for Group 1 and 2 elements. The test and application are based on the emission of light from atoms. Review these sections to answer the following:

a. What analytical technique utilizes the emission of light from excited atoms?
b. What elements in Groups 1 and 2 can be identified by this technique?
c. What types of compounds are used to provide color in fireworks?
d. What wavelengths within the visible spectrum would most likely contain emission lines for barium?

RESEARCH AND WRITING

57. Neon signs do not always contain neon gas. The various colored lights produced by the signs are due to the emission of a variety of low-pressure gases in different tubes. Research other kinds of gases used in neon signs, and list the colors that they emit.

58. Prepare a report about the photoelectric effect, and cite some of its practical uses. Explain the basic operation of each device or technique mentioned.

ALTERNATIVE ASSESSMENT

59. Performance A spectroscope is a device used to produce and analyze spectra. Construct a simple spectroscope, and determine the absorption spectra of several elemental gases. (Your teacher will provide you with the gas discharge tubes containing samples of different gases.)

Standards-Based Assessment

Record your answers on a separate piece of paper.

MULTIPLE CHOICE

1 For which of the following discoveries is Niels Bohr given credit?

 A discovering the electron

 B linking spectral lines with electron energy levels

 C explaining the details of bioluminescence

 D explaining the chemical behavior of atoms

Light	wavelength	frequency
Red	6.5×10^{-7} m	?
Blue	?	6.60×10^{14} Hz

speed of light	3×10^8 m/s
Planck's constant	6.26×10^{-34} J·s

For questions 2–4, refer to the tables above.

2 Using the table above, calculate the frequency of red light.

 A 4.6×10^{14} Hz

 B 3.0×10^8 Hz

 C 1.3×10^6 Hz

 D 9.8×10^4 Hz

3 Using the table above, calculate the wavelength of blue light.

 A 3.9×10^{-3} m

 B 2.2×10^{-7} m

 C 3.0×10^{-8} m

 D 4.5×10^{-7} m

4 How much energy in joules is found in a photon of yellow light with wavelength 5.9×10^{-7} m?

 A 1.3×10^{14} J

 B 3.9×10^{-19} J

 C 3.4×10^{-19} J

 D 3.4×10^{14} J

5 Which element has the noble gas notation $[Kr]5s^24d^2$?

 A Se

 B Zr

 C Sr

 D Mo

6 When a calcium salt is heated in a flame, a photon of light with an energy of 3.2×10^{-19} J is emitted. On the basis of this fact and the table below, what color would be expected for the calcium flame?

Frequency, s^{-1}	7.1×10^{14}	6.4×10^{14}	5.7×10^{14}
Wavelength, nm	422	469	526
Color	violet	blue	green
Frequency, s^{-1}	5.2×10^{14}	4.8×10^{14}	4.3×10^{14}
Wavelength, nm	577	625	698
Color	yellow	orange	red

 A yellow

 B yellow-orange

 C orange

 D red

7 Which of the following correctly expresses the electron configuration for bromine, Br?

 A $1s^22s^22p^63s^23p^63d^{10}4s^24p^5$

 B $1s^22s^22p^63s^23p^63d^84s^24p^63d^84s^24p^5$

 C $1s^22p^63s^23p^63d^{10}4s^24p^63d^{10}4s^24p^5$

 D $1s^22s^22p^63s^23p^63d^{10}4s^24p^63d^{10}4s^24p^6$

GRIDDED RESPONSE

8 A sample of a naturally occurring element contains the following proportions:

Natural Abundance	Atomic Mass
19.9%	10.0129369
80.1%	11.0093054

What is the average atomic mass for this element? Round to the nearest thousandth.

Test Tip

If time permits, take short mental breaks during the test to improve your concentration.

CHAPTER 5
The Periodic Law

BIG IDEA
The properties of the chemical elements are a periodic function of their atomic numbers.

ONLINE Chemistry
HMHScience.com

ONLINE LABS
- The Mendeleev Lab of 1869
- Reactivity of Halide Ions
- Periodicity of Properties of Oxides
- Exploring the Periodic Table

GO ONLINE

Why It Matters Video
HMHScience.com

Periodic Law

(t) ©NOAO/Photo Researchers, Inc

History of the Periodic Table

Key Terms

periodic law
periodic table
lanthanide
actinide

SECTION 1

Main Ideas

▶ Mendeleev's periodic table grouped elements by their properties.

▶ Moseley arranged elements by their atomic numbers.

▶ Modern periodic tables arrange the elements by both atomic number and properties.

Imagine the confusion among chemists during the middle of the nineteenth century. By 1860, more than 60 elements had been discovered. Chemists had to learn the properties of these elements as well as those of the many compounds that they formed—a difficult task. And to make matters worse, there was no method for accurately determining an element's atomic mass or the number of atoms of an element in a particular chemical compound. Different chemists used different atomic masses for the same elements, resulting in different compositions being proposed for the same compounds. This made it nearly impossible for one chemist to understand the results of another.

In September 1860, a group of chemists assembled at the First International Congress of Chemists in Karlsruhe, Germany, to settle the issue of atomic mass as well as some other matters that were making communication difficult. At the Congress, Italian chemist Stanislao Cannizzaro presented a convincing method for accurately measuring the relative masses of atoms. Cannizzaro's method enabled chemists to agree on standard values for atomic mass and initiated a search for relationships between atomic mass and other properties of the elements.

▶ **MAIN IDEA**

Mendeleev's periodic table grouped elements by their properties.

When the Russian chemist Dmitri Mendeleev heard about the new atomic masses discussed at Karlsruhe, he decided to include the new values in a chemistry textbook he was writing. In the book, Mendeleev hoped to organize the elements according to their properties. He went about this much as you might organize information for a research paper. He placed the name of each known element on a card, together with the atomic mass of the element and a list of its observed physical and chemical properties. He then arranged the cards according to various properties and looked for trends or patterns.

Mendeleev noticed that when the elements were arranged in order of increasing atomic mass, certain similarities in their chemical properties appeared at regular intervals. Such a repeating pattern is referred to as *periodic*. The second hand of a watch, for example, passes over any given mark at periodic, 60-second intervals. The circular waves created by a drop of water hitting a water surface, as shown in **Figure 1.1**, are also periodic.

FIGURE 1.1

Periodic Patterns The regularly spaced water waves represent a simple periodic pattern.

✓ **CRITICAL THINKING**

Relate Why are regularly spaced water waves referred to as a periodic pattern?

FIGURE 1.2

Mendeleev's First Periodic Table

In his first published periodic table, Mendeleev arranged the elements in vertical periods according to relative atomic mass. The atomic mass for each element is indicated by the number following the element's symbol. The unknown elements indicated by question marks at estimated atomic masses 45, 68, and 70 were later identified as scandium, Sc; gallium, Ga; and germanium, Ge.

но въ ней, мнѣ кажется, уже ясно выражается примѣнимость выставляемаго мною начала ко всей совокупности элементовъ, пай которыхъ извѣстенъ съ достовѣрностію. На этотъ разъ я и желалъ преимущественно найдти общую систему элементовъ. Вотъ этотъ опытъ:

			Ti = 50	Zr = 90	? = 180.
			V = 51	Nb = 94	Ta = 182.
			Cr = 52	Mo = 96	W = 186.
			Mn = 55	Rh = 104,4	Pt = 197,4
			Fe = 56	Ru = 104,4	Ir = 198.
		Ni = Co = 59		Pl = 106,6	Os = 199.
H = 1			Cu = 63,4	Ag = 108	Hg = 200.
	Be = 9,4	Mg = 24	Zn = 65,2	Cd = 112	
	B = 11	Al = 27,4	? = 68	Ur = 116	Au = 197?
	C = 12	Si = 28	? = 70	Su = 118	
	N = 14	P = 31	As = 75	Sb = 122	Bi = 210
	O = 16	S = 32	Se = 79,4	Te = 128?	
	F = 19	Cl = 35,5	Br = 80	I = 127	
Li = 7	Na = 23	K = 39	Rb = 85,4	Cs = 133	Tl = 204
		Ca = 40	Sr = 87,6	Ba = 137	Pb = 207.
		? = 45	Ce = 92		
		?Er = 56	La = 94		
		?Yt = 60	Di = 95		
		?In = 75,6	Th = 118?		

а потому приходится въ разныхъ рядахъ имѣть различное измѣненіе разностей, чего нѣтъ въ главныхъ числахъ предлагаемой таблицы. Или же придется предполагать при составленіи системы очень много недостающихъ членовъ. То и другое мало выгодно. Мнѣ кажется притомъ, наиболѣе естественнымъ составить

Mendeleev created a table in which elements with similar properties were grouped together—a periodic table of the elements. His first periodic table, shown in **Figure 1.2,** was published in 1869. Note that Mendeleev placed iodine, I (atomic mass 127), after tellurium, Te (atomic mass 128). Although this contradicted the pattern of listing the elements in order of increasing atomic mass, it allowed Mendeleev to place tellurium in a group of elements with which it shares similar properties. Reading horizontally across Mendeleev's table, this group includes oxygen, O; sulfur, S; and selenium, Se. Iodine could also then be placed in the group it resembles chemically, which includes fluorine, F; chlorine, Cl, and bromine, Br.

Mendeleev's procedure left several empty spaces in his periodic table (see **Figure 1.2**). In 1871, the Russian chemist boldly predicted the existence and properties of the elements that would fill three of the spaces. By 1886, all three elements had been discovered. Today these elements are known as scandium, Sc; gallium, Ga; and germanium, Ge. Their properties are strikingly similar to those predicted by Mendeleev.

The success of Mendeleev's predictions persuaded most chemists to accept his periodic table and earned him credit as the discoverer of the periodic law. Two questions remained, however. (1) Why could most of the elements be arranged in the order of increasing atomic mass, but a few could not? (2) What was the reason for chemical periodicity?

MAIN IDEA
Moseley arranged elements by their atomic numbers.

The first question was not answered until more than 40 years after Mendeleev's first periodic table was published. In 1911, the English scientist Henry Moseley, who was working with Ernest Rutherford, examined the spectra of 38 different metals. When analyzing his data, Moseley discovered a previously unrecognized pattern. The elements in the periodic table fit into patterns better when they were arranged in increasing order according to nuclear charge, or the number of protons in the nucleus. Moseley's work led to both the modern definition of atomic number and the recognition that atomic number, not atomic mass, is the basis for the organization of the periodic table.

Moseley's discovery was consistent with Mendeleev's ordering of the periodic table by properties rather than strictly by atomic mass. For example, according to Moseley, tellurium, with an atomic number of 52, belongs before iodine, which has an atomic number of 53. Today, Mendeleev's principle of chemical periodicity is correctly stated in what is known as the **periodic law:** The physical and chemical properties of the elements are periodic functions of their atomic numbers. In other words, when the elements are arranged in order of increasing atomic number, elements with similar properties appear at regular intervals.

MAIN IDEA
Modern periodic tables arrange the elements by both atomic number and properties.

The periodic table has undergone extensive change since Mendeleev's time. Chemists have discovered new elements and, in more recent years, synthesized new ones in the laboratory. Each of the more than 40 new elements, however, can be placed in a group of other elements with similar properties. **The periodic table** is an arrangement of the elements in order of their atomic numbers so that elements with similar properties fall in the same column, or group.

The Noble Gases

Perhaps the most significant addition to the periodic table came with the discovery of the noble gases. In 1894, English physicist John William Strutt (Lord Rayleigh) and Scottish chemist Sir William Ramsay discovered argon, Ar, a gas in the atmosphere that had previously escaped notice because of its total lack of chemical reactivity. Back in 1868, another noble gas, helium, He, had been discovered as a component of the sun. In 1895, Ramsay showed that helium also exists on Earth.

In order to fit argon and helium into the periodic table, Ramsay proposed a new group (see **Figure 1.3**). He placed this group between the groups now known as Group 17 (the fluorine family) and Group 1 (the lithium family). In 1898, Ramsay discovered two more noble gases, krypton, Kr, and xenon, Xe. The final noble gas, radon, Rn, was discovered in 1900 by the German scientist Friedrich Ernst Dorn.

FIGURE 1.3

Noble Gases The noble gases, also known as the Group 18 elements, are all rather unreactive. As you will read, the reason for this low reactivity also accounts for the special place occupied by the noble gases in the periodic table.

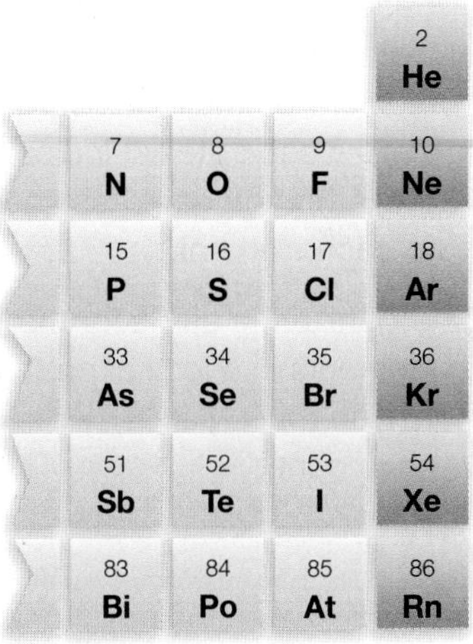

The Lanthanides

The next step in the development of the periodic table was completed in the early 1900s. It was then that the puzzling chemistry of the lanthanides was finally understood. **The lanthanides are the 14 elements with atomic numbers from 58 (cerium, Ce) to 71 (lutetium, Lu).** Because these elements are so similar in chemical and physical properties, the process of separating and identifying them was a tedious task that required the effort of many chemists.

The Actinides

Another major step in the development of the periodic table was the discovery of the actinides. **The actinides are the 14 elements with atomic numbers from 90 (thorium, Th) to 103 (lawrencium, Lr).** The lanthanides and actinides belong in Periods 6 and 7, respectively, of the periodic table, between the elements of Groups 3 and 4. To save space, the lanthanides and actinides are usually set off below the main portion of the periodic table.

QuickLAB — DESIGNING YOUR OWN PERIODIC TABLE

QUESTION

Can you design your own periodic table using information similar to that available to Mendeleev?

PROCEDURE

1. Write down the information available for each element on separate index cards. The following information is appropriate: a letter of the alphabet (A, B, C, etc.) to identify each element; atomic mass; state; density; melting point; boiling point; and any other readily observable physical properties. Do not write the name of the element on the index card, but keep a separate list indicating the letter you have assigned to each element.

2. Organize the cards for the elements in a logical pattern as you think Mendeleev might have done.

DISCUSSION

1. Keeping in mind that the information you have is similar to that available to Mendeleev in 1869, answer the following questions.

   a. Why are atomic masses given instead of atomic numbers?

   b. Can you identify each element by name?

2. How many groups of elements, or families, are in your periodic table? How many periods, or series, are in the table?

3. Predict the characteristics of any missing elements. When you have finished, check your work using your separate list of elements and a periodic table.

MATERIALS

- index cards

Periodicity

Periodicity with respect to atomic number can be observed in any group of elements in the periodic table. For example, consider the noble gases of Group 18. The first noble gas is helium, He. Helium has an atomic number of 2. The elements following helium in atomic number have completely different properties until the next noble gas, neon, Ne, is reached. Neon has an atomic number of 10. The remaining noble gases in order of increasing atomic number are argon (Ar, atomic number 18), krypton (Kr, atomic number 36), xenon (Xe, atomic number 54), and radon (Rn, atomic number 86). Thus, the differences in atomic number between successive noble gases are 8, 8, 18, 18, and 32, as shown in **Figure 1.4.**

Also shown in **Figure 1.4** are atomic-number differences between the elements of Group 1. These elements are all solid, silvery metals. As you can see, the differences in atomic number between the Group 1 metals follow the same pattern as the differences in atomic number between the noble gases: 8, 8, 18, 18, and 32.

Starting with the first member of Groups 13–17, a similar periodic tern is repeated. The atomic number of each successive element is 8, 8, 18, 18, and 32 higher than the atomic number of the element above it. In Section 2, you will see that the second mystery presented by Mendeleev's periodic table—the reason for periodicity—is explained by the arrangement of the electrons around the nucleus.

FIGURE 1.4

Patterns in the Periodic Table
In each of Groups 1 and 18, the differences between the atomic numbers of successive elements are 8, 8, 18, 18, and 32, respectively. Groups 2 and 13–17 follow a similar pattern.

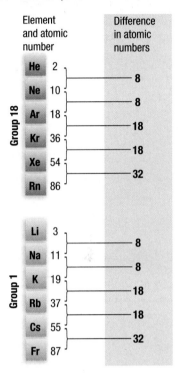

✔ SECTION 1 FORMATIVE ASSESSMENT

▶ Reviewing Main Ideas

1. **a.** Who is credited with developing a method that led to the determination of standard relative atomic masses?

   b. Who discovered the periodic law?

   c. Who established atomic numbers as the basis for organizing the periodic table?

2. State the periodic law.

3. Name three sets of elements that have been added to the periodic table since Mendeleev's time.

4. How do the atomic numbers of the elements within each of Groups 1, 2, and 13–18 of the periodic table vary? (Refer to **Figure 1.4** as a guide.)

✔ Critical Thinking

5. **RELATING IDEAS** Why are elements' atomic masses not in strict increasing order in the periodic table, even though the properties of the elements are similar? For example, by atomic mass, tellurium, Te, should be in group 17, and iodine, I, should be in Group 16, but grouping by properties has Te in Group 16 and I in Group 17.

SECTION 2

Main Idea

The periods of the periodic table are determined by electron configuration.

Electron Configuration and the Periodic Table

Key Terms
alkali metals

alkaline-earth metals

transition elements

main-group elements

halogens

The Group 18 elements of the periodic table (the noble gases) undergo few chemical reactions. This stability results from the gases' special electron configurations. Helium's highest occupied level, the $1s$ orbital, is completely filled with electrons. And the highest occupied levels of the other noble gases contain stable octets, ns^2np^6. Generally, the electron configuration of an atom's highest occupied energy level governs the atom's chemical properties.

▶ MAIN IDEA

The periods of the periodic table are determined by electron configuration.

While the elements are arranged vertically in the periodic table in groups that share similar chemical properties, they are also organized horizontally in rows, or *periods*. (There are a total of seven periods of elements in the modern periodic table.) As can be seen in **Figure 2.1**, the length of each period is determined by the number of electrons that can occupy the sublevels being filled in that period.

FIGURE 2.1

RELATIONSHIP BETWEEN PERIOD LENGTH AND SUBLEVELS BEING FILLED IN THE PERIODIC TABLE

Period number	Number of elements in period	Sublevels in order of filling
1	2	$1s$
2	8	$2s\,2p$
3	8	$3s\,3p$
4	18	$4s\,3d\,4p$
5	18	$5s\,4d\,5p$
6	32	$6s\,4f\,5d\,6p$
7	32	$7s\,5f\,6d\,7p$

In the first period, the $1s$ sublevel is being filled. The $1s$ sublevel can hold a total of two electrons. Therefore, the first period consists of two elements—hydrogen and helium. In the second period, the $2s$ sublevel, which can hold two electrons, and the $2p$ sublevel, which can hold six electrons, are being filled. Consequently, the second period totals eight elements. Similarly, filling of the $3s$ and $3p$ sublevels accounts for the eight elements of the third period. Filling $3d$ and $4d$ sublevels in addition to the s and p sublevels adds 10 elements to both the fourth and fifth periods. Therefore, each of these periods totals 18 elements. Filling $4f$ sublevels in addition to s, p, and d sublevels adds 14 elements to the sixth period, which totals 32 elements. And as new elements are created, the named elements in Period 7 could, in theory, be extended to 32 as well.

The period of an element can be determined from the element's electron configuration. For example, arsenic, As, has the electron configuration $[Ar]3d^{10}4s^24p^3$. The 4 in $4p^3$ indicates that arsenic's highest occupied energy level is the fourth energy level. Arsenic is thus in the fourth period in the periodic table. The period and electron configuration for each element can be found in the periodic table (on the next two pages). Based on the electron configurations of the elements, the periodic table can be divided into four blocks, the s-, p-, d-, and f-blocks. This division is illustrated in **Figure 2.2**. The name of each block is determined by whether an s, p, d, or f sublevel is being filled in successive elements of that block.

FIGURE 2.2

Sublevel Blocks Based on the electron configurations of the elements, the periodic table can be subdivided into four sublevel blocks.

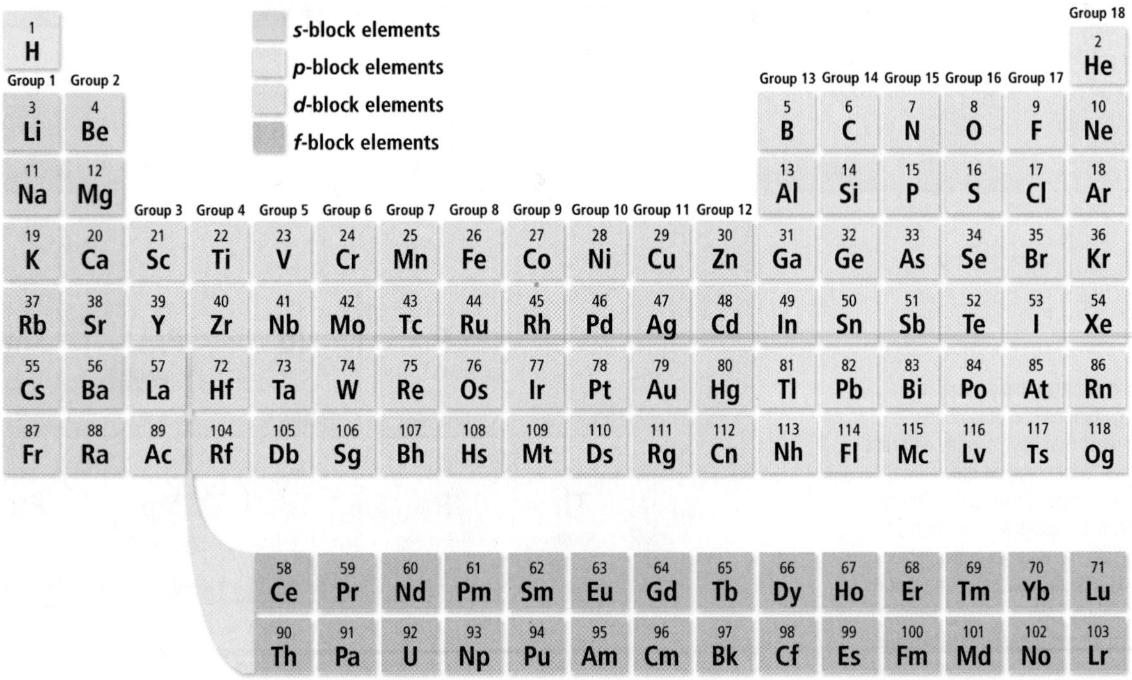

FIGURE 2.3

The Periodic Table of the Elements
In the modern periodic table, the elements are arranged by atomic number and form vertical groups and horizontal periods.

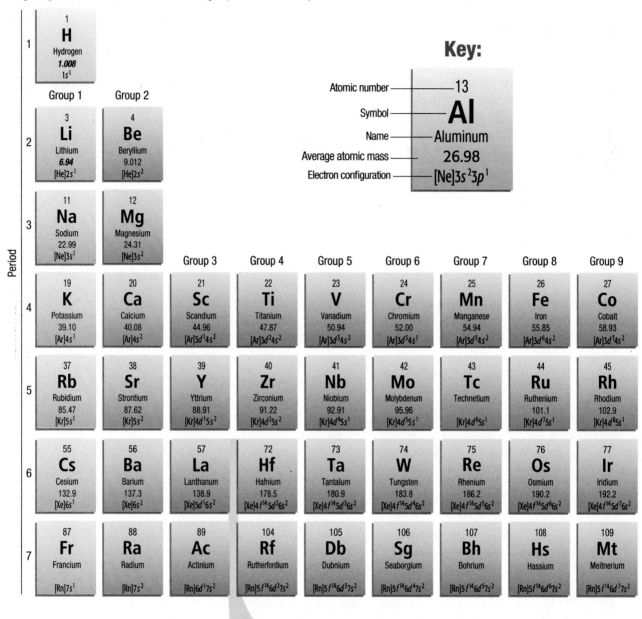

Atomic masses are averages based upon the naturally occurring composition of isotopes on Earth. For elements that have slightly different isotopic composition depending on the source, IUPAC now reports a range of values for atomic masses. These atomic masses are shown here in bold italics. The atomic masses in this table have been rounded to values sufficiently accurate for everyday calculations. Per IUPAC convention, no values are listed for elements whose isotopes lack a characteristic abundance in natural samples.

Hydrogen
Semiconductors
(also known as metalloids)

Metals
Alkali metals
Alkaline-earth metals
Transition metals
Other metals

Nonmetals
Halogens
Noble gases
Other nonmetals

Group 18

2
He
Helium
4.003
$1s^2$

Group 13	Group 14	Group 15	Group 16	Group 17
5	6	7	8	9
B	**C**	**N**	**O**	**F**
Boron	Carbon	Nitrogen	Oxygen	Fluorine
10.81	*12.01*	*14.007*	*15.999*	19.00
$[He]2s^22p^1$	$[He]2s^22p^2$	$[He]2s^22p^3$	$[He]2s^22p^4$	$[He]2s^22p^5$

10
Ne
Neon
20.18
$[He]2s^22p^6$

13	14	15	16	17	18
Al	**Si**	**P**	**S**	**Cl**	**Ar**
Aluminum	Silicon	Phosphorus	Sulfur	Chlorine	Argon
26.98	*28.085*	30.97	*32.06*	*35.45*	39.95
$[Ne]3s^23p^1$	$[Ne]3s^23p^2$	$[Ne]3s^23p^3$	$[Ne]3s^23p^4$	$[Ne]3s^23p^5$	$[Ne]3s^23p^6$

Group 10	Group 11	Group 12						
28	29	30	31	32	33	34	35	36
Ni	**Cu**	**Zn**	**Ga**	**Ge**	**As**	**Se**	**Br**	**Kr**
Nickel	Copper	Zinc	Gallium	Germanium	Arsenic	Selenium	Bromine	Krypton
58.69	63.55	65.38	69.72	72.63	74.92	78.96	79.90	83.80
$[Ar]3d^84s^2$	$[Ar]3d^{10}4s^1$	$[Ar]3d^{10}4s^2$	$[Ar]3d^{10}4s^24p^1$	$[Ar]3d^{10}4s^24p^2$	$[Ar]3d^{10}4s^24p^3$	$[Ar]3d^{10}4s^24p^4$	$[Ar]3d^{10}4s^24p^5$	$[Ar]3d^{10}4s^24p^6$
46	47	48	49	50	51	52	53	54
Pd	**Ag**	**Cd**	**In**	**Sn**	**Sb**	**Te**	**I**	**Xe**
Palladium	Silver	Cadmium	Indium	Tin	Antimony	Tellurium	Iodine	Xenon
106.4	107.9	112.4	114.8	118.7	121.8	127.6	126.9	131.3
$[Kr]4d^{10}$	$[Kr]4d^{10}5s^1$	$[Kr]4d^{10}5s^2$	$[Kr]4d^{10}5s^25p^1$	$[Kr]4d^{10}5s^25p^2$	$[Kr]4d^{10}5s^25p^3$	$[Kr]4d^{10}5s^25p^4$	$[Kr]4d^{10}5s^25p^5$	$[Kr]4d^{10}5s^25p^6$
78	79	80	81	82	83	84	85	86
Pt	**Au**	**Hg**	**Tl**	**Pb**	**Bi**	**Po**	**At**	**Rn**
Platinum	Gold	Mercury	Thallium	Lead	Bismuth	Polonium	Astatine	Radon
195.1	197.0	200.6	*204.38*	207.2	209.0			
$[Xe]4f^{14}5d^96s^1$	$[Xe]4f^{14}5d^{10}6s^1$	$[Xe]4f^{14}5d^{10}6s^2$	$[Xe]4f^{14}5d^{10}6s^26p^1$	$[Xe]4f^{14}5d^{10}6s^26p^2$	$[Xe]4f^{14}5d^{10}6s^26p^3$	$[Xe]4f^{14}5d^{10}6s^26p^4$	$[Xe]4f^{14}5d^{10}6s^26p^5$	$[Xe]4f^{14}5d^{10}6s^26p^6$
110	111	112	113	114	115	116	117	118
Ds	**Rg**	**Cn**	**Nh**	**Fl**	**Mc**	**Lv**	**Ts**	**Og**
Darmstadtium	Roentgenium	Copernicium	Nihonium	Flerovium	Moscovium	Livermorium	Tennessine	Oganesson
$[Rn]5f^{14}6d^97s^1$	$[Rn]5f^{14}6d^{10}7s^1$	$[Rn]5f^{14}6d^{10}7s^2$	$[Rn]5f^{14}6d^{10}7s^27p^1$	$[Rn]5f^{14}6d^{10}7s^27p^2$	$[Rn]5f^{14}6d^{10}7s^27p^3$	$[Rn]5f^{14}6d^{10}7s^27p^4$	$[Rn]5f^{14}6d^{10}7s^27p^5$	$[Rn]5f^{14}6d^{10}7s^27p^6$

63	64	65	66	67	68	69	70	71
Eu	**Gd**	**Tb**	**Dy**	**Ho**	**Er**	**Tm**	**Yb**	**Lu**
Europium	Gadolinium	Terbium	Dysprosium	Holmium	Erbium	Thulium	Ytterbium	Lutetium
152.0	157.3	158.9	162.5	164.9	167.3	168.9	173.1	175.0
$[Xe]4f^76s^2$	$[Xe]4f^75d^16s^2$	$[Xe]4f^96s^2$	$[Xe]4f^{10}6s^2$	$[Xe]4f^{11}6s^2$	$[Xe]4f^{12}6s^2$	$[Xe]4f^{13}6s^2$	$[Xe]4f^{14}6s^2$	$[Xe]4f^{14}5d^16s^2$
95	96	97	98	99	100	101	102	103
Am	**Cm**	**Bk**	**Cf**	**Es**	**Fm**	**Md**	**No**	**Lr**
Americium	Curium	Berkelium	Californium	Einsteinium	Fermium	Mendelevium	Nobelium	Lawrencium
$[Rn]5f^77s^2$	$[Rn]5f^76d^17s^2$	$[Rn]5f^97s^2$	$[Rn]5f^{10}7s^2$	$[Rn]5f^{11}7s^2$	$[Rn]5f^{12}7s^2$	$[Rn]5f^{13}7s^2$	$[Rn]5f^{14}7s^2$	$[Rn]5f^{14}6d^17s^2$

FIGURE 2.4

Group 1: Alkali Metals

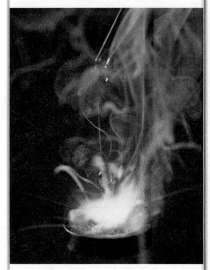

(a) Like other alkali metals, potassium reacts vigorously with water.

(b) Potassium must be stored in kerosene or oil to prevent it from reacting with moisture in the air.

The *s*-Block Elements: Groups 1 and 2

The elements of the *s*-block are chemically reactive metals. The Group 1 metals are more reactive than those of Group 2. The outermost energy level in an atom of each Group 1 element contains a single *s* electron. For example, the configurations of lithium and sodium are [He]$2s^1$ and [Ne]$3s^1$, respectively. As you will learn in Section 3, the ease with which the single electron is lost helps make the Group 1 metals extremely reactive. Using *n* for the number of the highest occupied energy level, the outer, or group, configurations of the Group 1 and 2 elements are written ns^1 and ns^2, respectively. For example, the configuration of Na is [Ne]$3s^1$, so the group configuration is written ns^1, where $n = 3$.

The elements of Group 1 of the periodic table (lithium, sodium, potassium, rubidium, cesium, and francium) are known as the **alkali metals.** In their pure state, all of the alkali metals have a silvery appearance and are soft enough to cut with a knife. However, because they are so reactive, alkali metals are not found in nature as free elements. They combine readily with most nonmetals. And they react vigorously with water to produce hydrogen gas and aqueous solutions of substances known as alkalis. Because of their extreme reactivity with air or moisture, alkali metals are usually stored in kerosene. Proceeding down the column, the elements of Group 1 melt at successively lower temperatures.

The elements of Group 2 of the periodic table (beryllium, magnesium, calcium, strontium, barium, and radium) are called the **alkaline-earth metals.** Atoms of alkaline-earth metals contain a pair of electrons in their outermost *s* sublevel. Consequently, the group configuration for Group 2 is ns^2. The Group 2 metals are harder, denser, and stronger than the alkali metals. They also have higher melting points. Although they are less reactive than the alkali metals, the alkaline-earth metals are also too reactive to be found in nature as free elements.

FIGURE 2.5

Group 2: Alkaline-Earth Metals

(a) Calcium, an alkaline-earth metal, is too reactive to be found in nature in its pure state.

(b) Instead, it exists in compounds, such as in the minerals that make up marble.

Hydrogen and Helium

Before discussing the other blocks of the periodic table, let's consider two special cases in the classification of the elements—hydrogen and helium. Hydrogen has an electron configuration of $1s^1$, but despite the ns^1 configuration, it does not share the same properties as the elements of Group 1. Although it is located above the Group 1 elements in many periodic tables, hydrogen is a unique element, with properties that do not closely resemble those of any group.

Like the Group 2 elements, helium has an ns^2 group configuration. Yet it is part of Group 18. Because its highest occupied energy level is filled by two electrons, helium possesses special chemical stability, exhibiting the unreactive nature of a Group 18 element. By contrast, the Group 2 metals have no special stability; their highest occupied energy levels are not filled because each metal has an empty available p sublevel.

CHECK FOR UNDERSTANDING

Apply Which is more important in determining an element's group: the electron configuration or the element's properties? Explain.

GO ONLINE

Learn It! Video
HMHScience.com

The Periodic Table and Electron Configurations

Sample Problem A (a) Without looking at the periodic table, identify the group, period, and block in which the element that has the electron configuration $[Xe]6s^2$ is located. (b) Without looking at the periodic table, write the electron configuration for the Group 1 element in the third period. Is this element likely to be more reactive or less reactive than the element described in (a)?

● **SOLVE**

    a. The element is in Group 2, as indicated by the group configuration of ns^2. It is in the sixth period, as indicated by the highest principal quantum number in its configuration, 6. The element is in the s-block.

    b. In a third-period element, the highest occupied energy level is the third main energy level, $n = 3$. The $1s$, $2s$, and $2p$ sublevels are completely filled (see **Figure 2.1**). A Group 1 element has a group configuration of ns^1, which indicates a single electron in its highest s sublevel. Therefore, this element has the following configuration:

$$1s^2 2s^2 2p^6 3s^1 \quad \text{or} \quad [Ne]3s^1$$

Because it is in Group 1 (the alkali metals), this element is likely to be more reactive than the element described in (a), which is in Group 2 (the alkaline-earth metals).

Practice   Answers in Appendix E

1. Without looking at the periodic table, identify the group, period, and block in which the element that has the electron configuration $[Kr]5s^1$ is located.

2. **a.** Without looking at the periodic table, write the group configuration for the Group 2 elements.

    b. Without looking at the periodic table, write the complete electron configuration for the Group 2 element in the fourth period.

    c. Refer to **Figure 2.3** to identify the element described in (b). Then, write the element's noble-gas notation.

FIGURE 2.6

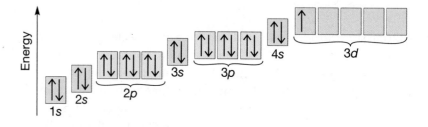

Group 3: Electron Configuration

The diagram shows the electron configuration of scandium, Sc, the Group 3 element of the fourth period. In general, the (n–1)d sublevel in Groups 3–12 is occupied by electrons after the ns sublevel is filled.

The d-Block Elements: Groups 3–12

For energy level n, there are n possible sublevels, so the d sublevel first appears when $n = 3$. This $3d$ sublevel is slightly higher in energy than the $4s$ sublevel, so these are filled in the order $4s3d$ (see **Figure 2.6**). This order of filling is also seen for higher values of n. Each d sublevel consists of five orbitals with a maximum of two electrons each, or up to 10 electrons possible in each d sublevel. In addition to the two ns electrons of Group 2, atoms of the Group 3 elements each have one electron in the d sublevel of the $(n–1)$ energy level. The group configuration for Group 3 is therefore $(n–1)d^1ns^2$. Atoms of the Group 12 elements have 10 electrons in the d sublevel plus two electrons in the ns sublevel. The group configuration for Group 12 is $(n–1)d^{10}ns^2$.

Some deviations from orderly d sublevel filling occur in Groups 4–11. As a result, elements in these d-block groups, unlike those in s-block and p-block groups, do not necessarily have identical outer electron configurations. For example, in Group 10, nickel, Ni, has the electron configuration $[Ar]3d^84s^2$. Palladium, Pd, has the configuration $[Kr]4d^{10}5s^0$. And platinum, Pt, has the configuration $[Xe]4f^{14}5d^96s^1$. Notice, however, that in each case the sum of the outer s and d electrons is equal to the group number.

The d-block elements are metals with typical metallic properties and are often referred to as transition elements. They are good conductors of electricity and have a high luster. They are typically less reactive than the alkali metals and the alkaline-earth metals. Some are so nonreactive that they do not easily form compounds and exist in nature as free elements. Palladium, platinum, and gold are among the least reactive of all the elements. Some d-block elements are shown in **Figure 2.7**.

✓ **CHECK FOR UNDERSTANDING**

Explain The word *transition* refers to change. What would be a reasonable explanation for referring to the d-block elements as transition elements?

FIGURE 2.7

Transition Elements

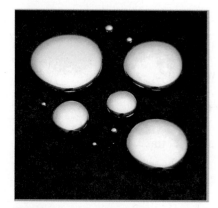

Mercury

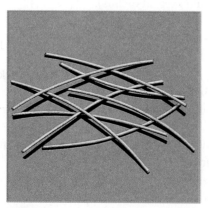

Tungsten

Vanadium

Materials Scientist

Materials scientists study the microstructure of materials, testing how they behave under various conditions.

Almost everything we use or wear is composed of materials. Materials can include metals, ceramics, polymers, semiconductors, and composites. Metals are good conductors of heat and electricity. They are strong but deformable. Ceramics are compounds that are typically made up of both metals and nonmetals. Usually, ceramics are insulators and are resistant to high temperatures. Examples of products that contain ceramics are dishes, building materials, bone and tooth replacements, and high-speed communications equipment. Polymers are generally organic compounds and have very large molecular structures. Polymer products include toys, storage containers, paints, and biomedical items; plastics (polymers) are everywhere. The electrical properties of semiconductors are between those of conductors and insulators. Computers, calculators, and cell phones are just a few examples of products that use semiconductors. Composites, such as ceramics and polymers, are found in flooring, tiles, bicycles, space shuttles, and insulation.

Materials science includes the study of the processing, structure, properties, and performance of materials. Processing involves manufacturing the material from its raw components. Structure refers to the arrangement of the material's components, from an atomic to a macro scale. Understanding the structure helps materials scientists develop new materials that have desirable properties. Typical properties of interest are mechanical, such as tensile strength or hardness; electrical, such as conductivity or resistivity; magnetic, such as magnetic susceptibility; optical, such as refractive index; thermal, such as heat capacity or thermal conductivity; and environmental, such as corrosion behavior. Performance testing and analysis ensure that the product has the desired properties. Because a property or a structural characterization of a material closely depends on the processing used, evaluation often improves the process used to make the material.

Careers in Materials Science

Materials scientists go by many different titles, such as process or production engineers, research scientists, metallurgists, polymer scientists, ceramic engineers, plant managers, and quality control engineers. They are employed in industries such as transportation, electronics, aerospace, and biomedical engineering or work for research laboratories, the government, or universities. Materials scientists also help determine what materials should be used in products based on desired properties, help synthesize new materials, and help produce these materials efficiently.

Because of the interdisciplinary nature of this field, many kinds of programs, disciplines, or majors can prepare a person for a career in materials science. An undergraduate degree in materials science and engineering, chemistry, physics, or engineering can lead to a career in this field. Many materials scientists obtain a more advanced degree, such as a master's degree in materials science and engineering or a doctorate (Ph.D.) in chemistry, physics, or engineering.

The materials field is exciting and expanding. The ability to create materials to meet specific needs is just starting to be realized, and many say we are living in the Materials Age.

Questions

1. Choose a product you might use in your daily life. Discuss the materials that compose the product and the properties that those materials give the product.

2. Find a profile of a materials scientist or engineer, and describe what that scientist or engineer does.

The Periodic Table and Electron Configurations

Sample Problem B An element has the electron configuration [Ar]$3d^6 4s^2$. Without looking at the periodic table, identify the period, block, and group in which this element is located. Then, consult the periodic table to identify this element and the others in its group.

 SOLVE

The number of the highest occupied energy level is 4, so the element is in the fourth period. There are six electrons in the d sublevel, which means that it is incompletely filled. The d sublevel can hold 10 electrons. Therefore, the element is in the d-block. For d-block elements, the number of electrons in the ns sublevel (2) plus the number of electrons in the $(n–1)d$ sublevel (6) equals the group number, 8. This Group 8 element is iron. The others in Group 8 are ruthenium, osmium, and hassium.

Practice

Answers in Appendix E

1. Without looking at the periodic table, identify the period, block, and group in which the element that has the electron configuration [Xe]$4f^{14} 5d^5 6s^2$ is located.
2. Without looking at the periodic table, write the outer electron configuration for the Group 12 element in the fifth period.

The *p*-Block Elements: Groups 13–18

The *p*-block elements consist of all the elements of Groups 13–18 except helium. Electrons add to a *p* sublevel only after the *s* sublevel in the same energy level is filled. Therefore, atoms of all *p*-block elements contain two electrons in the *ns* sublevel. **The *p*-block elements together with the *s*-block elements are called the main-group elements**, Groups 1–2; 13–18. For Group 13 elements, the added electron enters the *np* sublevel, giving a group configuration of $ns^2 np^1$. Atoms of Group 14 elements contain two electrons in the *p* sublevel, giving $ns^2 np^2$ for the group configuration. This pattern continues in Groups 15–18. In Group 18, the stable noble-gas configuration of $ns^2 np^6$ is reached. The relationships among group numbers and electron configurations for all the groups are summarized in **Figure 2.8,** on the next page.

For atoms of *p*-block elements, the total number of electrons in the highest occupied level is equal to the group number minus 10. For example, bromine is in Group 17. It has $17 - 10 = 7$ electrons in its highest energy level. Because atoms of *p*-block elements contain two electrons in the *ns* sublevel, we know that bromine has five electrons in its outer *p* sublevel. The electron configuration of bromine is [Ar]$3d^{10} 4s^2 4p^5$.

The properties of elements of the *p*-block vary greatly. At its right-hand end, the *p*-block includes all of the *nonmetals* except hydrogen and helium. All six of the *metalloids* (boron, silicon, germanium, arsenic, antimony, and tellurium) are also in the *p*-block. At the left-hand side and bottom of the block, there are eight *p*-block metals. The locations of the nonmetals, metalloids, and metals in the *p*-block are shown with distinctive colors in **Figure 2.3.**

FIGURE 2.8

RELATIONSHIPS AMONG GROUP NUMBERS, BLOCKS, AND ELECTRON CONFIGURATIONS

Group number	Group configuration	Block	Comments
1, 2	$ns^{1,\,2}$	s	One or two electrons in ns sublevel
3–12	$(n{-}1)d^{1-10}ns^{0-2}$	d	Sum of electrons in ns and $(n-1)d$ levels equals group number
13–18	ns^2np^{1-6}	p	Number of electrons in np sublevel equals group number minus 12

The elements of Group 17 (fluorine, chlorine, bromine, iodine, and astatine) are known as the **halogens** (see **Figure 2.9**). The halogens are the most reactive nonmetals. They react vigorously with most metals to form salts. As you will see, the reactivity of the halogens is based on the presence of seven electrons in their outer energy levels—one electron short of the stable noble-gas configuration. Fluorine and chlorine are gases at room temperature, bromine is a reddish liquid, and iodine is a dark purple solid. Astatine is a synthetic element prepared in very small quantities. Most of its properties are estimated, although it is known to be a solid.

The metalloids, or semiconducting elements, are located between nonmetals and metals in the *p*-block. They are mostly brittle solids with some properties of metals and some of nonmetals. The metalloid elements have electrical conductivity intermediate between that of metals, which are good conductors, and nonmetals, which are nonconductors.

The metals of the *p*-block are generally harder and denser than the *s*-block alkaline-earth metals but softer and less dense than the *d*-block metals. With the exception of bismuth, these metals are sufficiently reactive to be found in nature only in the form of compounds. Once obtained as free metals, however, they are stable in the presence of air.

FIGURE 2.9

The Halogens Fluorine, chlorine, bromine, and iodine are members of Group 17 of the periodic table, also known as the halogens. Locate the halogens in the *p*-block of the periodic table.

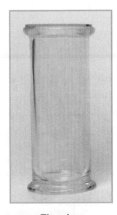

Fluorine

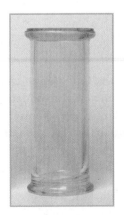

Chlorine

Bromine

Iodine

(bl), (cl) ©sciencephotos/Alamy

The Periodic Table and Electron Configurations

Sample Problem C Without looking at the periodic table, write the outer electron configuration for the Group 13 element in the third period. Then, name the element and identify it as a metal, nonmetal, or metalloid.

 SOLVE

The group number is higher than 12, so the element is in the p-block. The total number of electrons in the highest occupied s and p sublevels is therefore equal to the group number minus 10 ($13 - 10 = 3$). Two electrons are in the s sublevel, so one electron must be present in the $2p$ sublevel, which means that the outer electron configuration is $3s^2 3p^1$. The element is aluminum, Al, which is a metal.

Practice   Answers in Appendix E

1. **a.** Without looking at the periodic table, write the outer electron configuration for the Group 14 element in the fifth period.
   b. Name the element described in (a), and identify it as a metal, nonmetal, or metalloid.
2. **a.** Without looking at the periodic table, identify the period, block, and group of an element that has the electron configuration $[Ar]3d^{10}4s^2 4p^3$.
   b. Name the element described in (a), and identify it as a metal, nonmetal, or metalloid.

The f-Block Elements: Lanthanides and Actinides

In the periodic table, the f-block elements are wedged between Groups 3 and 4 in the sixth and seventh periods. The position of these inner transition elements reflects the fact that they involve the filling of the $4f$ sublevel. With seven $4f$ orbitals to be filled with two electrons each, there are a total of 14 f-block elements between lanthanum, La, and hafnium, Hf, in the sixth period. The lanthanides are shiny metals similar in reactivity to the Group 2 alkaline-earth metals.

There are also 14 f-block elements, the actinides, between actinium, Ac, and element 104, Rf, in the seventh period. In these elements the $5f$ sublevel is being filled with 14 electrons. The actinides are all radioactive. The first four actinides (thorium, Th, through neptunium, Np) have been found naturally on Earth. The remaining actinides are known only as laboratory-made elements.

The Periodic Table and Electron Configurations

Sample Problem D The electron configurations of atoms of four elements are written below. Name the block and group in which each of these elements is located in the periodic table. Then, use the periodic table to name each element. Identify each element as a metal, nonmetal, or metalloid. Finally, describe whether each element has high reactivity or low reactivity.

   a. $[Xe]4f^{14}5d^9 6s^1$ **c.** $[Ne]3s^2 3p^6$
   b. $[Ne]3s^2 3p^5$ **d.** $[Xe]4f^6 6s^2$

Continued ▶

SOLVE

a. The 4f sublevel is filled with 14 electrons. The 5d sublevel is partially filled with nine electrons. Therefore, this element is in the d-block. The element is the transition metal platinum, Pt, which is in Group 10 and has a low reactivity.

b. The incompletely filled p sublevel shows that this element is in the p-block. A total of seven electrons are in the ns and np sublevels, so this element is in Group 17, the halogens. The element is chlorine, Cl, and is highly reactive.

c. This element has a noble-gas configuration and thus is in Group 18 in the p-block. The element is argon, Ar, which is a nonreactive nonmetal and a noble gas.

d. The incomplete 4f sublevel shows that the element is in the f-block and is a lanthanide. Group numbers are not assigned to the f-block. The element is samarium, Sm. All of the lanthanides are reactive metals.

Practice   Answers in Appendix E

1. For each of the following, identify the block, period, group, group name (where appropriate), element name, element type (metal, nonmetal, or metalloid), and relative reactivity (high or low):
   a. $[He]2s^2 2p^5$ **b.** $[Ar]3d^{10} 4s^1$

 SECTION 2 **FORMATIVE ASSESSMENT**

▶ **Reviewing Main Ideas**

1. To illustrate the relationship between the elements' electron configurations and their placement in the periodic table, into what four blocks can the periodic table be divided?

2. What name is given to each of the following groups of elements in the periodic table?
   a. Group 1
   b. Group 2
   c. Groups 3–12
   d. Group 17
   e. Group 18

3. What are the relationships between group configuration and group number for elements in the s-, p-, and d-blocks?

4. Without looking at the periodic table, write the outer electron configuration for the Group 15 element in the fourth period.

5. Without looking at the periodic table, identify the period, block, and group of the element that has the electron configuration $[Ar]3d^7 4s^2$.

✓ **Critical Thinking**

6. **APPLYING MODELS** Period 7 contains elements in the s-, p-, d-, and f-blocks. Suppose that there were a Period 8 and it contained elements in the "g" block, where "g" had the angular momentum quantum number $\ell = 4$. If a hypothetical element in Period 8 had an atomic number of 120, into what group in the periodic table would the element fit, and what properties might it have (assuming it does not radioactively decay)?

▷ Atomic radii are related to electron configuration.

▷ Removing electrons from atoms to form ions requires energy.

▷ Adding electrons to atoms to form ions also involves energy.

▷ When atoms become ions, their radii change.

▷ Only the outer electrons are involved in forming compounds.

▷ Atoms have different abilities to capture electrons.

▷ The properties of *d*-block metals do not vary much.

GO ONLINE **Animated Chemistry**
HMHScience.com

Period Trends (Interaction)

Electron Configuration and Periodic Properties

Key Terms

atomic radius	ionization energy	anion
ion	electron affinity	valence electron
ionization	cation	electronegativity

So far, you have learned that the elements are arranged in the periodic table according to their atomic number and that there is a rough correlation between the arrangement of the elements and their electron configurations. In this section, the relationship between the periodic law and electron configurations will be further explored.

▶ MAIN IDEA

Atomic radii are related to electron configuration.

Ideally, the size of an atom is defined by the edge of its largest orbital. However, this boundary is fuzzy and varies under different conditions. Therefore, the conditions under which the atom exists must be specified to estimate its size. One way to express an atom's radius is to measure the distance between the nuclei of two identical atoms that are chemically bonded together and then divide this distance by two. **Atomic radius may be defined as one-half the distance between the nuclei of identical atoms that are bonded together.** This can be seen in **Figure 3.1** on the next page.

Period Trends

Figure 3.2 gives the atomic radii of the elements, and **Figure 3.3** (on the next spread) presents this information graphically. Note that there is a gradual decrease in atomic radii across the second period from lithium, Li, to neon, Ne. *The trend to smaller atoms across a period is caused by the increasing positive charge of the nucleus.* As electrons add to *s* and *p* sublevels in the same main energy level, they are gradually pulled closer to the more highly charged nucleus. This increased pull results in a decrease in atomic radii. The attraction of the nucleus is somewhat offset by repulsion among the increased number of electrons in the same outer energy level. As a result, the difference in radii between neighboring atoms in each period grows smaller, as shown in **Figure 3.2**.

Group Trends

Examine the atomic radii of the Group 1 elements in **Figure 3.2**. Notice that the radii of the elements increase as you read down the group.

FIGURE 3.1

Atomic Radii

Atomic Radii One method of determining atomic radius is to measure the distance between the nuclei of two identical atoms that are bonded together in an element or compound and then divide this distance by two. The atomic radius of a chlorine atom, for example, is about 100 picometers (pm).

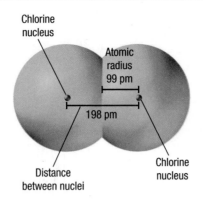

As electrons occupy sublevels in successively higher main energy levels farther from the nucleus, the sizes of the atoms increase. *In general, the atomic radii of the main-group elements increase down a group.*

Now examine the radii of the Group 13 elements. Although gallium, Ga, follows aluminum, Al, it has a slightly smaller atomic radius than does aluminum. This is because gallium, unlike aluminum, is preceded in its period by the 10 *d*-block elements. The expected increase in gallium's radius caused by the filling of the fourth main-energy level is outweighed by a shrinking of the electron cloud caused by a nuclear charge that is considerably higher than that of aluminum.

✔ **CHECK FOR UNDERSTANDING**

Explain Why is it necessary for the radii of atoms to be expressed as the distance between the nuclei of two identical atoms bonded together? (Refer to **Figure 3.1**.)

FIGURE 3.2

Decreasing Radii Atomic radii decrease from left to right across a period and increase down a group. Values are given in picometers (pm).

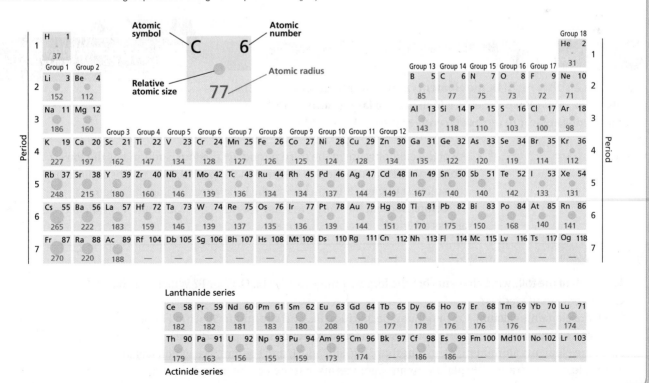

FIGURE 3.3

Periodic Trends The plot of atomic radius versus
atomic number shows period and group trends.

Atomic Radius vs. Atomic Number

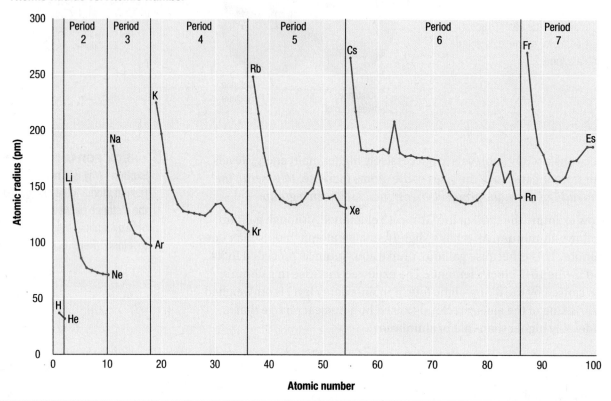

Atomic Radius

GO ONLINE

Learn It! Video
HMHScience.com

Sample Problem E Of the elements magnesium, Mg, chlorine, Cl,
sodium, Na, and phosphorus, P, which has the largest atomic radius?
Explain your answer in terms of trends in the periodic table.

● SOLVE   All of the elements are in the third period. Of the four, sodium has the lowest
atomic number and is the first element in the period. This means sodium has
the smallest nucleus and, therefore, the least attraction on the electrons.
Therefore, sodium has the largest atomic radius, because atomic radii decrease
across a period.

Practice   Answers in Appendix E

1. Which of the following elements has the largest atomic radius: Li, O, C, or F? Which has the
   smallest atomic radius?
2. Of the elements calcium, Ca, beryllium, Be, barium, Ba, and strontium, Sr, which has the
   largest atomic radius? Explain your answer in terms of trends in the periodic table.
3. Of the elements aluminum, Al, magnesium, Mg, silicon, Si, and sodium, Na, which has the
   smallest atomic radius? Explain your answer in terms of trends in the periodic table.

▶ MAIN IDEA

Removing electrons from atoms to form ions requires energy.

An electron can be removed from an atom if enough energy is supplied. Using A as a symbol for an atom of any element, the process can be expressed as follows.

$$A + \text{energy} \rightarrow A^+ + e^-$$

The A^+ represents an ion of element A with a single positive charge, referred to as a 1+ ion. **An ion is an atom or group of bonded atoms that has a positive or negative charge.** Sodium, for example, forms an Na^+ ion. **Any process that results in the formation of an ion is referred to as ionization.**

To compare the ease with which atoms of different elements give up electrons, chemists compare ionization energies. **The energy required to remove one electron from a neutral atom of an element is the ionization energy, IE (or first ionization energy, IE_1).** To avoid the influence of nearby atoms, measurements of ionization energies are made on isolated atoms in the gas phase. **Figure 3.4** gives the first ionization energies for the elements in kilojoules per mole (kJ/mol). **Figure 3.5**, on the next page, presents this information graphically.

FIGURE 3.4

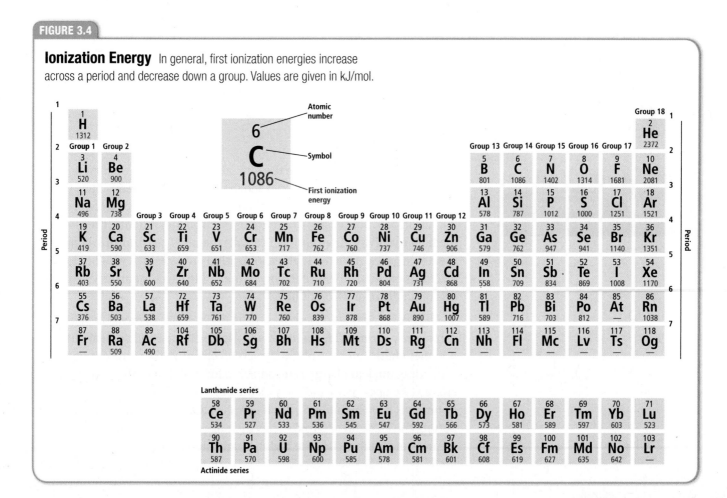

Ionization Energy In general, first ionization energies increase across a period and decrease down a group. Values are given in kJ/mol.

The Periodic Law **151**

FIGURE 3.5

Ionization Energy Plot of first ionization energy, IE_1, versus atomic number. As atomic number increases, both the period and the group trends become less pronounced.

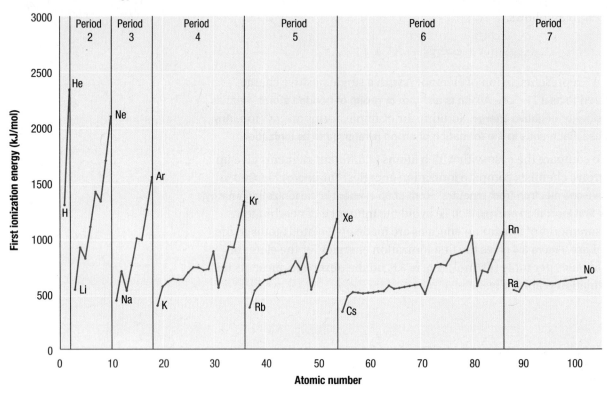

First Ionization Energy vs. Atomic Number

GO ONLINE
Animated
Chemistry
HMHScience.com

Period Trends

Period Trends

In **Figures 3.4** and **3.5,** examine the ionization energies for the first and last elements in each period. You can see that the Group 1 metals have the lowest first ionization energies in their respective periods. Therefore, they lose electrons most easily. This ease of electron loss is a major reason for the high reactivity of the Group 1 (alkali) metals. The Group 18 elements, the noble gases, have the highest ionization energies. They do not lose electrons easily. The low reactivity of the noble gases is partly based on this difficulty of electron removal.

In general, ionization energies of the main-group elements increase across each period. This increase is caused by increasing nuclear charge. A higher charge more strongly attracts electrons in the same energy level. Increasing nuclear charge is responsible for both increasing ionization energy and decreasing radii across the periods. Note that, in general, nonmetals have higher ionization energies than metals do. In each period, the element of Group 1 has the lowest ionization energy, and the element of Group 18 has the highest ionization energy.

Group Trends

Among the main-group elements, ionization energies generally decrease down the groups. Electrons removed from atoms of each succeeding element in a group are in higher energy levels, farther from the nucleus. Therefore, they are removed more easily. Also, as atomic number increases going down a group, more electrons lie between the nucleus and the electrons in the highest occupied energy levels. This partially shields the outer electrons from the effect of the nuclear charge. Together, these influences overcome the attraction of the electrons due to the increasing nuclear charge.

Removing Electrons from Positive Ions

With sufficient energy, electrons can be removed from positive ions as well as from neutral atoms. The energies for removal of additional electrons from an atom are referred to as *the second ionization energy* (IE_2), *third ionization energy* (IE_3), and so on. **Figure 3.6** shows the first five ionization energies for the elements of the first, second, and third periods. You can see that the second ionization energy is always higher than the first, the third is always higher than the second, and so on.

FIGURE 3.6

IONIZATION ENERGIES (IN kJ/MOL) FOR ELEMENTS OF PERIODS 1-3

	Period 1		Period 2							
	H	He	Li	Be	B	C	N	O	F	Ne
IE_1	1312	2372	520	900	801	1086	1402	1314	1681	2081
IE_2		5250	7298	1757	2427	2353	2856	3388	3374	3952
IE_3			11 815	14 849	3660	4621	4578	5300	6050	6122
IE_4				21 007	25 026	6223	7475	7469	8408	9370
IE_5					32 827	37 830	9445	10 990	11 023	12 178

	Period 3							
	Na	Mg	Al	Si	P	S	Cl	Ar
IE_1	496	738	578	787	1012	1000	1251	1521
IE_2	4562	1451	1817	1577	1903	2251	2297	2666
IE_3	6912	7733	2745	3232	2912	3361	3822	3931
IE_4	9544	10 540	11 578	4356	4957	4564	5158	5771
IE_5	13 353	13 628	14 831	16 091	6274	7013	6540	7238

CHECK FOR UNDERSTANDING

Explain Explain in your own words why ionization energies increase as successive electrons are removed from an ion.

This rise in ionization energies is understandable when you consider what is occurring. The first electron is removed from a neutral atom. However, the second electron is removed from a positive ion, so it takes more energy to remove it. Therefore, it is harder to remove each additional electron because it is being removed from an even more positive ion.

The electrons in the outermost energy level are called valence electrons. Those electrons in the lower levels are called core electrons. Once all of the valence electrons have been removed, it requires a lot more energy to remove successive core electrons. Look at the pattern in **Figure 3.6** again. The green boxes are the IE values to remove the first core electron, after all the valence electrons have been removed. Using Na (sodium) with the electron configuration $1s^2 2p^2 3s^1$ as an example, the 1s, 2s, and 2p electrons are the core electrons, and the 3s electron is the valence electron. Notice that it takes a lot more energy to remove the 2p electron from the core than it does the 3s valence electron. Also consider Mg (magnesium). Magnesium's third ionization energy is much greater than its first or second ionization energies. This is because Mg has two valance electrons, and so the third ionization energy is the energy required to remove a core electron. This pattern continues for the remainder of the elements in the third period.

Periodic Trends in Ionization Energy

Sample Problem F Consider two main-group elements, A and B. Element A has a first ionization energy of 520 kJ/mol. Element B has a first ionization energy of 1681 kJ/mol. Decide if each element is more likely to be in the *s*-block or *p*-block. Which element is more likely to form a positive ion?

● **SOLVE**

Element A has a lower ionization energy, which means that atoms of A lose electrons easily. Therefore, element A is most likely to be an *s*-block metal, because ionization energies increase across the periods.

Element B has a higher ionization energy, which means that atoms of B have difficulty losing electrons. Element B would most likely lie at the end of a period in the *p*-block.

Element A is more likely to form a positive ion, because it has a much lower ionization energy than element B does.

Practice   Answers in Appendix E

1. Consider four hypothetical main-group elements, Q, R, T, and X, that have the outer electron configurations indicated below. Then, answer the questions that follow.

   Q: $3d^{10}4s^24p^5$ R: $4s^1$ T: $4f^{14}5d^{10}6s^26p^4$ X: $4f^{14}5d^{10}6s^26p^1$

   a. Identify the block location of each hypothetical main-group element.
   b. Which of these elements are in the same period? Which are in the same group?
   c. Which element would you expect to have the highest first ionization energy? Which would have the lowest first ionization energy?
   d. Which element would you expect to have the highest second ionization energy?
   e. Which of the elements is most likely to form a 1+ ion?

▶ MAIN IDEA

Adding electrons to atoms to form ions also involves energy.

Neutral atoms can also acquire electrons. **The energy change that occurs when an electron is acquired by a neutral atom is called the atom's electron affinity.** Most atoms release energy when they acquire an electron.

$$A + e^- \rightarrow A^- + \text{energy}$$

On the other hand, some atoms must be "forced" to gain an electron by the addition of energy.

$$A + e^- + \text{energy} \rightarrow A^-$$

The quantity of energy absorbed would be represented by a positive number, but ions produced in this way are very unstable, and hence the electron affinity for them is very difficult to determine. An ion produced in this way will be unstable and will lose the added electron spontaneously.

Figure 3.7 shows the electron affinity in kilojoules per mole for the elements. Positive electron affinities, because they are so difficult to determine with any accuracy, are denoted in **Figure 3.7** by "(0)." **Figure 3.8**, on the next page, presents these data graphically.

Period Trends

Among the elements of each period, the halogens (Group 17) gain electrons most readily. This is shown in **Figure 3.7** by the large negative values of halogens' electron affinities and is a major reason for the high reactivity levels of Group 17 elements. In general, as electrons add to the same *p* sublevel of atoms with increasing nuclear charge, electron affinities become more negative across each period within the *p*-block.

FIGURE 3.7

Periodic Table of Electron Affinities (kJ/mol) The values listed in parentheses in this periodic table of electron affinities are approximate. Electron affinity is estimated to be −50 kJ/mol for each of the lanthanides and 0 kJ/mol for each of the actinides.

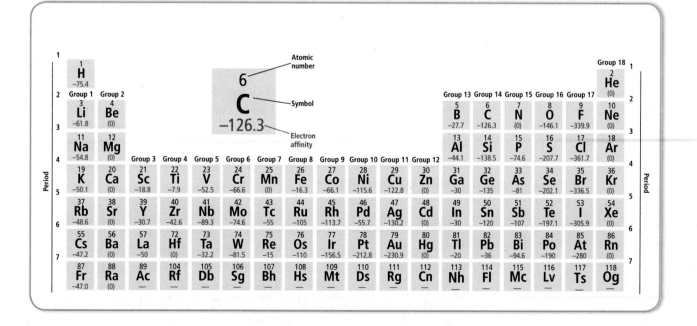

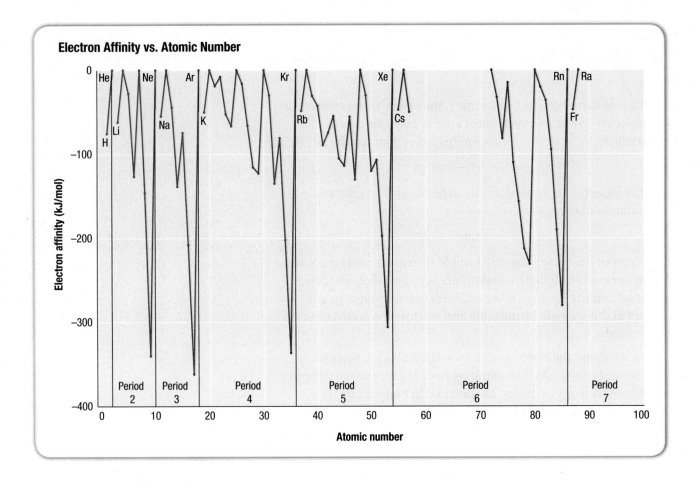

Electron Affinity vs. Atomic Number

FIGURE 3.8

Electron Affinity and Atomic Numbers The plot of electron affinity versus atomic number shows that most atoms release energy when they acquire an electron, as indicated by negative values.

An exception to this trend occurs between Groups 14 and 15. Compare the electron affinities of carbon ($[\text{He}]2s^22p^2$) and nitrogen ($[\text{He}]2s^22p^3$). Adding an electron to a carbon atom gives a half-filled p sublevel. This occurs more easily than forcing an electron to pair with another electron in an orbital of the already half-filled p sublevel of a nitrogen atom.

Group Trends

Trends for electron affinities within groups are not as regular as trends for ionization energies. As a general rule, electrons are added with greater difficulty down a group. This pattern is a result of two competing factors. The first is an increase in nuclear charge down a group, which increases electron affinities. The second is an increase in atomic radius down a group, which decreases electron affinities. In general, the size effect predominates. But there are exceptions, especially among the heavy transition metals, which tend to be the same size or even decrease in radius down a group.

Adding Electrons to Negative Ions

For an isolated ion in the gas phase, it is more difficult to add a second electron to an already negatively charged ion. Therefore, second electron affinities are all positive. Certain p-block nonmetals tend to form negative ions that have noble gas configurations. The halogens do so by adding one electron. For example, chlorine has the configuration $[\text{Ne}]3s^23p^5$.

An atom of chlorine achieves the configuration of the noble gas argon by adding an electron to form the ion Cl^- ($[Ne]3s^23p^6$). Adding another electron is so difficult that Cl^{2-} never occurs. Atoms of Group 16 elements are present in many compounds as 2– ions. For example, oxygen ($[He]2s^22p^4$) achieves the configuration of the noble gas neon by adding two electrons to form the ion O^{2-}($[He]2s^22p^6$).

▶ MAIN IDEA
When atoms become ions, their radii change.

Figure 3.9 shows the radii of some of the most common ions of the elements. Positive and negative ions have specific names.

A positive ion is known as a **cation.** The formation of a cation by the loss of one or more electrons always leads to a decrease in atomic radius, because the removal of the highest-energy-level electrons results in a smaller electron cloud. Also, the remaining electrons are drawn closer to the nucleus by its unbalanced positive charge.

A negative ion is known as an **anion.** The formation of an anion by the addition of one or more electrons always leads to an increase in atomic radius. This is because the total positive charge of the nucleus remains unchanged when an electron is added to an atom or an ion. So the electrons are not drawn to the nucleus as strongly as they were before the addition of the extra electron. The electron cloud also spreads out because of greater repulsion between the increased number of electrons.

Period Trends

Within each period of the periodic table, the metals at the left tend to form cations, and the nonmetals at the right tend to form anions. Cationic radii decrease across a period, because the electron cloud shrinks due to the increasing nuclear charge acting on the electrons in the same main energy level.

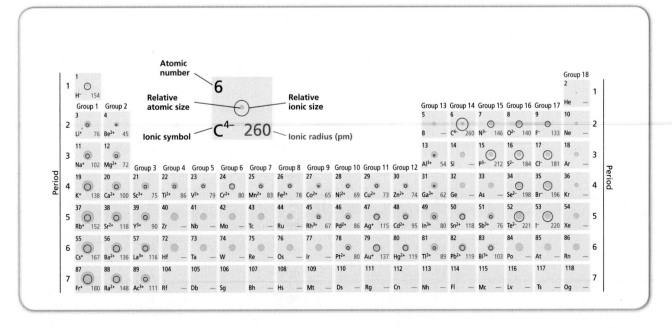

Starting with Group 15, in which atoms assume stable noble-gas configurations by gaining three electrons, anions are more common than cations. Anionic radii decrease across each period for the elements in Groups 15–18. The reasons for this trend are the same as the reasons that cationic radii decrease from left to right across a period.

Group Trends

The outer electrons in both cations and anions are in higher energy levels as one reads down a group. Thus, just as there is a gradual increase of atomic radii down a group, there is also a gradual increase of ionic radii.

▶ MAIN IDEA

Only the outer electrons are involved in forming compounds.

Chemical compounds form because electrons are lost, gained, or shared between atoms. The electrons that interact in this manner are those in the highest energy levels. These are the electrons most subject to the influence of nearby atoms or ions. **The electrons available to be lost, gained, or shared in the formation of chemical compounds are referred to as valence electrons.** Valence electrons are often located in incompletely filled main-energy levels. For example, the electron lost from the $3s$ sublevel of Na to form Na^+ is a valence electron.

For main-group elements, the valence electrons are the electrons in the outermost s and p sublevels. The inner electrons are in filled energy levels and are held too tightly by the nucleus to be involved in compound formation. The Group 1 and Group 2 elements have one and two valence electrons, respectively, as shown in **Figure 3.10.** The elements of Groups 13–18 have a number of valence electrons equal to the group number minus 10. In some cases, both the s and p sublevel valence electrons of the p-block elements are involved in compound formation **(Figure 3.10)**. In other cases, only the electrons from the p sublevel are involved.

FIGURE 3.10

VALENCE ELECTRONS IN MAIN-GROUP ELEMENTS

Group number	Group configuration	Number of valence electrons
1	ns^1	1
2	ns^2	2
13	ns^2p^1	3
14	ns^2p^2	4
15	ns^2p^3	5
16	ns^2p^4	6
17	ns^2p^5	7
18	ns^2p^6	8

▶ MAIN IDEA

Atoms have different abilities to capture electrons.

Valence electrons hold atoms together in chemical compounds. In many compounds, the negative charge of the valence electrons is concentrated closer to one atom than to another. This uneven concentration of charge has a significant effect on the chemical properties of a compound. It is therefore useful to have a measure of how strongly one atom attracts the electrons of another atom within a compound.

Linus Pauling, one of America's most famous chemists, devised a scale of numerical values reflecting the tendency of an atom to attract electrons. **Electronegativity is a measure of the ability of an atom in a chemical compound to attract electrons from another atom in the compound.** The most electronegative element, fluorine, is arbitrarily assigned an electronegativity of four. Other values are then calculated in relation to this value.

Period Trends

As shown in **Figure 3.11,** *electronegativities tend to increase across each period, although there are exceptions.* The alkali and alkaline-earth metals are the least electronegative elements. In compounds, their atoms have a low attraction for electrons. Nitrogen, oxygen, and the halogens are the most electronegative elements. Their atoms attract electrons strongly.

FIGURE 3.11

Periodic Table of Electronegativities Shown are the electronegativities of the elements according to the Pauling scale. The most-electronegative elements are located in the upper right of the *p*-block. The least-electronegative elements are located in the lower left of the *s*-block.

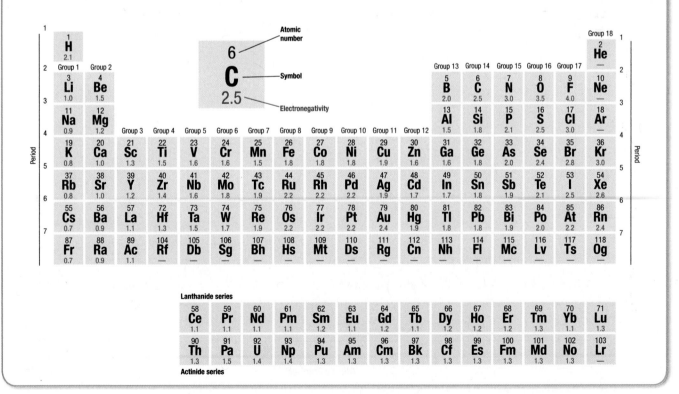

CHECK FOR UNDERSTANDING

Predict Metals generally have lower electronegativities than nonmetals. What type of ion would this suggest each would form?

Electronegativities tend to either decrease down a group or remain about the same. The noble gases are unusual in that some of them do not form compounds and therefore cannot be assigned electronegativities. When a noble gas does form a compound, its electronegativity is rather high, similar to the values for the halogens. The combination of the period and group trends in electronegativity results in the highest values belonging to the elements in the upper right of the periodic table. The lowest values belong to the elements in the lower left of the table. These trends are shown graphically in **Figure 3.12**.

▶ MAIN IDEA

The properties of *d*-block metals do not vary much.

The properties of the *d*-block elements (which are all metals) vary less and with less regularity than those of the main-group elements. This trend is indicated by the curves in **Figures 3.3** and **3.5**, which flatten where the *d*-block elements fall in the middle of Periods 4–6.

Recall that atoms of the *d*-block elements contain from zero to two electrons in the *s* orbital of their highest occupied energy level and one to ten electrons in the *d* sublevel of the next-lower energy level.

FIGURE 3.12

Electronegativity and Atomic Number The plot shows electronegativity versus atomic number for Periods 1–6.

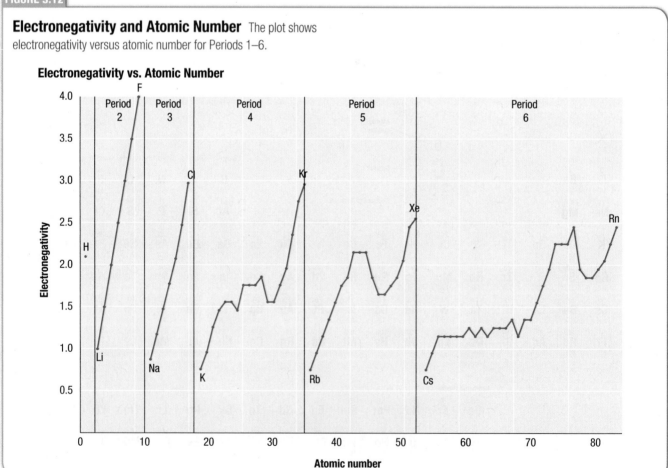

Periodic Trends in Electronegativity

Sample Problem G Of the elements gallium, Ga, bromine, Br, and calcium, Ca, which has the highest electronegativity? Explain your answer in terms of periodic trends.

 SOLVE

All of these elements are in the fourth period. Bromine has the highest atomic number and is farthest to the right in the period. Therefore, bromine should have the highest electronegativity because electronegativity increases across the periods.

Practice Answers in Appendix E

1. Consider five hypothetical main-group elements, E, G, J, L, and M, that have the outer electron configurations shown below.

$$E = 2s^2 2p^5 \qquad G = 4d^{10}5s^2 5p^5 \qquad J = 2s^2 2p^2$$
$$L = 5d^{10}6s^2 6p^5 \qquad M = 2s^2 2p^4$$

a. Identify the block location for each element. Then, determine which elements are in the same period and which are in the same group.
b. Which element would you expect to have the highest electron affinity? Which would you expect to form a 1– ion? Which should have the highest electronegativity?
c. Compare the ionic radius of the typical ion formed by the element G with the radius of the atom from which the ion was formed.
d. Which element(s) contains seven valence electrons?

Therefore, electrons in both the ns sublevel and the $(n–1)d$ sublevel are available to interact with their surroundings. As a result, electrons in the incompletely filled d sublevels are responsible for many characteristic properties of the d-block elements.

Atomic Radii

The atomic radii of the d-block elements generally decrease across the periods. However, this decrease is less than that for the main-group elements, because the electrons added to the $(n–1)d$ sublevel shield the outer electrons from the nucleus.

Also, note in **Figure 3.3** that the radii dip to a low and then increase slightly across each of the four periods that contain d-block elements. As the number of electrons in the d sublevel increases, the radii increase because of repulsion among the electrons.

In the sixth period, the f-block elements fall between lanthanum (Group 3) and hafnium (Group 4). Because of the increase in atomic number that occurs from lanthanum to hafnium, the atomic radius of hafnium is actually slightly less than that of zirconium, Zr, the element immediately above it. The radii of elements following hafnium in the sixth period vary with increasing atomic number in the usual manner.

Ionization Energy

As they do for the main-group elements, ionization energies of the *d*-block and *f*-block elements generally increase across the periods. In contrast to the decrease down the main groups, however, the first ionization energies of the *d*-block elements generally increase down each group. This is because the electrons available for ionization in the outer *s* sublevels are less shielded from the increasing nuclear charge by electrons in the incomplete $(n-1)d$ sublevels.

Ion Formation and Ionic Radii

Among all atoms of the *d*-block and *f*-block elements, electrons in the highest occupied sublevel, the *s* and *p* sublevels, are always removed first. For the *d*-block elements, this means that although newly added electrons occupy the *d* sublevels, the first electrons to be removed are those in the outermost *s* sublevels. For example, iron, Fe, has the electron configuration $[Ar]3d^6 4s^2$. First, it loses two 4*s* electrons to form Fe^{2+} ($[Ar]3d^6$). Fe^{2+} can then lose a 3*d* electron to form Fe^{3+} ($[Ar]3d^5$).

Most *d*-block elements commonly form 2+ ions in compounds. Some, such as iron and chromium, also commonly form 3+ ions. The Group 3 elements form only ions with a 3+ charge. Copper forms 1+ and 2+ ions, and silver usually forms only 1+ ions. As expected, the cations have smaller radii than the atoms do. Comparing 2+ ions across the periods shows a decrease in size that parallels the decrease in atomic radii.

Electronegativity

The *d*-block elements all have electronegativities between 1.1 and 2.5. Only the active metals of Groups 1 and 2 have lower electronegativities. The *d*-block elements also follow the general trend for electronegativity values to increase as radii decrease and vice versa. The *f*-block elements all have similar electronegativities, which range from 1.1 to 1.5.

 ## SECTION 3 FORMATIVE ASSESSMENT

▶ Reviewing Main Ideas

1. State the general period and group trends among main-group elements with respect to each of the following properties:
   a. atomic radii
   b. first ionization energy
   c. electron affinity
   d. ionic radii
   e. electronegativity

2. a. In general, how do the periodic properties of the *d*-block elements compare with those of the main-group elements?
   b. Explain the comparison made in (a).

3. For each main-group element, what is the relationship between its group number and the number of valence electrons that the group members have?

✔ Critical Thinking

4. **RELATING IDEAS** Graph the general trends (left to right and top to bottom) in the second ionization energy (IE_2) of an element as a function of its atomic number, over the range $Z = 3–20$. Label the minima and maxima on the graph with the appropriate element symbol.

The arrangement of elements in the periodic table reflects the arrangement of electrons in an atom. Each period begins with an atom that has an electron in a new energy level, and with the exception of the first period, each period ends with an atom that has a filled set of p orbitals.

To write the electron configuration of an element, you must fill the sublevels in order of increasing energy. If you follow the arrows in either of the two types of mnemonics shown below, you will get correct configurations for most elements.

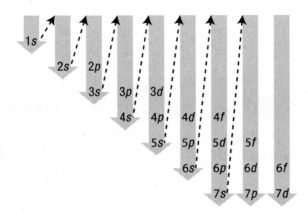
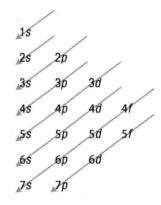

You also need to know how many orbitals are in each sublevel and that each orbital can contain two electrons of opposite spins. As shown in the following table, the sublevels s, p, d, and f have 1, 3, 5, and 7 available orbitals, respectively.

SUBLEVEL	s	p	d	f
No. of orbitals	1	3	5	7
No. of electrons	2	6	10	14

Sample Problem

Write the full electron configuration for phosphorus.

The atomic number of phosphorus is 15, so a phosphorus atom has 15 protons and 15 electrons. Assign each of the 15 electrons to the appropriate sublevels. The final sublevel can be unfilled and will contain the number of valence electrons.

$$\underbrace{1s^2}\ \underbrace{2s^2}\ \underbrace{2p^6}\ \underbrace{3s^2}\ \underbrace{3p^3}$$
$$2e^- + 2e^- + 6e^- + 2e^- + 3e^- = 15e^-$$

So, the full electron configuration of phosphorus is $1s^2 2s^2 2p^6 3s^2 3p^3$.

Practice   Answers in Appendix E

1. Write full electron configurations for the following elements.
   a. aluminum   c. tin
   b. neon   d. potassium

2. Use noble gas symbols to write shorthand electron configurations for the following elements.
   a. silicon   c. antimony
   b. rubidium   d. arsenic

CHAPTER 5 Summary

BIG IDEA The properties of the chemical elements are a periodic function of their atomic numbers.

SECTION 1 History of the Periodic Table

- The periodic law states that the physical and chemical properties of the elements are periodic functions of their atomic numbers.
- The periodic table is an arrangement of the elements in order of their atomic numbers so that elements with similar properties fall in the same column.
- The columns in the periodic table are referred to as groups.

KEY TERMS

periodic law
periodic table
lanthanide
actinide

SECTION 2 Electron Configuration and the Periodic Table

- The rows in the periodic table are called periods.
- Many chemical properties of the elements can be explained by the configurations of the elements' outermost electrons.
- The noble gases exhibit unique chemical stability because their highest occupied levels have an octet of electrons, ns^2np^6 (with the exception of helium, whose stability arises from its highest occupied level being completely filled with two electrons, $1s^2$).
- Based on the electron configurations of the elements, the periodic table can be divided into four blocks: the *s*-block, the *p*-block, the *d*-block, and the *f*-block.

KEY TERMS

alkali metals
alkaline-earth metals
transition elements
main-group elements
halogens

SECTION 3 Electron Configuration and Periodic Properties

- The groups and periods of the periodic table display general trends in the following properties of the elements: electron affinity, electronegativity, ionization energy, atomic radius, and ionic radius.
- The electrons in an atom that are available to be lost, gained, or shared in the formation of chemical compounds are referred to as valence electrons.
- In determining what the electron configuration of an ion is, assume electrons are removed from the orbitals with the highest value of *n* first.

KEY TERMS

atomic radius
ion
ionization
ionization energy
electron affinity
cation
anion
valence electron
electronegativity

CHAPTER 5 Review

GO ONLINE

Interactive Review
HMHScience.com

Review Games
Concept Maps

SECTION 1
History of the Periodic Table

▶ REVIEWING MAIN IDEAS

1. Describe the contributions made by the following scientists to the development of the periodic table:
   a. Stanislao Cannizzaro
   b. Dmitri Mendeleev
   c. Henry Moseley

2. State the periodic law.

3. How is the periodic law demonstrated within the groups of the periodic table?

SECTION 2
Electron Configuration and the Periodic Table

▶ REVIEWING MAIN IDEAS

4. a. How do the electron configurations within the same group of elements compare?
   b. Why are the noble gases relatively unreactive?

5. What determines the length of each period in the periodic table?

6. What is the relationship between the electron configuration of an element and the period in which that element appears in the periodic table?

7. a. What information is provided by the specific block location of an element?
   b. Identify, by number, the groups located within each of the four block areas.

8. a. Which elements are designated as the alkali metals?
   b. List four of their characteristic properties.

9. a. Which elements are designated as the alkaline-earth metals?
   b. How do their characteristic properties compare with those of the alkali metals?

10. a. Write the group configuration notation for each d-block group.
    b. How do the group numbers of those groups relate to the number of outer s and d electrons?

11. What name is sometimes used to refer to the entire set of d-block elements?

12. a. What types of elements make up the p-block?
    b. How do the properties of the p-block metals compare with those of the metals in the s- and d-blocks?

13. a. Which elements are designated as the halogens?
    b. List three of their characteristic properties.

14. a. Which elements are metalloids?
    b. Describe their characteristic properties.

15. Which elements make up the f-block in the periodic table?

16. a. What are the main-group elements?
    b. What trends can be observed across the various periods within the main-group elements?

PRACTICE PROBLEMS

17. Write the noble-gas notation for the electron configuration of each of the following elements, and indicate the period in which each belongs.
    a. Li   c. Cu   e. Sn
    b. O   d. Br

18. Without looking at the periodic table, identify the period, block, and group in which the elements with the following electron configurations are located. (Hint: See Sample Problem A.)
    a. $[Ne]3s^23p^4$
    b. $[Kr]4d^{10}5s^25p^2$
    c. $[Xe]4f^{14}5d^{10}6s^26p^5$

19. Based on the information given below, give the group, period, block, and identity of each element described. (Hint: See Sample Problem B.)
    a. $[He]2s^2$
    b. $[Ne]3s^1$
    c. $[Kr]5s^2$
    d. $[Ar]4s^2$
    e. $[Ar]3d^54s^1$

20. Without looking at the periodic table, write the expected outer electron configuration for each of the following elements. (Hint: See Sample Problem C.)
    a. Group 7, fourth period
    b. Group 3, fifth period
    c. Group 12, sixth period

21. Identify the block, period, group, group name (where appropriate), element name, element type, and relative reactivity for the elements with the following electron configurations. (Hint: See Sample Problem D.)
   a. $[Ne]3s^2 3p^1$
   b. $[Ar]3d^{10}4s^2 4p^6$
   c. $[Kr]4d^{10}5s^1$
   d. $[Xe]4f^1 5d^1 6s^2$

SECTION 3

Electron Configuration and Periodic Properties

▶ **REVIEWING MAIN IDEAS**

22. a. What is meant by *atomic radius*?
   b. What trend is observed among the atomic radii of main-group elements across a period?
   c. Explain this trend.

23. a. What trend is observed among the atomic radii of main-group elements down a group?
   b. Explain this trend.

24. Define each of the following terms:
   a. ion
   b. ionization
   c. first ionization energy
   d. second ionization energy

25. a. How do the first ionization energies of main-group elements vary across a period and down a group?
   b. Explain the basis for each trend.

26. a. What is electron affinity?
   b. What signs are associated with electron affinity values, and what is the significance of each sign?

27. a. Distinguish between a cation and an anion.
   b. How does the size of each compare with the size of the neutral atom from which it is formed?

28. a. What are valence electrons?
   b. Where are such electrons located?

29. For each of the following groups, indicate whether electrons are more likely to be lost or gained in compound formation and give the number of such electrons typically involved.
   a. Group 1   **d.** Group 16
   b. Group 2   **e.** Group 17
   c. Group 13   **f.** Group 18

30. a. What is electronegativity?
   b. Why is fluorine special in terms of electronegativity?

31. Identify the most- and least-electronegative groups of elements in the periodic table.

PRACTICE PROBLEMS

32. Of cesium, Cs, hafnium, Hf, and gold, Au, which element has the smallest atomic radius? Explain your answer in terms of trends in the periodic table. (Hint: See Sample Problem E.)

33. a. Distinguish between the first, second, and third ionization energies of an atom.
   b. How do the values of successive ionization energies compare?
   c. Why does this occur?

34. Without looking at the electron affinity table, arrange the following elements in order of *decreasing* electron affinities: C, O, Li, Na, Rb, and F.

35. a. Without looking at the ionization energy table, arrange the following elements in order of decreasing first ionization energies: Li, O, C, K, Ne, and F.
   b. Which of the elements listed in (a) would you expect to have the highest second ionization energy? Why?

36. a. Which of the following cations is least likely to form: Sr^{2+}, Al^{3+}, K^{2+}?
   b. Which of the following anions is least likely to form: I^-, Cl^-, O^{2-}?

37. Which element is the most electronegative among C, N, O, Br, and S? Which group does it belong to? (Hint: See Sample Problem G.)

38. The two ions K^+ and Ca^{2+} each have 18 electrons surrounding the nucleus. Which would you expect to have the smaller radius? Why?

Mixed Review

▶ **REVIEWING MAIN IDEAS**

39. Without looking at the periodic table, identify the period, block, and group in which each of the following elements is located.
   a. $[Rn]7s^1$
   b. $[Ar]3d^24s^2$
   c. $[Kr]4d^{10}5s^1$
   d. $[Xe]4f^{14}5d^96s^1$

40. a. Which elements are designated as the noble gases?
   b. What is the most significant property of these elements?

41. Which of the following does not have a noble-gas configuration: Na^+, Rb^+, O^{2-}, Br^- Ca^+, Al^{3+}, S^{2-}?

42. a. How many groups are in the periodic table?
   b. How many periods are in the periodic table?
   c. Which two blocks of the periodic table make up the main-group elements?

43. Write the noble-gas notation for the electron configuration of each of the following elements, and indicate the period and group in which each belongs.
   a. Mg
   b. P
   c. Sc
   d. Y

44. Use the periodic table to describe the chemical properties of the following elements:
   a. fluorine, F
   b. xenon, Xe
   c. sodium, Na
   d. gold, Au

45. For each element listed below, determine the charge of the ion that is most likely to be formed and the identity of the noble gas whose electron configuration is thus achieved.
   a. Li   **e.** Mg   **i.** Br
   b. Rb   **f.** Al   **j.** Ba
   c. O   **g.** P
   d. F   **h.** S

46. Describe some differences between the *s*-block metals and the *d*-block metals.

47. Why do the halogens readily form 1–ions?

48. Identify which trends in the diagrams below describe atomic radius, ionization energy, electron affinity, and electronegativity.

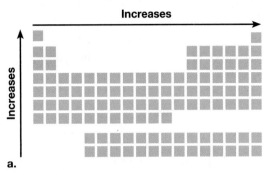

a.

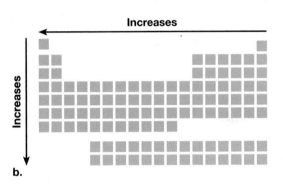

b.

c.

49. The electron configuration of argon differs from those of chlorine and potassium by one electron each. Compare the reactivity of these three elements.

CRITICAL THINKING

As a member on the newly inhabited space station Alpha, you are given the task of organizing information on newly discovered elements as it comes in from the laboratory. To date, five elements have been discovered and have been assigned names and symbols from the Greek alphabet. An analysis of the new elements has yielded the following data:

Element name	Atomic no.	Atomic mass	Properties
Epsilon ε	23	47.33	nonmetal, very reactive, produces a salt when combined with a metal, gaseous state
Beta β	13	27.01	metal, very reactive, soft solid, low melting point
Gamma γ	12	25.35	nonmetal, gaseous element, extremely unreactive
Delta Δ	4	7.98	nonmetal, very abundant, forms compounds with most other elements
Lambda Λ	9	16.17	metal, solid state, good conductor, high luster, hard and dense

50. **Applying Models** Create a periodic table based on the properties of the five new elements.

51. **Predicting Outcomes** Using your newly created periodic table, predict the atomic number of an element with an atomic mass of 11.29 that has nonmetallic properties and is very reactive.

52. **Predicting Outcomes** Predict the atomic number of an element having an atomic mass of 15.02 that exhibits metallic properties but is softer than lambda and harder than beta.

53. **Analyzing Information** Analyze your periodic table for trends, and describe those trends.

USING THE HANDBOOK

54. Review the boiling point and melting point data in the tables of the *Elements Handbook* (Appendix A). Make a list of the elements that exist as liquids or gases at the boiling point of water, 100°C.

55. Because transition metals have vacant *d* orbitals, they form a greater variety of colored compounds than do the metals of Groups 1 and 2. Review the section of the *Elements Handbook* (Appendix A) on transition metals, and answer the following:
    a. What colors are exhibited by chromium in its common oxidation states?
    b. What gems contain chromium impurities?
    c. What colors are often associated with the following metal ions: copper, cadmium, cobalt, zinc, and nickel?
    d. What transition elements are considered noble metals? What are the characteristics of a noble metal?

RESEARCH AND WRITING

56. Prepare a report tracing the evolution of the current periodic table since 1900. Cite the chemists involved and their major contributions.

57. Write a report describing the contributions of Glenn Seaborg toward the discovery of many of the actinide elements.

ALTERNATIVE ASSESSMENT

58. Construct your own periodic table or obtain a poster that shows related objects, such as fruits or vegetables, in periodic arrangement. Describe the organization of the table and the trends it illustrates. Use this table to make predictions about your subject matter.

Standards-Based Assessment

Record your answers on a separate piece of paper.

MULTIPLE CHOICE

[Periodic table figure]

For questions 1–3, refer to the figure above.

1 The alkaline earth metals are found in Group 2 of the periodic table. Which alkaline earth metal has the highest ionic radius based on its location on the periodic table?

A beryllium (Be)

B calcium (Ca)

C magnesium (Mg)

D radium (Ra)

2 Group 17 elements are the most reactive of the nonmetal elements because they —

A require only one electron to fill their outer energy level

B have the highest ionization energies

C have the largest atomic radii

D are the farthest to the right in the periodic table

3 Why do the alkali metals occupy Group 1 of the modern periodic table?

A The alkali metals have one valence electron in their outer shells.

B The alkali metals are highly reactive, which increases on descending Group 1.

C The alkali metals are more reactive than the alkaline earth metals in Group 2.

D The alkali metals have closer similarity than any other group.

4 Which of the following elements has the smallest atomic radius?

A $[Ar]\ 4s^2$

B $[Ar]\ 3d^{10}4s^2$

C $[Ne]\ 3s^1$

D $[Ar]\ 4s^1$

5 Which of the following *best* describes how ionic radius changes across the periodic table?

A It increases as you move down a group.

B It increases as you move up a group.

C It increases from left to right across a period.

D There is no identifiable pattern.

6 A student runs tests on an unknown substance and discovers the following properties.

State of matter at room temp	Gas
Number of valence electrons	8
Physical properties	Colorless and odorless

What other property does this element *most likely* have?

A highly reactive

B low electronegativity

C has many isotopes

D not found pure in nature

7 As you move left to right across Period 3 from Sc to Zn, the energy needed to remove an electron from an atom —

A generally increases

B generally decreases

C does not change

D varies unpredictably

GRIDDED RESPONSE

8 Determine which of the following electron configurations represents an element with lower reactivity compared to the other element. Record the period and group of that element in the grid, putting period number first, followed by a space, followed by the group number.

$1s^2 2s^2 2p^6 3s^2 3p^2$

$1s^2 2s^2 2p^6$

Test Tip

If you are short on time, quickly scan the unanswered questions to see which might be easiest to answer.

A BOOK EXPLAINING COMPLEX IDEAS USING ONLY THE 1,000 MOST COMMON WORDS

THE PIECES EVERYTHING IS MADE OF
A table for putting small pieces in order

You know that the periodic table is an arrangement of the elements in order of their atomic numbers so that elements with similar properties fall in the same column. Here's a look at how this arrangement of elements helps us understand the world on an atomic scale.

RANDALL MUNROE
XKCD.COM

THE STORY OF PUTTING THINGS IN ORDER

PEOPLE USED TO THINK THAT EVERYTHING AROUND US WAS BUILT FROM FOUR KINDS OF STUFF: EARTH, AIR, FIRE, AND WATER.

THEY WERE ALMOST RIGHT—BUT INSTEAD OF FOUR KINDS OF PIECES, THERE ARE MORE LIKE TEN DOZEN.

ALL THE THINGS WE CAN TOUCH (BUT NOT THINGS LIKE LIGHT) ARE MADE FROM THESE PIECES.

DON'T TOUCH MY FOOD!

THERE HE GOES TOUCHING THINGS AGAIN . . .

THERE ARE ALMOST TEN DOZEN THAT WE'EVE FOUND SO FAR, BUT THERE ARE PROBABLY MORE.

THIS TABLE PUTS THE PIECES IN ORDER BY WEIGHT, AND PUTS GROUPS OF PIECES THAT ARE LIKE EACH OTHER IN SOME WAY ABOVE AND BELOW EACH OTHER.

I GOT 4 NEW ONES!

PIECES OF PIECES

These pieces are made of even smaller pieces. Different kinds of pieces have different numbers of those smaller parts. There are three main kinds of these smaller parts—two heavy ones and a light one.

Over the past hundred years, we've learned that the idea of "where" doesn't always work well for very small things.

Light pieces

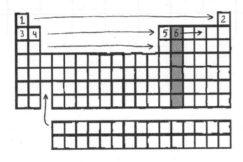

Heavy pieces

CENTER NUMBER

We number the pieces by counting how many of one kind of heavy part they have in their center, and use that number to put pieces in boxes in the table. The other heavy part doesn't matter to the count, so pieces with different numbers of that part may share the same box in the table.

TABLE SHAPE

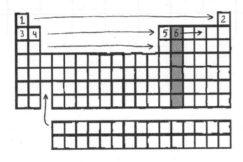

The boxes in this table are in order from left to right and top to bottom. It has this strange shape because pieces are in groups with other pieces that are a lot like them.

(The reason those groups are like each other has to do with the number of light parts around the outside of the piece—which is mostly the same as the piece's center number—and the way different numbers of light parts sort themselves around the outside of the piece.)

SHORT LIVES, STRANGE HEAT

Some kinds of pieces don't last very long, slowly breaking down into other pieces over time by throwing away bits of their centers in all directions, which makes them give off a kind of strange heat.

We count how long a kind of piece lasts by timing how long it takes for half of it to break down. We call this the piece's "half-life."

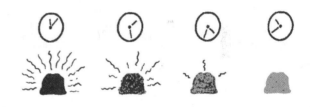

NAMES

Some of the things on this table have had names for a long time (like gold) but some of them were only found in the last few hundred years.

Many of the pieces in this table are named after people or places—and especially for people who helped to learn about them or the places where those people worked.

Here are a few of the things these pieces are named after.

THE PIECES EVERYTHING IS MADE OF

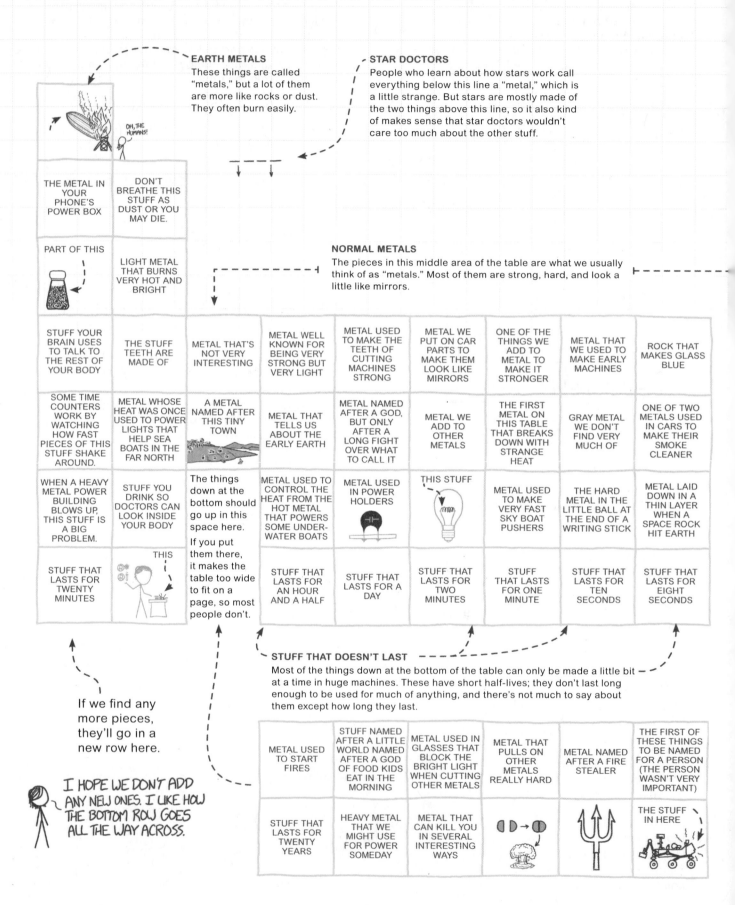

OH, THE HUMANS!

EARTH METALS
These things are called "metals," but a lot of them are more like rocks or dust. They often burn easily.

STAR DOCTORS
People who learn about how stars work call everything below this line a "metal," which is a little strange. But stars are mostly made of the two things above this line, so it also kind of makes sense that star doctors wouldn't care too much about the other stuff.

THE METAL IN YOUR PHONE'S POWER BOX

DON'T BREATHE THIS STUFF AS DUST OR YOU MAY DIE.

PART OF THIS

LIGHT METAL THAT BURNS VERY HOT AND BRIGHT

NORMAL METALS
The pieces in this middle area of the table are what we usually think of as "metals." Most of them are strong, hard, and look a little like mirrors.

STUFF YOUR BRAIN USES TO TALK TO THE REST OF YOUR BODY

THE STUFF TEETH ARE MADE OF

METAL THAT'S NOT VERY INTERESTING

METAL WELL KNOWN FOR BEING VERY STRONG BUT VERY LIGHT

METAL USED TO MAKE THE TEETH OF CUTTING MACHINES STRONG

METAL WE PUT ON CAR PARTS TO MAKE THEM LOOK LIKE MIRRORS

ONE OF THE THINGS WE ADD TO METAL TO MAKE IT STRONGER

METAL THAT WE USED TO MAKE EARLY MACHINES

ROCK THAT MAKES GLASS BLUE

SOME TIME COUNTERS WORK BY WATCHING HOW FAST PIECES OF THIS STUFF SHAKE AROUND.

METAL WHOSE HEAT WAS ONCE USED TO POWER LIGHTS THAT HELP SEA BOATS IN THE FAR NORTH

A METAL NAMED AFTER THIS TINY TOWN

METAL THAT TELLS US ABOUT THE EARLY EARTH

METAL NAMED AFTER A GOD, BUT ONLY AFTER A LONG FIGHT OVER WHAT TO CALL IT

METAL WE ADD TO OTHER METALS

THE FIRST METAL ON THIS TABLE THAT BREAKS DOWN WITH STRANGE HEAT

GRAY METAL WE DON'T FIND VERY MUCH OF

ONE OF TWO METALS USED IN CARS TO MAKE THEIR SMOKE CLEANER

WHEN A HEAVY METAL POWER BUILDING BLOWS UP, THIS STUFF IS A BIG PROBLEM.

STUFF YOU DRINK SO DOCTORS CAN LOOK INSIDE YOUR BODY

The things down at the bottom should go up in this space here.

If you put them there, it makes the table too wide to fit on a page, so most people don't.

METAL USED TO CONTROL THE HEAT FROM THE HOT METAL THAT POWERS SOME UNDER-WATER BOATS

METAL USED IN POWER HOLDERS

THIS STUFF

METAL USED TO MAKE VERY FAST SKY BOAT PUSHERS

THE HARD METAL IN THE LITTLE BALL AT THE END OF A WRITING STICK

METAL LAID DOWN IN A THIN LAYER WHEN A SPACE ROCK HIT EARTH

STUFF THAT LASTS FOR TWENTY MINUTES

THIS

STUFF THAT LASTS FOR AN HOUR AND A HALF

STUFF THAT LASTS FOR A DAY

STUFF THAT LASTS FOR TWO MINUTES

STUFF THAT LASTS FOR ONE MINUTE

STUFF THAT LASTS FOR TEN SECONDS

STUFF THAT LASTS FOR EIGHT SECONDS

STUFF THAT DOESN'T LAST
Most of the things down at the bottom of the table can only be made a little bit at a time in huge machines. These have short half-lives; they don't last long enough to be used for much of anything, and there's not much to say about them except how long they last.

If we find any more pieces, they'll go in a new row here.

I HOPE WE DON'T ADD ANY NEW ONES. I LIKE HOW THE BOTTOM ROW GOES ALL THE WAY ACROSS.

METAL USED TO START FIRES

STUFF NAMED AFTER A LITTLE WORLD NAMED AFTER A GOD OF FOOD KIDS EAT IN THE MORNING

METAL USED IN GLASSES THAT BLOCK THE BRIGHT LIGHT WHEN CUTTING OTHER METALS

METAL THAT PULLS ON OTHER METALS REALLY HARD

METAL NAMED AFTER A FIRE STEALER

THE FIRST OF THESE THINGS TO BE NAMED FOR A PERSON (THE PERSON WASN'T VERY IMPORTANT)

STUFF THAT LASTS FOR TWENTY YEARS

HEAVY METAL THAT WE MIGHT USE FOR POWER SOMEDAY

METAL THAT CAN KILL YOU IN SEVERAL INTERESTING WAYS

THE STUFF IN HERE

NOT METAL

The things toward the top right part of the table are things that aren't metal. Most of these things are very different from each other. Many of them come in the form of air. A few of them look like a kind of rock or water instead of air. They usually turn to air easily, and most of them are not very strong.

THE LINE

People don't agree exactly where the line between "metals" and "not metals" is, but it's somewhere around here, and runs down and to the right.

AIR, WATER, AND FIRE

The things in this area of the table do a lot of things. When you put them near things from the other end of the table, they can turn to different kinds of water, start fires, or make everything blow up.

QUIET AIR

This end of the table is pretty quiet. When you put these kinds of air with other things, they usually don't seem to notice.

THE AIR IN HERE

THE STUFF THAT KEEPS KITCHEN GLASS FROM BREAKING WHEN HOT	THE STUFF ALL KNOWN LIFE IS MADE FROM	THE PART OF AIR WE DON'T NEED TO BREATHE TO STAY ALIVE	THE PART OF AIR WE DO NEED TO BREATHE TO STAY ALIVE	GREEN BURNING AIR THAT KILLS	AIR IN BRIGHT SIGNS MADE FROM COLORED LIGHT
THIS METAL	THE ROCK THAT MAKES UP BEACHES, GLASS, AND COMPUTER BRAINS	BURNING WHITE ROCKS	SMELLY YELLOW ROCKS LIKE THIS	THE STUFF THEY PUT IN POOLS SO NOTHING BAD CAN GROW IN THEM	AIR THAT DOESN'T DO MUCH OF ANYTHING

THE GRAY METAL AT THE CENTER OF THE EARTH	BROWN METAL WE USE TO CARRY POWER AND VOICES	METAL USED TO MAKE THE BROWN METAL STRONGER (NOW USED FOR MANY OTHER THINGS)	WATERY METAL THAT MAKES DRINK CANS TEAR LIKE PAPER	METAL NAMED AFTER THIS PLACE	THE ROCK MOST WELL KNOWN FOR KILLING YOU IF YOU EAT IT	A ROCK THAT CAN CHANGE ONE KIND OF POWER INTO ANOTHER	RED WATER	AIR USED BY DOCTORS TO MAKE THIN BRIGHT LIGHTS FOR CUTTING EYES
ONE OF TWO METALS USED IN CARS TO MAKE THEIR SMOKE CLEANER		METAL USED IN PAINT UNTIL WE REALIZED IT MADE PEOPLE SICK	PART OF THE SILVER METAL YOU CAN HEAT UP AT HOME TO STICK PARTS TOGETHER	METAL PUT ON FOOD CANS TO KEEP WATER FROM MAKING HOLES IN THEM	METAL PUT IN THINGS TO KEEP THEM FROM BURNING	METAL THAT CAN BE FOUND IN LOTS OF PLACES, BUT MOST OF THEM AREN'T EARTH	STUFF THEY ADD TO THIS SO YOUR BRAIN GROWS RIGHT	AIR USED IN CAMERA FLASHES
A ROCK THAT PEOPLE WILL PAY AS MUCH FOR AS GOLD	GOLD	THIS	METAL WE USED FOR KILLING ANIMALS BUT STOPPED USING BECAUSE IT WAS TOO GOOD AT IT	METAL WELL KNOWN FOR BEING HEAVY	ROCK THAT LOOKS LIKE A COOL TINY CITY	THIS	STUFF NO ONE HAS SEEN CLEARLY BECAUSE IT BURNS UP TOO FAST	AIR THAT COMES FROM ROCKS UNDER HOUSES AND CAN MAKE YOU SICK
STUFF THAT LASTS FOR TEN SECONDS	STUFF THAT LASTS FOR HALF A MINUTE		STUFF THAT LASTS FOR A THIRD OF A MINUTE	STUFF THAT LASTS THREE SECONDS	STUFF THAT LASTS FOR LESS THAN A THIRD OF A SECOND	STUFF THAT LASTS FOR THE TIME IT TAKES YOU TO CLOSE AND OPEN YOUR EYES	STUFF THAT LASTS FOR THE TIME IT TAKES SOUND TO TRAVEL ONE FOOT

MONEY METAL

We use a lot of the things in this group as money—although not the bottom one, since it disappears very fast.

(Some people who know a lot about money actually think that having money that disappears over time could be good, but they probably don't mean quite this quickly.)

FEEL BETTER

This stuff is made from the rock that looks like a tiny city. If you feel like food is going to come out of your mouth, you can eat or drink some of this, and it might help you feel better.

SO MANY DIFFERENT PARTS OF THE WORLD!

METAL NAMED AFTER THIS PLACE	METAL THAT PULLS ON OTHER METALS WHEN IT GETS JUST A LITTLE COLDER THAN NORMAL AIR	ANOTHER METAL NAMED AFTER THIS TINY TOWN	METAL WHOSE NAME MEANS "HARD TO GET"	METAL NAMED AFTER THIS PLACE	ANOTHER METAL NAMED AFTER THIS TINY TOWN	THE NAME PEOPLE HERE USED FOR PEOPLE HERE	I'M SURE THIS IS A NICE TOWN, BUT COME ON.	METAL NAMED AFTER THIS PLACE
STUFF IN THE BOXES THAT TELL YOU WHEN YOUR HOUSE IS ON FIRE	METAL NAMED FOR HER	METAL NAMED AFTER THIS PLACE	METAL NAMED AFTER THIS PLACE	METAL NAMED FOR HIM	METAL NAMED FOR A MAN WHO HELPED BUILD THE FIRST HEAVY METAL POWER BUILDING	METAL NAMED FOR HIM THIS WAS MY IDEA.	METAL NAMED FOR HIM	METAL THAT LASTS FOR FOUR MINUTES

NAMED FOR THIS PLACE

CHAPTER 6
Chemical Bonding

BIG IDEA
Atoms form chemical bonds by sharing or transferring electrons.

ONLINE Chemistry
HMHScience.com

ONLINE LABS
- Conductivity as an Indicator of Bond Type
- Chemical Bonds
- Types of Bonding in Solids
- Repulsion Compulsion

GO ONLINE
Why It Matters Video
HMHScience.com

Chemical Bonding

(c) ©Alfred Pasieka/Photo Researchers, Inc; (br) ©Artville/Getty Images

Introduction to Chemical Bonding

Key Terms
chemical bond   nonpolar-covalent bond
ionic bonding   polar
covalent bonding   polar-covalent bond

Atoms seldom exist as independent particles in nature. The oxygen you breathe, the water you drink, and nearly all other substances consist of combinations of atoms that are held together by chemical bonds. **A chemical bond is a mutual electrical attraction between the nuclei and valence electrons of different atoms that binds the atoms together.**

Why are most atoms chemically bonded to each other? As independent particles, most atoms are at relatively high potential energy. Nature, however, favors arrangements in which potential energy is minimized. Most atoms are less stable existing by themselves than when they are combined. By bonding with each other, atoms decrease in potential energy, creating more stable arrangements of matter.

▶ MAIN IDEA

Atoms form compounds by gaining, losing, or sharing electrons.

When atoms bond, their valence electrons are redistributed in ways that make the atoms more stable. The way in which the electrons are redistributed determines the type of bonding. As discussed in the chapter "The Periodic Law," main-group metals tend to lose electrons to form positive ions, or *cations*, and nonmetals tend to gain electrons to form negative ions, or *anions*. **Chemical bonding that results from the electrical attraction between cations and anions is called ionic bonding.** In purely ionic bonding, atoms completely give up electrons to other atoms, as illustrated in **Figure 1.1** on the next page. In contrast to atoms joined by ionic bonding, atoms joined by covalent bonding share electrons. **Covalent bonding results from the sharing of electron pairs between two atoms** (see **Figure 1.1**). In a purely covalent bond, the shared electrons are "owned" equally by the two bonded atoms.

Ionic or Covalent?

Bonding between atoms of different elements is rarely purely ionic or purely covalent. It usually falls somewhere between these two extremes, depending on how strongly the atoms of each element attract electrons. Recall that electronegativity is a measure of an atom's ability to attract electrons. The degree to which bonding between atoms of two elements is ionic or covalent can be estimated by calculating the difference in the elements' electronegativities (see **Figure 1.2** on the next page).

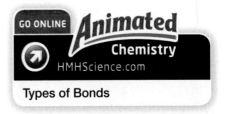

GO ONLINE **Animated Chemistry**
HMHScience.com

Types of Bonds

FIGURE 1.1

Ionic Bonding and Covalent Bonding In ionic bonding, atoms transfer electrons. The resulting positive and negative ions combine due to mutual electrical attraction. In covalent bonding, atoms share electron pairs to form independent molecules.

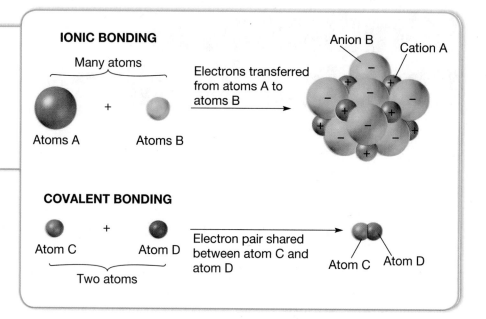

IONIC BONDING

Many atoms

Atoms A + Atoms B

Electrons transferred from atoms A to atoms B →

Anion B   Cation A

COVALENT BONDING

Atom C + Atom D

Two atoms

Electron pair shared between atom C and atom D →

Atom C   Atom D

FIGURE 1.2

Bonding and Electronegativity Differences in electronegativities reflect the character of bonding between elements. The electronegativity of the less-electronegative element is subtracted from that of the more-electronegative element. The greater the electronegativity difference, the more ionic is the bonding.

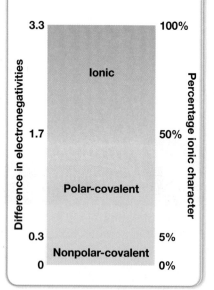

Difference in electronegativities

3.3 — 100%

Ionic

1.7 — 50%

Polar-covalent

0.3 — 5%

Nonpolar-covalent

0 — 0%

Percentage ionic character

For example, the electronegativity difference between fluorine, F, and cesium, Cs, is $4.0 - 0.7 = 3.3$. So, according to **Figure 1.2**, cesium-fluorine bonding is ionic. Fluorine atoms, which are highly electronegative, gain valence electrons, causing the atoms to become anions. Cesium atoms, which are less electronegative, lose valence electrons, causing the atoms to become cations.

Bonding between atoms with an electronegativity difference of 1.7 or less has an ionic character of 50% or less. These compounds are typically classified as covalent. Bonding between two atoms of the same element is completely covalent. Hydrogen, for example, exists in nature not as isolated atoms but as pairs of atoms held together by covalent bonds. **The hydrogen-hydrogen bond is a nonpolar-covalent bond, a covalent bond in which the bonding electrons are shared equally by the bonded atoms, resulting in a balanced distribution of electrical charge.** Bonds having 0% to 5% ionic character, corresponding to electronegativity differences of roughly 0 to 0.3, are generally considered nonpolar-covalent bonds. In bonds with significantly different electronegativities, the electrons are more strongly attracted by the more-electronegative atom. **Such bonds are polar, meaning that they have an uneven distribution of charge.** Covalent bonds having 5% to 50% ionic character, corresponding to electronegativity differences of 0.3 to 1.7, are classified as polar. **A polar-covalent bond is a covalent bond in which the bonded atoms have an unequal attraction for the shared electrons.**

Nonpolar- and polar-covalent bonds are compared in **Figure 1.3**, which illustrates the electron density distribution in hydrogen-hydrogen and hydrogen-chlorine bonds. The electronegativity difference between chlorine and hydrogen is $3.0 - 2.1 = 0.9$, indicating a polar-covalent bond. The electrons in this bond are closer to the more-electronegative chlorine atom than to the hydrogen atom. Thus, the chlorine end of the bond has a partial negative charge, indicated by the symbol $\delta-$. The hydrogen end of the bond then has an equal partial positive charge, $\delta+$.

 FIGURE 1.3

Electron Density Comparison of the electron density in
(a) a nonpolar hydrogen-hydrogen bond and **(b)** a polar hydrogen-
chlorine bond. Because chlorine is more electronegative than
hydrogen, the electron density in the hydrogen-chlorine bond is
greater around the chlorine atom.

Hydrogen nuclei

Hydrogen nucleus

Chlorine nucleus

$\delta+$ $\delta-$

(a) Nonpolar-covalent bond   **(b)** Polar-covalent bond

 CRITICAL THINKING

Explain Why is the density of the electron cloud greater around
the chlorine atom in the polar hydrogen-chlorine bond?

Classifying Bonds

Sample Problem A Use electronegativity differences and Figure 1.2 to classify bonding
between nitrogen, N, and the following elements: carbon, C; sodium, Na; and oxygen, O.
In each pair, which atom will be more negative?

● **SOLVE**

From the Periodic Table of Electronegativities in the chapter "The Periodic
Law," we know that the electronegativity of nitrogen is 3.0. The electronegativities of carbon, sodium, and oxygen are 2.5, 0.9, and 3.5, respectively. In each
pair, the atom with the larger electronegativity will be the more-negative atom.

Bonding between sulfur and	Electronegativity difference	Bond type	More-negative atom
carbon	$3.0 - 2.5 = 0.5$	polar-covalent	nitrogen
sodium	$3.0 - 0.9 = 2.1$	ionic	nitrogen
oxygen	$3.5 - 3.0 = 0.5$	polar-covalent	oxygen

Practice   Answers in Appendix E

Use electronegativity differences and **Figure 1.2** to classify bonding between oxygen, O, and the following
elements: potassium, K; phosphorus, P; and fluorine, F. Indicate the more-negative atom in each pair.

 SECTION 1 **FORMATIVE ASSESSMENT**

▶ Reviewing Main Ideas

1. What is the main distinction between ionic and covalent bonding?

2. How is electronegativity used in determining the ionic or covalent character of the bonding between two elements?

3. What type of bonding would be expected between the following atoms?
   a. Li and F
   b. Cu and S
   c. I and F

4. List the three pairs of atoms referred to in the previous question in order of increasing ionic character of the bonding between them.

✓ Critical Thinking

5. **INTERPRETING CONCEPTS** Compare the following two pairs of atoms: Cu and F; I and F.
   a. Which pair would have a bond with a greater percent ionic character?
   b. In which pair would F have the greater negative charge?

6. **INFERRING RELATIONSHIPS** The isolated K atom is larger than the isolated Br atom.
   a. What type of bond is expected between K and Br?
   b. Which ion in the compound KBr is larger?

Chemical Bonding   **173**

Covalent Bonding and Molecular Compounds

Key Terms

molecule
molecular compound
chemical formula
molecular formula
bond energy
electron-dot notation

Lewis structure
structural formula
single bond
multiple bond
resonance

Many chemical compounds, including most of the chemicals that are in living things and are produced by living things, are composed of molecules. **A molecule is a neutral group of atoms that are held together by covalent bonds.** A single molecule of a chemical compound is an individual unit capable of existing on its own. It may consist of two or more atoms of the same element, as in oxygen, or two or more different atoms, as in water or sugar (see **Figure 2.1**). **A chemical compound whose simplest units are molecules is called a molecular compound.**

The composition of a compound is given by its chemical formula. **A chemical formula indicates the relative numbers of atoms of each kind in a chemical compound by using atomic symbols and numerical subscripts.** The chemical formula of a molecular compound is referred to as a molecular formula. **A molecular formula shows the types and numbers of atoms combined in a single molecule of a molecular compound.** The molecular formula for water, for example, is H_2O. A single water molecule consists of one oxygen atom joined by separate covalent bonds to two hydrogen atoms. A molecule of oxygen, O_2, is an example of a diatomic molecule. A *diatomic molecule* contains only two atoms.

FIGURE 2.1

Covalently Bonded Molecules The models for **(a)** water, **(b)** oxygen, and **(c)** sucrose, or table sugar, represent a few examples of the many molecular compounds in and around us. Atoms within molecules may form one or more covalent bonds.

(a) Water molecule, H_2O

(b) Oxygen molecule, O_2

(c) Sucrose molecule, $C_{12}H_{22}O_{11}$

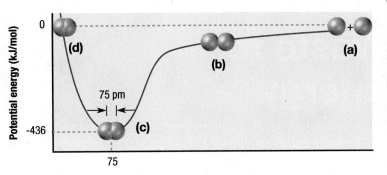

FIGURE 2.2

Potential Energy Changes during the Formation of a Hydrogen-Hydrogen Bond **(a)** The separated hydrogen atoms do not affect each other. **(b)** Potential energy decreases as the atoms are drawn together by attractive forces. **(c)** Potential energy is at a minimum when attractive forces are balanced by repulsive forces. **(d)** Potential energy increases when repulsion between like charges outweighs attraction between opposite charges.

MAIN IDEA

Covalent bonds form from shared electrons.

As you read in Section 1, nature favors chemical bonding because most atoms have lower potential energy when they are bonded to other atoms than they have when they are independent particles. In the case of covalent-bond formation, this idea is illustrated by a simple example, the formation of a hydrogen-hydrogen bond.

Picture two isolated hydrogen atoms separated by a distance large enough to prevent them from influencing each other. At this distance, the overall potential energy of the atoms is arbitrarily set at zero, as shown in part (a) of **Figure 2.2.**

Now consider what happens if the hydrogen atoms approach each other. Each atom has a nucleus containing a single positively charged proton. The nucleus of each atom is surrounded by a negatively charged electron in a spherical 1s orbital. As the atoms near each other, their charged particles begin to interact. As shown in **Figure 2.3**, the approaching nuclei and electrons are *attracted* to each other, which corresponds to a *decrease* in the total potential energy of the atoms. At the same time, the two nuclei *repel* each other, and the two electrons *repel* each other, which results in an *increase* in potential energy.

The relative strength of attraction and repulsion between the charged particles depends on the distance separating the atoms. When the atoms first "sense" each other, the electron-proton attraction is stronger than the electron-electron and proton-proton repulsions. Thus, the atoms are drawn to each other, and their potential energy is lowered, as shown in part (b) of **Figure 2.2.**

The attractive force continues to dominate, and the total potential energy continues to decrease until, eventually, a distance is reached at which the repulsion between the like charges equals the attraction of the opposite charges. This is shown in part (c) of **Figure 2.2.** At this point, which is represented by the bottom of the valley in the curve, potential energy is at a minimum, and a stable hydrogen molecule forms. A closer approach of the atoms, shown in part (d) of **Figure 2.2**, results in a sharp rise in potential energy as repulsion becomes increasingly greater than attraction.

FIGURE 2.3

Attractive and Repulsive Forces The arrows indicate the attractive and repulsive forces between the electrons (shown as electron clouds) and nuclei of two hydrogen atoms. Attraction between particles corresponds to a decrease in potential energy of the atoms, while repulsion corresponds to an increase.

✓ **CRITICAL THINKING**

Explain How do covalently bonded compounds stay together if both the nuclei and the electrons of the atoms involved repel each other?

Both nuclei repel each other, as do both electron clouds.

The nucleus of one atom attracts the electron cloud of the other atom, and vice versa.

Waste to Energy

S.T.E.M.

No one likes garbage piling up. It's unsightly, smelly, and unhealthful. You might think the garbage problem is solved once it's hauled away—out of sight, out of mind. But what happens to this waste after the garbage truck takes it away? In many places, it is simply dumped into a landfill and then covered with soil. The problem with this method is that trash contains toxic materials that eventually leach down into the groundwater and pollute the water table, making the water unfit for drinking or irrigation.

One solution to waste disposal is to incinerate, or burn, the combustible materials in the waste to produce thermal energy, which can be transformed into electrical energy. Combustible materials in waste include hydrocarbons, carbohydrates, and cellulose. These materials have the general formulas $C_nH_{(2n + 2)}$, $C_n(H_2O)_m$, and $(C_6H_{10}O_5)_n$, respectively. When each of these compounds burns, the products are water, carbon dioxide, and thermal energy. One problem with incineration is that carbon dioxide is a greenhouse gas that usually escapes into the atmosphere. Waste also contains toxic materials that can cause health problems. Technological advances have helped solve this problem. The incineration plant in the photo is equipped with devices that remove the pollutants dioxin and gaseous oxides of nitrogen.

Another waste-to-energy process is anaerobic digestion. *Anaerobic* means "in the absence of oxygen." Bacteria digest the waste, producing carbon dioxide and methane. Waste left unattended in a landfill undergoes this process spontaneously. The problem with this method of waste disposal is that both carbon dioxide and methane are greenhouse gases, and, in fact, methane adds to the greenhouse effect much more than carbon dioxide does.

One solution is to encourage anaerobic digestion in a closed container and use the methane to fuel production of electricity. There are four steps in the process, each carried out by a different type of bacteria:

1. Hydrolysis breaks down long-chain organic molecules by adding a water molecule to –COOC– bonds.

2. The products of the first step are broken down further by a fermentation process similar to the souring of milk.

3. The next stage converts stage 2 products into hydrogen, acetic acid, and carbon dioxide.

4. Finally, these molecules are converted to carbon dioxide and methane. The overall process can be summarized by the equation for the anaerobic digestion of glucose:

$$C_6H_{12}O_6 \rightarrow 3CO_2 + 3CH_4$$

An added bonus to this process: the bacteria do all this work for free!

Questions

1. This equation for the combustion of methane is unbalanced:

$$CH_4 + O_2 \rightarrow CO_2 + H_2O$$

Balance the equation and explain why burning methane to produce another greenhouse gas helps reduce global climate change.

2. Often, toxins and other pollutants are buried to get rid of them. Use evidence to explain if you think this approach is a viable long-term solution. Develop a model to help explain the rationale behind your argument.

MAIN IDEA

Bond lengths and energy vary from molecule to molecule.

In **Figure 2.2**, the bottom of the valley in the curve represents the balance between attraction and repulsion in a stable covalent bond. At this point, the electrons of each hydrogen atom of the hydrogen molecule are shared between the nuclei. As shown in **Figure 2.4**, the molecule's electrons can be pictured as occupying overlapping orbitals, moving about freely in either orbital.

The bonded atoms vibrate a bit, but as long as their potential energy remains close to the minimum, they are covalently bonded to each other. The distance between two bonded atoms at their minimum potential energy, that is, the average distance between two bonded atoms, is the *bond length*. The bond length of a hydrogen-hydrogen bond is 75 pm.

In forming a covalent bond, the hydrogen atoms release energy as they change from isolated individual atoms to parts of a molecule. The amount of energy released equals the difference between the potential energy at the zero level (separated atoms) and that at the bottom of the valley (bonded atoms) in **Figure 2.2**. The same amount of energy must be added to separate the bonded atoms. **Bond energy is the energy required to break a chemical bond and form neutral isolated atoms.** Scientists usually report bond energies in kilojoules per mole (kJ/mol), which indicates the energy required to break one mole of bonds in isolated molecules. For example, 436 kJ of energy is needed to break the hydrogen-hydrogen bonds in one mole of hydrogen molecules and form two moles of separated hydrogen atoms.

The energy relationships described here for the formation of a hydrogen-hydrogen bond apply generally to all covalent bonds. However, bond lengths and bond energies vary with the types of atoms that have combined. Even the energy of a bond between the same two types of atoms varies somewhat, depending on what other bonds the atoms have formed. These facts should be considered when examining the data in **Figure 2.5** on the next page. The first three columns in the table list bonds, bond lengths, and bond energies of atoms in specific diatomic molecules. The last three columns give average values of specified bonds in many different compounds.

✔ **CHECK FOR UNDERSTANDING**

Apply Does electronegativity play a role in the formation of covalent bonds? Explain.

FIGURE 2.4

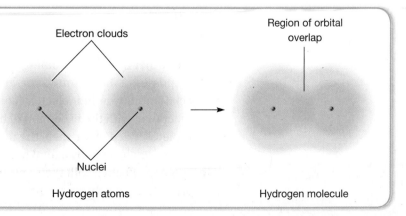

Overlapping Orbitals The orbitals of the hydrogen atoms in a hydrogen molecule overlap, allowing each electron to feel the attraction of both nuclei. The result is an increase in electron density between the nuclei.

Electron clouds

Region of orbital overlap

Nuclei

Hydrogen atoms

Hydrogen molecule

FIGURE 2.5

BOND LENGTHS AND BOND ENERGIES FOR SELECTED COVALENT BONDS

Bond	Average bond length (pm)	Average bond energy (kJ/mol)	Bond	Average bond length (pm)	Average bond energy (kJ/mol)
H—H	75	436	C—C	154	346
F—F	142	159	C—N	147	305
Cl—Cl	199	243	C—O	143	358
Br—Br	229	193	C—H	109	418
I—I	266	151	C—Cl	177	327
H—F	92	569	C—Br	194	285
H—Cl	127	432	N—N	145	163
H—Br	141	366	N—H	101	386
H—I	161	299	O—H	96	459

All individual hydrogen atoms contain a single, unpaired electron in a $1s$ atomic orbital. When two hydrogen atoms form a molecule, they share electrons in a covalent bond. As **Figure 2.6** shows, sharing electrons allows each atom to have the stable electron configuration of helium, $1s^2$. This tendency for atoms to achieve noble-gas configurations by bonding covalently extends beyond the simple case of a hydrogen molecule.

FIGURE 2.6

Bond Length and Stability

By sharing electrons in overlapping orbitals, each hydrogen atom in a hydrogen molecule experiences the effect of a stable $1s^2$ configuration.

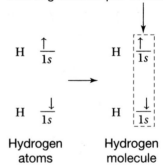

Bonding electron pair in overlapping orbitals

Hydrogen atoms → Hydrogen molecule

▶ MAIN IDEA

Atoms tend to form bonds to follow the octet rule.

Unlike other atoms, the noble-gas atoms exist independently in nature. They possess a minimum of energy existing on their own because of the special stability of their electron configurations. This stability results from the fact that, with the exception of helium and its two electrons in a completely filled outer shell, the noble-gas atoms' outer s and p orbitals are completely filled by a total of eight electrons. Other main-group atoms can effectively fill their outermost s and p orbitals with electrons by sharing electrons through covalent bonding.

Such bond formation follows the *octet rule:* Chemical compounds tend to form so that each atom, by gaining, losing, or sharing electrons, has an octet of electrons in its highest occupied energy level.

Let's examine how the bonding in a fluorine molecule illustrates the octet rule. An independent fluorine atom has seven electrons in its highest energy level ($[He]2s^2 2p^5$). Like hydrogen atoms, fluorine atoms bond covalently with each other to form diatomic molecules, F_2. When two fluorine atoms bond, each atom shares one of its valence electrons with its partner. The shared electron pair effectively fills each atom's outermost energy level with an octet of electrons, as illustrated in **Figure 2.7a**. **Figure 2.7b** shows another example of the octet rule, in which the chlorine atom in a molecule of hydrogen chloride, HCl, achieves an outermost octet by sharing an electron pair with an atom of hydrogen.

FIGURE 2.7

Octet Rule

(a) By sharing valence electrons in overlapping orbitals, each atom in a fluorine molecule feels the effect of neon's stable configuration, $[He]2s^2 2p^6$.
(b) In a hydrogen chloride molecule, the hydrogen atom effectively fills its $1s$ orbital with two electrons, while the chlorine atom experiences the stability of an outermost octet of electrons.

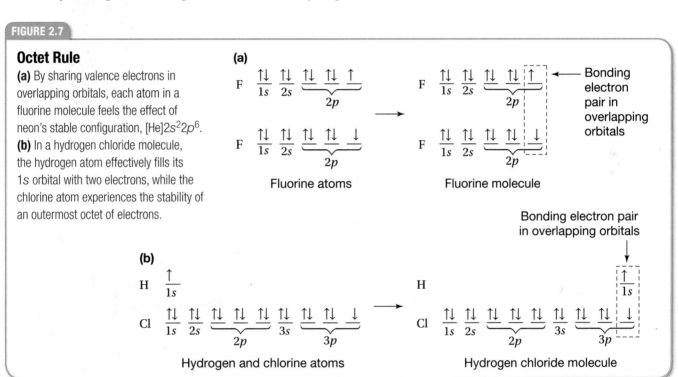

Exceptions to the Octet Rule

Most main-group elements tend to form covalent bonds according to the octet rule. However, there are exceptions. As you have seen, hydrogen forms bonds in which it is surrounded by only two electrons. Boron, B, has just three valence electrons ($[He]2s^2 2p^1$). Because electron pairs are shared in covalent bonds, boron tends to form bonds in which it is surrounded by six electrons. In boron trifluoride, BF_3, for example, the boron atom is surrounded by its own three valence electrons plus one from each of the three fluorine atoms bonded to it. Other elements can be surrounded by *more* than eight electrons when they combine with the highly electronegative elements fluorine, oxygen, and chlorine. In these cases of *expanded valence*, bonding involves electrons in *d* orbitals as well as in *s* and *p* orbitals. Examples of compounds that have an expanded valence include PCl_5 and SF_6, as shown in **Figure 5.4** (in Section 5).

x

x

FIGURE 2.8

Writing Electron-Dot Notations To write an element's electron-dot notation, determine the element's number of valence electrons. Then place a corresponding number of dots around the element's symbol, as shown.

Number of valence electrons	Electron-dot notation	Example
1	X·	Na·
2	·X·	·Mg·
3	·X̣·	·Ḅ·
4	·X̣·	·C̣·
5	·N̈·	·N̈·
6	:X̣·	:Ọ·
7	:X̣·	:F̈·
8	:N̈·	:N̈e·

▶ **MAIN IDEA**

Dots placed around an element's symbol can represent valence electrons.

Covalent-bond formation usually involves only the electrons in an atom's outermost energy levels, or the atom's valence electrons. To keep track of these electrons, it is helpful to use electron-dot notation. **Electron-dot notation** is an electron-configuration notation in which only the valence electrons of an atom of a particular element are shown, indicated by dots placed around the element's symbol. The inner-shell electrons are not shown. For example, the electron-dot notation for a fluorine atom (electron configuration $[He]2s^22p^5$) may be written as follows.

In general, a main-group element's number of valence electrons can be determined by adding the superscripts of the element's noble-gas notation. In this book, the electron-dot notations for elements with 1–8 valence electrons are written as shown in **Figure 2.8**.

GO ONLINE

Solve It! Cards
HMHScience.com

SOLUTION TUTOR
HMHScience.com

Electron-Dot Notation

Sample Problem B
  a. Write the electron-dot notation for hydrogen.
  b. Write the electron-dot notation for nitrogen.

 SOLVE

  a. A hydrogen atom has only one occupied energy level, the $n = 1$ level, which contains a single electron. Therefore, the electron-dot notation for hydrogen is written as follows.

$$H.$$

  b. The group notation for nitrogen's family of elements is ns^2np^3, which indicates that nitrogen has five valence electrons. Therefore, the electron-dot notation for nitrogen is written as follows.

▶ **MAIN IDEA**

Electron-dot notations can represent compounds.

Electron-dot notations are also useful for representing molecules. For example, a hydrogen molecule, H_2, is represented by combining the notations of two individual hydrogen atoms, as follows.

$$H:H$$

The pair of dots represents the shared electron pair of the hydrogen-hydrogen covalent bond. For a molecule of fluorine, F_2, the electron-dot notations of two fluorine atoms are combined.

$$:\overset{..}{\underset{..}{F}}:\overset{..}{\underset{..}{F}}:$$

Here, too, the pair of dots between the two symbols represents the shared pair of a covalent bond. In addition, each fluorine atom is surrounded by three pairs of electrons that are not shared in bonds. An *unshared pair*, also called a *lone pair*, is a pair of electrons that is not involved in bonding and that belongs exclusively to one atom.

The pair of dots representing a shared pair of electrons in a covalent bond is often replaced by a long dash. According to this convention, hydrogen and fluorine molecules are represented as follows.

$$H-H \quad :\overset{..}{\underset{..}{F}}-\overset{..}{\underset{..}{F}}:$$

These representations are all **Lewis structures,** formulas in which atomic symbols represent nuclei and inner-shell electrons, dot-pairs or dashes between two atomic symbols represent electron pairs in covalent bonds, and dots adjacent to only one atomic symbol represent unshared electrons. It is common to write Lewis structures that show only the electrons that are shared, using dashes to represent the bonds. A **structural formula** indicates the kind, number, arrangement, and bonds but not the unshared pairs of the atoms in a molecule. For example, $F-F$ and $H-Cl$ are structural formulas.

The Lewis structures (and therefore the structural formulas) for many molecules can be drawn if one knows the composition of the molecule and which atoms are bonded to each other. The following sample problem illustrates the basic steps for writing Lewis structures. The molecule described in this problem contains bonds with single, shared electron pairs. A single covalent bond, or a **single bond,** is a covalent bond in which one pair of electrons is shared between two atoms.

 Lewis Structures

Sample Problem C Draw the Lewis structure of iodomethane, CH_3I.

● **SOLVE**

    1. *Determine the type and number of atoms in the molecule.*
        The formula shows one carbon atom, one iodine atom, and three hydrogen atoms.

    2. *Write the electron-dot notation for each type of atom in the molecule.*
        Carbon is from Group 14 and has four valence electrons.
        Iodine is from Group 17 and has seven valence electrons.
        Hydrogen has one valence electron.

$$\cdot\overset{}{\underset{.}{C}}\cdot \quad :\overset{..}{\underset{..}{I}}: \quad H\cdot$$

Continued

3. *Determine the total number of valence electrons available in the atoms to be combined.*

$$
\begin{aligned}
\text{C} \quad & 1 \times 4e^- = 4e^- \\
\text{I} \quad & 1 \times 7e^- = 7e^- \\
\text{3H} \quad & 3 \times 1e^- = \underline{3e^-} \\
& \qquad\qquad\quad 14e^-
\end{aligned}
$$

4. *Arrange the atoms to form a skeleton structure for the molecule. If carbon is present, it is the central atom. Otherwise, the least-electronegative atom is central (except for hydrogen, which is never central). Then connect the atoms by electron-pair bonds.*

$$
\begin{array}{c}
\text{H} \\
\text{H}\!:\!\ddot{\text{C}}\!:\!\text{I} \\
\ddot{\text{H}}
\end{array}
$$

5. *Add unshared pairs of electrons to each nonmetal atom (except hydrogen) such that each is surrounded by eight electrons.*

$$
\begin{array}{c}
\text{H} \\
\text{H}\!:\!\ddot{\text{C}}\!:\!\ddot{\text{I}}\!: \\
\ddot{\text{H}}
\end{array}
\quad \text{or} \quad
\begin{array}{c}
\text{H} \\
| \\
\text{H}\!-\!\text{C}\!-\!\ddot{\text{I}}\!: \\
| \\
\text{H}
\end{array}
$$

6. *Count the electrons in the structure to be sure that the number of valence electrons used equals the number available. Be sure the central atom and other atoms besides hydrogen have an octet.* There are eight electrons in the four covalent bonds and six electrons in the three unshared pairs, giving the correct total of 14 valence electrons.

Practice

1. Draw the Lewis structure for ammonia, NH_3.
2. Draw the Lewis structure for hydrogen sulfide, H_2S.
3. Draw the Lewis structure for silane, SiH_4.
4. Draw the Lewis structure for phosphorus trifluoride, PF_3.

▶ **MAIN IDEA**

Some atoms can share multiple pairs of electrons.

Atoms of some elements, especially carbon, nitrogen, and oxygen, can share more than one electron pair. A double covalent bond, or simply a *double bond*, is a covalent bond in which two pairs of electrons are shared between two atoms. A double bond is shown either by two side-by-side pairs of dots or by two parallel dashes. All four electrons in a double bond "belong" to both atoms. In ethene, C_2H_4, for example, two electron pairs are simultaneously shared by two carbon atoms.

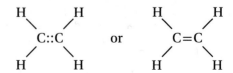

A triple covalent bond, or simply a *triple bond*, is a covalent bond in which three pairs of electrons are shared between two atoms. For example, elemental nitrogen, N_2, like hydrogen and the halogens, normally exists as diatomic molecules. In this case, however, each nitrogen atom, which has five valence electrons, acquires three electrons to complete an octet by sharing three pairs of electrons with its partner. This is illustrated in the Lewis structure and the formula structure for N_2, as shown below.

$$:N:::N: \quad \text{or} \quad :N{\equiv}N:$$

Figure 2.9 represents nitrogen's triple bond through orbital notation. Like the single bonds in hydrogen and halogen molecules, the triple bond in nitrogen molecules is nonpolar.

Carbon forms a number of compounds containing triple bonds. For example, the compound ethyne, C_2H_2, contains a carbon-carbon triple bond.

$$H:C:::C:H \quad \text{or} \quad H{-}C{\equiv}C{-}H$$

Double and triple bonds are referred to as multiple bonds, or multiple covalent bonds. Double bonds in general have greater bond energies and are shorter than single bonds. Triple bonds are even stronger and shorter. **Figure 2.10** compares average bond lengths and bond energies for some single, double, and triple bonds.

In writing Lewis structures for molecules that contain carbon, nitrogen, or oxygen, one must remember that multiple bonds between pairs of these atoms are possible. (A hydrogen atom, on the other hand, has only one electron and therefore always forms a single covalent bond.) The need for a multiple bond becomes obvious if there are not enough valence electrons to complete octets by adding unshared pairs. Sample Problem D on the next page shows how to deal with this situation.

FIGURE 2.9

Forming Triple Bonds In a molecule of nitrogen, N_2, each nitrogen atom is surrounded by six shared electrons plus one unshared pair of electrons. Thus, each nitrogen atom follows the octet rule in forming a triple covalent bond.

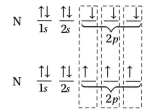

Nitrogen molecule

✔ **CHECK FOR UNDERSTANDING**

Explain Although silicon is in the same periodic group and shares many properties with carbon, it has a significantly greater bond length. Explain why this would make carbon a better building block than silicon for living organisms.

FIGURE 2.10

BOND LENGTHS AND BOND ENERGIES FOR SINGLE AND MULTIPLE COVALENT BONDS

Bond	Average bond length (pm)	Average bond energy (kJ/mol)	Bond	Average bond length (pm)	Average bond energy (kJ/mol)
C–C	154	346	C–O	143	358
C=C	134	612	C=O	120	732
C≡C	120	835	C≡O	113	1072
C–N	147	305	N–N	145	163
C=N	132	615	N=N	125	418
C≡N	116	887	N≡N	110	945

Lewis Structures

Sample Problem D Draw the Lewis structure for methanal, CH_2O, which is also known as formaldehyde.

● **SOLVE**

1. *Determine the number of atoms of each element present in the molecule.*
   The formula shows one carbon atom, two hydrogen atoms, and one oxygen atom.

2. *Write the electron-dot notation for each type of atom.*
   Carbon is from Group 14 and has four valence electrons. Oxygen, which is in Group 16, has six valence electrons. Hydrogen has only one electron.

$$\dot{\underset{\cdot}{C}}\cdot \qquad :\ddot{O}: \qquad H\cdot$$

3. *Determine the total number of valence electrons available in the atoms to be combined.*

$$
\begin{array}{lll}
C & 1 \times 4e^- = 4e^- \\
O & 1 \times 6e^- = 6e^- \\
2H & 2 \times 1e^- \underline{= 2e^-} \\
& \qquad\qquad 12e^-
\end{array}
$$

4. *Arrange the atoms to form a skeleton structure for the molecule, and connect the atoms by electron-pair bonds.*

$$
\begin{array}{c}
H \\
\ddot{} \\
H:C:O
\end{array}
$$

5. *Add unshared pairs of electrons to each nonmetal atom (except hydrogen) such that each is surrounded by eight electrons.*

$$
\begin{array}{c}
H \\
\ddot{} \\
H:C:\ddot{O}: \\
\ddot{}
\end{array}
$$

6a. *Count the electrons in the Lewis structure to be sure that the number of valence electrons used equals the number available.*
   The structure above has six electrons in covalent bonds and eight electrons in four lone pairs, for a total of 14 electrons. The structure has two valence electrons too many.

6b. *If too many electrons have been used, subtract one or more lone pairs until the total number of valence electrons is correct. Then move one or more lone electron pairs to existing bonds between non-hydrogen atoms until the outer shells of all atoms are completely filled.*
   Subtract the lone pair of electrons from the carbon atom. Then move one lone pair of electrons from the oxygen to the bond between carbon and oxygen to form a double bond. There are eight electrons in covalent bonds and four electrons in lone pairs, for a total of 12 valence electrons.

$$
\begin{array}{ccc}
H & & H \\
\ddot{} & & | \\
H:C::\ddot{O} & \text{or} & H-C=\ddot{O} \\
& & \ddot{}
\end{array}
$$

Practice

1. Draw the Lewis structure for carbon dioxide, CO_2.
2. Draw the Lewis structure for hydrogen cyanide, which contains one hydrogen atom, one carbon atom, and one nitrogen atom.

▶ MAIN IDEA
Resonance structures show hybrid bonds.

Some molecules and ions cannot be represented adequately by a single Lewis structure. One such molecule is ozone, O_3, which can be represented by either of the following Lewis structures.

$$\ddot{O}=\ddot{O}-\ddot{O}\colon \quad \text{or} \quad \colon\!\ddot{O}-\ddot{O}=\ddot{O}$$

Notice that each structure indicates that the ozone molecule has two types of O—O bonds, one single and one double. Chemists once speculated that ozone split its time existing as one of these two structures, constantly alternating, or "resonating," from one to the other. Experiments, however, revealed that the oxygen-oxygen bonds in ozone are identical. Therefore, scientists now say that ozone has a single structure that is the average of these two structures. Together the structures are referred to as resonance structures or resonance hybrids. **Resonance refers to bonding in molecules or ions that cannot be correctly represented by a single Lewis structure.** To indicate resonance, a double-headed arrow is placed between a molecule's resonance structures.

$$\ddot{O}=\ddot{O}-\ddot{O}\colon \longleftrightarrow \colon\!\ddot{O}-\ddot{O}=\ddot{O}$$

▶ MAIN IDEA
Some compounds are networks of bonded atoms.

The covalent compounds that you have read about so far consist of many identical molecules held together by forces acting between the molecules. (You will read more about these intermolecular forces in Section 5.) There are many covalently bonded compounds that do not contain individual molecules but instead can be pictured as continuous, three-dimensional networks of bonded atoms. You will read more about covalently bonded networks in the chapter "Chemical Formulas and Chemical Compounds."

✓ SECTION 2 FORMATIVE ASSESSMENT

▶ Reviewing Main Ideas

1. Define the following:
   a. bond length
   b. bond energy

2. State the octet rule.

3. How many pairs of electrons are shared in the following types of covalent bonds?
   a. a single bond
   b. a double bond
   c. a triple bond

4. Draw the Lewis valence electron dot structures to show the arrangement of electrons in the following atoms and molecules:
   a. C
   b. Al
   c. C_2HCl
   d. $SiCl_4$
   e. OF_2

✓ Critical Thinking

5. **APPLYING MODELS** Compare the molecules H_2NNH_2 and HNNH. Which molecule has the stronger N—N bond?

Main Ideas

- Ionic bonds form from attractions between positive and negative ions.

- Differences in attraction strength give ionic and molecular compounds different properties.

- Multiple atoms can bond covalently to form a single ion.

Ionic Bonding and Ionic Compounds

Key Terms

ionic compound

formula unit

lattice energy

polyatomic ion

Most of the rocks and minerals that make up Earth's crust consist of positive and negative ions held together by ionic bonding. A familiar example of an ionically bonded compound is sodium chloride, or common table salt, which is found in nature as rock salt. A sodium ion, Na^+, has a charge of $1+$. A chloride ion, Cl^-, has a charge of $1-$. There is an electrical force of attraction between oppositely charged ions. In sodium chloride, these ions combine in a one-to-one ratio—Na^+Cl^-—so that each positive charge is balanced by a negative charge. The chemical formula for sodium chloride is usually written simply as NaCl.

An **ionic compound** is composed of positive and negative ions that are combined so that the numbers of positive and negative charges are equal. Most ionic compounds exist as crystalline solids (see **Figure 3.1**). A crystal of any ionic compound is a three-dimensional network of positive and negative ions mutually attracted to one another. As a result, in contrast to a molecular compound, an ionic compound is not composed of independent, neutral units that can be isolated and examined. The chemical formula of an ionic compound merely represents the simplest ratio of the compound's combined ions that gives electrical neutrality.

The chemical formula of an ionic compound shows the ratio of the ions present in a sample of any size. **A formula unit is the simplest collection of atoms from which an ionic compound's formula can be written.** For example, one formula unit of sodium chloride, NaCl, is one sodium cation plus one chloride anion. (In the naming of a monatomic anion, the ending of the element's name becomes -*ide*.)

The ratio of ions in a formula unit depends on the charges of the ions combined. For example, to achieve electrical neutrality in the ionic compound calcium fluoride, two fluoride anions, F^-, each with a charge of $1-$, must balance the $2+$ charge of each calcium cation, Ca^{2+}. Therefore, the formula of calcium fluoride is CaF_2.

⏵ MAIN IDEA

Ionic bonds form from attractions between positive and negative ions.

Electron-dot notation can be used to demonstrate the changes that take place in ionic bonding. Ionic compounds do not ordinarily form by the combination of isolated ions, but consider for a moment a sodium atom and a chlorine atom approaching each other. The two atoms are neutral and have one and seven valence electrons, respectively.

$$Na\cdot \qquad\qquad :\overset{\cdot\cdot}{\underset{\cdot\cdot}{Cl}}:$$

Sodium atom   Chlorine atom

We have already seen that atoms of sodium and the other alkali metals readily lose one electron to form cations. And we have seen that atoms of chlorine and the other halogens readily gain one electron to form anions.

FIGURE 3.1

Ionic Compounds Sodium chloride (common table salt) is an ionic compound.

✔ **CRITICAL THINKING**

Explain How is the structure of sodium chloride typical of ionic compounds?

The combination of sodium and chlorine atoms to produce one formula unit of sodium chloride can thus be represented as follows.

$$\text{Na}^{\cdot} \quad + \quad :\overset{\cdot\cdot}{\underset{\cdot\cdot}{\text{Cl}}}: \quad \longrightarrow \quad \text{Na}^{+} \quad + \quad :\overset{\cdot\cdot}{\underset{\cdot\cdot}{\text{Cl}}}:^{-}$$

Sodium atom   Chlorine atom   Sodium cation   Chloride anion

The transfer of an electron from the sodium atom to the chlorine atom transforms each atom into an ion with a noble-gas configuration. In the combination of calcium with fluorine, two fluorine atoms are needed to accept the two valence electrons given up by one calcium atom.

$$.\text{Ca}^{\cdot} \quad + \quad :\overset{\cdot\cdot}{\underset{\cdot\cdot}{\text{F}}}: \quad + \quad :\overset{\cdot\cdot}{\underset{\cdot\cdot}{\text{F}}}: \quad \longrightarrow \quad \text{Ca}^{2+} \quad - \quad :\overset{\cdot\cdot}{\underset{\cdot\cdot}{\text{F}}}: \quad - \quad :\overset{\cdot\cdot}{\underset{\cdot\cdot}{\text{F}}}:^{-}$$

Calcium atom   Fluorine atoms   Calcium cation   Fluoride anions

Characteristics of Ionic Bonding

Recall that nature favors arrangements in which potential energy is minimized. In an ionic crystal, ions minimize their potential energy by combining in an orderly arrangement known as a *crystal lattice* (see **Figure 3.2**). The attractive forces at work within an ionic crystal include those between oppositely charged ions and those between the nuclei and electrons of adjacent ions. The repulsive forces include those between like-charged ions and those between electrons of adjacent ions. The distances between ions and their arrangement in a crystal represent a balance among all these forces. Sodium chloride's crystal structure is shown in **Figure 3.3** below.

FIGURE 3.2

Ions and Electrical Forces The ions in an ionic compound lower their potential energy by forming an orderly, three-dimensional array in which the positive and negative charges are balanced. The electrical forces of attraction between oppositely charged ions extend over long distances, causing a large decrease in potential energy.

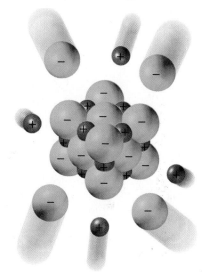

FIGURE 3.3

Crystal Structure of NaCl Two models of the crystal structure of sodium chloride are shown.

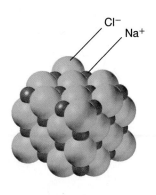

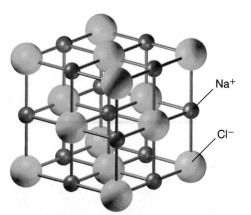

(a) To illustrate the ions' actual arrangement, the sodium and chloride ions are shown with their electron clouds just touching.

(b) In an expanded view, the distances between ions have been exaggerated in order to clarify the positioning of the ions in the structure.

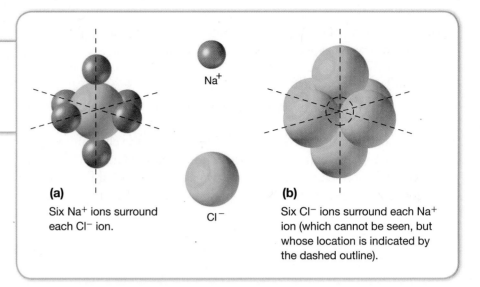

FIGURE 3.4

Crystal Structure of NaCl The figure shows the ions that most closely surround a chloride anion and a sodium cation within the crystal structure of NaCl.

Na$^+$

Cl$^-$

(a)
Six Na$^+$ ions surround each Cl$^-$ ion.

(b)
Six Cl$^-$ ions surround each Na$^+$ ion (which cannot be seen, but whose location is indicated by the dashed outline).

Figure 3.4 shows the crystal structure of sodium chloride in greater detail. Within the arrangement, each sodium cation is surrounded by six chloride anions. At the same time, each chloride anion is surrounded by six sodium cations. Attraction between the adjacent, oppositely charged ions is much stronger than repulsion by other ions of the same charge, which are farther away.

The three-dimensional arrangements of ions and the strengths of attraction between them vary with the sizes and charges of the ions and the numbers of ions of different charges. For example, in calcium fluoride, there are two anions for each cation. Each calcium cation is surrounded by eight fluoride anions. At the same time, each fluoride ion is surrounded by four calcium cations, as shown in **Figure 3.5**.

To compare bond strengths in ionic compounds, chemists compare the amounts of energy released when separated ions in a gas come together to form a crystalline solid. **Lattice energy is the energy released when one mole of an ionic crystalline compound is formed from gaseous ions.** Lattice energy values for a few common ionic compounds are shown in **Figure 3.6** (on the next page). The negative energy values indicate that energy is *released* when the crystals are formed.

FIGURE 3.5

Crystal Structure of CaF$_2$ In the crystal structure of calcium fluoride, CaF$_2$, each calcium cation is surrounded by eight fluoride anions, and each fluoride ion is surrounded by four calcium cations. This is the closest possible packing of the ions in which the positive and negative charges are balanced.

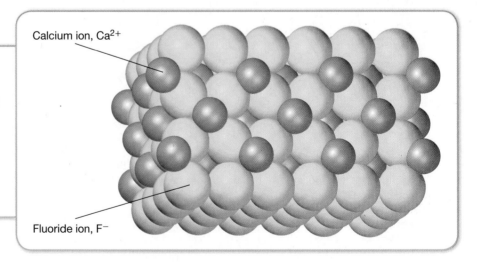

Calcium ion, Ca^{2+}

Fluoride ion, F$^-$

MAIN IDEA

Differences in attraction strength give ionic and molecular compounds different properties.

The force that holds ions together in ionic compounds is a very strong overall attraction between positive and negative charges. In a molecular compound, the covalent bonds of the atoms making up each molecule are also strong. But the forces of attraction *between* molecules are much weaker than the forces among formula units in ionic bonding. This difference in the strength of attraction between the basic units of molecular and ionic compounds gives rise to different properties in the two types of compounds.

The melting point, boiling point, and hardness of a compound depend on how strongly its basic units are attracted to each other. Because the forces of attraction between individual molecules are not very strong, many molecular compounds melt at low temperatures. In fact, many molecular compounds are already completely gaseous at room temperature. In contrast, the ions in ionic compounds are held together by strong attractive forces, so ionic compounds generally have higher melting and boiling points than do molecular compounds.

Ionic compounds are hard but brittle. Why? In an ionic crystal, even a slight shift of one row of ions relative to another causes a large buildup of repulsive forces, as shown in **Figure 3.7**. These forces make it difficult for one layer to move relative to another, causing ionic compounds to be hard. If one layer is moved, however, the repulsive forces make the layers part completely, causing ionic compounds to be brittle.

In the solid state, the ions cannot move, so the compounds are not electrical conductors. In the molten state, ionic compounds are electrical conductors because the ions can move freely to carry electrical current. Many ionic compounds can dissolve in water. When they dissolve, their ions separate from each other and become surrounded by water molecules. These ions are free to move through the solution, so such solutions are electrical conductors. Other ionic compounds do not dissolve in water, however, because the attractions between the water molecules and the ions cannot overcome the attractions between the ions.

FIGURE 3.6

LATTICE ENERGIES OF SOME COMMON IONIC COMPOUNDS

Compound	Lattice energy (kJ/mol)
NaCl	−787.5
NaBr	−751.4
CaF_2	−2634.7
LiCl	−861.3
LiF	−1032
MgO	−3760
KCl	−715

FIGURE 3.7

Ionic Properties **(a)** The attraction between positive and negative ions in a crystalline ionic compound causes layers of ions to resist motion.
(b) When struck with sufficient force, the layers shift so that ions of the same charge approach each other, causing repulsion. As a result, the crystal shatters along the planes.

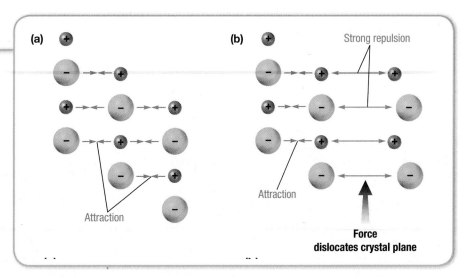

Chemical Bonding   **189**

MAIN IDEA

Multiple atoms can bond covalently to form a single ion.

Certain atoms bond covalently with each other to form a group of atoms that has both molecular and ionic characteristics. **A charged group of covalently bonded atoms is known as a polyatomic ion.** Polyatomic ions combine with ions of opposite charge to form ionic compounds. The charge of a polyatomic ion results from an excess of electrons (negative charge) or a shortage of electrons (positive charge). For example, an ammonium ion, a common positively charged polyatomic ion, contains one nitrogen atom and four hydrogen atoms and has a single positive charge. Its formula is NH_4^+, sometimes written as $[NH_4]^+$ to show that the group of atoms *as a whole* has a charge of 1+. The seven protons in the nitrogen atom plus the four protons in the four hydrogen atoms give the ammonium ion a total positive charge of 11+. An independent nitrogen atom has seven electrons, and four independent hydrogen atoms have a total of four electrons. When these atoms combine to form an ammonium ion, one of their electrons is lost, giving the polyatomic ion a total negative charge of 10−.

Lewis structures for the ammonium ion and some common negative polyatomic ions—the nitrate, sulfate, and phosphate ions—are shown below. To find the Lewis structure for a polyatomic ion, follow the steps of Sample Problem D, with the following exception. If the ion is negatively charged, add to the total number of valence electrons a number of electrons corresponding to the ion's negative charge. If the ion is positively charged, subtract from the total number of valence electrons a number of electrons corresponding to the ion's positive charge.

Ammonium ion   Nitrate ion   Sulfate ion   Phosphate ion

✔ CHECK FOR UNDERSTANDING

Why is it necessary to add or subtract electrons from the total number of valence electrons for polyatomic ions?

✔ SECTION 3 FORMATIVE ASSESSMENT

▶ Reviewing Main Ideas

1. Give two examples of an ionic compound.

2. Use electron-dot notation to demonstrate the formation of ionic compounds involving the following:
   a. Li and Cl
   b. Ca and I

3. Distinguish between ionic and molecular compounds in terms of the basic units that make up each.

4. Compound B has lower melting and boiling points than compound A. At the same temperature, compound B vaporizes faster than compound A. If one of these compounds is ionic and the other is molecular, which would you expect to be molecular? ionic? Explain your reasoning.

✔ Critical Thinking

5. **ANALYZING DATA** The melting points for the compounds Li_2S, Rb_2S, and K_2S are 900°C, 530°C, and 840°C, respectively. List these three compounds in order of increasing lattice energy.

Metallic Bonding

Key Terms

metallic bonding
malleability
ductility

Chemical bonding is different in metals than it is in ionic, molecular, or covalent-network compounds. This difference is reflected in the unique properties of metals. They are excellent electrical conductors in the solid state—much better conductors than even molten ionic compounds. This property is due to the highly mobile valence electrons of the atoms that make up a metal. Such mobility is not possible in molecular compounds, in which valence electrons are localized in electron-pair bonds between neutral atoms. Nor is it possible in solid ionic compounds, in which electrons are bound to individual ions that are held in place in crystal structures.

▶ MAIN IDEA
Metal electrons move freely in empty, overlapping orbitals.

The highest energy levels of most metal atoms are occupied by very few electrons. In *s*-block metals, for example, one or two valence electrons occupy the outermost orbital, and all three outermost *p* orbitals, which can hold a total of six electrons, are vacant. In addition to completely vacant outer *p* orbitals, *d*-block metals also possess many vacant *d* orbitals in the energy level just below their highest energy level.

Within a metal, the vacant orbitals in the atoms' outer energy levels overlap. This overlapping of orbitals allows the outer electrons of the atoms to roam freely throughout the entire metal. The electrons are *delocalized*, which means that they do not belong to any one atom but move freely about the metal's network of empty atomic orbitals. These mobile electrons form a *sea of electrons* around the metal atoms, which are packed together in a crystal lattice (see **Figure 4.1**). The chemical bonding that results from the attraction between metal atoms and the surrounding sea of electrons is called **metallic bonding**.

Metallic Properties

The freedom of electrons to move in a network of metal atoms accounts for the high electrical and thermal conductivity characteristic of all metals. In addition, metals are both strong absorbers and reflectors of light. Because they contain many orbitals separated by extremely small energy differences, metals can absorb a wide range of light frequencies. This absorption of light results in the excitation of the metal atoms' electrons to higher energy levels. However, in metals the electrons immediately fall back down to lower levels, emitting energy in the form of light at a frequency similar to the absorbed frequency. This re-radiated (or reflected) light is responsible for the metallic appearance or luster of metal surfaces.

FIGURE 4.1

Crystal Structure of Solid Sodium The model shows a portion of the crystal structure of solid sodium. The atoms are arranged so that each sodium atom is surrounded by eight other sodium atoms. The atoms are relatively fixed in position, while the electrons are free to move throughout the crystal, forming an electron sea.

FIGURE 4.2

Shaping Metals Unlike ionic crystalline compounds, most metals are malleable. This property allows iron, for example, to be shaped into useful tools.

Most metals are also easy to form into desired shapes. Two important properties related to this characteristic are malleability and ductility (see **Figure 4.2**). **Malleability** is the ability of a substance to be hammered or beaten into thin sheets. **Ductility** is the ability of a substance to be drawn, pulled, or extruded through a small opening to produce a wire. The malleability and ductility of metals are possible because metallic bonding is the same in all directions throughout the solid. When struck, one plane of atoms in a metal can slide past another without encountering resistance or breaking bonds. By contrast, recall from Section 3 that shifting the layers of an ionic crystal causes the bonds to break and the crystal to shatter.

Metallic Bond Strength

Metallic bond strength varies with the nuclear charge of the metal atoms and the number of electrons in the metal's electron sea. Both of these factors are reflected in a metal's *enthalpy of vaporization*. The amount of energy as heat required to vaporize the metal is a measure of the strength of the bonds that hold the metal together. The enthalpy of vaporization is defined as the amount of energy absorbed as heat when a specified amount of a substance vaporizes at constant pressure. Some enthalpies of vaporization for metals are given in **Figure 4.3**.

FIGURE 4.3

ENTHALPIES OF VAPORIZATION OF SOME METALS (kJ/mol)			
Period	Element		
Second	Li 147	Be 297	
Third	Na 97	Mg 128	Al 294
Fourth	K 77	Ca 155	Sc 333
Fifth	Rb 76	Sr 137	Y 365
Sixth	Cs 64	Ba 140	La 402

✓ SECTION 4 **FORMATIVE ASSESSMENT**

▶ Reviewing Main Ideas

1. Describe the electron-sea model of metallic bonding.

2. What is the relationship between metallic bond strength and enthalpy of vaporization?

3. Explain why most metals are malleable and ductile but ionic crystals are not.

✓ Critical Thinking

4. ORGANIZING IDEAS Explain why metals are good electrical conductors.

©Photri

Molecular Geometry

SECTION 5

Main Ideas

- Negative particles repel and move away from each other.
- Multiple orbitals can combine to form hybrid orbitals.
- Weak forces exist between molecules.

Key Terms

VSEPR theory	hybrid orbitals	hydrogen bonding
hybridization	dipole	London dispersion forces

The properties of molecules depend not only on the bonding of atoms but also on molecular geometry—the three-dimensional arrangement of a molecule's atoms in space. The polarity of each bond, along with the geometry of the molecule, determines *molecular polarity*, or the uneven distribution of molecular charge. As you will read, molecular polarity strongly influences the forces that act *between* molecules in liquids and solids.

A chemical formula reveals little information about a molecule's geometry. After performing many tests designed to reveal the shapes of various molecules, chemists developed two different, equally successful theories to explain certain aspects of their findings. One theory accounts for molecular-bond angles. The other is used to describe the orbitals that contain the valence electrons of a molecule's atoms.

MAIN IDEA

Negative particles repel and move away from each other.

As shown in **Figure 5.1,** diatomic molecules, like those of hydrogen, H_2, and hydrogen chloride, HCl, must be linear because they consist of only two atoms. To predict the geometries of more-complicated molecules, one must consider the locations of all electron pairs surrounding the bonded atoms. This is the basis of VSEPR theory.

The abbreviation VSEPR stands for "valence-shell, electron-pair repulsion," referring to the repulsion between pairs of valence electrons of the atoms in a molecule. **VSEPR theory** **states that repulsion between the sets of valence-level electrons surrounding an atom causes these sets to be oriented as far apart as possible.** How does the assumption that electrons in molecules repel each other account for molecular shapes? For now, let us consider only molecules with no unshared valence electron pairs on the central atom.

Let's examine the simple molecule BeF_2. The beryllium atom forms a covalent bond with each fluorine atom and does not follow the octet rule. It is surrounded by only the two electron pairs that it shares with the fluorine atoms.

$$:\ddot{\underset{\cdot\cdot}{\mathrm{F}}}:\mathrm{Be}:\ddot{\underset{\cdot\cdot}{\mathrm{F}}}:$$

According to VSEPR theory, the shared pairs will be as far away from each other as possible. As shown in **Figure 5.2a** on the next page, the distance between electron pairs is maximized if the bonds to fluorine are on opposite sides of the beryllium atom, 180° apart. Thus, all three atoms lie on a straight line. The molecule is linear.

FIGURE 5.1

Linear Molecules Ball-and-stick models illustrate the linearity of diatomic molecules.

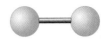

(a) Hydrogen, H_2

(a) A hydrogen molecule is represented by two identical balls (the hydrogen atoms) joined by a solid bar (the covalent bond).

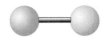

(b) Hydrogen chloride, HCl

(b) A hydrogen chloride molecule is composed of dissimilar atoms, but it is still linear.

FIGURE 5.2

Molecular Geometry Ball-and-stick models show the shapes of molecules according to VSEPR theory.

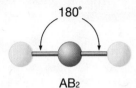

180°

AB₂

(a) Beryllium fluoride, BeF₂

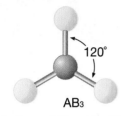

120°

AB₃

(b) Boron trifluoride, BF₃

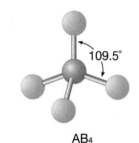

109.5°

AB₄

(c) Methane, CH₄

If we represent the central atom in a molecule by the letter A and the atoms bonded to the central atom by the letter B, then according to VSEPR theory, BeF_2 is an example of an AB_2 molecule, which is linear. Can you determine what an AB_3 molecule looks like? The three A—B bonds stay farthest apart by pointing to the corners of an equilateral triangle, giving 120° angles between the bonds. This trigonal-planar geometry is shown in **Figure 5.2b** for the AB_3 molecule boron trifluoride, BF_3.

The central atoms in AB_4 molecules follow the octet rule by sharing four electron pairs with B atoms, for a total of eight shared electrons. The distance between electron pairs is maximized if each A—B bond points to one of four corners of a tetrahedron. This geometry is shown in **Figure 5.2c** for the AB_4 molecule methane, CH_4. The same figure shows that in a tetrahedral molecule, each of the bond angles formed by the A atom and any two of the B atoms is equal to 109.5°.

The shapes of various molecules are summarized in the table on the next spread (**Figure 5.4**). B can represent a single type of atom, a group of identical atoms, or a group of different atoms in the same molecule. The shape of the molecule will still be based on the forms given in the table. However, different sizes of B groups distort the bond angles, making some bond angles larger or smaller than those given in the table.

VSEPR Theory and Molecular Geometry

Sample Problem E Use VSEPR theory to predict the molecular geometry of boron trichloride, BCl_3.

 SOLVE

First write the Lewis structure for BCl_3. Boron is in Group 13 and has three valence electrons.

·Ḃ·

Chlorine is in Group 17, so each chlorine atom has seven valence electrons.

:Ċl:

The total number of available valence electrons is therefore $24e^-$ ($3e^-$ from boron and $21e^-$ from chlorine). The following Lewis structure uses all $24e^-$.

:Cl:
:Cl:B:Cl:

This molecule is an exception to the octet rule because in this case B forms only three bonds. Boron trichloride is an AB_3 type of molecule. Therefore, according to VSEPR theory, it should have trigonal-planar geometry.

Practice   Answers in Appendix E

1. Use VSEPR theory to predict the molecular geometry of the following molecules:
   a. HI   **b.** CBr_4 **c.** CH_2Cl_2

VSEPR Theory and Unshared Electron Pairs

Ammonia, NH_3, and water, H_2O, are examples of molecules in which the central atom has both shared and unshared electron pairs (see **Figure 5.4** on the next page for their Lewis structures). How does VSEPR theory account for the geometries of these molecules?

The Lewis structure of ammonia shows that in addition to the three electron pairs it shares with the three hydrogen atoms, the central nitrogen atom has one unshared pair of electrons.

$$H \!:\! \ddot{N} \!:\! H$$
$$H$$

VSEPR theory postulates that the lone pair occupies space around the nitrogen atom just as the bonding pairs do. Thus, as in an AB_4 molecule, the electron pairs maximize their separation by assuming the four corners of a tetrahedron. Lone pairs do occupy space, but our description of the observed shape of a molecule refers to the *positions of atoms only*. Consequently, as shown in **Figure 5.3a,** the molecular geometry of an ammonia molecule is that of a pyramid with a triangular base. The general VSEPR formula for molecules such as ammonia is AB_3E, where E represents the unshared electron pair.

A water molecule has two unshared electron pairs. It is an AB_2E_2 molecule. Here, the oxygen atom is at the center of a tetrahedron, with two corners occupied by hydrogen atoms and two by the unshared pairs (**Figure 5.3b**). Again, VSEPR theory states that the lone pairs occupy space around the central atom but that the actual shape of the molecule is determined by the positions of the atoms only. In the case of water, this results in a "bent," or angular, molecule. In **Figure 5.3b,** the bond angles in ammonia and water are somewhat less than the 109.5° bond angles of a perfectly tetrahedral molecule, because the unshared electron pairs repel electrons more strongly than do bonding electron pairs.

FIGURE 5.3

Molecular Shape The locations of bonds and unshared electrons are shown for molecules of **(a)** ammonia and **(b)** water. Although unshared electrons occupy space around the central atoms, the shapes of the molecules depend only on the position of the molecules' atoms, as clearly shown by the ball-and-stick models.

CRITICAL THINKING

Explain Why would unshared electrons affect the geometry of a molecule?

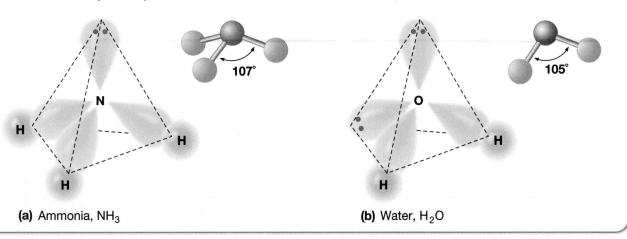

(a) Ammonia, NH_3

(b) Water, H_2O

Figure 5.4 also includes an example of an AB_2E-type molecule. This type of molecule results when a central atom forms two bonds and retains one unshared electron pair.

Finally, in VSEPR theory, double and triple bonds are treated in the same way as single bonds. And polyatomic ions are treated similarly to molecules. (Remember to consider *all* of the electron pairs present in any ion or molecule.) Thus, Lewis structures and **Figure 5.4** can be used together to predict the shapes of polyatomic ions as well as molecules with double or triple bonds.

VSEPR THEORY AND MOLECULAR GEOMETRY

	Molecular shape	Atoms bonded to central atom	Lone pairs of electrons	Type of molecule	Formula example	Lewis structure
Linear		2	0	AB_2	BeF_2	:F̈—Be—F̈:
Trigonal-planar		3	0	AB_3	BF_3	
Bent or Angular		2	1	AB_2E	ONF	
Tetrahedral		4	0	AB_4	CH_4	
Trigonal-pyramidal		3	1	AB_3E	NH_3	
Bent or Angular		2	2	AB_2E_2	H_2O	
Trigonal-bipyramidal		5	0	AB_5	PCl_5	
Octahedral		6	0	AB_6	SF_6	

Sample Problem F

a. Use VSEPR theory to predict the shape of a molecule of hydrogen bromide, HBr.

b. Use VSEPR theory to predict the shape of a phosphite ion, PO_3^-.

● **SOLVE**

a. The Lewis structure of hydrogen bromide shows a single hydrogen-bromine bond and no unshared electron pairs. To simplify the molecule's Lewis structure, we represent the covalent bonds with lines instead of dots.

$$H - \ddot{\text{Br}} :$$

This is an AB_2 molecule, which is linear.

b. The Lewis structure of a phosphite shows three oxygen atoms and an unshared pair of electrons surrounding a central phosphorus atom. Again, lines are used to represent the covalent bonds.

$$:\ddot{\text{O}} - \ddot{\text{P}} - \ddot{\text{O}}:$$
$$|$$
$$:\ddot{\text{O}}:$$

The phosphite ion is an AB_3E type. It has trigonal-pyramidal geometry, with the three oxygen atoms at the base of the pyramid and the phosphorus atom at the top.

Practice   Answers in Appendix E

1. Use VSEPR theory to predict the molecular geometries of the molecules whose Lewis structures are given below.

a.
$$:\ddot{\text{Br}}:$$
$$|$$
$$:\ddot{\text{Br}} - C - \ddot{\text{Br}}:$$
$$|$$
$$:\ddot{\text{Br}}:$$

b.
$$:\ddot{\text{Cl}}:$$
$$|$$
$$:\ddot{\text{Cl}} - B - \ddot{\text{Cl}}:$$

▶ **MAIN IDEA**

Multiple orbitals can combine to form hybrid orbitals.

VSEPR theory is useful for explaining the shapes of molecules. However, it does not reveal the relationship between a molecule's geometry and the orbitals occupied by its bonding electrons. To explain how the orbitals become rearranged when an atom forms covalent bonds, a different model is used. This model is called **hybridization,** which is the mixing of two or more atomic orbitals of similar energies on the same atom to produce new hybrid atomic orbitals of equal energies. Methane, CH_4, provides a good example of how hybridization is used to explain the geometry of molecular orbitals. The orbital notation for a carbon atom shows that it has four valence electrons, two in the $2s$ orbital and two in the $2p$ orbitals.

C $\underset{1s}{\uparrow\downarrow}$ $\underset{2s}{\uparrow\downarrow}$ $\underset{2p}{\underline{\uparrow\ \ \uparrow\ \ \_\_}}$

FIGURE 5.5

Hybridization of Carbon The sp^3 hybridization of carbon's outer orbitals combines one s and three p orbitals to form four sp^3 hybrid orbitals. Whenever hybridization occurs, the resulting hybrid orbitals are at an energy level between the levels of the orbitals that have combined.

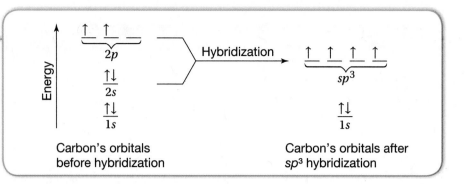

We know from experiments that a methane molecule has tetrahedral geometry. How does carbon form four equivalent, tetrahedrally arranged covalent bonds by orbital overlap with four other atoms?

Two of carbon's valence electrons occupy the $2s$ orbital, and two occupy the $2p$ orbitals. Recall that the $2s$ orbital and the $2p$ orbitals have different shapes. To achieve four equivalent bonds, carbon's $2s$ and three $2p$ orbitals *hybridize* to form four new, identical orbitals called sp^3 orbitals. The superscript 3 indicates that three p orbitals were included in the hybridization; the superscript 1 on the s is understood. The sp^3 orbitals all have the same energy, which is greater than that of the $2s$ orbital but less than that of the $2p$ orbitals, as shown in **Figure 5.5**. **Hybrid orbitals are orbitals of equal energy produced by the combination of two or more orbitals on the same atom.** The number of hybrid orbitals produced equals the number of orbitals that have combined. Bonding with carbon sp^3 orbitals is shown in **Figure 5.6a** for a molecule of methane.

Hybridization also explains the bonding and geometry of many molecules formed by Group 15 and 16 elements. The sp^3 hybridization of a nitrogen atom ($[He]2s^2 2p^3$) yields four hybrid orbitals—one orbital containing a pair of electrons and three orbitals that each contain an unpaired electron. Each unpaired electron is capable of forming a single bond, as shown for ammonia in **Figure 5.6b**. Similarly, two of the four sp^3 hybrid orbitals of an oxygen atom ($[He]2s^2 2p^4$) are occupied by two electron pairs, and two are occupied by unpaired electrons. Each unpaired electron can form a single bond, as shown for water in **Figure 5.6c**.

FIGURE 5.6

Hybrid Orbitals Bonds formed by the overlap of the $1s$ orbitals of hydrogen atoms and the sp^3 orbitals of **(a)** carbon, **(b)** nitrogen, and **(c)** oxygen. For the sake of clarity, only the hybrid orbitals of the central atoms are shown.

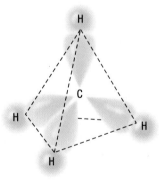

(a) Methane, CH_4

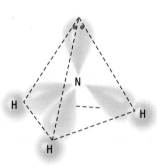

(b) Ammonia, NH_3

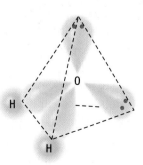

(c) Water, H_2O

FIGURE 5.7

GEOMETRY OF HYBRID ORBITALS

Atomic orbitals	Type of hybridization	Number of hybrid orbitals	Geometry
s, p	sp	2	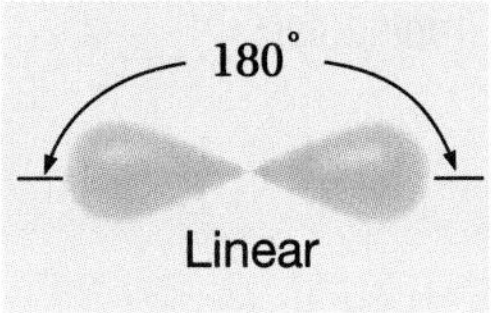 180° Linear
s, p, p	sp^2	3	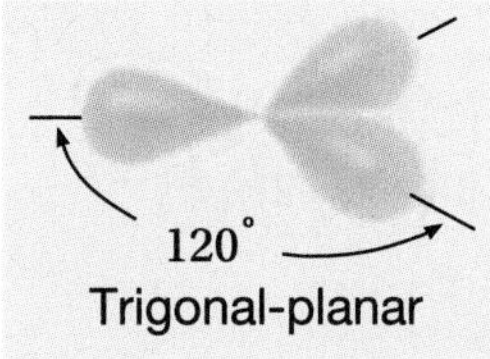 120° Trigonal-planar
s, p, p, p	sp^3	4	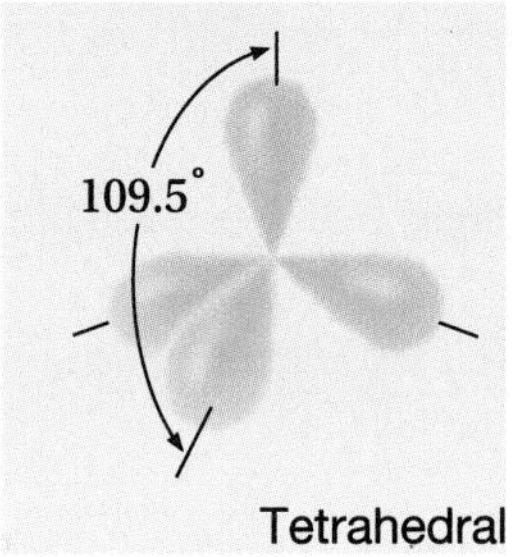 109.5° Tetrahedral

The linear geometry of molecules such as beryllium fluoride, BeF_2, is made possible by hybridization involving the s orbital and one available empty p orbital to yield sp hybrid orbitals. The trigonal-planar geometry of molecules such as boron fluoride, BF_3, is made possible by hybridization involving the s orbital, one singly occupied p orbital, and one empty p orbital to yield sp^2 hybrid orbitals (see **Figure 5.7**).

▶ **MAIN IDEA**

Weak forces exist between molecules.

As a liquid is heated, the kinetic energy of its particles increases. At the boiling point, the energy is sufficient to overcome the force of attraction between the liquid's particles. The particles pull away from each other and enter the gas phase. Boiling point is therefore a good measure of the force of attraction between particles of a liquid. The higher the boiling point, the stronger the forces between particles.

The forces of attraction between molecules are known as *intermolecular forces*. Intermolecular forces vary in strength but are generally weaker than bonds that join atoms in molecules, ions in ionic compounds, or metal atoms in solid metals. Compare the boiling points of the metals and ionic compounds in **Figure 5.8** (on the next page) with those of the molecular substances listed. Note that the values for ionic compounds and metals are much higher than those for molecular substances.

FIGURE 5.8

BOILING POINTS AND BONDING TYPES

Bonding type	Substance	bp (1 atm, °C)
Nonpolar-covalent (molecular)	H_2	−253
	O_2	−183
	Cl_2	−34
	Br_2	59
	CH_4	−164
	CCl_4	77
	C_6H_6	80
Polar-covalent (molecular)	PH_3	−88
	NH_3	−33
	H_2S	−61
	H_2O	100
	HF	20
	HCl	−85
	ICl	97
Ionic	NaCl	1413
	MgF_2	2239
Metallic	Cu	2567
	Fe	2750
	W	5660

Molecular Polarity and Dipole-Dipole Forces

The strongest intermolecular forces exist between polar molecules. Polar molecules act as tiny dipoles because of their uneven charge distribution. A **dipole** is created by equal but opposite charges that are separated by a short distance. The direction of a dipole is from the dipole's positive pole to its negative pole. A dipole is represented by an arrow with a head pointing toward the negative pole and a crossed tail situated at the positive pole. The dipole created by a hydrogen chloride molecule, which has its negative end at the more electronegative chlorine atom, is indicated as follows.

$$\overset{\longmapsto}{H-Cl}$$

The negative region in one polar molecule attracts the positive region in adjacent molecules, and so on throughout a liquid or solid. The forces of attraction between polar molecules are known as *dipole-dipole forces*. These forces are short-range forces, acting only between nearby molecules. The effect of dipole-dipole forces is reflected, for example, by the significant difference between the boiling points of iodine chloride, I—Cl, and bromine, Br—Br. The boiling point of polar iodine chloride is 97 °C, whereas that of nonpolar bromine is only 59 °C. The dipole-dipole forces responsible for the relatively high boiling point of ICl are illustrated schematically in **Figure 5.9** (on the next page).

FIGURE 5.9

Dipole-Dipole Forces

Ball-and-stick models illustrate the dipole-dipole forces between molecules of iodine chloride, ICl. In each molecule, the highly electronegative chlorine atom has a partial negative charge, leaving each iodine atom with a partial positive charge. Consequently, the negative and positive ends of neighboring molecules attract each other.

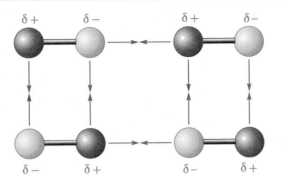

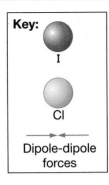

Key:

I

Cl

Dipole-dipole forces

The polarity of diatomic molecules such as ICl is determined by just one bond. For molecules containing more than two atoms, molecular polarity depends on both the polarity and the orientation of each bond. A molecule of water, for example, has two hydrogen-oxygen bonds in which the more-electronegative oxygen atom is the negative pole of each bond. Because the molecule is bent, the polarities of these two bonds combine to make the molecule highly polar, as shown in **Figure 5.10**. An ammonia molecule is also highly polar because the dipoles of the three nitrogen-hydrogen bonds are additive, combining to create a net molecular dipole. In some molecules, individual bond dipoles cancel one another, causing the resulting molecular polarity to be zero. Carbon dioxide and carbon tetrachloride are molecules of this type.

A polar molecule can *induce* a dipole in a nonpolar molecule by temporarily attracting its electrons. The result is a short-range intermolecular force that is somewhat weaker than the dipole-dipole force. The force of an induced dipole accounts for the slight solubility of nonpolar O_2 in water. The positive pole of a water molecule attracts the outer

FIGURE 5.10

Bond Polarities

(a) The bond polarities in a water or an ammonia molecule are additive, causing the molecule as a whole to be polar.
(b) In molecules of carbon tetrachloride and carbon dioxide, the bond polarities extend equally and symmetrically in different directions, canceling each other's effect and causing each molecule as a whole to be nonpolar.

✓ CRITICAL THINKING

Explain What explanation can you give for the fact that the boiling point of H_2O is significantly higher than the boiling point of either H_2 (g) or O_2 (g) alone?

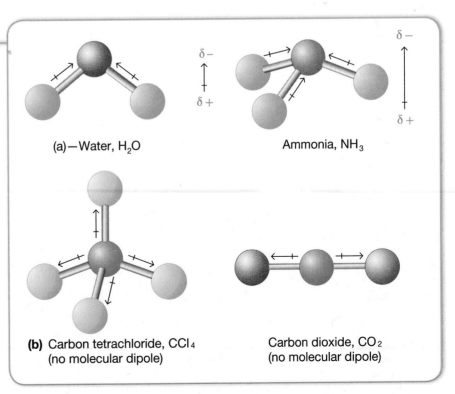

(a)—Water, H_2O

Ammonia, NH_3

(b) Carbon tetrachloride, CCl_4 (no molecular dipole)

Carbon dioxide, CO_2 (no molecular dipole)

FIGURE 5.11

Dipole-Induced Dipole Interaction
The positive pole of a water molecule causes a temporary change in the electron distribution of an oxygen molecule. The negative pole induced in the oxygen molecule is then attracted to the positive pole of the water molecule.

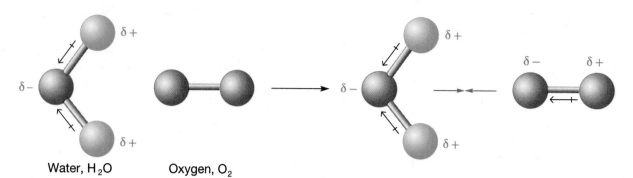

Water, H_2O Oxygen, O_2

electrons of an adjacent oxygen molecule. The oxygen molecule, then, has an induced negative pole on the side toward the water molecule and an induced positive pole on the opposite side. The result is an attraction to the water molecule, as shown in **Figure 5.11.**

Hydrogen Bonding

Some hydrogen-containing compounds, such as hydrogen fluoride (HF), water (H_2O), and ammonia (NH_3), have unusually high boiling points. This is explained by the presence of a particularly strong type of dipole-dipole force. In compounds containing H—F, H—O, or H—N bonds, the large electronegativity differences between hydrogen atoms and fluorine, oxygen, or nitrogen atoms make the bonds connecting them highly polar. This gives the hydrogen atom a positive charge that is almost half as large as that of a proton. Moreover, the small size of the hydrogen atom allows the atom to come very close to an unshared pair of electrons on an adjacent molecule. **The intermolecular force in which a hydrogen atom that is bonded to a highly electronegative atom is attracted to an unshared pair of electrons of an electronegative atom in a nearby molecule is known as hydrogen bonding.**

FIGURE 5.12

Hydrogen Bonding
Space-filling models illustrate hydrogen bonding between water molecules. The dotted lines indicate the attraction between electronegative oxygen atoms and electropositive hydrogen atoms of neighboring molecules.

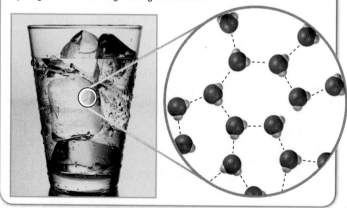

Hydrogen bonds are usually represented by dotted lines connecting the hydrogen-bonded hydrogen to the unshared electron pair of the electronegative atom to which it is attracted, as illustrated for water in **Figure 5.12.** The effect of hydrogen bonding can be seen by comparing the boiling points in **Figure 5.8.** Look at phosphine, PH_3, compared with hydrogen-bonded ammonia, NH_3. How does hydrogen sulfide, H_2S, compare with hydrogen-bonded water, H_2O?

In living organisms, hydrogen bonds play an extremely important role: that of stabilizing the structure of deoxyribonucleic acid (DNA). Hydrogen bonds are individually very weak, but the sum of millions of these bonds forms a very strong force holding two DNA strands together.

FIGURE 5.13

Temporary Dipoles When an instantaneous, temporary dipole develops in a helium atom, it induces a dipole in a neighboring atom.

Momentary dipole
in one helium atom

Weak
attractive
force

Dipole induced in
neighboring atom

London Dispersion Forces

Even noble-gas atoms and molecules that are nonpolar experience a weak intermolecular attraction. In any atom or molecule—polar or nonpolar—the electrons are in continuous motion. As a result, at any instant, the electron distribution may be slightly uneven. The momentary, uneven charge creates a positive pole in one part of the atom or molecule and a negative pole in another. This temporary dipole can then induce a dipole in an adjacent atom or molecule. The two are held together for an instant by the weak attraction between the temporary dipoles, as illustrated in **Figure 5.13. The intermolecular attractions resulting from the constant motion of electrons and the creation of instantaneous dipoles are called London dispersion forces, after Fritz London, who first proposed their existence in 1930.**

London forces act between all atoms and molecules. But they are the *only* intermolecular forces acting among noble-gas atoms and nonpolar molecules. This fact is reflected in the low boiling points of the noble gases and nonpolar molecular compounds listed in **Figure 5.8.** Because London forces are dependent on the motion of electrons, their strength increases with the number of electrons in the interacting atoms or molecules. In other words, London forces increase with increasing atomic or molar mass. This trend can be seen by comparing the boiling points of the gases helium, He, and argon, Ar; hydrogen, H_2, and oxygen, O_2; and chlorine, Cl_2, and bromine, Br_2.

SECTION 5 **FORMATIVE ASSESSMENT**

▶ **Reviewing Main Ideas**

1. What two theories can be used to predict molecular geometry?

2. Draw the Lewis structure and predict the molecular geometry of the following molecules:
   a. SO_2 **b.** CI_4 **c.** BCl_3

3. What factors affect the geometry of a molecule?

4. Explain what is meant by sp^3 hybridization.

5. What type of intermolecular force contributes to the high boiling point of water? Explain.

✓ **Critical Thinking**

6. **INFERRING RELATIONSHIPS** What experimental property directly correlates with the strength of the intermolecular forces? Briefly explain your answer.

Drawing Lewis dot structures can help you understand how valence electrons participate in bonding. Dots are placed around the symbol of an element to represent the element's valence electrons. For example, carbon has four valence electrons, and its Lewis dot structure is usually written as $\cdot\overset{\cdot}{\underset{\cdot}{C}}\cdot$. An atom of fluorine has seven valence electrons. Fluorine's Lewis dot structure can be written as $:\overset{\cdot\cdot}{\underset{\cdot\cdot}{F}}:$. When Lewis

structures for covalently bonded atoms are written, the dots may be placed as needed to show the electrons shared in each bond. Most atoms bond in a way that gives them a stable octet of s and p electrons in the highest energy level. So whenever possible, dots should be arranged in a way that represents a stable octet around each atom.

Problem-Solving TIPS

- Hydrogen is an exception to the octet rule, because hydrogen has only one electron and becomes stable with two electrons.
- Some elements, such as boron, can bond without achieving an octet, because they have three or fewer electrons to share.

Sample Problem

Draw the Lewis dot structure for a molecule of sulfur dichloride, SCl_2.

First, write the electron-dot notation for each atom.

$$:\overset{\cdot\cdot}{\underset{\cdot\cdot}{Cl}}: \qquad :\overset{\cdot\cdot}{\underset{\cdot\cdot}{Cl}}: \qquad :\overset{\cdot}{\underset{\cdot\cdot}{S}}:$$

Next, determine the total number of valence electrons in the atoms.

S	$1 \times 6e^-$	=	$6e^-$
2Cl	$2 \times 7e^-$	=	$14e^-$
	Total e^-	=	$20e^-$

Arrange the atoms to form a skeleton structure for the molecule, and place electron pairs between atoms to represent covalent bonds. You can predict the arrangement of atoms by figuring out how many covalent bonds each atom must form in order to achieve a stable octet. Each chlorine atom, which has 7 valence electrons, must form a single covalent bond. Sulfur, which has 6 valence electrons, must form two covalent bonds. The only possible structure is $Cl-S-Cl$.

Finally, insert dots representing the remaining electrons (16 in this case), in order to give each atom an octet.

$$:\overset{\cdot\cdot}{\underset{\cdot\cdot}{Cl}}\cdot\overset{\cdot\cdot}{\underset{\cdot\cdot}{S}}\cdot\overset{\cdot\cdot}{\underset{\cdot\cdot}{Cl}}:$$

Practice

1. Draw the electron-dot notations for a silicon atom and a strontium atom.
2. Draw Lewis structures for hydrogen sulfide, H_2S, and formic acid, HCO_2H.

CHAPTER 6 Summary

BIG IDEA Atoms form chemical bonds by sharing or transferring electrons.

SECTION 1 Introduction to Chemical Bonding

- Most atoms are chemically bonded to other atoms. The three major types of chemical bonding are ionic, covalent, and metallic.
- In general, atoms of metals bond ionically with atoms of non-metals, atoms of metals bond metallically with each other, and atoms of nonmetals bond covalently with each other.

KEY TERMS

chemical bond
ionic bonding
covalent bonding

nonpolar-covalent bond
polar
polar-covalent bond

SECTION 2 Covalent Bonding and Molecular Compounds

- Atoms in molecules are joined by covalent bonds. In a covalent bond, two atoms share one or more pairs of electrons.
- The octet rule states that many chemical compounds tend to form bonds so that each atom shares or has eight electrons in its highest occupied energy level.
- Bonding within many molecules and ions can be indicated by a Lewis structure. Molecules or ions that cannot be correctly represented by a single Lewis structure are represented by resonance structures.

KEY TERMS

molecule
molecular compound
chemical formula
molecular formula
bond energy
electron-dot notation

Lewis structure
structural formula
single bond
multiple bond
resonance

SECTION 3 Ionic Bonding and Ionic Compounds

- An ionic compound is a three-dimensional network of positive and negative ions mutually attracted to one another.
- Ionic compounds tend to be harder and more brittle and have higher boiling points than materials containing only covalently bonded atoms.

KEY TERMS

ionic compound
formula unit
lattice energy
polyatomic ion

SECTION 4 Metallic Bonding

- The "electron sea" formed in metallic bonding gives metals their properties of high electrical and thermal conductivity, malleability, ductility, and luster.

KEY TERMS

metallic bonding
malleability
ductility

SECTION 5 Molecular Geometry

- VSEPR theory is used to predict the shapes of molecules based on the fact that electron pairs strongly repel each other.
- Hybridization theory is used to predict the shapes of molecules, based on the fact that orbitals within an atom can mix to form orbitals of equal energy.
- Intermolecular forces include dipole-dipole forces and London dispersion forces. Hydrogen bonding is a special case of dipole-dipole forces.

KEY TERMS

VSEPR theory
hybridization
hybrid orbitals
dipole
hydrogen bonding
London dispersion forces

CHAPTER 6   **Review**

GO ONLINE
 Interactive Review
HMHScience.com

Review Games
Concept Maps

SECTION 1

Introduction to Chemical Bonding

 REVIEWING MAIN IDEAS

1. What is a chemical bond?

2. Identify and define the three major types of chemical bonding.

3. What is the relationship between electronegativity and the ionic character of a chemical bond?

4. **a.** What is the meaning of the term *polar* as applied to chemical bonding?
   b. Distinguish between polar-covalent and nonpolar-covalent bonds.

5. In general, what determines whether atoms will form chemical bonds?

PRACTICE PROBLEMS

6. Determine the electronegativity difference, the probable bond type, and the more-electronegative atom with respect to bonds formed between the following pairs of atoms. (Hint: See Sample Problem A.)
   a. H and I
   b. S and O
   c. K and Br
   d. Si and Cl
   e. K and Cl
   f. Se and S
   g. C and H

7. List the bonding pairs described in item 6 in order of increasing covalent character.

8. Use orbital notation to illustrate the bonding in each of the following molecules:
   a. chlorine, Cl_2
   b. oxygen, O_2
   c. hydrogen fluoride, HF

9. The lattice energy of sodium chloride, NaCl, is −787.5 kJ/mol. The lattice energy of potassium chloride, KCl, is −715 kJ/mol. In which compound is the bonding between ions stronger? Why?

SECTION 2

Covalent Bonding and Molecular Compounds

 REVIEWING MAIN IDEAS

10. What is a molecule?

11. **a.** What determines bond length?
    b. In general, how are bond energies and bond lengths related?

12. Describe the general location of the electrons in a covalent bond.

13. As applied to covalent bonding, what is meant by an unshared or lone pair of electrons?

14. Describe the octet rule in terms of noble-gas configurations and potential energy.

15. Determine the number of valence electrons in an atom of each of the following elements:
    a. H
    b. F
    c. Mg
    d. O
    e. Al
    f. N
    g. C

16. In a Lewis structure, which atom is usually the central atom?

17. Distinguish between single, double, and triple covalent bonds by defining each and providing an illustration of each type.

18. For Lewis structures, how is the need for multiple bonds generally determined?

PRACTICE PROBLEMS

19. Use Lewis valence electron dot structures to express the arrangement of valence electrons present in one atom of each of the following elements. (Hint: See Sample Problem B.)
    a. Li   **e.** C
    b. Ca   **f.** P
    c. Cl   **g.** Al
    d. O   **h.** S

20. Use electron-dot structures to demonstrate the formation of ionic compounds involving the following elements:
  a. Na and S
  b. Ca and O
  c. Al and S

21. Draw Lewis structures for each of the following molecules. (Hint: See Sample Problem D.)
  a. contains one C and four F atoms
  b. contains two H and one Se atom
  c. contains one N and three I atoms
  d. contains one Si and four Br atoms
  e. contains one C, one Cl, and three H atoms

22. Determine the type of hybrid orbitals formed by the boron atom in a molecule of boron fluoride, BF_3.

23. Draw Lewis structures for each of the following molecules. Show resonance structures, if they exist.
  a. O_2
  b. N_2
  c. CO
  d. SO_2

24. Draw Lewis structures for each of the following polyatomic ions. Show resonance structures, if they exist.
  a. OH^-
  b. $H_3C_2O_2^-$
  c. BrO_3^-

SECTION 3

Ionic Bonding and Ionic Compounds

▶ **REVIEWING MAIN IDEAS**

25. **a.** What is an ionic compound?
  b. In what form do most ionic compounds occur?

26. **a.** What is a formula unit?
  b. What are the components of one formula unit of CaF_2?

27. **a.** What is lattice energy?
  b. In general, what is the relationship between lattice energy and the strength of ionic bonding?

28. **a.** In general, how do ionic and molecular compounds compare in terms of melting points, boiling points, and ease of vaporization?
  b. What accounts for the observed differences in the properties of ionic and molecular compounds?
  c. Cite three physical properties of ionic compounds.

29. **a.** What is a polyatomic ion?
  b. Give two examples of polyatomic ions.
  c. In what form do such ions often occur in nature?

SECTION 4

Metallic Bonding

▶ **REVIEWING MAIN IDEAS**

30. **a.** How do the properties of metals differ from those of both ionic and molecular compounds?
  b. What specific property of metals accounts for their unusual electrical conductivity?

31. What properties of metals contribute to their tendency to form metallic bonds?

32. **a.** What is metallic bonding?
  b. How can the strength of metallic bonding be measured?

SECTION 5

Molecular Geometry

▶ **REVIEWING MAIN IDEAS**

33. **a.** How is the VSEPR theory used to classify molecules?
  b. What molecular geometry would be expected for F_2 and HF?

34. According to the VSEPR theory, what molecular geometries are associated with the following types of molecules?
  a. AB_2
  b. AB_3
  c. AB_4
  d. AB_5
  e. AB_6

35. Describe the role of each of the following in predicting molecular geometries:
  a. unshared electron pairs
  b. double bonds

36. a. What are hybrid orbitals?
  b. What determines the number of hybrid orbitals produced by the hybridization of an atom?

37. a. What are intermolecular forces?
  b. In general, how do these forces compare in strength with those in ionic and metallic bonding?
  c. What types of molecules have the strongest intermolecular forces?

38. What is the relationship between electronegativity and the polarity of a chemical bond?

39. a. What are dipole-dipole forces?
  b. What determines the polarity of a molecule?

40. a. What is meant by an induced dipole?
  b. What is a consequence of this type of intermolecular force?

41. a. What is hydrogen bonding?
  b. What accounts for its extraordinary strength?

42. What are London dispersion forces?

PRACTICE PROBLEMS

43. According to the VSEPR theory, what molecular geometries are associated with the following types of molecules?
  a. AB_3E
  b. AB_2E_2
  c. AB_2E

44. Use hybridization to explain the bonding in methane, CH_4.

45. For each of the following polar molecules, indicate the direction of the resulting dipole:
  a. H–F
  b. H–Cl
  c. H–Br
  d. H–I

46. Determine whether each of the following bonds would be polar or nonpolar:
  a. H–H
  b. H–O
  c. H–F
  d. Br–Br
  e. H–Cl
  f. H–N

47. On the basis of individual bond polarity and orientation, determine whether each of the following molecules would be polar or nonpolar:
  a. H_2O
  b. I_2
  c. CF_4
  d. NH_3
  e. CO_2

48. Draw a Lewis structure for each of the following molecules, and then use the VSEPR theory to predict the molecular geometry of each:
  a. SCl_2
  b. PI_3
  c. Cl_2O
  d. NH_2Cl
  e. $SiCl_3Br$
  f. ONCl

49. Draw a Lewis structure for each of the following polyatomic ions, and then use VSEPR theory to determine the geometry of each:
  a. NO_3^-
  b. NH_4^+
  c. SO_4^{2-}
  d. ClO_2^-

Mixed Review

▶ REVIEWING MAIN IDEAS

50. Arrange the following pairs from strongest to weakest attraction:
  a. polar molecule and polar molecule
  b. nonpolar molecule and nonpolar molecule
  c. polar molecule and ion
  d. ion and ion

51. Determine the geometry of the following molecules:
  a. CCl_4
  b. $BeCl_2$
  c. PH_3

52. What types of atoms tend to form the following types of bonding?
  a. ionic
  b. covalent
  c. metallic

53. What happens to the energy level and stability of two bonded atoms when they are separated and become individual atoms?

54. Draw the three resonance structures for sulfur trioxide, SO_3.

55. **a.** How do ionic and covalent bonding differ?
b. How does an ionic compound differ from a molecular compound?
c. How does an ionic compound differ from a metal?

56. Write the electron-dot notation for each of the following elements:
a. He
b. Cl
c. O
d. P
e. B

57. Write the structural formula for methanol, CH_3OH.

58. How many K^+ and S^{2-} ions would be in one formula unit of the ionic compound formed by these ions?

59. Explain metallic bonding in terms of the sparsely populated outermost orbitals of metal atoms.

60. Explain the role of molecular geometry in determining molecular polarity.

61. How does the energy level of a hybrid orbital compare with the energy levels of the orbitals from which it was formed?

62. Aluminum's enthalpy of vaporization is 284 kJ/mol. Beryllium's enthalpy of vaporization is 224 kJ/mol. In which element is the bonding stronger between atoms?

63. Determine the electronegativity difference, the probable bonding type, and the more-electronegative atom for each of the following pairs of atoms:
a. Zn and O
b. Br and I
c. S and Cl

64. Draw the Lewis structure for each of the following molecules:
a. PCl_3
b. CCl_2F_2
c. CH_3NH_2

65. Draw the Lewis structure for $BeCl_2$. (Hint: Beryllium atoms do not follow the octet rule.)

66. Draw a Lewis structure for each of the following polyatomic ions and determine their geometries:
a. NO_2^-
b. NO_3^-
c. NH_4^+

67. Why do most atoms tend to bond to other atoms?

CRITICAL THINKING

68. **Inferring Relationships** The length of a bond varies depending on the type of bond formed. Predict and compare the lengths of the carbon-carbon bonds in the following molecules. Explain your answer. (Hint: See Figure 2.10)

69. Why does F generally form covalent bonds with great polarity?

70. Explain what is wrong with the following Lewis structures, and then correct each one.

71. Ionic compounds tend to have higher boiling points than covalent substances do. Both ammonia, NH_3, and methane, CH_4, are covalent compounds, yet the boiling point of ammonia is 130 °C higher than that of methane. What might account for this large difference?

USING THE HANDBOOK

72. Figure 4.1 shows a model for a body-centered cubic crystal. Review the Properties tables for all of the metals in the *Elements Handbook* (Appendix A). What metals exist in body-centered cubic structures?

73. Group 14 of the *Elements Handbook* (Appendix A) contains a discussion of semiconductors and the band theory of metals. How does this model explain the electrical conductivity of metals?

RESEARCH AND WRITING

74. Prepare a report on the work of Linus Pauling.
   a. Discuss his work on the nature of the chemical bond.
   b. Linus Pauling was an advocate of the use of vitamin C as a preventative for colds. Evaluate Pauling's claims. Determine if there is any scientific evidence that indicates whether vitamin C helps prevent colds.

75. Covalently bonded solids, such as silicon, an element used in computer components, are harder than pure metals. Research theories that explain the hardness of covalently bonded solids and their usefulness in the computer industry. Present your findings to the class.

76. Natural rubber consists of long chains of carbon and hydrogen atoms covalently bonded together. When Charles Goodyear accidentally dropped a mixture of sulfur and rubber on a hot stove, the energy from the stove joined these chains together to make vulcanized rubber (named for Vulcan, the Roman god of fire). The carbon-hydrogen chains in vulcanized rubber are held together by two sulfur atoms that form covalent bonds between the chains. These covalent bonds are commonly called disulfide bridges. Explore other molecules that have such disulfide bridges. Present your findings to the class.

77. Searching for the perfect artificial sweetener—great taste with no Calories—has been the focus of chemical research for some time. Molecules such as sucralose, aspartame, and saccharine owe their sweetness to their size and shape. One theory holds that any sweetener must have three sites that fit into the proper taste buds on the tongue. This theory is appropriately known as the triangle theory. Research artificial sweeteners to develop a model to show how the triangle theory operates.

ALTERNATIVE ASSESSMENT

78. Devise a set of criteria that will allow you to classify the following substances as ionic or non-ionic: $CaCO_3$, Cu, H_2O, $NaBr$, and C (graphite). Show your criteria to your instructor.

79. **Performance Assessment** Identify 10 common substances in and around your home, and indicate whether you would expect these substances to contain ionic, covalent, or metallic bonds.

Standards-Based Assessment

Record your answers on a separate piece of paper.

MULTIPLE CHOICE

1 Between which two atoms are ionic bonds most likely to form? (Draw electron-dot structures to help you decide.)

 A K and F
 B O and O
 C C and H
 D N and O

2 Which of the following is a possible electron configuration ending for an element with the Lewis dot structure pictured below?

 A $4s^2 3d^{10} 4p^3$
 B $2s^2 2p^1$

   $\dot{X}:$

 C $3s^2 3p^6$
 D $5s^2 4d^3$

3 Which of the following correctly illustrates the Lewis structure for a covalent compound?

   H
 A H·C·H
   H

 B $:\!\overset{\cdot}{\underset{\cdot}{C}}\!:$

 C H:C:H

   H
 D H:C:H
   H

4 Lewis structures use dots to depict valence electrons. For the following elements, what pattern in the corresponding Lewis dot structures can you identify?

 lead (Pb) antimony (Sb) sulfur (S) chlorine (Cl)

 A The dot structure for each contains the same number of outer electrons.
 B The number of outer electrons increases by 2 for each element.
 C The number of outer electrons increases by 1 for each element.
 D The number of outer electrons corresponds to the total number of electrons in each element.

5 The Lewis structure of HCN contains

 A one double bond and one single bond.
 B one triple bond and one single bond.
 C two single bonds.
 D two double bonds.

6 Which of the following molecules contains a double bond?

 A $COCl_2$
 B C_2H_6
 C CF_4
 D SF_2

7 Which of the following represents the correct Lewis dot structure for sodium chloride?

 A Na + $:\!\overset{\cdot\cdot}{\underset{\cdot\cdot}{C}l}\!:$

 B $[Na]^-$ + $:\!\overset{\cdot\cdot}{\underset{\cdot\cdot}{C}l}\!:$

 C Na^+ + $[:\!\overset{\cdot\cdot}{\underset{\cdot\cdot}{C}l}\!:]^-$

 D $[Na]^-$ + $:\!\overset{\cdot\cdot}{\underset{\cdot\cdot}{C}l}\!:^+$

GRIDDED RESPONSE

8 The first step in constructing a Lewis dot structure for a molecule is to determine how many valence electrons are in all of the atoms contained in the molecule. How many total valence electrons are contained in the atoms of a molecule of butane, C_4H_{10}?

Test Tip
When several questions refer to the same graph, table, drawing, or passage, answer the questions you are sure of first.

CHAPTER 7
Chemical Formulas and Chemical Compounds

BIG IDEA
Chemical formulas represent the ratios of atoms in a chemical compound. Various rules are used to name ionic and covalent compounds.

 ONLINE Chemistry
HMHScience.com

ONLINE LABS
- Tests for Iron(II) and Iron(III)
- Water of Hydration
- Determining the Empirical Formula of Magnesium Oxide
- The Formula for Success

GO ONLINE

 Why It Matters Video
HMHScience.com

Formulas and Compounds

Chemical Names and Formulas

Key Terms

monatomic ion
binary compound
nomenclature

oxyanion
salt

Main Ideas

▶ Formulas tell the number and kinds of atoms in a compound.

▶ Monatomic ions are made of only one type of atom.

▶ Binary compounds contain atoms of two elements.

▶ Some covalent compounds are a network with no single molecules.

▶ Acids are solutions of water and a special type of compound.

The total number of natural and synthetic chemical compounds runs in the millions. For some of these substances, certain common names remain in everyday use. For example, calcium carbonate is better known as limestone, and sodium chloride is usually referred to simply as table salt. And everyone recognizes dihydrogen monoxide by its popular name, water.

Unfortunately, common names usually give no information about chemical composition. To describe the atomic makeup of compounds, chemists use systematic methods for naming compounds and writing chemical formulas. In this chapter, you will be introduced to some of the rules used to identify simple chemical compounds.

▶ **MAIN IDEA**

Formulas tell the number and kinds of atoms in a compound.

Recall that a chemical formula indicates the relative number of atoms of each kind in a chemical compound. For a molecular compound, the chemical formula reveals the number of atoms of each element contained in a single molecule of the compound, as shown below for the hydrocarbon octane. (*Hydrocarbons* are molecular compounds composed solely of carbon and hydrogen.)

$$C_8H_{18}$$

Subscript indicates that there are 8 carbon atoms in a molecule of octane.

Subscript indicates that there are 18 hydrogen atoms in a molecule of octane.

Unlike a molecular compound, an ionic compound consists of a lattice of positive and negative ions held together by mutual attraction. The chemical formula for an ionic compound represents one formula unit—the simplest ratio of the compound's positive ions (cations) and its negative ions (anions). The chemical formula for aluminum sulfate, an ionic compound consisting of aluminum cations and polyatomic sulfate anions, is written as shown on the next page.

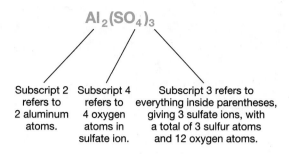

$$Al_2(SO_4)_3$$

Subscript 2 refers to 2 aluminum atoms.

Subscript 4 refers to 4 oxygen atoms in sulfate ion.

Subscript 3 refers to everything inside parentheses, giving 3 sulfate ions, with a total of 3 sulfur atoms and 12 oxygen atoms.

Note how the parentheses are used. They surround the polyatomic anion to identify it as a unit. The subscript 3 refers to the entire unit. Notice also that there is no subscript written next to the symbol for sulfur. When there is no subscript written next to an atom's symbol, the value of the subscript is understood to be 1.

▶ **MAIN IDEA**

Monatomic ions are made of only one type of atom.

By gaining or losing electrons, many main-group elements form ions with noble-gas configurations. For example, Group 1 metals lose one electron to give 1+ cations, such as Na^+. Group 2 metals lose two electrons to give 2+ cations, such as Mg^{2+}. **Ions formed from a single atom are known as monatomic ions.** The nonmetals of Groups 15, 16, and 17 gain electrons to form anions. For example, in ionic compounds, nitrogen forms the 3− anion N^{3-}. The three added electrons plus the five outermost electrons in nitrogen atoms give a completed outermost octet. Similarly, the Group 16 elements oxygen and sulfur form 2− anions, and the Group 17 halogens form 1− anions.

Not all main-group elements readily form ions, however. Rather than gain or lose electrons, atoms of carbon and silicon form covalent bonds in which they share electrons with other atoms. Other elements tend to form ions that do not have noble-gas configurations. For instance, it is difficult for the Group 14 metals tin and lead to lose four electrons to achieve a noble-gas configuration. Instead, they tend to lose the two electrons in their outer p orbitals but retain the two electrons in their outer s orbitals to form 2+ cations. (Tin and lead can also form molecular compounds in which all four valence electrons are involved in covalent bonding.)

Elements from the d-block form 2+, 3+, or, in a few cases, 1+ or 4+ cations. Many d-block elements form two ions of different charges. For example, copper forms 1+ and 2+ cations. Iron and chromium each form 2+ cations as well as 3+ cations. And vanadium forms 2+, 3+, and 4+ cations.

Naming Monatomic Ions

Monatomic cations are identified simply by the element's name, as illustrated by the examples at left. Naming monatomic anions is slightly more complicated. First, the ending of the element's name is dropped. Then the ending -*ide* is added to the root name, as illustrated by the examples on the next page.

✓ **CHECK FOR UNDERSTANDING**

Describe What characteristic of atoms determines whether they will exchange valence electrons (form an ionic compound) or share them (form a covalent compound)? Describe how this happens. Refer to the chapter "Chemical Bonding" for help.

Examples of Cations

K^+

Potassium cation

Mg^{2+}

Magnesium cation

The names and symbols of the common monatomic cations and anions are organized according to their charges in **Figure 1.1**. The names of many of the ions in the table include Roman numerals. These numerals are part of the *Stock system* of naming chemical ions and elements. You will read more about the Stock system and other systems of naming chemicals later in this chapter.

Examples of Anions	
Element	**Anion**
F	F⁻
Fluor*ine*	Fluor*ide* anion
N	N³⁻
Nitro*gen*	Nit*ride* anion

Examples of Anions	
Element	**Anion**
F	F^-
Fluor*ine*	Fluor*ide* anion
N	N^{3-}
Nitro*gen*	Nit*ride* anion

FIGURE 1.1

SOME COMMON MONATOMIC IONS

Main-group elements

1+		2+		3+	
lithium	Li^+	beryllium	Be^{2+}	aluminum	Al^{3+}
sodium	Na^+	magnesium	Mg^{2+}		
potassium	K^+	calcium	Ca^{2+}		
rubidium	Rb^+	strontium	Sr^{2+}		
cesium	Cs^+	barium	Ba^{2+}		

1−		2−		3−	
fluoride	F^-	oxide	O^{2-}	nitride	N^{3-}
chloride	Cl^-	sulfide	S^{2-}	phosphide	P^{3-}
bromide	Br^-				
iodide	I^-				

***d*-Block elements and others with multiple ions**

1+		2+		3+		4+	
copper(I)	Cu^+	vanadium(II)	V^{2+}	vanadium(III)	V^{3+}	vanadium(IV)	V^{4+}
silver	Ag^+	chromium(II)	Cr^{2+}	chromium(III)	Cr^{3+}	tin(IV)	Sn^{4+}
		manganese(II)	Mn^{2+}	iron(III)	Fe^{3+}	lead(IV)	Pb^{4+}
		iron(II)	Fe^{2+}	cobalt(III)	Co^{3+}		
		cobalt(II)	Co^{2+}				
		nickel(II)	Ni^{2+}				
		copper(II)	Cu^{2+}				
		zinc	Zn^{2+}				
		cadmium	Cd^{2+}				
		tin(II)	Sn^{2+}				
		mercury(II)	Hg^{2+}				
		lead(II)	Pb^{2+}				

✓ **CHECK FOR UNDERSTANDING**

Describe In your own words, describe how to determine the subscripts of a binary ionic compound by using the oxidation numbers of the ions.

▶ **MAIN IDEA**

Binary compounds contain atoms of two elements.

Compounds composed of two elements are known as **binary compounds**. In a binary ionic compound, the total numbers of positive charges and negative charges must be equal. Therefore, the formula for such a compound can be written given the identities of the compound's ions. For example, magnesium and bromine combine to form the ionic compound magnesium bromide. Magnesium, a Group 2 metal, forms the Mg^{2+} cation. Note that the $^{2+}$ in Mg^{2+} is written as a superscript. Bromine, a halogen, forms the Br^- anion when combined with a metal. In each formula unit of magnesium bromide, two Br^- anions are required to balance the 2+ charge of the Mg^{2+} cation. The compound's formula must therefore indicate one Mg^{2+} cation and two Br^- anions. The symbol for the cation is written first.

Ions combined: Mg^{2+}, Br^-, Br^- *Chemical formula:* $MgBr_2$

Note that the $_2$ in Br_2 is written as a subscript. The charges of the ions are not included in the formula. This is always the case when writing formulas for binary ionic compounds.

As an aid for determining subscripts in formulas for ionic compounds, the positive and negative charges can be "crossed over." Crossing over is a method of balancing the charges between ions in an ionic compound. For example, the formula for the compound formed by the aluminum ion, Al^{3+}, and the oxide ion, O^{2-}, is determined as follows.

1. *Write the symbols for the ions side by side. Write the cation first.*

$$Al^{3+} \quad O^{2-}$$

2. *Cross over the charges by using the absolute value of each ion's charge as the subscript for the other ion.*

$$Al_2^{3+} \quad O_3^{2-}$$

3. *Check the subscripts and divide them by their greatest common factor to give the smallest possible whole-number ratio of ions. Then write the formula.*

Multiplying the charge by the subscript shows that the charge on two Al^{3+} cations $(2 \times 3+ = 6+)$ equals the charge on three O^{2-} anions $(3 \times 2- = 6-)$. The greatest common factor of the subscripts is 1. The correct formula is therefore written as follows.

$$Al_2O_3$$

Naming Binary Ionic Compounds

The **nomenclature, or naming system,** of binary ionic compounds involves combining the names of the compound's positive and negative ions. The name of the cation is given first, followed by the name of the anion. For most simple ionic compounds, the ratio of the ions is not indicated in the compound's name, because it is understood based on the relative charges of the compound's ions.

The naming of a simple binary ionic compound is illustrated below for aluminum oxide. Notice that the known relative charges of each ion make specifying ratios in the name unnecessary.

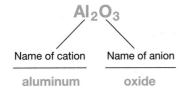

$$Al_2O_3$$

Name of cation   Name of anion

aluminum   oxide

GO ONLINE

Learn It! Video
HMHScience.com

Writing Formulas For Ionic Compounds

Sample Problem A Write the formulas for the binary ionic compounds formed between the following elements:

a. zinc and iodine   **b.** zinc and sulfur

 SOLVE

Write the symbols for the ions side by side. Write the cation first.
a. Zn^{2+} I^-
b. Zn^{2+} S^{2-}

Cross over the charges to give subscripts.
a. Zn_1^{2+} I_2^-
b. Zn_2^{2+} S_2^{2-}

Check the subscripts, and divide them by their greatest common factor to give the smallest possible whole-number ratio of ions. Then write the formula.

a. The subscripts are mathematically correct because they give equal total charges of $1 \times 2+ = 2+$ and $2 \times 1- = 2-$. The greatest common factor of the subscripts is 1.
The smallest possible whole-number ratio of ions in the compound is therefore 1:2.
The subscript 1 is not written, so the formula is ZnI_2.

b. The subscripts are mathematically correct because they give equal total charges of $2 \times 2+ = 4+$ and $2 \times 2- = 4-$. The greatest common factor of the subscripts is 2.
The smallest whole-number ratio of ions in the compound is therefore 1:1.
The correct formula is ZnS.

Practice   Answers in Appendix E

1. Write formulas for the binary ionic compounds formed between the following elements:
   a. potassium and iodine   **d.** aluminum and sulfur
   b. magnesium and chlorine   **e.** aluminum and nitrogen
   c. sodium and sulfur
2. Name the binary ionic compounds indicated by the following formulas:
   a. $AgCl$ **d.** SrF_2
   b. ZnO **e.** BaO
   c. $CaBr_2$ **f.** $CaCl_2$

The Stock System of Nomenclature

Some elements, such as iron, form two or more cations with different charges. To distinguish the ions formed by such elements, scientists use the Stock system of nomenclature. It is useful for distinguishing two different compounds formed by the same elements, as the lead oxides in **Figure 1.2.** This system uses a Roman numeral to indicate an ion's charge. The numeral in parentheses is placed *immediately* after the metal name.

$$Fe^{2+} \qquad Fe^{3+}$$
$$\text{iron(II)} \qquad \text{iron(III)}$$

Names of metals that commonly form only one cation do *not* include a Roman numeral.

$$Na^+ \qquad Ba^{2+} \qquad Al^{3+}$$
$$\text{sodium} \qquad \text{barium} \qquad \text{aluminum}$$

No element forms more than one monatomic anion.

Naming a binary ionic compound according to the Stock system is illustrated below.

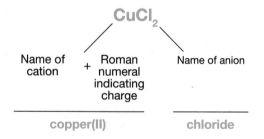

$CuCl_2$

Name of cation	+	Roman numeral indicating charge	Name of anion
copper(II)			chloride

Different Cations of a Metal
Different cations of the same metal form different compounds even when they combine with the same anion.

(a) lead(IV) oxide, PbO_2 **(b)** lead(II) oxide, PbO

Naming Ionic Compounds

Sample Problem B Write the formula and give the name for the compound formed by the ions Cu^{2+} and S^{2-}.

● **SOLVE**

Write the symbols for the ions side by side. Write the cation first.

$$Cu^{2+} \quad S^{2-}$$

Cross over the charges to give subscripts.

$$Cu_2^{2+} \quad S_2^{2-}$$

Check the subscripts, and write the formula.

The subscripts are correct because they give charges of $2 \times 2+ = 4+$ and $2 \times 2- = 4-$. The greatest common factor of the subscripts is 2, so the smallest whole-number ratio of the ions is 1:1. The formula is therefore CuS_3. As **Figure 1.1** shows, copper forms more than one ion. Therefore, the name of the 3+ copper ion must be followed by a Roman numeral indicating its charge. The compound's name is copper(II) sulfide.

Practice   Answers in Appendix E

1. Write the formula and give the name for the compounds formed between the following ions:
   a. Cu^{2+} and Br^- d. Hg^{2+} and S^{2-}
   b. Fe^{2+} and O^{2-} e. Sn^{2+} and F^-
   c. Pb^{2+} and Cl^- f. Fe^{3+} and O^{2-}

2. Give the names for the following compounds:
   a. CoI c. Cu_2Se
   b. FeS d. PbO_2

Compounds Containing Polyatomic Ions

Figure 1.3 on the next page lists some common polyatomic ions. Most are negatively charged, and most are **oxyanions—polyatomic ions that contain oxygen.** Some elements can combine with oxygen to form more than one type of oxyanion. For example, nitrogen can form NO_3^- or NO_2^-. The name given a compound containing such an oxyanion depends on the number of oxygen atoms in the oxyanion. The name of the ion with the greater number of oxygen atoms ends in *-ate*. The name of the ion with the lesser number of oxygen atoms ends in *-ite*.

$$NO_2^- \qquad NO_3^-$$
$$\text{nitrite} \qquad \text{nitrate}$$

FIGURE 1.3

SOME POLYATOMIC IONS

1+		2+	
ammonium	NH_4^+	dimercury*	Hg_2^{2+}

1−		2−		3−	
acetate	CH_3COO^-	carbonate	CO_3^{2-}	arsenate	AsO_4^{3-}
bromate	BrO_3^-	chromate	CrO_4^{2-}	phosphate	PO_4^{3-}
chlorate	ClO_3^-	dichromate	$Cr_2O_7^{2-}$		
chlorite	ClO_2^-	monohydrogen phosphate	HPO_4^{2-}		
cyanide	CN^-	oxalate	$C_2O_4^{2-}$		
dihydrogen phosphate	$H_2PO_4^-$	peroxide	O_2^{2-}		
hydrogen carbonate (bicarbonate)	HCO_3^-	sulfate	SO_4^{2-}		
hydrogen sulfate	HSO_4^-	sulfite	SO_3^{2-}		
hydroxide	OH^-				
hypochlorite	ClO^-				
nitrate	NO_3^-				
nitrite	NO_2^-				
perchlorate	ClO_4^-				
permanganate	MnO_4^-				

*The mercury(I) cation exists as two Hg^+ ions joined together by a covalent bond and is written as Hg_2^{2+}.

Sometimes, an element can form more than two types of oxyanions. In this case, the prefix *hypo-* is given to an anion that has one fewer oxygen atom than the -ite anion. The prefix *per-* is given to an anion that has one more oxygen atom than the -ate anion. This nomenclature is illustrated by the four oxyanions formed by chlorine.

ClO^-	ClO_2^-	ClO_3^-	ClO_4^-
hypochlorite	chlorite	chlorate	perchlorate

Compounds containing polyatomic ions are named in the same manner as binary ionic compounds. The name of the cation is given first, followed by the name of the anion. For example, the two compounds formed with silver by the nitrate and nitrite anions are named *silver nitrate*, $AgNO_3$, and *silver nitrite*, $AgNO_2$, respectively. When multiples of a polyatomic ion are present in a compound, the formula for the polyatomic ion is enclosed in parentheses.

Writing Formulas for Ionic Compounds

Sample Problem C Write the formula for tin(IV) sulfate.

 SOLVE

Write the symbols for the ions side by side. Write the cation first.

$$Sn^{4+} \quad SO_4^{2-}$$

Cross over the charges to give subscripts. Add parentheses around the polyatomic ion if necessary.

$$Sn_2^{4+} \quad (SO_4)_4^{2-}$$

Check the subscripts, and write the formula. The total positive charge is $2 \times 4+ = 8+$. The total negative charge is $4 \times 2- = 8-$. The charges are equal. The greatest common factor of the subscripts is 2, so the smallest whole-number ratio of ions in the compound is 1:2. The correct formula is therefore $Sn(SO_4)_2$.

Practice

1. Write formulas for the following ionic compounds:
   a. sodium iodide
   b. calcium chloride
   c. potassium sulfide
   d. lithium nitrate
   e. copper(II) sulfate
   f. sodium carbonate
   g. calcium nitrite
   h. potassium perchlorate

2. Give the names for the following compounds:
   a. Ag_2O
   b. $Ca(OH)_2$
   c. $KClO_3$
   d. NH_4Cl
   e. $Fe_2(CrO_4)_3$
   f. $KClO$

Naming Binary Molecular Compounds

Unlike ionic compounds, molecular compounds are composed of individual covalently bonded units, or molecules. Chemists use two nomenclature systems to name binary molecules. The newer system is the Stock system for naming molecular compounds, which requires an understanding of oxidation numbers. This system will be discussed in Section 2.

The old system of naming molecular compounds is based on the use of prefixes. For example, the molecular compound CCl_4 is named carbon *tetra*chloride. The prefix *tetra-* indicates that four chloride atoms are present in a single molecule of the compound. The two oxides of carbon, CO and CO_2, are named carbon *mon*oxide and carbon *di*oxide, respectively. These prefix-based names are often the most widely recognized names for some molecular compounds. However, either naming system is acceptable, unless specified otherwise.

FIGURE 1.4

NUMERICAL PREFIXES

Number	Prefix
1	mono-
2	di-
3	tri-
4	tetra-
5	penta-
6	hexa-
7	hepta-
8	octa-
9	nona-
10	deca-

In these names, the prefix *mon-* (from *mono-*) indicates one oxygen atom, and the prefix *di-* indicates two oxygen atoms. The prefixes used to specify the number of atoms in a molecule are listed in **Figure 1.4.**

The rules for the prefix system of nomenclature of binary molecular compounds are as follows.

1. The element that has the smaller group number is usually given first. If both elements are in the same group, the element whose period number is greater is given first. The element is given a prefix only if it contributes more than one atom to a molecule of the compound.

2. The second element is named by combining (a) a prefix indicating the number of atoms contributed by the element, (b) the root of the name of the element, and (c) the ending *-ide*. With few exceptions, the ending *-ide* indicates that a compound contains only two elements.

3. The *o* or *a* at the end of a prefix is usually dropped when the word following the prefix begins with another vowel. For example, one would write *monoxide* and *pentoxide* instead of *mono-oxide* and *penta-oxide*.

The prefix system is illustrated below.

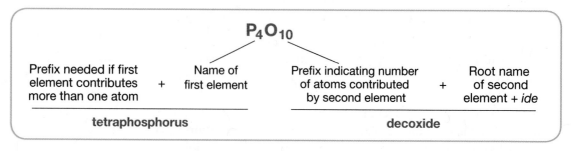

In general, the order of nonmetals in binary compound names and formulas is C, P, N, H, S, I, Br, Cl, O, and F.

FIGURE 1.5

BINARY COMPOUNDS OF NITROGEN AND OXYGEN

Formula	Prefix-system name
N_2O	dinitrogen monoxide
NO	nitrogen monoxide
NO_2	nitrogen dioxide
N_2O_3	dinitrogen trioxide
N_2O_4	dinitrogen tetroxide
N_2O_5	dinitrogen pentoxide

The prefix system is illustrated further in **Figure 1.5**, which lists the names of the six oxides of nitrogen. Note the application of rule 1, for example, in the name *nitrogen dioxide* for NO_2. No prefix is needed with *nitrogen* because only one atom of nitrogen is present in a molecule of NO_2. On the other hand, according to rule 2, the prefix *di-* in *dioxide* is needed to indicate the presence of two atoms of oxygen. Take a moment to review the prefixes in the other names in **Figure 1.5**.

✔ **CHECK FOR UNDERSTANDING**

Explain You have learned several ways to name compounds. Explain why it is necessary to have so many different methods of nomenclature.

GO ONLINE

Solve It! Cards
HMHScience.com

SOLUTION TUTOR
HMHScience.com

Naming Binary Molecular Compounds

Sample Problem D **a. Give the name for As_2O_5.**
b. Write the formula for oxygen difluoride.

● **SOLVE**

a. A molecule of the compound contains two arsenic atoms, so the first word in the name is *diarsenic*. The five oxygen atoms are indicated by adding the prefix *pent-* to the word *oxide*. The complete name is *diarsenic pentoxide*.

b. The first symbol in the formula is that for oxygen. Oxygen is first in the name because it is less electronegative than fluorine. Since there is no prefix, there must be only one oxygen atom. The prefix *di-* in *difluoride* shows that there are two fluorine atoms in the molecule. The formula is OF_2.

Practice   Answers in Appendix E

1. Name the following binary molecular compounds:
   a. SO_3
   b. ICl_3
   c. PBr_5
2. Write formulas for the following compounds:
   a. carbon tetraiodide
   b. phosphorus trichloride
   c. dinitrogen trioxide

▶ MAIN IDEA

Some covalent compounds are a network with no single molecules.

Some covalent compounds do not consist of individual molecules. Instead, each atom is joined to all its neighbors in a covalently bonded, three-dimensional network. There are no distinct units in these compounds, just as there are no such units in ionic compounds. The subscripts in a formula for a covalent-network compound indicate the smallest whole-number ratio of the atoms in the compound. Naming such compounds is similar to naming molecular compounds. Some common examples are given below.

SiC	SiO_2	Si_3N_4
silicon carbide	silicon dioxide	trisilicon tetranitride

▶ MAIN IDEA

Acids are solutions of water and a special type of compound.

An *acid* is a distinct type of molecular compound. Most acids used in the laboratory can be classified as either binary acids or oxyacids. *Binary acids* are acids that consist of two elements, usually hydrogen and one of the halogens— fluorine, chlorine, bromine, iodine. *Oxyacids* are acids that contain hydrogen, oxygen, and a third element (usually a nonmetal).

Acids were first recognized as a specific class of compounds based on their properties in solutions of water. Consequently, in chemical nomenclature, the term *acid* usually refers to a solution in water of one of these special compounds rather than to the compound itself. For example, *hydrochloric acid* refers to a water solution of the molecular compound hydrogen chloride, HCl. Some common binary and oxyacids are listed in **Figure 1.6. Figure 1.7** shows some common laboratory acids.

Many polyatomic ions are produced by the loss of hydrogen ions from oxyacids. A few examples of the relationship between oxyacids and oxyanions are shown below.

sulfuric acid	H_2SO_4	sulfate	SO_4^{2-}
nitric acid	HNO_3	nitrate	NO_3^-
phosphoric acid	H_3PO_4	phosphate	PO_4^{3-}

FIGURE 1.6

COMMON BINARY ACIDS AND OXYACIDS					
HF	hydrofluoric acid	HNO_2	nitrous acid	HClO	hypochlorous acid
HCl	hydrochloric acid	HNO_3	nitric acid	$HClO_2$	chlorous acid
HBr	hydrobromic acid	H_2SO_3	sulfurous acid	$HClO_3$	chloric acid
HI	hydriodic acid	H_2SO_4	sulfuric acid	$HClO_4$	perchloric acid
H_3PO_4	phosphoric acid	CH_3COOH	acetic acid	H_2CO_3	carbonic acid

FIGURE 1.7

Common Acids Some common laboratory acids are nitric acid, hydrochloric acid, and sulfuric acid. Acids should always be handled with care and according to instructions. They can burn holes in skin or clothing.

An ionic compound composed of a cation and the anion from an acid is often referred to as a **salt.** Table salt, NaCl, contains the anion from hydrochloric acid. Calcium sulfate, $CaSO_4$, is a salt containing an anion from sulfuric acid. Some salts contain anions in which one or more hydrogen atoms from the acid are retained. Such anions are named by adding the word *hydrogen* or the prefix *bi-* to the anion name. The best known such anion comes from carbonic acid, H_2CO_3.

$$HCO_3^-$$
hydrogen carbonate ion
bicarbonate ion

 SECTION 1 **FORMATIVE ASSESSMENT**

▶ **Reviewing Main Ideas**

1. What is the significance of a chemical formula?

2. Write formulas for the compounds formed between the following:
   a. aluminum and bromine
   b. sodium and oxygen
   c. magnesium and iodine
   d. Pb^{2+} and O^{2-}
   e. Sn^{2+} and I^-
   f. Fe^{3+} and S^{2-}
   g. Cu^{2+} and NO_3^-
   h. NH_4^+ and SO_4^{2-}

3. Name the following compounds by using the Stock system:
   a. NaI   **c.** CaO   **e.** CuBr
   b. MgS   **d.** K_2S **f.** $FeCl_2$

4. Write formulas for each of the following compounds:
   a. sodium hydroxide   **e.** carbon diselenide
   b. lead(II) nitrate   **f.** acetic acid
   c. iron(II) sulfate   **g.** chloric acid
   d. diphosphorus trioxide   **h.** sulfurous acid

✓ **Critical Thinking**

5. **RELATING IDEAS** Draw the Lewis structure, give the name, and predict VSEPR geometry of SCl_2.

▶ Specific rules are used to assign oxidation numbers.

▶ Many nonmetals have multiple oxidation numbers.

Oxidation Numbers

Key Terms

oxidation number
oxidation state

The charges on the ions composing an ionic compound reflect the electron distribution of the compound. **In order to indicate the general distribution of electrons among the bonded atoms in a molecular compound or a polyatomic ion, oxidation numbers, also called oxidation states, are assigned to the atoms composing the compound or ion.** Unlike ionic charges, oxidation numbers do not have an exact physical meaning. In fact, they are quite arbitrary in some cases. However, oxidation numbers are useful in naming compounds, in writing formulas, and in balancing chemical equations. And as is discussed in the chapter "Chemical Equations and Reactions", they are helpful in studying certain reactions.

▶ **MAIN IDEA**

Specific rules are used to assign oxidation numbers.

As a general rule in assigning oxidation numbers, shared electrons are assumed to belong to the more-electronegative atom in each bond. More-specific rules for determining oxidation numbers are provided by the following guidelines.

1. The atoms in a pure element have an oxidation number of zero. For example, the atoms in pure sodium, Na, oxygen, O_2, phosphorus, P_4, and sulfur, S_8, all have oxidation numbers of zero.

2. The more-electronegative element in a binary molecular compound is assigned the number equal to the negative charge it would have as an anion. The less-electronegative atom is assigned the number equal to the positive charge it would have as a cation.

3. Fluorine has an oxidation number of -1 in all of its compounds because it is the most-electronegative element.

4. Oxygen has an oxidation number of -2 in almost all compounds. Exceptions include when it forms peroxides, such as H_2O_2, in which its oxidation number is -1, and when it forms compounds with fluorine, such as OF_2, in which its oxidation number is $+2$.

5. Hydrogen has an oxidation number of $+1$ in all compounds containing elements that are more electronegative than it; it has an oxidation number of -1 in compounds with metals.

6. The algebraic sum of the oxidation numbers of all atoms in a neutral compound is equal to zero.

7. The algebraic sum of the oxidation numbers of all atoms in a polyatomic ion is equal to the charge of the ion.

8. A monatomic ion has an oxidation number equal to the charge of the ion. For example, the ions Na+, Ca²⁺, and Cl– have oxidation numbers of +1, +2, and −1, respectively.

Let's examine the assignment of oxidation numbers to the atoms in two molecular compounds, hydrogen fluoride, HF, and water, H_2O. Both compounds have polar-covalent bonds. In HF, the fluorine atom has an oxidation number of −1 (see Rule 3 on the previous page). Rule 5 tells us that hydrogen should have an oxidation number of +1. This makes sense because fluorine is more electronegative than hydrogen, and in a polar-covalent bond, shared electrons are assumed to belong to the more-electronegative element. For water, Rules 4 and 5 tell us that the oxidation number of oxygen is −2, and the oxidation number of each hydrogen atom is +1. Again, oxygen is more electronegative than hydrogen, so the shared electrons are assumed to belong to oxygen.

Because the sum of the oxidation numbers of the atoms in a compound must satisfy Rule 6 or 7 of the guidelines on the previous page, it is often possible to assign oxidation numbers to atoms that have more than one value when they are not known. This is illustrated in Sample Problem E.

Oxidation Numbers

Sample Problem E Assign oxidation numbers to each atom in the following compounds or ions:

a. CF_4

b. HNO_3

c. PO_4^{3-}

 SOLVE

a. Start by placing known oxidation numbers above the appropriate elements. From the guidelines, we know that fluorine always has an oxidation number of −1.

$$\overset{-1}{C}F_4$$

Multiply known oxidation numbers by the appropriate number of atoms, and place the totals underneath the corresponding elements. There are four fluorine atoms; $4 \times -1 = -4$.

$$\overset{-1}{C}F_4 \atop {}_{-4}$$

The compound CF_4 is molecular. According to the guidelines, the sum of the oxidation numbers must equal zero. The total of positive oxidation numbers is therefore +4.

$$\overset{-1}{C}F_4 \atop {}_{+4 \ -4}$$

Divide the total calculated oxidation number by the appropriate number of atoms. There is only one carbon atom in the molecule, so it must have an oxidation number of +4.

Continued ▶

$$\overset{+4\ -1}{CF_4}$$
$$\underset{+4\ -4}{}$$

b. Nitrogen and oxygen are each more electronegative than hydrogen, so hydrogen has an oxidation number of +1. Oxygen is not combined with a halogen, nor is HNO_3 a peroxide. Therefore, the oxidation number of oxygen is −2. Place these known oxidation numbers above the appropriate symbols. Place the total of the oxidation numbers underneath.

$$\overset{+1\ -2}{HNO_3}$$
$$\underset{+1\ -6}{}$$

The sum of the oxidation numbers must equal zero, and there is only one nitrogen atom in each molecule of HNO_3. Because $(+1)+(-6)=-5$, the oxidation number of each nitrogen atom must be +5.

c. To assign oxidation numbers to the elements in PO_4^{3-}, proceed as in parts (a) and (b). Remember, however, that the total of the oxidation numbers should equal the overall charge of the anion, 3−. The oxidation number of a single oxygen atom in the ion is −2. The total oxidation number due to the four oxygen atoms is −8. For the phosphate ion to have a 3− charge, phosphorous must be assigned an oxidation number of +5.

$$\overset{+5\ -2}{PO_4^{3-}}$$
$$\underset{+5\ -8}{}$$

Practice

1. Assign oxidation numbers to each atom in the following compounds or ions:

a. S_2O_3
b. $KClO_3$
c. Br_2
d. Na_2O_2
e. Cl_2O
f. $Ca(ClO_4)_2$
g. Na_2SO_4
h. P_2O_5
i. CO_3^{-2}
j. $(NH_4)_2S$

▶ MAIN IDEA

Many nonmetals have multiple oxidation numbers.

As shown in **Figure 2.1**, many nonmetals can have more than one oxidation number. (A more extensive list of oxidation numbers is given in Appendix Table B-15.) These numbers can sometimes be used in the same manner as ionic charges to determine formulas. Suppose, for example, you want to know the formula of a binary compound formed between sulfur and oxygen. From the common +4 and +6 oxidation states of sulfur, you could expect that sulfur might form SO_2 or SO_3. Both are known compounds. Of course, a formula must represent facts. Oxidation numbers alone cannot be used to prove the existence of a compound.

FIGURE 2.1

COMMON OXIDATION NUMBERS OF SOME NONMETALS THAT HAVE VARIABLE OXIDATION STATES*

Group 14	carbon	$-4, +2, +4$
Group 15	nitrogen phosphorus	$-3, +1, +2, +3, +4, +5$ $-3, +3, +5$
Group 16	sulfur	$-2, +4, +6$
Group 17	chlorine bromine iodine	$-1, +1, +3, +5, +7$ $-1, +1, +3, +5, +7$ $-1, +1, +3, +5, +7$

*In addition to the values shown, atoms of each element in its pure state are assigned an oxidation number of zero.

✔ CHECK FOR UNDERSTANDING

Explain Why do some elements have multiple oxidation states?

In Section 1, we introduced the use of Roman numerals to denote ionic charges in the Stock system of naming ionic compounds. The Stock system is actually based on oxidation numbers, and it can be used as an alternative to the prefix system for naming binary molecular compounds. In the prefix system, for example, SO_2 and SO_3 are named sulfur dioxide and sulfur trioxide, respectively. Their names according to the Stock system are sulfur(IV) oxide and sulfur(VI) oxide. The international body that governs nomenclature has endorsed the Stock system, which is more practical for complicated compounds. Prefix-based names and Stock-system names are still used interchangeably for many simple compounds, however. A few additional examples of names in both systems are given below.

	Prefix system	Stock system
PCl_3	phosphorus trichloride	phosphorus(III) chloride
PCl_5	phosphorus pentachloride	phosphorus(V) chloride
N_2O	dinitrogen monoxide	nitrogen(I) oxide
NO	nitrogen monoxide	nitrogen(II) oxide
PbO_2	lead dioxide	lead(IV) oxide
Mo_2O_3	dimolybdenum trioxide	molybdenum(III) oxide

✔ SECTION 2 FORMATIVE ASSESSMENT

▶ Reviewing Main Ideas

1. Assign oxidation numbers to each atom in the following compounds or ions:

   a. HF
   b. CI_4
   c. H_2O
   d. PI_3
   e. CS_2
   f. Na_2O_2
   g. H_2CO_3
   h. NO_2^-
   i. SO_4^{2-}

2. Name each of the following molecular compounds according to the Stock system:

   a. CI_4
   b. SO_3
   c. As_2S_3
   d. NCl_3

✔ Critical Thinking

3. **DRAWING CONCLUSIONS** Determine the oxidation numbers for iron oxide, Fe_3O_4. (Recall that oxidation numbers are not charges.)

Mass Spectrometry: Identifying Molecules

S.T.E.M.

Tests for locating oil deposits in the ground and detecting dioxins in our food supply are commonly performed today. These tests can be performed by using a technique known as *mass spectrometry*. Mass spectrometry is now used in many fields, such as medicine, chemistry, forensic science, and astronomy.

What is mass spectrometry? It is the most accurate technique available to measure the mass of an individual molecule or atom. Knowing the molecular mass is an essential part of identifying an unknown compound and determining the structure of a molecule of the compound. As the diagram of a mass spectrometer shows, the molecules in a gaseous sample are converted into ions. The ions then are separated and sorted according to their mass-to-charge ratio by a combination of electric and magnetic fields. The fields cause the ions' trajectories to change based on the ions' masses and charges. Then, the sorted ions are detected, and a mass spectrum is obtained. The mass spectrum is a graph of relative intensity (related to the number of ions detected) versus mass-to-charge ratio. Mass spectrometry uses a very small sample size (10^{-12} g) to obtain results.

The resulting spectrum is like a puzzle. It contains numerous peaks that correspond to fragments of the initial molecule. The largest peak (parent peak) corresponds to the molecular mass of the molecular ion. By analyzing the peaks, scientists can determine the identity and structure of a compound. Computers are used to help interpret the spectrum and identify the molecule by using online spectral database libraries.

Mass spectrometry has been an essential tool for scientists since its invention in the early 1900s. But its use was limited to small molecules from which ion creation was easy. Large biological molecules could not be studied, because they would break down or decompose during conventional ion-formation techniques. In the late 1980s, two groups developed ion-formation methods that are used today in commercial mass spectrometers. John Fenn (Virginia Commonwealth University) developed electrospray ionization mass spectrometry, and Koichi Tanaka (Shimadzu Corporation, Japan) developed matrix-assisted laser desorption ionization (MALDI) mass spectrometry. In 2002, both scientists received the Nobel Prize in Chemistry for their work. Their methods opened the field to the study of large molecules, allowing scientists to use mass spectrometry to study the structure of macromolecules, such as nucleic acids and steroids, and to identify the sequence of proteins.

Questions

1. Why is it necessary to convert the sample into ions in the mass spectrometer?

2. How have recent developments in mass spectrometry contributed to the field of medicine?

Scientists use mass spectrometers to identify and study the structure of molecules.

Ion separation and sorting

Ion detection

Ion creation

Heated filament

(−)

Magnets

Detector

(−) Negative grid

(+)

Gaseous sample

To vacuum pump

Mass spectrum

Using Chemical Formulas

Key Terms
formula mass
percentage composition

SECTION 3
Main Ideas

▶ Formula mass is the sum of the average atomic masses of a compound's elements.

▶ The molar mass of a compound is numerically equal to its formula mass.

▶ Molar mass is used to convert from moles to grams.

▶ Percentage composition is the number of grams in one mole of a compound.

As you have seen, a chemical formula indicates the elements as well as the relative number of atoms or ions of each element present in a compound. Chemical formulas also allow chemists to calculate a number of characteristic values for a given compound. In this section, you will learn how to use chemical formulas to calculate the *formula mass*, the *molar mass*, and the *percentage composition* by mass of a compound.

▶ MAIN IDEA

Formula mass is the sum of the average atomic masses of a compound's elements.

In an earlier chapter, we saw that hydrogen atoms have an average atomic mass of 1.007 94 u and that oxygen atoms have an average atomic mass of 15.9994 u. Like individual atoms, molecules, formula units, or ions have characteristic average masses. For example, we know from the chemical formula H_2O that a single water molecule is composed of exactly two hydrogen atoms and one oxygen atom. The mass of a water molecule is found by adding the masses of the three atoms in the molecule. (In the calculation, the average atomic masses have been rounded to two decimal places.)

$$\text{average atomic mass of H: 1.01 u}$$
$$\text{average atomic mass of O: 16.00 u}$$

$$2 \text{ H atoms} \times \frac{1.01 \text{ u}}{\text{H atom}} = 2.02 \text{ u}$$

$$1 \text{ O atom} \times \frac{16.00 \text{ u}}{\text{O atom}} = 16.00 \text{ u}$$

$$\text{average mass of } H_2O \text{ molecule} = 18.02 \text{ u}$$

The mass of a water molecule can be correctly referred to as a *molecular mass*. The mass of one NaCl formula unit, on the other hand, is not a molecular mass, because NaCl is an ionic compound. The mass of *any* unit represented by a chemical formula, whether the unit is a molecule, a formula unit, or an ion, is known as the formula mass. The **formula mass of any molecule, formula unit, or ion is the sum of the average atomic masses of all atoms represented in its formula.**

The procedure illustrated for calculating the formula mass of a water molecule can be used to calculate the mass of any unit represented by a chemical formula. In each of the problems that follow, the atomic masses from the periodic table in the back of the book have been rounded to two decimal places.

GO ONLINE

Learn It! Video
HMHScience.com

Formula Mass

Sample Problem F Find the formula mass of potassium chlorate, $KClO_3$.

 SOLVE

The mass of a formula unit of $KClO_3$ is found by summing the masses of one K atom, one Cl atom, and three O atoms. The required atomic masses can be found in the periodic table in the back of the book. In the calculation, each atomic mass has been rounded to two decimal places.

$$1 \text{ K atom} \times \frac{39.10 \text{ u}}{\text{K atom}} = 39.10 \text{ u}$$

$$1 \text{ Cl atom} \times \frac{35.45 \text{ u}}{\text{Cl atom}} = 35.45 \text{ u}$$

$$3 \text{ O atoms} \times \frac{16.00 \text{ u}}{\text{O atom}} = 48.00 \text{ u}$$

$$\text{formula mass of } KClO_3 = 122.55 \text{ u}$$

Practice   Answers in Appendix E

1. Find the formula mass of each of the following:
   a. H_2SO_4
   b. $Ca(NO_3)_2$
   c. PO_4^{3-}
   d. $MgCl_2$

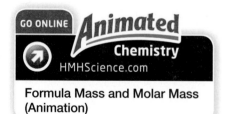

GO ONLINE

Animated Chemistry
HMHScience.com

Formula Mass and Molar Mass (Animation)

▶ **MAIN IDEA**

The molar mass of a compound is numerically equal to its formula mass.

In an earlier chapter, you learned that the molar mass of a substance is equal to the mass in grams of one mole, or approximately 6.022×10^{23} particles, of the substance. For example, the molar mass of pure calcium, Ca, is 40.08 g/mol because one mole of calcium atoms has a mass of 40.08 g.

The molar mass of a compound is calculated by adding the masses of the elements present in a mole of the molecules or formula units that make up the compound. For example, one mole of water molecules contains exactly two moles of H atoms and one mole of O atoms.

Rounded to two decimal places, a mole of hydrogen atoms has a mass of 1.01 g, and a mole of oxygen atoms has a mass of 16.00 g. The molar mass of water is calculated as follows.

$$2 \text{ mol H} \times \frac{1.01 \text{ g H}}{\text{mol H}} = 2.02 \text{ g H}$$

$$1 \text{ mol O} \times \frac{16.00 \text{ g O}}{\text{mol O}} = 16.00 \text{ g O}$$

$$\text{molar mass of H}_2\text{O} = 18.02 \text{ g/mol}$$

Figure 3.1 shows a mole of water as well as a mole of several other substances.

You may have noticed that *a compound's molar mass is numerically equal to its formula mass*. For instance, in Sample Problem F, the formula mass of $KClO_3$ was found to be 122.55 u. Therefore, because molar mass is numerically equal to formula mass, we know that the molar mass of $KClO_3$ is 122.55 g/mol.

FIGURE 3.1

Molar Mass Every compound has a characteristic molar mass. Shown here are one mole each of nitrogen (in balloon), water (in graduated cylinder), cadmium sulfide, CdS (yellow substance), and sodium chloride, NaCl (white substance).

GO ONLINE

SolveIt! Cards
HMHScience.com

Molar Mass

Sample Problem G What is the molar mass of barium nitrate, $Ba(NO_3)_2$?

● **SOLVE**

One mole of barium nitrate contains exactly one mole of Ba^{2+} ions and two moles of NO_3^- ions. The two moles of NO_3^- ions contain two moles of N atoms and six moles of O atoms. Therefore, the molar mass of $Ba(NO_3)_2$ is calculated as follows.

$$1 \text{ mol Ba} \times \frac{137.33 \text{ g Ba}}{\text{mol Ba}} = 137.33 \text{ g Ba}$$

$$2 \text{ mol N} \times \frac{14.01 \text{ g N}}{\text{mol N}} = 28.02 \text{ g N}$$

$$6 \text{ mol O} \times \frac{16.00 \text{ g O}}{\text{mol O}} = 96.00 \text{ g O}$$

$$\text{molar mass of Ba(NO}_3)_2 = 261.35 \text{ g/mol}$$

Practice   Answers in Appendix E

1. How many moles of atoms of each element are there in one mole of the following compounds?
   a. Al_2S_3
   b. $NaNO_3$
   c. $Ba(OH)_2$
2. Find the molar mass of each of the compounds listed in item 1.

FIGURE 3.2

Mass, Moles, and Molecules

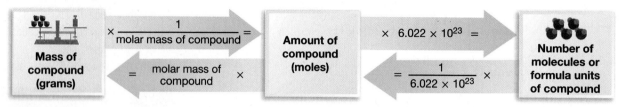

(a) This diagram shows the relationships between mass in grams, amount in moles, and number of molecules or atoms for a given compound.

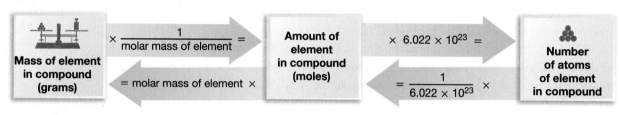

(b) Similar relationships exist for an element within a compound.

▶ **MAIN IDEA**

Molar mass is used to convert from moles to grams.

The molar mass of a compound can be used as a conversion factor to relate an amount in moles to a mass in grams for a given substance. Recall that molar mass usually has the units of grams per mole. To convert a known amount of a compound in moles to a mass in grams, multiply the amount in moles by the molar mass.

$$\text{amount in moles} \times \text{molar mass (g/mol)} = \text{mass in grams}$$

Conversions of this type for elements and compounds are summarized above in **Figure 3.2**. Becoming familiar with this process now will help you a great deal, as mass-to-mole and mole-to-mass conversions will be widely used in future chapters.

Molar Mass as a Conversion Factor

Sample Problem H What is the mass in grams of 3.20 mol of bromine gas?

❶ ANALYZE	**Given:** 3.20 mol Br_2
	Unknown: mass of Br_2 in grams

❷ PLAN   moles $Br_2 \longrightarrow$ grams Br_2
To convert amount of Br_2 in moles to mass of Br_2 in grams, multiply by the molar mass of Br_2.
$$\text{amount of } Br_2 \text{ (mol)} \times \text{molar mass of } Br_2 \text{ (g/mol)} = \text{mass of } Br_2 \text{ (g)}$$

Continued ▶

Molar Mass as a Conversion Factor (continued)

③ SOLVE

First, the molar mass of Br_2 must be calculated.

$$2 \text{ mol Br} \times \frac{35.00 \text{ g Br}}{\text{mol Br}} = 70.00 \text{ g (mass of one mole of } Br_2)$$

The molar mass of Br_2 is therefore 70.00 g/mol. Now do the calculation shown in step 2.

$$3.20 \text{ mol } Br_2 \times \frac{70.00 \text{ g } Br_2}{\text{mol } Br_2} = 224.00 \text{ g } Br_2$$

④ CHECK YOUR WORK

The answer is correctly given to three significant figures and is close to an estimated value of 221 g (3 mol × 70 g/mol).

To convert a known mass of a compound in grams to an amount in moles, the mass must be divided by the molar mass. Or you can invert the molar mass and multiply so that units are easily canceled.

$$\text{mass in grams} \times \frac{1}{\text{molar mass (g/mol)}} = \text{amount in moles}$$

GO ONLINE

Learn It! Video
HMHScience.com

Solve It! Cards
HMHScience.com

Molar Mass as a Conversion Factor

Sample Problem I Ibuprofen, $C_{13}H_{18}O_2$, is the active ingredient in many nonprescription pain relievers.

Its molar mass is 206.31 g/mol.

a. If the tablets in a bottle contain a total of 33 g of ibuprofen, how many moles of ibuprofen are in the bottle?

b. How many molecules of ibuprofen are in the bottle?

c. What is the total mass in grams of carbon in 33 g of ibuprofen?

① ANALYZE

Given: 33 g of $C_{13}H_{18}O_2$, molar mass 206.31 g/mol

Unknown:
a. moles $C_{13}H_{18}O_2$

b. molecules $C_{13}H_{18}O_2$

c. total mass of C

② PLAN

a. grams ⟶ moles
To convert mass of ibuprofen in grams to amount of ibuprofen in moles, multiply by the inverted molar mass of $C_{13}H_{18}O_2$.

$$\text{g } C_{13}H_{18}O_2 \times \frac{1 \text{ mol } C_{13}H_{18}O_2}{206.31 \text{ g } C_{13}H_{18}O_2} = \text{mol } C_{13}H_{18}O_2$$

b. moles ⟶ molecules
To find the number of molecules of ibuprofen, multiply amount of $C_{13}H_{18}O_2$ in moles by Avogadro's number.

$$\text{mol } C_{13}H_{18}O_2 \times \frac{6.022 \times 10^{23} \text{ molecules}}{\text{mol}} = \text{molecules } C_{13}H_{18}O_2$$

Continued

Molar Mass as a Conversion Factor (continued)

c. moles $C_{13}H_{18}O_2 \longrightarrow$ moles C $\longrightarrow$ grams C

To find the mass of carbon present in the ibuprofen, the two conversion factors needed are the amount of carbon in moles per mole of $C_{13}H_{18}O_2$ and the molar mass of carbon.

$$\text{mol } C_{13}H_{18}O_2 \times \frac{13 \text{ mol C}}{\text{mol } C_{13}H_{18}O_2} \times \frac{12.01 \text{ g C}}{\text{mol C}} = \text{g C}$$

③ SOLVE

a. $33 \text{ g } C_{13}H_{18}O_2 \times \dfrac{1 \text{ mol } C_{13}H_{18}O_2}{206.31 \text{ g } C_{13}H_{18}O_2} = 0.16 \text{ mol } C_{13}H_{18}O_2$

b. $0.16 \text{ mol } C_{13}H_{18}O_2 \times \dfrac{6.022 \times 10^{23} \text{ molecules}}{\text{mol}} = 9.6 \times 10^{22} \text{ molecules } C_{13}H_{18}O_2$

c. $0.16 \text{ mol } C_{13}H_{18}O_2 \times \dfrac{13 \text{ mol C}}{\text{mol } C_{13}H_{18}O_2} \times \dfrac{12.01 \text{ g C}}{\text{mol C}} = 25 \text{ g C}$

The bottle contains 0.16 mol of ibuprofen, which is 9.6×10^{22} molecules of ibuprofen.

The sample of ibuprofen contains 25 g of carbon.

④ CHECK YOUR WORK

Checking each step shows that the arithmetic is correct, significant figures have been used correctly, and units have canceled as desired.

Practice   Answers in Appendix E

1. How many moles of compound are there in the following?
    a. $6.60 \text{ g } (NH_4)_2SO_4$
    b. $4.5 \text{ kg } Ca(OH)_2$
2. How many molecules are there in the following.
    a. $25.0 \text{ g } H_2SO_4$
    b. 125 g of sugar, $C_{12}H_{22}O_{11}$
3. What is the mass in grams of 6.25 mol of copper(II) nitrate?

▶ MAIN IDEA

Percentage composition is the number of grams in one mole of a compound.

It is often useful to know the percentage by mass of a particular element in a chemical compound. For example, suppose the compound potassium chlorate, $KClO_3$, were to be used as a source of oxygen. It would be helpful to know the percentage of oxygen in the compound. To find the mass percentage of an element in a compound, one can divide the mass of the element in a sample of the compound by the total mass of the sample and then multiply this value by 100.

$$\frac{\text{mass of element in sample of compound}}{\text{mass of sample of compound}} \times 100 = \frac{\text{\% element in}}{\text{compound}}$$

The mass percentage of an element in a compound is the same regardless of the sample's size. Therefore, a simpler way to calculate the percentage of an element in a compound is to determine how many grams of the element are present in one mole of the compound. Then divide this value by the molar mass of the compound and multiply by 100.

$$\frac{\text{mass of element in 1 mol of compound}}{\text{molar mass of compound}} \times 100 = \begin{array}{c}\% \text{ element in} \\ \text{compound}\end{array}$$

The percentage by mass of each element in a compound is known as the **percentage composition** of the compound.

Percentage Composition

Sample Problem J Find the percentage composition of barium fluoride, BaF_2.

❶ ANALYZE	**Given:**	formula, BaF_2
	Unknown:	percentage composition of BaF_2

❷ PLAN

formula $\longrightarrow$ molar mass $\longrightarrow$ mass percentage of each element
The molar mass of the compound must be found. Then the mass of each element present in one mole of the compound is used to calculate the mass percentage of each element.

❸ SOLVE

$$1 \text{ mol Ba} \times \frac{137.3 \text{ g Ba}}{\text{mol Ba}} = 137.3 \text{ g Ba}$$

$$2 \text{ mol F} \times \frac{18.99 \text{ g F}}{\text{mol F}} = 32.98 \text{ g F}$$

molar mass of $BaF_2 = 175.3$

$$\frac{137.3 \text{ g Ba}}{175.3 \text{ g BaF}_2} \times 100 = 78.32\% \text{ Ba}$$

$$\frac{37.98 \text{ g F}}{175.3 \text{ g BaF}_2} \times 100 = 21.66\% \text{ F}$$

❹ CHECK YOUR WORK

A good check is to see if the results add up to about 100%. (Because of rounding, the total may not always be exactly 100%.)

Percentage Composition

Sample Problem K As some salts crystallize from a water solution, they bind water molecules in their crystal structure. Sodium carbonate forms such a *hydrate*, in which 10 water molecules are present for every formula unit of sodium carbonate. Find the mass percentage of water in sodium carbonate decahydrate, $Na_2CO_3 \bullet 10H_2O$, which has a molar mass of 286.19 g/mol.

Continued

Percentage Composition (continued)

① ANALYZE

Given: chemical formula, $Na_2CO_3 \cdot 10H_2O$
molar mass of $Na_2CO_3 \cdot 10H_2O$

Unknown: mass percentage of H_2O

② PLAN

chemical formula $\longrightarrow$ mass H_2O per mole of $Na_2CO_3 \cdot 10H_2O$ $\longrightarrow$ % water
The mass of water per mole of sodium carbonate decahydrate must first be found.
This value is then divided by the mass of one mole of $Na_2CO_3 \cdot 10H_2O$.

③ SOLVE

One mole of $Na_2CO_3 \cdot 10H_2O$ contains 10 mol H_2O. As noted earlier, the molar mass of H_2O is 18.02 g/mol. The mass of 10 mol H_2O is calculated as follows.

$$10 \text{ mol } H_2O \times \frac{18.02 \text{ g } H_2O}{\text{mol } H_2O} = 180.2 \text{ g } H_2O$$

mass of H_2O per mole of $Na_2CO_3 \cdot 10H_2O$ = 180.2 g

The molar mass of $Na_2CO_3 \cdot 10H_2O$ is 286.19 g/mol, so we know that 1 mol of the hydrate has a mass of 286.19 g. The mass percentage of 10 mol H_2O in 1 mol $Na_2CO_3 \cdot 10H_2O$ can now be calculated.

$$\text{mass percentage of } H_2O \text{ in } Na_2CO_3 \cdot 10H_2O = \frac{180.2 \text{ g } H_2O}{286.19 \text{ g } Na_2CO_3 \cdot 10H_2O} \times 100$$

$$= 62.97\% \ H_2O$$

④ CHECK YOUR WORK

Checking shows that the arithmetic is correct and that units cancel as desired.

Practice
Answers in Appendix E

1. Find the percentage compositions of the following:
   a. C_3H_8 **b.** $NaHSO_4$
2. Find the mass percentage of water in $ZnSO_4 \cdot 7H_2O$.
3. Magnesium hydroxide is 54.87% oxygen by mass. How many grams of oxygen are in 175 g of the compound? How many moles of oxygen is this?

SECTION 3 FORMATIVE ASSESSMENT

▶ Reviewing Main Ideas

1. Determine both the formula mass and molar mass of ammonium carbonate, $(NH_4)_2CO_3$.

2. How many moles of atoms of each element are there in one mole of $(NH_4)_2CO_3$?

3. What is the mass in grams of 3.25 mol $Fe_2(SO_4)_3$?

4. How many molecules of aspirin, $C_9H_8O_4$, are there in a 100.0 mg tablet of aspirin?

5. Calculate the percentage composition of $(NH_4)_2CO_3$.

✔ Critical Thinking

6. **RELATING IDEAS** A sample of hydrated copper (II) sulfate ($CuSO_4 \cdot nH_2O$) is heated to 150°C and produces 103.74 g anhydrous copper (II) sulfate and 58.55 g water. How many moles of water molecules are present in 1.0 mol of hydrated copper (II) sulfate?

Determining Chemical Formulas

SECTION 4

Main Ideas

▶ Empirical formulas show the whole-number ratio of elements in a compound.

▶ Molecular formulas give the types and numbers of atoms in a compound.

Key Terms

empirical formula

When a new substance is synthesized or is discovered, it is analyzed quantitatively to reveal its percentage composition. From these data, the empirical formula is then determined. **An empirical formula consists of the symbols for the elements combined in a compound, with subscripts showing the smallest whole-number mole ratio of the different atoms in the compound.** For an ionic compound, the formula unit is usually the compound's empirical formula. For a molecular compound, however, the empirical formula does not necessarily indicate the actual numbers of atoms present in each molecule. For example, the empirical formula of the gas diborane is BH_3, but the molecular formula is B_2H_6. In this case, the number of atoms given by the molecular formula corresponds to the empirical ratio multiplied by two.

▶ **MAIN IDEA**

Empirical formulas show the whole-number ratio of elements in a compound.

To determine a compound's empirical formula from its percentage composition, begin by converting percentage composition to a mass composition. Assume that you have a 100.0 g sample of the compound. Then calculate the amount of each element in the sample. For example, the percentage composition of diborane is 78.1% B and 21.9% H. Therefore, 100.0 g of diborane contains 78.1 g of B and 21.9 g of H.

Next, convert the mass composition of each element to a composition in moles by dividing by the appropriate molar mass.

$$78.1 \text{ g B} \times \frac{1 \text{ mol B}}{10.81 \text{ g B}} = 7.22 \text{ mol B}$$

$$21.9 \text{ g H} \times \frac{1 \text{ mol H}}{1.01 \text{ g H}} = 21.7 \text{ mol H}$$

These values give a mole ratio of 7.22 mol B to 21.7 mol H. However, this is not a ratio of least whole numbers. To find such a ratio, divide each number of moles by the least number in the existing ratio.

$$\frac{7.22 \text{ mol B}}{7.22} : \frac{21.7 \text{ mol H}}{7.22} = 1 \text{ mol B} : 3.01 \text{ mol H}$$

Because of rounding or experimental error, a compound's mole ratio sometimes consists of numbers close to whole numbers instead of exact whole numbers. In this case, the differences from whole numbers may be ignored and the nearest whole number taken. Thus, diborane contains atoms in the ratio 1 B : 3 H. The compound's empirical formula is BH_3.

Sometimes mass composition is known instead of percentage composition. To determine the empirical formula in this case, convert mass composition to composition in moles. Then calculate the least whole-number mole ratio of atoms. This process is shown in Sample Problem M.

Empirical Formulas

Sample Problem L Quantitative analysis shows that a compound contains 2.016% hydrogen, 32.60% sulfur, and 65.30% oxygen. Find the empirical formula of this compound.

❶ ANALYZE

Given: percentage composition: 2.016% H, 32.60% S, and 65.30% O

Unknown: empirical formula

❷ PLAN

percentage composition $\longrightarrow$ mass composition $\longrightarrow$ composition in moles $\longrightarrow$ least whole-number mole ratio of atoms

❸ SOLVE

Mass composition (mass of each element in 100.0 g sample):
2.016 g H, 32.60 g S, and 65.30 g O

Composition in moles: $2.016 \text{ g H} \times \dfrac{1 \text{ mol H}}{1.007 \text{ g H}} = 2.001 \text{ mol H}$

$32.60 \text{ g S} \times \dfrac{1 \text{ mol S}}{32.06 \text{ g S}} = 1.016 \text{ mol S}$

$65.30 \text{ g O} \times \dfrac{1 \text{ mol O}}{16.00 \text{ g O}} = 4.081 \text{ mol O}$

Least whole-number mole ratio of atoms:
The compound contains atoms in the ratio 2.001 mol H : 1.016 mol S : 4.081 mol O. To find the least whole-number mole ratio, divide each value by the least number in the ratio.

$$\dfrac{2.001 \text{ mol H}}{1.016} : \dfrac{1.016 \text{ mol S}}{1.016} : \dfrac{4.081 \text{ mol O}}{1.016} = 1.969 \text{ mol H} : 1 \text{ mol S} : 4.019 \text{ mol O}$$

Rounding each number in the ratio to the nearest whole number yields a mole ratio of 2 mol H : 1 mol S : 4 mol O. The empirical formula of the compound is H_2SO_4.

❹ CHECK YOUR WORK

Calculating the percentage composition of the compound based on the empirical formula determined in the problem reveals a percentage composition of 1.008% H, 32.69% S, and 65.24% O. These values agree reasonably well with the given percentage composition.

Empirical Formulas

GO ONLINE

Solve It! Cards
HMHScience.com

Sample Problem M Analysis of a 10.150 g sample of a compound known to contain only phosphorus and oxygen indicates a phosphorus content of 4.433 g. What is the empirical formula of this compound?

1 ANALYZE

Given: sample mass = 10.150 g

phosphorus mass = 4.433 g

Unknown: empirical formula

2 PLAN

Mass composition ⟶ composition in moles ⟶ smallest whole-number ratio of atoms

3 SOLVE

The mass of oxygen is found by subtracting the phosphorus mass from the sample mass.

sample mass − phosphorus mass = 10.150 g − 4.433 g = 5.717 g

Mass composition: 4.433 g P, 5.717 g O

Composition in moles:

$$4.433 \text{ g P} \times \frac{1 \text{ mol P}}{30.97 \text{ g P}} = 0.1431 \text{ mol P}$$

$$5.717 \text{ g O} \times \frac{1 \text{ mol O}}{16.00 \text{ g O}} = 0.3573 \text{ mol O}$$

Least whole-number mole ratio of atoms:

$$\frac{0.1431 \text{ mol P}}{0.1431} : \frac{0.3573 \text{ mol O}}{0.1431}$$

1 mol P : 2.497 mol O

The number of O atoms is not close to a whole number. But if we multiply each number in the ratio by 2, then the number of O atoms becomes 4.994 mol, which is close to 5 mol. The least whole-number mole ratio of P atoms to O atoms is 2 : 5. The compound's empirical formula is P_2O_5.

4 CHECK YOUR WORK

The arithmetic is correct, significant figures have been used correctly, and units cancel as desired. The formula is reasonable because +5 is a common oxidation state of phosphorus.

Practice   Answers in Appendix E

1. A compound is found to contain 6.1% hydrogen and 93.9% oxygen. Find its empirical formula.
2. Find the empirical formula of a compound found to contain 26.56% potassium, 35.41% chromium, and the remainder oxygen.
3. Analysis of 20.0 g of a compound containing only calcium and bromine indicates that 4.00 g of calcium are present. What is the empirical formula of the compound formed?

Molecular formulas give the types and numbers of atoms in a compound.

Remember that the *empirical formula* contains the least possible whole numbers that describe the atomic ratio. The *molecular formula* is the actual formula of a molecular compound. An empirical formula may or may not be a correct molecular formula. For example, diborane's empirical formula is BH_3. Any multiple of BH_3, such as B_2H_6, B_3H_9, B_4H_{12}, and so on, represents the same ratio of B atoms to H atoms. The molecular compounds ethene, C_2H_4, and cyclopropane, C_3H_6, also share an identical atomic ratio (2 H : 1 C), yet they are very different substances. How is the correct formula of a molecular compound found from an empirical formula?

The relationship between a compound's empirical formula and its molecular formula can be written as follows.

$$x\,(\text{empirical formula}) = \text{molecular formula}$$

The number represented by x is a whole-number multiple indicating the factor by which the subscripts in the empirical formula must be multiplied to obtain the molecular formula. (The value of x is sometimes 1.) The formula masses have a similar relationship.

$$x\,(\text{empirical formula mass}) = \text{molecular formula mass}$$

To determine the molecular formula of a compound, you must know the compound's formula mass. For example, experimentation shows the formula mass of diborane to be 27.67 u. The formula mass for the empirical formula, BH_3, is 13.84 u. Dividing the experimental formula mass by the empirical formula mass gives the value of x for diborane.

$$x = \frac{27.67 \text{ u}}{13.84 \text{ u}} = 2.000$$

The molecular formula of diborane is therefore B_2H_6.

$$2(BH_3) = B_2H_6$$

Recall that a compound's molecular formula mass is numerically equal to its molar mass, so a compound's molecular formula can also be found given the compound's empirical formula and its molar mass.

Molecular Formulas

Sample Problem N In Sample Problem M, the empirical formula of a compound of phosphorus and oxygen was found to be P_2O_5. Experimentation shows that the molar mass of this compound is 283.89 g/mol. What is the compound's molecular formula?

❶ ANALYZE

Given: empirical formula

Unknown: molecular formula

Continued ▶

Molecular Formulas (continued)

2 PLAN

x (empirical formula) = molecular formula

$$x = \frac{\text{molecular formula mass}}{\text{empirical formula mass}}$$

3 SOLVE

Molecular formula mass is numerically equal to molar mass. Thus, changing the g/mol unit of the compound's molar mass to u yields the compound's molecular formula mass.

molecular molar mass = 283.89 g/mol
molecular formula mass = 283.89 u

The empirical formula mass is found by adding the masses of each of the atoms indicated in the empirical formula.

mass of phosphorus atom = 30.97 u
mass of oxygen atom = 16.00 u
empirical formula mass of P_2O_5 = 2 × 30.97 u + 5 × 16.00 u = 141.94 u

Dividing the experimental formula mass by the empirical formula mass gives the value of x. The formula mass is numerically equal to the molar mass.

$$x = \frac{283.89 \text{ u}}{141.94 \text{ u}} = 2.0001$$

The compound's molecular formula is therefore P_4O_{10}.

$$2 \times (P_2O_5) = P_4O_{10}$$

4 CHECK YOUR WORK

Checking the arithmetic shows that it is correct.

Practice   Answers in Appendix E

1. Determine the molecular formula of the compound with an empirical formula of CH and a formula mass of 78.110 u.
2. A sample of a compound with a formula mass of 34.00 u is found to consist of 0.44 g H and 6.92 g O. Find its molecular formula.

SECTION 4 FORMATIVE ASSESSMENT

▶ Reviewing Main Ideas

1. A compound contains 36.48% Na, 25.41% S, and 38.11% O. Find its empirical formula.

2. Find the empirical formula of a compound containing 53.70% iron and 46.30% sulfur.

3. Analysis of a compound indicates that it contains 1.04 g K, 0.70 g Cr, and 0.86 g O. Find its empirical formula.

4. If 4.04 g of N combine with 11.46 g O to produce a compound with a formula mass of 108.0 u, what is the molecular formula of this compound?

✓ Critical Thinking

5. **RELATING IDEAS** A compound containing sodium, chlorine, and oxygen is 25.42% sodium by mass. A 3.25 g sample gives 4.33×10^{22} atoms of oxygen. What is the empirical formula?

Chemists can analyze an unknown substance by determining its percentage composition by mass. Percentage composition is determined by expressing the mass of each element in a sample of the substance as a percentage of the mass of the whole sample. The results of this analysis can then be compared with the percentage composition of known compounds to determine the probable identity of the unknown substance.

Sample Problem

Determine the percentage composition of potassium chlorate, $KClO_3$.

First, calculate the molar mass of $KClO_3$. The formula shows you that one mole of $KClO_3$ consists of 1 mol K atoms, 1 mol Cl atoms, and 3 mol O atoms. Thus, the molar mass of $KClO_3$ is molar mass K + molar mass Cl + 3(molar mass O) = 39.10 g K + 35.45 g Cl + 3(16.00 g O).

$$\text{molar mass } KClO_3 = 122.55 \text{ g}$$

The percentage composition of $KClO_3$ is determined by calculating the percentage of the total molar mass contributed by each element.

$$\frac{\text{mass of element in 1 mol of compound}}{\text{molar mass of compound}} \times 100 = \% \text{ element in compound}$$

$$\% \text{ K in } KClO_3 = \frac{39.10 \text{ g K}}{122.55 \text{ g } KClO_3} \times 100 = 31.91\%$$

$$\% \text{ Cl in } KClO_3 = \frac{35.45 \text{ g Cl}}{122.55 \text{ g } KClO_3} \times 100 = 28.93\%$$

$$\% \text{ O in } KClO_3 = \frac{48.00 \text{ g O}}{122.55 \text{ g } KClO_3} \times 100 = 39.17\%$$

Determine the percentage of nitrogen in ammonium sulfate, $(NH_4)_2SO_4$.

Even though you want to find the percentage of only one element, you must calculate the molar mass of $(NH_4)_2SO_4$. To do that, examine the formula to find the number of moles of each element in the compound. The two ammonium groups, indicated by $(NH_4)_2$, contain 2 mol N and 8 mol H per mole of $(NH_4)_2SO_4$. The sulfate group, SO_4, contains 1 mol S and 4 mol O per mole of $(NH_4)_2SO_4$.

$$
\begin{aligned}
2 \text{ mol N} &= 2 \times 14.01 \text{ g} = & 28.02 \text{ g} \\
8 \text{ mol H} &= 8 \times 1.01 \text{ g} = & 8.08 \text{ g} \\
1 \text{ mol S} &= 1 \times 32.06 = & 32.06 \text{ g} \\
4 \text{ mol O} &= 4 \times 16.00 = & 64.00 \text{ g} \\
\text{molar mass } (NH_4)_2SO_4 &= & 132.16 \text{ g}
\end{aligned}
$$

Now, you can determine the percentage of nitrogen in the compound as follows.

$$\% \text{ N in } (NH_4)_2SO_4 = \frac{28.02 \text{ g N}}{132.16 \text{ g } (NH_4)_2SO_4} \times 100 = 21.20\%$$

Practice

1. What is the percentage composition of sodium carbonate, Na_2CO_3?
2. What is the percentage of iodine in zinc iodate, $Zn(IO_3)_2$?

SECTION 1 Chemical Names and Formulas

KEY TERMS

- A positive monatomic ion is identified simply by the name of the appropriate element. A negative monatomic ion is named by dropping parts of the ending of the element's name and adding -ide to the root.

- The charge of each ion in an ionic compound may be used to determine the simplest chemical formula for the compound.

- Binary compounds are composed of two elements.

- Binary ionic compounds are named by combining the names of the positive and negative ions.

- The old system of naming binary molecular compounds uses prefixes. The new system, known as the *Stock system*, uses oxidation numbers.

monatomic ion
binary compound
nomenclature
oxyanion
salt

SECTION 2 Oxidation Numbers

KEY TERMS

- Oxidation numbers are useful in naming compounds, in writing formulas, and in balancing chemical equations.

- Compounds containing elements that have more than one oxidation state are named by using the Stock system.

- Stock-system names and prefix-system names are used interchangeably for many molecular compounds.

- Oxidation number rules allow assignment of oxidation numbers to each element.

- By knowing oxidation numbers, we can name compounds without knowing whether they are ionic or molecular.

oxidation number
oxidation state

SECTION 3 Using Chemical Formulas

KEY TERMS

- Formula mass, molar mass, and percentage composition can be calculated from the chemical formula for a compound.

- The percentage composition of a compound is the percentage by mass of each element in the compound.

- Molar mass is used as a conversion factor between amount in moles and mass in grams of a given compound or element.

formula mass
percentage composition

SECTION 4 Determining Chemical Formulas

KEY TERMS

- An empirical formula shows the least whole-number ratio of atoms in a given compound.

- Empirical formulas indicate how many atoms of each element are combined in the simplest unit of a chemical compound.

- A molecular formula can be found from the empirical formula if the molar mass is measured.

empirical formula

CHAPTER 7   Review

GO ONLINE
Interactive Review
HMHScience.com
Review Games
Concept Maps

SECTION 1

Chemical Names and Formulas

 REVIEWING MAIN IDEAS

1. a. What are monatomic ions?
   b. Give three examples of monatomic ions.

2. How does the chemical formula for the nitrite ion differ from the chemical formula for the nitrate ion?

3. Using the periodic table, write the symbol of the ion typically formed by each of the following elements:
   a. K   **d.** Cl
   b. Ca   **e.** Ba
   c. S   **f.** Br

4. Write the formula for and indicate the charge on each of the following ions:
   a. sodium ion
   b. aluminum ion
   c. chloride ion
   d. nitride ion
   e. iron(II) ion
   f. iron(III) ion

5. Name each of the following monatomic ions:
   a. K^+ **d.** Cl^-
   b. Mg^{2+} **e.** O^{2-}
   c. Al^{3+} **f.** Ca^{2+}

6. Write formulas for the binary ionic compounds formed between the following elements.
   (Hint: See Sample Problem A.)
   a. sodium and iodine
   b. calcium and sulfur
   c. zinc and chlorine
   d. barium and fluorine
   e. lithium and oxygen

7. Give the name of each of the following binary ionic compounds. (Hint: See Sample Problem B.)
   a. KCl   c. Li_2O
   b. $CaBr_2$ **d.** $MgCl_2$

8. Write the formulas for and give the names of the compounds formed by the following ions:
   a. Cr^{2+} and F^-
   b. Ni^{2+} and O^{2-}
   c. Fe^{3+} and O^{2-}

9. What determines the order in which the component elements of binary molecular compounds are written?

10. Name the following binary molecular compounds according to the prefix system. (Hint: See Sample Problem D.)
   a. CO_2 **d.** SeF_6
   b. CCl_4 **e.** As_2O_5
   c. PCl_5

11. Write formulas for each of the following binary molecular compounds. (Hint: See Sample Problem D.)
   a. carbon tetrabromide
   b. silicon dioxide
   c. tetraphosphorus decoxide
   d. diarsenic trisulfide

12. Distinguish between binary acids and oxyacids, and give two examples of each.

13. a. What is a salt?
   b. Give two examples of salts.

14. Name each of the following acids:
   a. HF   **d.** H_2SO_4
   b. HBr   **e.** H_3PO_4
   c. HNO_3

15. Give the molecular formula for each of the following acids:
   a. sulfurous acid
   b. chloric acid
   c. hydrochloric acid
   d. hypochlorous acid
   e. perchloric acid
   f. carbonic acid
   g. acetic acid

PRACTICE PROBLEMS

16. Write formulas for each of the following compounds:
   a. sodium fluoride
   b. calcium oxide
   c. potassium sulfide
   d. magnesium chloride
   e. aluminum bromide
   f. lithium nitride
   g. iron(II) oxide

17. Name each of the following ions:
    a. NH_4^+ **f.** CO_3^{2-}
    b. ClO_3^- **g.** PO_4^{3-}
    c. OH^- **h.** CH_3COO^-
    d. SO_4^{2-} **i.** HCO_3^-
    e. NO_3^- **j.** CrO_4^{2-}

18. Write the formula and charge for each of the following ions:
    a. ammonium ion   **g.** copper(II) ion
    b. acetate ion   **h.** tin(II) ion
    c. hydroxide ion   **i.** iron(III) ion
    d. carbonate ion   **j.** copper(I) ion
    e. sulfate ion   **k.** mercury(I) ion
    f. phosphate ion   **l.** mercury(II) ion

SECTION 2
Oxidation Numbers

 REVIEWING MAIN IDEAS

19. Name each of the following ions according to the Stock system:
    a. Fe^{2+} **d.** Pb^{4+}
    b. Fe^{3+} **e.** Sn^{2+}
    c. Pb^{2+} **f.** Sn^{4+}

20. Name each of the binary molecular compounds in item 11 by using the Stock system, when appropriate.

21. Write formulas for each of the following compounds:
    a. phosphorus(III) iodide
    b. sulfur(II) chloride
    c. carbon disulfide
    d. nitrogen(V) oxide

22. **a.** What are oxidation numbers?
    b. What useful functions do oxidation numbers serve?

PRACTICE PROBLEMS

23. Name each of the following ionic compounds by using the Stock system:
    a. $NaCl$
    b. KF
    c. CaS
    d. $Co(NO_3)_2$
    e. $FePO_4$
    f. Hg_2SO_4
    g. $Hg_3(PO_4)_2$

24. Assign oxidation numbers to each atom in the following compounds. (Hint: See Sample Problem E.)
    a. HI
    b. PBr_3
    c. GeS_2
    d. KH
    e. As_2O_5
    f. H_3PO_4

25. Assign oxidation numbers to each atom in the following ions. (Hint: See Sample Problem E.)
    a. NO_3^-
    b. ClO_4^-
    c. PO_4^{3-}
    d. $Cr_2O_7^{2-}$
    e. CO_3^{2-}

SECTION 3
Using Chemical Formulas

 REVIEWING MAIN IDEAS

26. **a.** Define *formula mass.*
    b. In what unit is formula mass expressed?

27. What is meant by the molar mass of a compound?

PRACTICE PROBLEMS

28. Determine the formula mass of each of the following compounds or ions. (Hint: See Sample Problem F.)
    a. glucose, $C_6H_{12}O_6$
    b. calcium acetate, $Ca(CH_3COO)_2$
    c. the ammonium ion, NH_4^+
    d. the chlorate ion, ClO_3^-

29. Determine the number of moles of each type of monatomic or polyatomic ion in one mole of the following compounds. For each polyatomic ion, determine the number of moles of each atom present in one mole of the ion.
    a. KNO_3
    b. Na_2SO_4
    c. $Ca(OH)_2$
    d. $(NH_4)_2SO_3$
    e. $Ca_3(PO_4)_2$
    f. $Al_2(CrO_4)_3$

30. Determine the molar mass of each compound listed in item 29. (Hint: See Sample Problem G.)

31. Determine the number of moles of compound in each of the following samples. (Hint: See Sample Problem I.)
   a. 4.50 g H_2O
   b. 471.6 g $Ba(OH)_2$
   c. 129.68 g $Fe_3(PO_4)_2$

32. Determine the percentage composition of each of the following compounds. (Hint: See Sample Problem J.)
   a. NaCl
   b. $AgNO_3$
   c. $Mg(OH)_2$

33. Determine the percentage by mass of water in the hydrate $CuSO_4 \bullet 5H_2O$. (Hint: See Sample Problem K.)

SECTION 4

Determining Chemical Formulas

 REVIEWING MAIN IDEAS

34. What three types of information can be used to find an empirical formula?

35. What is the relationship between the empirical formula and the molecular formula of a compound?

PRACTICE PROBLEMS

36. Determine the empirical formula of a compound containing 63.50% silver, 8.25% nitrogen, and 28.25% oxygen. (Hint: See Sample Problem L.)

37. Determine the empirical formula of a compound found to contain 52.11% carbon, 13.14% hydrogen, and 34.75% oxygen.

38. What is the molecular formula of the molecule that has an empirical formula of CH_2O and a molar mass of 120.12 g/mol?

39. A compound with a formula mass of 42.08 u is found to be 85.64% carbon and 14.36% hydrogen by mass. Find its molecular formula.

Mixed Review

 REVIEWING MAIN IDEAS

40. Chemical analysis shows that citric acid contains 37.51% C, 4.20% H, and 58.29% O. What is the empirical formula for citric acid?

41. Name each of the following compounds by using the Stock system:
   a. LiBr
   b. $Sn(NO_3)_2$
   c. $FeCl_2$
   d. MgO
   e. KOH
   f. Fe_2O_3
   g. $AgNO_3$
   h. $Fe(OH)_2$
   i. CrF_2

42. What is the mass in grams of each of the following samples?
   a. 1.000 mol NaCl
   b. 2.000 mol H_2O
   c. 3.500 mol $Ca(OH)_2$
   d. 0.625 mol $Ba(NO_3)_2$

43. Determine the formula mass and molar mass of each of the following compounds:
   a. XeF_4
   b. $C_{12}H_{24}O_6$
   c. Hg_2I_2
   d. CuCN

44. Write the chemical formulas for the following compounds:
   a. aluminum fluoride
   b. magnesium oxide
   c. vanadium(V) oxide
   d. cobalt(II) sulfide
   e. strontium bromide
   f. sulfur trioxide

45. How many atoms of each element are contained in a single formula unit of iron(III) formate, $Fe(CHO_2)_3 \bullet H_2O$? What percentage by mass of the compound is water?

46. Name each of the following acids, and assign oxidation numbers to the atoms in each:
   a. HNO_2
   b. H_2SO_3
   c. H_2CO_3
   d. HI

47. Determine the percentage composition of the following compounds:
   a. NaClO
   b. H_2SO_3
   c. C_2H_5COOH
   d. $BeCl_2$

48. Name each of the following binary compounds:
   a. MgI_2 e. SO_2
   b. NaF   f. PBr_3
   c. CS_2 g. $CaCl_2$
   d. N_2O_4 h. AgI

49. Assign oxidation numbers to each atom in the following molecules and ions:
   a. CO_2 e. H_2O_2
   b. NH_4^+ f. P_4O_{10}
   c. MnO_4^- g. OF_2
   d. $S_2O_3^{2-}$

50. A 175.0 g sample of a compound contains 56.15 g C, 9.43 g H, 74.81 g O, 13.11 g N, and 21.49 g Na. What is the compound's empirical formula?

CRITICAL THINKING

51. Analyzing Information Sulfur trioxide is produced in the atmosphere through a reaction of sulfur dioxide and oxygen. Sulfur dioxide is a primary air pollutant. Analyze the formula for sulfur trioxide. Then, use your analysis to list all of the chemical information that you can.

52. Analyzing Data In the laboratory, a sample of pure nickel was placed in a clean, dry, weighed crucible. The crucible was heated so that the nickel would react with the oxygen in the air. After the reaction appeared complete, the crucible was allowed to cool, and the mass was determined. The crucible was reheated and allowed to cool. Its mass was then determined again to be certain that the reaction was complete. The following data were collected:

Mass of crucible	= 30.02 g
Mass of nickel and crucible	= 31.07 g
Mass of nickel oxide and crucible	= 31.36 g

Determine the following information based on the data given above:

Mass of nickel	=
Mass of nickel oxide	=
Mass of oxygen	=

Based on your calculations, what is the empirical formula for the nickel oxide?

USING THE HANDBOOK

53. Review the common reactions of Group 1 metals in the *Elements Handbook* (Appendix A), and answer the following questions:
   a. Some of the Group 1 metals react with oxygen to form superoxides. Write the formulas for these compounds.
   b. What is the charge on each cation for the formulas that you wrote in (a)?
   c. How does the charge on the anion vary for oxides, peroxides, and superoxides?

54. Review the common reactions of Group 2 metals in the *Elements Handbook* (Appendix A), and answer the following questions:
   a. Some of the Group 2 metals react with oxygen to form oxides. Write the formulas for these compounds.
   b. Some of the Group 2 metals react with oxygen to form peroxides. Write the formulas for these compounds.
   c. Some of the Group 2 metals react with nitrogen to form nitrides. Write the formulas for these compounds.
   d. Most Group 2 elements form hydrides. What is hydrogen's oxidation state in these compounds?

55. Review the analytical tests for transition metals in the *Elements Handbook* (Appendix A), and answer the following questions:
   a. Determine the oxidation state of each metal in the precipitates shown for cadmium, zinc, and lead.
   b. Determine the oxidation state of each metal in the complex ions shown for iron, manganese, and cobalt.
   c. The copper compound shown is called a *coordination compound*. The ammonia shown in the formula exists as molecules that do not have a charge. Determine copper's oxidation state in this compound.

56. Review the common reactions of Group 15 elements in the *Elements Handbook* (Appendix A), and answer the following questions:

a. Write formulas for each of the oxides listed for the Group 15 elements.

b. Determine nitrogen's oxidation state in the oxides listed in (a).

RESEARCH AND WRITING

57. Nomenclature Biologists who name newly discovered organisms use a system that is structured very much like the one used by chemists in naming compounds. The system used by biologists is called the *Linnaean system of binomial nomenclature*, after its creator, Carolus Linnaeus. Research this system in a biology textbook, and then note similarities and differences between the Linnaeus system and chemical nomenclature.

58. Common Chemicals Find out the systematic chemical name and write the chemical formula for each of the following common compounds:

a. baking soda   **d.** limestone

b. milk of magnesia   **e.** lye

c. Epsom salts   **f.** wood alcohol

ALTERNATIVE ASSESSMENT

59. Performance Assessment Your teacher will supply you with a note card that has one of the following formulas on it: $NaCH_3COO \cdot 3H_2O$, $MgCl_2 \cdot 6H_2O$, $LiC_2H_3O_2 \cdot 2H_2O$, or $MgSO_4 \cdot 7H_2O$. Design an experiment to determine the percentage of water by mass in the hydrated salt assigned to you. Be sure to explain what steps you will take to ensure that the salt is completely dry. If your teacher approves your design, obtain the salt and perform the experiment. What percentage of water does the salt contain?

60. Both ammonia, NH_3, and ammonium nitrate, NH_4NO_3, are used in fertilizers as a source of nitrogen. Which compound has the higher percentage of nitrogen? Research the physical properties of both compounds, and find out how each compound is manufactured and used. Explain why each compound has its own particular application. (Consider factors such as the cost of raw ingredients, the ease of manufacture, and shipping costs.)

Standards-Based Assessment

Record your answers on a separate piece of paper.

MULTIPLE CHOICE

1 Which of the following compounds does not contain a polyatomic ion?

  A sodium carbonate

  B sodium sulfate

  C sodium sulfite

  D sodium sulfide

2 The correct formula for ammonium phosphate is

  A $(NH_4)_3PO_4$.

  B $(NH_4)_2PO_4$.

  C NH_4PO_4.

  D $NH_4(PO_4)_2$.

3 When writing the formula for a compound that contains a polyatomic ion,

  A write the anion's formula first.

  B use superscripts to show the number of polyatomic ions present.

  C use parentheses if the number of polyatomic ions is greater than 1.

  D always place the polyatomic ion in parentheses.

4 The correct name for CH_3COONH_4 is

  A ammonium carbonate.

  B ammonium hydroxide.

  C ammonium acetate.

  D ammonium nitrate.

5 Which of the following is the correct formula for iron (III) sulfate?

  A Fe_3SO_4

  B $Fe_3(SO_4)_2$

  C $Fe_2(SO_4)_3$

  D $3FeSO_4$

6 The molecular formula for acetylene is C_2H_2. The molecular formula for benzene is C_6H_6. The empirical formula for both is

  A CH.

  B C_2H_2.

  C C_6H_6.

  D $(CH)_2$.

7 What is the empirical formula for a compound represented by the chart below?

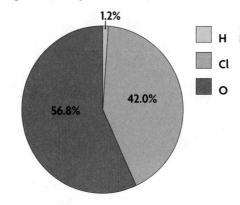

  A HClO

  B $HClO_2$

  C $HClO_3$

  D $HClO_4$

GRIDDED RESPONSE

8 What is the percentage composition of Na in NaCl?

Test Tip

Whenever possible, highlight or underline numbers or words critical to answering a question correctly.

CHAPTER 8
Chemical Equations and Reactions

BIG IDEA
Chemical equations use chemical formulas with coefficients to show how a reaction satisfies the law of conservation of mass.

 ONLINE Chemistry
HMHScience.com

SECTION 1
Describing Chemical Reactions

SECTION 2
Types of Chemical Reactions

SECTION 3
Activity Series of the Elements

ONLINE LABS
- Blueprint Paper
- Evidence for a Chemical Change
- Extraction of Copper from Its Ore
- Factors Affecting CO_2 Production in Yeast
- Getting a Reaction

GO ONLINE

 Why It Matters Video
HMHScience.com

Equations and Reactions

Describing Chemical Reactions

Key Terms

chemical equation
precipitate
coefficient

word equation
formula equation
reversible reaction

A *chemical reaction* is the process by which one or more substances are changed into one or more different substances. In any chemical reaction, the original substances are known as the *reactants*, and the resulting substances are known as the *products*. According to the law of conservation of mass, the total mass of reactants must equal the total mass of *products* for any given chemical reaction.

Chemical reactions are described by chemical equations. **A chemical equation represents, with symbols and formulas, the identities and relative molecular or molar amounts of the reactants and products in a chemical reaction.** For example, the following chemical equation shows that the reactant ammonium dichromate yields the products nitrogen, chromium(III) oxide, and water.

$$(NH_4)_2Cr_2O_7(s) \longrightarrow N_2(g) + Cr_2O_3(s) + 4H_2O(g)$$

This strongly exothermic reaction is shown in **Figure 1.1.**

▶ MAIN IDEA
Chemical reactions have physical indicators.

To know for certain that a chemical reaction has taken place requires evidence that one or more substances have undergone a change in identity. Absolute proof of such a change can be provided only by chemical analysis of the products. However, certain easily observed changes usually indicate that a chemical reaction has occurred.

1. *Evolution of energy as heat and light.* A change in matter that releases energy as both heat and light is strong evidence that a chemical reaction has taken place. For example, you can see in **Figure 1.1** that the decomposition of ammonium dichromate is accompanied by the evolution of energy as heat and light. And you can see evidence that a chemical reaction occurs between natural gas and oxygen if you burn gas for cooking in your house. Some reactions involve only heat or only light. But heat or light by itself is not necessarily a sign of chemical change, because many physical changes also involve either heat or light. However, heat and light are very strong indicators of a chemical change and should encourage you to investigate further.

2. *Color change.* A change in color is often an indication of a chemical reaction. Again, color change should not be the only physical indicator considered, because color changes can also be physical changes.

SECTION 1

Main Ideas

▶ Chemical reactions have physical indicators.

▶ Chemical equations must satisfy the law of conservation of mass.

▶ Chemical equations show relative amounts, masses, and progression of chemical reactions.

▶ Chemical equations can be balanced with step-by-step inspection.

FIGURE 1.1

Evolution of Energy as Heat and Light The decomposition of ammonium dichromate proceeds rapidly, releasing energy as light and heat.

FIGURE 1.2

Evidence of Reaction As shown in the photos, the production of a gas and the formation of a precipitate are two strong indicators that a chemical reaction has occurred.

(a) The reaction of vinegar and baking soda is evidenced by the production of bubbles of carbon dioxide gas.

(b) When water solutions of ammonium sulfide and cadmium nitrate are combined, the yellow precipitate cadmium sulfide forms.

3. *Production of a gas.* The evolution of gas bubbles when two substances are mixed is often evidence of a chemical reaction. For example, bubbles of carbon dioxide gas form immediately when baking soda is mixed with vinegar, as shown in **Figure 1.2a**.

4. *Formation of a precipitate.* Many chemical reactions take place between substances that are dissolved in liquids. If a solid appears after two solutions are mixed, a reaction has likely occurred. **A solid that is produced as a result of a chemical reaction in solution and that separates from the solution is known as a precipitate.** A precipitate-forming reaction is shown in **Figure 1.2b**.

▶ **MAIN IDEA**

Chemical equations must satisfy the law of conservation of mass.

A properly written chemical equation can summarize any chemical change. The following requirements will aid you in writing and reading chemical equations correctly.

1. *The equation must represent known facts.* All reactants and products must be identified, either through chemical analysis in the laboratory or from sources that give the results of experiments.

2. *The equation must contain the correct formulas for the reactants and products.* Remember what you've learned about symbols and formulas. Knowledge of the common oxidation states of the elements and of methods of writing formulas will enable you to write formulas for reactants and products if they are unavailable. Some elements are represented simply by their atomic symbols when they are in their elemental state. For example, iron is represented as Fe, and carbon is represented as C. The symbols are not given any subscripts because the elements do not form definite molecular structures. Two exceptions are sulfur, which is usually written S_8, and phosphorus, which is usually written P_4. In these cases, the formulas reflect each element's unique atomic arrangement in its natural state.

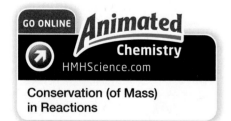

GO ONLINE **Animated Chemistry**
HMHScience.com

Conservation (of Mass) in Reactions

FIGURE 1.3

ELEMENTS THAT NORMALLY EXIST AS DIATOMIC MOLECULES

Element	Symbol	Molecular formula	Physical state at room temperature
Hydrogen	H	H_2	gas
Nitrogen	N	N_2	gas
Oxygen	O	O_2	gas
Fluorine	F	F_2	gas
Chlorine	Cl	Cl_2	gas
Bromine	Br	Br_2	liquid
Iodine	I	I_2	solid

Also remember some elements, listed in **Figure 1.3,** exist primarily as diatomic molecules, such as H_2 and O_2. Each of these elements is represented in an equation by its molecular formula.

3. *The law of conservation of mass must be satisfied.* Atoms are neither created nor destroyed in ordinary chemical reactions. Thus, the same number of atoms of each element must appear on each side of a correct chemical equation. To balance numbers of atoms, add coefficients where necessary. **A coefficient is a small whole number that appears in front of a formula in a chemical equation.** Placing a coefficient in front of a formula specifies the relative number of moles of the substance. If no coefficient is written, it's assumed to be 1.

Writing Word Equations

The first step in writing a chemical equation is to identify the facts to be represented. **It is often helpful to write a word equation, an equation in which the reactants and products in a chemical reaction are represented by words.** A word equation has only qualitative (descriptive) meaning. It does not give the whole story because it does not give the quantities of reactants used or products formed.

Consider the reaction of methane, the principal component of natural gas, with oxygen. When methane burns in air, it combines with oxygen to produce carbon dioxide and water vapor. In the reaction, methane and oxygen are the reactants. Carbon dioxide and water are the products. The word equation for the reaction is written as follows:

$$\text{methane} + \text{oxygen} \longrightarrow \text{carbon dioxide} + \text{water}$$

The arrow, $\longrightarrow$, is read as "react to yield" or "yield" (also "produce" or "form"). So the equation above is read, "methane and oxygen react to yield carbon dioxide and water," or simply, "methane and oxygen yield carbon dioxide and water."

Writing Formula Equations

The next step in writing a correct chemical equation is to replace the names of the reactants and products with appropriate symbols and formulas. Methane is a molecular compound composed of one carbon atom and four hydrogen atoms. Its chemical formula is CH_4. Recall that oxygen exists in nature as diatomic molecules; it is therefore represented as O_2. The correct formulas for carbon dioxide and water are CO_2 and H_2O, respectively.

A **formula equation** represents the reactants and products of a chemical reaction by their symbols or formulas. The formula equation for the reaction of methane and oxygen is written as follows:

$$CH_4(g) + O_2(g) \longrightarrow CO_2(g) + H_2O(g) \quad \text{(not balanced)}$$

The g in parentheses after each formula indicates that the corresponding substance is in the gaseous state. Like a word equation, a formula equation is a qualitative statement. It gives no information about the amounts of reactants or products.

Writing Balanced Equations

A formula equation meets two of the three requirements for a correct chemical equation. It represents the facts and shows the correct symbols and formulas for the reactants and products. To complete the process of writing a correct equation, the law of conservation of mass must be taken into account. The relative amounts of reactants and products represented in the equation must be adjusted so that the numbers and types of atoms are the same on both sides of the equation. This process is called *balancing an equation* and is carried out by inserting coefficients. Once it is balanced, a formula equation is a correctly written chemical equation.

Look again at the formula equation for the reaction of methane and oxygen.

$$CH_4(g) + O_2(g) \longrightarrow CO_2(g) + H_2O(g) \quad \text{(not balanced)}$$

To balance the equation, begin by counting atoms of elements that are combined with atoms of other elements and that appear only once on each side of the equation. In this case, we could begin by counting either carbon or hydrogen atoms. Usually, the elements hydrogen and oxygen are balanced only after balancing all other elements in an equation. (You will read more about the rules of balancing equations later in the chapter.) Thus, we begin by counting carbon atoms.

Inspecting the formula equation reveals that there is one carbon atom on each side of the arrow. Therefore, carbon is already balanced in the equation. Counting hydrogen atoms reveals that there are four hydrogen atoms in the reactants but only two in the products. Two additional hydrogen atoms are needed on the right side of the equation. They can be added by placing the coefficient 2 in front of the chemical formula H_2O.

$$CH_4(g) + O_2(g) \longrightarrow CO_2(g) + 2H_2O(g) \quad \text{(partially balanced)}$$

A coefficient multiplies the number of atoms of each element indicated in a chemical formula. Thus, $2H_2O$ represents *four* H atoms and *two* O atoms. To add two more hydrogen atoms to the right side of the equation, one may be tempted to change the subscript in the formula of water so that H_2O becomes H_4O. However, this would be a mistake because changing the subscripts of a chemical formula changes the *identity* of the compound. H_4O is not a product in the combustion of methane. In fact, there is no such compound. One must use only coefficients to change the relative number of atoms in a chemical equation because coefficients change the numbers of atoms without changing the identities of the reactants or products.

Now consider the number of oxygen atoms. There are four oxygen atoms on the right side of the arrow in the partially balanced equation. Yet there are only two oxygen atoms on the left side of the arrow. One can increase the number of oxygen atoms on the left side to four by placing the coefficient 2 in front of the molecular formula for oxygen. This results in a correct chemical equation, or *balanced formula equation*, for the burning of methane in oxygen.

$$CH_4(g) + 2O_2(g) \longrightarrow CO_2(g) + 2H_2O(g)$$

This reaction is further illustrated in **Figure 1.4.** As you study the molecular models, consider carefully the effects associated with changing the subscripts in formulas and those associated with changing coefficients. Also, be patient. Balancing equations is a skill that takes practice, and any chemist will admit to it being sometimes extremely complex.

✔ **CHECK FOR UNDERSTANDING**
Discuss Why are formula equations, using symbols and numbers, used more commonly in chemistry than word equations?

FIGURE 1.4

Chemical Equations

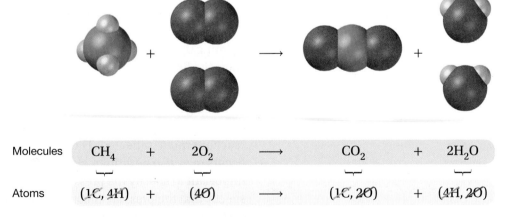

Molecules	CH_4	+	$2O_2$	$\longrightarrow$	CO_2	+	$2H_2O$
Atoms	(1C, 4H)	+	(4O)	$\longrightarrow$	(1C, 2O)	+	(4H, 2O)

(a) In a Bunsen burner, methane combines with oxygen in the air to form carbon dioxide and water vapor.

(b) The reaction is represented by both a molecular model and a balanced equation. Each shows that the number of atoms of each element in the reactants equals the number of atoms of each element in the products.

FIGURE 1.5

SYMBOLS USED IN CHEMICAL EQUATIONS

Symbol	Explanation
$\longrightarrow$	"Yields"; indicates result of reaction
$\underset{\longleftarrow}{\longrightarrow}$	Used in place of a single arrow to indicate a reversible reaction
(s)	A reactant or product in the solid state; also used to indicate a precipitate
$\downarrow$	Alternative to (s), but used only to indicate a precipitate
(l)	A reactant or product in the liquid state
(aq)	A reactant or product in an aqueous solution (dissolved in water)
(g)	A reactant or product in the gaseous state
$\uparrow$	Alternative to (g), but used only to indicate a gaseous product
$\xrightarrow{\Delta}$ or $\xrightarrow{heat}$	Reactants are heated
$\xrightarrow{2\ atm}$	Pressure at which reaction is carried out, in this case 2 atm
$\xrightarrow{Pressure}$	Pressure at which reaction is carried out exceeds normal atmospheric pressure
$\xrightarrow{0°C}$	Temperature at which reaction is carried out, in this case 0°C
$\xrightarrow{MnO_2}$	Formula of catalyst, in this case manganese dioxide, used to alter the rate of the reaction

Additional Symbols Used in Chemical Equations

Figure 1.5 above summarizes the symbols commonly used in chemical equations. As you can see, some things can be shown in different ways. For example, sometimes a gaseous product is indicated by an arrow pointing upward, $\uparrow$, instead of (g). A downward arrow, $\downarrow$, is often used to show the formation of a precipitate during a reaction in solution.

The conditions under which a reaction takes place are often indicated by placing information above or below the reaction arrow. The word *heat*, which is symbolized by a Greek capital delta (Δ), indicates that the reactants must be heated. The specific temperature at which a reaction occurs may also be written over the arrow. For some reactions, it is important to specify the pressure at which the reaction occurs or to specify that the pressure must be above normal. Many reactions are speeded up and can take place at lower temperatures in the presence of a *catalyst*. A catalyst is a substance that changes the rate of a chemical reaction but can be recovered unchanged. To show that a catalyst is present, the formula for the catalyst or the word *catalyst* is written over the reaction arrow.

In many reactions, as soon as the products begin to form, they immediately begin to react with each other and re-form the reactants. In other words, the reverse reaction also occurs. The reverse reaction may occur to a greater or lesser degree than the original reaction, depending on the specific reaction and the conditions. **A reversible reaction is a chemical reaction in which the products re-form the original reactants.** The reversibility of a reaction is indicated by writing two arrows pointing in opposite directions. For example, the reversible reaction between iron and water vapor is written as follows:

$$3Fe(s) + 4H_2O(g) \rightleftarrows Fe_3O_4(s) + 4H_2(g)$$

With an understanding of all the symbols and formulas used, it is possible to translate a chemical equation into a sentence. Consider the following equation:

$$2HgO(s) \xrightarrow{\Delta} 2Hg(l) + O_2(g)$$

Translated into a sentence, this equation reads, "When heated, solid mercury(II) oxide yields liquid mercury and gaseous oxygen."

It is also possible to write a chemical equation from a sentence describing a reaction. Consider the sentence, "Under pressure and in the presence of a platinum catalyst, gaseous ethene and hydrogen form gaseous ethane." This sentence can be translated into the following equation:

$$C_2H_4(g) + H_2(g) \xrightarrow{\text{pressure, Pt}} C_2H_6(g)$$

Throughout this chapter we will often include the symbols for physical states (*s*, *l*, *g*, and *aq*) in balanced formula equations. You should be able to interpret these symbols when they are used and to supply them when the necessary information is available.

GO ONLINE

Learn It! Video
HMHScience.com

Writing Word, Formula, and Balanced Chemical Equations

Sample Problem A Write word and formula equations for the chemical reaction that occurs when solid sodium oxide is added to water at room temperature and forms sodium hydroxide (dissolved in the water). Include symbols for physical states in the formula equation. Then balance the formula equation to give a balanced chemical equation.

 SOLVE

The word equation must show the reactants, sodium oxide and water, to the left of the arrow. The product, sodium hydroxide, must appear to the right of the arrow.

$$\text{sodium oxide} + \text{water} \longrightarrow \text{sodium hydroxide}$$

The word equation is converted to a formula equation by replacing the name of each compound with the appropriate chemical formula. To do this requires knowing that sodium forms a 1+ ion, that oxygen has a 2− charge, and that a hydroxide ion has a charge of 1−.

$$Na_2O + H_2O \longrightarrow NaOH \text{ (not balanced)}$$

Adding symbols for the physical states of the reactants and products and the coefficient 2 in front of NaOH produces a balanced chemical equation.

$$Na_2O(s) + H_2O(l) \longrightarrow 2NaOH(aq)$$

Sample Problem B Translate the following chemical equation into a sentence:

$$NaOH(aq) + Fe(NO_3)_3(aq) \longrightarrow FeOH_4(s) + NaNO_3(aq)$$

● **SOLVE**

Each reactant is an ionic compound and is named according to the rules for such compounds. Both reactants are in aqueous solution. One product is a precipitate, and the other remains in solution. The equation is translated as follows: Aqueous solutions of sodium hydroxide and iron nitrate react to produce a precipitate of iron hydroxide plus sodium nitrate in aqueous solution.

Practice   Answers in Appendix E

1. Write word and balanced chemical equations for the following reactions. Include symbols for physical states when indicated.
   a. Solid calcium reacts with solid sulfur to produce solid calcium sulfide.
   b. Hydrogen gas reacts with fluorine gas to produce hydrogen fluoride gas. (Hint: See **Figure 1.3**.)
   c. Solid aluminum metal reacts with aqueous zinc chloride to produce solid zinc metal and aqueous aluminum chloride.
2. Translate the following chemical equations into sentences:
   a. $3KOH(aq) + H_3PO_4(aq) \longrightarrow K_3PO_4(aq) + 3H_2O(l)$
   b. $FeS(s) + HCl(aq) \longrightarrow FeCl_2(s) + H_2S(g)$
3. Hydrazine, N_2H_4, is used as rocket fuel. Hydrazine reacts violently with oxygen to produce gaseous nitrogen and water. Write the balanced chemical equation.

▶ **MAIN IDEA**

Chemical equations show relative amounts, masses, and progression of chemical reactions.

Chemical equations are very useful in doing quantitative chemical work. The arrow in a balanced chemical equation is like an equal sign. And the chemical equation as a whole is similar to an algebraic equation in that it expresses an equality. Let's examine some of the quantitative information revealed by a chemical equation.

1. *The coefficients of a chemical reaction indicate relative, not absolute, amounts of reactants and products.* A chemical equation usually shows the least numbers of atoms, molecules, or ions that will satisfy the law of conservation of mass in a given chemical reaction.

Consider the equation for the formation of hydrogen chloride from hydrogen and chlorine.

$$H_2(g) + Cl_2(g) \longrightarrow 2HCl(g)$$

The equation indicates that 1 molecule of hydrogen reacts with 1 molecule of chlorine to produce 2 molecules of hydrogen chloride, resulting in the following molecular ratio of reactants and products.

1 molecule H_2 : 1 molecule Cl_2 : 2 molecules HCl

This ratio shows the least possible relative amounts of the reaction's reactants and products. To obtain greater relative amounts, we simply multiply each coefficient by the same number. For example, we could multiply each by a factor of 20. Thus, 20 molecules of hydrogen would react with 20 molecules of chlorine to yield 40 molecules of hydrogen chloride. The reaction can also be considered in terms of amounts in moles: 1 mol of hydrogen molecules reacts with 1 mol of chlorine molecules to yield 2 mol of hydrogen chloride molecules.

2. *The relative masses of the reactants and products of a chemical reaction can be determined from the reaction's coefficients.* Recall that an amount of an element or compound in moles can be converted to a mass in grams by multiplying by the appropriate molar mass. We know that 1 mol of hydrogen reacts with 1 mol of chlorine to yield 2 mol of hydrogen chloride. The relative masses of the reactants and products are calculated as follows.

$$1 \text{ mol } H_2 \times \frac{2.02 \text{ g } H_2}{\text{mol } H_2} = 2.02 \text{ g } H_2$$

$$1 \text{ mol } Cl_2 \times \frac{70.90 \text{ g } Cl_2}{\text{mol } Cl_2} = 70.90 \text{ g } Cl_2$$

$$2 \text{ mol } HCl \times \frac{36.46 \text{ g } HCl}{\text{mol } HCl} = 72.92 \text{ g } HCl$$

The chemical equation shows that 2.02 g of hydrogen will react with 70.90 g of chlorine to yield 72.92 g of hydrogen chloride.

3. *The reverse reaction for a chemical equation has the same relative amounts of substances as the forward reaction.* Because a chemical equation is like an algebraic equation, the equality can be read in either direction. Reading the hydrogen chloride formation equation, we can see that 2 molecules of hydrogen chloride break down to form 1 molecule of hydrogen plus 1 molecule of chlorine. Similarly, 2 mol (72.92 g) of hydrogen chloride yield 1 mol (2.02 g) of hydrogen and 1 mol (70.90 g) of chlorine. **Figure 1.6** summarizes the above ideas.

FIGURE 1.6

Interpreting Chemical Equations This representation of the reaction of hydrogen and chlorine to yield hydrogen chloride shows several ways to interpret the quantitative information of a chemical reaction.

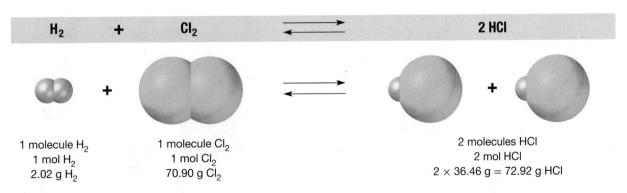

| H_2 | + | Cl_2 | ⇌ | 2 HCl |

1 molecule H_2
1 mol H_2
2.02 g H_2

1 molecule Cl_2
1 mol Cl_2
70.90 g Cl_2

2 molecules HCl
2 mol HCl
2×36.46 g $= 72.92$ g HCl

We have seen that a chemical equation provides useful quantitative information about a chemical reaction. However, there is also important information that is *not* provided by a chemical equation. For instance, an equation gives no indication of whether a reaction will actually occur. A chemical equation can be written for a reaction that may not even take place. Some guidelines about the types of simple reactions that can be expected to occur are given in later sections. And later chapters provide additional guidelines for other types of reactions. In all these guidelines, it is important to remember that experimentation forms the basis for confirming that a particular chemical reaction will occur.

In addition, chemical equations give no information about the speed at which reactions occur or about how the bonding between atoms or ions changes during the reaction. These aspects of chemical reactions are discussed in the chapter "Reaction Kinetics."

▶ MAIN IDEA

Chemical equations can be balanced with step-by-step inspection.

Most of the equations in the remainder of this chapter can be balanced by inspection. The following procedure demonstrates how to master balancing equations by inspection using a step-by-step approach. The equation for the decomposition of water (see **Figure 1.7**) will be used as an example.

1. *Identify the names of the reactants and the products, and write a word equation.* The word equation for the reaction shown in **Figure 1.7** is written as follows.

$$\text{water} \longrightarrow \text{hydrogen} + \text{oxygen}$$

2. *Write a formula equation by substituting correct formulas for the names of the reactants and the products.* We know that the formula for water is H_2O. And recall that both hydrogen and oxygen exist as diatomic molecules. Therefore, their correct formulas are H_2 and O_2, respectively.

$$H_2O(l) \longrightarrow H_2(g) + O_2(g) \text{ (not balanced)}$$

FIGURE 1.7

Decomposition of Water

When an electric current is passed through water that has been made slightly conductive, the water molecules break down to yield hydrogen (in tube at right) and oxygen (in tube at left). Bubbles of each gas are evidence of the reaction. Note that twice as much hydrogen as oxygen is produced.

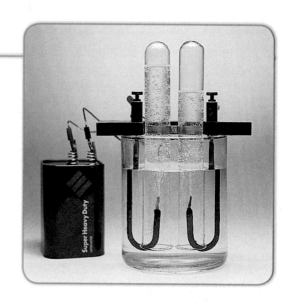

3. *Balance the formula equation according to the law of conservation of mass.* This last step is done by trial and error. Coefficients are changed, and the numbers of atoms are counted on both sides of the equation. When the numbers of each type of atom are the same for both the products and the reactants, the equation is balanced. The trial-and-error method of balancing equations is made easier by the use of the following guidelines.

- Balance the different types of atoms one at a time.
- First balance the atoms of elements that are combined and that appear only once on each side of the equation.
- Balance polyatomic ions that appear on both sides of the equation as single units. Look closely to see if these ions are enclosed in parentheses, and count the individual atoms accordingly.
- Balance H atoms and O atoms after atoms of all other elements have been balanced.

The formula equation in our example shows that there are two oxygen atoms on the right and only one on the left. To balance oxygen atoms, the number of H_2O molecules must be increased. Placing the coefficient 2 before H_2O gives the necessary two oxygen atoms on the left.

$$2H_2O(l) \longrightarrow H_2(g) + O_2(g) \quad \text{(partially balanced)}$$

The coefficient 2 in front of H_2O has upset the balance of hydrogen atoms. Placing the coefficient 2 in front of hydrogen, H_2, on the right, gives an equal number of hydrogen atoms (4) on both sides of the equation.

$$2H_2O(l) \longrightarrow 2H_2(g) + O_2(g)$$

4. *Count atoms to be sure that the equation is balanced.* Make sure that equal numbers of atoms of each element appear on both sides of the arrow.

$$2H_2O(l) \longrightarrow 2H_2(g) + O_2(g)$$
$$(4\cancel{H} + 2\cancel{O}) = (4\cancel{H}) + (2\cancel{O})$$

Occasionally at this point, the coefficients do not represent the least possible whole-number ratio of reactants and products. When this happens, the coefficients should be divided by their greatest common factor in order to obtain the least possible whole-number coefficients.

Balancing chemical equations by inspection becomes easier as you gain experience. Learn to avoid the most common mistakes: (1) writing incorrect chemical formulas for reactants or products and (2) trying to balance an equation by changing subscripts. Remember that subscripts cannot be added, deleted, or changed. Eventually, you will probably be able to skip writing the word equation and each separate step. You may even develop several "tricks" of your own for deciding how best to deal with certain compounds and polyatomic ions. Remember that there is no one, singular way to go about balancing a chemical equation, so you should not be afraid to use a method you feel works best for you. However, *do not* leave out the final step of counting atoms to be sure the equation is balanced.

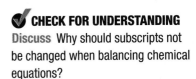

CHECK FOR UNDERSTANDING

Discuss Why should subscripts not be changed when balancing chemical equations?

Sample Problem C The reaction of zinc with aqueous hydrochloric acid produces a solution of zinc chloride and hydrogen gas. This reaction is shown in Figure 1.8. Write a balanced chemical equation for the reaction.

① ANALYZE

Write the word equation.

$$\text{zinc} + \text{hydrochloric acid} \longrightarrow \text{zinc chloride} + \text{hydrogen}$$

② PLAN

Write the formula equation.

$$Zn(s) + HCl(aq) \longrightarrow ZnCl_2(aq) + H_2(g) \text{ (not balanced)}$$

③ SOLVE

Adjust the coefficients. Note that chlorine and hydrogen each appear only once on each side of the equation. We balance chlorine first because it is combined on both sides of the equation. Also, recall from the guidelines on the previous page that hydrogen and oxygen are balanced only after all other elements in the reaction are balanced. To balance chlorine, we place the coefficient 2 before HCl. Two molecules of hydrogen chloride also yield the required two hydrogen atoms on the right. Finally, note that there is one zinc atom on each side in the formula equation. Therefore, no further coefficients are needed.

$$Zn(s) + 2HCl(aq) \longrightarrow ZnCl_2(aq) + H_2(g)$$

FIGURE 1.8

Reacting Zinc with HCl

Solid zinc reacts with hydrochloric acid to form aqueous zinc chloride and hydrogen gas.

④ CHECK YOUR WORK

Count atoms to check balance.

$$Zn(s) + 2HCl(aq) \longrightarrow ZnCl_2(aq) + H_2(g)$$

$$(1Zn) + (2H + 2Cl) = (1Zn + 2Cl) + (2H)$$

The equation is balanced.

Practice   Answers in Appendix E

1. Write word, formula, and balanced chemical equations for each of the following reactions:
   a. Solid magnesium and aqueous hydrochloric acid react to produce aqueous magnesium chloride and hydrogen gas.
   b. Aqueous nitric acid reacts with solid magnesium hydroxide to produce aqueous magnesium nitrate and water.
2. Solid calcium metal reacts with water to form aqueous calcium hydroxide and hydrogen gas. Write a balanced chemical equation for this reaction.

Balancing Chemical Equations

Sample Problem D Solid calcium carbide, CaC$_2$, reacts with water to produce acetylene gas and calcium hydroxide. Write a balanced chemical equation for this reaction.

 SOLVE

The reactants are calcium carbide and water. The products are acetylene and calcium hydroxide. The formula equation is written as follows.

$$CaC_2(s) + H_2O(l) \longrightarrow C_2H_2(g) + Ca(OH)_2(aq) \text{ (not balanced)}$$

Begin balancing the formula equation by counting calcium or carbon atoms. There is one Ca atom on the left and one on the right. The coefficient 1 is understood and does not have to appear in the equation. Ca is balanced.

$$CaC_2(s) + H_2O(l) \longrightarrow C_2H_2(g) + Ca(OH)_2(aq) \text{ (partially balanced)}$$

Now count carbon atoms. There are two C atoms on the left and two on the right. C is balanced.

$$CaC_2(s) + H_2O(l) \longrightarrow C_2H_2(g) + Ca(OH)_2(aq) \text{ (partially balanced)}$$

Balance oxygen atoms next because oxygen, unlike hydrogen, appears only once on each side of the equation. There is one O atom on the left and two on the right in Ca(OH)$_2$. Placing the coefficient 2 before H$_2$O balances the O atoms.

$$CaC_2(s) + 2H_2O(l) \longrightarrow C_2H_2(g) + Ca(OH)_2(aq)$$

This leaves the hydrogen atoms to be balanced. There are four H atoms on the left. On the right, there are two H atoms in acetylene and two H atoms in calcium hydroxide, totaling four H atoms. The H atoms are balanced.

$$CaC_2(s) \quad + \quad H_2O(l) \quad \longrightarrow \quad C_2H_4(g) \quad + \quad Ca(OH)_2(aq)$$
$$(1\cancel{Ca} + 2\cancel{C}) + \quad (4H + 2\cancel{O}) \quad \longrightarrow \quad (2\cancel{C} + 2H) \quad + \quad (1\cancel{Ca} + 2\cancel{O} + 2H)$$

The equation is balanced.

Balancing Chemical Equations

Sample Problem E Aluminum sulfate and calcium hydroxide are used in a water-purification process. When added to water, they dissolve and react to produce two insoluble products, aluminum hydroxide and calcium sulfate. These products settle out, taking suspended solid impurities with them. Write a balanced chemical equation for the reaction.

 SOLVE

Each of the reactants and products is an ionic compound. Recall that the formulas of ionic compounds are determined by the charges of the ions composing each compound. The formula reaction is thus written as follows.

$$Al_2(SO_4)_3 + Ca(OH)_2 \longrightarrow Al(OH)_3 + CaSO_4 \text{ (not balanced)}$$

Continued

Balancing Chemical Equations (continued)

There is one Ca atom on each side of the equation, so the calcium atoms are already balanced. There are two Al atoms on the left and one Al atom on the right. Placing the coefficient 2 in front of $Al(OH)_3$ produces the same number of Al atoms on each side of the equation.

$$Al_2(SO_4)_3 + Ca(OH)_2 \longrightarrow 2Al(OH)_3 + CaSO_4 \text{ (partially balanced)}$$

Next, checking SO_4^{2-} ions shows that there are three SO_4^{2-} ions on the left side of the equation and only one on the right side. Placing the coefficient 3 before $CaSO_4$ gives an equal number of SO_4^{2-} ions on each side.

$$Al_2(SO_4)_3 + Ca(OH)_2 \longrightarrow 2Al(OH)_3 + 3CaSO_4 \text{ (partially balanced)}$$

There are now three Ca atoms on the right, however. By placing the coefficient 3 in front of $Ca(OH)_2$, we once again have an equal number of Ca atoms on each side. This last step also gives six OH^- ions on both sides of the equation.

$$Al_2(SO_4)_3(aq) + 3Ca(OH)_2(aq) \longrightarrow 2Al(OH)_3(s) + 3CaSO_4(s)$$
$$(2Al + 3SO_4^{2-}) + (3Ca + 6OH^-) = (2Al + 6OH^-) + (3Ca + 3SO_4^{2-})$$

The equation is balanced.

Practice

1. Write balanced chemical equations for each of the following reactions:
   a. Solid calcium reacts with water to produce aqueous calcium hydroxide and hydrogen gas.
   b. When solid copper reacts with aqueous silver nitrate, the products are aqueous copper(II) nitrate and solid silver.
   c. In a blast furnace, the reaction between solid iron(III) oxide and carbon monoxide gas produces solid iron and carbon dioxide gas.

 ## SECTION 1 FORMATIVE ASSESSMENT

▶ Reviewing Main Ideas

1. Describe the differences between word equations, formula equations, and chemical equations.

2. Write word and formula equations for the reaction in which aqueous solutions of sulfuric acid and sodium hydroxide react to form aqueous sodium sulfate and water.

3. Translate the following chemical equations into sentences:
   a. $2K(s) + 2H_2O(l) \longrightarrow 2KOH(aq) + H_2(g)$
   b. $2Fe(s) + 3Cl_2(g) \longrightarrow 2FeCl_3(s)$

4. Write the word, formula, and chemical equations for the reaction between hydrogen sulfide gas and oxygen gas that produces sulfur dioxide gas and water vapor.

✔ Critical Thinking

5. **INTEGRATING CONCEPTS** The reaction of vanadium(II) oxide with iron(III) oxide results in the formation of vanadium(V) oxide and iron(II) oxide. Write the balanced chemical equation.

Carbon Monoxide Catalyst

S.T.E.M.

Colorless, odorless, and deadly, carbon monoxide, "the silent killer," causes the deaths of hundreds of Americans every year. When fuel does not burn completely in a combustion process, carbon monoxide is produced. Often this occurs in a malfunctioning heater, furnace, or fireplace. When the carbon monoxide is inhaled, it bonds to the hemoglobin in the blood, leaving the body oxygen-starved. Before people realize a combustion device is malfunctioning, it's often too late.

$$O_2Hb + CO \longrightarrow COHb + O_2$$

Carbon monoxide, CO, has almost 200 times the affinity to bind with the hemoglobin, Hb, in the blood as oxygen. This means that hemoglobin will bind to carbon monoxide rather than oxygen in the body. If enough carbon monoxide is present in the blood, it can be fatal.

Carbon monoxide poisoning can be prevented by installing filters that absorb the gas. After some time, however, filters become saturated, and then carbon monoxide can pass freely into the air. The best way to prevent carbon monoxide poisoning is not just to filter out the gas, but to eliminate it completely.

One solution to eliminate carbon monoxide was developed by NASA research chemists who were working on a problem with a space-based carbon dioxide laser. Carbon dioxide, of course, is not poisonous like carbon monoxide. In fact, it's what you exhale with each breath. The laser required a continuous supply of CO_2, but, as the laser operated, some of the CO_2 decomposed into carbon monoxide and oxygen. To address this problem, NASA scientists developed a catalyst made of tin oxide and platinum that oxidized the waste carbon monoxide back into carbon dioxide. The NASA scientists then realized that this catalyst had the potential to be used in many applications here on Earth, including removing carbon monoxide from houses and other buildings.

Typically, a malfunctioning heater circulates the carbon monoxide it produces through its air intake system back into a dwelling space. Installing the catalyst in the air intake would oxidize any carbon monoxide to nontoxic carbon dioxide before it reentered the room.

"The form of our catalyst is a very thin coating on some sort of a support, or substrate as we call it," says NASA chemist David Schryer. "And that support, or substrate, can be any one of a number of things. The great thing about a catalyst is that the only thing that matters about it is its surface. So a catalyst can be incredibly thin and still be very effective."

The idea of using catalysts to oxidize gases is not a new one. Catalytic converters in cars oxidize carbon monoxide and unburned hydrocarbons to minimize pollution. Many substances are oxidized into new materials for manufacturing purposes. But both of these types of catalytic reactions occur at very high temperatures. NASA's catalyst is special, because it's able to eliminate carbon monoxide at room temperature.

According to David Schryer, low-temperature catalysts constitute a whole new class of catalysts with abundant applications for the future.

Engineering Design

Design a pamphlet that tries to convince homeowners to install a catalyst into their home heating system to avoid carbon monoxide poisoning. Structure the information in your pamphlet to explain the advantages of the solution and give evidence to support your idea.

Types of Chemical Reactions

Key Terms
synthesis reaction
decomposition reaction
electrolysis
single-displacement reaction
double-displacement reaction
combustion reaction

Thousands of known chemical reactions occur in living systems, in industrial processes, and in chemical laboratories. Often it is necessary to predict the products formed in one of these reactions. Memorizing the equations for so many chemical reactions would be a difficult task. It is therefore more useful and realistic to classify reactions according to various similarities and regularities. This general information about reaction types can then be used to predict the products of specific reactions.

There are several ways to classify chemical reactions, and none are entirely satisfactory. The classification scheme described in this section provides an introduction to five basic types of reactions: synthesis, decomposition, single-displacement, double-displacement, and combustion reactions. In later chapters, you will be introduced to categories that are useful in classifying other types of chemical reactions.

▶ **MAIN IDEA**
Substances are combined in synthesis reactions.

In a **synthesis reaction,** also known as a composition reaction, two or more substances combine to form a new compound. This type of reaction is represented by the following general equation:

$$A + X \longrightarrow AX$$

A and X can be elements or compounds. AX is a compound. The following examples illustrate several kinds of synthesis reactions.

Reactions of Elements with Oxygen and Sulfur
One simple type of synthesis reaction is the combination of an element with oxygen to produce an *oxide* of the element. Almost all metals react with oxygen to form oxides. For example, when a thin strip of magnesium metal is placed in an open flame, it burns with bright white light. When the metal strip is completely burned, the product is a fine white powder of magnesium oxide. This chemical reaction, shown in **Figure 2.1** on the next page, is represented by the following equation:

$$2Mg(s) + O_2(g) \longrightarrow 2MgO(s)$$

The other Group 2 elements react in a similar manner, forming oxides with the formula MO, where M represents the metal. The Group 1 metals form oxides with the formula M_2O, for example, Li_2O. The Group 1 and Group 2 elements react similarly with sulfur, forming *sulfides* with the formulas M_2S and MS, respectively. Examples of these types of synthesis reactions are shown below.

$$16Rb(s) + S_8(s) \longrightarrow 8Rb_2S(s)$$

$$8Ba(s) + S_8(s) \longrightarrow 8BaS(s)$$

Some metals, such as iron, combine with oxygen to produce two different oxides.

$$2Fe(s) + O_2(g) \longrightarrow 2FeO(s)$$

$$4Fe(s) + 3O_2(g) \longrightarrow 2Fe_2O_3(s)$$

In the product of the first reaction, iron is in an oxidation state of +2. In the product of the second reaction, iron is in an oxidation state of +3. The particular oxide formed depends on the conditions surrounding the reactants. Both oxides are shown below in **Figure 2.2.**

Nonmetals also undergo synthesis reactions with oxygen to form oxides. Sulfur, for example, reacts with oxygen to form sulfur dioxide. And when carbon is burned in air, carbon dioxide is produced.

$$S_8(s) + 8O_2(g) \longrightarrow 8SO_2(g)$$

$$C(s) + O_2(g) \longrightarrow CO_2(g)$$

In a limited supply of oxygen, carbon monoxide is formed.

$$2C(s) + O_2(g) \longrightarrow 2CO(g)$$

Hydrogen reacts with oxygen to form dihydrogen monoxide, better known as water.

$$2H_2(g) + O_2(g) \longrightarrow 2H_2O(g)$$

FIGURE 2.1

Synthesis Reaction of Magnesium and Oxygen

(a) Magnesium, Mg, pictured here, undergoes a synthesis reaction with oxygen, O_2.

(b) The reaction produced magnesium oxide, MgO.

FIGURE 2.2

Synthesis Reactions of Iron and Oxygen Iron (Fe) and oxygen (O_2) combine to form two different oxides: FeO and Fe_2O_3.

(a) iron(II) oxide, FeO

(b) iron(III) oxide, Fe_2O_3

Reactions of Metals with Halogens

Most metals react with the Group 17 elements, the halogens, to form either ionic or covalent compounds. For example, Group 1 metals react with halogens to form ionic compounds with the formula MX, where M is the metal and X is the halogen. Examples of this type of synthesis reaction include the reactions of sodium with chlorine and potassium with iodine.

$$2Na(s) + Cl_2(g) \longrightarrow 2NaCl(s)$$

$$2K(s) + I_2(g) \longrightarrow 2KI(s)$$

Group 2 metals react with the halogens to form ionic compounds with the formula MX_2.

$$Mg(s) + F_2(g) \longrightarrow MgF_2(s)$$

$$Sr(s) + Br_2(l) \longrightarrow SrBr_2(s)$$

The halogens undergo synthesis reactions with many different metals. Fluorine in particular is so reactive that it combines with almost all metals. For example, fluorine reacts with sodium to produce sodium fluoride. Similarly, it reacts with cobalt to form cobalt(III) fluoride and with uranium to form uranium(VI) fluoride.

$$2Na(s) + F_2(g) \longrightarrow 2NaF(s)$$

$$2Co(s) + 3F_2(g) \longrightarrow 2CoF_3(s)$$

$$U(s) + 3F_2(g) \longrightarrow UF_6(g)$$

Sodium fluoride, NaF, is added to municipal water supplies in trace amounts to provide fluoride ions, which help to prevent tooth decay in the people who drink the water. Cobalt(III) fluoride, CoF_3, is a strong fluorinating agent. And natural uranium is converted to uranium(VI) fluoride, UF_6, as the first step in the production of uranium for use in nuclear power plants.

Synthesis Reactions with Oxides

Active metals are highly reactive metals. Oxides of active metals react with water to produce metal hydroxides. Calcium oxide, CaO, also known as lime or quicklime, is manufactured in large quantities. The addition of water to lime to produce $Ca(OH)_2$, which is also known as slaked lime, is a crucial step in the setting of cement.

$$CaO(s) + H_2O(l) \longrightarrow Ca(OH)_2(s)$$

Calcium hydroxide also is an ingredient in some stomach antacids, as shown in **Figure 2.3**. In the stomach, it reacts with hydrochloric acid, neutralizing its effects. These *neutralization* reactions are dealt with in more detail in the chapter on acids and bases.

Many oxides of nonmetals in the upper-right portion of the periodic table react with water to produce oxyacids. For example, sulfur dioxide, SO_2, reacts with water to produce sulfurous acid.

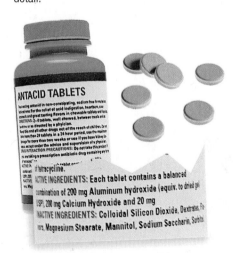

FIGURE 2.3

Calcium Hydroxide Calcium hydroxide, a base, can be used to *neutralize* hydrochloric acid in your stomach. The chapter "Acids and Bases" describes neutralization reactions in more detail.

$$SO_2(g) + H_2O(l) \longrightarrow H_2SO_3(aq)$$

In air polluted with SO_2, sulfurous acid further reacts with oxygen to form sulfuric acid, one of the main ingredients in *acid precipitation*, known more familiarly as *acid rain*.

$$2H_2SO_3(aq) + O_2(g) \longrightarrow 2H_2SO_4(aq)$$

Certain metal oxides and nonmetal oxides react with each other in synthesis reactions to form salts. For example, calcium sulfite is formed by the reaction of calcium oxide and sulfur dioxide.

$$CaO(s) + SO_2(g) \longrightarrow CaSO_3(s)$$

✔ **CHECK FOR UNDERSTANDING**

Apply Using your knowledge of synthesis reactions, explain the relationship between air pollution and acid rain.

▶ **MAIN IDEA**

Substances are broken down in decomposition reactions.

In a **decomposition reaction,** a single compound undergoes a reaction that produces two or more simpler substances. Decomposition reactions are the opposite of synthesis reactions and are represented by the following general equation.

$$AX \longrightarrow A + X$$

AX is a compound. A and X can be elements or compounds.

Most decomposition reactions take place only when energy in the form of electricity or heat is added. Examples of several types of decomposition reactions are given in the following sections.

Decomposition of Binary Compounds

The simplest kind of decomposition reaction is the decomposition of a binary compound into its elements. We have already examined one example of a decomposition reaction, the decomposition of water into hydrogen and oxygen. An electric current passed through water will decompose it into its constituent elements. The decomposition of a substance by an electric current is called **electrolysis.**

$$2H_2O(l) \xrightarrow{\text{electricity}} 2H_2(g) + O_2(g)$$

Notice the word *electricity* above the reaction arrow.

Oxides of the less-active metals, which are located in the lower center of the periodic table, decompose into their elements when heated. Joseph Priestley, one of the founders of modern chemistry, discovered oxygen through such a decomposition reaction in 1774, when he heated mercury(II) oxide to produce mercury and oxygen.

$$2HgO(s) \xrightarrow{\Delta} 2Hg(l) + O_2(g)$$

This reaction is shown in **Figure 2.4** on the following page.

FIGURE 2.4

Decomposition Reaction

When mercury(II) oxide (the red-orange substance in the bottom of the test tube) is heated, it decomposes into oxygen and metallic mercury, which can be seen as droplets on the inside wall of the test tube.

✔ **CRITICAL THINKING**

Apply What are the products of this reaction?

Decomposition of Metal Carbonates

When a metal carbonate is heated, it breaks down to produce a metal oxide and carbon dioxide gas. For example, calcium carbonate decomposes to produce calcium oxide and carbon dioxide.

$$CaCO_3(s) \xrightarrow{\Delta} CaO(s) + CO_2(g)$$

Decomposition of Metal Hydroxides

All metal hydroxides except those containing Group 1 metals decompose when heated to yield metal oxides and water. For example, calcium hydroxide decomposes to produce calcium oxide and water.

$$Ca(OH)_2(s) \xrightarrow{\Delta} CaO(s) + H_2O(g)$$

Decomposition of Metal Chlorates

When a metal chlorate is heated, it decomposes to produce a metal chloride and oxygen. For example, potassium chlorate, $KClO_3$, decomposes in the presence of the catalyst $MnO_2(s)$ to produce potassium chloride and oxygen.

$$2KClO_3(s) \xrightarrow[MnO_2(s)]{\Delta} 2KCl(s) + 3O_2(g)$$

Decomposition of Acids

Certain acids decompose into nonmetal oxides and water. Carbonic acid is unstable and decomposes readily at room temperature to produce carbon dioxide and water.

$$H_2CO_3(aq) \longrightarrow CO_2(g) + H_2O(l)$$

When heated, sulfuric acid decomposes into sulfur trioxide and water.

$$H_2SO_4(aq) \xrightarrow{\Delta} SO_3(g) + H_2O(l)$$

Sulfurous acid, H_2SO_3, decomposes to give sulfur dioxide and oxygen.

©Charles D. Winters

MAIN IDEA

One element replaces another in single-displacement reactions.

In a **single-displacement reaction,** also known as a replacement reaction, one element replaces a similar element in a compound. Many single-displacement reactions take place in aqueous solution. The amount of energy involved in this type of reaction is usually smaller than the amount involved in synthesis or decomposition reactions. Single-displacement reactions can be represented by the following general equations:

$$A + BX \longrightarrow AX + B$$
$$\text{or}$$
$$Y + BX \longrightarrow BY + X$$

A, B, X, and Y are elements. AX, BX, and BY are compounds.

Displacement of a Metal in a Compound by Another Metal

Aluminum is more active than lead. When solid aluminum is placed in aqueous lead(II) nitrate, $Pb(NO_3)_2(aq)$, the aluminum replaces the lead. Solid lead and aqueous aluminum nitrate are formed.

$$2Al(s) + 3Pb(NO_3)_2(aq) \longrightarrow 3Pb(s) + 2Al(NO_3)_3(aq)$$

Displacement of Hydrogen in Water by a Metal

The most-active metals, such as those in Group 1, react vigorously with water to produce metal hydroxides and hydrogen. For example, sodium reacts with water to form sodium hydroxide and hydrogen gas.

$$2Na(s) + 2H_2O(l) \longrightarrow 2NaOH(aq) + H_2(g)$$

Less-active metals, such as iron, react with steam to form a metal oxide and hydrogen gas.

$$3Fe(s) + 4H_2O(g) \longrightarrow Fe_3O_4(s) + 4H_2(g)$$

Displacement of Hydrogen in an Acid by a Metal

The more-active metals react with certain acidic solutions, such as hydrochloric acid and dilute sulfuric acid, replacing the hydrogen in the acid. The reaction products are a metal compound (a salt) and hydrogen gas. For example, when solid magnesium reacts with hydrochloric acid, as shown in **Figure 2.5,** the reaction products are hydrogen gas and aqueous magnesium chloride.

$$Mg(s) + 2HCl(aq) \longrightarrow H_2(g) + MgCl_2(aq)$$

Be careful as you study chemistry to remember that the term *salt* often has a wider definition than simply that of the table salt (sodium chloride) you put on food. Strictly speaking, a salt is any ionic compound formed in the neutralization of an acid by a base.

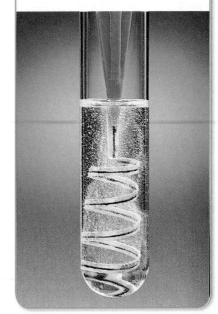

FIGURE 2.5

Single Displacement Reaction In this single-displacement reaction, the hydrogen in hydrochloric acid, HCl, is replaced by magnesium, Mg.

Displacement of Halogens

In another type of single-displacement reaction, one halogen replaces another halogen in a compound. Fluorine is the most-active halogen. As such, it can replace any of the other halogens in their compounds. Each halogen is less active than the one above it in the periodic table. Therefore, in Group 17 each element can replace any element below it but not any element above it. For example, while chlorine can replace bromine in potassium bromide, it cannot replace fluorine in potassium fluoride. The reaction of chlorine with potassium bromide produces bromine and potassium chloride, whereas the combination of fluorine and sodium chloride produces sodium fluoride and gaseous chlorine.

$$Cl_2(g) + 2KBr(aq) \longrightarrow 2KCl(aq) + Br_2(l)$$

$$F_2(g) + 2NaCl(aq) \longrightarrow 2NaF(aq) + Cl_2(g)$$

$$Br_2(l) + KCl(aq) \longrightarrow \text{no reaction}$$

▶ MAIN IDEA

In double-displacement reactions, two compounds exchange ions.

In **double-displacement reactions,** the ions of two compounds exchange places in an aqueous solution to form two new compounds. One of the compounds formed is usually a precipitate, an insoluble gas that bubbles out of the solution, or a molecular compound, usually water. The other compound is often soluble and remains dissolved in solution. A double-displacement reaction is represented by the following general equation.

$$AX + BY \longrightarrow AY + BX$$

A, X, B, and Y in the reactants represent ions. AY and BX represent ionic or molecular compounds.

Formation of a Precipitate

The formation of a precipitate occurs when the cations of one reactant combine with the anions of another reactant to form an insoluble or slightly soluble compound. For example, when an aqueous solution of potassium iodide is added to an aqueous solution of lead(II) nitrate, the yellow precipitate lead(II) iodide forms. This is shown in **Figure 2.6.**

$$2KI(aq) + Pb(NO_3)_2(aq) \longrightarrow PbI_2(s) + 2KNO_3(aq)$$

The precipitate forms as a result of the very strong attractive forces between the Pb^{2+} cations and the I^- anions. The other product is the water-soluble salt potassium nitrate, KNO_3. The potassium and nitrate ions do not take part in the reaction. They remain in solution as aqueous ions and therefore are often referred to as *spectator ions*. The guidelines that help identify which ions form a precipitate and which ions remain in solution are developed in a later chapter on ions in aqueous solutions.

FIGURE 2.6

Double-Displacement Reaction
The double-displacement reaction between aqueous lead(II) nitrate, $Pb(NO_3)_2(aq)$, and aqueous potassium iodide, $KI(aq)$, yields the precipitate lead(II) iodide, $PbI_2(s)$.

Formation of a Gas

In some double-displacement reactions, one of the products is an insoluble gas that bubbles out of the mixture. For example, iron(II) sulfide reacts with hydrochloric acid to form hydrogen sulfide gas and iron(II) chloride.

$$FeS(s) + 2HCl(aq) \longrightarrow H_2S(g) + FeCl_2(aq)$$

Formation of Water

In some double-displacement reactions, a very stable molecular compound, such as water, is one of the products. For example, hydrochloric acid reacts with an aqueous solution of sodium hydroxide to yield aqueous sodium chloride and water.

$$HCl(aq) + NaOH(aq) \longrightarrow NaCl(aq) + H_2O(l)$$

▶ **MAIN IDEA**
Combustion reactions involve oxygen.

In a **combustion reaction,** a substance combines with oxygen, releasing a large amount of energy in the form of light and heat. The burning of natural gas, propane, gasoline, and wood are all examples of combustion reactions. For example, propane, C_3H_8, combustion results in the production of carbon dioxide and water vapor.

$$C_3H_8(g) + 5O_2(g) \longrightarrow 3CO_2(g) + 4H_2O(g)$$

The combustion of hydrogen, shown in **Figure 2.7**, produces water vapor.

$$2H_2(g) + O_2(g) \longrightarrow 2H_2O(g)$$

FIGURE 2.7

Combustion Reaction of Hydrogen

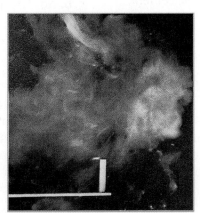

(a) The candle supplies heat to the hydrogen and oxygen in the balloon.

(b) The heat triggers the explosive combustion reaction.

✓ **CRITICAL THINKING**

Explain In combustion reactions, substances combined with oxygen usually result in a fire or explosion. What remains afterwards is usually ash or fine particles, which often do not contain all of the elements found in the reactants. Explain what happens to the missing elements in terms of conservation of matter.

QUESTION

How can molecular models and formula-unit ionic models be used to balance chemical equations and classify chemical reactions?

PROCEDURE

Examine the partial equations in Groups A–E. Using different-colored gumdrops to represent atoms of different elements, make models of the reactions by connecting the appropriate "atoms" with toothpicks. Use your models to (1) balance equations (a) and (b) in each group, (2) determine the products for reaction (c) in each group, and (3) complete and balance each equation (c). Finally, (4) classify each group of reactions by type.

Group A

a. $H_2 + Cl_2 \longrightarrow HCl$

b. $Mg + O_2 \longrightarrow MgO$

c. $BaO + H_2O \longrightarrow$ _____

Group B

a. $H_2CO_3 \longrightarrow CO_2 + H_2O$

b. $KClO_3 \longrightarrow KCl + O_2$

c. $H_2O \xrightarrow{\text{electricity}}$ _____

Group C

a. $Ca + H_2O \longrightarrow Ca(OH)_2 + H_2$

b. $KI + Br_2 \longrightarrow KBr + I_2$

c. $Zn + HCl \longrightarrow$ _____

Group D

a. $AgNO_3 + NaCl \longrightarrow AgCl + NaNO_3$

b. $FeS + HCl \longrightarrow FeCl_2 + H_2S$

c. $H_2SO_4 + KOH \longrightarrow$ _____

Group E

a. $CH_4 + O_2 \longrightarrow CO_2 + H_2O$

b. $CO + O_2 \longrightarrow CO_2$

c. $C_3H_8 + O_2 \longrightarrow$ _____

MATERIALS

- large and small gumdrops in at least four different colors
- toothpicks

SAFETY

Wear safety goggles and an apron.

✓ SECTION 2 FORMATIVE ASSESSMENT

▶ Reviewing Main Ideas

1. List five types of chemical reactions.

2. Classify each of the following reactions as a synthesis, decomposition, single-displacement, double-displacement, or combustion reaction:

   a. $N_2(g) + 3H_2(g) \longrightarrow 2NH_3(g)$

   b. $2Li(s) + 2H_2O(l) \longrightarrow 2LiOH(aq) + H_2(g)$

   c. $2NaNO_3(s) \longrightarrow 2NaNO_2(s) + O_2(g)$

   d. $2C_6H_{14}(l) + 19O_2(g) \longrightarrow 12CO_2(g) + 14H_2O(l)$

3. For each of the following reactions, identify the missing reactant(s) or products(s) and then balance the resulting equation. Note that each empty slot may require one or more substances.

   a. synthesis: _____ $\longrightarrow Li_2O$

   b. decomposition: $Mg(ClO_3)_2 \longrightarrow$ _____

   c. double displacement:
      $HNO_3 + Ca(OH)_2 \longrightarrow$ _____

   d. combustion: $C_5H_{12} + O_2 \longrightarrow$ _____

4. For each of the following reactions, write the missing product(s) and then balance the resulting equation. Identify each reaction by type.

   a. $Br_2 + KI \longrightarrow$ _____

   b. $NaClO_3 \xrightarrow{\Delta}$ _____

   c. $C_7H_{14} + O_2 \longrightarrow$ _____

   d. $CuCl_2 + Na_2S \longrightarrow$ _____

✓ Critical Thinking

5. **INFERRING RELATIONSHIPS** In an experiment, an iron sample is oxidized to iron(III) oxide by oxygen, which is generated in the thermal decomposition of potassium chlorate. Write the two chemical reactions in the correct sequence.

Activity Series of the Elements

Key Term

activity series

Main Idea

▶ An activity series helps determine what substances will displace others in chemical reactions.

The ability of an element to react is referred to as the element's *activity*. The more readily an element reacts with other substances, the greater its activity is. **An activity series is a list of elements organized according to the ease with which the elements undergo certain chemical reactions.** For metals, greater activity means a greater ease of *loss* of electrons, to form positive ions. For nonmetals, greater activity means a greater ease of *gain* of electrons, to form negative ions.

▶ **MAIN IDEA**

An activity series helps determine what substances will displace others in chemical reactions.

The order in which the elements are listed is usually determined by single-displacement reactions. The most-active element, placed at the top in the series, can replace each of the elements below it from a compound in a single-displacement reaction. An element farther down can replace any element below it but not any above it. For example, in the discussion of single-displacement reactions in Section 2, it was noted that each halogen will react to replace any halide listed below it in the periodic table. Therefore, an activity series for the Group 17 elements lists them in the same order, from top to bottom, as they appear in the periodic table. This is shown in **Figure 3.1** on the next page.

As mentioned in Section 1, the fact that a chemical equation can be written does not necessarily mean that the reaction it represents will actually take place. Activity series are used to help predict whether certain chemical reactions will occur. For example, according to the activity series for metals in **Figure 3.1**, aluminum displaces zinc chloride. Therefore, we could predict that the following reaction does occur.

$$2Al(s) + 3ZnCl_2(aq) \longrightarrow 3Zn(s) + 2AlCl_3(aq)$$

Cobalt, however, cannot displace sodium from its compound. Therefore, we write the following:

$$Co(s) + 2NaCl(aq) \longrightarrow \text{no reaction}$$

It is important to remember that like many other aids used to predict the products of chemical reactions, activity series are based on experiment. The information that they contain is used as a general guide for predicting reaction outcomes.

Such experimental observations are the basis for the activity series shown in **Figure 3.1**. For example, the activity series reflects the fact that some metals (potassium, for example) react vigorously with water and acids, replacing hydrogen to form new compounds. Other metals, such as iron or zinc, replace hydrogen in acids such as hydrochloric acid but react with water only when the water is hot enough to become steam. Nickel, however, will replace hydrogen in acids but will not react with steam at all. And gold will not react with individual acids or water, either as a liquid or as steam. If you look closely at the fairly unreactive metals in this activity series, you'll notice instantly that they represent the so-called precious metals that are very important to commerce. The ability of these metals to "stay intact" and not react with such things as water and acids, which are everywhere, should give you a clue as to why they have come to hold such great value by cultures all around the world.

FIGURE 3.1

ACTIVITY SERIES OF THE ELEMENTS

Activity of metals

Increased reactivity →

Li, Rb, K, Ba, Sr, Ca, Na	React with cold H_2O and acids, replacing hydrogen. React with oxygen, forming oxides.
Mg, Al, Mn, Zn, Cr, Fe, Cd	React with steam (but not cold water) and acids, replacing hydrogen. React with oxygen, forming oxides.
Co, Ni, Sn, Pb	Do not react with water. React with acids, replacing hydrogen. React with oxygen, forming oxides.
H_2, Sb, Bi, Cu, Hg	React with oxygen, forming oxides.
Ag, Pt, Au	Fairly unreactive, forming oxides only indirectly.

Activity of halogen nonmetals

F_2
Cl_2
Br_2
I_2

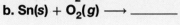

 Solve It! Cards
HMHScience.com

Activity Series

Sample Problem F Using the activity series shown in Figure 3.1, explain whether each of the possible reactions listed below will occur. For those reactions that will occur, predict what the products will be.

a. $Zn(s) + H_2O(l) \xrightarrow{50°C}$ _____

b. $Sn(s) + O_2(g) \longrightarrow$ _____

c. $Cd(s) + Pb(NO_3)_2(aq) \longrightarrow$ _____

d. $Cu(s) + HCl(aq) \longrightarrow$ _____

● **SOLVE**

a. This is a reaction between a metal and water at 50°C. Zinc reacts with water only when it is hot enough to be steam. Therefore, no reaction will occur.

b. Any metal more active than silver will react with oxygen to form an oxide. Tin is above silver in the activity series. Therefore, a reaction will occur, and the product will be a tin oxide, either SnO or SnO_2.

c. An element will replace any element below it in the activity series from a compound in aqueous solution. Cadmium is above lead, and therefore a reaction will occur to produce lead, Pb, and cadmium nitrate, $Cd(NO_3)_2$.

d. Any metal more active than hydrogen will replace hydrogen from an acid. Copper is not above hydrogen in the series. Therefore, no reaction will occur.

Practice   Answers in Appendix F

1. Using the activity series shown in **Figure 3.1**, predict whether each of the possible reactions listed below will occur. For the reactions that will occur, write the products and balance the equation.
   a. $Cr(s) + H_2O(l) \longrightarrow$ _____
   b. $Pt(s) + O_2(g) \longrightarrow$ _____
   c. $Cd(s) + 2HBr(aq) \longrightarrow$ _____
   d. $Mg(s) + steam \longrightarrow$ _____
2. Identify the element that displaces hydrogen from acids but cannot displace tin from its compounds.
3. According to **Figure 3.1**, what is the most-active transition metal?

✔ SECTION 3 FORMATIVE ASSESSMENT

▶ **Reviewing Main Ideas**

1. How is the activity series useful in predicting chemical behavior?

2. Based on the activity series, predict whether each of the following possible reactions will occur:
   a. $Ni(s) + H_2O(l) \longrightarrow$ _____
   b. $Br_2(l) + KI(aq) \longrightarrow$ _____
   c. $Au(s) + HCl(aq) \longrightarrow$ _____
   d. $Cd(s) + HCl(aq) \longrightarrow$ _____
   e. $Mg(s) + Co(NO_3)_2(aq) \longrightarrow$ _____

3. For each of the reactions in item 2 that will occur, write the products and balance the equation.

✔ **Critical Thinking**

4. **PREDICTING OUTCOMES** A mixture contains cobalt metal, copper metal, and tin metal. This mixture is mixed with nickel nitrate. Which metals, if any, will react? Write the chemical equation for any reaction.

Combustion Synthesis

S.T.E.M.

Aerospace materials, such as cutting tools, high-temperature superconductors, and rocket nozzles are made of composites, ceramics, and other advanced materials. Rocket nozzles require lightweight materials with high thermal conductivity at the low temperatures in space. Nozzles use nickel aluminide, NiAl, which has high-temperature strength and high thermal conductivity. NiAl is also low density and resists environmental effects. However, it can fracture at low temperatures.

Rocket nozzles that use NiAl are designed to be bimetallic, with an inner layer of NiAl and an outer layer of a metal alloy. The outer alloy layer helps prevent NiAl fractures at low temperature. The inner NiAl layer has good thermal conductivity and resists attack from the hot gases flowing through the nozzle.

Conventional techniques used to make these materials consist of a high-temperature furnace, operating from 500°C to 2000°C. The time required, minutes to hours, for the reaction and the difficulty in maintaining even heating can put flaws in the structures. This can cause stress points in the materials. These issues make conventional techniques hard to control.

A different technique, *combustion synthesis*, offers advantages that improve the fabrication process. Once the reactant mixture is ignited, a heat wave moves through the sample, producing the solid-state product. Combustion synthesis can reach 4000°C, twice what is possible with conventional high-temperature furnaces. It also allows reactions to be completed in just seconds. Therefore, this technique produces the desired material faster and requires less supplied energy than conventional techniques do. In addition, the intense and quick heating produces materials that are chemically homogeneous.

In a typical combustion synthesis procedure, the reactant powders are mixed and then pressed into a cylindrical pellet. The pellet is ignited by an intense heat source, such as an electrically heated coil or a laser. Because the combustion-synthesis reaction is very exothermic, the reaction is self-propagating, and the process does not need any further input of energy. This type of self-propagation is called a *reaction wave*, in which the reaction propagates through the starting material in a self-sustained manner. Therefore, compared with conventional high-temperature methods, this technique is an energy-saving process. In addition, the high temperatures and short reaction times can produce materials that would not be synthesized under conventional conditions.

Engineering Design

Describe why combustion synthesis would be especially useful in producing materials for use in the aerospace industry. What are potential drawbacks of these materials being made at lower temperatures? Why might stress faults be more important for aerospace materials than in household items? How could you test the difference between materials made at different temperatures?

Superconducting ceramics, like those used to make supercooled electromagnets, are formed using a combustion synthesis reaction.

A chemical equation is a written expression of an actual chemical reaction in which certain atoms, ions, or molecules become rearranged in a specific way. Therefore, the equation must represent exactly what happens in the reaction.

Recall that atoms are never created or destroyed in chemical reactions. A balanced chemical equation shows that all of the atoms present in reactants are still present in products.

Problem-Solving TIPS

- First, identify reactants and products. (You may find it helpful to write a word equation first.)
- Using correct formulas and symbols, write an unbalanced equation for the reaction.
- Balance atoms one element at a time by inserting coefficients.
- Identify elements that appear in only one reactant and one product, and balance the atoms of those elements first.
- If a polyatomic ion appears on both sides of the equation, treat it as a single unit.
- Double-check to be sure that the number of atoms of each element is the same on both sides of the equation.

Sample

When an aqueous solution of ammonium sulfate, $(NH_4)_2SO_4(aq)$, is combined with an aqueous solution of silver nitrate, $AgNO_3(aq)$, a precipitate of solid silver sulfate, $Ag_2SO_4(s)$, forms, leaving ammonium nitrate, $NH_4NO_3(aq)$, in solution. Balance the equation for this reaction.

As before, first write an equation with correct formulas for all reactants and products.

$$(NH_4)_2SO_4(aq) + AgNO_3(aq) \longrightarrow NH_4NO_3(aq) + Ag_2SO_4(s)$$

If you compare the number of silver atoms on each side, you can see that the equation is not balanced. This equation may look very complex, but it is really fairly simple. In many reactions involving polyatomic ions such as sulfate, nitrate, and ammonium, the ions do not change. In the equation above, you can see that NO_3 is present on both sides, as are SO_4 and NH_4. You can balance the equation by treating the groups as if they were single atoms. To balance the NH_4 groups, place a 2 in front of NH_4NO_3. This gives you two ammonium groups on the left and two on the right. Now, because you have two nitrate groups on the right, place a 2 in front of $AgNO_3$ to give two nitrate groups on the left. Finally, check silver atoms and sulfate groups, and you find that they balance.

$$(NH_4)_2SO_4(aq) + 2AgNO_3(aq) \longrightarrow 2NH_4NO_3(aq) + Ag_2SO_4(s)$$

Practice

1. When propane burns completely in air, the reaction forms carbon dioxide and water vapor. Balance the equation for this reaction.

$$C_3H_8 + O_2 \longrightarrow CO_2 + H_2O$$

2. Balance the following chemical equations:
   a. $KI(aq) + Cl_2(g) \longrightarrow KCl(aq) + I_2(s)$
   b. $Al(s) + H_2SO_4(aq) \longrightarrow Al_2(SO_4)_3(aq) + H_2(g)$

BIG IDEA Chemical equations use chemical formulas with coefficients to show how a reaction satisfies the law of conservation of mass.

SECTION 1 Describing Chemical Reactions

KEY TERMS

- Four observations that suggest a chemical reaction is taking place are the evolution of energy as heat and light, the production of gas, a change in color, and the formation of a precipitate.

- A balanced chemical equation represents, with symbols and formulas, the identities and relative amounts of reactants and products in a chemical reaction.

chemical equation
precipitate
coefficient
word equation
formula equation
reversible reaction

SECTION 2 Types of Chemical Reactions

KEY TERMS

- Synthesis reactions are represented by the general equation
$A + X \longrightarrow AX$.

- Decomposition reactions are represented by the general equation
$AX \longrightarrow A + X$.

- Single-displacement reactions are represented by the general equations
$A + BX \longrightarrow AX + B$ and $Y + BX \longrightarrow BY + X$.

- Double-displacement reactions are represented by the general equation
$AX + BY \longrightarrow AY + BX$.

- In a combustion reaction, a substance combines with oxygen, releasing energy in the form of heat and light.

synthesis reaction
decomposition reaction
electrolysis
single-displacement reaction
double-displacement reaction
combustion reaction

SECTION 3 Activity Series of the Elements

KEY TERMS

- Activity series list the elements in order of their chemical reactivity and are useful in predicting whether a chemical reaction will occur.

- Chemists determine activity series through experiments.

activity series

CHAPTER 8 **Review**

GO ONLINE

→ **Interactive** Review
HMHScience.com

Review Games
Concept Maps

SECTION 1

Describing Chemical Reactions

 REVIEWING MAIN IDEAS

1. List four observations that indicate that a chemical reaction may be taking place.

2. List the three requirements for a correctly written chemical equation.

3. **a.** What is meant by the term *coefficient* in relation to a chemical equation?
   b. How does the presence of a coefficient affect the number of atoms of each type in the formula that the coefficient precedes?

4. Give an example of a word equation, a formula equation, and a chemical equation.

5. What quantitative information is revealed by a chemical equation?

6. What limitations are associated with the use of both word and formula equations?

7. Define each of the following terms:
   a. aqueous solution
   b. catalyst
   c. reversible reaction

8. Write formulas for each of the following compounds:
   a. potassium hydroxide
   b. calcium nitrate
   c. sodium carbonate
   d. carbon tetrachloride
   e. magnesium bromide

9. What four guidelines are useful in balancing an equation?

10. How many atoms of each type are represented in each of the following?
    a. $3N_2$
    b. $2H_2O$
    c. $4HNO_3$
    d. $2Ca(OH)_2$
    e. $3Ba(ClO_3)_2$
    f. $5Fe(NO_3)_2$
    g. $4Mg_3(PO_4)_2$
    h. $2(NH_4)_2SO_4$
    i. $6Al_2(SeO_4)_3$
    j. $4C_3H_8$

PRACTICE PROBLEMS

11. Write the chemical equation that relates to each of the following word equations. Include symbols for physical states in the equation.
    a. solid zinc sulfide + oxygen gas $\longrightarrow$ solid zinc oxide + sulfur dioxide gas
    b. aqueous hydrochloric acid + aqueous barium hydroxide $\longrightarrow$ aqueous barium chloride + water
    c. aqueous nitric acid + aqueous calcium hydroxide $\longrightarrow$ aqueous calcium nitrate + water

12. Translate each of the following chemical equations into a sentence.
    a. $2ZnS(s) + 3O_2(g) \longrightarrow 2ZnO(s) + 2SO_2(g)$
    b. $CaH_2(s) + 2H_2O(l) \longrightarrow Ca(OH)_2(aq) + 2H_2(g)$
    c. $AgNO_3(aq) + KI(aq) \longrightarrow AgI(s) + KNO_3(aq)$

13. Balance each of the following:
    a. $H_2 + Cl_2 \longrightarrow HCl$
    b. $Al + Fe_2O_3 \longrightarrow Al_2O_3 + Fe$
    c. $Pb(CH_3COO)_2 + H_2S \longrightarrow PbS + CH_3COOH$

14. Identify and correct each error in the following equations, and then balance each equation.
    a. $Li + O_2 \longrightarrow LiO_2$
    b. $H_2 + Cl_2 \longrightarrow H_2Cl_2$
    c. $MgCO_3 \longrightarrow MgO_2 + CO_2$
    d. $NaI + Cl_2 \longrightarrow NaCl + I$

15. Write balanced chemical equations for each of the following sentences:
    a. Aluminum reacts with oxygen to produce aluminum oxide.
    b. Phosphoric acid, H_3PO_4, is produced through the reaction between tetraphosphorus decoxide and water.
    c. Iron(III) oxide reacts with carbon monoxide to produce iron and carbon dioxide.

16. Carbon tetrachloride is used as an intermediate chemical in the manufacture of other chemicals. It is prepared in liquid form by reacting chlorine gas with methane gas. Hydrogen chloride gas is also formed in this reaction. Write the balanced chemical equation for the production of carbon tetrachloride. (Hint: See Sample Problems C and D.)

17. For each of the following synthesis reactions, identify the missing reactant(s) or product(s) and then balance the resulting equation.
  a. $Mg +$ _____ $\longrightarrow MgO$
  b. _____ $+ O_2 \longrightarrow Fe_2O_3$
  c. $Li + Cl_2 \longrightarrow$ _____
  d. $Ca +$ _____ $\longrightarrow CaI_2$

Types of Chemical Reactions

▶ REVIEWING MAIN IDEAS

18. Define and give general equations for the five basic types of chemical reactions.

19. How are most decomposition reactions initiated?

20. A substance is decomposed by an electric current. What is the name of this type of reaction?

21. a. In what environment do many single-displacement reactions commonly occur?
  b. In general, how do single-displacement reactions compare with synthesis and decomposition reactions in terms of the amount of energy involved?

PRACTICE PROBLEMS

22. Complete each of the following synthesis reactions by writing both a word equation and a chemical equation.
  a. sodium + oxygen $\longrightarrow$ _____
  b. magnesium + fluorine $\longrightarrow$ _____

23. Complete and balance the equations for the following decomposition reactions:
  a. $HgO \xrightarrow{\Delta}$
  b. $H_2O(l) \xrightarrow{\text{electricity}}$
  c. $Ag_2O \xrightarrow{\Delta}$
  d. $CuCl_2 \xrightarrow{\text{electricity}}$

24. Complete and balance the equations for the following single-displacement reactions:
  a. $Zn + Pb(NO_3)_2 \longrightarrow$ _____
  b. $Al + Hg(CH_3COO)_2 \longrightarrow$ _____
  c. $Al + NiSO_4 \longrightarrow$ _____
  d. $Na + H_2O \longrightarrow$ _____

25. Complete and balance the equations for the following double-displacement reactions:
  a. $AgNO_3(aq) + NaCl(aq) \longrightarrow$ _____
  b. $Mg(NO_3)_2(aq) + KOH(aq) \longrightarrow$ _____
  c. $LiOH(aq) + Fe(NO_3)_3(aq) \longrightarrow$ _____

26. Complete and balance the equations for the following combustion reactions:
  a. $CH_4 + O_2 \longrightarrow$ _____
  b. $C_3H_6 + O_2 \longrightarrow$ _____
  c. $C_5H_{12} + O_2 \longrightarrow$ _____

27. Write and balance each of the following equations, and then identify each by type.
  a. hydrogen + iodine $\longrightarrow$ hydrogen iodide
  b. lithium + hydrochloric acid $\longrightarrow$
     lithium chloride + hydrogen
  c. sodium carbonate $\longrightarrow$
     sodium oxide + carbon dioxide
  d. mercury(II) oxide $\longrightarrow$ mercury + oxygen
  e. magnesium hydroxide $\longrightarrow$
     magnesium oxide + water

28. Identify the compound that could undergo decomposition to produce the following products, and then balance the final equation.
  a. magnesium oxide and water
  b. lead(II) oxide and water
  c. lithium chloride and oxygen
  d. barium chloride and oxygen
  e. nickel chloride and oxygen

29. In each of the following combustion reactions, identify the missing reactant(s), product(s), or both and then balance the resulting equation.
  a. $C_3H_8 +$ _____ $\longrightarrow$ _____ $+ H_2O$
  b. _____ $+ 8O_2 \longrightarrow 5CO_2 + 6H_2O$
  c. $C_2H_5OH +$ _____ $\longrightarrow$ _____ $+$ _____

30. Complete and balance the equations for the following reactions, and then identify each by type.
  a. zinc + sulfur $\longrightarrow$ _____
  b. silver nitrate + potassium iodide $\longrightarrow$ _____
  c. toluene, C_7H_8 + oxygen $\longrightarrow$ _____
  d. nonane, C_9H_{20} + oxygen $\longrightarrow$ _____

Activity Series of the Elements

▶ REVIEWING MAIN IDEAS

31. a. What is meant by the *activity* of an element?
  b. How does this description differ for metals and nonmetals?

32. a. What is an activity series of elements?
b. What is the basis for the ordering of the elements in the activity series?

33. What chemical principle is the basis for the activity series of metals?

PRACTICE PROBLEMS

34. Based on the activity series of metals and halogens, in **Figure 3.1**, which element within each pair is more likely to replace the other in a compound?
a. K and Na   **e.** Au and Ag
b. Al and Ni   **f.** Cl and I
c. Bi and Cr   **g.** Fe and Sr
d. Cl and F   **h.** I and F

35. Using the activity series in **Figure 3.1**, predict whether each of the possible reactions listed below will occur. For the reactions that will occur, write the products and balance the equation.
a. $Ni(s) + CuCl_2(aq) \longrightarrow$ _____
b. $Zn(s) + Pb(NO_3)_2(aq) \longrightarrow$ _____
c. $Cl_2(g) + KI(aq) \longrightarrow$ _____
d. $Cu(s) + FeSO_4(aq) \longrightarrow$ _____
e. $Ba(s) + H_2O(l) \longrightarrow$ _____

36. Use the activity series in **Figure 3.1** to predict whether each of the following synthesis reactions will occur, and write the chemical equations for those predicted to occur.
a. $Ca(s) + O_2(g) \longrightarrow$ _____
b. $Ni(s) + O_2(g) \longrightarrow$ _____
c. $Au(s) + O_2(g) \longrightarrow$ _____

Mixed Review

⏵ **REVIEWING MAIN IDEAS**

37. Ammonia reacts with oxygen to yield nitrogen and water.

$$4NH_3(g) + 3O_2(g) \longrightarrow 2N_2(g) + 6H_2O(l)$$

Given this chemical equation, as well as the number of moles of the reactant or product indicated below, determine the number of moles of all remaining reactants and products.
a. 3.0 mol O_2 **c.** 1.0 mol N_2
b. 8.0 mol NH_3 **d.** 0.40 mol H_2O

38. Complete the following synthesis reactions by writing both the word and chemical equation for each:
a. potassium + chlorine $\longrightarrow$ _____
b. hydrogen + iodine $\longrightarrow$ _____
c. magnesium + oxygen $\longrightarrow$ _____

39. Use the activity series in **Figure 3.1** to predict which metal—Sn, Mn, or Pt—would be the best choice as a container for an acid.

40. Aqueous sodium hydroxide is produced commercially by the electrolysis of aqueous sodium chloride. Hydrogen and chlorine gases are also produced. Write the balanced chemical equation for the production of sodium hydroxide. Include the physical states of the reactants and products.

41. Balance each of the following:
a. $Ca(OH)_2 + (NH_4)_2SO_4 \longrightarrow CaSO_4 + NH_3 + H_2O$
b. $C_2H_6 + O_2 \longrightarrow CO_2 + H_2O$
c. $Cu_2S + O_2 \longrightarrow Cu_2O + SO_2$
d. $Al + H_2SO_4 \longrightarrow Al_2(SO_4)_3 + H_2$

42. Use the activity series in **Figure 3.1** to predict whether each of the following reactions will occur, and write the balanced chemical equations for those predicted to occur.
a. $Al(s) + O_2(g) \longrightarrow$ _____
b. $Pb(s) + ZnCl_2(s) \longrightarrow$ _____

43. Complete and balance the equations for the following reactions, and identify the type of reaction that each equation represents.
a. $(NH_4)_2S(aq) + ZnCl_2(aq) \longrightarrow$ _____ $+ ZnS(s)$
b. $Al(s) + Pb(NO_3)_2(aq) \longrightarrow$ _____
c. $Ba(s) + H_2O(l) \longrightarrow$ _____
d. $Cl_2(g) + KBr(aq) \longrightarrow$
e. $NH_3(g) + O_2(g) \xrightarrow{\text{Pt}} NO(g) + H_2O(l)$
f. $H_2O(l) \longrightarrow H_2(g) + O_2(g)$

44. Write and balance each of the following equations, and then identify each by type.
a. copper + chlorine $\longrightarrow$ copper(II) chloride
b. calcium chlorate $\longrightarrow$
                calcium chloride + oxygen
c. lithium + water $\longrightarrow$
                lithium hydroxide + hydrogen
d. lead(II) carbonate $\longrightarrow$
                lead(II) oxide + carbon dioxide

45. How many moles of HCl can be made from 6.15 mol H_2 and an excess of Cl_2?

46. What product is missing in the following equation?

$$MgO + 2HCl \longrightarrow MgCl_2 + \underline{\qquad}$$

47. Balance the following equations:
a. $Pb(NO_3)_2(aq) + NaOH(aq) \longrightarrow$
$$Pb(OH)_2(s) + NaNO_3(aq)$$
b. $C_{12}H_{22}O_{11}(l) + O_2(g) \longrightarrow CO_2(g) + H_2O(l)$
c. $Al(OH)_3(s) + H_2SO_4(aq) \longrightarrow$
$$Al_2(SO_4)_3(aq) + H_2O(l)$$

CRITICAL THINKING

48. Inferring Relationships Activity series are prepared by comparing single-displacement reactions between metals. Based on observations, the metals can be ranked by their ability to react. However, reactivity can be explained by the ease with which atoms of metals lose electrons. Using information from the activity series, identify the locations in the periodic table of the most-reactive metals and the least-reactive metals. Using your knowledge of electron configurations and periodic trends, infer possible explanations for the metals' reactivity and position in the periodic table.

49. Analyzing Results Formulate an activity series for the hypothetical elements A, J, Q, and Z by using the following reaction information:
$$A + ZX \longrightarrow AX + Z$$
$$J + ZX \longrightarrow \text{no reaction}$$
$$Q + AX \longrightarrow QX + A$$

USING THE HANDBOOK

50. Find the common-reactions section for Group 1 metals in the *Elements Handbook* in Appendix A. Use this information to answer the following:
a. Write a balanced chemical equation for the formation of rubidium hydroxide from rubidium oxide.
b. Write a balanced chemical equation for the formation of cesium iodide.
c. Classify the reactions you wrote in (a) and (b).
d. Write word equations for the reactions you wrote in (a) and (b).

51. Find the common-reactions section for Group 13 in the *Elements Handbook* (Appendix A). Use this information to answer the following:
a. Write a balanced chemical equation for the formation of gallium bromide prepared from hydrobromic acid.
b. Write a balanced chemical equation for the formation of gallium oxide.
c. Classify the reactions you wrote in (a) and (b).
d. Write word equations for the reactions you wrote in (a) and (b).

RESEARCH AND WRITING

52. Trace the evolution of municipal water fluoridation. What advantages and disadvantages are associated with this practice?

53. Research how a soda-acid fire extinguisher works, and write the chemical equation for the reaction. Check your house and other structures for different types of fire extinguishers, and ask your local fire department to verify the effectiveness of each type of extinguisher.

ALTERNATIVE ASSESSMENT

54. Performance Assessment For one day, record situations that show evidence of a chemical change. Identify the reactants and the products, and determine whether there is proof of a chemical reaction. Classify each of the chemical reactions according to the common reaction types discussed in the chapter.

Standards-Based Assessment

Record your answers on a separate piece of paper.

MULTIPLE CHOICE

1 According to the law of conservation of mass, the total mass of the reacting substances is

A always more than the total mass of the products.
B always less than the total mass of the products.
C sometimes more and sometimes less than the total mass of the products.
D always equal to the total mass of the products.

2 To balance a chemical equation, you may adjust the

A coefficients.
B subscripts.
C formulas of the products.
D either the coefficients or the subscripts.

3 Which is the balanced chemical equation for the following formula equation: $(NH_4)_2S \rightarrow NH_3 + H_2S$?

A $2(NH_4)_2S \rightarrow 2NH_3 + H_2S_2$
B $2(NH_4)_2S \rightarrow 2NH_3 + H_2S$
C $(NH_4)_2S \rightarrow 2NH_3 + H_2S$
D $4(NH_4)_2S \rightarrow 2NH_3 + 2H_2S$

4 Determine the missing reactant for the following combustion reaction: $2\underline{\quad} + 15O_2 \rightarrow 14CO_2 + 6H_2O$.

A $C_{14}H_{12}$
B $C_{14}H_{12}O_4$
C C_7H_6
D $C_7H_6O_2$

5 Which of the following statements is true about the reaction $2F_2 + 2H_2O \rightarrow 4HF + O_2$?

A Two grams of O_2 are produced when 2 g of F_2 react with 2 g of H_2O.
B Two moles of HF are produced when 1 mol of F_2 reacts with 1 mol of H_2O.
C For every 2 mol O_2 produced, 6 mol HF are produced.
D For every 1 mol H_2O that reacts, 2 mol O_2 are produced.

6 Analyze the reaction of solid magnesium and water. Which pair of reactants and products in the table below represents the correct balanced equation for the reaction?

	Reactants	Products
1	$Mg(s) + H_2O(l)$	$Mg(OH)_2(aq)$
2	$Mg(s) + H_2O(l)$	$Mg(OH)_2(aq) + 2H_2(g)$
3	$Mg(s) + 2H_2O(l)$	$Mg(OH)_2(aq) + H_2(g)$
4	$Mg(s) + 2H_2O(l)$	$2Mg(OH)_2(aq) + 2H_2(g)$

A 1
B 2
C 3
D 4

7 A precipitation of iron(III) hydroxide is produced by reacting an aqueous solution of iron(III) chloride with an aqueous solution of sodium hydroxide. Which is the correct balanced chemical equation?

A $FeCl_3(aq) + 3NaOH(aq) \rightarrow Fe(OH)_3(s) + 3NaCl(s)$
B $3FeCl_3(aq) + 3NaOH(aq) \rightarrow 3Fe(OH)_3(s) + 3NaCl(s)$
C $3FeCl_3(aq) + NaOH(aq) \rightarrow Fe(OH)_3(s) + 3NaCl(s)$
D $FeCl_3(aq) + NaOH(aq) \rightarrow Fe(OH)_3(s) + NaCl(s)$

GRIDDED RESPONSE

8 Calcium hypochlorite, $Ca(OCl)_2$, is a bleaching agent produced from sodium hydroxide, calcium hydroxide, and chlorine. Sodium chloride and water are also produced in the reaction. What is the missing coefficient that will balance the chemical equation?

$\underline{\quad}NaOH + Ca(OH)_2 + 2Cl_2 \rightarrow Ca(OCl)_2 + 2NaCl + 2H_2O$

Test Tip
Focus on one question at a time unless you are asked to refer to previous answers.

CHAPTER 9
Stoichiometry

BIG IDEA
Reaction stoichiometry uses molar relationships to determine the amounts of unknown reactants or products from the amounts of known reactants or products.

ONLINE Chemistry
HMHScience.com

SECTION 1
Introduction to Stoichiometry

SECTION 2
Ideal Stoichiometric Calculations

SECTION 3
Limiting Reactants and Percentage Yield

ONLINE LABS
- Stoichiometry and Gravimetric Analysis

GO ONLINE

Why It Matters Video
HMHScience.com

Stoichiometry

Introduction to Stoichiometry

SECTION 1

Main Idea

▶ Ratios of substances in chemical reactions can be used as conversion factors.

Key Terms
composition stoichiometry
reaction stoichiometry
mole ratio

Much of our knowledge of chemistry is based on the careful quantitative analysis of substances involved in chemical reactions. **Composition stoichiometry deals with the mass relationships of elements in compounds. Reaction stoichiometry involves the mass relationships between reactants and products in a chemical reaction.** Reaction stoichiometry, the subject of this chapter, is based on chemical equations and the law of conservation of mass. All reaction stoichiometry calculations start with a balanced chemical equation. This equation gives the relative numbers of moles of reactants and products.

▶ MAIN IDEA

Ratios of substances in chemical reactions can be used as conversion factors.

The reaction stoichiometry problems in this chapter can be classified according to the information *given* in the problem and the information you are expected to find, the *unknown*. The *given* and the *unknown* may both be reactants, they may both be products, or one may be a reactant and the other a product. The masses are generally expressed in grams, but you will encounter both large-scale and micro-scale problems with other mass units, such as kg or mg. Stoichiometric problems are solved by using ratios from the balanced equation to convert the given quantity.

Problem Type 1: *Given* **and** *unknown* **quantities are amounts in moles.**

When you are given the amount of a substance in moles and asked to calculate the amount in moles of another substance in the chemical reaction, the general plan is

$$
\begin{array}{ccc}
\text{amount of} & & \text{amount of} \\
\textit{given}\ \text{substance (mol)} & \longrightarrow & \textit{unknown}\ \text{substance (mol)}
\end{array}
$$

Problem Type 2: *Given* **is an amount in moles, and** *unknown* **is a mass that is often expressed in grams.**

When you are given the amount in moles of one substance and asked to calculate the mass of another substance in the chemical reaction, the general plan is

$$
\begin{array}{ccccc}
\text{amount of} & & \text{amount of} & & \text{mass of} \\
\textit{given}\ \text{substance} & \longrightarrow & \textit{unknown}\ \text{substance} & \longrightarrow & \textit{unknown}\ \text{substance} \\
\text{(mol)} & & \text{(mol)} & & \text{(g)}
\end{array}
$$

Problem Type 3: *Given* **is a mass in grams, and** *unknown* **is an amount in moles.**

When you are given the mass of one substance and asked to calculate the amount in moles of another substance in the chemical reaction, the general plan is

mass of *given* substance (g) $\longrightarrow$ amount of *given* substance (mol) $\longrightarrow$ amount of *unknown* substance (mol)

Problem Type 4: *Given* **is a mass in grams, and** *unknown* **is a mass in grams.**

When you are given the mass of one substance and asked to calculate the mass of another substance in the chemical reaction, the general plan is

mass of *given* substance (g) $\longrightarrow$ amount of *given* substance (mol) $\longrightarrow$ amount of *unknown* substance (mol) $\longrightarrow$ mass of *unknown* substance (g)

Mole Ratio

Solving any reaction stoichiometry problem requires the use of a mole ratio to convert from moles or grams of one substance in a reaction to moles or grams of another substance. **A mole ratio is a conversion factor that relates the amounts in moles of any two substances involved in a chemical reaction.** This information is obtained directly from the balanced chemical equation. Consider, for example, the chemical equation for the electrolysis of melted aluminum oxide to produce aluminum and oxygen.

$$2Al_2O_3(l) \longrightarrow 4Al(s) + 3O_2(g)$$

Recall from your study of equations and reactions that the coefficients in a chemical equation satisfy the law of conservation of matter and represent the relative amounts in moles of reactants and products. Therefore, 2 mol of aluminum oxide decomposes to produce 4 mol of aluminum and 3 mol of oxygen gas. These relationships can be expressed in the following mole ratios.

$$\frac{2 \text{ mol Al}_2O_3}{4 \text{ mol Al}} \quad \text{or} \quad \frac{4 \text{ mol Al}}{2 \text{ mol Al}_2O_3}$$

$$\frac{2 \text{ mol Al}_2O_3}{3 \text{ mol O}_2} \quad \text{or} \quad \frac{3 \text{ mol O}_2}{2 \text{ mol Al}_2O_3}$$

$$\frac{4 \text{ mol Al}}{3 \text{ mol O}_2} \quad \text{or} \quad \frac{3 \text{ mol O}_2}{4 \text{ mol Al}}$$

For the decomposition of aluminum oxide, the appropriate mole ratio is used as a conversion factor to convert a given amount in moles of one substance to the corresponding amount in moles of another substance.

To determine the amount in moles of aluminum that can be produced from 13.0 mol of aluminum oxide, the mole ratio needed is that of Al to Al_2O_3.

$$13.0 \text{ mol Al}_2\text{O}_3 \times \frac{4 \text{ mol Al}}{2 \text{ mol Al}_2\text{O}_3} = 26.0 \text{ mol Al}$$

Mole ratios are exact, so they do not limit the number of significant figures in a calculation. The number of significant figures in the answer is therefore determined only by the number of significant figures of any measured quantities in a particular problem.

Molar Mass

Recall that the molar mass is the mass, in grams, of one mole of a substance. The molar mass is the conversion factor that relates the mass of a substance to the amount in moles of that substance. To solve reaction stoichiometry problems, you will need to determine molar masses using the periodic table.

Returning to the previous example, the decomposition of aluminum oxide, the rounded masses from the periodic table are the following.

$$1 \text{ mol Al}_2\text{O}_3 = 101.96 \text{ g} \qquad 1 \text{ mol Al} = 26.98 \text{ g} \qquad 1 \text{ mol O}_2 = 32.00 \text{ g}$$

These molar masses can be expressed by the following conversion factors.

$$\frac{101.96 \text{ g Al}_2\text{O}_3}{1 \text{ mol Al}_2\text{O}_3} \quad \text{or} \quad \frac{1 \text{ mol Al}_2\text{O}_3}{101.96 \text{ g Al}_2\text{O}_3}$$

$$\frac{26.98 \text{ g Al}}{1 \text{ mol Al}} \quad \text{or} \quad \frac{1 \text{ mol Al}}{26.98 \text{ g Al}}$$

$$\frac{32.00 \text{ g O}_2}{1 \text{ mol O}_2} \quad \text{or} \quad \frac{1 \text{ mol O}_2}{32.00 \text{ g O}_2}$$

To find the number of grams of aluminum equivalent to 26.0 mol of aluminum, the calculation would be as follows.

$$26.0 \text{ mol Al} \times \frac{26.98 \text{ g Al}}{1 \text{ mol Al}} = 701 \text{ g Al}$$

✔ SECTION 1 FORMATIVE ASSESSMENT

▶ Reviewing Main Ideas

1. What is stoichiometry?

2. For each equation, write all possible mole ratios.
   a. $2HgO(s) \longrightarrow 2Hg(l) + O_2(g)$
   b. $4NH_3(g) + 6NO(g) \longrightarrow 5N_2(g) + 6H_2O(l)$

3. How is a mole ratio used in stoichiometry?

✔ Critical Thinking

4. **RELATING IDEAS** What step must be performed before any stoichiometry problem is solved? Explain.

The Case of Combustion

P eople throughout history have transformed substances by burning them in air. Yet at the dawn of the scientific revolution, very little was known about the process of combustion. In attempting to explain this common phenomenon, chemists of the 18th century developed one of the first universally accepted theories in their field. But as one man would show, scientific theories do not always stand the test of time.

Changing Attitudes

Shunning the ancient Greek approach of logical argument based on untested premises, investigators of the 17th century began to understand the laws of nature by observing, measuring, and performing experiments on the world around them. However, this scientific method was incorporated into chemistry slowly. Although early chemists experimented extensively, most considered measurement to be unimportant. This viewpoint hindered the progress of chemistry for nearly a century.

A Flawed Theory

By 1700, combustion was assumed to be the decomposition of a material into simpler substances. People saw burning substances emitting smoke and energy as heat and light. To account for this emission, scientists proposed a theory that combustion depended on the emission of a substance called *phlogiston* (Greek, meaning "burned"), which appeared as a combination of energy as heat and light while the material was burning but which could not be detected beforehand.

The phlogiston theory was used to explain many chemical observations of the day. For example, a lit candle under a glass jar burned until the surrounding air became saturated with phlogiston, at which time the flame died because the air inside could not absorb more phlogiston.

A New Phase of Study

By the 1770s, the phlogiston theory had gained universal acceptance. At that time, chemists also began to experiment with air, which was generally believed to be an element.

Antoine Laurent Lavoisier helped establish chemistry as a science.

In 1772, when Daniel Rutherford found that a mouse kept in a closed container soon died, he explained the results based on the phlogiston theory. Like a burning candle, the mouse emitted phlogiston; when the air could hold no more phlogiston, the mouse died. Thus, Rutherford figured that the air in the container had become "phlogisticated air."

A couple of years later, Joseph Priestley obtained a reddish powder when he heated mercury in the air. He assumed that the powder was mercury devoid of phlogiston. But when he heated the powder, an unexpected result occurred: Metallic mercury, along with a gas that allowed a candle to burn, formed. Following the phlogiston theory, he believed this gas that supports combustion to be "dephlogisticated air."

©Stefano Bianchetti/Corbis

Nice Try, But . . .

Antoine Laurent Lavoisier was a meticulous scientist. He realized that Rutherford and Priestley had carefully observed and described their experiments but had not measured the mass of anything. Unlike his colleagues, Lavoisier knew the importance of using a balance. He measured the masses of reactants and products and compared them. He observed that the total mass of the reactants equaled the total mass of the products. Based on these observations, which supported what would become known as the *law of conservation of mass*, Lavoisier endeavored to explain the results of Rutherford and Priestley.

Lavoisier put some tin in a closed vessel and weighed the entire system. He then burned the tin. When he opened the vessel, air rushed into it as if something had been *removed* from the air in the vessel during combustion. He then measured the mass of the burned metal and observed that this mass was greater than the mass of the original tin. Curiously, this increase in mass equaled the mass of the air that had rushed into the vessel. To Lavoisier, this change in mass did not support the idea of phlogiston escaping the burning material. Instead, it indicated that during combustion, part of the air reacted with the tin.

After obtaining similar results by using various substances, Lavoisier concluded that air was not an element but a mixture composed principally of two gases, Priestley's "dephlogisticated air" (which Lavoisier renamed *oxygen*) and Rutherford's "phlogisticated air" (which was mostly nitrogen but had traces of other nonflammable atmospheric gases). When a substance burned, it chemically combined with oxygen, resulting in a product Lavoisier named an *oxide*. Lavoisier's theory of combustion persists today. He used the name *oxygen* because he thought that all acids contained oxygen. *Oxygen* means "acid former."

The Father of Chemistry

By emphasizing the importance of quantitative analysis, Lavoisier helped establish chemistry as a science. His work on combustion laid to rest the phlogiston theory and the theory that air is an element. He also explained why hydrogen burned in oxygen to form water, or hydrogen oxide. He later published one of the first chemistry textbooks, which established a common naming system of compounds and elements and helped unify chemistry worldwide. These accomplishments earned Lavoisier the reputation of being the father of chemistry.

Questions

1. Why does the mass of tin increase when tin is heated in air?

2. What was the composition of Priestley's "dephlogisticated air" and Rutherford's "phlogisticated air"?

TABLE OF SIMPLE SUBSTANCES
Simple substances belonging to all the kingdoms of nature, which may be considered as the elements of bodies.

New Names	Correspondent old Names
Light	Light.
Caloric	Heat. Principle or element of heat. Fire. Igneous fluid. Matter of fire and of heat.
Oxygen	Dephlogisticated air. Empyreal air. Vital air, or Base of vital air.
Azote	Phlogisticated air or gas. Mephitis, or its base.
Hydrogen	Inflammable air or gas, or the base of inflammable air.

Lavoisier's concept of simple substances was published in his book Elements of Chemistry *in 1789.*

Main Ideas

> Balanced equations give amounts of reactants and products under ideal conditions.

> Mole-to-gram calculations require two conversion factors.

> Gram-to-mole conversions require the molar mass of the given substance and the mole ratio.

> Mass-to-mass calculations use the mole ratio and the molar masses of the given and unknown substances.

Ideal Stoichiometric Calculations

A balanced chemical equation is the key step in all stoichiometric calculations, because the mole ratio is obtained directly from it. Solving any reaction stoichiometry problem must begin with a balanced equation.

Chemical equations help us plan the amounts of reactants to use in a chemical reaction without having to run the reaction in the laboratory. The reaction stoichiometry calculations described in this chapter are theoretical. They tell us the amounts of reactants and products for a given chemical reaction under *ideal conditions*, in which all reactants are completely converted into products. However, many reactions do not proceed such that all reactants are completely converted into products. Theoretical stoichiometric calculations allow us to determine the maximum amount of product that could be obtained in a reaction when the reactants are not pure or when byproducts are formed in addition to the expected products.

Solving stoichiometric problems requires practice. Practice by working the sample problems in the rest of this chapter. Using a logical, systematic approach will help you successfully solve these problems.

> **MAIN IDEA**

Balanced equations give amounts of reactants and products under ideal conditions.

In these stoichiometric problems, you are asked to calculate the amount in moles of one substance that will react with or be produced from the given amount in moles of another substance. The plan for a simple mole conversion problem is

$$\text{amount of } \textit{given} \text{ substance (mol)} \longrightarrow \text{amount of } \textit{unknown} \text{ substance (mol)}$$

This plan requires one conversion factor—the stoichiometric mole ratio of the *unknown* substance to the *given* substance from the balanced equation. To solve this type of problem, simply multiply the *known* quantity by the appropriate conversion factor (see **Figure 2.1**).

$$\textit{given} \text{ quantity} \times \text{conversion factor} = \textit{unknown} \text{ quantity}$$

FIGURE 2.1

Mole-to-Mole Conversions This is a solution plan for problems in which the given and unknown quantities are expressed in moles.

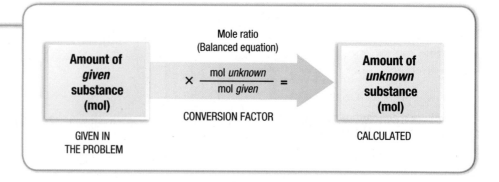

Stoichiometric Calculations Using Mole Ratios

GO ONLINE

Solve It! Cards
HMHScience.com

Learn It! Video
HMHScience.com

Sample Problem A In a spacecraft, the carbon dioxide exhaled by astronauts can be removed by its reaction with lithium hydroxide, LiOH, according to the following chemical equation.

$$CO_2(g) + 2LiOH(s) \longrightarrow Li_2CO_3(s) + H_2O(l)$$

How many moles of lithium hydroxide are required to react with 20 mol CO_2, the average amount exhaled by a person each day?

① ANALYZE

Given: amount of CO_2 = 20 mol

Unknown: amount of LiOH (mol)

② PLAN

amount of CO_2 (mol) $\longrightarrow$ amount of LiOH (mol)

This problem requires one conversion factor—the mole ratio of LiOH to CO_2. The mole ratio is obtained from the balanced chemical equation. Because you are given moles of CO_2, select a mole ratio that will cancel mol CO_2 and give you mol LiOH in your final answer. The correct ratio has the following units.

$$\frac{mol\ LiOH}{mol\ CO_2}$$

This ratio cancels mol CO_2 and gives the units mol LiOH in the answer.

$$mol\ CO_2 \times \overset{mol\ ratio}{\frac{mol\ LiOH}{mol\ CO_2}} = mol\ LiOH$$

③ SOLVE

Substitute the values in the equation in step 2, and compute the answer.

$$20\ \cancel{mol\ CO_2} \times \frac{2\ mol\ LiOH}{1\ \cancel{mol\ CO_2}} = 40\ mol\ LiOH$$

④ CHECK YOUR WORK

The answer is written correctly with one significant figure to match the number of significant figures in the given 20 mol CO_2, and the units cancel to leave mol LiOH, which is the unknown. The balanced equation shows that twice the amount in moles of LiOH reacts with CO_2. Therefore, the answer should be $2 \times 20 = 40$.

Practice Answers in Appendix E

1. Ammonia, NH_3, is widely used as a fertilizer and as an ingredient in many household cleaners. How many moles of ammonia are produced when 6 mol of hydrogen gas reacts with an excess of nitrogen gas?

2. The decomposition of potassium chlorate, $KClO_3$, into KCl and O_2 is used as a source of oxygen in the laboratory. How many moles of potassium chlorate are needed to produce 15 mol of oxygen gas?

MAIN IDEA

Mole-to-gram calculations require two conversion factors.

In these stoichiometric calculations, you are asked to calculate the mass (usually in grams) of a substance that will react with or be produced from a given amount in moles of a second substance. The plan for these mole-to-gram conversions is

| amount of given substance (mol) | $\longrightarrow$ | amount of unknown substance (mol) | $\longrightarrow$ | mass of unknown substance (g) |

This plan requires two conversion factors—the mole ratio of the *unknown* substance to the *given* substance and the molar mass of the *unknown* substance for the mass conversion. To solve this kind of problem, you simply multiply the known quantity, which is the amount in moles, by the appropriate conversion factors (see **Figure 2.2** on the next page).

(see **Figure 2.2** on the next page).

✔ **CHECK FOR UNDERSTANDING**

Explain Why might it be important for a chemist to be able to calculate, in advance, how much product a chemical reaction would yield?

Stoichiometric Calculations Using Mole Ratios

Sample Problem B In photosynthesis, plants use energy from the sun to produce glucose, $C_6H_{12}O_6$, and oxygen from the reaction of carbon dioxide and water. What mass, in grams, of glucose is produced when 3.00 mol of water reacts with carbon dioxide?

① ANALYZE

Given: amount of H_2O = 3.00 mol

Unknown: mass of $C_6H_{12}O_6$ produced (g)

② PLAN

You must start with a balanced equation.

$$6CO_2(g) + 6H_2O(l) \longrightarrow C_6H_{12}O_6(s) + 6O_2(g)$$

Given the amount in mol of H_2O, you need to get the mass of $C_6H_{12}O_6$ in grams. Two conversion factors are needed—the mole ratio of $C_6H_{12}O_6$ to H_2O and the molar mass of $C_6H_{12}O_6$.

$$\text{mol } H_2O \times \underbrace{\frac{\text{mol } C_6H_{12}O_6}{\text{mol } H_2O}}_{\text{mol ratio}} \times \underbrace{\frac{\text{g } C_6H_{12}O_6}{\text{mol } C_6H_{12}O_6}}_{\text{molar mass factor}} = \text{g } C_6H_{12}O_6$$

③ SOLVE

Use the periodic table to compute the molar mass of $C_6H_{12}O_6$.

$$C_6H_{12}O_6 = 180.18 \text{ g/mol}$$

$$3.00 \text{ mol } H_2O \times \frac{1 \text{ mol } C_6H_{12}O_6}{6 \text{ mol } H_2O} \times \frac{180.18 \text{ g } C_6H_{12}O_6}{1 \text{ mol } C_6H_{12}O_6} = 90.1 \text{ g } C_6H_{12}O_6$$

④ CHECK YOUR WORK

The answer is correctly rounded to three significant figures, to match those in 3.00 mol H_2O. The units cancel in the problem, leaving g $C_6H_{12}O_6$ as the units for the answer, which matches the unknown. The answer is reasonable because it is one-half of 180.

FIGURE 2.2

Mole-to-Gram Conversions This is a solution plan for problems in which the given quantity is expressed in moles and the unknown quantity is expressed in grams.

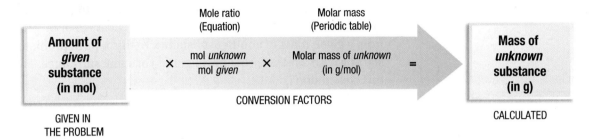

Stoichiometric Calculations Using Mole Ratios

Sample Problem C What mass of carbon dioxide, in grams, is needed to react with 3.00 mol H_2O in the photosynthetic reaction described in Sample Problem B?

1 ANALYZE

Given: amount of H_2O = 3.00 mol

Unknown: mass of CO_2 (g)

2 PLAN

The chemical equation from Sample Problem B is

$$6CO_2(g) + 6H_2O(l) \longrightarrow C_6H_{12}O_6(s) + 6O_2(g).$$

Two conversion factors are needed—the mole ratio of CO_2 to H_2O and the molar mass factor of CO_2.

3 SOLVE

$$\text{mol } H_2O \times \underset{\text{mol ratio}}{\frac{\text{mol } CO_2}{\text{mol } H_2O}} \times \underset{\text{molar mass factor}}{\frac{\text{g } CO_2}{\text{mol } CO_2}} = \text{g } CO_2$$

Use the periodic table to compute the molar mass of CO_2.

$$CO_2 = 44.01 \text{ g/mol}$$

4 CHECK YOUR WORK

$$3.00 \text{ mol } H_2O \times \frac{6 \text{ mol } CO_2}{6 \text{ mol } H_2O} \times \frac{44.01 \text{ g } CO_2}{1 \text{ mol } CO_2} = 132 \text{ g } CO_2$$

The answer is rounded correctly to three significant figures to match those in 3.00 mol H_2O. The units cancel to leave g CO_2, which is the unknown. The answer is close to an estimate of 120, which is 3 × 40.

Practice   Answers in Appendix E

1. When magnesium burns in air, it combines with oxygen to form magnesium oxide according to the following equation.

$$2Mg(s) + O_2(g) \longrightarrow 2MgO(s)$$

What mass in grams of magnesium oxide is produced from 2.00 mol of magnesium?

2. What mass in grams of glucose can be produced from a photosynthesis reaction that occurs using 10 mol CO_2?

$$6CO_2(g) + 6H_2O(l) \longrightarrow C_6H_{12}O_6(aq) + 6O_2(g)$$

MAIN IDEA

Gram-to-mole conversions require the molar mass of the given substance and the mole ratio.

In these stoichiometric calculations, you are asked to calculate the amount in moles of one substance that will react with or be produced from a given mass of another substance. In this type of problem, you are starting with a mass (probably in grams) of some substance. The plan for this conversion is

$$
\begin{array}{ccc}
\text{mass of} & \text{amount of} & \text{amount of} \\
\textit{given}\text{ substance} \longrightarrow & \textit{given}\text{ substance} \longrightarrow & \textit{unknown}\text{ substance} \\
\text{(g)} & \text{(mol)} & \text{(mol)}
\end{array}
$$

This route requires two additional pieces of data: the molar mass of the *given* substance and the mole ratio. The molar mass is determined by using masses from the periodic table. We will follow a procedure much like the one used previously by using the units of the molar mass conversion factor to guide our mathematical operations. Because the known quantity is a mass, the conversion factor will need to be 1 mol divided by molar mass. This conversion factor cancels units of grams and leaves units of moles (see **Figure 2.3** below).

You should take time at this point to look at each type of stoichiometric conversion and make note that in every type, you must begin with a correctly balanced chemical equation. It is important to remember that without a balanced equation, you will not have an accurate molar ratio and will not be able to calculate the correct molar mass to use in your conversions.

If you are still struggling with balancing equations, it is highly recommended that you continue to practice the process. The skill of balancing chemical equations will be used continually throughout the remainder of the course.

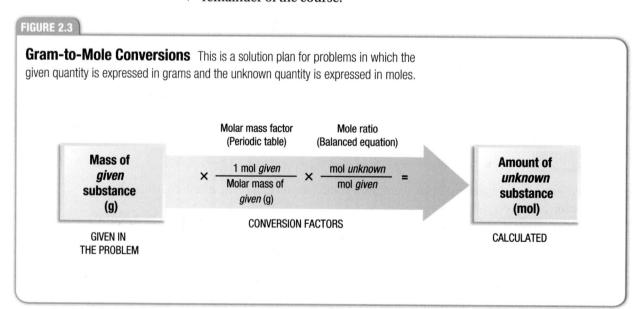

FIGURE 2.3

Gram-to-Mole Conversions This is a solution plan for problems in which the given quantity is expressed in grams and the unknown quantity is expressed in moles.

298   Chapter 9

Stoichiometric Calculations Using Mole Ratios

Sample Problem D The first step in the industrial manufacture of nitric acid is the catalytic oxidation of ammonia.

$$NH_3(g) + O_2(g) \longrightarrow NO(g) + H_2O(g) \text{ (unbalanced)}$$

The reaction is run using 824 g NH_3 and excess oxygen.

a. How many moles of NO are formed?
b. How many moles of H_2O are formed?

❶ ANALYZE

Given: mass of NH_3 = 824 g

Unknown: **a.** amount of NO produced (mol)

              b. amount of H_2O produced (mol)

❷ PLAN

First, write the balanced chemical equation.

$$4NH_3(g) + 5O_2(g) \longrightarrow 4NO(g) + 6H_2O(g)$$

Two conversion factors are needed to solve part (a)—the molar mass factor for NH_3 and the mole ratio of NO to NH_3. Part (b) starts with the same conversion factor as part (a), but then the mole ratio of H_2O to NH_3 is used to convert to the amount in moles of H_2O. The first conversion factor in each part is the molar mass factor of NH_3.

$$\textbf{a.} \quad g\,NH_3 \times \underset{\text{molar mass factor}}{\frac{1\,\text{mol}\,NH_3}{g\,NH_3}} \times \underset{\text{mol ratio}}{\frac{\text{mol}\,NO}{\text{mol}\,NH_3}} = \text{mol}\,NO$$

$$\textbf{b.} \quad g\,NH_3 \times \underset{\text{molar mass factor}}{\frac{1\,\text{mol}\,NH_3}{g\,NH_3}} \times \underset{\text{mol ratio}}{\frac{\text{mol}\,H_2O}{\text{mol}\,NH_3}} = \text{mol}\,H_2O$$

❸ SOLVE

Use the periodic table to compute the molar mass of NH_3.

$$1\,\text{mol}\,NH_3 = 17.04\,\text{g/mol}$$

$$\textbf{a.} \quad 824\,g\,NH_3 \times \frac{1\,\text{mol}\,NH_3}{17.04\,g\,NH_3} \times \frac{4\,\text{mol}\,NO}{4\,\text{mol}\,NH_3} = 48.4\,\text{mol}\,NO$$

$$\textbf{b.} \quad 824\,g\,NH_3 \times \frac{1\,\text{mol}\,NH_3}{17.04\,g\,NH_3} \times \frac{6\,\text{mol}\,H_2O}{4\,\text{mol}\,NH_3} = 72.5\,\text{mol}\,H_2O$$

❹ CHECK YOUR WORK

The answers are correctly given to three significant figures. The units cancel in the two problems to leave mol NO and mol H_2O, respectively, which are the unknowns.

Practice   Answers in Appendix E

Oxygen was discovered by Joseph Priestley in 1774 when he heated mercury(II) oxide to decompose it to form its constituent elements.

1. How many moles of mercury(II) oxide, HgO, are needed to produce 125 g of oxygen, O_2?
2. How many moles of mercury are produced?

FIGURE 2.4

Mass-to-Mass Conversions This is a solution plan for problems in which the given quantity is expressed in grams and the unknown quantity is also expressed in grams.

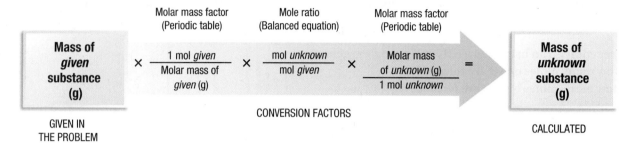

GIVEN IN THE PROBLEM · CONVERSION FACTORS · CALCULATED

> **MAIN IDEA**

Mass-to-mass calculations use the mole ratio and the molar masses of the given and unknown substances.

Mass-mass calculations are more practical than other mole calculations you have studied. You can never measure moles directly. You are generally required to calculate the amount in moles of a substance from its mass, which you can measure in the lab. Mass-mass problems can be viewed as the combination of the other types of problems. The plan for solving mass-mass problems is

mass of *given* substance (g)	$\longrightarrow$	amount of *given* substance (mol)	$\longrightarrow$	amount of *unknown* substance (mol)	$\longrightarrow$	mass of *unknown* substance (g)

Three additional pieces of data are needed to solve mass-mass problems: the molar mass of the *given* substance, the mole ratio, and the molar mass of the *unknown* substance (see **Figure 2.4** above).

GO ONLINE

 Solve It! Cards
HMHScience.com

 SOLUTION TUTOR
HMHScience.com

Stoichiometric Calculations Using Mole Ratios

Sample Problem E Tin(II) fluoride, SnF_2, is used in some toothpastes. It is made by the reaction of tin with hydrogen fluoride according to the following equation.

$$Sn(s) + 2HF(g) \longrightarrow SnF_2(s) + H_2(g)$$

How many grams of SnF_2 are produced from the reaction of 30.00 g HF with Sn?

1 ANALYZE

Given: amount of HF = 30.00 g

Unknown: mass of SnF_2 produced (g)

2 PLAN

The conversion factors needed are the molar masses of HF and SnF_2 and the mole ratio of SnF_2 to HF.

$$g\,HF \times \underset{\text{molar mass factor}}{\frac{mol\,HF}{g\,HF}} \times \underset{\text{mol ratio}}{\frac{mol\,SnF_2}{mol\,HF}} \times \underset{\text{molar mass factor}}{\frac{g\,SnF_2}{mol\,SnF_2}} = g\,SnF_2$$

Continued

Stoichiometric Calculations Using Mole Ratios (continued)

❸ SOLVE

Use the periodic table to compute the molar masses of HF and SnF_2.

$$1 \text{ mol HF} = 20.01 \text{ g}$$
$$1 \text{ mol SnF}_2 = 156.71 \text{ g}$$

$$30.00 \text{ g HF} \times \frac{1 \text{ mol HF}}{20.01 \text{ g HF}} \times \frac{1 \text{ mol SnF}_2}{2 \text{ mol HF}} \times \frac{156.71 \text{ g SnF}_2}{1 \text{ mol SnF}_2} = 117.5 \text{ g SnF}_2$$

❹ CHECK YOUR WORK

The answer is correctly rounded to four significant figures. The units cancel to leave g SnF_2, which matches the unknown. The answer is close to an estimated value of 120.

Practice   Answers in Appendix E

1. Laughing gas (nitrous oxide, N_2O) is sometimes used as an anesthetic in dentistry. It is produced when ammonium nitrate is decomposed according to the following reaction.

$$NH_4NO_3(s) \longrightarrow N_2O(g) + 2H_2O(l)$$

   a. How many grams of NH_4NO_3 are required to produce 33.0 g N_2O?
   b. How many grams of water are produced in this reaction?

2. When copper metal is added to silver nitrate in solution, silver metal and copper(II) nitrate are produced. What mass of silver is produced from 100. g Cu?

3. What mass of aluminum is produced by the decomposition of 5.0 kg Al_2O_3?

 SECTION 2 **FORMATIVE ASSESSMENT**

▶ **Reviewing Main Ideas**

1. Balance the following equation. Then, given the moles of reactant or product below, determine the corresponding amount in moles of each of the other reactants and products.

$$NH_3 + O_2 \longrightarrow N_2 + H_2O$$

   a. 4 mol NH_3 b. 4 mol N_2 c. 4.5 mol O_2

2. One reaction that produces hydrogen gas can be represented by the following unbalanced chemical equation:

$$Mg(s) + HCl(aq) \longrightarrow MgCl_2(aq) + H_2(g)$$

   a. What mass of HCl is consumed by the reaction of 2.50 moles of magnesium?

   b. What mass of each product is produced in part (a)?

3. Acetylene gas, C_2H_2, is produced as a result of the following reaction:

$$CaC_2(s) + 2H_2O(l) \longrightarrow C_2H_2(g) + Ca(OH)_2(aq)$$

   a. If 32.0 g CaC_2 is consumed in this reaction, how many moles of H_2O are needed?

   b. How many moles of each product would form?

4. When sodium chloride reacts with silver nitrate, silver chloride precipitates. What mass of AgCl is produced from 75.0 g $AgNO_3$?

✔ **Critical Thinking**

5. **RELATING IDEAS** Carbon and oxygen react to form carbon monoxide: $2C + O_2 \longrightarrow 2CO$. What masses of carbon and oxygen are needed to make 56.0 g CO? Which law does this illustrate?

SECTION 3

Main Ideas

▶ One reactant limits the product of a reaction.

▶ Comparing the actual and theoretical yields helps chemists determine the reaction's efficiency.

Limiting Reactants and Percentage Yield

Key Terms

limiting reactant   theoretical yield   percentage yield
excess reactant   actual yield

In the laboratory, a reaction is rarely carried out with exactly the required amount of each of the reactants. In many cases, one or more reactants are present in excess; that is, there is more than the exact amount required to react.

▶ **MAIN IDEA**

One reactant limits the product of a reaction.

Once one of the reactants is used up, no more product can be formed. The substance that is completely used up first in a reaction is called the limiting reactant. **The limiting reactant is the reactant that limits the amount of the other reactant that can combine and the amount of product that can form in a chemical reaction. The substance that is not used up completely in a reaction is called the excess reactant.** A limiting reactant may also be referred to as a *limiting reagent*.

Consider the reaction between carbon and oxygen:

$$C(s) + O_2(g) \longrightarrow CO_2(g)$$

According to the equation, one mole of carbon reacts with one mole of oxygen to form one mole of carbon dioxide. Suppose you could mix 5 mol C with 10 mol O_2 and allow the reaction to take place. **Figure 3.1** shows that there is more oxygen than is needed to react with the carbon. Carbon is the limiting reactant in this situation, and it limits the amount of CO_2 that is formed. Oxygen is the excess reactant, and 5 mol O_2 will be left over at the end of the reaction.

GO ONLINE

Animated Chemistry

HMHScience.com

Limiting Reactants

FIGURE 3.1

Limiting Reactants Carbon and oxygen always react in the same molar ratio to form carbon dioxide.

✔ **CRITICAL THINKING**

Explain Which substance is the limiting reactant in this chemical reaction? Explain your answer.

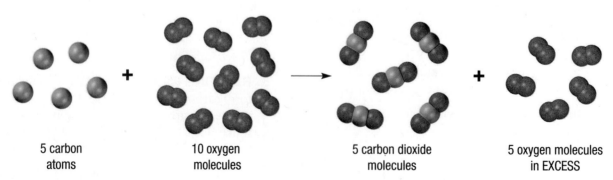

5 carbon atoms   +   10 oxygen molecules   →   5 carbon dioxide molecules   +   5 oxygen molecules in EXCESS

GO ONLINE

Solve It! Cards
HMHScience.com

Limiting Reactant

Sample Problem F **Calcium hydroxide, used to neutralize acid spills, reacts with hydrochloric acid according to the following equation:**

$$Ca(OH)_2 + 2HCl \longrightarrow CaCl_2 + 2H_2O$$

If you have spilled 6.3 mol of HCl and put 2.8 mol of $Ca(OH)_2$ on it, which substance is the limiting reactant?

1 ANALYZE

Given: amount of reactant $Ca(OH)_2$ = 2.8 mol
amount of reactant HCl = 6.3 mol

Unknown: limiting reactant

2 PLAN

Choose one of the reactants, in this case $Ca(OH)_2$. Use the mole ratio between the two reactants to compute the amount of the other reactant that would be needed to react with it. Compare that amount with the amount available.

$$\overset{\text{given}}{\text{mol } Ca(OH)_2} \times \overset{\text{mole ratio}}{\frac{2 \text{ mol HCl}}{1 \text{ mol } Ca(OH)_2}} = \text{mol HCl needed}$$

3 SOLVE

$$2.8 \text{ mol } Ca(OH)_2 \times \frac{2 \text{ mol HCl}}{1 \text{ mol } Ca(OH)_2} = 5.6 \text{ mol HCl needed}$$

The solution shows that more HCl (6.3 mol) is available than is needed (5.6 mol) to react with the 2.8 mol $Ca(OH)_2$ available. Therefore, HCl is present in excess, making $Ca(OH)_2$ the limiting reactant.

4 CHECK YOUR WORK

From the balanced equation, you can see that the reaction requires two times the number of moles of HCl as it does moles of $Ca(OH)_2$. Because the molar amount of HCl that you have, 6.3 mol, is more than is needed to react with 2.8 mol of $Ca(OH)_2$, the calculations show that $Ca(OH)_2$ is the limiting reactant.

Practice

1. Use the following equation for the oxidation of aluminum in the following problems.

$$4Al + 3O_2 \longrightarrow 2Al_2O_3$$

a. Which reactant is limiting if 0.32 mol Al and 0.26 mol O_2 are available?
b. If 3.17 g of Al and 2.55 g of O_2 are available, which reactant is limiting?
c. How many moles of Al_2O_3 are formed from the reaction of 6.38×10^{-3} mol of O_2 and 9.15×10^{-3} mol of Al?

Sample Problem G The black oxide of iron, Fe_3O_4, occurs in nature as the mineral magnetite. This substance can also be made in the laboratory by the reaction between red-hot iron and steam according to the following equation.

$$3Fe(s) + 4H_2O(g) \longrightarrow Fe_3O_4(s) + 4H_2(g)$$

a. When 36.0 g H_2O is mixed with 67.0 g Fe, which is the limiting reactant?
b. What mass in grams of black iron oxide is produced?
c. What mass in grams of excess reactant remains when the reaction is completed?

① ANALYZE

Given: mass of H_2O = 36.0 g
mass of Fe = 67.0 g

Unknown: limiting reactant

mass of Fe_3O_4, in grams

mass of excess reactant remaining

② PLAN

a. First, convert both given masses in grams to amounts in moles. Then, calculate the number of moles of one of the products. Because the problem asks for the mass of Fe_3O_4 formed, we will calculate moles of Fe_3O_4. The reactant yielding the lesser number of moles of product is the limiting reactant.

$$g\ Fe \times \overset{\text{molar mass factor}}{\frac{mol\ Fe}{g\ Fe}} \times \overset{\text{mol ratio}}{\frac{mol\ Fe_3O_4}{mol\ Fe}} = mol\ Fe_3O_4$$

$$g\ H_2O \times \overset{\text{molar mass factor}}{\frac{mol\ H_2O}{g\ H_2O}} \times \overset{\text{mol ratio}}{\frac{mol\ Fe_3O_4}{mol\ H_2O}} = mol\ Fe_3O_4$$

b. To find the maximum mass of Fe_3O_4 that can be produced, we must use the amount of Fe_3O_4 in moles from the limiting reactant in a simple stoichiometric problem.

$$mole\ Fe_3O_4\ \text{from limiting reactant} \times \overset{\text{molar mass factor}}{\frac{g\ Fe_3O_4}{mol\ Fe_3O_4}} = g\ Fe_3O_4\ produced$$

c. To find the amount of excess reactant remaining, we must first determine the amount of the excess reactant that is consumed. The calculated moles of the product (from the limiting reactant) is used to determine the amount of excess reactant that is consumed.

$$mol\ product \times \frac{mol\ excess\ reactant}{mol\ product} \times$$

$$\frac{g\ excess\ reactant}{mol\ excess\ reactant} = g\ excess\ reactant\ consumed$$

The amount of excess reactant remaining can then be found by subtracting the amount consumed from the amount originally present.

original g excess reactant − g excess reactant consumed
$$= g\ excess\ reactant\ remaining$$

Continued

Limiting Reactant (continued)

③ SOLVE

a. Use the periodic table to determine the molar masses of H_2O, Fe, and Fe_3O_4. Then, determine how many mol Fe_3O_4 can be produced from each reactant.

1 mol H_2O = 18.02 g

1 mol Fe = 55.85 g

1 mol Fe_3O_4 = 231.55 g

$$67.0 \text{ g Fe} \times \frac{1 \text{ mol Fe}}{55.85 \text{ g Fe}} \times \frac{1 \text{ mol Fe}_3O_4}{3 \text{ mol Fe}} = 0.400 \text{ mol Fe}_3O_4$$

$$36.0 \text{ g H}_2O \times \frac{1 \text{ mol H}_2O}{18.02 \text{ g H}_2O} \times \frac{1 \text{ mol Fe}_3O_4}{4 \text{ mol H}_2O} = 0.499 \text{ mol Fe}_3O_4$$

Fe is the limiting reactant, because the given amount of Fe can make only 0.400 mol Fe_3O_4, which is less than the 0.499 mol Fe_3O_4 that the given amount of H_2O would produce.

b. $0.400 \text{ mol Fe}_3O_4 \times \dfrac{231.55 \text{ g Fe}_3O_4}{1 \text{ mol Fe}_3O_4} = 92.6 \text{ g Fe}_3O_4$

c. $0.400 \text{ mol Fe}_3O_4 \times \dfrac{4 \text{ mol H}_2O}{1 \text{ mol Fe}_3O_4} \times \dfrac{18.02 \text{ g H}_2O}{1 \text{ mol H}_2O} = 28.8 \text{ g H}_2O \text{ consumed}$

$36.0 \text{ g H}_2O - 28.8 \text{ g H}_2O \text{ consumed} = 7.2 \text{ g H}_2O \text{ remaining}$

④ CHECK YOUR WORK

The mass of original reactants is $67.0 + 36.0 = 103.0$ g; the mass of Fe_3O_4 + unreacted water is $92.6 \text{ g} + 7.2 \text{ g} = 99.8$ g. The difference of 3.2 g is the mass of hydrogen that is produced with the Fe_3O_4.

Practice

Answers in Appendix E

1. Zinc and sulfur react to form zinc sulfide according to the following equation.

$$8Zn(s) + S_8(s) \longrightarrow 8ZnS(s)$$

a. If 2.00 mol of Zn is heated with 1.00 mol of S_8, identify the limiting reactant.

b. How many moles of excess reactant remain?

c. How many moles of the product are formed?

2. Carbon reacts with steam, H_2O, at high temperatures to produce hydrogen and carbon monoxide.

a. If 2.40 mol of carbon is exposed to 3.10 mol of steam, identify the limiting reactant.

b. How many moles of each product are formed?

c. What mass of each product is formed?

PROCEDURE

1. In the mixing bowl, combine the sugars and margarine together until smooth. (An electric mixer will make this process go much faster.)

2. Add the egg, salt, and vanilla. Mix well.

3. Stir in the baking soda, flour, and chocolate chips. Chill the dough for an hour in the refrigerator for best results.

4. Divide the dough into 24 small balls about 3 cm in diameter. Place the balls on an ungreased cookie sheet.

5. Bake at 350°F for about 10 minutes, or until the cookies are light brown.

   Yield: 24 cookies

DISCUSSION

1. Suppose you are given the following amounts of ingredients:

   1 dozen eggs

   24 tsp. of vanilla

   1 lb. (82 tsp.) of salt

   1 lb. (84 tsp.) of baking soda

   3 cups of chocolate chips

   5 lb. (11 cups) of sugar

   2 lb. (4 cups) of brown sugar

   1 lb. (4 sticks) of margarine

a. For each ingredient, calculate how many cookies could be prepared if all of that ingredient were consumed. (For example, the recipe shows that using 1 egg—with the right amounts of the other ingredients—yields 24 cookies. How many cookies can you make if the recipe is increased proportionately for 12 eggs?)

b. To determine the limiting reactant for the new ingredients list, identify which ingredient will result in the fewest number of cookies.

c. What is the maximum number of cookies that can be produced from the new amounts of ingredients?

MATERIALS

- 1/2 cup sugar
- 1/2 cup brown sugar
- 1 1/3 stick margarine (at room temperature)
- 1 egg
- 1/2 tsp. salt
- 1 tsp. vanilla
- 1/2 tsp. baking soda
- 1 1/2 cup flour
- 1 1/3 cup chocolate chips
- mixing bowl
- mixing spoon
- measuring spoons and cups
- cookie sheet
- oven preheated to 350°F

▶ MAIN IDEA

Comparing the actual and theoretical yields helps chemists determine the reaction's efficiency.

The amounts of products calculated in the ideal stoichiometry problems in this chapter so far represent theoretical yields. **The theoretical yield is the maximum amount of product that can be produced from a given amount of reactant.** In most chemical reactions, the amount of product obtained is less than the theoretical yield. There are many reasons for this result. Reactants may contain impurities or may form byproducts in competing side reactions. Also, in many reactions, all reactants are not converted to products. As a result, less product is produced than ideal stoichiometric calculations predict. **The measured amount of a product obtained from a reaction is called the actual yield of that product.**

Chemists are usually interested in the efficiency of a reaction. The efficiency is expressed by comparing the actual and theoretical yields. **The percentage yield is the ratio of the actual yield to the theoretical yield, multiplied by 100.**

✓ **CHECK FOR UNDERSTANDING**

Explain Explain why it might be necessary for a chemist in industry to find out how efficient a chemical reaction is.

$$\text{Percentage Yield} = \frac{\text{actual yield}}{\text{theoretical yield}} \times 100$$

Percentage Yield

Sample Problem H Dichlorine monoxide, Cl_2O, is sometimes used as a powerful chlorinating agent in research. It can be produced by passing chlorine gas over heated mercury(II) oxide according to the following equation:

$$HgO + Cl_2 \longrightarrow HgCl_2 + Cl_2O$$

What is the percentage yield, if the quantity of reactants is sufficient to produce 0.86 g of Cl_2O but only 0.71 g is obtained?

① ANALYZE

Given: actual yield of Cl_2O = 0.71 g
theoretical yield of Cl_2O = 0.86
mass of Cl_2 = excess

Unknown: percentage yield of Cl_2O

② PLAN

Compute the ratio of the actual yield to the theoretical yield.

$$\frac{\text{actual yield}}{\text{theoretical yield}} = \frac{\text{actual mass } Cl_2O}{\text{theoretical mass } Cl_2O}$$

Then multiply by 100 to find the percentage yield.

$$\frac{\text{actual mass } Cl_2O}{\text{theoretical mass } Cl_2O \times 100} = \% \text{ yield}$$

Continued ▶

Percentage Yield (continued)

③ SOLVE

$$\frac{0.71 \text{ g Cl}_2\text{O}}{0.86 \text{ g Cl}_2\text{O} \times 100} = 83\% \text{ yield}$$

④ CHECK YOUR WORK

The answer is correctly rounded to two significant figures to match those in 0.71 and 0.86 g Cl_2O. The units are correct as grams. The percentage yield is about $\frac{5}{6}$, which appears to be close to the ratio of actual yield to theoretical yield, $\frac{0.71}{0.86}$. The percentage yield is reasonable.

Practice   Answers in Appendix E

1. Some antacid medications use aluminum hydroxide to counteract the hydrochloric acid in the stomach.

$$Al(OH)_3 + 3HCl \longrightarrow AlCl_3 + 3H_2O$$

If a dose of antacid containing 28 g $Al(OH)_3$ reacts to produce 44 g $AlCl_3$, what is the percentage yield of $AlCl_3$?

2. Aluminum reacts with excess copper(II) sulfate according to the reaction given below. If 1.85 g of Al reacts and the percentage yield of Cu is 56.6%, what mass of Cu is produced?

$$Al(s) + CuSO_4(aq) \longrightarrow Al_2(SO_4)_3(aq) + Cu(s) \text{ (unbalanced)}$$

✔ SECTION 3 FORMATIVE ASSESSMENT

▶ Reviewing Main Ideas

1. Carbon disulfide burns in oxygen to yield carbon dioxide and sulfur dioxide according to the following chemical equation.

$$CS_2(l) + 3O_2(g) \longrightarrow CO_2(g) + 2SO_2(g)$$

   a. If 1.00 mol CS_2 reacts with 1.00 mol O_2, identify the limiting reactant.
   b. How many moles of excess reactant remain?
   c. How many moles of each product are formed?

2. Metallic magnesium reacts with steam to produce magnesium hydroxide and hydrogen gas.
   a. If 16.2 g Mg is heated with 12.0 g H_2O, what is the limiting reactant?
   b. How many moles of the excess reactant are left?
   c. How many grams of each product are formed?

3. Quicklime, CaO, can be prepared by roasting limestone, $CaCO_3$, according to the following reaction.

$$CaCO_3(s) \xrightarrow{\Delta} CaO(s) + CO_2(g).$$

When 2.00×10^3 g $CaCO_3$ is heated, the actual yield of CaO is 1.05×10^3 g. What is the percentage yield?

✔ Critical Thinking

4. **ANALYZING DATA** A chemical engineer calculated that 15.0 mol H_2 was needed to react with excess N_2 to prepare 10.0 mol NH_3. But the actual yield is 60.0%. Write a balanced chemical equation for the reaction. Is the amount of H_2 needed to make 10.0 mol NH_3 greater than, equal to, or less than 15 mol? How many moles of H_2 are needed?

An unbalanced chemical equation tells you what substances react and what products are produced. A balanced chemical equation gives you even more information. It tells you how many atoms, molecules, or ions react and how many atoms, molecules, or ions are produced. The coefficients in a balanced equation represent the relative amounts in moles of reactants and products. Using this information, you can set up a mole ratio. A mole ratio is a conversion factor that relates the amounts in moles of any two substances involved in a chemical reaction.

Problem-Solving TIPS

- When solving stoichiometric problems, always start with a balanced chemical equation.
- Identify the amount known from the problem (in moles or mass).
- If you are given the mass of a substance, use the molar mass factor as a conversion factor to find the amount in moles. If you are given the amount in moles of a substance, use the molar mass factor as a conversion factor to find the mass.

Sample Problem

If 3.61 g of aluminum reacts completely with excess $CuCl_2$, what mass of copper metal is produced? Use the balanced equation below.

$$2Al(s) + 3CuCl_2(aq) \longrightarrow 2AlCl_3(aq) + 3Cu(s)$$

You know the mass of aluminum that reacts. If you convert that mass to moles, you can apply the mole ratio of aluminum to copper in this reaction to find the moles of copper produced.

$$\text{mol Al} = 3.61 \text{ g Al} \times \frac{1 \text{ mol Al}}{26.98 \text{ g Al}} = 0.134 \text{ mol Al}$$

$$\text{mol Al} \times \frac{3 \text{ mol Cu}}{2 \text{ mol Al}} = \text{mol Cu}$$

$$0.134 \text{ mol Al} \times \frac{3 \text{ mol Cu}}{2 \text{ mol Al}} = 0.201 \text{ mol Cu}$$

Then, convert moles of Cu to mass of Cu by applying the following factor:

$$\text{mol Cu} \times \frac{\text{molar mass Cu}}{1 \text{ mol Cu}} = \text{mass Cu, or } 0.201 \text{ mol Cu} \times \frac{63.55 \text{ g Cu}}{1 \text{ mol Cu}} = 12.8 \text{ g Cu}$$

Practice

1. If 12.24 moles of O_2 reacts with excess SO_2, how many moles of SO_3 are formed? Use the balanced equation below.
$$2SO_2(g) + O_2(g) \longrightarrow 2SO_3(g)$$

2. If 78.50 g $KClO_3$ decomposes, what mass of O_2 is produced? Use the balanced equation below.
$$2KClO_3(s) \longrightarrow 2KCl(s) + 3O_2(g)$$

BIG IDEA Reaction stoichiometry uses molar relationships to determine the amounts of unknown reactants or products from the amounts of known reactants or products.

SECTION 1 Introduction to Stoichiometry

- Reaction stoichiometry involves the mass relationships between reactants and products in a chemical reaction.
- Relating one substance to another requires expressing the amount of each substance in moles.
- A mole ratio is the conversion factor that relates the amount in moles of any two substances in a chemical reaction. The mole ratio is derived from the balanced equation.
- Amount of a substance is expressed in moles, and mass of a substance is expressed by using mass units such as grams, kilograms, or milligrams.
- Mass and amount of substance are quantities, whereas moles and grams are units.
- A balanced chemical equation is necessary to solve any stoichiometric problem.

composition stoichiometry
reaction stoichiometry
mole ratio

SECTION 2 Ideal Stoichiometric Calculations

- In an ideal stoichiometric calculation, the mass or the amount of any reactant or product can be calculated if the balanced chemical equation and the mass or amount of any other reactant or product are known.

SECTION 3 Limiting Reactants and Percentage Yield

- In actual reactions, the reactants may be present in proportions that differ from the stoichiometric proportions required for a complete reaction in which all of each reactant is converted to product.
- The limiting reactant controls the maximum possible amount of product formed.
- For many reactions, the quantity of a product is less than the theoretical maximum for that product. Percentage yield shows the relationship between the theoretical yield and actual yield for the product of a reaction.

limiting reactant
excess reactant
theoretical yield
actual yield
percentage yield

GO ONLINE

Interactive Review
HMHScience.com

Review Games
Concept Maps

SECTION 1
Introduction to Stoichiometry

 REVIEWING MAIN IDEAS

1. **a.** Explain the concept of mole ratio as used in reaction stoichiometry problems.
    b. What is the source of this ratio?

2. For each of the following balanced chemical equations, write all possible mole ratios:
    a. $2Ca + O_2 \longrightarrow 2CaO$
    b. $Mg + 2HF \longrightarrow MgF_2 + H_2$

PRACTICE PROBLEMS

3. Given the chemical equation $Na_2CO_3(aq) + Ca(OH)_2 \longrightarrow 2NaOH(aq) + CaCO_3(s)$, determine to two decimal places the molar masses of all substances. Write molar masses as conversion factors.

SECTION 2
Ideal Stoichiometric Calculations

 REVIEWING MAIN IDEAS

4. **a.** What is molar mass?
    b. What is its role in reaction stoichiometry?

PRACTICE PROBLEMS

5. Hydrogen and oxygen react under a specific set of conditions to produce water according to the following: $2H_2(g) + O_2(g) \longrightarrow 2H_2O(g)$.
    a. How many moles of hydrogen would be required to produce 5.0 mol of water?
    b. How many moles of oxygen would be required? (Hint: See Sample Problem A.)

6. **a.** If 4.50 mol of ethane, C_2H_6, undergoes combustion according to the unbalanced equation $C_2H_6 + O_2 \longrightarrow CO_2 + H_2O$, how many moles of oxygen are required?
    b. How many moles of each product are formed?

7. Sodium chloride is produced from its elements through a synthesis reaction. What mass of each reactant would be required to produce 25.0 mol of sodium chloride?

8. In a blast furnace, iron(lll) oxide is used to produce iron by the following (unbalanced) reaction:
    $$Fe_2O_3(s) + CO(g) \longrightarrow Fe(s) + CO_2(g)$$
    a. If 4.00 kg Fe_2O_3 is available to react, how many moles of CO are needed?
    b. How many moles of each product are formed?

9. Methanol, CH_3OH, is an important industrial compound that is produced from the following (unbalanced) reaction: $CO(g) + H_2(g) \longrightarrow CH_3OH(g)$. What mass of each reactant would be needed to produce 100.0 kg of methanol? (Hint: See Sample Problem E.)

10. During lightning flashes, nitrogen combines with oxygen in the atmosphere to form nitrogen monoxide, NO, which then reacts further with O_2 to produce nitrogen dioxide, NO_2.
    a. What mass of NO_2 is formed when NO reacts with 384 g O_2?
    b. How many grams of NO are required to react with this amount of O_2?

11. As early as 1938, the use of NaOH was suggested as a means of removing CO_2 from the cabin of a spacecraft according to the following (unbalanced) reaction: $NaOH + CO_2 \longrightarrow Na_2CO_3 + H_2O$.
    a. If the average human body discharges 925.0 g CO_2 per day, how many moles of NaOH are needed each day for each person in the spacecraft?
    b. How many moles of each product are formed?

12. The double-replacement reaction between silver nitrate and sodium bromide produces silver bromide, a component of photographic film.
    a. If 4.50 mol of silver nitrate reacts, what mass of sodium bromide is required?
    b. What mass of silver bromide is formed?

13. In a soda-acid fire extinguisher, concentrated sulfuric acid reacts with sodium hydrogen carbonate to produce carbon dioxide, sodium sulfate, and water.
    a. How many moles of sodium hydrogen carbonate would be needed to react with 150.0 g of sulfuric acid?
    b. How many moles of each product would be formed?

14. Sulfuric acid reacts with sodium hydroxide according to the following:

$$H_2SO_4 + NaOH \longrightarrow Na_2SO_4 + H_2O$$

   a. Balance the equation for this reaction.

   b. What mass of H_2SO_4 would be required to react with 0.75 mol NaOH?

   c. What mass of each product is formed by this reaction? (Hint: See Sample Problem B.)

15. Copper reacts with silver nitrate through single replacement.

   a. If 2.25 g of silver is produced from the reaction, how many moles of copper(II) nitrate are also produced?

   b. How many moles of each reactant are required in this reaction? (Hint: See Sample Problem D.)

16. Aspirin, $C_9H_8O_4$, is produced through the following reaction of salicylic acid, $C_7H_6O_3$, and acetic anhydride, $C_4H_6O_3$: $C_7H_6O_3(s) + C_4H_6O_3(l) \longrightarrow C_9H_8O_4(s) + HC_2H_3O_2(l)$.

   a. What mass of aspirin (kg) could be produced from 75.0 mol of salicylic acid?

   b. What mass of acetic anhydride (kg) would be required?

   c. At 20°C, how many liters of acetic acid, $HC_2H_3O_2$, would be formed? The density of $HC_2H_3O_2$ is 1.05 g/mL.

SECTION 3

Limiting Reactants and Percentage Yield

▶ **REVIEWING MAIN IDEAS**

17. Distinguish between ideal and real stoichiometric calculations.

18. Distinguish between the limiting reactant and the excess reactant in a chemical reaction.

19. a. Distinguish between the theoretical yield and actual yield in stoichiometric calculations.

   b. How does the value of the theoretical yield generally compare with the value of the actual yield?

20. What is the percentage yield of a reaction?

21. Why are actual yields usually less than calculated theoretical yields?

PRACTICE PROBLEMS

22. Given the reactant amounts specified in each chemical equation, determine the limiting reactant in each case:

   a. $\text{HCl} + \text{NaOH} \longrightarrow \text{NaCl} + H_2O$
   2.0 mol   2.5 mol

   b. $\text{Zn} + 2\text{HCl} \longrightarrow \text{ZnCl}_2 + H_2$
   2.5 mol   6.0 mol

   c. $2\text{Fe(OH)}_3 + 3H_2SO_4 \longrightarrow \text{Fe}_2(\text{SO}_4)_3 + 6H_2O$
   4.0 mol   6.5 mol

   (Hint: See Sample Problem F.)

23. For each reaction specified in Problem 22, determine the amount in moles of excess reactant that remains. (Hint: See Sample Problem G.)

24. For each reaction specified in Problem 22, calculate the amount in moles of each product formed.

25. a. If 2.50 mol of copper and 5.50 mol of silver nitrate are available to react by single replacement, identify the limiting reactant.

   b. Determine the amount in moles of excess reactant remaining.

   c. Determine the amount in moles of each product formed.

   d. Determine the mass of each product formed.

26. Sulfuric acid reacts with aluminum hydroxide by double replacement.

   a. If 30.0 g of sulfuric acid reacts with 25.0 g of aluminum hydroxide, identify the limiting reactant.

   b. Determine the mass of excess reactant remaining.

   c. Determine the mass of each product formed. Assume 100% yield.

27. The energy used to power one of the Apollo lunar missions was supplied by the following overall reaction: $2N_2H_4 + (CH_3)_2N_2H_2 + 3N_2O_4 \longrightarrow 6N_2 + 2CO_2 + 8H_2O$. For the phase of the mission when the lunar module ascended from the surface of the moon, a total of 1200. kg N_2H_4 was available to react with 1000. kg $(CH_3)_2N_2H_2$ and 4500. kg N_2O_4.

   a. For this portion of the flight, which of the allocated components was used up first?

   b. How much water, in kilograms, was put into the lunar atmosphere through this reaction?

28. Calculate the indicated quantity for each of the various chemical reactions given:
    a. theoretical yield = 20.0 g, actual yield = 15.0 g, percentage yield = ?
    b. theoretical yield = 1.0 g, percentage yield = 90.0%, actual yield = ?
    c. theoretical yield = 5.00 g, actual yield = 4.75 g, percentage yield = ?
    d. theoretical yield = 3.45 g, percentage yield = 48.0%, actual yield = ?

29. The percentage yield for the reaction
$$PCl_3 + Cl_2 \longrightarrow PCl_5$$
is 83.2%. What mass of PCl_5 is expected from the reaction of 73.7 g PCl_3 with excess chlorine?

30. The Ostwald process for producing nitric acid from ammonia consists of the following steps:
$$4NH_3(g) + 5O_2(g) \longrightarrow 4NO(g) + 6H_2O(g)$$
$$2NO(g) + O_2(g) \longrightarrow 2NO_2(g)$$
$$3NO_2(g) + H_2O(g) \longrightarrow 2HNO_3(aq) + NO(g)$$
If the yield in each step is 94.0%, how many grams of nitric acid can be produced from 5.00 kg of ammonia?

Mixed Review

REVIEWING MAIN IDEAS

31. Magnesium is obtained from sea water. $Ca(OH)_2$ is added to sea water to precipitate $Mg(OH)_2$. The precipitate is filtered and reacted with HCl to produce $MgCl_2$. The $MgCl_2$ is electrolyzed to produce Mg and Cl_2. If 185.0 g of magnesium is recovered from 1000. g $MgCl_2$, what is the percentage yield for this reaction?

32. Phosphate baking powder is a mixture of starch, sodium hydrogen carbonate, and calcium dihydrogen phosphate. When mixed with water, phosphate baking powder releases carbon dioxide gas, causing a dough or batter to bubble and rise.
$$2NaHCO_3(aq) + Ca(H_2PO_4)_2(aq) \longrightarrow Na_2HPO_4(aq)$$
$$+ CaHPO_4(aq) + 2CO_2(g) + 2H_2O(l)$$
If 0.750 L CO_2 is needed for a cake and each kilogram of baking powder contains 168 g of $NaHCO_3$, how many grams of baking powder must be used to generate this amount of CO_2? The density of CO_2 at baking temperature is about 1.20 g/L.

33. Coal gasification is a process that converts coal into methane gas. If this reaction has a percentage yield of 85.0%, what mass of methane can be obtained from 1250 g of carbon?
$$2C(s) + 2H_2O(l) \longrightarrow CH_4(g) + CO_2(g)$$

34. If the percentage yield for the coal gasification process is increased to 95%, what mass of methane can be obtained from 2750 g of carbon?

35. Builders and dentists must store plaster of Paris, $CaSO_4 \bullet \frac{1}{2}H_2O$, in airtight containers to prevent it from absorbing water vapor from the air and changing to gypsum, $CaSO_4 \bullet 2H_2O$. How many liters of water vapor evolve when 2.00 kg of gypsum is heated at 110°C to produce plaster of Paris? At 110°C, the density of water vapor is 0.574 g/L.

36. Gold can be recovered from sea water by reacting the water with zinc, which is refined from zinc oxide. The zinc displaces the gold in the water. What mass of gold can be recovered if 2.00 g of ZnO and an excess of sea water are available?
$$2ZnO(s) + C(s) \longrightarrow 2Zn(s) + CO_2(g)$$
$$2Au^{3+}(aq) + 3Zn(s) \longrightarrow 3Zn^{2+}(aq) + 2Au(s)$$

CRITICAL THINKING

37. **Relating Ideas** The chemical equation is a good source of information concerning a reaction. Explain the relationship between the actual yield of a reaction product and the chemical equation of the product.

38. **Analyzing Results** Very seldom are chemists able to achieve a 100% yield of a product from a chemical reaction. However, the yield of a reaction is usually important because of the expense involved in producing less product. For example, when magnesium metal is heated in a crucible at high temperatures, the product magnesium oxide, MgO, is formed. Based on your analysis of the reaction, describe some of the actions that you would take to increase your percentage yield. The reaction is as follows:
$$2Mg(s) + O_2(g) \longrightarrow 2MgO(s)$$

39. **Analyzing Results** In the lab, you run an experiment that appears to have a percentage yield of 115%. Propose reasons for this result. Can an actual yield ever exceed a theoretical yield? Explain your answer.

40. **Relating Ideas** Explain the stoichiometry of blowing air on a smoldering campfire to keep the coals burning.

USING THE HANDBOOK

41. The steel-making process described in the Transition Metal section of the *Elements Handbook* (Appendix A) shows the equation for the formation of iron carbide. Use this equation to answer the following questions:

    a. If 3.65×10^3 kg of iron is used in a steel-making process, what is the minimum mass of carbon needed to react with all of the iron?

    b. What is the theoretical mass of iron carbide that is formed?

42. The reaction of aluminum with oxygen to produce a protective coating for the metal's surface is described in the discussion of aluminum in Group 13 of the *Elements Handbook* (Appendix A). Use this equation to answer the following questions:

    a. What mass of aluminum oxide would theoretically be formed if a 30.0 g piece of aluminum foil reacted with excess oxygen?

    b. Why would you expect the actual yield from this reaction to be far less than the mass you calculated in item (a)?

43. The reactions of oxide compounds to produce carbonates, phosphates, and sulfates are described in the section on oxides in Group 16 of the *Elements Handbook* (Appendix A). Use those equations to answer the following questions:

    a. What mass of CO_2 is needed to react with 154.6 g MgO?

    b. What mass of magnesium carbonate is produced?

    c. When 45.7 g P_4O_{10} is reacted with an excess of calcium oxide, what mass of calcium phosphate is produced?

RESEARCH AND WRITING

44. Research the history of the Haber process for the production of ammonia. What was the significance of this process in history? How is this process related to the discussion of reaction yields in this chapter?

ALTERNATIVE ASSESSMENT

45. **Performance** Just as reactants combine in certain proportions to form a product, colors can be combined to create other colors. Artists do this all the time to find just the right color for their paintings. Using poster paint, determine the proportions of primary pigments used to create the following colors. Your proportions should be such that anyone could mix the color perfectly.

46. **Performance** Write two of your own sample problems that are descriptions of how to solve a mass-mass problem. Assume that your sample problems will be used by other students to learn how to solve mass-mass problems.

Standards-Based Assessment

Record your answers on a separate piece of paper.

MULTIPLE CHOICE

1 Nitrogen gas reacts with hydrogen gas to produce ammonia according to the following equation.

$$N_2\,(g) + 3H_2\,(g) \rightarrow 2NH_3\,(g)$$

What is the mass of ammonia produced from 6.5 grams of the hydrogen reactant, assuming there is sufficient nitrogen to react?

A 4 g NH_3
B 8 g NH_3
C 37 g NH_3
D 55 g NH_3

2 The "phlogiston theory" was the idea that combustion depended on the presence of a substance called *phlogiston*. Phlogiston was colorless, odorless, and, apparently, massless, but without it, a substance would not burn. Why might it be inaccurate to call phlogiston a scientific theory?

A It didn't explain anything.
B It was difficult to test, because phlogiston was undetectable.
C It had no supporters.
D It couldn't be proven false.

3 Which mole ratio for the equation $6Li + N_2 \rightarrow 2Li_3N$ is *incorrect*?

A $\dfrac{6 \text{ mol Li}}{2 \text{ mol N}_2}$

B $\dfrac{1 \text{ mol N}_2}{6 \text{ mol Li}}$

C $\dfrac{2 \text{ mol Li}_3N}{1 \text{ mol N}_2}$

D $\dfrac{2 \text{ mol Li}_3N}{6 \text{ mol Li}}$

4 For the reaction below, how many moles of N_2 are required to produce 18 mol NH_3?

$$N_2 + 3H_2 \rightarrow 2NH_3$$

A 4.5
B 9.0
C 18
D 36

5 What mass of CO_2 can be produced from 25.0 g $CaCO_3$ given the decomposition reaction below?

$$CaCO_3 \rightarrow CaO + CO_2$$

A 11.0 g
B 22.0 g
C 25.0 g
D 56.0 g

6 What is the maximum number of moles of $AlCl_3$ that can be produced from 5.0 mol Al and 6.0 mol Cl_2?

$$2Al + 3Cl_2 \rightarrow 2AlCl$$

A 2.0 mol $AlCl_3$
C 5.0 mol $AlCl_3$
B 4.0 mol $AlCl_3$
D 6.0 mol $AlCl_3$

7 Silicon dioxide reacts with carbon to produce silicon carbide and carbon monoxide. A chemist performs this reaction in the lab and writes her data in the table shown here.

Reactants	Amount Used	Products	Amount Yielded
$SiO_2(s)$	25 g	$SiC(s)$	15 g
$C(s)$	15 g	$CO(g)$	22 g

What is the chemist's percent yield for carbon monoxide?

A 90%
B 95%
C 98.5%
D 100%

GRIDDED RESPONSE

8 What mass in grams of NaCl can be produced by the reaction of 0.75 mol Cl_2?

$$2Na + Cl_2 \rightarrow 2NaCl$$

Test Tip
Carefully read questions that ask for the one choice that is incorrect. Often these questions include words such as *not*, *except*, or *all but*.

CHAPTER 10
States of Matter

BIG IDEA
The kinetic-molecular theory of matter explains the properties of solids, liquids, and gases in terms of the energy of particles and the forces acting between them.

ONLINE Chemistry
HMHScience.com

SECTION 1
The Kinetic-Molecular Theory of Matter

SECTION 2
Liquids

SECTION 3
Solids

SECTION 4
Changes of State

SECTION 5
Water

ONLINE LABS
- Viscosity of Liquids
- Evaporation and Ink Solvents
- "Wet" Dry Ice
- Constructing a Heating/Cooling Curve

GO ONLINE

Why It Matters Video
HMHScience.com

States of Matter

The Kinetic-Molecular Theory of Matter

SECTION 1

Main Ideas

▸ The kinetic-molecular theory explains the constant motion of gas particles.

▸ The kinetic-molecular theory explains the physical properties of gases.

▸ Real gases do not behave according to the kinetic-molecular theory.

Key Terms
kinetic-molecular theory   elastic collision   effusion
ideal gas   diffusion   real gas

In the chapter "Matter and Change," you read that matter exists on Earth in the forms of solids, liquids, and gases. Although it is not usually possible to observe individual particles directly, scientists have studied large groups of these particles as they occur in solids, liquids, and gases.

In the late 19th century, scientists developed the kinetic-molecular theory of matter to account for the behavior of the atoms and molecules that make up matter. **The kinetic-molecular theory is based on the idea that particles of matter are always in motion.** The theory can be used to explain the properties of solids, liquids, and gases in terms of the energy of particles and the forces that act between them. In this section, you will study the theory as it applies to gas molecules.

▸ MAIN IDEA

The kinetic-molecular theory explains the constant motion of gas particles.

The kinetic-molecular theory can help you understand the behavior of gas molecules and the physical properties of gases. The theory provides a model of what is called an ideal gas. **An ideal gas is a hypothetical gas that perfectly fits all the assumptions of the kinetic-molecular theory.**

The kinetic-molecular theory of gases is based on the following five assumptions:

1. *Gases consist of large numbers of tiny particles that are far apart relative to their size.* These particles, usually molecules or atoms, typically occupy a volume that is about 1000 times greater than the volume occupied by an equal number of particles in the liquid or solid state. Thus, molecules of gases are much farther apart than molecules of liquids or solids. Most of the volume occupied by a gas is empty space, which is the reason that gases have a lower density than liquids and solids do. This also explains the fact that gases are easily compressed.

2. *Collisions between gas particles and between particles and container walls are elastic collisions.* **An elastic collision is one in which there is no net loss of total kinetic energy.** Kinetic energy is transferred between two particles during collisions. However, the total kinetic energy of the two particles remains the same as long as temperature is constant.

FIGURE 1.1

Elastic Collisions Diatomic gas particles travel in a straight-line motion until they collide with each other or the walls of their container.

3. *Gas particles are in continuous, rapid, random motion. They therefore possess kinetic energy, which is energy of motion.* Gas particles move in all directions, as shown in **Figure 1.1**. The kinetic energy of the particles overcomes the attractive forces between them, except near the temperature at which the gas condenses and becomes a liquid.

4. *There are no forces of attraction between gas particles.* You can think of ideal gas molecules as behaving like small billiard balls. When they collide, they do not stick together but immediately bounce apart.

5. *The temperature of a gas depends on the average kinetic energy of the particles of the gas.* The kinetic energy of any moving object, including a particle, is given by the following equation:

> **Kinetic Energy** $\qquad KE = \frac{1}{2}mv^2$

In the equation, m is the mass of the particle, and v is its speed. Because all the particles of a specific gas have the same mass, their kinetic energies depend only on their speeds. The average speeds and kinetic energies of gas particles increase with an increase in temperature and decrease with a decrease in temperature.

All gases at the same temperature have the same average kinetic energy. Therefore, at the same temperature, lighter gas particles, such as hydrogen molecules, have higher average speeds than do heavier gas particles, such as oxygen molecules.

● **MAIN IDEA**

The kinetic-molecular theory explains the physical properties of gases.

The kinetic-molecular theory applies only to ideal gases. Although ideal gases do not actually exist, many gases behave nearly ideally if pressure is not very high and temperature is not very low. As you will see, the kinetic-molecular theory accounts for the physical properties of gases.

Expansion

Gases do not have a definite shape or volume. They completely fill any container in which they are enclosed, and they take its shape. A gas transferred from a one-liter vessel to a two-liter vessel will expand to fill the larger volume. The kinetic-molecular theory explains these facts. According to the theory, gas particles move rapidly in all directions (assumption 3), with no significant attraction between them (assumption 4).

Fluidity

Because the attractive forces between gas particles are insignificant (assumption 4), gas particles glide easily past one another. This ability to flow causes gases to behave as liquids do. Because liquids and gases flow, they are both referred to as *fluids*.

Low Density

The density of a gaseous substance at atmospheric pressure is about 1/1000 the density of the same substance in the liquid or solid state. The reason is that the particles are so much farther apart in the gaseous state (assumption 1).

Compressibility

During compression, the gas particles, which are initially very far apart (assumption 1), are crowded closer together. The volume of a given sample of a gas can be greatly decreased. Steel cylinders containing gases under pressure are widely used in industry. When they are full, such cylinders may contain more than 100 times as many particles of gas as nonpressurized containers of the same size could contain.

Diffusion and Effusion

Gases spread out and mix with one another, even without being stirred. If the stopper is removed from a container of ammonia in a room, ammonia gas will mix uniformly with the air and spread throughout the room. The random and continuous motion of the ammonia molecules (assumption 3) carries them throughout the available space. Such spontaneous mixing of the particles of two substances caused by their random motion is called **diffusion.**

Gases diffuse readily into one another and mix together due to the rapid motion of the molecules and the empty space between the molecules. The gas molecules in each of the two flasks in **Figure 1.2a** continuously move about in separate flasks because the stopcock is closed. When the stopcock is open, the gas molecules continuously diffuse back and forth from one flask to the other through the opening in the stopcock, as shown in **Figure 1.2b.**

Diffusion is a process by which particles of a gas spread out spontaneously and mix with other gases. In contrast, **effusion** is a process by which gas particles pass through a tiny opening into a vacuum.

FIGURE 1.2

Diffusion Gases diffuse readily into one another. The space between the molecules allows different gases to mix together easily.

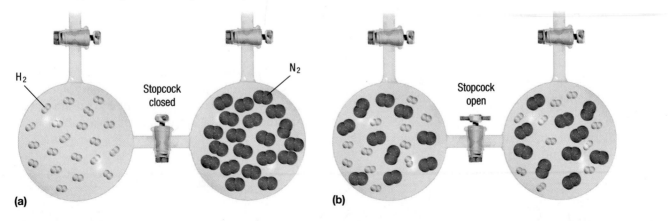

(a)　　　　　　　　　　　　　　　　(b)

FIGURE 1.3

Real Gases

(a) Gas molecules in a car-engine cylinder expand to fill the cylinder.

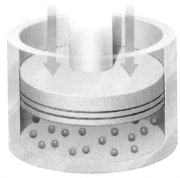

(b) As pressure is exerted on them, the gas molecules move closer together, reducing their volume.

✔ **CRITICAL THINKING**

Describe What will eventually happen to a gas if it is compressed enough?

The rates of effusion of different gases are directly proportional to the velocities of their particles. Because of this proportionality, molecules of low mass effuse faster than molecules of high mass.

▶ **MAIN IDEA**

Real gases do not behave according to the kinetic-molecular theory.

Because particles of gases occupy space and exert attractive forces on each other, all real gases deviate to some degree from ideal gas behavior. A **real gas** is a gas that does not behave completely according to the assumptions of the kinetic-molecular theory. At very high pressures and low temperatures, the gas particles will be closer together, and their kinetic energy will be insufficient to completely overcome the attractive forces. At such conditions, the gas deviates from ideal behavior. At very low temperatures or very high pressures, gases condense to the liquid phase. **Figure 1.3** shows what happens to a gas in a car engine's cylinder as the pressure is increased. Increase the pressure sufficiently, and the gas will begin to deviate from ideal behavior.

The kinetic-molecular theory is more likely to hold true for gases whose particles have little attraction for each other. The noble gases, such as helium, He, and neon, Ne, show essentially ideal gas behavior over a wide range of temperatures and pressures. The particles of these gases are monatomic and thus nonpolar. The particles of gases such as nitrogen, N_2, and hydrogen, H_2, are nonpolar diatomic molecules. The behavior of these gases most closely approximates that of the ideal gas under certain conditions. The more polar the molecules of a gas are, the greater the attractive forces between them and the more the gas will deviate from ideal gas behavior. For example, highly polar gases, such as ammonia (NH_3) and water vapor, deviate from ideal behavior to a larger degree than nonpolar gases.

✔ ## SECTION 1 FORMATIVE ASSESSMENT

▶ **Reviewing Main Ideas**

1. Use the kinetic-molecular theory to explain the following properties of gases: expansion, fluidity, low density, compressibility, and diffusion.

2. Describe the conditions under which a real gas is most likely to behave ideally.

3. Which of the following gases would you expect to deviate significantly from ideal behavior: He, O_2, H_2, H_2O, N_2, HCl, or NH_3?

4. How does the kinetic-molecular theory explain the pressure exerted by gases?

5. What happens to gas particles when a gas is compressed?

6. What happens to gas particles when a gas is heated?

✔ **Critical Thinking**

7. **DRAWING CONCLUSIONS** Molecules of hydrogen escape from Earth, but molecules of oxygen and nitrogen are held to the surface and remain in the atmosphere. Explain.

Liquids

Key Terms

fluid
surface tension

capillary action
vaporization

evaporation
freezing

When you think of Earth's oceans, lakes, and rivers and the many liquids you use every day, it is hard to believe that liquids are the *least* common state of matter in the universe. Liquids are less common than solids and gases because a substance can exist in the liquid state only within a relatively narrow range of temperatures and pressures. In this section, you will examine the properties of the liquid state and compare them with those of the solid state and the gas state. These properties will be discussed in terms of the kinetic-molecular theory.

▶ MAIN IDEA

The intermolecular forces of liquids determine their properties.

A liquid can be described as a form of matter that has a definite volume and takes the shape of its container. The properties of liquids can be understood by applying the kinetic-molecular theory.

As in a gas, particles in a liquid are in constant motion. However, the particles in a liquid are closer together than the particles in a gas are. Therefore, the attractive forces between particles in a liquid are more effective than those between particles in a gas. This attraction between liquid particles is caused by intermolecular forces, such as dipole-dipole forces, London dispersion forces, and hydrogen bonding.

Liquids are more ordered than gases because of the stronger intermolecular forces and the lower mobility of the liquid particles. According to the kinetic-molecular theory of liquids, the particles are not bound together in fixed positions but move about constantly. This particle mobility explains why liquids and gases are referred to as fluids. A **fluid** is a substance that can flow and therefore take the shape of its container. Most liquids naturally flow downhill because of gravity. However, some liquids can flow in other directions as well. For example, liquid helium near absolute zero is able to flow uphill.

Relatively High Density

At normal atmospheric pressure, most substances are hundreds of times denser in a liquid state than in a gaseous state. This higher density is a result of the close arrangement of liquid particles. Most substances are only slightly less dense (about 10%) in a liquid state than in a solid state, however. Water is one of the few substances that becomes less dense when it solidifies, as will be discussed further in Section 5.

At the same temperature and pressure, different liquids can differ greatly in density. **Figure 2.1** shows some liquids and solids with different densities. The densities differ to such an extent that the liquids form layers.

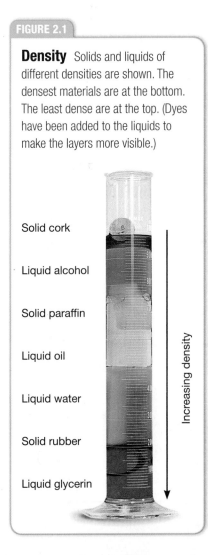

FIGURE 2.1

Density Solids and liquids of different densities are shown. The densest materials are at the bottom. The least dense are at the top. (Dyes have been added to the liquids to make the layers more visible.)

Solid cork

Liquid alcohol

Solid paraffin

Liquid oil

Liquid water

Solid rubber

Liquid glycerin

Increasing density

Relative Incompressibility

When liquid water at 20°C is compressed by a pressure of 1000 atm, its volume decreases by only 4%. Such behavior is typical of all liquids and is similar to the behavior of solids. In contrast, a gas under a pressure of 1000 atm would have only about 1/1000 of its volume at normal atmospheric pressure. Liquids are much less compressible than gases because liquid particles are more closely packed together. Like gases, liquids can transmit pressure equally in all directions.

Ability to Diffuse

As described in Section 1, gases diffuse and mix with other gas particles. Liquids also diffuse and mix with other liquids, as shown in **Figure 2.2.** Any liquid gradually diffuses throughout any other liquid in which it can dissolve. The constant, random motion of particles causes diffusion in liquids, as it does in gases. Yet diffusion is much slower in liquids than in gases because liquid particles are closer together. Also, the attractive forces between the particles of a liquid slow their movement. As the temperature of a liquid is increased, diffusion occurs more rapidly. The reason is that the average kinetic energy, and therefore the average speed of the particles, is increased.

Surface Tension

A property common to all liquids is **surface tension,** a force that tends to pull adjacent parts of a liquid's surface together, thereby decreasing surface area to the smallest possible size. Surface tension results from the attractive forces between particles of a liquid. The higher the force of attraction, the higher the surface tension.

FIGURE 2.2

Diffusion of Liquids   Like gases, the two liquids in this beaker diffuse over time. The green liquid food coloring from the drop will eventually form a uniform solution with the water.

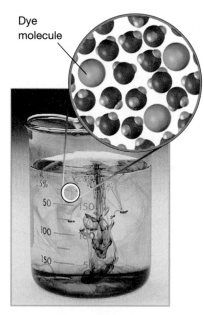

Water has a higher surface tension than most liquids. This is due in large part to the hydrogen bonds water molecules can form with each other. The molecules at the surface of the water are a special case. They can form hydrogen bonds with the other water molecules beneath them and beside them but not with the molecules in the air above them. As a result, the surface water molecules are drawn together and toward the body of the liquid, creating a high surface tension. Surface tension causes liquid droplets to take on a spherical shape, because a sphere has the smallest possible surface area for a given volume. An example of this phenomenon is shown in **Figure 2.3.**

Capillary action, the attraction of the surface of a liquid to the surface of a solid, is a property closely related to surface tension. A liquid will rise quite high in a very narrow tube and will wet the tube if a strong attraction exists between the liquid molecules and the molecules that make up the surface of the tube. This attraction tends to pull the liquid molecules upward along the surface and against the pull of gravity. This process continues until the attractive forces between the liquid molecules and the surface of the tube are balanced by the weight of the liquid. Capillary action can occur between water molecules and paper fibers, as shown in **Figure 2.4.** Capillary action is at least partly responsible for the transportation of water from the roots of a plant to its leaves. The same process is responsible for the concave liquid surface, called a *meniscus*, that forms in a test tube or graduated cylinder.

Evaporation and Boiling

The process by which a liquid or solid changes to a gas is **vaporization.** Evaporation is a form of vaporization. **Evaporation** is the process by which particles escape from the surface of a nonboiling liquid and enter the gas state.

FIGURE 2.3

Surface Tension As a result of surface tension, liquids form roughly spherical drops. The net attractive forces between the particles pull the molecules on the surface of the drop inward. The molecules are pulled very close together, which minimizes the surface area.

Attractions on a typical molecule in a liquid   Attractions on a surface molecule

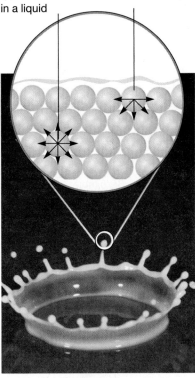

FIGURE 2.4

Polar Attraction

(a) Water-soluble ink is placed near the bottom of a piece of chromatography paper in shallow water.

(b) The black ink separates into its component colors due to the different attraction between each component and water.

✓ **CRITICAL THINKING**

Apply Using the principles of capillary action, describe why water-soluble ink rises up the chromatography paper, which is set into a small amount of water.

(cr) ©Ted Kinsman/Photo Researchers, Inc.

FIGURE 2.5

Evaporation Liquid bromine, Br$_2$, evaporates near room temperature. The resulting brownish-red gas diffuses into the air above the surface of the liquid.

Evaporated Br$_2$(g) molecule diffusing into air

N$_2$(g) molecule   O$_2$(g) molecule

Br$_2$(l) molecule

A small amount of liquid bromine was added to the bottle shown in **Figure 2.5.** Within a few minutes, the air above the liquid bromine turned brownish-red because some bromine molecules escaped from the surface of the liquid. These molecules became gas molecules, or bromine vapor, which mixed with the air. A similar phenomenon occurs if you apply perfume to your wrist. Within seconds, you become aware of the perfume's fragrance. Scent molecules evaporate from your skin and diffuse through the air, where your nose detects them.

Evaporation occurs because the particles of a liquid have different kinetic energies. Some surface particles with higher-than-average energies can overcome the intermolecular forces that bind them to the liquid. They can then escape into the gas state.

Evaporation is a crucial process in nature. Evaporation removes fresh water from the surface of the ocean, leaving behind a higher concentration of salts. In tropical areas, evaporation occurs at a higher rate, causing the surface water to be saltier. All water that falls to Earth in the form of rain and snow previously evaporated from oceans, lakes, and rivers. Evaporation of perspiration plays an important role in keeping you cool. Perspiration, which is mostly water, cools since the higher-energy water molecules escape by evaporation. This means the average energy of the remaining liquid water molecules is less, thus cooler.

Boiling is the change of a liquid to bubbles of vapor that appear throughout the liquid. Boiling differs from evaporation, as you will see in Section 4.

Formation of Solids

When a liquid is cooled, the average energy of its particles decreases. If the energy is low enough, attractive forces pull the particles into an even more orderly arrangement. The substance then becomes a solid. **The physical change of a liquid to a solid by removal of energy as heat is called freezing or solidification.** Perhaps the best-known example of freezing is the change of liquid water to solid water, or ice, at 0°C. Another familiar example is the solidification of paraffin at room temperature. All liquids freeze, although not necessarily at temperatures you normally encounter. Ethanol, for example, freezes near −114°C.

✓ SECTION 2 **FORMATIVE ASSESSMENT**

▶ Reviewing Main Ideas

1. Describe the liquid state according to the kinetic-molecular theory.

2. List the properties of liquids.

3. How does the kinetic-molecular theory explain the following properties of liquids: (a) relatively high density, (b) ability to diffuse, and (c) ability to evaporate?

4. Explain why liquids in a test tube form a meniscus.

5. Compare vaporization and evaporation.

✓ Critical Thinking

6. **INTERPRETING CONCEPTS** The evaporation of liquid water from the surface of Earth is an important step in the water cycle. How do water molecules obtain enough kinetic energy to escape into the gas state?

©Charles D. Winters/Photo Researchers, Inc

Solids

Key Terms

crystalline solid
crystal
amorphous solid

melting
melting point
supercooled liquid

crystal structure
unit cell

Main Ideas

The particles in a solid hold relatively fixed positions.

Crystal particles are arranged in a three-dimensional lattice.

The particles in amorphous solids are not arranged in a regular pattern.

The common expression "solid as a rock" suggests something that is hard or unyielding and has a definite shape and volume. In this section, you will examine the properties of solids and compare them with those of liquids and gases. The properties of solids are explained in terms of the kinetic-molecular theory, as are the other states of matter.

▶ MAIN IDEA
The particles in a solid hold relatively fixed positions.

The particles of a solid are more closely packed than those of a liquid or gas. Intermolecular forces between particles are thus much more effective in solids. All interparticle attractions, such as dipole-dipole attractions, London dispersion forces, and hydrogen bonding, exert stronger effects in solids than in the corresponding liquids or gases. Attractive forces tend to hold the particles of a solid in relatively fixed positions, with only vibrational movement around fixed points. Because the motions of the particles are restricted in this way, solids are more ordered than liquids and are much more ordered than gases. The importance of order and disorder in physical and chemical changes will be discussed in the chapter "Reaction Energy." Compare the physical appearance and molecular arrangement of the substances in **Figure 3.1** in solid, liquid, and gas form.

✔ CRITICAL THINKING

Analyze Analyze the pictures below, and describe in detail what each picture is showing.

FIGURE 3.1

States of Matter
Particles of substances in three different states are shown.

Arrangement of particles in a solid

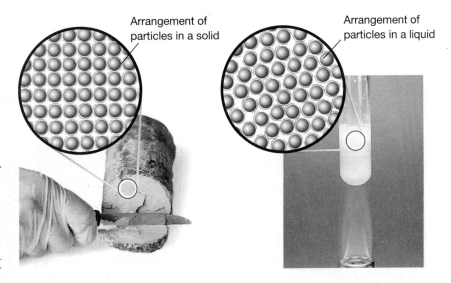

Arrangement of particles in a liquid

Arrangement of particles in a gas

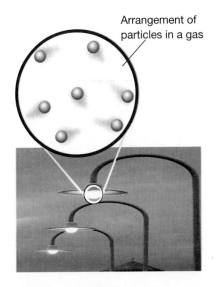

(br) ©Roberto Orecchia/Alamy

There are two types of solids: crystalline solids and amorphous solids. **Most solids are crystalline solids—they consist of crystals. A crystal is a substance in which the particles are arranged in an orderly, geometric, repeating pattern.** Noncrystalline solids, including glass and plastics, are called amorphous solids. **An amorphous solid is one in which the particles are arranged randomly.** The two types of solids will be discussed in more detail later in this section.

Definite Shape and Volume

Unlike liquids and gases, solids can maintain a definite shape without a container. In addition, crystalline solids are geometrically regular. Even the fragments of a shattered crystalline solid have distinct geometric shapes that reflect their internal structure. Amorphous solids maintain a definite shape, but they do not have the distinct geometric shapes of crystalline solids. For example, glass can be molded into any shape. If glass is shattered, the fragments can have a variety of irregular shapes.

The volume of a solid changes only slightly with a change in temperature or pressure. Solids have definite volume because their particles are packed closely together. There is very little empty space into which the particles can be compressed. Crystalline solids generally do not flow, because their particles are held in relatively fixed positions.

Definite Melting Point

Melting is the physical change of a solid to a liquid by the addition of energy as heat. The temperature at which a solid becomes a liquid is its melting point. At this temperature, the kinetic energies of the particles within the solid overcome the attractive forces holding them together. The particles can then break out of their positions in crystalline solids, which have definite melting points. In contrast, amorphous solids, such as glass and plastics, have no definite melting point. They have the ability to flow over a range of temperatures. Therefore, amorphous solids are sometimes classified as **supercooled liquids, which are substances that retain certain liquid properties even at temperatures at which they appear to be solid.** These properties exist because the particles in amorphous solids are arranged randomly, much like the particles in a liquid. Unlike the particles in a true liquid, however, the particles in amorphous solids are not constantly changing their positions.

High Density and Incompressibility

In general, substances are most dense in the solid state. Solids tend to be slightly denser than liquids and much denser than gases. The higher density results from the fact that the particles of a solid are more closely packed than those of a liquid or a gas. Solid hydrogen is the least dense solid; its density is about 1/320 that of the densest element, osmium, Os.

Solids are generally less compressible than liquids. For practical purposes, solids can be considered incompressible. Some solids, such as wood and cork, may *seem* compressible, but they are not. They contain pores that are filled with air. When subjected to intense pressure, the pores are compressed, not the solid matter in the wood or cork itself.

©Andrew Syred/Photo Researchers, Inc.

FIGURE 3.2

Crystal Lattice of Sodium Chloride

(a) This is a scanning electron micrograph (SEM) of sodium chloride crystals.

Sodium ion, Na⁺

Chloride ion, Cl⁻

(b) The crystal structure of sodium chloride is made up of individual unit cells represented regularly in three dimensions. Here, one unit cell is outlined in red.

FIGURE 3.3

Crystal Systems in Minerals Shown are the seven basic crystal systems and representative crystals of each.

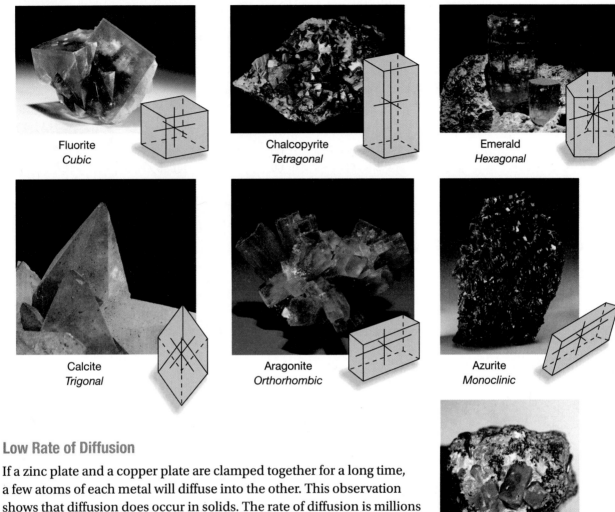

Fluorite
Cubic

Chalcopyrite
Tetragonal

Emerald
Hexagonal

Calcite
Trigonal

Aragonite
Orthorhombic

Azurite
Monoclinic

Low Rate of Diffusion

If a zinc plate and a copper plate are clamped together for a long time, a few atoms of each metal will diffuse into the other. This observation shows that diffusion does occur in solids. The rate of diffusion is millions of times faster in liquids than in solids, however.

▶ **MAIN IDEA**

Crystal particles are arranged in a three-dimensional lattice.

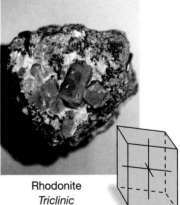

Rhodonite
Triclinic

Crystalline solids exist either as single crystals or as groups of crystals fused together. **The total three-dimensional arrangement of particles of a crystal is called a crystal structure.** The arrangement of particles in the crystal can be represented by a coordinate system called a lattice. **The smallest portion of a crystal lattice that shows the three-dimensional pattern of the entire lattice is called a unit cell.** Each crystal lattice contains many unit cells packed together. **Figure 3.2** (on the previous page) shows the relationship between a crystal lattice and its unit cell. A crystal and its unit cells can have any one of seven types of symmetry. This fact enables scientists to classify crystals by their shape. Diagrams and examples of each type of crystal symmetry are shown in **Figure 3.3**.

FIGURE 3.4

MELTING AND BOILING POINTS OF REPRESENTATIVE CRYSTALLINE SOLIDS

Type of substance	Formula	Melting point (°C)	Boiling point at 1 atm (°C)
ionic	NaCl	801	1413
	MgF_2	1266	2239
covalent network	$(SiO_2)_x$	1610	2230
	C_x (diamond)	3500	3930
metallic	Hg	−39	357
	Cu	1083	2567
	Fe	1535	2750
	W	3410	5660
covalent molecular (nonpolar)	H_2	−259	−253
	O_2	−218	−183
	CH_4	−182	−164
	CCl_4	−23	77
	C_6H_6	−6	80
covalent molecular (polar)	NH_3	−78	−33
	H_2O	0	100

Binding Forces in Crystals

Crystal structures can also be described in terms of the types of particles in the crystals and the types of chemical bonding between the particles. According to this method of classification, there are four types of crystals. These types are listed in **Figure 3.4.** Refer to this table as you read the following discussion.

1. *Ionic crystals.* The ionic crystal structure consists of positive and negative ions arranged in a regular pattern. The ions can be monatomic or polyatomic. Generally, ionic crystals form when Group 1 or Group 2 metals combine with Group 16 or Group 17 nonmetals or nonmetallic polyatomic ions. The strong binding forces between the positive and negative ions in the crystal structure give the ionic crystals certain properties. For example, these crystals are hard and brittle, have high melting points, and are good insulators.

2. *Covalent network crystals.* In covalent network crystals, each atom is covalently bonded to its nearest neighboring atoms. The covalent bonding extends throughout a network that includes a very large number of atoms. Three-dimensional covalent network solids include diamond, C_x, quartz, $(SiO_2)_x$ (see **Figure 3.5** on the next page), silicon carbide, $(SiC)_x$, and many oxides of transition metals. Such solids are essentially giant molecules. The subscript x in these formulas indicates that the component within the parentheses extends indefinitely. The network solids are nearly always very hard and brittle. They have rather high melting points and are usually nonconductors or semiconductors.

3. *Metallic crystals.* The metallic crystal structure consists of metal cations surrounded by a sea of delocalized valence electrons. The electrons come from the metal atoms and belong to the crystal as a whole. This explains the high electrical conductivity of metals.

4. *Covalent molecular crystals.* The crystal structure of a covalent molecular substance consists of covalently bonded molecules held together by intermolecular forces. If the molecules are nonpolar—for example, hydrogen, H_2, methane, CH_4, and benzene, C_6H_6—then there are only weak London dispersion forces between molecules. In a polar covalent molecular crystal, molecules are held together by dispersion forces, by somewhat stronger dipole-dipole forces, and sometimes by even stronger hydrogen bonding—for example, water, H_2O, and ammonia, NH_3. The forces that hold polar or nonpolar molecules together in the structure are much weaker than the covalent chemical bonds between the atoms within each molecule. Covalent molecular crystals thus have low melting points. They are easily vaporized, are relatively soft, and are good insulators. Ice crystals, the most familiar molecular crystals, are discussed in Section 5.

▶ MAIN IDEA

The particles in amorphous solids are not arranged in a regular pattern.

The word *amorphous* comes from the Greek for "without shape." Unlike the atoms that form crystals, the atoms that make up amorphous solids, such as glasses and plastics, are not arranged in a regular pattern.

Glasses are made by cooling certain molten materials in a way that prevents them from crystallizing. The properties that result make glasses suitable for many uses, including windows, light bulbs, transformer cores, and optical fibers that carry telephone conversations.

Plastics, another type of amorphous solid, are easily molded at high temperatures and pressures. They are used in many structural materials.

Other, more recently created amorphous solids have been placed in many important applications. Amorphous semiconductors are used in electronic devices, including solar cells, copiers, laser printers, and flat-panel displays for computer monitors and television screens.

©Scott Camazine/Photo Researchers, Inc

FIGURE 3.5

Covalent Network Crystals
Covalent network crystals include three-dimensional network solids, such as this quartz, $(SiO_2)_x$, shown here with its three-dimensional atomic structure.

✔ SECTION 3 FORMATIVE ASSESSMENT

▶ **Reviewing Main Ideas**

1. Describe the solid state according to the kinetic-molecular theory.

2. What is the difference between an amorphous solid and a crystalline solid?

3. Account for each of the following properties of solids: (a) the definite volume, (b) the relatively high density, (c) the extremely low rate of diffusion.

4. Compare and contrast the four types of crystals.

5. Why do crystalline solids shatter into regularly shaped fragments when broken?

✔ **Critical Thinking**

6. **RELATING IDEAS** Explain why ionic crystals melt at much higher temperatures than typical covalent molecular crystals.

Main Ideas

▶ Substances in equilibrium change back and forth between states at equal speeds.

▶ A liquid boils when it has absorbed enough energy to evaporate.

▶ Freezing occurs when a substance loses enough heat energy to solidify.

▶ Under certain conditions, water can exist in all three phases at the same time.

Changes of State

Key Terms

phase	boiling point	deposition
condensation	molar enthalpy of vaporization	phase diagram
equilibrium	freezing	triple point
equilibrium vapor pressure	freezing point	critical point
volatile liquid	molar enthalpy of fusion	critical temperature
boiling	sublimation	critical pressure

Matter on Earth can exist in any of three states—gas, liquid, or solid—and can change from one state to another. **Figure 4.1** lists the possible changes of state. In this section, you will examine these changes of state and the factors that cause them.

▶ **MAIN IDEA**

Substances in equilibrium change back and forth between states at equal speeds.

Some liquid chemical substances, such as rubbing alcohol, have an odor that is very easily detected. This is because some molecules at the upper surface of the liquid have enough energy to overcome the attraction of neighboring molecules, leave the liquid phase, and evaporate. **A phase is any part of a system that has uniform composition and properties.** In a closed bottle of rubbing alcohol, gas molecules under the cap strike the liquid surface and reenter the liquid phase through *condensation*. **Condensation is the process by which a gas changes to a liquid.** A gas in contact with its liquid or solid phase is often called a *vapor*.

If the temperature of the liquid remains constant and the cap remains closed, the rate at which molecules move from the liquid to vapor remains constant. Near the beginning of the evaporation process, very few molecules are in the gas phase, so the rate of condensation is very low.

GO ONLINE **Animated Chemistry**
HMHScience.com

Changes of State

FIGURE 4.1

POSSIBLE CHANGES OF STATE		
Change of state	**Process**	**Example**
solid ⟶ liquid	melting	ice ⟶ water
solid ⟶ gas	sublimation	dry ice ⟶ CO_2 gas
liquid ⟶ solid	freezing	water ⟶ ice
liquid ⟶ gas	vaporization	liquid bromine ⟶ bromine vapor
gas ⟶ liquid	condensation	water vapor ⟶ water
gas ⟶ solid	deposition	water vapor ⟶ ice

FIGURE 4.2

Liquid-Vapor Equilibrium A liquid-vapor equilibrium develops in a closed system.

(a) At first, there is only liquid present, but molecules are beginning to evaporate.

(b) Evaporation continues at a constant rate. Some vapor molecules are beginning to condense to liquid.

(c) Equilibrium has been reached between the rate of condensation and the rate of evaporation.

As more liquid evaporates, the increasing number of gas molecules causes the rate of condensation to increase until the rate of condensation equals the rate of evaporation and a state of equilibrium is established (see **Figure 4.2**). **Equilibrium is a dynamic condition in which two opposing changes occur at equal rates in a closed system.** Even though molecules are constantly moving between liquid and gas phases, there is no net change in the amount of substance in either phase.

Equilibrium Vapor Pressure of a Liquid

Vapor molecules in equilibrium with a liquid in a closed system exert a pressure proportional to the concentration of molecules in the vapor phase. The pressure exerted by a vapor in equilibrium with its corresponding liquid at a given temperature is called the **equilibrium vapor pressure** of the liquid.

The increase in equilibrium vapor pressure with increasing temperature can be explained in terms of the kinetic-molecular theory for the liquid and gaseous states. Increasing the temperature of a liquid increases the average kinetic energy of the liquid's molecules. This increases the number of molecules that have enough energy to escape from the liquid phase into the vapor phase. The resulting increased evaporation rate increases the number of molecules in the vapor phase, which in turn increases the equilibrium vapor pressure.

Every liquid has a specific equilibrium vapor pressure at a given temperature. The stronger these attractive forces are, the smaller is the percentage of liquid particles that can evaporate at any given temperature. A low percentage of evaporation results in a low equilibrium vapor pressure. **Volatile liquids,** which are liquids that evaporate readily, have relatively weak forces of attraction between their particles.

Ether is a typical volatile liquid. Nonvolatile liquids, such as molten ionic compounds, do not evaporate readily and have relatively strong attractive forces between their particles.

▶ MAIN IDEA

A liquid boils when it has absorbed enough energy to evaporate.

Equilibrium vapor pressures can be used to explain and define the concept of **boiling,** which is the conversion of a liquid to a vapor within the liquid as well as at its surface.

If the temperature of the liquid is increased, the equilibrium vapor pressure also increases. The **boiling point** of a liquid is the temperature at which the equilibrium vapor pressure of the liquid equals the atmospheric pressure. The lower the atmospheric pressure is, the lower the boiling point is.

At the boiling point, all of the energy absorbed is used to evaporate the liquid, and the temperature remains constant as long as the pressure does not change. If the pressure above the liquid being heated is increased, the temperature of the liquid will rise until the vapor pressure equals the new pressure and the liquid boils once again. A pressure cooker is sealed so that steam pressure builds up over the surface of the boiling water inside. The boiling temperature of the water increases, resulting in shorter cooking times. A device called a *vacuum evaporator* causes boiling at lower-than-normal temperatures. Vacuum evaporators used to prepare evaporated and sweetened condensed milk remove water from milk and sugar solutions. Under reduced pressure, the water boils away at a temperature low enough to avoid scorching the milk or sugar.

At normal atmospheric pressure (1 atm, 760 torr, or 101.3 kPa), water boils at exactly 100°C. This is the *normal* boiling point of water.

FIGURE 4.3

Boiling Point The vapor pressure of any liquid increases as its temperature increases. A liquid boils when its vapor pressure equals the pressure of the atmosphere.

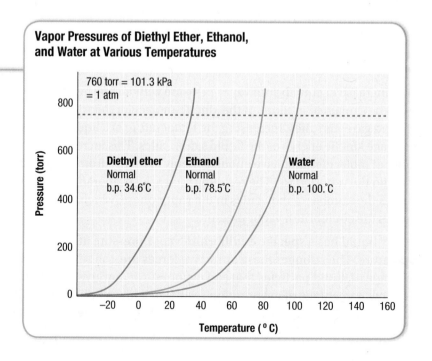

Vapor Pressures of Diethyl Ether, Ethanol, and Water at Various Temperatures

FIGURE 4.4

Energy Distribution

The number of molecules in a liquid with various kinetic energies is represented at two different temperatures.

CRITICAL THINKING

Analyze Look at the graph, and describe what is happening in the shaded area at the lower right.

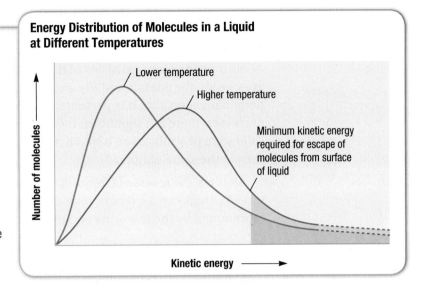

Energy Distribution of Molecules in a Liquid at Different Temperatures

Lower temperature

Higher temperature

Minimum kinetic energy required for escape of molecules from surface of liquid

Number of molecules

Kinetic energy

Figure 4.3 (see previous page) shows that the normal boiling point of each liquid occurs when its equilibrium vapor pressure equals 760 torr. Energy must be added continuously in order to keep a liquid boiling. The temperature of a liquid and its vapor at the boiling point remains constant despite the continuous addition of energy. The added energy is used to overcome the attractive forces between molecules of the liquid during the liquid-to-gas change and is stored in the vapor as potential energy.

Molar Enthalpy of Vaporization

The amount of energy as heat that is needed to vaporize one mole of liquid at the liquid's boiling point at constant pressure is called the liquid's **molar enthalpy of vaporization,** ΔH_v. Molar enthalpy of vaporization measures the attraction between particles of the liquid. The stronger the attraction is, the more energy is required to overcome it, resulting in a higher molar enthalpy of vaporization. Each liquid has a characteristic molar enthalpy of vaporization. Liquid water's molar enthalpy of vaporization is very high, due to its extensive hydrogen bonding. This makes water an effective cooling agent. When water evaporates, the escaping molecules carry away with them a great deal of energy as heat. **Figure 4.4** shows the distribution of the kinetic energies of molecules in a liquid at two different temperatures. At higher temperatures, a greater portion of the surface molecules have the kinetic energy required to escape and become vapor.

▶ MAIN IDEA

Freezing occurs when a substance loses enough heat energy to solidify.

The physical change of a liquid to a solid is called **freezing.** Freezing involves a loss of energy in the form of heat by the liquid.

$$\text{liquid} \rightarrow \text{solid} + \text{energy}$$

In the case of a pure crystalline substance, this change occurs at constant temperature. **The normal freezing point is the temperature at which the solid and liquid are in equilibrium at 1 atm (760 torr, or 101.3 kPa) pressure.** At the freezing point, particles of the liquid and the solid have the same average kinetic energy, and the energy lost during freezing is the potential energy that was present in the liquid. At the same time energy decreases, there is a significant increase in particle order, because the solid state of a substance is much more ordered than the liquid state, even at the same temperature.

Melting, the reverse of freezing, also occurs at constant temperature. As a solid melts, it continuously absorbs energy as heat, as represented by the following equation.

$$\text{solid} + \text{energy} \longrightarrow \text{liquid}$$

For pure crystalline solids, the melting point and freezing point are the same. At equilibrium, melting and freezing proceed at equal rates. The following general equilibrium equation can be used to represent these states.

$$\text{solid} + \text{energy} \rightleftharpoons \text{liquid}$$

At normal atmospheric pressure, the temperature of a system containing ice and liquid water will remain at 0.°C as long as both ice and water are present, no matter what the surrounding temperature. Adding energy in the form of heat to such a system shifts the equilibrium to the right. That shift increases the proportion of liquid water and decreases that of ice. Only after all the ice has melted will the addition of energy increase the temperature of the system.

Molar Enthalpy of Fusion

The amount of energy as heat required to melt one mole of solid at the solid's melting point is the solid's molar enthalpy of fusion, ΔH_f. The energy absorbed increases the solid's potential energy as its particles are pulled apart, overcoming the attractive forces holding them together. At the same time, there is a significant decrease in particle order as the substance makes the transformation from solid to liquid. Similar to the molar enthalpy of vaporization, the magnitude of the molar enthalpy of fusion depends on the attraction between the solid particles.

Sublimation and Deposition

At sufficiently low temperature and pressure conditions, a liquid cannot exist. Under such conditions, a solid substance exists in equilibrium with its vapor instead of its liquid, as represented by the following equation.

$$\text{solid} + \text{energy} \rightleftharpoons \text{vapor}$$

The change of state from a solid directly to a gas is known as sublimation. The reverse process is called **deposition, the change of state from a gas directly to a solid.** Among the common substances that sublime at ordinary temperatures are dry ice (solid CO_2) and iodine.

Ordinary ice sublimes slowly at temperatures lower than its melting point (0.°C). This explains how a thin layer of snow can eventually disappear, even if the temperature remains below 0.°C. Sublimation occurs in frost-free refrigerators when the temperature in the freezer compartment is periodically raised to cause any ice that has formed to sublime. A blower then removes the water vapor that has formed. The formation of frost on a cold surface is a familiar example of deposition.

▶ MAIN IDEA

Under certain conditions, water can exist in all three phases at the same time.

A **phase diagram** is a graph of pressure versus temperature that shows the conditions under which the phases of a substance exist. A phase diagram also reveals how the states of a system change with changing temperature or pressure.

Figure 4.5 shows the phase diagram for water over a range of temperatures and pressures. Note the three curves, AB, AC, and AD. Curve AB indicates the temperature and pressure conditions at which ice and water vapor can coexist at equilibrium. Curve AC indicates the temperature and pressure conditions at which liquid water and water vapor coexist at equilibrium. Similarly, curve AD indicates the temperature and pressure conditions at which ice and liquid water coexist at equilibrium. Because ice is less dense than liquid water, an increase in pressure lowers the melting point. (Most substances have a positive slope for this curve.) Point A is the triple point of water. The **triple point** of a substance indicates the temperature and pressure conditions at which the solid, liquid, and vapor of the substance can coexist at equilibrium. Point C is the critical point of water. The **critical point** of a substance indicates the critical temperature and critical pressure. The **critical temperature** (t_c) is the temperature above which the substance cannot exist in the liquid state.

FIGURE 4.5

Phase Diagram This phase diagram shows the relationships between the physical states of water and its pressure and temperature.

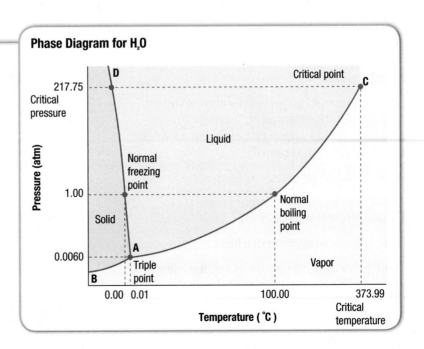

Phase Diagram for H₂O

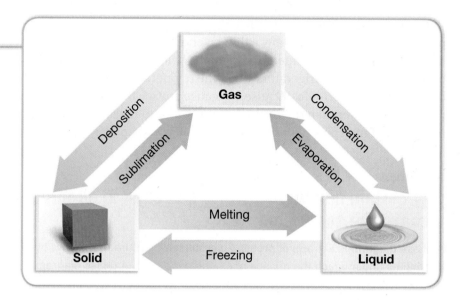

FIGURE 4.6

Changes of State Solids, liquids, and gases can undergo various changes of state. The changes shown in green are exothermic, and those shown in blue are endothermic.

The critical temperature of water is 373.99°C. Above this temperature, water cannot be liquefied, no matter how much pressure is applied. The **critical pressure** (P_c) is the lowest pressure at which the substance can exist as a liquid at the critical temperature. The critical pressure of water is 217.75 atm.

The phase diagram in **Figure 4.5** on the previous page indicates the normal boiling point and the normal freezing point of water. It also shows how boiling point and freezing point change with pressure. As shown by the slope of line AD, ice melts at a higher temperature with decreasing pressure. Below the triple point, the temperature of sublimation decreases with decreasing pressure. **Figure 4.6** summarizes the changes of state of solids, liquids, and gases.

✔ SECTION 4 FORMATIVE ASSESSMENT

▶ Reviewing Main Ideas

1. What is equilibrium?

2. What happens when a liquid-vapor system at equilibrium experiences an increase in temperature? What happens when it experiences a decrease in temperature?

3. What would be an example of deposition?

4. What is the equilibrium vapor pressure of a liquid? How is it measured?

5. What is the boiling point of a liquid?

6. In the phase diagram for water, what is meant by the triple point and the critical point?

✔ Critical Thinking

7. **INTERPRETING GRAPHICS** Refer to the phase diagram for water (**Figure 4.5**) to answer the following questions.

   a. Describe all the changes a sample of solid water would undergo when heated from −10°C to its critical temperature at a pressure of 1.00 atm.

   b. Describe all the changes a sample of water vapor would undergo when cooled from 110°C to 5°C at a pressure of 1.00 atm.

   c. At approximately what pressure will water be a vapor at 0°C?

   d. Within what range of pressures will water be a liquid at temperatures above its normal boiling point?

Water

Water is a familiar substance in all three physical states: solid, liquid, and gas. On Earth, water is by far the most abundant liquid. Oceans, rivers, and lakes cover about 75% of Earth's surface. Significant quantities of water are also frozen in glaciers. Water is an essential component of all organisms; 70% to 90% of the mass of living things is water. The chemical reactions of most life processes take place in water, and water is frequently a reactant or product in such reactions. In order to better understand the importance of water, let us take a closer look at its structure and its properties.

SECTION 5

Main Ideas

▶ The properties of water in all phases are determined by its structure.

▶ The molar enthalpy of water determines many of its physical characteristics.

▶ Water playes a unique role in chemical and biological systems.

▶ **MAIN IDEA**
The properties of water in all phases are determined by its structure.

Water molecules consist of two atoms of hydrogen and one atom of oxygen united by polar-covalent bonds. Research shows that a water molecule is bent. The structure can be represented as follows.

$$H \overset{\overset{\displaystyle \cdot\cdot \atop O \atop \cdot\cdot}{}}{\underset{105°}{\frown}} H$$

The angle between the two hydrogen-oxygen bonds is about 105°. This is close to the angle expected for sp^3 hybridization of the oxygen-atom orbitals.

The molecules in solid or liquid water are linked by hydrogen bonding. The number of linked molecules decreases with increasing temperature, because increases in kinetic energy make hydrogen bond formation difficult. Nevertheless, there are usually from four to eight molecules per group in liquid water, as shown in **Figure 5.1.** If it were not for these molecular groups, water would be a gas at room temperature. Nonpolar molecules, such as methane, CH_4, that are similar in size and mass to water molecules do not undergo hydrogen bonding. Such substances are gases at room temperature.

FIGURE 5.1

Liquid Water   Within the water molecule, oxygen and hydrogen are covalently bonded to each other. Hydrogen bonds hold the molecules together in groups.

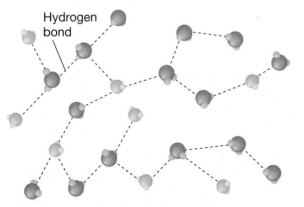

Hydrogen bond

FIGURE 5.2

Solid Water Ice contains the same types of bonding as liquid water. However, the structure of the hydrogen bonding is much more rigid and open than it is in liquid water.

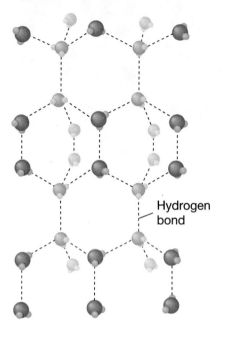

Hydrogen bond

Ice consists of water molecules in the hexagonal arrangement shown in **Figure 5.2**. The empty spaces between molecules in this pattern account for the relatively low density of ice. As ice is heated, the increased energy of the molecules causes them to move and vibrate more vigorously. When the melting point is reached, the energy of the molecules is so great that the rigid open structure of the ice crystals breaks down, and ice turns into liquid water.

Figure 5.1 and **Figure 5.2** also show that the hydrogen bonds between molecules of liquid water at 0°C are fewer and more disordered than those between molecules of ice at the same temperature. Because the rigid open structure of ice has broken down, water molecules can crowd closer together. Thus, liquid water is denser than ice.

As the liquid water is warmed from 0°C, the water molecules crowd still closer together. Water molecules are as tightly packed as possible at 3.98°C. At temperatures above 3.98°C, the increasing kinetic energy of the water molecules causes them to overcome molecular attractions. The molecules move farther apart as the temperature continues to rise. As the temperature approaches the boiling point, groups of liquid water molecules absorb enough energy to break up into separate molecules. Because of hydrogen bonding between water molecules, a high kinetic energy is needed, causing water's boiling point to be relatively high (100°C) compared to other liquids that have similar molar masses.

▶ **MAIN IDEA**

The molar enthalpy of water determines many of its physical characteristics.

At room temperature, pure liquid water is transparent, odorless, tasteless, and almost colorless. Any observable odor or taste is caused by impurities, such as dissolved minerals, liquids, or gases.

As shown by its phase diagram in **Figure 4.5** (in Section 4), water freezes and ice melts at 0°C at a pressure of 1 atm (101.3 kPa). The molar enthalpy of fusion of ice is 6.009 kJ/mol. That value is relatively large compared with the molar enthalpy of fusion of other solids. As you have read, water has the unusual property of expanding in volume as it freezes, because its molecules form an open rigid structure. As a result, ice at 0°C has a density of only about 0.917 g/cm^3, but liquid water at 0°C has a density of 0.999 84 g/cm^3.

This lower density explains why ice floats in liquid water. The insulating effect of floating ice is particularly important in the case of large bodies of water. If ice were more dense than liquid water, it would sink to the bottom of lakes and ponds, where it would be less likely to melt completely. The water of such bodies of water in temperate climates would eventually freeze solid, killing nearly all the living things in it.

Under a pressure of 1 atm (101.3 kPa), water boils at 100°C. At this temperature, water's molar enthalpy of vaporization is 40.79 kJ/mol. Both the boiling point and the molar enthalpy of vaporization of water are quite high compared with those of nonpolar substances of comparable molecular mass, such as methane. The values are high because of the strong hydrogen bonding that must be overcome for boiling to occur. The high molar enthalpy of vaporization makes water useful for household steam-heating systems. The steam (vaporized water) stores a great deal of energy as heat. When the steam condenses in radiators, great quantities of energy are released. In living organisms, the high molar enthalpy of vaporization helps them to resist dehydration when sources of water intake are restricted and provides a large degree of evaporative cooling to carry excess heat away from their bodies. This property especially allows warm-blooded organisms to better regulate their internal temperatures, reduce cell death from water loss, and maintain homeostasis.

Using Molar Enthalpy of Vaporization

GO ONLINE

Learn It! Video
HMHScience.com

Solve It! Cards
HMHScience.com

Sample Problem A How much energy is absorbed when 47.0 g of ice melts at STP? How much energy is absorbed when this same mass of liquid water boils?

① ANALYZE

Given: mass of $H_2O(s)$ = 47.0 g
mass of $H_2O(l)$ = 47.0 g
molar enthalpy of fusion of ice = 6.009 kJ/mol
molar enthalpy of vaporization = 40.79 kJ/mol

Unknown: energy absorbed when ice melts; energy absorbed when liquid water boils

② PLAN

First, convert the mass of water from grams to moles.

$$47.0 \text{ g } H_2O \times \frac{1 \text{ mol } H_2O}{18.02 \text{ g } H_2O} = 2.61 \text{ mol } H_2O$$

Then, use the molar enthalpy of fusion of a solid to calculate the amount of energy absorbed when the solid melts. Multiply the number of moles by the amount of energy needed to melt one mole of ice at its melting point (the molar enthalpy of fusion of ice). Using the same method, calculate the amount of energy absorbed when water boils by using the molar enthalpy of vaporization.

amount of substance (mol) × molar enthalpy of fusion or vaporization (kJ/mol) = energy (kJ)

③ SOLVE

2.61 mol × 6.009 kJ/mol = 15.7 kJ (on melting)
2.61 mol × 40.79 kJ/mol = 106 kJ (on vaporizing or boiling)

④ CHECK YOUR WORK

Units have canceled correctly. The answers have the proper number of significant figures and are reasonably close to estimated values of 18 (3 × 6) and 120 (3 × 40), respectively.

Practice   Answers in Appendix E

1. What quantity of energy is released when 506 g of liquid water freezes?
2. What mass of steam is required to release 4.97×10^5 kJ of energy on condensation?

FIGURE 5.3

The Big Blue Marble Earth appears blue from outer space because two-thirds of its surface is covered in liquid water.

▶ MAIN IDEA

Water plays a unique role in chemical and biological systems.

In a later chapter, you will learn about some complex molecules that make life on Earth possible. As important as proteins, carbohydrates, and DNA are, life as we know it would be impossible without water. For such a small molecule, water plays a large role in biological systems. All of water's physical and chemical properties make water the perfect substance for supporting life on Earth. Those same properties are also important in determining the unique role of water in chemical systems.

Physical Properties

Looking at depictions of the Earth from outer space, like the one in **Figure 5.3**, some have described our planet as resembling a "big blue marble." Earth appears blue because liquid water covers two-thirds of its surface. Water, in fact, is one of the few naturally occurring liquids on this planet. Not only that, but water also is the only substance that occurs naturally in all three common physical states (solid, liquid, and gas) on Earth's surface. This quality makes possible the water cycle, the natural cycle of evaporation and condensation that carries water from the oceans to the clouds and then to the land.

Water's ability to remain a liquid under a wide range of temperatures is crucial to life as well. Earth's surface can experience wide fluctuations in temperature without the oceans freezing or boiling. In addition, the high specific heat capacity of water makes the oceans a climate moderator. Because a large quantity of energy as heat is required to raise the temperature of water, the oceans warm and cool much more slowly than land areas. As a result, coastal areas have warmer winters and cooler summers than areas farther inland. Ocean currents also transport warm water from tropical regions toward the poles and transport cool water in the opposite direction. This redistribution of energy as heat also has a moderating effect on climate.

But as you learned on the previous page, perhaps water's most impressive property is that its volume increases as it freezes. Ice, therefore, floats on liquid water. This property prevents the millions of organisms that live in water from perishing in winter. As shown in **Figure 5.4**, even an apparently frozen-over lake is still mostly liquid water.

FIGURE 5.4

Ice Floats As the photo shows, the scuba diver can move freely in the water even when its surface is frozen enough for others to walk on it. Animals and humans living in colder climates depend on aquatic organisms as a primary food source. Because ice floats, this source always remains available to them. .

Water's Role in Biological Systems

Water dissolves many substances, especially polar molecules and ionic substances. So, water plays a vital role in living systems. For example, most of the chemical reactions essential to life take place in aqueous solutions within the cells of organisms. Also, some compounds, known as electrolytes, break apart to form ions that play key roles in biological functions. For example, sodium and potassium ions are used by complex animals to regulate processes such as muscle function. Many sports drinks, such as the one in **Figure 5.5**, claim to replenish electrolytes.

The fact that water is such a powerful solvent also contributes to its role as a transport medium in living things. Water provides organisms with a way to transport materials into and out of the cells that need them. In the human body, for example, blood consists of materials suspended in plasma, a clear fluid that is about 90 percent water. Many substances dissolve in plasma and can be transported throughout the body. Plants also use water to transport nutrients through their vascular system.

Finally, water itself participates in many biochemical reactions. Along with carbon dioxide from the air, water is an essential reactant in photosynthesis, the process by which plants convert energy from the sun into chemical energy that organisms can use. Water also participates in reactions that assemble molecules for energy storage and disassemble them when they are needed to fuel cell processes.

Water's Role in Chemical Systems

A chemical system is any group of substances that is studied to see what the inputs, outputs, and reactions among the components are. Because of its unique properties, water plays an important role in chemical systems in both the natural world and the designed world.

Water's properties as a solvent make our oceans salty, enable geochemical cycles to move substances around Earth, and enable water to shape Earth's surface as water dissolves and deposits minerals. Water is used as a coolant in power plants because water's high specific heat capacity allows it to absorb a lot of heat from other substances. The participation of water in reactions is also important in many chemical systems. For example, the reaction of water and carbon dioxide to form carbonic acid is critical to the pH and the chemistry of the oceans and atmosphere.

FIGURE 5.5

Electrolyte Solutions The labels of many sports drinks note that the drink contains electrolytes.

✔ SECTION 5 FORMATIVE ASSESSMENT

▶ Reviewing Main Ideas

1. Why is a water molecule polar?

2. How is the structure of water responsible for some of water's unique characteristics?

3. Describe the arrangement of molecules in liquid water and in ice.

4. Why does ice float? Why is this phenomenon important to living things?

5. Is more energy required to melt one gram of ice at 0°C or to boil one gram of water at 100°C? How do you know?

✔ Critical Thinking

6. **RELATING IDEAS** Describe what might be the result if water could freeze at a higher temperature. How might this affect chemical and biological systems that contain water?

When one mole of a liquid freezes to a solid, energy is released as attractive forces between particles pull the disordered particles of the liquid into a more orderly crystalline solid. When the solid melts to a liquid, the solid must absorb the same quantity of energy in order to separate the particles of the crystal and overcome the attractive forces opposing separation. This quantity of energy used to melt or freeze one mole of a substance at its melting point is called its molar enthalpy of fusion, ΔH_f.

Problem-Solving TIPS

- The enthalpy of fusion of a substance can be given as either joules per gram or kilojoules per mole.
- *Molar* enthalpy of fusion is most commonly used in calculations.
- The enthalpy of fusion is the energy absorbed or given off as heat when a substance melts or freezes at the melting point of the substance.
- There is no net change in temperature as the change of state occurs.

Samples

7.30 kJ of energy is required to melt 0.650 mol of ethylene glycol ($C_2H_6O_2$) at its melting point. Calculate the molar enthalpy of fusion, ΔH_f, of ethylene glycol and the energy absorbed.

$$\text{molar enthalpy of fusion} = \Delta H_f = \frac{\text{energy absorbed}}{\text{moles of substance}}$$

$$\Delta H_{f, \text{ ethylene glycol}} = \frac{7.30 \text{ kJ}}{0.065 \text{ mol}} = 11.2 \frac{\text{kJ}}{\text{mol}}$$

Determine the quantity of energy that will be needed to melt 2.50×10^5 kg of iron at its melting point, 1536°C. The ΔH_f of iron is 13.807 kJ/mol.

To calculate the number of moles of iron, use the equation below.

$$\text{moles of substance} = \frac{\text{mass of substance}}{\text{molar mass of substance}}$$

Next, use the following equation for energy as heat absorbed.

$$\text{energy absorbed} = \Delta H_f \times \text{moles of substance}$$

Now, substitute the calculation for moles of substance, and solve.

$$\text{energy absorbed} = \Delta H_f \times \frac{\text{grams of substance}}{\text{molar mass of substance}}$$

$$= 13.807 \frac{\text{kJ}}{\text{mol}} \times \frac{2.50 \times 10^8 \text{ g Fe}}{55.847 \text{ g Fe/mol Fe}}$$

$$\text{energy absorbed} = 6.18 \times 10^7 \text{ kJ}$$

Practice   Answers in Appendix E

1. Calculate the molar enthalpy of fusion of silver if 1.940 mol of silver requires 22.60 kJ of energy to change from a solid to a liquid at its melting point, 961°C.
2. What quantity of energy in kJ must be absorbed by 6.47 mol of solid acetic acid, $C_2H_4O_2$, to melt it at its melting point, 16.7°C? The ΔH_f for acetic acid is 11.54 kJ/mol.

CHAPTER 10 Summary

BIG IDEA The kinetic-molecular theory of matter explains the properties of solids, liquids, and gases in terms of the energy of particles and the forces acting between them.

SECTION 1 The Kinetic-Molecular Theory of Matter

- The kinetic-molecular theory of matter can be used to explain the properties of gases, liquids, and solids.
- The kinetic-molecular theory of gases describes a model of an ideal gas.
- Gases consist of large numbers of tiny, fast-moving particles that are far apart relative to their size.

KEY TERMS

kinetic-molecular theory
ideal gas
elastic collision

diffusion
effusion
real gas

SECTION 2 Liquids

- The particles of a liquid are closer together and more ordered than those of a gas and are less ordered than those of a solid.
- Liquids have a definite volume and a fairly high density, and they are relatively incompressible. Like gases, liquids can flow and thus are considered to be fluids.

KEY TERMS

fluid
surface tension
capillary action

vaporization
evaporation
freezing

SECTION 3 Solids

- The particles of a solid are not nearly as free to move about as those of a liquid or a gas are.
- Solids have a definite shape and may be crystalline or amorphous. They have a definite volume and are generally nonfluid.
- A crystal structure is the total three-dimensional array of points that describes the arrangement of the particles of a crystal.
- Unlike crystalline solids, amorphous solids do not have a highly ordered structure or a regular shape.

KEY TERMS

crystalline solid
crystal
amorphous solid
melting
melting point
supercooled liquid
crystal structure
unit cell

SECTION 4 Changes of State

- A liquid in a closed system will gradually reach a liquid-vapor equilibrium as the rate at which molecules condense equals the rate at which they evaporate.
- When two opposing changes occur at equal rates in the same closed system, the system is said to be in dynamic equilibrium.

KEY TERMS

phase
condensation
equilibrium
equilibrium vapor pressure
volatile liquid
boiling
boiling point
molar enthalpy of vaporization

freezing
freezing point
molar enthalpy of fusion
sublimation
deposition
phase diagram
triple point
critical point
critical temperature
critical pressure

SECTION 5 Water

- The structure and the hydrogen bonding in water are responsible for its relatively high melting point, molar enthalpy of fusion, boiling point, and molar enthalpy of vaporization.
- Water's properties make it important to life on Earth.

CHAPTER 10 **Review**

GO ONLINE

Interactive Review
HMHScience.com

Review Games
Concept Maps

SECTION 1

The Kinetic-Molecular Theory of Matter

 REVIEWING MAIN IDEAS

1. What idea is the kinetic-molecular theory based on?

2. What is an ideal gas?

3. State the five basic assumptions of the kinetic-molecular theory.

4. How do gases compare with liquids and solids in terms of the distance between their molecules?

5. What is the relationship between the temperature, speed, and kinetic energy of gas molecules?

6. **a.** What is diffusion?
   b. What factors affect the rate of diffusion of one gas through another?

SECTION 2

Liquids

 REVIEWING MAIN IDEAS

7. What is a fluid?

8. What is surface tension?

9. Give two reasons that evaporation is a crucial process in nature.

SECTION 3

Solids

REVIEWING MAIN IDEAS

10. List six properties of solids, and explain each in terms of the kinetic-molecular theory of solids.

11. List four common examples of amorphous solids.

12. List and describe the four types of crystals in terms of the nature of their component particles and the type of bonding between them.

SECTION 4

Changes of State

REVIEWING MAIN IDEAS

13. Using **Figure 4.3,** estimate the approximate equilibrium vapor pressure of each of the following at the specified temperature.
    a. water at 80°C
    b. diethyl ether at 20°C
    c. ethanol at 60°C

14. **a.** What is sublimation?
    b. Give two examples of common substances that sublime at ordinary temperatures.

15. What is meant by the normal freezing point of a substance?

16. Explain how the attractive forces between the particles in a liquid are related to the equilibrium vapor pressure of that liquid.

17. Explain the relationship between atmospheric pressure and the actual boiling point of a liquid.

18. Explain the relationship between the molar enthalpy of fusion of a solid and the strength of attraction between that solid's particles.

PRACTICE PROBLEMS

19. **a.** The molar enthalpy of vaporization for water is 40.79 kJ/mol. Express this enthalpy of vaporization in joules per gram.
    b. The molar enthalpy of fusion for water is 6.009 kJ/mol. Express this enthalpy of fusion in joules per gram.

20. Calculate the molar enthalpy of vaporization of a substance, given that 0.433 mol of the substance absorbs 36.5 kJ of energy when it is vaporized.

21. Given that a substance has a molar mass of 259.0 g/mol and a 71.8 g sample of the substance absorbs 4.307 kJ when it melts,
    a. calculate the number of moles in the sample.
    b. calculate the molar enthalpy of fusion.

22. a. Calculate the number of moles in a liquid sample of a substance that has a molar enthalpy of fusion of 3.811 kJ/mol, given that the sample releases 83.2 kJ when it freezes.
  b. Calculate the molar mass of this substance if the mass of the sample is 5519 g.

SECTION 5
Water

▶ REVIEWING MAIN IDEAS

23. Describe the structure of a water molecule.

24. a. List at least eight physical properties of water.
  b. Referencing three of these properties, explain the unique role of water in biological and chemical systems.

PRACTICE PROBLEMS

25. Which contains more molecules of water: 5.00 cm³ of ice at 0°C or 5.00 cm³ of liquid water at 0.°C? How many more? What is the ratio of the numbers of molecules in these two samples?

26. a. What volume and mass of steam at 100.°C and 1.00 atm would release the same amount of energy during condensation as 100. cm³ of liquid water would release during freezing?
  b. What do you note, qualitatively, about the relative volumes and masses of steam and liquid water required to release the same amount of heat? (Hint: See Sample Problem A.)

Mixed Review

▶ REVIEWING MAIN IDEAS

27. Find the molar enthalpy of vaporization for a substance, given that 3.21 mol of the substance absorbs 28.4 kJ of energy as heat when the substance changes from a liquid to a gas.

28. Water's molar enthalpy of fusion is 6.009 kJ/mol. Calculate the amount of energy as heat required to melt 7.95×10^5 g of ice.

29. A certain substance has a molar enthalpy of vaporization of 31.6 kJ/mol. How much of it is in a sample that requires 57.0 kJ to vaporize?

30. Given that water has a molar enthalpy of vaporization of 40.79 kJ/mol, how many grams of water could be vaporized by 0.545 kJ?

31. Calculate the amount of energy released as heat by the freezing of 13.3 g of a liquid substance, given that the substance has a molar mass of 82.9 g/mol and a molar enthalpy of fusion of 4.60 kJ/mol.

32. What volume and mass of steam at 100.°C and 760. torr would release the same amount of energy as heat during condensation as 65.5 cm³ of liquid water would release during freezing?

33. The following liquid-vapor system is at equilibrium at a given temperature in a closed system.

$$\text{liquid} + \text{energy} \rightleftharpoons \text{vapor}$$

Suppose the temperature is increased, and equilibrium is established at the higher temperature. How does the final value of each of the following compare with its initial value? (In each case, answer either higher, lower, or the same.)
  a. the rate of evaporation
  b. the rate of condensation
  c. the final concentration of vapor molecules
  d. the final number of liquid molecules

34. Given a sample of water at any point on curve AB in **Figure 4.5,** what effect would each of the following changes have on that sample?
  a. adding energy at constant pressure
  b. decreasing the volume at constant temperature
  c. removing energy at constant pressure
  d. increasing the volume at constant temperature

35. Using the phase diagram for CO₂, describe all the phase changes that would occur when CO₂ is heated from −100°C to −10°C at a constant pressure of 6 atm.

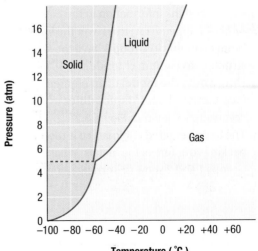

CO₂ Phase Diagram

CRITICAL THINKING

36. Interpreting Concepts During the freezing of a substance, energy is being removed from that substance. Yet the temperature of the liquid-solid system remains constant. Explain this phenomenon.

37. Applying Models At normal atmospheric pressure, the temperature of an ice-water system remains at 0°C as long as both ice and liquid water are present, regardless of the surrounding temperature. Explain why this occurs.

38. Predicting Outcomes Given a sample of water at any point on curve AD in **Figure 4.5,** how could more of the liquid water in that sample be converted into a solid without changing the temperature? Explain your reasoning.

39. Interpreting Diagrams Refer to the phase diagram in question 35.
  a. Explain what happens when solid CO_2 ("dry ice") warms up to room temperature at normal atmospheric pressure.
  b. Is there a pressure below which liquid CO_2 cannot exist? Estimate that pressure from the graph.

USING THE HANDBOOK

40. The *Elements Handbook* (Appendix A) contains a table of properties for each group that includes information on the crystal structures of the elements. Most metals crystallize in one of three lattice arrangements: body-centered cubic, face-centered cubic, or hexagonal close-packed. **Figure 3.2** shows a model of the face-centered cubic lattice for sodium chloride. Use this figure and the information in the *Elements Handbook* (Appendix A) to answer the following.
  a. What elements in Group 2 have the same lattice structure as sodium chloride?
  b. How would the model of an element in a face-centered cubic lattice differ from the compound shown in **Figure 3.2**?
  c. The body-centered cubic lattice is the least-efficient packing structure of the metals. What elements in Groups 1 and 2 show this arrangement?

RESEARCH AND WRITING

41. Ceramics are formed from silicates found in the soil. Artists use them to create pottery, but engineers and scientists have created ceramics with superconductive properties. Investigate the growing field of superconductive ceramics.

42. Liquid crystals are substances that possess the combined properties of both liquids and crystals. Write a report on these substances and the various uses we are finding for them.

ALTERNATIVE ASSESSMENT

43. Compile separate lists of crystalline and amorphous solids found in your home. Compare your lists with those of your classmates.

44. After consulting with your teacher, design an experiment to grow crystals of various safe, common household materials. Record the conditions under which each type of crystal is best grown.

Standards-Based Assessment

Record your answers on a separate piece of paper.

MULTIPLE CHOICE

1 Pure liquids boil at higher temperatures under high pressures than they do under low pressures, because —

A liquid molecules are closer together at higher pressures

B it takes a higher temperature for the vapor pressure to equal the higher external pressure

C vapor molecules are farther apart at higher pressures

D the vapor diffuses more rapidly at higher pressures

2 Water boils at 100°C. Ethanol boils at 78.5°C. Which of the following statements is *true*?

A Water has the higher vapor pressure at 78.5°C.

B Ethanol has the higher vapor pressure at 78.5°C.

C Both have the same vapor pressure at 78.5°C.

D Vapor pressure is not related to boiling point.

3 Which of the following is *not* a typical property of solids?

A very low melting point

B high density

C easily compressible

D low rate of diffusion

4 The kinetic-molecular theory states that ideal gas molecules —

A are in constant, rapid, random motion

B slow down as temperature increases

C exert forces of attraction and repulsion on each other

D have high densities compared with liquids and solids

Use the graph of vapor pressures to answer questions 5 and 6.

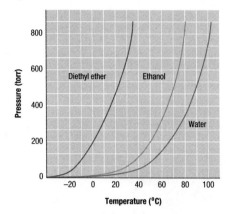

5 Estimate the boiling point of ethanol at an applied (external) pressure of 200 torr.

A 10°C

B 40°C

C 50°C

D 80°C

6 From what you know of the properties of water, estimate which value best corresponds to average atmospheric pressure.

A 200 torr

B 460 torr

C 600 torr

D 760 torr

GRIDDED RESPONSE

7 It is found that 60.0 J of energy is required to melt 15 g of a substance. The molar mass of the substance is 120 g/mol. Calculate the enthalpy of fusion of the substance in kilojoules per mole.

Test Tip

Test questions are not necessarily arranged in order of increasing difficulty. If you are unable to answer a question, mark it and move on to other questions

CHAPTER 11
Gases

BIG IDEA
The gas laws describe mathematical relationships among the pressure, temperature, volume, and quantity of gases.

ONLINE Chemistry
HMHScience.com

ONLINE LABS
- Mass and Density of Air at Different Pressures
- Boyle's Law
- Molar Volume of a Gas
- Generating and Collecting O_2
- Generating and Collecting H_2
- Testing for Dissolved Oxygen
- Why Are All the Fish Dying?

GO ONLINE
Why It Matters Video
HMHScience.com

Gases

(c) ©Pictor International/ImageState/Alamy; (b) ©Corbis

Gases and Pressure

Main Ideas

▶ Collisions of air molecules generate pressure.

▶ Pressure depends on force and area.

▶ The total pressure of a gas mixture is the sum of the pressures of the gases in it.

Key Terms

pressure
newton
barometer

millimeters of mercury
atmosphere of pressure
pascal

partial pressure
Dalton's law of partial pressures

In the chapter "States of Matter," you read about the kinetic-molecular theory, which is based on the idea that particles of matter are always in motion. In this section, you will study the implications of the kinetic-molecular theory of gases.

You have learned that the temperature of a gas is related to the kinetic energy of the gas molecules. Now you will learn about other properties of gases, including pressure, volume, and amount of gas present, and about the relationships among these properties.

▶ **MAIN IDEA**

Collisions of air molecules generate pressure.

If you pump air into an automobile tire, the pressure in the tire will increase. The pressure increase is caused by the increase in the number of collisions of molecules of air with the inside walls of the tire. The collisions cause an outward push, or force, against the inside walls. Gas molecules exert pressure on any surface with which they collide. The pressure exerted by a gas depends on volume, temperature, and the number of molecules present. **Pressure (P) is defined as the force per unit area on a surface.** The equation defining pressure is shown in **Figure 1.1**.

FIGURE 1.1

Pressure and Area of Contact
Because force is constant, the pressure the ballet dancer exerts against the floor depends on the area of contact.

$$\text{Pressure} = \frac{\text{Force}}{\text{Area}}$$

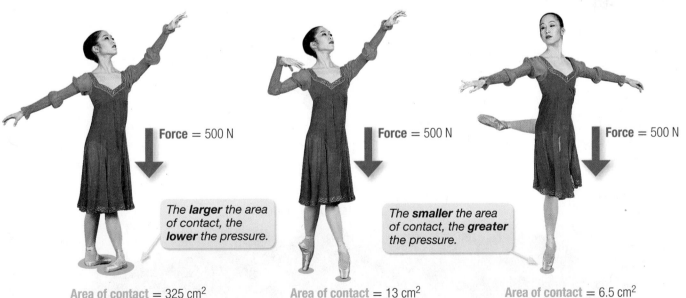

Force = 500 N

*The **larger** the area of contact, the **lower** the pressure.*

Force = 500 N

*The **smaller** the area of contact, the **greater** the pressure.*

Force = 500 N

Area of contact = 325 cm²

(a) **Pressure** = $\dfrac{500\ \text{N}}{325\ \text{cm}^2}$ = 1.5 N/cm²

Area of contact = 13 cm²

(b) **Pressure** = $\dfrac{500\ \text{N}}{13\ \text{cm}^2}$ = 38.5 N/cm²

Area of contact = 6.5 cm²

(c) **Pressure** = $\dfrac{500\ \text{N}}{6.5\ \text{cm}^2}$ = 77 N/cm²

MAIN IDEA
Pressure depends on force and area.

The SI unit for force is the newton (N). **The newton is the force that will increase the speed of a one-kilogram mass by one meter per second each second that the force is applied.** At Earth's surface, gravity has an acceleration of 9.8 m/s². Consider a ballet dancer with a mass of 51 kg, as shown in **Figure 1.1** (on the previous page). A mass of 51 kg exerts a force of 500 N (51 kg × 9.8 m/s²) on Earth's surface. No matter how the dancer stands, she exerts the same force—500 N—against the floor. But the pressure exerted against the floor depends on the area of contact.

When the dancer rests her weight on the soles of both feet, as shown in **Figure 1.1a**, the area of contact with the floor is about 325 cm². The pressure, or force per unit area, when she stands in this manner is 500 N/325 cm², or roughly 1.5 N/cm². When she stands on her toes, as in **Figure 1.1b**, the total area of contact with the floor is only 13 cm². The pressure exerted is then equal to 500 N/13 cm²—roughly 38 N/cm². And when she stands on one toe, as in **Figure 1.1c**, the pressure exerted is twice that, or about 77 N/cm². Thus, the same force applied to a smaller area results in a greater pressure.

Atmospheric Pressure

The atmosphere—the shell of air surrounding Earth—exerts pressure. **Figure 1.2** shows that atmospheric pressure at sea level is about equal to the weight of a 1.03 kg mass per square centimeter of surface, or 10.1 N/cm². The pressure of the atmosphere can be thought of as caused by the weight of the gases that compose the atmosphere. The atmosphere contains about 78% nitrogen, 21% oxygen, and 1% other gases, including argon and carbon dioxide. Atmospheric pressure is the sum of the individual pressures of the various gases in the atmosphere.

✔ **CHECK FOR UNDERSTANDING**

Explain Why is it easier to pop a balloon with a sharp object than by squeezing it between your hands? Use the term "pressure" in your explanation.

FIGURE 1.2

Atmospheric Pressure Air molecules collide with Earth's surface, creating pressure.

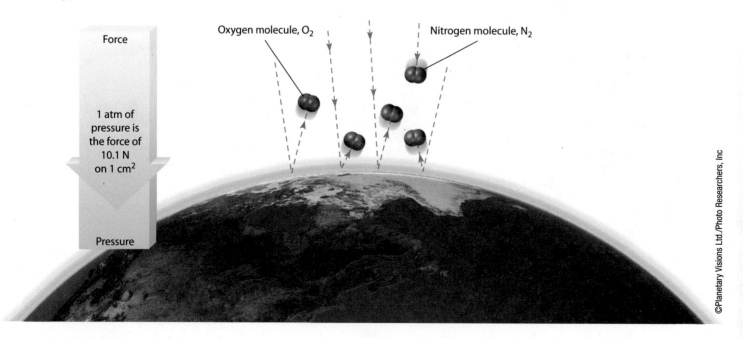

©Planetary Visions Ltd./Photo Researchers, Inc

The Barometer

A **barometer** is a device used to measure atmospheric pressure. The first type of barometer, illustrated in **Figure 1.3,** was introduced by Evangelista Torricelli during the early 1600s. Torricelli wondered why water pumps could raise water to a maximum height of only about 34 feet. He thought that the height must depend somehow on the weight of water compared with the weight of air. He reasoned that liquid mercury, which is about 14 times as dense as water, could be raised only 1/14 as high as water. To test this idea, Torricelli sealed a long glass tube at one end and filled it with mercury. Holding the open end with his thumb, he inverted the tube into a dish of mercury without allowing any air to enter the tube. When he removed his thumb, the mercury column in the tube dropped to a height of about 30 in. (760 mm) above the surface of the mercury in the dish, just as he predicted.

How a Barometer Works

The space above the mercury in the tube of a barometer is nearly a vacuum. The mercury in the tube pushes downward because of gravitational force. The column of mercury in the tube is stopped from falling beyond a certain point because the atmosphere exerts a pressure on the surface of the mercury outside the tube. This pressure is transmitted through the fluid mercury and is exerted upward on the column of mercury.

The exact height of the mercury in the tube depends on the atmospheric pressure, or force per unit area. The pressure is measured in terms of the mercury column's height in the barometer tube.

From experiments like Torricelli's, it is known that at sea level at 0°C, the average pressure of the atmosphere can support a 760 mm column of mercury. The atmospheric pressure at any given place depends on the elevation and the weather conditions. If the atmospheric pressure is greater than the average at sea level, the height of the mercury column in a barometer will be greater than 760 mm. If the atmospheric pressure is less, the height of the mercury column will be less than 760 mm.

Using a Manometer

All gases exert pressure. A device called a manometer can be used to measure the pressure of an enclosed gas sample (see **Figure 1.4**). The difference in the height of mercury in the two arms of the U-tube is a measure of the oxygen gas pressure in the container.

FIGURE 1.3

Torricelli's Barometer Torricelli discovered that the pressure of the atmosphere supports a column of mercury about 760 mm above the surface of the mercury in the dish.

Vacuum

Pressure exerted by the column of mercury

Nitrogen molecule, N_2

Oxygen molecule, O_2

760 mm

Atmospheric pressure

Surface of mercury

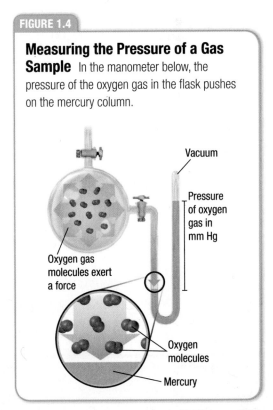

FIGURE 1.4

Measuring the Pressure of a Gas Sample In the manometer below, the pressure of the oxygen gas in the flask pushes on the mercury column.

Vacuum

Pressure of oxygen gas in mm Hg

Oxygen gas molecules exert a force

Oxygen molecules

Mercury

Consider a can filled with air. The atmosphere exerts a pressure on the can. The air inside the can pushes outward and balances the atmosphere's inward-pushing force. If a vacuum pump removes the air from the can, the outward force is removed, and the atmospheric pressure crushes the can.

Units of Pressure

A number of different units are used to measure pressure. Because atmospheric pressure is often measured by a mercury barometer, pressure can be expressed in terms of the height of a mercury column. **Thus, the common unit of pressure is millimeters of mercury, symbolized mm Hg.** A pressure of 1 mm Hg is also called 1 torr to honor Torricelli for his invention of the barometer. The average atmospheric pressure at sea level at 0°C is 760 mm Hg. Pressures are often measured in units of atmospheres. **One atmosphere of pressure (atm) is defined as being exactly equivalent to 760 mm Hg.** In SI, pressure is expressed in derived units called pascals. The unit is named for Blaise Pascal, a French mathematician and philosopher who studied pressure during the seventeenth century. **One pascal (Pa) is defined as the pressure exerted by a force of one newton (1 N) acting on an area of one square meter.** In many cases, it is more convenient to express pressure in kilopascals (kPa). The standard atmosphere (1 atm) is equal to $1.013\,25 \times 10^5$ Pa, or 101.325 kPa. Several pressure units and common uses for them are summarized in **Figure 1.5.**

✓ **CHECK FOR UNDERSTANDING**
Apply Why is 760 mm of mercury equal to 1 atmosphere?

Standard Temperature and Pressure

To compare gas volumes, one must know the temperature and pressure at which they are measured. *For purposes of comparison, scientists have agreed on standard conditions of 1 atm pressure and 0°C.* These conditions are called standard temperature and pressure, abbreviated STP.

FIGURE 1.5

UNITS OF PRESSURE			
Unit	Symbol	Definition/relationship	Application
pascal	Pa	SI pressure unit $$1\ Pa = \frac{1\ N}{m^2}$$	scientific (kPa)
millimeter of mercury	mm Hg	pressure that supports a 1 mm mercury column in a barometer	blood pressure monitors
torr	torr	1 torr = 1 mm Hg	vacuum pumps

atmosphere	atm	average atmospheric pressure at sea level and 0°C
		1 atm = 760 mm Hg
		      = 760 torr
		      = $1.013\,25 \times 10^5$ Pa
		      = 101.325 kPa
			atmospheric pressure

pounds per square inch	psi	1 psi = $6.892\,86 \times 10^3$ Pa 1 atm = 14.700 psi	tire gauges

Converting Between Units of Pressure

Sample Problem A The average atmospheric pressure in Denver, Colorado, is 0.830 atm. Express this pressure in (a) millimeters of mercury (mm Hg) and (b) kilopascals (kPa).

① ANALYZE

Given: P of atmosphere = 0.830 atm
760 mm Hg = 1 atm (definition); 101.325 kPa = 1 atm (definition)

Unknown: a. P of atmosphere in mm Hg **b.** P of atmosphere in kPa

② PLAN

a. atm → mm Hg; $1 \text{ atm} \times \dfrac{760 \text{ mm Hg}}{1 \text{ atm}} = \text{mm Hg}$

b. atm → kPa; $1 \text{ atm} \times \dfrac{101.325 \text{ kPa}}{1 \text{ atm}} = \text{kPa}$

③ SOLVE

a. $P = 0.830 \text{ atm} \times \dfrac{760 \text{ mm Hg}}{1 \text{ atm}} = 631 \text{ mm Hg}$

b. $P = 0.830 \text{ atm} \times \dfrac{101.325 \text{ kPa}}{1 \text{ atm}} = 84.1 \text{ kPa}$

④ CHECK YOUR WORK

Units have canceled to give the desired units, and answers are expressed to the correct number of significant figures. The known pressure and the calculated pressures are about 80% of the atmospheric pressure, in the new units.

Practice   Answers in Appendix E

1. Convert a pressure of 1.75 atm to kPa and to mm Hg.
2. The critical pressure of carbon dioxide is 72.7 atm. What is this value in units of pascals?

▶ **MAIN IDEA**

The total pressure of a gas mixture is the sum of the pressures of the gases in it.

John Dalton, the English chemist who proposed the atomic theory, also studied gas mixtures. He found that the pressure exerted by each gas in an unreactive mixture is independent of that exerted by other gases present. The pressure of each gas in a mixture is called the **partial pressure** of that gas. **Dalton's law of partial pressures** states that the total pressure of a gas mixture is the sum of the partial pressures of the component gases. The law is true regardless of the gases present in the mixture. Dalton's law may be expressed as follows.

Dalton's law	$P_T = P_1 + P_2 + P_3 + \ldots$

In this equation, P_T is the total pressure of the mixture. P_1, P_2, P_3, and so on are the partial pressures of component gases 1, 2, 3, and so on.

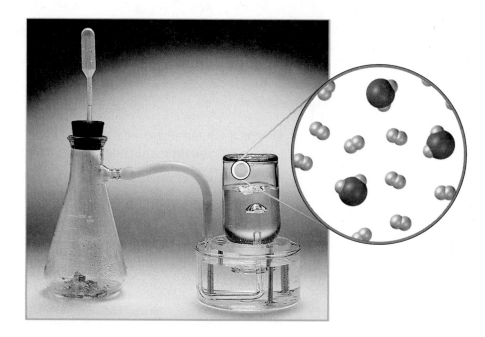

FIGURE 1.6

Collecting Gas by Displacement

Hydrogen can be collected by water displacement by reacting zinc with sulfuric acid. The hydrogen gas produced displaces the water in the gas-collecting bottle to the right. It now also contains some water vapor.

✔ CRITICAL THINKING

Infer As the gas accumulates in the collecting bottle, what will happen to the water it displaces?

Dalton's Law and the Kinetic-Molecular Theory

You can understand Dalton's law in terms of the kinetic-molecular theory. Each of the rapidly moving particles of gases in a mixture has an equal chance to collide with the container walls. Therefore, each gas exerts a pressure independent of that exerted by the other gases present. The total pressure is the result of the total number of collisions per unit of wall area in a given time.

Vapor Pressure of Water

Gases produced in the laboratory are often collected over water, as shown in **Figure 1.6.** The gas produced by the reaction displaces the water, which is more dense, in the collection bottle. You need to apply Dalton's law of partial pressures in calculating the pressures of gases collected in this way. A gas collected by water displacement is not pure but is always mixed with water vapor. That is because water molecules at the liquid surface evaporate and mix with the gas molecules. In a closed system, water vapor, like other gases, exerts a pressure known as *vapor pressure*.

Suppose you wished to determine the total pressure of the gas and water vapor inside a collection bottle. You would raise the bottle until the water levels inside and outside the bottle were the same. At that point, the total pressure inside the bottle would be the same as the atmospheric pressure, P_{atm}. According to Dalton's law of partial pressures, the following is true:

$$P_{atm} = P_{gas} + P_{H_2O}$$

To calculate the partial pressure of the dry gas collected, you would read the atmospheric pressure, P_{atm}, from a barometer in the laboratory. Subtract the vapor pressure of the water at the given temperature from the total pressure. The vapor pressure of water varies with temperature. You need to look up the value of P_{H_2O} at the temperature of the experiment in a standard reference table (see Appendix B).

Calculating Partial Pressure

Sample Problem B A student collects oxygen gas by water displacement at a temperature of 16°C. The total volume is 188 mL at a pressure of 92.3 kPa. What is the partial pressure of oxygen collected? The vapor pressure of water at 16°C is 1.82 kPa.

1 ANALYZE

Given: $P_{total} = 92.3$ kPa

$P_{H_2O} = 1.82$ kPa at 16°C

Unknown: $P_{O_2} = ?$ kPa

2 PLAN

The pressure of oxygen collected is calculated by subtracting the partial pressure of water vapor from the total pressure, according to Dalton's law of partial pressures.

$$P_{O_2} = P_{total} - P_{H_2O\ vapor}$$

3 SOLVE

Substituting values for P_{atm} and P_{H_2O} gives P_{O_2}:

$$P_{O_2} = P_{total} - P_{H_2O\ vapor} = 92.3 \text{ kPa} - 1.82 \text{ kPa} = 90.5 \text{ kPa}$$

4 CHECK YOUR WORK

As expected, the units are kPa. The number of significant figures is correct at one decimal place. The pressure of the collected oxygen and the water vapor adds up to the total pressure of the system.

Practice   Answers in Appendix E

1. A chemist collects a sample of $H_2S(g)$ over water at a temperature of 27°C. The total pressure of the gas that has displaced a volume of 15 mL of water is 207.33 kPa. What is the pressure of the H_2S gas collected?

SECTION 1 FORMATIVE ASSESSMENT

▶ Reviewing Main Ideas

1. Define *pressure*.

2. What units are used to express pressure measurements?

3. What are standard conditions for gas measurements?

4. Convert the following pressures to pressures in standard atmospheres:
   a. 151.98 kPa
   b. 456 torr

5. A sample of nitrogen gas is collected over water at a temperature of 23.0°C. What is the pressure of the nitrogen gas if atmospheric pressure is 785 mm Hg?

6. Why can you calculate the total pressure of a mixture of gases by adding together the partial pressures of the component gases?

✔ Critical Thinking

7. **EVALUATING METHODS** Clean rooms used for sterile biological research are sealed and operate at slightly above atmospheric pressure. Explain why.

8. **INFERRING RELATIONSHIPS** Why do ears "pop" when driving in the mountains, flying in the airplane, or riding the elevator in a skyscraper?

The Gas Laws and Scuba Diving

An understanding of Dalton's law and Henry's law is essential to safe scuba diving. Dalton's law states that the total pressure of a gas mixture is equal to the sum of the partial pressures of the component gases. Henry's law predicts that the solubility of a gas in a liquid is a direct function of the partial pressure of that gas.

For every 33 ft of sea water that a diver descends, he or she feels one additional atmosphere of pressure because of the increasing weight of water overhead. Most divers use compressed air tanks to breathe underwater. The air in these tanks, which contains approximately 78% nitrogen and 21% oxygen, is the same as the air that we breathe. Once the compressed air enters the diver's lungs, it is subjected to the pressure caused by the water. The increase in the air pressure leads to an increase in the partial pressures of the nitrogen and oxygen in air, as predicted by Dalton's law. Henry's law predicts that this increase in partial pressures will increase the solubility of nitrogen and oxygen in the diver's tissues and bloodstream.

The increase in the partial pressure of oxygen is not problematic under typical diving conditions, because a diver's body can metabolize the extra oxygen that is present in the bloodstream. At extreme depths, however, increased pressure of oxygen becomes a problem. Extended exposure to high concentrations of oxygen can result in *oxygen toxicity*. This condition can damage the lungs and nervous system. Divers avoid oxygen toxicity by breathing gas mixtures that contain more helium and less oxygen than compressed air does.

Compressed air mixtures contain nitrogen. The body does not metabolize nitrogen, however, so it can accumulate in a diver's tissues and bloodstream. The extra nitrogen can affect the nerve cells, causing *nitrogen narcosis*. Divers suffering from nitrogen narcosis become disoriented and experience symptoms similar to intoxication. To decrease the probability of contracting nitrogen narcosis, divers can use gas mixtures that contain less nitrogen than compressed air does.

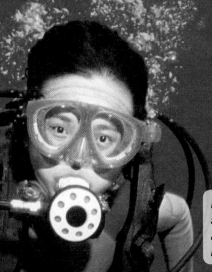

In order to dive safely, scuba divers must be aware of some of the basic gas laws.

Dissolved nitrogen can also be harmful if a diver ascends too quickly. As Henry's law predicts, nitrogen becomes less soluble in the blood as the pressure decreases. This decrease in solubility causes nitrogen to leave the diver's tissues and blood. Normally, the excess nitrogen is discharged through the lungs.

However, if the diver comes up too rapidly, the nitrogen will form bubbles in the tissues and blood vessels. This condition is known as *decompression sickness*, or "the bends." If the bubbles block blood flow, a wide range of effects may occur, including fatigue, dizziness, nausea, reduced vision, numbness, severe joint pain, and even paralysis. For this reason, divers are very careful to ascend slowly after diving.

Engineering Design

Gas laws also apply to astronauts. Research the conditions and dangers involved in space walks. How do astronauts prepare for a space walk? Why are the preparations important? Do astronauts experience dangers during and after space walks that are similar to dangers faced by divers as related to gas laws? Based on your research, suggest new or improved features in spacesuits or other equipment that would help astronauts on space walks.

The Gas Laws

SECTION 2

Main Ideas

▶ Gas volume and pressure are indirectly proportional.

▶ Gas volume and temperature are directly related.

▶ Gas pressure and temperature are directly related.

▶ Gas pressure, temperature, and volume are interrelated.

Key Terms

Boyle's law
absolute zero

Charles's law
Gay-Lussac's law

combined gas law

Scientists have been studying physical properties of gases for hundreds of years. In 1662, Robert Boyle discovered that gas pressure and volume are related mathematically. The observations of Boyle and others led to the development of the gas laws. The gas laws are simple mathematical relationships among the volume, temperature, pressure, and amount of a gas.

▶ **MAIN IDEA**

Gas volume and pressure are indirectly proportional.

Robert Boyle discovered that doubling the pressure on a sample of gas at constant temperature reduces its volume by one-half. Reducing the pressure on a gas by one-half allows the volume of the gas to double. As one variable increases, the other decreases. **Figure 2.1** shows that as the volume of gas in the syringe decreases, the pressure of the gas increases.

You can use the kinetic-molecular theory to understand why this pressure-volume relationship holds. The pressure of a gas is caused by moving molecules hitting the container walls. Suppose the volume of a container is decreased, but the same number of gas molecules is present at the same temperature. There will be more molecules per unit volume. The number of collisions with a given unit of wall area per unit time will increase as a result. Therefore, pressure will also increase.

FIGURE 2.1

Volume and Pressure The volume of gas in the syringe shown in **(a)** is reduced when the plunger is pushed down. The gas pressure in **(b)** is increased as the volume is reduced, because the molecules collide more frequently with the walls of the container in the smaller volume.

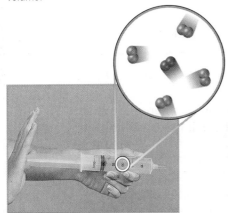

(a) Lower pressure/ Increased volume

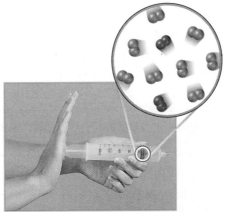

(b) Higher pressure/ Decreased volume

FIGURE 2.2

Volume vs. Pressure for a Gas at Constant Temperature

CRITICAL THINKING

Interpret What is happening to the volume of the gas as the pressure increases?

Graphing Boyle's Law

Plotting the values of volume versus pressure for a gas at constant temperature gives a curve like that in **Figure 2.2**. The general volume-pressure relationship that is illustrated is called Boyle's law. **Boyle's law** states that the volume of a fixed mass of gas varies inversely with the pressure at constant temperature.

Mathematically, Boyle's law can be expressed as follows:

$$PV = k$$

P is the pressure, V is the volume, and k is a constant. Since P and V vary inversely, their product remains the same. The inverse relationship between changes of pressure and volume can be expressed as shown below.

Boyle's law	$P_1 V_1 = P_2 V_2$

P_1 and V_1 represent initial conditions, and P_2 and V_2 represent a different set of conditions. Given three of the four values P_1, V_1, P_2, and V_2, you can use this equation to calculate the fourth value for a system at constant temperature.

GO ONLINE

Learn It! Video
HMHScience.com

Using Boyle's Law

Sample Problem C A sample of oxygen gas has a volume of 150.0 mL when its pressure is 0.947 atm. What will the volume of the gas be at a pressure of 0.987 atm if the temperature remains constant?

1 ANALYZE

Given:
V_1 of O_2 = 150.0 mL
P_1 of O_2 = 0.947 atm
P_2 of O_2 = 0.987 atm

Unknown: V_2 of O_2 in mL

2 PLAN

Rearrange the equation for Boyle's law ($P_1 V_1 = P_2 V_2$) to obtain V_2.

$$V_2 = \frac{P_1 V_1}{P_2}$$

3 SOLVE

Substitute values for P_1, V_1, and P_2 to obtain the new volume, V_2.

$$V_2 = \frac{(0.947 \text{ atm})(150.0 \text{ mL } O_2)}{0.987 \text{ atm}} = 144 \text{ mL } O_2$$

4 CHECK YOUR WORK

When the pressure is increased slightly at constant temperature, the volume decreases slightly, as expected. Units cancel to give milliliters, a volume unit.

Practice   Answers in Appendix E

1. A balloon filled with helium gas has a volume of 500 mL at a pressure of 1 atm. The balloon is released and reaches an altitude of 6.5 km, where the pressure is 0.5 atm. If the temperature has remained the same, what volume does the gas occupy at this height?

▶ MAIN IDEA
Gas volume and temperature are directly related.

Balloonists, such as those in the photo at the beginning of this chapter, are making use of a physical property of gases: if pressure is constant, gases expand when heated. When the temperature increases, the volume of a fixed number of gas molecules must increase if the pressure is to stay constant. At the higher temperature, the gas molecules move faster. They collide with the walls of the container more frequently and with more force. The volume of a flexible container must then increase in order for the pressure to remain the same.

The quantitative relationship between volume and temperature was discovered by the French scientist Jacques Charles in 1787. Charles found that plotting the volume of a gas versus the temperature in degrees Celsius gave a straight line that extrapolated to zero volume when the gas temperature reached −273°C. He found this was true for all gases. This temperature , −273.15°C to be exact, is referred to as absolute zero. **Absolute zero, the lowest possible achievable temperature, is assigned the value of zero on the Kelvin temperature scale.** This fact gives the following relationship between the two temperature scales.

$$K = 273.15 + °C$$

For calculations in this book, 273.15 is rounded off to 273.

Working with kelvins has its advantages with gases. When the temperature of a gas is given in kelvins, doubling the temperature doubles the volume. Likewise, lowering the temperature causes a decrease in the volume of a gas, as shown in **Figure 2.3.**

FIGURE 2.3

The Relationship between Temperature and Volume

(a) Air-filled balloons are cooled with liquid nitrogen.

(b) The balloons shrink in liquid nitrogen at −196°C.

(c) The balloons expand when the air inside warms up.

✔ CRITICAL THINKING
Explain Use the kinetic-molecular theory to explain what happens to the balloons.

FIGURE 2.4

Volume vs. Temperature for a Gas at Constant Pressure

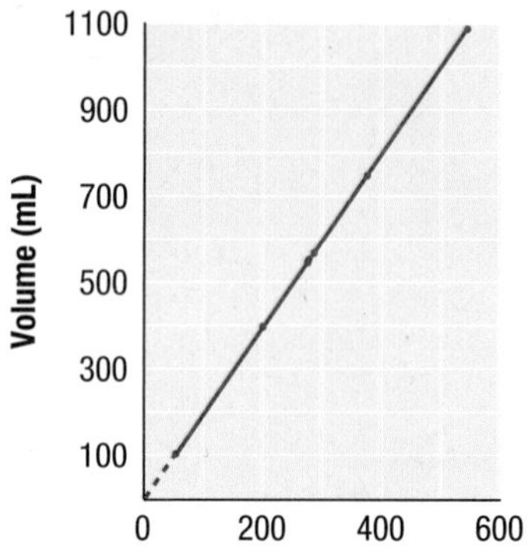

✓ **CRITICAL THINKING**

Interpret What is happening to the volume of the gas as the temperature increases?

Graphing Charles's Law

The relationship between temperature in kelvins and gas volume is known as Charles's law. **Charles's law** states that the volume of a fixed mass of gas at constant pressure varies directly with the temperature in kelvins. Charles's law is plotted in **Figure 2.4** and may be expressed as follows:

$$V = kT \text{ or } \frac{V}{T} = k$$

The value of T is the temperature in kelvins, and k is a constant. The ratio V/T for any set of volume-temperature values always equals the same k. The form of Charles's law that can be applied directly to most volume-temperature problems involving gases is as follows:

Charles's law	$\dfrac{V_1}{T_1} = \dfrac{V_2}{T_2}$

V_1 and T_1 represent initial conditions, and V_2 and T_2 represent a different set of conditions. When three of the four values T_1, V_1, T_2, and V_2 are known, you can use this equation to calculate the fourth value for a system at constant pressure.

Using Charles's Law

Sample Problem D A container of oxygen has a volume of 349 mL at a temperature of 22°C. What volume will the gas occupy at 50°C if the pressure remains constant?

1 ANALYZE

Given: V_1 of O_2 = 349 mL

T_1 of O_2 = 22.0°C + 273 = 295 K; T_2 of O_2 = 50.0°C + 273 = 323 K

Unknown: V_2 at T_2 Kelvin = ? mL O_2

2 PLAN

The gas remains at constant pressure, so increasing the temperature will increase the volume. Rearrange the Charles's law equation to solve for V_2, substitute known quantities, and calculate.

3 SOLVE

Substitute values for V_1, T_1, and T_2 to obtain the new volume.

$$V_2 = \frac{V_1 T_2}{T_1} = \frac{349 \text{ mL O}_2 \times 323 \text{ K}}{295 \text{ K}} = 382 \text{ mL O}_2$$

4 CHECK YOUR WORK

As expected, the units cancel to give mL O_2. There are three significant figures. The temperature increased, so the volume must also increase.

Practice   Answers in Appendix E

1. A balloon full of air has a volume of 2.75 L at a temperature of 18°C. What is the balloon's volume at 45°C?

2. A sample of argon has a volume of 0.43 mL at 24°C. At what temperature in degrees Celsius will it have a volume of 0.57 mL?

MAIN IDEA

Gas pressure and temperature are directly related.

You have just learned about the quantitative relationship between volume and temperature at constant pressure. What would you predict about the relationship between pressure and temperature at constant volume? You have seen that pressure is the result of collisions of molecules with container walls. The energy and frequency of collisions depend on the average kinetic energy of molecules. For a fixed quantity of gas at constant volume, the pressure should be directly proportional to the temperature in kelvins, which depends directly on average kinetic energy.

That prediction turns out to be correct. We see that for every kelvin of temperature change, the pressure of a confined gas changes by a predictable amount. Joseph Gay-Lussac is given credit for recognizing this in 1802. The data plotted in Figure 2.5 illustrate **Gay-Lussac's law:** The pressure of a fixed mass of gas at constant volume varies directly with the temperature in kelvins. Mathematically, Gay-Lussac's law is expressed as follows.

$$P = kT \text{ or } \frac{P}{T} = k$$

The value of T is the temperature in kelvins, and k is a constant that depends on the quantity of gas and the volume. For a given mass of gas at constant volume, the ratio P/T is the same for any set of pressure-temperature values. Unknown values can be found using the relationship.

Gay-Lussac's law	$\dfrac{P_1}{T_1} = \dfrac{P_2}{T_2}$

P_1 and T_1 represent initial conditions, and P_2 and T_2 represent a different set of conditions. When values are known for three of the four quantities, the fourth value can be calculated for a system at constant volume.

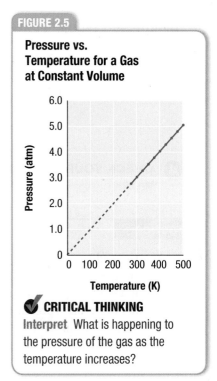

FIGURE 2.5

Pressure vs. Temperature for a Gas at Constant Volume

(Graph: Pressure (atm) on y-axis from 0 to 6.0, Temperature (K) on x-axis from 0 to 500, showing a linear increasing line.)

✔ **CRITICAL THINKING**

Interpret What is happening to the pressure of the gas as the temperature increases?

Using Gay-Lussac's Law

Sample Problem E A cylinder of gas has a pressure of 4.40 atm at 25°C. At what temperature in °C will it reach a pressure of 6.50 atm?

1 ANALYZE

Given:
$P_{1 \text{ of gas}} = 4.40 \text{ atm}$

$T_{1 \text{ of gas}} = 25°C + 273 = 298 \text{ K}; \ P_{2 \text{ of gas}} = 6.50 \text{ atm}$

Unknown: T_2 of gas in °C

2 PLAN

Rearrange the Gay-Lussac's law equation to solve for T_2.

Continued

③ **SOLVE**	Substitute known values for T_1, P_2, and P_1 to calculate the new temperature.	

$$T_2 = \frac{T_1 P_2}{P_1} = \frac{298 \text{ K} \times 6.50 \text{ atm}}{4.40 \text{ atm}} = 440. \text{ K}$$

Convert back to °C.

$$440. \text{ K} = (440. - 273) \, °C = 167°C$$

④ **CHECK YOUR WORK**	The units cancel to give Kelvin temperature, which was converted to °C. The number of significant figures is correct because the data were given to three significant figures. The pressure increases, so the temperature must also increase.

Practice

1. At 120.0°C, the pressure of a sample of nitrogen is 1.07 atm. What will the pressure be at 205°C, assuming constant volume?

2. A cylinder of compressed gas has a pressure of 4.882 atm on one day. The next day, the same cylinder of gas has a pressure of 4.690 atm, and its temperature is 8°C. What was the temperature on the previous day in °C?

3. A mylar balloon is filled with helium gas to a pressure of 107 kPa when the temperature is 22°C. If the temperature changes to 45°C, what will be the pressure of the helium in the balloon?

▶ **MAIN IDEA**

Gas pressure, temperature, and volume are interrelated.

A gas sample often undergoes changes in temperature, pressure, and volume all at the same time. When this happens, three variables must be dealt with at once. Boyle's law, Charles's law, and Gay-Lussac's law can be combined into a single expression that is useful in such situations. The **combined gas law expresses the relationship between pressure, volume, and temperature of a fixed amount of gas.** The combined gas law can be expressed as follows:

$$\frac{PV}{T} = k$$

In the equation, k is constant and depends on the amount of gas. The combined gas law can also be written as follows:

Combined gas law $\quad \dfrac{P_1 V_1}{T_1} = \dfrac{P_2 V_2}{T_2}$

The subscripts in the equation above indicate two different sets of conditions, and T represents the temperature in Kelvins.

From this expression, any value can be calculated if the other five are known. Note that each of the gas laws can be obtained from the combined gas law when the proper variable is constant. For example, Boyle's law is obtained when the temperature is constant. Because $T_1 = T_2$, T_1 and T_2 will cancel out on both sides of the combined gas law equation, giving Boyle's law.

$$P_1 V_1 = P_2 V_2$$

✔ **CHECK FOR UNDERSTANDING**
Assess What advantage does the combined gas law have over the three individual gas laws?

Using the Combined Gas Law

GO ONLINE

Solve It! Cards
HMHScience.com

Sample Problem F A helium-filled balloon has a volume of 50.0 L at 25°C and 1.08 atm. What volume will it have at 0.855 atm and 10.0°C?

1 ANALYZE

Given: V_1 of He = 50.0 L

T_1 of He = 25°C + 273 = 298 K; T_2 of He = 10°C + 273 = 283 K

P_1 of He = 1.08 atm; P_2 of He = 0.855 atm

Unknown: V_2 of He

2 PLAN

Because the gas remains at constant pressure, an increase in temperature will cause an increase in volume. To obtain V_2, rearrange the equation for Charles's law.

$$\frac{P_1V_1}{T_1} = \frac{P_2V_2}{T_2} \rightarrow V_2 = \frac{P_1V_1T_2}{P_2T_1}$$

3 SOLVE

Substitute the known values to obtain the new volume, V_2.

$$V_2 = \frac{(1.08\ \text{atm})(50.0\ \text{L He})(283\ \text{K})}{(0.855\ \text{atm})(298\ \text{K})} = 60.0\ \text{L He}$$

4 CHECK YOUR WORK

The pressure factor 1.80/0.855 predicts a larger volume, and the temperature factor 283/298 predicts a smaller volume. The pressure factor predominates, increasing the volume from 50.0 L to 60.0 L. Units cancel appropriately. The answer is correctly expressed to three significant figures.

Practice   Answers in Appendix E

1 The volume of a gas is 27.5 mL at 22.0°C and 0.974 atm. What will the volume be at 15.0°C and 0.993 atm?

2. A 700.0 mL gas sample at STP is compressed to a volume of 200.0 mL, and the temperature is increased to 30.0°C. What is the new pressure of the gas in Pa?

 SECTION 2 **FORMATIVE ASSESSMENT**

▶ **Reviewing Main Ideas**

1. Relate the effect of temperature and pressure on a gas to the model of a gas given by the kinetic-molecular theory.

2. A sample of helium gas has a volume of 200.0 mL at 0.960 atm. What pressure, in atmospheres, is needed to reduce the volume at constant temperature to 50.0 mL?

3. A sample of nitrogen gas occupies 1.55 L at 27.0°C and 1.00 atm. What will the volume be at −100.0°C and the same pressure?

4. A gas occupies 2.0 m³ at 100.0 K and exerts a pressure of 100.0 kPa. What volume will the gas occupy if the temperature is increased to 400.0 K and the pressure is increased to 200.0 kPa?

✔ **Critical Thinking**

5. **ANALYZING RESULTS** A student has the following data: V_1 = 822 mL, T_1 = 75°C, and T_2 = −25°C. He calculates V_2 and gets −274 mL. Is this value correct? Explain why or why not.

6. **APPLYING MODELS** Explain Charles's law in terms of the kinetic-molecular theory.

Chemistry's First Law

The notion that "nature abhors a vacuum"—meaning that there is no such thing as "empty space"—was proposed by the ancient Greek philosopher Aristotle, whose word was unchallenged for nearly 2000 years. Then, in the mid 1600s, a new breed of thinkers known as *natural philosophers*—what we now know as "scientists"—began testing the long-held assumption that all space must contain matter. These investigations were some of the earliest experiments with gases, and they led to the discovery of the first empirical principle of chemistry, Boyle's law.

Overturning an Ancient Assumption

The first scientist to demonstrate the existence of a vacuum was Evangelista Torricelli. In 1643, he showed that when a glass tube that was 3 ft. long and about 1 in. in diameter was sealed at one end, filled with mercury, and inverted in a container full of mercury, the mercury in the tube fell to a height of about 30 in. above the level of mercury in the container. Some thinkers remained skeptical, but it was generally accepted that the space between the mercury and the sealed end of the tube was indeed a vacuum.

Torricelli then turned his attention to how the mercury in the glass tube of his apparatus was supported. The fact that liquids exert a pressure on objects immersed in them inspired him to hypothesize that a "sea of air" surrounded Earth. He further hypothesized that the air exerted pressure on the mercury in the container and thus supported the mercury in the column.

Support for the New Theory

Although the idea of an atmosphere that has weight and exerts a pressure on the objects within it seems obvious today, it was a radical theory at the time. To test the effects of the atmosphere, Robert Boyle, one of the period's great scientists, had his talented assistant, Robert Hooke, create a piece of equipment that would revolutionize the study of air. The apparatus was an improved version of a pump designed by the German experimenter Otto von Guericke; the pump had a large receptacle in which a partial vacuum could be created.

Boyle placed Torricelli's setup, known today as a barometer, in the receptacle of the pump and observed the mercury column as he reduced the pressure around it. The height of the mercury decreased as the pressure surrounding the mercury in the container dropped, strongly supporting Torricelli's atmospheric theory.

Using Hooke's pump, Boyle performed additional studies that verified the idea that air exerted pressure and had weight. Boyle's experiments also led to the important conclusion that air was elastic: that is, it could expand and contract. Boyle discovered the fundamental law that bears his name during an investigation into air's elasticity.

An Ingenious Experiment

In response to a criticism of his findings, Boyle performed an experiment to show that air could be compressed to a pressure greater than that of the atmosphere. First, he prepared a glass J-tube with the short end sealed off and the long end left open. Then, he poured mercury into the tube, making sure that the levels in the two ends were the same. He then let air travel freely between the ends to ensure that each column was at atmospheric pressure.

Then, Boyle poured more mercury into the long end of the tube until it was about 30 in. above the level of mercury in the short end. He observed that the volume of the trapped air was halved. He continued to add mercury until the total pressure on the trapped air was about 4 times that of the atmosphere. Noting that the air had been compressed to a volume about one-fourth of what it originally was, Boyle discovered the inverse relationship between air's pressure and volume.

A Long-Standing Contribution

Boyle went on to show that the relationship between air pressure and volume, $P \propto 1/V$ (at constant temperature), held not only when the gas was compressed but also when it was allowed to expand. Future investigators would show that the law is a principle that applies to gases in general. Along with the findings of other researchers, such as Jacques Charles, Joseph Gay-Lussac, and Amadeo Avogadro, Boyle's discovery led chemists to the famous ideal gas law, $PV = nRT$, which serves as a starting point in the study of chemistry today.

(t) ©Johnathan Ampersand Esper/Aurora/Getty Images; (b) ©Rod McLean/Alamy Images

Questions

1. Why was it necessary for Boyle to seal one end of his J-tube?

2. What would have happened if Boyle had allowed the temperature of the trapped air sample to change as he added mercury to the tube?

We can measure the difference between the atmospheric pressure on a mountaintop and the atmospheric pressure at sea level thanks to the work of Torricelli and Boyle.

Gas Volumes and the Ideal Gas Law

Key Terms

Gay-Lussac's law of combining volumes of gases

Avogadro's law

standard molar volume of a gas

ideal gas law

ideal gas constant

In this section, you will study the relationships between the volumes of gases that react with each other. You will also learn about the relationship between molar amount of gas and volume and about a single gas law that unifies all the basic gas laws into a single equation.

▶ **MAIN IDEA**

Gases react in whole-number ratios.

In the early 1800s, French chemist Joseph Gay-Lussac studied gas-volume relationships involving a chemical reaction between hydrogen and oxygen. He observed that 2 L of hydrogen can react with 1 L of oxygen to form 2 L of water vapor at constant temperature and pressure.

hydrogen gas	+	oxygen gas	→	water vapor
2 L (2 volumes)		1 L (1 volume)		2 L (2 volumes)

In other words, this reaction shows a simple and definite 2 : 1 : 2 relationship between the volumes of the reactants and the product. Two volumes of hydrogen react with 1 volume of oxygen to produce 2 volumes of water vapor. The 2 : 1 : 2 relationship for this reaction applies to any proportions for volume—for example, 2 mL, 1 mL, and 2 mL; 600 L, 300 L, and 600 L; or 400 cm^3, 200 cm^3, and 400 cm^3.

Gay-Lussac also noticed simple and definite proportions by volume in other reactions of gases, such as in the reaction between hydrogen gas and chlorine gas.

hydrogen gas	+	chlorine gas	→	hydrogen chloride gas
1 L (1 volume)		1 L (1 volume)		2 L (2 volumes)

In 1808, in what is known today as **Gay-Lussac's law of combining volumes of gases,** the scientist summarized the results of his experiments by stating that at constant temperature and pressure, the volumes of gaseous reactants and products can be expressed as ratios of small whole numbers. This simple observation, combined with the insight of Avogadro, provided more understanding of how gases react and combine with each other.

MAIN IDEA

Equal volumes of gases under the same conditions contain equal numbers of molecules.

Recall an important point of Dalton's atomic theory: atoms are indivisible. Dalton also thought that the particles of gaseous elements exist in the form of isolated single atoms. He believed that one atom of one element always combines with one atom of another element to form a single particle of the product. However, some of the volume relationships observed by Gay-Lussac could not be accounted for by Dalton's theory. For example, in reactions such as the formation of water vapor, mentioned on the preceding page, it would seem that the oxygen atoms involved would have to divide into two parts.

In 1811, Avogadro found a way to explain Gay-Lussac's simple ratios of combining volumes without violating Dalton's idea of indivisible atoms. He did this by rejecting Dalton's idea that reactant elements are always in monatomic form when they combine to form products. He reasoned that these molecules could contain more than one atom. **Avogadro's law** states that equal volumes of gases at the same temperature and pressure contain equal numbers of molecules. **Figure 3.1** illustrates Avogadro's law. It follows that at the same temperature and pressure, the volume of any given gas varies directly with the number of molecules. Avogadro's law also indicates that gas volume is directly proportional to the amount of gas, at a given temperature and pressure, as shown in the following equation:

Avogadro's law	$V = kn$

Here, n is the amount of gas, in moles, and k is a constant.

Avogadro's reasoning applies to the combining volumes for the reaction of hydrogen and oxygen to form water vapor. Dalton had guessed that the formula of water was HO, because this formula seemed to be the most likely formula for such a common compound. But Avogadro's reasoning established that water must contain twice as many H atoms as O atoms, consistent with the formula H_2O. As shown below, the coefficients in a chemical reaction involving gases indicate the relative numbers of molecules, the relative numbers of moles, and the relative volumes.

$$2H_2(g) \quad + \quad O_2(g) \quad \rightarrow \quad 2H_2O(g)$$

2 molecules	1 molecule	2 molecules
2 mol	1 mol	2 mol
2 volumes	1 volume	2 volumes

The simplest hypothetical formula for oxygen indicated two oxygen atoms, which turns out to be correct. The simplest possible molecule of water indicated two hydrogen atoms and one oxygen atom per molecule, which is also correct. Experiments eventually showed that all elements that are gases near room temperature, except the noble gases, normally exist as diatomic molecules.

FIGURE 3.1

Avogadro's Law

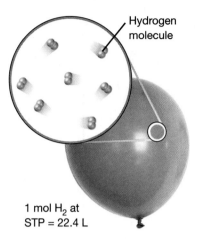

1 mol H_2 at
STP = 22.4 L

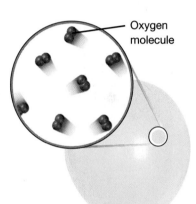

1 mol O_2 at
STP = 22.4 L

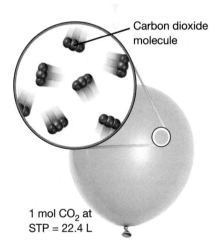

1 mol CO_2 at
STP = 22.4 L

✔ CRITICAL THINKING

Conclude By observing the figures above, what statement could you make about what these three gases at STP have in common?

Gases **367**

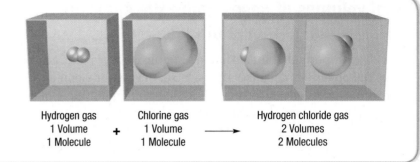

FIGURE 3.2

Avogadro's Law Hydrogen molecules combine with chlorine molecules in a 1:1 volume ratio to produce two volumes of hydrogen chloride. Avogadro's law thus demonstrates that hydrogen and chlorine gases are diatomic.

Hydrogen gas
1 Volume
1 Molecule

+

Chlorine gas
1 Volume
1 Molecule

⟶

Hydrogen chloride gas
2 Volumes
2 Molecules

Consider the reaction of hydrogen and chlorine to produce hydrogen chloride, illustrated in **Figure 3.2.** According to Avogadro's law, equal volumes of hydrogen and chlorine contain the same number of molecules. Avogadro's idea of diatomic gases applies to this reaction also. He concluded that the hydrogen and chlorine components must each consist of two or more atoms joined together. The simplest assumption was that hydrogen and chlorine molecules are composed of two atoms each. That assumption leads to the following balanced equation:

$$H_2(g) \quad + \quad Cl_2(g) \quad \rightarrow \quad 2HCl(g)$$

1 volume   1 volume   2 volumes

1 molecule   1 molecule   2 molecules

The simplest hypothetical formula for hydrogen chloride, HCl, indicates that the molecule contains one hydrogen atom and one chlorine atom. Given the ratios of the combined volumes, the simplest formulas for hydrogen and chlorine must be H_2 and Cl_2, respectively.

▶ **MAIN IDEA**

All gases have a volume of 22.4 L under standard conditions.

Recall that one mole of a molecular substance contains a number of molecules equal to Avogadro's constant (6.022×10^{23}). One mole of oxygen, O_2, contains 6.022×10^{23} diatomic oxygen molecules and has a mass of 31.9988 g. One mole of helium, a monatomic gas, contains the same number of helium atoms and has a mass of 4.002 602 g.

According to Avogadro's law, one mole of any gas will occupy the same volume as one mole of any other gas at the same temperature and pressure, despite mass differences. The volume occupied by one mole of a gas at STP is known as the **standard molar volume of a gas.** It has been found to be 22.414 10 L. For calculations in this book, we use 22.4 L as the standard molar volume.

You can use standard molar volume to determine volume/mass relationships of gases participating in a chemical reaction. For example, 22.4 L of oxygen reacts with 44.8 L of hydrogen to produce 44.8 L of water vapor at STP. This means that 1 mole of oxygen reacts with 2 moles of hydrogen to produce 2 moles of water vapor. Likewise, 31.998 g of oxygen reacts with 4.032 grams of hydrogen to produce 36.030 g of water vapor.

Calculating with Avogadro's Law

Sample Problem G **a.** What volume does 0.0685 mol of gas occupy at STP?
b. What quantity of gas, in moles, is contained in 2.21 L at STP?

 SOLVE

a. Multiply the amount in moles by the conversion factor, $\dfrac{22.4\ L}{1\ mol}$.

$$V = 0.0685\ \cancel{mol} \times \dfrac{22.4\ L}{1\ \cancel{mol}} = 1.53\ L$$

b. Multiply the volume in liters by the conversion factor, $\dfrac{1\ mol}{22.4\ L}$.

$$Moles = 2.21\ \cancel{L} \times \dfrac{1\ mol}{22.4\ \cancel{L}} = 0.0987\ mol$$

Practice Answers in Appendix E

1. At STP, what is the volume of 7.08 mol of nitrogen gas?
2. A sample of hydrogen gas occupies 14.1 L at STP. How many moles of the gas are present?

▶ **MAIN IDEA**

In a chemical equation, the coefficients can indicate moles, molecules, or volume.

You can apply the discoveries of Gay-Lussac and Avogadro to calculate the stoichiometry of reactions involving gases. For gaseous reactants or products, the coefficients in chemical equations not only indicate molar amounts and mole ratios but also reveal volume ratios, assuming conditions remain the same. For example, consider the reaction of carbon monoxide with oxygen to give carbon dioxide.

$$2CO(g) \quad + \quad O_2(g) \quad \rightarrow \quad 2CO_2(g)$$

2 molecules	1 molecule	2 molecules
2 mol	1 mol	2 mol
2 volumes	1 volume	2 volumes

The possible volume ratios can be expressed in the following ways.

a. $\dfrac{2\ volumes\ CO}{1\ volume\ O_2}$ or $\dfrac{1\ volume\ O_2}{2\ volumes\ CO}$

b. $\dfrac{2\ volumes\ CO}{2\ volumes\ CO_2}$ or $\dfrac{2\ volumes\ CO_2}{2\ volumes\ CO}$

c. $\dfrac{1\ volume\ O_2}{2\ volumes\ CO_2}$ or $\dfrac{2\ volumes\ CO_2}{1\ volume\ O_2}$

GO ONLINE

Solve It! Cards
HMHScience.com

Sample Problem H Propane, C_3H_8, is a gas that is sometimes used as a fuel for cooking and heating. The complete combustion of propane occurs according to the following balanced equation.

$$C_3H_8(g) + 5O_2(g) \rightarrow 3CO_2(g) + 4H_2O(g)$$

(a) What will be the volume, in liters, of oxygen required for the complete combustion of 0.350 L of propane? (b) What will be the volume of carbon dioxide produced in the reaction? Assume that all volume measurements are made at the same temperature and pressure.

❶ ANALYZE

Given: balanced chemical equation

V of propane = 0.350 L

Unknown: **a.** V of O_2 in L

     b. V of CO_2 in L

❷ PLAN

a. V of $C_3H_8 \rightarrow V$ of O_2

b. V of $C_3H_8 \rightarrow V$ of CO_2

All volumes are to be compared at the same temperature and pressure. Therefore, volume ratios can be used like mole ratios to find the unknowns.

❸ SOLVE

a. V of $O_2 = 0.350 \text{ L } C_3H_8 \times \dfrac{5 \text{ L } O_2}{1 \text{ L } C_3H_8} = 1.75 \text{ L } O_2$

b. V of $CO_2 = 0.350 \text{ L } C_3H_8 \times \dfrac{3 \text{ L } CO_2}{1 \text{ L } C_3H_8} = 1.05 \text{ L } CO_2$

❹ CHECK YOUR WORK

Each result is correctly given to three significant figures. The answers are reasonably close to estimated values of 2, calculated as 0.4×5, and 1.2, calculated as 0.4×3, respectively.

Practice   Answers in Appendix E

1. Assuming all volume measurements are made at the same temperature and pressure, what volume of hydrogen gas is needed to react completely with 4.55 L of oxygen gas to produce water vapor?

2. What volume of oxygen gas is needed to react completely with 0.626 L of carbon monoxide gas, CO, to form gaseous carbon dioxide? Assume all volume measurements are made at the same temperature and pressure.

3. Nitric acid can be produced by the reaction of gaseous nitrogen dioxide with water, according to the following balanced chemical equation.

$$3NO_2(g) + H_2O(l) \rightarrow 2HNO_3(l) + NO(g)$$

If 708 L of NO_2 gas react with water, what volume of NO gas will be produced? Assume the gases are measured under the same conditions before and after the reaction.

▶ MAIN IDEA

Pressure, volume, and temperature are related to the number of moles of a gas.

You have learned about equations describing the relationships between two or three of the four variables—pressure, volume, temperature, and moles—needed to describe a gas sample. All the gas laws you have learned thus far can be combined into a single equation. **The ideal gas law is the mathematical relationship among pressure, volume, temperature, and the number of moles of a gas.** It is the equation of state for an ideal gas, because the state of a gas can be defined by its pressure, volume, temperature, and number of moles. It is stated as shown below, where R is a constant.

Ideal gas law	$PV = nRT$

The ideal gas law reduces to Boyle's law, Charles's law, Gay-Lussac's law, or Avogadro's law when the appropriate variables are held constant.

The number of molecules or moles present will always affect at least one of the other three quantities. The collision rate of molecules per unit area of container wall depends on the number of molecules present. If the number of molecules is increased for a sample at constant volume and temperature, the collision rate increases. Therefore, the pressure increases, as shown by the model in **Figure 3.3a.** Consider what would happen if the pressure and temperature were kept constant while the number of molecules increased. According to Avogadro's law, the volume would increase. As **Figure 3.3b** shows, an increase in volume keeps the pressure constant at constant temperature. Increasing the volume keeps the collision rate per unit of wall area constant.

FIGURE 3.3

The Ideal Gas Law

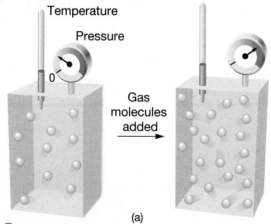

(a)

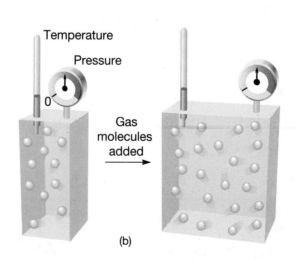

(b)

✔ CRITICAL THINKING

Analyze When volume and temperature are constant and the number of molecules increases, what happens to the gas pressure?

Analyze When pressure and temperature are constant and the number of molecules increases, what happens to the gas volume?

MAIN IDEA

The ideal gas law relates pressure to volume to temperature.

In the equation representing the ideal gas law, the constant R is known as the **ideal gas constant.** Its value depends on the units chosen for pressure, volume, and temperature. Measured values of P, V, T, and n for a gas at near-ideal conditions can be used to calculate R. Recall that the volume of one mole of an ideal gas at STP (1 atm and 273.15 K) is 22.414 10 L. Substituting these values and solving the ideal gas law equation for R gives the following.

$$R = \frac{PV}{nT} = \frac{(1\text{ atm})\,(22.414\ 10\text{ L})}{(1\text{ mol})\,(273.15\text{ K})} = 0.082\ 057\ 84\ \frac{\text{L} \cdot \text{atm}}{\text{mol} \cdot \text{K}}$$

For calculations in this text, R is rounded to 0.0821 L • atm/(mol•K). Use this value in ideal gas law calculations when the volume is in liters, the pressure is in atmospheres, and the temperature is in kelvins. See **Figure 3.4** for the value of R when other units for n, P, V, and T are used.

Finding P, V, T, or n from the Ideal Gas Law

The ideal gas law can be applied to determine the existing conditions of a gas sample when three of the four variables, P, V, T, and n, are known. It can also be used to calculate the molar mass or density of a gas sample.

Be sure to match the units of the known quantities and the units of R. In this book, you will be using $R = 0.0821$ L•atm/(mol•K). Your first step in solving any ideal gas law problem should be to check the known values to be sure you are working with the correct units. If necessary, you must convert volumes to liters, pressures to atmospheres, temperatures to kelvins, and masses to numbers of moles before using the ideal gas law.

✓ **CHECK FOR UNDERSTANDING**

Identify What variable in the ideal gas law does not change units?

FIGURE 3.4

NUMERICAL VALUES OF GAS CONSTANT, R

Units of R	Numerical value of R	Unit of P	Unit of V	Unit of T	Unit of n
$\dfrac{\text{L} \cdot \text{mm Hg}}{\text{mol} \cdot \text{K}}$	62.4	mm Hg	L	K	mol
$\dfrac{\text{L} \cdot \text{atm}}{\text{mol} \cdot \text{K}}$	0.0821	atm	L	K	mol
$\dfrac{\text{J}}{\text{mol} \cdot \text{K}}$ *	8.314	Pa	m^3	K	mol
$\dfrac{\text{L} \cdot \text{kPa}}{\text{mol} \cdot \text{K}}$	8.314	kPa	L	K	mol

Note: 1 L•atm = 101.325 J; 1 J = 1 Pa•m^3
*SI units

Using the Ideal Gas Law

Sample Problem I What is the pressure in atmospheres exerted by a 0.500 mol sample of nitrogen gas in a 10.0 L container at 298 K?

GO ONLINE

Learn It! Video
HMHScience.com

Solve It! Cards
HMHScience.com

SOLUTION TUTOR
HMHScience.com

1 ANALYZE

Given: V of N_2 = 10.0 L

n of N_2 = 0.500 mol

T of N_2 = 298 K

Unknown: P of N_2 in atm

2 PLAN

$n, V, T \rightarrow P$

The gas sample undergoes no change in conditions. Therefore, the ideal gas law can be rearranged and used to find the pressure as follows:

$$P = \frac{nRT}{V}$$

3 SOLVE

$$P = \frac{(0.500 \text{ mol}) \left(\dfrac{0.0821 \text{ L} \cdot \text{atm}}{\text{mol} \cdot \text{K}} \right)(298 \text{ K})}{10.0 \text{ L}} = 1.22 \text{ atm}$$

4 CHECK YOUR WORK

All units cancel correctly to give the result in atmospheres. The answer is properly limited to three significant figures. It is also close to an estimated value of 1.5, computed as $(0.5 \times 0.1 \times 300)/10$.

Practice   Answers in Appendix E

1. What pressure, in atmospheres, is exerted by 0.325 mol of hydrogen gas in a 4.08 L container at 35°C?

2. A gas sample occupies 8.77 L at 20°C. What is the pressure, in atmospheres, given that there are 1.45 mol of gas in the sample?

✔ SECTION 3 FORMATIVE ASSESSMENT

▶ Reviewing Main Ideas

1. State Avogadro's law, and explain its significance.

2. What volume (in milliliters) at STP will be occupied by 0.0035 mol of methane, CH_4?

3. State the ideal gas law equation, and tell what each term means.

4. What would be the units for R if P is in pascals, T is in kelvins, V is in liters, and n is in moles?

5. A 4.44 L container holds 15.4 g of oxygen at 22.55°C. What is the pressure?

6. A tank of hydrogen gas has a volume of 22.9 L and holds 14.0 mol of the gas at 12°C. What is the pressure of the gas in atmospheres?

✔ Critical Thinking

7. **ANALYZING DATA** Nitrous oxide is sometimes used as a source of oxygen gas:

$$2N_2O(g) \rightarrow 2N_2(g) + O_2(g)$$

What volume of each product will be formed from 2.22 L N_2O? At STP, what is the density of the product gases when they are mixed?

SECTION 4

Main Idea

The rates of effusion and diffusion for gases depend on the velocities of their molecules.

Diffusion and Effusion

Key Term

Graham's law of effusion

The constant motion of gas molecules causes them to spread out to fill any container in which they are placed. The gradual mixing of two or more gases due to their spontaneous, random motion is known as diffusion, illustrated in **Figure 4.1.** *Effusion* is the process whereby the molecules of a gas confined in a container randomly pass through a tiny opening in the container. In this section, you will learn how the rate of effusion can be used to estimate the molar mass of a gas.

▶ MAIN IDEA

The rates of effusion and diffusion for gases depend on the velocities of their molecules.

The rates of effusion and diffusion depend on the relative velocities of gas molecules. The velocity of a gas varies inversely with the square root of its molar mass. Lighter molecules move faster than heavier molecules at the same temperature.

Recall that the average kinetic energy of the molecules in any gas depends only on the temperature and equals $\frac{1}{2}mv^2$. For two different gases, A and B, at the same temperature, the following relationship is true:

$$\tfrac{1}{2}M_A v_A{}^2 = \tfrac{1}{2}M_B v_B{}^2$$

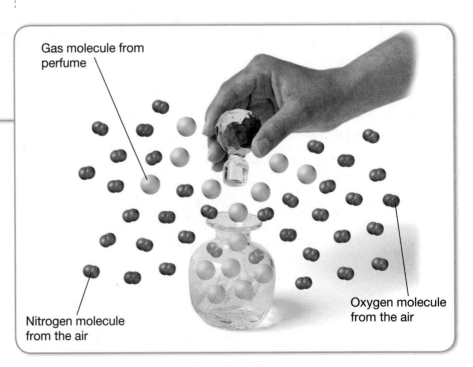

Gas molecule from perfume

Oxygen molecule from the air

Nitrogen molecule from the air

FIGURE 4.1

Diffusion When a bottle of perfume is opened, some of its molecules diffuse into the air and mix with the molecules of the air. At the same time, molecules from the air, such as nitrogen and oxygen, diffuse into the bottle and mix with the gaseous scent molecules.

✔ CRITICAL THINKING

Deduce As diffusion occurs, what would you expect to see happen to the different molecules in the figure at the right?

From the equation relating the kinetic energy of two different gases at the same conditions, one can derive an equation relating the rates of effusion of two gases with their molecular mass. This equation is shown below.

$$\frac{\text{rate of effusion of A}}{\text{rate of effusion of B}} = \frac{\sqrt{M_B}}{\sqrt{M_A}}$$

In the mid-1800s, the Scottish chemist Thomas Graham studied the effusion and diffusion of gases. The above equation is a mathematical statement of some of Graham's discoveries. It describes the rates of effusion. It can also be used to find the molar mass of an unknown gas. **Graham's law of effusion** states that the rates of effusion of gases at the same temperature and pressure are inversely proportional to the square roots of their molar masses.

*Quick*LAB   DIFFUSION

QUESTION
Do different gases diffuse at different rates?

PROCEDURE
Record all of your results in a data table.

1. Outdoors or in a room separate from the one in which you will carry out the rest of the investigation, pour approximately 10 mL of the household ammonia into one of the 250 mL beakers and cover it with a watch glass. Pour roughly the same amount of perfume or cologne into the second beaker. Cover it with a watch glass also.

2. Take the two samples you just prepared into a large, draft-free room. Place the samples about 12 to 15 ft apart and at the same height. Position someone as the observer midway between the two beakers. Remove both watch glass covers at the same time.

3. Note whether the observer smells the ammonia or the perfume first. Record how long this takes. Also, record how long it takes the vapor of the other substance to reach the observer. Air the room after you have finished.

DISCUSSION
1. What do the times that the two vapors took to reach the observer show about the two gases?

2. What factors other than molecular mass (which determines diffusion rate) could affect how quickly the observer smells each vapor?

MATERIALS
- household ammonia
- perfume or cologne
- two 250 mL beakers
- two watch glasses
- 10 mL graduated cylinder
- clock or watch with second hand

SAFETY
     Wear safety goggles and an apron.

Ammonia

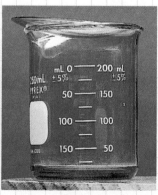

Perfume

Graham's Law of Effusion

Sample Problem J Compare the rates of effusion of hydrogen and oxygen at the same temperature and pressure.

❶ ANALYZE

Given: identities of two gases, H_2 and O_2

Unknown: relative rates of effusion

❷ PLAN

molar mass ratio → ratio of rates of effusion
The ratio of the rates of effusion of two gases at the same temperature and pressure can be found from Graham's Law.

$$\frac{\text{rate of effusion of A}}{\text{rate of effusion of B}} = \frac{\sqrt{M_B}}{\sqrt{M_A}}$$

❸ SOLVE

$$\frac{\text{rate of effusion of } H_2}{\text{rate of effusion of } O_2} = \frac{\sqrt{M_{O_2}}}{\sqrt{M_{H_2}}} = \frac{\sqrt{32.00 \text{ g/mol}}}{\sqrt{2.02 \text{ g/mol}}} = \sqrt{\frac{32.00 \text{ g/mol}}{2.02 \text{ g/mol}}} = 3.98$$

Hydrogen effuses 3.98 times faster than oxygen.

❹ CHECK YOUR WORK

The result is correctly reported to three significant figures. It is also approximately equivalent to an estimated value of 4, calculated as $\sqrt{32}/\sqrt{2}$.

Practice Answers in Appendix E

1. Compare the rate of effusion of carbon dioxide with that of hydrogen chloride at the same temperature and pressure.

2. A sample of hydrogen effuses through a porous container about 9 times faster than an unknown gas. Estimate the molar mass of the unknown gas.

3. If a molecule of neon gas travels at an average of 400. m/s at a given temperature, estimate the average speed of a molecule of butane gas, C_4H_{10}, at the same temperature.

SECTION 4 FORMATIVE ASSESSMENT

▶ Reviewing Main Ideas

1. Compare diffusion with effusion.

2. State Graham's law of effusion.

3. Estimate the molar mass of a gas that effuses at 1.6 times the effusion rate of carbon dioxide.

4. Determine the molecular mass ratio of two gases whose rates of effusion have a ratio of 16 : 1.

5. List the following gases in order of increasing average molecular velocity at 25°C: H_2O, He, HCl, BrF, and NO_2.

✔ Critical Thinking

6. **ANALYZING INFORMATION** An unknown gas effuses at one-half the speed of oxygen. What is the molar mass of the unknown? The gas is known to be either HBr or HI. Which gas is it?

Math Tutor

Algebraic Rearrangements of Gas Laws

When you solve problems in chemistry, it's usually a bad idea to just start entering numbers into a calculator. Instead, doing a little pencil-and-paper work beforehand will help you eliminate errors. When using the gas laws, you do not need to memorize all of the equations because they are easily derived from the equation for the combined gas law.

Study the table below. In each of Boyle's, Charles's, and

Gay-Lussac's laws, one of the quantities—T, P, or V—does not change. By simply eliminating that factor from the equation, you obtain the equation for one particular gas law.

The conditions stated in the problem should make clear which factors change and which are held constant. This information will tell you which law's equation to use.

GAS LAW	HELD CONSTANT	CANCELLATION	RESULT
combined gas law	none	$\dfrac{P_1 V_1}{T_1} = \dfrac{P_2 V_2}{T_2}$	$\dfrac{P_1 V_1}{T_1} = \dfrac{P_2 V_2}{T_2}$
Boyle's law	temperature	$\dfrac{P_1 V_1}{\cancel{T_1}} = \dfrac{P_2 V_2}{\cancel{T_2}}$	$P_1 V_1 = P_2 V_2$
Charles's law	pressure	$\dfrac{\cancel{P_1} V_1}{T_1} = \dfrac{\cancel{P_2} V_2}{T_2}$	$\dfrac{V_1}{T_1} = \dfrac{V_2}{T_2}$
Gay-Lussac's law	volume	$\dfrac{P_1 \cancel{V_1}}{T_1} = \dfrac{P_2 \cancel{V_2}}{T_2}$	$\dfrac{P_1}{T_1} = \dfrac{P_2}{T_2}$

Sample Problem

A cylinder of nitrogen gas has a volume of 35.00 L at a pressure of 11.50 atm. What pressure will the nitrogen have if the contents of the cylinder are allowed to flow into a sealed reaction chamber whose volume is 140.0 L and if the temperature remains constant?

 ANALYZE

Start with the combined gas law, and cancel the temperature, which does not change.

$$\frac{P_1 V_1}{\cancel{T_1}} = \frac{P_2 V_2}{\cancel{T_2}}; P_1 V_1 = P_2 V_2$$

You want to know the new pressure in the chamber, so solve for P_2.

$$\frac{P_1 V_1}{V_2} = \frac{P_2 \cancel{V_2}}{\cancel{V_2}}; \frac{P_1 V_1}{V_2} = P_2$$

 SOLVE

The resulting equation to use in solving the problem is

$$P_2 = \frac{P_1 V_1}{V_2} = \frac{(11.50 \text{ atm})(35.00 \text{ L})}{140.0 \text{ L}} = 2.875 \text{ atm.}$$

Practice   Answers in Appendix E

1. A sample of gas has a pressure P_1 at a temperature T_1. Write the equation that you would use to find the temperature, T_2, at which the gas has a pressure of P_2.
2. An ideal gas occupies a volume of 785 mL at a pressure of 0.879 atm. What volume will the gas occupy at the pressure of 0.994 atm?

BIG IDEA The gas laws describe mathematical relationships among the pressure, temperature, volume, and quantity of gases.

SECTION 1 Gases and Pressure

- The kinetic-molecular theory of gases describes an ideal gas. The behavior of real gases is nearly ideal except at very high pressures and low temperatures.
- A barometer measures atmospheric pressure.
- Dalton's law of partial pressures states that in a mixture of unreacting gases, the total pressure equals the sum of the partial pressures of each gas.

KEY TERMS

pressure
newton
barometer
millimeters of mercury
atmosphere of pressure

pascal
partial pressure
Dalton's law of partial pressures

SECTION 2 The Gas Laws

- Boyle's law states the inverse relationship between the volume and the pressure of a gas:

$$PV = k$$

- Charles's law illustrates the direct relationship between a gas's volume and its temperature in kelvins:

$$V = kT$$

- Gay-Lussac's law represents the direct relationship between a gas's pressure and its temperature in kelvins:

$$P = kT$$

- The combined gas law, as its name implies, combines the previous relationships into the following mathematical expression:

$$\frac{PV}{T} = k$$

KEY TERMS

Boyle's law
absolute zero
Charles's law
Gay-Lussac's law
combined gas law

SECTION 3 Gas Volumes and the Ideal Gas Law

- Gay-Lussac's law of combining volumes states that the volumes of reacting gases and their products at the same temperature and pressure can be expressed as ratios of whole numbers.
- Avogadro's law states that equal volumes of gases at the same temperature and pressure contain equal numbers of molecules.
- The volume occupied by one mole of an ideal gas at STP is called the standard molar volume, which is 22.414 10 L.
- Charles's law, Boyle's law, and Avogadro's law can be combined to create the ideal gas law:

$$PV = nRT$$

KEY TERMS

Gay-Lussac's law of combining volumes of gases
Avogadro's law

standard molar volume of a gas
ideal gas law
ideal gas constant

SECTION 4 Diffusion and Effusion

- Gases diffuse, or become more spread out, due to their constant random molecular motion.
- Graham's law of effusion states that the relative rates of effusion of gases at the same temperature and pressure are inversely proportional to the square roots of their molar masses.

KEY TERM

Graham's law of effusion

CHAPTER 11 **Review**

GO ONLINE

 Interactive Review
HMHScience.com

Review Games
Concept Maps

SECTION 1
Gases and Pressure

▶ **REVIEWING MAIN IDEAS**

1. State the assumptions that the kinetic-molecular theory makes about the characteristics of gas particles.

2. What is an ideal gas?

3. **a.** Why does a gas in a closed container exert pressure?
   b. What is the relationship between the area a force is applied to and the resulting pressure?

4. **a.** Why does a column of mercury in a tube that is inverted in a dish of mercury have a height of about 760 mm at sea level?
   b. The density of water is approximately 1/13.5 the density of mercury. What height would be maintained by a column of water inverted in a dish of water at sea level?
   c. What accounts for the difference in the heights of the mercury and water columns?

5. **a.** Identify three units used to express pressure.
   b. Convert one atmosphere to millimeters of mercury.
   c. What is a pascal?
   d. What is the SI equivalent of one standard atmosphere of pressure?

6. **a.** Explain what is meant by the partial pressure of each gas within a mixture of gases.
   b. How do the partial pressures of gases in a mixture affect each other?

PRACTICE PROBLEMS

7. If the atmosphere can support a column of mercury 760. mm high at sea level, what height of a hypothetical liquid whose density is 1.40 times the density of mercury could be supported?

8. Convert each of the following into a pressure reading expressed in torrs.
   a. 1.25 atm
   b. 2.48×10^{-3} atm
   c. 4.75×10^4 atm
   d. 7.60×10^6 atm

9. Convert each of the following into the unit specified.
   a. 125 mm Hg into atmospheres
   b. 3.20 atm into pascals
   c. 5.38 kPa into millimeters of mercury

10. Three of the primary components of air are carbon dioxide, nitrogen, and oxygen. In a sample containing a mixture of only these gases at exactly 1 atm, the partial pressures of carbon dioxide and nitrogen are given as $P_{CO_2} = 0.285$ torr and $P_{N_2} = 593.525$ torr. What is the partial pressure of oxygen?

11. A gas sample is collected over water at a temperature of 35.0°C when the barometric pressure reading is 742.0 torr. What is the partial pressure of the dry gas?

SECTION 2
The Gas Laws

▶ **REVIEWING MAIN IDEAS**

12. How are the volume and pressure of a gas at constant temperature related?

13. Explain why pressure increases as a gas is compressed into a smaller volume.

14. How are the absolute temperature and volume of a gas at constant pressure related?

15. How are the pressure and absolute temperature of a gas at constant volume related?

16. Explain Gay-Lussac's law in terms of the kinetic-molecular theory.

17. State the combined gas law.

PRACTICE PROBLEMS

18. Use Boyle's law to solve for the missing value in each of the following:
   a. $P_1 = 350.0$ torr, $V_1 = 200.0$ mL, $P_2 = 700.0$ torr, $V_2 = ?$
   b. $V_1 = 2.4 \times 10^5$ L, $P_2 = 180$ mm Hg, $V_2 = 1.8 \times 10^3$ L, $P_1 = ?$

19. Use Charles's law to solve for the missing value in each of the following:
   a. $V_1 = 80.0$ mL, $T_1 = 27°C$, $T_2 = 77°C$, $V_2 = ?$
   b. $V_1 = 125$ L, $V_2 = 85.0$ L, $T_2 = 127°C$, $T_1 = ?$
   c. $T_1 = -33°C$, $V_2 = 54.0$ mL, $T_2 = 160.0°C$, $V_1 = ?$

20. A sample of air has a volume of 140.0 mL at 67°C. At what temperature would its volume be 50.0 mL at constant pressure?

21. The pressure exerted on a 240.0 mL sample of hydrogen gas at constant temperature is increased from 0.428 atm to 0.724 atm. What will the final volume of the sample be?

22. A sample of hydrogen at 47°C exerts a pressure of 0.329 atm. The gas is heated to 77°C at constant volume. What will its new pressure be?

23. A sample of gas at 47°C and 1.03 atm occupies a volume of 2.20 L. What volume would this gas occupy at 107°C and 0.789 atm?

24. The pressure on a gas at −73°C is doubled, but its volume is held constant. What will the final temperature be in degrees Celsius?

25. A flask contains 155 cm^3 of hydrogen that was collected under a pressure of 22.5 kPa. What pressure would have been required for the volume of the gas to have been 90.0 cm^3, assuming the same temperature?

26. A gas has a volume of 450.0 mL. If the temperature is held constant, what volume would the gas occupy if the pressure were
  a. doubled? (Hint: Express P_2 in terms of P_1.)
  b. reduced to one-fourth of its original value?

27. A sample of oxygen that occupies 1.00×10^6 mL at 575 mm Hg is subjected to a pressure of 1.25 atm. What will the final volume of the sample be if the temperature is held constant?

28. To what temperature must a sample of nitrogen at 27°C and 0.625 atm be taken so that its pressure becomes 1.125 atm at constant volume?

29. A gas has a volume of 1.75 L at −23°C and 150.0 kPa. At what temperature would the gas occupy 1.30 L at 210.0 kPa?

30. A gas at 7.75×10^4 Pa and 17°C occupies a volume of 850.0 cm^3. At what temperature, in degrees Celsius, would the gas occupy 720.0 cm^3 at 8.10×10^4 Pa?

31. A meteorological balloon contains 250.0 L He at 22°C and 740.0 mm Hg. If the volume of the balloon can vary according to external conditions, what volume would it occupy at an altitude at which the temperature is −52°C and the pressure is 0.750 atm?

32. The balloon in the previous problem will burst if its volume reaches 400.0 L. Given the initial conditions specified in that problem, determine at what temperature, in degrees Celsius, the balloon will burst if its pressure at that bursting point is 0.475 atm.

33. The normal respiratory rate for a human being is 15.0 breaths per minute. The average volume of air for each breath is 505 cm^3 at 20.0°C and 9.95×10^4 Pa. What is the volume of air at STP that an individual breathes in one day? Give your answer in cubic meters.

Gas Volumes and the Ideal Gas Law

▶ **REVIEWING MAIN IDEAS**

34. a. What are the restrictions on the use of Gay-Lussac's law of combining volumes?
  b. At the same temperature and pressure, what is the relationship between the volume of a gas and the number of molecules present?

35. a. In a balanced chemical equation, what is the relationship between the molar ratios and the volume ratios of gaseous reactants and products?
  b. What restriction applies to the use of the volume ratios in solving stoichiometry problems?

36. According to Avogadro,
  a. what is the relationship between gas volume and number of moles at constant temperature and pressure?
  b. what is the mathematical expression denoting this relationship?

37. What is the relationship between the number of molecules and the mass of 22.4 L of different gases at STP?

38. a. In what situations is the ideal gas law most suitable for calculations?
  b. When using this law, why do you have to pay particular attention to units?

39. a. Write the equation for the ideal gas law.
  b. What relationship is expressed in the ideal gas law?

PRACTICE PROBLEMS

40. Suppose a 5.00 L sample of O_2 at a given temperature and pressure contains 1.08×10^{23} molecules. How many molecules would be contained in each of the following at the same temperature and pressure?
  a. 5.0 L H_2
  b. 5.0 L CO_2
  c. 10.0 L NH_3

41. How many moles are contained in each of the following at STP?
  a. 22.4 L N_2
  b. 5.60 L Cl_2
  c. 0.125 L Ne
  d. 70.0 mL NH_3

42. Find the mass, in grams, of each of the following at STP.
  a. 11.2 L H_2
  b. 2.80 L CO_2
  c. 15.0 mL SO_2
  d. 3.40 cm^3 F_2

43. Find the volume, in liters, of each of the following at STP.
  a. 8.00 g O_2
  b. 3.50 g CO
  c. 0.0170 g H_2S
  d. 2.25×10^5 kg NH_3

44. Acetylene gas, C_2H_2, undergoes combustion to produce carbon dioxide and water vapor. If 75.0 L CO_2 is produced,
  a. how many liters of C_2H_2 are required?
  b. what volume of H_2O vapor is produced?
  c. what volume of O_2 is required?

45. Assume that 0.504 g of H_2 gas at STP reacts with excess CuO according to the following equation:
$$CuO(s) + H_2(g) \rightarrow Cu(s) + H_2O(g)$$
Make sure the equation is balanced before beginning your calculations.
  a. How many liters of H_2 react?
  b. How many moles of Cu are produced?
  c. How many grams of Cu are produced?

46. If 13.2 g of methane, CH_4, undergoes complete combustion at 0.961 atm and 140°C, how many liters of each product would be present at the same temperature and pressure? How many grams of each product will be present?

47. If air is 20.9% oxygen by volume,
  a. how many liters of air are needed for complete combustion of 25.0 L of octane vapor, C_8H_{18}?
  b. what volume of each product is produced?

48. Methanol, CH_3OH, is made by causing carbon monoxide and hydrogen gases to react at high temperature and pressure. If 4.50×10^2 mL CO and 8.25×10^2 mL H_2 are mixed,
  a. which reactant is present in excess?
  b. how much of that reactant remains after the reaction?
  c. what volume of CH_3OH is produced, assuming the same pressure?

49. Calculate the pressure, in atmospheres, exerted by each of the following:
  a. 2.50 L HF containing 1.35 mol at 320.0 K
  b. 4.75 L NO_2 containing 0.86 mol at 300.0 K
  c. 5.50×10^4 mL CO_2 containing 2.15 mol at 57°C

50. Calculate the volume, in liters, occupied by each of the following:
  a. 2.00 mol H_2 at 300.0 K and 1.25 atm
  b. 0.425 mol NH_3 at 37°C and 0.724 atm
  c. 4.00 g O_2 at 57°C and 0.888 atm

51. Determine the number of moles of gas contained in each of the following:
  a. 1.25 L at 250.0 K and 1.06 atm
  b. 0.80 L at 27°C and 0.925 atm
  c. 7.50×10^2 mL at −50.0°C and 0.921 atm

52. Find the mass of each of the following.
  a. 5.60 L O_2 at 1.75 atm and 250.0 K
  b. 3.50 L NH_3 at 0.921 atm and 27°C
  c. 125 mL SO_2 at 0.822 atm and −5°C

SECTION 4
Diffusion and Effusion

▶ REVIEWING MAIN IDEAS

53. Describe in your own words the process of diffusion.

54. At a given temperature, what factor determines the rates at which different molecules undergo diffusion and effusion?

55. Ammonia, NH_3, and alcohol, C_2H_6O, are released together across a room. Which will you smell first?

PRACTICE PROBLEMS

56. Quantitatively compare the rates of effusion for the following pairs of gases at the same temperature and pressure:
   a. hydrogen and nitrogen
   b. fluorine and chlorine

57. What is the ratio of the average velocity of hydrogen molecules to that of neon atoms at the same temperature and pressure?

58. At a certain temperature and pressure, chlorine molecules have an average velocity of 324 m/s. What is the average velocity of sulfur dioxide molecules under the same conditions?

Mixed Review

▶ REVIEWING MAIN IDEAS

59. A mixture of three gases, A, B, and C, is at a total pressure of 6.11 atm. The partial pressure of gas A is 1.68 atm; that of gas B is 3.89 atm. What is the partial pressure of gas C?

60. A child receives a balloon filled with 2.30 L of helium from a vendor at an amusement park. The temperature outside is 311 K. What will the volume of the balloon be when the child brings it home to an air-conditioned house at 295 K? Assume that the pressure stays the same.

61. A sample of argon gas occupies a volume of 295 mL at 36°C. What volume will the gas occupy at 55°C, assuming constant pressure?

62. A sample of carbon dioxide gas occupies 638 mL at 0.893 atm and 12°C. What will the pressure be at a volume of 881 mL and a temperature of 18°C?

63. At 84°C, a gas in a container exerts a pressure of 0.503 atm. Assuming the size of the container has not changed, at what temperature in degrees Celsius would the pressure be 1.20 atm?

64. A weather balloon at Earth's surface has a volume of 4.00 L at 304 K and 755 mm Hg. If the balloon is released and the volume reaches 4.08 L at 728 mm Hg, what is the temperature?

65. A gas has a pressure of 4.62 atm when its volume is 2.33 L. If the temperature remains constant, what will the pressure be when the volume is changed to 1.03 L? Express the final pressure in torrs.

66. At a deep-sea station that is 200 m below the surface of the Pacific Ocean, workers live in a highly pressurized environment. How many liters of gas at STP must be compressed on the surface to fill the underwater environment with 2.00×10^7 L of gas at 20.0 atm? Assume that temperature remains constant.

67. An unknown gas effuses at 0.850 times the effusion rate of nitrogen dioxide, NO_2. Estimate the molar mass of the unknown gas.

68. A container holds 265 mL of chlorine gas, Cl_2. If the gas sample is at STP, what is its mass?

69. Suppose that 3.11 mol of carbon dioxide is at a pressure of 0.820 atm and a temperature of 39°C. What is the volume of the sample, in liters?

70. Compare the rates of diffusion of carbon monoxide, CO, and sulfur trioxide, SO_3.

71. A gas sample that has a mass of 0.993 g occupies 0.570 L. Given that the temperature is 281 K and the pressure is 1.44 atm, what is the molar mass of the gas?

72. How many moles of helium gas would it take to fill a balloon to a volume of 1000.0 cm³ when the temperature is 32°C and the atmospheric pressure is 752 mm Hg?

73. A gas sample is collected at 16°C and 0.982 atm. If the sample has a mass of 7.40 g and a volume of 3.96 L, find the volume of the gas at STP and the molar mass.

CRITICAL THINKING

74. Applying Models
   a. Why do we say the graph in **Figure 2.2** illustrates an inverse relationship?
   b. Why do we say the data plotted in **Figure 2.4** indicate a direct relationship?

75. Inferring Conclusions If all gases behaved as ideal gases under all conditions of temperature and pressure, solid or liquid forms of these substances would not exist. Explain.

76. Relating Ideas Pressure is defined as force per unit area. Yet Torricelli found that the diameter of the barometer dish and the surface area of contact between the mercury in the tube and in the dish did not affect the height of mercury that was supported. Explain this seemingly inconsistent observation in view of the relationship between pressure and surface area.

77. Evaluating Methods In solving a problem, what types of conditions involving temperature, pressure, volume, or number of moles would allow you to use
a. the combined gas law?
b. the ideal gas law?

78. Evaluating Ideas Gay-Lussac's law of combining volumes holds true for relative volumes at any proportionate size. Use Avogadro's law to explain why this proportionality exists.

79. Interpreting Graphics The graph below shows velocity distribution curves for the same gas under two different conditions, A and B. Compare the behavior of the gas under conditions A and B in relation to each of the following:
a. temperature
b. average kinetic energy
c. average molecular velocity
d. gas volume
e. gas pressure

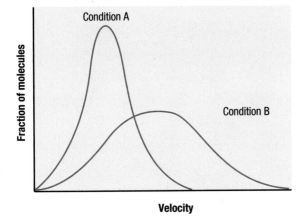

80. Interpreting Concepts The diagrams below represent equal volumes of four different gases.

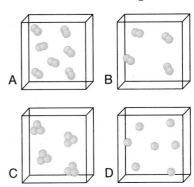

Use the diagrams to answer the following questions:
a. Are these gases at the same temperature and pressure? How do you know?
b. If the molar mass of gas B is 38 g/mol and that of gas C is 46 g/mol, which gas sample is denser?
c. To make the densities of gas samples B and C equal, which gas should expand in volume?
d. If the densities of gas samples A and C are equal, what is the relationship between their molar masses?

RESEARCH AND WRITING

81. Design and conduct a meteorological study to examine the interrelationships among barometric pressure, temperature, humidity, and other weather variables. Prepare a report explaining your results.

82. Conduct library research on attempts made to approach absolute zero and on the interesting properties that materials exhibit near that temperature. Write a report on your findings.

83. How do scuba divers use the laws and principles that describe the behavior of gases to their advantage? What precautions do they take to prevent the bends?

84. Explain the processes involved in the liquefaction of gases. Name some substances that are gases under normal room conditions and that are typically used in the liquid form. Explain why this is so.

85. Write a summary describing how Gay-Lussac's work on combining volumes relates to Avogadro's study of gases. Explain how certain conclusions about gases followed logically from consideration of the work of both scientists.

USING THE HANDBOOK

86. Review the melting point data in the properties tables for each group of the *Elements Handbook* (Appendix A). What elements on the periodic table exist as gases at room temperature?

87. Review in the *Elements Handbook* (Appendix A) the listing of the top 10 chemicals produced in the United States. Which of the top 10 chemicals are gases?

88. Most elements from Groups 1, 2, and 13 will react with water, acids, or bases to produce hydrogen gas. Review the common reactions information in the *Elements Handbook* (Appendix A), and answer the following questions:
  a. What is the equation for the reaction of barium with water?
  b. What is the equation for the reaction between cesium and hydrochloric acid?
  c. What is the equation for the reaction of gallium with hydrofluoric acid?
  d. What mass of barium would be needed to react with excess water to produce 10.1 L H_2 at STP?
  e. What masses of cesium and hydrochloric acid would be required to produce 10.1 L H_2 at STP?

89. Group 1 metals react with oxygen to produce oxides, peroxides, or superoxides. Review the equations for these common reactions in the *Elements Handbook* (Appendix A), and answer the following:
  a. How do oxides, peroxides, and superoxides differ?
  b. What mass of product will be formed from a reaction of 5.00 L O_2 with excess sodium? The reaction occurs at 27°C and 1 atm.

ALTERNATIVE ASSESSMENT

90. The air pressure of car tires should be checked regularly for safety reasons and for prevention of uneven tire wear. Find out the units of measurement on a typical tire gauge, and determine how gauge pressure relates to atmospheric pressure.

91. During a typical day, record every instance in which you encounter the diffusion or effusion of gases (for example, when smelling perfume).

92. **Performance** Qualitatively compare the molecular masses of various gases by noting how long it takes you to smell them from a fixed distance. Work only with materials that are not dangerous, such as flavor extracts, fruit peels, and onions.

93. **Performance** Design an experiment to gather data to verify the ideal gas law. If your teacher approves of your plan, carry it out. Illustrate your data with a graph, and determine if the data are consistent with the ideal gas law.

Standards-Based Assessment

Record your answers on a separate piece of paper.

MULTIPLE CHOICE

1 When the temperature of a gas is increased within a closed container, pressure increases due to which of the following?

A The frequency of collisions between molecules and the container walls decreases.

B The frequency of collisions between molecules and the container walls increases.

C The spaces between the molecules of gas decrease.

D The gas turns into a liquid.

2 Gas A and gas B (both unreactive) are allowed to mix. The total pressure is found to be 3.50 atm. If gas B was measured initially at 1.25 atm, what is the partial pressure of gas A?

A 4.75 atm

B −2.25 atm

C 2.25 atm

D 1.25 atm

3 Dalton's law of partial pressure explains why, when gases are collected over water,

A water vapor forms that mixes with the other gases.

B water vapor pressure must be subtracted to determine the final pressure of the other gases.

C the gas pressures add up to a total pressure.

D all of the above

4 Calculate the volume of 12.0 g of helium at 100°C and 1.2 atm.

A 0.013 L

B 76.5 L

C 7,750 L

D 56.0 L

5 5.0 L of a gas goes from 1.0 atm to 1.3 atm. Calculate the final volume of this gas.

A 6.5 L

B 0.26 L

C 4.1 L

D 3.8 L

The graph below shows a plot of volume versus pressure for a particular gas sample at constant temperature. Use it to answer questions 6 and 7.

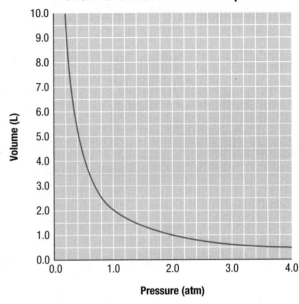

6 What is the volume of this gas at 4.0 atm pressure?

A 0.68 L

B 1.0 L

C 0.5 L

D 4.0 L

7 At what pressure would this gas occupy a volume of 5.0 L?

A 0.4 atm

B 0.33 atm

C 2.0 atm

D 0.5 atm

GRIDDED RESPONSE

8 A gas has a volume of 5 L at 120 K. What is its volume (in liters) at 100 K? (Round to nearest thousandth.)

Test Tip

If you are permitted to, draw a line through each incorrect answer choice as you eliminate it.

CHAPTER 12
Solutions

BIG IDEA
Solutions are homogeneous mixtures of a solute in a solvent. Chemical and physical factors affect how much of one substance will dissolve in another.

SECTION 1
Types of Mixtures

SECTION 2
The Solution Process

SECTION 3
Concentration of Solutions

ONLINE Chemistry
HMHScience.com

ONLINE LABS
- Separation of Pen Inks by Paper Chromatography
- A Close Look at Soaps and Detergents
- The Counterfeit Drugs
- The Fast Food Arson
- The Untimely Death
- Testing Reaction Combinations of H_2 and O_2
- S.T.E.M. Allergic to Color

GO ONLINE

Why It Matters Video
HMHScience.com

Solutions

Types of Mixtures

Key Terms

soluble   solute   electrolyte

solution   suspension   nonelectrolyte

solvent   colloid

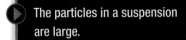

SECTION 1

Main Ideas

▶ Solutions are homogeneous mixtures.

▶ The particles in a suspension are large.

▶ Colloids have particles of intermediate size.

▶ Electrolytes are ionic solutions that conduct electricity.

It is easy to determine that some materials are mixtures because you can see their component parts. For example, soil is a mixture of substances, including small rocks and decomposed animal and plant matter. You can see this by picking up some soil in your hand and looking at it closely. Milk, on the other hand, does not appear to be a mixture, but in fact it is. Milk is composed principally of fats, proteins, milk sugar, and water. If you look at milk under a microscope, it will look something like **Figure 1.1a.** You can see round lipid (fat) droplets that measure from 1 to 10 µm in diameter. Irregularly shaped casein (protein) particles that are about 0.2 µm wide can also be seen. Both milk and soil are examples of *heterogeneous mixtures* because their composition is not uniform.

Salt (sodium chloride) and water form a *homogeneous mixture*. The sodium and chloride ions are interspersed among the water molecules, and the mixture appears uniform throughout, as illustrated in **Figure 1.1b.**

▶ MAIN IDEA

Solutions are homogeneous mixtures.

Suppose a sugar cube is dropped into a glass of water. You know from experience that the sugar will dissolve. Sugar is described as "soluble in water." **By soluble, we mean capable of being dissolved.** As it dissolves, a sugar lump gradually disappears as sugar molecules leave the surface of their crystals and mix with water molecules. Eventually, all the sugar molecules become uniformly distributed among the water molecules, as indicated by the equally sweet taste of any part of the mixture. All visible traces of the solid sugar are gone. Such a mixture is called a solution.

A solution is a homogeneous mixture of two or more substances uniformly dispersed throughout a single phase.

FIGURE 1.1

Heterogeneous and Homogeneous Mixtures

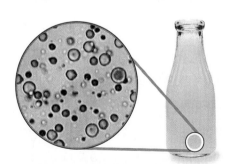

Sodium ion, Na⁺

Water molecule

Chloride ion, Cl⁻

(a) Milk is a heterogeneous mixture that consists of visible particles in a nonuniform arrangement.

(b) Salt water is an example of a homogeneous mixture. Ions and water molecules are in a random arrangement.

FIGURE 1.2

Solutes and Solvents The solute in a solution can be a solid, liquid, or gas.

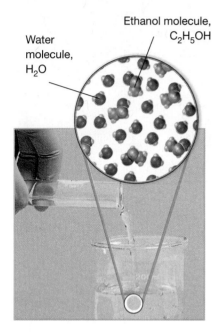

Water molecule, H_2O

Ethanol molecule, C_2H_5OH

(a) The ethanol-water solution is made from a liquid solute in a liquid solvent.

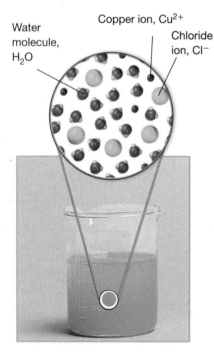

Water molecule, H_2O

Copper ion, Cu^{2+}

Chloride ion, Cl^-

(b) The copper(II) chloride–water solution is made from a solid solute in a liquid solvent. Note that the composition of each solution is uniform.

Components of Solutions

In a solution, atoms, molecules, or ions are thoroughly mixed, resulting in a mixture that has the same composition and properties throughout. In the simplest type of solution, such as a sugar-water solution, the particles of one substance are randomly mixed with the particles of another substance. **The dissolving medium in a solution is called the solvent, and the substance dissolved in a solution is called the solute.** The solute is generally designated as that component of a solution that is of lesser quantity. In the ethanol-water solution shown in **Figure 1.2**, ethanol is the solute, and water is the solvent. Occasionally, these terms have little meaning. For example, in a 50%-50% solution of ethanol and water, it would be difficult and unnecessary to say which is the solvent and which the solute.

In a solution, the dissolved solute particles are so small that they cannot be seen. They remain mixed with the solvent indefinitely, as long as the existing conditions remain unchanged. If the solutions in **Figure 1.2** are poured through filter paper, both the solute and the solvent will pass through the paper. The solute-particle dimensions are those of atoms, molecules, and ions—which range from about 0.01 to 1 nm in diameter.

Types of Solutions

Solutions may exist as gases, liquids, or solids. Some possible solute-solvent combinations of gases, liquids, and solids in solutions are summarized in **Figure 1.3**. Note each has a defined solvent and solute.

Many alloys, such as brass (made from zinc and copper) and sterling silver (made from silver and copper), are solid solutions in which the atoms of two or more metals are uniformly mixed. By properly choosing the proportions of each metal in the alloy, many desirable properties can be obtained. For example, alloys can have more strength and greater resistance to corrosion than the pure metals. Pure gold (24K), for instance, is too soft to use in jewelry. Alloying it with silver and copper greatly increases its strength and hardness while retaining its appearance and corrosion resistance. **Figure 1.4** (on the next page) compares solutions of pure gold and a gold alloy. 14-karat gold is a solution because the gold, silver, and copper are uniformly mixed at the atomic level.

FIGURE 1.3

SOME SOLUTE-SOLVENT COMBINATIONS FOR SOLUTIONS

Solute state	Solvent state	Example
gas	gas	oxygen in nitrogen
gas	liquid	carbon dioxide in water
liquid	liquid	alcohol in water
liquid	solid	mercury in silver and tin (dental amalgam)
solid	liquid	sugar in water
solid	solid	copper in nickel (Monel™ alloy)

FIGURE 1.4

Pure Gold vs. Gold Alloy Pure gold is too soft to use in jewelry. Alloying it with other metals increases its strength and hardness while retaining its appearance and corrosion resistance.

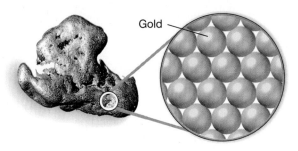

Gold

(a) 24-karat gold is pure gold.

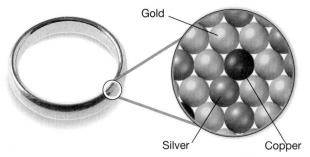

Gold

Silver   Copper

(b) 14-karat gold is an alloy of gold with silver and copper. 14-karat gold is 14/24, or 58.3%, gold.

▶ MAIN IDEA
The particles in a suspension are large.

If the particles in a solvent are so large that they settle out unless the mixture is constantly stirred or agitated, the mixture is called a **suspension.** Think of a jar of muddy water. If left undisturbed, particles of soil collect on the bottom of the jar. The soil particles are denser than the solvent, water. Gravity pulls them to the bottom of the container. Particles over 1000 nm in diameter—1000 times as large as atoms, molecules, or ions—form suspensions. The particles in suspension can be separated from heterogeneous mixtures by passing the mixture through a filter.

▶ MAIN IDEA
Colloids have particles of intermediate size.

Particles that are intermediate in size between those in solutions and suspensions form mixtures known as colloidal dispersions, or simply **colloids.** Particles between 1 nm and 1000 nm in diameter may form colloids. After large soil particles settle out of muddy water, the water is often still cloudy because colloidal particles remain dispersed in the water. If the cloudy mixture is poured through a filter, the colloidal particles will pass through the filter, and the mixture will remain cloudy. The particles in a colloid are small enough to be suspended throughout the solvent by the constant movement of the surrounding molecules. The colloidal particles make up the *dispersed phase*, and water is the *dispersing medium*. Many common things you use regularly, such as milk, hair spray, and paint, are colloids. Similar to solutions, colloids can be classified according to their dispersed phase and dispersed medium. For example, a solid might be dispersed in a liquid, as is the case with many paints, or a gas might be dispersed in a liquid, as is the case with foams such as whipped cream. The different types of colloids have common names you may recognize. For example, an *emulsion* is a liquid in a liquid, like milk. And clouds and fog, liquids dispersed in gas, are *liquid aerosols*. **Figure 1.5** on the next page lists these different types of colloids and gives some examples of each one.

FIGURE 1.5

CLASSES OF COLLOIDS

Class of colloid	Phases	Example
sol	solid dispersed in liquid	paints, mud
gel	solid network extending throughout liquid	gelatin
liquid emulsion	liquid dispersed in a liquid	milk, mayonnaise
foam	gas dispersed in liquid	shaving cream, whipped cream
solid aerosol	solid dispersed in gas	smoke, airborne particulate matter, auto exhaust
liquid aerosol	liquid dispersed in gas	fog, mist, clouds, aerosol spray
solid emulsion	liquid dispersed in solid	cheese, butter

FIGURE 1.6

Tyndall Effect A beam of light distinguishes a colloid from a solution. The particles in a colloid will scatter light, making the beam visible. The mixture of gelatin and water in the jar on the right is a colloid. The mixture of water and sodium chloride in the jar on the left is a true solution.

Tyndall Effect

Many colloids appear homogeneous because the individual particles cannot be seen. The particles are, however, large enough to scatter light. You have probably noticed that a headlight beam is visible from the side on a foggy night. Known as the *Tyndall effect*, this occurs when light is scattered by colloidal particles dispersed in a transparent medium. The Tyndall effect is a property that can be used to distinguish between a solution and a colloid, as demonstrated in **Figure 1.6.**

The distinctive properties of solutions, colloids, and suspensions are summarized in **Figure 1.7.** The individual particles of a colloid can be detected under a microscope if a bright light is cast on the specimen at a right angle. The particles, which appear as tiny specks of light, are seen to move rapidly in a random motion. This motion is due to collisions of rapidly moving molecules and is called *Brownian motion*, after its discoverer, Robert Brown. Brownian motion is not simply a casual curiosity for interesting lighting effects. In fact, it is one of the strongest macroscopic observations that science has for assuming matter is ultimately composed of particulate atoms and molecules. Only small, randomly moving particles could produce such effects.

FIGURE 1.7

PROPERTIES OF SOLUTIONS, COLLOIDS, AND SUSPENSIONS

Solutions	Colloids	Suspensions
Homogeneous	Heterogeneous	Heterogeneous
Particle size: 0.01–1 nm; can be atoms, ions, molecules	Particle size: 1–1000 nm, dispersed; can be aggregates or large molecules	Particle size: over 1000 nm, suspended; can be large particles or aggregates
Do not separate on standing	Do not separate on standing	Particles settle out
Cannot be separated by filtration	Cannot be separated by filtration	Can be separated by filtration
Do not scatter light	Scatter light (Tyndall effect)	May scatter light but are not transparent

OBSERVING SOLUTIONS, SUSPENSIONS, AND COLLOIDS

PROCEDURE

1. Prepare seven mixtures, each containing 250 mL of water and one of the following substances.

    a. 12 g of sucrose

    b. 3 g of soluble starch

    c. 5 g of clay

    d. 2 mL of food coloring

    e. 2 g of sodium borate

    f. 50 mL of cooking oil

    g. 3 g of gelatin

    Making the gelatin mixture: Soften the gelatin in 65 mL of cold water, and then add 185 mL of boiling water.

2. Observe the seven mixtures and their characteristics. Record the appearance of each mixture after stirring.

3. Transfer to individual test tubes 10 mL of each mixture that does not separate after stirring. Shine a flashlight on each mixture in a dark room. Make note of the mixtures in which the path of the light beam is visible.

DISCUSSION

1. Using your observations, classify each mixture as a solution, suspension, or colloid.

2. What characteristics did you use to classify each mixture?

MATERIALS

- balance
- 7 beakers, 400 mL
- clay
- cooking oil
- flashlight
- gelatin, plain
- hot plate (to boil H_2O)
- red food coloring
- sodium borate ($Na_2B_4O_7 \cdot 10H_2O$)
- soluble starch
- stirring rod
- sucrose
- test-tube rack
- water

SAFETY

Wear safety goggles and an apron.

▶ **MAIN IDEA**

Electrolytes are ionic solutions that conduct electricity.

Substances that dissolve in water are classified according to whether they yield molecules or ions in solution. When an ionic compound dissolves, the positive and negative ions separate from each other and are surrounded by water molecules. These solute ions are free to move, making it possible for an electric current to pass through the solution. **A substance that dissolves in water to give a solution that conducts electric current is called an electrolyte.** Sodium chloride, NaCl, is an electrolyte, as is any soluble ionic compound. Certain highly polar molecular compounds, such as hydrogen chloride, HCl, are also electrolytes because HCl molecules form the ions H_3O^+ and Cl^- when dissolved in water.

By contrast, a solution containing neutral solute molecules does not conduct electric current because it does not contain mobile, charged particles. **A substance that dissolves in water to give a solution that does not conduct an electric current is called a nonelectrolyte.** Sugar is a nonelectrolyte.

FIGURE 1.8

Electrolytes and Nonelectrolytes

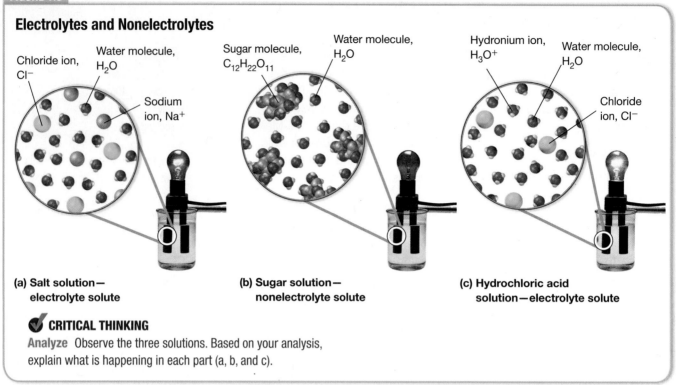

(a) Salt solution—
    electrolyte solute

(b) Sugar solution—
    nonelectrolyte solute

(c) Hydrochloric acid
    solution—electrolyte solute

✔ CRITICAL THINKING

Analyze Observe the three solutions. Based on your analysis, explain what is happening in each part (a, b, and c).

Figure 1.8 shows an apparatus for testing the conductivity of solutions. Electrodes are attached to a power supply and make contact with the test solution. If the test solution provides a conducting path, the light bulb will glow. A nonconducting solution is like an open switch between the electrodes, and there is no current in the circuit. The light bulb glows brightly if a solution that is a good conductor is tested. For a moderately conductive solution, the light bulb is dim. If a solution is a poor conductor, the light bulb does not glow at all; such solutions contain solutes that are nonelectrolytes.

✔ SECTION 1 FORMATIVE ASSESSMENT

▶ Reviewing Main Ideas

1. Classify the following as either a heterogeneous or homogeneous mixture. Explain your answers.
   a. orange juice   b. tap water

2. a. What are substances called whose water solutions conduct electricity?
   b. Why does a salt solution conduct electricity?
   c. Why does a sugar-water solution not conduct electricity?

3. Make a drawing of the particles in an NaCl solution to show why this solution conducts electricity. Make a drawing of the particles in an NaCl crystal to show why pure salt does not conduct.

4. Describe one way to prove that a mixture of sugar and water is a solution and that a mixture of sand and water is not a solution.

5. Name the solute and solvent in the following:
   a. 14-karat gold
   b. corn syrup
   c. carbonated, or sparkling, water

✔ Critical Thinking

6. **ANALYZING INFORMATION** If you allow a container of sea water to sit in the sun, the liquid level gets lower and lower, and finally crystals appear. What is happening?

The Solution Process

Key Terms

solution equilibrium
saturated solution
unsaturated solution
supersaturated solution

solubility
hydration
immiscible
miscible

Henry's Law
effervescence
solvated
enthalpy of solution

Main Ideas

Several factors affect dissolving.

Solubility is a measure of how well one substance dissolves in another.

A change in energy accompanies solution formation.

▶ **MAIN IDEA**

Several factors affect dissolving.

If you have ever tried to dissolve sugar in iced tea, you know that temperature has something to do with how quickly a solute dissolves. What other factors affect how quickly you can dissolve sugar in iced tea?

Increasing the Surface Area of the Solute

Sugar dissolves as sugar molecules leave the crystal surface and mix with water molecules. The same is true for any solid solute in a liquid solvent: molecules or ions of the solute are attracted by the solvent.

Because the dissolution process occurs at the surface of the solute, it can be sped up if the surface area of the solute is increased. Crushing sugar that is in cubes or large crystals increases its surface area. In general, the more finely divided a substance is, the greater the surface area per unit mass and the more quickly it dissolves. **Figure 2.1** shows a model of solutions that are made from the same solute but have different amounts of surface area exposed to the solvent.

FIGURE 2.1

Rates of Dissolution The rate at which a solid solute dissolves can be increased by increasing the surface area. A powdered solute has a greater surface area exposed to solvent particles and therefore dissolves faster than a solute in large crystals.

Small surface area exposed to solvent—slow rate

Solvent particle

Solute

$CuSO_4 \cdot 5H_2O$ large crystals

Large surface area exposed to solvent—faster rate

$CuSO_4 \cdot 5H_2O$ powdered (increased surface area)

Agitating a Solution

Very close to the surface of a solute, the concentration of dissolved solute is high. Stirring or shaking helps to disperse the solute particles and bring fresh solvent into contact with the solute surface. Thus, the effect of stirring is similar to that of crushing a solid—contact between the solvent and the solute surface is increased.

Heating a Solvent

You probably have noticed that sugar and other materials dissolve more quickly in warm water than in cold water. As the temperature of the solvent increases, solvent molecules move faster, and their average kinetic energy increases. Therefore, at higher temperatures, collisions between the solvent molecules and the solute are more frequent and of higher energy than at lower temperatures. This separates and disperses the solute molecules.

▶ MAIN IDEA

Solubility is a measure of how well one substance dissolves in another.

If you add spoonful after spoonful of sugar to tea, eventually no more sugar will dissolve. For every combination of solvent with a solid solute at a given temperature, there is a limit to the amount of solute that can be dissolved. The point at which this limit is reached for any solute-solvent combination is difficult to predict precisely and depends on the nature of the solute, the nature of the solvent, and the temperature.

The following model describes why there is a limit. When solid sugar is added to water, sugar molecules leave the solid surface and move about at random. Some of these dissolved molecules may collide with the crystal and remain there (recrystallize). As more solid dissolves, these collisions become more frequent. Eventually, molecules are returning to the crystal at the same rate at which they are going into solution, and a dynamic equilibrium is established between dissolution and crystallization. Ionic solids behave similarly, as shown in **Figure 2.2.**

Solution equilibrium is the physical state in which the opposing processes of dissolution and crystallization of a solute occur at equal rates.

FIGURE 2. 2

Solution Equilibrium A saturated solution in a closed system is at equilibrium. The solute is recrystallizing at the same rate that it is dissolving, even though it appears that there is no activity in the system.

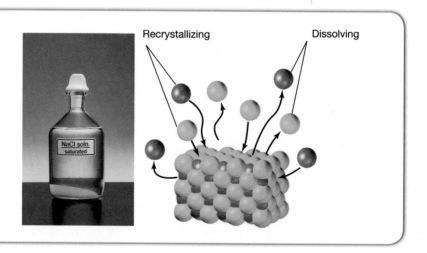

Recrystallizing   Dissolving

NaCl soln.
saturated

FIGURE 2.3

Saturation Point The graph shows the range of solute masses that will produce an unsaturated solution. Once the saturation point is exceeded, the system will contain undissolved solute.

Mass of Solute Added vs. Mass of Solute Dissolved

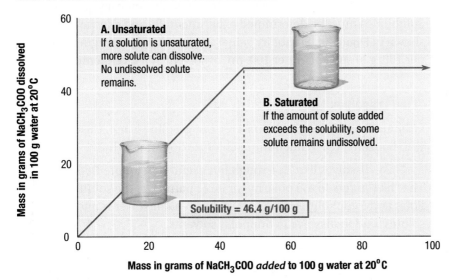

A. Unsaturated
If a solution is unsaturated, more solute can dissolve. No undissolved solute remains.

B. Saturated
If the amount of solute added exceeds the solubility, some solute remains undissolved.

Solubility = 46.4 g/100 g

y-axis: Mass in grams of $NaCH_3COO$ dissolved in 100 g water at 20°C

x-axis: Mass in grams of $NaCH_3COO$ *added* to 100 g water at 20°C

Saturated Versus Unsaturated Solutions

A solution that contains the maximum amount of dissolved solute is described as a **saturated solution.** How can you tell that the $NaCH_3COO$ solution pictured in **Figure 2.3** is saturated? If more sodium acetate is added to the solution, it falls to the bottom and does not dissolve because an equilibrium has been established between ions leaving and entering the solid phase. If more water is added to the saturated solution, then more sodium acetate will dissolve in it. At 20°C, 46.4 g of $NaCH_3COO$ is the maximum amount that will dissolve in 100 g of water. **A solution that contains less solute than a saturated solution under the existing conditions is an unsaturated solution.**

Supersaturated Solutions

When a saturated solution of a solute whose solubility increases with temperature is cooled, the excess solute usually comes out of solution, leaving the solution saturated at the lower temperature. But sometimes, if the solution is left to cool undisturbed, the excess solute does not separate, and a supersaturated solution is produced. **A supersaturated solution is a solution that contains more dissolved solute than a saturated solution contains under the same conditions.** A supersaturated solution may remain unchanged for a long time if it is not disturbed, but once crystals begin to form, the process continues until equilibrium is reestablished at the lower temperature. An example of a supersaturated solution is one prepared from a saturated solution of sodium thiosulfate, $Na_2S_2O_3$, or sodium acetate, $NaCH_3COO$. Solute is added to hot water until the solution is saturated, and the hot solution is filtered. The filtrate is left to stand undisturbed as it cools. Dropping a small crystal of the solute into the supersaturated solution ("seeding") or disturbing the solution causes a rapid formation of crystals by the excess solute.

Solubility Values

The **solubility** of a substance is the amount of that substance required to form a saturated solution with a specific amount of solvent at a specified temperature. The solubility of sugar, for example, is 204 g per 100. g of water at 20.°C. The temperature must be specified because solubility varies with temperature. For gases, the pressure must also be specified. Solubilities must be determined experimentally and can vary widely, as shown in **Figure 2.4.** Solubility values are usually given as grams of solute per 100. g of solvent or per 100. mL of solvent at a given temperature.

"Like Dissolves Like"

Lithium chloride is soluble in water, but gasoline is not. Gasoline mixes with benzene, C_6H_6, but lithium chloride does not. Why?

"Like dissolves like" is a rough but useful rule for predicting solubility. The "like" refers to the polarity (or ionic nature) of the solute and solvent. Polar and ionic solutes tend to dissolve in polar solvents and nonpolar solutes tend to dissolve in nonpolar solvents.

FIGURE 2.4

SOLUBILITY OF SOLUTES AS A FUNCTION OF TEMPERATURE (IN g SOLUTE/100 g H_2O)

Substance	Temperature (°C)					
	0	20	40	60	80	100
$AgNO_3$	122	216	311	440	585	733
$Ba(OH)_2$	1.67	3.89	8.22	20.94	101.4	—
$C_{12}H_{22}O_{11}$	179	204	238	287	362	487
$Ca(OH)_2$	0.189	0.173	0.141	0.121	—	0.07
$Ce_2(SO_4)_3$	20.8	10.1	—	3.87	—	—
KCl	28.0	34.2	40.1	45.8	51.3	56.3
KI	128	144	162	176	192	206
KNO_3	13.9	31.6	61.3	106	167	245
LiCl	69.2	83.5	89.8	98.4	112	128
Li_2CO_3	1.54	1.33	1.17	1.01	0.85	0.72
NaCl	35.7	35.9	36.4	37.1	38.0	39.2
$NaNO_3$	73	87.6	102	122	148	180
CO_2 (gas)	0.335	0.169	0.0973	0.058	—	—
O_2 (gas)	0.00694	0.00537	0.00308	0.00227	0.00138	0.00

FIGURE 2.5

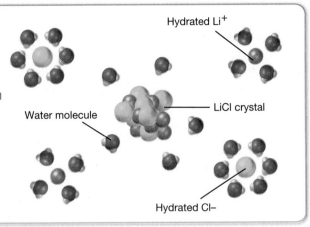

Hydration When LiCl dissolves, the ions are hydrated. The attraction between ions and water molecules is strong enough that each ion in solution is surrounded by water molecules.

Dissolving Ionic Compounds in Aqueous Solution

The polarity of water molecules plays an important role in the formation of solutions of ionic compounds in water. The slightly charged parts of water molecules attract the ions in the ionic compounds and surround them to keep them separated from the other ions in the solution. Suppose we drop a few crystals of lithium chloride into a beaker of water. At the crystal surface, water molecules come into contact with Li^+ and Cl^- ions. The positive region of the water molecules is attracted to Cl^- ions, while the negative region is attracted to Li^+ ions. The attraction between water molecules and the ions is strong enough to draw the ions away from the crystal surface and into solution, as illustrated in **Figure 2.5.** **This solution process with water as the solvent is referred to as hydration.** The ions are said to be *hydrated.* As hydrated ions diffuse into the solution, other ions are exposed and drawn away from the crystal surface by the solvent. The entire crystal gradually dissolves, and hydrated ions become uniformly distributed in the solution.

When crystallized from aqueous solutions, some ionic substances form crystals that incorporate water molecules. These crystalline compounds, known as *hydrates,* retain specific ratios of water molecules, as shown in **Figure 2.6,** and are represented by formulas such as $CuSO_4 \bullet 5H_2O$. Heating the crystals of a hydrate can drive off the water of hydration and leave the anhydrous salt. When a crystalline hydrate dissolves in water, the water of hydration returns to the solvent. The behavior of a solution made from a hydrate is no different from the behavior of one made from the anhydrous form. Dissolving either results in a system containing hydrated ions and water.

Nonpolar Solvents

Ionic compounds are generally not soluble in nonpolar solvents such as carbon tetrachloride, CCl_4, and toluene, $C_6H_5CH_3$. The nonpolar solvent molecules do not attract the ions of the crystal strongly enough to overcome the forces holding the crystal together.

Would you expect lithium chloride to dissolve in toluene? No, LiCl is not soluble in toluene. LiCl is ionic, and $C_6H_5CH_3$ is nonpolar, so there is not much intermolecular attraction between them.

FIGURE 2.6

Hydrate Hydrated copper(II) sulfate has water as part of its crystal structure. Heating releases the water and produces the anhydrous form of the substance, which has the formula $CuSO_4$.

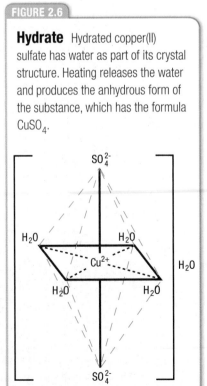

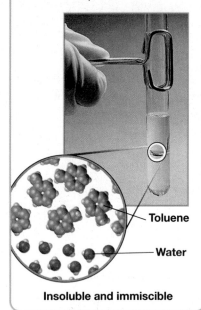

FIGURE 2.7

Immiscibility

Toluene and water are immiscible. The components of this system exist in two distinct phases.

Toluene

Water

Insoluble and immiscible

✓ **CHECK FOR UNDERSTANDING**

Apply Give an example of an everyday mixture that is immiscible.

Liquid Solutes and Solvents

When you shake a bottle of salad dressing, oil droplets become dispersed in the water. As soon as you stop shaking the bottle, the strong attraction of hydrogen bonding between the water molecules squeezes out the oil droplets, forming separate layers. **Liquids that are not soluble in each other are immiscible.** Toluene and water, shown in **Figure 2.7,** are another example of immiscible substances.

Nonpolar substances, such as fats, oils, and greases, are generally quite soluble in nonpolar liquids, such as carbon tetrachloride, toluene, and gasoline. The only attractions between the nonpolar molecules are London forces, which are quite weak. The intermolecular forces existing in the solution are therefore very similar to those in pure substances. Thus, the molecules can mix freely with one another.

Liquids that dissolve freely in one another in any proportion are said to be miscible. Benzene and carbon tetrachloride are miscible. The nonpolar molecules of these substances exert no strong forces of attraction or repulsion, so the molecules mix freely. Ethanol and water, shown in **Figure 2.8,** also mix freely, but for a different reason. The —OH group on an ethanol molecule is somewhat polar. This group can form hydrogen bonds with water as well as with other ethanol molecules. The intermolecular forces in the mixture are so similar to those in the pure liquids that the liquids are mutually soluble in all proportions.

Gasoline is a solution composed mainly of nonpolar hydrocarbons and is also an excellent solvent for fats, oils, and greases. The major intermolecular forces acting between the nonpolar molecules are weak London forces.

Ethanol is intermediate in polarity between water and carbon tetrachloride. It is not as good as water as a solvent for polar or ionic substances. Sodium chloride is only slightly soluble in ethanol. On the other hand, ethanol is a better solvent than water for less-polar substances because the molecule has a nonpolar region.

FIGURE 2.8

Miscibility

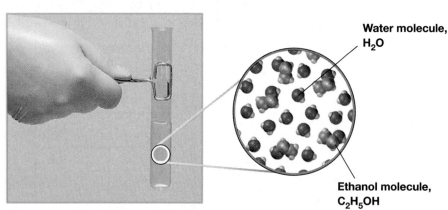

Water molecule, H_2O

Ethanol molecule, C_2H_5OH

(a) Water and ethanol are miscible. The components of this system exist in a single phase with a uniform arrangement.

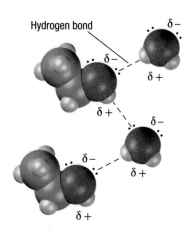

Hydrogen bond

$\delta -$ $\delta -$ $\delta +$ $\delta +$ $\delta -$ $\delta -$ $\delta +$ $\delta +$

(b) Hydrogen bonding between the solute and solvent enhances the solubility of ethanol in water.

Effects of Pressure on Solubility

Changes in pressure have very little effect on the solubilities of liquids or solids in liquid solvents. However, increases in pressure increase gas solubilities in liquids.

When a gas is in contact with the surface of a liquid, gas molecules can enter the liquid. As the amount of dissolved gas increases, some molecules begin to escape and reenter the gas phase. An equilibrium is eventually established between the rates at which gas molecules enter and leave the liquid phase. As long as this equilibrium is undisturbed, the solubility of the gas in the liquid is unchanged at a given pressure.

$$gas + solvent \rightleftharpoons solution$$

Increasing the pressure of the solute gas above the solution puts stress on the equilibrium. Molecules collide with the liquid surface more often. The increase in pressure is partially offset by an increase in the rate of gas molecules entering the solution. In turn, the increase in the amount of dissolved gas causes an increase in the rate at which molecules escape from the liquid surface and become vapor. Eventually, equilibrium is restored at a higher gas solubility. An increase in gas pressure causes the equilibrium to shift so that more molecules are in the liquid phase.

Henry's Law

Henry's law, named after the English chemist William Henry, states: The solubility of a gas in a liquid is directly proportional to the partial pressure of that gas on the surface of the liquid. Henry's law applies to gas-liquid solutions at constant temperature.

Recall that when a mixture of ideal gases is confined in a constant volume at a constant temperature, each gas exerts the same pressure it would exert if it occupied the space alone. Assuming that the gases do not react in any way, each gas dissolves to the extent it would dissolve if no other gases were present.

In carbonated beverages, the solubility of CO_2 is increased by increasing the pressure. At the bottling plant, carbon dioxide gas is forced into the solution of flavored water at a pressure of 5–10 atm. The gas-in-liquid solution is then sealed in bottles or cans. When the cap is removed, the pressure is reduced to 1 atm, and some of the carbon dioxide escapes as gas bubbles. **The rapid escape of a gas from a liquid in which it is dissolved is known as effervescence.** This is shown in **Figure 2.9.**

FIGURE 2.9

Partial Pressure

(a) There are no gas bubbles in the unopened bottle of soda because the pressure of CO_2 applied during bottling keeps the carbon dioxide gas dissolved in the liquid.

CO_2 under high pressure above solvent

Soluble CO_2 molecules

(b) When the cap on the bottle is removed, the pressure of CO_2 on the liquid is reduced, and CO_2 can escape from the liquid. The soda effervesces when the bottle is opened and the pressure is reduced.

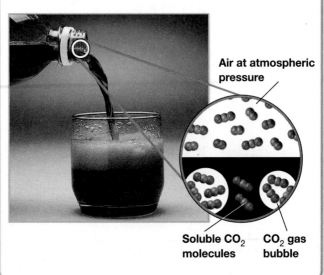

Air at atmospheric pressure

Soluble CO_2 molecules

CO_2 gas bubble

FIGURE 2.10

Temperature and Solubility of Gases
The solubility of gases in water decreases with increasing temperature. Which gas has the greater solubility at 30°C—CO_2 or SO_2?

Solubility vs. Temperature Data for Some Gases

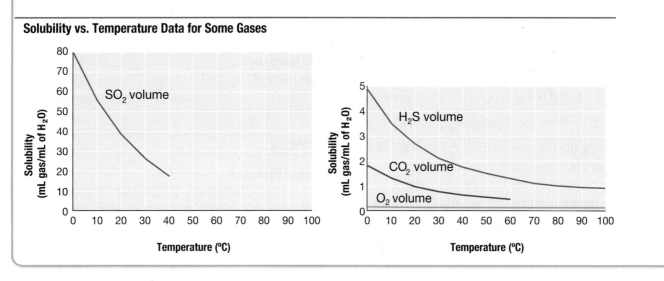

FIGURE 2.11

Temperature and Solubility of Solids
Solubility curves for various solid solutes generally show increasing solubility with increases in temperature. From the graph, you can see that the solubility of $NaNO_3$ is affected more by temperature than is NaCl.

Solubility vs. Temperature for Some Solid Solutes

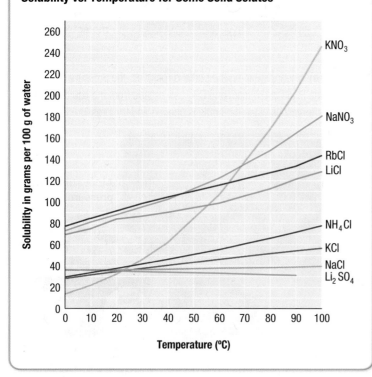

Effects of Temperature on Solubility

First, let's consider gas solubility. Increasing the temperature always decreases gas solubility. As the temperature increases, the average kinetic energy of the molecules in solution increases. A greater number of solute molecules are able to escape from the attraction of solvent molecules and return to the gas phase. At higher temperatures, therefore, equilibrium is reached with fewer gas molecules in solution, and gases are less soluble, as shown in **Figure 2.10**.

The effect of temperature on the solubility of solids in liquids is more difficult to predict. Often, increasing the temperature increases the solubility of solids. However, an equivalent temperature increase can result in a large increase in solubility for some solvents and only a slight change for others.

Compare the effect of temperature on the solubility of NaCl with that on the solubility of potassium nitrate, KNO_3 (**Figure 2.11**). About 14 g of potassium nitrate dissolves in 100 g of water at 0°C. The solubility of potassium nitrate increases by more than 150 g KNO_3 per 100 g H_2O when the temperature is raised to 80°C.

Under similar circumstances, the solubility of sodium chloride increases by only about 2 g NaCl per 100 g H_2O. Sometimes, solubility of a solid *decreases* with an increase in temperature. For example, between 0°C and 60.°C the solubility of cerium sulfate, $Ce_2(SO_4)_3$, decreases by about 17 g/100 g.

▶ **MAIN IDEA**
A change in energy accompanies solution formation.

The formation of a solution is accompanied by an energy change. If you dissolve some potassium iodide, KI, in water, you will find that the outside of the container feels cold to the touch. But if you dissolve some sodium hydroxide, NaOH, in the same way, the outside of the container feels hot. The formation of a solid-liquid solution can apparently either absorb energy (KI in water) or release energy as heat (NaOH in water).

During solution formation, changes occur in the forces between solvent and solute particles. Before dissolving begins, solvent and solute molecules are held to one another by intermolecular forces (solvent-solvent or solute-solute). Energy is required to separate each from their neighbors. **A solute particle that is surrounded by solvent molecules is said to be solvated. The net amount of energy absorbed as heat by the solution when a specific amount of solute dissolves in a solvent is the enthalpy of solution. Figure 2.12** should help you understand this process better. From the model, you can see that the enthalpy of solution is negative (energy is released) when the sum of attractions from Steps 1 and 2 is less than that of Step 3. The enthalpy of solution is positive (energy is absorbed) when the sum of attractions from Steps 1 and 2 is greater than that of Step 3.

FIGURE 2.12

Enthalpy of Solution The graph shows the changes in the enthalpy that occur during the formation of a solution. How would the graph differ for a system with an endothermic heat of solution?

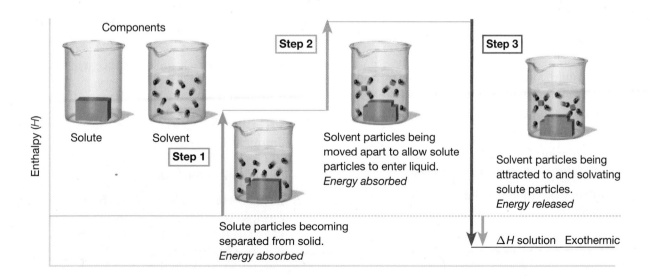

FIGURE 2.13

ENTHALPIES OF SOLUTION (kJ/MOL SOLUTE AT 25°C)

Substance	Enthalpy of solution	Substance	Enthalpy of solution
$AgNO_3(s)$	+22.59	$KOH(s)$	−57.61
$CH_3COOH(l)$	−1.51	$MgSO_4(s)$	+15.9
$HCl(g)$	−74.84	$NaCl(s)$	+3.88
$HI(g)$	−81.67	$NaNO_3(s)$	+20.50
$KCl(s)$	+17.22	$NaOH(s)$	−44.51
$KClO_3(s)$	+41.38	$NH_3(g)$	−30.50
$KI(s)$	+20.33	$NH_4Cl(s)$	+14.78
$KNO_3(s)$	+34.89	$NH_4NO_3(s)$	+25.69

You know that heating decreases the solubility of a gas, so dissolution of gases is exothermic. How do the values for the enthalpies of solution in **Figure 2.13** support this idea of exothermic solution processes for gaseous solutes?

In the gaseous state, molecules are so far apart that there are virtually no intermolecular forces of attraction between them. Therefore, the solute-solute interaction has little effect on the enthalpy of a solution of a gas. Energy is released when a gas dissolves in a liquid because attraction between solute gas and solvent molecules outweighs the energy needed to separate solvent molecules.

✔ SECTION 2 FORMATIVE ASSESSMENT

▶ **Reviewing Main Ideas**

1. Why would you expect a packet of sugar to dissolve faster in hot tea than in iced tea?

2. a. Explain how you would prepare a saturated solution of sugar in water.
   b. How would you make it a supersaturated solution of sodium acetate in water?

3. Explain why ethanol will dissolve in water and carbon tetrachloride will not.

4. When a solute molecule is solvated, is energy released or absorbed?

5. If a warm bottle of soda and a cold bottle of soda are opened, which will effervesce more and why?

✔ **Critical Thinking**

6. **PREDICTING OUTCOMES** You get a small amount of lubricating oil on your clothing. Which would work better to remove the oil—water or toluene? Explain.

7. **INTERPRETING CONCEPTS** A "fizz saver" pumps air under pressure into a soda bottle to keep gas from escaping. Will this keep CO_2 in the soda bottle? Explain your answer.

Artificial Blood

A patient lies bleeding on a stretcher. The doctor leans over to check the patient's wounds and barks an order to a nearby nurse: "Get him a unit of artificial blood, stat!" Although this may sound like something from a science fiction movie, the scenario may soon be commonplace thanks to a synthetic mixture that can perform one of the main functions of human blood—transporting oxygen.

The hemoglobin inside red blood cells collects oxygen in our lungs, transports it to all the tissues of the body, and then takes carbon dioxide back to the lungs. A blood substitute could accomplish the same task, but it uses nonpolar chemicals called *perfluorocarbons* instead of hemoglobin to transport the oxygen. The perfluorocarbons are carried in a water-based saline solution, but because nonpolar substances and water do not mix well, a bonding chemical called a *surfactant* is added to hold the mixture together. The perfluorocarbons are sheared into tiny droplets and then coated with the bonding molecules. One end of these molecules attaches to the perfluorocarbon, and the other end attaches to the water, creating a milky emulsion. Blood-substitute mixtures are being researched and, if approved for treatment in the U.S., could be administered to future patients in the same way regular blood is. The perfluorocarbons are eventually exhaled through the lungs in the same way other products of respiration are.

Blood substitutes only function to carry gases to and from tissues; they cannot clot or perform any of the immune-system functions that blood does. Still, substitutes have several advantages over real blood. They could have a much longer shelf life. They could also eliminate many of the risks associated with blood transfusions. Because the substitute can dissolve larger amounts of oxygen than real blood can, smaller amounts of the mixture are needed.

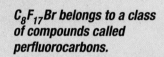

$C_8F_{17}Br$ belongs to a class of compounds called perfluorocarbons.

The collapse of the circulatory system from inadequate oxygen supply, commonly referred to as "shock," could be more effectively prevented with blood substitutes. Blood substitutes also would be useful for treating the effects of decompression sickness scuba divers experience when the higher pressures underwater allow more nitrogen to become dissolved in the blood.

Question

Do Internet research to find more information about artificial blood. Then write a letter to a friend explaining what artificial blood is, what it does in the body, and how it might benefit a family member.

Concentration of Solutions

Key Terms
concentration   molarity   molality

The concentration of a solution is a measure of the amount of solute in a given amount of solvent or solution. Some medications are solutions of drugs—a one-teaspoon dose at the correct concentration might cure the patient, while the same dose in the wrong concentration might kill the patient.

In this section, we introduce two different ways of expressing the concentrations of solutions: molarity and molality.

Sometimes, solutions are referred to as "dilute" or "concentrated," but these are not very definite terms. "Dilute" just means that there is a relatively small amount of solute in a solvent. "Concentrated," on the other hand, means that there is a relatively large amount of solute in a solvent. Note that these terms are unrelated to the degree to which a solution is saturated. A saturated solution of a substance that is not very soluble might be very dilute.

▶ **MAIN IDEA**

Molarity is moles of solute per liter of solution.

Molarity is the number of moles of solute in one liter of solution. For example, a one-molar solution of sodium hydroxide, NaOH, contains one mole of NaOH in every liter of solution. The symbol for molarity is M, and the concentration of a one-molar solution of sodium hydroxide is written as 1 M NaOH.

One mole of NaOH has a mass of 40.0 g. If this quantity of NaOH is dissolved in enough water to make exactly 1.00 L of solution, the solution is a 1.00 M solution. If 20.0 g of NaOH, which is 0.500 mol, is dissolved in enough water to make 1.00 L of solution, a 0.500 M NaOH solution is produced. This relationship between molarity, moles, and volume may be expressed in the following ways.

GO ONLINE *Animated* **Chemistry** HMHScience.com

Solution Dilution

> **Molarity (M)** $$\text{molarity} = \frac{\text{amount of solute (mol)}}{\text{volume of solution (L)}}$$

$$= \frac{0.500 \text{ mol NaOH}}{1.00 \text{ L}} = 0.500 \text{ M NaOH}$$

If we diluted 1 L of the 0.500 M NaOH solution to 2 L, we could find the new concentration simply by using the ratio $M_1V_1 = M_2V_2$. Here, M_1 and V_1 are the molarity and volume of the original solution, and M_2 and V_2 are the molarity and volume of the new solution. We solve for M_2 as follows:

$$\frac{(0.500 \text{ M})(1 \text{ L})}{(2 \text{ L})} = 0.250 \text{ M}$$

Solutions are often diluted just before use, because those of greater molarity take up less lab space. Chemists can have solutions of greater molarity and lower volume in stock and then dilute them to ones of higher volume and lower molarity for use.

Note that a 1 M solution is *not* made by adding 1 mol of solute to 1 L of *solvent*. Instead, 1 mol of solute is first dissolved in less than 1 L of solvent. The resulting solution is carefully diluted with more solvent to bring the *total volume* to 1 L, as shown in **Figure 3.1**.

FIGURE 3.1

Preparing a 0.5000 M Solution The preparation of a 0.5000 M solution of $CuSO_4 \cdot 5H_2O$ starts with calculating the mass of solute needed.

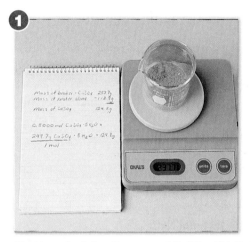

1 Start by calculating the mass of $CuSO_4 \cdot 5H_2O$ needed. Making a liter of this solution requires 0.5000 mol of solute. Convert the moles to mass by multiplying by the molar mass of $CuSO_4 \cdot 5H_2O$. This mass is calculated to be 124.9 g.

2 Add some solvent to the solute to dissolve it, and then pour it into a 1.0-L volumetric flask.

3 Rinse the weighing beaker with more solvent to remove all the solute, and pour the rinse into the flask. Add water until the volume of the solution nears the neck of the flask.

4 Put the stopper in the flask, and swirl the solution thoroughly.

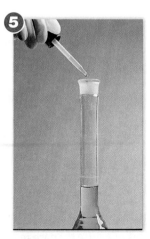

5 Carefully fill the flask to the 1.0-L mark with water.

6 Restopper the flask, and invert it at least 10 times to ensure complete mixing.

7 The resulting solution has 0.5000 mol of solute dissolved in 1.000 L of solution, which is a 0.5000 M concentration.

Calculating with Molarity

Sample Problem A You have 3.50 L of solution that contains 90.0 g of sodium chloride, NaCl. What is the molarity of that solution?

① ANALYZE

Given: solute mass = 90.0 g NaCl
solution volume = 3.50 L

Unknown: molarity of NaCl solution

② PLAN

Molarity is the number of moles of solute per liter of solution. The solute is described in the problem by mass, not the amount in moles. You need one conversion (grams to moles of solute) using the inverted molar mass of NaCl to arrive at your answer.

$$\text{grams of solute} \longrightarrow \text{number of moles of solute} \longrightarrow \text{molarity}$$

$$\text{g NaCl} \times \frac{\text{mol NaCl}}{\text{g NaCl}} = \text{mol NaCl}$$

$$\frac{\text{amount of solute (mol)}}{V \text{ solution (L)}} = \text{molarity of solution (M)}$$

③ SOLVE

You will need the molar mass of NaCl.
NaCl = 58.44 g/mol

$$90.0 \text{ g NaCl} \times \frac{1 \text{ mol NaCl}}{58.44 \text{ g NaCl}} = 1.54 \text{ mol NaCl}$$

$$\frac{1.54 \text{ mol NaCl}}{3.50 \text{ L of solution}} = 0.440 \text{ M NaCl}$$

④ CHECK YOUR WORK

Because each factor involved is limited to three significant digits, the answer should have three significant digits—which it does. The units cancel correctly to give the desired moles of solute per liter of solution, which is molarity.

Calculating with Molarity

Sample Problem B You have 0.8 L of a 0.5 M HCl solution. How many moles of HCl does this solution contain?

① ANALYZE

Given: volume of solution = 0.8 L
concentration of solution = 0.5 M HCl

Unknown: moles of HCl in a given volume

② PLAN

The molarity indicates the moles of solute that are in one liter of solution. Given the volume of the solution, the number of moles of solute can then be found.

concentration (mol of HCl/L of solution) × volume (L of solution) = mol of HCl

Continued

Calculating with Molarity (continued)

③ SOLVE

$$\frac{0.5 \text{ mol HCl}}{1.0 \text{ L of solution}} \times 0.8 \text{ L of solution} = 0.4 \text{ mol HCl}$$

④ CHECK YOUR WORK

The answer is correctly given to one significant digit. The units cancel correctly to give the desired unit, mol. There should be less than 0.5 mol HCl, because less than 1 L of solution was used.

Calculating with Molarity

Sample Problem C A 23.4 g sample of potassium chromate is needed to carry out a reaction in aqueous solution of silver chromate. All you have on hand is 5 L of a 6.0 M K_2CrO_4 solution. What volume of the solution is needed to give you the 23.4 g K_2CrO_4 needed for the reaction?

① ANALYZE

Given: volume of solution = 5 L
concentration of solution = 6.0 M K_2CrO_4
mass of solute = 23.4 g K_2CrO_4

Unknown: volume of K_2CrO_4 solution in L

② PLAN

The molarity indicates the moles of solute that are in 1 L of solution. Given the mass of solute needed, the amount in moles of solute can then be found. Use the molarity and the amount, in moles, of K_2CrO_4 to determine the volume of K_2CrO_4 that will provide 23.4 g.

$$\text{grams of solute} \longrightarrow \text{moles solute}$$
$$\text{moles solute and molarity} \longrightarrow \text{liters of solution needed}$$

③ SOLVE

To get the moles of solute, you'll need to calculate the molar mass of K_2CrO_4.

$$1 \text{ mol } K_2CrO_4 = 194.2 \text{ g } K_2CrO_4$$

$$23.4 \text{ g } K_2CrO_4 \times \frac{1 \text{ mol } K_2CrO_4}{194.2 \text{ g } K_2CrO_4} = 0.120 \text{ mol } K_2CrO_4$$

Use the molarity of the solution to convert. Since you know 6.0 mol of K_2CrO_4 is in 1 L of solution, you will need:

$$0.120 \text{ mol } K_2CrO_4 \times \frac{1 \text{ L}}{6.0 \text{ mol}} =$$
$$= 0.020 \text{ L of } K_2CrO_4 \text{ solution}$$

④ CHECK YOUR WORK

The answer is correctly given to two significant digits. The units cancel correctly to give the desired unit, liters of solution.

Practice Answers in Appendix E

1. What is the molarity of a solution composed of 5.85 g of potassium iodide, KI, dissolved in enough water to make 0.125 L of solution?
2. How many moles of H_2SO_4 are present in 0.500 L of a 0.150 M H_2SO_4 solution?
3. What volume of 3.00 M NaCl is needed for a reaction that requires 146.3 g of NaCl?

◀ **MAIN IDEA**

Molality is moles of solute per kilogram of solvent.

Molality is the concentration of a solution expressed in moles of solute per kilogram of solvent. A solution that contains 1 mol of solute, sodium hydroxide, NaOH, for example, dissolved in exactly 1 kg of solvent is a one-molal solution. The symbol for molality is m, and the concentration of this solution is written as 1 m NaOH.

One mole of NaOH has a molar mass of 40.0 g, so 40.0 g of NaOH dissolved in 1 kg of water results in a one-molal NaOH solution. If 20.0 g of NaOH, which is 0.500 mol of NaOH, is dissolved in exactly 1 kg of water, the concentration of the solution is 0.500 m NaOH.

molality (m)	$\text{molality} = \dfrac{\text{moles solute}}{\text{mass of solvent (kg)}}$

$$\frac{0.500 \text{ mol NaOH}}{1.00 \text{ kg H}_2\text{O}} = 0.500 \ m \text{ NaOH}$$

If 80.0 g of sodium hydroxide, which is 2.00 mol, is dissolved in 1 kg of water, a 2.00 m solution of NaOH is produced. The molality of any solution can be found by dividing the number of moles of solute by the mass in kilograms of the solvent in which it is dissolved. Note that if the amount of solvent is expressed in grams, the mass of solvent must be converted to kilograms by multiplying by the following conversion factor:

$$\frac{1 \text{ kg}}{1000 \text{ g}}$$

Figure 3.2 shows how a 0.5000 m solution of $CuSO_4 \cdot 5H_2O$ is prepared, in contrast with the 0.5000 M solution in **Figure 3.1**.

FIGURE 3.2

Preparation of a 0.5000 m Solution The preparation of a 0.5000 m solution of $CuSO_4 \cdot 5H_2O$ also starts with the calculation of the mass of solute needed.

1

Calculate the mass of $CuSO_4 \cdot 5H_2O$ needed. Making this solution will require 0.5000 mol of $CuSO_4 \cdot 5H_2O$ per kilogram of solvent (1000 g). This mass is calculated to be 124.9 g.

2

Add 1.000 kg of solvent to the solute in the beaker. Because the solvent is water, 1.000 kg will equal 1000 mL.

3

Mix thoroughly.

4

The resulting solution has 0.5000 mol of solute dissolved in 1.000 kg of solvent.

Concentrations are expressed as molalities when studying properties of solutions related to vapor pressure and freezing point and boiling point changes. Molality is used because it does not change with changes in temperature. Below is a comparison of the equations for molarity and molality.

| Molarity (*M*) | $\text{molarity} = \dfrac{\text{amount of A (mol)}}{\text{volume of solution (L)}}$ |
| Molality (*m*) | $\text{molality} = \dfrac{\text{amount of A (mol)}}{\text{mass of solvent (kg)}}$ |

GO ONLINE
Solve It! Cards
HMHScience.com

Calculating with Molality

Sample Problem D A solution was prepared by dissolving 81.3 g of ethylene glycol ($C_2H_6O_2$). Find the molal concentration of this solution.

❶ ANALYZE

Given: solute mass = 81.3 g $C_2H_6O_2$
solvent mass = 166 g H_2O

Unknown: molal concentration of $C_2H_6O_2$

❷ PLAN

To find molality, you need moles of solute and kilograms of solvent. The given grams of ethylene glycol must be converted to moles. The mass in grams of solvent must be converted to kilograms.

$$\text{mol } C_2H_6O_2 = \dfrac{\text{g } C_2H_6O_2}{\text{molar mass } C_2H_6O_2}$$

$$\text{kg } H_2O = \text{g } H_2O \times \dfrac{1 \text{ kg}}{1000 \text{ g}}$$

$$\text{molality } C_2H_6O_2 = \dfrac{\text{mol } C_2H_6O_2}{\text{kg } H_2O}$$

❸ SOLVE

Use the periodic table to compute the molar mass of $C_2H_6O_2$.
$C_2H_6O_2 = 62.08$ g/mol

$$81.3 \text{ g } C_2H_6O_2 \times \dfrac{1 \text{ mol } C_2H_6O_2}{62.08 \text{ g } C_2H_6O_2} = 1.31 \text{ mol } C_2H_6O_2$$

$$\dfrac{166 \text{ g } H_2O}{1000 \text{ g/kg}} = 0.166 \text{ kg } H_2O$$

$$\dfrac{1.31 \text{ mol } C_2H_6O_2}{0.166 \text{ kg } H_2O} = 7.89 \ m \ C_2H_6O_2$$

❹ CHECK YOUR WORK

The answer is correctly given to three significant digits. The unit mol solute/kg solvent is correct for molality.

Calculating with Molality

Sample Problem E Solutions of urea, CH_4N_2O, in water, H_2O, are used in industries such as agriculture and automobiles. What mass of urea must be dissolved in 2250 g of water to prepare a 1.50 m solution?

① ANALYZE

Given: molality of solution = 1.50 m CH_4N_2O
            mass of solvent = 2250 g H_2O

Unknown: mass of solute

② PLAN

Your first step should be to convert the grams of solvent to kilograms. The molality gives you the moles of solute, which can be converted to the grams of solute using the molar mass of CH_4N_2O.

③ SOLVE

Use the periodic table to compute the molar mass of CH_4N_2O.
CH_4N_2O = 60.06 g/mol

$$2250 \text{ g } \cancel{CH_4N_2O} \times \frac{1 \text{ kg}}{2250 \text{ g } \cancel{CH_4N_2O}} = 2.250 \text{ kg } CH_4N_2O$$

$$2.250 \cancel{\text{kg}} \times \frac{1.5 \text{ mol } CH_4N_2O}{1 \cancel{\text{kg}}} = 3.375 \text{ mol } CH_4N_2O$$

$$3.375 \text{ mol } \cancel{CH_4N_2O} \times \frac{60.06 \text{ g } CH_4N_2O}{\text{mol } I_2} = 203 \text{ g } CH_4N_2O$$

④ CHECK YOUR WORK

The answer has three significant digits and the units for mass of I_2.

Practice

1. What is the molality of acetone in a solution composed of 255 g of acetone, $(CH_3)_2CO$, dissolved in 200. g of water?
2. What mass of anhydrous calcium chloride ($CaCl_2$) should be dissolved in 590.0 g of water to produce a 0.82 m solution?

✓ SECTION 3 FORMATIVE ASSESSMENT

▶ Reviewing Main Ideas

1. What quantity represents the ratio of the number of moles of solute for a given volume of solution?

2. We dissolve 5.00 grams of sugar, $C_{12}H_{22}O_{11}$, in water to make 1.000 L of solution. What is the concentration of this solution expressed as a molarity?

✓ Critical Thinking

3. **ANALYZING DATA** You evaporate all of the water from 100 mL of NaCl solution and obtain 11.3 grams of NaCl. What was the molarity of the NaCl solution?

4. **RELATING IDEAS** Suppose you know the molarity of a solution. What additional information would you need to calculate the molality of the solution?

You can use the relationship below to calculate the concentration in molarity of any solution.

$$\text{molarity of solution (M)} = \frac{\text{moles of solute (mol)}}{\text{volume of solution (L)}}$$

Suppose you dissolve 20.00 g of NaOH in some water and dilute the solution to a volume of 250.0 mL (0.2500 L). You don't know the molarity of this solution until you know how many moles of NaOH were dissolved. The number of moles of a substance can be found by dividing the mass of the substance by the mass of 1 mol (molar mass) of the substance.

The molar mass of NaOH is 40.00, so the number of moles of NaOH dissolved is

$$20.00 \text{ g NaOH} \times \frac{1 \text{ mol NaOH}}{40.00 \text{ g NaOH}} = 0.5000 \text{ mol NaOH}$$

Now you know that the solution has 0.5000 mol NaOH dissolved in 0.2500 L of solution, so you can calculate molarity.

$$\text{molarity of NaOH} = \frac{\text{mol NaOH}}{\text{L solution}} = \frac{0.5000 \text{ mol NaOH}}{0.2500 \text{ L solution}}$$

$$= 2.000 \text{ mol/L} = 2.000 \text{ M NaOH}$$

Problem-Solving TIPS

- Remember that balances measure mass and not moles, so you often have to convert between mass and moles of solute when making or using solutions.

Sample Problem

A 0.5000 L volume of a solution contains 36.49 g of magnesium chloride, $MgCl_2$. What is the molarity of the solution?

You know the volume of the solution, but you need to find the number of moles of the solute $MgCl_2$ by the following conversion:

$$\text{mass MgCl}_2 \times \frac{1 \text{ mol MgCl}_2}{\text{molar mass MgCl}_2} = \text{mol MgCl}_2$$

$$36.49 \text{ g MgCl}_2 \times \frac{1 \text{ mol MgCl}_2}{95.20 \text{ g MgCl}_2} = 0.3833 \text{ mol MgCl}_2$$

Now you can calculate mol $MgCl_2$ per liter of solution (molarity).

$$\frac{0.3833 \text{ mol MgCl}_2}{0.5000 \text{ L solution}} = 0.7666 \text{ M MgCl}_2$$

Practice

1. What is the molarity of a 50.0 mL solution that contains 0.0350 mol of sodium sulfate, Na_2SO_4?
2. What is the molarity of a 400.0 mL solution that contains 45.00 g of cadmium nitrate, $Cd(NO_3)_2$?

CHAPTER 12 **Summary**

BIG IDEA Solutions are homogeneous mixtures of a solute in a solvent. Chemical and physical factors affect how much of one substance will dissolve in another.

SECTION 1 Types of Mixtures

- Solutions are homogeneous mixtures.
- Mixtures are classified as solutions, suspensions, or colloids, depending on the size of the solute particles in the mixture.
- The dissolved substance is the solute. Solutions that have water as a solvent are aqueous solutions.
- Solutions can consist of solutes and solvents that are solids, liquids, or gases.
- Suspensions settle out upon standing. Colloids do not settle out, and they scatter light that is shined through them.
- Most ionic solutes and some molecular solutes form aqueous solutions that conduct an electric current. These solutes are called electrolytes.
- Nonelectrolytes are solutes that dissolve in water to form solutions that do not conduct electric currents.

KEY TERMS

soluble
solution
solvent
solute
suspension
colloid
electrolyte
nonelectrolyte

SECTION 2 The Solution Process

- A solute dissolves at a rate that depends on the surface area of the solute, how vigorously the solution is mixed, and the temperature of the solvent.
- The solubility of a substance indicates how much of that substance will dissolve in a specified amount of solvent under certain conditions.
- The solubility of a substance depends on the temperature.
- The solubility of gases in liquids increases with increases in pressure.
- The solubility of gases in liquids decreases with increases in temperature.
- The overall energy absorbed as heat by the system when a specified amount of solute dissolves during solution formation is called the enthalpy of solution.

KEY TERMS

solution equilibrium
saturated solution
unsaturated solution
supersaturated solution
solubility

hydration
immiscible
miscible
Henry's law
effervescence
solvated
enthalpy of solution

SECTION 3 Concentration of Solutions

- Two useful expressions of concentration are molarity and molality.
- The molar concentration of a solution represents the ratio of moles of solute to liters of solution.
- The molal concentration of a solution represents the ratio of moles of solute to kilograms of solvent.

KEY TERMS

concentration
molarity
molality

CHAPTER 12 **Review**

GO ONLINE

Interactive Review
HMHScience.com

Review Games
Concept Maps

SECTION 1
Types of Mixtures

▶ REVIEWING MAIN IDEAS

1. **a.** What is the Tyndall effect?
   b. Identify one example of this effect.

2. Given an unknown mixture consisting of two or more substances, explain how you could determine whether that mixture is a true solution, a colloid, or a suspension.

3. Explain why a suspension is considered a heterogeneous mixture.

4. Does a solution have to involve a liquid? Explain your answer.

5. What is the difference between an electrolyte and a nonelectrolyte?

SECTION 2
The Solution Process

▶ REVIEWING MAIN IDEAS

6. **a.** What is solution equilibrium?
   b. What factors determine the point at which a given solute-solvent combination reaches equilibrium?

7. **a.** What is a saturated solution?
   b. What visible evidence indicates that a solution is saturated?
   c. What is an unsaturated solution?

8. **a.** What is meant by the solubility of a substance?
   b. What condition(s) must be specified when expressing the solubility of a substance?

9. **a.** What rule of thumb is useful for predicting whether one substance will dissolve in another?
   b. Describe what the rule means in terms of various combinations of polar and nonpolar solutes and solvents.

10. **a.** How does pressure affect the solubility of a gas in a liquid?
    b. What law is a statement of this relationship?

c. If the pressure of a gas above a liquid is increased, what happens to the amount of the gas that will dissolve in the liquid, if all other conditions remain constant?

d. Two bottles of soda are opened. One is a cold bottle, and the other is at room temperature. Which system will show more effervescence and why?

11. Based on **Figure 2.11,** determine the solubility of each of the following in grams of solute per 100 g H_2O.
    a. $NaNO_3$ at 10°C
    b. KNO_3 at 60°C
    c. NaCl at 50°C

12. Based on **Figure 2.11**, at what temperature would each of the following solubility levels be observed?
    a. 50 g KCl in 100 g H_2O
    b. 100 g $NaNO_3$ in 100 g H_2O
    c. 60 g KNO_3 in 100 g H_2O

13. The enthalpy of solution for $AgNO_3$ is +22.8 kJ/mol.
    a. Write the equation that represents the dissolution of $AgNO_3$ in water.
    b. Is the dissolution process endothermic or exothermic? Is the crystallization process endothermic or exothermic?
    c. As $AgNO_3$ dissolves, what change occurs in the temperature of the solution?
    d. When the system is at equilibrium, how do the rates of dissolution and crystallization compare?
    e. If the solution is then heated, how will the rates of dissolution and crystallization be affected? Why?
    f. How will the increased temperature affect the amount of solute that can be dissolved?
    g. If the solution is allowed to reach equilibrium and is then cooled, how will the system be affected?

14. What opposing forces are at equilibrium in the sodium chloride system shown in **Figure 2.2**?

SECTION 3
Concentration of Solutions

▶ REVIEWING MAIN IDEAS

15. On which property of solutions does the concept of concentration rely?

16. In what units is molarity expressed?

17. Under what circumstances might we prefer to express solution concentrations in terms of
   a. molarity?
   b. molality?

18. If you dissolve 2.00 mol KI in 1.00 L of water, will you get a 2.00 M solution? Explain.

PRACTICE PROBLEMS

19. a. Suppose you wanted to dissolve 106 g of Na_2CO_3 in enough H_2O to make 6.00 L of solution.
   (1) What is the molar mass of Na_2CO_3?
   (2) What is the molarity of this solution?
   b. What is the molarity of a solution of 14.0 g NH_4Br in enough H_2O to make 150. mL of solution?

20. a. Suppose you wanted to prepare 1.00 L of a 3.50 M aqueous solution of H_2SO_4.
   (1) What is the solute?
   (2) What is the solvent?
   (3) How many grams of solute are needed to make this solution?
   b. How many grams of solute are needed to make 2.50 L of a 1.75 M solution of $Ba(NO_3)_2$?

21. How many moles of NaOH are contained in 65.0 mL of a 2.20 M solution of NaOH in H_2O? (Hint: See Sample Problem B.)

22. A solution is made by dissolving 26.42 g of $(NH_4)_2SO_4$ in enough H_2O to make 50.00 mL of solution.
   a. What is the molar mass of $(NH_4)_2SO_4$?
   b. What is the molarity of this solution?

23. Suppose you wanted to find out how many milliliters of 1.0 M $AgNO_3$ are needed to provide 169.9 g of $AgNO_3$.
   a. What is the first step in solving the problem?
   b. What is the molar mass of $AgNO_3$?
   c. How many milliliters of solution are needed?

24. a. Balance this equation:
$$H_3PO_4 + Ca(OH)_2 \longrightarrow Ca_3(PO_4)_2 + H_2O$$
   b. What mass of each product results if 750 mL of 6.00 M H_3PO_4 reacts completely according to the equation?

25. How many milliliters of 0.750 M H_3PO_4 are required to react with 250 mL of 0.150 M $Ba(OH)_2$ if the products are barium phosphate and water?

26. 75.0 mL of an $AgNO_3$ solution reacts with enough Cu to produce 0.250 g of Ag by single displacement. What is the molarity of the initial $AgNO_3$ solution if $Cu(NO_3)_2$ is the other product?

27. Determine the number of grams of solute needed to make each of the following molal solutions:
   a. a 4.50 m solution of H_2SO_4 in 1.00 kg H_2O
   b. a 1.00 m solution of HNO_3 in 2.00 kg H_2O

28. A solution is prepared by dissolving 17.1 g of sucrose, $C_{12}H_{22}O_{11}$, in 275 g of H_2O.
   a. What is the molar mass of sucrose?
   b. What is the molality of that solution?

29. How many kilograms of H_2O must be added to 75.5 g of $Ca(NO_3)_2$ to form a 0.500 m solution?

30. A solution made from ethanol, C_2H_5OH, and water is 1.75 m ethanol. How many grams of C_2H_5OH are contained per 250. g of water?

Mixed Review

▶ REVIEWING MAIN IDEAS

31. Na_2SO_4 is dissolved in water to make 450 mL of a 0.250 M solution.
   a. What is the molar mass of Na_2SO_4?
   b. How many moles of Na_2SO_4 are needed?

32. Citric acid is one component of some soft drinks. Suppose that 2.00 L of solution are made from 150. mg of citric acid, $C_6H_8O_7$.
   a. What is the molar mass of citric acid?
   b. What is the molarity of citric acid in the solution?

33. Suppose you wanted to know how many grams of KCl would be left if 350 mL of a 2.0 M KCl solution were evaporated to dryness.
   a. What is the molar mass of KCl?
   b. How would heating the solution affect the mass of KCl remaining?
   c. How many grams of KCl would remain?

34. Sodium metal reacts violently with water to form NaOH and release hydrogen gas. Suppose that 10.0 g of Na react completely with 1.00 L of water and the final solution volume is 1.00 L.

    a. What is the molar mass of NaOH?

    b. Write a balanced equation for the reaction.

    c. What is the molarity of the NaOH solution formed by the reaction?

35. In cars, ethylene glycol, $C_2H_6O_2$, is used as a coolant and antifreeze. A mechanic fills a radiator with 6.5 kg of ethylene glycol and 1.5 kg of water.

    a. What is the molar mass of ethylene glycol?

    b. What is the molality of the water in the solution?

36. Plot a solubility graph for $AgNO_3$ from the following data, with grams of solute (by increments of 50) per 100 g of H_2O on the vertical axis and with temperature in °C on the horizontal axis.

Grams solute per 100 g H_2O	Temperature (°C)
122	0
216	30
311	40
440	60
585	80
733	100

    a. How does the solubility of $AgNO_3$ vary with the temperature of the water?

    b. Estimate the solubility of $AgNO_3$ at 35°C, 55°C, and 75°C.

    c. At what temperature would the solubility of $AgNO_3$ be 275 g per 100 g of H_2O?

    d. If 100 g of $AgNO_3$ were added to 100 g of H_2O at 10°C, would the resulting solution be saturated or unsaturated? What would occur if 325 g of $AgNO_3$ were added to 100 g of H_2O at 35°C?

37. If a saturated solution of KNO_3 in 100 g of H_2O at 60°C is cooled to 20°C, approximately how many grams of the solute will precipitate out of the solution? (Use **Figure 2.4.**)

38. a. Suppose you wanted to dissolve 294.3 g of H_2SO_4 in 1.000 kg of H_2O.

    (1) What is the solute?

    (2) What is the solvent?

    (3) What is the molality of this solution?

    b. What is the molality of a solution of 63.0 g HNO_3 in 0.250 kg H_2O?

ALTERNATIVE ASSESSMENT

39. Predicting Outcomes You have been investigating the nature of suspensions, colloids, and solutions and have collected the following observational data on four unknown samples. From the data, infer whether each sample is a solution, suspension, or colloid.

		DATA TABLE 1 *Samples*		
Sample	Color	Clarity (clear or cloudy)	Settle out	Tyndall effect
1	green	clear	no	no
2	blue	cloudy	yes	no
3	colorless	clear	no	yes
4	white	cloudy	no	yes

Based on your inferences in Data Table 1, you decide to conduct one more test of the particles. You filter the samples and then reexamine the filtrate. You obtain the data found in Data Table 2. Infer the classifications of the filtrate based on the data in Data Table 2.

		DATA TABLE 2 *Filtrate of Samples*		
Sample	Color	Clarity (clear or cloudy)	On filter paper	Tyndall effect
1	green	clear	nothing	no
2	blue	cloudy	gray solid	yes
3	colorless	clear	none	yes
4	colorless	clear	white solid	no

40. Review the information on alloys in the *Elements Handbook* (Appendix A).
  a. Why is aluminum such an important component of alloys?
  b. What metals make up bronze?
  c. What metals make up brass?
  d. What is steel?
  e. What is the composition of the mixture called *cast iron*?

41. **Table 5A** of the *Elements Handbook* (Appendix A) contains carbon monoxide concentration data expressed as parts per million (ppm). The OSHA (Occupational Safety and Health Administration) limit for worker exposure to CO is 200 ppm for an eight-hour period.
  a. At what concentration do harmful effects occur in less than one hour?
  b. By what factor does the concentration in item (a) exceed the maximum limit set by OSHA?

RESEARCH AND WRITING

42. Find out about the chemistry of emulsifying agents. How do these substances affect the dissolution of immiscible substances such as oil and water? As part of your research on this topic, find out why eggs are an emulsifying agent for baking mixtures.

ALTERNATIVE ASSESSMENT

43. Make a comparison of the electrolyte concentration in various brands of sports drinks. Using the labeling information for sugar, calculate the molarity of sugar in each product or brand. Construct a poster to show the results of your analysis of the product labels.

44. Write a set of instructions on how to prepare a solution that is 1 M $CuSO_4$, using $CuSO_4 \cdot 5H_2O$ as the solute. How do the instructions differ if the solute is anhydrous $CuSO_4$? Your instructions should include a list of all materials needed.

Standards-Based Assessment

Record your answers on a separate piece of paper.

MULTIPLE CHOICE

1 Which one of the following statements is false?

A Gases are generally more soluble in water under high pressures than under low pressures.

B As temperature increases, the solubilities of solids in water increase.

C Water dissolves many ionic solutes because of its ability to hydrate ions in solution.

D Many solids dissolve more quickly in a cold solvent than in a warm solvent.

2 Two liquids are likely to be immiscible if

A both have polar molecules.

B both have nonpolar molecules.

C one is polar and the other is nonpolar.

D one is water and the other is methyl alcohol, CH_3OH.

3 The solubility of a gas in a liquid would be increased by

A the addition of an electrolyte.

B the addition of an emulsifier.

C agitation of the solution.

D an increase in its partial pressure.

4 Which of the following types of compounds is most likely to be a strong electrolyte?

A a polar compound

B a nonpolar compound

C a covalent compound

D an ionic compound

5 A saturated solution can become supersaturated under which of the following conditions?

A It contains electrolytes.

B A heated saturated solution is allowed to cool.

C More solvent is added.

D More solute is added.

6 Molarity is expressed in units of

A moles of solute per liter of solution.

B liters of solution per mole of solute.

C moles of solute per liter of solvent.

D liters of solvent per mole of solute.

7 What mass of NaOH is contained in 2.5 L of a 0.010 M solution?

A 0.010 g

B 1.0 g

C 2.5 g

D 0.40 g

GRIDDED RESPONSE

8 If 75.0 mL of an $AgNO_3$ solution reacts with enough Cu to produce 0.250 g Ag by single displacement, what is the molarity of the initial $AgNO_3$ solution if $Cu(NO_3)_2$ is the other product? (Give your answer to three significant figures.)

Test Tip

Before choosing an answer to a question, try to answer the question without looking at the answer choices on the test.

CHAPTER 13
Ions in Aqueous Solutions and Colligative Properties

BIG IDEA
Ionic compounds dissociate in aqueous solutions. Colligative properties of a solution depend only on the number of solute particles present.

 ONLINE Chemistry
HMHScience.com

GO ONLINE

 Why It Matters Video
HMHScience.com

Colligative Properties

Compounds in Aqueous Solutions

SECTION 1

Main Ideas

▸ Ions separate from each other when ionic compounds are dissolved in water.

▸ A molecular compound ionizes in a polar solvent.

▸ An electrolyte's strength depends on how many dissolved ions it contains.

Key Terms

dissociation   ionization   strong electrolyte
net ionic equation   hydronium ion   weak electrolyte
spectator ions

Solid compounds can be ionic or molecular. An ionic solid consists of oppositely charged ions. The attraction between the ions of opposite charge is responsible for its stability. In a molecular solid, molecules are composed of covalently bonded atoms. The solid is held together by noncovalent, intermolecular forces. When they dissolve in water, ionic compounds and molecular compounds behave differently.

▸ MAIN IDEA

Ions separate from each other when ionic compounds are dissolved in water.

When a compound that is made of ions dissolves in water, the ions separate from one another, as shown in **Figure 1.1. This separation of ions that occurs when an ionic compound dissolves is called dissociation.** For example, dissociation of sodium chloride and calcium chloride in water can be represented by the following equations. (As usual, (s) indicates a solid species, and (aq) indicates a species in an aqueous solution. Note that each equation is balanced for charge as well as for atoms.)

$$NaCl(s) \xrightarrow{H_2O} Na^+(aq) + Cl^-(aq)$$
$$CaCl_2(s) \xrightarrow{H_2O} Ca^{2+}(aq) + 2Cl^-(aq)$$

Notice the number of ions produced per formula unit in the equations above. One formula unit of sodium chloride gives two ions in solution, whereas one formula unit of calcium chloride gives three ions in solution.

FIGURE 1.1

Dissociation
When NaCl dissolves in water, the ions separate as they leave the crystal.

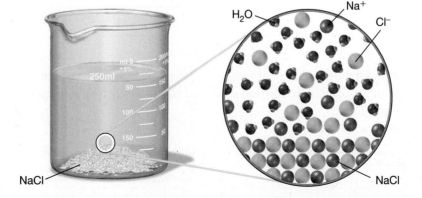

Assuming 100% dissociation, a solution that contains 1 mol of sodium chloride contains 1 mol of Na^+ ions and 1 mol of Cl^- ions. In this book, you can assume 100% dissociation for all soluble ionic compounds. The dissociation of NaCl can be represented as follows.

$$NaCl(s) \xrightarrow{H_2O} Na^+(aq) + Cl^-(aq)$$

1 mol → 1 mol + 1 mol

A solution that contains 1 mol of calcium chloride contains 1 mol of Ca^{2+} ions and 2 mol of Cl^- ions—a total of 3 mol of ions.

$$CaCl_2(s) \xrightarrow{H_2O} Ca^{2+}(aq) + 2Cl^-(aq)$$

1 mol → 1 mol + 2 mol

Calculating Moles of Dissolved Ions

GO ONLINE

Learn It! Video
HMHScience.com

Sample Problem A Write the equation for the dissolution of aluminum sulfate, $Al_2(SO_4)_3$, in water. How many moles of aluminum ions and sulfate ions are produced by dissolving 1 mol of aluminum sulfate? What is the total number of moles of ions produced by dissolving 1 mol of aluminum sulfate?

① ANALYZE

Given: amount of solute = 1 mol $Al_2(SO_4)_3$

solvent identity = water

Unknown: **a.** moles of aluminum ions and sulfate ions

b. total number of moles of solute ions produced

② PLAN

The coefficients in the balanced dissociation equation will reveal the mole relationships, so you can use the equation to determine the number of moles of solute ions produced.

$$Al_2(SO_4)_3(s) \xrightarrow{H_2O} 2Al^{3+}(aq) + 3SO_4^{2-}(aq)$$

③ SOLVE

a. 1 mol $Al_2(SO_4)_3 \longrightarrow$ 2 mol Al^{3+} + 3 mol SO_4^{2-}

b. 2 mol Al^{3+} + 3 mol SO_4^{2-} = 5 mol of solute ions

④ CHECK YOUR WORK

The equation is correctly balanced. Because one formula unit of $Al_2(SO_4)_3$ has 5 ions, 1 mol of $Al_2(SO_4)_3$ produces 5 mol of ions.

Practice   Answers in Appendix E

1. Write the equation for the dissolution of each of the following in water, and then determine the number of moles of each ion produced as well as the total number of moles of ions produced.
   a. 1 mol ammonium chloride
   b. 1 mol sodium sulfide
   c. 0.5 mol barium nitrate

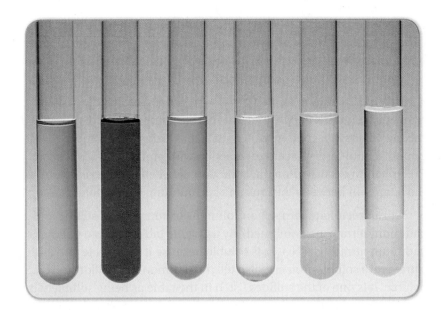

FIGURE 1.2

Solubility of Ionic Compounds Ionic compounds can be soluble or insoluble in water. $NiCl_2$, $KMnO_4$, $CuSO_4$, and $Pb(NO_3)_2$ are soluble in water. AgCl and CdS are insoluble in water.

Precipitation Reactions

Although no ionic compound is completely insoluble, compounds of very low solubility can be considered insoluble for most practical purposes. Some examples of ionic compounds that are soluble and insoluble in water are shown in **Figure 1.2**. It is difficult to write solubility rules that cover all possible conditions. However, we can write some general guidelines to help predict whether a compound made of a certain combination of ions is soluble. These general solubility guidelines are given in **Figure 1.3**.

By looking at the table, you can tell that most sodium compounds are soluble. Sodium carbonate, Na_2CO_3, is soluble because it contains sodium. Its dissociation equation is as follows.

$$Na_2CO_3(s) \xrightarrow{\ H_2O\ } 2Na^+(aq) + CO_3^{2-}(aq)$$

GO ONLINE

Animated **Chemistry**
HMHScience.com

Precipitation Reactions

FIGURE 1.3

GENERAL SOLUBILITY GUIDELINES

1. Sodium, potassium, and ammonium compounds are soluble in water.

2. Nitrates, acetates, and chlorates are soluble.

3. Most chlorides are soluble, except those of silver, mercury(I), and lead. Lead(II) chloride is soluble in hot water.

4. Most sulfates are soluble, except those of barium, strontium, lead, calcium, and mercury(I).

5. Most carbonates, phosphates, and silicates are insoluble, except those of sodium, potassium, and ammonium.

6. Most sulfides are insoluble, except those of calcium, strontium, sodium, potassium, and ammonium.

Is calcium phosphate, $Ca_3(PO_4)_2$, soluble or insoluble? According to **Figure 1.3,** most phosphates are insoluble. Calcium phosphate is not one of the exceptions listed, so it is insoluble. Dissociation equations cannot be written for insoluble compounds.

The information in **Figure 1.3** is also useful in predicting what will happen if solutions of two different soluble compounds are mixed. If the mixing results in a combination of ions that forms an insoluble compound, a double-displacement reaction with precipitation will occur. Precipitation occurs when the attraction between the ions is greater than the attraction between the ions and surrounding water molecules.

Will a precipitate form when solutions of ammonium sulfide and cadmium nitrate are combined? By using the table, you can tell that cadmium nitrate, $Cd(NO_3)_2$, is soluble because it is a nitrate and all nitrates are soluble. You can also tell that ammonium sulfide, $(NH_4)_2S$, is soluble. It is one of the sulfides listed in the table as being soluble. Their dissociation equations are as follows.

$$(NH_4)_2S(s) \xrightarrow{H_2O} 2NH_4^+(aq) + S^{2-}(aq)$$

$$Cd(NO_3)_2(s) \xrightarrow{H_2O} Cd^{2+}(aq) + 2NO_3^-(aq)$$

FIGURE 1.4

Precipitation Ammonium sulfide is a soluble compound that dissociates in water to form NH_4^+ and S^{2-} ions. Cadmium nitrate is a soluble compound that dissociates in water to form NO_3^- and Cd^{2+} ions. Precipitation of cadmium sulfide occurs when the two solutions are mixed.

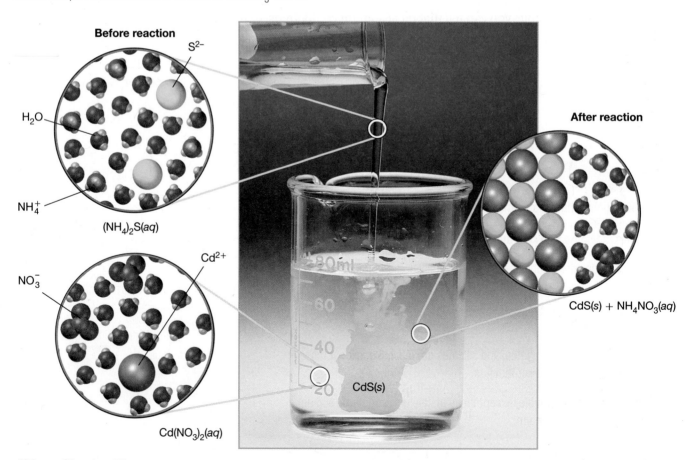

Before reaction

S^{2-}

H_2O

NH_4^+

$(NH_4)_2S(aq)$

NO_3^-

Cd^{2+}

$Cd(NO_3)_2(aq)$

After reaction

$CdS(s) + NH_4NO_3(aq)$

$CdS(s)$

The two possible products of a double-displacement reaction between $(NH_4)_2S$ and $Cd(NO_3)_2$ are ammonium nitrate, NH_4NO_3, and cadmium sulfide, CdS. The question marks indicate that the states are unknown.

$$(NH_4)_2S(aq) + Cd(NO_3)_2(aq) \longrightarrow 2NH_4NO_3(?) + CdS(?)$$

To decide whether a precipitate can form, you must know the solubilities of these two compounds. Consulting **Figure 1.3**, you can see that NH_4NO_3 is soluble in water. However, CdS is insoluble. You can therefore predict that when solutions of ammonium sulfide and cadmium nitrate are combined, ammonium nitrate will not precipitate and cadmium sulfide will. As illustrated in **Figure 1.4**, on the previous page, crystals of CdS form when the solutions are mixed. In the following equation, the designations (aq) and (s) show that $NH_4NO_3(aq)$ remains in solution and $CdS(s)$ precipitates.

$$(NH_4)_2S(aq) + Cd(NO_3)_2(aq) \longrightarrow 2NH_4NO_3(aq) + CdS(s)$$

Net Ionic Equations

Reactions of ions in aqueous solution are usually represented by net ionic equations rather than formula equations. **A net ionic equation includes only those compounds and ions that undergo a chemical change in a reaction in an aqueous solution.** They do not include any ions or substances that do not actually participate in the chemical reaction. To write a net ionic equation, you first convert the chemical equation into a complete ionic equation. All soluble ionic compounds are shown as dissociated ions in solution. The precipitates are shown as solids. The precipitation of cadmium sulfide described previously can be shown by the following overall ionic equation.

$$Cd^{2+}(aq) + 2NO_3^-(aq) + 2NH_4^+(aq) + S^{2-}(aq) \longrightarrow$$
$$CdS(s) + 2NO_3^-(aq) + 2NH_4^+(aq)$$

Notice that the aqueous ammonium ion, $NH_4^+(aq)$, and the aqueous nitrate ion, $NO_3^-(aq)$, appear on both sides of this equation. Therefore, they have not undergone any chemical change and are still present in their original form. **Ions that do not take part in a chemical reaction and are found in solution both before and after the reaction are spectator ions.**

To convert an ionic equation into a net ionic equation, the spectator ions are canceled on both sides of the equation. Eliminating the NH_4^+ and NO_3^- ions from the overall ionic equation above gives the following net ionic equation.

$$Cd^{2+}(aq) + S^{2-}(aq) \longrightarrow CdS(s)$$

This net ionic equation applies not only to the reaction between $(NH_4)_2S$ and $Cd(NO_3)_2$ but also to *any* reaction in which a precipitate of cadmium sulfide forms when the ions are combined in solution. For example, it is also the net ionic equation for the precipitation of CdS when $CdSO_4$ and Na_2S react.

✔ **CHECK FOR UNDERSTANDING**

Interpret In your own words, state why it is helpful to write net ionic equations for chemical reactions.

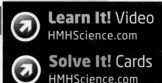
Writing Net Ionic Equations

Sample Problem B Identify the precipitate that forms when aqueous solutions of zinc nitrate and ammonium sulfide are combined. Write the equation for the possible double-displacement reaction. Then write the formula equation, complete ionic equation, and net ionic equation for the reaction.

1 ANALYZE

Given: identity of reactants: zinc nitrate and ammonium sulfide reaction
medium: aqueous solution

Unknown: **a.** equation for the possible double-displacement reaction

   b. identity of the precipitate   **c.** formula equation

   d. complete ionic equation   **e.** net ionic equation

2 PLAN

Write the possible double-displacement reaction between $Zn(NO_3)_2$ and $(NH_4)_2S$. Use **Figure 1.3** to determine if any of the products are insoluble and will precipitate. Write a formula equation and a complete ionic equation, and then cancel the spectator ions to produce a net ionic equation.

3 SOLVE

a. The equation for the possible double-displacement reaction is as follows.

$$Zn(NO_3)_2(aq) + (NH_4)_2S(aq) \longrightarrow ZnS(?) + 2NH_4NO_3(?)$$

b. **Figure 1.3** reveals that because it is not soluble, zinc sulfide is a precipitate. Ammonium nitrate is soluble according to the table.

c. The formula equation is as follows.

$$Zn(NO_3)_2(aq) + (NH_4)_2S(aq) \longrightarrow ZnS(s) + 2NH_4NO_3(aq)$$

d. The complete ionic equation is as follows.

$$Zn^{2+}(aq) + 2NO_3^-(aq) + 2NH_4^+(aq) + S^{2-}(aq) \longrightarrow ZnS(s) + 2NH_4^+(aq) + 2NO_3^-(aq)$$

e. The ammonium and nitrate ions appear on both sides of the equation as spectator ions. The net ionic equation is as follows.

$$Zn^{2+}(aq) + S^{2-}(aq) \longrightarrow ZnS(s)$$

Practice   Answers in Appendix E

1. Will a precipitate form if solutions of potassium sulfate and barium nitrate are combined? If so, write the net ionic equation for the reaction.

2. Will a precipitate form if solutions of potassium nitrate and magnesium sulfate are combined? If so, write the net ionic equation for the reaction.

3. Will a precipitate form if solutions of barium chloride and sodium sulfate are combined? If so, identify the spectator ions and write the net ionic equation.

4. Write the net ionic equation for the precipitation of nickel(II) sulfide.

▶ MAIN IDEA
A molecular compound ionizes in a polar solvent.

A few molecular compounds can form ions in solution. **Ions are formed from solute molecules by the action of the solvent in a process called ionization.** The more general meaning of this term is the creation of ions where there were none. Note that *ionization* is different from *dissociation*. When an ionic compound dissolves, the ions that were already present separate from one another. When a molecular compound dissolves and ionizes in a polar solvent, ions are formed where none existed in the undissolved compound. Like all ions in aqueous solution, the ions formed by such a molecular solute are hydrated. The energy to break the covalent bonds to form ions comes from the energy released as the ions become hydrated.

In general, the extent to which a solute ionizes in solution depends on the strength of the bonds within the molecules of the solute and the strength of attraction between the solute and solvent molecules. If the strength of a bond within the solute molecule is weaker than the attractive forces of the solvent molecules, then the covalent bond of the solute breaks and the molecule is separated into ions. Hydrogen chloride, HCl, is a molecular compound that ionizes in aqueous solution. In aqueous solution, the HCl bond is broken, and a positively charged hydrogen ion and a negatively charged chloride ion are formed. The ions are each surrounded by water molecules, which enables them to stay separated.

$$\text{HCl} \xrightarrow{\text{H}_2\text{O}} \text{H}^+(aq) + \text{Cl}^-(aq)$$

The Hydronium Ion

Some molecular compounds, especially those that contain a hydrogen atom covalently bonded to an atom of high electronegativity, can ionize in an aqueous solution to release H^+. The H^+ ion attracts other molecules or ions so strongly that it does not normally exist alone. The ionization of hydrogen chloride in water is better described as a chemical reaction in which a proton is transferred directly from HCl to a water molecule, where it becomes covalently bonded to oxygen and forms H_3O^+.

$$\text{H}_2\text{O}(l) + \text{HCl}(g) \longrightarrow \text{H}_3\text{O}^+(aq) + \text{Cl}^-(aq)$$

This process is represented in **Figure 1.5. The H_3O^+ ion is known as the hydronium ion.** The reaction of the H^+ ion to form the hydronium ion produces much of the energy needed to ionize a molecular solute.

FIGURE 1.5

Ionization When hydrogen chloride gas dissolves in water, it ionizes to form an H^+ ion and a Cl^- ion. The H^+ ion immediately bonds to a water molecule, forming a hydronium ion. The aqueous solution of hydrogen chloride is called hydrochloric acid.

Ions in Aqueous Solutions and Colligative Properties   **425**

FIGURE 1.6

Electrolytes Strong electrolytes, such as NaCl, yield only ions when they dissolve in aqueous solution. Weak electrolytes, such as HF, exist as both ions and nonionized molecules in aqueous solution. Nonelectrolytes, such as sucrose, $C_{12}H_{22}O_{11}$, do not form any ions in aqueous solution.

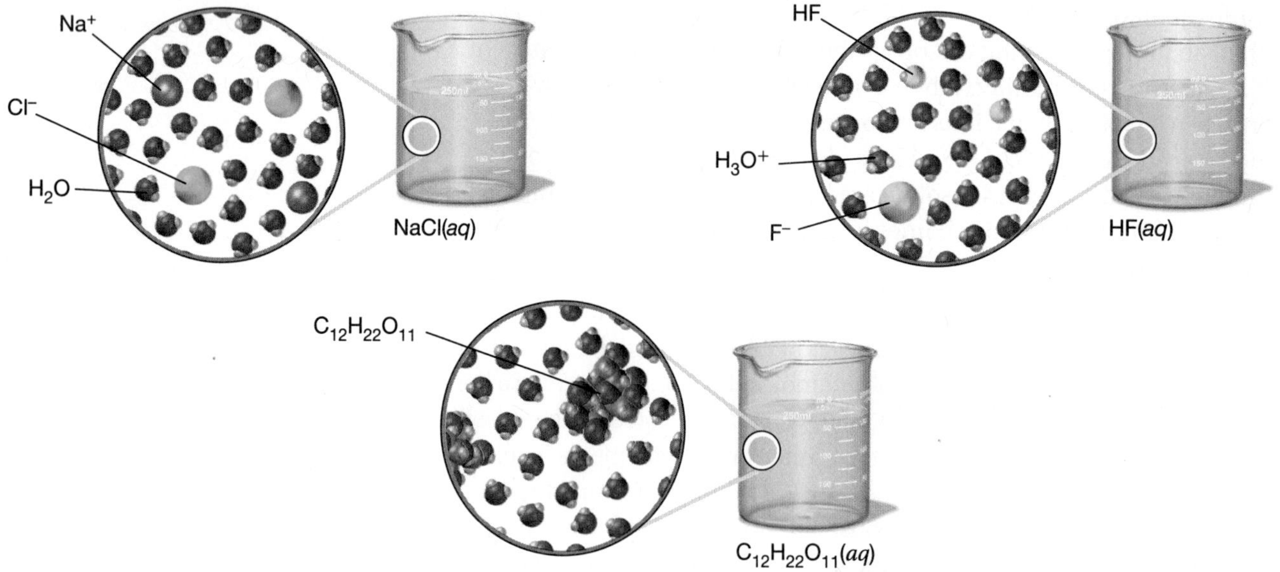

Na^+

Cl^-

H_2O

NaCl(aq)

HF

H_3O^+

F^-

HF(aq)

$C_{12}H_{22}O_{11}$

$C_{12}H_{22}O_{11}(aq)$

▶ **MAIN IDEA**

An electrolyte's strength depends on how many dissolved ions it contains.

Substances that yield ions and conduct an electric current in solution are electrolytes. Substances that do not yield ions and do not conduct an electric current in solution are nonelectrolytes. Hydrogen chloride is one of a series of compounds composed of hydrogen and the members of Group 17 (known as the halogens). The hydrogen halides are all molecular compounds with single polar-covalent bonds. All are gases, all are very soluble in water, and all are electrolytes. Hydrogen chloride, hydrogen bromide, and hydrogen iodide strongly conduct an electric current in an aqueous solution. However, hydrogen fluoride only weakly conducts an electric current at the same concentration. The strength with which substances conduct an electric current is related to their ability to form ions in solution, as shown in **Figure 1.6.**

Strong Electrolytes

Hydrogen chloride, hydrogen bromide, and hydrogen iodide are 100% ionized in dilute aqueous solution. **A strong electrolyte is any compound whose dilute aqueous solutions conduct electricity well; this is due to the presence of all or almost all of the dissolved compound in the form of ions.** Hydrogen chloride, hydrogen bromide, and hydrogen iodide are all acids in aqueous solution. These acids, several other acids, and all soluble ionic compounds are strong electrolytes.

All electrolytes that yield only ions when they dissolve are strong electrolytes. This includes all soluble ionic compounds, like NaCl, and a limited number of molecular compounds , like HCl.

Weak Electrolytes

Some molecular compounds form aqueous solutions that contain dissolved ions and some dissolved molecules that are not ionized. Hydrogen fluoride, HF, dissolves in water to give an acidic solution known as hydrofluoric acid. However, the hydrogen-fluorine bond is much stronger than the bonds between hydrogen and the other halogens. When hydrogen fluoride dissolves, some molecules ionize. But the reverse reaction—the transfer of H^+ ions back to F^- ions to form hydrogen fluoride molecules—also takes place.

$$HF(aq) + H_2O(l) \rightleftarrows H_3O^+(aq) + F^-(aq)$$

Thus, the concentration of dissolved intact HF is much greater than the concentration of H_3O^+ and F^- ions.

Hydrogen fluoride is an example of a weak electrolyte. **A weak electrolyte is any compound whose dilute aqueous solutions conduct electricity poorly; this is due to the presence of a small amount of the dissolved compound in the form of ions.** This is in contrast to a nonelectrolyte, such as the molecular compound sucrose, which dissolves but does not produce any ions in solution. Another example of a weak electrolyte is acetic acid, CH_3COOH. Only a small percentage of the acetic acid molecules ionize in aqueous solution.

$$CH_3COOH(aq) + H_2O(l) \rightleftarrows CH_3COO^-(aq) + H_3O^+(aq)$$

The description of an electrolyte as strong or weak must not be confused with concentrated or dilute. Strong and weak electrolytes differ in the *degree of ionization or dissociation.* Concentrated and dilute solutions differ in the *amount of solute dissolved* in a given quantity of a solvent. Hydrochloric acid is always a strong electrolyte. This is true even in a solution that is 0.000 01 M—a very dilute solution. By contrast, acetic acid is always considered a weak electrolyte, even in a 10 M solution—a very concentrated solution.

SECTION 1 FORMATIVE ASSESSMENT

▶ Reviewing Main Ideas

1. Write the equation for the dissolution of $Sr(NO_3)_2$ in water. How many moles of strontium ions and nitrate ions are produced by dissolving 0.5 mol of strontium nitrate?

2. Will a precipitate form if solutions of magnesium acetate and strontium chloride are combined?

3. What determines whether a molecular compound will be ionized in water?

4. Explain why HCl is a strong electrolyte and HF is a weak electrolyte.

✓ Critical Thinking

5. **PREDICTING OUTCOMES** For each of the following pairs, tell which solution contains the larger total concentration of ions.
   a. 0.10 M HCl and 0.05 M HCl
   b. 0.10 M HCl and 0.10 M HF
   c. 0.10 M HCl and 0.10 M CaCl$_2$

The Riddle of Electrolysis

Historical Perspective

When Michael Faraday performed his electrochemical experiments, little was known about the relationship between matter and electricity. Chemists were still debating the existence of atoms, and the discovery of the electron was more than 50 years in the future. Combining his talents in electrical and chemical investigation, Faraday pointed researchers to the intimate connection between chemical reactions and electricity while setting the stage for the development of a new branch of chemistry.

Electrifying Experiments

In 1800, Italian physicist Alessandro Volta introduced his *voltaic pile,* better known as the battery. The stack of alternating zinc and silver disks provided scientists with a source of electric current for the first time.

That same year, chemists discovered a new phenomenon using Volta's device. They immersed the two poles of a battery at different locations in a container of water. The current caused the water to decompose into its elemental components, with hydrogen evolving at the positive pole of the battery and oxygen evolving at the negative pole. Similar experiments using solutions of certain solids dissolved in water resulted in the decomposition of the solids, with the two products of the solids' breakdown also evolving at opposite poles of the battery. This electrochemical decomposition was later named *electrolysis.*

The Roots of Electrolytic Theory

The discovery of electrolysis led two pioneering chemists to ponder the connection between chemical forces and electricity. One of the chemists was Humphry Davy, who thought that chemical bonding must be driven by the same forces that drive electrical attractions.

The Swedish chemist Jöns Jacob Berzelius took Davy's idea a step further. He postulated that matter consisted of combinations of "electropositive" and "electronegative" substances, classifying the parts by the pole at which they accumulated during electrolysis.

These ideas inspired two early electrolytic theories, each of which ultimately proved incorrect but contributed to our present understanding of the phenomenon. The *contact theory* proposed that electrolytic current was due merely to the contact of the battery's metals with the electrolytic solution. The *chemical theory,* on the other hand, attributed the current to undefined changes in the solution's components.

Chlorine being produced by electrolysis.

Cathode

Anode

Faraday Provides a Spark

Although Michael Faraday is best remembered for his work in electromagnetism, he began his career as Humphry Davy's laboratory assistant at the Royal Institution in London and went on to be the professor of chemistry there for over 30 years. In the 1830s, Faraday devised several ingenious experiments to determine whether the current in an electrolytic solution is dependent solely on the contact of the battery's poles with the solution. In a typical setup, one of the poles was separated from the solution, and electricity was permitted to enter the solution by way of a spark. In all cases, Faraday observed current in the electrolytic cell despite one or both of the poles not being in direct contact with the electrolytic solution. In 1833, he made the hypothesis that the process of electrolysis was due to the intrinsic properties of the metals in solution and the effect of current on these properties.

Although the battery's poles were, in fact, later shown to play a part in the current, Faraday had established the active role of the electrolytic solution in electrolysis. And in realizing that electricity affected the chemical nature of the solution, he anticipated the ideas of oxidation and reduction despite the concepts of electrons and ions being unknown at the time.

Faraday's Legacy

Faraday continued to study the role of the electrolytic solution, or electrolyte, as he named it, in electrolysis. He also coined most of the other modern terms of electrolysis, including *electrode, ion, anode, cathode, anion,* and *cation.* These investigations culminated in the discovery of his basic laws of electrolysis.

Electrolytic processes are used every day for such things as depositing a thin layer of a valuable metal (like gold or silver) over a metal of lower quality (such as iron or brass), extracting pure metals from impure ones, and refining them. These processes are known as *electroplating, electrorefining,* and *electrometallurgy.*

Still valid, these principles put electrolysis on a quantitative footing, leading to our current understanding of the phenomenon. They also bolstered the atomic theory, which was still seriously contested by many chemists at the time. And perhaps most important, Faraday's experiments inspired his successors to further clarify the chemical nature of solutions.

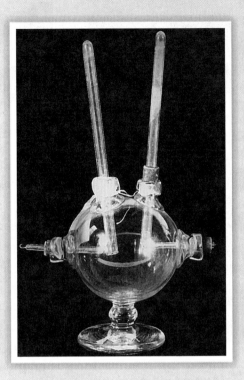

Michael Faraday used this instrument in his studies of electrolysis.

This ultimately led to Svante Arrhenius's theory of electrolytic dissociation and the evolution of a new division in the chemical field, known today as *physical chemistry.*

Questions

1. To which scientist does this feature give the most credit for the initial understanding of the basic nature of electrolysis? Briefly summarize his contributions in this area.

2. How are amounts of hydrogen and oxygen gas made from the electrolytic decomposition of water related to the chemical formula of water?

SECTION 2

Main Ideas

▶ Lowering vapor pressure depends on nonelectrolyte solute concentration.

▶ A solution with a nonelectrolyte solute will have a lower freezing point than the pure solvent.

▶ A solution with a nonelectrolyte solute will have a higher boiling point than the pure solvent.

▶ Osmotic pressure is determined by the concentration of dissolved solute particles.

▶ The total molality of all dissolved particles determines changes in colligative properties.

Colligative Properties of Solutions

Key Terms

colligative properties	freezing-point depression, Δt_f	semipermeable membrane
nonvolatile substance	molal boiling-point constant, K_b	osmosis
molal freezing-point constant, K_f	boiling-point elevation, Δt_b	osmotic pressure

The presence of solutes affects the properties of the solutions. Some of these properties are not dependent on the nature of the dissolved substance but only on how many dissolved particles are present. **Properties that depend on the concentration of solute particles but not on their identity are called colligative properties.** The magnitude of the colligative properties depends on the molal concentration, m.

▶ **MAIN IDEA**

Lowering vapor pressure depends on nonelectrolyte solute concentration.

The boiling point and freezing point of a solution differ from those of the pure solvent. The graph in **Figure 2.1** shows that a nonvolatile solute raises

---

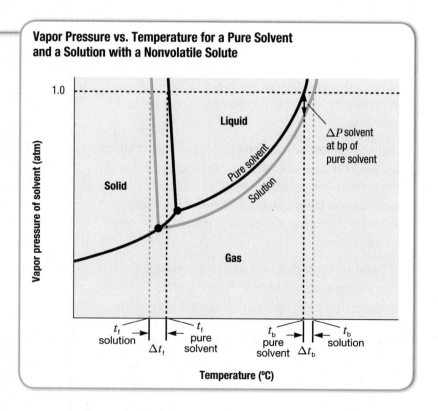

FIGURE 2.1

Vapor-Pressure Lowering Vapor pressure as a function of temperature is shown for a pure solvent and for a solution of a nonvolatile solute in that solvent. The vapor pressure of the solution is lower than the vapor pressure of the pure solvent. This can be seen by noting the decrease in pressure between the pure solvent and the solution at the temperature that is the boiling point of the pure solvent. The solute thus reduces the freezing point and elevates the boiling point.

Vapor Pressure vs. Temperature for a Pure Solvent and a Solution with a Nonvolatile Solute

FIGURE 2.2

Vapor-Pressure Lowering: Pure Solvent vs. Solution

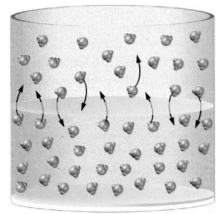

Pure water

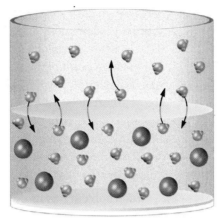

Aqueous solution of nonvolatile solute

 Used to represent $C_{12}H_{22}O_{11}$, sucrose

Used to represent H_2O, water

the boiling point and lowers the freezing point. **A nonvolatile substance is one that has little tendency to become a gas under existing conditions.**

To understand why a nonvolatile solute changes the boiling point and freezing point, you must consider equilibrium vapor pressure. Vapor pressure is the pressure caused by molecules in the gas phase that are in equilibrium with the liquid phase. Experiments show that the vapor pressure of a solvent containing a nonvolatile solute is lower than the vapor pressure of the pure solvent at the same temperature, as shown in **Figure 2.2.** As the number of solute particles increases in a given volume of solution, the proportion of solvent (water) molecules decreases. Fewer water molecules will be available to escape from the liquid. As a result, the tendency of water molecules to leave the solution and enter the vapor phase decreases. Thus, the vapor pressure of the solution is less than the vapor pressure of pure water.

Nonelectrolyte solutions of the same molality have the same concentration of particles. Nonelectrolyte solutes with the same molarity in the same solvent lower the vapor pressure the same amount. For example, a 1 m aqueous solution of the nonelectrolyte glucose, $C_6H_{12}O_6$, lowers the vapor pressure of water by 5.5×10^{-4} atm at 25°C. A 1 m solution of sucrose, $C_{12}H_{22}O_{11}$, another nonelectrolyte, also lowers the vapor pressure by 5.5×10^{-4} atm. Because vapor-pressure lowering depends on the concentration of a nonelectrolyte solute and is independent of solute identity, it is a colligative property.

Refer to the graph in **Figure 2.1.** Because the vapor pressure has been lowered, the solution remains liquid over a larger temperature range. This lowers the freezing point and raises the boiling point. It follows that changes in boiling point and freezing point also depend on the concentration of solute and are therefore colligative properties.

▶ MAIN IDEA

A solution with a nonelectrolyte solute will have a lower freezing point than the pure solvent.

The freezing point of a 1 m solution of any nonelectrolyte solute in water is found by experiment to be 1.86°C lower than the freezing point of water. That is, when 1 mol of a nonelectrolyte solute is dissolved in 1 kg of water, the freezing point of the solution is −1.86°C instead of 0.00°C. When 2 mol of a nonelectrolyte solute is dissolved in 1 kg of water, the freezing point of the solution is −3.72°C. This is 2 × (−1.86°C). In fact, for any concentration of a nonelectrolyte solute in water, the decrease in freezing point can be estimated by using the value of −1.86°C/m. **This value, called the molal freezing-point constant (K_f) is the freezing-point depression of the solvent in a 1-molal solution of a nonvolatile, nonelectrolyte solute.**

Each solvent has its own characteristic molal freezing-point constant. The values of K_f for some common solvents are given in **Figure 2.3.** These values are most accurate for dilute solutions at 1 atmosphere of pressure. The table shows the values of a related quantity called K_b, which you will study next.

As stated earlier, the freezing point of a solution containing 1 mol of a nonelectrolyte solute in 1 kg water is 1.86°C lower than the normal freezing point of water. **The freezing-point depression, Δt_f, is the difference between the freezing points of the pure solvent and a solution of a nonelectrolyte in that solvent, and it is directly proportional to the molal concentration of the solution.** As shown by the previous example, if the molal concentration is doubled, the freezing-point depression is doubled. Freezing-point depression can be calculated by the following equation.

> **Freezing-Point Depression** $\qquad \Delta t_f = K_f m$

K_f is expressed as °C/m, m is expressed in mol solute/kg solvent (molality), and Δt_f is expressed in °C. Sample Problems C and D show how this relationship can be used to determine the freezing-point depression and molal concentration of a solution.

✓ CHECK FOR UNDERSTANDING

Interpret In your own words, describe the process by which ice cream is made at home and explain how the process relates to freezing-point depression.

FIGURE 2.3

MOLAL FREEZING-POINT AND BOILING-POINT CONSTANTS

Solvent	Normal f.p. (°C)	Molal f.p. constant, K_f (°C/m)	Normal b.p. (°C)	Molal b.p. constant, K_b (°C/m)
Acetic acid	16.6	−3.90	117.9	3.07
Camphor	178.8	−39.7	207.4	5.61
Ether	−116.3	−1.79	34.6	2.02
Naphthalene	80.2	−6.94	217.7	5.80
Phenol	40.9	−7.40	181.8	3.60
Water	0.00	−1.86	100.0	0.51

Calculating Freezing-Point Depression

GO ONLINE
Solve It! Cards
HMHScience.com

Sample Problem C What is the freezing-point depression of a solution of 210.0 g of glycerol, $C_3H_8O_3$, in 350. g of water? What is the actual freezing point of the solution?

① ANALYZE

Given: solute mass and chemical formula = 210.0 g of glycerol, $C_3H_8O_3$

solvent mass and identity = 350. g water

Unknown: **a.** freezing-point depression

b. freezing point of the solution

② PLAN

Look up the molal freezing-point constant, K_f, for water in **Figure 2.3.** To use the equation for freezing-point depression, $\Delta t_f = K_f m$, you need to determine the molality of the solution.

$$\text{mass of solute (g)} \times \frac{1\ \text{mol solute}}{\text{molar mass of solute (g)}} = \text{amount of solute (mol)}$$

$$\frac{\text{amount of solute (mol)}}{\text{mass of solvent (g)}} \times \frac{1000\ \text{g water}}{1\ \text{kg water}} = \text{molality}$$

$$\Delta t_f = K_f m$$

$$\text{f.p. solution} = \text{f.p. solvent} + \Delta t_f$$

③ SOLVE

$$210.0\ \text{g } C_3H_8O_3 \times \frac{1\ \text{mol } C_3H_8O_3}{92.11\ \text{g } C_3H_8O_3} = 2.279\ \text{mol } C_3H_8O_3$$

$$\frac{2.279\ \text{mol } C_3H_8O_3}{350.\ \text{g water}} \times \frac{1000\ \text{g water}}{\text{kg water}} = \frac{6.511\ \text{mol } C_3H_8O_3}{\text{kg water}} = 6.511\ m$$

a. $\Delta t_f = 6.511\ m \times (-1.86°C/m) = -12.1°C$
b. f.p. solution $= 0.000°C + (-12.1°C) = -12.1°C$

Calculating Molal Concentration

GO ONLINE
SOLUTION TUTOR
HMHScience.com

Sample Problem D A water solution containing an unknown quantity of a nonelectrolyte solute is found to have a freezing point of −0.23°C. What is the molal concentration of the solution?

① ANALYZE

Given: freezing point of solution = −0.23°C

Unknown: molality of the solution

② PLAN

Water is the solvent, so you will need the value of K_f, the molal-freezing-point constant for water, from **Figure 2.3.** The Δt_f for this solution is the difference between the f.p. of water and the f.p. of the solution. Use the equation for freezing-point depression to calculate molality.

$$\Delta t_f = \text{f.p. of solution} - \text{f.p. of pure solvent}$$

$$\Delta t_f = K_f m \qquad \text{Solve for molality, } m.$$

$$m = \frac{\Delta t_f}{K_f}$$

Continued ▶

Calculating Molal Concentration (continued)

③ SOLVE

$$\Delta t_f = -0.23°C - 0.00°C = -0.23°C$$

$$m = \frac{-0.23°C}{-1.86°C/m} = 0.12\ m$$

④ CHECK YOUR WORK   As shown by the unit cancellation, the answer gives the molality, as desired. The answer is properly limited to two significant digits.

Practice   Answers in Appendix E

1. A solution consists of 10.3 g of the nonelectrolyte glucose, $C_6H_{12}O_6$, dissolved in 250. g of water. What is the freezing-point depression of the solution?
2. In a laboratory experiment, the freezing point of an aqueous solution of glucose is found to be $-0.325°C$. What is the molal concentration of this solution?
3. What is the freezing point of a solution of 60.0 g of glucose, $C_6H_{12}O_6$, dissolved in 80.0 g of water?
4. The freezing point of an aqueous solution that contains a nonelectrolyte is $-9.0°C$.
    a. What is the freezing-point depression of the solution?
    b. What is the molal concentration of the solution?

▶ MAIN IDEA

A solution with a nonelectrolyte solute will have a higher boiling point than the pure solvent.

As discussed previously, the boiling point of a liquid is the temperature at which the vapor pressure of the liquid is equal to the prevailing atmospheric pressure. Therefore, a change in the vapor pressure of the liquid will cause a corresponding change in the boiling point. In other words, if the vapor pressure is lowered, the boiling point is raised. If the vapor pressure is increased, the boiling point decreases. The vapor pressure of a solution containing a nonvolatile solute is lower than the vapor pressure of the pure solvent. This means that more energy as heat will be required to raise the vapor pressure of the solution to equal the atmospheric pressure. Thus, the boiling point of a solution is higher than the boiling point of the pure solvent.

The **molal boiling-point constant (K_b)** is the boiling-point elevation of the solvent in a 1-molal solution of a nonvolatile, nonelectrolyte solute. The boiling-point elevation of a 1-molal solution of any nonelectrolyte solute in water has been found by experiment to be $0.51°C$. Thus, the molal boiling-point constant for water is $0.51°C/m$.

For different solvents, the molal boiling-point constants have different values. Some other values for K_b are included in **Figure 2.3**. Like the freezing-point constants, these values are most accurate for dilute solutions.

The **boiling-point elevation, Δt_b,** is the difference between the boiling points of the pure solvent and a nonelectrolyte solution of that solvent, and it is directly proportional to the molal concentration of the solution.

Boiling-point elevation can be calculated by the following equation.

> **Boiling-Point Elevation** $\Delta t_b = K_b m$

When K_b is expressed in °C/m and m is expressed in mol of solute/kg of solvent, Δt_b is the boiling-point elevation in °C.

Calculating Boiling-Point Elevation

Sample Problem E What is the boiling-point elevation of a solution containing 34.3 g of the nonelectrolyte compound glucose, $C_6H_{12}O_6$, dissolved in 107 g of water?

❶ ANALYZE

Given:
solute mass = 34.3 g

solute molar mass = 180.16 g/mol

solvent mass and identity = 107 g of water

Unknown: boiling-point elevation

❷ PLAN

Find the molal boiling-point constant, K_b, for water in **Figure 2.3**. To use the equation for boiling-point elevation, $\Delta t_b = K_b m$, you need to determine the molality of the solution.

$$\text{mass of solute (g)} \times \frac{1 \text{ mol solute}}{\text{molar mass solute (g)}} = \text{amount of solute (mol)}$$

$$\frac{\text{amount of solute (mol)}}{\text{mass of solvent (g)}} \times \frac{1000 \text{ g water}}{1 \text{ kg water}} = \text{molality}$$

$$\Delta t_b = K_b m$$

❸ SOLVE

$$34.3 \text{ g of solute} \times \frac{1 \text{ mol solute}}{180.16 \text{ g of solute}} = 0.190 \text{ mol of solute}$$

$$\frac{0.190 \text{ mol of solute}}{107 \text{ g water}} \times \frac{1000 \text{ g water}}{1 \text{ kg water}} = 1.776 \frac{\text{mol solute}}{\text{kg water}} = 1.776 \, m$$

$$\Delta t_b = 0.51°C/m \times 1.775 \, m = 0.905°C$$

Practice

1. A solution contains 50.0 g of sucrose, $C_{12}H_{22}O_{11}$, a nonelectrolyte, dissolved in 500.0 g of water. What is the boiling-point elevation?
2. Determine the boiling point of a solution of 72.4 g of glycerol dissolved in 122.5 g of water.
3. If the boiling-point elevation of an aqueous solution containing a nonvolatile electrolyte is 1.02°C, what is the molality of the solution?
4. The boiling point of an aqueous solution containing a nonvolatile electrolyte is 100.75°C.
   a. What is the boiling-point elevation?
   b. What is the molality of the solution?

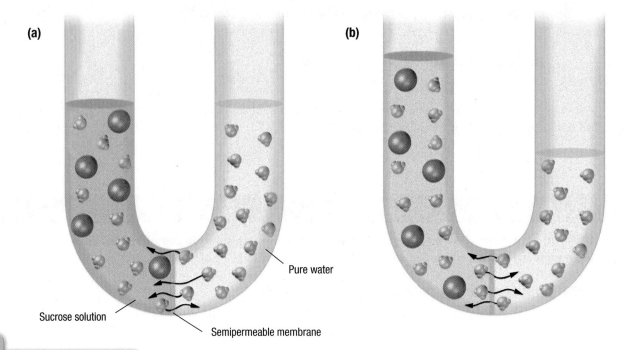

(a)   **(b)**

Pure water

Sucrose solution

Semipermeable membrane

FIGURE 2.4

Osmotic Pressure **(a)** When pure water and an aqueous sucrose solution are separated by a semipermeable membrane, the net movement of water molecules through the membrane is from the pure water side into the aqueous solution. **(b)** The level of the solution rises until pressure exerted by the height of the solution equals the osmotic pressure, at which point no net movement of water molecules occurs.

▶ **MAIN IDEA**

Osmotic pressure is determined by the concentration of dissolved solute particles.

Figure 2.4 illustrates another colligative property. In the figure, an aqueous sucrose solution is separated from pure water by a semipermeable membrane. A **semipermeable membrane** allows the passage of some particles while blocking the passage of others. The level of the sucrose solution will rise until a certain height is reached. What causes the level of the solution to rise?

The semipermeable membrane allows water molecules, but not sucrose molecules, to pass through. The sucrose molecules on the solution side allow fewer water molecules to strike the membrane than to strike on the pure water side in the same amount of time. Thus, the rate at which water molecules leave the pure water side is greater than the rate at which they leave the solution side. This causes the level of the solution to rise. The level rises until the pressure exerted by the height of the solution is large enough to force water molecules back through the membrane from the solution at a rate equal to that at which they enter from the pure water side.

The movement of solvent through a semipermeable membrane from the side of lower solute concentration to the side of higher solute concentration is **osmosis.** Osmosis occurs whenever two solutions of different concentrations are separated by a semipermeable membrane. **Osmotic pressure** is the external pressure that must be applied to stop osmosis. In the example given above, osmosis caused the level of the solution to rise until the height of the solution provided the pressure necessary to stop osmosis. Because osmotic pressure is dependent on the concentration of solute particles and not on the type of solute particles, it is a colligative property. The greater the concentration of a solution, the greater the osmotic pressure of the solution.

Regulation of osmosis is vital to the life of a cell because cell membranes are semipermeable. Cells lose water and shrink when placed in a solution of higher concentration. They gain water and swell when placed in a solution of lower concentration. In vertebrates, cells are protected from swelling and shrinking by blood and lymph that surround the cells. Blood and lymph are equal in concentration to the concentration inside the cell.

▶ MAIN IDEA

The total molality of all dissolved particles determines changes in colligative properties.

Early investigators were puzzled by experiments in which certain substances depressed the freezing point or elevated the boiling point of a solvent more than expected. For example, a 0.1 m solution of sodium chloride, NaCl, lowers the freezing point of the solvent nearly twice as much as a 0.1 m solution of sucrose. A 0.1 m solution of calcium chloride, $CaCl_2$, lowers the freezing point of the solvent nearly three times as much as a 0.1 m solution of sucrose. The effect on boiling points is similar.

To understand why this is so, contrast the behavior of sucrose with that of sodium chloride in aqueous solutions. Sugar is a nonelectrolyte. Each sucrose molecule dissolves to produce only one particle in solution, so 1 mol of sucrose dissolves to produce only 1 mol of particles in solution. NaCl, however, is a strong electrolyte. Each mole of NaCl dissolves to produce 2 mol of particles in solution: 1 mol of sodium ions and 1 mol of chloride ions. **Figure 2.5** compares the production of particles in solution for three different solutes. As you can see, electrolytes produce more than 1 mol of solute particles for each mole of compound dissolved.

FIGURE 2.5

Colligative Properties Compare the number of particles produced per formula unit for these three solutes. Colligative properties depend on the total concentration of particles.

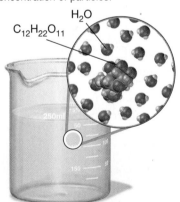
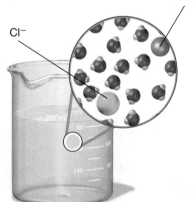
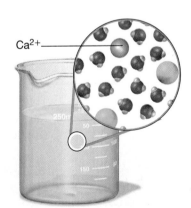

Sucrose solution

Sodium chloride solution

Calcium chloride solution

$C_{12}H_{22}O_{11} \xrightarrow{H_2O} C_{12}H_{22}O_{11}(aq)$

$NaC \xrightarrow{H_2O} Na^+(aq) + Cl^-(aq)$

$CaCl_2 \xrightarrow{H_2O} Ca^{2+}(aq) + 2Cl^-(aq)$

Calculated Values for Electrolyte Solutions

Remember that colligative properties depend on the total concentration of solute particles regardless of their identity. The changes in colligative properties caused by electrolytes will be proportional to the total molality of all dissolved particles, not to formula units. For the same molal concentrations of sucrose and sodium chloride, you would expect the effect on colligative properties to be twice as large for sodium chloride as for sucrose. What about barium nitrate, $Ba(NO_3)_2$? Each mole of barium nitrate yields 3 mol of ions in solution.

$$Ba(NO_3)_2(s) \longrightarrow Ba^{2+}(aq) + 2NO_3^-(aq)$$

You would expect a $Ba(NO_3)_2$ solution of a given molality to lower the freezing point of its solvent three times as much as a nonelectrolytic solution of the same molality.

Freezing-Point Depression of Electrolytes

Sample Problem F What is the expected change in the freezing point of water in a solution of 62.5 g of barium nitrate, $Ba(NO_3)_2$, in 1.00 kg of water?

❶ ANALYZE

Given: solute mass and formula = 62.5 g $Ba(NO_3)_2$

solvent mass and identity = 1.00 kg water

$\Delta t_f = K_f m$

Unknown: expected freezing-point depression

❷ PLAN

The molality can be calculated by converting the solute mass to moles and then dividing by the number of kilograms of solvent. That molality is in terms of formula units of $Ba(NO_3)_2$ and must be converted to molality in terms of dissociated ions in solution. It must be multiplied by the number of moles of ions produced per mole of formula unit. This adjusted molality can then be used to calculate the freezing-point depression.

$$\frac{\text{mass of solute (g)}}{\text{mass of solvent (kg)}} \times \frac{1 \text{ mass solute}}{\text{molar mass solute (g)}} = \text{molality of solution} \left(\frac{\text{mol}}{\text{kg}} \right)$$

$$\text{molality of solution} \left(\frac{\text{mol}}{\text{kg}} \right) \times \text{molality conversion} \left(\frac{\text{mol ions}}{\text{mol}} \right) \times K_f \left(\frac{°C \bullet \text{kg } H_2O}{\text{mol ions}} \right)$$

$$= \text{expected freezing-point depression (°C)}$$

This problem is similar to Sample Problem E, except that the solute is ionic rather than a nonionizing molecular solute. The number of particles in solution will therefore equal the number of ions of the solute.

❸ SOLVE

$$\frac{62.5 \text{ g } Ba(NO_3)_2}{1.00 \text{ kg } H_2O} \times \frac{\text{mol } Ba(NO_3)_2}{261.35 \text{ g } Ba(NO_3)_2} = \frac{0.239 \text{ mol } Ba(NO_3)_2}{\text{kg } H_2O}$$

Continued ▶

Freezing-Point Depression of Electrolytes (continued)

$$Ba(NO_3)_2(s) \longrightarrow Ba^{2+}(aq) + 2NO_3^-(aq)$$

Each formula unit of barium nitrate yields three ions in solution.

$$\frac{0.239 \text{ mol Ba(NO}_3)_2}{\text{kg H}_2\text{O}} \times \frac{3 \text{ mol ions}}{\text{mol Ba(NO}_3)_2} \times -\frac{1.86°C \bullet \text{kg H}_2\text{O}}{\text{mol ions}} = -1.33°C$$

4 CHECK YOUR WORK

The units cancel properly to give the desired answer in °C. The answer is correctly given to three significant digits. The mass of the solute is approximately one-fourth its molar mass and would give 0.75 mol of ions in the 1 kg of solvent, so the estimated answer of $0.75 \times (-1.86°C) = -1.4°C$ supports our computation.

Practice   Answers in Appendix E

1. What is the expected freezing-point depression for a solution that contains 2.0 mol of magnesium sulfate dissolved in 1.0 kg of water?
2. What is the expected boiling-point elevation of water for a solution that contains 150 g of sodium chloride dissolved in 1.0 kg of water?
3. The freezing point of an aqueous sodium chloride solution is −0.20°C. What is the molality of the solution?

Actual Values for Electrolyte Solutions

It is important to remember that the values just calculated are only *expected* values. As stated earlier, a $0.1 \, m$ solution of sodium chloride lowers the freezing point *nearly* twice as much as a $0.1 \, m$ solution of sucrose. The actual values of the colligative properties for all strong electrolytes are *almost* what would be expected based on the number of particles they produce in solution. Some specific examples are given in **Figure 2.6.** The freezing-point depression of a compound that produces two ions per formula unit is almost twice that of a nonelectrolytic solution. The freezing-point depression of a compound that produces three ions per formula unit is almost three times that of a nonelectrolytic solution.

FIGURE 2.6

MOLAL FREEZING-POINT DEPRESSIONS FOR AQUEOUS SOLUTIONS OF IONIC SOLUTES

Solute	Concentration (m)	Δt_f, observed (°C)	Δt_f, nonelectrolyte solution (°C)	$\dfrac{\Delta t_f, \text{ observed}}{\Delta t_f, \text{ nonelectrolyte solution (°C)}}$
KCl	0.1	−0.345	−0.186	1.85
	0.01	−0.0361	−0.0186	1.94
	0.001	−0.00366	−0.00186	1.97
MgSO₄	0.1	−0.225	−0.186	1.21
	0.01	−0.0285	−0.0186	1.53
	0.001	−0.00338	−0.00186	1.82
BaCl₂	0.1	−0.470	−0.186	2.53
	0.01	−0.0503	−0.0186	2.70
	0.001	−0.00530	−0.00186	2.84

FIGURE 2.7

Freezing-Point Depression
The salts applied to icy roads lower the freezing point of water and melt the ice.

Look at the values given for KCl solutions in **Figure 2.6**, on the previous page. The freezing-point depression of a 0.1 *m* KCl solution is only 1.85 times greater than that of a nonelectrolyte solution. However, as the concentration decreases, the freezing-point depression comes closer to the value that is twice that of a nonelectrolyte solution (see **Figure 2.7**).

The differences between the expected and calculated values are caused by the attractive forces that exist between dissociated ions in aqueous solution. The attraction between the hydrated ions in the solution is small compared with those in the crystalline solid. However, forces of attraction do interfere with the movements of the aqueous ions. Only in very dilute solutions is the average distance between the ions large enough and the attraction between ions small enough for the solute ions to move about almost completely freely.

Peter Debye and Erich Hückel introduced a theory in 1923 to account for this attraction between ions in dilute aqueous solutions. According to this theory, the attraction between dissociated ions of ionic solids in dilute aqueous solutions is caused by an ionic atmosphere that surrounds each ion. This means that each ion is, on average, surrounded by more ions of opposite charge than of like charge. A cluster of hydrated ions can act as a single unit rather than as individual ions. Thus, the effective total concentration is less than expected, based on the number of ions known to be present.

Ions of higher charge attract other ions very strongly. They therefore cluster more and have lower effective concentrations than ions with smaller charge. For example, ions formed by $MgSO_4$ have charges of 2^+ and 2^-. Ions formed by KCl have charges of 1^+ and 1^-. Note in **Figure 2.6** that $MgSO_4$ in a solution does not depress the freezing point as much as the same concentration of KCl.

✓ SECTION 2 FORMATIVE ASSESSMENT

▶ Reviewing Main Ideas

1. What colligative properties are displayed by each of the following situations?
   a. Antifreeze is added to a car's cooling system to prevent freezing when the air temperature is below 0°C.
   b. Ice melts on sidewalks after salt has been spread on them.

2. Two moles of a nonelectrolyte solute are dissolved in 1 kg of an unknown solvent. The solution freezes at 7.8°C *below* its normal freezing point. What is the molal freezing-point constant of the unknown solvent? Suggest a possible identity of the solvent.

3. If two solutions of equal amounts in a U-tube are separated by a semipermeable membrane, will the level of the more-concentrated solution or the less-concentrated solution rise?

4. a. Calculate the expected freezing-point depression of a 0.200 *m* KNO_3 solution.
   b. Will the value you calculated match the actual freezing-point depression for this solution? Why or why not?

✓ Critical Thinking

5. **INFERRING RELATIONSHIPS** The freezing-point depressions of aqueous solutions A, B, and C are −2.3°C, −1.2°C, and −4.1°C, respectively. Predict the order of the boiling-point elevations of these solutions, from lowest to highest. Explain your ranking.

The presence of a nonvolatile solute causes the freezing point of a solution to be lower and the boiling point to be higher than those of the pure solvent. The freezing-point depression, Δt_f, is the amount that the freezing point is lowered. It is calculated by using the formula $\Delta t_f = K_f m$. The boiling-point elevation, Δt_b, is the amount that the boiling point is elevated. It is found by using the equation $\Delta t_b = K_b m$. To determine Δt_f or Δt_b, you need to know its *molal* concentration, m (moles of solute per kilogram of solvent). You also need to know the molal freezing-point constant, K_f, or the molal boiling-point constant, K_b. The values for K_f and K_b depend on the solvent and are given in **Figure 2.3.** When these equations are used for electrolytes, the molality represents the total number of moles of ions in solution.

Problem-Solving TIPS

- Make sure that you find the molal concentration, not the molar concentration.
- For electrolytes, calculate the total number of moles of ions in solution.

Sample Problem

What is the theoretical boiling point of a solution of 247 g of potassium chloride, KCl, dissolved in 2.90 kg of water? Potassium chloride is a strong electrolyte.

First, determine the molality of the KCl that dissolved.

$$\text{mass of solute (g)} \times \frac{1 \text{ mol solute}}{\text{molar mass of solute (g)}} = \text{amount of solute (mol)}$$

$$247 \text{ g KCl} \times \frac{1 \text{ mol KCl}}{74.55 \text{ g KCl}} = 3.31 \text{ mol KCl}$$

$$\text{molality KCl}(m) = \frac{\text{mol solute particles}}{\text{mass of solvent (kg)}} = \frac{3.31 \text{ mol KCl}}{2.90 \text{ kg H}_2\text{O}} = 1.14 \text{ } m \text{ KCl}$$

Because KCl is an electrolyte, the total moles of ions in solution must now be determined. The equation $KCl(s) \longrightarrow K^+(aq) + Cl^-(aq)$ shows that 1 mol KCl will yield 2 mol of ions.

To find the total molality of particles in solution, multiply the molality of the solute by the moles of ions produced by the dissociation: $2 \times 1.14 \text{ } m \text{ KCl} = 2.28 \text{ } m$.

Next, use the equation $\Delta t_b = K_b m$, where K_b for water is $0.51°C/m$ and the value for m is 2.28.

$$\Delta t_b = (0.51°C/m)(2.28 \text{ } m) = 1.16°C$$

The new boiling point is equal to the sum of the boiling point of the solvent and Δt_b.

$$\text{boiling point of solution} = 100°C + 1.16°C = 101.16°C$$

Practice

1. What is the freezing point of a solution containing 28.0 g of the strong electrolyte calcium chloride, $CaCl_2$, dissolved in 295 g of water?

2. What is the boiling point of a solution composed of 850 g of ethylene glycol, $C_2H_6O_2$, mixed with 1100 g of water?

BIG IDEA Ionic compounds dissociate in aqueous solutions. Colligative properties of a solution depend only on the number of solute particles present.

SECTION 1 Compounds in Aqueous Solutions

KEY TERMS

- The separation of ions that occurs when an ionic solid dissolves is called dissociation.

- When two different ionic solutions are mixed, a precipitate may form if ions from the two solutions react to form an insoluble compound.

- A net ionic equation for a reaction in aqueous solution includes only compounds and ions that change chemically in the reaction. Spectator ions are ions that do not take part in such a reaction.

- Formation of ions from molecular compounds is called ionization. Acids are molecular compounds that form ions in aqueous solutions. In an acid, a polar covalently bonded H atom is ionized in aqueous solutions.

- An H_3O^+ ion is called a hydronium ion.

- All, or almost all, of a dissolved strong electrolyte exists as ions in an aqueous solution, whereas a relatively small amount of a dissolved weak electrolyte exists as ions in an aqueous solution.

dissociation
net ionic equation
spectator ions
ionization
hydronium ion
strong electrolyte
weak electrolyte

SECTION 2 Colligative Properties of Solutions

KEY TERMS

- Colligative properties of solutions depend only on the total number of solute particles present. Boiling-point elevation, freezing-point depression, vapor-pressure lowering, and osmotic pressure are colligative properties.

- The molal boiling-point and freezing-point constants are used to calculate boiling-point elevations and freezing-point depressions of solvents containing nonvolatile solutes.

- Electrolytes have a greater effect on the freezing and boiling points of solvents than nonelectrolytes do.

- Except in very dilute solutions, the values of colligative properties of electrolyte solutions are less than expected because of the attraction between ions in solution.

colligative properties
nonvolatile substance
molal freezing-point constant, K_f
freezing-point depression, Δt_f
molal boiling-point constant, K_b
boiling-point elevation, Δt_b
semipermeable membrane
osmosis
osmotic pressure

CHAPTER 13 **Review**

GO ONLINE

Interactive Review
HMHScience.com

Review Games
Concept Maps

SECTION 1

Compounds in Aqueous Solutions

 REVIEWING MAIN IDEAS

1. How many moles of ions are contained in 1 L of a 1 M solution of KCl? of $Mg(NO_3)_2$?

2. Use **Figure 1.3** to predict whether each of the following compounds is considered soluble or insoluble:
   a. KCl
   b. $NaNO_3$
   c. AgCl
   d. $BaSO_4$
   e. $Ca_3(PO_4)_2$
   f. $Pb(ClO_3)_2$
   g. $(NH_4)_2S$
   h. $PbCl_2$ (in cold water)
   i. FeS
   j. $Al_2(SO_4)_3$

3. What is a net ionic equation?

4. a. What is ionization?
   b. Distinguish between ionization and dissociation.

5. a. Define and distinguish between strong electrolytes and weak electrolytes.
   b. Give two examples of each type.

6. What determines the strength of a solute as an electrolyte?

7. Distinguish between the use of the terms *strong* and *weak* and the use of the terms *dilute* and *concentrated* when describing electrolyte solutions.

PRACTICE PROBLEMS

8. Write the equation for the dissolution of each of the following ionic compounds in water. (Hint: See Sample Problem A.)
   a. KI   c. $MgCl_2$
   b. $NaNO_3$ d. Na_2SO_4

9. For the compounds listed in the previous problem, determine the number of moles of each ion produced as well as the total number of moles of ions produced when 1 mol of each compound dissolves in water.

10. Write the equation for the dissolution of each of the following in water, and then indicate the total number of moles of solute ions formed.
    a. 0.50 mol strontium nitrate
    b. 0.50 mol sodium phosphate

11. Using **Figure 1.3**, write the balanced chemical equation, write the overall ionic equation, identify the spectator ions and possible precipitates, and write the net ionic equation for each of the following reactions. (Hint: See Sample Problem B.)
    a. mercury(II) chloride (aq) + potassium sulfide $(aq) \longrightarrow$
    b. sodium carbonate (aq) + calcium chloride $(aq) \longrightarrow$
    c. copper(II) chloride (aq) + ammonium phosphate $(aq) \longrightarrow$

12. Identify the spectator ions in the reaction between KCl and $AgNO_3$ in an aqueous solution.

13. Copper(II) chloride and lead(II) nitrate react in aqueous solutions by double displacement. Write the balanced chemical equation, the overall ionic equation, and the net ionic equation for this reaction. If 13.45 g of copper(II) chloride react, what is the maximum amount of precipitate that could be formed?

SECTION 2

Colligative Properties of Solutions

 REVIEWING MAIN IDEAS

14. How does the presence of a nonvolatile solute affect each of the following properties of the solvent in which the solute is dissolved?
    a. vapor pressure
    b. freezing point
    c. boiling point
    d. osmotic pressure

15. Using **Figure 2.1** as a guide, make a graph of vapor pressure versus temperature that shows the comparison of pure water, a solution with x concentration of solute, and a solution with $2x$ concentration of solute. What is the relationship between Δt_f for the x solution and Δt_f for the $2x$ solution?

16. a. Why does the level of the more-concentrated solution rise when two solutions of different concentrations are separated by a semipermeable membrane?

b. When does the level of the solution stop rising?

c. When the level stops rising, is there movement of water molecules across the membrane?

17. a. Compare the effects of nonvolatile electrolytes with the effects of nonvolatile nonelectrolytes on the freezing and boiling points of solvents in which they are dissolved.

b. Why are such differences observed?

18. Why does the actual freezing-point depression of an electrolytic solution differ from the freezing-point depression calculated on the basis of the concentration of particles?

PRACTICE PROBLEMS

19. Determine the freezing-point depression of H_2O in each of the following solutions. (Hint: See Sample Problem C.)

a. 1.50 m solution of $C_{12}H_{22}O_{11}$ (sucrose) in H_2O

b. 171 g of $C_{12}H_{22}O_{11}$ in 1.00 kg H_2O

c. 77.0 g of $C_{12}H_{22}O_{11}$ in 400. g H_2O

20. Given the following freezing-point depressions, determine the molality of each solution of an unknown nonelectrolyte in water. (Hint: See Sample Problem D.)

a. −0.930°C

b. −3.72°C

c. −8.37°C

21. A solution contains 20.0 g of $C_6H_{12}O_6$ (glucose) in 250. g of water.

a. What is the freezing-point depression of the solvent?

b. What is the freezing point of the solution?

22. How many grams of antifreeze, $C_2H_4(OH)_2$, would be required per 500. g of water to prevent the water from freezing at a temperature of −20.0°C?

23. Pure benzene, C_6H_6, freezes at 5.45°C. A solution containing 7.24 g $C_2Cl_4H_2$ in 115 g of benzene (specific gravity = 0.879) freezes at 3.55°C. Based on these data, what is the molal freezing-point constant for benzene?

24. If 1.500 g of a solute that has a molar mass of 125.0 g were dissolved in 35.00 g of camphor, what would be the resulting freezing point of the solution?

25. Determine the boiling-point elevation of H_2O in each of the following solutions. (Hint: See Sample Problem E.)

a. 2.5 m solution of $C_6H_{12}O_6$ (glucose) in H_2O

b. 3.20 g $C_6H_{12}O_6$ in 1.00 kg H_2O

c. 20.0 g $C_{12}H_{22}O_{11}$ (sucrose) in 500. g H_2O

26. Given the following boiling points, determine the molality of each water solution.

a. 100.25°C

b. 101.53°C

c. 102.805°C

27. Given 1.00 m aqueous solutions of each of the following electrolytic substances, determine the expected change in the freezing point of the solvent. (Hint: See Sample Problem F.)

a. KI

b. $CaCl_2$

c. $Ba(NO_3)_2$

28. What is the expected change in the freezing point of water for a 0.015 m aqueous solution of $AlCl_3$?

29. What is the expected freezing point of a solution containing 85.0 g NaCl dissolved in 450. g of water?

30. Determine the expected boiling point of a solution made by dissolving 25.0 g of barium chloride in 0.150 kg of water.

31. The change in the boiling point of water for an aqueous solution of potassium iodide is 0.65°C. Determine the molal concentration of potassium iodide.

32. The freezing point of an aqueous solution of barium nitrate is −2.65°C. Determine the molal concentration of barium nitrate.

33. Calculate the expected freezing point of a solution containing 1.00 kg H_2O and 0.250 mol NaCl.

34. Experimental data for a 1.00 m MgI_2 aqueous solution indicate an actual change in the freezing point of water of −4.78°C. Find the expected change in the freezing point of water. Suggest a possible reason for the discrepancy between the experimental and expected values.

Mixed Review

▶ REVIEWING MAIN IDEAS

35. Given 0.01 m aqueous solutions of each of the following, arrange the solutions in order of increasing change in the freezing point of the solution.
  a. NaI
  b. $CaCl_2$
  c. K_3PO_4
  d. $C_6H_{12}O_6$ (glucose)

36. What is the molal concentration of an aqueous calcium chloride solution that freezes at −2.43°C?

37. a. Write the balanced formula equation that shows the possible products of a double-displacement reaction between calcium nitrate and sodium chloride.
  b. Using **Figure 1.3,** determine whether there is a precipitate.
  c. Does this reaction occur?

38. Write a balanced equation to show what occurs when hydrogen bromide dissolves and reacts with water. Include a hydronium ion in the equation.

39. Write the equation for the dissolution of each of the following in water, and then indicate the total number of moles of solute ions formed.
  a. 0.275 mol of potassium sulfide
  b. 0.15 mol of aluminum sulfate

40. Calculate the expected change in the boiling point of water in a solution made up of 131.2 g of silver nitrate, $AgNO_3$, in 2.00 kg of water.

41. Nitrous acid, HNO_2, is a weak electrolyte. Nitric acid, HNO_3, is a strong electrolyte. Write equations to represent the ionization of each in water. Include the hydronium ion, and show the appropriate kind of arrow in each equation.

42. Find the boiling point of an aqueous solution containing a nonelectrolyte that freezes at −6.51°C.

43. Write a balanced equation for the dissolution of sodium carbonate, Na_2CO_3, in water. Find the number of moles of each ion produced when 0.20 mol of sodium carbonate dissolves. Then, find the total number of moles of ions.

44. Given the reaction below and the information in **Figure 1.3,** write the net ionic equation for the reaction.

potassium phosphate (aq) + lead(II) nitrate (aq)

45. Find the expected freezing point of a water solution that contains 268 g of aluminum nitrate, $Al(NO_3)_3$, in 8.50 kg of water.

CRITICAL THINKING

46. Applying Models
  a. You are conducting a freezing-point determination in the laboratory by using an aqueous solution of KNO_3. The observed freezing point of the solution is −1.15°C. Using a pure water sample, you recorded the freezing point of the pure solvent on the same thermometer as 0.25°C. Determine the molal concentration of KNO_3. Assume that there are no forces of attraction between ions.
  b. You are not satisfied with the result in part (a) because you suspect that you should not ignore the effect of ion interaction. You take a 10.00 mL sample of the solution. After carefully evaporating the water from the solution, you obtain 0.415 g KNO_3. Determine the actual molal concentration of KNO_3 and the percentage difference between the concentration observed in the freezing-point determination and the actual concentration of KNO_3. Assume that the solution's density is 1.00 g/mL.

47. Analyzing Information The observed freezing-point depression for electrolyte solutions is sometimes not as much as the calculated value. Why does this occur? Is the difference greater for concentrated solutions or dilute solutions?

48. Analyzing Information The osmotic pressure of a dilute solution can be calculated as follows:

$\pi = MRT$
π = osmotic pressure
M = concentration in moles per liter
R = ideal gas constant
T = absolute temperature of the solution

How does the osmotic-pressure equation compare with the ideal gas law?

49. Common reactions for Group 13 elements are found in the *Elements Handbook* (Appendix A). Review this material, and answer the following:

a. Write net ionic equations for each of the example reactions listed under "Common Reactions" for Group 13.

b. Which reactions did not change when written in net ionic form? Why?

50. Common reactions for Group 14 elements are found in the *Elements Handbook* (Appendix A). Review this material, and answer the following:

a. Write net ionic equations for each of the example reactions listed under "Common Reactions" for Group 14.

b. Which reactions did not change when written in net ionic form? Why?

RESEARCH AND WRITING

51. Find out how much salt a large northern city, such as New York City or Chicago, uses on its streets in a typical winter. What environmental problems result from this use of salt? What substitutes for salt are being used to melt ice and snow?

52. Research the role of electrolytes and electrolytic solutions in your body. Find out how electrolytes work in the functioning of nerves and muscles. What are some of the health problems that can arise from an imbalance of electrolytes in body fluids?

ALTERNATIVE ASSESSMENT

53. Performance Determine the freezing point of four different mixtures of water and ethylene glycol (use commercial antifreeze). What mixture has the lowest freezing point?

54. Performance Find the optimum mixture of salt and ice for reducing the temperature of the chilling bath for an ice-cream freezer. Use your data to write a set of instructions on how to prepare the chilling bath for making ice cream.

55. Performance Using a low-voltage dry cell, assemble a conductivity apparatus. Secure several unknown aqueous solutions of equal molality from your instructor, and use the apparatus to distinguish the electrolytes from the nonelectrolytes. Among those identified as electrolytes, rank their relative strengths as conductors from good to poor.

56. Performance Using equal volumes of the unknown solutions from the preceding activity, explain how you could use the freezing-point depression concept to distinguish the electrolytes from the nonelectrolytes. Explain how you could determine the number of ions contained per molecule among the solutes identified as electrolytes. Design and conduct an experiment to test your theories.

Standards-Based Assessment

Record your answers on a separate piece of paper.

MULTIPLE CHOICE

1 Identify which of the following substances would be soluble in water in all cases.

  A lead(II) iodide

  B sodium nitrate

  C silver carbonate

  D barium sulfate

2 Identify the reaction in which a precipitate occurs.

  A $NaOH + HCl \rightarrow$

  B $NaNO_3 + KI \rightarrow$

  C $MgBr_2 + AgNO_3 \rightarrow$

  D None of the above form precipitates.

3 Identify the precipitate in the following reaction:

$Ca(OH)_2(aq) + FeCl_3(aq) \rightarrow$

  A $Ca(OH)_2$

  B $FeCl_3$

  C $Fe(OH)_3$

  D $CaCl_2$

4 Which of the following must not be split up when writing net ionic equations?

  A molecular substances, liquids, and solids

  B solids, liquids, and ionic substances

  C ionic substances, soluble substances, and gases

  D soluble substances, molecular substances, and solids

5 Which of the following is not incorporated into a net ionic equation?

  A solids

  B liquids

  C spectator ions

  D precipitates

6 Which of the following statements accurately describes precipitates and precipitation reactions?

  A *Dissolve* means the same thing as *dissociate*.

  B *Ionize* means the same thing as *dissociate*.

  C A substance can dissolve without dissociating.

  D Electrolytes form whenever solids are added to water.

7 Which of the following is the best representation of the precipitation reaction that occurs when aqueous solutions of sodium carbonate and calcium chloride are mixed?

  A $Na^+(aq) + Cl^-(aq) \rightarrow 2NaCl(s)$

  B $Ca^{2+}(aq) + CO_3^{2-}(aq) \rightarrow CaCO_3(s)$

  C $2Na^+(aq) + CO_3^{2-}(aq) + Ca^{2+}(aq) + 2Cl^-(aq)$
$\rightarrow CaCO_3(s) + 2NaCl(s)$

  D No precipitation reaction occurs.

GRIDDED RESPONSE

8 An aqueous solution of an unknown quantity of a nonelectrolyte solute is found to have a freezing point of $-0.58°C$. What is the molar concentration of the solution?

Test Tip

Before choosing an answer to a question, try to answer the question without looking at the answer choices on the test.

CHAPTER 14
Acids and Bases

BIG IDEA
Acids are substances that donate hydrogen ions in aqueous solutions. Bases are substances that accept hydrogen ions in aqueous solutions.

 ONLINE Chemistry
HMHScience.com

SECTION 1
Properties of Acids and Bases

SECTION 2
Acid-Base Theories

SECTION 3
Acid-Base Reactions

ONLINE LABS
- Is It an Acid or a Base?
- Effects of Acid Rain on Plants
- I've Got a Secret

GO ONLINE

 Why It Matters Video
HMHScience.com

Acids and Bases

Properties of Acids and Bases

Key Terms

binary acid
oxyacid

Arrhenius acid
Arrhenius base

strong acid
weak acid

SECTION 1

Main Ideas

▶ Acids are identified by their properties.

▶ Some acids are useful in industry.

▶ The properties of bases differ from those of acids.

▶ Arrhenius acids and bases produce ions in solution.

How many foods can you think of that are sour? Chances are that almost all the foods you thought of, like those in **Figure 1.1a,** owe their sour taste to an acid. Sour milk contains *lactic acid*. Vinegar, which can be produced by fermenting juices, contains *acetic acid*. *Phosphoric acid* gives a tart flavor to many carbonated beverages. Most fruits contain some kind of acid. Lemons, oranges, grapefruits, and other citrus fruits contain *citric acid*. Apples contain *malic acid*, and grape juice contains *tartaric acid*.

Many substances known as bases are commonly found in household products, such as those in **Figure 1.1b.** Household ammonia is an ammonia-water solution that is useful for all types of general cleaning. Sodium hydroxide, NaOH, known by the common name *lye*, is present in some commercial cleaners. Milk of magnesia is a suspension in water of magnesium hydroxide, $Mg(OH)_2$, which is not very water-soluble. It is used as an antacid to relieve discomfort caused by excess hydrochloric acid in the stomach. Aluminum hydroxide, $Al(OH)_3$, and sodium hydrogen carbonate, $NaHCO_3$, are also bases commonly found in antacids.

FIGURE 1.1

Common Acids and Bases

Benzoic acid, $HC_7H_5O_2$
Sorbic acid, $HC_6H_7O_2$
Phosphoric acid, H_3PO_4
Carbonic acid, H_2CO_3

Citric acid, $H_3C_6H_5O_7$
Ascorbic acid, $H_2C_6H_6O_6$

(a) Fruits and fruit juices contain acids such as citric acid and ascorbic acid. Carbonated beverages contain benzoic acid, phosphoric acid, and carbonic acid.

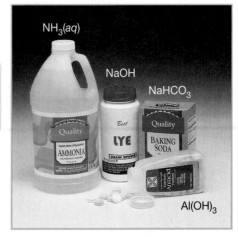

$NH_3(aq)$

NaOH

$NaHCO_3$

$Al(OH)_3$

(b) Many household cleaners contain bases such as ammonia and sodium hydroxide. Antacids contain bases such as aluminum hydroxide.

FIGURE 1.2

Acid Indicator A strip of pH paper dipped into vinegar turns red, showing that vinegar is an acid.

▶ **MAIN IDEA**

Acids are identified by their properties.

Acids were first recognized as a distinct class of compounds because of the common properties of their aqueous solutions. These properties are listed below.

1. *Aqueous solutions of acids have a sour taste.* Taste, however, should NEVER be used as a test to evaluate any chemical substance. Many acids, especially in concentrated solutions, are corrosive; that is, they destroy body tissue and clothing. Many are also poisons.

2. *Acids change the color of acid-base indicators.* When pH paper is used as an indicator, the paper turns certain colors in acidic solution. This reaction is demonstrated in **Figure 1.2**.

3. *Some acids react with active metals and release hydrogen gas, H_2.* Recall that metals can be ordered in terms of an activity series. Metals above hydrogen in the series undergo single-displacement reactions with certain acids. Hydrogen gas is formed as a product, as shown by the reaction of barium with sulfuric acid.

$$Ba(s) + H_2SO_4(aq) \longrightarrow BaSO_4(s) + H_2(g)$$

4. *Acids react with bases to produce salts and water.* When chemically equivalent amounts of acids and bases react, the three properties just described disappear because the acid is "neutralized." The reaction products are water and an ionic compound called a *salt*.

5. *Acids conduct electric current.* Some acids completely separate into ions in water and are strong electrolytes. Other acids are weak electrolytes.

Acid Nomenclature

A **binary acid** is an acid that contains only two different elements: hydrogen and one of the more electronegative elements. Many common inorganic acids are binary acids. The hydrogen halides—HF, HCl, HBr, and HI—are all binary acids. Names for some binary acids are given in **Figure 1.3.**

FIGURE 1.3

NAMES OF BINARY ACIDS		
Formula	Acid name	Molecule name
HF	hydrofluoric acid	hydrogen fluoride
HCl	hydrochloric acid	hydrogen chloride
HBr	hydrobromic acid	hydrogen bromide
HI	hydriodic acid	hydrogen iodide
H_2S	hydrosulfuric acid	hydrogen sulfide

In pure form, each compound listed in the table is a gas. Aqueous solutions of these compounds are known by the acid names. Specific rules for naming binary compounds are listed below.

Binary Acid Nomenclature

1. The name of a binary acid begins with the prefix *hydro-*.

2. The root of the name of the second element follows this prefix.

3. The name then ends with the suffix *-ic.*

An **oxyacid** is an acid that is a compound of hydrogen, oxygen, and a third element, usually a nonmetal. Nitric acid, HNO_3, is an oxyacid. The structures of two other oxyacids are shown in **Figure 1.4.** Oxyacids are one class of ternary acids, which are acids that contain three different elements. Usually, the elements in an oxyacid formula are written as one or more hydrogen atoms followed by a polyatomic anion. But as you can see from the structures, the H atoms are bonded to O atoms. The names of oxyacids follow a pattern, and the names of their anions are based on the names of the acids. Some common oxyacids and their anions are given in **Figure 1.5.** Many of these names should be familiar to you.

FIGURE 1.4

Oxyacid Structure Although the chemical formula shows hydrogen atoms and a polyatomic ion, notice that the hydrogens are bonded to the oxygen in an oxyacid.

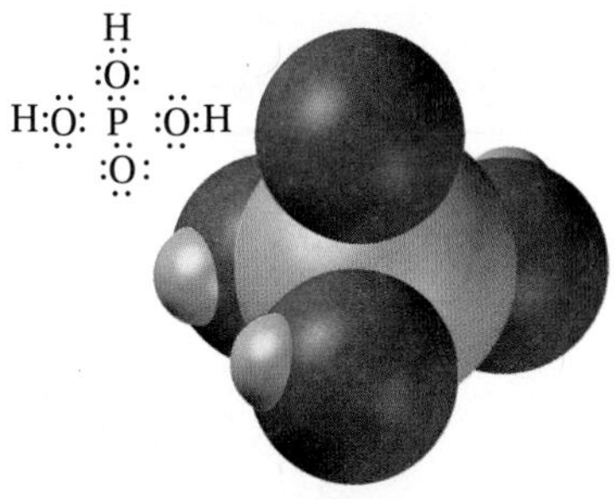

(a) Structure of H_3PO_4

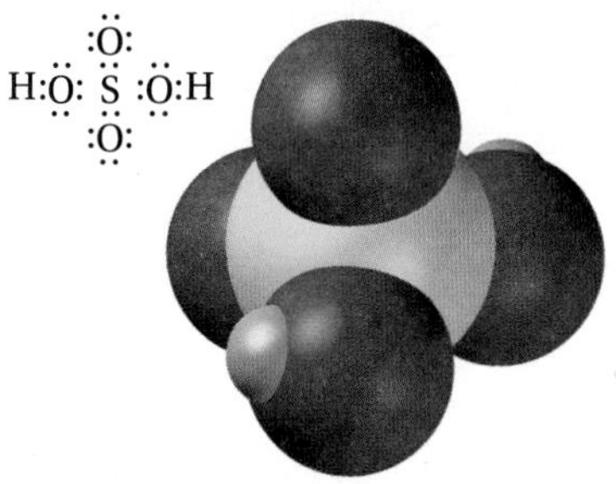

(b) Structure of H_2SO_4

FIGURE 1.5

NAMES OF COMMON OXYACIDS AND OXYANIONS

Formula	Acid name	Anion
CH_3COOH	acetic acid	CH_3COO^-, acetate
H_2CO_3	carbonic acid	CO_3^{2-}, carbonate
$HClO$	hypochlorous acid	ClO^-, hypochlorite
$HClO_2$	chlorous acid	ClO_2^-, chlorite
$HClO_3$	chloric acid	ClO_3^-, chlorate
$HClO_4$	perchloric acid	ClO_4^-, perchlorate
HIO_3	iodic acid	IO_3^-, iodate
HNO_2	nitrous acid	NO_2^-, nitrite
HNO_3	nitric acid	NO_3^-, nitrate
H_3PO_3	phosphorous acid	PO_3^{3-}, phosphite
H_3PO_4	phosphoric acid	PO_4^{3-}, phosphate
H_2SO_3	sulfurous acid	SO_3^{2-}, sulfite
H_2SO_4	sulfuric acid	SO_4^{2-}, sulfate

MAIN IDEA

Some acids are useful in industry.

The properties of acids make them important chemicals both in the laboratory and in industry. Sulfuric acid, nitric acid, phosphoric acid, hydrochloric acid, and acetic acid are all common industrial acids.

Sulfuric Acid

Sulfuric acid is the most commonly produced industrial chemical in the world. More than 37 million metric tons of it are made each year in the United States alone. Sulfuric acid is used in large quantities in petroleum refining and metallurgy as well as in the manufacture of fertilizer. It is also essential to a vast number of industrial processes, including the production of metals, paper, paint, dyes, detergents, and many chemical raw materials. Sulfuric acid is the acid used in automobile batteries.

Because it attracts water, concentrated sulfuric acid is an effective dehydrating (water-removing) agent. It can be used to remove water from gases with which it does not react. Sugar and certain other organic compounds are also dehydrated by sulfuric acid. Skin contains organic compounds that are attacked by concentrated sulfuric acid, which can cause serious burns.

Nitric Acid

Pure nitric acid is a volatile, unstable liquid. Dissolving the acid in water makes the acid more stable. Solutions of nitric acid are widely used in industry. Nitric acid also stains proteins yellow. The feather in **Figure 1.6** was stained by nitric acid. The acid has a suffocating odor, stains skin, and can cause serious burns. It is used in making explosives, many of which are nitrogen-containing compounds. It is also used to make rubber, plastics, dyes, and pharmaceuticals. Initially, nitric acid solutions are colorless; however, upon standing, they gradually become yellow because of slight decomposition to brown nitrogen dioxide gas.

FIGURE 1.6

Nitric Acid and Proteins
Concentrated nitric acid stains a feather yellow.

Phosphoric Acid

Phosphorus, along with nitrogen and potassium, is an essential element for plants and animals. The bulk of phosphoric acid produced each year is used directly for manufacturing fertilizers and animal feed. Dilute phosphoric acid has a pleasant but sour taste and is not toxic. It is used as a flavoring agent in beverages and as a cleaning agent for dairy equipment. Phosphoric acid is also important in the manufacture of detergents and ceramics.

Hydrochloric Acid

The stomach produces HCl to aid in digestion. Industrially, hydrochloric acid is important for "pickling" iron and steel. Pickling is the immersion of metals in acid solutions to remove surface impurities. This acid is also used in industry as a general cleaning agent, in food processing, in the activation of oil wells, in the recovery of magnesium from sea water, and in the production of other chemicals.

Concentrated solutions of hydrochloric acid, commonly referred to as *muriatic acid*, can be found in hardware stores. It is used to maintain the correct acidity in swimming pools and to clean masonry.

Acetic Acid

Pure acetic acid is a clear, colorless, and pungent-smelling liquid known as *glacial acetic acid*. This name is derived from the fact that pure acetic acid has a freezing point of 17°C. It can form crystals in a cold room. The fermentation of certain plants produces vinegars containing acetic acid. White vinegar contains 4% to 8% acetic acid.

Acetic acid is important industrially in synthesizing chemicals used in the manufacture of plastics. It is a raw material in the production of food supplements—for example, lysine, an essential amino acid. Acetic acid is also used as a fungicide.

▶ MAIN IDEA

The properties of bases differ from those of acids.

How do bases differ from acids? You can answer this question by comparing the following properties of bases with those of acids.

1. *Aqueous solutions of bases taste bitter*. You may have noticed this fact if you have ever gotten soap, a basic substance, in your mouth. Taste should NEVER be used to test a substance to see if it is a base, because many bases are caustic; they attack the skin, causing severe burns.

2. *Bases change the color of acid-base indicators*. As **Figure 1.7** shows, an acid-base indicator changes to a different color in a basic solution than in an acidic solution.

3. *Dilute aqueous solutions of bases feel slippery*. You encounter this property of aqueous bases whenever you wash with soap.

FIGURE 1.7

Base Indicator pH paper turns blue in the presence of this solution of sodium hydroxide.

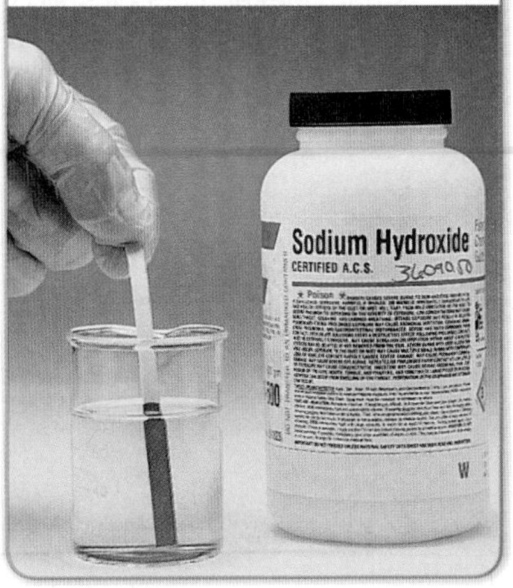

4. *Bases react with acids to produce salts and water.* It could also be said that "neutralization" of the base occurs when these two substances react to produce a salt and water.

5. *Bases conduct electric current.* Like acids, bases form ions in aqueous solutions and are thus electrolytes.

Unlike acids, there are no special rules for naming basic compounds. The names of bases follow the conventions for chemical compounds outlined in the chapter "Chemical Formulas and Chemical Compounds."

---

*Quick*LAB HOUSEHOLD ACIDS AND BASES

QUESTION
Which of the household substances are acids, and which are bases?

PROCEDURE
Record all your results in a data table.

1. To make an acid-base indicator, extract juice from red cabbage. First, cut up some red cabbage and place it in a large beaker. Add enough water so that the beaker is half full. Then, bring the mixture to a boil. Let it cool, and then pour off and save the cabbage juice. This solution is an acid-base indicator.

2. Assemble foods, beverages, and cleaning products to be tested.

3. If the substance being tested is a liquid, pour about 5 mL into a small beaker. If it is a solid, place a small amount into a beaker and moisten it with about 5 mL of water.

4. Add a drop or two of the red cabbage juice to the solution being tested, and note the color. The solution will turn red if it is acidic and green if it is basic.

DISCUSSION

1. Are the cleaning products acids, bases, or neither?

2. What are acid/base characteristics of foods and beverages?

3. Did you find consumer warning labels on basic or acidic products?

MATERIALS
- dishwashing liquid, dishwasher detergent, laundry detergent, laundry stain remover, fabric softener, and bleach
- mayonnaise, baking powder, baking soda, white vinegar, cider vinegar, lemon juice, soft drinks, mineral water, and milk
- fresh red cabbage
- hot plate
- beaker, 500 mL or larger
- beakers, 50 mL
- spatula
- tap water
- tongs

SAFETY
  Wear safety goggles, gloves, and an apron.

Red cabbage can be used to make an acid-base indicator by extracting its anthocyanin pigment.

▶ MAIN IDEA

Arrhenius acids and bases produce ions in solution.

Svante Arrhenius, a Swedish chemist who lived from 1859 to 1927, understood that aqueous solutions of acids and bases conducted electric current. Arrhenius therefore theorized that acids and bases must produce ions in solution. **An Arrhenius acid is a chemical compound that increases the concentration of hydrogen ions, H^+, in aqueous solution.** In other words, an acid will ionize in solution, increasing the number of hydrogen ions present. **An Arrhenius base is a substance that increases the concentration of hydroxide ions, OH^-, in aqueous solution.** Some bases are ionic hydroxides. These bases dissociate in solution to release hydroxide ions into the solution. Other bases are substances that react with water to remove a hydrogen ion, leaving hydroxide ions in the solution.

Aqueous Solutions of Acids

The acids described by Arrhenius are molecular compounds with ionizable hydrogen atoms. Their water solutions are known as *aqueous acids*. All aqueous acids are electrolytes.

Because acid molecules are sufficiently polar, water molecules attract one or more of their hydrogen ions. Negatively charged anions are left behind. As explained in a previous chapter, the hydrogen ion in aqueous solution is typically represented as H_3O^+, the hydronium ion. The ionization of an HNO_3 molecule is shown by the following equation. **Figure 1.8** also shows how the hydronium ion forms when nitric acid reacts with water.

$$HNO_3(l) + H_2O(l) \longrightarrow H_3O^+(aq) + NO_3^-(aq)$$

Similarly, ionization of a hydrogen chloride molecule in hydrochloric acid can be represented in the following way.

$$HCl(g) + H_2O(l) \longrightarrow H_3O^+(aq) + Cl^-(aq)$$

FIGURE 1.8

Arrhenius Acids Arrhenius's observations form the basis of a definition of acids. Arrhenius acids, such as the nitric acid shown here, produce hydronium ions in aqueous solution.

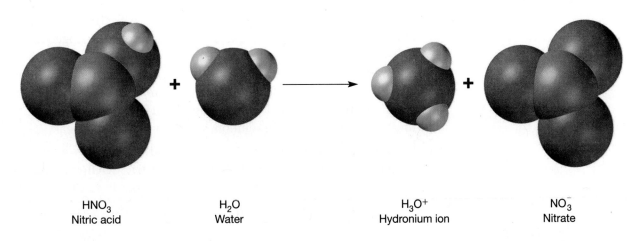

HNO_3	H_2O	H_3O^+	NO_3^-
Nitric acid	Water	Hydronium ion	Nitrate

FIGURE 1.9

COMMON AQUEOUS ACIDS

Strong acids	Weak acids
$HI + H_2O \longrightarrow H_3O^+ + I^-$	$HSO_4^- + H_2O \rightleftharpoons H_3O^+ + SO_4^{2-}$
$HClO_4 + H_2O \longrightarrow H_3O^+ + ClO_4^-$	$H_3PO_4 + H_2O \rightleftharpoons H_3O^+ + H_2PO_4^-$
$HBr + H_2O \longrightarrow H_3O^+ + Br^-$	$HF + H_2O \rightleftharpoons H_3O^+ + F^-$
$HCl + H_2O \longrightarrow H_3O^+ + Cl^-$	$CH_3COOH + H_2O \rightleftharpoons H_3O^+ + CH_3COO^-$
$H_2SO_4 + H_2O \longrightarrow H_3O^+ + HSO_4^-$	$H_2CO_3 + H_2O \rightleftharpoons H_3O^+ + HCO_3^-$
$HClO_3 + H_2O \longrightarrow H_3O^+ + ClO_3^-$	$H_2S + H_2O \rightleftharpoons H_3O^+ + HS^-$
	$HCN + H_2O \rightleftharpoons H_3O^+ + CN^-$
	$HCO_3^- + H_2O \rightleftharpoons H_3O^+ + CO_3^{2-}$

Strength of Acids

A **strong acid** is one that ionizes completely in aqueous solution. A strong acid is a strong electrolyte. Perchloric acid, $HClO_4$, hydrochloric acid, HCl, and nitric acid, HNO_3, are examples of strong acids. In water, 100% of the acid molecules are ionized. The strength of an acid depends on the polarity of the bond between hydrogen and the element to which it is bonded and the ease with which that bond can be broken. Acid strength increases with increasing polarity and decreasing bond energy.

An acid that releases few hydrogen ions in aqueous solution is a **weak acid.** The aqueous solution of a weak acid contains hydronium ions, anions, and dissolved acid molecules. Hydrocyanic acid is an example of a weak acid. In aqueous solution, both the ionization of HCN and the reverse reaction occur simultaneously. In a 1 M solution of HCN, there will be only two H^+ ions and two CN^- ions out of 100,000 molecules. The other 99,998 molecules remain as HCN.

$$HCN(aq) + H_2O(l) \rightleftharpoons H_3O^+(aq) + CN^-(aq)$$

Common aqueous acids are listed in **Figure 1.9.** Each strong acid ionizes completely in aqueous solution to give up one hydrogen ion per molecule. Notice that the number of hydrogen atoms in the formula does not indicate acid strength. Molecules with multiple hydrogen atoms may not readily give them up. The fact that phosphoric acid has three hydrogen atoms per molecule does not mean that it is a strong acid. None of these ionize completely in solution, so phosphoric acid is weak.

Organic acids, which contain the acidic carboxyl group —COOH, are generally weak acids. For example, acetic acid, CH_3COOH, ionizes slightly in water to give hydronium ions and acetate ions, CH_3COO^-.

$$CH_3COOH(aq) + H_2O(l) \rightleftharpoons H_3O^+(aq) + CH_3COO^-(aq)$$

A molecule of acetic acid contains four hydrogen atoms. However, only one of the hydrogen atoms is ionizable. The hydrogen atom in the carboxyl group in acetic acid is the one that is "acidic" and forms the hydronium ion. This acidic hydrogen can be seen in the structural diagram in **Figure 1.10.**

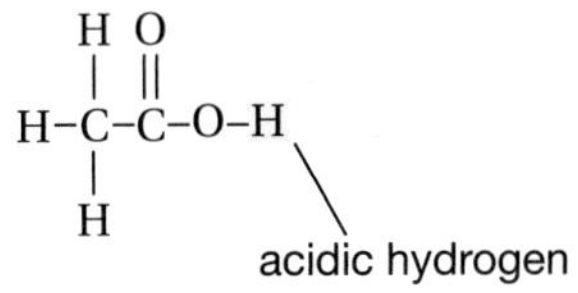

Aqueous Solutions of Bases

Most bases are ionic compounds containing metal cations and the hydroxide anion, OH^-. Because these bases are ionic, they dissociate when dissolved in water. When a base completely dissociates in water to yield aqueous OH^- ions, the solution is considered a strong base. Sodium hydroxide, NaOH, is a common laboratory base. It is water-soluble and dissociates as shown by the equation below.

$$NaOH(s) \xrightarrow{H_2O} Na^+(aq) + OH^-(aq)$$

As you will remember from learning about the periodic table, Group 1 elements are the alkali metals. This group gets its name from the fact that the hydroxides of Li, Na, K, Rb, and Cs all form alkaline (basic) solutions.

Not all bases are ionic compounds. A base commonly used in household cleaners is ammonia, NH_3, which is molecular. Ammonia is a base because it produces hydroxide ions when it reacts with water molecules, as shown in the equation below.

$$NH_3(aq) + H_2O(l) \rightleftharpoons NH_4^+(aq) + OH^-(aq)$$

Strength of Bases

As with acids, the strength of a base also depends on the extent to which the base dissociates, or adds hydroxide ions to the solution. For example, potassium hydroxide, KOH, is a strong base because it completely dissociates into its ions in dilute aqueous solutions.

$$KOH(s) \xrightarrow{H_2O} K^+(aq) + OH^-(aq)$$

Strong bases are strong electrolytes, just as strong acids are strong electrolytes. **Figure 1.11** lists some strong bases.

FIGURE 1.10

Acetic Acid Acetic acid contains four hydrogen atoms, but only one of them is "acidic" and forms the hydronium ion in solution.

✔ **CHECK FOR UNDERSTANDING**
Differentiate What is the difference between the strength and the concentration of an acid or base?

FIGURE 1.11

COMMON AQUEOUS BASES

Strong bases	Weak bases
$Ca(OH)_2 \longrightarrow Ca^{2+} + 2OH^-$	$NH_3 + H_2O \rightleftharpoons NH_4^+ + OH^-$
$Sr(OH)_2 \longrightarrow Sr^{2+} + 2OH^-$	$C_6H_5NH_2 + H_2O \rightleftharpoons C_6H_5NH_3^+ + OH^-$
$Ba(OH)_2 \longrightarrow Ba^{2+} + 2OH^-$	
$NaOH \longrightarrow Na^+ + OH^-$	
$KOH \longrightarrow K^+ + OH^-$	
$RbOH \longrightarrow Rb^+ + OH^-$	
$CsOH \longrightarrow Cs^+ + OH^-$	

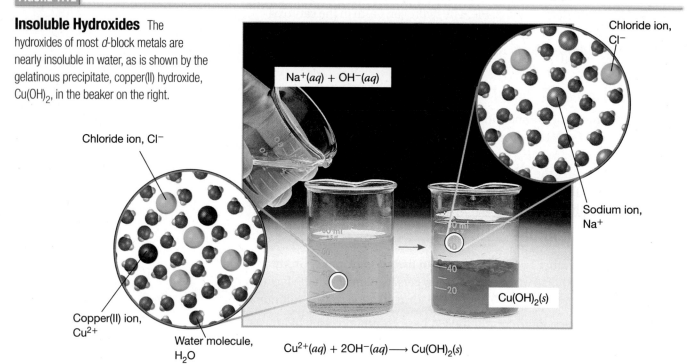

FIGURE 1.12

Insoluble Hydroxides The hydroxides of most *d*-block metals are nearly insoluble in water, as is shown by the gelatinous precipitate, copper(II) hydroxide, $Cu(OH)_2$, in the beaker on the right.

Chloride ion, Cl^-

Copper(II) ion, Cu^{2+}

Water molecule, H_2O

$Na^+(aq) + OH^-(aq)$

Chloride ion, Cl^-

Sodium ion, Na^+

$Cu(OH)_2(s)$

$$Cu^{2+}(aq) + 2OH^-(aq) \longrightarrow Cu(OH)_2(s)$$

Bases that are not very soluble do not produce a large number of hydroxide ions when added to water. Some metal hydroxides, such as $Cu(OH)_2$, are not very soluble in water, as seen in **Figure 1.12**. They cannot produce concentrated alkaline solutions. The alkalinity of aqueous solutions depends on the concentration of OH^- ions in solution. It is unrelated to the number of hydroxide ions in the undissolved compound.

Now consider ammonia, which is highly soluble but is a weak electrolyte. The concentration of OH^- ions in an ammonia solution is relatively low. Ammonia is therefore a *weak base*. Many organic compounds that contain nitrogen atoms are also weak bases. For example, codeine, $C_{18}H_{21}NO_3$, a pain reliever and common cough suppressant found in prescription cough medicine, is a weak base.

✔ SECTION 1 FORMATIVE ASSESSMENT

▶ Reviewing Main Ideas

1. a. What are five general properties of aqueous acids?

   b. Name some common substances that have one or more of these properties.

2. Name the following acids.
   a. HBrO   **b.** $HBrO_3$

3. Write the chemical formulas for the following common bases.
   a. lithium hydroxide
   b. sodium hydroxide

4. a. What are five general properties of aqueous bases?

   b. Name some common substances that have one or more of these properties.

5. a. Why are strong acids also strong electrolytes?

   b. Is every strong electrolyte also a strong acid?

✔ Critical Thinking

6. RELATING IDEAS A classmate states, "All compounds containing H atoms are acids, and all compounds containing OH groups are bases." Do you agree? Give examples.

Acid Water—A Hidden Menace

Many people are unaware of the pH of the tap water in their home until they are confronted with such phenomena as a blue ring materializing around a porcelain sink drain, a water heater suddenly giving out, or tropical fish that keep dying. Each of these events could be due to acidic water. Acidic water can also cause the amount of lead in the water to rise.

The possibility of lead poisoning from home water supplies is a concern. Many older homes still have lead pipes in their plumbing, though most modern homes use copper piping. Copper pipe joints, however, are often sealed with lead-containing solder. Highly acidic water can leach out both the lead from the solder joints and copper from the pipes themselves, which turns the sink drain blue. In addition, people who are in the habit of filling their tea kettles and coffee pots in the morning without letting the tap run awhile first could be adding copper and lead ions to their tea or coffee.

Lead poisoning is of particular concern in young children. The absorption rate of lead in the intestinal tract of a child is much higher than in that of an adult, and lead poisoning can permanently impair a child's rapidly growing nervous system. The good news is that lead poisoning and other effects of acidic water in the home can be easily prevented by following these tips:

1. Monitor the pH of your water on a regular basis, especially if you have well water. This can easily be done with pH test kits (see photograph) that are sold in hardware or pet stores—many tropical fish are intolerant of water with a pH that is either too high (basic) or too low (acidic). The pH of municipal water supplies is already regulated, but regularly checking your water's pH yourself is a good idea.

2. In the morning, let your water tap run for about half a minute before you fill your kettle or drink the water. If the water is acidic, the first flush of water will have the highest concentration of lead and copper ions.

3. Install an alkali-injection pump, a low-cost, low-maintenance solution that can save your plumbing and lessen the risk of lead poisoning from your own water supply. The pump injects a small amount of an alkali (usually potassium carbonate or sodium carbonate) into your water-pressure tank each time your well's pump starts. This effectively neutralizes the acidity of your water.

Question

Suppose that you have tested the drinking water in your home and found it to be too acidic. Design a solution to correct this problem. In your solution, explain the steps you will take to make the water less acidic and what evidence you will collect to show that your solution has worked.

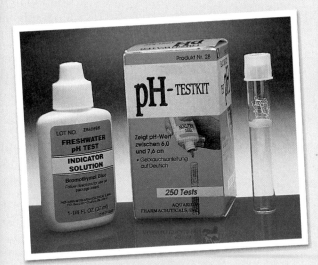

The pH of your home's water supply can be easily monitored using a test kit, such as the one shown here.

Main Ideas

▶ Brønsted-Lowry acids and bases donate or accept protons.

▶ A Lewis acid or base accepts or donates a pair of electrons.

Acid-Base Theories

Key Terms

Brønsted-Lowry acid
Brønsted-Lowry base
Brønsted-Lowry acid-base reaction
monoprotic acid

polyprotic acid
diprotic acid
triprotic acid
Lewis acid

Lewis base
Lewis acid-base reaction

For most uses, scientists found the Arrhenius definition of acids and bases to be adequate. However, as scientists further investigated acid-base behavior, they found that some substances acted as acids or bases when they were not in a water solution. Because the Arrhenius definition requires that the substances be aqueous, the definitions of acids and bases had to be revised.

▶ **MAIN IDEA**

Brønsted-Lowry acids and bases donate or accept protons.

In 1923, the Danish chemist J. N. Brønsted and the English chemist T. M. Lowry independently expanded the Arrhenius acid definition. A **Brønsted-Lowry acid** is a molecule or ion that is a proton donor. Because H^+ is a proton, all acids as defined by Arrhenius donate protons to water and are Brønsted-Lowry acids as well. Substances other than molecules, such as certain ions, can also donate protons. Such substances are not Arrhenius acids but are included in the category of Brønsted-Lowry acids.

Hydrogen chloride acts as a Brønsted-Lowry acid when it reacts with ammonia. The HCl transfers protons to NH_3 much as it does in water.

$$HCl + NH_3 \longrightarrow NH_4^+ + Cl^-$$

A proton is transferred from the hydrogen chloride molecule, HCl, to the ammonia molecule, NH_3. The ammonium ion, NH_4^+, is formed. Electron-dot formulas show the similarity of this reaction to the reaction of HCl with water.

$$H{:}\ddot{\underset{\cdot\cdot}{C}}l{:} + H{:}\ddot{\underset{\cdot\cdot}{O}}{:} \longrightarrow \left[H{:}\ddot{\underset{\underset{\displaystyle H}{}}{O}}{:}H \right]^+ + {:}\ddot{\underset{\cdot\cdot}{C}}l{:}^-$$

$$H{:}\ddot{\underset{\cdot\cdot}{C}}l{:} + H{:}\ddot{\underset{\underset{\displaystyle H}{}}{N}}{:}H \longrightarrow \left[H{:}\overset{\displaystyle H}{\underset{\underset{\displaystyle H}{}}{N}}{:}H \right]^+ + {:}\ddot{\underset{\cdot\cdot}{C}}l{:}^-$$

In both reactions, hydrogen chloride is a Brønsted-Lowry acid.

FIGURE 2.1

Brønsted-Lowry Acid-Base
Reactions Hydrogen chloride gas escapes from a hydrochloric acid solution and combines with ammonia gas that has escaped from an aqueous ammonia solution. The resulting cloud is solid ammonium chloride that is dispersed in air.

Water can also act as a Brønsted-Lowry acid. Consider, for example, the following reaction, in which the water molecule donates a proton to the ammonia molecule.

$$H_2O(l) + NH_3(aq) \rightleftharpoons NH_4^+(aq) + OH^-(aq)$$

$$H\!:\!\ddot{O}\!:\; + \; H\!:\!\ddot{N}\!:\!H \rightleftharpoons \left[H\!:\!\overset{H}{\underset{H}{\ddot{N}}}\!:\!H \right]^+ + \left[:\!\ddot{\underset{H}{O}}\!: \right]^-$$

A **Brønsted-Lowry base** is a molecule or ion that is a proton acceptor. In the reaction between hydrochloric acid and ammonia, ammonia accepts a proton from the hydrochloric acid. It is a Brønsted-Lowry base. The Arrhenius hydroxide bases, such as NaOH, are not, strictly speaking, Brønsted-Lowry bases. Instead, it is the OH^- ion produced in solution that is the Brønsted-Lowry base. It is the species that can accept a proton.

In a **Brønsted-Lowry acid-base reaction,** protons are transferred from one reactant (the acid) to another (the base). **Figure 2.1** shows the reaction between the Brønsted-Lowry acid HCl and the Brønsted-Lowry base NH_3.

Monoprotic and Polyprotic Acids

An acid that can donate only one proton (hydrogen ion) per molecule is known as a **monoprotic acid.** Perchloric acid, $HClO_4$, hydrochloric acid, HCl, and nitric acid, HNO_3, are all monoprotic. The following equation shows how a molecule of the monoprotic acid HCl donates a proton to a water molecule. The HCl ionizes to form H_3O^+ ions and Cl^- ions. The Cl^- has no hydrogens to lose, so HCl has only one ionization step.

$$HCl(g) + H_2O(l) \longrightarrow H_3O^+(aq) + Cl^-(aq)$$

A **polyprotic acid** is an acid that can donate more than one proton per molecule. Sulfuric acid, H_2SO_4, and phosphoric acid, H_3PO_4, are examples of polyprotic acids. The ionization of a polyprotic acid occurs in stages. The acid loses its hydrogen ions one at a time. Sulfuric acid ionizes in two stages. In its first ionization, sulfuric acid is a strong acid. It is completely converted to hydrogen sulfate ions, HSO_4^-.

$$H_2SO_4(l) + H_2O(l) \longrightarrow H_3O^+(aq) + HSO_4^-(aq)$$

The hydrogen sulfate ion is itself a weak acid. It establishes the following equilibrium in solution.

$$HSO_4^-(aq) + H_2O(l) \rightleftharpoons H_3O^+(aq) + SO_4^{2-}(aq)$$

All stages of ionization of a polyprotic acid occur in the same solution. Sulfuric acid solutions therefore contain H_3O^+, HSO_4^-, and SO_4^{2-} ions. Note that in sulfuric acid solutions, there are many more hydrogen sulfate and hydronium ions than there are sulfate ions.

Sulfuric acid is the type of polyprotic acid that can donate two protons per molecule, and it is therefore known as a **diprotic acid.** Ionizations of a monoprotic acid and a diprotic acid are shown in **Figure 2.2**.

FIGURE 2.2

Monoprotic and Diprotic Acids Hydrochloric acid, HCl, is a strong monoprotic acid. A dilute HCl solution contains hydronium ions and chloride ions. Sulfuric acid, H_2SO_4, is a strong diprotic acid. A dilute H_2SO_4 solution contains hydrogen sulfate ions from the first ionization, sulfate ions from the second ionization, and hydronium ions from both ionizations.

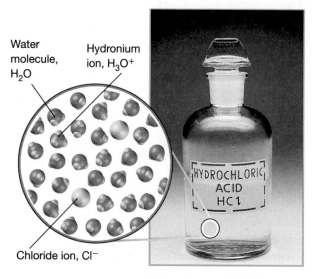
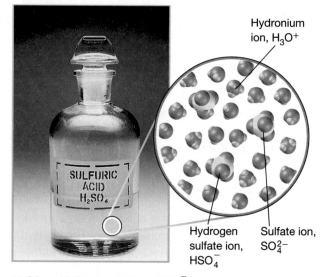

Water molecule, H_2O
Hydronium ion, H_3O^+
Chloride ion, Cl^-

Hydronium ion, H_3O^+
Hydrogen sulfate ion, HSO_4^-
Sulfate ion, SO_4^{2-}

$$HCl + H_2O \longrightarrow H_3O^+ + Cl^-$$

$$H_2SO_4 + H_2O \longrightarrow H_3O^+ + HSO_4^-$$
$$HSO_4^- + H_2O \rightleftharpoons H_3O^+ + SO_4^{2-}$$

✔ **CRITICAL THINKING**

Explain Using the Brønsted-Lowry definition, is it possible to have an acid without an accompanying base?

Phosphoric acid is the type of polyprotic acid known as a **triprotic acid**—an acid able to donate three protons per molecule. The equations for these reactions are shown below.

$$H_3PO_4(aq) + H_2O(l) \rightleftharpoons H_3O^+(aq) + H_2PO_4^-(aq)$$

$$H_2PO_4^-(aq) + H_2O(l) \rightleftharpoons H_3O^+(aq) + HPO_4^{2-}(aq)$$

$$HPO_4^{2-}(aq) + H_2O(l) \rightleftharpoons H_3O^+(aq) + PO_4^{3-}(aq)$$

A solution of phosphoric acid contains H_3O^+, H_3PO_4, $H_2PO_4^-$, HPO_4^{2-}, and PO_4^{3-}. As with most polyprotic acids, the concentration of ions formed in the first ionization is the greatest. There are lesser concentrations of the respective ions from each succeeding ionization. Phosphoric acid is a weak acid in each step of its ionization.

▶ MAIN IDEA

A Lewis acid or base accepts or donates a pair of electrons.

The Arrhenius and Brønsted-Lowry definitions describe most acids and bases. Both definitions assume that the acid contains or produces hydrogen ions. A third acid classification, based on bonding and structure, includes, as acids, substances that do not contain hydrogen at all. This definition of acids was introduced in 1923 by G. N. Lewis, the American chemist whose name was given to electron-dot structures. Lewis's definition emphasizes the role of electron pairs in acid-base reactions. A **Lewis acid** is an atom, ion, or molecule that accepts an electron pair to form a covalent bond.

The Lewis definition is the broadest of the three acid definitions you have read about so far. It applies to any species that can accept an electron pair to form a covalent bond with another species. A bare proton (hydrogen ion) is a Lewis acid in reactions in which it forms a covalent bond, as shown below.

$$H^+(aq) + :NH_3(aq) \longrightarrow [H{-}NH_3]^+(aq) \text{ or } [NH_4]^+(aq)$$

The formula for a Lewis acid need not include hydrogen. Even a silver ion can be a Lewis acid, accepting electron pairs from ammonia to form covalent bonds.

$$Ag^+(aq) + 2:NH_3(aq) \longrightarrow [H_3N{-}Ag{-}NH_3]^+(aq) \text{ or } [Ag(NH_3)_2]^+$$

A compound in which the central atom has three valence electrons and forms three covalent bonds can react as a Lewis acid. It does so by accepting a pair of electrons to form a fourth covalent bond, completing an electron octet. Boron trifluoride, for example, is an excellent Lewis acid. It forms a fourth covalent bond with many molecules and ions. Its reaction with a fluoride ion is shown below.

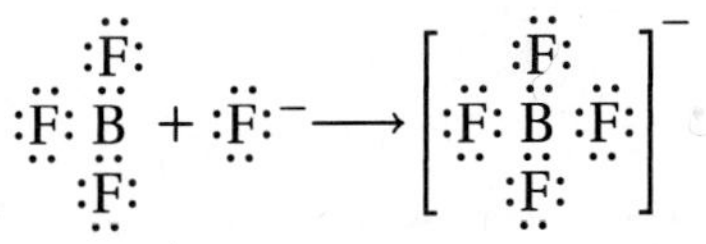

$$BF_3(aq) + F^-(aq) \longrightarrow BF_4^-(aq)$$

FIGURE 2.3

ACID-BASE DEFINITIONS

Type	Acid	Base
Arrhenius	H^+ or H_3O^+ producer	OH^- producer
Brønsted-Lowry	proton (H^+) donor	proton (H^+) acceptor
Lewis	electron-pair acceptor	electron-pair donor

The Lewis definition of acids can apply to species in any phase. For example, boron trifluoride is a Lewis acid in the gas-phase combination with ammonia.

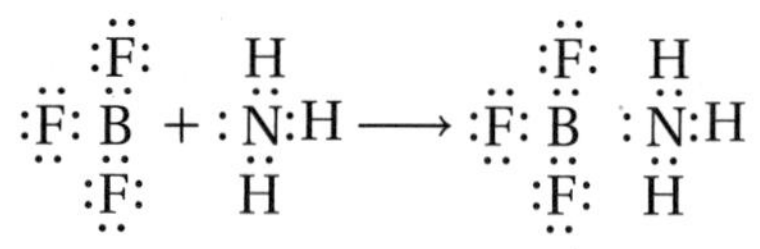

$$\overset{\displaystyle :\!\overset{..}{F}\!:}{\underset{\displaystyle :\!\overset{..}{F}\!:}{:\!\overset{..}{F}\!:\!B}} + \overset{\displaystyle H}{\underset{\displaystyle H}{:N\!:H}} \longrightarrow \overset{\displaystyle :\!\overset{..}{F}\!:}{\underset{\displaystyle :\!\overset{..}{F}\!:}{:\!\overset{..}{F}\!:\!B}} \quad \overset{\displaystyle H}{\underset{\displaystyle H}{:N\!:H}}$$

A **Lewis base** is an atom, ion, or molecule that donates an electron pair to form a covalent bond. An anion is a Lewis base in a reaction in which it forms a covalent bond by donating an electron pair. In the example of boron trifluoride reacting with the fluoride anion, F^- donates an electron pair to boron trifluoride. F^- acts as a Lewis base.

$$BF_3(aq) + :\overset{..}{F}\!:^- (aq) \longrightarrow BF_4^-(aq)$$

A **Lewis acid-base reaction** is the formation of one or more covalent bonds between an electron-pair donor and an electron-pair acceptor.

Note that although the three acid-base definitions differ, many compounds may be categorized as acids or bases according to all three descriptions. For example, ammonia is an Arrhenius base because OH^- ions are created when ammonia is in solution, it is a Brønsted-Lowry base because it accepts a proton in an acid-base reaction, and it is a Lewis base in all reactions in which it donates its lone pair to form a covalent bond. A comparison of the three acid-base definitions is given in **Figure 2.3.**

SECTION 2 FORMATIVE ASSESSMENT

▶ Reviewing Main Ideas

1. Label each reactant in the reaction below as a proton donor or a proton acceptor and as acidic or basic.

$$H_2CO_3 + H_2O \rightleftharpoons HCO_3^- + H_3O^+$$

2. For the reaction below, label each reactant as an electron-pair acceptor or electron-pair donor and as a Lewis acid or a Lewis base.

$$AlCl_3 + Cl^- \longrightarrow AlCl_4^-$$

✔ Critical Thinking

3. **ANALYZING INFORMATION** For the following three reactions, identify the reactants that are Arrhenius bases, Brønsted-Lowry bases, and/or Lewis bases. State which type(s) of bases each reactant is. Explain your answers.

a. $NaOH(s) \longrightarrow Na^+(aq) + OH^-(aq)$

b. $HF(aq) + H_2O(l) \longrightarrow F^-(aq) + H_3O^+(aq)$

c. $H^+(aq) + NH_3(aq) \longrightarrow NH_4^+(aq)$

Acid-Base Reactions

SECTION 3

Main Ideas

▶ Brønsted-Lowry reactions involve conjugate acid-base pairs.

▶ Some substances act as either acids or bases.

▶ Neutralization reactions produce water and a salt.

Key Terms

conjugate base
conjugate acid
amphoteric

neutralization
salt

In the previous sections, you learned about three acid-base theories: Arrhenius, Brønsted-Lowry, and Lewis. The Brønsted-Lowry theory is especially useful for describing acid-base reactions that take place in aqueous solutions. This section will use the Brønsted-Lowry description to explore reactions between acids and bases.

▶ **MAIN IDEA**

Brønsted-Lowry reactions involve conjugate acid-base pairs.

The Brønsted-Lowry definitions of acids and bases provide a basis for studying proton-transfer reactions. Suppose that a Brønsted-Lowry acid gives up a proton; the remaining ion or molecule can re-accept that proton and can act as a base. Such a base is known as a conjugate base. **Thus, the species that remains after a Brønsted-Lowry acid has given up a proton is the conjugate base of that acid.** For example, the fluoride ion is the conjugate base of hydrofluoric acid.

$$HF(aq) + H_2O(l) \rightleftharpoons F^-(aq) + H_3O^+(aq)$$
$$\text{acid} \qquad\qquad\qquad\quad \text{conjugate base}$$

In this reaction, the water molecule is a Brønsted-Lowry base. It accepts a proton from HF to form H_3O^+, which is an acid. The hydronium ion is the conjugate acid of water. **The species that is formed when a Brønsted-Lowry base gains a proton is the conjugate acid of that base.**

$$HF(aq) + H_2O(l) \rightleftharpoons F^-(aq) + H_3O^+(aq)$$
$$\qquad\qquad \text{base} \qquad\qquad\qquad \text{conjugate acid}$$

In general, Brønsted-Lowry acid-base reactions are equilibrium systems, meaning that both the forward and reverse reactions occur. They involve two acid-base pairs, known as conjugate acid-base pairs.

$$HF(aq) + H_2O(l) \rightleftharpoons F^-(aq) + H_3O^+(aq)$$
$$\text{acid}_1 \quad\; \text{base}_2 \qquad \text{base}_1 \qquad \text{acid}_2$$

The subscripts designate the two conjugate acid-base pairs: (1) HF and F^- and (2) H_3O^+ and H_2O. In every conjugate acid-base pair, the acid has one more proton than its conjugate base.

Strength of Conjugate Acids and Bases

The extent of the reaction between a Brønsted-Lowry acid and base depends on the relative strengths of the acids and bases involved. Consider the following example. Hydrochloric acid is a strong acid. It gives up protons readily. Therefore, the Cl^- ion has little tendency to attract and retain a proton. Consequently, the Cl^- ion is an extremely weak base.

$$HCl(g) \quad + \quad H_2O(l) \quad \longrightarrow \quad H_3O^+(aq) \quad + \quad Cl^-(aq)$$

stronger acid   stronger base   weaker acid   weaker base

This observation leads to an important conclusion: *the stronger an acid is, the weaker its conjugate base; the stronger a base is, the weaker its conjugate acid.*

Using Strength to Predict Reactions

This concept allows strengths of different acids and bases to be compared to predict the outcome of a reaction. As an example, consider the reaction of perchloric acid, $HClO_4$, and water.

$$HClO_4(aq) \quad + \quad H_2O(l) \quad \longrightarrow \quad H_3O^+(aq) \quad + \quad ClO_4^-(aq)$$

stronger acid   stronger base   weaker acid   weaker base

The hydronium ion is too weak an acid to compete successfully with perchloric acid in donating a proton; $HClO_4$ is the stronger acid. In this reaction, the perchlorate ion, ClO_4^-, and H_2O are both bases. Because $HClO_4$ is a very strong acid, ClO_4^- is an extremely weak base. Therefore, H_2O competes more strongly than ClO_4^- to acquire a proton. The reaction proceeds such that the stronger acid reacts with the stronger base to produce the weaker acid and base.

Now consider a comparable reaction between water and acetic acid.

$$CH_3COOH(aq) + \quad H_2O(l) \quad \longleftarrow \quad H_3O^+(aq) \quad + CH_3COO^-(aq)$$

weaker acid   weaker base   stronger acid   stronger base

The H_3O^+ ion concentration in this solution is much lower than it was in the $HClO_4$ solution because acetic acid is a weak acid. The CH_3COOH molecule does not compete successfully with the H_3O^+ ion in donating protons to a base. The acetate ion, CH_3COO^-, is a stronger base than H_2O. Therefore, the H_2O molecule does not compete successfully with the CH_3COO^- ion in accepting a proton. The H_3O^+ ion is the stronger acid, and the CH_3COO^- ion is the stronger base. Thus, the reverse reaction (to the left) is more favorable.

Note that in the reactions for both perchloric acid and acetic acid, the favored direction is toward the weaker acid and the weaker base. This observation leads to a second important general conclusion: *proton-transfer reactions favor the production of the weaker acid and the weaker base.* For an acid-base reaction to form products completely, the reactants must be much stronger as acids and bases than the products.

The table in **Figure 3.1** shows that a very strong acid, such as $HClO_4$, has a very weak conjugate base, ClO_4^-. The strongest base listed in the table, the hydride ion, H^-, has the weakest conjugate acid, H_2. In aqueous solutions, all of the strong acids are 100% ionized, forming hydronium ions along with their anion. The acids below hydronium ion in **Figure 3.1** do not ionize 100% in water. Water will react as an acid if a very strong base, such as hydride ion, is present.

FIGURE 3.1

RELATIVE STRENGTHS OF ACIDS AND BASES

Conjugate acid	Formula	Conjugate base	Formula
hydriodic acid*	HI	iodide ion	I^-
perchloric acid*	$HClO_4$	perchlorate ion	ClO_4^-
hydrobromic acid*	HBr	bromide ion	Br^-
hydrochloric acid*	HCl	chloride ion	Cl^-
sulfuric acid*	H_2SO_4	hydrogen sulfate ion	HSO_4^-
chloric acid*	$HClO_3$	chlorate ion	ClO_3^-
nitric acid*	HNO_3	nitrate ion	NO_3^-
hydronium ion	H_3O^+	water	H_2O
chlorous acid	$HClO_2$	chlorite ion	ClO_2^-
hydrogen sulfate ion	HSO_4^-	sulfate ion	SO_4^{2-}
phosphoric acid	H_3PO_4	dihydrogen phosphate ion	$H_2PO_4^-$
hydrofluoric acid	HF	fluoride ion	F^-
acetic acid	CH_3COOH	acetate ion	CH_3COO^-
carbonic acid	H_2CO_3	hydrogen carbonate ion	HCO_3^-
hydrosulfuric acid	H_2S	hydrosulfide ion	HS^-
dihydrogen phosphate ion	$H_2PO_4^-$	monohydrogen phosphate ion	HPO_4^{2-}
hypochlorous acid	HClO	hypochlorite ion	ClO^-
ammonium ion	NH_4^+	ammonia	NH_3
hydrogen carbonate ion	HCO_3^-	carbonate ion	CO_3^{2-}
monohydrogen phosphate ion	HPO_4^{2-}	phosphate ion	PO_4^{3-}
water	H_2O	hydroxide ion	OH^-
ammonia	NH_3	amide ion†	NH_2^-
hydrogen	H_2	hydride ion†	H^-

Increasing acid strength

Increasing base strength

* Strong acids
† Strong bases

FIGURE 3.2

$$CaH_2(s) + 2H_2O(l) \longrightarrow Ca(OH)_2(aq) + 2H_2(g)$$

Water as an Acid Calcium hydride, CaH_2, reacts vigorously with water to produce hydrogen gas. Water acts as an acid in this reaction because the hydride ion is a very strong base.

✔ **CHECK FOR UNDERSTANDING**

Identify Identify the conjugate acid and base in the reaction of calcium hydride with water.

▶ **MAIN IDEA**

Some substances act as either acids or bases.

You have probably noticed that water can be either an acid or a base. **Any species that can react as either an acid or a base is described as amphoteric.** For example, consider the first ionization of sulfuric acid, in which water acts as a base.

$$H_2SO_4(aq) + H_2O(l) \longrightarrow H_3O^+(aq) + HSO_4^-(aq)$$
$$\text{acid}_1 \qquad\quad \text{base}_2 \qquad\quad \text{acid}_2 \qquad\quad \text{base}_1$$

However, water acts as an acid in the following reaction.

$$NH_3(g) + H_2O(l) \rightleftharpoons NH_4^+(aq) + OH^-(aq)$$
$$\text{base}_1 \qquad \text{acid}_2 \qquad\quad \text{acid}_1 \qquad \text{base}_2$$

Likewise, water is acting as an acid in the reaction shown in **Figure 3.2**.

Thus, water can act as either an acid or a base and is amphoteric. Such a substance acts as either an acid or a base depending on the strength of the acid or base with which it is reacting—if it's a stronger acid than the substance, the substance will act as a base. If, however, it's a stronger base than the substance, the substance will act as an acid.

FIGURE 3.3

O—H Bonds and Acid Strength

Each oxyacid of chlorine contains one chlorine atom and one hydrogen atom. They differ in the number of oxygen atoms they contain. The effect of the increasing O—H bond polarity can be seen in the increasing acid strength from hypochlorous acid to perchloric acid.

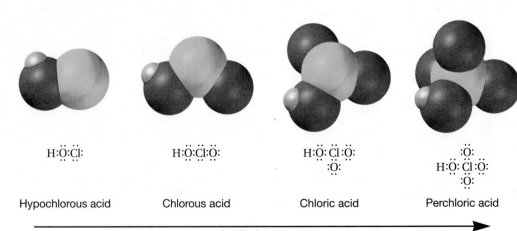

H:Ö:Cl:	H:Ö:Cl:Ö:	H:Ö: Cl:Ö:	:Ö:
Hypochlorous acid	Chlorous acid	Chloric acid	Perchloric acid

Acidity increases →

–OH in a Molecule

Molecular compounds containing –OH groups can be acidic or amphoteric. The covalently bonded –OH group in an acid is referred to as a *hydroxyl group*. For the compound to be acidic, a water molecule must be able to attract a hydrogen atom from a hydroxyl group. This occurs more easily when the O–H bond is very polar. Any feature of a molecule that increases the polarity of the O–H bond increases the acidity of a molecular compound. The small, more-electronegative atoms of nonmetals at the upper right in the periodic table form compounds with acidic hydroxyl groups. All oxyacids are molecular electrolytes that contain one or more of these O–H bonds. Such compounds include chloric and perchloric acids.

Figure 3.3 (on the previous page) shows the electron-dot formulas of the four oxyacids of chlorine. Notice that all of the oxygen atoms are bonded to the chlorine atom. Each hydrogen atom is bonded to an oxygen atom. Aqueous solutions of these molecules are acids because the O–H bonds are broken as the hydrogen is pulled away by water molecules.

The behavior of a compound is affected by the number of oxygen atoms bonded to the atom connected to the –OH group. The larger the number of such oxygen atoms is, the more acidic the compound is. The electronegative oxygen atoms draw electron density away from the O–H bond and make it more polar. For example, chromium forms three different compounds containing –OH groups, as shown below.

basic	*amphoteric*	*acidic*
$Cr(OH)_2$	$Cr(OH)_3$	H_2CrO_4
chromium(II) hydroxide	chromium(III) hydroxide	chromic acid

Notice that as the number of oxygen atoms increases, so does the acidity of the compound.

Consider also the compounds shown in **Figure 3.4.** In acetic acid, but not in ethanol, a second oxygen atom is bonded to the carbon atom connected to the –OH group. That explains why acetic acid is acidic but ethanol is not, even though the same elements form each compound.

▶ **MAIN IDEA**

Neutralization reactions produce water and a salt.

Neutralization reactions commonly occur in nature. One example is when an antacid tablet such as milk of magnesia, $Mg(OH)_2$, neutralizes stomach acid, HCl. The products are $MgCl_2$ and H_2O. Some neutralization reactions produce gases. Sodium bicarbonate, $NaHCO_3$, and tartaric acid, $H_2C_4H_4O_6$, are two components in baking powder. When water is added, the two compounds produce carbon dioxide. The escaping carbon dioxide causes foods, such as biscuits, to rise.

©Jerry Mason/Photo Researchers, Inc

FIGURE 3.4

Polarity and Acids

(a) CH_3COOH
Acetic acid is acidic. The second oxygen atom on the carbon draws electron density away from the –OH group, making the O–H bond more polar.

(b) C_2H_5OH
Ethanol is essentially neutral. It has no second oxygen atom, so the O–H bond is less polar than in acetic acid, and it is a much weaker acid.

GO ONLINE **Animated Chemistry**
HMHScience.com

Neutralization Reactions

Strong Acid-Strong Base Neutralization

An acid-base reaction occurs in aqueous solution between hydrochloric acid, a strong acid that completely ionizes to produce H_3O^+, and sodium hydroxide, a strong base that completely dissociates to produce OH^-. The formula equation for this reaction is written as follows.

$$HCl(aq) + NaOH(aq) \longrightarrow NaCl(aq) + H_2O(l)$$

In an aqueous solution containing 1 mol of sodium hydroxide, NaOH dissociates as represented by the following equation.

$$NaOH(aq) \longrightarrow Na^+(aq) + OH^-(aq)$$

A solution containing 1 mol of hydrochloric acid ionizes as represented by the following equation.

$$HCl(aq) + H_2O(l) \longrightarrow H_3O^+(aq) + Cl^-(aq)$$

If the two solutions are mixed, as in **Figure 3.5,** a reaction occurs between the aqueous H_3O^+ and OH^- ions. Notice that sodium chloride, NaCl, and water are produced. The full ionic equation is shown below.

$$H_3O^+(aq) + Cl^-(aq) + Na^+(aq) + OH^-(aq) \longrightarrow$$
$$Na^+(aq) + Cl^-(aq) + 2H_2O(l)$$

FIGURE 3.5

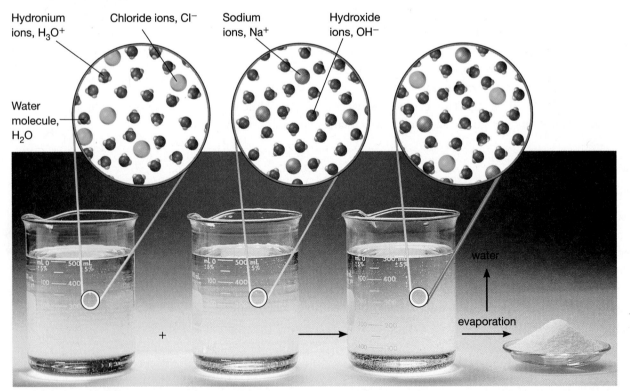

Neutralization When aqueous hydrochloric acid, HCl, reacts with aqueous sodium hydroxide, NaOH, the reaction produces aqueous sodium chloride, NaCl. Ions that are present in each solution are represented by the models.

Hydronium ions, H_3O^+

Chloride ions, Cl^-

Sodium ions, Na^+

Hydroxide ions, OH^-

Water molecule, H_2O

water

evaporation

Because they appear on both sides of the overall ionic equation, Na^+ and Cl^- are spectator ions. The only participants in the reaction are the hydronium ion and the hydroxide ion, as shown in the following net ionic equation.

$$H_3O^+(aq) + OH^-(aq) \longrightarrow 2H_2O(l)$$

There are equal numbers of H_3O^+ and OH^- ions in this reaction, and they are fully converted to water. In aqueous solutions, **neutralization** is the reaction of hydronium ions and hydroxide ions to form water molecules.

A neutralization reaction also produces a salt. **A salt** is an ionic compound composed of a cation from a base and an anion from an acid.

Acid Rain

Many industrial processes produce gases such as NO, NO_2, CO_2, SO_2, and SO_3. These compounds can dissolve in atmospheric water to produce acidic solutions that fall to the ground in the form of rain or snow. For example, sulfur from the burning of oil and coal forms sulfur dioxide, SO_2. The SO_2 is then converted to SO_3, sulfur trioxide, which reacts with water in the atmosphere to produce sulfuric acid, as shown below.

$$SO_3(g) + H_2O(l) \longrightarrow H_2SO_4(aq)$$

Rainwater is normally slightly acidic due to carbon dioxide in the atmosphere, but sometimes rain is very acidic and is called *acid rain*. **Figure 3.6** shows a forest that was damaged by severe acid rain. Acid rain can erode statues and affect ecosystems, such as water environments and forests. In the 1970s, scientists found that acid rain was causing the fish populations in some lakes and streams to decline. When fish are completely eliminated from lakes and streams because of acid rain, the biodiversity of the ecosystem decreases. Because of amendments to the Clean Air Act in 1990, a limit was set on the amount of SO_2 that power plants are permitted to emit. This limit has decreased but not eliminated acid rain in the United States.

FIGURE 3.6

Acid Precipitation Acid precipitation causes extensive environmental damage.

SECTION 3 FORMATIVE ASSESSMENT

▶ **Reviewing Main Ideas**

1. Complete and balance the equations for the following acid-base reactions:
   a. $H_2CO_3 + Sr(OH)_2 \longrightarrow$
   b. $HClO_4 + NaOH \longrightarrow$
   c. $HBr + Ba(OH)_2 \longrightarrow$
   d. $NaHCO_3 + H_2SO_4 \longrightarrow$

2. Consider the equation for acetic acid plus water.

$$CH_3COOH + H_2O \longrightarrow CH_3COO^- + H_3O^+$$

a. Refer to **Figure 3.1** to compare the strengths of the two acids in the equation. Do the same for the two bases.

b. Determine which direction—forward or reverse—is favored in the reaction.

✔ **Critical Thinking**

3. **INFERRING RELATIONSHIPS** Explain how the presence of several oxygen atoms in a compound containing an −OH group can make the compound acidic.

Many chemical reactions that occur in water solutions are reactions involving ions. Soluble ionic compounds dissociate into ions when they dissolve, and some molecular compounds, including acids, ionize when they dissolve. An ionic equation represents the species actually present more accurately than an equation that uses full formulas.

Problem-Solving TIPS

- All soluble ionic compounds are dissociated into ions. Therefore, soluble ionic compounds are shown as the separated ions in the full ionic equation. Strong acids and bases are also shown as the separated ions in the full ionic equation because they are 100% ionized.
- Ions that do not take part in the reaction are called *spectator ions*. In other words, spectator ions stay in solution and will be labeled "(aq)" on both sides of the equation. Eliminating spectator ions reduces the "clutter" of the full ionic equation and produces a net ionic equation that shows only the species that actually react.

Sample Problem

Write the net ionic equation for the reaction of aqueous ammonium sulfate and aqueous barium nitrate to produce a precipitate of barium sulfate. The balanced formula equation is $(NH_4)_2SO_4(aq) + Ba(NO_3)_2(aq) \longrightarrow 2NH_4NO_3(aq) + BaSO_4(s)$

Rewrite the equation in full ionic form; because ammonium sulfate and barium nitrate are soluble, they are written as separated ions:

$$2NH_4^+(aq) + SO_4^{2-}(aq) + Ba^{2+}(aq) + 2NO_3^-(aq) \longrightarrow 2NH_4^+(aq) + 2NO_3^-(aq) + BaSO_4(s)$$

Eliminating spectator ions, NH_4^+ and NO_3^-, yields the net ionic equation:

$$SO_4^{2-}(aq) + Ba^{2+}(aq) \longrightarrow BaSO_4(s)$$

Write full and net ionic equations for the reaction that occurs when hydrochloric acid solution is combined with silver nitrate solution.

Hydrochloric acid is a strong acid, so it is completely ionized in solution. Silver nitrate is a soluble ionic compound, so its ions are separated in solution. Although most chlorides are soluble, silver chloride is not, so silver chloride will precipitate. The balanced formula equation is

$$HCl(aq) + AgNO_3(aq) \longrightarrow AgCl(s) + HNO_3(aq)$$

The full ionic equation is

$$H_3O^+(aq) + Cl^-(aq) + Ag^+(aq) + NO_3^-(aq) \longrightarrow H_3O^+(aq) + NO_3^-(aq) + AgCl(s)$$

Eliminate spectator ions to obtain the net ionic equation:

$$Cl^-(aq) + Ag^+(aq) \longrightarrow AgCl(s)$$

Practice   Answers in Appendix E

1. Aqueous copper(II) sulfate reacts with aqueous sodium sulfide to produce a black precipitate of copper(II) sulfide. Write the formula equation, the full ionic equation, and the net ionic equation for this reaction.
2. Write full and net ionic equations for the reaction that occurs when a solution of cadmium chloride, $CdCl_2$, is mixed with a solution of sodium carbonate, Na_2CO_3. Cadmium carbonate is insoluble.

BIG IDEA Acids are substances that donate hydrogen ions in aqueous solutions. Bases are substances that accept hydrogen ions in aqueous solutions.

SECTION 1 **Properties of Acids and Bases**

KEY TERMS

- Acids have a sour taste and react with active metals. Acids change the colors of acid-base indicators, react with bases to produce salts and water, and conduct electricity in aqueous solutions.

- Bases have a bitter taste, feel slippery to the skin in dilute aqueous solutions, change the colors of acid-base indicators, react with acids to produce salts and water, and conduct electricity in aqueous solution.

- An Arrhenius acid contains hydrogen and ionizes in aqueous solution to form hydrogen ions. An Arrhenius base produces hydroxide ions in aqueous solution.

- The strength of an Arrhenius acid or base is determined by the extent to which the acid or base ionizes or dissociates in aqueous solutions.

binary acid
oxyacid
Arrhenius acid
Arrhenius base
strong acid
weak acid

SECTION 2 **Acid-Base Theories**

KEY TERMS

- A Brønsted-Lowry acid is a proton donor. A Brønsted-Lowry base is a proton acceptor.

- A Lewis acid is an electron-pair acceptor. A Lewis base is an electron-pair donor.

- Acids are described as monoprotic, diprotic, or triprotic depending on whether they can donate one, two, or three protons per molecule, respectively, in aqueous solutions. Polyprotic acids include both diprotic and triprotic acids.

Brønsted-Lowry acid
Brønsted-Lowry base
Brønsted-Lowry acid-base reaction
monoprotic acid
polyprotic acid
diprotic acid
triprotic acid
Lewis acid
Lewis base
Lewis acid-base reaction

SECTION 3 **Acid-Base Reactions**

KEY TERMS

- In every Brønsted-Lowry acid-base reaction, there are two conjugate acid-base pairs.

- A strong acid has a weak conjugate base; a strong base has a weak conjugate acid.

- Proton-transfer reactions favor the production of the weaker acid and weaker base.

- The acidic or basic behavior of a molecule containing −OH groups depends on the electronegativity of other atoms in the molecule and on the number of oxygen atoms bonded to the atom that is connected to the −OH group.

- A neutralization reaction produces water and an ionic compound called a salt.

- Acid rain can create severe ecological problems.

conjugate base
conjugate acid
amphoteric
neutralization
salt

CHAPTER 14 Review

GO ONLINE

Interactive Review
HMHScience.com

Review Games
Concept Maps

SECTION 1
Properties of Acids and Bases

▶ REVIEWING MAIN IDEAS

1. Compare the general properties of acids with the general properties of bases.

2. **a.** Distinguish between binary acids and oxyacids in terms of their component elements and the systems used in naming them.
   b. Give three examples of each type of acid.

3. Identify and describe the characteristic properties of five common acids used in industry. Give some examples of the typical uses of each.

4. Although HCl(*aq*) exhibits properties of an Arrhenius acid, pure HCl gas and HCl dissolved in a nonpolar solvent exhibit none of the properties of an Arrhenius acid. Explain why.

5. **a.** What distinguishes strong acids from weak acids?
   b. Give two examples each of strong acids and weak acids.

6. H_3PO_4, which contains three hydrogen atoms per molecule, is a weak acid, whereas HCl, which contains only one hydrogen atom per molecule, is a strong acid. Explain why.

7. **a.** What compounds are strong Arrhenius bases?
   b. Give an example of an aqueous solution of a strong base and one of a weak base.

PRACTICE PROBLEMS

8. Name each of the following binary acids:
   a. HCl   **b.** H_2S

9. Name each of the following oxyacids:
   a. HNO_3 **c.** $HClO_3$
   b. H_2SO_3 **d.** HNO_2

10. Write formulas for the following binary acids and common bases:
    a. hydrofluoric acid   **c.** sodium bicarbonate
    b. hydriodic acid   **d.** aluminum hydroxide

11. Write formulas for the following oxyacids:
    a. perbromic acid
    b. chlorous acid
    c. phosphoric acid
    d. hypochlorous acid

SECTION 2
Acid-Base Theories

▶ REVIEWING MAIN IDEAS

12. Distinguish between a monoprotic, a diprotic, and a triprotic acid. Give an example of each.

13. Which of the three acid definitions is the broadest? Explain.

PRACTICE PROBLEMS

14. **a.** Write the balanced equations that describe the two-step ionization of sulfuric acid in a dilute aqueous solution.
    b. How do the degrees of ionization in the two steps compare?

15. Dilute HCl(*aq*) and KOH(*aq*) are mixed in chemically equivalent quantities. Write the following:
    a. formula equation for the reaction
    b. full ionic equation
    c. net ionic equation

16. Repeat item 15, but mix H_3PO_4(*aq*) and NaOH(*aq*).

17. Write the formula equation and net ionic equation for each of the following reactions:
    a. $Zn(s) + HCl(aq) \longrightarrow$
    b. $Al(s) + H_2SO_4(aq) \longrightarrow$

18. Write the formula equation and net ionic equation for the reaction between Ca(*s*) and HCl(*aq*).

SECTION 3
Acid-Base Reactions

▶ REVIEWING MAIN IDEAS

19. Define and give an equation to illustrate each of the following substances:
    a. a conjugate base
    b. a conjugate acid

20. a. What is the relationship between the strength of an acid and the strength of its conjugate base?

b. What is the relationship between the strength of a base and the strength of its conjugate acid?

21. a. What trend is there in the favored direction of proton-transfer reactions?

b. What determines the extent to which a proton-transfer reaction occurs?

22. a. What is meant by the term *amphoteric*?

b. Give an example of a substance or ion that has amphoteric characteristics.

23. For each reaction listed, identify the proton donor or acid and the proton acceptor or base. Label each conjugate acid-base pair.

a. $CH_3COOH(aq) + H_2O(l) \rightleftharpoons$
$$H_3O+(aq) + CH_3COO^-(aq)$$

b. $HCO_3^-(aq) + H_2O(l) \rightleftharpoons$
$$H_2CO_3(aq) + OH^-(aq)$$

c. $HNO_3 + SO_4^{2-} \longrightarrow HSO_4^- + NO_3^-$

24. Using the information given in **Figure 3.1**, determine the following relative to HF, H_2S, HNO_3, and CH_3COOH:

a. strongest acid

b. weakest acid

c. strongest conjugate base among the four conjugate bases produced by the acids listed

d. weakest conjugate base among the four conjugate bases produced by the acids listed

25. Explain why the conjugate base of a strong acid is a weak base and the conjugate acid of a strong base is a weak acid.

PRACTICE PROBLEMS

26. Complete the following neutralization reactions. Balance each reaction, and then write the overall ionic and net ionic equation for each.

a. $HCl(aq) + NaOH(aq) \longrightarrow$

b. $HNO_3(aq) + KOH(aq) \longrightarrow$

c. $Ca(OH)_2(aq) + HNO_3(aq) \longrightarrow$

d. $Mg(OH)_2(aq) + HCl(aq) \longrightarrow$

27. Write the formula equation, the overall ionic equation, and the net ionic equation for the neutralization reaction involving aqueous solutions of H_3PO_4 and $Mg(OH)_2$. Assume that the solutions are sufficiently dilute so that no precipitates form.

28. Write the balanced chemical equation for each of the following reactions between water and the non-metallic oxide to form an acid.

a. $CO_2(g) + H_2O(l) \longrightarrow$

b. $SO_3(g) + H_2O(l) \longrightarrow$

c. $N_2O_5(g) + H_2O(l) \longrightarrow$

29. Write the formula equation, the overall ionic equation, and the net ionic equation for a neutralization reaction that would form each of the following salts.

a. $RbClO_4$ **c.** $CaCl_2$

b. $BaSO_4$ **d.** K_2SO_4

30. Zinc reacts with 100.0 mL of 6.00 M cold, aqueous sulfuric acid through single replacement.

a. How many grams of zinc sulfate can be produced?

b. How many liters of hydrogen gas could be released at STP?

31. A 211 g sample of barium carbonate, $BaCO_3$, reacts with a solution of nitric acid to give barium nitrate, carbon dioxide, and water. If the acid is present in excess, what mass and volume of dry carbon dioxide gas at STP will be produced?

32. A seashell that is composed largely of calcium carbonate reacts with a solution of HCl. As a result, 1500 mL of dry CO_2 gas at STP is produced. The other products are $CaCl_2$ and H_2O.

a. How many grams of $CaCO_3$ are consumed in the reaction?

b. What volume of 2.00 M HCl solution is used in this reaction?

33. *Acid precipitation* is the term generally used to describe rain or snow that is more acidic than it normally is. One cause of acid precipitation is the formation of sulfuric and nitric acids from various sulfur and nitrogen oxides produced in volcanic eruptions, forest fires, and thunderstorms. In a typical volcanic eruption, for example, 3.50×10^8 kg SO_2 may be produced. If this amount of SO_2 were converted to H_2SO_4 according to the two-step process given below, how many kilograms of H_2SO_4 would be produced from such an eruption?

$$SO_2 + \frac{1}{2}O_2 \longrightarrow SO_3$$
$$SO_3 + H_2O \longrightarrow H_2SO_4$$

Mixed Review

▶ **REVIEWING MAIN IDEAS**

34. Suppose that dilute $HNO_3(aq)$ and $LiOH(aq)$ are mixed in chemically equivalent quantities. Write the following for the resulting reaction:
 a. formula equation
 b. overall ionic equation
 c. net ionic equation

35. Write the balanced chemical equation for the reaction between hydrochloric acid and magnesium metal.

36. Write equations for the three-step ionization of phosphoric acid, H_3PO_4. Compare the degree of ionization for the three steps.

37. Name or give the molecular formula for each of the following acids:
 a. HF
 b. acetic acid
 c. phosphorous acid
 d. $HClO_4$
 e. H_3PO_4
 f. hydrobromic acid
 g. HClO
 h. H_2CO_3
 i. sulfuric acid

CRITICAL THINKING

38. Analyzing Conclusions In the 18th century, Antoine Lavoisier experimented with oxides, such as CO_2 and SO_2. He observed that they formed acidic solutions. His observations led him to infer that to exhibit acidic behavior, a substance must contain oxygen. However, today that inference is known to be incorrect. Provide evidence to refute Lavoisier's conclusion.

USING THE HANDBOOK

39. Group 16 of the *Elements Handbook* (Appendix A) contains a section covering the acid-base chemistry of oxides. Review this material, and answer the following questions:
 a. What types of compounds form acidic oxides?
 b. What is an acid anhydride?
 c. What are three examples of compounds that are classified as acid anhydrides?
 d. What types of compounds form basic oxides? Why are they basic oxides?

40. a. Look at Table 7A in the *Elements Handbook* (Appendix A). What periodic trends regarding the acid-base character of oxides do you notice?
 b. How is the nature of the product affected by the concentrations of the reactants?

RESEARCH AND WRITING

41. Explain how sulfuric acid production serves as a measure of a country's economy. Write a report on your findings.

42. Performance Conduct library research to find out about the buffering of solutions. Include information on why solutions are buffered and what kinds of materials are used as buffers. Write a brief report on your findings.

43. Research how to determine whether the soil around your house is acidic or basic using pH paper obtained from your teacher. Write a brief description of what you should do. Then follow the directions, and test the soil. Find one type of plant that would grow well in the type of soil around your home and one that would not grow well.

ALTERNATIVE ASSESSMENT

44. Antacids are designed to neutralize excess hydrochloric acid secreted by the stomach during digestion. Carbonates, bicarbonates, and hydroxides are the active ingredients in the most widely used antacids. These ingredients act to drive the neutralization reactions. Examine the labels of several common antacids, and identify the active ingredients.

45. Design an experiment that compares three brands of antacids in terms of the speed of symptom relief and amount of acid neutralized.

Standards-Based Assessment

Record your answers on a separate piece of paper.

MULTIPLE CHOICE

1 Which is the correct name for the base $CuOH_2$?

  A copper hydroxide

  B copper(II) hydroxide

  C copper(I) hydroxide

  D copper hydroxide(I)

2 Which of the following formula-name pairs below is written correctly?

  A $Na(OH)_1$ = sodium hydroxide

  B NH_4OH = ammonium hydroxide

  C $Sr(OH)_2$ = strontium(II) hydroxide

  D $Cu(OH)_2$ = copper(I) hydroxide

3 The following table shows some common bases.

Hydroxides
sodium hydroxide
potassium hydroxide
ammonium hydroxide
lithium hydroxide

How is the hydroxide part of a chemical formula for the bases in the table expressed?

  A OH

  B NH_3

  C O

  D H

4 The following table shows some oxides.

Oxides
lithium oxide
calcium oxide
barium oxide
ferrous oxide

How is the oxide part of a chemical formula for the bases in the table expressed?

  A OH

  B NH_3

  C O

  D H

5 There are two classes of acids: organic and inorganic. The following table shows both organic and inorganic acids.

Acids
citric acid
hydrochloric acid
hydrofluoric acid
nitric acid

Which one of the acids in the table is an organic acid?

  A citric acid

  B hydrochloric acid

  C hydrofluoric acid

  D nitric acid

6 Which of the following properties is a common property of acids?

  A pH values < 7

  B insoluble in water

  C does not conduct electricity

  D does not react with metals

7 Which of the following statements is true for the reaction below?

$$HF(aq) + HPO_4^{2-}(aq) \rightleftharpoons F^-(aq) + H_2PO_4^-(aq)$$

  A HF is the base.

  B HPO_4^{2-} is the acid.

  C F^- is the conjugate base.

  D $H_2PO_4^-$ is the conjugate base.

GRIDDED RESPONSE

8 How many hydrogen atoms in CH_3COOH can be ionized?

Test Tip

Double check (with a calculator, if permitted) all mathematical computations involved in answering a question.

CHAPTER 15
Acid-Base Titration and pH

BIG IDEA
A solution's pH is a measure of its hydronium ion concentration and is used to rate its acidity.

ONLINE Chemistry
HMHScience.com

SECTION 1
Aqueous Solutions and the Concept of pH

SECTION 2
Determining pH and Titrations

ONLINE LABS
- Hydronium Ion Concentration and pH
- Wetlands Acid Spill
- How Much Calcium Carbonate Is in an Eggshell?
- Titration with an Acid and a Base
- Shampoo Chemistry

GO ONLINE

Why It Matters Video
HMHScience.com

Acids and Bases

©Steffen Hauser/botanikfoto/Alamy Images; (br) ©Corbis

Aqueous Solutions and the Concept of pH

SECTION 1

Main Ideas

▶ Self-ionization of water forms hydronium and hydroxide ions.

▶ The concentrations of hydronium and hydroxide ions determine pH and pOH.

▶ The sum of a solution's pH and pOH is always 14.

Key Terms

self-ionization of water
pH
pOH

▶ MAIN IDEA

Self-ionization of water forms hydronium and hydroxide ions.

You have already seen that acids and bases form hydronium ions and hydroxide ions, respectively, in aqueous solutions. However, these ions formed from the solute are not the only such ions present in an aqueous solution. Hydronium ions and hydroxide ions are also provided by the solvent, water.

Self-Ionization of Water

Careful electrical conductivity experiments have shown that pure water is an extremely weak electrolyte. Water undergoes self-ionization, as shown in the model in **Figure 1.1**. In the **self-ionization of water, two water molecules produce a hydronium ion and a hydroxide ion by transfer of a proton.** The following equilibrium takes place.

$$H_2O(l) + H_2O(l) \rightleftharpoons H_3O^+(aq) + OH^-(aq)$$

Conductivity measurements show that concentrations of H_3O^+ and OH^- in pure water are each only 1.0×10^{-7} mol/L of water at 25°C.

FIGURE 1.1

Self-Ionization of Water Water undergoes self-ionization to a slight extent. A proton is transferred from one water molecule to another. A hydronium ion, H_3O^+, and a hydroxide ion, OH^-, are produced.

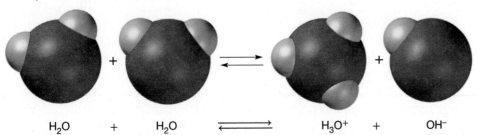

H_2O + H_2O ⇌ H_3O^+ + OH^-

FIGURE 1.2

K_W **AT SELECTED TEMPERATURES**

Temperature (°C)	K_w
0	1.2×10^{-15}
10	3.0×10^{-15}
25	1.0×10^{-14}
50	5.3×10^{-14}

There is a standard notation to show concentration in moles per liter. The formula of the particular ion or molecule is enclosed in brackets, [ ]. For example, the symbol $[H_3O^+]$ means "hydronium ion concentration in moles per liter," or "molar hydronium ion concentration." In water at 25°C, $[H_3O^+] = 1.0 \times 10^{-7}$ M, and $[OH^-] = 1.0 \times 10^{-7}$ M.

The mathematical product of $[H_3O^+]$ and $[OH^-]$ remains constant in water and dilute aqueous solutions at constant temperature. This constant mathematical product is called the *ionization constant of water*, K_w, and is expressed by the following equation.

$$K_w = [H_3O^+][OH^-]$$

For example, in water and dilute aqueous solutions at 25°C, the following relationship is valid.

$$K_w = [H_3O^+][OH^-] = (1.0 \times 10^{-7})(1.0 \times 10^{-7}) = 1.0 \times 10^{-14}$$

The ionization of water increases as temperature increases. Therefore, the ion product, K_w, also increases as temperature increases, as shown in **Figure 1.2**. However, at any given temperature, K_w is always a constant value. The value 1.0×10^{-14} is assumed to be constant within the ordinary range of room temperatures. In this chapter, you can assume that these conditions are present unless otherwise stated.

Neutral, Acidic, and Basic Solutions

Because the hydronium ion and hydroxide ion concentrations are the same in pure water, it is *neutral*. In fact, any solution in which $[H_3O^+] = [OH^-]$ is neutral. Recall that acids increase the concentration of H_3O^+ in aqueous solutions, as shown in **Figure 1.3a**. Solutions in which the $[H_3O^+]$ is greater than the $[OH^-]$ are *acidic*. Bases increase the concentration of OH^- in aqueous solutions, as shown in **Figure 1.3b**. In *basic* solutions, the $[OH^-]$ is greater than the $[H_3O^+]$.

FIGURE 1.3

Identifying Acids and Bases

(a) Addition of dry ice, carbon dioxide, to water increases the $[H_3O^+]$, which is shown by the color change of the indicator bromthymol blue to yellow. The white mist is formed by condensation of water vapor because the dry ice is cold.

(b) Addition of sodium peroxide to water increases the $[OH^-]$, which is shown by the color change of the indicator phenolphthalein to pink.

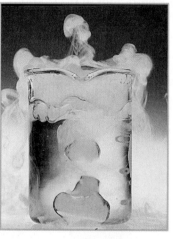

(a)

(b)

As stated earlier, the $[H_3O^+]$ and the $[OH^-]$ of a neutral solution at 25°C both equal 1.0×10^{-7} M. Therefore, if the $[H_3O^+]$ is increased to greater than 1.0×10^{-7} M, the solution becomes acidic. A solution containing 1.0×10^{-5} mol H_3O^+ ion/L at 25°C is acidic because 1.0×10^{-5} is greater than 1.0×10^{-7}. If the $[OH^-]$ is increased to greater than 1.0×10^{-7} M, the solution becomes basic. A solution containing 1.0×10^{-4} mol OH^- ions/L at 25°C is basic because 1.0×10^{-4} is greater than 1.0×10^{-7}.

Calculating $[H_3O^+]$ and $[OH^-]$

Recall that strong acids and bases are considered completely ionized or dissociated in weak aqueous solutions. A review of strong acids and bases is given in **Figure 1.4**. Because NaOH is a strong base, 1 mol of it will yield 1 mol of OH^- in an aqueous solution.

$$NaOH(s) \xrightarrow{H_2O} Na^+(aq) + OH^-(aq)$$
$$\text{1 mol} \qquad \text{1 mol} \qquad \text{1 mol}$$

Therefore, a 1.0×10^{-2} M NaOH solution has an $[OH^-]$ of 1.0×10^{-2} M, as shown by the following.

$$\frac{1.0 \times 10^{-2}\ \text{mol NaOH}}{\text{1 L solution}} \times \frac{\text{1 mol OH}^-}{\text{1 mol NaOH}} = \frac{1.0 \times 10^{-2}\ \text{mol OH}^-}{\text{1 L solution}}$$

$$= 1.0 \times 10^{-2}\ \text{M OH}^-$$

Notice that the $[OH^-]$ is greater than 1.0×10^{-7} M. This solution is basic.

Because the K_w of an aqueous solution is a relatively constant 1.0×10^{-14} at ordinary room temperatures, the concentration of either ion can be determined if the concentration of the other ion is known. The $[H_3O^+]$ of this solution is calculated as follows.

$$K_w = [H_3O^+][OH^-] = 1.0 \times 10^{-14}$$

$$[H_3O^+] = \frac{1.0 \times 10^{-14}}{[OH^-]} = \frac{1.0 \times 10^{-14}}{1.0 \times 10^{-2}} = 1.0 \times 10^{-12}\ \text{M}$$

The $[OH^-]$, 1.0×10^{-2} M, is greater than the $[H_3O^+]$, 1.0×10^{-12} M, as is true for all basic solutions.

Now consider a 2.0×10^{-4} M HCl solution. Because HCl is a strong acid, the $[H_3O^+]$ is 2.0×10^{-4} M, as shown by the following.

$$HCl(g) + H_2O(l) \longrightarrow H_3O^+(aq) + Cl^-(aq)$$
$$\text{1 mol} \quad \text{1 mol} \qquad \text{1 mol} \qquad \text{1 mol}$$

$$\frac{2.0 \times 10^{-4}\ \text{mol HCl}}{\text{1 L solution}} \times \frac{\text{1 mol H}_3\text{O}^+}{\text{1 mol HCl}} = \frac{2.0 \times 10^{-4}\ \text{mol H}_3\text{O}^+}{\text{1 L solution}}$$

$$= 2.0 \times 10^{-4}\ \text{M H}_3\text{O}^+$$

Notice that the $[H_3O^+]$ is greater than 1.0×10^{-7} M. This solution is acidic. The $[OH^-]$ of this solution is calculated as follows.

$$K_w = [H_3O^+][OH^-] = 1.0 \times 10^{-14}$$

$$[OH^-] = \frac{1.0 \times 10^{-14}}{[H_3O^+]} = \frac{1.0 \times 10^{-14}}{2.0 \times 10^{-4}} = 5.0 \times 10^{-11}\ \text{M}$$

The $[H_3O^+]$ is greater than the $[OH^-]$ for all acidic solutions.

FIGURE 1.4

COMMON STRONG ACIDS AND BASES

Strong Acids	Strong Bases
HCl	LiOH
HBr	NaOH
HI	KOH
$HClO_4$	RbOH
$HClO_3$	CsOH
HNO_3	$Ca(OH)_2$
H_2SO_4	$Sr(OH)_2$
	$Ba(OH)_2$

You may have realized that in order for K_w to remain constant, an increase in either the $[H_3O^+]$ or the $[OH^-]$ in an aqueous solution causes a decrease in the concentration of the other ion. Sample Problem A also shows calculation of the $[H_3O^+]$ and $[OH^-]$ of an acidic solution.

Calculating Hydronium and Hydroxide Concentrations

GO ONLINE

Learn It! Video
HMHScience.com

Solve It! Cards
HMHScience.com

Sample Problem A A 1.0×10^{-4} M solution of HNO_3 has been prepared for a laboratory experiment.   **a.** Calculate the $[H_3O^+]$ of this solution.   **b.** Calculate the $[OH^-]$.

❶ ANALYZE

Given: Concentration of the solution
$= 1.0 \times 10^{-4}$ M HNO_3

Unknown: **a.** $[H_3O^+]$ **b.** $[OH^-]$

❷ PLAN

HNO_3 is a strong acid, which means that it is essentially 100% ionized in dilute solutions. One molecule of acid produces one hydronium ion. The concentration of the hydronium ions thus equals the concentration of the acid. Because the ion product, $[H_3O^+] [OH^-]$, is a constant, $[OH^-]$ can easily be determined by using the value for $[H_3O^+]$.

a. $HNO_3(l) + H_2O(l) \longrightarrow H_3O^+(aq) + NO_3^-(aq)$ (assuming 100% ionization)
$\quad$ 1 mol $\qquad$ 1 mol $\qquad\quad$ 1 mol $\qquad$ 1 mol

$$\text{molarity of } HNO_3 = \frac{\text{mol } HNO_3}{1 \text{ L solution}}$$

$$\frac{\text{mol } HNO_3}{\text{L solution}} \times \frac{1 \text{ mol } H_3O^+}{1 \text{ mol } HNO_3} = \frac{\text{mol } H_3O^+}{\text{L solution}} = \text{molarity of } H_3O^+$$

b. $[H_3O^+] [OH^-] = 1.0 \times 10^{-14}$

$$[OH^-] = \frac{1.0 \times 10^{-14}}{[H_3O^+]}$$

❸ SOLVE

a. $\dfrac{1.0 \times 10^{-4} \text{ mol } HNO_3}{1 \text{ L solution}} \times \dfrac{1 \text{ mol } H_3O^+}{1 \text{ mol } HNO_3} = \dfrac{1.0 \times 10^{-4} \text{ M } H_3O^+}{1 \text{ L solution}} = 1.0 \times 10^{-4}$ M H_3O^+

b. $[OH^-] = \dfrac{1.0 \times 10^{-14}}{[H_3O^+]} = \dfrac{1.0 \times 10^{-14}}{1.0 \times 10^{-4}} = 1.0 \times 10^{-10}$ M

❹ CHECK YOUR WORK

Because the $[H_3O^+]$, 1.0×10^{-4}, is greater than 1.0×10^{-7}, the $[OH^-]$ must be less than 1.0×10^{-7}. The answers are correctly expressed to two significant digits.

Practice   Answers in Appendix E

1. Determine the hydronium and hydroxide ion concentrations in a solution that is:

$\quad$ **a.** 1×10^{-4} M HCl.
$\quad$ **b.** 1.0×10^{-3} M HNO_3.
$\quad$ **c.** 3.0×10^{-2} M NaOH.
$\quad$ **d.** 1.0×10^{-4} M $Ca(OH)_2$.

▶ MAIN IDEA

The concentrations of hydronium and hydroxide ions determine pH and pOH.

Expressing acidity or basicity in terms of the concentration of H_3O^+ or OH^- can be cumbersome because the values tend to be very small. A more convenient quantity, called pH, also indicates the hydronium ion concentration of a solution. The letters *pH* stand for the French words *pouvoir hydrogène*, meaning "hydrogen power." **The pH of a solution is defined as the negative of the common logarithm of the hydronium ion concentration, [H_3O^+].** The pH is expressed by the following equation.

> **pH**
> $$pH = -\log [H_3O^+]$$

The common logarithm of a number is the power to which 10 must be raised to equal the number. A neutral solution at 25°C has a [H_3O^+] of 1×10^{-7} M. The logarithm of 1×10^{-7} is -7.0. The pH is determined as follows.

$$pH = -\log [H_3O^+] = -\log (1 \times 10^{-7}) = -(-7.0) = 7.0$$

The relationship between pH and [H_3O^+] is shown on the scale in **Figure 1.5**.

Likewise, **the pOH** of a solution is defined as the negative of the common logarithm of the hydroxide ion concentration, [OH^-].

> **pOH**
> $$pOH = -\log [OH^-]$$

A neutral solution at 25°C has a [OH^-] of 1×10^{-7} M and a pOH of 7.0.

Remember that the values of [H_3O^+] and [OH^-] are related by K_w. The negative logarithm of K_w at 25°C, 1×10^{-14}, is 14.0. Notice that the sum of the pH and the pOH of a neutral solution at 25°C is also equal to 14.0. The following relationship is true at 25°C.

$$pH + pOH = 14.0$$

✔ **CRITICAL THINKING**

Explain **Figure 1.5** shows the pH scale with which most people are familiar. Can there be pH measurements greater than 14 or less than zero? Explain.

FIGURE 1.5

The pH Scale As the concentration of hydronium ions increases, the solution becomes more acidic, and the pH decreases. As the concentration of hydronium ions decreases, the solution becomes more basic, and the pH increases.

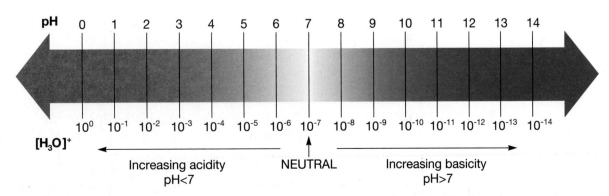

FIGURE 1.6

APPROXIMATE pH RANGE OF SOME COMMON MATERIALS (AT 25°C)

Material	pH	Material	pH
Gastric juice	1.0–3.0	Bread	5.0–6.0
Lemons	1.8–2.4	Rainwater	5.5–5.8
Vinegar	2.4–3.4	Potatoes	5.6–6.0
Soft drinks	2.0–4.0	Milk	6.3–6.6
Apples	2.9–3.3	Saliva	6.5–7.5
Grapefruit	2.9–3.4	Pure water (25 °C)	7.0
Oranges	3.0–4.0	Blood	7.3–7.5
Cherries	3.2–4.7	Eggs	7.6–8.0
Tomatoes	4.0–4.4	Seawater	8.0–8.5
Bananas	4.5–5.7	Milk of magnesia	10.5

At 25°C, the range of pH values of aqueous solutions generally falls between 0 and 14, as shown in **Figure 1.6.**

Suppose the $[H_3O^+]$ in a solution is greater than the $[OH^-]$, as is true for acidic solutions. For example, the pH of an acidic solution at 25°C with a $[H_3O^+]$ of 1×10^{-6} M is 6.0.

$$pH = -\log [H_3O^+] = -\log (1 \times 10^{-6}) = -(-6.0) = 6.0$$

FIGURE 1.7

$[H_3O^+]$, $[OH^-]$, pH, AND pOH OF SOLUTIONS

Solution	General condition	At 25°C
Neutral	$[H_3O^+] = [OH^-]$ pH = pOH	$[H_3O^+] = [OH^-] = 1 \times 10^{-7}$ M pH = pOH = 7.0
Acidic	$[H_3O^+] > [OH^-]$ pH < pOH	$[H_3O^+] > 1 \times 10^{-7}$ M $[OH^-] < 1 \times 10^{-7}$ M pH < 7.0 pOH > 7.0
Basic	$[H_3O^+] < [OH^-]$ pH > pOH	$[H_3O^+] < 1 \times 10^{-7}$ M $[OH^-] > 1 \times 10^{-7}$ M pH > 7.0 pOH < 7.0

The pH of this solution is less than 7. This is the case for all acidic solutions at 25°C. The following calculation shows that the pOH is greater than 7.0, as is true for all acidic solutions at 25°C.

$$pOH = 14.0 - pH = 14.0 - 6.0 = 8.0$$

Similar calculations show that the pH of a basic solution at 25°C is more than 7.0 and the pOH is less than 7.0. These and other relationships are listed in **Figure 1.7** (on the previous page). As the temperature changes, the exact values will change because the value of K_w changes. However, the relationship $pH + pOH = pK_w$ will remain the same.

● MAIN IDEA

The sum of a solution's pH and pOH is always 14.

If either the $[H_3O^+]$ or pH of a solution is known, the other can be calculated. Because pH represents a logarithm, the number to the *left of the decimal* only locates the decimal point. It isn't included when counting significant figures. So there must be as many significant figures to the *right of the decimal* as there are in the number whose logarithm was found.

GO ONLINE

Solve It! Cards
HMHScience.com

Learn It! Video
HMHScience.com

Calculating pH

Sample Problem B What is the pH of a 1.0×10^{-5} M LiOH solution?

① ANALYZE

Given: Identity and concentration of solution = 1.0×10^{-5} M LiOH

Unknown: pH of solution

② PLAN

concentration of base $\longrightarrow$ concentration of OH^-
$\longrightarrow$ concentration of H_3O^+ $\longrightarrow$ pH

LiOH is completely dissociated when it is dissolved in water. A 1.0×10^{-5} M LiOH solution therefore produces a $[OH^-]$ equal to 1.0×10^{-5} M. The ion product of $[H_3O^+]$ and $[OH^-]$ is a constant, 1.0×10^{-14}. By substitution, the $[H_3O^+]$ can be determined. The pH can then be calculated.

③ SOLVE

$$[H_3O^+][OH^-] = 1.0 \times 10^{-14}$$

$$[H_3O^+] = \frac{1.0 \times 10^{-14}}{[OH^-]} = \frac{1.0 \times 10^{-14}}{1.0 \times 10^{-5}} = 1.0 \times 10^{-9} \text{ M}$$

$$pH = -\log [H_3O^+] = -\log (1.0 \times 10^{-9}) = 9.00$$

④ CHECK YOUR WORK

The answer correctly indicates that NaOH forms a basic solution, pH > 7. There are 2 significant figures in the answer, to the right of the decimal point.

Practice Answers in Appendix E

1. Determine the pH of the following solutions:
   a. 1×10^{-6} M $HClO_4$
   b. 1.0×10^{-5} M HNO_3
   c. 1×10^{-3} M RbOH
   d. 1.0×10^{-2} M KOH

For example, a $[H_3O^+]$ value of 1×10^{-7} has *one* significant figure. Therefore, the pH, or $-\log$, of this value must have one digit to the right of the decimal. Thus, pH = 7.0 has the correct number of significant figures.

Calculating pH from $[H_3O^+]$

You have already seen the simplest pH problems. In these problems, the $[H_3O^+]$ of the solution is an integral power of 10, such as 1 M or 0.01 M. The pH of this type of solution is the exponent of the hydronium ion concentration with the sign changed. For example, the pH of a solution in which $[H_3O^+]$ is 1×10^{-5} M is 5.0.

Using a Calculator to Calculate pH from $[H_3O^+]$

Most problems involve hydronium ion concentrations that are not equal to integral powers of 10. These problems require a calculator. Most scientific calculators have a "log" key. Consult the instructions for your particular calculator.

GO ONLINE

SOLUTION TUTOR

HMHScience.com

Calculating pH

Sample Problem C What is the pH of a solution if the $[H_3O^+]$ is 3.4×10^{-5} M?

❶ ANALYZE

Given: $[H_3O^+] = 3.4 \times 10^{-5}$ M

Unknown: pH of solution

❷ PLAN

$[H_3O^+] \longrightarrow \text{pH}$

The only difference between this problem and previous pH problems is that you will determine the logarithm of 3.4×10^{-5} using your calculator. You can convert numbers to logarithms on most calculators by using the "log" key.

❸ SOLVE

$$\text{pH} = -\log [H_3O^+]$$
$$= -\log (3.4 \times 10^{-5})$$
$$= 4.47$$

On most calculators, this problem is entered in the following steps.

❹ CHECK YOUR WORK

The pH of a 1×10^{-5} M H_3O^+ solution is 5.0. A solution that has a greater concentration of hydronium ions will be more acidic and will have a pH less than 5. Because the concentration has two significant figures, the pH will have two figures following the decimal point.

Practice   Answers in Appendix E

1. What is the pH of a solution if the $[H_3O^+]$ is 6.7×10^{-4} M?
2. What is the pH of a solution with a hydronium ion concentration of 2.5×10^{-2} M?
3. Determine the pH of a 2.5×10^{-6} M HNO_3 solution.
4. Determine the pH of a 2.0×10^{-2} M $Sr(OH)_2$ solution.

An estimate of pH can be used to check your calculations. For example, suppose the $[H_3O^+]$ of a solution is 3.4×10^{-5} M. Because 3.4×10^{-5} lies between 1×10^{-4} and 1×10^{-5}, the pH of the solution must be between 4 and 5. Sample Problem C (on the previous page) shows the actual calculation of the pH value for a solution with $[H_3O^+] = 3.4 \times 10^{-5}$ M.

Calculating $[H_3O^+]$ and $[OH^-]$ from pH

You have now learned to calculate the pH of a solution given its $[H_3O^+]$. Suppose you are given the pH of a solution instead. How can you determine its hydronium ion concentration?

You already know the following equation.

$$pH = -\log [H_3O^+]$$

Remember that the base of common logarithms is 10. Therefore, the antilog of a common logarithm is 10 raised to that number.

$$\log [H_3O^+] = -pH$$
$$[H_3O^+] = \text{antilog} (-pH)$$
$$[H_3O^+] = 10^{-pH}$$

The simplest cases are those in which pH values are integers. The exponent of 10 that gives the $[H_3O^+]$ is the negative of the pH. For an aqueous solution that has a pH of 2.0, for example, the $[H_3O^+]$ is equal to 1×10^{-2} M. Likewise, when the pH is 0, the $[H_3O^+]$ is 1 M because $10^0 = 1$. Sample Problem D shows how to convert a pH value that is a positive integer. Sample Problem E shows how to use a calculator to convert a pH that is not an integral number.

GO ONLINE

Solve It! Cards
HMHScience.com

SOLUTION TUTOR

HMHScience.com

Calculating Hydronium Concentration Using pH

Sample Problem D Determine the hydronium ion concentration of an aqueous solution that has a pH of 4.0.

 ANALYZE

Given: pH = 4.0

Unknown: $[H_3O^+]$

 PLAN

$$pH \longrightarrow [H_3O+]$$

This problem requires that you rearrange the pH equation and solve for the $[H_3O^+]$. Because 4.0 has one digit to the right of the decimal, the answer must have one significant figure.

$$pH = -\log [H_3O^+]$$
$$\log [H_3O^+] = -pH$$
$$[H_3O^+] = \text{antilog} (-pH)$$
$$[H_3O^+] = 1 \times 10^{-pH}$$

❸ **SOLVE**

$$[H_3O^+] = 1 \times 10^{-pH} = 1 \times 10^{-4} \text{ M}$$

 CHECK YOUR WORK

A solution with a pH of 4.0 is acidic. The answer, 1×10^{-4} M, is greater than 1.0×10^{-7} M, which is correct for an acidic solution.

Calculating Hydronium and Hydroxide Concentrations

Sample Problem E The pH of a solution is measured and determined to be 8.43.
a. What is the hydronium ion concentration?
b. What is the hydroxide ion concentration?
c. Is the solution acidic or basic?

① ANALYZE

Given: pH of the solution = 8.43

Unknown: **a.** $[H_3O^+]$ **b.** $[OH^-]$ **c.** Is the solution acidic or basic?

② PLAN

$$pH \longrightarrow [H_3O^+] \longrightarrow [OH^-]$$

This problem is very similar to previous pH problems. You will need to substitute values into the $pH = -\log [H_3O^+]$ equation and use a calculator. Once the $[H_3O^+]$ is determined, the ion-product constant $[H_3O^+] [OH^-] = 1.0 \times 10^{-14}$ may be used to calculate $[OH^-]$.

③ SOLVE

a. $pH = -\log [H_3O^+]$

$\log [H_3O^+] = -pH$

$[H_3O^+] = $ antilog $(-pH) = $ antilog $(-8.43) = 1.0 \times 10^{-8.43} = 3.7 \times 10^{-9}\ M\ H_3O^+$

On most calculators, this is entered in one of the following two ways.

| 8 | . | 4 | 3 | +/- | 2nd | 10^x | or | 8 | . | 4 | 3 | +/- | 2nd | LOG |

7b. $[H_3O^+] [OH^-] = 1.0 \times 10^{-14}$

$$[OH^-] = \frac{1.0 \times 10^{-14}}{[H_3O^+]}$$

$$= \frac{1.0 \times 10^{-14}}{3.7 \times 10^{-9}} = 2.7 \times 10^{-6}\ M\ OH^-$$

c. A pH of 8.43 is slightly greater than a pH of 7. This means that the solution is slightly basic.

④ CHECK YOUR WORK

Because the solution is slightly basic, a hydroxide ion concentration slightly greater than 10^{-7} M is predicted. A hydronium ion concentration slightly less than 10^{-7} M is also predicted. The answers agree with these predictions.

Practice

1. The pH of a solution is determined to be 5.0. What is the hydronium ion concentration of this solution?
2. The pH of a solution is determined to be 11.0. What is the hydronium ion concentration of this solution?
3. The pH of an aqueous solution is measured as 2.60. Calculate the $[H_3O^+]$ and the $[OH^-]$.
4. The pH of an aqueous solution is 3.67. Determine $[H_3O^+]$.

FIGURE 1.8

RELATIONSHIP OF $[H_3O^+]$ TO $[OH^-]$ AND pH (AT 25°C)			
Solution	$[H_3O^+]$	$[OH^-]$	pH
1.0×10^{-2} M KOH	1.0×10^{-12}	1.0×10^{-2}	12.00
1.0×10^{-2} M NH$_3$	2.4×10^{-11}	4.2×10^{-4}	10.63
Pure H$_2$O	1.0×10^{-7}	1.0×10^{-7}	7.00
1.0×10^{-3} M HCl	1.0×10^{-3}	1.0×10^{-11}	3.00
1.0×10^{-1} M CH$_3$COOH	1.3×10^{-3}	7.5×10^{-12}	2.87

pH Calculations and the Strength of Acids and Bases

So far, we have discussed the pH of solutions that contain only strong acids or strong bases. We must also consider weak acids and weak bases. **Figure 1.8** lists the $[H_3O^+]$, the $[OH^-]$, and the pH for several solutions.

KOH, the solute in the first solution listed, is a soluble ionic compound and a strong base. The molarity of a KOH solution directly indicates the $[OH^-]$, and the $[H_3O^+]$ can be calculated. Once the $[H_3O^+]$ is known, the pH can be calculated as in Sample Problem C. If the pH of this solution is measured experimentally, it will be the same as this calculated value. Methods for experimentally determining the pH of solutions will be presented in Section 2. Hydrochloric acid, HCl, is a strong acid, and similar calculations can be made for solutions that contain HCl.

Solutions of weak acids, such as acetic acid, CH$_3$COOH, present a different problem. The $[H_3O^+]$ cannot be calculated directly from the molar concentration because not all of the acetic acid molecules are ionized. The same problem occurs for weak bases such as ammonia, NH$_3$. The pH of these solutions must be measured experimentally. The $[H_3O^+]$ and $[OH^-]$ can then be calculated from the measured pH values.

SECTION 1 FORMATIVE ASSESSMENT

▶ Reviewing Main Ideas

1. What is the concentration of hydronium and hydroxide ions in pure water at 25°C?

2. Why does the pH scale generally range from 0 to 14 in aqueous solutions?

3. Why does a pH of 7 represent a neutral solution at 25°C?

4. A solution contains 4.5×10^{-3} M HCl. Determine the following:
   a. $[H_3O^+]$ **b.** $[OH^-]$ **c.** pH

5. A Ca(OH)$_2$ solution has a pH of 8.0. Determine the following for the solution:
   a. $[H_3O^+]$ **b.** $[OH^-]$ **c.** $[Ca(OH)_2]$

✓ Critical Thinking

6. **PREDICTING OUTCOMES** Arrange the following solutions in order from lowest to highest pH: 0.10 M HCl, 0.10 M H$_2$SO$_4$, and 0.10 M HF.

S.T.E.M.

Liming Streams

Scientists have documented many examples of the effects of increased acidity on freshwater lakes and streams. Although natural rainwater is slightly acidic, most natural lakes and streams have a pH between 6 and 8. This is because other factors, like the underlying geology and soils, help keep pH within reasonable values. Some lakes and streams, however, have become acidified due to human activities that cause acid rain and from leaching from soils and rock strata and runoff from agriculture and mining.

Acid rain is precipitation with higher than natural levels of acid caused by human activities, often containing a mixture of nitrous, nitric, sulfurous, and sulfuric acids. These acids come from reactions of sulfur compounds from industrial and mining pollution, from reactions of nitrogen compounds from fertilizer, and from the emissions from power plants and motor vehicles burning fossil fuels. Acid rain has a pH of 5.6 or lower. Runoff and rock leaching can have even lower pH. In areas where soil and rock strata lack the buffering capacity to neutralize the pH of runoff or acid rain, lakes and streams can become so acidic that fish and other aquatic organisms die.

There are several natural mechanisms that help regulate the acidity of streams and lakes. Some streams flow over limestone deposits, which are alkaline and tend to naturally neutralize the acid in the water. This process increases a lake or stream's *acid neutralizing capacity*, or ANC. When limestone dissolves, it produces calcium and carbonate ions. Calcium ions are a nutrient for many organisms. Carbonate ions react with acid, forming bicarbonate to neutralize the acid and raise the pH. The change in pH also converts aluminum, also harmful to fish, in the water to an inert compound that is not toxic to fish. Some lakes and streams, however, are located in geological environments with few natural basic components. In these places, acid rain and runoff have a greater effect on the water.

One way to counter acidification is liming, a method of treating acid in streams and lakes that have pH levels above normal due to acid rain and other human activities. Liming involves adding a base, such as calcium carbonate ($CaCO_3$) in a form such as limestone, to counteract acidification in lakes and streams. Limestone is often used because it is a natural material, can be ground into sand-sized grains, and gives a long-lasting treatment by dissolving slowly.

Calcium carbonate can also be applied to the surface of soil to improve its buffering capacity against sudden changes in pH. An issue to be decided for each location is whether to use a one-time, one-place application of calcium carbonate or a system that continuously adds calcium carbonate to multiple sites. But any solution has its drawbacks. Just as a lake or stream can become too acidic, overliming can cause the water to become too alkaline.

Activity

Design a method to counteract the acidification of lakes and streams. As part of your design, explain the overall neutralization reaction of the acid in the water, what substances could be used for the treatment, how the proposed treatment could be delivered or distributed, and what factors should be monitored to support your method. Also consider if liming is an effective, long-term solution to the problem of the acidification of freshwater sources. Describe what would be necessary for a more permanent solution.

Determining pH and Titrations

Key Terms

acid-base indicators
transition interval
pH meter
titration
equivalence point

end point
standard solution
primary standard

▸ **MAIN IDEA**

Indicators can determine pH, pOH, and strength.

An approximate value for the pH of a solution can be obtained using acid-base indicators. **Acid-base indicators are compounds whose colors are sensitive to pH.** In other words, the color of an indicator changes as the pH of a solution changes.

Indicators change colors because they are either weak acids or weak bases. A weak-acid indicator (H*In*) can be represented by the equation below, which is modeled in **Figure 2.1.**

$$HIn \rightleftharpoons H^+ + In^-$$

(*In*⁻ is the symbol of the anion part of the indicator.) The colors displayed result from the fact that H*In* and *In*⁻ are different colors.

A strip of neutral litmus paper contains both the weak acid and its conjugate base. When placed in an acidic solution, the indicator acts as a Brønsted base and accepts protons from the acid to produce more of the weak acid, H*In*. H*In* has a red color, as shown in **Figure 2.1.**

When placed in a basic solution, the OH⁻ ions combine with H⁺ ions that come from the indicator. In the affected area of the strip, the indicator is now present largely in the form of its anion, *In*⁻. The anion has a bluish color, and so the litmus turns blue.

FIGURE 2.1

Acid-Base Indicators When placed in an acidic solution, the nonionized form, H*In*, predominates, and the litmus paper turns red. When placed in a basic solution, the ionized form, *In*⁻, predominates and the litmus paper turns blue.

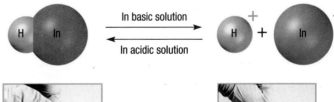

Nonionized form

Ionized form

©GIPhotoStock/Science Source

FIGURE 2.2

pH of Common Materials The pH of a solution can be determined by comparing the color it turns pH paper with the scale of the paper. The colors of pH paper at various pH values are shown, as are the pH values for some common materials.

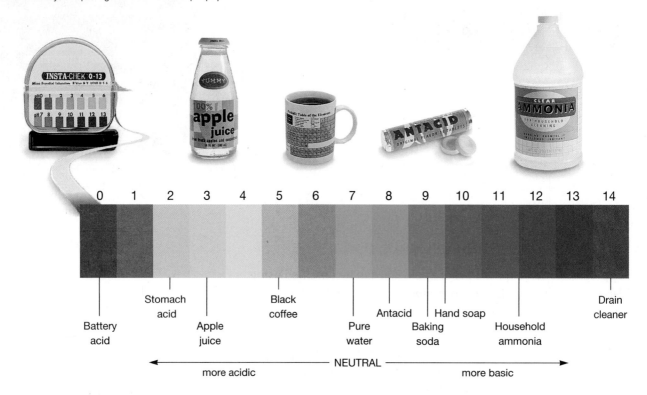

more acidic — NEUTRAL — more basic

Battery acid | Stomach acid | Apple juice | Black coffee | Pure water | Antacid | Baking soda | Hand soap | Household ammonia | Drain cleaner

---

Indicators come in many different colors. The exact pH range over which an indicator changes color also varies. The pH range over which an indicator changes color is called its **transition interval. Figure 2.4** gives the color changes and transition intervals for a number of common indicators.

Different indicators change color at different pH values. The color depends on the relative amounts of H*In* and *In*⁻ at a given pH. Methyl red changes from red to yellow between pH 4.4 and 6.2. At pH 4.4, the indicator exists mostly as H*In* molecules, which appear red in the solution. Above pH 6.2, the indicator exists mostly as *In*⁻ ions, which appear yellow. A similar situation exists with other indicators. Phenol red at 6.4 or below is yellow as H*In*. Above 8.0, it is in the *In*⁻ form, which is red. In the transition interval, significant amounts of both forms are present, so the color is due to the mixture of H*In* and *In*⁻.

Universal indicators are made by mixing several different indicators. Paper soaked in universal indicator solution is called pH paper. This paper can turn almost any color of the rainbow and provides a fairly accurate way of distinguishing the pH of solutions, as shown in **Figure 2.2.**

If a more precise value for the pH of a solution is needed, a pH meter, shown in **Figure 2.3,** should be used. **A pH meter determines the pH of a solution by measuring the voltage between the two electrodes that are placed in the solution.** The voltage changes as the hydronium ion concentration in the solution changes.

FIGURE 2.3

pH Meters A pH meter precisely measures the pH of a solution.

©Photo Researchers, Inc

FIGURE 2.4

COLOR RANGES OF VARIOUS INDICATORS USED IN TITRATIONS

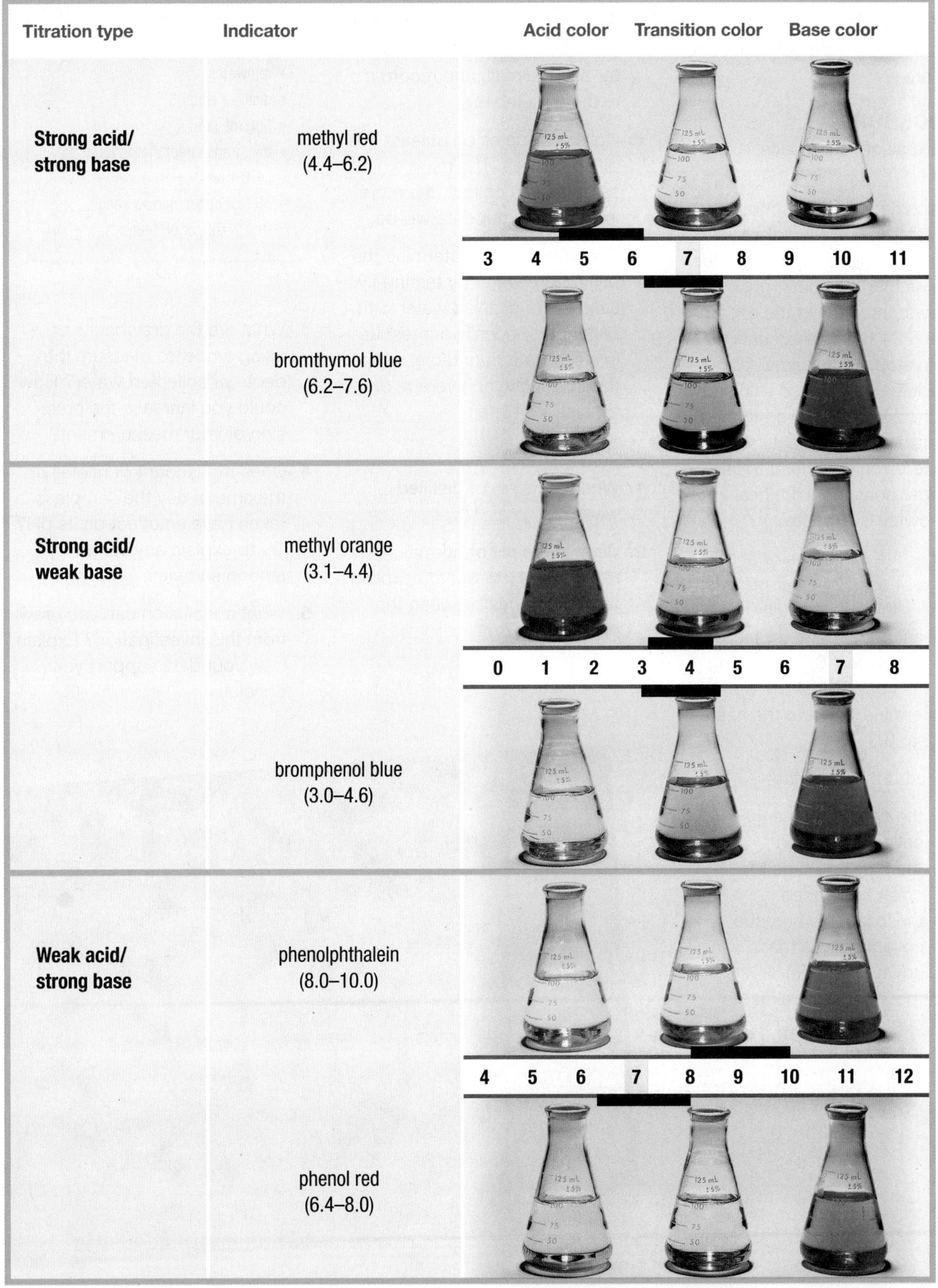

Titration type	Indicator	Acid color	Transition color	Base color
Strong acid/ strong base	methyl red (4.4–6.2)			
		3 4 5 6 7 8 9 10 11		
	bromthymol blue (6.2–7.6)			
Strong acid/ weak base	methyl orange (3.1–4.4)			
		0 1 2 3 4 5 6 7 8		
	bromphenol blue (3.0–4.6)			
Weak acid/ strong base	phenolphthalein (8.0–10.0)			
		4 5 6 7 8 9 10 11 12		
	phenol red (6.4–8.0)			

QUESTION
Do you have acid precipitation in your area?

PROCEDURE
Record all of your results in a data table.

1. Each time it rains, set out five clean jars to collect the rainwater. If the rain continues for more than 24 hours, put out new containers at the end of each 24-hour period until the rain stops. (The same procedure can be used with snow if the snow is allowed to melt before measurements are taken. You may need to use larger containers if a heavy snowfall is expected.)

2. After the rain stops or at the end of each 24-hour period, use a thin, plastic ruler to measure the depth of the water to the nearest 0.1 cm. Using the pH paper, test the water to determine its pH to the nearest 0.2 to 0.3.

3. Record the following:
   a. the date and time the collection started
   b. the date and time the collection ended
   c. the location where the collection was made (town and state)
   d. the amount of rainfall in centimeters
   e. the pH of the rainwater

4. Find the average pH of each collection that you have made for each rainfall, and record it in the data table.

5. Collect samples on at least five different days. The more samples you collect, the more informative your data will be.

6. For comparison, determine the pH of pure water by testing five samples of distilled water with pH paper. Record your results in a separate data table, and then calculate an average pH for distilled water.

DISCUSSION
1. What is the pH of distilled water?

2. What is the pH of normal rainwater? How do you explain any differences between the pH readings?

MATERIALS
- rainwater
- distilled water
- 500 mL jars
- thin, transparent metric ruler ($\pm$ 0.1 cm)
- pH test paper: narrow range, $\pm$ 0.2–0.3, or pH meter

3. What are the drawbacks of using a ruler to measure the depth of collected water? How could you increase the precision of your measurement?

4. Does the amount of rainfall or the time of day the sample is taken have an effect on its pH? Try to explain any variability among samples.

5. What conclusion can you draw from this investigation? Explain how your data support your conclusion.

GO ONLINE

Animated
Chemistry
HMHScience.com

Titration

MAIN IDEA

Titration is used to determine exact concentrations.

As you know, neutralization reactions occur between acids and bases. The OH^- ion acquires a proton from the H_3O^+ ion, forming two molecules of water. The following equation summarizes this reaction.

$$H_3O^+(aq) + OH^-(aq) \longrightarrow 2H_2O(l)$$

This equation shows that one mol of hydronium ions and one mol of hydroxide ions are chemically equivalent amounts. They combine in a one-to-one mole ratio. Neutralization occurs when hydronium ions and hydroxide ions are supplied in equal numbers by reactants, as shown in **Figure 2.5.**

One liter of a 0.10 M HCl solution contains 0.10 mol of hydronium ions. Now suppose that 0.10 mol of solid NaOH is added to 1 L of 0.10 M HCl solution. The NaOH dissolves and supplies 0.10 mol of hydroxide ions to the solution. HCl and NaOH are present in chemically equivalent amounts. Hydronium and hydroxide ions, which are present in equal numbers, combine to form water. NaCl, the salt produced in the reaction, is the product of this neutralization of a strong acid and a strong base. The resulting solution is neutral.

Because acids and bases react, the progressive addition of an acid to a base (or a base to an acid) can be used to compare the concentrations of the acid and the base. **Titration is the controlled addition and measurement of the amount of a solution of known concentration required to react completely with a measured amount of a solution of unknown concentration.** Titration provides a sensitive means of determining the chemically equivalent amounts of acid and base.

✔ **CRITICAL THINKING**
Assess From your own experiences, describe three everyday reasons to test for pH.

FIGURE 2.5

Neutralization The solution on the left turns pH paper red because it is acidic. The solution on the right turns pH paper blue because it is basic. When equal numbers of H_3O^+ and OH^- from the acidic and basic solutions react, the resulting solution is neutral. The neutral solution turns pH paper green.

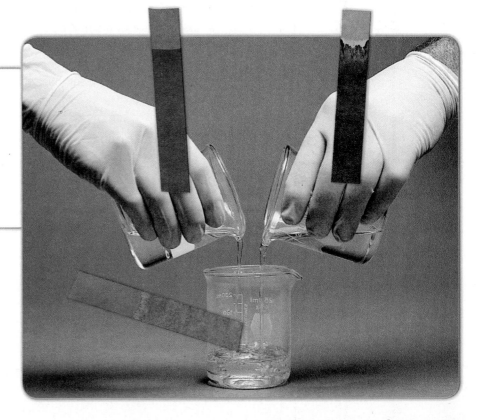

Equivalence Point

The point at which the two solutions used in a titration are present in chemically equivalent amounts is the **equivalence point.** Indicators and pH meters can be used to determine the equivalence point. The pH will change rapidly as the equivalence point is approached. If an indicator is used, it must change color over a range that includes the pH of the equivalence point, as shown in **Figure 2.6. The point in a titration at which an indicator changes color is called the end point of the indicator.**

Some indicators, such as litmus, change color at about pH 7. However, the color-change interval for litmus is broad, pH 5.5–8.0. This broad range makes it difficult to determine an accurate pH. Bromthymol blue is better because it has a smaller transition interval, pH 6.2–7.6 (see **Figure 2.4**). Indicators that undergo transition at about pH 7 are used to determine the equivalence point of strong-acid/strong-base titrations because the neutralization of strong acids with strong bases produces a salt solution with a pH of 7.

Indicators that change color at pH lower than 7 are useful in determining the equivalence point of strong-acid/weak-base titrations. Methyl orange is an example of this type. The equivalence point of a strong-acid/weak-base titration is acidic because the salt formed is itself a weak acid. Thus the salt solution has a pH lower than 7 at the equivalence point.

Indicators that change color at pH higher than 7 are useful in determining the equivalence point of weak-acid/strong-base titrations. Phenolphthalein is an example. These reactions produce salt solutions whose pH is greater than 7. This occurs because the salt formed is a weak base.

You may be wondering what type of indicator is used to determine the equivalence point of weak-acid/weak-base titrations. The surprising answer is "none at all." The pH at the equivalence point of a weak-acid/weak-base titration could be acidic, basic, or neutral, depending on the relative acid-base strengths. Because the pH value does not change dramatically as the equivalence point is approached, it is not practical to carry out weak-acid/weak-base titrations.

FIGURE 2.6

End Point Indicators change color at the end point of a titration with a base.

(a) Phenolphthalein turns pink at the end point.

(b) Methyl red turns red at the end point.

(br), (bl) ©Richard Megna/Fundamental Photographs

FIGURE 2.7

Equivalence
Points

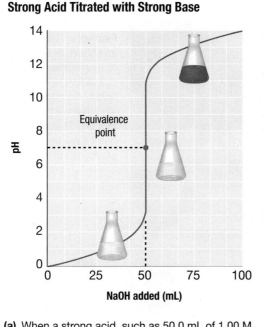

Strong Acid Titrated with Strong Base

(a) When a strong acid, such as 50.0 mL of 1.00 M HCl, is titrated with a strong base, such as 1.00 M NaOH, the equivalence point occurs at pH 7.00.

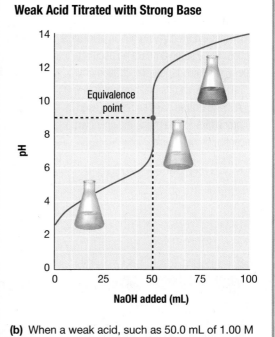

Weak Acid Titrated with Strong Base

(b) When a weak acid, such as 50.0 mL of 1.00 M CH_3COOH, is titrated with a strong base, such as 1.00 M NaOH, the initial pH is higher, and the equivalence point occurs at a pH above 7.00.

In a titration, successive additions of an aqueous base are made to a measured volume of an aqueous acid. As base is added, the pH changes from a lower numerical value to a higher one. The change in pH occurs slowly at first, then rapidly through the equivalence point, and then slowly again as the solution becomes more basic. Near the equivalence point, one drop can cause a pH change of 3 to 5 pH units! Typical pH curves for strong-acid/strong-base and weak-acid/strong-base titrations are shown in **Figure 2.7.**

▶ **MAIN IDEA**

A standard solution is used to titrate unknowns.

Figure 2.8 on the following pages shows the proper method of carrying out a titration. If the concentration of one solution is known precisely, the concentration of the other solution in a titration can be calculated from the chemically equivalent volumes. The solution that contains the precisely known concentration of a solute is known as a **standard solution.** It is often called simply the "known" solution.

To be certain of the concentration of the known solution, that solution must first be compared with a solution of a primary standard. A **primary standard** is a highly purified solid compound used to check the concentration of the known solution in a titration. The known solution is prepared first to give approximately the desired concentration. The known solution concentration is then determined precisely by titrating a carefully measured quantity of the primary standard.

FIGURE 2.8

Titration Techniques Following is the proper method for carrying out an acid-base titration. To be sure you have an accurate value, you should repeat the titration until you have three results that agree within 0.05 mL. A standardized base solution is used in this procedure to determine the unknown concentration of an acid.

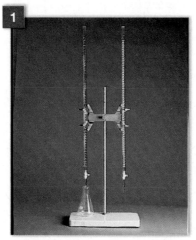

1

First set up two clean burets as shown. Decide which buret to use for the acid and which to use for the base. Rinse the acid buret three times with the acid that will be used in the titration. Then, rinse the base buret three times with the base solution to be used.

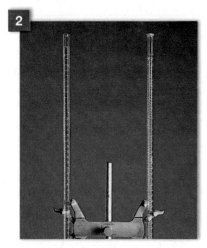

2

Fill the first buret to a point above the 0 mL calibration mark with the acid of unknown concentration.

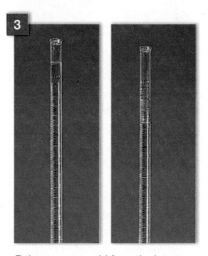

3

Release some acid from the buret to remove any air bubbles from the tip and to lower the volume to the calibrated portion of the buret.

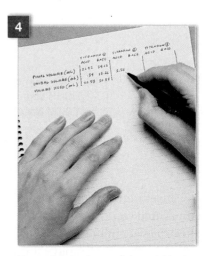

4

Record the volume of the acid in the buret to the nearest 0.01 mL as the initial volume. Remember to read the volume at the bottom of the meniscus.

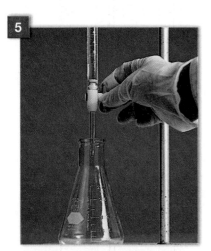

5

Allow the approximate volume of acid that was determined by your teacher or lab procedure to flow into a clean Erlenmeyer flask.

6

Subtract the initial volume reading on the buret from the final reading. This is the exact volume of the acid released into the flask. Record it to the nearest 0.01 mL.

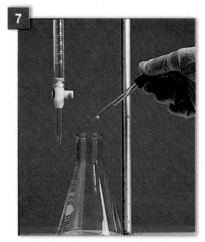

7

Add three drops of the appropriate indicator (in this case phenolphthalein) to the flask.

8

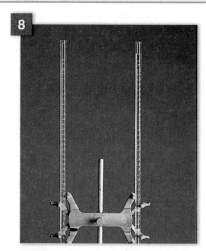

Fill the other buret with the standard base solution to a point above the calibration mark. The concentration of the standard base is known to a certain degree of precision because the base was previously titrated with an exact mass of solid acid, which is the primary standard.

9

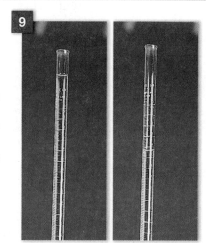

Release some base from the buret to remove any air bubbles and to lower the volume to the calibrated portion of the buret.

10

Record the volume of the base to the nearest 0.01 mL as your initial volume. Remember to read the volume at the bottom of the meniscus.

11

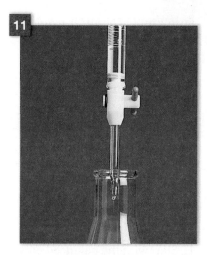

Place the Erlenmeyer flask under the base buret as shown. Notice that the tip of the buret extends into the mouth of the flask.

12

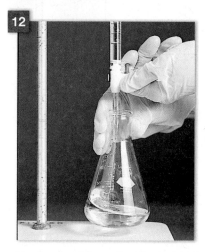

Slowly release base from the buret into the flask while constantly swirling the contents of the flask. The pink color of the indicator should fade with swirling.

13

The titration is nearing the end point when the pink color stays for longer periods of time. At this point, add base drop by drop.

14

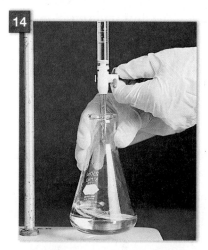

The equivalence point is reached when a very light pink color remains after 30 seconds of swirling.

15

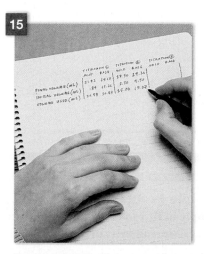

Subtract the initial volume reading on the buret from the final reading. This is the exact volume of the base released into the flask. Record it to the nearest 0.01 mL.

The known solution can be used to determine the molarity of another solution by titration. Suppose 20.00 mL of 5.00×10^{-3} M NaOH is required to reach the end point in the titration of 10.00 mL of HCl of unknown concentration. How can these titration data be used to determine the molarity of the acidic solution?

Begin with the balanced neutralization reaction equation. From the equation, determine the chemically equivalent amounts of HCl and NaOH.

$$HCl(aq) + NaOH(aq) \longrightarrow NaCl(aq) + H_2O(l)$$
$$\text{1 mol} \qquad \text{1 mol} \qquad \qquad \text{1 mol} \qquad \text{1 mol}$$

Calculate the number of moles of NaOH used in the titration.

$$\frac{5.00 \times 10^{-3} \text{ mol NaOH}}{1 \text{ L}} \times \frac{1 \text{ L}}{1000 \text{ mL}} \times 20.00 \text{ mL} = 1.00 \times 10^{-4} \text{ mol}$$
$$\text{NaOH used}$$

Because 1 mol of NaOH is needed to neutralize 1 mol of HCl, the amount of HCl in the titration must be 1.00×10^{-4} mol. This is confirmed by the following equation.

$$1.00 \times 10^{-4} \text{ mol NaOH} \times \frac{1 \text{ mol HCl}}{1 \text{ mol NaOH}} = 1.00 \times 10^{-4} \text{ mol HCl}$$

This amount of acid must be in the 10.0 mL of the HCl solution used for the titration. The molarity of the HCl solution can now be calculated.

$$\frac{1.00 \times 10^{-4} \text{ mol HCl}}{10.00 \text{ mL}} \times \frac{1000 \text{ mL}}{1 \text{ L}} = \frac{1.00 \times 10^{-2} \text{ mol HCl}}{1 \text{ L}}$$
$$= 1.00 \times 10^{-2} \text{ M HCl}$$

Sample Problem F illustrates the following four steps.

1. Start with the balanced equation for the neutralization reaction, and determine the chemically equivalent amounts of the acid and base.

2. Determine the moles of acid (or base) from the known solution used during the titration.

3. Determine the moles of solute of the unknown solution used during the titration.

4. Determine the molarity of the unknown solution.

GO ONLINE

SolveIt! Cards
HMHScience.com

Calculating the Molarity of an Acid Solution

Sample Problem F In a titration, 27.4 mL of 0.0154 M Ba(OH)$_2$ is added to a 20.0 mL sample of HCl solution of unknown concentration until the equivalence point is reached. What is the molarity of the acid solution?

1 ANALYZE

Given: volume and concentration of known solution = 27.4 mL of 0.0154 M Ba(OH)$_2$; volume of unknown HCl solution = 20.0 mL

Unknown: molarity of acid solution

Continued

2 PLAN

1. balanced neutralization equation ⟶ chemically equivalent amounts

$$Ba(OH)_2 + 2HCl \longrightarrow BaCl_2 + 2H_2O$$
$$1\ mol \qquad 2\ mol \qquad 1\ mol \qquad 2\ mol$$

2. volume of known basic solution used (mL) ⟶ amount of base used (mol)

$$\frac{mol\ Ba(OH)_2}{1\ \cancel{L}} \times mL\ of\ Ba(OH)_2\ solution \times \frac{1\ \cancel{L}}{1000\ \cancel{mL}} = mol\ Ba(OH)_2$$

3. moles of base used, mole ratio ⟶ moles of acid used from unknown solution

$$mol\ \cancel{Ba(OH)_2} \times \frac{2\ mol\ HCl}{1\ mol\ \cancel{Ba(OH)_2}}\ in\ known\ solution = mol\ HCl\ in\ unknown\ solution$$

4. volume of unknown, moles of solute in unknown ⟶ molarity of unknown

$$\frac{amount\ of\ solute\ in\ unknown\ solution\ (mol)}{volume\ of\ unknown\ solution\ (\cancel{mL})} \times \frac{1000\ \cancel{mL}}{1\ L} = molarity\ of\ unknown\ solution$$

3 SOLVE

1. The mole ratio from the equation is 1 mol $Ba(OH)_2$ for every 2 mol HCl.

2. $\dfrac{0.0154\ mol\ Ba(OH)_2}{1\ \cancel{L}} \times \dfrac{1\ \cancel{L}}{1000\ \cancel{mL}} \times 27.4\ \cancel{mL} = 4.22 \times 10^{-4}\ mol\ Ba(OH)_2$

3. $4.22 \times 10^{-4}\ mol\ \cancel{Ba(OH)_2} \times \dfrac{2\ mol\ HCl}{1\ mol\ \cancel{Ba(OH)_2}} = 8.44 \times 10^{-4}\ mol\ HCl$

4. $\dfrac{8.44 \times 10^{-4}\ mol\ HCl}{20.0\ \cancel{mL}} \times \dfrac{1000\ \cancel{mL}}{1\ L} = \dfrac{4.22 \times 10^{-2}\ mol\ HCl}{1\ L} = 4.22 \times 10^{-2}\ M\ HCl$

Practice   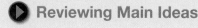 Answers in Appendix E

1. A 15.5 mL sample of 0.215 M KOH solution required 21.2 mL of aqueous acetic acid solution in a titration experiment. Calculate the molarity of the acetic acid solution.
2. By titration, 17.6 mL of aqueous H_2SO_4 neutralized 27.4 mL of 0.0165 M LiOH solution. What was the molarity of the aqueous acid solution?

✓ SECTION 2 FORMATIVE ASSESSMENT

▶ Reviewing Main Ideas

1. Name an appropriate indicator for titrating the following:

a. a strong acid and a weak base

b. a strong base and a weak acid

2. If 20.0 mL of 0.0100 M aqueous HCl is required to neutralize 30.0 mL of an aqueous solution of NaOH, determine the molarity of the NaOH solution.

3. Suppose that 20.0 mL of 0.010 M $Ca(OH)_2$ is required to neutralize 12.0 mL of aqueous HCl solution. What is the molarity of the HCl solution?

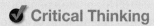 Critical Thinking

4. PREDICTING OUTCOMES Sketch the titration curve for 50.0 mL of 0.10 M NH_3 that is titrated with 0.10 M HCl.

When you work with acids and bases, you often need to state the hydronium ion concentration, $[H_3O^+]$, of a solution. One common practice is to use the negative logarithm of $[H_3O^+]$. This quantity is called *pH*. For example, pure water has a $[H_3O^+]$ of 1.0×10^{-7} M. So the pH of pure water is $-\log(1.0 \times 10^{-7}$ M$) = 7.00$. A solution of 0.10 M HCl has a pH of 1.00, or pH $= -\log(1.0 \times 10^{-1}) = 1.00$. The term *pOH* is also used for the negative logarithm of the hydroxide ion concentration, $[OH^-]$. The pOH of pure water is also 7.00.

Problem-Solving TIPS

- For pure water at 25°C, $[H_3O^+] = [OH^-] = 1.00 \times 10^{-7}$ M.
- The ionization constant of water, K_w, is the product of $[H_3O^+]$ and $[OH^-]$, so
  $K_w = [H_3O^+][OH^-] = (1.00 \times 10^{-7})(1.00 \times 10^{-7}) = 1.00 \times 10^{-14}$ at 25°C.
- If you know either $[H_3O^+]$ or $[OH^-]$, you can determine the other concentration.
- In terms of pH and pOH, pH + pOH = 14.00 for an aqueous solution at 25°C.
- Because pH calculations involve scientific notation and changes in signs, you should always check to see if answers make sense.

Sample Problem

What is the pH of a 0.0046 M solution of KOH?

KOH is completely dissociated into equal numbers of $K^+(aq)$ and $OH^-(aq)$. The concentration of OH^- is the same as the concentration of dissolved KOH, 0.0046 M. So $[OH^-] = 4.6 \times 10^{-3}$ M, and pOH $= -\log(4.6 \times 10^{-3}$ M$) = 2.34$.
For an aqueous solution at 25°C, pH + pOH = 14.00, so pH + 2.34 = 14.00.
Therefore, the pH of 0.0046 M KOH solution = 14.00 − 2.34 = 11.66.

What is the hydronium ion concentration, $[H_3O^+]$, of a solution with a pH of 4.08?
What is the pOH of the solution?

In this solution, $\log[H_3O^+] = -4.08$

$[H_3O^+] = $ antilog $(-4.08) = 0.000\,083$ M $= 8.3 \times 10^{-5}$ M

The pOH of the solution is 14.00 − pH = 14.00 − 4.08 = 9.92.

Practice   Answers in Appendix E

1. What is the pH of a 0.000 85 M solution of nitric acid, HNO_3, which is a strong acid?
2. What is the hydroxide ion concentration of an aqueous solution that has a pH of 9.95?

CHAPTER 15 **Summary**

BIG IDEA A solution's pH is a measure of its hydronium ion concentration and is used to rate its acidity.

SECTION 1 Aqueous Solutions and the Concept of pH

KEY TERMS

- Pure water undergoes self-ionization to give 1.0×10^{-7} M H_3O^+ and 1.0×10^{-7} M OH^- at 25°C.

- $pH = -\log[H_3O^+]$; $pOH = -\log[OH^-]$; at 25°C, $pH + pOH = 14.0$.

- At 25°C, acids have a pH of less than 7, bases have a pH of greater than 7, and neutral solutions have a pH of 7.

- If a solution contains a strong acid or a strong base, the $[H_3O^+]$, $[OH^-]$, and pH can be calculated from the molarity of the solution. If a solution contains a weak acid or a weak base, the $[H_3O^+]$ and the $[OH^-]$ must be calculated from an experimentally measured pH.

self-ionization of water
pH
pOH

SECTION 2 Determining pH and Titrations

KEY TERMS

- The pH of a solution can be measured using either a pH meter or acid-base indicators.

- Titration uses a solution of known concentration to determine the concentration of a solution of unknown concentration.

- To determine the end point of a titration, one should choose indicators that change color over ranges that include the pH of the equivalence point.

- When the molarity and volume of a known solution used in a titration are known, then the molarity of a given volume of an unknown solution can be found.

acid-base indicators
transition interval
pH meter
titration
equivalence point
end point
standard solution
primary standard

CHAPTER 15 **Review**

GO ONLINE

Interactive Review
HMHScience.com

Review Games
Concept Maps

SECTION 1

Aqueous Solutions and the Concept of pH

 REVIEWING MAIN IDEAS

1. Why is pure water a very weak electric conductor?

2. What does it mean when the formula of a particular ion or molecule is enclosed in brackets?

3. **a.** What is the $[H_3O^+]$ of pure water at 25°C?
   b. Is this true at all temperatures? Why or why not?

4. **a.** What is always true about the $[H_3O^+]$ value of acidic solutions?
   b. What is true about the $[H_3O^+]$ value of acidic solutions at 25°C?

5. **a.** Describe what is meant by the pH of a solution.
   b. Write the equation for determining pH.
   c. Explain and illustrate what is meant by the common logarithm of a number.

6. Identify each of the following solutions that are at 25°C as acidic, basic, or neutral:
   a. $[H_3O^+] = 1.0 \times 10^{-7}$ M
   b. $[H_3O^+] = 1.0 \times 10^{-10}$ M
   c. $[OH^-] = 1.0 \times 10^{-7}$ M
   d. $[OH^-] = 1.0 \times 10^{-11}$ M
   e. $[H_3O^+] = [OH^-]$
   f. pH = 3.0
   g. pH = 13.0

7. Arrange the following common substances in order of increasing pH:
   a. eggs   **f.** potatoes
   b. apples   **g.** lemons
   c. tomatoes **h.** milk of magnesia
   d. milk   **i.** seawater
   e. bananas

PRACTICE PROBLEMS

8. Calculate the $[H_3O^+]$ and $[OH^-]$ for each of the following. (Hint: See Sample Problem A.)
   a. 0.030 M HCl
   b. 1.0×10^{-4} M NaOH
   c. 5.0×10^{-3} M HNO₃
   d. 0.010 M Ca(OH)₂

9. Determine the pH of each of the following solutions. (Hint: See Sample Problem B.)
   a. 1.0×10^{-2} M HCl   **c.** 1.0×10^{-5} M HI
   b. 1.0×10^{-3} M HNO₃   **d.** 1.0×10^{-4} M HBr

10. Given the following $[OH^-]$ values, determine the pH of each solution.
    a. 1.0×10^{-6} M   **c.** 1.0×10^{-2} M
    b. 1.0×10^{-9} M   **d.** 1.0×10^{-7} M

11. Determine the pH of each solution.
    a. 1.0×10^{-2} M NaOH
    b. 1.0×10^{-3} M KOH
    c. 1.0×10^{-4} M LiOH

12. Determine the pH of solutions with each of the following $[H_3O^+]$. (Hint: See Sample Problem C.)
    a. 2.0×10^{-5} M
    b. 4.7×10^{-7} M
    c. 3.8×10^{-3} M

13. Given the following pH values, determine the $[H_3O^+]$ for each solution. (Hint: See Sample Problem D.)
    a. 3.0   **c.** 11.0
    b. 7.00   **d.** 5.0

14. Given the following pH values, determine the $[OH^-]$ for each solution.
    a. 7.00   **c.** 4.00
    b. 11.00   **d.** 6.00

15. Determine $[H_3O^+]$ for solutions with the following pH values. (Hint: See Sample Problem E.)
    a. 4.23
    b. 7.65
    c. 9.48

16. A nitric acid solution is found to have a pH of 2.70. Determine each of the following:
    a. $[H_3O^+]$
    b. $[OH^-]$
    c. the number of moles of HNO₃ required to prepare 5.50 L of this solution
    d. the mass of HNO₃ in the solution in part (c)
    e. the milliliters of concentrated acid needed to prepare the solution in part (c)
       (Concentrated nitric acid is 69.5% HNO₃ by mass and has a density of 1.42 g/mL.)

SECTION 2
Determining pH and Titrations

▶ **REVIEWING MAIN IDEAS**

17. What is meant by the transition interval of an indicator?

18. Explain how changes in pH affect the color of an indicator.

19. a. Without using an indicator, how can you determine the equivalence point of a titration experiment or the pH of a solution?
b. What can be observed about the rate of change of the pH of a solution near the end point of a titration?

20. a. What is meant by the end point of a titration?
b. What is the role of an indicator in the titration process?
c. On what basis is an indicator selected for a particular titration experiment?

21. For each of the four possible types of acid-base titration combinations (strong-strong, strong-weak, etc.), indicate the approximate pH at the end point. Also name a suitable indicator for detecting that end point.

22. Use **Figures 2.7a** and **2.7b** to sketch the pH curve of a strong acid being titrated by a weak base.

23. An unknown solution is colorless when tested with phenolphthalein but causes the indicator phenol red to turn red. Use this information to find the approximate pH of this solution.

PRACTICE PROBLEMS

24. For each of the following acid-base titration combinations, determine the number of moles of the first substance listed that would be the chemically equivalent amount of the second substance.
a. NaOH with 1.0 mol HCl
b. HNO_3 with 0.75 mol KOH
c. $Ba(OH)_2$ with 0.20 mol HF
d. H_2SO_4 with 0.90 mol $Mg(OH)_2$

25. Suppose that 15.0 mL of 2.50×10^{-2} M aqueous H_2SO_4 is required to neutralize 10.0 mL of an aqueous solution of KOH. What is the molarity of the KOH solution? (Hint: See Sample Problem F.)

26. In a titration experiment, a 12.5 mL sample of 1.75×10^{-2} M $Ba(OH)_2$ just neutralized 14.5 mL of HNO_3 solution. Calculate the molarity of the HNO_3 solution.

Mixed Review

▶ **REVIEWING MAIN IDEAS**

27. a. What is the $[OH^-]$ of a 4.0×10^{-4} M solution of $Ca(OH)_2$?
b. What is the $[H_3O+]$ of the solution?

28. Given the following $[H_3O^+]$ values, determine the pH of each solution.
a. 1.0×10^{-7} M
c. 1.0×10^{-12} M
b. 1.0×10^{-3} M
d. 1.0×10^{-5} M

29. What is the $[H_3O^+]$ for a solution that has a pH of 6.0?

30. Suppose that a 5.0×10^{-5} M solution of $Ba(OH)_2$ is prepared. What is the pH of the solution?

31. a. Calculate the pH of a solution that has an $[H_3O^+]$ of 8.4×10^{-11} M.
b. Calculate the $[H_3O^+]$ of a solution that has a pH of 2.50.

32. a. What is the concentration of OH^- in a 5.4×10^{-5} M solution of magnesium hydroxide, $Mg(OH)_2$?
b. Calculate the concentration of H_3O+ for this solution.

33. a. Calculate the molarity of H_3O^+ in a solution that has a pH of 8.90.
b. Calculate the concentration of OH^- for this solution.

34. What is the pH of a solution in which $[OH^-]$ equals 6.9×10^{-10} M?

35. In a titration, 25.9 mL of 3.4×10^{-3} M $Ba(OH)_2$ neutralized 16.6 mL of HCl solution. What is the molarity of the HCl solution?

36. Find the molarity of a $Ca(OH)_2$ solution given that 428 mL of the solution is neutralized in a titration by 115 mL of 6.7×10^{-3} M HNO_3.

37. Suppose that 10.1 mL of HNO_3 is neutralized by 71.4 mL of a 4.2×10^{-3} M solution of KOH in a titration. Calculate the concentration of the HNO_3 solution.

CRITICAL THINKING

38. Interpreting Graphics The following titration curve resulted from the titration of an unknown acid with 0.10 M NaOH. Analyze the curve. Make inferences related to the type of acidic solution titrated.

Titration of an Unknown Acid

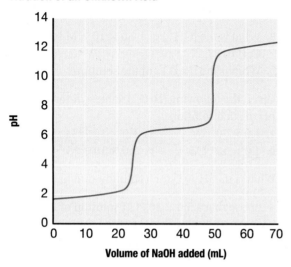

USING THE HANDBOOK

39. The normal pH of blood is about 7.4. When the pH shifts above or below that level, the results are acidosis or alkalosis. Review the section on blood pH in Group 14 of the *Elements Handbook* (Appendix A), and answer the following.
  a. What chemical species keep H_3O^+ in blood at the appropriate pH?
  b. What condition results when there is an excess of CO_2 in the blood?
  c. What is hyperventilation, and how does it affect blood pH?

RESEARCH AND WRITING

40. Examine the labels of at least five brands of shampoo. Note what is written there, if anything, regarding the pH of the shampoo. Do library research to find out why such pH ranges are chosen and why other ranges might be harmful to hair or eyes.

41. Acid rain is an environmental issue that crosses state and national boundaries. Conduct library research on this topic, and write a brief report. Include a description of the areas in the United States affected by acid rain and the geographical source of the sulfur and nitrogen oxides that are responsible for acid rain in each region.

ALTERNATIVE ASSESSMENT

42. Performance Use pH paper to determine the approximate pH of various brands of orange juice, which contains citric acid.

43. Performance Design and conduct an experiment to extract possible acid-base indicators from sources such as red cabbage, berries, and flower petals. Use known acidic, basic, and neutral solutions to test the action of each indicator that you are able to isolate.

Standards-Based Assessment

Record your answers on a separate piece of paper.

MULTIPLE CHOICE

1 Distilled water contains —

  A H_2O
  B H_3O^+
  C OH^-
  D all of the above

2 What is the pH of a 0.0010 M solution of HNO_3?

  A 1.0
  B 3.0
  C 4.0
  D 5.0

3 If the pH of a solution of the strong base NaOH is known, which property of the solution can be calculated?

  A molar concentration
  B $[OH^-]$
  C $[H_3O^+]$
  D all of the above

4 A neutral aqueous solution —

  A has a 7.0 M H_3O^+ concentration
  B contains neither hydronium ions nor hydroxide ions
  C has an equal number of hydronium ions and hydroxide ions
  D none of the above

5 Identify the salt that forms when a solution of H_2SO_4 is titrated with a solution of $Ca(OH)_2$.

  A calcium sulfate
  B calcium hydroxide
  C calcium oxide
  D calcium phosphate

6 The pH of a solution is 6.32. What is the pOH?

  A 6.32
  B 4.8×10^{-7}
  C 7.68
  D 2.1×10^{-8}

7 The K_w value for water can be affected by —

  A dissolving a salt in the solution
  B changes in temperature
  C changes in the hydroxide ion concentration
  D the presence of a strong acid

GRIDDED RESPONSE

8 The hydroxide ion concentration in a solution is 1.6×10^{-11} M. What is the pOH of the solution? (Express your answer to two decimal places.)

Test Tip

If you are permitted to, draw a line through each incorrect answer choice as you eliminate it.

CHAPTER 16

Reaction Energy

BIG IDEA
Energy is released or absorbed in chemical reactions. The tendency in nature is for chemical reactions to proceed in the direction of the lowest energy state.

ONLINE Chemistry
HMHScience.com

SECTION 1
Thermochemistry

SECTION 2
Driving Force of Reactions

ONLINE LABS
- Calorimetry and Hess's Law
- Evaluating Fuels
- Energy in Foods
- S.T.E.M. A Burning Interest

GO ONLINE
Why It Matters Video
HMHScience.com

Reactions

(b) NASA; (t) ©Charles D. Winters

Thermochemistry

Key Terms

thermochemistry
calorimeter
temperature
joule

heat
specific heat
enthalpy change
enthalpy of reaction

thermochemical equation
molar enthalpy of formation
enthalpy of combustion
Hess's law

Virtually every chemical reaction is accompanied by a change in energy. The energy absorbed or released, as light and heat for example, during a chemical reaction is referred to as *chemical energy*, because it appears when a chemical reaction occurs. Chemical energy is a form of potential energy, because it is energy a substance has available to do work during a chemical reaction. Think of it in these terms: a burning log is releasing energy as heat, but that energy was contained in the chemical bonds of the log before it began to burn.

As chemical reactions usually absorb or release energy as heat, i.e., *thermal energy*, we call **the study of the transfers of energy as heat that accompany chemical reactions and physical changes thermochemistry.** It is a fundamental law of science that energy can neither be created nor destroyed; it can only change forms. This is the *law of conservation of energy* and serves as the basis for the study of thermochemistry.

▶ MAIN IDEA
Temperature and heat are related but not identical.

The energy absorbed or released as heat in a chemical or physical change is measured in a calorimeter. In one kind of calorimeter, known quantities of reactants are sealed in a reaction chamber, which is immersed in a known quantity of water in an insulated vessel. Therefore, the energy given off (or absorbed) during the reaction is equal to the energy absorbed (or given off) by the known quantity of water. The amount of energy is determined from the temperature change of the known mass of water. Temperature change is measured, because energy cannot be measured directly. Temperature, however, which is affected by the transfer of energy as heat, is directly measurable. To understand this, let us look at the definitions of heat and temperature and at how temperature is measured.

Temperature is a measure of the average kinetic energy of the particles in a sample of matter. The greater the kinetic energy of the particles in a sample, the higher the temperature is and the hotter it feels. To assign a numerical value to temperature, it is necessary to define a temperature scale. For calculations in thermochemistry, we use the Celsius and Kelvin scales. Celsius and Kelvin temperatures are related by the equation K = 273.15 + °C. For most calculations in this book, 273.15 is rounded to 273.

The ability to measure temperature is thus based on energy transfer. The amount of energy transferred as heat is usually measured in joules. **A joule is the SI unit of heat as well as all other forms of energy.** The joule, abbreviated J, is derived from the units for mass, distance, and time.

$$J = \frac{kg \times m^2}{s^2}$$

SECTION 1

Main Ideas

▷ Temperature and heat are related but not identical.

▷ Energy transfer varies from reaction to reaction.

▷ Heat energy is transferred during a reaction.

▷ Enthalpy of formation is the energy change when elements form one mole of a compound.

▷ Compounds with large negative heats of formation tend to be stable.

▷ Enthalpy changes in combustion.

▷ Change in enthalpy is calculated using Hess's law.

▷ Hess's Law can be used to determine reaction enthalpies not measurable directly.

FIGURE 1.1

Transfer of Energy The direction of energy transfer as heat is determined by the temperature differences between the objects within a system. The energy is transferred as heat from the hotter brass bar to the cooler water. This energy transfer will continue until the bar and the water reach the same temperature.

Heat can be thought of as the energy transferred between samples of matter because of a difference in their temperatures. Energy transferred as heat always moves spontaneously from matter at a higher temperature to matter at a lower temperature. As shown in **Figure 1.1,** the temperature of the cool water in the beaker increases as energy flows into it. Likewise, the temperature of the hot brass bar decreases as energy flows away from it. When the temperature of the water equals the temperature of the brass bar, energy is no longer transferred as heat within the system.

▶ MAIN IDEA

Energy transfer varies from reaction to reaction.

The quantity of energy transferred as heat during a temperature change depends on the nature of the material changing temperature, the mass of the material changing temperature, and the size of the temperature change. One gram of iron heated to 100.0°C and cooled to 50.0°C in a calorimeter transfers 22.5 J of energy to the surrounding water. But one gram of silver transfers 11.8 J of energy under the same conditions. The difference depends on the metals' differing capacities for absorbing this energy. A quantity called specific heat can be used to compare heat absorption capacities for different materials. **Specific heat is the amount of energy required to raise the temperature of one gram of a substance by one degree Celsius (1°C) or one kelvin (1 K) (because the sizes of the degree divisions on both scales are equal).** Values of specific heat can be given in units of joules per gram per degree Celsius, J/(g • °C), joules per gram per kelvin, J/(g • K), or calories per gram per degree Celsius, cal/(g • °C). **Figure 1.2** gives the specific heats of some common substances. Notice the extremely high specific heat of water, one of the highest of common substances. This is why water plays such a crucial role in regulating temperature.

FIGURE 1.2

SPECIFIC HEATS OF SOME COMMON SUBSTANCES AT 298.15 K

Substance	Specific heat J/(g•K)
Water (l)	4.18
Water (s)	2.06
Water (g)	1.87
Ammonia (g)	2.09
Benzene (l)	1.74
Ethanol (l)	2.44
Ethanol (g)	1.42
Aluminum (s)	0.897
Calcium (s)	0.647
Carbon, graphite (s)	0.709
Copper (s)	0.385
Gold (s)	0.129
Iron (s)	0.449
Mercury (l)	0.140
Lead (s)	0.129

Specific heat is measured under constant pressure conditions, so its symbol, c_p, has a subscripted p as a reminder. In the equation, c_p is the specific heat at a given pressure, q is the energy lost or gained, m is the mass of the sample, and ΔT represents the change in temperature.

$$c_p = \frac{q}{m \times \Delta T}$$

This equation can be rearranged to give an equation that can be used to find the quantity of energy gained or lost with a change in temperature.

Energy Lost or Gained $q = c_p \times m \times \Delta T$

GO ONLINE

Learn It! Video
HMHScience.com

Solve It! Cards
HMHScience.com

SOLUTION TUTOR

HMHScience.com

Specific Heat

Sample Problem A A 4.0-g sample of glass was heated from 274 K to 314 K, a temperature increase of 40. K, and was found to have absorbed 32 J of energy as heat.

a. What is the specific heat of this type of glass?

b. How much energy will the same glass sample gain when it is heated from 314 K to 344 K?

Continued

Specific Heat (continued)

① ANALYZE

Given:
$m = 4.0 \text{ g}$

$\Delta T = 40. \text{ K}$

$q = 32 \text{ J}$

Unknown: **a.** $c_p = $ in $\text{J}/(\text{g} \cdot \text{K})$ and **b.** q when $\Delta T = 344 \text{ K} - 314 \text{ K}$

② PLAN

a. The specific heat, c_p, of the glass is calculated using the equation given for specific heat.

$$c_p = \frac{q}{m \times \Delta T}$$

b. The rearranged specific heat equation is used to find the energy gained when the glass was heated.

$$q = c_p \times m \times \Delta T$$

③ SOLVE

a. $c_p = \dfrac{32 \text{ J}}{(4.0 \text{ g})(40. \text{ K})} = 0.20 \text{ J}/(\text{g} \cdot \text{K})$

b. $q = \dfrac{0.20 \text{ J}}{(\text{g} \cdot \text{K})}(4.0 \text{ g})(344 \text{ K} - 314 \text{ K})$

$q = \dfrac{0.20 \text{ J}}{(\text{g} \cdot \text{K})}(4.0 \text{ g})(30 \text{ K}) = 24 \text{ J}$

④ CHECK YOUR WORK

The units combine or cancel correctly to give the specific heat in $\text{J}/(\text{g} \cdot \text{K})$ and the energy in J.

Practice   Answers in Appendix E

1. Determine the specific heat of a material if a 35-g sample absorbed 96 J as it was heated from 293 K to 313 K.
2. If 980 kJ of energy are added to 6.2 L of water at 291 K, what will the final temperature of the water be?

▶ MAIN IDEA

Heat energy is transferred during a reaction.

The energy absorbed as heat during a chemical reaction at constant pressure is represented by ΔH. The H is the symbol for a quantity called *enthalpy*. It is not practical to talk just about enthalpy as a quantity, because we have no way to directly measure the enthalpy of a system. Only *changes* in enthalpy can be measured. The Greek letter Δ ("delta") stands for "change in." Therefore, ΔH is read as "change in enthalpy." An **enthalpy change** is the amount of energy absorbed by a system as heat during a process at constant pressure. The enthalpy change is always the difference between the enthalpies of the products and the reactants. The following equation expresses an enthalpy change for a reaction.

Enthalpy $$\Delta H = H_{\text{products}} - H_{\text{reactants}}$$

The **enthalpy of reaction** is the quantity of energy transferred as heat during a chemical reaction. You can think of enthalpy of reaction as the difference between the stored energy of the reactants and the products. Enthalpy of reaction is sometimes called "heat of reaction."

Enthalpy of Reaction in Exothermic Reactions

If a mixture of hydrogen and oxygen is ignited, water will form, and energy will be released explosively. The released energy comes from the reactants as they form products. Because energy is released, the reaction is *exothermic*, and the energy of the product, water, must be less than the energy of the reactants. The following chemical equation for this reaction shows that when 2 mol of hydrogen gas at room temperature are burned, 1 mol of oxygen gas is consumed and 2 mol of water vapor are formed.

$$2H_2(g) + O_2(g) \longrightarrow 2H_2O(g)$$

The equation does not tell you that energy is evolved as heat during the reaction. Experiments have shown that 483.6 kJ of energy are evolved when 2 mol of gaseous water are formed from its elements at 298.15 K.

Modifying the chemical equation to show the amount of energy as heat released during the reaction gives the following expression.

$$2H_2(g) + O_2(g) \longrightarrow 2H_2O(g) + 483.6 \text{ kJ}$$

This expression is an example of a **thermochemical equation,** an equation that includes the quantity of energy released or absorbed as heat during the reaction as written. In any thermochemical equation, we must always interpret the coefficients as *numbers of moles* and never as *numbers of molecules*. The quantity of energy released as heat in this or any other reaction depends on the amounts of reactants and products. The quantity of energy as heat released during the formation of water from H_2 and O_2 is proportional to the quantity of water formed. Producing twice as much water vapor would require twice as many moles of reactants and would release 2×483.6 kJ of energy as heat, as shown in the following thermochemical equation (which is simply the previous thermochemical equation multiplied by two).

$$4H_2(g) + 2O_2(g) \longrightarrow 4H_2O(g) + 967.2 \text{ kJ}$$

Producing one-half as much water requires one-half as many moles of reactants and releases only one-half as much energy, or $\frac{1}{2} \times 483.6$ kJ. The thermochemical equation for this reaction is as follows.

$$H_2(g) + \frac{1}{2}O_2(g) \longrightarrow H_2O(g) + 241.8 \text{ kJ}$$

Enthalpy of Reaction in Endothermic Reactions

The situation is reversed in an *endothermic* reaction—products have a larger enthalpy than reactants. The decomposition of water vapor is endothermic; it is the reverse of the reaction that forms water vapor. The amount of energy as heat absorbed by water molecules to form hydrogen and oxygen equals the amount of energy as heat released when the elements combine to form the water. The equation changes accordingly.

FIGURE 1.3

Enthalpy in Exothermic
Reactions In an exothermic chemical reaction, the enthalpy change is negative because energy is released into the system as heat.

✔ **CRITICAL THINKING**

Interpret Data What is the connection between the negative ΔH and the slope of the red line in the graph?

GO ONLINE *Animated* Chemistry
HMHScience.com

Endothermic and Exothermic Reactions

Exothermic Reaction Pathway

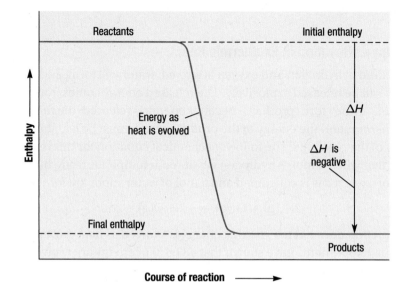

So for an endothermic reaction, enthalpy now appears on the reactant side of the thermochemical equation. However, it hasn't changed value.

$$2H_2O(g) + 483.6\ kJ \longrightarrow 2H_2(g) + O_2(g)$$

The physical states of reactants and products must always be included in thermochemical equations because they influence the overall amount of energy as heat gained or lost. For example, the energy needed to decompose water would be greater than 483.6 kJ if we started with ice, because extra energy would be needed to go from ice to liquid and then to vapor.

Thermochemical Equations

Thermochemical equations are usually written by designating the value of ΔH, rather than by writing the energy as a reactant or product. For an exothermic reaction, ΔH is always negative because the system loses energy. So the thermochemical equation for the formation of 2 mol of gaseous water would be written as

$$2H_2(g) + O_2(g) \longrightarrow 2H_2O(g) \quad \Delta H = -483.6\ kJ$$

Figure 1.3 graphically shows the course of an exothermic reaction. The initial enthalpy of the reactants is greater than the final enthalpy of the products. This means energy as heat is evolved, or given off, during the reaction; this is described as a negative enthalpy change.

For an endothermic reaction, ΔH is always positive because the system gains energy. Thus, the endothermic decomposition of 2 mol of gaseous water has the following thermochemical equation.

$$2H_2O(g) \longrightarrow 2H_2(g) + O_2(g) \quad \Delta H = +483.6\ kJ$$

FIGURE 1.4

Enthalpy in Endothermic Reactions In an endothermic chemical reaction, the enthalpy change is positive because energy is absorbed into the system as heat.

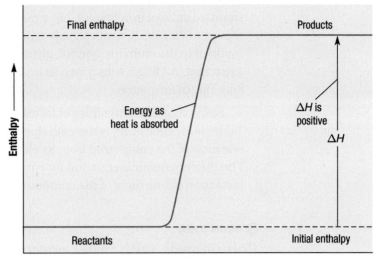

Endothermic Reaction Pathway

The course of an endothermic reaction is illustrated in **Figure 1.4.** Since energy as heat is absorbed, the enthalpy of the reactants is lower than the final enthalpy of the products, and ΔH is positive. In general, when looking at all thermochemical equations, consider the following.

1. The coefficients in a balanced thermochemical equation represent the numbers of *moles* of reactants and products and never the numbers of *molecules*. They can be fractions when necessary.

2. The physical state of the product or reactant involved in a reaction is an important factor and, therefore, must be included in the thermochemical equation.

3. The change in enthalpy represented by a thermochemical equation is directly proportional to the number of moles of substances undergoing a change. For example, if 2 mol of water are decomposed, twice as much enthalpy, 483.6 kJ, is needed than for the decomposition of 1 mol of water.

4. The value of the enthalpy change, ΔH, is usually not significantly influenced by changing temperature.

▶ **MAIN IDEA**

Enthalpy of formation is the energy change when elements form one mole of a compound.

The formation of water from hydrogen and oxygen is a composition reaction—the formation of a compound from its elements in their standard form. Thermochemical data are often recorded as the enthalpies of such composition reactions. **The molar enthalpy of formation is the enthalpy change that occurs when one mole of a compound is formed from its elements in their standard state at 25°C and 1 atm.**

To make comparisons meaningful, enthalpies of formation are given for the standard states of reactants and products—these are the states found at atmospheric pressure and, usually, room temperature (298.15 K). Thus, the standard state of water is liquid, not gas or solid. The standard state of iron is solid, not a molten liquid. To signify that a value represents measurements on substances in their standard states, a ^{0} sign is added to the enthalpy symbol, giving ΔH^0 for the standard enthalpy of a reaction. Adding a subscript f, as in ΔH_f^0, further indicates a standard enthalpy of formation.

Some standard enthalpies of formation are given in Appendix Table B–14. Each entry is the enthalpy of formation for the synthesis of *one mole* of the compound from its elements in their standard states. The thermochemical equation for each enthalpy of formation shows the formation of one mole of the compound from its elements.

▶ MAIN IDEA

Compounds with large negative heats of formation tend to be stable.

If a large amount of energy as heat is released when a compound is formed, the compound has a large negative enthalpy of formation. Such compounds are very stable.

Elements in their standard states are defined as having $\Delta H_f^0 = 0$. The ΔH_f^0 of carbon dioxide is -393.5 kJ/mol of gas produced. Therefore, carbon dioxide is more stable than the elements from which it was formed. You can see in Appendix Table B–14 that the majority of the enthalpies of formation are negative.

Compounds with relatively positive values of enthalpies of formation, or only slightly negative values, are typically unstable. For example, hydrogen iodide, HI, is a colorless gas that decomposes somewhat when stored at room temperature. It has a relatively high positive enthalpy of formation of $+26.5$ kJ/mol. As it decomposes, violet iodine vapor, I_2, becomes visible throughout the container of the gas.

Compounds with a high positive enthalpy of formation are sometimes very unstable and may react or decompose violently. Mercury fulminate, $HgC_2N_2O_2$, has a very large enthalpy of formation of $+270$ kJ/mol. Its instability makes it useful as a detonator for explosives.

▶ MAIN IDEA

Enthalpy changes in combustion.

Combustion reactions produce a large amount of energy in the form of light and heat when a substance is combined with oxygen. The enthalpy change that occurs during the complete combustion of one mole of a substance is called the **enthalpy of combustion** of the substance. Enthalpy of combustion is defined in terms of *one mole of reactant*, whereas the enthalpy of formation is defined in terms of *one mole of product*.

FIGURE 1.5

Combustion Calorimeter A weighed sample is ignited by an electric spark and burned in the sample dish in an atmosphere of pure oxygen. The energy generated by the combustion reaction warms the steel bomb and the water surrounding it. The thermometer measures the initial and final temperatures of the water, and this temperature change is then used to calculate the energy evolved by the reaction as heat.

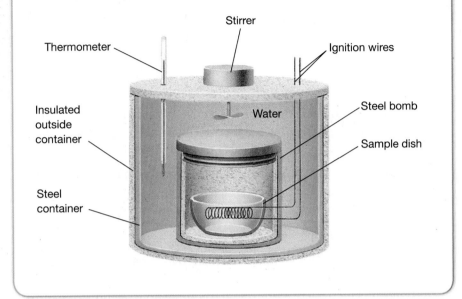

✔ **CRITICAL THINKING**

Deduce What is the relationship between calories as a measurement of heat energy and the Calorie content found in the food you eat?

All substances are in their standard states. The general enthalpy notation, ΔH, applies to enthalpies of reaction, but the addition of a subscripted c, ΔH_c, refers specifically to enthalpy of combustion. A list of enthalpies of combustion can be found in Appendix Table B–5. A combustion calorimeter is a common instrument used to determine enthalpies of combustion. **Figure 1.5** shows a fixed-volume calorimeter. A similar apparatus under constant pressure is used to obtain enthalpy measurements.

▶ **MAIN IDEA**

Change in enthalpy is calculated using Hess's law.

Thermochemical equations can be rearranged and added to give enthalpy changes for reactions not included in the data tables. **The basis for calculating enthalpies of reaction is known as Hess's law: The overall enthalpy change in a reaction is equal to the sum of enthalpy changes for the individual steps in the process.** The energy difference between reactants and products is independent of the route taken to get from one to the other. In fact, measured enthalpies of reaction can be combined to calculate enthalpies of reaction that are difficult or impossible to actually measure.

To demonstrate how to apply Hess's law, we will work through the calculation of the enthalpy of formation for the formation of methane gas from its elements. The calculation takes several steps.

Our calculation will consider how methane gas, CH_4, forms from its elements, hydrogen gas and solid carbon (graphite), at 298.15 K (25°C).

$$C(s) + 2H_2(g) \longrightarrow CH_4(g) \quad \Delta H_f^0 = ?$$

In order to calculate the change in enthalpy for this reaction, we can use the combustion reactions of the elements, carbon and hydrogen, and of methane.

$$C(s) + O_2(g) \longrightarrow CO_2(g) \qquad \Delta H_c^0 = -393.5 \text{ kJ}$$

$$H_2(g) + \frac{1}{2}O_2(g) \longrightarrow H_2O(l) \qquad \Delta H_c^0 = -285.8 \text{ kJ}$$

$$CH_4(g) + 2O_2(g) \longrightarrow CO_2(g) + 2H_2O(l) \qquad \Delta H_c^0 = -890.8 \text{ kJ}$$

The general principles for combining thermochemical equations follow.

1. If a reaction is reversed, the sign of ΔH is also reversed.

2. Multiply the coefficients of the known equations so that, when added together, they give the desired thermochemical equation. Multiply the ΔH by the same factor as the corresponding equation.

In this case, we must reverse the combustion equation for methane and remember to change the sign of ΔH from negative to positive. This will change the exothermic reaction to an endothermic one.

$$CO_2(g) + 2H_2O(l) \longrightarrow CH_4(g) + 2O_2(g) \quad \Delta H^0 = +890.8 \text{ kJ}$$

Now we notice that 2 moles of water are used as a reactant; therefore, 2 moles of water will be needed as a product. Remember that mass is conserved in chemical reactions. In the combustion reaction for hydrogen as it is written, it only produces one mole of water. We must multiply the coefficients of this combustion reaction and the value of ΔH by 2 in order to obtain the desired quantity of water.

$$2H_2(g) + O_2(g) \longrightarrow 2H_2O(l) \quad \Delta H_c^0 = 2(-285.8 \text{ kJ})$$

We are now ready to add the three equations together using Hess's law to give the enthalpy of formation of methane and the balanced equation.

$$C(s) + O_2(g) \longrightarrow CO_2(g) \qquad \Delta H_c^0 = -393.5 \text{ kJ}$$

$$2H_2(g) + O_2(g) \longrightarrow 2H_2O(l) \qquad \Delta H_c^0 = 2(-285.8 \text{ kJ})$$

$$CO_2(g) + 2H_2O(l) \longrightarrow CH_4(g) + 2O_2(g) \qquad \Delta H^0 = +890.8 \text{ kJ}$$

$$\overline{C(s) + 2H_2(g) \longrightarrow CH_4(g) \qquad \Delta H_f^0 = -74.3 \text{ kJ}}$$

Hess's law says that the enthalpy difference between reactants and products is independent of pathway. Therefore, any enthalpy of reaction may be calculated using enthalpies of formation for all the substances in the reaction of interest, without knowing anything else about how the reaction occurs. Mathematically, the overall equation for enthalpy change will be in the form of the equation shown below.

Total Enthalpy Change

$$\Delta H^0 = \text{sum of } [(\Delta H_f^0 \text{ of products}) \times (\text{mol of products})] - \text{sum of } [(\Delta H_f^0 \text{ of reactants}) \times (\text{mol of reactants})]$$

An example using Hess's law is shown in Sample Problem B.

Sample Problem B Calculate the enthalpy of reaction for the combination of methane and oxygen to form ethenone, CH_2CO, and water, as given in the following equation.

$$2CH_4(g) + 2O_2(g) \longrightarrow CH_2CO(g) + 3H_2O$$

Use the following two reactions and enthalpy data to make your calculation.

$$CH_2CO(g) + 2O_2(g) \longrightarrow 2CO_2(g) + H_2O(g) \qquad \Delta H = -981.1 \text{ kJ}$$

$$CH_4(g) + 2O_2(g) \longrightarrow CO_2(g) + 2H_2O(g) \qquad \Delta H = -802.3 \text{ kJ}$$

---

❶ ANALYZE

Given:　　$CH_2CO(g) + 2O_2(g) \longrightarrow 2CO_2(g) + H_2O(g) \qquad \Delta H = -981.1 \text{ kJ}$

　　　　　　$CH_4(g) + 2O_2(g) \longrightarrow CO_2(g) + 2H_2O(g) \qquad \Delta H = -802.3 \text{ kJ}$

Unknown:　$\Delta H^0 \; 2CH_4(g) + 2O_2(g) \longrightarrow CH_2CO(g) + 3H_2O$

---

❷ PLAN

ΔH can be found by adding all the ΔH values of the component reactions as specified in Hess's law. The desired equation has $2CH_4$ and $2O_2(g)$ as reactants and CH_2CO and $3H_2O$ as the products.

$$2CH_4(g) + 2O_2(g) \longrightarrow CH_2CO(g) + 3H_2O(g)$$

We need an equation with CH_4 as a product. The first reaction for the combustion of CH_4 has CH_4 reacting with O_2 to give CO_2 and $2H_2O$.

$$CH_4(g) + 2O_2(g) \longrightarrow CO_2(g) + 2H_2O(g) \qquad \Delta H_c^0 = -802.3 \text{ kJ}$$

The other equation should have CH_2CO and H_2O as products, so we can reverse the second equation for the formation of H_2O and CO_2 from CH_2CO and O_2.

$$2CO_2(g) + H_2O(l) \longrightarrow CH_2CO(g) + 2O_2(g) \qquad \Delta H^0 = +981.1 \text{ kJ}$$

---

❸ SOLVE

$$2CO_2(g) + H_2O(g) \longrightarrow CH_2CO(g) + 2O_2(g)$$
$$2CH_4(g) + 4O_2(g) \longrightarrow 2CO_2(g) + 4H_2O(g)$$

$$\overline{2\cancel{CO_2}(g) + H_2O(g) + 2CH_4(g) + \overset{2}{\cancel{4}}O_2(g) \longrightarrow}$$
$$CH_2CO(g) + 2\cancel{O_2}(g) + 2\cancel{CO_2}(g) + \overset{3}{\cancel{4}}H_2O(g)$$
$$2CH_4(g) + 2O_2(g) \longrightarrow CH_2CO(g) + 3H_2O(g)$$
$$-(-981.1 \text{ kJ})$$
$$\underline{+(2 \times -802.3 \text{ kJ})}$$
$$-623.5 \text{ kJ}$$

Note the multiplication by 2, the cancellation of O_2 and CO_2, and the partial cancellation of H_2O.

Continued

Enthalpy of Reaction (continued)

4 CHECK YOUR WORK

The desired equation is obtained when the two equations are added.
The enthalpy of reaction also can be calculated from the enthalpies of formation of the reactants and products as described in the following word equation.

$$\Delta H^0 = \text{sum of } [(\Delta H_f^0 \text{ of products}) \times (\text{mol of products})] - \text{sum of } [(\Delta H_f^0 \text{ of reactants}) \times (\text{mol of reactants})]$$

Evaluate your solution by considering if the correct units, kilojoules, were used consistently. Rules for adding and rounding measurements give a solution with four significant figures, which the calculated answer contains. Double-check that the unnecessary reactants and products canceled correctly and that the equation multiplied by 2 had all values adjusted appropriately. Finally, check the reasonableness of the answer by rounding the values and approximating the answer.

$$-1600 \text{ kJ} + 1000 \text{ kJ} = -600 \text{ kJ}$$

-600 KJ is a reasonable approximation.

Practice   Answers in Appendix E

1. Calculate the ΔH for the reaction of fluorine gas, $F_2(g)$ with $H_2O(l)$ water to form $2HF(g)$ and $O_2(g)$.
2. Carbon occurs in two distinct forms. It can be the soft, black material found in pencils and lock lubricants, called graphite, or it can be the hard, brilliant gem we know as diamond. Calculate ΔH^0 for the conversion of graphite to diamond for the following reaction.

$$C_{graphite}(s) \longrightarrow C_{diamond}(s)$$

The combustion reactions you will need follow.

$$C_{graphite}(s) + O_2(g) \longrightarrow CO_2(g) \quad \Delta H_c^0 = -394 \text{ kJ}$$
$$C_{diamond}(s) + O_2(g) \longrightarrow CO_2(g) \quad \Delta H_c^0 = -396 \text{ kJ}$$

▶ MAIN IDEA

Hess's law can be used to determine reaction enthalpies not measurable directly.

When carbon is burned in a limited supply of oxygen, carbon monoxide is produced. In this reaction, carbon is probably first oxidized to carbon dioxide. Then part of the carbon dioxide is reduced with carbon to give some carbon monoxide. Because these two reactions occur simultaneously and we get a mixture of CO and CO_2, it is not possible to directly measure the enthalpy of formation of $CO(g)$ from C(s) and $O_2(g)$.

$$C(s) + \frac{1}{2}O_2(g) \longrightarrow CO(g) \quad \Delta H_f^0 = ?$$

However, we do know the enthalpy of formation of carbon dioxide and the enthalpy of combustion of carbon monoxide.

$$C(s) + O_2(g) \longrightarrow CO_2(g) \quad \Delta H_f^0 = -393.5 \text{ kJ/mol}$$
$$CO(g) + \frac{1}{2}O_2(g) \longrightarrow CO_2(g) \quad \Delta H_c^0 = -283.0 \text{ kJ/mol}$$

We reverse the second equation because we need CO as a product. Adding gives the desired enthalpy of formation of carbon monoxide.

$$C(s) + O_2(g) \longrightarrow \cancel{CO_2(g)} \qquad \Delta H^0 = -393.5 \text{ kJ}$$
$$\cancel{CO_2(g)} \longrightarrow CO(g) + \frac{1}{2}O_2(g) \qquad \Delta H^0 = +283.0 \text{ kJ}$$

$$\overline{C(s) + \frac{1}{2}O_2(g) \longrightarrow CO(g) \qquad \Delta H_f^0 = -110.5 \text{ kJ}}$$

FIGURE 1.6

Enthalpy of a Two-Step Reaction This diagram shows the enthalpy of reaction for carbon dioxide, CO_2, and carbon monoxide, CO.

Enthalpies of Reaction

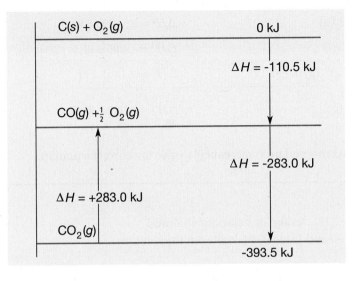

Look closely at **Figure 1.6.** This diagram is a model for a reaction that takes place in two distinct steps. If we plot the reactions based on their relative energy, you can see the relationship among the values obtained for the enthalpy of formation of carbon monoxide. The formation of CO_2 is plotted at a level corresponding to -393.5 kJ/mol. The diagram shows the reverse of the combustion reaction ($+283.0$ kJ/mol) is added to that level. From the diagram, you see the difference between the two. This represents the formation of CO. The value of this is -110.5 kJ/mol.

GO ONLINE

Solve It! Cards
HMHScience.com

Enthalpy of Formation

Sample Problem C Calculate the enthalpy of formation of ethyne (acetylene), C_2H_2, using the information on enthalpies of formation in Appendix Table B–14 and the information on enthalpies of combustion in Appendix Table B–5. Solve by combining the known thermochemical equations.

1 ANALYZE

Given:

$$C(s) + O_2(g) \longrightarrow CO_2(g) \qquad \Delta H_f^0 = -393.5 \text{ kJ}$$

$$H_2(g) + \frac{1}{2}O_2(g) \longrightarrow H_2O(l) \qquad \Delta H_f^0 = -285.8 \text{ kJ}$$

$$C_5H_2(g) + \frac{5}{2}O_2(g) \longrightarrow 2CO_2(g) + H_2O(l) \qquad \Delta H_c^0 = -1301.1 \text{ kJ}$$

Unknown: ΔH_f^0 for $2C(s) + H_2(g) \longrightarrow C_2H_2(g)$

 Continued

Enthalpy of Formation (continued)

2 PLAN

Combine the given equations according to Hess's law. We need C_2H_2 as a product, so we reverse the equation for combustion of C_2H_2 and the sign for ΔH_c^0. Multiply the equation for formation of CO_2 by 2 to give 2C as a reactant. Multiply the equation for formation of H_2O by 6 to give $6H_2$ as a reactant.

3 SOLVE

$$2C(s) + 2O_2(g) \longrightarrow 2CO_2(g) \qquad\qquad \Delta H^0 = 2(-393.5\ kJ)$$

$$H_2(g) + \frac{1}{2}O_2(g) \longrightarrow H_2O(l) \qquad\qquad \Delta H^0 = -285.8\ kJ$$

$$2CO_2(g) + H_2O(l) \longrightarrow C_2H_2(g) + \frac{5}{2}O_2(g) \qquad \Delta H^0 = +1301.1\ kJ$$

$$\overline{2C(s) + H_2(g) \longrightarrow C_2H_2(g) \qquad\qquad\qquad \Delta H_f^0 = +228.3\ kJ}$$

4 CHECK YOUR WORK

The unnecessary reactants and products cancel to give the correct equation.

Practice Answers in Appendix E

1. Calculate the enthalpy of formation of butane, C_4H_{10}, using the balanced chemical equation and information in Appendix Table B–5 and Table B–14. Write out the solution according to Hess's law.
2. Calculate the enthalpy of combustion of 1 mol decane, $C_{10}H_{22}(l)$, to form CO_2 and H_2O. ΔH_f^0 for decane is -300.9 kJ/mol using the balanced chemical equation and Appendix Table B–14.
3. Calculate the enthalpy of formation for sulfur dioxide, SO_2, from its elements, sulfur and oxygen. Use the balanced chemical equation and the following information.

$$S(s) + \frac{3}{2}O_2(g) \longrightarrow SO_3(g) \qquad \Delta H_c^0 = -395.2\ kJ$$

$$2SO_2(g) + O_2(g) \longrightarrow 2SO_3(g) \qquad \Delta H^0 = -198.2\ kJ$$

✓ SECTION 1 FORMATIVE ASSESSMENT

▶ Reviewing Main Ideas

1. What is meant by *enthalpy change*?
2. What is meant by *enthalpy of reaction*?
3. Describe the relationship between a compound's stability and its enthalpy of formation.
4. What is the importance of Hess's law to thermodynamic calculations?
5. How much energy would be absorbed as heat by 75 g of iron when heated from 295 K to 301 K?
6. A hot, just-minted copper coin is placed in 101 g of water to cool. The water temperature changes by 8.39°C, and the temperature of the coin changes by 68.0°C. What is the mass of the coin?

✓ Critical Thinking

7. **INTEGRATING CONCEPTS** Isooctane (C_8H_{18}) is a major component of gasoline.
   a. Using the following thermodynamic data, calculate the change in enthalpy for the combustion of 1.0 mol of isooctane.

   $$H_2(g) + \frac{1}{2}O_2(g) \longrightarrow H_2O(g)\ \Delta H^0 = -241.8\ kJ$$
   $$C(s) + O_2(g) \longrightarrow CO_2(g)\ \Delta H^0 = -393.5\ kJ$$
   $$8C(s) + 9H_2(g) \longrightarrow C_8H_{18}(l)\ \Delta H^0 = -224.13\ kJ$$

   b. One gallon of isooctane has a mass of 2.6 kg. What is the heat of (enthalpy of) combustion of one gallon of this compound?

Energy Density of Fuels

S.T.E.M.

How much energy is in your gas tank? As you know, enthalpy of reaction, ΔH, is a measure of energy released or absorbed in the course of a chemical reaction. It would seem, then, that ignoring all other factors, the best fuel would be the one with the most negative ΔH.

It's not that simple. Other factors, such as if burning the fuels produces toxins or greenhouse gases, cannot be ignored. Also confusing are the different ways in which ΔH is measured and the units in which it is reported. Energy of combustion is often expressed as energy density, or the amount of energy that can be extracted from a given amount of matter. When it is important to minimize the mass of fuel, energy densities are compared in units of MJ/kg. When volume of fuel is a concern, comparisons are made in units of MJ/L. Almost any fuel can be made to look like the best source if you aren't paying close attention.

The table compares fuels in three different ways. The kJ/mol column shows ΔH for the reactions that release the energy of each fuel. The second and third columns show two ways of expressing energy density.

ENTHALPIES OF COMBUSTION			
Fuel	MJ/kg	MJ/L	kJ/mol
Hydrogen	142	0.010	286
Methane	56	0.036	889
Gasoline	44	32.4	~ 5,000
Coal	~ 30	~ 39	~ 1,390
Ethanol	26.4	20.6	1,300

Methane and hydrogen compare favorably with gasoline in terms of energy released for a given mass of fuel. Methane and hydrogen, however, are gases, and gasoline is a liquid. The low densities of gases explain why the values in the MJ/L are so low for methane and hydrogen. These fuels must be compressed or liquefied to store a useful amount of energy in a reasonable volume. This isn't practical for the gas tank of a vehicle.

A comparison of ethanol and gasoline is more useful. The table shows that gasoline appears to be better than ethanol in terms of energy density and enthalpy of combustion. Ethanol, however, is a renewable resource because it can be produced from plants grown on farms. Comparing two fuels is complex and at times controversial.

Clearly, there are considerations other than energy density that need to be taken into account. There is no clear consensus on how to compare fuels, but here are some questions you can ask:

- Are the combustion products hazardous?
- How much energy is used in producing each fuel?
- How does each fuel affect vehicle engine performance?
- Who benefits financially from production of the fuel?
- Why is the choice of fuel politically controversial?
- Is it ethical to take land out of food production when people are starving in other countries?

Questions

1. How does coal compare with gasoline in energy per liter and energy per kilogram? Why?

2. Which fuels listed in the table produce greenhouse gases, and why?

©Jim West/Alamy

Driving Force of Reactions

Key Terms

entropy   free energy   free-energy change

The change in energy of a reaction system is one of two factors that allow chemists to predict whether a reaction will occur spontaneously and to explain how it occurs. The randomness of the particles in a system is the second factor affecting whether a reaction will occur spontaneously.

▶ **MAIN IDEA**

Reactions generally move to a lower-energy state.

The great majority of chemical reactions in nature are exothermic. As these reactions proceed, energy is liberated, and the products have less energy than the original reactants. The products are also more resistant to change, more stable, than the original reactants. In nature, reactions tend to proceed in a direction that leads to a lower-energy state.

But can endothermic reactions, ones in which energy is absorbed and products are less stable than the original reactants, occur spontaneously? We might expect this only with the assistance of an outside influence, such as continued heating. However, some endothermic reactions *do* occur spontaneously. Thus, we can conclude that something other than enthalpy change must help determine whether a reaction will occur.

▶ **MAIN IDEA**

Entropy measures randomness in a system.

A naturally occurring endothermic process is melting. An ice cube melts spontaneously at room temperature as energy is transferred from the warm air to the ice. The well-ordered arrangement of water molecules in the ice crystal is lost, and the less-ordered liquid phase of higher energy content is formed. A system that can go from one state to another without a decrease in enthalpy does so with an increase in entropy.

Look at the physical states of the reactants in the chemical equation for the decomposition of ammonium nitrate.

$$2NH_4NO_3(s) \longrightarrow 2N_2(g) + 4H_2O(l) + O_2(g)$$

On the left side are 2 mol of solid ammonium nitrate. The right side of the equation shows 3 mol of gaseous molecules plus 4 mol of a liquid. The arrangement of particles on the right side of the equation is more random than the arrangement on the left side of the equation and hence is less ordered. **Figures 2.1a** and **2.1b** show the reactant and products of this decomposition reaction.

FIGURE 2.1

Decomposition and Entropy

When ammonium nitrate, NH_4NO_3, decomposes, the entropy of the reaction system increases as **(a)** one solid reactant becomes **(b)** three products: $N_2(g)$, $H_2(g)$, $H_2O(l)$.

✔ CRITICAL THINKING

Explain Why does adding energy to a system increase its entropy?

(a) The ammonium nitrate starts as a solid.

(b) It becomes two gaseous products and one liquid product.

There is a tendency in nature to proceed in a direction that increases the randomness of a system. A random system is one that lacks a regular arrangement of its parts. This tendency toward randomness is called entropy. **Entropy, S, can be defined in a simple qualitative way as a measure of the degree of randomness of the particles, such as molecules, in a system.** To understand the concept of entropy, consider solids, liquids, and gases. In a solid, the particles are fixed in position in their small regions of space, but they are vibrating back and forth. Even so, we can determine with fair precision the location of the particles. The degree of randomness is low, so the entropy is low. When the solid melts, the particles are still very close together, but they can move about somewhat. The system is more random, it is more difficult to describe the location of the particles, and the entropy is higher. When the liquid evaporates, the particles are moving rapidly and are much farther apart. Locating an individual particle is more difficult, the system is much more random, and the entropy of the gas is higher than that of the liquid. A general rule is that the entropy of liquids is greater than that of solids and the entropy of gases is greater than that of liquids.

The entropy of a pure crystalline solid at absolute zero is zero. As energy is added, the randomness of the molecular motion increases. Measurements of energy absorbed and calculations are used to determine the absolute entropy or standard molar entropy, and values are then recorded in tables. These molar values are reported as kJ/(mol • K). Entropy change, which can also be measured, is defined as the difference between the entropy of the products and the reactants. Therefore, an increase in entropy is represented by a positive value for ΔS, and a decrease in entropy is represented by a negative value for ΔS.

The process of forming a solution almost always involves an increase in entropy because there is an increase in randomness. This is true for mixing gases, dissolving a liquid in another liquid, and dissolving a solid in a liquid.

FIGURE 2.2

Mixtures and Entropy When a solid dissolves in a liquid, the entropy of the system increases.

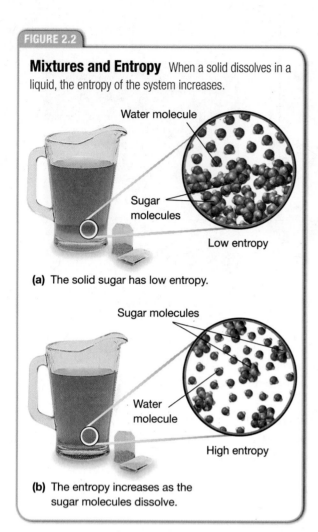

Water molecule

Sugar molecules

Low entropy

(a) The solid sugar has low entropy.

Sugar molecules

Water molecule

High entropy

(b) The entropy increases as the sugar molecules dissolve.

Figure 2.2 illustrates the entropy change that takes place when solid sugar is dissolved in tea (an aqueous solution). In the sugar-water system shown in **Figure 2.2a,** the solid sugar has just been added to the tea, but most of it has not yet dissolved. The entropy is low because the majority of the sugar molecules are in one region at the bottom of the pitcher and the majority of the water molecules can be found everywhere else in the pitcher. After the sugar dissolves in the tea, shown in **Figure 2.2b,** the sugar molecules are thoroughly mixed throughout the tea solution. Sugar molecules and water molecules might be found anywhere in the solution, so the entropy, the randomness, of the system increases. This would give ΔS a positive value for this solid-liquid system. You can imagine the same series of events happening for a system of gases mixing with each other or a system of liquids mixing. In each case, ΔS would have a positive value once the solution was formed.

▶ **MAIN IDEA**

Free-energy changes determine if a reaction is spontaneous.

Processes in nature are driven in two directions: toward least enthalpy and toward greatest entropy. When these two oppose each other, the dominant factor determines the direction of change. As a way to predict which factor will dominate for a given system, a function has been defined to relate the enthalpy and entropy factors at a given temperature and constant pressure. **This combined enthalpy-entropy function is called the free energy, G, of the system; it is also called Gibbs free energy.** This function simultaneously assesses the tendencies for enthalpy and entropy to change. Natural processes proceed in the direction that lowers the free energy of a system.

Only the *change* in free energy can be measured. It can be defined in terms of changes in enthalpy and entropy. **At a constant pressure and temperature, the free-energy change, ΔG, of a system is defined as the difference between the change in enthalpy, ΔH, and the product of the Kelvin temperature and the entropy change, which is defined as $T\Delta S$.**

Free Energy Change $\quad\quad \Delta G^0 = \Delta H^0 - T\Delta S^0$

Note that this expression is for substances in their standard states. The product $T\Delta S$ and the quantities ΔG and ΔH have the same units, usually kJ. The units of ΔS for use in this equation are usually kJ/K. If $\Delta G < 0$, the reaction is spontaneous.

ΔH and ΔS in the free-energy equation can have positive or negative values. This leads to four possible combinations of terms.

Figure 2.3 shows that if ΔH is negative and ΔS is positive, then both terms on the right in the free-energy equation are negative. Both factors contribute to the process being spontaneous. Therefore, ΔG will always be negative, and the reaction is definitely spontaneous. On the other hand, if ΔH is positive (endothermic process) and ΔS is negative (decrease in randomness), then the reaction, as written, is not spontaneous. When the enthalpy and entropy changes are operating in different directions, sometimes one will predominate, and sometimes the other will predominate. There are reactions in which the enthalpy change is negative and the entropy change is negative. The enthalpy factor leads to a spontaneous process, but the negative entropy change opposes this. This is true in the following reaction. The entropy decreases because there is a decrease in moles of gas.

$$C_2H_4(g) + H_2(g) \longrightarrow C_2H_6(g)$$

There is a fairly large decrease in entropy, $\Delta S^0 = -0.1207 \text{ kJ/(mol} \bullet \text{K)}$. However, the reaction is strongly exothermic, with $\Delta H^0 = -136.9 \text{ kJ/mol}$. The reaction proceeds at 298 K because the enthalpy term predominates.

$$\Delta G^0 = \Delta H^0 - T\Delta S^0 = -136.9 \text{ kJ/mol} - 298 \text{ K}[-0.1207 \text{ kJ/(mol} \bullet \text{K)}]$$
$$= -100.9 \text{ kJ/mol}$$

We can contrast this with the common commercial process for the manufacture of syngas, a mixture of CO and H_2. (This gas mixture is the starting point for the synthesis of a number of large-volume commercial chemicals, such as methanol, CH_3OH.)

$$CH_4(g) + H_2O(g) \longrightarrow CO(g) + 3H_2(g)$$

This reaction is endothermic, with $\Delta H^0 = +206.1 \text{ kJ/mol}$ and $\Delta S^0 = +0.215 \text{ kJ/(mol} \bullet \text{K)}$, at standard conditions. The resulting ΔG is positive at room temperature. This tells us that the reaction will not occur at room temperature even though the entropy change is favorable.

$$\Delta G^0 = \Delta H^0 - T\Delta S^0 = +206.1 \text{ kJ/mol} - 298 \text{ K}[+0.215 \text{ kJ/(mol} \bullet \text{K)}]$$
$$= +142.0 \text{ kJ/mol}$$

WHY IT MATTERS

Diamonds Are Forever? S.T.E.M.

Carbon occurs in different forms, two of which are graphite and diamond. Using thermodynamic data, the change in free energy for diamond converting to graphite under standard thermodynamic conditions is −3 kJ/mol. That is, since ΔG is negative for this reaction, diamond should spontaneously change to graphite at 25°C and 1 atm. So why doesn't all of our diamond jewelry change to graphite? The reaction rate is too slow for this spontaneous change to be observed. Therefore, at 25°C and 1 atm, although diamonds are not "forever," they will last a very long time.

FIGURE 2.3

RELATING ENTHALPY, ENTROPY, AND FREE-ENERGY CHANGES TO REACTION OCCURRENCE

ΔH	ΔS	ΔG
− value (exothermic)	+ value (more random)	always negative
− value (exothermic)	− value (less random)	negative at *lower* temperatures
+ value (endothermic)	+ value (more random)	negative at *higher* temperatures
+ value (endothermic)	− value (less random)	never negative

Calculating Free Energy Change

Sample Problem D For the reaction $NH_4Cl(s) \longrightarrow NH_3(g) + HCl(g)$, at 298.15 K, $\Delta H^0 = 176$ kJ/mol, and $\Delta S^0 = 0.285$ kJ/(mol • K). Calculate ΔG^0, and tell whether this reaction is spontaneous in the forward direction at 298.15 K.

① ANALYZE

Given: $\Delta H^0 = 176$ kJ/mol at 298.15 K
$\Delta S^0 = 0.285$ kJ/(mol • K) at 298.15 K

Unknown: ΔG^0 at 298.15 K

② PLAN

$\Delta S, \Delta H, T \rightarrow \Delta G$

The value of ΔG can be calculated according to the following equation.

③ SOLVE

$$\Delta G^0 = \Delta H^0 - T\Delta S^0$$

$$\Delta G^0 = 176 \text{ kJ/mol} - 298 \text{ K} [0.285 \text{ kJ/(mol} \bullet \text{K})]$$
$$\Delta G^0 = 176 \text{ kJ/mol} - 84.9 \text{ kJ/mol}$$
$$\Delta G^0 = 91.1 \text{ kJ/mol}$$

④ CHECK YOUR WORK

The answer is reasonably close to an estimated value of 110, calculated as $200 - (300 \times 0.3)$. The positive value of ΔG shows that this reaction does not occur spontaneously at 298.15 K.

Practice   Answers in Appendix E

1. For the vaporization reaction $Br_2(l) \longrightarrow Br_2(g)$, $\Delta H^0 = 31.0$ kJ/mol, and $\Delta S^0 = 93.0$ J/(mol • K). At what temperature will this process be spontaneous?

 SECTION 2 **FORMATIVE ASSESSMENT**

▶ **Reviewing Main Ideas**

1. What kind of enthalpy change favors a spontaneous reaction?

2. What is entropy, and how does it relate to spontaneity of reactions?

3. List several changes that result in an entropy increase.

4. Define *free energy*, and explain how its change is calculated.

5. Explain the relationship between free-energy change and spontaneity of reactions.

6. In the reaction in Sample Problem D, why does the entropy increase?

✔ **Critical Thinking**

7. **APPLYING MODELS** Most biological enzymes become denatured when they are heated and lose their ability to catalyze reactions. This process (original enzyme $\longrightarrow$ denatured enzyme) is endothermic and spontaneous. Which structure, the original enzyme or the denatured enzyme, is more ordered? Explain your reasoning using thermodynamic concepts.

You may have seen a popular comic strip in which a little boy takes a long, twisting path between the school-bus stop and home. No matter which path the boy takes, the result is always the same: He goes from the bus stop to the door of his house. Hess's law covers a similar situation in thermochemistry. No matter which or how many steps occur in the process of changing one or more substances into one or more other substances, the overall change in enthalpy is always the same. Hess's law can be used, for example, to predict the enthalpy change, ΔH^0, of a reaction without actually carrying out the reaction.

Sample Problem

Determine ΔH for the burning of carbon disulfide in oxygen.

$$CS_2(l) + 3O_2(g) \longrightarrow CO_2(g) + 2SO_2(g); \Delta H^0 = ?$$

Use the following information:

$$C(s) + O_2(g) \longrightarrow CO_2(g) \qquad \Delta H^0_f = -393.5 \text{ kJ/mol}$$

$$S(s) + O_2(g) \longrightarrow SO_2(g) \qquad \Delta H^0_f = -296.8 \text{ kJ/mol}$$

$$C(s) + 2S(s) \longrightarrow CS_2(l) \qquad \Delta H^0_f = 87.9 \text{ kJ/mol}$$

Rearrange the given equations in a way that will put the reactants of the above equation on the left and the products on the right.

1. $C(s) + O_2(g) \longrightarrow CO_2(g) \qquad \Delta H^0_f = -393.5 \text{ kJ/mol}$
2. $2S(s) + 2O_2(g) \longrightarrow 2SO_2(g) \qquad \Delta H^0 = 2(-296.8 \text{ kJ})$
3. $CS_2(l) \longrightarrow C(s) + 2S(s) \qquad \Delta H^0 = -87.9 \text{ kJ}$

SUM: $CS_2(l) + 3O_2(g) \longrightarrow CO_2(g) + 2SO_2(g)$

Notice that equation 2 is double the original equation $S(s) + O_2(g) \longrightarrow SO_2(g)$. The reason for this is that $2SO_2$ are needed on the product side to match the $2SO_2$ in $CS_2(l) + 3O_2(g) \longrightarrow CO_2(g) + 2SO_2(g)$. The third equation is the reverse of the original, putting CS_2 on the reactant side of the final equation. The sign of ΔH is likewise reversed. The value of ΔH^0 is the sum of the ΔH^0 values for the three added equations.

$$\Delta H^0 = -393.5 \text{ kJ} + 2(-296.8 \text{ kJ}) + (-87.9 \text{ kJ})$$

$$\Delta H^0 = -1075.0 \text{ kJ}$$

Practice   Answers in Appendix E

1. Calculate ΔH^0 for the complete oxidation of sulfur to sulfur trioxide.
$$S(s) + \frac{3}{2}O_2(g) \longrightarrow SO_3(g)$$
Use the following information.
$$S(s) + O_2(g) \longrightarrow SO_2(g) \qquad \Delta H^0_f = -296.8 \text{ kJ/mol}$$
$$SO_2(g) + \frac{1}{2}O_2(g) \longrightarrow SO_3(g) \qquad \Delta H = -99.2 \text{ kJ/mol}$$

2. Calculate ΔH^0 for the reaction in which zinc sulfide ore is roasted to obtain zinc oxide.
$$ZnS(s) + \frac{3}{2}O_2(g) \longrightarrow ZnO(s) + SO_2(g)$$
Use the following information.
$$Zn(s) + \frac{1}{2}O_2(g) \longrightarrow ZnO(s) \qquad \Delta H^0_f = -348.0 \text{ kJ/mol}$$
$$Zn(s) + S(s) \longrightarrow ZnS(s) \qquad \Delta H^0_f = -203.0 \text{ kJ/mol}$$
$$S(s) + O_2(g) \longrightarrow SO_2(g) \qquad \Delta H^0_f = -296.8 \text{ kJ/mol}$$

CHAPTER 16 Summary

BIG IDEA Energy is released or absorbed in chemical reactions. The tendency in nature is for chemical reactions to proceed in the direction of the lowest energy state.

SECTION 1 Thermochemistry

- Thermochemistry is the study of the changes in energy that accompany chemical reactions and physical changes.
- A thermochemical equation is an equation that includes the quantity of energy released or absorbed in addition to the reactants and products.
- An enthalpy change is the amount of energy absorbed as heat by a system in a process carried out at constant pressure.
- The enthalpy of reaction is the enthalpy change that occurs during a chemical reaction.
- The enthalpy change is negative for exothermic reactions and positive for endothermic reactions.
- Compounds with highly negative enthalpies of formation tend to be stable; compounds with highly positive or only slightly negative enthalpies of formation tend to be unstable.
- The standard molar enthalpy of formation is the enthalpy change that occurs when one mole of a compound is formed from its elements in their standard states at 25°C and 1 atm.
- The enthalpy change that occurs in a combustion reaction is called the enthalpy of combustion.
- Enthalpies of reaction can be calculated by using enthalpies of formation of reactants and products.

KEY TERMS

thermochemistry
calorimeter
temperature
joule
heat
specific heat
enthalpy change
enthalpy of reaction
thermochemical equation
molar enthalpy of formation
enthalpy of combustion
Hess's law

SECTION 2 Driving Force of Reactions

- The tendency throughout nature is for a reaction to proceed in the direction that leads to a lower energy state and higher entropy (or disorder).
- Entropy is a measure of the randomness of a system.
- Free-energy change combines the effects of entropy and enthalpy changes and temperature of a system, and it is a measure of the overall tendency toward natural change.
- A reaction is spontaneous if it is accompanied by a decrease in free energy. It is not spontaneous if there is an increase in free energy.

KEY TERMS

entropy
free energy
free-energy change

CHAPTER 16 **Review**

GO ONLINE

Interactive Review
HMHScience.com

Review Games
Concept Maps

SECTION 1

Thermochemistry

 REVIEWING MAIN IDEAS

1. How does the enthalpy of the products of a reaction system compare with the enthalpy of the reactants when the reaction is
   a. endothermic? b. exothermic?

2. a. Distinguish between enthalpies of reaction, formation, and combustion.
   b. On what basis are enthalpies of formation and combustion defined?

3. Write the equation that can be used to calculate the enthalpy of reaction from enthalpies of formation.

4. What does the law of conservation of energy state?

5. State Hess's law. How is it used?

6. Describe a combustion calorimeter. What information can it give?

PRACTICE PROBLEMS

7. How much energy is needed to raise the temperature of a 55 g sample of aluminum from 22.4°C to 94.6°C? Refer to **Figure 1.2** for the specific heat of aluminum. (Hint: See Sample Problem A.)

8. If 3.5 kJ of energy are added to a 28.2 g sample of iron at 20.°C, what is the final temperature of the iron in kelvins? The specific heat of iron is 0.449 J/(g • K).

9. You need 70.2 J to raise the temperature of an unknown mass of ammonia, $NH_3(g)$, from 23.0°C to 24.0°C. If the specific heat of ammonia is 2.09 J/(g • K), calculate the unknown mass of ammonia.

10. Calculate c_p for indium metal, given that 1.0 mol In absorbs 53 J while increasing in temperature from 297.5 K to 299.5 K.

11. For each equation listed below, determine the ΔH and type of reaction (endothermic or exothermic).
    a. $C(s) + O_2(g) \longrightarrow CO_2(g) + 393.51$ kJ
    b. $CH_4(g) + 2O_2(g) \longrightarrow$
       $\qquad CO_2(g) + 2H_2O(l) + 890.31$ kJ
    c. $CaCO_3(s) + 176$ kJ $\longrightarrow CaO(s) + CO_2(g)$
    d. $H_2O(g) \longrightarrow H_2O(l) + 44.02$ kJ

12. Rewrite each equation below with the ΔH value included with either the reactants or the products, and identify the reaction as endothermic or exothermic.
    a. $H_2(g) + \frac{1}{2}O_2(g) \longrightarrow H_2O(l)$;
       $\Delta H^0 = -285.8$ kJ
    b. $2Mg(s) + O_2(g) \longrightarrow 2MgO(s)$;
       $\Delta H^0 = -1200$ kJ
    c. $I_2(s) \longrightarrow I_2(g); \Delta H^0 = +62.4$ kJ
    d. $3CO(g) + Fe_2O_3(s) \longrightarrow 2Fe(s) + 3CO_2(g)$;
       $\Delta H^0 = -24.7$ kJ

13. Use Appendix Table B–14 to write the reaction illustrating the formation of each of the following compounds from its elements. Write the ΔH as part of each equation, and indicate the ΔH for the reverse reaction.
    a. $CaCl_2(s)$
    b. $C_2H_2(g)$ (ethyne, or acetylene)
    c. $SO_2(g)$

14. The reaction $2Fe_2O_3(s) + 3C(s) \longrightarrow 4Fe(s) + 3CO_2(g)$ is involved in the smelting of iron. Use ΔH_f values given in Appendix Table B–14 to calculate the enthalpy change for the production of 1 mol of iron.

15. Use enthalpy-of-formation data given in Appendix Table B–14 to calculate the enthalpy of reaction for each of the following. Solve each by combining the known thermochemical equations. Verify each result by using the general equation for finding enthalpies of reaction from enthalpies of formation. (Hint: See Sample Problem B.)
    a. $CaCO_3(s) \longrightarrow CaO(s) + CO_2(g)$
    b. $Ca(OH)_2(s) \longrightarrow CaO(s) + H_2O(g)$
    c. $Fe_2O_3(s) + 3CO(g) \longrightarrow 2Fe(s) + 3CO_2(g)$

16. For glucose, $C_6H_{12}O_6(s)$, $\Delta H_f = -1263$ kJ/mol. Calculate the enthalpy change when 1 mol of $C_6H_{12}O_6(s)$ combusts to form $CO_2(g)$ and $H_2O(l)$.

17. Calculate the standard enthalpies of reaction for combustion reactions in which ethane, C_2H_6, and benzene, C_6H_6, are the respective reactants and $CO_2(g)$ and $H_2O(l)$ are the products in each. Solve each by combining the known thermochemical equations using the ΔH_f values in Appendix Table B–14. Verify the result by using the general equation for finding enthalpies of reaction from enthalpies of formation.
    a. $C_2H_6(g) + O_2(g) \longrightarrow$
    b. $C_6H_6(l) + O_2(g) \longrightarrow$

18. The enthalpy of formation of ethanol, C_2H_5OH, is −277.0 kJ/mol at 298.15 K. Calculate the enthalpy of combustion of one mole of ethanol, assuming that the products are $CO_2(g)$ and $H_2O(l)$. (Hint: See Sample Problem C.)

Driving Force of Reactions

▶ REVIEWING MAIN IDEAS

19. Would entropy increase or decrease for changes in state in which the reactant is a gas or liquid and the product is a solid? What sign would the entropy change have?

20. How does an increase in temperature affect the entropy of a system?

21. What combination of ΔH and ΔS values always produces a negative free-energy change?

22. Explain the relationship between temperature and the tendency for reactions to occur spontaneously.

PRACTICE PROBLEMS

23. A reaction has $\Delta H = -356$ kJ and $\Delta S = -36$ J/K. Calculate ΔG at 25°C to confirm that the reaction is spontaneous.

24. A reaction has $\Delta H = 98$ kJ and $\Delta S = 292$ J/K. Investigate the spontaneity of the reaction at 298 K (25°C). Would increasing the temperature have any effect on the spontaneity of the reaction?

25. A reaction has $\Delta H = -76$ kJ and $\Delta S = -117$ J/K. Calculate ΔG for the reaction at 298.15 K. Is the reaction spontaneous?

26. The gas-phase reaction of H_2 with CO_2 to produce H_2O and CO has $\Delta H = 11.0$ kJ and $\Delta S = 41.0$ J/K. Is the reaction spontaneous at 298.15 K? What is ΔG?

27. Based on the following values, compute ΔG values for each reaction and predict whether the reaction will occur spontaneously. (Hint: See Sample Problem D.)
   a. $\Delta H = +125$ kJ, $T = 293$ K,
      $\Delta S = 0.0350$ kJ/K
   b. $\Delta H = -85.2$ kJ, $T = 127$°C,
      $\Delta S = 0.125$ kJ/K
   c. $\Delta H = -275$ kJ, $T = 773$ K,
      $\Delta S = 0.450$ kJ/K

28. The ΔS^0 for the reaction shown, at 298.15 K, is 0.003 00 kJ/(mol • K). Calculate the ΔG^0 for this reaction, and determine whether it will occur spontaneously at 298.15 K.

$$C(s) + O_2(g) \longrightarrow CO_2(g) + 393.51 \text{ kJ}$$

Mixed Review

▶ REVIEWING MAIN IDEAS

29. Describe how chemical energy is a form of potential energy.

30. How might you change reaction conditions to induce an endothermic reaction that does not occur naturally?

31. The diagram below represents an interpretation of Hess's law for the following reaction.

$$Sn(s) + 2Cl_2(g) \longrightarrow SnCl_4(l)$$

Use the diagram to determine ΔH for each step and the net reaction.

$$Sn(s) + Cl_2(g) \longrightarrow SnCl_2(s) \qquad \Delta H = ?$$
$$SnCl_2(s) + Cl_2(g) \longrightarrow SnCl_4(l) \qquad \Delta H = ?$$
$$Sn(s) + 2Cl_2(g) \longrightarrow SnCl_4(l) \qquad \Delta H = ?$$

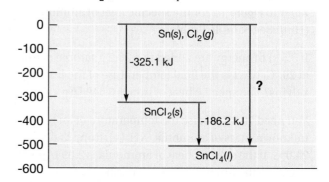

32. The standard enthalpy of formation for sulfur dioxide gas is −296.8 kJ/mol. Calculate the amount of energy given off in kJ when 30.0 g of $SO_2(g)$ is formed from its elements.

33. The thermite reaction used in some welding applications has the following enthalpy and entropy changes at 298.15 K. Assuming ΔS and ΔH are constant, calculate ΔG at 448 K.

$$Fe_2O_3 + 2Al(s) \longrightarrow 2Fe(s) + Al_2O_3(s)$$

$$\Delta H^0 = -851.5 \text{ kJ}, \Delta S^0 = -38.5 \text{ J/K}$$

34. Rewrite each equation below with the ΔH value included in either the reactants or products, and identify the reaction as endothermic or exothermic.
  a. $2SO_2(g) + O_2(g) \longrightarrow 2SO_3(g);$
  $\Delta H = -197.8 \text{ kJ}$
  b. $2NO_2(g) \longrightarrow 2NO(g) + O_2(g);$
  $\Delta H = +114.2 \text{ kJ}$
  c. $C_2H_4(g) + 3O_2(g) \longrightarrow 2CO_2(g) + 2H_2O(l);$
  $\Delta H = -1411.0 \text{ kJ}$

35. Calculate the change in enthalpy for the following reaction.

$$4FeO(s) + O_2(g) \longrightarrow 2Fe_2O_3(s)$$

Use the enthalpy-of-formation data listed in Appendix Table B–14.

36. The reaction to synthesize methanol (CH_3OH) industrially is

$$CO(g) + 2H_2(g) \longrightarrow CH_3OH(g).$$

The $\Delta H^0_{reaction} = -90.7 \text{ kJ}$, and the $\Delta S^0_{reaction} = -220.8 \text{ J/K}$. At what temperatures is the reaction nonspontaneous?

37. What is the main characteristic of a calorimeter in a bomb calorimeter experiment, and why is this characteristic essential?

CRITICAL THINKING

38. Relating Ideas Given the entropy change for the first two reactions below, calculate the entropy change for the third reaction below.

$S_8(s) + 8O_2(s) \longrightarrow 8SO_2(g)$	$\Delta S = 89 \text{ J/K}$
$2SO_2(s) + O_2(s) \longrightarrow 2SO_3(g)$	$\Delta S = -188 \text{ J/K}$
$S_8(s) + 12O_2(s) \longrightarrow 8SO_3(g)$	$\Delta S = ?$

39. Interpreting Concepts Look at the two pictures below. Which picture appears to have more order? Why? Are there any similarities between the amount of order the marbles have and the entropy of particles?

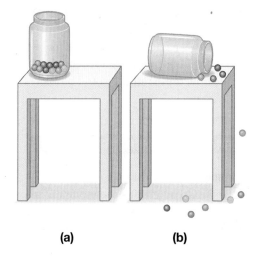

(a)   (b)

40. Inferring Conclusions A reaction is endothermic and has a $\Delta H = 8 \text{ kJ}$. This reaction occurs spontaneously at 25°C. What must be true about the entropy change?

41. Inferring Conclusions If both ΔH and ΔS are negative, how does temperature affect spontaneity?

42. Inferring Relationships If the reaction $X \longrightarrow Y$ is spontaneous, what can be said about the reaction $Y \longrightarrow X$?

43. Interpreting Concepts Absolute enthalpy cannot be determined; only change in energy can be measured. However, absolute entropy can be determined. Explain why an absolute entropy can be determined.

44. Obtain information on alternative units of measure used to express values of energy as heat and other forms of energy. Also, find out how the quantities relate to SI units. Include information specifically on English units, such as the British thermal unit (Btu), and on typical Btu ratings of household appliances. Calculate how these ratings would be expressed in joules instead.

ALTERNATIVE ASSESSMENT

45. Performance Design a simple calorimeter investigation to determine the molar enthalpy of fusion of water. Use the following materials: a large plastic-foam cup with cover, a thermometer, a balance, water at room temperature, and an ice cube. Allow your teacher to review your design. Then carry out the investigation, and write a laboratory report including your calculations and a comparison of your quantitative results with known values. Try to account for any disagreements between the experimental and actual values.

46. Performance Design an experiment to measure the molar heat capacities of zinc and copper. If your teacher approves the design, obtain the materials needed and conduct the experiment. When you are finished, compare your experimental values with those from a chemical handbook or other reference source.

47. Performance Develop a procedure to measure the ΔH of the reaction shown below. If your teacher approves your procedure, test your procedure by measuring the ΔH value of the reaction. Determine the accuracy of your method by comparing your ΔH with the accepted ΔH value.

$$CH_3COONa(s) \longrightarrow Na^+(aq) + CH_3COO^-(aq)$$

Standards-Based Assessment

Record your answers on a separate piece of paper.

MULTIPLE CHOICE

1 Which of the following conditions will favor a spontaneous reaction?

  A an increase in entropy and a decrease in enthalpy

  B an increase in both entropy and enthalpy

  C a decrease in both entropy and enthalpy

  D a decrease in entropy and an increase in enthalpy

2 Two metals of equal mass but different specific heats absorb the same amount of heat. Which metal undergoes the smaller change in temperature?

  A the metal with the higher specific heat

  B the metal with the lower specific heat

  C Both undergo the same change in temperature.

  D cannot determine from the information given

3 Which of the following processes has a negative ΔS?

  A evaporating 1 mol of a liquid

  B raising the temperature of 1 L of water from 295 K to 350 K

  C freezing of 1 mol of a liquid

  D none of the above

4 At a constant pressure, the following reaction is exothermic: $2NO_2(g) \rightarrow N_2O_4(g)$. Which of the following statements is true about the reaction (as written)?

  A The reaction is always spontaneous.

  B The reaction is spontaneous at low temperatures but not at high temperatures.

  C The reaction is spontaneous at high temperatures but not at low temperatures.

  D The reaction is never spontaneous.

5 Increasing the temperature of a substance —

  A increases its kinetic energy

  B increases its potential energy

  C increases its specific heat

  D makes the molecules move more slowly

6 Identify the correct pairing of term and definition.

  A enthalpy—temperature

  B endothermic—reaction in which energy is released

  C specific heat—amount of energy required to raise 1 g of a substance 1 degree Celsius (or 1 Kelvin)

  D joule—the unit that measures temperature

7 Identify the conditions in which a spontaneous chemical reaction is expected in all cases.

  A if ΔH is negative and ΔS is negative

  B if ΔH is negative and ΔS is positive

  C if ΔH is positive and ΔS is negative

  D if ΔH is positive and ΔS is positive

GRIDDED RESPONSE

8 The gasification of coal is a method of producing methane by the following reaction:

$$C(s) + 2H_2(g) \rightarrow CH_4(g) \qquad \Delta H = ?$$

Find ΔH (kJ/mol) by using the enthalpy changes in the following combustion reactions:

$$C(s) + O_2(g) \longrightarrow CO_2(g) \qquad \Delta H = -394 \text{ kJ}$$

$$H_2(g) + \frac{1}{2}O_2(g) \longrightarrow H_2O(l) \qquad \Delta H = -286 \text{ kJ}$$

$$CH_4(g) + 2O_2(g) \longrightarrow CO_2(g) + 2H_2O(l)$$
$$\Delta H = -891 \text{ kJ}$$

Test Tip

If you are permitted to, draw a line through each incorrect answer choice as you eliminate it.

CHAPTER 17
Reaction Kinetics

BIG IDEA
For chemical reactions to occur, the particles of the reactants must collide with sufficient kinetic energy and in the proper orientation.

 ONLINE Chemistry
HMHScience.com

ONLINE LABS
- Clock Reactions
- Rate of a Chemical Reaction
- A Leaky Reaction
- Reaction Action

GO ONLINE

 Why It Matters Video
HMHScience.com

Reaction Kinetics

The Reaction Process

SECTION 1

Main Ideas

▶ Some reactions have intermediate steps.

▶ Molecular collisions need the right energy and orientation to react.

▶ Reactions occur only if there is enough energy.

▶ In a transition state, bonds are breaking as new bonds form.

Key Terms

reaction mechanism
intermediate

homogeneous reaction
collision theory

activation energy
activated complex

By studying many types of experiments, chemists have found that chemical reactions occur at widely differing rates. For example, in the presence of air, iron rusts very slowly, whereas the methane in natural gas burns rapidly when ignited. The speed of a chemical reaction depends on the energy pathway that a reaction follows and the changes that take place on the molecular level when substances interact. In this chapter, you will study the factors that affect how fast chemical reactions take place.

▶ **MAIN IDEA**

Some reactions have intermediate steps.

If you mix aqueous solutions of HCl and NaOH, an extremely rapid neutralization reaction occurs, as shown in **Figure 1.1.**

$$H_3O^+(aq) + Cl^-(aq) + Na^+(aq) + OH^-(aq) \longrightarrow$$
$$2H_2O(l) + Na^+(aq) + Cl^-(aq)$$

The reaction is practically instantaneous; the rate is limited only by the speed with which the H_3O^+ and OH^- ions can diffuse through the water to meet each other. On the other hand, reactions between ions of the same charge and between molecular substances are not instantaneous. Negative ions repel each other, as do positive ions. The electron clouds of molecules also repel each other strongly at very short distances. Therefore, only ions or molecules with very high kinetic energy can overcome repulsive forces and get close enough to react. In this section, we will limit our discussion to reactions between molecules.

Colorless hydrogen gas consists of pairs of hydrogen atoms bonded together as diatomic molecules, H_2. Violet-colored iodine vapor is also diatomic, consisting of pairs of iodine atoms bonded together as I_2 molecules. A chemical reaction between these two gases at elevated temperatures produces hydrogen iodide, HI, a colorless gas. Hydrogen iodide molecules, in turn, tend to decompose and re-form hydrogen and iodine molecules, producing the violet gas shown in **Figure 1.2** on the next page. The following chemical equations describe these two reactions.

$$H_2(g) + I_2(g) \longrightarrow 2HI(g)$$

$$2HI(g) \longrightarrow H_2(g) + I_2(g)$$

Such equations indicate only which molecular species disappear as a result of the reactions and which species are produced. **They do not show the reaction mechanism, the step-by-step sequence of reactions by which the overall chemical change occurs.**

FIGURE 1.1

Instantaneous Reaction As NaOH solution is poured into HCl solution, a very rapid neutralization reaction occurs. Excess NaOH turns the phenolphthalein indicator pink.

©Charles D. Winters

FIGURE 1.2

Intermediates Colorless hydrogen iodide gas, HI, decomposes into colorless hydrogen gas and violet iodine gas. Some of the hydrogen gas and iodine gas will re-form HI.

Although only the net chemical change is directly observable for most chemical reactions, experiments can often be designed that suggest the probable sequence of steps in a reaction mechanism. Each reaction step is usually a simple process. The equation for each step represents the *actual* atoms, ions, or molecules that participate in that step. Even a reaction that appears from its balanced equation to be a simple process may actually be the result of several simple steps.

For many years, the formation of hydrogen iodide, as shown in **Figure 1.2**, was considered a simple one-step process. It was thought to involve the interaction of two molecules, H_2 and I_2, in the forward reaction and two HI molecules in the reverse reaction. Experiments eventually showed, however, that a direct reaction between H_2 and I_2 does not take place.

Alternative mechanisms for the reaction were proposed based on the experimental results. The steps in each reaction mechanism had to add together to give the overall equation. Note that two of the species in the mechanism steps—I and H_2I—do not appear in the net equation. **Species that appear in some steps but not in the net equation are known as intermediates.** (Notice that they cancel each other out in the following mechanisms.) The first possible mechanism has the following two-step pathway.

$$\text{Step 1:} \quad I_2 \rightleftharpoons 2\cancel{I}$$
$$\text{Step 2:} \quad \underline{2\cancel{I} + H_2 \rightleftharpoons 2HI}$$
$$I_2 + H_2 \rightleftharpoons 2HI$$

The second possible mechanism has a three-step pathway.

$$\text{Step 1:} \quad I_2 \rightleftharpoons 2\cancel{I}$$
$$\text{Step 2:} \quad \cancel{I} + H_2 \rightleftharpoons H_2\cancel{I}$$
$$\text{Step 3:} \quad \underline{H_2\cancel{I} + \cancel{I} \rightleftharpoons 2HI}$$
$$I_2 + H_2 \rightleftharpoons 2HI$$

The reaction between hydrogen gas and iodine vapor to produce hydrogen iodide gas is an example of a **homogeneous reaction,** a reaction whose reactants and products exist in a single phase—in this case, the gas phase. This reaction system is also an example of a homogeneous chemical system, because all reactants and products in all intermediate steps are in the same phase.

✔ CHECK FOR UNDERSTANDING

Propose Based on your knowledge of reaction mechanisms, propose at least one reason that a chemist working in industry might need to know all of the steps in a chemical reaction.

▶ **MAIN IDEA**

Molecular collisions need the right energy and orientation to react.

In order for reactions to occur between substances, their particles (molecules, atoms, or ions) must collide. Furthermore, these collisions must result in interactions. **The set of assumptions regarding collisions and reactions is known as collision theory.** Chemists use this theory to interpret many of their observations about chemical reactions.

Consider what might happen on a molecular scale in one step of a homogeneous reaction system. We will analyze a proposed first step in a hypothetical decomposition reaction.

$$AB + AB \rightleftharpoons A_2 + 2B$$

According to the collision theory, the two AB molecules must collide in order to react. Furthermore, they must collide with a favorable orientation and with enough energy to overcome electron-cloud repulsion and disrupt the bonds of the AB molecules. If they do so, AB bonds break, and A_2 bonds form, leading to the formation of the products, one A_2 molecule and two B atoms. An effective collision is modeled in **Figure 1.3a.**

If a collision is too gentle, the two molecules simply rebound from each other. This effect is illustrated in **Figure 1.3b.** Similarly, a collision in which the reactant molecules have an unfavorable orientation has little effect. The colliding molecules rebound without reacting. A collision that has poor orientation is shown in **Figure 1.3c.**

A chemical reaction produces new bonds formed between specific atoms in the colliding molecules. Unless the collision brings the correct atoms close together and in the proper orientation, the molecules will not react. For example, if a chlorine molecule collides with the oxygen end of a nitrogen monoxide molecule, the following reaction may occur.

$$NO(g) + Cl_2(g) \longrightarrow NOCl(g) + Cl(g)$$

This reaction will not occur if the chlorine molecule strikes the nitrogen end of the molecule.

Thus, collision theory provides two reasons that a collision between reactant molecules may fail to produce a new chemical species: the collision is not energetic enough to supply the required energy, or the colliding molecules are not oriented in a way that enables them to react with each other.

FIGURE 1.3

Collision Patterns

Three possible collision patterns for AB molecules are shown. Not every collision produces a chemical reaction.

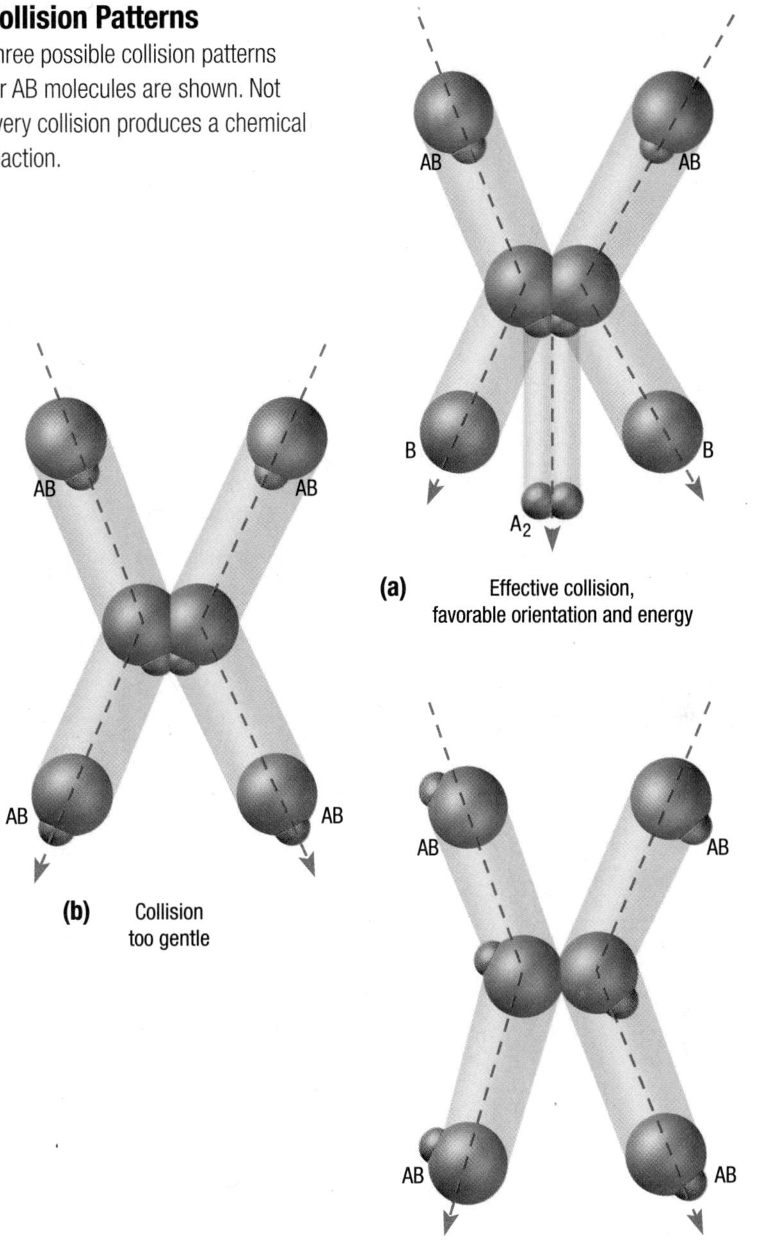

(a) Effective collision, favorable orientation and energy

(b) Collision too gentle

(c) Collision that has poor orientation

▶ MAIN IDEA

Reactions occur only if there is enough energy.

Consider the reaction for the formation of water from the diatomic gases oxygen and hydrogen according to the following equation:

$$2H_2(g) + O_2(g) \longrightarrow 2H_2O(l)$$

The enthalpy of formation is quite high: $\Delta H_f^0 = -285.8$ kJ/mol at 298.15 K. The free-energy change is also large: $\Delta G^0 = -237.1$ kJ/mol. Why, then, don't oxygen and hydrogen combine spontaneously and immediately to form water when they are mixed at room temperature?

Hydrogen and oxygen gases exist as diatomic molecules. When the molecules approach each other, the electron clouds repel each other. For a reaction to occur, the colliding molecules must have enough kinetic energy to overcome the electron-cloud repulsion. The bonds of these molecular species must be broken in order for new bonds to be formed between oxygen and hydrogen atoms. Bond breaking is an endothermic process, and bond forming is exothermic. Even though the net process for forming water is exothermic, an initial input of energy is needed to overcome the repulsion forces that occur between reactant molecules when they are brought very close together. This initial energy input activates the reaction.

Once an exothermic reaction is started, the energy released is enough to sustain the reaction by activating other molecules. Thus, the reaction rate keeps increasing. It is limited only by the time required for reactant particles to acquire the energy and make contact. Energy from an outside source may start exothermic reactants along the pathway of reaction. A generalized reaction pathway for an exothermic reaction is shown as the forward reaction in **Figure 1.4.** The minimum amount of energy needed to activate this reaction is the activation energy represented by E_a. **Activation energy is the minimum energy required to transform the reactants into an activated complex.**

FIGURE 1.4

Reaction Pathways The difference between the activation energies for the reverse and forward reactions of a reversible reaction equals the energy change in the reaction, ΔE. The quantity for ΔE is the same for both directions but is negative for the exothermic direction and positive for the endothermic direction.

Reaction Pathways for Forward and Reverse Reactions

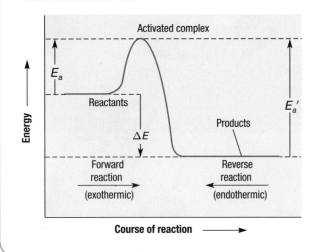

The reverse reaction, decomposition of water molecules, is endothermic, because the water molecules lie at an energy level lower than that of the hydrogen and oxygen molecules. The water molecules require a larger activation energy before they can decompose to re-form oxygen and hydrogen. The energy needed to activate an endothermic reaction is greater than that required for the original exothermic change and is represented by E_a' in **Figure 1.4.** The difference between E_a' and E_a is equal to the energy change in the reaction, ΔE. This energy change has the same numerical value for the forward reaction as it has for the reverse reaction but with the opposite sign.

● MAIN IDEA

In a transition state, bonds are breaking as new bonds form.

When molecules collide, some of their high kinetic energy is converted into internal potential energy within the colliding molecules. If enough energy is converted, molecules with suitable orientation become activated. New bonds can then form. In this brief interval of bond breakage and bond formation, the collision complex is in a *transition state*. Some partial bonding exists in this transitional structure. **A transitional structure that results from an effective collision and that persists while old bonds are breaking and new bonds are forming is called an activated complex.**

Figure 1.5 graphically breaks down the reaction pathway of the formation of hydrogen iodide gas into three steps. Beginning with the reactants, H_2 and I_2, a certain amount of activation energy, E_{a1}, is needed to form the activated complex that leads to the formation of the intermediates H_2 and $2I$. Then more activation energy, E_{a2}, is needed to form the activated complex leading to the intermediates H_2I and I. In order to arrive at the final product, $2HI$, another increase in activation energy is necessary, as seen by the highest peak, labeled E_{a3}.

An activated complex is formed when an effective collision raises the internal energies of the reactants to their minimum level for reaction, as in **Figure 1.4** (see previous page). Both forward and reverse reactions go through the same activated complex. A bond broken in the activated complex for the forward reaction must be re-formed in the activated complex for the reverse reaction. Observe that an activated complex occurs at a high-energy position along the reaction pathway.

The kinetic-molecular theory states that the speeds and the kinetic energies of the molecules increase as the temperature increases. An increase in speed causes more collisions, which can cause an increase in the number of reactions. However, an increase in the reaction rate depends on more than simply the number of collisions, as **Figure 1.3** (earlier in the section) illustrates. The collisions between molecules must possess sufficient energy to form an activated complex, or a reaction will not take place. Raising the temperature of a reaction means more molecules that have enough energy to exceed activation energy, increasing the reaction rate.

In its brief existence, the activated complex has partial bonding that is characteristic of both reactant and product. It may then re-form the original bonds and separate back into the reactant particles, or it may form new bonds and separate into product particles. The activated complex, unlike the relatively stable intermediate products, is a very short-lived molecular complex in which bonds are in the process of being broken and formed.

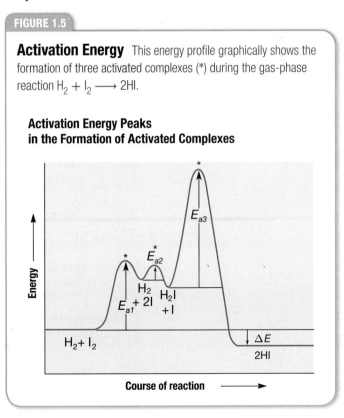

FIGURE 1.5

Activation Energy This energy profile graphically shows the formation of three activated complexes (*) during the gas-phase reaction $H_2 + I_2 \longrightarrow 2HI$.

Activation Energy Peaks in the Formation of Activated Complexes

GO ONLINE

Learn It! Video
HMHScience.com

Sample Problem A Copy the energy diagram below, and label the reactants, products, ΔE, E_a, and E_a'. Determine the value of $\Delta E_{forward}$, $\Delta E_{reverse}$, E_a, and E_a'.

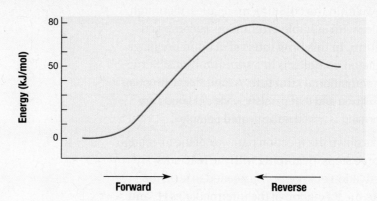

● **SOLVE**

The energy level of reactants is always at the left-hand end of such a curve, and the energy level of products is always at the right-hand end. The energy change in the reaction, ΔE, is the difference between these two energy levels. The activation energy differs in the forward and reverse directions. It is the minimum energy needed to achieve effective reaction in either direction. As E_a, it is the difference between the reactant energy level and the peak in the curve. As E_a', it is the difference between the product energy level and the peak in the curve.

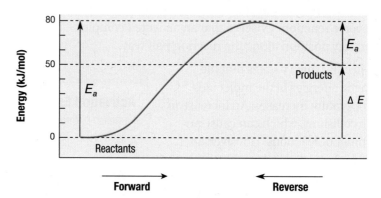

$\Delta E_{forward}$ = energy of products − energy of reactants
$\Delta E_{forward}$ = 50 kJ/mol − 0 kJ/mol = +50 kJ/mol

$\Delta E_{reverse}$ = energy of reactants − energy of products
$\Delta E_{reverse}$ = 0 kJ/mol − 50 kJ/mol = −50 kJ/mol

E_a = energy of activated complex − energy of reactants
E_a = 80 kJ/mol − 0 kJ/mol = 80 kJ/mol

E_a' = energy of activated complex − energy of products
E_a' = 80 kJ/mol − 50 kJ/mol = 30 kJ/mol

Continued

Energy Diagrams (continued)

Practice Answers in Appendix E

1. a. Use the method shown in the sample problem to redraw and label the following energy diagram. Determine the value of $\Delta E_{forward}$, $\Delta E_{reverse}$, E_a, and $E_a{'}$.
b. Is the forward reaction shown in the diagram exothermic or endothermic? Explain your answer.

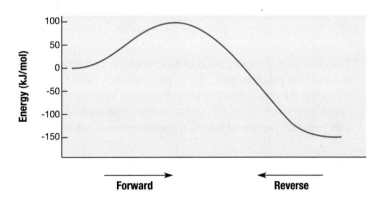

2. a. Draw and label an energy diagram similar to the one shown in the sample problem for a reaction in which $E_a = 125$ kJ/mol and $E_a{'} = 86$ kJ/mol. Place the reactants at energy level zero.
b. Calculate the values of $\Delta E_{forward}$ and $\Delta E_{reverse}$.
c. Is this reaction endothermic or exothermic? Explain your answer.
3. a. Draw and label an energy diagram for a reaction in which $E_a = 154$ kJ/mol and $\Delta E = 136$ kJ/mol.
b. Calculate the activation energy, $E_a{'}$, for the reverse reaction.

✔ SECTION 1 FORMATIVE ASSESSMENT

▶ Reviewing Main Ideas

1. What is meant by *reaction mechanism*?

2. What factors determine whether a molecular collision produces a reaction?

3. What is activation energy?

4. What is an activated complex?

5. How is activation energy of the forward and reverse reactions related to the energy of reaction?

6. What is the difference between an activated complex and an intermediate?

7. Explain why, even though a collision may have energy in excess of the activation energy, a reaction may not occur.

✔ Critical Thinking

8. ANALYZING INFORMATION Which corresponds to the faster rate: a mechanism with a small activation energy or one with a large activation energy? Explain your answer.

Reaction Rate

Key Terms

reaction rate	catalysis	order
chemical kinetics	homogeneous catalyst	rate-determining step
heterogeneous reaction	heterogeneous catalyst	
catalyst	rate law	

The change in concentration of reactants per unit time as a reaction proceeds is called the reaction rate. The study of reaction rates is concerned with the factors that affect the rate and with the mathematical expressions that reveal the specific dependencies of the rate on concentration. **The area of chemistry that is concerned with reaction rates and reaction mechanisms is called chemical kinetics.**

▶ **MAIN IDEA**

Several factors can influence reaction rates.

For reactions to occur, particles must come into contact in a favorable orientation and with enough energy for activation. Thus, the rate of a reaction depends on the collision frequency of the reactants and on the collision efficiency. Any change in reaction conditions that affects the collision frequency, the collision efficiency, or the collision energy affects the reaction rate. At least five important factors influence the rate of a chemical reaction.

Nature of Reactants

Substances vary greatly in their tendencies to react. For example, hydrogen combines vigorously with chlorine under certain conditions. Under the same conditions, it may react only slowly with nitrogen. Sodium and oxygen combine much more rapidly than iron and oxygen under similar conditions. Bonds are broken, and other bonds are formed in reactions. The rate of reaction depends on the particular reactants and reaction conditions.

Surface Area

Gaseous mixtures and dissolved particles can mix and collide freely; therefore, reactions involving them can occur rapidly. In heterogeneous reactions, the reaction rate depends on the area of contact of the reaction substances. **Heterogeneous reactions involve reactants in two different phases.** These reactions can occur only when the two phases are in contact. Thus, the surface area of a solid reactant is an important factor in determining rate. An increase in surface area increases the rate of heterogeneous reactions.

Solid zinc reacts with aqueous hydrochloric acid to produce zinc chloride and hydrogen gas according to the following equation:

$$Zn(s) + 2HCl(aq) \rightarrow ZnCl_2(aq) + H_2(g)$$

This reaction occurs at the surface of the zinc solid. A cube of zinc measuring 1 cm on each edge presents only 6 cm² of contact area. The same amount of zinc in the form of a fine powder might provide a contact area thousands of times greater than the original area. Consequently, the reaction rate of the powdered solid is much faster.

A lump of coal burns slowly when kindled in air. The rate of burning can be increased by breaking the lump into smaller pieces, exposing more surface area. If the piece of coal is powdered and then ignited while suspended in air, it burns explosively. This is the cause of some explosions in coal mines.

Temperature

An increase in temperature increases the average kinetic energy of the particles in a substance; this can result in a greater number of effective collisions when the substance is allowed to react with another substance. If the number of effective collisions increases, the reaction rate will increase.

To be effective, the energy of the collisions must be equal to or greater than the activation energy. At higher temperatures, more particles possess enough energy to form the activated complex when collisions occur. Thus, a rise in temperature produces an increase in collision energy as well as in collision frequency.

Decreasing the temperature of a reaction system has the opposite effect. The average kinetic energy of the particles decreases, so they collide less frequently and with less energy, producing fewer effective collisions. Beginning near room temperature, the reaction rates of many common reactions roughly double with each 10 K (10°C) rise in temperature. This rule of thumb should be used with caution, however. The actual rate increase with a given rise in temperature must be determined experimentally.

Concentration

Pure oxygen has five times the concentration of oxygen molecules that air has at the same pressure; consequently, a substance that oxidizes in air oxidizes more vigorously in pure oxygen. For example, in **Figure 2.1,** the light produced when the lump of charcoal is burned in pure oxygen is much more intense than the light produced when the charcoal lump is heated in air until combustion begins. The oxidation of charcoal is a heterogeneous reaction system in which one reactant is a gas. The reaction rate depends not only on the amount of exposed charcoal surface but also on the concentration of the reacting species, O_2.

In homogeneous reaction systems, reaction rates depend on the concentration of the reactants. Predicting the mathematical relationship between rate and concentration is difficult, because most chemical reactions occur in a series of steps and only one of these steps determines the reaction rate. If the number of effective collisions increases, the rate increases as well. In general, an increase in rate is expected if the concentration of one or more of the reactants is increased.

FIGURE 2.1

Concentration and Reaction Rate A greater concentration increases the number of effective collisions, so the reaction rate increases.

(a) Pure oxygen has five times the concentration of oxygen molecules compared to air, so the charcoal will burn more intensely.

(b) Air contains substances in addition to oxygen, so oxygen molecules have fewer chances to collide with the charcoal to react.

FIGURE 2.2

Collisions and Reaction Rates

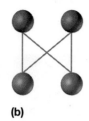
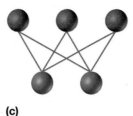
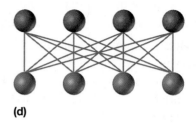

(a)　　　　(b)　　　　　(c)　　　　　　(d)

Consider the model depicted in **Figure 2.2.** In the system with only two molecules, shown in **Figure 2.2a,** only one collision can possibly occur. When there are four molecules in the system, as in **Figure 2.2b,** there can be four possible collisions. With temperature and pressure under constant conditions, as the number of molecules in the system increases, so does the total number of possible collisions between them. **Figures 2.2c** and **d** show a five- and eight-molecule system, allowing six and sixteen possible collisions, respectively. Lowering the concentration should have the opposite effect. The actual effect of concentration changes on reaction rate, however, must be determined experimentally.

Presence of Catalysts

Some chemical reactions proceed quite slowly. Sometimes their reaction rates can be increased dramatically by the presence of a catalyst. **A catalyst is a substance that changes the rate of a chemical reaction without itself being consumed. The action of a catalyst is called catalysis.** The catalysis of the decomposition reaction of hydrogen peroxide by manganese dioxide is shown in **Figure 2.3.** A catalyst provides a reaction mechanism with an alternate pathway, which has a lower activation energy. Think of it as driving through a tunnel in a mountain, rather than driving up the mountain and down the other side. The catalyst may be effective in forming an alternative activated complex that requires a lower activation energy—as suggested in the energy profiles of the decomposition of hydrogen peroxide, H_2O_2, shown on the next page in **Figure 2.4**—via the following equation:

$$2H_2O_2(l) \rightarrow O_2(g) + 2H_2O(l)$$

Catalysts do not appear among the final products of reactions they accelerate. They may participate in one step along a reaction pathway and be regenerated in a later step. In large, cost-sensitive reaction systems, catalysts are recovered and reused. **A catalyst that is in the same phase as all the reactants and products in a reaction system is called a homogeneous catalyst. When its phase is different from that of the reactants, it is called a heterogeneous catalyst.** Metals are often used as heterogeneous catalysts. The catalysis of many reactions is promoted by adsorption of reactants on the metal surfaces, which increases the concentration of the reactants. In the chapter "Biochemistry," you will learn about enzymes, biological catalysts to facilitate chemical reactions in living organisms.

Reaction Rate and Catalysts

The reaction rate of the decomposition of hydrogen peroxide, H_2O_2, can be increased by using a catalyst. The catalyst used here is manganese dioxide, MnO_2, a black solid. A 30% H_2O_2 solution is added dropwise onto the MnO_2 in the beaker and rapidly decomposes to O_2 and H_2O. Both the oxygen and water appear as gases, because the energy released by the reaction causes much of the water to vaporize.

✔ **CRITICAL THINKING**

Describe Research and describe at least two important chemical reactions in the human body that require catalysts.

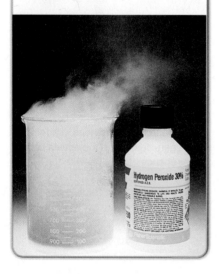

FIGURE 2.4

Reaction Pathways and Catalysts
A catalyst reduces the activation energy for a chemical reaction.

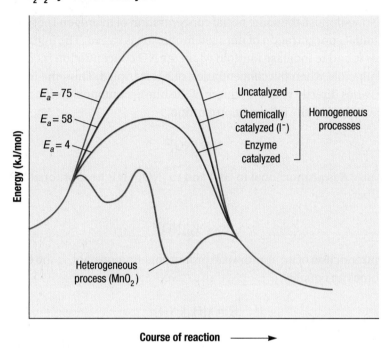

Comparison of Pathways for the Decomposition of H$_2$O$_2$ by Various Catalysts

$E_a = 75$ — Uncatalyzed
$E_a = 58$ — Chemically catalyzed (I$^-$) } Homogeneous processes
$E_a = 4$ — Enzyme catalyzed

Energy (kJ/mol)

Heterogeneous process (MnO$_2$)

Course of reaction →

GO ONLINE **Animated** Chemistry
HMHScience.com
Catalysts

▶ MAIN IDEA
Concentration and reaction rate are related.

The relationship between the rate of a reaction and the concentration of one reactant is determined experimentally by first keeping the concentrations of other reactants and the temperature of the system constant. Then the reaction rate is measured for various concentrations of the reactant in question. A series of such experiments reveals how the concentration of each reactant affects the reaction rate.

Hydrogen gas reacts with nitrogen monoxide gas at constant volume and at an elevated constant temperature, via the following equation.

$$2H_2(g) + 2NO(g) \rightarrow N_2(g) + 2H_2O(g)$$

Four moles of reactant gases produce three moles of product gases; thus, the pressure of the system diminishes as the reaction proceeds. The rate of the reaction can, therefore, be determined by measuring the change of pressure in the vessel with time.

Suppose a series of experiments is conducted using the same initial concentration of nitrogen monoxide but different initial concentrations of hydrogen. The initial reaction rate is found to vary directly with the hydrogen concentration: doubling the concentration of H$_2$ doubles the rate, tripling the concentration of H$_2$ triples the rate, and so on.

CHECK FOR UNDERSTANDING

Describe The feature on this page, "Why It Matters: Explosives," describes why TNT and dynamite explosions occur very quickly. Describe a chemical reaction with a very slow reaction rate.

We can represent this proportion mathematically. If R represents the reaction rate and $[H_2]$ is the concentration of hydrogen in moles per liter, the mathematical relationship between rate and concentration can be expressed as follows:

$$R \propto [H_2]$$

The $\propto$ is a symbol that is read "is proportional to."

Now suppose the same initial concentration of hydrogen is used, but the initial concentration of nitrogen monoxide is varied. The initial reaction rate is found to increase fourfold when the NO concentration is doubled and ninefold when the concentration of NO is tripled. Thus, the reaction rate varies directly with the square of the nitrogen monoxide concentration, as described by the following proportion:

$$R \propto [NO]^2$$

Because R is proportional to $[H_2]$ and to $[NO]^2$, it is proportional to their product:

$$R \propto [H_2][NO]^2$$

By introduction of an appropriate proportionality constant, k, the expression becomes an equality:

$$R = k[H_2][NO]^2$$

An equation that relates reaction rate and concentrations of reactants is called the **rate law** for the reaction. It is applicable for a specific reaction at a given temperature. A rise in temperature increases the reaction rates of reactions, so the value of k usually increases as the temperature increases.

Using the Rate Law

The general form for the rate law is given by the following equation:

$$R = k[A]^n[B]^m$$

The reaction rate is represented by R, k is the specific rate constant, and $[A]$ and $[B]$ represent the molar concentrations of reactants. The respective powers to which the concentrations are raised are represented by n and m. The rate law is applicable for a specific reaction at a given set of conditions and must be determined from experimental data.

The power to which a reactant concentration is raised is called the **order** in that reactant. The value of n is said to be the order of the reaction with respect to $[A]$, so the reaction is said to be "nth order in A." Similarly, for the value of m, the reaction is said to be "mth order in B." The orders, or powers, n and m, are usually small integers or zero.

An order of *one* for a reactant means the reaction rate is directly proportional to the concentration of that reactant. An order of *two* means the reaction rate is directly proportional to the *square* of the reactant concentration. An order of *zero* means that the rate does not depend on the concentration of the reactant, *as long as some of the reactant is present*. The sum of all of the reactant orders is called the *order of the reaction*, or *overall order*. The overall order of the reaction is equal to the sum of the reactant orders, or $n + m$. Some examples of observed rate laws are shown below. Some of these reactions involve nitrogen oxides, which are highly reactive gases that contribute to the formation of smog that can blanket an entire city, as shown in **Figure 2.5**.

FIGURE 2.5

Smog A cloud of polluted air, commonly known as smog, settles over a city. Smog is common in industrialized areas, where highly reactive gases and particulate matter are released into the air. The rate of the reaction that produces smog is determined by the amount of sunlight present.

$$3NO(g) \rightarrow N_2O(g) + NO_2(g)$$

$R = k[NO]^2$

second order in NO, second order overall

$$NO_2(g) + CO(g) \rightarrow NO(g) + CO_2(g)$$

$R = k[NO_2]^2$
second order in NO_2,
zero order in CO,
second order overall

$$2NO_2(g) \rightarrow 2NO(g) + O_2(g)$$

$R = k[NO_2]^2$
second order in NO_2,
second order overall

$$2H_2O_2(aq) \rightarrow 2H_2O(l) + O_2(g)$$

$R = k[H_2O_2]$
first order in H_2O_2,
first order overall

Important to understand is that orders in the rate law must be determined from experiment and cannot be predicted from the reaction stoichiometry.

Rate Constant

The *rate constant* (k) is the proportionality constant relating the rate of the reaction to the concentrations of reactants. It is important to remember the following about the value of k:

1. Once the reaction orders (powers) are known, the value of k can be determined from experimental data.
2. The value of k is for a *specific reaction*; k has a different value for other reactions, even at the same conditions.
3. The units of k depend on the *overall order of the reaction*.
4. The value of k *does not change* for different concentrations of reactants or products. So the value of k for a reaction remains the same throughout the reaction and does not change with time.
5. The value of k is for the reaction *at a specific temperature*; if we increase the temperature of the reaction, the value of k increases.
6. The value of k changes (becomes larger) if a *catalyst* is present.

Determining Rate Law and Rate Constant

GO ONLINE

Learn It! Video
HMHScience.com

Solve It! Cards
HMHScience.com

Sample Problem B Three experiments that have identical conditions were performed to measure the initial rate of the reaction

$$2HI(g) \rightarrow H_2(g) + I_2(g)$$

The results for the three experiments in which only the HI concentration was varied are as follows:

Experiment	[HI] (M)	Rate (M/s)
1	0.015	1.1×10^{-3}
2	0.030	4.4×10^{-3}
3	0.045	9.9×10^{-3}

Write the rate law for the reaction. Find the value and units of the specific rate constant, k.

① ANALYZE

The general rate law for this reaction has the form $R = k[HI]^n$. We need to deduce the value of the power n.

② PLAN

Find the ratio of the reactant concentrations between two experiments, such as 1 and 2, $\frac{[HI]_2}{[HI]_1}$. Then, see how the ratio of concentration affects the ratio of rates, $\frac{R_2}{R_1}$.

③ SOLVE

Concentration ratio: $\frac{[HI]_2}{[HI]_1} = \frac{0.030 \text{ M}}{0.015 \text{ M}} = 2.0$; rate ratio: $\frac{R_2}{R_1} = \frac{4.4 \times 10^{-3} \text{ M/s}}{1.1 \times 10^{-3} \text{ M/s}} = 4.0$

Thus, when the concentration changes by a factor of 2, the rate changes by a factor of 4, or 2^2, so the rate law is $R = k[HI]^2$.

To find the value of k, we can rearrange the rate law and substitute known values for any one experiment. Do the following for Experiment 1:

$$k = \frac{R}{[HI]^2} = \frac{1.1 \times 10^{-3} \text{ M/s}}{(0.015 \text{ M})^2} = 4.9 \text{ M}^{-1}\text{s}^{-1}$$

④ CHECK YOUR WORK

By comparing items 1 and 3 in the table, we see that when [HI] is tripled, the rate changes by a factor of 9, or 3^2. This rate change confirms that the order is 2. The same value of k can be calculated from any other experiment. Thus, the rate law and k are correct.

Practice   Answers in Appendix E

1. For the reaction $3A \rightarrow C$, the initial concentration of A was 0.2 M, and the reaction rate was 1.0 M/s. When [A] was doubled, the reaction rate increased to 4.0 M/s. Determine the rate law for the reaction.

2. The rate law for a reaction is found to be rate = $k[X]^3$. By what factor does the rate increase if [X] is tripled?

Determining Rate Law and Rate Constant

Sample Problem C Three experiments were performed to measure the initial rate of the reaction

$$A + B \rightarrow C$$

Conditions were identical in the three experiments except that the concentrations of reactants varied. The results are as follows:

Experiment	[A] (M)	[B] (M)	Rate (M/s)
1	2.4	4.8	6.0×10^{-9}
2	2.4	2.4	3.0×10^{-9}
3	7.2	4.8	5.4×10^{-8}

Write the rate law for the reaction. Find the value and units of the specific rate constant, k.

① ANALYZE

The general rate law for this reaction has the form $R = k[A]^n[B]^m$. We need to calculate the values of the powers n and m.

② PLAN

Find the ratio of the reactant concentrations between two experiments that have the same [A] but different [B]. Then, see how this ratio affects the ratio of rates, $\frac{R_2}{R_1}$; this ratio of rates lets us find the value of m. A similar approach of comparing two experiments that have the same [B] but a different [A] lets us find the value of n.

③ SOLVE

First compare Experiments 1 and 2, which have the same [A], to find m:

Concentration ratio: $\frac{[B]_1}{[B]_2} = \frac{4.8\,M}{2.4\,M} = 2.0$; rate ratio: $\frac{R_1}{R_2} = \frac{6.0 \times 10^{-9}\,M/s}{3.0 \times 10^{-9}\,M/s} = 2.0$

Thus, when the concentration of B changes by a factor of 2, the rate changes by a factor of 2, or 2^1. So m is 1, and the reaction is first order in B.
Then, compare Experiments 1 and 3, which have the same [B], to find n:

Concentration ratio: $\frac{[A]_3}{[A]_1} = \frac{7.2\,M}{2.4\,M} = 3.0$; rate ratio: $\frac{R_3}{R_1} = \frac{5.4 \times 10^{-8}\,M/s}{6.0 \times 10^{-9}\,M/s} = 9.0$

Thus, when the concentration of A changes by a factor of 3, the rate changes by a factor of 9, or 3^2. So n is 2, and the reaction is second order in A.
The rate law is $R = k[A]^2[B]$.
To find the value of k, we can rearrange the rate law and substitute known values for any one experiment. Do the following for Experiment 1:

$$k = \frac{R}{[A]^2[B]} = \frac{6.0 \times 10^{-9}\,M/s}{(2.4\,M)^2(4.8\,M)} = 2.2 \times 10^{-10}\,M^{-2}s^{-1}$$

④ CHECK YOUR WORK

The same value of k can be calculated from the data for any other experiment. So the rate law and the calculation of k are correct.

Rate Laws and Reaction Pathway

The rate law depends on the reaction mechanism. For a reaction that occurs in a *single step*, the reaction rate of that step is proportional to the product of the reactant concentrations, each of which is raised to its stoichiometric coefficient. For example, suppose one molecule of gas A collides with one molecule of gas B to form two molecules of substance C, according to the following equation:

$$A + B \rightarrow 2C$$

One particle of each reactant is involved in each collision. Thus, doubling the concentration of either reactant will double the collision frequency. It will also double the reaction rate *for this step*. Therefore, the rate for this step is directly proportional to the concentration of A and B. The rate law for this one-step forward reaction follows:

$$R_{forward} = k_{forward}[A][B]$$

Now suppose the reaction is reversible. In the reverse step, two molecules of C must decompose to form one molecule of A and one of B, or $2C \rightarrow A + B$.

Thus, the reaction rate for this reverse step is directly proportional to $[C] \times [C]$. The rate law for the reverse step is $R_{reverse} = k_{reverse}[C]^2$.

The power to which the molar concentration of each reactant is raised in the rate laws above corresponds to the coefficient for the reactant in the balanced chemical equation. Such a relationship holds *only* if the reaction follows a simple one-step path, that is, if the reaction occurs at the molecular level exactly as written in the chemical equation.

If a chemical reaction proceeds in a sequence of steps, the rate law is determined from the slowest step because it has the lowest rate. **This slowest-rate step is called the rate-determining step for the chemical reaction.**

Consider the reaction of nitrogen dioxide and carbon monoxide.

$$NO_2(g) + CO(g) \rightarrow NO(g) + CO_2(g)$$

The reaction is believed to be a two-step process represented by the following mechanism:

Step 1: $NO_2 + NO_2 \rightarrow NO_3 + NO$ slow

Step 2: $NO_3 + CO \rightarrow NO_2 + CO_2$ fast

In the first step, shown in **Figure 2.6,** two molecules of NO_2 collide, forming the intermediate species NO_3. This molecule then collides with one molecule of CO and reacts quickly to produce one molecule each of NO_2 and CO_2. The first step is the slower of the two and is therefore the rate-determining step. We can write the rate law from this rate-determining step, which has two molecules of NO_2 as the reactants.

$$R = k[NO_2]^2$$

The rate law does not include [CO], because CO reacts after the rate-determining step and its concentration does not affect the rate.

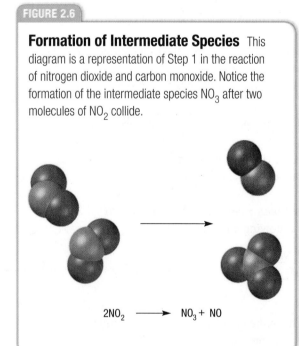

FIGURE 2.6

Formation of Intermediate Species This diagram is a representation of Step 1 in the reaction of nitrogen dioxide and carbon monoxide. Notice the formation of the intermediate species NO_3 after two molecules of NO_2 collide.

$$2NO_2 \longrightarrow NO_3 + NO$$

Determining Rate-Determining Step and Law and Rate Constant

Sample Problem D Nitrogen dioxide and fluorine react in the gas phase according to the following equation.

$$2NO_2(g) + F_2(g) \rightarrow 2NO_2F(g)$$

The rate law is $k\,[NO_2][F_2]$.

A proposed mechanism for this reaction follows.

Step 1: $NO_2 + F_2 \rightarrow NO_2F + F$ (slow)

Step 2: $F + NO_2 \rightarrow NO_2F$ (fast)

Identify the rate-determining step.

● **SOLVE**   If we combine these two steps, the intermediate, F, cancels out, and we are left with the original equation. Since the rate law is first order in both NO and F_2, they react in the slower rate-determining step. Thus, Step 1 is the rate-determining step.

Determining Effects on Reaction Rate

Sample Problem E A reaction involving reactants X and Y was found to occur by a one-step mechanism: $X + 2Y \rightarrow XY_2$. Write the rate law for this reaction, and then determine the effect of each of the following on the reaction rate:

a. doubling the concentration of X

b. doubling the concentration of Y

c. using one-third the concentration of Y

● **SOLVE**   Because the equation represents a single-step mechanism, the rate law can be written from the equation (otherwise, it could not be). The rate will vary directly with the concentration of X, which has an implied coefficient of 1 in the equation. And the rate will vary directly with the square of the concentration of Y, which has the coefficient of 2: $R = k[X][Y]^2$.

a. Doubling the concentration of X will double the rate ($R = k[2X][Y]^2$).

b. Doubling the concentration of Y will increase the rate fourfold ($R = k[X][2Y]^2$).

c. Using one-third the concentration of Y will reduce the rate to one-ninth of its original value ($R = k[X][\frac{1}{3}Y]^2$).

Practice   Answers in Appendix E

1. The rate of a hypothetical reaction involving L and M is found to double when the concentration of L is doubled and to increase fourfold when the concentration of M is doubled. Write the rate law for this reaction.

2. At temperatures below 498 K, the following reaction takes place.

$$NO_2(g) + CO(g) \rightarrow CO_2(g) + NO(g)$$

Doubling the concentration of NO_2 quadruples the rate of CO_2 formed if the CO concentration is held constant. However, doubling the concentration of CO has no effect on the rate of CO_2 formation. Write a rate-law expression for this reaction.

QuickLAB FACTORS INFLUENCING REACTION RATE

QUESTION

How do the type of reactants, surface area of reactants, concentration of reactants, and catalysts affect the rates of chemical reactions?

PROCEDURE

Remove all combustible material from the work area. Wear safety goggles and an apron. Record all your results in a data table.

1. Add 10 mL of vinegar to each of three test tubes. To one test tube, add a 3 cm piece of magnesium ribbon; to a second, add a 3 cm zinc strip; and to a third, add a 3 cm copper strip. (All metals should be the same width.) If necessary, polish the metals with sandpaper until they are shiny.

2. Using tongs, hold a paper clip in the hottest part of the burner flame for 30 s. Repeat with a ball of steel wool 2 cm in diameter.

3. To one test tube, add 10 mL of vinegar; to a second, add 5 mL of vinegar plus 5 mL of water; and to a third, add 2.5 mL of vinegar plus 7.5 mL of water. To each of the three test tubes, add a 3 cm piece of magnesium ribbon.

4. Using tongs, hold a sugar cube and try to ignite it with a match. Then try to ignite it in a burner flame. Rub paper ash on a second cube, and try to ignite it with a match.

DISCUSSION

1. What are the rate-influencing factors in each step of the procedure?

2. What were the results from each step of the procedure? How do you interpret each result?

MATERIALS

- Bunsen burner
- paper ash
- copper foil strip
- graduated cylinder, 10 mL
- magnesium ribbon
- matches
- paper clip
- sandpaper
- steel wool
- 2 sugar cubes
- white vinegar
- zinc strip
- 6 test tubes, 16 × 150 mm
- tongs

SAFETY

  Wear safety goggles and an apron.

✔ SECTION 2 FORMATIVE ASSESSMENT

▶ Reviewing Main Ideas

1. What is studied in the branch of chemistry that is known as chemical kinetics?

2. List five important factors that influence the rate of chemical reactions.

3. What is a catalyst? Explain the effect of a catalyst on the rate of chemical reactions. How does a catalyst influence the activation energy required by a particular reaction?

4. What is meant by a rate law for a chemical reaction?

✔ Critical Thinking

5. **RELATING IDEAS** Using the ideas of reaction kinetics, explain the purpose of food refrigeration.

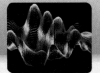

New Generation Catalysts S.T.E.M.

To see an important example of *heterogeneous catalysis*, you do not need to look any farther than the streets near your home. The *catalytic converter,* an important part of a vehicle's exhaust system, uses metal catalysts to reduce harmful gaseous pollutants.

In an automobile engine, hydrocarbon molecules in gasoline or diesel fuel undergo a combustion reaction with oxygen from air to make carbon dioxide, CO_2, and water. The correct stoichiometric ratio of fuel to oxygen is required for the fuel to be completely burned in the reaction. Additional reaction products are formed when not enough oxygen or excess oxygen is present. These products include carbon monoxide, CO, and NO_x compounds, such as nitric oxide, NO, and nitrogen dioxide, NO_2. There is also leftover unburned fuel, which is called a volatile organic compound (VOC).

The Clean Air Act, last amended in 1990, regulates automobile emissions of CO, NO_x, and VOCs. In addition to being harmful themselves, NO_x compounds, CO, and VOCs react with sunlight to make ozone, O_3. In the lower atmosphere, ozone is a major part of photochemical smog. NO_x gases can also mix with rainwater to produce acid rain.

Catalytic converters use precious-metal catalysts to change the gases coming from the engine into less-harmful gases. A combination of rhodium and platinum, and sometimes palladium, is used to convert nitrogen compounds back into N_2 and O_2. This combination also converts CO into CO_2 and converts VOCs into CO_2 and water. The catalysts need O_2 from the air and temperatures above approximately 500°F to work properly. The temperatures are achieved from the normal operation of the car engine.

Up to 90% of CO, NO_x, and VOCs are typically eliminated from automobile exhaust by a catalytic converter. Although catalytic converters are beneficial to our environment, they could still be improved. To this end, researchers at the Department of Energy's Oak Ridge National Laboratory (ORNL) in Tennessee are developing a new generation of catalysts to remove pollutants from engine exhausts. In particular, they are working on the problem of inhibition in catalytic converters. This happens when pollutant molecules occupy too many of the active sites on catalytic surfaces, which has the effect of clogging the converter. A combination of copper, cobalt, and cerium oxides shows promise in solving this problem.

Another problem ORNL is working on is low-temperature exhaust gases. The improved efficiency of newer engines has reduced the waste heat lost through the exhaust system. The problem is that catalysts currently in use operate better at high temperature. The mixed metal oxide catalyst described above may hold promise for working at lower temperatures.

ORNL is also working on an improved catalyst to speed up the synthesis of nylon, an important polymer used for cloth, cookware, machinery, and electronics. Researchers have discovered that a catalyst made of a mixture of manganese and cerium oxides is very selective for carbon-hydrogen bonds. These bonds must be broken to take cyclohexane to the next step in the synthesis of nylon. In addition to being selective, the catalyst is very porous. This gives it a large surface area, which speeds up the process, resulting in more nylon being made in less time.

Questions

1. Catalysts lower the activation energy of chemical reactions. How does this benefit the environment?

2. Chlorine free radicals are produced in the upper atmosphere when ultraviolet radiation interacts with chlorofluorocarbons (CFCs). The free radicals catalyze the conversion of ozone to oxygen. How is this catalysis harmful to humans?

Scientist Sheng Dai at the Department of Energy's Oak Ridge National Laboratory

Factors such as surface area and temperature affect the rate of reactions because they affect the frequency and energy of collisions between particles. The concentrations of reactants can also affect the frequency of collisions. If other factors are kept constant, the rates of most chemical reactions will be determined by the concentrations of reactants. Thus, it is possible to write an equation called a *rate law* that relates the rate of a reaction to the concentrations of reactants.

Sample Problem

Fluorine gas reacts with chlorine dioxide according to the following equation.

$$F_2(g) + 2ClO_2(g) \longrightarrow 2FClO_2(g)$$

Use the following experimental data to write a rate law for this reaction.

TRIAL	CONCENTRATION OF F_2	CONCENTRATION OF ClO_2	RATE (MOL/L•S)
1	0.10 M	0.10 M	1.1×10^{-3}
2	0.20 M	0.10 M	2.2×10^{-3}
3	0.10 M	0.20 M	2.2×10^{-3}
4	0.20 M	0.20 M	4.4×10^{-3}

To write the rate law, first examine the data to see how the rate of reaction changes as the concentrations of the reactants change.

- When $[F_2]$ doubles and $[ClO_2]$ remains constant, the rate of reaction doubles from 1.1×10^{-3} mol/L•s to 2.2×10^{-3} mol/L•s. So the rate is directly proportional to $[F_2]$, or $R \propto [F_2]$.
- When $[ClO_2]$ doubles and $[F_2]$ remains constant, the rate of reaction also doubles from 1.1×10^{-3} mol/L•s to 2.2×10^{-3} mol/L•s. So the rate is directly proportional to $[ClO_2]$, or $R \propto [ClO_2]$.
- Because rate is proportional to both $[F_2]$ and $[ClO_2]$, you can write the rate law $R = k[F_2][ClO_2]$. The data from Trial 4 help confirm the rate law, because when both $[F_2]$ and $[ClO_2]$ double, the rate increases by a factor of four, from 1.1×10^{-3} mol/L•s to 4.4×10^{-3} mol/L•s.

Practice

1. Nitrogen monoxide and oxygen react to produce nitrogen dioxide according to the following equation:

$$O_2(g) + 2NO(g) \longrightarrow 2NO_2(g)$$

Use the data in the following table to write a rate law for this reaction.

TRIAL	$[O_2]$	[NO]	REACTION RATE (MOL/L•S)
1	1.20×10^{-2} M	1.40×10^{-2} M	3.30×10^{-3}
2	2.40×10^{-2} M	1.40×10^{-2} M	6.60×10^{-3}
3	1.20×10^{-2} M	2.80×10^{-2} M	1.32×10^{-2}

2. Hydrogen reacts with ethyne, C_2H_2, to produce ethane, C_2H_6, as shown below:

$$2H_2(g) + C_2H_2(g) \longrightarrow C_2H_6(g)$$

Use the data in the following table to write a rate law for this reaction.

TRIAL	$[H_2]$	$[C_2H_2]$	REACTION RATE (MOL/L•MIN)
1	0.20 M	0.20 M	1.5×10^{-4}
2	0.40 M	0.20 M	3.0×10^{-4}
3	0.20 M	0.40 M	1.5×10^{-4}

CHAPTER 17 Summary

BIG IDEA For chemical reactions to occur, the particles of the reactants must collide with sufficient kinetic energy and in the proper orientation.

SECTION 1 The Reaction Process

- The step-by-step process by which an overall chemical reaction occurs is called the *reaction mechanism*.
- In order for chemical reactions to occur, the particles of the reactants must collide.
- Activation energy is needed to merge valence electrons and to loosen bonds sufficiently for molecules to react.
- An activated complex is formed when an effective collision between molecules of reactants raises the internal energy to the minimum level necessary for a reaction to occur.

KEY TERMS

reaction mechanism
intermediate
homogeneous reaction
collision theory
activation energy
activated complex

SECTION 2 Reaction Rate

- The rate of reaction is influenced by the following factors: nature of reactants, surface area, temperature, concentration of reactants, and the presence of catalysts.
- The rates at which chemical reactions occur can sometimes be experimentally measured and expressed in terms of mathematical equations called *rate laws*.
- Rate laws are determined by studying how reaction rate depends on concentration.

KEY TERMS

reaction rate
chemical kinetics
heterogeneous reaction
catalyst
catalysis
homogeneous catalyst
heterogeneous catalyst
rate law
order
rate-determining step

GO ONLINE

Interactive Review
HMHScience.com

Review Games
Concept Maps

SECTION 1

The Reaction Process

 REVIEWING MAIN IDEAS

1. **a.** What is the collision theory?
   b. According to this theory, what two conditions must be met for a collision between reactant molecules to be effective in producing new chemical species?

2. **a.** What condition must be met for an activated complex to result from the collision of reactant particles?
   b. Where, in terms of energy, does the activated complex occur along a typical reaction pathway?

3. In a reversible reaction, how does the activation energy required for the exothermic change compare with the activation energy required for the endo-thermic change?

4. Would you expect the following equation to represent the mechanism by which propane, C_3H_8, burns? Why or why not?

$$C_3H_8(g) + 5O_2(g) \longrightarrow 3CO_2(g) + 4H_2O(g)$$

5. The decomposition of nitrogen dioxide, $2NO_2 \longrightarrow 2NO + O_2$, occurs in a two-step sequence at elevated temperatures. The first step is $NO_2 \longrightarrow NO + O$. Predict a possible second step that, when combined with the first step, gives the complete reaction.

PRACTICE PROBLEMS

6. For each of the energy diagrams provided below, label the reactants, products, ΔE, E_a, and E_a'. Also determine the values of ΔE for the forward and reverse reactions, and determine the values of E_a and E_a'. (Hint: See Sample Problem A.)

(a)

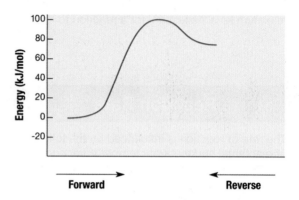

(b)

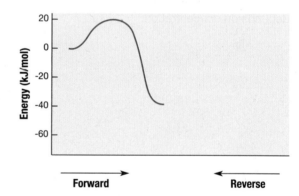

(c)

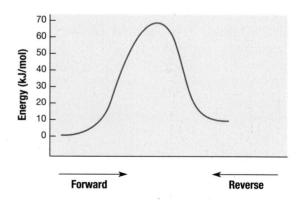

7. Draw and label energy diagrams that depict the following reactions, and determine all remaining values. Place the reactants at energy level zero.
   a. $\Delta E_{forward} = -10\ kJ/mol$, $E_a' = 40\ kJ/mol$
   b. $\Delta E_{forward} = -95\ kJ/mol$, $E_a = 20\ kJ/mol$
   c. $\Delta E_{reverse} = -40\ kJ/mol$, $E_a' = 30\ kJ/mol$

SECTION 2
Reaction Rate

 REVIEWING MAIN IDEAS

8. Define the rate-determining step for a chemical reaction.

9. Write the general equation for the rate law, and label the various factors.

PRACTICE PROBLEMS

10. a. Determine the overall balanced equation for a reaction that has the following proposed mechanism, and write an acceptable rate law. (Hint: See Sample Problem C.)
    Step 1: $B_2 + B_2 \longrightarrow E_3 + D$ slow
    Step 2: $E_3 + A \longrightarrow B_2 + C_2$ fast
    b. Give the order of the reaction with respect to each reactant.
    c. What is the overall order of the reaction?

11. A reaction that involves reactants A and B is found to occur in the one-step mechanism $2A + B \longrightarrow A_2B$. Write the rate law for this reaction, and predict the effect of doubling the concentration of either reactant on the overall reaction rate. (Hint: See Sample Problem C.)

12. A chemical reaction is expressed by the balanced chemical equation $A + 2B \longrightarrow C$. Three reaction-rate experiments yield the following data.

Experiment number	Initial [A]	Initial [B]	Initial rate of formation of C
1	0.20 M	0.20 M	2.0×10^{-4} M/min
2	0.20 M	0.40 M	8.0×10^{-4} M/min
3	0.40 M	0.40 M	1.6×10^{-3} M/min

a. Determine the rate law for the reaction.
b. Calculate the value of the specific rate constant.
c. If the initial concentrations of both A and B are 0.30 M, at what initial rate is C formed?
d. What is the order of the reaction with respect to A?
e. What is the order of the reaction with respect to B?

Mixed Review

 REVIEWING MAIN IDEAS

13. Draw and label energy diagrams that depict the following reactions, and determine all remaining values. Place the reactants at energy level zero.
    a. $\Delta E = +30\ kJ/mol$ $E_a' = 20\ kJ/mol$
    b. $\Delta E = -30\ kJ/mol$ $E_a = 20\ kJ/mol$

14. A particular reaction is found to have the following rate law:

$$R = k[A][B]^2$$

How is the rate affected by each of the following changes?
    a. The initial concentration of A is cut in half.
    b. The initial concentration of B is tripled.
    c. The concentration of A is doubled, but the concentration of B is cut in half.
    d. A catalyst is added.

15. For each of the following pairs, choose the substance or process that you would expect to react more rapidly.
    a. granulated sugar or powdered sugar
    b. zinc in HCl at 298.15 K or zinc in HCl at 320 K
    c. 5 g of thick platinum wire or 5 g of thin platinum wire

16. The following data relate to the reaction $A + B \longrightarrow C$. Find the order with respect to each reactant.

[A] (M)	[B] (M)	Rate (M/s)
0.08	0.06	0.012
0.08	0.03	0.006
0.04	0.06	0.003

CRITICAL THINKING

17. Predicting Outcomes The balanced equation for a rapid homogeneous reaction between two gases is as follows: $4A + B \longrightarrow 2C + 2D$. Because the simultaneous collision of four molecules of one reactant with one molecule of the other reactant is extremely improbable, what would you predict about the nature of the reaction mechanism for this reaction system?

18. Evaluating Ideas
   a. How can you justify calling the reaction pathway that is shown in **Figure 1.4** the minimum-energy pathway for reaction?
   b. What significance is associated with the maximum-energy region of this minimum-energy pathway?

19. Applying Models Explain why there is a danger of explosion in places such as coal mines, sawmills, and grain elevators, where large amounts of dry, powdered combustible materials are present.

20. Evaluating Methods What property would you measure to determine the reaction rate for the following reaction? Justify your choice.

$$2NO_2(g) \longrightarrow N_2O_4(g)$$

RESEARCH AND WRITING

21. Look for situations around your house in which processes are speeded up by an increase in temperature or slowed down by a decrease in temperature. Make a list, and discuss the different processes.

ALTERNATIVE ASSESSMENT

22. Boilers are sometimes used to heat large buildings. Deposits of $CaCO_3$, $MgCO_3$, and $FeCO_3$ can hinder the boiler operation. Aqueous solutions of hydrochloric acid are commonly used to remove these deposits. The general equation for the reaction is written below.

$$MCO_3(s) + 2H_3O^+(aq) \longrightarrow$$
$$M^{2+}(aq) + 3H_2O(l) + CO_2(g)$$

In the equation, M stands for Ca, Mg, or Fe. Design an experiment to determine the effect of various HCl concentrations on the rates of this reaction. Present your design to the class.

Standards-Based Assessment

Record your answers on a separate piece of paper.

MULTIPLE CHOICE

1 A transition structure that results from an effective energetic collision between reactants is the —

A order of the reaction
B rate law
C overall reaction
D activated complex

2 How does the potential energy of the activated complex compare with the energies of the reactants and products?

A It is less than both the energy of the reactants and the energy of the products.
B It is less than the energy of the reactants but greater than the energy of the products.
C It is greater than the energy of the reactants but less than the energy of the products.
D It is greater than both the energy of the reactants and the energy of the products.

3 If a collision between molecules is very gentle, the molecules are —

A more likely to be oriented favorably
B less likely to be oriented favorably
C likely to react
D likely to rebound without reacting

4 Which of the explanations below describes why catalysts can increase reaction rates?

A Adding a catalyst adds more molecules.
B Adding a catalyst adds heat to the reaction.
C Adding a catalyst adds electricity to the reaction.
D Adding a catalyst provides an alternate reaction mechanism having a lower potential-energy barrier between reactants and products.

5 A rate law relates —

A reaction rate and temperature
B reaction rate and concentration
C temperature and concentration
D energy and concentration

6 In a graph of how energy changes with reaction progress, the activated complex appears at the —

A left end of the curve
B right end of the curve
C bottom of the curve
D peak of the curve

7 A certain reaction is zero order in reactant A and second order in reactant B. What happens to the reaction rate when the concentrations of both reactants are doubled?

A The reaction rate remains the same.
B The reaction rate increases by a factor of two.
C The reaction rate increases by a factor of four.
D The reaction rate increases by a factor of eight.

GRIDDED RESPONSE

8 Using the graph below, determine the value of ΔE for the reaction pathway shown.

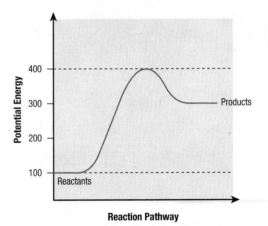

Test Tip

If you are permitted to, draw a line through each incorrect answer choice as you eliminate it.

Standards-Based Assessment   **561**

CHAPTER 18
Chemical Equilibrium

BIG IDEA
A reaction system is at equilibrium when forward and reverse reactions occur simultaneously and at the same rate. Several factors can influence equilibrium.

 ONLINE Chemistry
HMHScience.com

ONLINE LABS
- Equilibrium
- Measuring K_a for Acetic Acid
- Buffer Capacity in Commercial Beverages
- Solubility Product Constant— Algal Blooms
- Striking a Balance

GO ONLINE

 Why It Matters Video
HMHScience.com

Acids and Bases

The Nature of Chemical Equilibrium

Key Terms

reversible reaction
chemical equilibrium

equilibrium constant
chemical equilibrium expression

SECTION 1

Main Ideas

▶ All reactions are reversible under certain conditions.

▶ Some reactions favor products, and others reactants.

▶ At equilibrium, the concentrations of reactants and products remain constant.

In systems that are in equilibrium, opposing processes occur at the same time and at the same rate. For example, when an excess of sugar is placed in water, some sugar molecules go into solution, and others remain undissolved. At equilibrium, molecules of sugar are crystallizing at the same rate that molecules from the crystal are dissolving. The rate of evaporation of a liquid in a closed vessel can eventually be equaled by the rate of condensation of its vapor. The resulting equilibrium vapor pressure is a characteristic of the liquid at the prevailing temperature. The preceding examples are physical equilibria. In this chapter, we will expand on the concept of equilibrium to include chemical reactions. You will learn how a system at equilibrium responds when equilibrium conditions are altered by changing concentration, pressure, and temperature.

▶ MAIN IDEA

All reactions are reversible under certain conditions.

Theoretically, every reaction can proceed in two directions, forward and reverse. Thus, essentially all chemical reactions are considered to be reversible under suitable conditions. **A chemical reaction in which the products can react to re-form the reactants is called a reversible reaction.**

Mercury(II) oxide decomposes when heated.

$$2HgO(s) \xrightarrow{\Delta} 2Hg(l) + O_2(g)$$

Mercury and oxygen combine to form mercury(II) oxide when heated gently.

$$2Hg(l) + O_2(g) \xrightarrow{\Delta} 2HgO(s)$$

Figure 1.1 shows both of these reactions taking place. Suppose mercury(II) oxide is heated in a closed container from which neither the mercury nor the oxygen can escape. Once decomposition has begun, the mercury and oxygen released can recombine to form mercury(II) oxide again. Thus, both reactions can proceed at the same time. Under these conditions, the rate of the synthesis reaction will eventually equal that of the decomposition reaction. At equilibrium, mercury and oxygen will combine to form mercury(II) oxide at the same rate that mercury(II) oxide decomposes into mercury and oxygen. The amounts of mercury(II) oxide, mercury, and oxygen can then be expected to remain constant as long as these conditions persist: a state of dynamic equilibrium has been reached.

FIGURE 1.1

Reversible Reactions When heated, mercury(II) oxide decomposes into its elements, mercury and oxygen. Liquid mercury reacts with oxygen to re-form mercury(II) oxide. Together, these reactions represent a reversible chemical process.

✔ CRITICAL THINKING

Relate What is the relationship between reversible reactions and photosynthesis? Explain the importance of this connection.

(br) ©Charles D. Winters

GO ONLINE Animated
Chemistry
HMHScience.com

Dynamic Equilibrium

In such a state of dynamic equilibrium, both reactions continue, but there is no net change in the composition of the system. **A reversible chemical reaction is in chemical equilibrium when the rate of its forward reaction equals the rate of its reverse reaction and the concentrations of its products and reactants remain unchanged.** The chemical equation for the reaction at equilibrium is written using double arrows to indicate the overall reversibility of the reaction.

$$2HgO(s) \rightleftharpoons 2Hg(l) + O_2(g)$$

▶ MAIN IDEA

Some reactions favor products, and others reactants.

Many chemical reactions are reversible under ordinary conditions of temperature and concentration. They will reach a state of equilibrium unless at least one of the substances involved escapes or is removed from the reaction system. In some cases, however, the forward reaction is so predominant that essentially all reactants will react to form products. Here, the products of the forward reaction are favored, meaning that at equilibrium there is a much higher concentration of products than of reactants. Hence, we can say that the equilibrium "lies to the right," because products predominate, and products conventionally are written on the right side of a chemical equation. An example of such a system is the formation of sulfur trioxide from sulfur dioxide and oxygen.

$$2SO_2(g) + O_2(g) \rightleftharpoons 2SO_3(g)$$

Notice that the equation is written showing an inequality of the two arrow lengths. The forward reaction is represented by the longer arrow to imply that the product is favored in this reaction.

In other cases, the forward reaction is barely under way when the rate of the reverse reaction becomes equal to that of the forward reaction, and equilibrium is established. In these cases, the amounts of reactants remain high, and the amounts of products are low. Here, we say that the equilibrium "lies to the left," because the reactants are the predominant species. An example of such a system is the acid-base reaction between carbonic acid and water.

$$H_2CO_3(aq) + H_2O(l) \rightleftharpoons H_3O^+(aq) + HCO_3^-(aq)$$

In still other cases, both forward and reverse reactions occur to nearly the same extent before chemical equilibrium is established. Neither reaction is favored, and considerable concentrations of both reactants and products are present at equilibrium. An example is the dissociation of sulfurous acid in water.

$$H_2SO_3(aq) + H_2O(l) \rightleftharpoons H_3O^+(aq) + HSO_3^-(aq)$$

Chemical reactions ordinarily are used to convert available reactants into more desirable products. Chemists try to convert as much of these reactants as possible into products. The extent to which reactants are converted to products is indicated by the numerical value of the equilibrium constant, which will be described in the next section.

✔ CHECK FOR UNDERSTANDING

Explain The two terms *dynamic* and *equilibrium* seem to contradict each other at first. *Dynamic* means that changes are occurring, but *equilibrium* means that no overall change is happening. Given this, explain why the combination of the two, *dynamic equilibrium*, is correct.

▶ MAIN IDEA

At equilibrium, the concentrations of reactants and products remain constant.

Suppose two substances, A and B, react to form products C and D. In turn, C and D react to produce A and B. Under appropriate conditions, equilibrium occurs for this reversible reaction. This hypothetical equilibrium reaction is described by the following general equation.

$$nA + mB \rightleftarrows xC + yD$$

Initially, the concentrations of C and D are zero, and those of A and B are maximum. **Figure 1.2** shows that, over time, the rate of the forward reaction decreases as A and B are used up. Meanwhile, the rate of the reverse reaction increases as C and D are formed. When these two reaction rates become equal, equilibrium is established. The individual concentrations of A, B, C, and D undergo no further change if conditions remain the same.

Once equilibrium is attained, the concentrations of products and reactants remain constant, so a ratio of their concentrations should also remain constant. The ratio of the mathematical product $[C]^x \times [D]^y$ to the mathematical product $[A]^n \times [B]^m$ for this reaction has a definite value at a given temperature. It is the equilibrium constant of the reaction and is designated by the letter K. The following equation describes the equilibrium constant for the hypothetical equilibrium system. The brackets ([ ]) indicate the concentration of each substance as expressed in mol/L. The superscripts are the coefficients of each substance in the balanced chemical equation.

Equilibrium Constant $$K = \frac{[C]^x[D]^y}{[A]^n[B]^m}$$

FIGURE 1.2

Equilibrium Reaction

Systems Shown are reaction rates for the hypothetical equilibrium reaction system $A + B \rightleftarrows C + D$. From the time A and B are mixed together at t_0, the rate of the forward reaction declines and the rate of the reverse reaction increases until both forward and reverse reaction rates are equal at t_1, when the equilibrium condition begins.

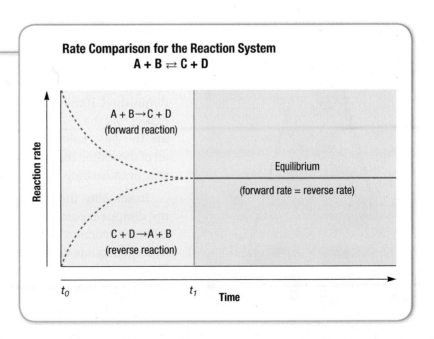

Rate Comparison for the Reaction System
A + B ⇌ C + D

$A + B \rightarrow C + D$
(forward reaction)

Equilibrium
(forward rate = reverse rate)

$C + D \rightarrow A + B$
(reverse reaction)

Reaction rate

t_0 t_1 Time

The concentrations of substances on the right side of the chemical equation appear in the numerator of the ratio, with each concentration raised to a power equal to the coefficient of that substance in the balanced chemical equation. These substances are the products of the forward reaction. The concentrations of substances on the left side of the chemical equation are in the denominator of the ratio, with each concentration raised to a power equal to the coefficient of that substance in the balanced chemical equation. These substances are the reactants of the forward reaction. The constant K is independent of the initial concentrations. It is, however, dependent on the temperature of the system.

The Equilibrium Constant

The numerical value of K for a particular equilibrium system is obtained experimentally. The chemist must analyze the equilibrium mixture and determine the concentrations of all substances. The value of K for a given equilibrium reaction at a given temperature shows the extent to which the reactants are converted into the products of the reaction. If the value of K is small, the forward reaction occurs only very slightly before equilibrium is established, and the reactants are favored. A large value of K indicates an equilibrium in which the original reactants are largely converted to products. Only the concentrations of substances that can actually change are included in K. This means that *pure* solids and liquids are omitted, because their concentrations cannot change.

In general, then, the **equilibrium constant**, K, is the ratio of the mathematical product of the concentrations of substances formed at equilibrium to the mathematical product of the concentrations of reacting substances. Each concentration is raised to a power equal to the coefficient of that substance in the chemical equation. The equation for K is referred to as the **chemical equilibrium expression**.

The H_2, I_2, HI Equilibrium System

An excellent example of an equilibrium system occurs with the reaction between H_2 and I_2 vapor in a sealed flask at an elevated temperature. A typical look at this reaction can be seen in **Figure 1.3**. If the reaction were observed, its rate could be followed by making note of how quickly the violet color of the iodine vapor diminished. If colorless H_2 gas is present in excess, we might expect that the reaction would continue until all of the I_2 is used up. The violet color of the flask would decrease in intensity until all of the iodine reacts. At that time, the beaker would be colorless, because both HI and the excess H_2 are colorless gases.

In actuality, the color fades to a constant intensity but does not disappear completely, because the reaction is reversible. Once the reaction between H_2 and I_2 reaches a certain point, hydrogen iodide decomposes to re-form hydrogen and iodine. The rate of this reverse reaction increases as the concentration of hydrogen iodide increases.

FIGURE 1.3

H_2, I_2, HI Equilibrium System The violet color of the reactant iodine gas, I_2, gives an indication of the progress of the reaction between hydrogen and iodine. Both H_2 (reactant) and HI (product) are colorless gases. The darker the purple color in the flask, the less I_2 gas reacted, so the more reactants remain.

The rate of the forward reaction decreases accordingly. The concentrations of hydrogen and iodine decrease as they react. As the rates of the opposing reactions become equal, equilibrium is established. The constant color achieved indicates that equilibrium exists among hydrogen, iodine, and hydrogen iodide. The net chemical equation for the reaction system at equilibrium follows.

$$H_2(g) + I_2(g) \rightleftharpoons 2HI(g)$$

From this chemical equation, the following chemical equilibrium expression can be written. The concentration of HI is raised to the power of 2, because the coefficient of HI in the balanced chemical equation is 2.

$$K = \frac{[HI]^2}{[H_2][I_2]}$$

Chemists have carefully measured the concentrations of H_2, I_2, and HI in equilibrium mixtures at various temperatures. In some experiments, the flasks were filled with hydrogen iodide at known pressure. The flasks were held at fixed temperatures until equilibrium was established. In other experiments, hydrogen and iodine were the original substances. Experimental data, together with the calculated values for K, are listed in **Figure 1.4**. Experiments 1 and 2 began with hydrogen iodide. Experiments 3 and 4 began with hydrogen and iodine. Note the close agreement obtained for the numerical values of the equilibrium constant in all cases.

At 425°C, the equilibrium constant for this equilibrium reaction system has the average value of 54.34. This value for K is constant for any system of H_2, I_2, and HI at equilibrium at this temperature. If the calculation for K yields a different result, there must be a reason. Either the H_2, I_2, and HI system has not reached equilibrium, or the system is not at 425°C.

The balanced chemical equation for an equilibrium system is necessary to write the expression for the equilibrium constant. The data in **Figure 1.4** show that the validity of this expression is confirmed when the actual values of the equilibrium concentrations of reactants and products are determined experimentally. The values of K are calculated from these concentrations. No information concerning the kinetics of the reacting systems is required.

FIGURE 1.4

TYPICAL EQUILIBRIUM CONCENTRATIONS OF H_2, I_2, AND HI IN MOL/L AT 425°C

Experiment	$[H_2]$	$[I_2]$	$[HI]$	$K = \frac{[HI]^2}{[H_2][I_2]}$
1	0.4953×10^{-3}	0.4953×10^{-3}	3.655×10^{-3}	54.46
2	1.141×10^{-3}	1.141×10^{-3}	8.410×10^{-3}	54.33
3	3.560×10^{-3}	1.250×10^{-3}	15.59×10^{-3}	54.62
4	2.252×10^{-3}	2.336×10^{-3}	16.85×10^{-3}	53.97

Once the value of the equilibrium constant is known, the equilibrium-constant expression can be used to calculate concentrations of reactants or products at equilibrium. Suppose an equilibrium system at 425°C is found to contain 0.015 mol/L each of H_2 and I_2. To find the concentration of HI in this system, rearrange the chemical equilibrium expression as shown in the two equations that follow.

$$K = \frac{[HI]^2}{[H_2][I_2]}$$

$$[HI] = \sqrt{K[H_2][I_2]}$$

Using the known K value and the given concentrations for H_2 and I_2, if you solve the equation for [HI], you will observe the following result:

$$[HI] = \sqrt{0.015 \times 0.015 \times 54.34}$$

$$[HI] = 0.11 \text{ mol/L}$$

When calculating concentrations at equilibrium, always be sure to note the temperature at which the reaction is taking place. Values for K do change with changing temperature.

GO ONLINE

Solve It! Cards
HMHScience.com

SOLUTION
TUTOR
HMHScience.com

Equilibrium Constant

Sample Problem A An equilibrium mixture of N_2, O_2, and NO gases at 1500 K is determined to consist of 6.4×10^{-3} mol/L of N_2, 1.7×10^{-3} mol/L of O_2, and 1.1×10^{-5} mol/L of NO. What is the equilibrium constant for the system at this temperature?

① ANALYZE

Given: $[N_2] = 6.4 \times 10^{-3}$ mol/L

$[O_2] = 1.7 \times 10^{-3}$ mol/L

$[NO] = 1.1 \times 10^{-5}$ mol/L

Unknown: K

② PLAN

The balanced chemical equation is $N_2(g) + O_2(g) \rightleftarrows 2NO(g)$.

The chemical equilibrium expression is $K = \dfrac{[NO]^2}{[N_2][O_2]}$.

③ SOLVE

Substitute the given values for the concentrations into the equilibrium expression.

$$K = \frac{(1.1 \times 10^{-5} \text{ mol/L})^2}{(6.4 \times 10^{-3} \text{ mol/L})(1.7 \times 10^{-3} \text{ mol/L})} = 1.1 \times 10^{-5}$$

Continued ▶

Equilibrium Constant (continued)

The value of K is small, which is consistent with more N_2 and O_2 being present at equilibrium than NO. The answer has the correct number of significant figures and is close to an estimated value of 8×10^{-6}, calculated as:

$$\frac{(1 \times 10^{-5})^2}{(6 \times 10^{-3})(2 \times 10^{-3})}$$

Practice   Answers in Appendix E

1. At equilibrium, a mixture of N_2, H_2, and NH_3 gas at 500°C is determined to consist of 0.602 mol/L of N_2, 0.420 mol/L of H_2, and 0.113 mol/L of NH_3. What is the equilibrium constant for the reaction $N_2(g) + 3H_2(g) \rightleftharpoons 2NH_3(g)$ at this temperature?

2. The reaction $AB_2C(g) \rightleftharpoons B_2(g) + AC(g)$ reached equilibrium at 900 K in a 5.00-L vessel. At equilibrium, 0.084 mol of AB_2C, 0.035 mol of B_2, and 0.059 mol of AC were detected. What is the equilibrium constant at this temperature for this system? (Don't forget to convert amounts to concentrations.)

3. A reaction between gaseous sulfur dioxide and oxygen gas to produce gaseous sulfur trioxide takes place at 600°C. At that temperature, the concentration of SO_2 is found to be 1.50 mol/L, the concentration of O_2 is 1.25 mol/L, and the concentration of SO_3 is 3.50 mol/L. Using the balanced chemical equation, calculate the equilibrium constant for this system.

 SECTION 1 **FORMATIVE ASSESSMENT**

▶ Reviewing Main Ideas

1. What is meant by *chemical equilibrium*?

2. What is an equilibrium constant?

3. How does the value of an equilibrium constant relate to the relative quantities of reactants and products at equilibrium?

4. What is meant by a *chemical equilibrium expression*?

5. Hydrochloric acid, HCl, is a strong acid that dissociates completely in water to form H_3O^+ and Cl^-. Should the value of K for the reaction $HCl(aq) + H_2O(l) \rightleftharpoons H_3O^+(aq) + Cl^-(aq)$ be 1×10^{-2}, 1×10^{-5}, or "very large"? Justify your answer.

6. Write the chemical equilibrium expression for the following reaction:
$4HCl(g) + O_2(g) \rightleftharpoons 2Cl_2(g) + 2H_2O(g)$

7. At equilibrium at 2500 K, $[HCl] = 0.0625$ mol/L and $[H_2] = [Cl_2] = 0.00450$ mol/L for the reaction $H_2(g) + Cl_2(g) \rightleftharpoons 2HCl(g)$. Find the value of K.

8. An equilibrium mixture at 425°C is found to consist of 1.83×10^{-3} mol/L of H_2, 3.13×10^{-3} mol/L of I_2, and 1.77×10^{-2} mol/L of HI. Calculate the equilibrium constant, K, for the reaction $H_2(g) + I_2(g) \rightleftharpoons 2HI(g)$.

9. For the reaction $H_2(g) + I_2(g) \rightleftharpoons 2HI(g)$ at 425°C, calculate [HI], given $[H_2] = [I_2] = 4.79 \times 10^{-4}$ mol/L and $K = 54.3$.

✓ Critical Thinking

10. **INFERRING RELATIONSHIPS** Use the data from Experiment 1 in **Figure 1.4** to calculate the value of K for the following reaction:

$$2HI(g) \rightleftharpoons H_2(g) + I_2(g)$$

Do you see a relationship between the value you obtained and the value in the table?

Fixing the Nitrogen Problem

Historical Perspective

Each year, the chemical industry synthesizes tons of nitrogenous fertilizers, increasing agricultural production around the globe. But prior to 1915, people had to rely solely on natural resources for fertilizer, and the dwindling supply of these materials caused widespread fear of world starvation. A crisis was averted, however, through the discovery of an answer to the "nitrogen problem," a term used at the time to describe the shortage of useful nitrogen despite its abundance in the atmosphere.

The Malthusian Threat

In 1798, Thomas Malthus published his famous "Essay on Population," a report predicting that the world's food supplies could not keep up with the growing human population and that

famine, death, and misery were inevitable. Malthus's warning seemed to be echoed in the 1840s by the great Irish potato famine. In fact, the rest of Europe likely would have suffered serious food shortages as well had crop yields per acre not been increased through the use of fertilizers containing nitrogen.

Few living organisms can utilize the gas that forms 78% of the atmosphere; they need nitrogen that has been combined with other elements, or "fixed," to survive.

But soils often lack enough of the microorganisms that fix nitrogen for plants, so fertilizers containing usable nitrogen compounds are added. In 1898, two-thirds of the world's supply of these compounds came from Chile, where beds of sodium nitrate, or Chile saltpeter, were abundant. But, as the chemist William Crookes emphasized in his speech to the British Association that year, these reserves were limited; it was up to his colleagues to discover alternatives and prevent Malthus's dire forecast from coming true.

Nitrogen is released when living organisms die. It is also released from animal wastes and plant material. Some bacteria are able to break the bond holding the nitrogen molecule together, freeing the nitrogen atoms to combine with hydrogen to form ammonia. Plants can absorb the nitrogen in this form from the soil. Animals then benefit from the nitrogen by eating the plants.

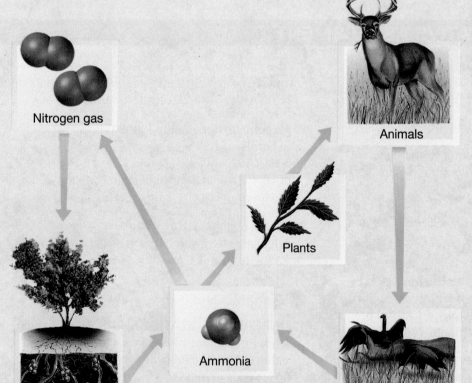

Nitrogen gas

Animals

Plants

Ammonia

Decomposition

Nitrogen-fixing bacteria on plant roots

The Haber-Nernst Controversy

As early as the 1890s, chemists had shown that ammonia, a practical source of fixed nitrogen, could be synthesized at high temperatures and at atmospheric pressure from elemental hydrogen and nitrogen. The problem was that the end product was present in such minute amounts that the process was not industrially practical.

In 1904, the German chemist Fritz Haber seemed to confirm this assessment. He tried reacting hydrogen and nitrogen at temperatures up to 1020°C using pure iron as well as other metals as a catalyst. He found that the amount of ammonia was a mere 0.005% to 0.012% at equilibrium.

Haber had apparently closed the door on the synthesis of ammonia from its elements. But in 1906, Walther Nernst, using his new heat theorem, calculated the reaction's theoretical ammonia concentration at equilibria corresponding to several pressures. He found that his value at atmospheric pressure disagreed significantly with Haber's, and he publicly challenged Haber's values.

Haber was convinced that he was right. He ran the reaction at increased pressure to attain an amount of ammonia that could be measured more accurately.

Haber and his assistants confirmed their original findings, and Nernst later conceded a mathematical error. But more important, the new round of experiments indicated that a reasonable amount of ammonia might be attained at pressures of 200 atm (20,000 kPa) using a uranium or osmium catalyst.

Scaling Up

Large-scale equipment that could withstand such high pressures was unheard of at the time, and osmium and uranium were far too scarce to be cost-effective for industry. Nevertheless, in 1909, the German firm BASF bought the rights to Haber's findings and put its gifted chemical engineer Karl Bosch in charge of creating an industrial-scale system that would make the process profitable.

Today, ammonia is produced on an industrial scale in plants like this one.

After nearly five years, Bosch and the company's chief chemist, Alwin Mittasch, succeeded in developing a suitable reactor that could handle the reaction's high pressures. They also discovered that a catalyst of iron containing small amounts of impurities was an effective replacement for the rare metals used by Haber.

An Eerie Epilogue

By September 1913, BASF was producing 20 metric tons of ammonia a day using the Haber-Bosch process. Eventually, enough ammonia was produced by the chemical industry to free Germany and the world of dependence on Chile saltpeter for fertilizer. Chemists had thwarted the Malthusian threat. Yet, the victory proved bittersweet; the new ammonia synthesis also became the basis for the production of nitric acid, used to make many of the explosives employed in the wars that rocked Europe and the rest of the globe in the first half of the twentieth century.

Questions

1. What is the major use for ammonia?

2. What did Haber find when he tried to synthesize ammonia at increased pressure?

Shifting Equilibrium

Key Term

common-ion effect

In systems that have attained chemical equilibrium, the relative amounts of reactants and products stay the same. But changes in pressure, concentration, or temperature can alter the equilibrium position and thereby change the relative amounts of reactants and products. By shifting an equilibrium in the desired direction, chemists can often improve the yield of the product they are seeking.

▶ **MAIN IDEA**

Equilibrium shifts to relieve stress on the system.

In 1888, the French chemist Henri Louis Le Châtelier developed a principle that provides a means of predicting the influence of stress factors on equilibrium systems. Le Châtelier's principle states that *if a system at equilibrium is subjected to a stress, the equilibrium is shifted in the direction that tends to relieve the stress.* This principle is true for all dynamic equilibria, chemical as well as physical. Changes in pressure, concentration, and temperature illustrate Le Châtelier's principle.

Changes in Pressure

A change in pressure affects only equilibrium systems in which gases are involved. For changes in pressure to affect the system, the *total* number of moles of gas on the left side of the equation must be different from the *total* number of moles of gas on the right side of the equation.

Let us consider the Haber-Bosch process for the synthesis of ammonia. Note that there is a total of four molecules of gas on the reactant side of the equation and two molecules of gas on the product side of the equation.

$$N_2(g) + 3H_2(g) \rightleftarrows 2NH_3(g)$$

First, consider an increase in pressure as the applied stress. Can the system shift in a way that reduces the stress? Yes. An increase in pressure causes increases in the concentrations of all species. The system can reduce the number of molecules, and hence the total pressure, by shifting the equilibrium to the right. For each four molecules of reactants, nitrogen and hydrogen, there are two molecules of product, ammonia. By producing more NH_3, and using up N_2 and H_2, the system can reduce the total number of molecules. This leads to a decrease in pressure. Although the new equilibrium pressure is still higher than before, it is not as high as the pressure caused by the initial stress. Even though changes in pressure may shift the equilibrium position, they do not affect the value of the equilibrium constant.

The introduction of an inert gas, such as helium, into a gaseous reaction mixture also increases the total pressure. But it does not change the partial pressures of the reaction gases present. Therefore, increasing pressure by adding a gas that is not a reactant or a product *cannot* affect the equilibrium position of the reaction system.

✔ **CHECK FOR UNDERSTANDING**

Explain Why would increasing the pressure by using an inert gas not change the equilibrium of a reaction?

Changes in Concentration

An increase in the concentration of a reactant is a stress on the equilibrium system. Consider the following hypothetical reaction.

$$A + B \rightleftarrows C + D$$

An increase in the concentration of A creates a stress. To relieve the stress, some of the added A reacts with B to form products C and D. The equilibrium is reestablished with a higher concentration of A than before the addition but with a lower concentration of B. Similarly, an increase in the concentration of B drives the reaction to the right. An increase in the concentration of either C or D shifts the equilibrium to the left. A decrease in the concentration of C or D has the same effect on the position of the equilibrium as does an increase in the concentration of A or B; the equilibrium shifts to the right. **Figure 2.1** gives an example of such an instance by showing what effects an increase of N_2 has on the equilibrium in the Haber process.

Ammonia produced in the Haber-Bosch process is continuously removed by condensing it to liquid ammonia. This condensation removes most of the product from the gas phase in which the reaction occurs. The resulting decrease in the partial pressure of NH_3 gas in the reaction vessel is a stress and is the same as a decrease in product concentration, which also shifts the equilibrium to the right.

Changes in concentration have no effect on the value of the equilibrium constant. Although concentrations of both reactants and products do change, the new concentrations give the same value of the equilibrium constant when equilibrium is reestablished.

Many chemical processes involve heterogeneous reactions in which reactants or products are in different phases. The concentrations of pure solids and liquids do not change and by convention are not written in the equilibrium expression. Also, in a system involving acids and bases, when a solvent such as water is in an equilibrium equation, it is not included in the equilibrium expression. In an earlier chapter, the expression for K_w used this convention, and the concentration of water is not included in the expression. The reaction representing the self-ionization of water is

$$2H_2O(l) \rightleftarrows H_3O^+(aq) + OH^-(aq)$$

and the equation for K_w is $K_w = [H_3O^+][OH^-]$.

The following equation describes the equilibrium system established by the decomposition of solid calcium carbonate.

$$CaCO_3(s) \rightleftarrows CaO(s) + CO_2(g)$$

FIGURE 2.1

Concentration's Effect on Equilibrium

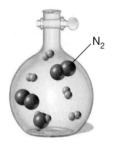

(a) N_2, H_2, and NH_3 are in equilibrium within a closed system.

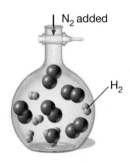

(b) Addition of more N_2 causes a stress on the initial equilibrium.

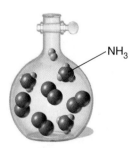

$$N_2(g) + 3H_2(g) \rightleftarrows 2NH_3(g)$$

(c) The new equilibrium position for this system has a higher concentration of N_2, a lower concentration of H_2, and a higher concentration of NH_3 than initially.

The products are a solid and a gas. Because both $CaCO_3$ and CaO are solids, they are not in the equilibrium constant expression. This leads to the following expression for the equilibrium constant.

$$K = [CO_2]$$

Carbon dioxide is the only substance in the system that appears in the equilibrium expression. Because the total number of moles of gas on the left side of the equation is different from the total number of moles on the right side of the equation, pressure changes will affect the equilibrium. High pressure favors the reverse reaction, which causes CO_2 molecules to react with the solid CaO to form solid $CaCO_3$. Low pressure favors the formation of CO_2 from the decomposition of $CaCO_3$. Because both CaO and $CaCO_3$ are solids, changing their amounts will not change the equilibrium concentration of CO_2.

Changes in Temperature

Reversible reactions are exothermic in one direction and endothermic in the other. Remember that equilibrium constants are for a given temperature, because changing the temperature changes the relative amounts of reactants and products.

Increasing the temperature is, in effect, the addition of energy in the form of heat. According to Le Châtelier's principle, the stress of the added heat will be lessened by shifting the equilibrium in the direction that removes heat (lowers the temperature). This means that energy must be absorbed so the reaction that is endothermic occurs until a new equilibrium is established. Likewise, the removal of energy as a result of lowering the temperature causes the exothermic reaction to take place.

The synthesis of ammonia by the Haber-Bosch process is exothermic, as indicated by the energy as heat shown on the product side of the equation.

$$N_2(g) + 3H_2(g) \rightleftharpoons 2NH_3(g) + 92 \text{ kJ}$$

A high temperature favors the decomposition of ammonia, the endothermic reaction. But at low temperatures, the forward reaction is too slow to be commercially useful. The temperature used represents a compromise between kinetic and equilibrium requirements. It is high enough that equilibrium is established rapidly but low enough that the equilibrium concentration of ammonia is still significant. Moderate temperature (about 500°C) and very high pressure (700–1000 atm) produce a satisfactory yield of ammonia.

The production of colorless dinitrogen tetroxide gas, N_2O_4, from dark red-brown NO_2 gas is also an exothermic reaction. **Figure 2.2** shows how temperature affects the equilibrium of this system. **Figure 2.2b** shows the NO_2/N_2O_4 equilibrium mixture at 25°C. When the temperature of the system is lowered to 0°C, the system experiences a stress (removal of energy as heat). To counteract this stress, the system shifts to the right, in the direction of the exothermic reaction. This increases the amount of colorless N_2O_4 gas and decreases the amount of brown NO_2 gas; see **Figure 2.2a**. Because more N_2O_4 and less NO_2 are present, K is increased.

FIGURE 2.2

Temperature Effects on Equilibrium Different temperatures can cause an equilibrium system to shift and seek a new equilibrium position.

(a) When energy as heat is taken away from the system, the exothermic reaction is favored, so more N_2O_4 is produced. N_2O_4 is colorless, so the bottle appears lighter.

0°C

(b) At increasing temperatures, more of the endothermic reaction can occur, so more of the brown NO_2 forms.

25°C

(c) At even higher temperatures, still more of the brown NO_2 forms, and the color in the bottle appears even darker.

100°C

$$2NO_2(g) \rightleftharpoons N_2O_4(g) + \text{energy as heat}$$
(brown)   (colorless)

When the system is heated to 100°C, the added energy is the stress, and the equilibrium shifts to the left, or in the direction of the endothermic reaction. This shift decreases the amount of colorless N_2O_4 gas and increases the amount of brown NO_2 gas, see **Figure 2.2c**. Because less N_2O_4 gas and more NO_2 are present, K is decreased. The change in temperature changes the value of K. For a system in which the forward reaction is an exothermic reaction, increasing temperature decreases the value of K.

For an endothermic reaction, such as the decomposition of calcium carbonate, energy as heat shows up on the reactant side of the equation.

$$556 \text{ kJ} + CaCO_3(s) \rightleftharpoons CaO(s) + CO_2(g)$$

An increase in temperature caused by adding energy to the system causes the value of K to increase and the equilibrium to shift to the right.

Catalysts speed up the rate of reactions. So what happens to equilibrium concentrations if a catalyst is present? Nothing! When a catalyst is added to an equilibrium system, it speeds up both the forward and reverse reactions. The equilibrium concentrations are achieved faster, but the concentrations and K remain the same.

▶ **MAIN IDEA**

Some ionic reactions seem to go to completion.

Some reactions involving compounds formed by the chemical interaction of ions in solutions appear to go to completion in the sense that the ions are almost completely removed from solution. The extent to which reacting ions are removed from solution depends on the solubility of the compound formed and, if the compound is soluble, on the degree of ionization. Thus, a product that escapes as a gas, precipitates as a solid, or forms a weak electrolyte effectively removes from solution virtually all of the reacting ions that compose it.

Formation of a Gas

Reactions that form a gas as a product are one example of reactions that go to completion. When a strong acid is added to an aqueous solution of baking soda, or sodium bicarbonate, carbon dioxide is formed. The net ionic equation shows that ions are removed.

$$H_3O^+ + HCO_3^- \rightarrow 2H_2O(l) + CO_2(g)$$

This reaction goes practically to completion because one of the products, CO_2, escapes as a gas if the container is open to the air and the other, water, is a weak electrolyte.

✔ CHECK FOR UNDERSTANDING
Explain Why would formation of a gas stop a reversible reaction from remaining in equilibrium?

Formation of a Precipitate

When solutions of sodium chloride and silver nitrate are mixed, a white precipitate of silver chloride immediately forms, as shown in **Figure 2.3.** The full ionic equation for this reaction follows.

$$Na^+(aq) + Cl^-(aq) + Ag^+(aq) + NO_3^-(aq) \rightarrow Na^+(aq) + NO_3^-(aq) + AgCl(s)$$

If chemically equivalent amounts of the two solutes are mixed, only Na^+ ions and NO_3^- ions remain in solution in appreciable quantities. Almost all of the Ag^+ ions and Cl^- ions combine and precipitate from the solution as $AgCl$, because $AgCl$ is only very slightly soluble in water. The solution is now a saturated solution of $AgCl$. Thus, the reaction effectively goes to completion, because an essentially insoluble product is formed.

FIGURE 2.3

Precipitate Formation When a clear sodium chloride solution is combined with a clear solution of silver nitrate, an insoluble white precipitate of silver chloride is formed.

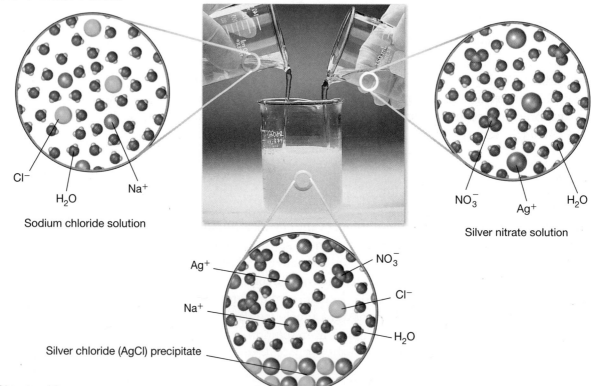

Cl⁻
H₂O
Na⁺
Sodium chloride solution

NO₃⁻
Ag⁺
H₂O
Silver nitrate solution

Ag⁺
NO₃⁻
Na⁺
Cl⁻
H₂O
Silver chloride (AgCl) precipitate

Formation of a Weak Electrolyte

Neutralization reactions between H_3O^+ ions from aqueous acids and OH^- ions from aqueous bases result in the formation of water molecules, which are only slightly ionized. A reaction between HCl and NaOH illustrates this process. Aqueous HCl supplies H_3O^+ ions and Cl^- ions to the solution, and aqueous NaOH supplies Na^+ ions and OH^- ions, as shown in the following overall ionic equation:

$$H_3O^+(aq) + Cl^-(aq) + Na^+(aq) + OH^-(aq) \rightarrow Na^+(aq) + Cl^-(aq) + 2H_2O(l)$$

Neglecting the spectator ions, the net ionic equation is as follows:

$$H_3O^+(aq) + OH^-(aq) \rightarrow 2H_2O(l)$$

Because it is only slightly ionized, the water exists almost entirely as molecules. Thus, hydronium ions and hydroxide ions are almost entirely removed from the solution. The reaction effectively goes to completion because the product is a weak electrolyte.

▶ MAIN IDEA

Common ions often produce precipitates.

An equilibrium reaction may be driven in the desired direction by applying Le Châtelier's principle. Suppose hydrogen chloride gas is bubbled into a saturated solution of sodium chloride. Hydrogen chloride is extremely soluble in water, and it is completely ionized.

$$HCl(g) + H_2O(l) \rightarrow H_3O^+(aq) + Cl^-(aq)$$

The equilibrium for a saturated solution of sodium chloride is described by the following equation.

$$NaCl(s) \rightleftharpoons Na^+(aq) + Cl^-(aq)$$

As the hydrogen chloride dissolves in sufficient quantity, it increases the concentration of Cl^- ions in the solution, which is a stress on the equilibrium system. The system can compensate, according to Le Châtelier's principle, by combining some of the added Cl^- ions with an equivalent amount of Na^+ ions. This causes some solid NaCl to precipitate out, relieving the stress of added chloride. The new equilibrium has a greater concentration of Cl^- ions but a decreased concentration of Na^+ ions. However, the product of $[Na^+]$ and $[Cl^-]$ still has the same value as before. This phenomenon, in which the addition of an ion common to two solutes brings about precipitation or the formation of a weak electrolyte, is an example of the common-ion effect.

The common-ion effect is also observed when one ion species of a weak electrolyte is added in excess to a solution. Acetic acid, CH_3COOH, is such an electrolyte. A 0.1 M CH_3COOH solution is only about 1.3% ionized as hydronium ions and acetate ions, CH_3COO^-. The ionic equilibrium is shown by the following equation:

$$CH_3COOH(aq) + H_2O(l) \rightleftharpoons H_3O^+(aq) + CH_3COO^-(aq)$$

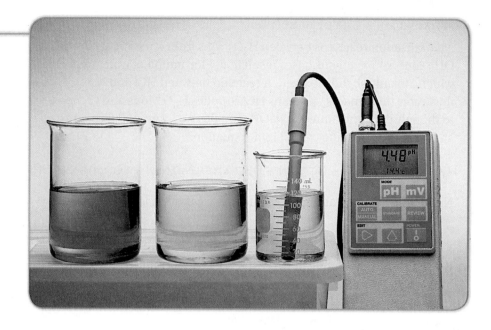

FIGURE 2.4

Common-Ion Effect The solution of CH_3COOH on the left is combined with the solution of $NaCH_3COO$ in the center. Both contain the common ion CH_3COO^-. They produce the solution on the right, which is only slightly acidic due to the decreased ionization of the acid. The colors of the solutions are due to the addition of an acid-base indicator.

Addition of sodium acetate, $NaCH_3COO$ (an ionic salt soluble in water), to a solution containing acetic acid increases the acetate ion concentration. The equilibrium then shifts in the direction that uses up some of the added acetate ions in accordance with Le Châtelier's principle. More molecules of acetic acid are formed, and the concentration of hydronium ions is reduced. In general, the addition of a salt with an ion in common with the weak electrolyte reduces the ionization of the electrolyte. **Figure 2.4** shows a 0.25 M CH_3COOH solution on the left that has a pH of about 2.7. Mixing that with the 0.10 M $NaCH_3COO$ solution in the center produces the solution on the right, which has a pH of about 4.5, indicating lower $[H_3O^+]$ and thus lowered acetic acid ionization.

✓ SECTION 2 **FORMATIVE ASSESSMENT**

▶ **Reviewing Main Ideas**

1. Name three ways the chemical equilibrium can be disturbed.

2. Describe three situations in which ionic reactions go to completion.

3. Describe the common-ion effect.

4. Identify the common ion in each of the following situations.

   a. 5 g of NaCl is added to a 2.0 M solution of HCl

   b. 50 mL of 1.0 M $NaCH_3COO$ is added to 1.0 M CH_3COOH

   c. 1 g of NH_4Cl is added to 100 mL of aqueous NH_3

5. Predict the effect that decreasing pressure would have on each of the following reaction systems at equilibrium.

   a. $H_2(g) + Cl_2(g) \rightleftharpoons 2HCl(g)$

   b. $NH_4Cl(s) \rightleftharpoons NH_3(g) + HCl(g)$

   c. $2H_2O_2(aq) \rightleftharpoons 2H_2O(l) + O_2(g)$

   d. $3O_2(g) \rightleftharpoons 2O_3(g)$

✓ **Critical Thinking**

6. **PREDICTING OUTCOMES** Carbon dioxide and water react to form bicarbonate ion and hydronium ion. Hyperventilation (rapid breathing) causes more carbon dioxide to be exhaled than normal. How will hyperventilation affect the pH of blood? Explain.

578   Chapter 18

Equilibria of Acids, Bases, and Salts

Key Terms
acid ionization constant
buffered solution
hydrolysis

Main Ideas

The ionization constant is a measure of acid and base strength in solution.

Buffers resist changes in pH.

Water is a weak electrolyte.

Hydrolysis of anions and cations can produce non-neutral solutions.

▶ MAIN IDEA
The ionization constant is a measure of acid and base strength in solution.

About 1.3% of the solute molecules in a 0.1 M acetic acid solution are ionized at room temperature. The remaining 98.7% of the acetic acid molecules, CH_3COOH, remain nonionized. Thus, the solution contains three species of particles in equilibrium: CH_3COOH molecules, H_3O^+ ions, and acetate ions, CH_3COO^-. From the equilibrium equation for the ionization of acetic acid, the equilibrium constant equation can be written.

$$CH_3COOH + H_2O \rightleftharpoons H_3O^+ + CH_3COO^-$$

$$K = \frac{[H_3O^+][CH_3COO^-]}{[CH_3COOH][H_2O]}$$

By convention, the concentration of water is not included in the equilibrium expression. Water is the solvent, and water molecules greatly exceed the number of acetic acid molecules. We can assume that the molar concentration of H_2O molecules remains constant in such a solution without introducing a measurable error. Thus, because both K and $[H_2O]$ are constant, the product $K[H_2O]$ is constant.

$$K[H_2O] = \frac{[H_3O^+][CH_3COO^-]}{[CH_3COOH]}$$

The left side of the equation can be simplified by setting $K[H_2O] = K_a$.

$$K_a = \frac{[H_3O^+][CH_3COO^-]}{[CH_3COOH]}$$

The term K_a is called the **acid ionization constant.** The acid ionization constant, K_a, like the equilibrium constant, K, is constant for a specified temperature but has a new value for each new temperature.

The acid ionization constant for a weak acid is small since the concentration of ions is small. To determine the numerical value of the ionization constant for acetic acid at a specific temperature, the equilibrium concentrations of H_3O^+ ions, CH_3COO^- ions, and CH_3COOH molecules must be known. The ionization of a molecule of CH_3COOH in water yields one H_3O^+ ion and one CH_3COO^- ion. These concentrations can therefore be found experimentally by measuring the pH of the solution.

FIGURE 3.1

IONIZATION OF ACETIC ACID				
Molarity	% ionized	$[H_3O^+]$	$[CH_3COOH]$	K_a
0.100	1.33	0.00133	0.0987	1.79×10^{-5}
0.0500	1.89	0.000945	0.0491	1.82×10^{-5}
0.0100	4.17	0.000417	0.00958	1.81×10^{-5}
0.00500	5.86	0.000293	0.00471	1.82×10^{-5}
0.00100	12.6	0.000126	0.000874	1.82×10^{-5}

FIGURE 3.2

Buffered Solution

(a) The beaker on the left contains a buffered solution and an indicator and has a pH of about 5. The beaker on the right contains mostly water with a trace amount of acid and an indicator. The pH meter shows a pH of 5.00 for this solution.

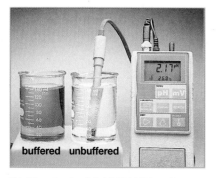

(b) After 5 mL of 0.10 M HCl is added to both beakers, the beaker on the left does not change color, indicating no substantial change in its pH. However, the beaker on the right undergoes a definite color change, and the pH meter shows a pH of 2.17.

Ionization data and constants for some dilute acetic acid solutions at 25°C are given in **Figure 3.1**. Notice that the numerical value of K_a is almost identical for each solution molarity shown. The numerical value of K_a for CH_3COOH at 25°C can be determined by substituting numerical values for concentration into the equilibrium equation.

$$K_a = \frac{[H_3O^+][CH_3COO^-]}{[CH_3COOH]}$$

At constant temperature, an increase in the concentration of CH_3COO^- ions through the addition of sodium acetate, $NaCH_3COO$, disturbs the equilibrium, as predicted by Le Châtelier's principle. This disturbance causes a decrease in $[H_3O^+]$ and an increase in $[CH_3COOH]$. Eventually, the equilibrium is reestablished with the *same* value of K_a. But there is a higher concentration of nonionized acetic acid molecules and a lower concentration of H_3O^+ ions than before the extra CH_3COO^- was added. Changes in the hydronium ion concentration affect pH. In this example, the reduction in $[H_3O^+]$ means an increase in the pH of the solution.

▶ MAIN IDEA

Buffers resist changes in pH.

The solution just described contains both a weak acid, CH_3COOH, and a salt of the weak acid, $NaCH_3COO$. The solution can react with either an acid or a base. When small amounts of acids or bases are added, the pH of the solution remains nearly constant. The weak acid and the common ion, CH_3COO^-, act as a "buffer" against significant changes in the pH of the solution. Because it can resist changes in pH, this solution is a **buffered solution.** Figure 3.2 shows how a buffered and an unbuffered solution react to the addition of an acid.

Suppose a small amount of acid is added to the acetic acid–sodium acetate solution. Acetate ions react with most of the added hydronium ions to form nonionized acetic acid molecules.

$$CH_3COO^-(aq) + H_3O^+(aq) \rightarrow CH_3COOH(aq) + H_2O(l)$$

The hydronium ion concentration and the pH of the solution remain practically unchanged.

Suppose a small amount of a base is added to the original solution. The OH⁻ ions of the base react with and remove hydronium ions to form nonionized water molecules. Acetic acid molecules then ionize and mostly replace the hydronium ions neutralized by the added OH⁻ ions.

$$CH_3COOH(aq) + H_2O(l) \rightarrow H_3O^+(aq) + CH_3COO^-(aq)$$

The pH of the solution again remains practically unchanged.

A solution of a weak base containing a salt of the base behaves in a similar manner. The hydroxide ion concentration and the pH of the solution remain essentially constant with small additions of acids or bases. Suppose a base is added to an aqueous solution of ammonia that also contains ammonium chloride. Ammonium ions donate a proton to the added hydroxide ions to form nonionized water molecules.

$$NH_4^+(aq) + OH^-(aq) \rightarrow NH_3(aq) + H_2O(l)$$

If a small amount of an acid is added to the solution instead, hydroxide ions from the solution accept protons from the added hydronium ions to form nonionized water molecules. Ammonia molecules in the solution then ionize and mostly replace the hydroxide ions neutralized by added H_3O^+.

$$NH_3(aq) + H_2O(l) \rightarrow NH_4^+(aq) + OH^-(aq)$$

Buffer action has many important applications in chemistry and physiology. Human blood is naturally buffered to maintain a pH of between 7.3 and 7.5. This is essential, because large changes in pH would lead to serious disturbances of normal body functions. **Figure 3.3** shows an example of one of the many medicines buffered to prevent large and potentially damaging changes in pH.

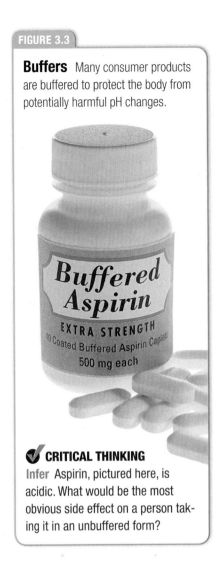

Buffers Many consumer products are buffered to protect the body from potentially harmful pH changes.

✔ **CRITICAL THINKING**
Infer Aspirin, pictured here, is acidic. What would be the most obvious side effect on a person taking it in an unbuffered form?

⬤ **MAIN IDEA**

Water is a weak electrolyte.

In the chapter "Acid-Base Titration and pH," you learned that the self-ionization of water is an equilibrium reaction.

$$H_2O(l) + H_2O(l) \rightleftharpoons H_3O^+(aq) + OH^-(aq)$$

Equilibrium is established with a very low concentration of H_3O^+ and OH⁻ ions. The expression for the equilibrium constant, $K_w = [H_3O^+][OH^-]$, is derived from the balanced chemical equation. The numerical value of K_w, obtained experimentally, is 1.0×10^{-14} at 25°C.

The self-ionization of water may seem inconsequential at first, since the percent of ionization is very low and the resulting product neutral; however, it has a major impact on the equilibrium achieved in the aqueous solutions of salts. Because salts dissociate into their constituent ions when dissolved, these ions can, and often do, interact with the ions produced by water's self-ionization. The result is a solution that can be acidic, basic, or neutral depending on the salt that forms.

▶ MAIN IDEA

Hydrolysis of anions and cations can produce non-neutral solutions.

Salts are formed during neutralization reactions between acids and bases. When a salt dissolves in water, it produces positive ions (cations) of the base from which it was formed and negative ions (anions) of the acid from which it was formed. Therefore, the solution might be expected to be neutral. The aqueous solutions of some salts, such as NaCl and KNO₃, are neutral, having a pH of 7. However, when sodium carbonate dissolves in water, the resulting solution turns red litmus paper blue, indicating a pH greater than 7. Ammonium chloride produces an aqueous solution that turns blue litmus paper red, indicating a pH less than 7. Salts formed from combining strong or weak acids and bases are shown in **Figure 3.4.**

The variation in pH values can be accounted for by examining the ions formed when each of these salts dissociates. If the ions formed are from weak acids or bases, they react chemically with the water molecules, and the pH of the solution will have a value other than 7. **A reaction between water molecules and ions of a dissolved salt is hydrolysis.** If the anions of a weak acid react with water, the hydrolysis results in a more basic solution. If the cations of a weak base react with water molecules, the hydrolysis results in a more acidic solution.

Anion Hydrolysis

In the Brønsted sense, the anion of the salt is the conjugate base of the acid from which it was formed. It is also a proton acceptor. If the acid is weak, its conjugate base (the anion) will be strong enough to remove protons from some water molecules, proton donors, to form OH⁻ ions.

OH^-

FIGURE 3.4

Hydrolysis The universal indicator shows that the pH of salt solutions varies, depending on the strength of the acid and the base that formed the salt.

(a) NaCl is formed from a strong acid and a strong base; the color of the indicator shows the pH is neutral.

(b) The indicator shows the pH of the sodium acetate solution is basic. This was formed from a strong base and a weak acid.

(c) The strong acid and weak base combination in ammonium chloride produces an acidic solution, as shown by the reddish tint of the indicator.

(d) The weak acid and weak base that form ammonium acetate are of comparable strength. A solution of ammonium acetate is essentially neutral.

582 Chapter 18

An equilibrium is established in which the net effect of the anion hydrolysis is an increase in the hydroxide ion concentration, [OH$^-$], of the solution.

The equilibrium equation for a typical weak acid in water, HA, forming hydronium ion and an anion, A$^-$, is as follows:

$$HA(aq) + H_2O(l) \rightleftharpoons H_3O^+(aq) + A^-(aq)$$

From this equation, the generalized expression for K_a can be written. Note that as before, water does not appear in the general equilibrium equation.

$$K_a = \frac{[H_3O^+][A^-]}{[HA]}$$

The hydrolysis reaction between water and the anion, A$^-$, that is produced by the ionization of the weak acid, HA, is represented by the general equilibrium equation that follows:

$$A^-(aq) + H_2O(l) \rightleftharpoons HA(aq) + OH^-(aq)$$

Neutral water has equal concentrations of H$_3$O$^+$ and OH$^-$. Since HA is a weak acid, the anion A$^-$ has a strong attraction for protons. Adding A$^-$ to water in effect attracts (removes) H$_3$O$^+$ in water to form HA. This causes OH$^-$ to increase relative to H$_3$O$^+$ as represented in the equation above. The lower the value of K_a, the stronger the attraction A$^-$ will have for protons and the larger the concentration of OH$^-$. In other words, the weaker the acid, HA, the stronger its conjugate base, A$^-$.

Aqueous solutions of sodium carbonate are strongly basic. The sodium ions, Na$^+$, in sodium carbonate do not undergo hydrolysis in aqueous solution, but the carbonate ions, CO$_3^{2-}$, react as a Brønsted base. A CO$_3^{2-}$ anion acquires a proton from a water molecule to form the weak Brønsted acid HCO$_3^-$ and the OH$^-$ ion.

$$CO_3^{2-}(aq) + H_2O(l) \rightleftharpoons HCO_3^-(aq) + OH^-(aq)$$

The OH$^-$ ion concentration increases until equilibrium is established. Consequently, the H$_3$O$^+$ ion concentration decreases so that the product [H$_3$O$^+$][OH$^-$] remains equal to the ionization constant, K_w, of water at the temperature of the solution. Thus, the pH is *higher* than 7, and the solution is basic.

Cation Hydrolysis

In the Brønsted sense, the cation of the salt is the conjugate acid of the base from which it was formed. It is also a proton donor. If the base is weak, the cation is an acid strong enough to donate a proton to a water molecule, a proton acceptor, to form H$_3$O$^+$ ions. An equilibrium is established in which the net effect of the cation hydrolysis is an increase in the hydronium ion concentration, [H$_3$O$^+$], of the solution.

✔ **CHECK FOR UNDERSTANDING**

Explain In the Cross-Disciplinary Connection feature "Blood Buffers" above, *hypo*ventilation is described as the opposite of *hyper*ventilation. Based on information in the feature, explain why one treatment for hyperventilation is breathing with a paper bag placed over the mouth and nose.

The following equilibrium equation for a typical weak base, B, is used to derive the generalized expression for K_b, the base dissociation constant.

$$B(aq) + H_2O(l) \rightleftharpoons BH^+(aq) + OH^-(aq)$$

$$K_b = \frac{[BH^+][OH^-]}{[B]}$$

The hydrolysis between water and the cation, BH^+, from the dissociation of the weak base, B, is shown by the general equilibrium equation:

$$BH^+(aq) + H_2O(l) \rightleftharpoons H_3O^+(aq) + B(aq)$$

In the forward reaction, the cation BH^+ donates a proton to the water molecule to form the hydronium ion. Because H_3O^+ ions are formed, the solution must become more acidic, as shown in the equation above. The extent of H_3O^+ ion formation depends on the relative strength of the base B. The weaker the base, the greater the concentration of H_3O^+ ions will be. Therefore, the weaker the base, the stronger its conjugate acid.

Ammonium chloride, NH_4Cl, dissociates in water to produce NH_4^+ ions and Cl^- ions. Chloride ions are the conjugate base of the strong acid HCl, so they do not hydrolyze in water. Ammonium ions, however, are the conjugate acid of a weak base, NH_3. Ammonium ions donate protons to water molecules. Equilibrium is established with an increased $[H_3O^+]$, so pH is *lower* than 7.

Hydrolysis in Acid-Base Reactions

Many assume that a neutralization reaction between an acid and a base always results in a neutral solution. However, this is not necessarily the case. Hydrolysis can help explain why the end point of a neutralization reaction can occur at a pH other than 7.

FIGURE 3.5

Titration Curve of a Weak Acid and Strong Base At point 1, only acetic acid is present. The pH depends on the weak acid alone. At 2, there is a mixture of CH_3COOH and CH_3COO^-. Adding NaOH changes the pH slowly. At point 3, all acid has been converted to CH_3COO^-. This hydrolyzes to produce a slightly basic solution. At 4, the pH is due to the excess OH^- that has been added.

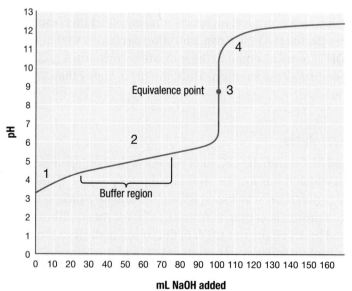

Titration Curve for 100 mL of 0.100 M CH_3COOH Titrated with 0.100 M NaOH

The hydrolysis properties of salts are determined by the relative strengths of the acids and bases from which the salts form. We can place these salts into four general categories: strong acid–strong base, strong acid–weak base, weak acid–strong base, and weak acid–weak base.

Salts of strong acids and strong bases produce neutral solutions because neither the cation of a strong base nor the anion of a strong acid hydrolyzes appreciably in aqueous solutions. An example of this is the reaction between HCl(*aq*), which is a strong acid, and NaOH(*aq*), which is a strong base. Neither the Na^+ cation of the strong base nor the Cl^- anion of the strong acid undergoes hydrolysis in water solutions. Therefore, aqueous solutions of NaCl are neutral. KNO_3 is the salt of the strong acid HNO_3 and the strong base KOH and, in solution, also has a pH of 7.

Aqueous solutions of salts formed from weak acids and strong bases are basic at the equivalence point (see **Figure 3.5**). Anions of the dissolved salt are hydrolyzed by the water molecules, and the pH of the solution is raised, indicating that the hydroxide-ion concentration has increased. Aqueous solutions of sodium acetate, $NaCH_3COO$, are basic. The acetate ions, CH_3COO^-, undergo hydrolysis because they are the anions of the weak acid acetic acid. The cations of the salt are from a strong base, NaOH, and do not hydrolyze, because NaOH is 100% dissociated.

Figure 3.6 shows that salts of strong acids and weak bases are acidic at the equivalence point. Cations of the dissolved salt are hydrolyzed in the water solvent, and the pH of the solution is lowered, indicating that the hydronium ion concentration has increased. In this case, the cations of the salt undergo hydrolysis because they are the positive ions from a weak base. The anions of the salt are the negative ions from a strong acid and do not hydrolyze appreciably. Ammonium chloride, NH_4Cl, is a salt that produces an acidic solution.

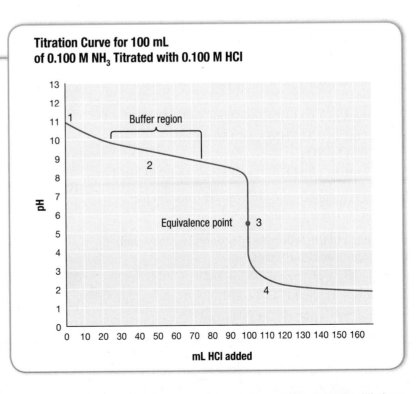

FIGURE 3.6

Titration Curve of a Strong Acid and a Weak Base At point 1 on the titration curve, only aqueous ammonia is present. The pH is determined by the base alone. At 2, there is a mixture of NH_3 and NH_4^+. Adding HCl changes the pH slowly. At point 3, all aqueous ammonia has been converted to NH_4^+. At 4, the pH is determined by the excess H_3O^+ that is being added.

Titration Curve for 100 mL of 0.100 M NH_3 Titrated with 0.100 M HCl

Salts of weak acids and weak bases can produce either acidic, neutral, or basic aqueous solutions, depending on the salt dissolved. This is because both ions of the dissolved salt are hydrolyzed extensively. If both ions are hydrolyzed equally, the solution remains neutral. The ions in ammonium acetate, NH_4CH_3COO, hydrolyze equally, producing a neutral solution (see **Figure 3.4d** in this section).

In salts formed from a weak acid and weak base, the cation and anion both undergo hydrolysis. For example, when aluminum sulfide is placed in water, Al^{3+} reacts with OH^-, forming $Al(OH)_3$, and S^{2-} reacts with H^+, forming H_2S. The reaction is shown by the following chemical equation.

$$Al_2S_3(s) + 6H_2O(l) \rightarrow 2Al(OH)_3(s) + 3H_2S(g)$$

Since $Al(OH)_3$ is a precipitate and H_2S is a gas, both leave the solution.

As you can see, there are several variations on neutralization reactions, each based on whether the reactants are strong or weak acids and bases. It is good practice to start your determination of the pH of one of these solutions by looking closely at the balanced equation for the reaction. By taking this first step and determining the strength or weakness of the reactants, you can make a generalized prediction of what the pH of the product solution will be at the equivalence point.

SECTION 3 FORMATIVE ASSESSMENT

▶ Reviewing Main Ideas

1. What is meant by an *acid ionization constant*?

2. How is an acid ionization equilibrium expression written?

3. What is meant by the term *buffered solution*?

4. Which of the following combinations of solutions would form buffers when they are mixed?
   a. 50 mL of 1.0 M HCl and 50 mL of 1.0 M NaCl
   b. 25 mL of 0.5 M HNO_2 and 50 mL of 1.0 M $NaNO_2$
   c. 25 mL of 1.0 M HNO_2 and 25 mL of 1.0 M NaCl

5. What is meant by the *ion product constant* for water? What is its value at 25°C?

6. For each of the following reactions, identify each conjugate acid-base pair.
   a. $H_2CO_3 + H_2O \rightleftharpoons HCO_3^- + H_3O^+$
   b. $H_2O + H_2O \rightleftharpoons H_3O^+ + OH^-$
   c. $H_2S + NH_3 \rightleftharpoons HS^- + NH_4^+$
   d. $H_2PO_4^- + H_2O \rightleftharpoons H_3PO_4 + OH^-$

7. What is hydrolysis? Compare cation and anion hydrolysis.

8. Which of the following ions hydrolyze in aqueous solution?
   a. NO_3^- e. CH_3COO^-
   b. F^- f. SO_4^{2-}
   c. NH_4^+ g. CO_3^{2-}
   d. K^+ h. PO_4^{3-}

9. Identify the following solutions as acidic, basic, or neutral.
   a. 0.5 M KI c. 0.25 M NH_4NO_3
   b. 0.10 M $Ba(OH)_2$ d. 0.05 M K_2CO_3

10. Identify the acid and base from which each of the following salts was formed.
    a. K_2CrO_4 c. CaF_2
    b. $Ca(CH_3COO)_2$ d. $(NH_4)_2SO_4$

✓ Critical Thinking

11. **RELATING IDEAS** Describe how to make a buffer solution using a strong base and one other reagent.

Solubility Equilibrium

Key Term
solubility product constant

Ionic solids dissolve in water until they are in equilibrium with their ions. An equilibrium expression can be written from the balanced chemical equation of the solid's dissociation. Concentrations of the ions can be determined from the balanced chemical equation and solubility data. The ion concentrations can then be used to determine the value of the equilibrium constant. The numerical value for the equilibrium constant can be used to predict whether precipitation occurs when solutions of various concentrations are combined.

▶ **MAIN IDEA**

The equilibrium product constant (K_{sp}) describes how soluble a substance is.

A saturated solution contains the maximum amount of solute possible at a given temperature in equilibrium with an undissolved excess of the substance. A saturated solution is not necessarily a concentrated solution. The concentration can be low, if the solubility of the solute is low.

A general rule is often used to express solubilities qualitatively. By this rule, a substance is said to be *soluble* if the solubility is *greater than* 1 g per 100 g of water and slightly soluble if less than that. Even substances we have previously referred to as "insoluble" are slightly soluble. We will describe the degree of solubility with an equilibrium constant.

The equilibrium principles developed in this chapter apply to all saturated solutions of slightly soluble salts. Silver chloride is a slightly soluble salt. It reaches saturation when the Ag^+ and Cl^- concentrations are 1.3×10^{-5} M, or about 2×10^{-4} g of AgCl in 100 mL. When mixed, all ions in excess of this concentration eventually precipitate as AgCl.

Consider the equilibrium system in a saturated solution of silver chloride containing an excess of the solid AgCl. This system is represented by the following equilibrium equation.

$$AgCl(s) \rightleftharpoons Ag^+(aq) + Cl^-(aq)$$

This is a heterogeneous reaction. Recall that the convention is to write its equilibrium expression without the solid species, AgCl. The resulting equilibrium expression is known as the solubility product constant, K_{sp}.

$$K_{sp} = [Ag^+][Cl^-]$$

The solubility product constant of a substance is the product of the molar concentrations of its ions in a saturated solution, each raised to the power that is the coefficient of that ion in the balanced chemical equation.

Like all such equilibrium expressions, the solubility product constant is expressing an equilibrium and, in the case of AgCl, is equal to the product of the concentrations of its ions in solution. It depends on the form of the equilibrium expression.

For example, calcium fluoride is another slightly soluble salt. The equilibrium in a saturated CaF_2 solution is described by the equation

$$CaF_2(s) \rightleftharpoons Ca^{2+}(aq) + 2F^-(aq)$$

The solubility product constant has the following form.

$$K_{sp} = [Ca^{2+}][F^-]^2$$

Notice that K_{sp} is the product of the molar concentration of Ca^{2+} ions and the molar concentration of F^- ions squared, as required by the balanced chemical equilibrium expression.

The numerical value of K_{sp} can be determined from solubility data. These data indicate that a maximum of 1.9×10^{-4} g of AgCl can dissolve in 100 g of water at 25°C. One mole of AgCl has a mass of 143.32 g. The solubility of AgCl can therefore be expressed in moles per liter of water, which is very nearly equal to moles per liter of solution.

$$\frac{1.9 \times 10^{-4} \text{ g AgCl}}{100. \text{ g } H_2O} \times \frac{1 \text{ g } H_2O}{1 \text{ mL } H_2O} \times \frac{1000 \text{ mL}}{1 \text{ L}} \times \frac{1 \text{ mol AgCl}}{143.32 \text{ g AgCl}}$$

$$= 1.3 \times 10^{-5} \text{ mol/L}$$

Silver chloride dissociates in solution, contributing equal numbers of Ag^+ and Cl^- ions. The ion concentrations in the saturated solution are therefore 1.3×10^{-5} mol/L.

$$[Ag^+] = 1.3 \times 10^{-5}$$
$$[Cl^-] = 1.3 \times 10^{-5}$$

and

$$K_{sp} = [Ag^+][Cl^-]$$
$$K_{sp} = (1.3 \times 10^{-5})(1.3 \times 10^{-5}) = 1.7 \times 10^{-10}$$

This result agrees with the solubility product constant of AgCl at 25°C.

The solubility of CaF_2 is 1.6×10^{-3} g/100 g of water at 25°C. Expressed in moles per liter, as before, this concentration is 2.05×10^{-4} mol/L. CaF_2 dissociates in solution to yield twice as many F^- ions as Ca^{2+} ions. The ion concentrations in the saturated solution are 2.05×10^{-4} for the calcium ion and $2(2.05 \times 10^{-4})$, or 4.1×10^{-4}, for the fluoride ion. Note that at equilibrium at 25°C, $[Ca^{2+}]$ equals the solubility of 2.05×10^{-4} mol/L, but $[F^-]$ equals twice the solubility, or 4.1×10^{-4} mol/L. The number of moles of positive and negative ions per mole of compound must always be accounted for when using K_{sp} and solubilities.

$$K_{sp} = [Ca^{2+}][F^-]^2$$
$$K_{sp} = (2.05 \times 10^{-4})(4.1 \times 10^{-4})^2$$
$$K_{sp} = 3.45 \times 10^{-11}$$

Thus, the solubility product constant of CaF_2 is 5.3×10^{-9} at 25°C.

Comparing Solubility and K_{sp}

It is difficult to measure very small concentrations of a solute with precision. For this reason, solubility data from different sources may report different values of K_{sp} for a substance. Thus, calculations of K_{sp} ordinarily should be limited to two significant figures. Representative values of K_{sp} at 25°C for some slightly soluble compounds are listed in **Figure 4.1**. Assume that all data used in K_{sp} calculations have been taken at 25°C unless otherwise specified.

At this point, you should note the difference between the solubility of a given solid and its solubility product constant. Remember that the *solubility product constant* is an equilibrium constant representing the product of the molar concentrations of its ions, raised to the power of their coefficients in the solubility equilibrium expression, in a saturated solution. The solubility represents the maximum mass of solute that can dissolve in a given volume at a given temperature. Solubilities are often expressed in grams of solute per 100 g of water.

FIGURE 4.1

SOLUBILITY PRODUCT CONSTANTS, K_{SP}, AT 25°C

Salt	Ion product	K_{sp}	Salt	Ion product	K_{sp}
$AgCH_3COO$	$[Ag^+][CH_3COO^-]$	1.9×10^{-3}	$CuCl$	$[Cu^+][Cl^-]$	1.2×10^{-6}
$AgBr$	$[Ag^+][Br^-]$	5.0×10^{-13}	CuS	$[Cu^{2+}][S^{2-}]$	6.3×10^{-36}
Ag_2CO_3	$[Ag^+]^2[CO_3^{2-}]$	8.1×10^{-12}	FeS	$[Fe^{2+}][S^{2-}]$	6.3×10^{-18}
$AgCl$	$[Ag^+][Cl^-]$	1.8×10^{-10}	$Fe(OH)_2$	$[Fe^{2+}][OH^-]^2$	8.0×10^{-16}
AgI	$[Ag^+][I^-]$	8.3×10^{-17}	$Fe(OH)_3$	$[Fe^{3+}][OH^-]^3$	4.0×10^{-38}
Ag_2S	$[Ag^+]^2[S^{2-}]$	6.3×10^{-50}	HgS	$[Hg^{2+}][S^{2-}]$	1.6×10^{-52}
$Al(OH)_3$	$[Al^{3+}][OH^-]^3$	1.3×10^{-33}	$MgCO_3$	$[Mg^{2+}][CO_3^{2-}]$	3.5×10^{-8}
$BaCO_3$	$[Ba^{2+}][CO_3^{2-}]$	5.1×10^{-9}	$Mg(OH)_2$	$[Mg^{2+}][OH^-]^2$	1.8×10^{-11}
$BaSO_4$	$[Ba^{2+}][SO_4^{2-}]$	1.1×10^{-10}	MnS	$[Mn^{2+}][S^{2-}]$	2.5×10^{-13}
CdS	$[Cd^{2+}][S^{2-}]$	8.0×10^{-27}	$PbCl_2$	$[Pb^{2+}][Cl^-]^2$	1.6×10^{-5}
$CaCO_3$	$[Ca^{2+}][CO_3^{2-}]$	2.8×10^{-9}	$PbCrO_4$	$[Pb^{2+}][CrO_4^{2-}]$	2.8×10^{-13}
CaF_2	$[Ca^{2+}][F^-]^2$	5.3×10^{-9}	$PbSO_4$	$[Pb^{2+}][SO_4^{2-}]$	1.6×10^{-8}
$Ca(OH)_2$	$[Ca^{2+}][OH^-]^2$	5.5×10^{-6}	PbS	$[Pb^{2+}][S^{2-}]$	8.0×10^{-28}
$CaSO_4$	$[Ca^{2+}][SO_4^{2-}]$	9.1×10^{-6}	SnS	$[Sn^{2+}][S^{2-}]$	1.0×10^{-25}
$CoCO_3$	$[Co^{2+}][CO_3^{2-}]$	1.4×10^{-13}	$SrSO_4$	$[Sr^{2+}][SO_4^{2-}]$	3.2×10^{-7}
CoS	$[Co^{2+}][S^{2-}]$	4.0×10^{-21}	ZnS	$[Zn^{2+}][S^{2-}]$	1.6×10^{-24}

On the other hand, the *solubility* of a substance is a value and not a product of values. Solubility is an equilibrium position that represents the amount of the solid required to form a saturated solution with a specific amount of solvent. It has an infinite number of possible values at a given temperature and is dependent on other conditions, such as the presence of a common ion. Another way to distinguish the two is that solubility speaks of the substance as a whole, while the solubility product constant deals with its constituent parts.

GO ONLINE

SolveIt! Cards
HMHScience.com

Solubility Product Constant

Sample Problem B Calculate the solubility product constant, K_{sp}, for copper(I) chloride, CuCl, given that the solubility of this compound at 25°C is 1.08×10^{-2} g/100. g H_2O.

❶ ANALYZE

Given: solubility of CuCl = 1.08×10^{-2} g CuCl/100. g H_2O

Unknown: K_{sp}

❷ PLAN

Start by converting the solubility of CuCl in g/100 g H_2O to mol/L. You will need the molar mass of CuCl to get moles CuCl from grams CuCl. Then use the solubility of the $[Cu^+]$ and $[Cl^-]$ ions in the K_{sp} expression and solve for K_{sp}.

$$\frac{g\ CuCl}{100\ g\ H_2O} \times \frac{1\ g\ H_2O}{1\ mL\ H_2O} \times \frac{1000\ mL}{1\ L} \times \frac{1\ mol\ CuCl}{g\ CuCl} = \text{solubility in mol/L}$$

$$CuCl(s) \rightleftharpoons Cu^+(aq) + Cl^-(aq)$$

$$K_{sp} = [Cu^+][Cl^-]$$

$$[Cu^+] = [Cl^-] = \text{solubility in mol/L}$$

❸ SOLVE

The molar mass of CuCl is 99.00 g/mol.

$$\text{solubility in mol/L} = \frac{1.08 \times 10^{-2}\ g\ CuCl}{100.\ g\ H_2O} \times \frac{1\ g\ H_2O}{1\ mL} \times \frac{1000\ mL}{1\ L} \times \frac{1\ mol\ CuCl}{99.00\ g\ CuCl} =$$

$$1.09 \times 10^{-3}\ \text{mol/L CuCl}$$

$$[Cu^+] = [Cl^-] = 1.09 \times 10^{-3}\ \text{mol/L}$$

$$K_{sp} = (1.09 \times 10^{-3})(1.09 \times 10^{-3}) = 1.19 \times 10^{-6}$$

❹ CHECK YOUR WORK

The answer contains the proper number of significant figures and is close to the K_{sp} value given in **Figure 4.1**.

Practice   Answers in Appendix E

1. Calculate the solubility product constant, K_{sp}, of lead(II) chloride, $PbCl_2$, which has a solubility of 1.0 g/100 g H_2O at 20°C.

2. A 5.0 gram sample of Ag_2SO_4 will dissolve in 1.0 L of water. Calculate the solubility product constant for this salt.

MAIN IDEA

Solubility of a slightly soluble salt is found using the solubility product constant.

Once known, the solubility product constant can be used to determine the solubility of a slightly soluble salt. Suppose you wish to know how many moles of barium carbonate, $BaCO_3$, can be dissolved in 1 L of water at 25°C. From **Figure 4.1**, K_{sp} for $BaCO_3$ has the numerical value 5.1×10^{-9}. The equilibrium equation is written as follows:

$$BaCO_3(s) \rightleftharpoons Ba^{2+}(aq) + CO_3^{2-}(aq)$$

Given the value for K_{sp}, we can write the solubility equilibrium expression as follows:

$$K_{sp} = [Ba^{2+}][CO_3^{2-}] = 5.1 \times 10^{-9}$$

Therefore, $BaCO_3$ dissolves until the product of the molar concentrations of Ba^{2+} ions and CO_3^{2-} ions equals 5.1×10^{-9}. The solubility equilibrium equation shows that Ba^{2+} ions and CO_3^{2-} ions enter the solution in equal numbers as the salt dissolves. Thus, they have the same concentration. Let $[Ba^{2+}] = x$. Then $[CO_3^{2-}] = x$ also.

$$[Ba^{2+}][CO_3^{2-}] = K_{sp} = 5.1 \times 10^{-9}$$
$$(x)(x) = x^2 = 5.1 \times 10^{-9}$$
$$x = \sqrt{5.1 \times 10^{-9}}$$

The molar solubility of $BaCO_3$ is 7.1×10^{-5} mol/L.

Thus, the solution concentration is 7.1×10^{-5} M for Ba^{2+} ions and 7.1×10^{-5} M for CO_3^{2-} ions.

Calculating Solubility

Sample Problem C Calculate the solubility of lead sulfate, $PbSO_4$, in mol/L, using the K_{sp} value for this compound listed in Figure 4.1.

1 ANALYZE

Given: $K_{sp} = 1.6 \times 10^{-8}$

Unknown: solubility of $PbSO_4$

2 PLAN

$$PbSO_4 \rightleftharpoons Pb^{2+}(aq) + SO_4^{2-}(aq)$$
$$K_{sp} = [Pb^{2+}][SO_4^{2-}]$$
$$[Pb^{2+}] = [SO_4^{2-}], \text{ so let } [Pb^{2+}] = x \text{ and } [SO_4^{2-}] = x$$

3 SOLVE

$$PbSO_4 \rightleftharpoons Pb^{2+}(aq) + SO_4^{2-}(aq)$$
$$K_{sp} = x^2$$
$$x^2 = 1.6 \times 10^{-8}$$
$$x = \sqrt{1.6 \times 10^{-8}}$$
$$\text{Solubility of } PbSO_4 = \sqrt{1.6 \times 10^{-8}} = 1.3 \times 10^{-4}\,\text{mol/L}$$

4 CHECK YOUR WORK

The answer has the proper number of significant figures and is of the expected order of magnitude.

Continued

Chemical Equilibrium   **591**

Practice   Answers in Appendix E

1. Calculate the solubility of ferrous hydroxide, $Fe(OH)_2$, in mol/L, given the K_{sp} value listed in **Figure 4.1.**
2. Determine the concentration of strontium ions in a saturated solution of strontium sulfate, $SrSO_4$, if the K_{sp} for $SrSO_4$ is 3.2×10^{-7}.

▶ **MAIN IDEA**

Solubility constants predict precipitate formation.

In an earlier example, $BaCO_3$ served as the source of both Ba^{2+} and CO_3^{2-} ions. Because each mole of $BaCO_3$ yields one mole of Ba^{2+} ions and one mole of CO_3^{2-} ions, the concentrations of the two ions were equal. However, the equilibrium condition does not require that the two ion concentrations be equal. Equilibrium will still be established so that the ion product $[Ba^{2+}][CO_3^{2-}]$ does not exceed the value of K_{sp} for the system.

Similarly, if the ion product $[Ca^{2+}][F^-]^2$ is less than the value of K_{sp} at a particular temperature, the solution is unsaturated. If the ion product is greater than the value for K_{sp}, CaF_2 precipitates. This precipitation reduces the concentrations of Ca^{2+} and F^- ions until equilibrium is established.

Suppose that unequal quantities of $BaCl_2$ and Na_2CO_3 are dissolved in water and the solutions are then mixed. If the ion product $[Ba^{2+}][CO_3^{2-}]$ exceeds the K_{sp} of $BaCO_3$, a precipitate of $BaCO_3$ forms. After precipitation, the ion concentrations are such that $[Ba^{2+}][CO_3^{2-}]$ equals the K_{sp}.

FIGURE 4.2

Precipitation Reactions

Silver nitrate, $AgNO_3$, produces Ag^+ and NO_3^- ions in solution, so no precipitate forms.

Adding silver nitrate to a solution of potassium bromide causes a precipitation of silver bromide, KBr.

While potassium iodide, KI, and lead(II) nitrate, $Pb(NO_3)_2$ ions are soluble, when they mix, lead iodide, PbI_2, precipitates.

While potassium chromate is an exception to the rule that chromates are insoluble, when it is added to silver nitrate, a silver chromate precipitate will form.

While sulfates are generally very soluble, barium sulfate, $BaSO_4$, is an exception to the rule. So adding a barium-containing compound is often a test for the presence of sulfate ions.

All hydroxides, except for a few, are insoluble, as seen when nickel(II) hydroxide, $Ni(OH)_2$, forms from mixing solutions containing nickel(II) chloride, $NiCl_2$, and sodium hydroxide, NaOH.

Substances differ greatly in their tendencies to form precipitates when mixed in moderate concentrations. The photos in **Figure 4.2** show the behavior of some anions in the presence of certain cations. Note that not all the combinations have produced precipitates. The solubility product can be used to predict whether a precipitate forms when two solutions are mixed.

Precipitation Calculations

Sample Problem D **Will a precipitate form if 20.0 mL of 0.010 M BaCl$_2$ is mixed with 20.0 mL of 0.0050 M Na$_2$SO$_4$?**

① ANALYZE

Given: concentration of $BaCl_2$ = 0.010 M

volume of $BaCl_2$ = 20.0 mL

concentration of Na_2SO_4 = 0.0050 M

volume of Na_2SO_4 = 20.0 mL

Unknown: whether a precipitate forms

② PLAN

The two possible new pairings of ions are NaCl and $BaSO_4$. Of these, only $BaSO_4$ is a slightly soluble salt. It will precipitate if the ion product $[Ba^{2+}][SO_4^{2-}]$ in the mixed solution exceeds K_{sp} for $BaSO_4$. From the list of solubility products in **Figure 4.2**, the K_{sp} is found to be 1.1×10^{-10}. The solubility equilibrium equation follows:

$$BaSO_4(s) \rightleftharpoons Ba^{2+}(aq) + SO_4^{2-}(aq)$$

The solubility equilibrium expression is written as follows:

$$K_{sp} = [Ba^{2+}][SO_4^{2-}] = 1.1 \times 10^{-10}$$

First $[Ba^{2+}]$ and $[SO_4^{2-}]$ in the above solution must be found. Then the ion product is calculated and compared with the K_{sp}.

③ SOLVE

Calculate the mole quantities of Ba^{2+} and SO_4^{2-} ions.

$$0.020 \, \cancel{L} \times \frac{0.010 \, \text{mol Ba}^{2+}}{1 \, \cancel{L}} = 0.000 \, 20 \, \text{mol Ba}^{2+}$$

$$0.020 \, \cancel{L} \times \frac{0.0050 \, \text{mol SO}_4^{2-}}{1 \, \cancel{L}} = 0.000 \, 10 \, \text{mol SO}_4^{2-}$$

Calculate the total volume of solution containing Ba^{2+} and SO_4^{2-} ions.

$$0.020 \, \text{L} + 0.020 \, \text{L} = 0.040 \, \text{L}$$

Calculate the Ba^{2+} and SO_4^{2-} ion concentrations in the combined solution.

$$\frac{0.000 \, 20 \, \text{mol Ba}^{2+}}{0.040 \, \text{L}} = 5.0 \times 10^{-3} \, \text{mol/L Ba}^{2+}$$

$$\frac{0.000 \, 10 \, \text{mol SO}_4^{2-}}{0.040 \, \text{L}} = 2.5 \times 10^{-3} \, \text{mol/L SO}_4^{2-}$$

Calculate the ion product.

$$[Ba^{2+}][SO_4^{2-}] = (5.0 \times 10^{-3})(2.5 \times 10^{-3})$$

$$= 1.25 \times 10^{-5}$$

The ion product, which rounds to 1.3×10^{-5}, is greater than the value of K_{sp}, 1.1×10^{-10}, so precipitation occurs.

Continued

Precipitation Calculations (continued)

④ CHECK YOUR WORK The answer contains the appropriate number of significant figures and is close to an estimated value of 1×10^{-5}, calculated as $(5 \times 10^{-3})(2 \times 10^{-3})$; because $10^{-5} > 10^{-10}$, precipitation should occur.

Practice   Answers in Appendix E

1. Does a precipitate form when 100. mL of 0.0025 M $AgNO_3$ and 150. mL of 0.0020 M NaBr solutions are mixed?
2. Does a precipitate form when 20. mL of 0.038 M $Pb(NO_3)_2$ and 30. mL of 0.018 M KCl solutions are mixed?

▶ **MAIN IDEA**

K_{sp} cannot be used for solutions of soluble compounds.

The solubility product principle can be very useful when applied to solutions of slightly soluble substances. It *cannot* be applied to solutions of soluble substances. This is because the positive and negative ions attract each other, and this attraction becomes appreciable when the ions are close together. Sometimes it is necessary to consider two equilibria simultaneously. For example, if either ion hydrolyzes, the salt will be more soluble than predicted when only the solubility product constant is used. The solubility product is also sensitive to changes in solution temperature to the extent that the solubility of the dissolved substance is affected by such changes. All of these factors limit the conditions under which the solubility product principle can be applied.

✔ SECTION 4 FORMATIVE ASSESSMENT

▶ **Reviewing Main Ideas**

1. What is a solubility product constant? How are such constants determined?

2. How are solubility product constants used to calculate solubilities?

3. What is an ion product?

4. How are calculations to predict possible precipitation carried out?

5. What is the value of K_{sp} for Ag_2SO_4 if 5.40 g is soluble in 1.00 L of water?

6. Determine whether a precipitate will form if 20.0 mL of 1.00×10^{-7} M $AgNO_3$ is mixed with 20.0 mL of 2.00×10^{-9} M NaCl at 25°C.

✔ **Critical Thinking**

7. **ANALYZING DATA** A solution is 0.20 M in each of the following: $Ca(NO_3)_2$, $Cr(NO_3)_3$, and $La(NO_3)_3$. Solid NaF is added to the solution until the [F⁻] of the solution is 1.0×10^{-4} M. Given the values of K_{sp} below, describe what will happen.

$$CaF_2 = 3.9 \times 10^{-11}$$
$$CrF_3 = 6.6 \times 10^{-11}$$
$$LaF_3 = 4.0 \times 10^{-17}$$

The equilibrium constant expression is derived from the balanced equilibrium equation. The equation defines an equilibrium constant, K, as a function of the concentrations of products and reactants at equilibrium.

Consider an equilibrium process in which reactants A and B form products C and D.

$$nA + mB \rightleftharpoons xC + yD$$

The terms n, m, x, and y are the coefficients of the balanced equation.

$$K = \frac{[C]^x[D]^y}{[A]^n[B]^m}$$

Problem-Solving TIPS

- Always use a balanced chemical equation to write an equilibrium-constant equation.
- To write an equation, place the product concentrations in the numerator and the reactant concentrations in the denominator. Raise each substance's concentration to the power equal to the substance's coefficient in the balanced chemical equation.
- The concentration of any solid or pure liquid that takes part in the reaction is left out, because these concentrations never change.

Sample Problem

Write an equation for the equilibrium constant of the reaction in which nitrogen monoxide changes to dinitrogen monoxide and nitrogen dioxide.

To write an equation for an equilibrium constant, you must start with a balanced chemical equation for the equilibrium reaction. By writing the formulas of the compounds mentioned in the description, you get the unbalanced equilibrium equation $NO(g) \rightleftharpoons N_2O(g) + NO_2(g)$.

Balancing the equation requires a coefficient of 3 in front of NO, giving $3NO(g) \rightleftharpoons N_2O(g) + NO_2(g)$. Next, write an equilibrium equation. Remember that each concentration in the equilibrium equation is raised to a power equal to its coefficient in the balanced chemical equation. The product concentrations, $[N_2O]$ and $[NO_2]$, are placed in the numerator. The coefficient of each of the products is 1, so the exponent of each concentration is 1. There is only one reactant, so its concentration, $[NO]$, is written in the denominator. Its coefficient is 3 in the balanced chemical equation, so the concentration of NO is raised to the third power. The exponents with a value of 1 do not have to be written. The resulting equation is

$$K = \frac{[N_2O]^1[NO_2]^1}{[NO]^3} = \frac{[N_2O][NO_2]}{[NO]^3}$$

Practice

1. Write equations for the equilibrium constant of each of the following hypothetical reactions:

   a. $A(aq) + 2B(aq) \rightleftharpoons AB_2(aq)$

   b. $2DE_2(g) \rightleftharpoons D_2(g) + 2E_2(g)$

2. Use the equilibrium concentrations below to calculate the equilibrium constant for the following decomposition reaction:

$$2BrF_5(g) \rightleftharpoons Br_2(g) + 5F_2(g)$$

$[BrF_5] = 0.000137$ mol/L, $[Br_2] = 0.00050$ mol/L, and $[F_2] = 0.0025$ mol/L

CHAPTER 18 **Summary**

BIG IDEA A reaction system is at equilibrium when forward and reverse reactions occur simultaneously and at the same rate. Several factors can influence equilibrium.

SECTION 1 The Nature of Chemical Equilibrium

KEY TERMS

- A reaction system in which the forward and reverse reactions occur simultaneously and at the same rate is said to be at *equilibrium*. Both reactions continue, but there is no net change in the composition of the system.

- At equilibrium, the ratio of the product of the molar concentrations of substances formed to the product of the molar concentrations of reactants, each raised to the appropriate power, has a definite numerical value, *K*, which is the equilibrium constant at a given temperature.

reversible reaction

chemical equilibrium

equilibrium constant

chemical equilibrium expression

SECTION 2 Shifting Equilibrium

KEY TERM

- According to Le Châtelier's principle, when a stress (a change in concentration, pressure, or temperature) is applied to a system at equilibrium, the equilibrium is shifted in the direction that relieves the stress.

- The common-ion effect occurs when a solution containing ions in common with those in an equilibrium system involving ions as reactants or products is added to the system. Le Châtelier's principle explains the response of the system to the stress.

common-ion effect

SECTION 3 Equilibria of Acids, Bases, and Salts

KEY TERMS

- The equilibrium expression for the ionization constant of the weak acid HA follows:

$$K_a = \frac{[H_3O^+][A^-]}{[HA]}$$

- Salts formed from strong bases and weak acids produce aqueous solutions that are basic because of *anion hydrolysis*.

- Salts formed from strong acids and weak bases produce aqueous solutions that are acidic because of *cation hydrolysis*.

- Salts formed from strong acids and strong bases do not hydrolyze in water, and their solutions are neutral.

- Salts formed from weak acids and weak bases may produce neutral, acidic, or basic solutions, depending on the relative strengths of the weak acid and weak base.

acid ionization constant

buffered solution

hydrolysis

SECTION 4 Solubility Equilibrium

KEY TERM

- Ions of salts that are slightly soluble form saturated aqueous solutions at low concentrations. The solubility equilibrium expression for such salts yields a constant—the solubility product constant, K_{sp}.

solubility product constant

CHAPTER 18 **Review**

The Nature of Chemical Equilibrium

▶ **REVIEWING MAIN IDEAS**

1. Describe and explain how the concentrations of A, B, C, and D change from the time when A and B are first combined to the point at which equilibrium is established for the reaction $A + B \rightleftharpoons C + D$.

2. **a.** Write the general expression for an equilibrium constant based on the equation
   $$nA + mB + \ldots \rightleftharpoons xC + yD + \ldots$$
   b. What information is provided by the value of K for a given equilibrium system at a specified temperature?

3. In general, which reaction is favored (forward or reverse) if the value of K at a specified temperature is
   a. very small?
   b. very large?

PRACTICE PROBLEMS

4. Determine the value of the equilibrium constant for each reaction from the equilibrium concentrations given. (Concentrations are in mol/L.) (Hint: See Sample Problem A.)
   a. $A + B \rightleftharpoons C$; $[A] = 2.0$; $[B] = 3.0$; $[C] = 4.0$
   b. $D + 2E \rightleftharpoons F + 3G$; $[D] = 1.5$; $[E] = 2.0$; $[F] = 1.8$; $[G] = 1.2$
   c. $N_2(g) + 3H_2(g) \rightleftharpoons 2NH_3(g)$; $[N_2] = 0.45$; $[H_2] = 0.14$; $[NH_3] = 0.62$

5. An equilibrium mixture at a specific temperature is found to consist of 1.2×10^{-3} mol/L HCl, 3.8×10^{-4} mol/L O_2, 5.8×10^{-2} mol/L H_2O, and 5.8×10^{-2} mol/L Cl_2 according to the following:
   $$4HCl(g) + O_2(g) \rightleftharpoons 2H_2O(g) + 2Cl_2(g).$$
   Determine the value of the equilibrium constant for this system.

6. At 450°C, the value of the equilibrium constant for the following system is 6.59×10^{-3}. If $[NH_3] = 1.23 \times 10^{-4}$ M and $[H_2] = 2.75 \times 10^{-2}$ M at equilibrium, determine the concentration of N_2 at that point.
   $$N_2(g) + 3H_2(g) \rightleftharpoons 2NH_3(g)$$

7. The value of the equilibrium constant for the reaction below is 40.0 at a specified temperature. What would be the value of that constant for the reverse reaction under the same conditions?
   $$H_2(g) + I_2(g) \rightleftharpoons 2HI(g)$$

Shifting Equilibrium

▶ **REVIEWING MAIN IDEAS**

8. Predict whether each of the following pressure changes would favor the forward or reverse reaction.
   $$2NO(g) + O_2(g) \rightleftharpoons 2NO_2(g)$$
   a. increased pressure
   b. decreased pressure

9. In heterogeneous reaction systems, what types of substances do not appear in the equilibrium constant expression? Why?

10. Explain the effect of a catalyst on an equilibrium system.

11. Predict the effect of each of the following on the indicated equilibrium system in terms of the direction of equilibrium shift (forward, reverse, or neither).
    $$H_2(g) + Cl_2(g) \rightleftharpoons 2HCl(g) + 184 \text{ kJ}$$
    a. addition of Cl_2
    b. removal of HCl
    c. increased pressure
    d. decreased temperature
    e. removal of H_2
    f. decreased pressure
    g. addition of a catalyst
    h. increased temperature
    i. decreased system volume

12. How would the changes in (a) through (i) of item 11 affect the new equilibrium concentration of HCl and the value of K at the new equilibrium?

13. Explain why changes in the concentrations of the reactants and products at equilibrium have no effect on the value of the equilibrium constant.

14. What relative pressure (high or low) would result in the production of the maximum level of CO_2 according to the following equation? Why?

$$2CO(g) + O_2(g) \rightleftharpoons 2CO_2(g)$$

15. What relative conditions (reactant concentrations, pressure, and temperature) would favor a high equilibrium concentration of the underlined substance in each of the following equilibrium systems?

a. $2CO(g) + O_2(g) \rightleftharpoons \underline{2CO_2(g)} + 167 \text{ kJ}$

b. $Cu^{2+}(aq) + 4NH_3(aq) \rightleftharpoons \underline{Cu(NH_3)_4^{2+}(aq)} + 42 \text{ kJ}$

c. $2HI(g) + 12.6 \text{ kJ} \rightleftharpoons H_2(g) + \underline{I_2(g)}$

d. $4HCl(g) + O_2(g) \rightleftharpoons 2H_2O(g) + \underline{2Cl_2(g)} + 113 \text{ kJ}$

e. $PCl_5(g) + 88 \text{ kJ} \rightleftharpoons PCl_3(g) + \underline{Cl_2(g)}$

16. The reaction between hemoglobin, Hb, and oxygen, O_2, in red blood cells is responsible for transporting O_2 to body tissues. This process can be represented by the following equilibrium reaction:

$$Hb(aq) + O_2(g) \rightleftharpoons HbO_2(aq)$$

What will happen to the concentration of oxygenated hemoglobin, HbO_2, at high altitude, where the pressure of oxygen is 0.1 atm instead of 0.2 atm, as it is at sea level?

17. What two factors determine the extent to which reacting ions are removed from solution?

18. Identify the three conditions under which ionic reactions can run to completion, and write an equation for each.

SECTION 3
Equilibria of Acids, Bases, and Salts

REVIEWING MAIN IDEAS

19. a. Write the ion product constant expression for water.
b. What is the value of this constant at 25°C?

20. List and distinguish between the four general categories of salts, based on their hydrolysis properties, and give an example of each.

21. Explain why the pH of a solution containing both acetic acid and sodium acetate is higher than that of a solution containing the same concentration of acetic acid alone.

22. The ionization constant, K_a, for acetic acid is 1.8×10^{-5} at 25°C. Explain the significance of this value.

23. a. From the development of K_a described in Section 3, show how you would express an ionization constant, K_b, for the weak base NH_3.
b. In this case, $K_b = 1.8 \times 10^{-5}$. What is the significance of this numerical value to equilibrium?

SECTION 4
Solubility Equilibrium

REVIEWING MAIN IDEAS

24. Explain why a saturated solution is not necessarily a concentrated solution.

25. What rule of thumb is used to distinguish between soluble and slightly soluble substances?

26. What is the relative ion concentration of an ionic substance typically involved in solubility equilibrium systems?

27. What is the relationship between K_{sp} and the product of the ion concentrations in terms of determining whether a solution of those ions is saturated?

PRACTICE PROBLEMS

28. The ionic substance EJ dissociates to form E^{2+} and J^{2-} ions. The solubility of EJ is 8.45×10^{-6} mol/L. What is the value of the solubility product constant? (Hint: See Sample Problem B.)

29. Calculate the solubility product constant K_{sp} for each of the following, based on the solubility information provided.
a. $BaSO_4 = 2.4 \times 10^{-4}$ g/100. g H_2O at 20°C
b. $Ca(OH)_2 = 0.173$ g/100. g H_2O at 20°C

30. Calculate the molar solubility of a substance MN that ionizes to form M^{2+} and N^{2-} ions, given that $K_{sp} = 8.1 \times 10^{-6}$. (Hint: See Sample Problem C.)

31. Use the K_{sp} values given in **Figure 4.2** to evaluate the solubility of each of the following in moles per liter.
   a. AgBr
   b. CoS

32. A 25.0 mL sample of 0.0500 M $Pb(NO_3)_2$ is combined with 25.0 mL of 0.0400 M Na_2SO_4 at 25°C.
   a. Write the solubility equilibrium equation at 25°C.
   b. Write the solubility equilibrium expression for the net reaction.

33. The ionic substance T_3U_2 ionizes to form T^{2+} and U^{3-} ions. The solubility of T_3U_2 is 3.8×10^{-10} mol/L. What is the value of the solubility product constant?

34. A solution of AgI contains 2.7×10^{-10} mol/L Ag^+. What is the maximum I^- concentration that can exist in this solution?

35. Calculate whether a precipitate will form if 0.35 L of 0.0044 M $Ca(NO_3)_2$ and 0.17 L of 0.000 39 M NaOH are mixed at 25°C. (See **Figure 4.2** for K_{sp} values.) (Hint: See Sample Problem D.)

36. Determine whether a precipitate will form if 1.70 g of solid $AgNO_3$ and 14.5 g of solid NaCl are dissolved in 200. mL of water to form a solution at 25°C.

37. If 2.50×10^{-2} g of solid $Fe(NO_3)_3$ is added to 100. mL of a 1.0×10^{-4} M NaOH solution, will a precipitate form?

Mixed Review

▶ **REVIEWING MAIN IDEAS**

38. Calcium carbonate is only slightly soluble in water.
   a. Write the equilibrium equation for calcium carbonate in solution.
   b. Write the solubility product constant expression, K_{sp}, for the equilibrium in a saturated solution of $CaCO_3$.

39. Calculate the concentration of Hg^{2+} ions in a saturated solution of $HgS(s)$. How many Hg^{2+} ions are in 1000 L of the solution?

40. Calculate the equilibrium constant, K, for the following reaction at 900°C.
$$H_2(g) + CO_2(g) \rightleftharpoons H_2O(g) + CO(g)$$
The components were analyzed, and it was found that $[H_2] = 0.061$ mol/L, $[CO_2] = 0.16$ mol/L, $[H_2O] = 0.11$ mol/L, and $[CO] = 0.14$ mol/L.

41. A solution in equilibrium with solid barium phosphate is found to have a barium ion concentration of 5.0×10^{-4} M and a K_{sp} of 3.4×10^{-23}. Calculate the concentration of phosphate ion.

42. At 25°C, the value of K is 1.7×10^{-13} for the following reaction.
$$2N_2O(g) + O_2(g) \rightleftharpoons 4NO(g)$$
It is determined that $[N_2O] = 0.0035$ mol/L and $[O_2] = 0.0027$ mol/L. Using this information, what is the concentration of $NO(g)$ at equilibrium?

43. Tooth enamel is composed of the mineral hydroxyapatite, $Ca_5(PO_4)_3OH$, which has a K_{sp} of 6.8×10^{-37}. The molar solubility of hydroxyapatite is 2.7×10^{-5} mol/L. When hydroxyapatite is reacted with fluoride, the OH^- is replaced with the F^- ion on the mineral, forming fluorapatite, $Ca_5(PO_4)_3F$. (The latter is harder and less susceptible to cavities.) The K_{sp} of fluorapatite is 1×10^{-60}. Calculate the molar solubility of fluorapatite in water. Given your calculations, can you support the fluoridation of drinking water?

44. Determine whether a precipitate will form when 0.96 g Na_2CO_3 is combined with 0.20 g $BaBr_2$ in a 10. L solution $(K_{sp} = 2.8 \times 10^{-9})$.

45. For the formation of ammonia, the equilibrium constant is calculated to be 5.2×10^{-5} at 25°C. After analysis, it is determined that $[N_2] = 2.00$ M and $[H_2] = 0.80$ M. How many grams of ammonia are in the 10. L reaction vessel at equilibrium? Use the following equilibrium equation.
$$N_2(g) + 3H_2(g) \rightleftharpoons 2NH_3(g)$$

CRITICAL THINKING

46. **Relating Ideas** Let s equal the solubility, in mol/L, of AB_2. In terms of s, what is the molar concentration of A? of B? What is the K_{sp} of AB_2?

47. Predicting Outcomes When gasoline burns in an automobile engine, nitric oxide is formed from oxygen and nitrogen. Nitric oxide is a major air pollutant. High temperatures, such as those found in a combustion engine, are needed for the following reaction:

$$N_2(g) + O_2(g) \rightleftarrows 2NO(g)$$

K for the reaction is 0.01 at 2000°C. If 4.0 mol of N_2, 0.1 mol of O_2, and 0.08 mol of NO are placed in a 1.0-L vessel at 2000°C, predict which reaction will be favored.

USING THE HANDBOOK

48. An equilibrium system helps maintain the pH of the blood. Review the material on the carbon dioxide–bicarbonate ion equilibrium system in Group 14 of the *Elements Handbook* (Appendix A), and answer the following.
   a. Write the equation for the equilibrium system that responds to changes in H_3O^+ concentration.
   b. Use Le Châtelier's principle to explain how hyperventilation affects this system.
   c. How does this system maintain pH when acid is added?

49. The reactions used to confirm the presence of transition metal ions often involve the formation of precipitates. Review the analytical tests for the transition metals in the *Elements Handbook* (Appendix A). Use that information and **Figure 4.2** to determine the minimum concentration of Zn^{2+} needed to produce a precipitate that confirms the presence of Zn. Assume enough sulfide ion reagent is added to the unknown solution in the test tube to produce a sulfide ion concentration of 1.4×10^{-20} M.

RESEARCH AND WRITING

50. Find photos of several examples of stalagmites and stalactites in various caves. Investigate the equilibrium processes involved in the formation of stalagmites and stalactites.

51. Carry out library research on the use of catalysts in industrial processes. Explain what types of catalysts are used for specific processes, such as the Haber-Bosch process.

ALTERNATIVE ASSESSMENT

52. Research nitrogen narcosis in the library. What causes nitrogen narcosis, and how does it relate to Le Châtelier's principle?

Standards-Based Assessment

Record your answers on a separate piece of paper.

MULTIPLE CHOICE

1 A chemical reaction is in equilibrium when —

A forward and reverse reactions have ceased

B the equilibrium constant equals 1

C forward and reverse reaction rates are equal

D no reactants remain

2 Which change can cause the value of the equilibrium constant to change?

A temperature

B concentration of a reactant

C concentration of a product

D none of the above

3 Consider the following reaction:

$$2C(s) + O_2(g) \rightleftharpoons 2CO(g)$$

The equilibrium constant expression for this reaction is —

A $\dfrac{[CO]^2}{[O_2]}$

B $\dfrac{[CO]^2}{[O_2][C]^2}$

C $\dfrac{2[CO]}{[O_2][2C]}$

D $\dfrac{[CO]}{[O_2]^2}$

4 If an exothermic reaction has reached equilibrium, then increasing the temperature will —

A favor the forward reaction

B favor the reverse reaction

C favor both the forward and reverse reactions

D have no effect on the equilibrium

5 Le Châtelier's principle states that —

A at equilibrium, the forward and reverse reaction rates are equal

B stresses include changes in concentrations, pressure, and temperature

C to relieve stress, solids and solvents are omitted from equilibrium constant expressions

D chemical equilibria respond to reduce applied stress

6 The graph below shows the neutralization curve for 100 mL of 0.100 M acid with 0.100 M base. Which letter represents the equivalence point?

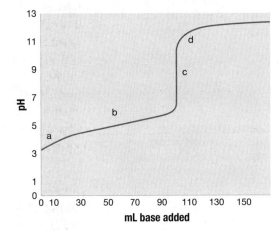

A a

B b

C c

D d

GRIDDED RESPONSE

7 The solubility product of calcium chromate, $CaCrO_4$, is 7.1×10^{-4}. What is the solubility of this compound in mol/L? (Give your answer to two significant figures.)

CHAPTER 19
Oxidation-Reduction Reactions

BIG IDEA
In oxidation-reduction reactions, atoms and ions change oxidation states, either by losing electrons (oxidizing) or gaining electrons (reducing).

ONLINE Chemistry
HMHScience.com

ONLINE LABS
- Rust Race
- Oxidation-Reduction Reactions
- Reduction of Manganese in Permanganate Ion

GO ONLINE

Why It Matters Video
HMHScience.com

Equations and Reactions

(t) ©Dean Fox/SuperStock; (b) NASA

Oxidation and Reduction

Key Terms

oxidation
oxidized
reduction
reduced
oxidation-reduction reaction
redox reaction
half-reaction

SECTION 1

Main Ideas

▶ Atoms can change their oxidation states.

▶ Oxidation occurs when valence electrons are lost.

▶ Reduction occurs when valence electrons are gained.

▶ Oxidation and reduction are paired reactions.

▶ **MAIN IDEA**

Atoms can change their oxidation states.

Chemists classify reactions according to different criteria. You have learned of a few already. For example, a precipitation reaction can be any reaction that takes place in solution in which one of the products is insoluble. An acid-base reaction commonly refers to an acid reacting with a base to produce water and a salt, a neutralization. What distinguishes an oxidation-reduction reaction is that it involves a transfer of electrons, a change in an atom's oxidation state. You previously learned the rules for assigning oxidation states, summarized below in **Figure 1.1**.

FIGURE 1.1

RULES FOR ASSIGNING OXIDATION NUMBERS	
Rule	**Example**
1. The oxidation number of any pure element is 0.	The oxidation number of Na(s) is 0.
2. The oxidation number of a monatomic ion equals the charge on the ion.	The oxidation number of Cl^- is -1.
3. The more-electronegative element in a binary compound is assigned the number equal to the charge it would have if it were an ion.	The oxidation number of O in NO is -2.
4. The oxidation number of fluorine in a compound is always -1.	The oxidation number of F in LiF is -1.
5. Oxygen has an oxidation number of -2 unless it is combined with F, in which case it is $+1$ or $+2$, or it is in a peroxide, in which case it is -1.	The oxidation number of O in NO_2 is -2.
6 Hydrogen's oxidation state in most of its compounds is $+1$ unless it is combined with a metal, in which case it is -1.	The oxidation number of H in LiH is -1.
7. In compounds, Group 1 and 2 elements and aluminum have oxidation numbers of $+1$, $+2$, and $+3$, respectively.	The oxidation number of Ca in $CaCO_3$ is $+2$.
8. The sum of the oxidation numbers of all atoms in a neutral compound is 0.	The oxidation number of C in $CaCO_3$ is $+4$.
9. The sum of the oxidation numbers of all atoms in a polyatomic ion equals the charge of the ion.	The oxidation number of P in $H_2PO_4^-$ is $+5$.

FIGURE 1.2

Oxidation States of Chromium Compounds Chromium provides a very visual example of oxidation numbers. Different oxidation states of chromium have dramatically different colors. Solutions with the same oxidation state show less dramatic differences.

✔ CRITICAL THINKING

Relate Examine the tables of ions and their oxidation numbers, **Figures 1.1** and **1.3,** in the chapter "Chemical Formulas and Chemical Compounds." Compare the elements that have multiple ions or oxidation states with the placement of those elements on the periodic table. What relationship is there between the ability to form multiple ions and where those elements are generally found on the periodic table?

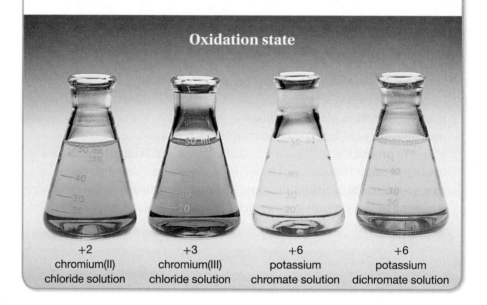

Oxidation state

+2	+3	+6	+6
chromium(II) chloride solution	chromium(III) chloride solution	potassium chromate solution	potassium dichromate solution

FIGURE 1.3

Oxidation in NaCl Synthesis
Sodium and chlorine react violently to form NaCl. The synthesis of NaCl from its elements illustrates the oxidation-reduction process.

▶ MAIN IDEA

Oxidation occurs when valence electrons are lost.

Processes in which the atoms or ions of an element experience an increase in oxidation state are oxidation processes. The combustion of metallic sodium in an atmosphere of chlorine gas is shown in **Figure 1.3.** The sodium ions and chloride ions produced during this strongly exothermic reaction form a cubic crystal lattice in which sodium cations form ionic bonds to chloride anions. The chemical equation for this reaction is written as follows.

$$2Na(s) + Cl_2(g) \longrightarrow 2NaCl(s)$$

The formation of sodium ions illustrates an oxidation process because each sodium atom loses an electron to become a sodium ion. The oxidation state is represented by placing an oxidation number above the symbol of the atom and the ion.

$$\overset{0}{Na} \longrightarrow \overset{+1}{Na^+} + e^-$$

The oxidation state of sodium has changed from 0 to the +1 state of the ion (Rules 1 and 7, **Figure 1.1**). **A species whose oxidation number increases is oxidized.** The sodium atom is *oxidized* to a sodium ion.

▶ MAIN IDEA
Reduction occurs when valence electrons are gained.

Processes in which the oxidation state of an element decreases are **reduction processes.** Consider the behavior of chlorine in its reaction with sodium. Each chlorine atom accepts an electron and becomes a chloride ion. The oxidation state of chlorine decreases from 0 to −1 for the chloride ion (Rules 1 and 2, **Figure 1.1**).

$$\overset{0}{Cl_2} + 2e^- \longrightarrow \overset{-1}{2Cl^-}$$

A species that undergoes a decrease in oxidation state is **reduced.** The chlorine atom is reduced to the chloride ion.

▶ MAIN IDEA
Oxidation and reduction are paired reactions.

Electrons are released in oxidation and acquired in reduction. Therefore, for oxidation to occur during a chemical reaction, reduction must also occur. Furthermore, the number of electrons produced in oxidation must equal the number of electrons acquired in reduction. Recall that electrons are negatively charged and that for charge to be conserved, the number of electrons lost must equal the number of electrons gained. Mass is conserved in any chemical reaction. Therefore, like mass, the electrons exchanged during oxidation and reduction are conserved.

But why do we say a substance is *reduced* when it *gains* electrons? Remember that when electrons are gained, their negative electrical charge will cause the overall oxidation number to drop, that is, be reduced.

A transfer of electrons causes changes in the oxidation states of one or more elements. **Any chemical process in which elements undergo changes in oxidation number is an oxidation-reduction reaction. This name is often shortened to redox reaction.** An example of a redox reaction can be seen in **Figure 1.4,** in which copper is being oxidized and NO_3^- from nitric acid is being reduced. **The part of the reaction involving oxidation or reduction alone can be written as a half-reaction.** The overall equation for a redox reaction is the sum of two half-reactions. Because the number of electrons involved is the same for oxidation and reduction, they cancel each other out and do not appear in the overall chemical equation.

Equations for the reaction between nitric acid and copper illustrate the relationship between half-reactions and the overall redox reaction.

$$\overset{0}{Cu} \longrightarrow \overset{+2}{Cu^{2+}} + 2e^- \qquad \text{(oxidation half-reaction)}$$

$$\overset{+5}{2NO_3^-} \overset{-2}{} + 2e^- + \overset{+1}{4H^+} \longrightarrow \overset{+4}{2NO_2} \overset{-2}{} + \overset{+1}{2H_2O} \overset{-2}{} \qquad \text{(reduction half-reaction)}$$

$$\overset{0}{Cu} + \overset{+5}{2NO_3^-} + 4H^+ \longrightarrow \overset{+2}{Cu^{2+}} + \overset{+4}{2NO_2} + 2H_2O \qquad \text{(redox reaction)}$$

Notice that electrons lost in oxidation appear on the product side of the oxidation half-reaction. Electrons are gained in reduction and appear as reactants in the reduction half–reaction.

FIGURE 1.4

Oxidation of Copper Copper is oxidized and nitrogen dioxide is produced when this penny is placed in a concentrated nitric acid solution.

Distinguishing Redox Reactions

Combining the half-reactions gives a full picture of what occurs. Metallic copper reacts in nitric acid, and in so doing, one copper atom is oxidized from Cu to Cu^{2+} as two nitrogen atoms are reduced from a $+5$ oxidation state to a $+4$ oxidation state. Both atoms and electrons are conserved. This balanced chemical equation shows this.

$$Cu + 4HNO_3 \longrightarrow Cu(NO_3)_2 + 2NO_2 + 2H_2O$$

Remember that redox reactions are only those involving atoms that change oxidation states. If none of the atoms in a reaction change oxidation state, the reaction is *not* a redox reaction. For example, sulfur dioxide gas, SO_2, dissolves in water to form an acidic solution containing a low concentration of sulfurous acid, H_2SO_3.

$$\overset{+4\,-2}{SO_2} + \overset{+1\,-2}{H_2O} \longrightarrow \overset{+1\,+4\,-2}{H_2SO_3}$$

No atoms change oxidation states, so this is *not* a redox reaction.

When a solution of sodium chloride is added to a solution of silver nitrate, an ion–exchange reaction occurs, and white silver chloride precipitates.

$$\overset{+1}{Na^+} + \overset{-1}{Cl^-} + \overset{+1}{Ag^+} + \overset{+5\,-2}{NO_3^-} \longrightarrow \overset{+1}{Na^+} + \overset{+5\,-2}{NO_3^-} + \overset{+1\,-1}{AgCl}$$

The oxidation state of each monatomic ion remains unchanged. Again, this reaction is *not* an oxidation–reduction reaction.

Redox Reactions and Covalent Bonds

The synthesis of NaCl from its elements involves ionic bonding. Substances with covalent bonds also undergo redox reactions. An oxidation number, unlike an ionic charge, has no physical meaning. That is, the oxidation number assigned to a particular atom is based on its electronegativity relative to the other atoms to which it is bonded in a given molecule; it is not based on any real charge on the atom. For example, an ionic charge of $1-$ results from the complete gain of one electron by an atom or other neutral species, whereas an oxidation state of -1 means an increased attraction for a bonding electron. A change in oxidation number does not require a change in actual charge.

When hydrogen burns in chlorine, a covalent bond forms from the sharing of two electrons. The two bonding electrons in the HCl molecule are not shared equally. Rather, the pair of electrons is more strongly attracted to the chlorine atom because of its higher electronegativity.

$$\overset{0}{H_2} + \overset{0}{Cl_2} \longrightarrow \overset{+1\,-1}{2HCl}$$

As specified by Rule 3 in **Figure 1.1,** chlorine in HCl is assigned an oxidation number of -1. Thus, the oxidation number for the chlorine atoms changes from 0, its oxidation number in the elemental state, to -1; chlorine atoms are reduced. As specified by Rule 1, the oxidation number of each hydrogen atom in the hydrogen molecule is 0. As specified by Rule 6, the oxidation state of the hydrogen atom in the HCl molecule is $+1$; the hydrogen atom is oxidized.

Thinking of Oxidation States

When you think of atoms changing oxidation states, don't think that either atom has totally lost or totally gained any electrons. In the case of the formation of hydrogen chloride, for example, hydrogen simply has donated a share of its bonding electron to the chlorine; it has not completely transferred that electron. The assignment of oxidation numbers allows an approximation of the electron distribution of a molecule. An element can have different oxidation numbers in different compounds. This difference in oxidation numbers can reveal the difference in electron distribution of the compounds.

Reactants and products in redox reactions are not limited to monatomic ions and uncombined elements. Elements in molecular compounds or polyatomic ions can also be oxidized and reduced if they have more than one nonzero oxidation state. An example of this is provided in the reaction between the copper penny and nitric acid in which the nitrate ion, NO_3^-, is converted to nitrogen dioxide, NO_2. Nitrogen is reduced in this reaction. Usually, we refer to the oxidation or reduction of the entire molecule or ion. Instead of saying that the nitrogen atom is reduced, we say the nitrate ion is reduced to nitrogen dioxide.

$$\cdots + \overset{+5}{N}O_3^- \longrightarrow \overset{+4}{N}O_2 + \cdots$$

SECTION 1 FORMATIVE ASSESSMENT

► Reviewing Main Ideas

1. What differentiates an oxidation-reduction reaction from other types of reactions, such as precipitation reactions or acid-base reactions?

2. Label each of the following half-reactions as either an oxidation or a reduction half-reaction:

a. $\overset{0}{Br_2} + 2e^- \longrightarrow 2\,\overset{-1}{Br^-}$

b. $\overset{0}{Na} \longrightarrow \overset{+1}{Na^+} + e^-$

c. $2\overset{-1}{Cl^-} \longrightarrow \overset{0}{Cl_2} + 2e^-$

d. $\overset{0}{Cl_2} + 2e^- \longrightarrow 2\,\overset{-1}{Cl^-}$

e. $\overset{+1}{Na^+} + e^- \longrightarrow \overset{0}{Na}$

f. $\overset{0}{Fe} \longrightarrow \overset{+2}{Fe^{2+}} + 2e^-$

g. $\overset{+2}{Cu^{2+}} + 2e^- \longrightarrow \overset{0}{Cu}$

h. $\overset{+3}{Fe^{3+}} + e^- \longrightarrow \overset{+2}{Fe^{2+}}$

3. Which of the following equations represent redox reactions?

a. $2KNO_3(s) \longrightarrow 2KNO_2(s) + O_2(g)$

b. $H_2(g) + CuO(s) \longrightarrow Cu(s) + H_2O(l)$

c. $NaOH(aq) + HCl(aq) \longrightarrow NaCl(aq) + H_2O(l)$

d. $H_2(g) + Cl_2(g) \longrightarrow 2HCl(g)$

e. $SO_3(g) + H_2O(l) \longrightarrow H_2SO_4(aq)$

4. For each redox equation identified in the previous question, determine which element is oxidized and which is reduced.

✔ Critical Thinking

5. ANALYZING INFORMATION Use the following equations for the redox reaction between Al^{3+} and Na to answer the questions below.

$$\overset{0}{3Na} \longrightarrow 3\overset{+1}{Na^+} + 3e^- \qquad \text{(oxidation)}$$

$$\overset{+3}{Al^{3+}} + 3e^- \longrightarrow \overset{0}{Al} \qquad \text{(reduction)}$$

$$\overset{0}{3Na} + \overset{+3}{Al^{3+}} \longrightarrow 3\overset{+1}{Na^+} + \overset{0}{Al} \qquad \text{(redox reaction)}$$

a. Explain how this reaction illustrates that charge is conserved in a redox reaction.

b. Explain how this reaction illustrates that mass is conserved in a redox reaction.

c. Explain why electrons do not appear as reactants or products in the combined equation.

Production of Aluminum

S.T.E.M.

Aluminum, the third most abundant element after oxygen and silicon, is the most abundant metallic element in Earth's crust. However, aluminum always occurs combined with other elements, usually oxygen, silicon, and iron. You have to work very hard to produce pure aluminum metal.

Aluminum, Al, was first discovered in 1825, and for more than 60 years was considered a very expensive rarity. Because aluminum was considered rare but was extremely resistant to corrosion, it was selected as the material for the lightning arrestor atop the Washington Monument in Washington, D.C. A pyramid 23 cm tall, weighing 2.83 kg, was cast. At the time, it was the largest single piece of aluminum ever cast and was placed on the monument amid great ceremony on December 6, 1884.

In 1886, American Charles Hall and Frenchman Paul Héroult independently invented the chemical process for producing pure aluminum from its ore. What is now called the Hall-Héroult process is still used for aluminum production.

Aluminum ore—the relatively common mineral, bauxite—is a mixture of aluminum oxide (alumina), silica (sand), and iron oxides. Alumina is first separated from the impurities.

Next, the Hall-Héroult process converts alumina to molten aluminum metal: in a large pot lined with carbon, alumina is dissolved in a bath of a molten cryolite, NA_3AlF_6, at a temperature of about 1000°C

Electrolytic process of manufacturing aluminum

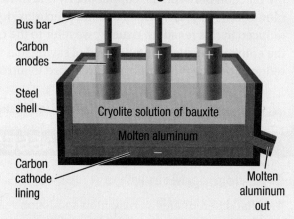

Bus bar

Carbon anodes

Steel shell

Cryolite solution of bauxite

Molten aluminum

Carbon cathode lining

Molten aluminum out

An electric current, 4–6 volts, 100,000–230,000 amperes, is passed through the molten cryolite, decomposing the dissolved alumina to aluminum and oxygen. The aluminum sinks to the bottom of the reaction vessel, and the oxygen reacts with the carbon lining, forming carbon dioxide, which bubbles off into the air. The overall reaction is:

$$2Al_2O_3 + 3C + 12e^- \longrightarrow 4Al + 3CO_3$$

The Hall-Héroult process has made aluminum products affordable. And yet aluminum used to be more expensive than gold!

Questions

1. Many industries use redox reactions to make products such as aluminum, steel, and lead storage batteries for cars and trucks. Explain why it has been so important to scale the Hall-Héroult process up to quantities of many tons per electrolytic cell for modern uses.

2. Identify which material is oxidized and which is reduced by the electric current in the Hall-Héroult process.

Balancing Redox Equations

Main Idea

▷ Oxidation and reduction reactions are balanced separately and then added together.

Equations for simple redox reactions can be balanced by inspection. Most redox equations, however, require more systematic methods. The equation-balancing process requires the use of oxidation numbers. In a balanced equation, both charge and mass are conserved. Although oxidation and reduction half-reactions occur together, their reaction equations are balanced separately and then combined to give the balanced redox-reaction equation.

▷ MAIN IDEA
Oxidation and reduction reactions are balanced separately and then added together.

The *half-reaction method,* or ion-electron method, for balancing redox equations consists of seven steps. Oxidation numbers are assigned to all atoms and polyatomic ions to determine which species are part of the redox process. The oxidation and reduction equations are balanced separately for mass and charge. They are then added together to produce a complete balanced equation. These seven steps are applied to balance the reaction of hydrogen sulfide and nitric acid. Sulfuric acid, nitrogen dioxide, and water are the products of the reaction.

1. **Write the formula equation if it is not given in the problem. Then write the ionic equation.**

   Formula equation: $H_2S + HNO_3 \longrightarrow H_2SO_4 + NO_2 + H_2O$

   Ionic equation: $H_2S + H^+ + NO_3^- \longrightarrow 2H^+ + SO_4^{2-} + NO_2 + H_2O$

2. **Assign oxidation numbers. Delete substances containing only elements that do not change oxidation state.**

$$\overset{+1\ -2}{H_2S} + \overset{+1}{H^+} + \overset{+5\ -2}{NO_3^-} \longrightarrow \overset{+1}{2H^+} + \overset{+6\ -2}{SO_4^{2-}} + \overset{+4\ -2}{NO_2} + \overset{+1\ -2}{H_2O}$$

The sulfur changes oxidation state from -2 to $+6$. The nitrogen changes oxidation state from $+5$ to $+4$. The other substances are deleted.

$$\overset{+1\ -2}{H_2S} + \overset{+5\ -2}{NO_3^-} \longrightarrow \overset{+6\ -2}{SO_4^{2-}} + \overset{+4\ -2}{NO_2}$$

The remaining species are used in step 3.

3. **Write the half-reaction for oxidation.** In this example, the sulfur is being oxidized.

$$\overset{-2}{H_2S} \longrightarrow \overset{+6}{SO_4^{2-}}$$

- **Balance the atoms.** To balance the oxygen in this half-reaction, 4 water, H_2O, molecules must be added to the left side. This gives 10 extra hydrogen atoms on that side of the equation. Therefore, 10 hydrogen ions are added to the right side. In basic solution, OH^- ions and water may be used to balance atoms.

$$\overset{-2}{H_2S} + 4H_2O \longrightarrow \overset{+6}{SO_4^{2-}} + 10H^+$$

- **Balance the charge.** Electrons are added to the side having the greater positive net charge. The left side of the equation has no net charge; the right side has a net charge of 8+. For the charges to balance, each side must have the same net charge. Therefore, 8 electrons are added to the product side so that it has no charge and balances with the reactant side of the equation. Notice that the oxidation of sulfur from a state of -2 to $+6$ indicates a loss of 8 electrons.

$$\overset{-2}{H_2S} + 4H_2O \longrightarrow \overset{+6}{SO_4^{2-}} + 10H^+ + 8e^-$$

The oxidation half-reaction is now balanced.

4. **Write the half-reaction for reduction.** In this example, nitrogen is being reduced from a +5 state to a +4 state.

$$\overset{+5}{NO_3^-} \longrightarrow \overset{+4}{NO_2}$$

- **Balance the atoms.** One water, H_2O, molecule must be added to the product side of the reaction to balance the oxygen atoms. Therefore, two hydrogen ions must be added to the reactant side to balance the hydrogen atoms.

$$\overset{+5}{NO_3^-} + 2H^+ \longrightarrow \overset{+4}{NO_2} + H_2O$$

- **Balance the charge.** Electrons are added to the side having the greater positive net charge. The left side of the equation has a net charge of 1+. Therefore, 1 electron must be added to this side to balance the charge.

$$\overset{+5}{NO_3^-} + 2H^+ + e^- \longrightarrow \overset{+4}{NO_2} + H_2O$$

The reduction half-reaction is now balanced.

5. **Conserve charge by adjusting the coefficients in front of the electrons so that the number lost in oxidation equals the number gained in reduction.** Write the ratio of the number of electrons lost to the number of electrons gained.

$$\frac{e^- \text{ lost in oxidation}}{e^- \text{ gained in reduction}} = \frac{8}{1}$$

This ratio is already in its lowest terms. If it were not, it would need to be reduced. Multiply the oxidation half-reaction by 1 (it remains unchanged) and the reduction half-reaction by 8. The number of electrons lost now equals the number of electrons gained.

$$1\left(\overset{-2}{H_2S} + 4H_2O \longrightarrow \overset{+6}{SO_4^{2-}} + 10H^+ + 8e^-\right)$$
$$8\left(\overset{+5}{NO_3^-} + 2H^- + e^- \longrightarrow \overset{+4}{NO_2} + H_2O\right)$$

6. **Combine the half-reactions, and cancel out anything common to both sides of the equation.**

$$\overset{-2}{H_2S} + 4H_2O \longrightarrow \overset{+6}{SO_4^{2-}} + 10H^+ + 8e^-$$
$$\overset{+5}{8NO_3^-} + 16H^+ + 8e^- \longrightarrow \overset{+4}{8NO_2} + 8H_2O$$

$$\overset{+5}{8NO_3^-} + \overset{6}{16H^+} + 8e^- + \overset{-2}{H_2S} + 4H_2O \longrightarrow$$
$$\overset{+4}{8NO_2} + \overset{4}{8H_2O} + \overset{+6}{SO_4^{2-}} + 10H^+ + 8e^-$$

Each side of the above equation has $10H^+$, $8e^-$, and $4H_2O$. These cancel each other out and do not appear in the balanced equation.

$$\overset{+5}{8NO_3^-} + \overset{-2}{H_2S} + 6H^+ \longrightarrow \overset{+4}{8NO_2} + 4H_2O + \overset{+6}{SO_4^{2-}}$$

7. **Combine ions to form the compounds shown in the original formula equation. Check to ensure that all other ions balance.** The NO_3^- ion appeared as nitric acid in the original equation. There are only 6 hydrogen ions to pair with the 8 nitrate ions. Therefore, 2 hydrogen ions must be added to complete this formula. If 2 hydrogen ions are added to the left side of the equation, 2 hydrogen ions must also be added to the right side of the equation.

$$8HNO_3 + H_2S \longrightarrow 8NO_2 + 4H_2O + SO_4^{2-} + 2H^+$$

The sulfate ion appeared as sulfuric acid in the original equation. The hydrogen ions added to the right side are used to complete the formula for sulfuric acid.

$$8HNO_3 + H_2S \longrightarrow 8NO_2 + 4H_2O + H_2SO_4$$

A final check must be made to ensure that all elements are correctly balanced.

FIGURE 2.1

Redox Titration As a $KMnO_4$ solution is titrated into an acidic solution of $FeSO_4$, deep purple MnO_4^- ions are reduced to colorless Mn^{2+} ions. When all Fe^{2+} ions are oxidized, MnO_4^- ions are no longer reduced to colorless Mn^{2+} ions. Thus, the first faint appearance of the MnO_4^- color indicates the end point of the titration.

GO ONLINE

Learn It! Video
HMHScience.com

Solve It! Cards
HMHScience.com

Sample Problem A Write a balanced equation for the reaction shown in Figure 2.1 (on the previous page). A deep purple solution of potassium permanganate is titrated with a colorless solution of iron(II) sulfate and sulfuric acid. The products are iron(III) sulfate, manganese(II) sulfate, potassium sulfate, and water—all of which are colorless.

 SOLVE

1. *Write the formula equation if it is not given in the problem. Then write the ionic equation.*

$$KMnO_4 + FeSO_4 + H_2SO_4 \longrightarrow Fe_2(SO_4)_3 + MnSO_4 + K_2SO_4 + H_2O$$

$$K^+ + MnO_4^- + Fe^{2+} + SO_4^{2-} + 2H^+ + SO_4^{2-} \longrightarrow$$
$$2Fe^{3+} + 3SO_4^{2-} + Mn^{2+} + SO_4^{2-} + 2K^+ + SO_4^{2-} + H_2O$$

2. *Assign oxidation numbers to each element and ion. Delete substances containing an element that does not change oxidation state.*

$$\overset{+1}{K^+} + \overset{+7}{Mn}\overset{-2}{O}_4^- + \overset{+2}{Fe^{2+}} + \overset{+6}{S}\overset{-2}{O}_4^{2-} + \overset{+1}{2H^+} + \overset{+6}{S}\overset{-2}{O}_4^{2-} \longrightarrow$$
$$\overset{+3}{2Fe^{3+}} + \overset{+6}{3S}\overset{-2}{O}_4^{2-} + \overset{+2}{Mn^{2+}} + \overset{+6}{S}\overset{-2}{O}_4^{2-} + \overset{+1}{2K^+} + \overset{+6}{S}\overset{-2}{O}_4^{2-} + \overset{+1}{H_2}\overset{-2}{O}$$

Only ions or molecules whose oxidation numbers change are retained.

$$\overset{+7}{Mn}\overset{-2}{O}_4^- + \overset{+2}{Fe^{2+}} \longrightarrow \overset{+3}{Fe^{3+}} + \overset{+2}{Mn^{2+}}$$

3. *Write the half-reaction for oxidation.* The iron shows the increase in oxidation number. Therefore, it is oxidized.

$$\overset{+2}{Fe^{2+}} \longrightarrow \overset{+3}{Fe^{3+}}$$

• *Balance the mass.* The mass is already balanced.

• *Balance the charge.*

$$\overset{+2}{Fe^{2+}} \longrightarrow \overset{+3}{Fe^{3+}} + e^-$$

4. *Write the half-reaction for reduction.* Manganese shows a change in oxidation number from +7 to +2. It is reduced.

$$\overset{+7}{Mn}O_4^- \longrightarrow \overset{+2}{Mn^{2+}}$$

• *Balance the mass.* Water and hydrogen ions must be added to balance the oxygen atoms in the permanganate ion.

$$\overset{+7}{Mn}O_4^- + 8H^+ \longrightarrow \overset{+2}{Mn^{2+}} + 4H_2O$$

• *Balance the charge.*

$$\overset{+7}{Mn}O_4^- + 8H^+ + 5e^- \longrightarrow \overset{+2}{Mn^{2+}} + 4H_2O$$

5. *Adjust the coefficients to conserve charge.*

$$\frac{e^- \text{ lost in oxidation}}{e^- \text{ gained in reduction}} = \frac{1}{5}$$

$$5(Fe^{2+} \longrightarrow Fe^{3+} + e^-)$$
$$1(MnO_4^- + 8H^+ + 5e^- \longrightarrow Mn^{2+} + 4H_2O)$$

Continued

6. *Combine the half-reactions, and cancel.*

$$5Fe^{2+} \longrightarrow 5Fe^{3+} + 5e^-$$
$$MnO_4^- + 8H^+ + 5e^- \longrightarrow Mn^{2+} + 4H_2O$$
$$\overline{MnO_4^- + 5Fe^{2+} + 8H^+ + \cancel{5e^-} \longrightarrow Mn^{2+} + 5Fe^{3+} + 4H_2O + \cancel{5e^-}}$$

7. *Combine ions to form compounds from the original equation.* The iron(III) product appears in the original equation as $Fe_2(SO_4)_3$. Every iron(III) sulfate molecule requires two iron ions. Therefore, the entire equation must be multiplied by 2 to provide an even number of iron ions.

$$2(5Fe^{2+} + MnO_4^- + 8H^+ \longrightarrow 5Fe^{3+} + Mn^{2+} + 4H_2O)$$
$$10Fe^{2+} + 2MnO_4^- + 16H^+ \longrightarrow 10Fe^{3+} + 2Mn^{2+} + 8H_2O$$

The iron(II), iron(III), manganese(II), and 2 hydrogen ions in the original equation are paired with sulfate ions. Iron(II) sulfate requires 10 sulfate ions, and sulfuric acid requires 8 sulfate ions. To balance the equation, 18 sulfate ions must be added to each side. On the product side, 15 of these ions form iron(III) sulfate, and 2 of them form manganese(II) sulfate. That leaves 1 sulfate ion unaccounted for. The permanganate ion requires the addition of 2 potassium ions to each side. These 2 potassium ions form potassium sulfate on the product side of the reaction.

$$10FeSO_4 + 2KMnO_4 + 8H_2SO_4 \longrightarrow 5Fe_2(SO_4)_3 + 2MnSO_4 + K_2SO_4 + 8H_2O$$

Final inspection shows that atoms and charges are balanced.

Practice   Answers in Appendix E

1. Copper reacts with hot, concentrated sulfuric acid to form copper(II) sulfate, sulfur dioxide, and water. Write and balance the equation for this reaction.
2. Write and balance the equation for the reaction between nitric acid and potassium iodide. The products are potassium nitrate, iodine, nitrogen monoxide, and water.

✓ SECTION 2 FORMATIVE ASSESSMENT

▶ Reviewing Main Ideas

1. What two quantities are conserved in redox equations?

2. Why do we add H^+ and H_2O to some half-reactions and OH^- and H_2O to others?

3. Balance the following redox reaction:
$$Na_2SnO_2 + Bi(OH)_3 \longrightarrow Bi + Na_2SnO_3 + H_2O$$

✓ Critical Thinking

4. RELATING IDEAS When heated, elemental phosphorus, P_4, produces phosphine, PH_3, and phosphoric acid, H_3PO_4. How many grams of phosphine are produced if 56 g P_4 have reacted?

▶ The more active an element is, the better it acts as an oxidizer or reducer.

▶ Some substances can be oxidizers and reducers in the same reaction.

Oxidizing and Reducing Agents

Key Terms
reducing agent
oxidizing agent
disproportionation

A **reducing agent** is a substance that has the potential to cause another substance to be reduced. Reducing agents lose electrons; they attain a more positive oxidation state during an oxidation-reduction reaction. Therefore, the reducing agent is the oxidized substance.

An **oxidizing agent** is a substance that has the potential to cause another substance to be oxidized. Oxidizing agents gain electrons and attain a more negative oxidation state during an oxidation-reduction reaction. The oxidizing agent is the reduced substance. **Figure 3.1** helps clarify the terms describing the oxidation-reduction process.

▶ MAIN IDEA
The more active an element is, the better it acts as an oxidizer or reducer.

✓ **CHECK FOR UNDERSTANDING**
Describe In your own words, describe the relationship between the relative strength of oxidizing and reducing agents and their placement on the activity series table (given in the chapter "Chemical Equations and Reactions").

Different substances can be compared and rated by their relative potential as reducing and oxidizing agents. For example, the order of the elements in the activity series, seen in the chapter on chemical equations and reactions, is related to each element's tendency to lose electrons. Elements in this series lose electrons to the positively charged ions of any element below them in the series. The more active an element is, the greater its tendency to lose electrons and the better a reducing agent it is. The greater the distance is between two elements in the list, the more likely it is that a redox reaction will take place between them. These elements and some other familiar substances are arranged in **Figure 3.2** according to their activity as oxidizing and reducing agents.

FIGURE 3.1

OXIDATION-REDUCTION TERMINOLOGY		
Term	Change in oxidation number	Change in electron population
Oxidation	increases	loss of electrons
Reduction	decreases	gain of electrons
Oxidizing agent	decreases	gains electrons
Reducing agent	increases	loses electrons

The fluorine atom is the most highly electronegative atom. It is also the most active oxidizing agent. Because of its strong attraction for its own electrons, the fluoride ion is the weakest reducing agent. The negative ion of a strong oxidizing agent is a weak reducing agent.

The positive ion of a strong reducing agent is a weak oxidizing agent. As shown in **Figure 3.2,** Li atoms are strong reducing agents because Li is a very active metal. When Li atoms oxidize, they produce Li^+ ions, which are unlikely to reacquire electrons, so Li^+ ions are weak oxidizing agents.

The left column of each pair also shows the relative abilities of these metals to displace other metals from compounds. Zinc, for example, is above copper, so zinc is a more active reducing agent. It displaces copper ions from solutions of copper compounds, as shown in **Figure 3.3.** A copper(II) ion, however, is a more active oxidizing agent than a zinc ion.

Nonmetals and some important ions also are included in the series in **Figure 3.2.** Any reducing agent is oxidized by the oxidizing agents below it. Observe that F_2 displaces Cl^-, Br^-, and I^- ions from their solutions. Cl_2 displaces Br^- and I^- ions, and Br_2 displaces I^- ions. The equation for the displacement of Br^- by Cl_2 is as follows.

$$Cl_2 + 2Br^{-2}(aq) \longrightarrow 2Cl^-(aq) + Br_2$$
$$\overset{-1}{2Br^-} \longrightarrow \overset{0}{Br_2} + 2e^- \qquad \text{(oxidation)}$$
$$\overset{0}{Cl_2} + 2e^- \longrightarrow \overset{-1}{2Cl^-} \qquad \text{(reduction)}$$

In every redox reaction, there is one reducing agent and one oxidizing agent. In the preceding example, Br^- is the reducing agent, and Cl_2 is the oxidizing agent.

FIGURE 3.3

Reduction of Copper by Zinc

Zinc displaces copper ions from a copper(II) sulfate solution. Metallic copper precipitates.

FIGURE 3.2

RELATIVE STRENGTH OF OXIDIZING AND REDUCING AGENTS

Reducing agents	Oxidizing agents
Li	Li^+
K	K^+
Ca	Ca^{2+}
Na	Na^+
Mg	Mg^{2+}
Al	Al^{3+}
Zn	Zn^{2+}
Cr	Cr^{3+}
Fe	Fe^{2+}
Ni	Ni^{2+}
Sn	Sn^{2+}
Pb	Pb^{2+}
H_2	H_3O^+
H_2S	S
Cu	Cu^{2+}
I^-	I_2
MnO_4^{2-}	MnO_4^-
Fe^{2+}	Fe^{3+}
Hg	Hg_2^{2+}
Ag	Ag^+
NO_2^-	NO_3^-
Br^-	Br_2
Mn^{2+}	MnO_2
SO_2	H_2SO_4 (conc.)
Cr^{3+}	$Cr_2O_7^{2-}$
Cl^-	Cl_2
Mn^{2+}	MnO_4^-
F^-	F_2

Increasing strength

Increasing strength

✓ **CRITICAL THINKING**

Analyze Examine **Figure 3.2** closely. Various oxidation states of iron (Fe) appear in both the top and bottom half and left and right columns of the table. What pattern becomes apparent when you compare the oxidation numbers in each case and iron's function as an oxidizing or reducing agent?

QuickLAB • REDOX REACTIONS

PROCEDURE

Record your results in a data table.

1. Put 10 mL of hydrogen peroxide in a test tube. Add a small amount of manganese dioxide (equal to the size of about half a pea). What is the result?

2. Insert a glowing wooden splint into the test tube (see diagram). What is the result? If oxygen is produced, a glowing wooden splint inserted into the test tube will glow brighter.

3. Fill the 250 mL beaker halfway with the copper(II) chloride solution.

4. Cut aluminum foil into 2 cm × 12 cm strips.

5. Add the aluminum strips to the copper(II) chloride solution. Use a glass rod to stir the mixture, and observe for 12 to 15 minutes. What is the result?

DISCUSSION

1. Write balanced equations showing what happened in each of the reactions.

2. Write a conclusion for the two experiments.

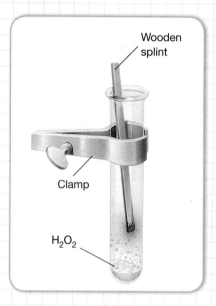

Wooden splint

Clamp

H_2O_2

MATERIALS
- aluminum foil
- beaker, 250 mL
- 1 M copper(II) chloride solution, $CuCl_2$
- 3% hydrogen peroxide
- manganese dioxide
- metric ruler
- scissors
- test-tube clamp
- test tube, 16 × 150 mm
- wooden splint

SAFETY

 Wear safety goggles and an apron.

▶ MAIN IDEA

Some substances can be oxidizers and reducers in the same reaction.

Some substances can be both reduced and oxidized easily. For example, peroxide ions, O_2^{2-}, have a relatively unstable covalent bond between the two oxygen atoms. The electron-dot formula is written as follows.

$$\left[:\ddot{O}:\ddot{O}:\right]^{2-}$$

Each oxygen atom has an oxidation number of −1. The peroxide ion structure represents an intermediate oxidation state between O_2 and O^{2-}. Therefore, the peroxide ion is highly reactive.

Hydrogen peroxide, H_2O_2, is a covalent compound. It decomposes into water and molecular oxygen, as shown in the equation below.

$$2\overset{-1}{H_2O_2} \longrightarrow 2\overset{-2}{H_2O} + \overset{0}{O_2}$$

FIGURE 3.4

Disproportionation in Nature A bombardier beetle can repel large predators such as frogs with a chemical defense mechanism that uses the disproportionation of hydrogen peroxide.

Notice that in this reaction, hydrogen peroxide is both oxidized and reduced. Oxygen atoms that become part of gaseous oxygen molecules are oxidized. The oxidation number of these oxygen atoms increases from −1 to 0. Oxygen atoms that become part of water are reduced. The oxidation number of these oxygen atoms decreases from −1 to −2. **A process in which a substance acts as both an oxidizing agent and a reducing agent is called disproportionation.** A substance that undergoes disproportionation is both *self-oxidizing* and *self-reducing*.

The bombardier beetle defends itself by spraying its enemies with an unpleasant hot chemical mixture, as shown in **Figure 3.4**. The catalyzed disproportionation of hydrogen peroxide produces hot oxygen gas. This gas gives the insect an ability to eject irritating chemicals from its abdomen with explosive force.

✔ SECTION 3 FORMATIVE ASSESSMENT

▶ Reviewing Main Ideas

1. Describe the oxidation and reduction strengths of alkali metals and halogens.

2. Look at the photo. The test tube on the left shows a copper coil placed in a solution of zinc(II) sulfate. The test tube on the right shows a zinc coil placed in a solution of copper(II) sulfate. Both solutions have a similar concentration. Explain why a reaction happens in one test tube and not the other. What is the product of the reaction?

3. Would Cl_2 be reduced by I^-? Explain.

4. In each pair, which is the stronger oxidizing agent: Cu^{2+} or Al^{3+}, I_2 or S, F_2 or Li^+?

5. What is meant by *disproportionation*?

✔ Critical Thinking

6. **ORGANIZING IDEAS** In general, where in the periodic table are the elements found that in elemental form are the strongest oxidizing agents? Explain.

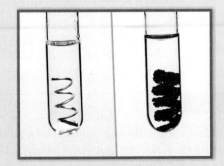

A redox equation must conserve both mass and charge. So to balance a redox equation, you must balance both atoms and charge (electrons). The problem-solving tips and sample below show how to balance an equation for a redox reaction in *basic* solution.

Problem-Solving TIPS

To balance redox equations for reactions in *basic* solution:
- Add OH^- and H_2O to balance oxygen and hydrogen in the redox half-reactions.
- Add OH^- ions to the side of the equation that needs oxygen atoms. Make sure you add enough OH^- ions so that the number of oxygen atoms added is twice the number needed.
- Then, add enough H_2O molecules to the other side of the equation to balance the hydrogen atoms.

Sample Problem

The following unbalanced equation represents a redox reaction that takes place in a basic solution containing KOH. Balance the redox equation.

$$Br_2(l) + KOH(aq) \longrightarrow KBr(aq) + KBrO_3(aq)$$

Write the full ionic equation, assign oxidation numbers, and eliminate species whose oxidation numbers do not change. The result is the following equation:

$$\overset{0}{Br_2} \longrightarrow \overset{-1}{Br^-} + \overset{+5}{BrO_3^-}$$

Divide this equation into half-reactions. Note that Br_2 is the reactant in both half-reactions.

Reduction: $Br_2 \longrightarrow Br^-$ Oxidation: $Br_2 \longrightarrow BrO_3^-$

Add H_2O and OH^- to balance atoms in basic solution. Then, add electrons to balance charge.

Reduction: $Br_2 + 2e^- \longrightarrow 2Br^-$ (no need to add H_2O or OH^-)
Oxidation: $12OH^- + Br_2 \longrightarrow 2BrO_3^- + 6H_2O + 10e^-$

To balance transferred electrons, you must multiply the reduction half-reaction by 5 so that both reactions have $10e^-$.

$$5 \times (Br_2 + 2e^- \longrightarrow 2Br^-) = 5Br_2 + 10e^- \longrightarrow 10Br^-$$

Combining the two half-reactions gives

$$5Br_2 + 12OH^- + Br_2 + 10e^- \longrightarrow 10Br^- + 2BrO_3^- + 6H_2O + 10e^-$$

Combining and canceling common species gives

$$6Br_2 + 12OH^- \longrightarrow 10Br^- + 2BrO_3^- + 6H_2O$$

Returning the potassium ions to the equation gives

$$6Br_2 + 12KOH \longrightarrow 10KBr + 2KBrO_3 + 6H_2O, \text{ or } 3Br_2 + 6KOH \longrightarrow 5KBr + KBrO_3 + 3H_2O$$

Practice

1. Balance the following equation for a redox reaction that takes place in basic solution:
$$MnO_2(s) + NaClO_3(aq) + NaOH(aq) \longrightarrow NaMnO_4(aq) + NaCl(aq) + H_2O(l)$$

2. Balance the following equation for a redox reaction that takes place in basic solution:
$$N_2O(g) + KClO(aq) + KOH(aq) \longrightarrow KCl(aq) + KNO_2(aq) + H_2O(l)$$

BIG IDEA In oxidation-reduction reactions atoms and ions change oxidation states, either by losing electrons (oxidizing) or gaining electrons (reducing).

SECTION 1 **Oxidation and Reduction**

KEY TERMS

- Oxidation numbers are assigned by the set of rules listed in **Figure 1.1**. Oxidation numbers are based on the distribution of electrons in a molecule.

- Oxidation-reduction reactions consist of two half-reactions that must occur simultaneously.

- Oxidation-reduction reactions are identified by examining the changes in the oxidation numbers of atoms in the reactants and products.

- Oxidation involves the loss of electrons, and reduction involves the gain of electrons.

- A species whose oxidation number increases is oxidized. A species whose oxidation number decreases is reduced.

oxidation
oxidized
reduction
reduced
oxidation-reduction reaction
redox reaction
half-reaction

SECTION 2 **Balancing Redox Equations**

- Charge and mass are conserved in a balanced redox equation.

- In the half-reaction method for balancing equations, the atoms and charge of oxidation and reduction equations are balanced separately. Then, they are combined to give a complete balanced equation.

- In a half-reaction, the charge on the reactant side must equal the charge on the product side, but these charges do not need to be zero.

- For the half-reaction method, the atoms in each half-reaction are balanced by adding H^+ ions and H_2O molecules in acidic solutions. If the solution is basic, OH^- ions and H_2O molecules are added to balance the atoms in each half-reaction.

- The number of electrons lost in the oxidation half-reaction must equal the number of electrons gained in the reduction half-reaction. The two half-reactions must be multiplied by appropriate factors to ensure that the same number of electrons are transferred.

SECTION 3 **Oxidizing and Reducing Agents**

KEY TERMS

- The substance that is *reduced* in redox reactions is the *oxidizing agent* because it *acquires* electrons from the substance that is oxidized.

- The substance that is *oxidized* in a redox reaction is the *reducing agent* because it *supplies* the electrons to the substance that is reduced.

- Strong reducing agents are substances that easily give up electrons.

- Disproportionation is a process in which a substance is both an oxidizing agent and a reducing agent.

reducing agent
oxidizing agent
disproportionation

GO ONLINE

⟳ **Interactive** Review   Review Games
HMHScience.com   Concept Maps

SECTION 1

Oxidation and Reduction

▶ **REVIEWING MAIN IDEAS**

1. **a.** Distinguish between the processes of oxidation and reduction.
   b. Write an equation to illustrate each process.

2. Which of the following are redox reactions?
   a. $2Na + Cl_2 \longrightarrow 2NaCl$
   b. $C + O_2 \longrightarrow CO_2$
   c. $2H_2O \longrightarrow 2H_2 + O_2$
   d. $NaCl + AgNO_3 \longrightarrow AgCl + NaNO_3$
   e. $NH_3 + HCl \longrightarrow NH_4^+ + Cl^-$
   f. $2KClO_3 \longrightarrow 2KCl + 3O_2$
   g. $H_2 + Cl_2 \longrightarrow 2HCl$
   h. $H_2SO_4 + 2KOH \longrightarrow K_2SO_4 + 2H_2O$
   i. $Zn + CuSO_4 \longrightarrow ZnSO_4 + Cu$

3. For each oxidation-reduction reaction in the previous question, identify what is oxidized and what is reduced. Can an oxidation-reduction reaction also be another type of reaction?

PRACTICE PROBLEMS

4. Each of the following atom/ion pairs undergoes the oxidation-number change indicated below. For each pair, determine whether oxidation or reduction has occurred and then write the electronic equation indicating the corresponding number of electrons lost or gained.
   a. $K \longrightarrow K^+$ **e.** $H_2 \longrightarrow H^+$
   b. $S \longrightarrow S^{2-}$ **f.** $O_2 \longrightarrow O^{2-}$
   c. $Mg \longrightarrow Mg^{2+}$ **g.** $Fe^{3+} \longrightarrow Fe^{2+}$
   d. $F^- \longrightarrow F_2$ **h.** $Mn^{2+} \longrightarrow MnO_4^-$

5. Identify the following reactions as redox or nonredox:
   a. $2NH_4Cl(aq) + Ca(OH)_2(aq) \longrightarrow$
   $2NH_3(aq) + 2H_2O(l) + CaCl_2(aq)$
   b. $2HNO_3(aq) + 3H_2S(g) \longrightarrow$
   $2NO(g) + 4H_2O(l) + 3S(s)$
   c. $[Be(H_2O)_4]^{2+}(aq) + H_2O(l) \longrightarrow$
   $H_3O^+(aq) + [Be(H_2O)_3OH]^+(aq)$

6. Arrange the following in order of increasing oxidation number of the xenon atom: $CsXeF_8$, Xe, XeF_2, $XeOF_2$, XeO_3, and XeF.

7. Determine the oxidation number of each atom indicated in the following:
   a. H_2 **f.** HNO_3
   b. H_2O **g.** H_2SO_4
   c. Al **h.** $Ca(OH)_2$
   d. MgO **i.** $Fe(NO_3)_2$
   e. Al_2S_3 **j.** O_2

SECTION 2

Balancing Redox Equations

▶ **REVIEWING MAIN IDEAS**

8. Label the following half-reactions as either reduction or oxidation half-reactions.
   a. $H_2S \longrightarrow S + 2H^+ + 2e^-$
   b. $SO_2 + 2H_2O + 4e^- \longrightarrow S + 4OH^-$
   c. $ClO_3^- + 6H^+ + 6e^- \longrightarrow Cl^- + 3H_2O$
   d. $Mn(CN)_6^{4-} \longrightarrow Mn(CN)_6^{3-} + e^-$

9. What are the oxidation states of the elements that changed oxidation states in the half-reactions in the above question?

10. Balance the equation for the following reaction in a basic solution. Give balanced equations for both half-reactions and a balanced equation for the overall reaction.
    $$KMnO_4 + NaIO_3 \longrightarrow MnO_2 + NaIO_4$$

PRACTICE PROBLEMS

11. For each requested step, use the half-reaction method to balance the oxidation-reduction equation below. (Hint: See Sample Problem A.)
    $$K + H_2O \longrightarrow KOH + H_2$$
    a. Write the ionic equation, and assign oxidation numbers to all atoms to determine what is oxidized and what is reduced.
    b. Write the equation for the reduction, and balance it for both atoms and charge.
    c. Write the equation for the oxidation, and balance it for both atoms and charge.
    d. Multiply the coefficients of the oxidation and reduction equations so that the number of electrons lost equals the number of electrons gained. Add the two equations.
    e. Add species as necessary to balance the overall formula equation.

12. Use the method in the previous problem to balance each of the reactions below.

a. $HI + HNO_2 \longrightarrow NO + I_2 + H_2O$

b. $FeCl_3 + H_2S \longrightarrow FeCl_2 + HCl + S$

13. Balance the equation for the reaction in which hot, concentrated sulfuric acid reacts with zinc to form zinc sulfate, hydrogen sulfide, and water.

SECTION 3

Oxidizing and Reducing Agents

▶ **REVIEWING MAIN IDEAS**

14. a. Identify the most active reducing agent among all common elements.

b. Why are all of the elements in its group in the periodic table very active reducing agents?

c. Identify the most active oxidizing agent among the common elements.

15. Use **Figure 3.1** to identify the strongest and weakest reducing agents among the substances listed within each of the following groupings:

a. Ca, Ag, Sn, Cl^-

b. Fe, Hg, Al, Br^-

c. F^-, Pb, Mn^{2+}, Na

16. Use **Figure 3.1** to respond to each of the following:

a. Would Al be oxidized by Ni^{2+}?

b. Would Cu be oxidized by Ag^+?

c. Would Pb be oxidized by Na^+?

d. Would F_2 be reduced by Cl^-?

e. Would Br_2 be reduced by Cl^-?

Mixed Review

▶ **REVIEWING MAIN IDEAS**

17. Identify the following reactions as redox or nonredox:

a. $Mg(s) + ZnCl_2(aq) \longrightarrow Zn(s) + MgCl_2(aq)$

b. $2H_2(g) + OF_2(g) \longrightarrow H_2O(g) + 2HF(g)$

c. $2KI(aq) + Pb(NO_3)_2(aq) \longrightarrow$
$\qquad PbI_2(s) + 2KNO_3(aq)$

d. $CaO(s) + H_2O(l) \longrightarrow Ca(OH)_2(aq)$

e. $3CuCl_2(aq) + 2(NH_4)_3PO_4(aq) \longrightarrow$
$\qquad 6NH_4Cl(aq) + Cu_3(PO_4)_2(s)$

f. $CH_4(g) + 2O_2(g) \longrightarrow CO_2(g) + 2H_2O(g)$

18. Arrange the following in order of decreasing oxidation number of the nitrogen atom: N_2, NH_3, N_2O_4, N_2O, N_2H_4, and NO_3^-.

19. Balance the following redox equations:

a. $SbCl_5 + KI \longrightarrow KCl + I_2 + SbCl_3$

b. $Ca(OH)_2 + NaOH + ClO_2 + C \longrightarrow$
$\qquad NaClO_2 + CaCO_3 + H_2O$

20. Balance the following equations in basic solution:

a. $PbO_2 + KCl \longrightarrow KClO + KPb(OH)_3$

b. $KMnO_4 + KIO_3 \longrightarrow MnO_2 + KIO_4$

c. $K_2MnO_4 \longrightarrow MnO_2 + KMnO_4$

21. Balance the following equations in acidic solution:

a. $MnO_4^- + Cl^- \longrightarrow Mn^{2+} + HClO$

b. $NO_3^- + I_2 \longrightarrow IO_3^- + NO_2$

c. $NO_2^- \longrightarrow NO + NO_3^-$

CRITICAL THINKING

22. Interpreting Graphics Given the activity table below, determine whether a reaction will occur or not. If the reaction will occur, give the products.

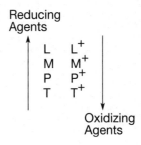

a. L and M^+

b. P and M^+

c. P and T^+

23. Drawing Conclusions A substance has an element in one of its highest possible oxidation states. Is this substance more likely to be an oxidizing agent or a reducing agent? Explain your reasoning.

24. Drawing Conclusions Use **Figure 3.2** to decide if a redox reaction would occur between the two species, and if so, write the balanced equation. Explain your reasoning.

a. Cl_2 and Br_2

b. Sn^{2+} and Zn

25. Drawing Conclusions An element that disproportionates must have at least how many different oxidation states? Explain your reasoning.

26. Several reactions of aluminum are shown in the common reactions section for Group 13 of the *Elements Handbook* (Appendix A). Use these reactions to answer the following:
    a. Which of the five reactions shown are oxidation-reduction reactions? How do you know?
    b. For each redox reaction you listed in item **a,** identify what is oxidized and what is reduced.
    c. Write half-reactions for each equation you listed in item **a.**

27. Aluminum is described in Group 13 of the *Elements Handbook* (Appendix A) as a self-protecting metal. This property of aluminum results from a redox reaction.
    a. Write the redox equation for the oxidation of aluminum.
    b. Write the half-reactions for this reaction, and show the number of electrons transferred.
    c. What problems are associated with the buildup of aluminum oxide on electrical wiring made of aluminum?

28. Oxidizing agents are used in the cleaning industry. Research three different oxidizing agents used in this area, and write a report on the advantages and disadvantages of these compounds.

29. Oxidizing and reducing agents play important roles in biological systems. Research the role of one of these agents in a biological process. Write a report describing the process and the role of oxidation and reduction.

30. Boilers are used to convert water to steam in electric power plants. Dissolved oxygen in the water promotes corrosion of the steel used in boiler parts. Explain how dissolved oxygen is removed from the water in boilers.

31. **Performance** For one day, record situations that show evidence of oxidation-reduction reactions. Identify the reactants and the products, and determine whether there is proof that a chemical reaction has taken place.

Standards-Based Assessment

Record your answers on a separate piece of paper.

MULTIPLE CHOICE

1 In the following chemical reaction, which substance is reduced?

$$Mg + 2HCl \rightarrow MgCl_2 + H_2$$

A Mg

B H^+

C Cl^-

D Mg^{2+}

2 Which of the following equations shows a redox reaction?

A $NaI + KBr \rightarrow NaBr + KI$

B $2HCl + NaOH \rightarrow NaCl + H_2O$

C $Zn + 2HCl \rightarrow ZnCl_2 + H_2$

D $BaCl_2 + Na_2SO_4 \rightarrow BaSO_4 + 2NaCl$

3 The oxidation number of the sulfur atom in the SO_4^{2-} ion is —

A $+2$

B -2

C $+6$

D $+4$

4 In the following reaction, which is the oxidizing agent?

$$AgNO_2 + Cl_2 + 2KOH \rightarrow AgNO_3 + 2KCl + H_2O$$

A $AgNO_2$

B Cl_2

C KOH

D KCl

5 A half-reaction —

A involves a change in the oxidation state of an element

B always contains H_2O molecules

C always contains H^+ ions

D all of the above

6 What are the oxidation states (in increasing order) of the element that undergoes disproportionation in the following reaction?

$$Cl_2 + H_2O \rightarrow HCl + HOCl$$

A $-1, 0, +2$

B $-1, 0, +1$

C $-2, -1, 0$

D none of the above

7 Which of the statements best describes the following reaction?

$$2Pb(NO_3)_2 \rightarrow 2PbO + 4NO_2 + O_2$$

A This reaction is a decomposition reaction and not a redox reaction.

B This reaction is between a strong acid and a strong base.

C This reaction is a precipitation reaction.

D This reaction is a redox reaction in which the nitrogen is reduced and the oxygen is oxidized.

GRIDDED RESPONSE

8 Determine the oxidation number for barium in the superconductor $YBa_2Cu_3O_7$. Yttrium (Y) has an oxidation number of $+3$. Give only an integer oxidation number.

CHAPTER 20
Electrochemistry

BIG IDEA
Electrochemical cells separate oxidation from reduction reactions and either produce or are driven by an electric current.

ONLINE Chemistry
HMHScience.com

ONLINE LABS
- Electric Charge
- Voltaic Cells
- Micro-Voltaic Cells
- Electroplating for Corrosion Protection
- S.T.E.M. Lab Store Charge

GO ONLINE

  Why It Matters Video
HMHScience.com

Electrochemistry

(t) ©Jet Propulsion Laboratory/NASA

Introduction to Electrochemistry

Key Terms

electrochemistry   half-cell   cathode
electrode   anode

Oxidation-reduction reactions involve energy changes. Because these reactions involve electron transfer, the net *release* or net *absorption* of energy can occur in the form of electrical energy rather than as heat. This property allows for a great many practical applications of redox reactions. **The branch of chemistry that deals with electricity-related applications of oxidation-reduction reactions is called electrochemistry.**

▶ MAIN IDEA

Electrochemical cells separate oxidation reactions from reduction reactions.

Oxidation-reduction reactions involve a transfer of electrons. If the two substances are in contact with one another, a transfer of energy as heat accompanies the electron transfer. In **Figure 1.1,** a zinc strip is in contact with a copper(II) sulfate solution. The zinc strip loses electrons to the copper(II) ions in solution. Copper(II) ions accept the electrons and fall out of solution as copper atoms. As electrons are transferred between zinc atoms and copper(II) ions, energy is released as heat, as indicated by the rise in temperature.

FIGURE 1.1

Temperature Change with Electron Transfer Energy as heat given off when electrons are transferred directly from Zn atoms to Cu^{2+} ions causes the temperature of the aqueous $CuSO_4$ solution to rise.

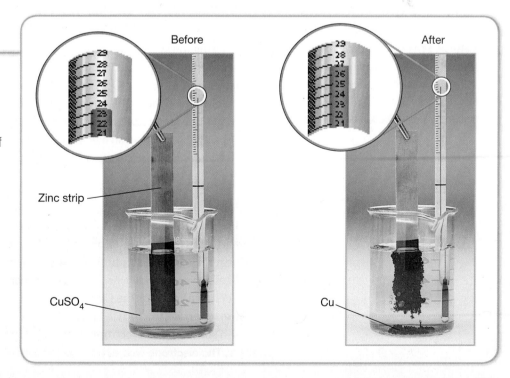

Before   After

Zinc strip

$CuSO_4$ Cu

FIGURE 1.2

Electrochemical Cell

An electrochemical cell consists of two electrodes. Each electrode is in contact with an electrolyte; the electrode and the electrolyte make up a half-cell. The two electrodes are connected by a wire, and a porous barrier separates the two electrolytes.

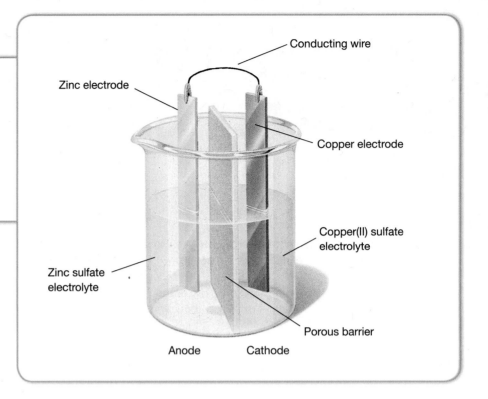

Conducting wire

Zinc electrode

Copper electrode

Copper(II) sulfate electrolyte

Zinc sulfate electrolyte

Porous barrier

Anode   Cathode

CHECK FOR UNDERSTANDING

Identify In an electrochemical cell, at which electrode does oxidation take place? At which electrode does reduction take place?

If, however, we separate the substance that is oxidized from the substance that is reduced, the electron transfer is accompanied by a transfer of electrical energy instead of energy as heat. One means of separating oxidation and reduction half-reactions is with a *porous barrier,* or *salt bridge.* This barrier prevents the metal atoms of one half-reaction from mixing with the ions of the other half-reaction. Ions in the two solutions can move through the porous barrier, which keeps a charge from building up on the electrodes. Electrons can be transferred from one side to the other through an external connecting wire. Electric current moves in a closed-loop path, or *circuit*, so this movement of electrons through the wire is balanced by the movement of ions in solution.

Altering the system in **Figure 1.1** as just described would simply involve separating the copper and zinc, as shown in **Figure 1.2**. The Zn strip is in an aqueous solution of $ZnSO_4$. The Cu strip is in an aqueous solution of $CuSO_4$. Both solutions conduct electricity, because they are electrolytes. **An electrode is a conductor used to establish electrical contact with a nonmetallic part of a circuit, such as an electrolyte.** In **Figure 1.2**, the Zn and Cu strips are electrodes. **A single electrode immersed in a solution of its ions is a half-cell.**

The Half-Cells

In the half-cell that contains the Zn electrode in aqueous $ZnSO_4$ solution, the half-reaction is $Zn(s) \longrightarrow Zn^{2+}(aq) + 2e^-$. The Zn metal loses two electrons to form Zn^{2+} ions in solution, and therefore oxidation is taking place in this half-cell. **The electrode where oxidation occurs is called the anode.** In the half-cell that contains the Cu electrode in aqueous $CuSO_4$ solution, the half-reaction is $Cu^{2+}(aq) + 2e^- \longrightarrow Cu(s)$. In this half-reaction, the Cu^{2+} ions in solution gain electrons to become Cu solid; that is, reduction is taking place. **The electrode where reduction occurs is called the cathode.**

The Complete Cell

Recall that oxidation cannot occur separately from reduction. Both must occur in an electrochemical reaction. The two half-cells taken together make an electrochemical cell. In the Zn/Cu electrochemical cell, the electrons move from the Zn electrode through the wire and down the Cu electrode to the Cu^{2+} ions at the electrode-solution interface. The Cu^{2+} ions are reduced to solid Cu, and the resulting Cu atoms attach themselves to the surface of the Cu electrode. For this reaction, a charge is carried through the barrier by a combination of $Zn^{2+}(aq)$ ions moving from the anode to the cathode and the $SO_4^{2-}(aq)$ ions moving from the cathode to the anode.

An electrochemical cell may be represented by the following notation:

anode electrode |anode solution ||cathode solution | cathode electrode

The double line represents the salt bridge, or porous barrier, between the two half-cells. For the present cell, the cell notation is

$$Zn(s)\,|\,Zn^{2+}(aq)\,||\,Cu^{2+}(aq)\,|\,Cu(s)$$

The electrochemical reaction can be found by adding the anode half-reaction to the cathode half-reaction. This overall (or net) reaction is the following redox reaction:

$$Zn(s) + Cu^{2+}(aq) \longrightarrow Zn^{2+}(aq) + Cu(s)$$

Although the two half-reactions occur at the same time, they occur at different places in the cell. Thus, for the reaction to proceed, electrons must pass through the wire that connects the two half-cells.

An electrochemical cell that consists of the Zn and Cu reaction described above is called the *Daniell cell*, named for the English chemist John Frederic Daniell. The Daniell cell can generate enough electricity to light up the light bulb shown in **Figure 1.3.** In electrochemical cells, either a chemical reaction produces electrical energy, or an electric current produces a chemical change.

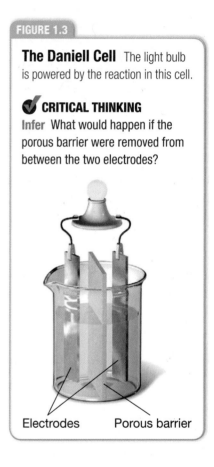

FIGURE 1.3

The Daniell Cell The light bulb is powered by the reaction in this cell.

✓ **CRITICAL THINKING**
Infer What would happen if the porous barrier were removed from between the two electrodes?

Electrodes   Porous barrier

SECTION 1 FORMATIVE ASSESSMENT

▶ **Reviewing Main Ideas**

1. Why is the use of a salt bridge, or porous barrier, necessary in an electrochemical cell?

2. Given the $Cu^{2+}(aq)\,|\,Cu(s)$ and $Mg^{2+}(aq)\,|\,Mg(s)$ half-reactions, where $Cu^{2+}(aq)\,|\,Cu(s)$ is the cathode reaction,
   a. write the overall reaction.
   b. write the cell notation.

3. Write the half-reaction in which $I^-(aq)$ changes to $I_2(s)$. Would this reaction occur at the anode or cathode?

✓ **Critical Thinking**

4. **RELATING IDEAS** Is the net chemical result of an electrochemical cell a redox reaction? Explain your answer.

Batteries and fuel cells are two types of voltaic cells.

Exposure to water and oxygen causes iron to corrode.

The electric potential of a voltaic cell depends on the strengths of the oxidizing and reducing agents.

Voltaic Cells

Key Terms

voltaic cell

reduction potential

electrode potential

standard electrode potential

Voltaic cells use spontaneous oxidation-reduction reactions to convert chemical energy into electrical energy. Voltaic cells are also called galvanic cells. The most common application of voltaic cells is in batteries.

▶ MAIN IDEA

Batteries and fuel cells are two types of voltaic cells.

Figure 2.1 shows an example of a voltaic cell: the Zn || Cu electrochemical cell discussed in the previous section.

Electrons given up at the anode pass along the external connecting wire to the cathode. The movement of electrons through the wire must be balanced by the movement of ions in the solution. Thus, in **Figure 2.1,** sulfate ions in the $CuSO_4$ solution can move through the barrier into the $ZnSO_4$ solution.

The dry cells pictured in **Figure 2.2** are common sources of electrical energy. Like the wet cell previously described, dry cells are voltaic cells. The three most common types of dry cells are the zinc-carbon battery, the alkaline battery, and the mercury battery. They differ in the substances being oxidized and reduced.

FIGURE 2.1

Voltaic Cell In a voltaic cell, electrons spontaneously flow from anode to cathode. The copper strip gains mass as copper ions become copper atoms. The zinc strip loses mass as the zinc atoms become zinc ions.

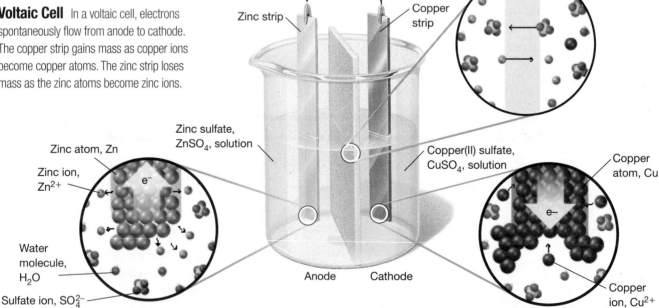

Zinc strip

Copper strip

Porous barrier

Zinc atom, Zn

Zinc ion, Zn^{2+}

Water molecule, H_2O

Sulfate ion, SO_4^{2-}

Zinc sulfate, $ZnSO_4$, solution

Copper(II) sulfate, $CuSO_4$, solution

Copper atom, Cu

Copper ion, Cu^{2+}

Anode   Cathode

Zinc atoms losing two electrons to become ions

Copper(II) ions gaining two electrons to become atoms

Zinc-Carbon Dry Cells

Batteries such as those used in flashlights are zinc-carbon dry cells. These cells consist of a zinc container, which serves as the anode, filled with a moist paste of MnO_2, carbon black, NH_4Cl, and $ZnCl_2$, as illustrated in **Figure 2.3a.** When the external circuit is closed, zinc atoms are oxidized at the negative electrode, or anode.

$$\overset{0}{Zn}(s) \longrightarrow \overset{+2}{Zn^{2+}}(aq) + 2e^-$$

Electrons move across the circuit and reenter the cell through the carbon rod. The carbon rod is the cathode or positive electrode. Here MnO_2 is reduced in the presence of H_2O according to the following half-reaction.

$$2\overset{+4}{Mn}O_2(s) + H_2O(l) + 2e^- \longrightarrow \overset{+3}{Mn_2}O_3(s) + 2OH^-(aq)$$

Alkaline Batteries

The batteries found in a television remote or other small electronic device are frequently alkaline dry cells. These cells do not have a carbon rod cathode, as in the zinc-carbon cell. The absence of the carbon rod allows them to be smaller. **Figure 2.3b** shows a model of an alkaline battery. This cell uses a paste of Zn metal and potassium hydroxide instead of a solid metal anode. The half-reaction at the anode is as follows.

$$\overset{0}{Zn}(s) + 2OH^-(aq) \longrightarrow \overset{+2}{Zn}(OH)_2(s) + 2e^-$$

The reduction half-reaction, the reaction at the cathode, is exactly the same as that for the zinc-carbon dry cell.

FIGURE 2.2

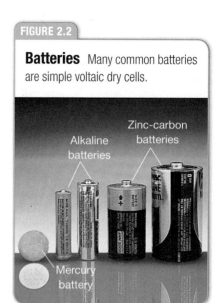

Batteries Many common batteries are simple voltaic dry cells.

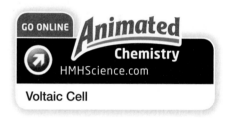

GO ONLINE *Animated* **Chemistry** HMHScience.com

Voltaic Cell

FIGURE 2.3

Zinc and Alkaline Dry Cells

✓ **CRITICAL THINKING**

Distinguish What is the difference between a zinc-carbon dry cell and an alkaline battery?

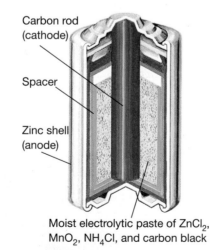

Carbon rod (cathode)

Spacer

Zinc shell (anode)

Moist electrolytic paste of $ZnCl_2$, MnO_2, NH_4Cl, and carbon black

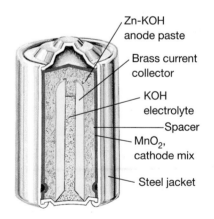

Zn-KOH anode paste

Brass current collector

KOH electrolyte

Spacer

MnO_2, cathode mix

Steel jacket

(a) Zinc Dry Cell
In a zinc dry cell, zinc is oxidized to Zn^{2+} at the anode, and manganese(IV) is reduced to manganese(III) at the cathode.

(b) Alkaline Dry Cell
KOH makes the electrolyte paste in this battery basic. Thus, it is called an alkaline dry cell.

FIGURE 2.4

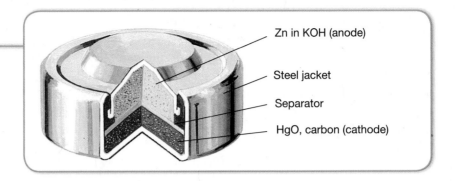

Mercury Batteries It is important that mercury batteries be recycled and not just discarded, because mercury is a poisonous substance.

Mercury Batteries

The tiny batteries found in hearing aids, calculators, and camera flashes are mercury batteries, as shown in **Figure 2.4.** The anode half-reaction is identical to that found in the alkaline dry cell. However, the cathode, or reduction, half-reaction is different. The cathode half-reaction is described by the following equation.

$$\overset{+2}{HgO}(s) + H_2O(l) + 2e^- \longrightarrow \overset{0}{Hg}(l) + 2OH^-(aq)$$

Fuel Cells

A fuel cell is a voltaic cell in which the reactants are being continuously supplied and the products are being continuously removed. Therefore, unlike a battery, a fuel cell could, in principle, work forever, changing chemical energy into electrical energy.

Fuel cells based on the reactions listed below and shown in **Figure 2.5** are used in the United States space program.

$$\text{Cathode: } O_2(g) + 2H_2O(l) + 4e^- \longrightarrow 4OH^-(aq)$$

$$\text{Anode: } 2H_2(g) + 4OH^-(aq) \longrightarrow 4e^- + 4H_2O(l)$$

$$\text{Net reaction: } 2H_2 + O_2 \longrightarrow 2H_2O$$

Fuel cells are very efficient and have very low emissions.

FIGURE 2.5

Fuel Cells The reactions in this fuel cell take place at carbon electrodes that contain metal catalysts. The water formed is removed as a gas.

 CRITICAL THINKING

Analyze Why would a fuel cell have less of an impact on the environment than other types of cells?

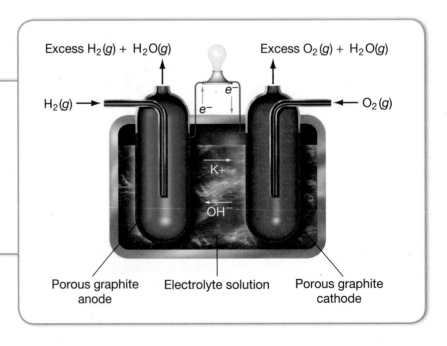

MAIN IDEA
Exposure to water and oxygen causes iron to corrode.

Corrosion is an electrochemical process that has a large economic impact. Approximately 20% of all the iron and steel produced is used to repair or replace corroded structures. One of the metals most commonly affected by corrosion is iron. Rust, hydrated iron(III) oxide, forms by the following overall reaction.

$$4Fe(s) + 3O_2(g) + xH_2O(l) \longrightarrow 2Fe_2O_3 \bullet xH_2O(s)$$

The amount of hydration of the iron oxide, noted by the coefficient x in the equation above, varies and affects the color of the rust formed.

The mechanism for the corrosion of iron contains the following electrochemical reactions.

$$\text{Anode: } Fe(s) \longrightarrow Fe^{2+}(aq) + 2e^-$$

$$\text{Cathode: } O_2(g) + 2H_2O(l) + 4e^- \longrightarrow 4OH^-(aq)$$

The anode and cathode reactions occur at different regions of the metal surface. The electric circuit is completed by electron flow through the metal itself, which acts like the wire in an electrochemical cell. The water on the surface of the metal serves as the salt bridge. Thus, for corrosion to occur, water and oxygen must be present with the iron.

As shown in **Figure 2.6**, when the iron is exposed to water and oxygen, such as in spots where paint is chipped, the iron metal at the anodic site is oxidized to Fe^{2+} ions. The electrons released at this site travel along the metal (like the wire of a cell) to the cathodic region, where oxygen is reduced. The Fe^{2+} ions travel along the moisture toward the cathodic regions. At the cathode, the Fe^{2+} ions are further oxidized to Fe^{3+} ions and form rust, which is hydrated iron oxide, $Fe_2O_3 \bullet xH_2O$.

$$2Fe^{2+}(aq) + (3 + x)H_2O(l) \longrightarrow Fe_2O_3 \bullet xH_2O(s) + 6H^+(aq) + 2e^-$$

✔ **CHECK FOR UNDERSTANDING**
Extend Express the process of rusting in electrochemical-cell notation.

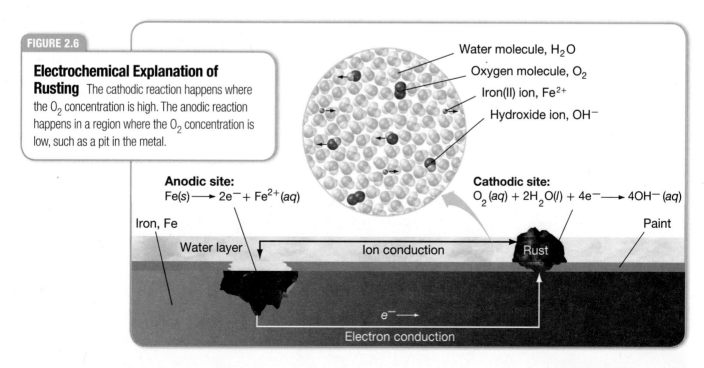

FIGURE 2.6

Electrochemical Explanation of Rusting The cathodic reaction happens where the O_2 concentration is high. The anodic reaction happens in a region where the O_2 concentration is low, such as a pit in the metal.

Water molecule, H_2O
Oxygen molecule, O_2
Iron(II) ion, Fe^{2+}
Hydroxide ion, OH^-

Anodic site:
$Fe(s) \longrightarrow 2e^- + Fe^{2+}(aq)$

Iron, Fe

Water layer

Ion conduction

Cathodic site:
$O_2(aq) + 2H_2O(l) + 4e^- \longrightarrow 4OH^-(aq)$

Paint

Rust

$e^- \longrightarrow$

Electron conduction

FIGURE 2.7

Sacrificial Anode The Alaskan pipeline is cathodically protected by a parallel zinc cable.

Preventing Corrosion

How can corrosion be prevented? One way is to paint the metal to protect it. Another way, which makes use of the electrochemical properties of metals, is to coat steel with zinc in a process called *galvanizing*. Zinc is more easily oxidized than iron; therefore, zinc will react before the iron is oxidized. This is called *cathodic protection*, and the more easily oxidized metal used is called a *sacrificial anode*.

The Alaskan oil pipeline, shown in **Figure 2.7,** is an example of steel that is cathodically protected. However, instead of coating, zinc is connected to the pipe by a wire. The zinc will oxidize before the iron in the steel does. As the zinc anode corrodes, it gives electrons to the cathode, the steel, and as the zinc anode does so, it prevents the steel from corroding. As the zinc reacts, it needs to be replaced. As long as zinc metal that is able to corrode is present, the steel will be protected from corrosion.

▶ MAIN IDEA

The electric potential of a voltaic cell depends on the strengths of the oxidizing and reducing agents.

In a voltaic cell, the oxidizing agent at the cathode pulls the electrons through the wire away from the reducing agent at the anode. The "pull," or driving force on the electrons, is called the *electric potential*. Electric potential, or voltage, is expressed in units of volts (V), which is the potential energy per unit charge. Current is the movement of the electrons and is expressed in units of amperes, or amps (A).

Electrical potential is analogous to gravitational potential. Just as water flows from a position of higher gravitational potential to a position of lower gravitational potential, electrons flow from higher electrical potential to lower electrical potential.

Electrode Potentials

Reconsider the voltaic cell shown in **Figure 2.1.** There are two electrodes, Zn and Cu. These two metals each have different tendencies for accepting electrons. **This tendency for the half-reaction of either copper or zinc to occur as a reduction half-reaction in an electrochemical cell can be quantified as a reduction potential.** There are two half-cells in **Figure 2.1:** a strip of zinc placed in a solution of $ZnSO_4$ and a strip of copper placed in a solution of $CuSO_4$. **The difference in potential between an electrode and its solution is known as electrode potential.** When these two half-cells are connected and the reaction begins, a difference in potential is observed between the electrodes. This potential difference, or voltage, is proportional to the energy required to move a certain electric charge between the electrodes. A voltmeter connected across the Zn ‖ Cu voltaic cell measures a potential difference of about 1.10 V when the solution concentrations of Zn^{2+} and Cu^{2+} ions are each 1 M.

The potential difference measured across the complete voltaic cell is easily measured and equals the sum of the electrode potentials for the two half-reactions. Individual electrode potential cannot be measured directly, because there can be no transfer of electrons unless both the anode and the cathode are connected to form a complete circuit. A relative value for the potential of a half-reaction can be determined by connecting it to a standard half-cell as a reference. This standard half-cell, shown in **Figure 2.8**, is called a standard hydrogen electrode, or SHE. It consists of a platinum electrode dipped into a 1.00 M acid solution surrounded by hydrogen gas at 1 atm pressure and 25°C. Other electrodes are ranked according to their ability to reduce hydrogen in the SHE.

The anodic reaction for the standard hydrogen electrode is described by the forward half-reaction in the following equilibrium equation.

$$\overset{0}{H_2}(g) \rightleftharpoons 2\overset{+1}{H^+}(aq) + 2e^-$$

The cathodic half-reaction is the reverse. An arbitrary potential of 0.00 V is assigned to both of these half-reactions. **The potential of a half-cell under standard conditions measured relative to the standard hydrogen electrode is a standard electrode potential, E^0.** Electrode potentials are expressed as *potentials for reduction*, which provide a reliable indication of the tendency of a substance to be reduced. **Figure 2.9** shows how the SHE is used to find the electrode potentials of the zinc and copper half-cells. Half-reactions for some common electrodes and their standard electrode potentials are listed in **Figure 2.10** on the next page.

Effective oxidizing agents, such as Cu^{2+} and F_2, have positive E^0 values. Half-reactions with negative reduction potentials prefer oxidation over reduction. Effective reducing agents, such as Li and Zn, have negative E^0 values, indicating that the metal or other electrode is more willing to give up electrons than hydrogen.

When a half-reaction is written as an oxidation reaction, the sign of its electrode potential is reversed, as shown for the half-reactions for zinc.

$$Zn^{2+} + 2e^- \longrightarrow Zn \qquad E^0 = -0.76\text{ V}$$
$$Zn \longrightarrow Zn^{2+} + 2e^- \qquad E^0 = +0.76\text{ V}$$

The potential difference across the zinc/hydrogen cell is -0.76 V, so zinc is considered to have an electrode potential of -0.76. The negative number indicates that electrons flow from the zinc electrode, where zinc is oxidized, to the hydrogen electrode, reducing aqueous hydrogen ions.

FIGURE 2.8

Standard Hydrogen Electrode (SHE) A hydrogen electrode is the standard reference electrode for measuring electrode potentials. The electrode surface in contact with the solution is actually a layer of hydrogen adsorbed onto the surface of the platinum.

✔ **CRITICAL THINKING**

Evaluate What is the advantage of using a standard electrode compared to all other electrodes?

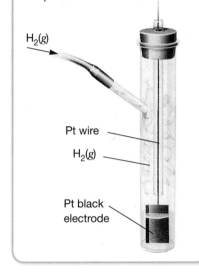

$H_2(g)$

Pt wire

$H_2(g)$

Pt black electrode

FIGURE 2.9

Finding Electrode Potentials
The electrode potentials of zinc and copper half-cells are measured by coupling them with a standard hydrogen electrode.

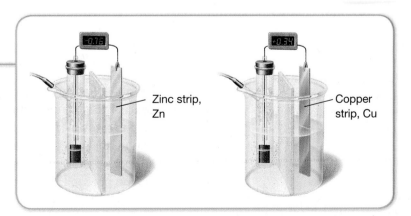

Zinc strip, Zn

Copper strip, Cu

FIGURE 2.10

STANDARD REDUCTION POTENTIALS

Half-cell reaction	Standard electrode potential, E^0 (in volts)	Half-cell reaction	Standard electrode potential, E^0 (in volts)
$F_2 + 2e^- \rightleftharpoons 2F^-$	+2.87	$Fe^{3+} + 3e^- \rightleftharpoons Fe$	−0.04
$MnO_4^- + 8H^+ + 5e^- \rightleftharpoons Mn^{2+} + 4H_2O$	+1.49	$Pb^{2+} + 2e^- \rightleftharpoons Pb$	−0.13
$Au^{3+} + 3e^- \rightleftharpoons Au$	+1.42	$Sn^{2+} + 2e^- \rightleftharpoons Sn$	−0.14
$Cl_2 + 2e^- \rightleftharpoons 2Cl^-$	+1.36	$Ni^{2+} + 2e^- \rightleftharpoons Ni$	−0.23
$Cr_2O_7^{2-} + 14H^+ + 6e^- \rightleftharpoons 2Cr^{3+} + 7H_2O$	+1.33	$Co^{2+} + 2e^- \rightleftharpoons Co$	−0.28
$MnO_2 + 4H^+ + 2e^- \rightleftharpoons Mn^{2+} + 2H_2O$	+1.21	$Cd^{2+} + 2e^- \rightleftharpoons Cd$	−0.40
$Br_2 + 2e^- \rightleftharpoons 2Br^-$	+1.07	$Fe^{2+} + 2e^- \rightleftharpoons Fe$	−0.41
$Hg^{2+} + 2e^- \rightleftharpoons Hg$	+0.85	$S + 2e^- \rightleftharpoons S^{2-}$	−0.51
$Ag^+ + e^- \rightleftharpoons Ag$	+0.80	$Cr^{3+} + 3e^- \rightleftharpoons Cr$	−0.74
$Hg_2^{2+} + 2e^- \rightleftharpoons 2Hg$	+0.80	$Zn^{2+} + 2e^- \rightleftharpoons Zn$	−0.76
$Fe^{3+} + e^- \rightleftharpoons Fe^{2+}$	+0.77	$Al^{3+} + 3e^- \rightleftharpoons Al$	−1.66
$MnO_4^- + e^- \rightleftharpoons MnO_4^{2-}$	+0.56	$Mg^{2+} + 2e^- \rightleftharpoons Mg$	−2.37
$I_2 + 2e^- \rightleftharpoons 2I^-$	+0.54	$Na^+ + e^- \rightleftharpoons Na$	−2.71
$Cu^{2+} + 2e^- \rightleftharpoons Cu$	+0.34	$Ca^{2+} + 2e^- \rightleftharpoons Ca$	−2.76
$Cu^{2+} + e^- \rightleftharpoons Cu^+$	+0.16	$Ba^{2+} + 2e^- \rightleftharpoons Ba$	−2.90
$S + 2H^+(aq) + 2e^- \rightleftharpoons H_2S(aq)$	+0.14	$K^+ + e^- \rightleftharpoons K$	−2.93
$2H^+(aq) + 2e^- \rightleftharpoons H_2$	0.00	$Li^+ + e^- \rightleftharpoons Li$	−3.04

A copper half-cell coupled with the standard hydrogen electrode gives a potential difference measurement of +0.34 V. This positive number indicates that $Cu^{2+}(aq)$ ions are more readily reduced than $H^+(aq)$ ions.

Standard electrode potentials can be used to predict if a redox reaction will occur spontaneously. A spontaneous reaction will have a positive value for E^0_{cell}, which is calculated using the following equation.

$$E^0_{cell} = E^0_{cathode} - E^0_{anode}$$

✔ **CHECK FOR UNDERSTANDING**

Compare How is subtracting the value for the half-cell reaction at the anode the same as reversing the reaction?

The half-reaction that has the more negative standard reduction potential will be the anode. Oxidation occurs at the anode, so the anode half-cell reaction will be the reverse of the reduction reaction found in **Figure 2.10**. Thus, the total potential of a cell is calculated by *subtracting* the standard reduction potential for the reaction at the anode (E^0_{anode}) from the standard reduction potential for the reaction at the cathode ($E^0_{cathode}$).

Calculating Cell Potentials

Sample Problem A Write the overall cell reaction, and calculate the cell potential for a voltaic cell consisting of the following half-cells: an iron (Fe) electrode in a solution of $Fe(NO_3)_3$ and a silver (Ag) electrode in a solution of $AgNO_3$.

① ANALYZE

Given: A half-cell consists of Fe(s) with $Fe(NO_3)_3(aq)$, and a second half-cell consists of Ag(s) with $AgNO_3(aq)$.

Unknown: E^0_{cell}

② PLAN

1. Look up E^0 for each half-reaction (written as reductions) in **Figure 2.10**.

$Fe^{3+}(aq) + 3e^- \longrightarrow Fe(s)$ $E^0 = -0.04$ V $Ag^+(aq) + e^- \longrightarrow Ag(s)$
$E^0 = +0.80$ V

2. Determine the cathode and anode.

Fe in $Fe(NO_3)_3$ is the anode because it has a lower reduction potential than Ag. Ag in $Ag(NO_3)$ is therefore the cathode.

③ SOLVE

1. Determine the overall cell reaction. Multiply the Ag half-reaction by 3 so that the number of electrons lost in that half-reaction equals the number of electrons gained in the oxidation of iron. Reverse the iron half-reaction to be an oxidation half-reaction.

$$3Ag^+(aq) + Fe(s) \longrightarrow 3Ag(s) + Fe^{3+}(aq)$$

2. Calculate the cell potential by $E^0_{cell} = E^0_{cathode} - E^0_{anode}$. Note that when a half-reaction is multiplied by a constant, the E^0 value is not multiplied by that constant but remains the same.

$$E^0_{cell} = E^0_{cathode} - E^0_{anode} = +0.80 \text{ V} - (-0.04 \text{ V}) = +0.84 \text{ V}$$

④ CHECK YOUR WORK

The calculated value for E^0_{cell} is positive, which confirms that it is a voltaic cell, as the problem states.

Practice   Answers in Appendix E

1. For each pair of half-cells, determine the overall electrochemical reaction that proceeds spontaneously and the E^0 value.
   a. $Cr_2O_7^{2-}/Cr^{3+}$ and Ni^{2+}/Ni
   b. SHE and Fe^{2+}/Fe^{3+}

✓ SECTION 2 FORMATIVE ASSESSMENT

▶ Reviewing Main Ideas

1. What is a voltaic cell?

2. What is electrode potential, and how is it used to calculate information about an electrochemical cell?

3. Given the Na^+/Na and K^+/K half-cells, determine the overall electrochemical reaction that proceeds spontaneously and the E^0 value.

4. Given the MnO_2/Mn^{2+} and Cr^{3+}/Cr half-cells, determine the overall electrochemical reaction that occurs spontaneously and the E^0 value.

✓ Critical Thinking

5. **EVALUATING IDEAS** A sacrificial anode is allowed to corrode. Why is the use of a sacrificial anode a way to prevent corrosion?

Advances in Battery Technology

S.T.E.M.

You have a new smartphone or short-range wireless earphones, and you want them to keep operating hour after hour. But you also want those devices to be small and lightweight. How are you going to keep them operating, without using a battery possibly bigger and heavier than the device itself?

The cells found in newer devices use lithium ions and carbon as the active materials, enabling the batteries to be compact and lightweight.

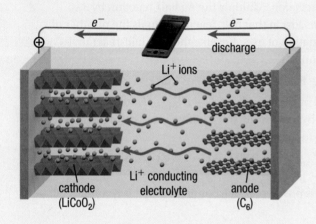

Lithium-ion batteries have a long shelf life, continue operating through many charge-discharge cycles, can be manufactured in many configurations, and contain fewer toxic metals than most other batteries. The basic concept of the lithium-ion battery was developed decades ago, but the technology is constantly being improved.

The safety of lithium-ion batteries has been an issue due to the high flammability of their electrolyte, a lithium salt in an organic solvent. These batteries also have a tendency to produce short circuits as the cells are charged and discharged through many cycles or if the cells become damaged. Today's lithium-ion batteries are not as dangerous as the older, metal-based designs, but blunt force can still cause them to short-circuit, disintegrate, or release harmful gas. Failures are rare, but the results can be dramatic—a pierced battery pack once caused a battery-powered car to catch fire. Lithium-ion battery packs in laptop or tablet computers occasionally develop short circuits and overheat.

A recently developed material may help prevent overheating in batteries. A quickly reversible TRPS (thermoresponsive polymer switching) material could be added to batteries to prevent thermal runaway. The TRPS material consists of electrochemically stable graphene-covered spikelike nickel nanoparticles in a polymer matrix with a high thermal expansion coefficient. The polymer composite films have high electrical conductivity: up to $50\,S\,cm^{-1}$ at room temperature. When the material reaches the transition temperature, its conductivity decreases within one second by seven to eight orders of magnitude. It returns again to normal once the temperature falls. This approach results in 10^3–10^4 times greater sensitivity to temperature changes than previous switching devices.

Along with a concern for safety, chemists and engineers have further challenges, including developing ways to manufacture the millions of cells needed for new devices.

Questions

1. Seemingly minor changes in the chemical technology of lithium-ion batteries are being made to improve their lifetime, safety, fast-charging capability, energy density, and other features. What other features of these batteries could be improved? Explain how these improvements might expand their usefulness in products people use every day.

2. Consider how a longer-lasting battery would affect all mobile devices (laptops, phones, music players, and so on). There is a large industry built around the manufacture and sale of charging accessories, such as special cases for phones that can also act as a charger. How would improvements in battery life and flammability affect the sales of these products?

Electrolytic Cells

Main Ideas

▶ Nonspontaneous redox reactions occur in electrolytic cells.

▶ Electrolysis uses electrical energy to cause a nonspontaneous chemical reaction to occur.

Key Terms

electrolytic cell   electroplating   electrolysis

Some oxidation-reduction reactions do not occur spontaneously but can be driven by electrical energy. **If electrical energy is required to produce a redox reaction and bring about a chemical change in an electrochemical cell, it is an electrolytic cell.** Most commercial uses of redox reactions make use of electrolytic cells.

▶ **MAIN IDEA**

Nonspontaneous redox reactions occur in electrolytic cells.

A comparison of electrolytic and voltaic cells can be seen in **Figure 3.1.** The voltaic cell shown has a copper cathode and a zinc anode. If a battery is connected so that the positive terminal contacts the copper electrode and the negative terminal contacts the zinc electrode, the electrons move in the opposite direction. The battery forces the cell to reverse its reaction; the zinc electrode becomes the cathode, and the copper electrode becomes the anode. The half-reaction at the anode, in which copper metal is oxidized, can be written as follows:

$$\overset{0}{\text{Cu}} \longrightarrow \overset{+2}{\text{Cu}^{2+}} + 2e^-$$

The reduction half-reaction of zinc at the cathode is written as follows:

$$\overset{+2}{\text{Zn}^{2+}} + 2e^- \longrightarrow \overset{0}{\text{Zn}}$$

FIGURE 3.1

Voltaic versus Electrolytic Cells

The direction in which the electrons move reverses if a voltaic cell is connected to a direct-current source to become an electrolytic cell.

✓ **CRITICAL THINKING**

Analyze Can any voltaic cell become an electrolytic cell?

Voltaic Cell

Copper strip

Zinc strip

Zinc sulfate, ZnSO$_4$, solution

Copper(II) sulfate, CuSO$_4$, solution

Anode   Cathode

Electrolytic Cell

Cathode   Anode

There are two main differences between voltaic and electrolytic cells.

1. Electrolytic cells are connected to a battery or other direct-current source. A voltaic cell is a source of electrical energy.

2. In an electrolytic cell, electrical energy from an external source causes *nonspontaneous* redox reactions. In a voltaic cell, *spontaneous* redox reactions produce electricity. In an electrolytic cell, electrical energy turns to chemical energy; in a voltaic cell, the reverse occurs.

✓ **CHECK FOR UNDERSTANDING**
List State the two important differences between a voltaic and an electrolytic cell.

Electroplating

An electrolytic process in which a metal ion is reduced and deposited as solid metal on a surface is called **electroplating.** An electroplating cell contains a solution of a salt of the plating metal, an object to be plated (the cathode), and a piece of the plating metal (the anode). A silver-plating cell contains a solution of a soluble silver salt and a silver anode. The cathode is the object to be plated. The silver anode is connected to the positive electrode of a battery or to some other source of direct current. The object to be plated is connected to the negative electrode.

Figure 3.2 shows silver being electroplated onto a bracelet. Silver ions are reduced at the cathode according to the following half-reaction and deposited as metallic silver when electrons flow through the circuit.

$$\overset{+1}{Ag^+} + e^- \longrightarrow \overset{0}{Ag}$$

At the anode, metallic silver is oxidized by the following half-reaction.

$$\overset{0}{Ag} \longrightarrow \overset{+1}{Ag^+} + e^-$$

In effect, silver is transferred from the anode to the cathode of the cell.

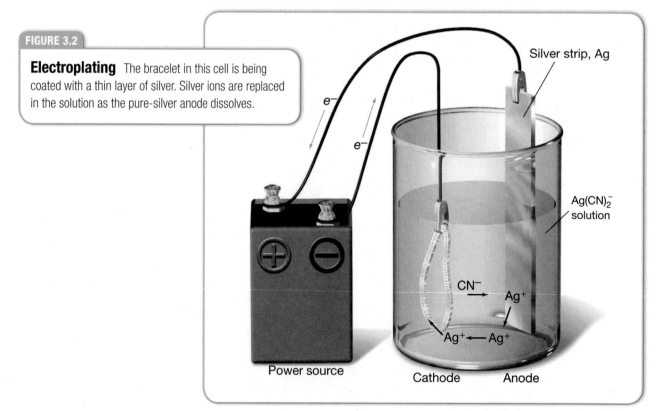

FIGURE 3.2

Electroplating The bracelet in this cell is being coated with a thin layer of silver. Silver ions are replaced in the solution as the pure-silver anode dissolves.

Silver strip, Ag

e^-

e^-

$Ag(CN)_2^-$ solution

CN^-

Ag^+

$Ag^+ \leftarrow Ag^+$

Power source

Cathode

Anode

Rechargeable Cells

A rechargeable cell combines the oxidation-reduction chemistry of both voltaic cells and electrolytic cells. When a rechargeable cell converts chemical energy to electrical energy, it operates as a voltaic cell. But when the cell is recharged, it operates as an electrolytic cell, converting electrical energy to chemical energy.

The standard 12 V automobile battery, shown in **Figure 3.3,** is a set of six rechargeable cells. The anode in each cell is lead submerged in a solution of H_2SO_4. The anode half-reaction is described below.

$$Pb(s) + SO_4^{2-}(aq) \longrightarrow PbSO_4(s) + 2e^-$$

At the cathode, PbO_2 is reduced according to the following equation.

$$PbO_2(s) + 4H^+(aq) + SO_4^{2-}(aq) + 2e^- \longrightarrow PbSO_4(s) + 2H_2O(l)$$

The net oxidation-reduction reaction for the discharge cycle is:

$$Pb(s) + PbO_2(s) + 2H_2SO_4(aq) \longrightarrow 2PbSO_4(s) + 2H_2O(l)$$

A car's battery produces the electric energy needed to start its engine. Sulfuric acid, present as its ions, is consumed, and lead(II) sulfate accumulates as a white powder on the electrodes. Once the car is running, the half-reactions are reversed by a voltage produced by the alternator. The Pb, PbO_2, and H_2SO_4 are regenerated. A battery can be recharged as long as all reactants necessary for the electrolytic reaction are present and all reactions are reversible.

The lead storage battery is one of the oldest types of rechargeable batteries. It is designed to deliver a high amount of current in a short period of time, as, for example, when an engine needs to be started. If the battery has been in use too long without being recharged by the alternator, it will not be able to deliver the starting current. In such cases, cars require a "jump start" from another source.

FIGURE 3.3

Rechargeable Batteries

The rechargeable cells of a car battery produce electricity from reactions between lead(IV) oxide, lead, and sulfuric acid.

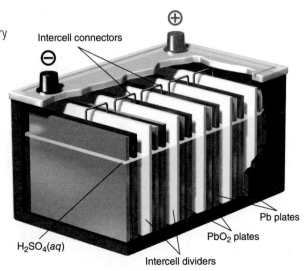

Intercell connectors

Pb plates

PbO_2 plates

$H_2SO_4(aq)$

Intercell dividers

> **MAIN IDEA**

Electrolysis uses electrical energy to cause a nonspontaneous chemical reaction to occur.

Electroplating and recharging a battery are examples of electrolysis. **Electrolysis** is the process of passing a current through a cell for which the cell potential is negative and causing an oxidation-reduction reaction to occur. That is, electrical energy is used to force a nonspontaneous chemical reaction to occur. For this cell reaction to occur, the external voltage must be greater than the potential that would be produced by the spontaneous reverse cell reaction.

Electrolysis is of great industrial importance. It is used to purify many metals from the ores in which they are found chemically combined in Earth's crust.

Electrolysis of Water

The electrolysis of water, shown in **Figure 3.4,** leads to the cell reaction in which water is broken down into its elements, H_2 and O_2. Recall that hydrogen gas and oxygen gas combine spontaneously to form water and are used to power fuel cells, which produce electricity. Therefore, the reverse process (electrolysis of water) is nonspontaneous and requires electrical energy. The two half-reactions occur at the anode and cathode.

$$\text{Anode: } 6H_2O(l) \longrightarrow 4e^- + O_2(g) + 4H_3O^+(aq)$$

$$\text{Cathode: } 4H_2O(l) + 4e^- \longrightarrow 2H_2(g) + 4OH^-(aq)$$

> **FIGURE 3.4**

Electrolysis
Electrical energy from the battery is used to break down water. Hydrogen forms at the cathode (left tube), and oxygen forms at the anode (right tube).

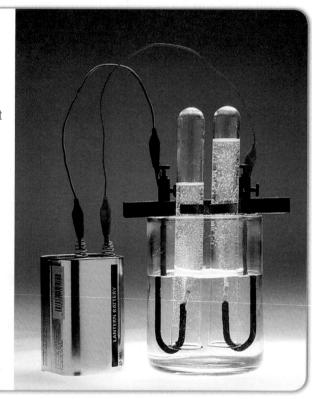

Aluminum Production by Electrolysis

Aluminum is the most abundant metal in Earth's crust. It is a relatively reactive metal; therefore, in nature, it is found as its oxide in an ore called *bauxite*. Aluminum is now very useful commercially, but it was not until 1886 that a process to obtain pure aluminum metal was discovered. Charles M. Hall (from the United States) and Paul Héroult (from France) simultaneously, but independently, determined a practical method for producing aluminum; it is an electrolytic process called the Hall-Héroult process.

Bauxite ore contains not only aluminum oxide (Al_2O_3) but also oxides of iron, silicon, and titanium. Therefore, the aluminum oxide (called alumina) must first be separated from the other compounds in the ore. The pure hydrated alumina ($Al_2O_3 \bullet nH_2O$) is obtained by treating bauxite with sodium hydroxide, which dissolves the alumina but does not dissolve the other compounds in the ore. The alumina solution is then separated from the remaining solid compounds and reprecipitated to obtain pure alumina. The purified alumina is dissolved in molten cryolite, Na_3AlF_6, at 970°C in an electrochemical cell, and the aluminum ions are reduced to aluminum metal. The liquid aluminum is denser than the molten cryolite and alumina; therefore, the molten aluminum metal settles to the bottom of the cell and is drained off periodically.

The electrolytic solution contains a large number of aluminum-containing ions, and the chemistry of the electrochemical reaction is not completely understood. Scientists still debate the exact species that participate in the half-reactions, but the overall cell reaction is

$$2Al_2O_3(l) + 3C(s) \longrightarrow 4Al(l) + 3CO_2(g),$$

where carbon is the anode and steel is the cathode in the cell.

The aluminum metal produced in this process is 99.5% pure. The Hall-Héroult process made the production of aluminum economically feasible. However, this process is the largest single user of electrical energy in the United States—nearly 5% of the national total. Recycling aluminum saves almost 95% of the cost of production. Aluminum recycling is one of the most economically worthwhile recycling programs that has been developed.

✔ CHECK FOR UNDERSTANDING

Distinguish Why is it so critical for people to recycle aluminum?

✔ SECTION 3 FORMATIVE ASSESSMENT

▶ Reviewing Main Ideas

1. Describe an electrolytic cell.

2. Explain the process of electroplating.

3. What is a rechargeable cell?

4. Give an example of how electrolytic cells are used in industry.

✔ Critical Thinking

5. **APPLYING CONCEPTS** Copper ore contains zinc metal, which is oxidized along with Cu during the electrolytic purification process. However, the Zn^{2+} ions are not then reduced when the Cu^{2+} ions are reduced to Cu at the cathode to obtain purified copper metal. Explain how Zn can be oxidized with Cu but their ions not be reduced together.

You have learned that electrons are transferred in all oxidation-reduction reactions. Electrons from a substance being oxidized are transferred to another substance being reduced. A voltaic cell is a simple device that physically separates the oxidation reaction from the reduction reaction, thus forcing electrons released during oxidation to travel through a wire to reach the site of reduction. If a device, such as a light bulb or a motor, is placed in the circuit, the moving electrons can perform useful work. The device will continue to operate until the circuit is broken or the reaction ceases to occur spontaneously.

The potential (voltage) of a given voltaic cell depends on how strongly the oxidation process tends to give up electrons and how strongly the reduction process tends to take them. The greater these two combined tendencies, the higher the potential of the cell. Potentials have been measured for each half-reaction. In a voltaic cell, the process with the more-negative reduction potential will proceed as the oxidation reaction at the anode of the cell. The more-positive reaction will proceed as reduction at the cathode. The sample problem shows how to find the potential of a voltaic cell.

Problem-Solving TIPS

- In a voltaic cell, the process that has the more-negative reduction potential will proceed as the oxidation reaction at the anode of the cell.

Sample Problem

Calculate the potential of a voltaic cell in which Hg^{2+} ions are reduced to Hg metal while Zn metal is oxidized to Zn^{2+} ions.

Reduction takes place at the cathode, so the cathode half-reaction is

$$Hg^{2+}(aq) + 2e^- \longrightarrow Hg(l)$$

Oxidation takes place at the anode, so the anode half-reaction is

$$Zn(s) \longrightarrow Zn^{2+}(aq) + 2e^-$$

To use the equation for cell potential, rewrite the anode half-reaction as a reduction reaction, $Zn^{2+}(aq) + 2e^- \longrightarrow Zn(s)$.

Use **Figure 2.10** in the current chapter to find the standard reduction potential for each half-reaction. Then, calculate the cell potential.

$$Hg^{2+}(aq) + 2e^- \longrightarrow Hg(l) \ E^0{}_{cathode} = +0.85 \text{ V}$$

$$Zn^{2+}(aq) + 2e^- \longrightarrow Zn(s) \ E^0{}_{anode} = -0.76 \text{ V}$$

$$E^0{}_{cell} = E^0{}_{cathode} - E^0{}_{anode} = +0.85 \text{ V} - (-0.76 \text{ V}) = 1.61 \text{ V}$$

Practice   Answers in Appendix E

1. Calculate the potential of a voltaic cell in which aluminum metal is oxidized to Al^{3+} ions while Cu^{2+} ions are reduced to Cu^+ ions.
2. Calculate the potential of a cell in which the reaction is $Pb(s) + Br_2(l) \longrightarrow Pb^{2+}(aq) + 2Br^-(aq)$.

CHAPTER 20 Summary

BIG IDEA Electrochemical cells separate oxidation from reduction reactions and either produce or are driven by an electric current.

SECTION 1 Introduction to Electrochemistry

- Electrochemistry is the branch of chemistry that deals with electricity-related applications of redox reactions.
- The electrode immersed in an electrolyte solution is a half-cell.
- The anode is the electrode where oxidation takes place. The cathode is the electrode where reduction occurs.
- The cell consists of electrodes connected by a wire along which the electrons travel and a salt bridge (or porous barrier) through which ions transfer to balance the charge.
- An electrochemical cell is a system of electrodes and electrolytes in which either chemical reactions produce electrical energy or electric current produces chemical change.

KEY TERMS

electrochemistry
electrode
half-cell
anode
cathode

SECTION 2 Voltaic Cells

- A voltaic cell, sometimes called a galvanic cell, uses a spontaneous redox reaction to produce electrical energy. Examples of voltaic cells are batteries and fuel cells.
- Fuel cells are voltaic cells in which the reactants are continuously supplied and the products are continuously removed.
- The potential difference must be measured across a complete cell because no transfer of electrons can occur unless both the anode and cathode are connected to form a complete circuit. Thus, the standard electrode potential for a half-cell is measured against the standard hydrogen electrode (SHE).
- Standard reduction potentials, E^0, are stated as reduction half-reactions. In **Fig. 2.10**, better oxidizing agents are on the left and have higher reduction potentials. Better reducing agents are on the right and have lower reduction potentials.
- A voltaic cell has an E^0_{cell} value that is positive.
- Corrosion occurs when iron is exposed to oxygen and water. One of the best methods to prevent corrosion is by the use of sacrificial anodes.

KEY TERMS

voltaic cell
reduction potential
electrode potential
standard electrode potential

SECTION 3 Electrolytic Cells

- Electrolytic cells are cells in which electrical energy from an external source causes a nonspontaneous reaction to occur.
- An electrolytic cell has an E^0_{cell} value that is negative.
- Electrolysis has great economic impact. Applications of electrolytic cells are electroplating of metallic surfaces, rechargeable batteries, aluminum production, and purification of metals.

KEY TERMS

electrolytic cell
electroplating
electrolysis

SECTION 1

Introduction to Electrochemistry

▶ REVIEWING MAIN IDEAS

1. In the half-cell $Zn^{2+}(aq) + 2e^- \longrightarrow Zn(s)$, what is the electrode, and is this half-reaction an anodic reaction or a cathodic reaction?

2. What role does the porous barrier play?

3. For each of the following pairs of half-cells, write the overall reaction and the cell notation. Assume the first half-cell given in each pair is the cathodic half-cell.
   a. Ag^+/Ag, Co^{2+}/Co
   b. Au^{3+}/Au, Zn^{2+}/Zn
   c. Hg^{2+}/Hg, K^+/K

4. Describe the components of an electrochemical cell and how the electrical charge travels through these components.

SECTION 2

Voltaic Cells

▶ REVIEWING MAIN IDEAS

5. Describe a voltaic cell, and give two examples of a voltaic cell.

6. What is the essential advantage of a fuel cell over batteries in the generation of electrical energy?

7. Explain why corrosion is a voltaic cell.

8. Discuss the advantages and disadvantages of corrosion-prevention methods.

9. Which half-reaction would more likely be an oxidation reaction: one with a standard reduction potential of -0.42 V, or one with a standard reduction potential of $+0.42$ V?

10. Why are dry-cell batteries called *dry cells*, even though their chemistry involves water?

11. a. Explain what is meant by the potential difference between the two electrodes in an electrochemical cell.
    b. How is this potential difference measured? What units are used?

12. The standard hydrogen electrode is assigned an electrode potential of 0.00 V. Explain why this voltage is assigned.

13. a. What information is provided by the standard reduction potential of a given half-cell?
    b. What does the relative value of the reduction potential of a given half-reaction indicate about its oxidation-reduction tendency?

14. When the cell $Ba(s)\,|\,Ba^{2+}(aq)\,||\,Sn^{2+}(aq)\,|\,Sn(s)$ is running, what observations can be made?

PRACTICE PROBLEMS

15. For each of the following pairs of half-cells, determine the overall electrochemical reaction that proceeds spontaneously:
    a. Na^+/Na, Ni^{2+}/Ni
    b. F_2/F^-, S/H_2S
    c. Br_2/Br^-, Cr^{3+}/Cr
    d. MnO_4^-/Mn^{2+}, Co^{2+}/Co

16. Determine the values of E^0 for the cells in the previous problem.

17. Suppose chemists had chosen to make the $I_2 + 2e^- \longrightarrow 2I^-$ half-cell the standard electrode and had assigned it a potential of zero volts.
    a. What would be the E^0 value for the $Br_2 + 2e^- \longrightarrow 2Br^-$ half-cell?
    b. What would be the E^0 value for the $Al^{3+} + 3e^- \longrightarrow Al$ half-cell?
    c. How much change would be observed in the E^0 value for the reaction involving $Br_2 + I^-$ if the I_2 half-cell is the standard?

18. If a strip of Ni were dipped into a solution of $AgNO_3$, what would be expected to occur? Explain, using E^0 values and equations.

SECTION 3

Electrolytic Cells

▶ REVIEWING MAIN IDEAS

19. What reaction happens at the cathode in an electrolysis process?

20. Explain why water cannot be used in the electro-chemical cell during the production of aluminum.

21. Calculate the voltage of a cell in which the overall reaction is the electrolysis of molten cadmium chloride into its elements.

22. According to electrochemical data, can Ni be plated onto a zinc metal object using a nickel nitrate solution? Explain.

23. Distinguish between a voltaic cell and an electrolytic cell in terms of the nature of the reaction involved.

24. **a.** What is electroplating?
    b. Identify the anode and cathode in such a process.

Mixed Review

▶ REVIEWING MAIN IDEAS

25. Predict whether each of the following reactions will occur spontaneously as written by determining the E^0 value for potential reaction. Write and balance the overall equation for each reaction that does occur spontaneously.
    a. $Mg + Sn^{2+} \longrightarrow$
    b. $K + Al^{3+} \longrightarrow$
    c. $Li^+ + Zn \longrightarrow$
    d. $Cu + Cl_2 \longrightarrow$

26. Why is it possible for alkaline batteries to be smaller than zinc-carbon dry cells?

27. Draw a diagram of a voltaic cell whose two half-reactions consist of Ag in $AgNO_3$ and Ni in $NiSO_4$. Identify the anode and cathode, and indicate the directions in which the electrons and ions are moving.

28. Can a solution of $Sn(NO_3)_2$ be stored in an aluminum container? Explain, using E^0 values.

29. A voltaic cell is made up of a cadmium electrode in a solution of $CdSO_4$ and a zinc electrode in a solution of $ZnSO_4$. The two half-cells are separated by a porous barrier.
    a. Which is the cathode, and which is the anode?
    b. In which direction are the electrons flowing?
    c. Write balanced equations for the two half-reactions, and write a net equation for the combined reaction.

30. Would the following pair of electrodes make a good battery? Explain.
    $Cd \longrightarrow Cd^{2+} + 2e^-$
    $Fe \longrightarrow Fe^{2+} + 2e^-$

31. **a.** What would happen if an aluminum spoon were used to stir a solution of $Zn(NO_3)_2$?
    b. Could a strip of Zn be used to stir a solution of $Al(NO_3)_3$? Explain, using E^0 values.

32. How do the redox reactions for each of the following types of batteries differ?
    a. zinc-carbon
    b. alkaline
    c. mercury

33. **a.** Why are some standard reduction potentials positive and some negative?
    b. Compare the E^0 value for a metal with the reactivity of that metal.

CRITICAL THINKING

34. **Applying Models** Explain how the oxidation-reduction chemistry of both the voltaic cell and the electrolytic cell are combined in the chemistry of rechargeable cells.

35. **Applying Ideas** In lead-acid batteries, such as your car battery, the degree of discharge of the battery can be determined by measuring the density of the battery fluid. Explain how this is possible.

36. **Applying Ideas** In lead-acid batteries, the battery cannot be recharged indefinitely. Explain why not.

37. **Interpreting Graphics** A voltaic cell is pictured below. Identify the species that is oxidized if current is allowed to flow.

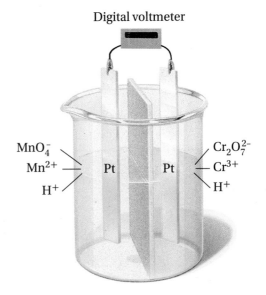

Digital voltmeter

MnO_4^-
Mn^{2+}
H^+
Pt
Pt
$Cr_2O_7^{2-}$
Cr^{3+}
H^+

38. Aluminum is described in Group 13 of the *Elements Handbook* (Appendix A) as a self-protecting metal and can be used in preventing corrosion of iron structures. Using electrochemical data, explain how aluminum protects iron structures.

RESEARCH AND WRITING

39. Go to the library, and find out about the electroplating industry in the United States. What are the top three metals used for plating, and how many metric tons of each are used for electroplating each year in the United States?

40. Investigate the types of batteries being considered for electric cars. Write a report on the advantages and disadvantages of these types of batteries.

ALTERNATIVE ASSESSMENT

41. Performance Take an inventory of the types of batteries used in your home. Find out the voltage supplied by each battery and what electrochemical reaction each uses. Suggest why that electrochemical reaction is used in each case.

42. In our portable society, batteries have become a necessary power supply. As consumers, we want to purchase batteries that will last as long as possible. Advertisements tell us that some batteries last longer than others, but do they really? Design an investigation to answer the question. Is there a difference in longevity between the major brands of AA batteries? Add a cost-effectiveness component to your design.

43. When someone who has a silver filling in a tooth bites down on an aluminum gum wrapper, saliva acts as an electrolyte. The system is an electrochemical cell that produces a small jolt of pain. Explain what occurs, using half-cell reactions and E^0 values.

Standards-Based Assessment

Record your answers on a separate piece of paper.

MULTIPLE CHOICE

1 The electrode at which reduction occurs is —

A always the anode

B always the cathode

C either the anode or the cathode

D always the half-cell

Use the table of standard reduction potentials below to answer the following questions.

Half-cell reaction	Standard reduction potential, E^0 (in volts)
$Au^{3+} + 3e^- \rightleftharpoons Au$	+1.50
$Cu^{2+} + 2e^- \rightleftharpoons Cu$	+0.34
$Fe^{2+} + 2e^- \rightleftharpoons Fe$	−0.41
$Sn^{2+} + 2e^- \rightleftharpoons Sn$	−0.14
$Zn^{2+} + 2e^- \rightleftharpoons Zn$	−0.76
$Mg^{2+} + 2e^- \rightleftharpoons Mg$	−2.37

2 A voltaic cell contains a strip of zinc metal in a solution containing zinc ions in one half-cell. The second is a strip of tin metal in a solution containing tin ions. According to the table above, when this cell operates —

A Sn is oxidized and Zn^{2+} is reduced

B Sn is reduced and Zn^{2+} is oxidized

C Sn^{2+} is oxidized and Zn is reduced

D Sn^{2+} is reduced and Zn is oxidized

3 According to the table above, which metal, Zn or Au, can reduce Sn^{2+} ions to Sn metal when placed in an aqueous solution of Sn^{2+} ions?

A Zn

B Au

C Both Zn and Au can reduce Sn^{2+} ions.

D Neither Zn nor Au can reduce Sn^{2+} ions.

4 When silver is electroplated onto another metal, Ag^+ is —

A oxidized at the anode

B reduced at the anode

C oxidized at the cathode

D reduced at the cathode

5 In the production of aluminum by the Hall-Héroult process, is the aluminum metal produced at the cathode or the anode?

A Al^{3+} is reduced to Al metal at the anode.

B Al is oxidized to Al^{3+} at the anode.

C Al^{3+} is reduced to Al metal at the cathode.

D Al is oxidized to Al^{3+} at the anode.

6 Someone asks you which type of AA battery is the best—an alkaline, a nickel-cadmium, or a mercury battery. Assuming all batteries are manufactured equally well, why might you find it difficult to give a satisfactory answer?

A The batteries could be old.

B The batteries are of different types.

C There is no control group.

D The condition that "best" refers to was not defined.

7 Which metal would **best** provide cathodic protection from corrosion for an iron bridge?

A Au

B Sn

C Cu

D Mg

GRIDDED RESPONSE

8 Use the table of reduction potentials at the top left to answer this question. The standard potential of the cell Sn | Sn^{2+} || Cr^{3+} | Cr is −0.60 V. What is the standard reduction potential, in volts, of the Cr^{3+}/Cr electrode?

Test Tip

Remember that if you eliminate two of the four answer choices, your chances of choosing the correct answer will double.

A BOOK EXPLAINING
COMPLEX IDEAS USING
ONLY THE 1,000 MOST
COMMON WORDS

POWER BOXES

Making power from different metals

You've learned that batteries generate power through electrochemical reactions. Here's a look at their insides.

RANDALL MUNROE
XKCD.COM

THE STORY OF HOW POWER BOXES WORK

IT'S HARD TO UNDERSTAND HOW POWER BOXES WORK, BECAUSE THEY'RE FULL OF WATER AND METAL DOING THINGS THAT ARE TOO SMALL TO SEE. IDEAS FROM OUR NORMAL LIVES DON'T REALLY HELP US TO THINK ABOUT WHAT THEY'RE DOING.

TO TRY TO EXPLAIN HOW THEY WORK, WE HAVE TO MAKE UP NEW IDEAS. THESE IDEAS AREN'T REAL—WE CAN'T SEE THE "REAL" THINGS—BUT THE IDEAS CAN EXPLAIN AN IMPORTANT IDEA ABOUT HOW THEY WORK.

I CAN'T SEE THE IDEA!

RIGHT, JUST WAIT.

A LOT OF LEARNING WE DO WORKS THIS WAY. THE IDEAS ON THIS PAGE ARE PRETTY FAR AWAY FROM "REAL," BUT THEY SHOULD HELP EXPLAIN PART OF HOW POWER BOXES WORK.

I'M STILL IN THE DARK.

BUT IT'S SO CLEAR!

IDEAS FOR THINKING ABOUT POWER BOXES

A power box has two sides, one holding a carrier wanter and the other holding a carrier maker. Between them is a wall that lets carriers through. The carrier maker would make carriers that cover the carrier wanter. But eating carriers puts pieces of power in the carrier wanter, and you can't have too many pieces of power together, because they push each other away. This stops the carrier wanter from eating too many carriers.

● PIECE OF POWER

◯ POWER CARRIER

◉ POWER
(in power carrier)

CARRIER MAKER

This metal wants to get rid of carriers. If it gets a piece of power inside it, it will send it away in a carrier made from its surface.

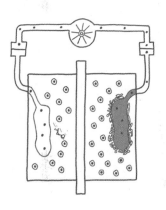

CARRIER WANTER

This metal wants to be covered in carriers. It will grab them if they come near and stick them to its surface, and the power from the carrier will go inside them.

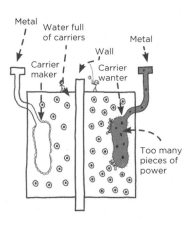

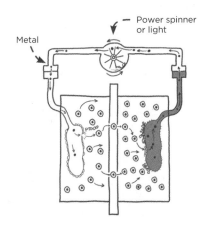

FULL

The two sides of a power box have a wall between them. This wall lets carriers through, but not pieces of power. It also stops the carrier wanter and carrier maker from touching, which would make the carriers all move to the carrier wanter without sending any power anywhere.

Extra pieces of power gather in the carrier wanter, but they can't go anywhere at first.

RUNNING

When you join the two sides with a stick of metal, the pieces of power can get from the carrier wanter to the carrier maker.

If you put a machine in their way—like a light or a power spinner—they can push on it and make it run, just like water pushing on a water wheel.

When the pieces of power get to the carrier maker, it uses them to make new carriers.

EMPTY

After a while, the carrier wanter gets covered in empty carriers, and the carrier maker gets used up. There's nothing left to push the power pieces through the metal path; the power box is dead.

With some power boxes, you can turn the wheel and push power back into the power box. This fills the power box back up.

POWER BOXES

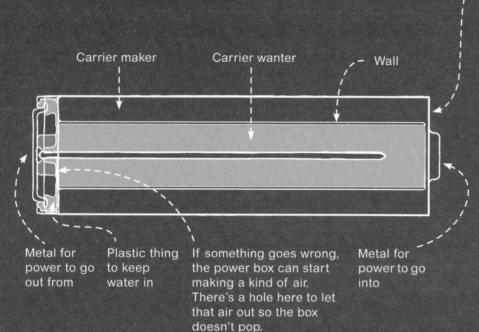

Carrier maker   Carrier wanter   Wall

Metal for power to go out from

Plastic thing to keep water in

If something goes wrong, the power box can start making a kind of air. There's a hole here to let that air out so the box doesn't pop.

Metal for power to go into

SMALL POWER BOX

This kind of power box is used in a lot of places. It powers hand lights, face hair cutters, and things kids play with.

In this kind of power box, the carrier wanter and carrier maker are made from different kinds of metal. The stuff in between is water with a kind of white stuff in it which lets the carriers move across. If the power box breaks, that stuff can come out. Don't worry, it's safe to clean up; it won't hurt your skin.

All power boxes run out of power after a while. With some kinds, you can put power back in and use them again and again, but you can't really do that with the kind shown here.

YOU CAN DROP THESE TO SEE IF THEY'RE DEAD

The carrier wanter in these boxes is made from metal dust. When it gets covered in carriers, it becomes stronger and sticks together, so the dust can't move around. This makes dead power boxes fly back up when you drop them, but full ones just hit the ground and stop.

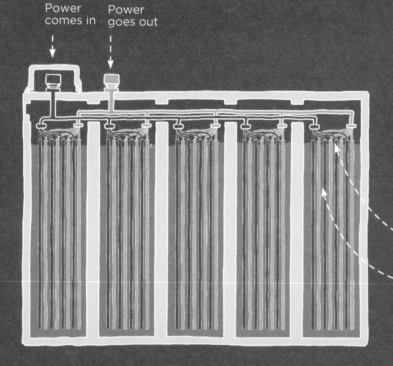

Power comes in   Power goes out

CAR POWER BOX

These power boxes are used in cars. They use two kinds of heavy metal as the carrier wanter and the carrier maker, which is why they're so heavy.

The power carrier water in between the two sides can burn your skin.

The carrier maker and the carrier wanter are two different kinds of metal, but there's something strange about this power box: When the carrier wanter gets covered in carriers, and the carrier maker makes them, they both turn into the same kind of metal.

If you cut one of these open, it would look like this—but never cut these open. They can blow up.

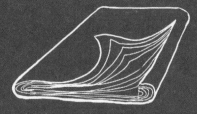

LIGHT METAL

In these power boxes, the carrier wanter and carrier maker are both made of very light metals. To make this kind of carrier maker and wanter work together, they're laid down in sheets almost touching each other, like two long sheets of paper laid flat and then rolled up.

HAND COMPUTER POWER BOX

These power boxes hold more power for their size than any other. We first made them to power helper machines in people's chests. Those machines need to hold a lot of power, since people don't like it if you take them out too often.

When we started making lots of hand computers, we got better at making these power boxes, since lots of people wanted their computers to work all day without having to get power from the wall.

Of course, people also wanted their hearts to work, but more people have hand computers than heart boxes.

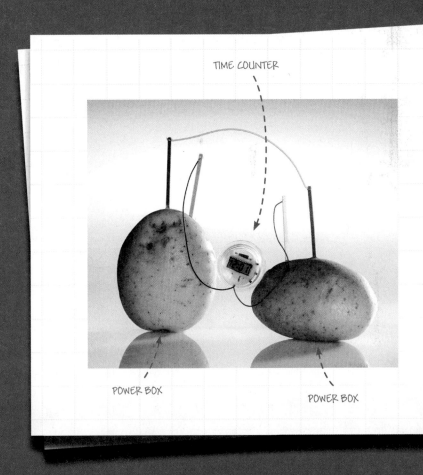

TIME COUNTER

POWER BOX

POWER BOX

CHAPTER 21
Nuclear Chemistry

BIG IDEA
When an atomic nucleus becomes unstable, it emits radiation in the form of particles and energy to regain stability. Nuclei often change identity during radioactive decay.

ONLINE Chemistry
HMHScience.com

ONLINE LABS
- Simulation of Nuclear Decay Using Pennies and Paper
- Radioactivity
- Detecting Radioactivity

GO ONLINE

Why It Matters Video
HMHScience.com

Nuclear Chemistry

The Nucleus

Key Terms

nucleon
nuclide
mass defect

nuclear binding energy
nuclear shell model
magic number

nuclear reaction
transmutation

Main Ideas

An atom's mass is less than the masses of its parts.

Stable nuclides cluster over a range of neutron-proton ratios known as the band of stability.

Nuclear reactions affect the nucleus of an atom.

Atomic nuclei are made of protons and neutrons, which are collectively called **nucleons. In nuclear chemistry, an atom is referred to as a nuclide and is identified by the number of protons and neutrons in its nucleus.** We identify nuclides in two ways. When a symbol such as $^{228}_{88}$Ra is used, the superscript is the mass number, and the subscript is the atomic number. The same nuclide can also be written as radium-228, where the mass number is written following the element name.

▶ MAIN IDEA

An atom's mass is less than the masses of its parts.

The mass of an atom is not equal to the total mass of an equal number of isolated parts. Consider a $^{4}_{2}$He atom. The combined mass of two protons, two neutrons, and two electrons is calculated below.

2 protons: $(2 \times 1.007\ 276\ u) = 2.014\ 552\ u$
2 neutrons: $(2 \times 1.008\ 665\ u) = 2.017\ 330\ u$
2 electrons: $(2 \times 0.000\ 548\ 6\ u) = \underline{0.001\ 097\ u}$
                total combined mass: 4.032 979 u

However, the atomic mass of a $^{4}_{2}$He atom has been measured to be 4.002 602 u. The measured mass, 4.002 602 u, is 0.030 377 u *less* than the combined mass, 4.032 979 u, calculated above. **This difference between the mass of an atom and the sum of the masses of its particles is the mass defect.**

Nuclear Binding Energy

What causes the loss in mass? According to Albert Einstein's equation $E = mc^2$, mass can be converted to energy, and energy to mass. The mass defect is caused by the conversion of mass to energy upon formation of the nucleus. The mass units of the mass defect can be converted to energy units by using Einstein's equation. First, convert 0.030 377 u to kilograms to match the mass units for energy, kg • m^2/s^2.

$$0.030\ 377\ u \times \frac{1.6605 \times 10^{-27}\ kg}{1\ u} = 5.0441 \times 10^{-29}\ kg$$

The energy equivalent can now be calculated.

$$E = mc^2$$
$$E = (5.0441 \times 10^{-29}\ kg)(3.00 \times 10^8\ m/s)^2$$
$$= 4.54 \times 10^{-12}\ kg \bullet m^2/s^2 = 4.54 \times 10^{-12}\ J$$

This is the nuclear binding energy, the energy released when a nucleus is formed from nucleons. Think of it as the amount of energy needed to break apart the nucleus, or as a measure of the stability of a nucleus.

FIGURE 1.1

Binding Energy This graph shows the relationship between binding energy per nucleon and mass number. The binding energy per nucleon is a measure of the stability of a nucleus.

✓ **CRITICAL THINKING**

Interpret Which nucleon has the greater binding energy, Fe or U?

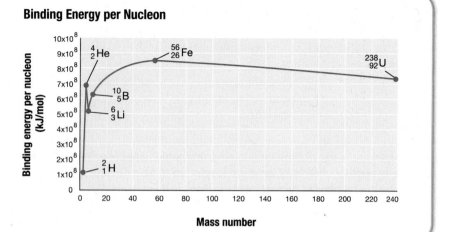

Binding Energy per Nucleon

Binding Energy per Nucleon

The binding energy per nucleon is used to compare the stability of different nuclides, as shown in **Figure 1.1**. The *binding energy per nucleon* is the binding energy of the nucleus divided by its number of nucleons. The higher the binding energy per nucleon, the more tightly the nucleons are held together. Elements with intermediate atomic masses have the greatest binding energies per nucleon and are therefore the most stable.

▶ **MAIN IDEA**

Stable nuclides cluster over a range of neutron-proton ratios known as the band of stability.

Stable nuclides have certain characteristics. When the number of protons in stable nuclei is plotted against the number of neutrons, as shown in **Figure 1.2**, a belt-like graph is obtained. This stable nuclei cluster over a range of neutron-proton ratios is referred to as the *band of stability*. Among atoms having low atomic numbers, the most stable nuclei are those with a neutron-proton ratio of approximately 1:1. For example, $^4_2$He, a stable isotope of helium with two neutrons and two protons, has a neutron-proton ratio of 1:1. As the atomic number increases, the stable neutron-proton ratio increases to about 1.5:1. For example, $^{206}_{82}$Pb, with 124 neutrons and 82 protons, has a neutron-proton ratio of 1.51:1.

This trend can be explained by the relationship between the nuclear force and the electrostatic forces between protons. Protons in a nucleus repel all other protons through electrostatic repulsion, but the short range of the nuclear force allows them to attract only protons very close to them, as shown in **Figure 1.3**.

As the number of protons in a nucleus increases, the repulsive electro-static force between protons increases faster than the nuclear force. More neutrons are required to increase the nuclear force and stabilize the nucleus. At atomic number 83, bismuth, and beyond, the repulsive force of the protons is so great that no stable nuclides exist, because the nuclear force cannot overcome the repulsive force between protons.

CROSS-DISCIPLINARY CONNECTION

Quarks   **S.T.E.M.**

Many subatomic particles have been identified. Leptons and quarks are the elementary particles of matter. The electron is a lepton. Protons and neutrons are made of quarks. There are six types of quarks that differ in mass and charge. They are named *up, down, strange, charm, bottom,* and *top*. Protons consist of two up quarks and one down quark, and neutrons consist of two down quarks and one up quark. Although individual quarks have not been isolated, their existence explains the patterns of nuclear binding and decay.

The Standard Model for particle physics predicted the interactions of quarks with another predicted particle, named the Higgs boson, which gives quarks and other fundamental particles their mass. The 2013 Nobel Prize for Physics recognized work confirming the discovery of this predicted particle.

FIGURE 1.2

Band of Stability The neutron-proton ratios of stable nuclides cluster together in a region known as the band of stability. As the number of protons increases, the ratio increases from 1:1 to about 1.5:1.

FIGURE 1.3

Competing Forces Proton A attracts proton B through the nuclear force but repels it through the electrostatic force. Proton A mainly repels proton C through the electrostatic force, because the nuclear force reaches only a few nucleon diameters.

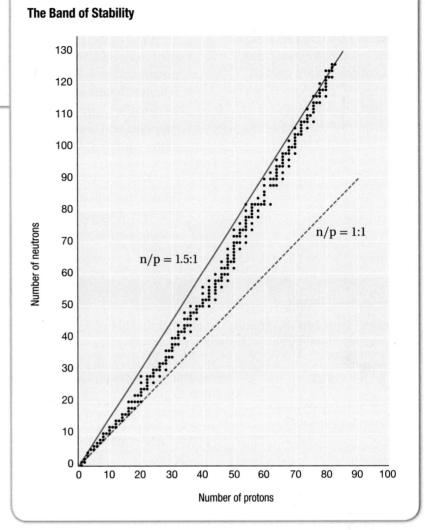

The Band of Stability

Stable nuclei tend to have even numbers of nucleons. Of the stable nuclides, more than half have even numbers of both protons and neutrons. Only five nuclides have odd numbers of both. This indicates that stability of a nucleus is greatest when the nucleons—like electrons—are paired.

The most stable nuclides are those having 2, 8, 20, 28, 50, 82, or 126 protons, neutrons, or total nucleons. This extra stability at certain numbers supports a theory that nucleons—like electrons—exist at certain energy levels. **According to the nuclear shell model, nucleons exist in different energy levels, or shells, in the nucleus. The numbers of nucleons that represent completed nuclear energy levels—2, 8, 20, 28, 50, 82, and 126—are called magic numbers.**

The nuclear shell model suggests that there might be an "island of stability" for elements that lie beyond uranium in the periodic table. The explanation is that although smaller nuclides may be quite unstable individually, once enough are assembled to fill an entire shell, those nuclides may be stable enough to stay together for minutes or even hours. Minutes and hours are a long time in the usually nanosecond lifetimes of the larger, laboratory-synthesized elements.

▶ MAIN IDEA

Nuclear reactions affect the nucleus of an atom.

✓ CHECK FOR UNDERSTANDING

Compare How does a nuclear reaction compare to a chemical reaction?

Unstable nuclei undergo spontaneous changes that change their numbers of protons and neutrons. In this process, they give off large amounts of energy and increase their stability. These changes are a type of nuclear reaction. **A nuclear reaction is a reaction that affects the nucleus of an atom.** In equations representing nuclear reactions, the total of the atomic numbers and the total of the mass numbers must be equal on both sides of the equation. An example is shown below.

$$\,^{9}_{4}\text{Be} + \,^{4}_{2}\text{He} \rightarrow \,^{12}_{6}\text{C} + \,^{1}_{0}n$$

Notice that when the atomic number changes, the identity of the element changes. **A transmutation is a change in the identity of a nucleus as a result of a change in the number of its protons.**

GO ONLINE

Solve It! Cards
HMHScience.com

Balancing Nuclear Reactions

Sample Problem A Identify the product that balances the following nuclear reaction: $\,^{212}_{84}\text{Po} \rightarrow \,^{4}_{2}\text{He} + \,\underline{\;?\;}$

① ANALYZE

The total mass number and atomic number must be equal on both sides of the equation.

$$\,^{212}_{84}\text{Po} \rightarrow \,^{4}_{2}\text{He} + \,\underline{\;?\;}$$

mass number: $212 - 4 = 208$ atomic number: $84 - 2 = 82$

② SOLVE

The nuclide has a mass number of 208 and an atomic number of 82, $\,^{208}_{82}\text{Pb}$.

The balanced nuclear equation is $\,^{212}_{84}\text{Po} \rightarrow \,^{4}_{2}\text{He} + \,^{208}_{82}\text{Pb}$

Practice Answers in Appendix E

Using $\,^{1}_{0}n$ to represent a neutron and $\,^{\;\;0}_{-1}e$ to represent an electron, complete the following nuclear equations:

1. $\,^{253}_{99}\text{Es} + \,^{4}_{2}\text{He} \rightarrow \,^{1}_{0}n + \,\underline{\;?\;}$

2. $\,^{142}_{61}\text{Pm} + \,\underline{\;?\;} \rightarrow \,^{142}_{60}\text{Nd}$

✓ SECTION 1 **FORMATIVE ASSESSMENT**

▶ Reviewing Main Ideas

1. Define *mass defect*.

2. How is nuclear stability related to the neutron-proton ratio?

3. Complete and balance the following nuclear equations:

a. $\,^{187}_{75}\text{Re} + \,\underline{\;?\;} \rightarrow \,^{188}_{75}\text{Re} + \,^{1}_{1}\text{H}$

b. $\,^{9}_{4}\text{Be} + \,^{4}_{2}\text{He} \rightarrow \,\underline{\;?\;} + \,^{1}_{0}n$

c. $\,^{22}_{11}\text{Na} + \,\underline{\;?\;} \rightarrow \,^{22}_{10}\text{Ne}$

✓ Critical Thinking

4. INTERPRETING GRAPHICS Examine **Figure 1.2**, and predict whether $\,^{9}_{3}\text{Li}$ is a stable isotope of lithium. Explain your answer.

Radioactive Decay

Key Terms

radioactive decay	gamma ray
nuclear radiation	half-life
radioactive nuclide	decay series
alpha particle	parent nuclide
beta particle	daughter nuclide
positron	artificial transmutation
electron capture	transuranium element

Main Ideas

▶ Radioactive decay leads to more-stable nucleons.

▶ Half-life is the time needed for one-half of an amount of radioactive nuclei to decay.

▶ Radioactive nuclides become stable nuclides through a series of decays.

▶ Nuclides can become radioactive artificially.

In 1896, Henri Becquerel was studying the possible connection between light emission of some uranium compounds after exposure to sunlight and x-ray emission. He wrapped a photographic plate in a lightproof covering and placed a uranium compound on top of it. He then placed them in sunlight. The photographic plate was exposed even though it was protected from visible light, suggesting that it had been exposed by x-rays. When he tried to repeat his experiment, cloudy weather prevented him from placing the experiment in sunlight. To his surprise, the plate was still exposed. This meant that sunlight was not needed to produce the rays that exposed the plate. The rays were produced by radioactive decay. **Radioactive decay is the spontaneous disintegration of a nucleus into a slightly lighter nucleus, accompanied by emission of particles, electromagnetic radiation, or both. The radiation that exposed the plate was nuclear radiation, particles or electromagnetic radiation emitted from the nucleus during radioactive decay.**

Uranium is a **radioactive nuclide, an unstable nucleus that undergoes radioactive decay.** Studies by Marie Curie and Pierre Curie found that of the elements known in 1896, only uranium and thorium were radioactive. In 1898, the Curies discovered two new radioactive metallic elements, polonium and radium. Since that time, many other radioactive nuclides have been identified. In fact, all of the nuclides beyond atomic number 83 are unstable and thus radioactive.

▶ **MAIN IDEA**
Radioactive decay leads to more-stable nucleons.

A nuclide's type and rate of decay depend on the nucleon content and energy level of the nucleus. Some common types of radioactive nuclide emissions are summarized in **Figure 2.1**.

GO ONLINE **Animated Chemistry**
HMHScience.com

Types of Radioactive Decay

FIGURE 2.1

RADIOACTIVE NUCLIDE EMISSIONS

Type	Symbol	Charge	Mass (u)
Alpha particle	$_{2}^{4}\text{He}$	2+	4.001 5062
Beta particle	$_{-1}^{0}\beta$	1−	0.000 5486
Positron	$_{+1}^{0}\beta$	1+	0.000 5486
Gamma ray	γ	0	0

FIGURE 2.2

Alpha Emission An alpha particle, identical to a helium nucleus, is emitted during the radioactive decay of some very heavy nuclei.

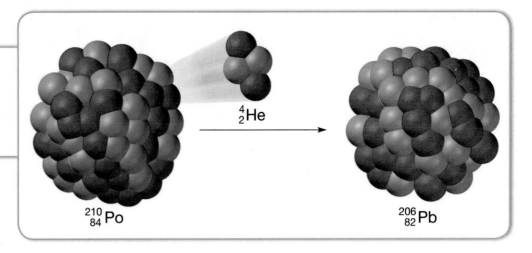

$^{210}_{84}$Po

$^{4}_{2}$He

$^{206}_{82}$Pb

Alpha Emission

An **alpha particle** (α) is two protons and two neutrons bound together and is emitted from the nucleus during some kinds of radioactive decay. Alpha particles are helium nuclei and have a charge of 2+. They are often represented with the symbol $^{4}_{2}$He. Alpha emission is restricted almost entirely to very heavy nuclei. In these nuclei, both the number of neutrons and the number of protons need to be reduced in order to increase the stability of the nucleus. An example of alpha emission is the decay of $^{210}_{84}$Po into $^{206}_{82}$Pb, shown in **Figure 2.2.** The atomic number decreases by two, and the mass number decreases by four.

$$^{210}_{84}\text{Po} \longrightarrow {}^{206}_{82}\text{Pb} + {}^{4}_{2}\text{He}$$

Beta Emission

Nuclides above the band of stability are unstable because their neutron-proton ratio is too large. To decrease the number of neutrons, a neutron can be converted into a proton and an electron. The electron is emitted from the nucleus as a beta particle. A **beta particle** (β) is an electron emitted from the nucleus during some kinds of radioactive decay.

$$^{1}_{0}n \longrightarrow {}^{1}_{1}p + {}^{0}_{-1}\beta$$

An example of beta emission, shown in **Figure 2.3,** is the decay of $^{14}_{6}$C into $^{14}_{7}$N. Notice that the atomic number increases by one and the mass number stays the same and neutron to proton ratio decreases.

$$^{14}_{6}\text{C} \longrightarrow {}^{14}_{7}\text{N} + {}^{0}_{-1}\beta$$

Positron Emission

Nuclides below the band of stability are unstable because their neutron-proton ratio is too small. To decrease the number of protons, a proton can be converted into a neutron by emitting a positron. A **positron** is a particle that has the same mass as an electron but has a positive charge and is emitted from the nucleus during some kinds of radioactive decay.

$$^{1}_{1}p \longrightarrow {}^{1}_{0}n + {}^{0}_{+1}\beta$$

✓ **CHECK FOR UNDERSTANDING**
Infer Why would alpha emission occur in only more-massive nuclei?

FIGURE 2.3

Beta Emission Beta emission causes the transmutation of $^{14}_{6}$C into $^{14}_{7}$N. Beta emission is a type of radioactive decay in which a neutron is converted to a proton with the emission of a beta particle.

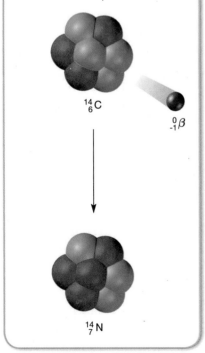

$^{14}_{6}$C

$^{0}_{-1}\beta$

$^{14}_{7}$N

An example of positron emission is the decay of $^{38}_{19}K$ into $^{38}_{18}Ar$. Notice that the atomic number decreases by one but the mass number stays the same and neutron to proton ratio increases.

$$^{38}_{19}K \longrightarrow {}^{38}_{18}Ar + {}^{0}_{+1}\beta$$

Electron Capture

Another type of decay for nuclides that have a neutron-proton ratio that is too small is electron capture. **In electron capture, an inner orbital electron is captured by the nucleus of its own atom.** The inner orbital electron combines with a proton, and a neutron is formed.

$$^{0}_{-1}e + {}^{1}_{1}p \longrightarrow {}^{1}_{0}n$$

An example of electron capture is the radioactive decay of $^{106}_{47}Ag$ into $^{106}_{46}Pd$. Just as in positron emission, the atomic number decreases by one, but the mass number stays the same and neutron to proton ratio increases.

$$^{106}_{47}Ag + {}^{0}_{-1}e \longrightarrow {}^{106}_{46}Pd$$

Gamma Emission

Gamma rays (γ) are high-energy electromagnetic waves emitted from a nucleus as it changes from an excited state to a ground energy state.
Figure 2.4 shows the position of gamma rays in the electromagnetic spectrum. The emission of gamma rays supports the nuclear shell model. In this model, gamma rays are produced when nuclear particles undergo transitions in nuclear-energy levels. This is similar to the emission of photons (light or x-rays) when an electron drops to a lower energy level. Gamma emission usually occurs immediately following other types of decay, when other types of decay leave the nucleus in an excited state.

FIGURE 2.4

Gamma Rays in the EM Spectrum Gamma rays, like visible light, are a form of electromagnetic radiation. They have a shorter wavelength and are higher in energy than visible light.

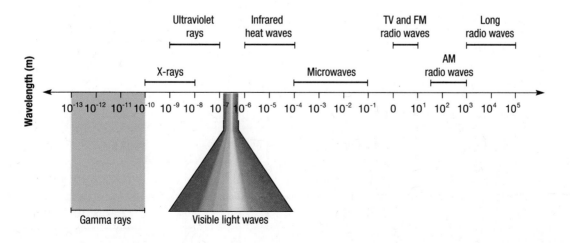

FIGURE 2.5

Half-Life The half-life of radium-226 is 1599 years. Half of the remaining radium-226 decays by the end of each additional half-life.

✔ **CRITICAL THINKING**

Model Describe half-life using a bag of oranges, assuming each orange to be an individual atom.

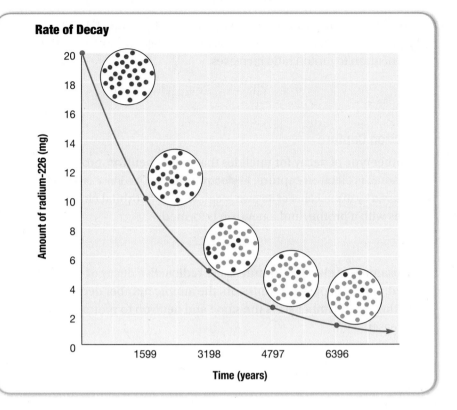

Rate of Decay

Amount of radium-226 (mg) / Time (years)

▶ **MAIN IDEA**

Half-life is the time needed for one-half of an amount of radioactive nuclei to decay.

No two radioactive isotopes decay at the same rate. **Half-life, $t_{1/2}$, is the time required for half the atoms of a radioactive nuclide to decay.** Look at the graph of the decay of radium-226 in **Figure 2.5.** Radium-226 has a half-life of 1599 years. Half of a given amount of radium-226 decays in 1599 years. In another 1599 years, half of the remaining radium-226 decays. This process continues until there is a negligible amount of radium-226. Each radioactive nuclide has its own half-life. More-stable nuclides decay slowly and have longer half-lives. Less-stable nuclides decay very quickly and have shorter half-lives, sometimes just a fraction of a second. Some representative radioactive nuclides, along with their half-lives, are given in **Figure 2.6.**

FIGURE 2.6

REPRESENTATIVE RADIOACTIVE NUCLIDES AND THEIR HALF-LIVES

Nuclide	Half-life	Nuclide	Half-life
$^{3}_{1}\text{H}$	12.32 years	$^{214}_{84}\text{Po}$	163.7 μs
$^{14}_{6}\text{C}$	5715 years	$^{218}_{84}\text{Po}$	3.0 min
$^{32}_{15}\text{P}$	14.28 days	$^{218}_{85}\text{At}$	1.6 s
$^{40}_{19}\text{K}$	1.3×10^{9} years	$^{238}_{92}\text{U}$	4.46×10^{9} years
$^{60}_{27}\text{Co}$	5.27 years	$^{239}_{94}\text{Pu}$	2.41×10^{4} years

GO ONLINE

Learn It! Video
HMHScience.com

Solve It! Cards
HMHScience.com

Sample Problem B Phosphorus-32 has a half-life of 14.3 days. How many milligrams of phosphorus-32 remain after 57.2 days if you start with 4.0 mg of the isotope?

❶ ANALYZE

Given: original mass of phosphorus-32 = 4.0 mg
half-life of phosphorus-32 = 14.3 days
time elapsed = 57.2 days

Unknown: amount of phosphorus-32 remaining

❷ PLAN

To determine the number of milligrams of phosphorus-32 remaining, we must first find the number of half-lives that have passed in the time elapsed. Then the amount of phosphorus-32 is determined by reducing the original amount by half for every half-life that has passed.

$$\text{number of half-lives} = \text{time elapsed (days)} \times \frac{1 \text{ half-life}}{14.3 \text{ days}}$$

amount of phosphorus-32 remaining =
$$\text{original amount of phosphorus-32} \times \frac{1}{2} \text{ for each half-life}$$

❸ SOLVE

$$\text{number of half-lives} = 57.2 \text{ days} \times \frac{1 \text{ half-life}}{14.3 \text{ days}} = 4 \text{ half-lives}$$

$$\text{amount of phosphorus-32 remaining} = 4.0 \text{ mg} \times \frac{1}{2} \times \frac{1}{2} \times \frac{1}{2} \times \frac{1}{2} = 0.25 \text{ mg}$$

❹ CHECK YOUR WORK

A period of 57.2 days is four half-lives for phosphorus-32. At the end of one half-life, 2.0 mg of phosphorus-32 remains; 1.0 mg remains at the end of two half-lives; 0.50 mg remains at the end of three half-lives; and 0.25 mg remains at the end of four half-lives.

Practice   Answers in Appendix E

1. The half-life of polonium-210 is 138.4 days. How many milligrams of polonium-210 remain after 415.2 days if you start with 2.0 mg of the isotope?
2. Assuming a half-life of 1599 years, how many years will be needed for the decay of $\frac{15}{16}$ of a given amount of radium-226?
3. The half-life of radon-222 is 3.824 days. After what time will one-fourth of a given amount of radon remain?
4. The half-life of cobalt-60 is 5.27 years. How many milligrams of cobalt-60 remain after 52.7 years if you start with 10.0 mg?
5. A sample contains 4.0 mg of uranium-238. After 4.46×10^9 years, the sample will contain 2.0 mg of uranium-238. What is the half-life of uranium-238?

● MAIN IDEA

Radioactive nuclides become stable nuclides through a series of decays.

One nuclear reaction is not always enough to produce a stable nuclide. A **decay series** is a series of radioactive nuclides produced by successive radioactive decay until a stable nuclide is formed. The heaviest nuclide of each decay series is called the **parent nuclide.** The nuclides produced by the decay of the parent nuclides are called **daughter nuclides.** All naturally occurring nuclides with atomic numbers greater than 83 are radioactive and belong to one of three natural decay series. The parent nuclides are uranium-238, uranium-235, and thorium-232.

The transmutations of the uranium-238 decay series are charted in **Figure 2.7.** Locate the parent nuclide, uranium-238, on the chart. As the nucleus of uranium-238 decays, it emits an alpha particle. The mass number of the nuclide, and thus the vertical position on the graph, decreases by four. The atomic number, and thus the horizontal position, decreases by two. The daughter nuclide is an isotope of thorium.

$$^{238}_{92}U \rightarrow {}^{234}_{90}Th + {}^{4}_{2}He$$

FIGURE 2.7

Uranium-238 Decay Series This chart shows the transmutations that occur as $^{238}_{92}U$ decays to the final, stable nuclide, $^{206}_{82}Pb$. Decay usually follows the solid arrows. The dotted arrows represent alternative routes of decay.

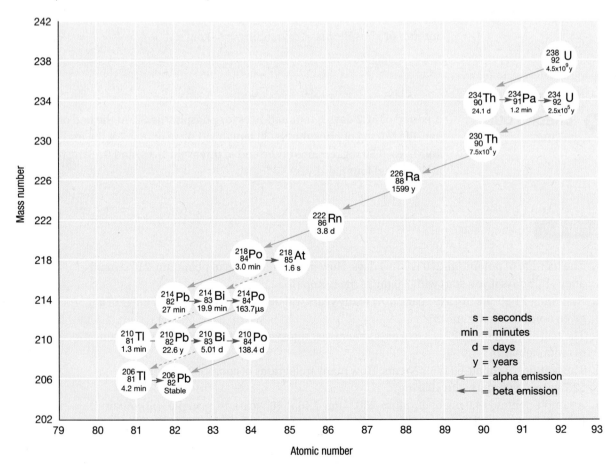

The half-life of $^{234}_{90}$Th, about 24 days, is indicated on the chart. It decays by giving off beta particles. This increases its atomic number, and thus its horizontal position, by one. The mass number, and thus its vertical position, remains the same.

$$^{234}_{90}\text{Th} \rightarrow \; ^{234}_{91}\text{Pa} + \; ^{0}_{-1}\beta$$

The remaining atomic number and mass number changes shown on the decay chart are also explained in terms of the particles given off. In the final step, $^{210}_{84}$Po loses an alpha particle to form $^{206}_{82}$Pb. This is a stable, nonradioactive isotope of lead. Notice that $^{206}_{82}$Pb contains 82 protons, a magic number. It contains the extra-stable nuclear configuration of a completed nuclear shell.

▶ MAIN IDEA

Nuclides can become radioactive artificially.

Artificial radioactive nuclides are radioactive nuclides not found naturally on Earth. They are made by **artificial transmutations,** bombardment of nuclei with charged and uncharged particles. Because neutrons have no charge, they can easily penetrate the nucleus of an atom. However, positively charged alpha particles, protons, and other ions are repelled by the nucleus. Because of this repulsion, great quantities of energy are required to bombard nuclei with these particles. The necessary energy may be supplied by accelerating these particles in the magnetic or electrical field of a particle accelerator. **Figure 2.8** shows an example of an accelerator.

✔ CHECK FOR UNDERSTANDING

Hypothesize The neutrons released by atoms are moving incredibly fast. Why do you think scientists found they needed to slow down these neutrons for them to produce artificial transmutations?

FIGURE 2.8

Particle Accelerator This is an aerial view of the Fermi National Accelerator Laboratory (Fermilab), in Illinois. The particle accelerators are underground. The Tevatron ring, the larger particle accelerator, has a circumference of 4 mi. The smaller ring (top left) is a new accelerator, the Main Injector.

FIGURE 2.9

REACTIONS FOR THE FIRST PREPARATION OF SEVERAL TRANSURANIUM ELEMENTS

Atomic number	Name	Symbol	Nuclear reaction
93	neptunium	Np	$^{238}_{92}U + ^{1}_{0}n \rightarrow ^{239}_{92}U$ $^{239}_{92}U \rightarrow ^{239}_{93}Np + ^{0}_{-1}\beta$
94	plutonium	Pu	$^{238}_{93}Np \rightarrow ^{238}_{94}Pu + ^{0}_{-1}\beta$
95	americium	Am	$^{239}_{94}Pu + 2^{1}_{0}n \rightarrow ^{241}_{95}Am + ^{0}_{-1}\beta$
96	curium	Cm	$^{239}_{94}Pu + ^{4}_{2}He \rightarrow ^{242}_{96}Cm + ^{1}_{0}n$
97	berkelium	Bk	$^{241}_{95}Am + ^{4}_{2}He \rightarrow ^{243}_{97}Bk + 2^{1}_{0}n$
98	californium	Cf	$^{242}_{96}Cm + ^{4}_{2}He \rightarrow ^{245}_{98}Cf + ^{1}_{0}n$
99	einsteinium	Es	$^{238}_{92}U + 15^{1}_{0}n \rightarrow ^{253}_{99}Es + 7^{0}_{-1}\beta$
100	fermium	Fm	$^{238}_{92}U + 17^{1}_{0}n \rightarrow ^{255}_{100}Fm + 8^{0}_{-1}\beta$
101	mendelevium	Md	$^{253}_{99}Es + ^{4}_{2}He \rightarrow ^{256}_{101}Md + ^{1}_{0}n$
102	nobelium	No	$^{246}_{96}Cm + ^{12}_{6}C \rightarrow ^{254}_{102}No + 4^{1}_{0}n$
103	lawrencium	Lr	$^{252}_{98}Cf + ^{10}_{5}B \rightarrow ^{258}_{103}Lr + 4^{1}_{0}n$

FIGURE 2.10

Manufactured Elements Artificial transmutations filled the gaps in the periodic table, shown in red, and extended the periodic table with the transuranium elements, shown in blue. The production of elements that would occupy the lighter blue boxes in the table have yet to be confirmed.

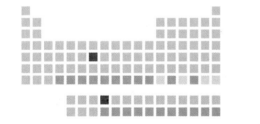

Artificial Radioactive Nuclides

Radioactive isotopes of all the natural elements have been produced by artificial transmutation. In addition, production of technetium and promethium by artificial transmutation has filled gaps in the periodic table. Their positions are shown in red in **Figure 2.10.**

Artificial transmutations are also used to produce the transuranium elements. **Transuranium elements are elements with more than 92 protons in their nuclei.** All of these elements are radioactive. The nuclear reactions for the synthesis of several transuranium elements are shown in **Figure 2.9.** Currently, 22 artificially prepared transuranium elements have been named. Others have been reported but not confirmed. Their positions in the periodic table are shown in blue in **Figure 2.10.**

✓ SECTION 2 FORMATIVE ASSESSMENT

▶ Reviewing Main Ideas

1. Define *radioactive decay*.

2. **a.** What are the different types of common radioactive decay?

   b. List the types of radioactive decay that convert one nuclide into another.

3. What fraction of a given sample of a radioactive nuclide remains after four half-lives?

4. When does a decay series end?

✓ Critical Thinking

5. **INTERPRETING CONCEPTS** Distinguish between natural and artificial radioactive nuclides.

Nuclear Radiation

Main Ideas

▶ Ionizing radiation can harm living tissues.

▶ Film and electronic methods can detect radiation.

▶ Radioactivity has important applications.

▶ Storage and disposal of nuclear waste pose important concerns.

Key Terms

roentgen
rem
film badge

Geiger-Müller counter
scintillation counter
radioactive dating

radioactive tracer
nuclear waste

In Becquerel's experiment, nuclear radiation from the uranium compound penetrated the lightproof covering and exposed the film. Different types of nuclear radiation have different penetrating abilities. Nuclear radiation includes alpha particles, beta particles, and gamma rays.

Alpha particles can travel only a few centimeters in air and have a low penetrating ability due to their large mass and charge. They cannot penetrate skin. However, they can cause damage if ingested or inhaled. Beta particles, which are emitted electrons, travel at speeds close to the speed of light and have a penetrating ability about 100 times greater than that of alpha particles. Beta particles can travel a few meters in air. Gamma rays have the greatest penetrating ability. **Figure 3.1** gives the penetrating abilities and shielding requirements of some types of nuclear radiation.

▶ **MAIN IDEA**

Ionizing radiation can harm living tissues.

Nuclear radiation can transfer the energy from nuclear decay to the electrons of atoms or molecules and cause ionization. **The roentgen (R) is a unit used to measure nuclear radiation exposure; it is equal to the amount of gamma and x-ray radiation that produces 2×10^9 ion pairs when it passes through 1 cm^3 of dry air.** Ionization can damage living tissue. Radiation damage to human tissue is measured in rems (roentgen equivalent in man). **A rem is a unit used to measure the dose of any type of ionizing radiation that factors in the effect that the radiation has on human tissue.** Long-term exposure to radiation can cause DNA mutations that result in cancer and other genetic defects. DNA can be mutated directly by interaction with radiation or indirectly by interaction with previously ionized molecules.

FIGURE 3.1

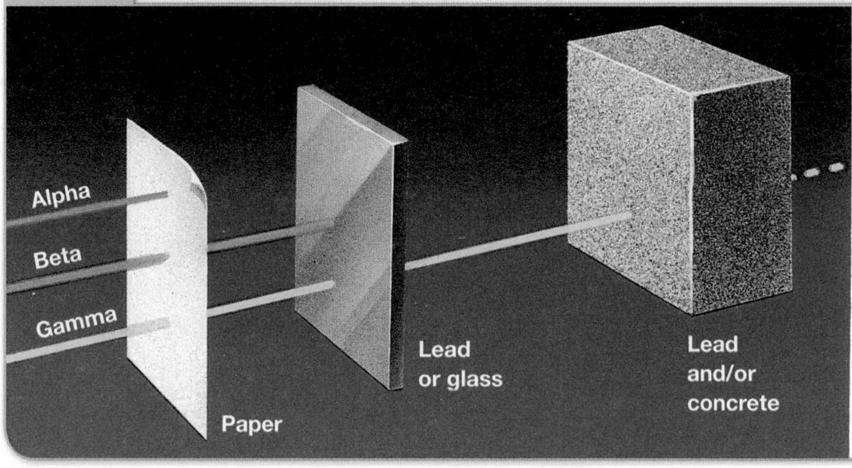

Radiation Energy The different penetrating abilities of alpha particles, beta particles, and gamma rays require different levels of shielding. Alpha particles can be shielded with just a sheet of paper. Lead or glass is often used to shield beta particles. Gamma rays are the most penetrating and require shielding with thick layers of lead or concrete, or both.

Everyone is exposed to background radiation. The estimated average exposure for people living in the United States is thought to be about 0.1 rem per year. However, actual exposure varies. The maximum permissible dose of radiation exposure for a person in the general population is 0.5 rem per year. Airline crews and those who live at high altitudes have increased exposure levels because of increased cosmic-ray levels at high altitudes. Radon-222 trapped inside homes also causes increased exposure. Because it is a gas, radon released from certain rocks can move up through the soil into homes through holes in the foundation. Radon trapped in homes increases the risk of lung cancer, especially among smokers.

▶ MAIN IDEA
Film and electronic methods can detect radiation.

Film badges, Geiger-Müller counters, and scintillation counters are three devices commonly used to detect and measure nuclear radiation. A film badge and a Geiger-Müller counter are shown in **Figure 3.2**. As previously mentioned, nuclear radiation exposes film just as visible light does. This property is used in film badges. **Film badges use exposure of film to measure the approximate radiation exposure of people working with radiation. Geiger-Müller counters are instruments that detect radiation by counting electric pulses carried by gas ionized by radiation.** Geiger-Müller counters are typically used to detect beta-particles, x-rays, and gamma radiation. Radiation can also be detected when it transfers its energy to substances that *scintillate*, or absorb ionizing radiation and emit visible light. **Scintillation counters are instruments that convert scintillating light to an electric signal for detecting radiation.**

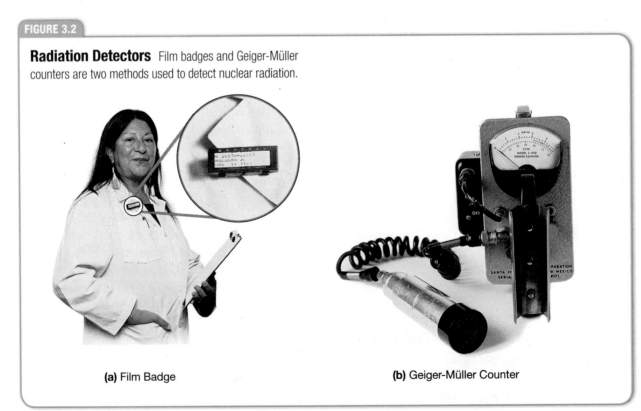

FIGURE 3.2

Radiation Detectors Film badges and Geiger-Müller counters are two methods used to detect nuclear radiation.

(a) Film Badge

(b) Geiger-Müller Counter

▶ MAIN IDEA
Radioactivity has important applications.

Many applications use the fact that the physical and chemical properties of stable isotopes are similar to those of radioactive isotopes of the same element. A few uses of radioactive nuclides are discussed below.

Radioactive Dating

Radioactive dating is the process by which the approximate age of an object is determined based on the amount of certain radioactive nuclides present. Such an estimate is based on the fact that radioactive substances decay with known half-lives. Age is estimated by measuring either the accumulation of a daughter nuclide or the disappearance of the parent nuclide.

Carbon-14 is radioactive and has a half-life of approximately 5715 years. It can be used to estimate the age of organic material up to about 50 000 years old. Nuclides with longer half-lives are used to estimate the age of older objects; methods using nuclides with long half-lives have been used to date minerals and lunar rocks more than 4 billion years old.

Radioactive Nuclides in Medicine

In medicine, radioactive nuclides, such as the artificial radioactive nuclide cobalt-60, are used to destroy certain types of cancer cells. **Many radioactive nuclides are also used as radioactive tracers, which are radioactive atoms that are incorporated into substances so that movement of the substances can be followed by radiation detectors.** Detection of radiation from radioactive tracers can be used to diagnose cancer and other diseases. See **Figure 3.3.**

Radioactive Nuclides in Agriculture

In agriculture, radioactive tracers in fertilizers are used to determine the effectiveness of the fertilizer. The amount of radioactive tracer absorbed by a plant indicates the amount of fertilizer absorbed. Nuclear radiation is also used to prolong the shelf life of food. For example, gamma rays from cobalt-60 can be used to kill bacteria and insects that spoil and infest food.

▶ MAIN IDEA
Storage and disposal of nuclear waste pose important concerns.

In nuclear fission, the nucleus of a very heavy atom, such as uranium, is split into two or more lighter nuclei. The products include the nuclei as well as the nucleons formed from the fragments' radioactive decay. Fission is the process that powers nuclear reactors, including those on nuclear-powered submarines and aircraft carriers.

Fusion is the opposite process. In fusion, very high temperatures and pressures combine light atoms, such as hydrogen, to make heavier atoms, such as helium. Fusion is the primary process that fuels the sun and the stars. Creating and maintaining a fusion reaction is very complex.

FIGURE 3.3

Radioactive Tracers
Radioactive nuclides, such as technetium-99, can be used to detect bone cancer. In this procedure, technetium-99 accumulates in areas of abnormal bone metabolism. Detection of the nuclear radiation then shows the location of bone cancer.

✔ **CRITICAL THINKING**
Recall What would be the dangers of using radioactivity in medicine? In agriculture?

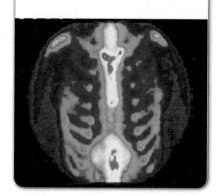

Both fission and fusion release enormous amounts of energy that can be converted into energy as heat and electrical energy. **Energy-producing nuclear processes, however, also produce nuclear waste, or unusable end materials that contain radioisotopes.** Fission produces more waste than fusion. As new processes are developed to use energy from fission and fusion, a more vexing question arises: how to contain, store, and dispose of nuclear waste.

Containment and Storage of Nuclear Waste

Every radioactive substance has a half-life, which is the amount of time needed for half of a given material to decay. Radioactive waste from medical research, for example, usually has a half-life that is a few months or less. Some of the waste that is produced in a nuclear reactor will take hundreds of thousands of years to decay, and it needs to be contained so that living organisms can be shielded from radioactivity. There are two main types of containment: on-site storage and off-site disposal.

The most common form of nuclear waste is spent fuel rods from nuclear power plants. These fuel rods can be contained above the ground by placing them in water pools or in dry casks. Each nuclear reactor in the United States has large pools of water where spent rods can be stored, and some of the radioactive materials will decay. When these pools are full, the rods are moved to dry casks, which are usually made of concrete and steel. Both storage pools and casks are meant for only temporary storage before moving the waste to permanent underground facilities.

Disposal of Nuclear Waste

Disposal of nuclear waste is done with the intention of never retrieving the materials. Because of this, building disposal sites takes careful planning. Currently, there are 131 disposal sites in 39 states around the United States. Plans to find a permanent disposal site for all the nation's nuclear waste are still not fully realized. Any proposed site has to contend with the concerns of nearby residents regarding the potential environmental and human impacts. Some have suggested either blowing up the waste or sending it into space, but such solutions are still speculative.

 SECTION 3 **FORMATIVE ASSESSMENT**

▶ Reviewing Main Ideas

1. What is required to shield alpha particles? Why are these materials effective?

2. a. What is the average exposure of people living in the United States to environmental background radiation?

   b. How does this relate to the maximum permissible dose?

3. What device is used to measure the radiation exposure of people working with radiation?

4. Explain why nuclear radiation can be used to preserve food.

✔ Critical Thinking

5. INFERRING CONCLUSIONS Explain how nuclear waste is contained, stored, and disposed of and how each method affects the environment.

Nuclear Fission and Nuclear Fusion

Key Terms

nuclear fission
chain reaction
critical mass

nuclear reactor
nuclear power plant
shielding

control rod
moderator
nuclear fusion

MAIN IDEA
In fission, atoms split into nearly equal parts.

Recall that nuclei of intermediate mass are the most stable. **In nuclear fission, a very heavy nucleus splits into more-stable nuclei of intermediate mass.** This process releases enormous amounts of energy. Nuclear fission may occur spontaneously or when nuclei are bombarded by particles. When uranium-235 is bombarded with slow neutrons, a uranium nucleus can capture one of the neutrons, making it very unstable. The nucleus splits into medium-mass nuclei with the emission of more neutrons. The mass of the products is less than the mass of the reactants. The missing mass is converted to energy.

Nuclear Chain Reaction

When fission of an atom bombarded by neutrons produces more neutrons, a chain reaction can occur. **A chain reaction is a reaction in which the material that starts the reaction is also one of the products and can start another reaction.** As shown in **Figure 4.1,** two or three neutrons can be given off when uranium-235 fission occurs. These neutrons can cause the fission of other uranium-235 nuclei. Again, neutrons are emitted, which can cause the fission of still other uranium-235 nuclei.

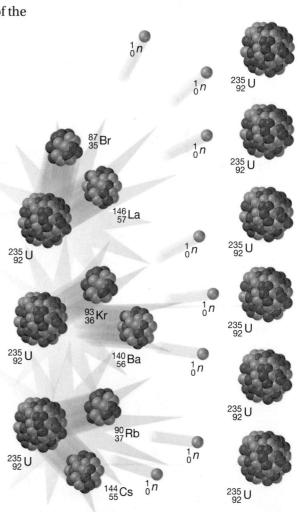

FIGURE 4.1

Nuclear Chain Reactions Fission induction of uranium-235 by bombardment with neutrons can lead to a chain reaction when a critical mass of uranium-235 is present.

A chain reaction continues until all of the uranium-235 atoms have split or until the neutrons fail to strike other uranium-235 nuclei. If the mass of the uranium-235 sample is below a certain minimum, too many neutrons escape without striking other nuclei, and the chain reaction stops. **The minimum amount of nuclide that provides the number of neutrons needed to sustain a chain reaction is called the critical mass.** Uncontrolled chain reactions give the explosive energy to atomic bombs. **Nuclear reactors** use controlled-fission chain reactions to produce energy and radioactive nuclides.

Nuclear Power Plants

Nuclear power plants use energy as heat from nuclear reactors to produce electrical energy. They have five main components: shielding, fuel, control rods, moderator, and coolant. The components, shown in **Figure 4.2,** are surrounded by shielding. **Shielding** is radiation-absorbing material that is used to decrease exposure to radiation, especially gamma rays, from nuclear reactors. Uranium-235 is typically used as the fissile fuel to produce energy as heat, which is absorbed by the coolant. **Control rods** are neutron-absorbing rods that help control the reaction by limiting the number of free neutrons. Because fission of uranium-235 is more efficiently induced by slow neutrons, a **moderator** is used to slow down the fast neutrons produced by fission. Nuclear power plants can provide competitively priced electricity without emitting greenhouse gases or particulates. Concerns about nuclear power include storage and disposal of spent radioactive fuel, as well as public perception.

FIGURE 4.2

Nuclear Power Plant In this model of a nuclear power plant, pressurized water is heated by fission of uranium-235. This water is circulated to a steam generator. The steam drives a turbine to produce electricity. Cool water from a lake or river is then used to condense the steam into water. The warm water from the condenser may be cooled in cooling towers before being reused or returned to the lake or river.

✔ CRITICAL THINKING

Defend How is a nuclear power plant similar to a fossil fuel plant? Which do you believe has more dangerous wastes? Support your opinion with at least three facts.

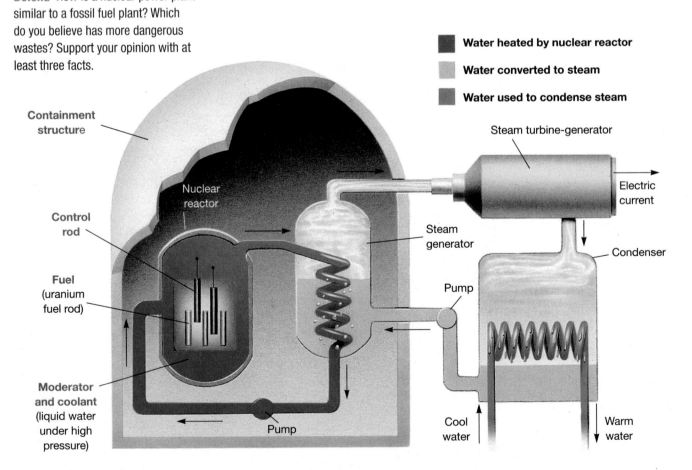

Water heated by nuclear reactor

Water converted to steam

Water used to condense steam

Containment structure

Steam turbine-generator

Electric current

Nuclear reactor

Control rod

Steam generator

Condenser

Fuel (uranium fuel rod)

Pump

Moderator and coolant (liquid water under high pressure)

Pump

Cool water

Warm water

FIGURE 4.3

Nuclear Fusion Fusion of hydrogen nuclei into more-stable helium nuclei provides the energy of our sun and other stars.

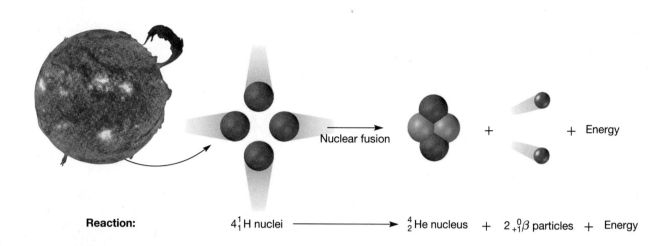

Reaction: $4\,_1^1H$ nuclei $\longrightarrow$ $_2^4He$ nucleus $+$ $2\,_{+1}^0\beta$ particles $+$ Energy

▶ MAIN IDEA
Nuclei combine in nuclear fusion.

The high stability of nuclei with intermediate masses can also be used to explain nuclear fusion. In **nuclear fusion,** low-mass nuclei combine to form a heavier, more stable nucleus. Nuclear fusion releases even more energy per gram of fuel than nuclear fission. In our sun and stars that are similar to the sun, hydrogen nuclei combine at extremely high temperature and pressure to form a helium nucleus with a loss of mass and release of energy. The net reaction is illustrated in **Figure 4.3.**

If fusion reactions can be controlled, they could be used for energy generation. Researchers are currently studying ways to contain the reacting plasma that is required for fusion. A plasma is an extremely hot mixture of positive nuclei and electrons. There is no known material that can withstand the initial temperatures, about 10^8 K, required to induce fusion. Scientists use strong magnetic fields to suspend the charged plasma inside a container but away from the walls. Additionally, a large amount of energy is needed to initiate fusion reactions. For fusion to be a practical energy source, more energy needs to be generated by the reaction than is needed to initiate it.

✔ **CHECK FOR UNDERSTANDING**
Compare How is nuclear fusion different from nuclear fission?

✔ SECTION 4 **FORMATIVE ASSESSMENT**

▶ Reviewing Main Ideas

1. Distinguish between nuclear fission and nuclear fusion.

2. Define *chain reaction.*

3. List the five main components of a nuclear power plant.

✔ Critical Thinking

4. RELATING IDEAS Explain how fusion is one of our sources of energy.

An Unexpected Finding

Historical Perspective

The discovery of the artificial transmutation of uranium in 1934 triggered great excitement in science. Chemists who were preoccupied with identifying what they thought were the final missing elements of the periodic table suddenly had to consider the existence of elements beyond atomic number 92. Physicists began to probe the stability of the nucleus more deeply. By 1939, nuclear investigators in both fields had collaborated to provide a stunning explanation for the mysterious results of uranium's forced transformation.

This apparatus from Otto Hahn's lab was used to produce fission reactions.

Neutrons in Italy

In 1934, the element with the most known protons was uranium, with 92. But that year, Italian physicist Enrico Fermi thought he had synthesized elements with higher atomic numbers. After bombarding a sample of uranium with neutrons, Fermi and his coworkers recorded measurements that seemed to indicate that some uranium nuclei had absorbed neutrons and then undergone beta decay:

$$^{238}_{92}U + ^{1}_{0}n \longrightarrow ^{239}_{92}U \longrightarrow$$
$$^{239}_{93}? + ^{0}_{-1}\beta$$

His report noted further subsequent beta decays, by which he hypothesized the existence of a whole new series of "transuranic" elements, now called *transuranes:*

$$^{238}_{92}U \longrightarrow ^{239}_{93}? + ^{0}_{-1}\beta \longrightarrow$$
$$^{238}_{94}?? + ^{0}_{-1}\beta \longrightarrow ^{238}_{95}??? + ^{0}_{-1}\beta$$

Unfortunately, Fermi and his group of scientists could not verify the existence of the transuranes because, according to Fermi, "We did not know enough chemistry to separate the products of uranium disintegration from one another."

Curiosity in Berlin

Fermi's experiments caught the attention of a physicist in Berlin, Lise Meitner. Knowing that she could not perform the difficult task of chemically separating radionuclides either, Meitner persuaded a colleague, radiochemist Otto Hahn, to help her explain Fermi's results. Joined by expert chemical analyst Fritz Strassmann, Meitner's team began investigating neutron-induced uranium decay at the end of 1934.

From the onset, Meitner's team, as well as all other scientists at the time, operated under two false assumptions. The first involved the makeup of the bombarded nuclei. In every nuclear reaction that had been observed, the resulting nucleus had never differed from the original by more than a few protons or neutrons. Thus, scientists assumed that the products of neutron bombardment were radioisotopes of elements that were at most a few places in the periodic table before or beyond the atoms being bombarded (as Fermi had presumed in hypothesizing the transuranes).

The second assumption concerned the periodicity of the transuranes. Because the elements Ac, Th, Pa, and U chemically resemble the transition elements in the third row of the periodic table, La, Hf, Ta, and W, scientists thought that

©akg images

elements beyond U would correspondingly resemble those following W. Thus, the transuranes were thought to be homologues of Re, Os, Ir, Pt, and the other transition elements in the third row. This belief was generally unquestioned and seemed to be confirmed. In fact, by 1937 Hahn was sure that the chemical evidence of transuranes confirmed their location in the periodic table.

Meitner's Exile

By 1938, the political situation in Germany had become dangerous for Meitner. Because she was of Jewish descent, she was targeted by the Nazis and fled to Sweden to escape persecution. Meanwhile in Berlin, Hahn and Strassmann, who were critical of the Nazis, had to be careful.

Despite being censored by the Nazis, Meitner's team continued to communicate through letters. Meitner could not formulate a satisfying physical explanation for the chemical results of Hahn and Strassmann, and she insisted that her partners reexamine their findings. Because of her colleagues' great respect for her talent and expertise, they quickly performed control experiments to test their results.

A Shocking Discovery

Prompted by Meitner, Hahn and Strassmann realized they had been looking in the wrong place to find the cause of their results. In analyzing a fraction of a solution assay that they had previously ignored, they found the critical evidence they had been seeking.

The analysis indicated that barium appeared to be a result of neutron bombardment of uranium. Suspecting the spectacular truth but lacking confidence, Hahn wrote to Meitner for an explanation. After consultation with her nephew, Otto Frisch, Meitner proposed that the uranium nuclei had been broken apart into elemental fragments, one of which was barium, Ba. On January 3, 1939, she wrote to Hahn to congratulate him on the groundbreaking result.

Thus, the "transuranes" turned out to be merely radioisotopes of known elements—atomic fragments of uranium atoms that had burst apart when struck by neutrons.

The politics of World War II prevented Lise Meitner from receiving the Nobel Prize in Physics for explaining nuclear fission.

For the discovery of this unexpected phenomenon, which Meitner named nuclear fission, the talented Hahn was awarded the 1944 Nobel Prize in Chemistry. Because of wartime politics, however, Lise Meitner did not receive the corresponding award in physics. It was not until well after her death in 1968 that she was properly recognized for her role in clarifying the process that she first explained and named.

Questions

1. What type of element did Fermi expect to find when uranium absorbed a neutron and then ejected a beta particle?

2. What were the products of uranium disintegrations?

The rate at which a sample of a radioactive nuclide decays is expressed in terms of half-life. This quantity is the time required for half of the atoms of a sample of a given nuclide to decay. For example, it takes 37.2 min for half of the nuclei of chlorine-38 to decay to argon-38. After 37.2 min, 0.50 g of a 1.0 g sample of chlorine-38 will remain, and there will be 0.50 g of argon-38. After two half-lives (74.4 min), the fraction of chlorine-38 that remains will be $\frac{1}{2}$ of $\frac{1}{2}$, or $\frac{1}{4}$.

After n half-lives, the fraction of a radioactive nuclide that remains is $\left(\frac{1}{2}\right)^n$, or 2^{-n}.

If you know the amount of nuclide that was present initially and the amount of nuclide that remains, you can determine the number of half-lives that have passed.

Problem-Solving TIPS

- Familiarize yourself with the values of some common powers of two (2^n, $n = 1, 2, 3, 4, 5, 6$, etc). This will allow you to determine the number of half-lives quickly.

Sample Problem

The half-life of polonium-218 is 3.04 min. A sample of polonium contains 0.00558 g of $^{218}_{84}$Po. What mass of $^{218}_{84}$Po will remain after 18.24 min?

First, you must determine the number of half-lives that have passed in 18.24 min.

$$\text{number of half-lives} = \frac{\text{time elapsed}}{\text{half-life}} = \frac{18.24 \text{ min}}{3.04 \text{ min}} = 6.00 \text{ half-lives}$$

Then, to determine the mass of polonium-218 remaining, apply the following relationship:

$$\text{mass remaining} = \text{starting mass} \times \text{fraction remaining}$$

$$\text{mass } ^{218}_{84}\text{Po remaining} = 0.00558 \text{ g} \times \left(\frac{1}{2}\right)^6 = 0.00558 \text{ g} \times \frac{1}{64} = 8.72 \times 10^{-5} \text{ g } ^{218}_{84}\text{Po}$$

The half-life of potassium-40 is 1.3×10^9 years. A volcanic rock contains $\frac{1}{8}$ of the amount of potassium-40 found in newly formed rocks. When was the rock formed?

First, determine the number of half-lives that have passed.

$$\text{fraction remaining} = \frac{1}{8} = \left(\frac{1}{2}\right) \times \left(\frac{1}{2}\right) \times \left(\frac{1}{2}\right)$$

Therefore, three half-lives have passed. The time since the rock was formed is

$$3 \text{ half-lives} \times \left(1.3 \times 10^9 \frac{\text{y}}{\text{half-life}}\right) = 3.9 \times 10^9 \text{ y.}$$

Practice

1. A sample of chromium contains 8.9×10^{-5} g of the radioactive nuclide chromium-51, which has a half-life of 28 days. What mass of chromium-51 will remain in the sample after 168 days?

2. The half-life of lead-202 is 53 000 years. A sample of lead contains only $\frac{1}{256}$ of the expected amount of lead-202. How old is the lead sample?

BIG IDEA When an atomic nucleus becomes unstable, it emits radiation in the form of particles and energy to regain stability. Nuclei often change identity during radioactive decay.

SECTION 1 The Nucleus

KEY TERMS

- The difference between the sum of the masses of the nucleons and electrons in an atom and the actual mass of an atom is the mass defect, or nuclear binding energy.
- Nuclear stability tends to be greatest when nucleons are paired, when there are magic numbers of nucleons, and when there are certain neutron-proton ratios.
- Nuclear reactions, which are represented by nuclear equations, can involve the transmutation of nuclides.

nucleon
nuclide
mass defect
nuclear binding energy

nuclear shell model
magic number
nuclear reaction
transmutation

SECTION 2 Radioactive Decay

KEY TERMS

- Radioactive nuclides decay to form more stable nuclides.
- Alpha, beta, positron, and gamma emissions are types of radioactive decay. Electron capture is also a type of radioactive decay. The type of decay is related to the nucleon content and the energy level of the nucleus.
- The half-life of a radioactive nuclide is the length of time that it takes for half of a given number of atoms of the nuclide to decay.
- Artificial transmutations are used to produce artificial radioactive nuclides, which include the transuranium elements.

radioactive decay
nuclear radiation
radioactive nuclide
alpha particle
beta particle
positron
electron capture

gamma ray
half-life
decay series
parent nuclide
daughter nuclide
artificial transmutation
transuranium element

SECTION 3 Nuclear Radiation

KEY TERMS

- Alpha particles, beta particles, and gamma rays have different penetrating abilities and shielding requirements.
- Film badges, Geiger-Müller counters, and scintillation detectors are used to detect radiation.
- Everyone is exposed to environmental background radiation.
- Radioactive nuclides have many uses, including radioactive dating, disease detection, and therapy.
- Nuclear waste must be contained, stored, and disposed of in a way that minimizes harm to people and the environment.

roentgen
rem
film badge
Geiger-Müller counter
scintillation counter

radioactive dating
radioactive tracer
nuclear waste

SECTION 4 Nuclear Fission and Nuclear Fusion

KEY TERMS

- Nuclear fission and nuclear fusion are nuclear reactions in which the splitting and fusing of nuclei produce more stable nuclei and release enormous amounts of energy.
- Controlled fission reactions produce energy and radioactive nuclides.
- Fusion reactions produce the sun's energy in the form of heat and light. If fusion reactions could be controlled, they would produce more usable energy per gram of fuel than fission reactions.

nuclear fission
chain reaction
critical mass
nuclear reactor
nuclear power plant

shielding
control rod
moderator
nuclear fusion

CHAPTER 21 Review

GO ONLINE

Interactive Review
HMHScience.com

Review Games
Concept Maps

SECTION 1
The Nucleus

 REVIEWING MAIN IDEAS

1. a. How does mass defect relate to nuclear binding energy?
  b. How does binding energy per nucleon vary with mass number?
  c. How does binding energy per nucleon affect the stability of a nucleus?

2. Describe three ways in which the number of protons and the number of neutrons in a nucleus affect the stability of the nucleus.

PRACTICE PROBLEMS

3. The mass of a $^{20}_{10}Ne$ atom is 19.992 44 u. Calculate the atom's mass defect.

4. The mass of a $^{7}_{3}Li$ atom is 7.016 00 u. Calculate the atom's mass defect.

5. Calculate the nuclear binding energy of one lithium-6 atom. The measured atomic mass of lithium-6 is 6.015 u.

6. Calculate the binding energies of the following two nuclei, and indicate which nucleus releases more energy when formed. You will need information from the periodic table and the text.
  a. atomic mass 34.988011 u, $^{35}_{19}K$
  b. atomic mass 22.989767 u, $^{23}_{11}Na$

7. a. What is the binding energy per nucleon for each nucleus in the previous problem?
  b. Which nucleus is more stable?

8. The mass of $^{7}_{3}Li$ is 7.016 00 u. Calculate the binding energy per nucleon for $^{7}_{3}Li$.

9. Calculate the neutron-proton ratios for the following nuclides:
  a. $^{12}_{6}C$ **c.** $^{206}_{82}Pb$
  b. $^{3}_{1}H$ **d.** $^{134}_{50}Sn$

10. a. Locate the nuclides in problem 9 on the graph in **Figure 1.2**. Which ones lie within the band of stability?
  b. For the stable nuclides, determine whether their neutron-proton ratio tends toward 1:1 or 1.5:1.

11. Balance the following nuclear equations. (Hint: See Sample Problem A.)
  a. $^{43}_{19}K \longrightarrow {}^{43}_{20}Ca +$ _?_
  b. $^{233}_{92}U \longrightarrow {}^{229}_{90}Th +$ _?_
  c. $^{11}_{6}C +$ _?_ $\longrightarrow {}^{11}_{5}B$
  d. $^{13}_{7}N \longrightarrow + {}^{1}_{0}\beta^{+} +$ _?_

12. Write the nuclear equation for the release of an alpha particle by $^{210}_{84}Po$.

13. Write the nuclear equation for the release of a beta particle by $^{210}_{82}Pb$.

SECTION 2
Radioactive Decay

 REVIEWING MAIN IDEAS

14. Beyond what point on the periodic table are all of the naturally occuring elements radioactive?

15. What changes in atomic number and mass number occur in each of the following types of radioactive decay?
  a. alpha emission
  b. beta emission
  c. positron emission
  d. electron capture

16. Which types of radioactive decay cause the transmutation of a nuclide? (Hint: Review the definition of *transmutation*.)

17. Explain how beta emission, positron emission, and electron capture affect the neutron-proton ratio.

18. Write the nuclear reactions that show particle conversion for the following types of radioactive decay:
  a. beta emission
  b. positron emission
  c. electron capture

19. Compare electrons, beta particles, and positrons.

20. a. What are gamma rays?
  b. How do scientists think gamma rays are produced?

21. How does the half-life of a nuclide relate to the stability of the nuclide?

22. List the three parent nuclides of the natural decay series.

23. How are artificial radioactive isotopes produced?

24. Neutrons are more effective for bombarding atomic nuclei than protons or alpha particles are. Why?

25. Why are all of the transuranium elements radioactive? (Hint: See Section 1.)

PRACTICE PROBLEMS

26. The half-life of plutonium-239 is 24 110 years. Of an original mass of 100. g, how much plutonium-239 remains after 96 440 years? (Hint: See Sample Problem B.)

27. The half-life of thorium-227 is 18.72 days. How many days are required for three-fourths of a given amount of thorium-227 to decay?

28. Exactly $\frac{1}{16}$ of a given amount of protactinium-234 remains after 26.76 hours. What is the half-life of protactinium-234?

29. How many milligrams of a 15.0 mg sample of radium-226 remain after 6396 years? The half-life of radium-226 is 1599 years.

SECTION 3

Nuclear Radiation

▶ **REVIEWING MAIN IDEAS**

30. Why can a radioactive material affect photographic film even though the film is completely wrapped in black paper?

31. How does the penetrating ability of gamma rays compare with that of alpha particles and beta particles?

32. How does nuclear radiation damage biological tissue?

33. Explain how film badges, Geiger-Müller counters, and scintillation detectors are used to detect radiation and measure radiation exposure.

34. How is the age of an object that contains a radioactive nuclide estimated?

SECTION 4

Nuclear Fission and Nuclear Fusion

▶ **REVIEWING MAIN IDEAS**

35. How is the fission of a uranium-235 nucleus induced?

36. How does the fission of uranium-235 produce a chain reaction?

37. Describe the purposes of the five major components of a nuclear power plant.

38. Describe the reaction that produces the sun's energy.

39. What is one problem that must be overcome before controlled fusion reactions that produce energy are a reality?

Mixed Review

▶ **REVIEWING MAIN IDEAS**

40. Balance the following nuclear reactions:
    a. $^{239}_{93}\text{Np} \longrightarrow ^{0}_{-1}\beta + \underline{?}$
    b. $^{9}_{4}\text{Be} + ^{4}_{2}\text{He} \longrightarrow \underline{?}$
    c. $^{32}_{15}\text{P} + \underline{?} \longrightarrow ^{33}_{15}\text{P}$
    d. $^{236}_{92}\text{U} \longrightarrow ^{94}_{36}\text{Kr} + \underline{?} + 3\,^{1}_{0}n$

41. After 4797 years, how much of the original 0.250 g of radium-226 remains? The half-life of radium-226 is 1599 years.

42. The parent nuclide of the thorium decay series is $^{232}_{90}\text{Th}$. The first four decays are as follows: alpha emission, beta emission, beta emission, and alpha emission. Write the nuclear equations for this series of emissions.

43. The half-life of radium-224 is 3.66 days. What was the original mass of radium-224 if 0.0500 g remains after 7.32 days?

44. Calculate the neutron-proton ratios for the following nuclides, and determine where they lie in relation to the band of stability.
    a. $^{235}_{92}\text{U}$ c. $^{56}_{26}\text{Fe}$
    b. $^{16}_{8}\text{O}$ d. $^{156}_{60}\text{Nd}$

45. Calculate the binding energy per nucleon of $^{238}_{92}\text{U}$ in joules. The atomic mass of a $^{238}_{92}\text{U}$ nucleus is 238.050 784 u.

46. The energy released by the formation of a nucleus of $^{56}_{26}$Fe is 7.89×10^{-11} J. Use Einstein's equation $E = mc^2$ to determine how much mass (in kilograms) is lost in this process.

47. Calculate the binding energy for one mole of deuterium atoms. The measured mass of deuterium is 2.0140 u.

CRITICAL THINKING

48. Why do we compare binding energy per nuclear particle of different nuclides instead of the total binding energy per nucleus of different nuclides?

49. Why is the constant rate of decay of radioactive nuclei so important in radioactive dating?

50. Which of the following nuclides of carbon is more likely to be stable? State reasons for your answer.

   a. $^{11}_{6}$C   **b.** $^{12}_{6}$C

51. Which of the following nuclides of iron is more likely to be stable? State reasons for your answer.

   a. $^{56}_{26}$Fe   **b.** $^{59}_{26}$Fe

52. Use the data shown below to determine the following:

   a. the isotopes that would be best for dating ancient rocks

   b. the isotopes that could be used as tracers

   State reasons for your answers.

Element	Half-Life
potassium-40	1.28×10^9 y
potassium-42	12.36 h
uranium-238	4.468×10^9 y
uranium-239	23.47 min

RESEARCH AND WRITING

53. Investigate the history of the Manhattan Project.

54. Research the 2011 Fukashima reactor accident in Japan. What factors combined to cause the accident?

55. Find out about the various fusion-energy research projects that are being conducted in the United States and other parts of the world. What obstacles in finding an economical method of producing energy must still be overcome?

ALTERNATIVE ASSESSMENT

56. Using the library, research the medical uses of radioactive isotopes such as cobalt-60 and technetium-99. Evaluate the benefits and risks of using radioisotopes in the diagnosis and treatment of medical conditions. Report your findings to the class.

Standards-Based Assessment

Record your answers on a separate piece of paper.

MULTIPLE CHOICE

1 Complete the nuclear equation shown below:

$$\underline{?} \rightarrow {}^{187}_{76}\text{Os} + {}^{0}_{-1}\beta$$

A ${}^{187}_{77}\text{Os}$

B ${}^{187}_{75}\text{Os}$

C ${}^{187}_{77}\text{Ir}$

D ${}^{187}_{75}\text{Re}$

2 The mass of the nucleus is —

A greater than the mass of the protons and neutrons that make up the nucleus

B equal to the mass of the protons and neutrons that make up the nucleus

C less than the mass of the protons and neutrons that make up the nucleus

D converted to energy

3 Which type of radiation has the *most* penetrating ability?

A an alpha particle

B a beta particle

C a gamma ray

D a neutron

4 Which of the following nuclear equations is correctly balanced?

A ${}^{37}_{18}\text{Ar} + {}^{0}_{-1}e \rightarrow {}^{37}_{17}\text{Cl}$

B ${}^{6}_{3}\text{Li} + 2{}^{1}_{0}n \rightarrow {}^{4}_{2}\text{He} + {}^{3}_{1}\text{H}$

C ${}^{254}_{99}\text{Es} + {}^{4}_{2}\text{He} \rightarrow {}^{258}_{101}\text{Md} + 2{}^{1}_{0}n$

D ${}^{14}_{7}\text{N} + {}^{4}_{2}\text{He} \rightarrow {}^{17}_{8}\text{O} + {}^{2}_{1}\text{H}$

5 It takes 5.2 min for a 4.0 g sample of francium-210 to decay until only 1.0 g is left. What is the half-life of francium-210?

A 1.3 min

B 2.6 min

C 5.2 min

D 7.8 min

6 In the early 20th century, experiments by Max Planck explained the photoelectric effect in terms of light quanta called photons. In the 1920s, Niels Bohr explained the emission spectra of atoms with photons, and Erwin Schrödinger and Louis de Broglie described electrons in terms of waves. The concept that results from these experiments is that light waves sometimes have particle properties and sometimes have wave properties. This concept illustrates that —

A even strong scientific theories can be open to change

B a scientific theory, if posited, will never change

C scientists change theories with very little evidence if it helps them explain a phenomenon

D light will most likely never be better understood than how it was understood 300 years ago

7 Between 1800 and 1935, the concept of the atom changed by steps from the first evidence of indivisible particles to the structured atom with protons and neutrons in a tiny, dense nucleus and electrons orbiting it. The atomic theory changed over time because —

A over time, scientists were able to use the same tools with more success

B the development of new technologies, such as cathode rays and scintillation counters, made observations of subatomic particles possible

C about every 50 years, someone would discover a new theory of atoms

D as more scientists worked on the question of what an atom really is, change was inevitable

GRIDDED RESPONSE

8 The half-life of thorium-234 is 24 days. If you have a 42.0 g sample of thorium-234, how much, in grams, will remain after 72 days?

Test Tip
Keeping a positive attitude during any test will help you focus on the test and likely improve your score.

A BOOK EXPLAINING COMPLEX IDEAS USING ONLY THE 1,000 MOST COMMON WORDS

RANDALL MUNROE
XKCD.COM

HEAVY METAL POWER BUILDING

Making heat from heavy metals

You know that nuclear reactors use controlled-fission chain reactions to produce energy and radioactive nuclides—and that nuclear power plants use heat from nuclear reactors to produce electrical energy. Here's a look at the process that turns nuclear fission into electric current.

THE STORY OF THE HEAVY METAL POWER BUILDING

THESE BUILDINGS USE SPECIAL KINDS OF HARD-TO-FIND HEAVY METAL TO MAKE POWER. SOME OF THE METALS THEY USE CAN BE FOUND IN THE GROUND, BUT ONLY IN A FEW PLACES. OTHER KINDS CAN BE MADE BY PEOPLE—BUT ONLY WITH THE HELP OF A POWER BUILDING THAT'S ALREADY RUNNING.

THESE METALS MAKE HEAT ALL THE TIME, EVEN WHEN THEY'RE JUST SITTING. THEY MAKE TWO KINDS OF HEAT: NORMAL HEAT—LIKE HEAT FROM A FIRE—AND A DIFFERENT, SPECIAL KIND OF HEAT. THIS SPECIAL HEAT IS LIKE LIGHT THAT YOU CAN'T SEE. (AT LEAST, YOU CAN'T SEE IT MOST OF THE TIME. IF THERE'S A WHOLE LOT OF IT, ENOUGH TO KILL YOU QUICKLY, YOU CAN SEE IT. IT LOOKS BLUE.)

NORMAL HEAT CAN BURN YOU, BUT THE SPECIAL HEAT FROM THESE METALS CAN BURN YOU IN A DIFFERENT WAY.

I'M ON FIRE!   ME TOO

IF YOU SPEND TOO MUCH TIME NEAR THIS HEAT, YOUR BODY CAN START GROWING WRONG. SOME OF THE FIRST PEOPLE WHO TRIED TO LEARN ABOUT THESE METALS DIED THAT WAY.

I'M BURNING UP

RIP

THE SPECIAL HEAT IS MADE WHEN TINY PIECES OF THE METAL BREAK DOWN. THIS LETS OUT A LOT OF HEAT, FAR MORE THAN ANY NORMAL FIRE COULD. BUT FOR MANY KINDS OF METAL, IT HAPPENS VERY SLOWLY. A PIECE OF METAL AS OLD AS THE EARTH MIGHT BE ONLY HALF BROKEN DOWN BY NOW.

WITHIN THE LAST HUNDRED YEARS, WE LEARNED SOMETHING VERY STRANGE: WHEN SOME OF THESE METALS FEEL SPECIAL HEAT, THEY BREAK DOWN FASTER. IF YOU PUT A PIECE OF THIS METAL CLOSE TO ANOTHER PIECE, IT WILL MAKE HEAT, WHICH WILL MAKE THE OTHER PIECE BREAK DOWN FASTER AND MAKE MORE HEAT.

IF YOU PUT TOO MUCH OF THE METAL TOGETHER LIKE THIS, IT GETS HOTTER AND HOTTER SO FAST THAT IT CAN ALL BREAK DOWN AT ONCE, LETTING OUT ALL ITS HEAT IN LESS THAN A SECOND. THIS IS HOW A SMALL MACHINE CAN BURN AN ENTIRE CITY.

BOOM!

TO MAKE POWER, PEOPLE TRY TO PUT PIECES OF THIS METAL CLOSE ENOUGH TOGETHER THAT THEY MAKE HEAT FAST, BUT NOT SO CLOSE THAT THEY GO OUT OF CONTROL AND BLOW UP. THIS IS VERY HARD, BUT THERE IS SO MUCH HEAT AND POWER STORED IN THIS METAL THAT SOME PEOPLE HAVE WANTED TO TRY ANYWAY.

OUTSIDE POWER LINE

Even though the building makes power, without outside power it will stop running.

This is important, because it means that if there's a very big problem, you can stop things from the outside by turning off the power.

POWER BUILDING

This building holds the metal and makes power. Water comes in, and it uses the metal to heat the water, then makes power from the hot water. (There's a bigger picture of it on the next page.)

COOLING BUILDING

After they're done with it, the sea water is very hot. They put it in this building to let it cool down a little so it's not too hot when they put it back in the sea.

They pour the water out into the air, where it falls like rain. As it falls, the air cools it down. This warms up the air, which makes it rise, and new cold air moves in from the outside to take its place.

HOT METAL SIDE   **POWER SIDE**

POWER LINE BOX

Sometimes animals get in here and break something, and it makes the entire building stop working.

Used water comes out here. The used water is clean, but it's still warm. Animals like to hang around here when it's cold out.

Cold water gets pulled in here. Sometimes fish get stuck in it and they have to turn off the power building to figure out what's wrong.

MAKING POWER WITH WATER

The building makes power by heating water. This means they need lots of cold water, which is why they're usually built near the sea or a big river.

They don't let the water from the sea touch the water that goes near the hot metal itself. Instead, they let the metal heat up water that runs through metal lines. Then the heat from those lines heats water in another water carrier, which goes over to the other part of the building. Then *that* water heats the water from the sea.

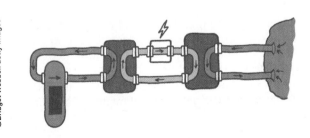

HEAVY METAL POWER BUILDING

CONTROL STICKS

These sticks control how hot the metal gets. When they're pushed down, the ends go in between the pieces of metal and block the special heat.

Sometimes, these are held up by outside power, so if the power stops, the sticks all fall down and stop the heat.

WALL
For keeping problems inside.

USED METAL ROOM
The water blocks the strange heat from the metal while it cools back down.

HOT WET AIR

METAL LIFTER

PART LIFTER

CONTROL ROOM

HOLE IN WALL
New metal goes in here.

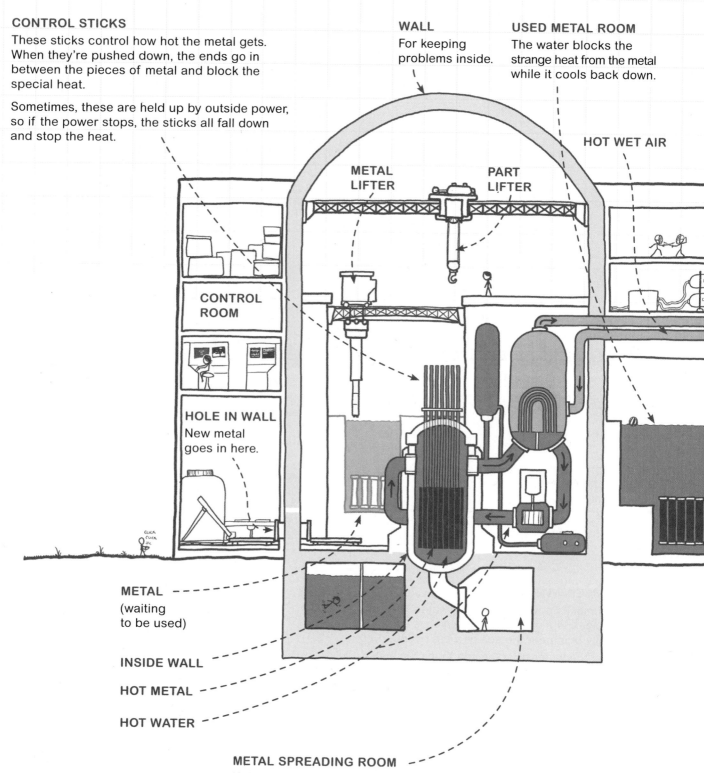

METAL
(waiting to be used)

INSIDE WALL

HOT METAL

HOT WATER

METAL SPREADING ROOM

If there are problems and everything is on fire, the special metal can get so hot that it starts moving like water. Sometimes, it can get hot enough to burn a hole through the floor. If that happens, this room is here so the watery metal can fall down and then spread out over the floor.

It's good if the metal can spread out, since when it's all close together, it keeps making itself hotter. If this room ever gets used, it means everything has gone very, very wrong.

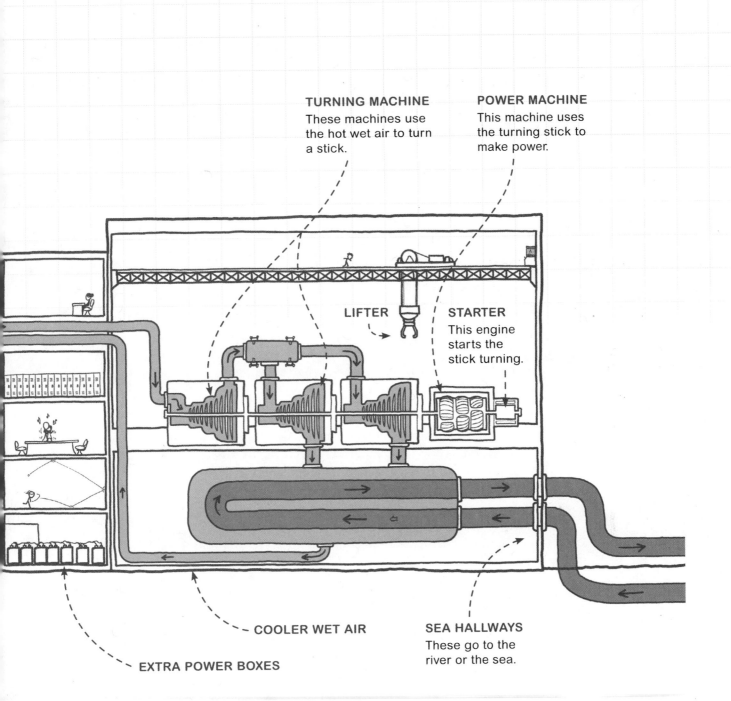

TURNING MACHINE
These machines use the hot wet air to turn a stick.

POWER MACHINE
This machine uses the turning stick to make power.

LIFTER

STARTER
This engine starts the stick turning.

COOLER WET AIR

SEA HALLWAYS
These go to the river or the sea.

EXTRA POWER BOXES

CHAPTER 22
Organic Chemistry

BIG IDEA
Carbon's ability to form four covalent bonds either to itself or other atoms leads to compounds with unique structures. Many carbon compounds are important to life.

 ONLINE Chemistry
HMHScience.com

ONLINE LABS
- Carbon
- A Cloth of Many Colors
- Polymers and Toy Balls
- Polymers
- The Slime Challenge
- S.T.E.M. Lab Cleaning Up Oil Spills

GO ONLINE

 Why It Matters Video
HMHScience.com

Organic Chemistry

©David Luzzi, Univ. of Pennsylvania/Photo Researchers, Inc; (br) ©PhotoDisc/C Squared Studios/Getty Images

Organic Compounds

Key Terms

organic compound   isomer   geometric isomer
catenation   structural formula
hydrocarbon   structural isomer

All organic compounds contain carbon atoms. However, not all carbon-containing compounds are classified as organic. There are a few exceptions, such as Na_2CO_3, CO, and CO_2, that are considered inorganic. **We can define organic compounds as covalently bonded compounds containing carbon, excluding carbonates and oxides. Figure 1.1** shows a few familiar items that contain organic compounds.

SECTION 1

Main Ideas

▶ The uniqueness of carbon bonding results in many organic compounds.

▶ Structural formulas show the numbers, types, and arrangement of the atoms in a molecule.

▶ Isomers can be structural or geometric.

▶ MAIN IDEA

The uniqueness of carbon bonding results in many organic compounds.

The diversity of organic compounds results from the uniqueness of carbon's structure and bonding. Carbon's electronic structure allows it to bind to itself to form chains and rings, to bind covalently to other elements, and to bind to itself and other elements in different arrangements.

FIGURE 1.1

Organic Compounds Aspirin, polyethylene in plastic bags, citric acid in fruit, and amino acids in animals are all examples of organic compounds.

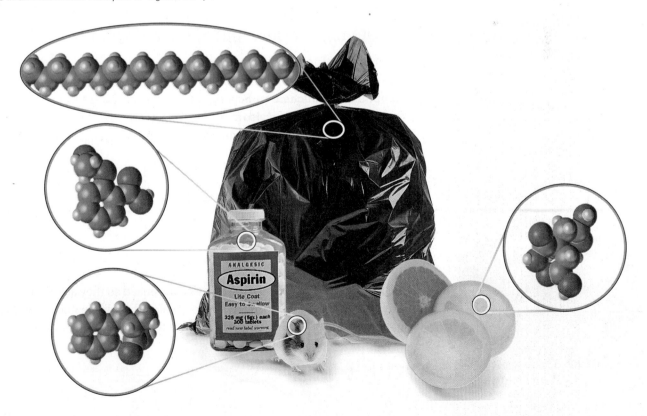

FIGURE 1.2

Carbon-Carbon Bonds

Carbon-Carbon Bonds Compare the shape of a fatty acid found in cream with that of fructose, found in fruit. In the fatty acid, the carbon atoms are in chains. In fructose, carbon atoms form a ring.

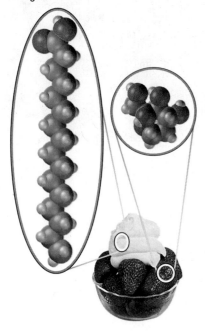

FIGURE 1.3

Carbon and Other Elements

In firefly luciferin, carbon atoms bind to hydrogen, oxygen, nitrogen, and sulfur. Luciferin is responsible for the light emitted from the tail of a firefly.

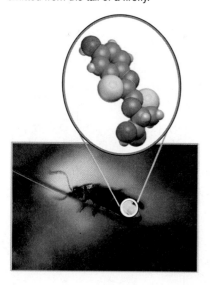

Carbon-Carbon Bonding

Carbon atoms are unique in their ability to form long chains and rings of covalently bonded atoms. **This type of bonding is known as catenation, the covalent bonding of an element to itself to form chains or rings.** In addition, carbon atoms in these structures can be linked by single, double, or triple covalent bonds. Examples of molecules containing carbon-atom rings and chains are shown in **Figure 1.2**.

Carbon Bonding to Other Elements

Besides being able to bind to each other, carbon atoms bind readily to elements with similar electronegativities. Organic compounds consist of carbon and these other elements. **Hydrocarbons are composed of only carbon and hydrogen; they are the simplest organic compounds.** Other organic compounds contain hydrocarbon backbones to which other elements, primarily O, N, S, and the halogens, are attached. **Figure 1.3** shows a molecule in which carbon atoms are bound to other elements.

Arrangement of Atoms

The bonding capabilities of carbon also allow for different arrangements of atoms. This means that some compounds may contain the same atoms but have different properties because the atoms are arranged differently. For example, the molecular formula C_2H_6O represents both ethanol and dimethyl ether. **Compounds that have the same molecular formula but different structures are called isomers.**

▶ MAIN IDEA

Structural formulas show the numbers, types, and arrangement of the atoms in a molecule.

Organic chemists use structural formulas to represent organic compounds. This is necessary in order to show the difference between isomers of a compound. **A structural formula indicates the number and types of atoms present in a molecule and also shows the bonding arrangement of the atoms.** An example of a structural formula for an isomer of C_4H_{10} is the following.

$$
\begin{array}{ccccc}
 & H & & H & & H \\
 & | & & | & & | \\
H- & C & - & C & - & C & -H \\
 & | & & | & & | \\
 & H & & H-C-H & & H \\
 & & & | & & \\
 & & & H & &
\end{array}
$$

Structural formulas are sometimes condensed so they are easier to read. In one type, the hydrogen single covalent bonds are not shown. The atoms are understood to bind to the atom they are written beside.

The following structural and condensed structural formulas represent the same molecule.

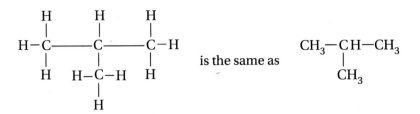

is the same as

Remember that the structural formula does not accurately show the three-dimensional shape of the molecule. Three-dimensional shape is depicted with drawings or models, as shown for ethanol in **Figure 1.4.**

FIGURE 1.4

Structural and Condensed Formulas The structure of ethanol can be represented in different ways. Ball-and-stick and space-filling models represent the three-dimensional shape of the molecule.

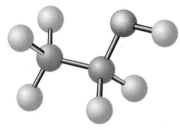

Ball-and-stick model

Space-filling model

▶ **MAIN IDEA**

Isomers can be structural or geometric.

You have learned that isomers are compounds that have the same molecular formula but different structural formulas. Isomers can be further classified by structure and geometry.

Structural Isomers

Structural isomers, also called "constitutional isomers," are isomers in which the atoms are bonded together in different orders. For example, the atoms of the molecular formula C_4H_{10} can be arranged in two different ways.

butane   2-methylpropane

Notice that the formula for butane shows a continuous chain of four carbon atoms, but the formula of 2-methylpropane shows a continuous chain of three carbon atoms, with the fourth carbon atom attached to the second carbon atom of the chain. Structural isomers can have different properties. For example, butane and 2-methylpropane have different melting points, boiling points, and densities, as shown in **Figure 1.5.**

✔ **CHECK FOR UNDERSTANDING**
Explain Why would using structural formulas help chemists understand the shapes of geometric isomers?

FIGURE 1.5

PHYSICAL PROPERTIES OF THE STRUCTURAL ISOMERS BUTANE AND 2-METHYLPROPANE			
	Melting point (°C)	Boiling point (°C)	Density at 20°C (g/mL)
butane	−138.4	−0.5	0.5788
2-methylpropane	−159.4	−11.633	0.549

FIGURE 1.6

Geometric Isomers in Nature

Males of the Iowa strain of the European corn borer respond most strongly to mixtures of the female sex attractant pheromone that are 96% *cis* isomer. But males of the New York strain respond most strongly to mixtures containing 97% *trans* isomer.

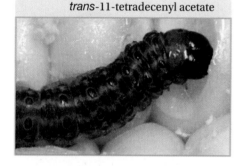

cis-11-tetradecenyl acetate

trans-11-tetradecenyl acetate

Geometric Isomers

Geometric isomers are isomers in which the order of atom bonding is the same but the arrangement of atoms in space is different. Consider the molecule 1,2-dichloroethene, which contains a double bond. The double bond prevents free rotation and holds groups to either side of the molecule. This means there can be two different 1,2-dichloroethene geometric isomers, as shown below.

$$
\begin{array}{cc}
Cl \quad\quad Cl \\
\diagdown \quad\quad \diagup \\
C = C \\
\diagup \quad\quad \diagdown \\
H \quad\quad H
\end{array}
\qquad\qquad
\begin{array}{cc}
H \quad\quad Cl \\
\diagdown \quad\quad \diagup \\
C = C \\
\diagup \quad\quad \diagdown \\
Cl \quad\quad H
\end{array}
$$

cis   *trans*

The geometric isomer with the two chlorine atoms on the same side of the molecule is called *cis*. The isomer with the chlorine atoms on opposite sides of the molecule is called *trans*. This particular isomeric form has been in the news a great deal in recent years, due to research showing the harmfulness of trans fats in the human diet. **Figure 1.6** shows an example of geometric isomers that occur in nature.

The difference in properties between two geometric isomers can be very small or very large, depending on the type of bonding in them. Sometimes, the arrangement of the atoms in the *trans* formation enables the molecules to pack together more easily and so increases the melting point of the isomer. Similarly, if the arrangement increases the intramolecular forces between two molecules, as a consequence of the polarity of the bonds, the boiling point of that isomer will be higher, because the molecules are held together more strongly.

✓ SECTION 1 FORMATIVE ASSESSMENT

▶ Reviewing Main Ideas

1. Which of the following represent the same molecule?

a.
$$
\begin{array}{ccccc}
H & H & H & H & H \\
| & | & | & | & | \\
H-C-C-C-C-C-H \\
| & | & | & | & | \\
H & H & H & H & H
\end{array}
$$

b. $CH_3-CH_2-CH_2-CH_3$

c. $CH_3-CH_2-CH_2$
$$
\qquad\qquad |
$$
$$
\qquad\quad CH_2
$$
$$
\qquad\quad |
$$
$$
\qquad\quad CH_3
$$

d. C_5H_{12}

2. What are three characteristics of carbon that contribute to the diversity of organic compounds?

3. Define the term *isomer*, and distinguish between structural and geometric isomers.

4. Which of the following types of molecular representations can be used to show differences between isomers? Explain why each can or cannot.

    a. molecular formula

    b. structural formula

    c. three-dimensional drawing or model

✓ Critical Thinking

5. INTERPRETING CONCEPTS Can molecules that have molecular formulas C_4H_{10} and $C_4H_{10}O$ be isomers of one another? Why or why not?

©Scott Camazine/Photo Researchers, Inc

The Beginnings of Organic Chemistry

Friedrich Wöhler was the first person to synthesize an organic compound from inorganic chemicals.

Today, *organic chemistry* refers to the study of carbon compounds. However, organic chemistry was originally thought of as unique among all chemical sciences, because it emphasized the study of compounds that came from living organisms. Chemists of the early 19th century viewed organic compounds as fundamentally different from inorganic compounds, such as rocks and minerals, because organic compounds seemed to come only from living things. But because living organisms are built from carbon-containing molecules, organic chemistry later came to mean the study of carbon compounds, including those that are manufactured artificially.

Like modern researchers, early chemists were interested in the workings of the body. They tried to characterize the chemicals in blood, tissue, and urine. Urea, the molecule that the human body excretes to get rid of ammonia waste, was first isolated from urine in 1773. Although scientists could successfully isolate urea and other organic compounds, they did not know how to synthesize—that is, make from other, simpler chemicals—organic compounds. This tended to confirm a commonly held belief, called *vitalism*, that organic compounds could only be made inside living organisms with the help of a special life force known as the "vital force."

In 1828, the young German chemist Friedrich Wöhler announced that he had been able to make urea from inorganic chemicals. Wöhler had been attempting to prepare ammonium cyanate, NH_4OCN, from inorganic compounds, such as silver cyanate and ammonium chloride. But Wöhler unintentionally synthesized urea as a byproduct of the reactions that he carried out. Wöhler made an exciting discovery—the first example of organic synthesis—by using the same principles of qualitative analysis used by chemists today.

The remainder of the 19th century saw the syntheses of many other organic compounds. In 1845, acetic acid was prepared in several steps from charcoal. Many other organic molecules, such as dyes and glucose (blood sugar), were synthesized in the last half of the 19th century. Gradually, as more natural products were prepared in chemistry laboratories, the concept of vitalism was abandoned.

Interestingly, the newly synthesized organic compounds made their biggest "splash," you might say, in the dye industry. When he was only 18 years old, the chemist William Perkin discovered that an extraction from coal tar produced a very dark purple color. He found that the color would not wash out of clothing, and so he realized that it could be used as a practical synthetic dye. The discovery, coming as it did in the mid-19th century, coincided with advances in textile manufacturing. Perkin's color, called *mauveine* or *mauve*, became an instant hit. Purple had long been a color associated with aristocracy, and one not easily captured and held in a cloth for any length of time. Perkin's dye brought this color to everyone.

Today, urea, acetic acid, and many other organic chemicals are produced in huge quantities. Organic chemists can synthesize complex drug molecules, such as penicillin and taxol, which were once available only from natural sources. Using methods of organic synthesis, chemists can also prepare completely new drugs, polymers, flavors, and dyes that are not present in nature.

Questions

1. What do people usually mean by the term *organic* when they use it to describe food, such as fruits and vegetables?

2. Think of three things that you use in your everyday life that an organic chemist might be able to make.

- Alkanes contain only single bonds.

- Cycloalkanes have a ringed structure.

- Organic compounds have systematic names.

- The properties of alkanes are related to the lengths of their carbon chains.

- Unsaturated hydrocarbons have at least one carbon-carbon double bond.

Hydrocarbons

Key Terms

saturated hydrocarbon	natural gas	alkyne
alkane	petroleum	aromatic hydrocarbon
cycloalkane	unsaturated hydrocarbon	benzene
alkyl group	alkene	

Hydrocarbons are compounds that contain only carbon and hydrogen. They make up the simplest class of organic compounds. All other organic compounds can be viewed as hydrocarbons in which one or more hydrogen atoms have been replaced by other atoms or groups of atoms.

Hydrocarbons are grouped mainly by the type of bonding between carbon atoms. **Saturated hydrocarbons are hydrocarbons in which each carbon atom in the molecule forms four single covalent bonds with other atoms.**

▶ **MAIN IDEA**

Alkanes contain only single bonds.

Hydrocarbons that contain only single bonds are **alkanes.** In **Figure 2.1,** the molecular formulas, structural formulas, and space-filling models are given for alkanes with one to four carbon atoms. If you examine the molecular formulas for successive alkanes in **Figure 2.1,** you will see a clear pattern. Each member of the series differs from the preceding one by one carbon atom and two hydrogen atoms. For example, propane, C_3H_8, differs from ethane, C_2H_6, by one carbon atom and two hydrogen atoms, a —CH_2— group.

$$
\begin{array}{cc}
\text{H} \quad \text{H} & \text{H} \quad \text{H} \quad \text{H} \\
| \quad | & | \quad | \quad | \\
\text{H}-\text{C}-\text{C}-\text{H} & \text{H}-\text{C}-\text{C}-\text{C}-\text{H} \\
| \quad | & | \quad | \quad | \\
\text{H} \quad \text{H} & \text{H} \quad \text{H} \quad \text{H} \\
\text{ethane} & \text{propane}
\end{array}
$$

Compounds that differ in this fashion belong to a *homologous series.* A homologous series is one in which adjacent members differ by a constant unit. It is not necessary to remember the molecular formulas for all members of a homologous series. Instead, a general molecular formula can be used to determine the formulas. Look at the molecular formulas for ethane and propane, C_2H_6 and C_3H_8. They both fit the formula C_nH_{2n+2}. For ethane, $n = 2$, so there are two carbon atoms and $(2 \times 2) + 2 = 6$ hydrogen atoms. For propane, $n = 3$, so there are three carbon atoms and $(2 \times 3) + 2 = 8$ hydrogen atoms. Now consider a molecule for which we do not know the molecular formula. Suppose a member of this series has 30 carbon atoms in its molecules. Then $n = 30$, and there are $(2 \times 30) + 2 = 62$ hydrogen atoms. The formula is $C_{30}H_{62}$. Incidentally, an alkane with this formula, known as *squalane,* does exist and is a component in some moisturizers.

FIGURE 2.1

ALKANES WITH ONE TO FOUR CARBON ATOMS

Molecular formulas	Structural formulas	Space-filling models
CH_4	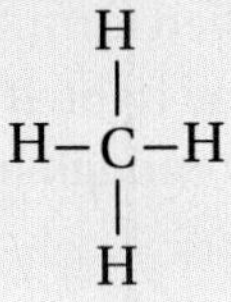 H | H–C–H | H methane	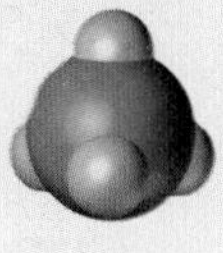
C_2H_6	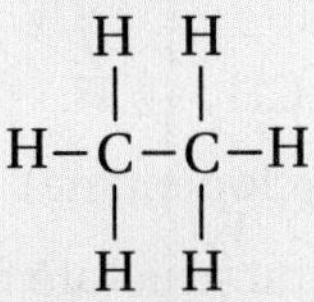 H H | | H–C–C–H | | H H ethane	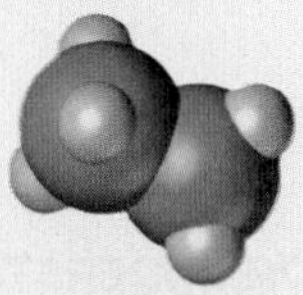
C_3H_8	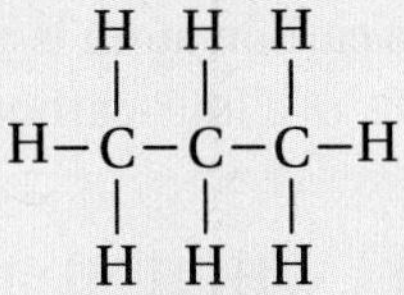 H H H | | | H–C–C–C–H | | | H H H propane	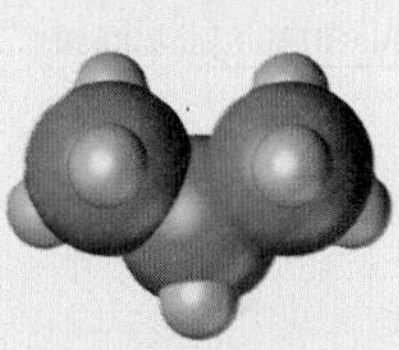
C_4H_{10}	H H H H | | | | H–C–C–C–C–H | | | | H H H H butane H H H | | | H–C———C———C–H | | | H H–C–H H | H 2-methylpropane	

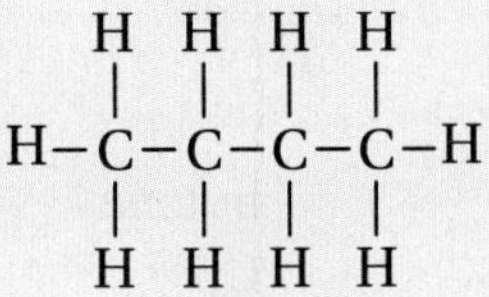

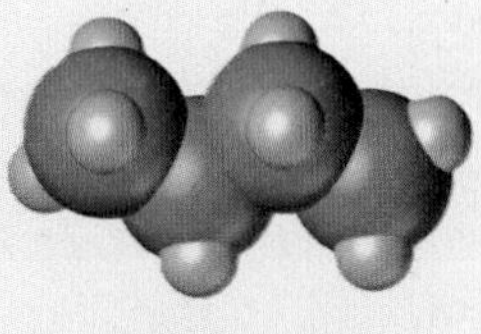

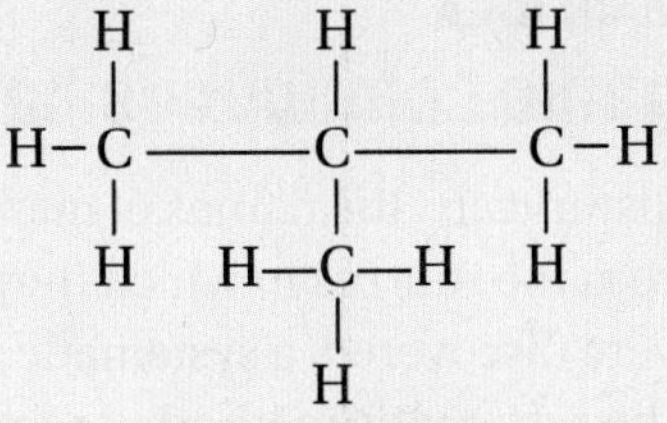

   Notice that for alkanes with three or fewer carbon atoms, only one molecular structure is possible. However, in alkanes with more than three carbon atoms, the chains can be straight or branched. Thus, alkanes with four or more carbon atoms have structural isomers. There are two possible structural isomers for alkanes with four carbon atoms, butane and 2-methylpropane.

   The number of structural isomers increases greatly as the number of carbon atoms in alkanes increases. There are three isomeric C_5H_{12} alkanes, five isomeric C_6H_{14} alkanes, and nine isomeric C_7H_{16} alkanes. There are nearly 37 million possible isomers of $C_{25}H_{52}$, although most have never been prepared or isolated.

▶ MAIN IDEA
Cycloalkanes have a ringed structure.

Cycloalkanes are alkanes in which the carbon atoms are arranged in a ring, or cyclic, structure. The structural formulas for cycloalkanes are often drawn in a simplified form. In these skeletal representations, such as the one below on the right, it is understood that there is a carbon atom at each corner and enough hydrogen atoms to complete the four bonds to each carbon atom.

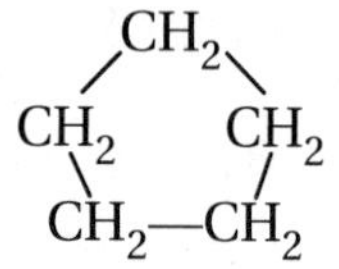

$$CH_2$$
$$CH_2 \quad CH_2$$
$$CH_2 - CH_2$$
cyclopentane   *or*   cyclopentane

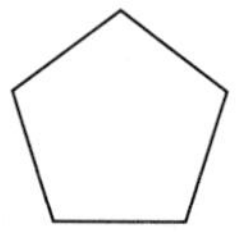

The general structure for cycloalkanes, C_nH_{2n}, shows that they have $2 \times n$ hydrogen atoms, two fewer hydrogen atoms than noncyclic alkanes, C_nH_{2n+2}, have. This is because cycloalkanes have no free ends where a carbon atom is attached to three hydrogen atoms. Another example, of a four-carbon alkane and cycloalkane, is shown below.

$$H \quad H \quad H \quad H$$
$$H - C - C - C - C - H$$
$$H \quad H \quad H \quad H$$
butane
C_4H_{10}

$$H \quad H$$
$$H - C - C - H$$
$$H - C - C - H$$
$$H \quad H$$
cyclobutane
C_4H_8

✔ CHECK FOR UNDERSTANDING

Infer Even though they don't follow the general formula C_nH_{2n+2}, why are cycloalkanes still alkanes?

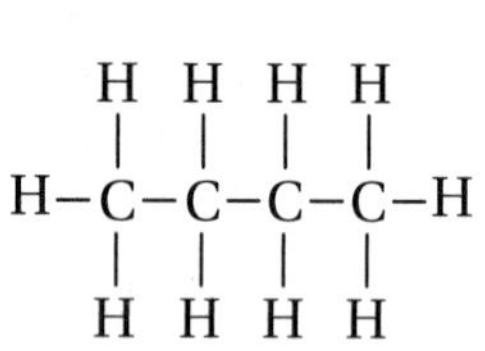

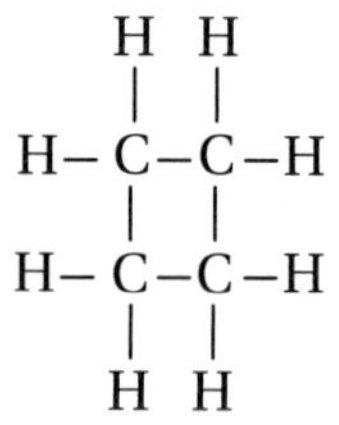

FIGURE 2.2

CARBON-ATOM CHAIN PREFIXES

Number of carbon atoms	Prefix
1	meth-
2	eth-
3	prop-
4	but-
5	pent-
6	hex-
7	hept-
8	oct-
9	non-
10	dec-

▶ MAIN IDEA
Organic compounds have systematic names.

Historically, the names of many organic compounds were derived from the sources in which they were found. As more organic compounds were discovered, a systematic naming method became necessary. The systematic method used primarily in this book was developed by the International Union of Pure and Applied Chemistry, IUPAC.

Unbranched-Chain Alkane Nomenclature

To name an unbranched alkane, find the prefix in **Figure 2.2** that corresponds to the number of carbon atoms in the chain of the hydrocarbon. Then add the suffix *-ane* to the prefix. An example is shown below.

$$\overset{1}{CH_3} - \overset{2}{CH_2} - \overset{3}{CH_2} - \overset{4}{CH_2} - \overset{5}{CH_2} - \overset{6}{CH_2} - \overset{7}{CH_3}$$
heptane

The molecule has a chain seven carbon atoms long, so the prefix *hept-* is added to the suffix *-ane* to form *heptane*.

FIGURE 2.3

SOME STRAIGHT-CHAIN ALKYL GROUPS

Alkane	Name	Alkyl group	Name
CH_4	methane	$-CH_3$	methyl
CH_3-CH_3	ethane	$-CH_2-CH_3$	ethyl
$CH_3-CH_2-CH_3$	propane	$-CH_2-CH_2-CH_3$	propyl
$CH_3-CH_2-CH_2-CH_3$	butane	$-CH_2-CH_2-CH_2-CH_3$	butyl
$CH_3-CH_2-CH_2-CH_2-CH_3$	pentane	$-CH_2-CH_2-CH_2-CH_2-CH_3$	pentyl

Branched-Chain Alkane Nomenclature

The naming of branched-chain alkanes also follows a systematic method. The hydrocarbon branches of alkanes are alkyl groups. **Alkyl groups are groups of atoms that are formed when one hydrogen atom is removed from an alkane molecule.** Alkyl groups are named by replacing the suffix -*ane* of the parent alkane with the suffix -*yl*. Some examples of alkyl groups are shown in **Figure 2.3.** Alkyl group names are used when naming branched-chain alkanes. We will present only the method for naming simple branched-chain alkanes with only straight-chain alkyl groups. Consider the following molecule.

$$
\begin{array}{c}
\quad\quad\quad\quad\quad CH_3\ \ CH_3 \\
\quad\quad\quad\quad\quad\ |\quad\ \ | \\
CH_3-CH_2-CH_2-CH-CH-CH-CH_2-CH_3 \\
\quad\quad\quad\quad\quad\quad\quad\quad\quad\quad |\\
\quad\quad\quad\quad\quad\quad\quad\quad\quad CH-CH_3 \\
\quad\quad\quad\quad\quad\quad\quad\quad\quad\ |\\
\quad\quad\quad\quad\quad\quad\quad\quad\quad CH_3
\end{array}
$$

To name this molecule, locate the parent hydrocarbon. The parent hydrocarbon is the longest continuous chain that contains the most straight-chain branches. In this molecule, there are two chains that are eight carbon atoms long. The parent hydrocarbon is the chain that contains the most straight-chain branches. Do not be tricked by the way the molecule is drawn. The longest chain may be shown bent.

$$
\begin{array}{c}
\quad\quad\quad\quad\quad CH_3\ \ CH_3 \\
\quad\quad\quad\quad\quad\ |\quad\ \ | \\
CH_3-CH_2-CH_2-CH-CH-CH-CH_2-CH_3 \\
\quad\quad\quad\quad\quad\quad\quad\quad\quad\quad |\\
\quad\quad\quad\quad\quad\quad\quad\quad\quad CH-CH_3 \\
\quad\quad\quad\quad\quad\quad\quad\quad\quad\ |\\
\quad\quad\quad\quad\quad\quad\quad\quad\quad CH_3
\end{array}
$$

NOT

$$
\begin{array}{c}
\quad\quad\quad\quad\quad CH_3\ \ CH_3 \\
\quad\quad\quad\quad\quad\ |\quad\ \ | \\
CH_3-CH_2-CH_2-CH-CH-CH-CH_2-CH_3 \\
\quad\quad\quad\quad\quad\quad\quad\quad\quad\quad |\\
\quad\quad\quad\quad\quad\quad\quad\quad\quad CH-CH_3 \\
\quad\quad\quad\quad\quad\quad\quad\quad\quad\ |\\
\quad\quad\quad\quad\quad\quad\quad\quad\quad CH_3
\end{array}
$$

To name the parent hydrocarbon, add the suffix *-ane* to the prefix *oct-* (for a carbon-atom chain with eight carbon atoms) to form *octane.* Now identify and name the alkyl groups.

$$CH_3-CH_2-CH_2-\underset{\underset{\underset{CH_3}{|}}{\underset{CH-CH_3}{|}}}{CH}-\overset{\overset{CH_3}{|}}{CH}-\overset{\overset{CH_3}{|}}{CH}-CH_2-CH_3$$

The three —CH_3 groups are methyl groups. The —CH_2—CH_3 group is an ethyl group. Arrange the names in alphabetical order in front of the name of the parent hydrocarbon.

ethyl methyloctane

To show that there are three methyl groups present, attach the prefix *tri-* to the name *methyl* to form *trimethyl.*

ethyl trimethyloctane

Now, we need to show the locations of the alkyl groups on the parent hydrocarbon. Number the octane chain so that the alkyl groups have the lowest numbers possible.

$$\overset{8}{C}H_3-\overset{7}{C}H_2-\overset{6}{C}H_2-\underset{\underset{\underset{1CH_3}{|}}{\underset{2CH-CH_3}{|}}}{\overset{5}{C}H}-\overset{\overset{CH_3}{|}}{\overset{4}{C}H}-\overset{\overset{CH_3}{|}}{\overset{3}{C}H}-CH_2-CH_3$$

NOT

$$\overset{1}{C}H_3-\overset{2}{C}H_2-\overset{3}{C}H_2-\underset{\underset{\underset{8CH_3}{|}}{\underset{7CH-CH_3}{|}}}{\overset{4}{C}H}-\overset{\overset{CH_3}{|}}{\overset{5}{C}H}-\overset{\overset{CH_3}{|}}{\overset{6}{C}H}-CH_2-CH_3$$

Place the location number of *each* of the alkyl groups in front of its name. Separate the numbers from the names of the alkyl groups with hyphens. The ethyl group is on carbon 3.

3-ethyl trimethyloctane

Because there are three methyl groups, there will be three numbers, separated by commas, in front of *trimethyl.*

3-ethyl-2,4,5-trimethyloctane

The full name is 3-ethyl-2,4,5-trimethyloctane.

The procedure for naming simple branched-chain alkanes can be summarized as shown in the list on the next page.

Alkane Nomenclature

1. **Name the parent hydrocarbon.** Find the longest continuous chain of carbon atoms that have straight-chain branches. Add the suffix *-ane* to the prefix corresponding to the number of carbon atoms in the chain.

2. **Add the names of the alkyl groups.** Add the names of the alkyl groups in front of the name of the parent hydrocarbon in alphabetical order. When there is more than one branch of the same alkyl group present, attach the appropriate numerical prefix to the name: *di* = 2, *tri* = 3, *tetra* = 4, and so on. Do so after the names have been put in alphabetical order.

3. **Number the carbon atoms in the parent hydrocarbon.** If one or more alkyl groups are present, number the carbon atoms in the continuous chain to give the lowest numbers possible in the name. If there are two equivalent lowest positions with two different alkyl groups, give the lowest number to the alkyl group that comes first in the name. (This will be the alkyl group that is first in alphabetical order, *before* any prefixes are attached.)

4. **Insert position numbers.** Put the position numbers of each alkyl group in front of the name of that alkyl group.

5. **Punctuate the name.** Use hyphens to separate the position numbers from the names. If there is more than one number in front of a name, use commas to separate the numbers.

GO ONLINE

Learn It! Video
HMHScience.com

Solve It! Cards
HMHScience.com

Naming Alkanes

Sample Problem A **Name the following simple branched-chain alkane:**

$$CH_3 - CH - CH_2 - CH - CH - CH_3$$
$$\qquad\; | \qquad\qquad\quad | \quad\; |$$
$$\qquad CH_3 \qquad\quad CH_3\; CH_3$$

● SOLVE

1. Identify and name the parent hydrocarbon.

Because the longest continuous chain contains six carbon atoms, the parent hydrocarbon is *hexane*.

2. Identify and name the alkyl groups attached to the chain.

There is only one type of alkyl group, with one carbon atom. Alkyl groups with one carbon atom are methyl groups. Add the name *methyl* in front of the name of the continuous chain. Add the prefix *tri-* to show that there are three methyl groups present.

trimethylhexane

  Continued

3. Number the carbon atoms in the continuous chain so that the alkyl groups have the lowest numbers possible.

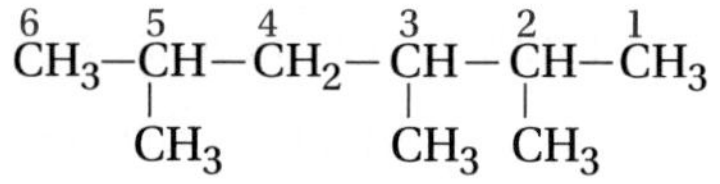

$$\overset{6}{C}H_3-\overset{5}{C}H-\overset{4}{C}H_2-\overset{3}{C}H-\overset{2}{C}H-\overset{1}{C}H_3$$

(with CH₃ below the 5-position, and CH₃, CH₃ below the 3- and 2-positions)

4. The methyl groups are on the carbon atoms numbered 2, 3, and 5. Put the numbers of the positions of the alkyl groups, separated by commas, in front of the name of the alkyl group. Separate the numbers from the name with a hyphen.

2,3,5-trimethylhexane

Practice   Answers in Appendix E

Name the following molecules:

1. 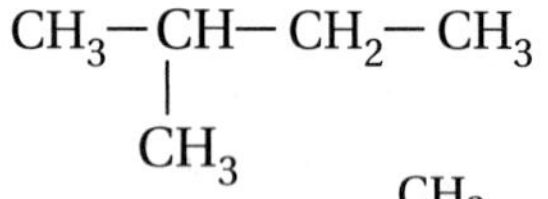 CH₃—CH—CH₂—CH₃
          |
         CH₃

2. 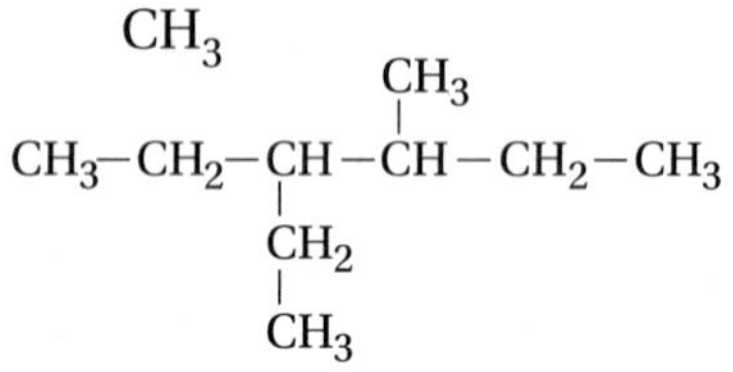 CH₃—CH₂—CH—CH—CH₂—CH₃
                    | |
                   CH₂ CH₃
                    |
                   CH₃

(CH₃ is above the fourth carbon)

▶ MAIN IDEA

The properties of alkanes are related to the lengths of their carbon chains.

Properties for some straight-chain alkanes are listed in **Figure 2.4**. The trends in these properties can be explained by examining the structure of alkanes. The carbon-hydrogen bonds of alkanes are nonpolar. The only forces of attraction between nonpolar molecules are weak intermolecular forces, or London dispersion forces. The strength of London dispersion forces increases as the mass of a molecule increases.

FIGURE 2.4

PROPERTIES OF STRAIGHT-CHAIN ALKANES

Molecular formula	IUPAC name	Boiling point (°C)	State at room temperature
CH_4	methane	−164	gas
C_2H_6	ethane	−88.6	
C_3H_8	propane	−42.1	
C_4H_{10}	butane	−0.5	
C_5H_{12}	pentane	36.1	liquid
C_8H_{18}	octane	125.7	
$C_{10}H_{22}$	decane	174.1	
$C_{17}H_{36}$	heptadecane	301.8	solid
$C_{20}H_{42}$	eicosane	343.	

Physical States

The physical states at which some alkanes exist at room temperature and atmospheric pressure are found in **Figure 2.4.** Alkanes that have the lowest molecular mass—those with one to four carbon atoms—are gases. **Natural gas is a fossil fuel composed primarily of alkanes containing one to four carbon atoms.** These alkanes are gases because they are very small molecules. Therefore, they have weak London dispersion forces between them and are not held together tightly. Larger alkanes are liquids. Gasoline and kerosene consist mostly of liquid alkanes. Stronger London dispersion forces hold these molecules close enough together to form liquids. Alkanes that have a very high molecular mass are solids, corresponding to a greater increase in London dispersion forces. Paraffin wax contains solid alkanes. It can be used in candles, as shown in **Figure 2.5.**

Boiling Points

The boiling points of alkanes, also shown in **Figure 2.4,** increase with molecular mass. As London dispersion forces increase, more energy is required to pull the molecules apart. This property is used in the separation of petroleum, a major source of alkanes. **Petroleum is a complex mixture of different hydrocarbons that varies greatly in composition.** The hydrocarbon molecules in petroleum contain from 1 to more than 50 carbon atoms. This range allows the separation of petroleum into different portions that have different boiling-point ranges, as shown in **Figure 2.6.** In *fractional distillation,* components of a mixture are separated on the basis of boiling point, by condensation of vapor in a fractionating column. **Figure 2.7** shows an example of refinery towers in which the process takes place. During its fractional distillation, petroleum is heated to about 370°C. Nearly all components of the petroleum are vaporized at this temperature. As the vapors rise in the fractionating column, or tower, they are gradually cooled. Alkanes that have higher boiling points have higher condensation temperatures and condense for collection lower in the tower. For example, lubricating oils, which have higher condensation temperatures than gasoline has, are collected lower in the fractionating tower.

FIGURE 2.5

Solid Alkanes Paraffin wax, used in candles, contains solid alkanes. Molecules of paraffin wax contain 26 to 30 carbon atoms.

FIGURE 2.7

Fractional Distillation
Fractional distillation takes place in petroleum refinery towers.

FIGURE 2.6

PETROLEUM FRACTIONS		
Fraction	Size range of molecules	Boiling-point range (°C)
Gasoline	$C_4–C_{12}$	up to 200
Kerosene	$C_{10}–C_{14}$	180–290
Middle distillate, such as heating oil, gas-turbine fuel, diesel	$C_{12}–C_{20}$	185–345
Wide-cut gas oil, such as lubricating oil, waxes	$C_{20}–C_{36}$	345–540
Asphalt	above C_{36}	residues

Unsaturated hydrocarbons have at least one carbon-carbon double bond.

Hydrocarbons that do not contain the maximum amount of hydrogen are referred to as *unsaturated*. **Unsaturated hydrocarbons** are hydrocarbons in which not all carbon atoms have four single covalent bonds. An unsaturated hydrocarbon has one or more double bonds or triple bonds. Carbon atoms can easily form double and triple bonds to other carbon atoms, so multiple bonds between carbon atoms are common in organic compounds.

Alkenes

Alkenes are hydrocarbons that contain double covalent bonds. Some examples of alkenes are given in **Figure 2.8**. Notice that because alkenes have a double bond, the simplest alkene, ethene, has two carbon atoms.

Carbon atoms linked by double bonds cannot bind as many atoms as those that are linked by only single bonds. An alkene with one double bond has two fewer hydrogen atoms than the corresponding alkane.

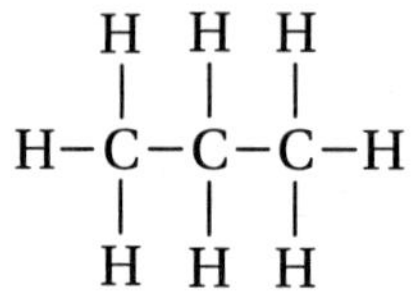

$$C_3H_8 \qquad\qquad C_3H_6$$

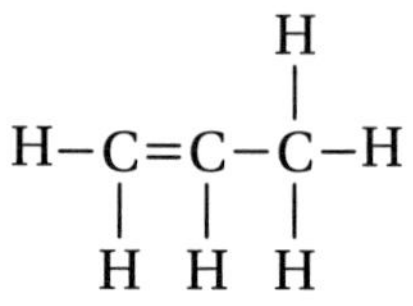

Thus, the general formula for noncyclic alkenes with one double bond is C_nH_{2n}.

Because alkenes have a double bond, they can have geometric isomers, as shown in the examples below.

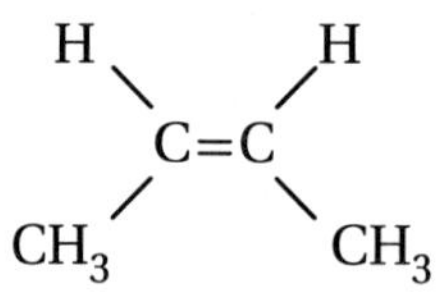

cis-2-butene 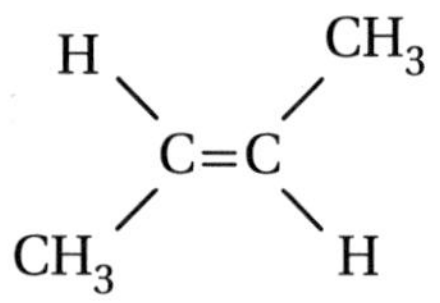   *trans*-2-butene

CHECK FOR UNDERSTANDING
Identify Is the compound $C_{10}H_{20}$ an alkane or an alkene? Can you know for sure?

FIGURE 2.8

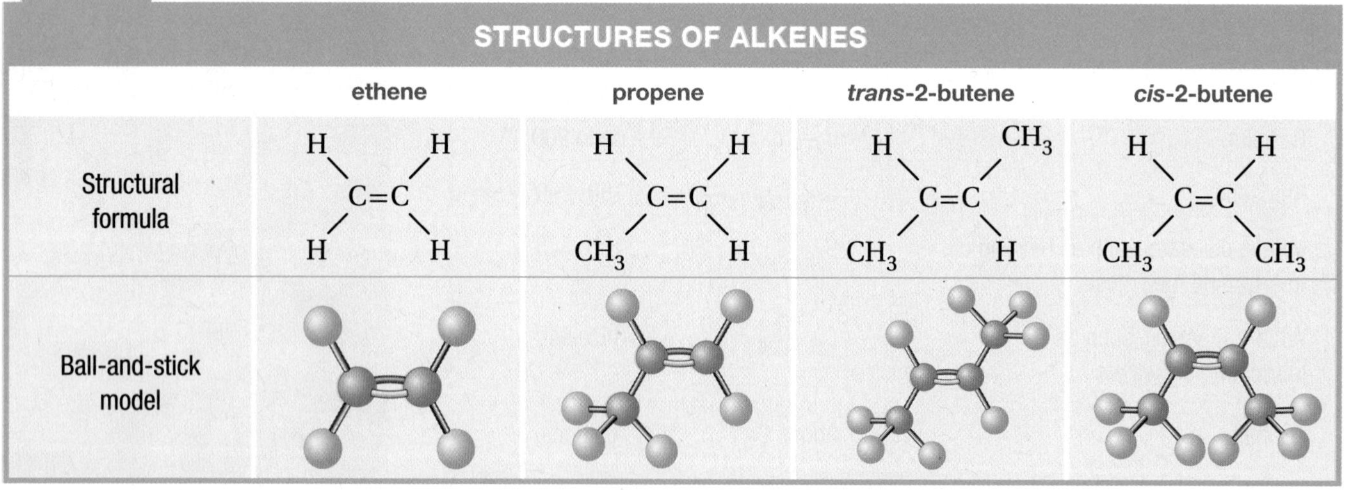

STRUCTURES OF ALKENES

	ethene	propene	*trans*-2-butene	*cis*-2-butene
Structural formula				
Ball-and-stick model				

Systematic Names of Alkenes

The rules for naming a simple alkene are similar to those for naming an alkane. The parent hydrocarbon is the longest continuous chain of carbon atoms *that contains the double bond.*

$$CH_2=\overset{\overset{\displaystyle CH_2-CH_3}{|}}{C}-CH_2-CH_2-CH_3 \qquad \textit{NOT} \qquad CH_2=\overset{\overset{\displaystyle CH_2-CH_3}{|}}{C}-CH_2-CH_2-CH_3$$

pentene   hexene

The carbon atoms in the chain are numbered so that the first carbon atom in the double bond has the lowest number.

$$\overset{1}{C}H_2=\overset{\overset{\displaystyle CH_2-CH_3}{|}}{\underset{2}{C}}-\overset{3}{C}H_2-\overset{4}{C}H_2-\overset{5}{C}H_3$$

1-pentene

The position number and name of the alkyl group are placed in front of the double-bond position number. This alkyl group has two carbon atoms, an ethyl group. It is on the second carbon atom of the parent hydrocarbon.

2-ethyl-1-pentene

If there is more than one double bond, the suffix is modified to indicate the number of double bonds: 2 = -*adiene*, 3 = -*atriene*, and so on.

$$CH_2=CH-CH_2-CH=CH_2$$

1,4-pentadiene

The procedure for naming alkenes can be summarized as follows.

Alkene Nomenclature

Use the rules for alkane nomenclature listed earlier in this section, with the following exceptions.

1. **Name the parent hydrocarbon.** Locate the longest continuous chain that *contains the double bond(s)*. If there is only one double bond, add the suffix -*ene* to the prefix corresponding to the number of carbon atoms in this chain. If there is more than one double bond, modify the suffix to indicate the number of double bonds. For example, 2 = -*adiene*, 3 = -*atriene*, and so on.

2. **Add the names of the alkyl groups.**

3. **Number the carbon atoms in the parent hydrocarbon.** Number the carbon atoms in the chain so that the first carbon atom in the double bond nearest the end of the chain has the lowest number. If numbering from both ends gives equivalent positions for two double bonds, then number from the end nearest the first alkyl group.

4. **Insert position numbers.** Place double-bond position numbers immediately before the name of the parent hydrocarbon alkene. Place alkyl group position numbers immediately before the name of the corresponding alkyl group.

5. **Punctuate the name.**

GO ONLINE

Solve It! Cards
HMHScience.com

Sample Problem B Name the following alkene.

$$CH_3$$
$$|$$
$$CH_3-CH-C=CH_2$$
$$|$$
$$CH_2-CH_3$$

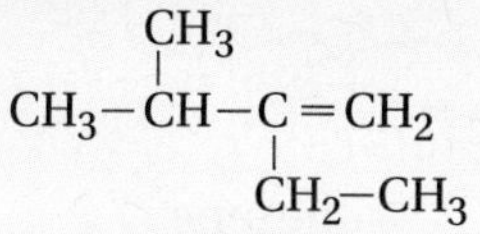

① ANALYZE

1. Identify and name the parent hydrocarbon.

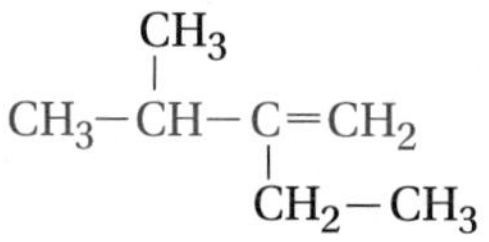

$$CH_3$$
$$|$$
$$CH_3-CH-C=CH_2$$
$$|$$
$$CH_2-CH_3$$

The parent hydrocarbon has four carbon atoms and one double bond, so it is named *butene*.

2. Identify and name the alkyl groups.

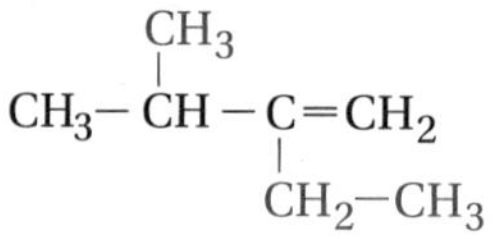

$$CH_3$$
$$|$$
$$CH_3-CH-C=CH_2$$
$$|$$
$$CH_2-CH_3$$

The alkyl groups are *ethyl* and *methyl*.
Place their names in front of the name of the parent hydrocarbon in alphabetical order.

ethyl methyl butene

3. Number the carbon chain to give the double bond the lowest position.

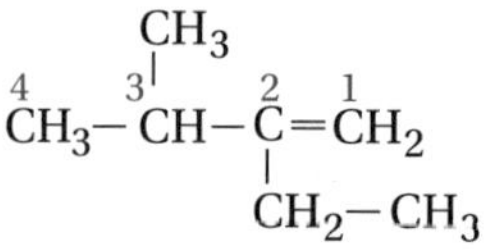

$$CH_3$$
$$\overset{4}{CH_3}-\overset{3}{CH}-\overset{2}{C}=\overset{1}{CH_2}$$
$$|$$
$$CH_2-CH_3$$

② SOLVE

Place the position number of the double bond in front of butene. Place the position numbers of the alkyl groups in front of each alkyl group. Separate the numbers from the name with hyphens. The full name is

2-ethyl-3-methyl-1-butene.

Practice Answers in Appendix E

Name the following alkenes:

1. $CH_3-CH_2-CH_2-CH=CH-CH_3$

$$CH_3$$
$$|$$
2. 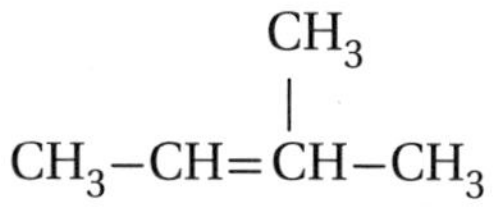 $CH_3-CH=CH-CH_3$

$$CH_3$$
$$|$$
3. $CH_3-CH-CH=CH-CH_2-CH_3$

$$CH_3$$
$$|$$
$$CH$$ $$CH_3$$ 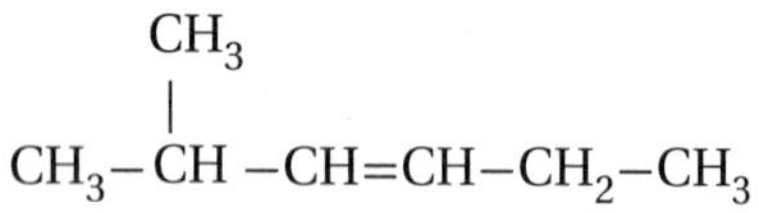
$$\|$$ $$|$$
4. 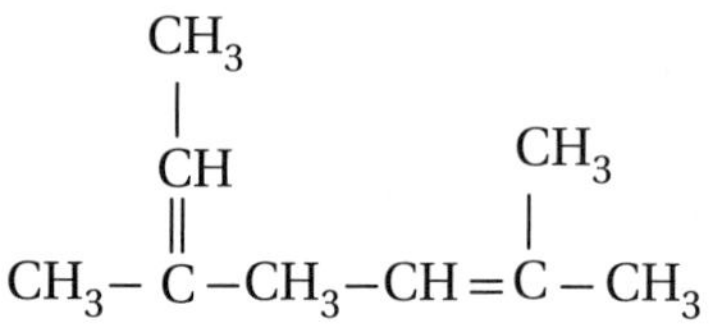 $CH_3-C-CH_3-CH=C-CH_3$

FIGURE 2.9

Alkenes in Nature α-farnesene is a solid alkene found in the natural wax covering of apples. Can you determine the IUPAC name for this large alkene?

α-farnesene

Properties and Uses of Alkenes

Alkenes are nonpolar and show trends in properties similar to those of alkanes in boiling points and physical states. For example, α-farnesene has 15 carbon atoms and 4 double bonds, as shown in **Figure 2.9.** This large alkene is a solid at room temperature and atmospheric pressure. It is found in the natural wax covering of apples. Ethene, the smallest alkene, is a gas. Ethene is commonly called *ethylene.*

Ethene is the hydrocarbon commercially produced in the greatest quantity in the United States. It is used in the synthesis of many plastics and commercially important alcohols. Ethene is also an important plant hormone. Induction of flowering and the ripening of fruit, as shown in **Figure 2.10,** are effects of ethene hormone action that can be manipulated by commercial growers.

Alkynes

Hydrocarbons with triple covalent bonds are alkynes. Like the double bond of alkenes, the triple bond of alkynes requires that the simplest alkyne have two carbon atoms.

$$H-C\equiv C-H$$

ethyne

The general formula for the alkynes is C_nH_{2n-2}. Alkynes have four fewer hydrogen atoms than the corresponding alkanes and two fewer hydrogen atoms than the corresponding alkenes. The simplest alkyne is ethyne, more commonly known as *acetylene.*

C_2H_6
ethane

C_2H_4
ethene

C_2H_2
ethyne

FIGURE 2.10

Fruit Ripening Ethene is a plant hormone that triggers fruit ripening. At ordinary conditions, ethene is a gas.

Systematic Naming of Alkynes

Alkyne nomenclature is almost the same as alkene nomenclature. The only difference is that the *-ene* suffix of the corresponding alkene is replaced with *-yne*. A complete list of rules follows.

Alkyne Nomenclature

Use the rules for alkane nomenclature listed earlier in this section, with the following exceptions.

1. **Name the parent hydrocarbon.** Locate the longest continuous chain that *contains the triple bond(s)*. If there is only one triple bond, add the suffix *-yne*. If there is more than one triple bond, modify the suffix. For example, 2 = *–adiyne*, 3 = *–atriyne*, and so on.

2. **Add the names of the alkyl groups.**

3. **Number the carbon atoms in the parent hydrocarbon.** Number the carbon atoms in the chain so that the first carbon atom in the triple bond nearest the end of the chain has the lowest number.

4. **Insert position numbers.** Place the position numbers of the triple bond immediately before the name of the parent hydrocarbon alkyne. Place alkyl group position numbers immediately before the name of the corresponding alkyl group.

5. **Punctuate the name.**

Two examples of correctly named alkynes are given below.

$$CH_3-CH_2-CH_2-C{\equiv}CH \qquad\qquad CH{\equiv}C-\underset{\underset{\displaystyle CH_3}{|}}{CH}-CH_3$$

1-pentyne   3-methyl-1-butyne

Properties and Uses of Alkynes

Alkynes are nonpolar and exhibit the same trends in boiling points and physical states as other hydrocarbons. The smallest alkyne, ethyne, is a gas. The combustion of ethyne when it is mixed with pure oxygen produces the intense heat of welding torches, as shown in **Figure 2.11.** As mentioned, the common name of ethyne is acetylene, so these welding torches are commonly called *oxyacetylene torches.*

FIGURE 2.11

Alkynes Ethyne is the fuel used in oxyacetylene torches. Oxyacetylene torches can reach temperatures of over 3000°C.

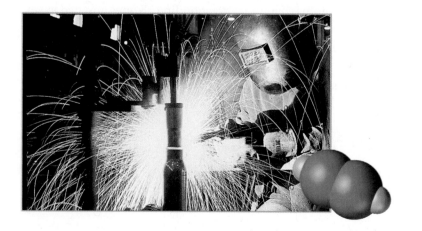

(br) ©Kevin Anderson/Getty Images

Aromatic Hydrocarbons

Aromatic hydrocarbons are hydrocarbons that have six-membered carbon rings and delocalized electrons. **Benzene** is the primary aromatic hydrocarbon. The molecular formula of benzene is C_6H_6. One possible structural formula is a six-carbon-atom ring with three double bonds.

However, benzene does not behave chemically like an alkene. The entire molecule lies in the same plane, as shown in **Figure 2.12**. Benzene contains six equivalent C–C bonds, and the structure of the benzene ring allows electrons to be spread through delocalized p-orbitals over the whole ring. The structural and skeletal formulas below show benzene as a resonance hybrid, representing the delocalization of electrons.

Aromatic hydrocarbons can be thought of as derivatives of benzene. The simplest have one benzene ring, as shown in the following example.

methylbenzene

FIGURE 2.12

Aromatic Hydrocarbons
Electron orbitals in benzene overlap to form continuous p-orbitals that allow the delocalized electrons to spread uniformly over the entire ring.

✔ **CHECK FOR UNDERSTANDING**
Defend How does the circle in the middle of the benzene ring better represent the type of bonding in benzene?

✔ SECTION 2 FORMATIVE ASSESSMENT

▶ Reviewing Main Ideas

1. List the basic structural features that characterize each of the following hydrocarbons:
   a. alkanes
   b. alkenes
   c. alkynes
   d. aromatic hydrocarbons

2. Draw all of the condensed structural formulas that can represent C_5H_{12}.

3. Give the systematic name for each compound in your answers to item 2.

4. Give examples of a property or use of three hydrocarbons.

5. Name the following compounds:
   a. $CH_3- CH_2- CH_3$
      |
      $CH_3- CH-CH-CH_2-CH_3$
   b. $CH_2=CH-CH=CH_2$
   c. $CH_3-C{\equiv}C-CH_2-CH_3$

✔ Critical Thinking

6. **ANALYZING INFORMATION** Write the structural formulas for an alkane, an alkene, and an alkyne that have five carbon atoms each. Why are these three hydrocarbons not considered isomers?

Organic Chemistry **695**

Functional Groups

Key Terms

functional group	ether	amine
alcohol	aldehyde	carboxylic acid
alkyl halide	ketone	ester

▶ **MAIN IDEA**

Functional groups can classify organic compounds.

A **functional group** is an atom or group of atoms that is responsible for the specific properties of an organic compound. A functional group undergoes the same types of chemical reactions in every molecule in which it is found. Therefore, compounds with similar groups are classified together.

The compounds in **Figure 3.1** have four carbon atoms, but they have very different physical properties due to their different functional groups. Some functional groups and their characteristic general formulas are shown in **Figure 3.2.** Many of the names may be familiar to you.

FIGURE 3.1

COMPARING CLASSES OF ORGANIC COMPOUNDS

Name	Structural formula	Melting point (°C)	Boiling point (°C)	Density (g/mol)
butane	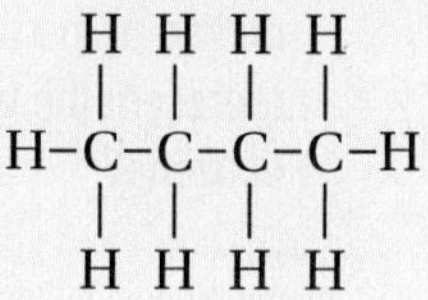 H H H H │ │ │ │ H–C–C–C–C–H │ │ │ │ H H H H	−138.4	−0.5	0.5788
1-butanol	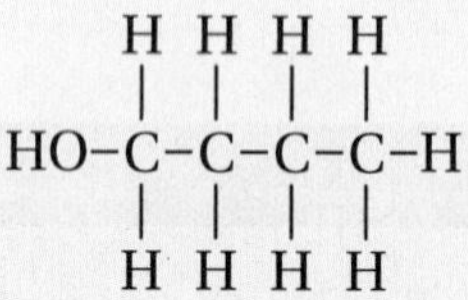 H H H H │ │ │ │ HO–C–C–C–C–H │ │ │ │ H H H H	−89.5	117.2	0.8098
butanoic acid	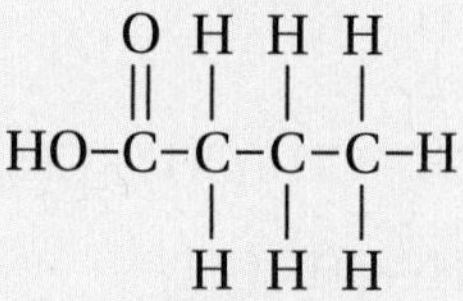 O H H H ║ │ │ │ HO–C–C–C–C–H │ │ │ H H H	−4.5	163.5	0.9577
2-butanone	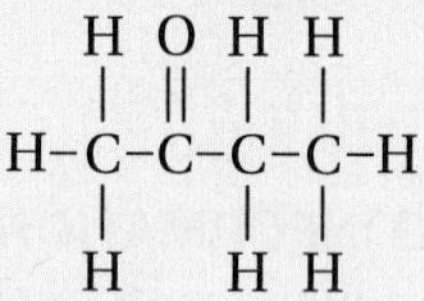 H O H H │ ║ │ │ H–C–C–C–C–H │ │ │ H H H	−86.3	79.6	0.8054
diethyl ether	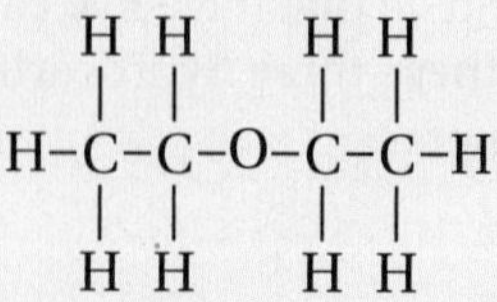 H H H H │ │ │ │ H–C–C–O–C–C–H │ │ │ │ H H H H	−116.2	34.5	0.7138

FIGURE 3.2

CLASSES OF ORGANIC COMPOUNDS

Class	Functional group	General formula
alcohol	$-OH$	$R-OH$
alkyl halide	$-X(X = F, Cl, Br, I)$	$R-X$
ether	$-O-$	$R-O-R'$
aldehyde	$\overset{\displaystyle O}{\overset{\displaystyle \|}{-C-H}}$	$\overset{\displaystyle O}{\overset{\displaystyle \|}{R-C-H}}$
ketone	$\overset{\displaystyle O}{\overset{\displaystyle \|}{-C-}}$	$\overset{\displaystyle O}{\overset{\displaystyle \|}{R-C-R'}}$
amine	$\underset{\displaystyle \|}{-N-}$	$\underset{\displaystyle \underset{\displaystyle R'}{\|}}{R-N-R''}$
carboxylic acid	$\overset{\displaystyle O}{\overset{\displaystyle \|}{-C-OH}}$	$\overset{\displaystyle O}{\overset{\displaystyle \|}{R-C-OH}}$
ester	$\overset{\displaystyle O}{\overset{\displaystyle \|}{-C-O-}}$	$\overset{\displaystyle O}{\overset{\displaystyle \|}{R-C-O-R'}}$

GO ONLINE **Animated Chemistry**
HMHScience.com

Functional Groups

✓ **CHECK FOR UNDERSTANDING**
Compare What is the difference between an aldehyde and a ketone?

Alcohols

Alcohols are organic compounds that contain one or more hydroxyl groups. The general formula for a class of organic compounds consists of the functional group and the letter R, which stands for the rest of the molecule. The general formula for alcohols is $R-OH$. Customarily, alcohols get their names by appending the suffix *-ol* to the hydrocarbon. For example, *butane* becomes *butanol*.

Hydrogen bonding in alcohols explains some of their properties and uses. Cold creams, lipsticks, body lotions, and similar products generally include the alcohol 1,2,3-propanetriol, commonly called *glycerol*, to keep them moist. A model for glycerol is shown in **Figure 3.3**. Multiple hydroxyl groups allow glycerol to form many hydrogen bonds with water molecules.

Alcohols are sometimes used today as alternative fuels and as octane enhancers in fuel for automobiles. Ethanol is combined with gasoline, for example, in a one-to-nine ratio to produce gasohol. Some experts have promoted the use of gasohol as a fuel for automobiles because it burns more cleanly and efficiently. However, there are also disadvantages. The combustion of ethanol produces only about 60% as much energy per gram as the combustion of gasoline does. The presence of ethanol also causes increased water absorption in the fuel.

FIGURE 3.3

Alcohols Glycerol contains three hydroxyl groups. This structure allows it to form multiple hydrogen bonds with water. Glycerol is added to skin products as a moisturizer.

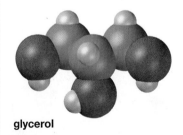

glycerol

Alkyl Halides

Alkyl halides are organic compounds in which one or more halogen atoms—fluorine, chlorine, bromine, or iodine—are substituted for one or more hydrogen atoms in a hydrocarbon. Because —X is often used to represent any halogen, an alkyl halide may be represented by the general formula R—X.

Alkyl halides are some of the most widely used organic chemicals. A family of alkyl halides that has received widespread attention in recent years is the chlorofluorocarbons, or CFCs. CFCs are alkyl halides that contain both chlorine and fluorine. The formulas for two widely used CFCs, Freon-11 and Freon-12, are shown below.

$$\begin{array}{c} \text{Cl} \\ | \\ \text{F}-\text{C}-\text{Cl} \\ | \\ \text{Cl} \end{array} \qquad\qquad \begin{array}{c} \text{F} \\ | \\ \text{Cl}-\text{C}-\text{F} \\ | \\ \text{Cl} \end{array}$$

trichlorofluoromethane (Freon-11)   dichlorodifluoromethane (Freon-12)

CFCs, which have been used as liquid refrigerants, contribute to the destruction of ozone in the upper atmosphere. When released into the atmosphere, CFCs can break down and release free chlorine atoms.

$$CCl_2F_2 \xrightarrow{\text{solar radiation}} Cl + CClF_2$$

The released chlorine atoms attack molecules of ozone, O_3, found in the upper atmosphere. The ozone is converted to diatomic oxygen.

$$Cl + O_3 \longrightarrow ClO + O_2$$

Chlorine atoms are eventually regenerated in various ways, including the reaction of ClO with O.

$$ClO + O \longrightarrow Cl + O_2$$

This makes it possible for a single chlorine atom to destroy thousands of ozone molecules. Because CFCs are a major cause of ozone depletion, more than 100 nations signed an agreement in 1987 to reduce the amount of CFCs produced.

Another alkyl halide is tetrafluoroethene, C_2F_4. It is joined in long chains to make a material with the trade name Teflon®. Because of the unreactive carbon-fluorine bond, Teflon is inactive and stable to about 325°C. It also has a low coefficient of friction, which means that other objects slide smoothly over its surface. These properties enable Teflon to be used in heat-resistant machine parts that cannot be lubricated. It is also used in making utensils with "nonstick" surfaces, such as the frying pan in **Figure 3.4.**

Ethers

Ethers are organic compounds in which two hydrocarbon groups are bonded to the same atom of oxygen. They can be represented by the general formula R—O—R'. In this formula, R' may be the same hydrocarbon group as R or a different one. Like alkanes, ethers are not very reactive compounds, so they are commonly used as solvents.

FIGURE 3.4

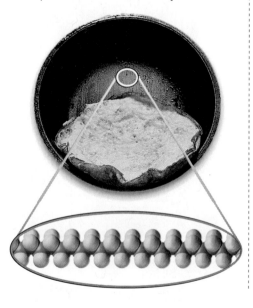

Alkyl Halides The nonstick coating on this pan is made of Teflon, an alkyl halide.

FIGURE 3.5

Aldehydes and Ketones Many common odors and flavors come from aldehydes and ketones.

irone

cinnamaldehyde

raspberry ketone

vanillin

benzaldehyde

✓ **CRITICAL THINKING**

Infer Why do you need structural formulas in order to be sure what kind of compound a substance is?

Aldehydes and Ketones

Aldehydes and ketones contain the *carbonyl group*, shown below.

$$-\overset{\displaystyle \overset{O}{\|}}{C}-$$

The difference between aldehydes and ketones is the location of the carbonyl group. **Aldehydes** are organic compounds in which the carbonyl group is attached to a carbon atom at the end of a carbon-atom chain. **Ketones** are organic compounds in which the carbonyl group is attached to carbon atoms within the chain. These differences can be seen in their general formulas, shown below.

$$R-\overset{\displaystyle \overset{O}{\|}}{C}-H \qquad\qquad R-\overset{\displaystyle \overset{O}{\|}}{C}-R'$$

aldehyde   ketone

Aldehydes and ketones are often responsible for odors and flavors. **Figure 3.5** gives some examples.

Amines

Amines are organic compounds that can be considered to be derivatives of ammonia, NH_3. Amines are common in nature. They often form during the breakdown of proteins in animal cells.

The unshared electron pair on the nitrogen atom makes amines act as weak bases in aqueous solutions, as shown below.

$$R-\overset{\displaystyle \overset{..}{N}}{\underset{\displaystyle R'}{|}}-R'' + H-O-H \rightleftharpoons R-\overset{\displaystyle \overset{H^+}{|}}{\underset{\displaystyle R'}{|}}N-R'' + OH^-$$

Carboxylic Acids

FIGURE 3.6

Carboxylic Acids Citric acid, found in citrus fruits, contains three carboxylic acid groups, shown in red on the structural formula.

citric acid

Carboxylic acids are organic compounds that contain the carboxyl functional group. A member of this class of organic compounds can be represented by the general formula shown below.

$$\underset{\substack{\| \\ R-C-OH}}{O}$$

Carboxylic acids, like inorganic acids, react to lose a hydrogen ion and become a negatively charged ion in water.

$$\underset{\substack{\| \\ R-C-OH}}{O} \underset{H_2O}{\rightleftarrows} \underset{\substack{\| \\ R-C-O^-}}{O} + H^+$$

Carboxylic acids are much weaker than many inorganic acids, such as hydrochloric, sulfuric, and nitric acids. Acetic acid, the weak acid in vinegar, is a carboxylic acid.

A number of carboxylic acids occur naturally in plants and animals. For example, citrus fruits, shown in **Figure 3.6**, contain citric acid. Benzoic, propanoic, and sorbic acids are used as preservatives. All three acids kill microorganisms that cause foods to spoil.

Esters

Esters are organic compounds that have carboxylic acid groups in which the hydrogen of the hydroxyl group has been replaced by an alkyl group. Esters are considered *derivatives* of carboxylic acids because of their structural similarity to carboxylic acids. The general formula for an ester is given below.

$$\underset{\substack{\| \\ R-C-O-R'}}{O}$$

✓ SECTION 3 FORMATIVE ASSESSMENT

▶ Reviewing Main Ideas

1. Give the general formula and class of organic compounds for each of the following:
   a. CH_3-OH
   b. CH_3-O-CH_3
   c. $Br-CH_2-CH_2-CH_3$
   d. $CH_3-CH_2-\underset{\substack{\| \\ .C}}{O}-OH$
   e. $CH_3-\underset{\substack{\| \\ C}}{O}-H$
   f. $CH_3-CH_2-NH_2$
   g. $CH_3-\underset{\substack{\| \\ C}}{O}-O-CH_2-CH_3$
   h. $CH_3-\underset{\substack{\| \\ C}}{O}-CH_3$

2. Compare the boiling points of alcohols, ethers, and alkanes, and explain one reason for the differences.

3. How are aldehydes and ketones alike? How are they different?

4. How do the strengths of organic acids compare with the strengths of most inorganic acids?

✓ Critical Thinking

5. **APPLYING MODELS** Identify the functional groups in vanillin, shown in **Figure 3.5.**

Organic Reactions

Key Terms

substitution reaction   elimination reaction   copolymer
addition reaction   polymer
condensation reaction   monomer

SECTION 4

Main Ideas

▶ Atoms replace one another in substitution reactions.

▶ Addition reactions increase a molecule's saturation.

▶ Molecules combine in condensation reactions.

▶ A smaller molecule breaks off from a larger one in an elimination reaction.

▶ Polymers are large molecules made of smaller monomers.

▶ Addition reactions produce addition polymers.

▶ Condensation reactions often make polymers.

▶ **MAIN IDEA**

Atoms replace one another in substitution reactions.

A **substitution reaction** is one in which one or more atoms replace another atom or group of atoms in a molecule. The reaction between an alkane, such as methane, and a halogen, such as chlorine, to form an alkyl halide is an example of a substitution reaction. Notice that in this reaction, a chlorine atom replaces a hydrogen atom on the methane molecule.

$$
\underset{\text{methane}}{H-\overset{\displaystyle H}{\underset{\displaystyle H}{C}}-H} \;+\; \underset{\text{chlorine}}{Cl-Cl} \longrightarrow \underset{\text{chloromethane}}{H-\overset{\displaystyle H}{\underset{\displaystyle H}{C}}-Cl} \;+\; \underset{\text{hydrogen chloride}}{H-Cl}
$$

Additional compounds can be formed by replacing the other hydrogen atoms remaining in the methane molecule. The products are dichloromethane, trichloromethane, and tetrachloromethane. Trichloromethane is also known as chloroform, and tetrachloromethane is also known as carbon tetrachloride. CFCs are formed by further substitution reactions between chloroalkanes and HF.

$$
C-\overset{\displaystyle Cl}{\underset{\displaystyle Cl}{C}}-Cl \;+\; H-F \;\xrightarrow{\ SbF_5\ }\; Cl-\overset{\displaystyle Cl}{\underset{\displaystyle Cl}{C}}-F \;+\; H-Cl
$$

$$
Cl-\overset{\displaystyle Cl}{\underset{\displaystyle Cl}{C}}-F \;+\; H-F \;\xrightarrow{\ SbF_5\ }\; Cl-\overset{\displaystyle F}{\underset{\displaystyle Cl}{C}}-F \;+\; H-Cl
$$

▶ **MAIN IDEA**

Addition reactions increase a molecule's saturation.

An **addition reaction** is one in which two parts of a molecule are added to an unsaturated molecule, increasing the saturation of the molecule. A common type of addition reaction is hydrogenation. In *hydrogenation*, hydrogen atoms are added to an unsaturated molecule. Vegetable oils are triesters of unsaturated fatty acids, long chains of carbon atoms that have many double bonds. When hydrogen gas reacts with oil, hydrogen atoms can add to the double bonds in the oil molecule. Remember the degree of saturation refers to a carbon molecule's number of double bonds. The fewer the double bonds, the higher is the degree of saturation.

FIGURE 4.1

Hydrogenated Fats The fatty acid shown in the model for vegetable oil contains a double bond. During hydrogenation, which is used to produce margarine and vegetable shortening, addition of hydrogen atoms removes double bonds from fatty acids.

$$\left(\begin{array}{c} \text{H H H H H H H} \\ | \ | \ | \ | \ | \ | \ | \\ \text{C-C=C-C-C=C-C} \\ | \qquad | \qquad | \\ \text{H} \qquad \text{H} \qquad \text{H} \end{array}\right) + \text{H}_2 \xrightarrow{\text{catalyst}} \left(\begin{array}{c} \text{H H H H H H H} \\ | \ | \ | \ | \ | \ | \ | \\ \text{-C-C=C-C-C-C-C-} \\ | \qquad | \ | \ | \ | \\ \text{H} \qquad \text{H H H H} \end{array}\right)$$

An example of hydrogen addition is shown above. The molecule still consists of long chains of carbon atoms, but it contains far fewer double bonds. This changes the material from an oil, which is a liquid, into a fat, which is a solid. When you see the word *hydrogenated* on a food product, you know that an oil has been converted to a fat by this process. Examples of an oil and hydrogenated fats are shown in **Figure 4.1.**

▶ **MAIN IDEA**

Molecules combine in condensation reactions.

A **condensation reaction** is one in which two molecules or parts of the same molecule combine. A small molecule, such as water, is usually removed during the reaction. An example is the reaction between two amino acids, which contain both amine and carboxyl groups. One hydrogen from the amine group of one amino acid combines with the hydroxyl from the carboxyl group of the other amino acid to form a molecule of water. When repeated many times, this reaction forms a protein molecule.

$$\underset{\text{amino acid}}{\text{H}-\text{N}-\overset{\text{H}}{\underset{R}{\text{C}}}-\overset{\text{O}}{\text{C}}-\text{OH}} + \underset{\text{amino acid}}{\text{H}-\text{N}-\overset{\text{H}}{\underset{R'}{\text{C}}}-\overset{\text{O}}{\text{C}}-\text{OH}} \longrightarrow \underset{\text{dipeptide}}{\text{H}-\text{N}-\overset{\text{H}}{\underset{R}{\text{C}}}-\overset{\text{O}}{\text{C}}-\text{N}-\overset{\text{H}}{\underset{R'}{\text{C}}}-\overset{\text{O}}{\text{C}}-\text{OH}} + \underset{\text{water}}{\text{H}_2\text{O}}$$

FIGURE 4.2

Elimination Reaction Sucrose is dehydrated when it reacts with concentrated sulfuric acid. Elimination of water produces a compound that is mostly carbon.

▶ MAIN IDEA

A smaller molecule breaks off from a larger one in an elimination reaction.

An **elimination reaction** is one in which a simple molecule, such as water or ammonia, is formed from adjacent carbon atoms of a larger molecule. A simple example of an elimination reaction is the heating of ethanol in the presence of concentrated sulfuric acid. Under these conditions, a hydrogen atom bonded to one carbon atom and a hydroxyl group bonded to the second carbon atom are removed from the ethanol molecule. A molecule of water is formed as a result.

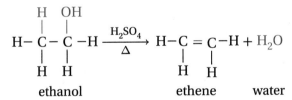

ethanol   ethene   water

Another example of an elimination reaction is the dehydration of sucrose with concentrated sulfuric acid, shown in **Figure 4.2.**

▶ MAIN IDEA

Polymers are large molecules made of smaller monomers.

Polymers are large molecules made of many small units joined to each other through organic reactions. The small units are **monomers.** A polymer can be made from identical or different monomers. A polymer made from two or more different monomers is a **copolymer.**

Polymers are all around us. The foods we eat and the clothes we wear are made of polymers. Some of the most common natural polymers include starch, cellulose, and proteins. Some synthetic polymers may be familiar to you as plastics and synthetic fibers.

✔ **CHECK FOR UNDERSTANDING**

Distinguish How is an elimination reaction different from a condensation reaction?

● MAIN IDEA
Addition reactions produce addition polymers.

An *addition polymer* is a polymer formed by addition reactions between monomers that contain a double bond. For example, molecules of ethene can polymerize with each other to form polyethene, commonly called polyethylene.

$$n\mathrm{CH_2}{=}\mathrm{CH_2} \xrightarrow{\text{catalyst}} {-}\!\!\left(\mathrm{-CH_2}{-}\mathrm{CH_2}\right)\!\!\frac{}{n}$$

ethene   polyethylene

The letter n shows that the addition reaction can be repeated multiple times to form a polymer n monomers long. In fact, this reaction can be repeated hundreds or thousands of times.

Various forms of polyethylene, shown in **Figure 4.3,** have different molecular structures. High-density polyethylene (HDPE) is a linear polymer. It has a high density because linear molecules can pack together closely. One use of HDPE is in plastic containers such as milk and juice bottles, because HDPE tends to remain stiff and rigid.

● MAIN IDEA
Condensation reactions often make polymers.

A *condensation polymer* is a polymer formed by condensation reactions. Monomers of condensation polymers must contain two functional groups. This allows each monomer to link with two other monomers by condensation reactions. Condensation polymers are usually copolymers with two monomers in an alternating order.

FIGURE 4.3

Polyethylene Properties of the different forms of polyethylene are reflected in their uses. Linear molecules of polyethylene can pack together very closely, as shown in the model of high-density polyethylene (HDPE). The branches of branched polyethylene keep the molecules from packing tightly, as shown in the low-density polyethylene (LDPE) structure. The cross-links of cross-linked polyethylene (cPE) make it very strong.

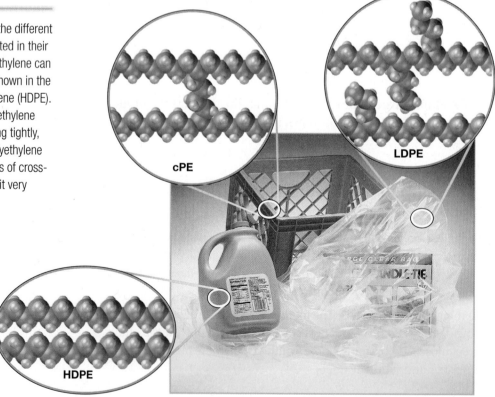

cPE

LDPE

HDPE

Polyamides and Polyesters

One example of a condensation polymer is shown below. A carboxylic acid with two carboxyl groups, adipic acid, and an amine with two amine groups, hexanediamine, react with each other to form water.

$$n\text{H}-\overset{\overset{\displaystyle \text{H}}{|}}{\text{N}}-\text{CH}_2-\text{CH}_2-\text{CH}_2-\text{CH}_2-\text{CH}_2-\text{CH}_2-\overset{\overset{\displaystyle \text{H}}{|}}{\text{N}}-\text{H} + n\text{HO}-\overset{\overset{\displaystyle \text{O}}{\|}}{\text{C}}-\text{CH}_2-\text{CH}_2-\text{CH}_2-\text{CH}_2-\overset{\overset{\displaystyle \text{O}}{\|}}{\text{C}}-\text{OH} \longrightarrow$$

hexanediamine   adipic acid

$$\left(-\overset{\overset{\displaystyle \text{H}}{|}}{\text{N}}-\text{CH}_2-\text{H}_2-\text{CH}_2-\text{CH}_2-\text{CH}_2-\text{CH}_2-\overset{\overset{\displaystyle \text{H}}{|}}{\text{N}}-\overset{\overset{\displaystyle \text{O}}{\|}}{\text{C}}-\text{CH}_2-\text{CH}_2-\text{CH}_2-\text{CH}_2-\overset{\overset{\displaystyle \text{O}}{\|}}{\text{C}}-\right)_{\!\!n} + n\text{H}_2\text{O}$$

nylon 66   water

The product contains two kinds of monomers, the adipic acid monomer and the hexanediamine monomer. This copolymer is known as nylon 66 because each of the monomers contains six carbon atoms. Nylon 66 is one of the most widely used of all synthetic polymers.

Polyesters are another common type of condensation polymer. They are formed from dialcohols and dicarboxylic acids, which undergo a condensation reaction to form an ester group, linking the alcohol end of a monomer to the acid end of a monomer. Polyesters have many uses, such as in tires, in food packaging, and as fibers in permanent-press fabrics.

Chemists have synthesized many unique polymers, using reactions that take advantage of the chemistry associated with the functional groups on the monomers. And they have managed to craft materials containing certain desired properties by doing so.

✔ SECTION 4 FORMATIVE ASSESSMENT

▶ Reviewing Main Ideas

1. Can an addition reaction occur between chlorine and ethane? Why or why not?

2. Does an addition reaction increase or decrease the saturation of a molecule?

3. What functional groups does the molecule of water that results in the condensation reaction between two amino acids come from?

4. Explain how elimination reactions could be considered the opposite of addition reactions.

5. Why can a molecule that has only one functional group *not* undergo a condensation reaction to form a polymer?

6. Would it be possible to have an addition polymer synthesized from a monomer that has only single bonds? Why or why not?

✔ Critical Thinking

7. **APPLYING MODELS** Polyvinyl chloride (PVC) is a polymer that is widely used in pipes and flooring. It is an addition polymer made from chloroethene, commonly known as *vinyl chloride*.

   a. Draw the structure of vinyl chloride. Then, look up the structure or check it with your teacher.

   b. Write the reaction for the polymerization of vinyl chloride to form polyvinyl chloride (PVC).

An empirical formula shows the simplest whole-number ratio among the elements in a compound. For example, the simplest ratio among the atoms in benzene, C_6H_6, can be expressed by the empirical formula CH (or C_1H_1). Empirical formulas may be calculated from simple analytical data, as shown in the example below.

Problem-Solving TIPS

- Sometimes, you can deduce the mole ratios of the elements in a compound just by examining the moles of each element. If not, divide the moles of each element by the moles of the least-abundant element in the compound.

Sample Problem

Find the empirical formula of acetone, a common organic solvent, the composition by mass of which is 62.04% carbon, 10.41% hydrogen, and 27.55% oxygen.

The easiest way to calculate an empirical formula from percentage composition is to consider a 100.00 g sample of the compound. In this case, a 100.00 g sample would contain 62.04 g of carbon, 10.41 g of hydrogen, and 27.55 g of oxygen. Convert each mass to moles so that you can compare the mole ratio of the three elements.

$$62.04 \text{ g C} \times \frac{1 \text{ mol C}}{12.01 \text{ g C}} = 5.166 \text{ mol C}$$

$$10.41 \text{ g H} \times \frac{1 \text{ mol H}}{1.008 \text{ g H}} = 10.33 \text{ mol H}$$

$$27.55 \text{ g O} \times \frac{1 \text{ mol O}}{16.00 \text{ g O}} = 1.722 \text{ mol O}$$

$$\frac{5.166 \text{ mol C}}{1.722} : \frac{10.33 \text{ mol H}}{1.722} : \frac{1.722 \text{ mol O}}{1.722}$$

$$3.000 \text{ mol C} : 5.999 \text{ mol H} : 1.000 \text{ mol O}$$

As you can see, the empirical formula of this compound is C_3H_6O.

Practice

1. Urea was the first organic compound to be synthesized in the laboratory. Urea's composition by mass is 20.00% carbon, 6.71% hydrogen, 46.65% nitrogen, and 26.64% oxygen. What is the empirical formula of urea?
2. An organic compound sometimes used in the manufacture of perfumes is 29.78% carbon, 4.17% hydrogen, and 66.05% bromine, by mass. What is the empirical formula of this compound?
3. The composition by mass of lactic acid is 40.00% carbon, 6.71% hydrogen, and 53.28% oxygen. What is the empirical formula of lactic acid?

BIG IDEA Carbon's ability to form four covalent bonds either to itself or other atoms leads to compounds with unique structures. Many carbon compounds are important to life.

SECTION 1 Organic Compounds

KEY TERMS

- The ability of carbon to bond to other elements and to allow different arrangements of atoms contributes to the diversity of carbon compounds.
- Isomers are compounds that have the same molecular formula but different structures. In structural isomers, the atoms are bonded together in different orders. In geometric isomers, the order of atom bonding is the same, but the atoms are oriented differently in space.

organic compound
catenation
hydrocarbon
isomer

structural formula
structural isomer
geometric isomer

SECTION 2 Hydrocarbons

KEY TERMS

- Alkanes are saturated hydrocarbons; they contain only single bonds. Physical trends in alkanes correspond to trends in alkane size and amount of branching.
- Organic compounds are named according to a systematic method.
- Unsaturated hydrocarbons have one or more multiple carbon-carbon bonds. These include alkenes, alkynes, and aromatic hydrocarbons.

saturated hydrocarbon
alkane
cycloalkane
alkyl group
natural gas
petroleum

unsaturated hydrocarbon
alkene
alkyne
aromatic hydrocarbon
benzene

SECTION 3 Functional Groups

KEY TERMS

- Functional groups determine the properties of the organic compounds that contain them.
- Alcohols contain the hydroxyl functional group.
- Alkyl halides contain one or more halogen atoms.
- Two alkyl groups are joined to an oxygen atom in ethers.
- Both aldehydes and ketones contain the carbonyl group.
- Amines are derivatives of ammonia.
- Carboxylic acids contain carboxyl groups.
- In esters, the hydrogen atom of a carboxylic acid group has been replaced with an alkyl group.

functional group
alcohol
alkyl halide
ether

aldehyde
ketone
amine
carboxylic acid
ester

SECTION 4 Organic Reactions

KEY TERMS

- In substitution reactions, an atom or group of atoms is replaced. In addition reactions, an atom or group of atoms is added to a double or triple bond.
- In a condensation reaction, two molecules combine. In an elimination reaction, a small molecule forms from a large molecule.
- Polymers are large molecules made of many repeating units called *monomers*. A copolymer consists of two or more different monomers.

substitution reaction
addition reaction
condensation reaction
elimination reaction

polymer
monomer
copolymer

CHAPTER 22 **Review**

GO ONLINE

Interactive Review
HMHScience.com

Review Games
Concept Maps

SECTION 1

Organic Compounds

 REVIEWING MAIN IDEAS

1. a. What is catenation?
   b. How does catenation contribute to the diversity of organic compounds?

2. a. What information about a compound is provided by a structural formula?
   b. How are structural formulas used in organic chemistry?

3. Can molecules with the molecular formulas C_4H_{10} and $C_4H_{10}O$ be structural isomers of one another? Why or why not?

4. Can molecules with only single bonds (and no rings) have geometric isomers? Why or why not?

SECTION 2

Hydrocarbons

 REVIEWING MAIN IDEAS

5. What are hydrocarbons, and what is their importance?

6. a. What do the terms *saturated* and *unsaturated* mean when applied to hydrocarbons?
   b. What other meanings do these terms have in chemistry?
   c. Classify alkenes, alkanes, alkynes, and aromatic hydrocarbons as either saturated or unsaturated.

7. Classify each of the following as an alkane, alkene, alkyne, or aromatic hydrocarbon.

a.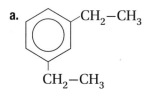

b. $CH_3-CH=CH_2$

c. $CH\equiv C-\overset{\overset{\displaystyle CH_3}{|}}{CH}-CH_2-CH_3$

d. $CH_3-\overset{\overset{\displaystyle}{CH}}{\underset{\underset{\displaystyle CH_3}{|}}{}}-CH_2-CH_2-CH_2-CH_2-CH_3$

8. Give the general formula for the members of the following:
   a. alkane series
   b. alkene series
   c. alkyne series

9. a. What is a homologous series?
   b. By what method are straight-chain hydrocarbons named?
   c. Name the straight-chain alkane with the molecular formula $C_{10}H_{22}$.

10. What are cycloalkanes?

11. a. What trend occurs in the boiling points of alkanes?
   b. How would you explain this trend?
   c. How is the trend in alkane boiling points used in petroleum fractional distillation?

12. Give examples of ethene's commercial uses.

13. Give one use for ethyne.

14. What is the name of the parent hydrocarbon of simple aromatic hydrocarbons?

PRACTICE PROBLEMS

15. Name the following molecules. (Hint: See Sample Problem A.)

a. $CH_3-CH_2-CH_2-CH_2-CH_2-CH_2-CH_3$

b. $CH_3-\overset{\overset{\displaystyle CH_3}{|}}{\underset{\underset{\displaystyle CH_3}{\underset{|}{C}}}{}}-CH_2-\overset{\overset{\displaystyle CH}{}}{\underset{\underset{\displaystyle CH_3}{|}}{}}-CH-CH_3$

c. $CH_3-\overset{\overset{\displaystyle CH_3}{\overset{|}{C}}}{\underset{\underset{\displaystyle CH_3}{|}}{}}-CH_2-CH_2-\overset{\overset{\displaystyle CH_2-CH_2-CH_2-CH_3}{|}}{CH}-CH_2-CH_2-CH_2-CH_3$

16. Give the complete, uncondensed structural formula for each of the following alkanes. (Hint: See Sample Problem A.)
   a. decane
   b. 3,3-dimethylpentane

17. Give the condensed structural formula for 2,2,4,4-tetramethylpentane.

18. For each of the following, determine whether the alkane is named correctly. If it is not, give the correct name.
   a. 1-methylpropane
   b. nonane
   c. 4-methylhexane
   d. 4-ethyl-2-methylhexane

19. Name the following alkenes. (Hint: See Sample Problem B.)
   a. $CH_2=CH-CH_2-CH_2-CH_3$

   b.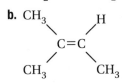

   c.

   $$CH_2=CH-\overset{\overset{\displaystyle CH_3}{|}}{\underset{\underset{\displaystyle CH_3}{|}}{\underset{\underset{\displaystyle CH_2}{|}}{C}}}-CH_2-CH_3$$

   d.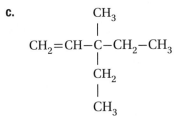

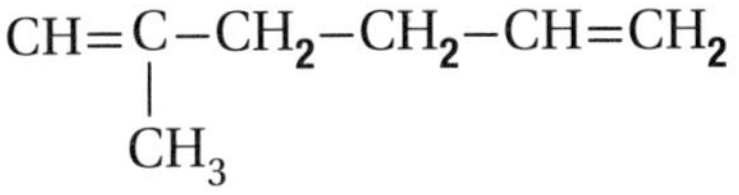

20. Name the following alkynes:
   a. $CH\equiv C-CH_3$

   b. 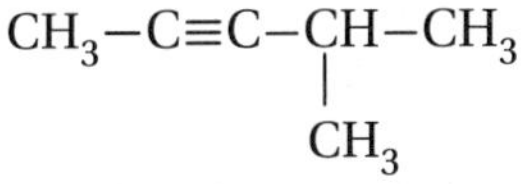 $CH_3-C\equiv C-\overset{\overset{\displaystyle CH_3}{|}}{CH}-CH_3$

   c. $CH_3-\overset{\overset{\displaystyle CH_3}{|}}{CH}-C\equiv C-\overset{\overset{\displaystyle CH_3}{|}}{CH}-CH_3$

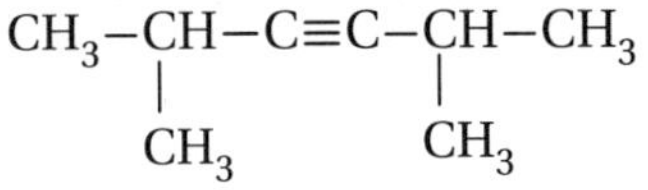

   d. $CH\equiv C-CH_2-CH_2-CH_2-C\equiv CH$

SECTION 3
Functional Groups

▶ **REVIEWING MAIN IDEAS**

21. Write the general formula for the following:
   a. alcohol
   b. ether
   c. alkyl halide

22. Based on the boiling points of water and methanol, in which would you expect to observe a greater degree of hydrogen bonding? Explain your answer.

23. a. Why is glycerol used in moisturizing skin lotions?
   b. How does this relate to the chemical structure of glycerol?

24. Write the general formula for each of the following:
   a. aldehyde   **d.** ester
   b. ketone   **e.** amine
   c. carboxylic acid

25. Aldehydes and ketones both contain the same functional group. Why are they classified as separate classes of organic compounds?

26. How are esters related to carboxylic acids?

27. What element do amines contain besides carbon and hydrogen?

28. Explain why an amine acts as a base.

29. What classes of organic compounds contain oxygen?

SECTION 4
Organic Reactions

▶ **REVIEWING MAIN IDEAS**

30. What type of chemical reaction would you expect to occur between 2-octene and hydrogen bromide, HBr?

31. How many molecules of chlorine, Cl_2, can be added to a molecule of 1-propene? a molecule of 1-propyne?

32. Compare substitution and addition reactions.

33. In a chemical reaction, two small molecules are joined, and a water molecule is produced. What type of reaction took place?

34. What are two reactions by which polymers can be formed?

35. What is the structural requirement for a molecule to be a monomer in an addition polymer?

36. Which of the following reactions is a substitution reaction?
   a. $CH_2=CH_2 + Cl_2 \longrightarrow Cl-CH_2-CH_2-Cl$
   b. $CH_3-CH_2-CH_2-CH_3 + Cl_2 \longrightarrow$
   $Cl-CH_2-CH_2-CH_2-CH_3 + HCl$
   c.

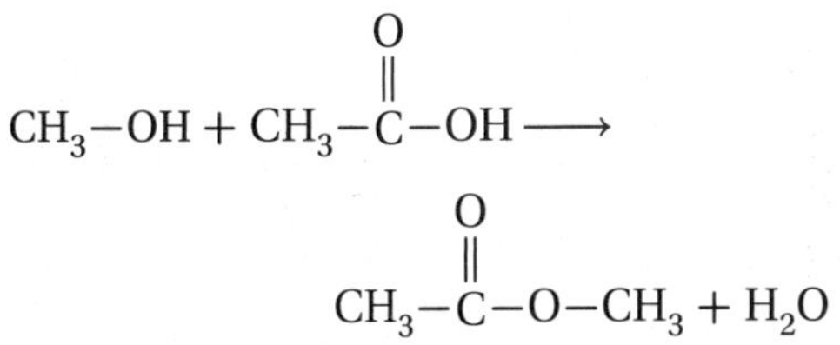

   $$CH_3-OH + CH_3-\overset{\overset{\displaystyle O}{||}}{C}-OH \longrightarrow$$

   $$CH_3-\overset{\overset{\displaystyle O}{||}}{C}-O-CH_3 + H_2O$$

37. Which of the following reactions is an addition reaction?

a. $CH_3-CH_2-CH=CH_2 + Br_2 \longrightarrow$
$$CH_3-CH_2-\underset{\underset{Br}{|}}{CH}-CH_2-Br$$

b.

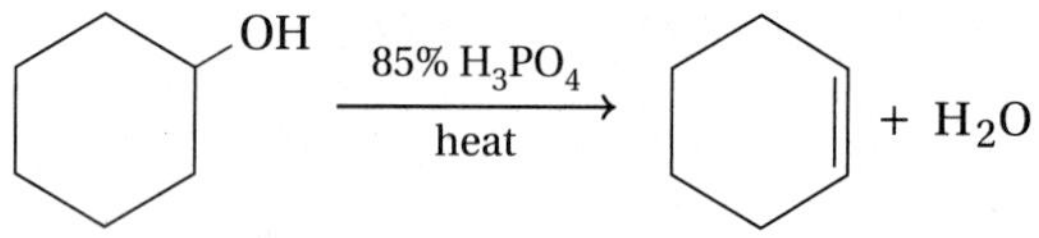

$\xrightarrow[\text{heat}]{85\% \ H_3PO_4}$ $+ H_2O$

c.
$$CH_3-\overset{\overset{O}{\|}}{C}-OH + CH_3-OH \longrightarrow$$
$$CH_3-\overset{\overset{O}{\|}}{C}-O-CH_3 + H_2O$$

38. Which of the following reactions is a condensation reaction?

a.
$$CH_3C\equiv CH + HBr \xrightarrow{\text{ether}} CH_3-\underset{\underset{Br}{|}}{C}=CH_2$$

b.

$+ Br_2 \xrightarrow{CCl_4}$

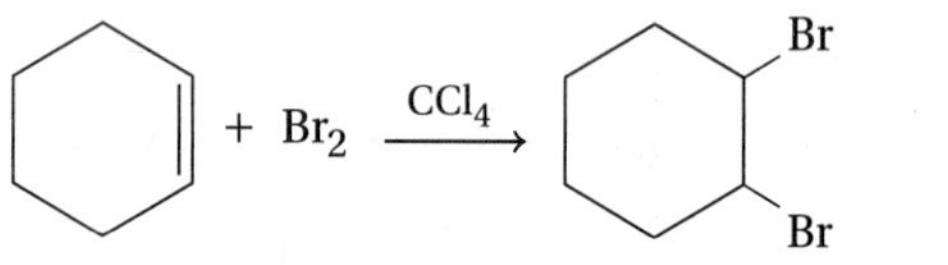

c. $CH_3-CH_2-OH + CH_3-CH_2-OH \xrightarrow{H_2SO_4}$
$$CH_3-CH_2-O-CH_2-CH_3 + H_2O$$

39. Which of the following reactions is an elimination reaction?

a. $CH_2=CH-CH_2-CH_3 + Cl_2 \longrightarrow$
$$Cl-CH_2-\underset{\underset{Cl}{|}}{CH}-CH_2-CH_3$$

b. $CH_3-\underset{\overset{|}{OH}}{CH}-CH_3 \xrightarrow{H_3O^+} CH_3-CH=CH_2 + H_2O$

c. $CH_3CH_3 + Cl_2 \xrightarrow[\text{heat}]{\text{light or}} CH_3CH_2Cl + HCl$

Mixed Review

▶ **REVIEWING MAIN IDEAS**

40. Classify each of the following reactions as an elimination reaction or a condensation reaction:

a. $CH_3-\overset{\overset{Br}{|}}{C}=CH_2 + NaNH_2 \longrightarrow$
$$CH_3C\equiv CH + NaBr + NH_3$$

b. $CH_3-CH_2-\underset{\overset{|}{OH}}{CH}-CH_3 \xrightarrow[\text{heat}]{85\% \ H_3PO_4}$
$$CH_3-CH=CH-CH_3 + H_2O$$

c. $CH_3-CH_2-OH + CH_3-\overset{\overset{O}{\|}}{C}-OH \longrightarrow$
$$CH_3-CH_2-O-\overset{\overset{O}{\|}}{C}-CH_3 + H_2O$$

d.

$-\overset{\overset{O}{\|}}{C}H + CH_3-\overset{\overset{O}{\|}}{C}-CH_3 \xrightarrow{OH^-}$

$-CH=CH-\overset{\overset{O}{\|}}{C}-CH_3 + H_2O$

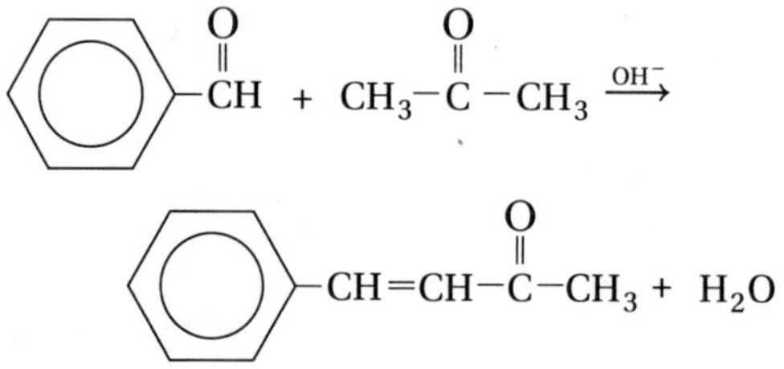

41. Classify each of the following reactions as a substitution reaction or an addition reaction:

a. $CH_3-CH_2-CH_2-CH_2-OH + HCl \xrightarrow[\text{heat}]{ZnCl_2}$
$$CH_3-CH_2-CH_2-CH_2-Cl + H_2O$$

b. $CH_2=CH_2 + HBr \xrightarrow[25°C]{\text{ether}} CH_3-CH_2-Br$

c. $CH\equiv CH + HCl \xrightarrow{HgCl_2} CH_2=CH-Cl$

d.

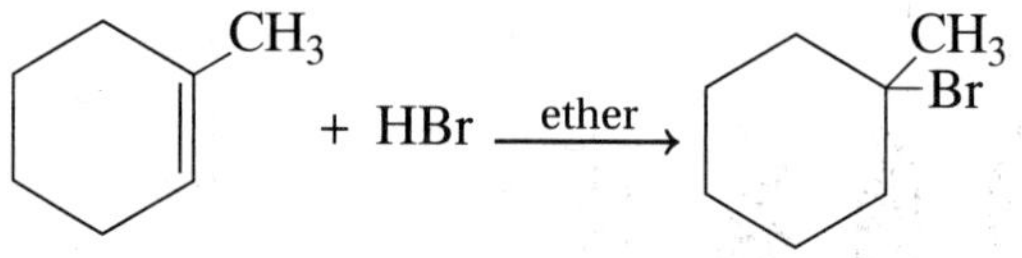

$+ HBr \xrightarrow{\text{ether}}$

42. Identify each of the following reactions as an addition, substitution, elimination, or condensation reaction:

a. 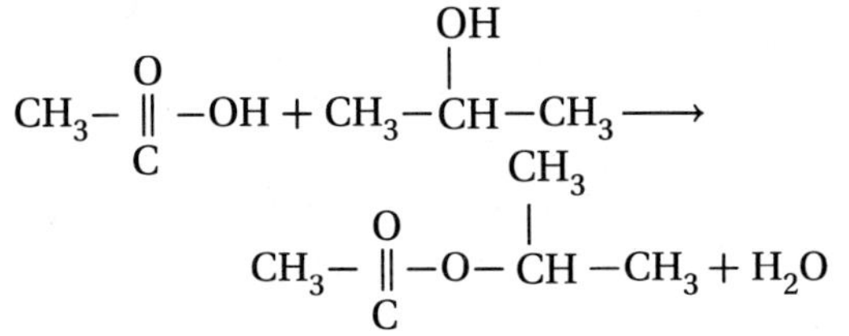 $CH_3-\overset{\displaystyle O}{\underset{\displaystyle C}{\|}}-OH + CH_3-\overset{\displaystyle OH}{\underset{\displaystyle CH_3}{|}}CH-CH_3 \longrightarrow$

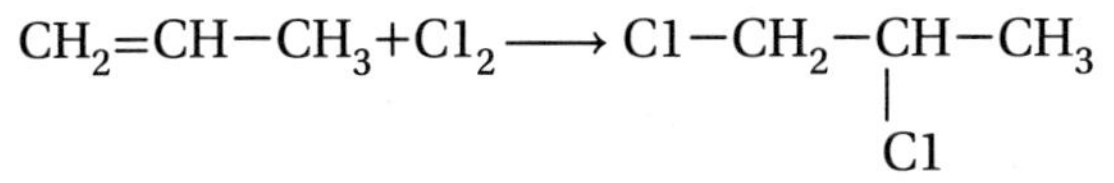

$CH_3-\overset{\displaystyle O}{\underset{\displaystyle C}{\|}}-O-\overset{\displaystyle CH_3}{\underset{}{|}}CH-CH_3 + H_2O$

b. $CH_2=CH-CH_3 + Cl_2 \longrightarrow Cl-CH_2-\overset{}{\underset{\displaystyle Cl}{|}}CH-CH_3$

c.

$\bigcirc + Cl_2 \xrightarrow[\text{heat}]{\text{light or}} \overset{\displaystyle Cl}{\bigcirc} + HCl$

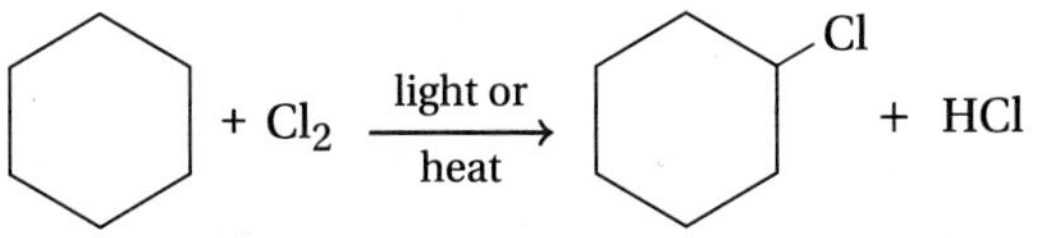

d.

$\overset{\displaystyle CH_3 \; OH}{\bigcirc} \xrightarrow[\text{50°C}]{H_3O^+,\ THF} \overset{\displaystyle CH_3}{\bigcirc} + H_2O$

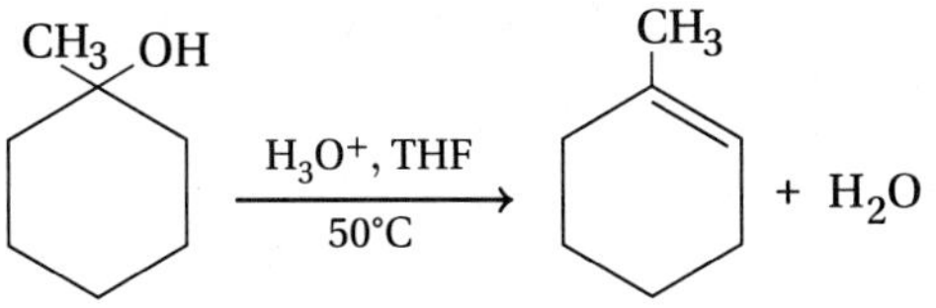

43. Give the molecular formula for each type of hydrocarbon. Assume each contains seven carbon atoms.
  a. an alkane
  b. an alkene
  c. an alkyne

44. a. Alkyne nomenclature is very similar to the nomenclature of what other group of hydrocarbons?
  b. How do these nomenclatures differ?

45. a. What are delocalized electrons?
  b. What is their effect on the reactivity of aromatic hydrocarbons?

CRITICAL THINKING

46. Inferring Conclusions Why are organic compounds with covalent bonds usually less stable when heated than inorganic compounds with ionic bonds?

47. Inferring Relationships The element that appears in the greatest number of compounds is hydrogen. The element found in the second greatest number of compounds is carbon. Why are there more hydrogen compounds than carbon compounds?

48. Relating Ideas As the number of carbon atoms in an alkane molecule increases, does the percentage by mass of hydrogen increase, decrease, or remain the same?

49. Applying Ideas How does ethylene glycol protect radiator fluid in an automobile from both freezing in the winter and boiling over in the summer?

USING THE HANDBOOK

50. The top 10 chemicals produced in the United States are listed in Table 7B of the *Elements Handbook* (Appendix A). Review this material, and answer the following:
  a. Which of the top ten compounds are organic?
  b. Write structural formulas for the compounds you listed in item (a).
  c. To what homologous series do each of these compounds belong?

51. The reaction of methane with oxygen produces two different oxides of carbon. Review this material in the *Elements Handbook* (Appendix A), and answer the following:
  a. What condition determines whether the product of the methane reaction is CO_2 or CO?
  b. If a home heating system is fueled by natural gas, what difference does it make if the combustion produces CO_2 or CO?

52. Silicon is similar to carbon in forming long-chain compounds. Review the material on silicon in the *Elements Handbook* (Appendix A), and answer the following.
  a. How does a long-chain silicon compound differ in composition from a long-chain carbon compound?
  b. The simplest alkane is methane. Methyl groups are found in all alkanes. What is a common subunit of a silicate? What is the geometry of that subunit?

53. Mercury in the environment poses a hazard to living organisms. Review the section on mercury poisoning in the *Elements Handbook* (Appendix A).
  a. Draw a structural formula for the organic mercury compound described in that section.
  b. What is the IUPAC name for this compound?

RESEARCH AND WRITING

54. *Chemical and Engineering News* publishes a list once a year of the top 50 chemicals. Find out which chemicals on the current year's list are hydrocarbons, and report your findings to the class.

55. Consult reference materials at the library, and read about products made from hydrocarbons. Keep a list of the number of petroleum-related products you use in a single day.

56. The widespread use of synthetic polymers in modern society has led to a number of new environmental problems. Find out what some of these problems are and what can be done to reduce them.

ALTERNATIVE ASSESSMENT

57. Performance Models are often used to visualize the three-dimensional shape of molecules. Using gumdrops as atoms and toothpicks to bond them together, construct models of different hydrocarbons. Use large gumdrops for carbon and smaller gumdrops for hydrogen.

58. Performance Using your gumdrop models, demonstrate why alkenes can have geometric isomers while alkanes (except cycloalkanes) cannot.

59. Performance Devise a set of experiments to study how well biodegradable plastics break down. If your teacher approves your plan, conduct an experiment to test the procedure on products labeled "biodegradable."

60. Performance You are asked to identify three samples whose labels are missing. The samples are benzoic acid, ethyl alcohol, and hexanediamine, the latter being an extremely caustic substance that you should only handle with gloves and proper ventilation. Develop an experiment that would allow you to identify each sample.

61. Keep a list of the food you consume in a single day. Compare the content labels from those foods, and then list the most commonly used chemicals in them. With the aid of your teacher and some reference books, try to classify the organic chemicals by their functional groups.

62. As a class or small group, research the preservatives used in various foods. Examine their chemical structures. Determine a way to test for organic functional groups of possibly hazardous preservatives.

Standards-Based Assessment

Record your answers on a separate piece of paper.

MULTIPLE CHOICE

1 During a condensation polymerization reaction —

A single bonds replace all double bonds that are present in the monomer

B water is often produced

C alcohol groups are formed

D an aldehyde group is changed to a ketone group

2 In naming an organic compound, we —

A should remember that naming the location of all functional groups is optional

B do not consider the number of carbon atoms in the molecule as a factor

C begin by identifying and naming the longest hydrocarbon chain

D ignore side chains when we name the molecule

3 Hydrocarbons may be saturated or unsaturated. Which of the following statements is true of hydrocarbons?

A Saturated hydrocarbon molecules contain at least one non-carbon atom.

B Saturated hydrocarbon molecules contain a double bond.

C Saturated hydrocarbon molecules contain only single bonds from carbon or other atoms.

D Saturated hydrocarbons do not exist naturally.

4 Examine the following structural formula:

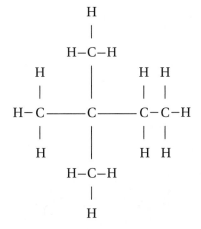

The correct name for this compound is —

A 2,2-dimethylbutane

B 1,1,1-trimethylpropane

C 2-ethyl-2-methylpropane

D 3,3-dimethylbutane

5 Proteins are made up of a sequence of molecules called amino acids. Generally, what type of molecule is removed during the reaction that combines amino acids?

A amine group

B H_2O

C $C_6H_{12}O_6$

D alcohol group

6 Which of the following hydrocarbons is an alkane?

A C_2H_2

B C_5H_{10}

C C_7H_{12}

D $C_{14}H_{30}$

7 Which of the following compounds *cannot* have different isomers?

A C_7H_{16}

B C_5H_{10}

C C_3H_8

D $C_6H_{12}O_6$

GRIDDED RESPONSE

8 A hydrocarbon that is named as an octane would have how many carbon atoms in the longest of its chains?

Test Tip

If you become short on time, quickly scan the unanswered questions to see which might be easier to answer.

CHAPTER 23
Biological Chemistry

BIG IDEA
The organic molecules in living things are classified into four major groups: carbohydrates, lipids, proteins, and nucleic acids.

ONLINE Chemistry
HMHScience.com

SECTION 1
Carbohydrates and Lipids

SECTION 2
Amino Acids and Proteins

SECTION 3
Metabolism

SECTION 4
Nucleic Acids

ONLINE LABS
- All Fats Are Not Equal
- Identifying Organic Compounds in Foods
- The Neighborhood Burglaries
- Blood Typing
- The Murder and the Blood Sample

GO ONLINE

Why It Matters Video
HMHScience.com

Biological Chemistry

Carbohydrates and Lipids

Key Terms

carbohydrate
monosaccharide
disaccharide

condensation reaction
hydrolysis
polysaccharide

lipid
fatty acid
saponification

Main Ideas

▶ Carbohydrates contain carbon, hydrogen, and oxygen atoms.

▶ Lipids have a high percentage of carbon and hydrogen atoms.

Biochemistry is the study of the chemicals and reactions that occur in living organisms. Biochemical compounds are often large and complex organic molecules, but their chemistry is similar to that of the smaller organic molecules. In this chapter, you will study many important biochemical molecules and learn why they are needed to stay healthy. Two of the most common types of molecules that you may know about are *carbohydrates* and *lipids*. These molecules are important parts of the food that you eat and provide most of the energy that your body needs.

▶ **MAIN IDEA**

Carbohydrates contain carbon, hydrogen, and oxygen atoms.

Sugars, starches, and *cellulose* belong to the large group of biochemical molecules called carbohydrates. **Carbohydrates are molecules, composed of carbon, hydrogen, and oxygen atoms in a 1:2:1 ratio, that provide nutrients to the cells of living organisms.** Their general formula is $C_m(H_2O)_n$. They are produced by plants through a process called *photosynthesis.* Cellulose provides structure and support for plants, and starch stores energy in plants. Because animals cannot make their own carbohydrates, they must get them from food. Carbohydrates provide nearly all of the energy that is available in most plant-derived food. Carbohydrates are also referred to as saccharides. This comes from the Greek word for sugar. It is also the basis for the name *saccharin*, a popular artificial sweetener.

Monosaccharides

A monosaccharide is a simple sugar that is the basic subunit of a carbohydrate. A single monosaccharide molecule contains three to seven carbon atoms. Monosaccharide compounds are typically sweet-tasting, white solids at room temperature. Because they have polar hydroxyl (−OH) groups in their molecular structures, they are very soluble in water. The most common monosaccharides are *glucose* (also called *dextrose*) and *fructose*. Although both of these monosaccharides have the formula $C_6(H_2O)_6$, their structural formulas differ. As **Figure 1.1** shows, glucose in a water solution forms a ring made up of five carbon atoms and one oxygen atom, and fructose in a water solution forms a ring made up of four carbon atoms and one oxygen atom. Notice that both compounds have five −OH groups in their structures.

FIGURE 1.1

Monosaccharides Glucose and fructose both have 6 C, 12 H, and 6 O atoms. The arrangement of the C, H, and O atoms determines the shape and properties of each sugar.

glucose

fructose

FIGURE 1.2

Sugar Beets Most of the sugar produced throughout the world comes from sugar beets, such as those shown here, or from sugar cane.

Glucose is the most abundant monosaccharide in nature. It is also the most important monosaccharide nutritionally, because glucose provides energy for cellular activities. The carbohydrates we eat are broken down into glucose, which may be used immediately by cells or stored in the liver, as glycogen, for later use.

Fructose, also called *fruit sugar*, is found in most fruits, honey, and corn syrup. The sweetest naturally occurring sugar, fructose is sweeter than table sugar. Because fructose is not regulated by insulin, as glucose is, it does not trigger the release of the hormone *leptin* that causes us to feel "full." Some research links fructose consumption to unhealthy weight gain.

Disaccharides

Generally, when someone asks for "sugar," the person is asking for the disaccharide *sucrose*, $C_{12}H_{22}O_{11}$. **A disaccharide is a sugar that consists of two monosaccharide units that are joined together.** Like monosaccharides, disaccharides have polar hydroxyl groups in their molecular structures and therefore are water soluble. Sucrose forms when a glucose molecule bonds to a fructose molecule. Commercially available sugar comes from sugar cane or sugar beets (see **Figure 1.2**). Another important disaccharide is *lactose*. Lactose is made up of a sugar called *galactose* and glucose. Human milk is 7% to 8% lactose, but cow's milk is only 4% to 5% lactose. Infant formula is enriched with lactose to simulate human milk.

Carbohydrate Reactions

Carbohydrates undergo two important kinds of reactions: condensation reactions and hydrolysis reactions. **A condensation reaction is a reaction in which two molecules or parts of the same molecule combine.** **Figure 1.3** shows a condensation reaction in which a molecule of glucose combines with a molecule of fructose to yield a molecule of sucrose and a molecule of water.

Disaccharides and longer-chain polysaccharides can be broken down into smaller sugar units by hydrolysis. **Hydrolysis is a chemical reaction between water and another substance to form two or more new substances.** Sucrose will undergo a hydrolysis reaction with water to form glucose and fructose. This hydrolysis reaction occurs in many common processes.

FIGURE 1.3

Condensation Reaction The disaccharide sucrose is formed by a condensation reaction between glucose and fructose.

✔ **CRITICAL THINKING**

Infer Why could this reaction also be called a dehydration synthesis reaction?

glucose   fructose   sucrose   water

Cooking sucrose with high-acid foods, such as berries and fruits, causes it to break down into a mixture of equal parts glucose and fructose. This new mixture provides the sweet taste in jams and jellies, which is sweeter than the starting sugar. When lactose is broken down, glucose and galactose are formed. Some people do not produce the enzyme needed to break down the milk sugar in dairy products. This condition is called *lactose intolerance*. People who have this may feel ill when they drink milk or eat foods that have milk in them.

Polysaccharides

When many monosaccharides or disaccharides combine in a series of condensation reactions, they form a polysaccharide. **A polysaccharide is a carbohydrate made up of long chains of simple sugars.** Cellulose, starch, and glycogen are *polymers* of glucose, or polysaccharides, that contain many glucose monomer units.

As shown in **Figure 1.4,** the glucose molecules in cellulose chains are arranged in such a way that hydrogen bonds link the hydroxyl groups of adjacent glucose molecules to form insoluble fibrous sheets. These sheets of cellulose make up plant cell walls. More than 50% of the total organic matter in the world is cellulose. People cannot digest cellulose, but when we eat fiber, which is cellulose, it speeds the movement of food through the digestive tract. Microorganisms that can digest cellulose are present in the digestive tracts of some animals. Cows and other herbivores have extra stomachs that hold the plants they eat for long periods of time, during which these microorganisms can break down the cellulose.

Starch is the storage form of glucose in plants. Starch from foods such as potatoes and cereal grains makes up about two-thirds of the food eaten by people throughout the world. Starch in food is broken down into glucose during digestion. Glucose is broken down further in metabolic reactions.

✔ **CHECK FOR UNDERSTANDING**
Recall How is the structure of polysaccharides related to that of monosaccharides?

FIGURE 1.4

Glucose Monomers Glucose is the monosaccharide subunit for glycogen, cellulose, and starch. Notice that these three polymers differ in their arrangement of glucose monomers.

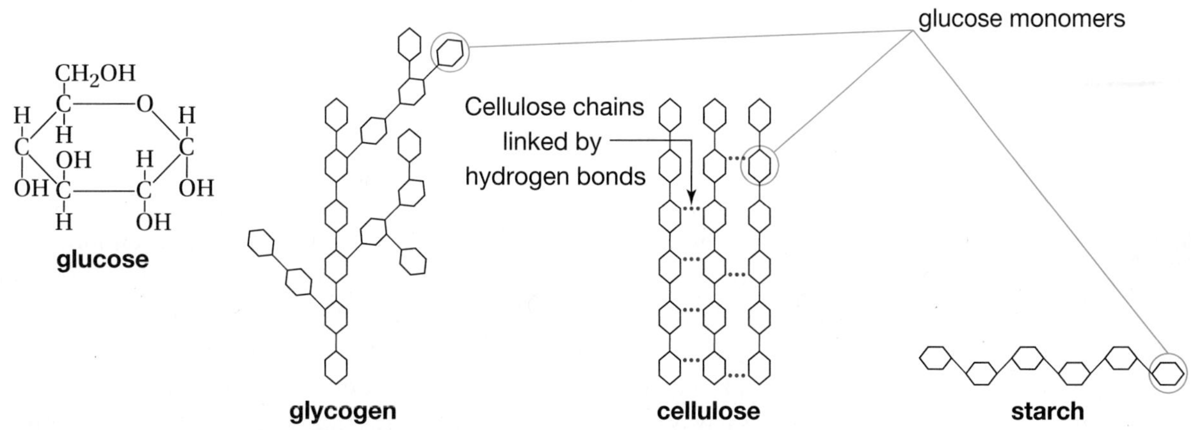

Cellulose chains linked by hydrogen bonds

glucose monomers

glucose

glycogen

cellulose

starch

▶ MAIN IDEA

Lipids have a high percentage of carbon and hydrogen atoms.

Lipids are another important class of nutrients in our diet. They are found in dairy products, grains, meats, and oils. **A lipid is a type of biochemical that does not dissolve in water, has a high percentage of C and H atoms, and is soluble in nonpolar solvents.** As a class, lipids are not nearly as similar to each other as carbohydrates are. Long-chain fatty acids, phospholipids, steroids, and cholesterol are lipids.

Fatty Acids and Triglycerides

Fatty acids consist of a long, nonpolar hydrocarbon "tail" and a polar carboxylic acid functional group at the "head." Fatty acids are the simplest lipid molecules. They have *hydrophilic* polar heads, but their hydrocarbon chains make them insoluble in water. Fatty acids can also be saturated or unsaturated. *Saturated fatty acids* have no carbon–carbon double bonds, while *unsaturated fatty acids* have one or more double bonds in the hydrocarbon chain. The lipid shown below is oleic acid, which is found in animal fat.

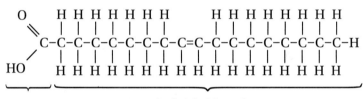

hydrophilic region   hydrophobic region

Fats and oils make up the most common group of lipids in your diet. These molecules are known as *triglycerides*. They are formed by condensation reactions in which three fatty acid molecules bond to one glycerol (a type of alcohol) molecule. Fats, such as butter and lard, come from animals, while oils come from plant sources, such as coconuts, peanuts, corn, and olives, as shown in **Figure 1.5**. Because they have a large amount of saturated fatty acids, fats are solids at room temperature. Oils have more unsaturated fatty acids than fats, so they are liquids. Like other animals, humans make fat, which is stored in *adipose* tissue until it is needed as an energy source. Fat has about twice as much energy per gram as carbohydrates or proteins do. Thus, fat is an efficient form of energy storage.

Fats have another important commercial value based on their ability to react with sodium hydroxide, NaOH, commonly known as *lye*. **When a fat combines with NaOH, an acid-base reaction called saponification occurs, and a salt and water form.** The salt formed is called a *soap* and consists of the long carboxylic acid chain anion and sodium ion as the cation. A molecule of soap has a charged ionic head and a nonpolar hydrocarbon tail. This structure allows the ionic head of a soap molecule to dissolve in water and the nonpolar tail to dissolve in nonpolar greases. This property gives the soap its cleaning ability. The chemistry of this reaction is also used as a way of classifying lipids. Lipids that react with a base to form soap are called *saponifiable lipids*, which include fats, oils, and fatty acids.

✓ CHECK FOR UNDERSTANDING

Distinguish What is the difference between saturated and unsaturated fatty acids?

FIGURE 1.5

Foods High in Fats and Oils Fats, such as lard and butter, are obtained from animals. Oils are found in many different plants.

Other Important Lipids

Compound saponifiable lipids play an important role in biochemical processes. These lipids are structurally similar to triglycerides in that at least one fatty acid is bonded to the central glycerol or glycerol-like unit. These molecules may also have phosphate groups, sugar units, or nitrogen-containing groups. Phospholipids, shown in **Figure 1.6,** are compound saponifiable lipids and are the main structural component of cell membranes. Phospholipids are arranged in a *bilayer*, or double layer, at the surface of the cell. As **Figure 1.6** shows, the hydrophilic heads of the phospholipids are on the outside surfaces of the bilayer. The heads are in contact with water-containing solutions inside the cell and surrounding the cell. The hydrophobic tails point toward the interior of the membrane, away from water-containing solutions. The cell membrane forms a boundary between the cell and its external environment. Only certain substances may pass through the cell membrane. This enables the cell to maintain a stable internal environment.

Nonsaponifiable lipids are nonpolar compounds that do not form soap. They include *steroids*, many *vitamins*, and *bile acids*. *Cholesterol* is a steroid present in animal cell membranes and is a precursor of many hormones.

FIGURE 1.6

Phospholipids

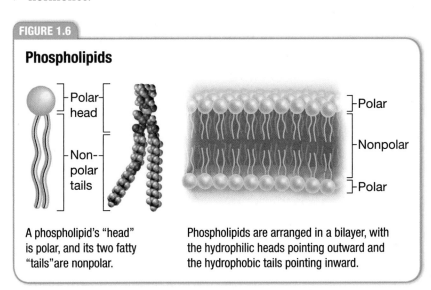

A phospholipid's "head" is polar, and its two fatty "tails" are nonpolar.

Phospholipids are arranged in a bilayer, with the hydrophilic heads pointing outward and the hydrophobic tails pointing inward.

✔ SECTION 1 FORMATIVE ASSESSMENT

▶ Reviewing Main Ideas

1. Describe two functions of carbohydrates in living systems.

2. Carbohydrates make up about 2% of the mass of the human body, yet we need about 1 tsp of glucose every 15 min to maintain energy for our cells. Where does all of this glucose come from?

3. What is the difference between saponifiable and nonsaponifiable lipids?

✔ Critical Thinking

4. **ANALYZING RELATIONSHIPS** Glucose is soluble in water. Why is cellulose, which is made up of glucose, insoluble in water?

5. **EVALUATING IDEAS** Carbohydrates make up 75% of the mass of dried plant material. Cotton is at least 95% carbohydrate. Why do humans not include cotton in their diet?

SECTION 2

Main Ideas

- Amino acids contain an amino and an acid group.
- Proteins are chains of 50 or more amino acid monomers.
- Enzymes are biological catalysts.

Amino Acids and Proteins

Key Terms

amino acid
protein
enzyme
denaturation

Proteins are polymers made up of smaller monomers known as *amino acids*. Although only 20 types of amino acids are found in human proteins, more than 700 types of amino acids occur in nature. Combinations of these 20 amino acids make up the more than 9000 different proteins found in the human body. However, our bodies can synthesize only 11 of the 20 amino acids that we need. The other nine, called the *essential amino acids,* have to be supplied by the food that we eat. A deficiency of these can cause illness and, in some cases, death.

MAIN IDEA

Amino acids contain an amino and an acid group.

Amino acids are organic molecules that contain two functional groups: a basic $-NH_2$ amino group and an acidic $-COOH$ carboxylic acid group. All of the 20 amino acids have the general structure shown in **Figure 2.1.** The *R* represents a side chain that is different for each amino acid. The *R*-groups of the amino acids present in a protein determine the protein's biological activity. The structures of four amino acids—cysteine, valine, glutamic acid, and histidine—are shown below.

FIGURE 2.1

Amino Acid Structure Amino acids have the same basic structure. The *R* represents a side chain.

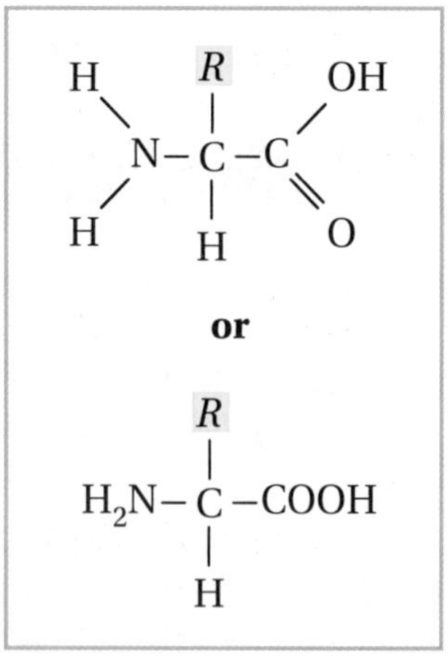

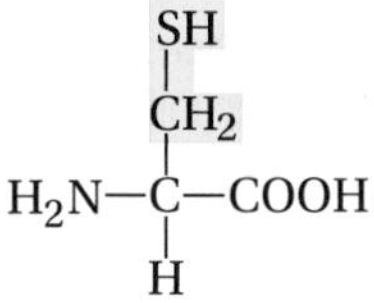

cysteine

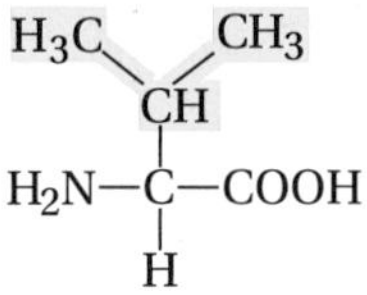

valine

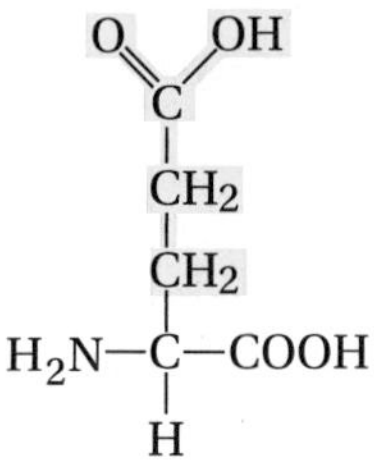

glutamic acid

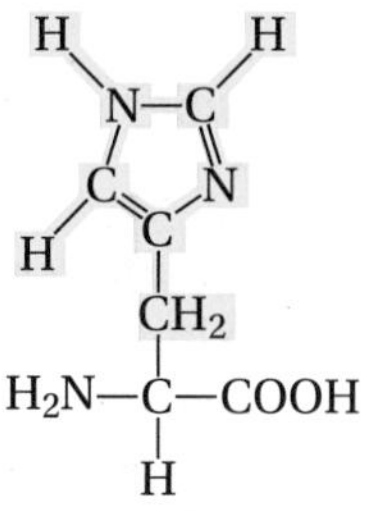

histidine

Amino Acid Reactions

Two amino acids can react with each other in an acid-base type of reaction. The basic amino group of one amino acid reacts with the acidic carboxylic acid group of another amino acid to form a *peptide*, and a molecule of water is lost. This reaction, shown below, is classified as a condensation reaction, or a *dehydration synthesis,* and the two amino acid molecules join together. The bond formed is called a *peptide bond,* and the product is a *dipeptide*, because it is made up of two amino acid units. Longer chains are called *polypeptides*, and chains of 50 or more amino acids are called *proteins*.

Peptide bonds can be broken by enzymes called *proteases*. These enzymes are found in cells and tissues where they aid in the digestion of proteins from food or where they degrade unneeded or damaged proteins.

▶ MAIN IDEA

Proteins are chains of 50 or more amino acid monomers.

Proteins are found in all living cells and are the most complex and varied class of biochemical molecules. A **protein is an organic biological polymer, made up of polypeptide chains of 50 or more amino acids, that is an important building block of all cells.** These chains may be branched and cross-linked as well. *Protein* comes from the Greek *proteios*: "of first importance." This name emphasizes the importance of proteins in living organisms.

Proteins are the second most common molecules found in the body (after water) and make up about 10% to 20% of the mass of a cell. Made up of specific sequences of amino acids, proteins have molecular masses that range from 6000 to more than 9 million unified atomic mass units. Nitrogen accounts for about 15% of the mass of a protein molecule, which makes the structure of a protein quite different from that of a carbohydrate or lipid. Most proteins also contain sulfur, phosphorus, or other elements, such as iron, zinc, and copper.

The importance of proteins in living organisms comes from their many different functions. Besides being the body's main food source for nitrogen and sulfur, proteins have many important catalytic, structural, regulatory, and antibody-defense functions. Some examples of proteins are *keratin*, which is the main component of hair and fingernails; *enzymes*, which catalyze biochemical reactions; *hemoglobin*, which carries oxygen in the blood; *insulin,* which regulates glucose levels; and *antibodies*, which protect the body from foreign substances. Many genetic disorders, such as cystic fibrosis and sickle-cell anemia (discussed later in this section), result from malformed or missing proteins.

✔ **CHECK FOR UNDERSTANDING**
Recognize What makes the structures of proteins quite different from those of carbohydrates?

FIGURE 2.2

Dipeptide A scanning electron micrograph showing crystals of the amino acid glycine, one of the building blocks of proteins.

Arrangement of Amino Acids in Peptides and Proteins

Each peptide, polypeptide, or protein is made up of a special sequence of amino acids. A simple set of three-letter abbreviations is used to represent each amino acid in these kinds of molecules. For example, the dipeptide from glycine, shown in **Figure 2.2,** and glutamic acid would be written as Gly–Glu. The dipeptide Glu–Gly is an isomer of Gly–Glu. Both have the same numbers of C, H, O, and N atoms but in a different order. For the tripeptide Val–Asn–His, made up of valine, asparagine, and histidine, there are five isomers. There are 120 possible isomers for a pentapeptide of five different amino acids. Even though there are only 20 types of amino acids in proteins found in the human body, an incredibly large number of polypeptide and protein molecules are possible. Even for a small protein made up of 100 amino acids, the number of possible combinations of the 20 amino acids is 20^{100}. Polypeptide and protein function depend not only on the kinds and number of amino acids but also on their order. Later, you will see that even the difference of only one amino acid in a polypeptide or protein chain can cause a big change in a protein's activity in a cell.

Amino-Acid Side-Chain Reactions

The properties of amino acids—and ultimately polypeptides and proteins—depend on the properties of the side chains present. For example, the side chain of *glutamic acid* is acidic, and the side chain of *histidine* is basic. The side chains of *asparagine* and several other amino acids are polar. In addition, both glutamic acid and asparagine can form hydrogen bonds, shown in **Figure 2.3.** Some amino-acid side chains can form ionic or covalent bonds with other side chains. *Cysteine* is a unique amino acid, because the —SH group in cysteine can form a covalent bond with another cysteine side chain. **Figure 2.3** shows that two cysteine units—at different points on a protein molecule—can bond to form a *disulfide bridge.* Such bonding can link two separate polypeptides or can cause one long protein to bond onto itself to form a loop. In fact, curly hair is a result of the presence of many disulfide bridges in hair protein.

FIGURE 2.3

Disulfide Bridge Three kinds of interactions between side chains on a polypeptide molecule are shown here. These interactions help determine the shape of a protein.

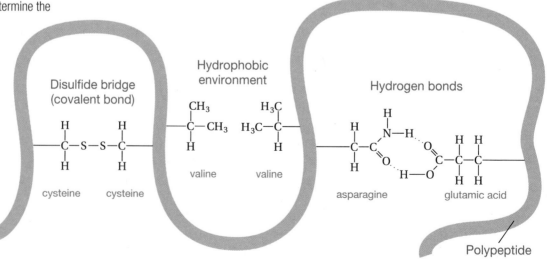

(tr) ©Dr. Jeremy Burgess/Photo Researchers, Inc

Shape and Structure of Protein Molecules

The interaction of amino-acid side chains determines the shape and structure of proteins, which in turn are important to the proteins' biological functions. In a polypeptide chain or protein, the sequence of the amino acids is called the *primary* (1°) *structure*. The *secondary* (2°) *structure* describes how the chain is coiled or otherwise arranged in space. For example, the alpha (α) helix is a secondary structure that resembles a coiled spring. Another type of secondary structure is the beta (β) pleated sheet, which has accordion-like folds. These secondary structures form because hydrogen bonding occurs between a hydrogen atom attached to the nitrogen atom in one peptide bond and the oxygen atom of another peptide bond farther down the backbone of the protein.

In a protein, the amino-acid side chains project out in such a way that they often interact with other side chains located at various positions along the protein backbone. These interactions give the protein its characteristic three-dimensional shape, which is called its *tertiary* (3°) *structure*. The side-chain interactions can include hydrogen bonding, salt bridges, and cysteine–cysteine disulfide bonds. Hydrophobic interactions that occur between nonpolar side chains also contribute to a protein's tertiary structure. Because nonpolar side groups are repulsed by the water found in cells and body fluids, these groups tend to be found in the interior of the protein, where contact with water is minimal. Polar and ionic side chains tend to be on the protein surface, where they are in contact with water. In some proteins, different polypeptides, each of which has its own 3° structure, come together. In the case of hemoglobin, four different polypeptides make up the *quaternary* (4°) *structure*. The four structural levels of proteins are shown in **Figure 2.4.**

✔ CRITICAL THINKING

Predict Why might a protein's environment have a great effect on its structure?

FIGURE 2.4

The Four Structural Levels of Proteins The functions of proteins are determined by their complex structures.

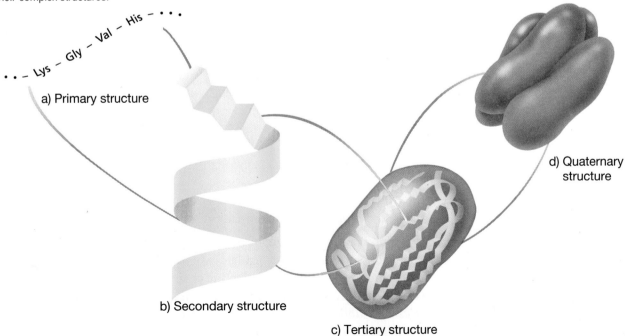

a) Primary structure

b) Secondary structure

c) Tertiary structure

d) Quaternary structure

FIGURE 2.5

BIOLOGICAL FUNCTIONS OF PROTEINS

Type of protein	Function	Examples
storage	storage of amino acids	*Casein* protein in milk supplies amino acids for baby mammals. Egg-white protein, or *ovalbumin*, is a source of amino acids for developing embryos. Plants store proteins in seeds.
transport	transport of substances	Proteins transport molecules across cell membranes. *Hemoglobin* in blood transports oxygen.
structural	support	Spiders produce silk fibers, which are proteins, to make webs. *Collagen* and *elastin* give connective tissues strength and flexibility. *Keratin* is found in hair, feathers, horns, hooves, and nails.
contractile	movement	*Actin* and *myosin* fibers cause movement in muscles. Contractile fibers in cilia and flagella help propel single-celled organisms.
enzymatic	catalysis of chemical reactions	Enzymes break down large molecules in food within the digestive system.
hormonal	coordination of processes in an organism	Pancreatic insulin helps regulate blood-sugar levels.
receptor	response of cell to chemical stimuli	Nerve-cell membranes have chemical receptors that detect chemical signals released by other nerve cells.
defensive	protection against disease	Antibodies attack pathogenic viruses and bacteria.

Biological Functions of Proteins

From **Figure 2.5,** you can see that almost everything that occurs in a living organism depends on one or more proteins. Scientists have discovered that the specific function of a protein is related to the protein's shape. The shape of a protein can generally be described as fibrous or globular. *Fibrous proteins* are insoluble in water and are long, thin, and physically strong. *Globular proteins* are generally soluble in water and are twisted and folded into a globe-like shape.

Fibrous proteins give strength and protection to structures in living organisms. *Keratin* is a fibrous protein whose secondary structure is almost entirely alpha helical in shape. The keratin in nails and hooves is much stiffer than the keratin in fur or wool because of the large number of side-chain interactions that occur between the nail and hoof proteins. *Collagen*, found in bone and tendons, is a triple helix of three intertwined alpha helices, which gives these tissues their strength. *Fibrin* found in silk has a beta-pleated sheet structure. *Elastins* in blood tissue, *fibrins* in blood clots, and *myosins* found in muscle tissue are other kinds of fibrous proteins.

Globular proteins regulate body functions, catalyze reactions, and transport substances. The regulatory hormone *insulin* is a small protein of 51 amino acids in two polypeptide chains. *Myoglobin* transports oxygen in the muscles, and *hemoglobin* transports oxygen in the blood. *Casein*, found in milk and used for food, is also a globular protein. It contains phosphorus, which is needed for bone growth.

Amino Acid Substitution

A protein's amino acid sequence determines its three-dimensional structure, which in turn determines its function. Even a single substitution of one amino acid for another can change the shape and function of a protein. For example, the genetic disease sickle-cell anemia can happen when one amino acid—glutamic acid—is replaced by a another—valine. This change in only 1 of 146 amino acids in one of the two protein chains in the hemoglobin molecule causes a major change in the shape of the molecule. This change in the shape of the hemoglobin molecule causes the red blood cells to sickle when oxygen levels are relatively low (as is the case in most body tissues). The sickle cells tend to clog small blood vessels, which prevents the transport of enough oxygen to tissue cells. As a result, people who have sickle-cell anemia suffer from shortness of breath. **Figure 2.6** shows the shape of normal red blood cells and sickle cells. The sickle-cell gene is more common in some groups of people than it is in others. In areas where the disease malaria is common, scientists have discovered that sickle cells are more resistant to malarial infection than other cells are. So people who have sickle-cell trait are more resistant to malaria than other people are.

FIGURE 2.6

Sickle-Cell Anemia

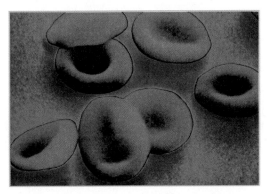

(a) The round, flat shape of healthy red blood cells shows they have normal hemoglobin molecules.

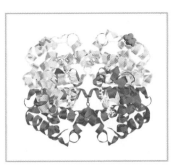

(b) Hemoglobin consists of four polypeptide chains; a fragment of one chain is shown in green.

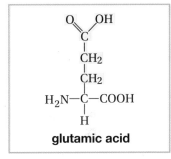

glutamic acid

(c) Each of the chains is a polymer of 141 or 146 amino acid units, such as the glutamic acid monomer shown here.

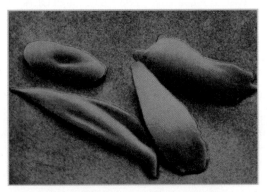

(d) Because of their shape, sickle cells clog small blood vessels.

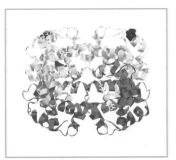

(e) A genetic mutation causes one glutamic acid to be replaced by valine in the hemoglobin molecules, as shown in red.

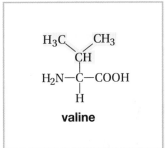

valine

(f) The sickle shape of the cell comes from the different shape of the hemoglobin caused by the substitution of valine for glutamic acid.

Dr. Charles Drew and Blood Transfusions

Prior to the 1900s, severe bleeding often resulted in death. But today, blood is stored at blood banks, where people "deposit" blood so that they or others can "withdraw" it when needed. Charles Drew was a pioneer in the work of blood transfusions, especially in the use of plasma and the development of blood banks.

Charles Drew was a pioneer in the development of blood banks.

The Need for Blood

While in medical school, Drew realized that many lives could be saved if blood could be stored for transfusions. Before 1937, most patients needing blood received it directly from a donor at the time it was needed. In 1938, Drew and physician John Scudder from Britain studied the chemistry of blood to try to find a way to preserve blood. Drew recognized that extracting blood plasma could help solve the problems of storing blood.

There are two main components of blood: blood cells and plasma. Red blood cells, white blood cells, and platelets make up 45% of the volume of blood, while plasma makes up 55% of blood. Plasma is amber colored and is about 90% water. It has more than 100 solutes, including nutrients, antibodies, hormones, and proteins. Drew discovered that plasma could be used as an emergency substitute for blood without testing for blood type, because the ABO blood types are removed with the red blood cells. He also found that plasma could be dehydrated and stored.

During World War II, Drew was the medical supervisor for the "Blood for Britain" program. He also coordinated the American blood-storage program by setting up collection centers, standardizing blood-bank equipment, and establishing record-keeping procedures and criteria to ensure the safety of blood products. When the United States entered the war, the blood supply was ready, and stored blood and plasma saved several thousand lives.

A Safer Blood Supply

With the emergence of HIV and AIDS in the 1980s, the methods of blood transfusion needed to be modified. Some transfused blood was found to carry HIV in a number of people. Before modifications were put into place, as many as 50% of hemophiliacs in the United States could have been infected with HIV because of their frequent transfusions. Although current screening procedures to detect HIV, hepatitis, and other diseases have almost completely removed the risk of transfusing infected blood, some people choose to bank their own blood before undergoing surgery.

Blood Substitutes

The AIDS epidemic has sped up attempts to find an artificial blood substitute. Perfluorocarbons (PFCs), which are made by replacing the hydrogen atoms of hydrocarbons with fluorine atoms, are possible substitutes. Oxygen binds to PFCs 10 to 20 times more readily than it binds to plasma or water, and products using PFCs have a shelf life of up to two years. Another substitute is a hemoglobin-based oxygen carrier (HBOC). HBOCs may be able to transport oxygen until a body is able to replenish its red blood cells. If these products are successful, they could provide a supply of blood substitutes that do not require typing and do not depend on donors.

Questions

1. What was Dr. Drew's contribution to medicine?

2. Why are scientists searching for blood substitutes?

● MAIN IDEA

Enzymes are biological catalysts.

An **enzyme** is a protein that catalyzes a biochemical reaction. Enzymes make up the largest and most highly specialized class of proteins. All living organisms have enzymes; as many as 3000 enzymes can be found in a single cell. Most enzymes are water-soluble, globular proteins. Remember that catalysts speed up a reaction by lowering the activation energy and are not changed in the reaction. An enzyme also does not change the amount of product that is formed in a reaction. Enzymes catalyze both decomposition and synthesis reactions.

Enzymes are also very efficient. For example, the enzyme *carbonic anhydrase* acts on carbonic acid to break down as many as 36 million molecules in 1 minute. Carbon dioxide is carried from all the parts of the body to the lungs as carbonic acid in the blood. In the lungs, carbonic anhydrase breaks down carbonic acid into CO_2 and water vapor, which then exit the lungs as a person exhales.

Enzyme Specificity

In addition to being highly efficient, enzymes are very specific. For example, the enzyme peroxidase is responsible only for the decomposition of hydrogen peroxide to water and oxygen. Hydrogen peroxide is fairly stable in the bottle, but when you put it on a minor cut, the peroxidase enzyme in the blood catalyzes its decomposition. Bubbling occurs as a result of the gaseous oxygen from the decomposing hydrogen peroxide. As you can see in **Figure 2.7,** enzymes act by binding to a specific *substrate* molecule. Hydrogen peroxide is the substrate in the reaction just discussed. The shape of the enzyme is such that a molecule of hydrogen peroxide can fit into the enzyme at a specific part of the enzyme molecule, called the *active site*. The resulting compound is called the *enzyme–substrate complex*. In this complex, hydrogen–oxygen bonds break, and oxygen–oxygen bonds form. Then the enzyme releases the products and is ready to react with another substrate molecule. This model of enzyme action is called the *lock-and-key model.*

FIGURE 2.7

Lock-and-Key Enzyme Model

(a) The substrate comes into contact with the active site.

(b) The activated complex forms, and a reaction occurs.

(c) The products form, but the enzyme remains unchanged.

FIGURE 2.8

Activation Energy and Enzymes
Enzymes decrease the activation energy of a chemical reaction.

✓ CRITICAL THINKING

Interpret In **Figure 2.8**, how can you tell that the enzyme does not change the total amount of energy required for or released by the reaction?

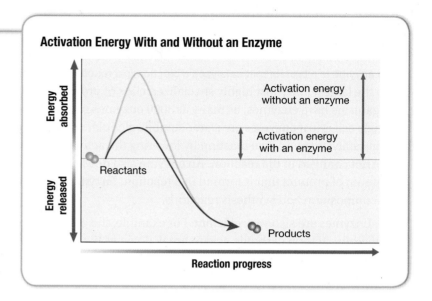

Activation Energy With and Without an Enzyme

FIGURE 2.9

Temperature and Enzyme Activity
Enzymes have maximum activity within a narrow temperature range. Denaturation occurs at temperatures above 50°C to 60°C and causes a decrease in activity.

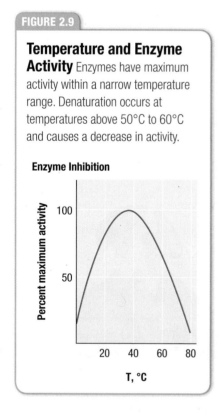

Enzyme Inhibition

Enzymes and Reaction Rates

The presence of an enzyme in a chemical reaction can increase the rate of a reaction by a factor of up to 10^{20}. Recall that a reaction can only occur when two atoms or molecules collide with enough energy to overcome the *activation energy* and have the proper orientation to change reactants into products. As you can see from the graph in **Figure 2.8,** an enzyme that catalyzes a chemical reaction causes an increase in the rate of the reaction by reducing the activation energy. The enzyme lowers the activation energy by forming the enzyme–substrate complex, which makes breaking bonds in the reactants and forming new bonds in the products easier. The net amount of energy required for the reaction or released by the reaction is not changed by the action of an enzyme.

Temperature and Enzyme Activity

Proteins, including enzymes, are also affected by changes in temperature. The graph in **Figure 2.9** shows the relatively narrow range of temperatures within which enzymes typically have maximum activity. Enzymes in the human body work optimally at the normal body temperature of 37°C (98.6°F). At temperatures above 50°C to 60°C, enzymes typically show a decline in activity. High heat can denature, or alter, the shape of a protein, which in turn alters the protein's function. **Denaturation is a change in a protein's characteristic three-dimensional shape due to changes in its secondary, tertiary, and quaternary structure.** If you have ever cooked an egg, you have caused protein denaturation. The white of an egg is a solution of the protein albumin. When the egg is placed in a hot frying pan, a dramatic change takes place, and the semitransparent solution turns into a white solid. Because the primary structure is retained in denaturation, the nutritional value of the egg white is not affected. The process is not reversible, however; cooling a fried egg does not reverse the denaturation. When food is cooked, the three-dimensional structure of the protein is altered, making the food easier to digest.

pH and Enzyme Activity

Enzymes also typically have maximum activity within a relatively narrow range of pH. The optimal pH for normal cell enzyme functions is almost neutral, about 7.3 to 7.4. Changes in pH can cause changes in protein structure and shape. For example, adding acid or base can interfere with the side-chain interactions and thus change the shape of a protein. Most enzymes become *inactivated*, or no longer work, because of denaturation when the pH changes. When milk sours (because lactic acid has formed), it curdles, and curds of the protein casein form. Yogurt is made by growing acid-producing bacteria in skim milk, which causes the casein to denature, which in turn gives yogurt its consistency.

The digestion of dietary protein by enzymes begins in the stomach. When food is swallowed, the stomach lining produces HCl and *pre-enzymes,* inactive forms of protein-digesting enzymes. These pre-enzymes travel from the stomach lining into the stomach before they become activated by the stomach's low pH of 1.5 to 2.0. This process is important because it prevents the active form of the enzymes from digesting the stomach lining. A layer of mucus protects the lining of the stomach from the enzymes it contains. Once activated, the enzymes catalyze the breakdown of the proteins in food into shorter polypeptide segments. *Pepsin* is a stomach enzyme found in adults. The partially digested protein in food travels into the small intestine, where the pH is 7 to 8. Under these conditions, the enzyme *trypsin* becomes active. It catalyzes the hydrolysis of the polypeptide segments into amino acids, which are absorbed through the intestinal wall and enter the bloodstream. The body uses these newly acquired amino acids to make new protein molecules. **Figure 2.10** shows how the protein in raw fish looks before and after it is soaked in acidic lime juice. Because the acidic lime juice denatures protein in the fish, the acid-treated fish looks very different. Marinades made with wine or vinegar are also used to flavor meats. As a result, many of the proteins in the meat are denatured, making it more tender.

✓ CHECK FOR UNDERSTANDING
Conclude Why might highly acidic foods cause problems in digestion?

Acid Denaturation of Protein
The fish treated with lime has turned white because the acidic lime juice denatures the protein in raw fish.

✓ SECTION 2 **FORMATIVE ASSESSMENT**

▶ Reviewing Main Ideas

1. Which elements do amino acids and proteins have in common with carbohydrates and lipids?

2. What is the difference between an amino acid and a protein?

3. Explain the difference between fibrous proteins and globular proteins.

4. Why are only small amounts of enzymes found in the body?

✓ Critical Thinking

5. **RELATING IDEAS** Explain how the ball-like structure of globular proteins allows them to be water soluble.

6. **INFERRING CONCLUSIONS** If an essential amino acid is in short supply in the diet, it can become a limiting reactant in building any protein that contains the amino acid. Explain why, under these conditions, the only way that the body could make that protein would be to destroy one of its proteins that contain the limiting amino acid.

- ATP is an energy source for cells.

- Complex compounds get broken down and energy gets released in catabolism.

- Smaller compounds get converted to larger ones during anabolism.

Metabolism

Key Terms

metabolism

autotroph

adenosine triphosphate (ATP)

heterotroph

adenosine diphosphate (ADP)

catabolism

anabolism

Metabolism is the sum of all the chemical processes that occur in an organism. Complex molecules are broken down into smaller ones through *catabolism*, and simple molecules are used to build bigger ones through a process called *anabolism*. A *metabolic pathway* is a series of linked chemical reactions that occur within a cell and result in a specific product. The major metabolic pathways for most organisms are very similar. So one can study the metabolic pathways in simple organisms to get information about reactions in more complex organisms, including humans.

▶ MAIN IDEA

ATP is an energy source for cells.

Cells require energy to make the proteins, carbohydrates, lipids, and nucleic acids that are necessary for life. In addition, the body needs energy as heat to keep warm, mechanical energy to move muscles and pump blood, and electrical energy to move ions across cell membranes. The original source for almost all of the energy needed by living systems is the sun. **Autotrophs are living organisms that use sunlight (or other energy), water, and CO_2 to make carbon-containing biomolecules, including carbohy-**drates. The most common form of this process, called *photosynthesis*, occurs in the cells of plants and algae, such as those shown in **Figure 3.1,** within structures called *chloroplasts*. Chloroplasts contain *chlorophyll*, an organic molecule that absorbs solar energy. This energy is captured in two compounds, one of which is adenosine triphosphate (ATP). **ATP (adenosine triphosphate) is a high-energy molecule that plant cells use to make carbohydrates.** The other compound, *NADPH*, is also used in carbohydrate-forming reactions.

A less-common type of autotrophic metabolism, called *chemosynthesis*, is found in microbes living around deep-sea hydrothermal vents. These organisms obtain nutrients in the absence of sunlight by metabolizing nitrogen and sulfur compounds produced by geothermal activity beneath the oceans.

Animals, however, cannot use the sun's energy to convert CO_2 into food. Animals must get the energy that they need to sustain life by consuming plants and other animals. **Living organisms, including most microorganisms, that depend on plants or other animals for food are called heterotrophs.** Heterotrophs use the energy obtained in the breakdown of complex molecules to drive chemical reactions in cells. The carbohydrates, lipids, and amino acids that heterotrophs consume undergo several energy-yielding reactions as they break down into simpler molecules. Some of this energy is stored in ATP molecules, which cells use to drive a wide variety of metabolic reactions.

©Perennou Nuridsany/Photo Researchers, Inc

FIGURE 3.1

Chlorophyll The cells of algae and green plants contain chlorophyll, the green pigment that absorbs light energy from the sun.

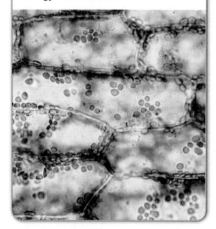

FIGURE 3.2

The ATP Cycle ATP is formed by photosynthesis or catabolism. Cell activities that require energy are powered by ATP hydrolysis. The "P_i" represents a phosphate group.

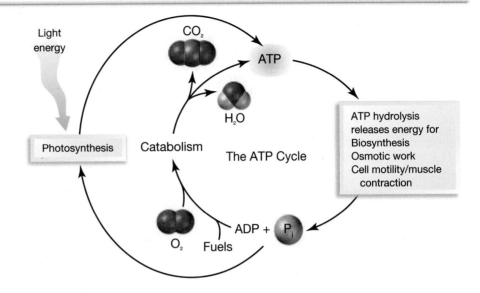

The ATP Cycle

Adenosine diphosphate (ADP) is the molecular building block from which ATP is made. The cycle between ATP and ADP is the primary energy-exchange mechanism in the body. **Figure 3.2** provides an overview of the ATP cycle in cells. In this cycle, ATP carries energy from energy-storing molecules, carbohydrates, lipids, and proteins to specific energy-requiring processes in cells. When ATP is hydrolyzed to ADP, in a process called *phosphorylation*, energy is released to power the cell's activities. The molecular structures of ATP and ADP are closely related, as shown in **Figure 3.3**.

The difference in the number of phosphate groups between ATP and ADP molecules is the key to the energy exchange in metabolic reactions. The chemical equation below shows the hydrolysis reaction by which ATP is converted into ADP and a phosphate group (represented by the gold-colored ball in **Figure 3.2**). The free energy for this reaction is –31 kJ, which is the amount of energy available to do work.

$$\text{ATP}^{4-}(aq) + \text{H}_2\text{O}(l) \longrightarrow \text{ADP}^{3-}(aq) + \text{H}_2\text{PO}_4^-(aq) \quad \Delta G = -31 \text{ kJ}$$

✔ **CHECK FOR UNDERSTANDING**
Identify What is the primary difference between an ATP and an ADP molecule?

FIGURE 3.3

Hydrolysis of ATP The hydrolysis of ATP produces ADP and releases energy.

Adenosine triphosphate (ATP)

Adenosine diphosphate (ADP)

FIGURE 3.4

Catabolic and Anabolic Pathways Catabolic pathways release free energy in the form of ATP and NADH. Anabolic pathways consume energy released by catabolic pathways.

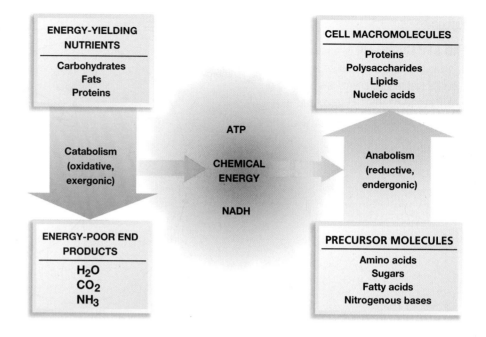

▶ **MAIN IDEA**

Complex compounds get broken down and energy gets released in catabolism.

The energy that your body needs to maintain its temperature and drive its biochemical reactions is provided through *catabolic* processes, or *cellular respiration*. **Figure 3.4** illustrates the relationship between the pathways of catabolism and anabolism. **Catabolism is the part of metabolism in which complex compounds break down into simpler ones and is accompanied by the release of energy.** First, enzymes break down the complex compounds in food—carbohydrates, fats, and proteins—into simpler molecules, releasing the energy stored in their carbon–carbon bonds.

Carbohydrate digestion begins in the mouth, where the enzyme *amylase* in saliva begins to break down polysaccharides. The food then passes through the esophagus, then the stomach, and into the small intestine. Here, more enzymes are secreted to complete the hydrolysis of carbohydrates to form glucose and other monosaccharides.

Digestion of fats occurs only in the small intestine. Protein digestion begins in the stomach and is completed in the small intestine. During digestion, fats are broken down into fatty acids and glycerol. Proteins are broken down into amino acids.

These products are absorbed across the wall of the small intestine into the blood and are transported to cells. Once in the cells, glucose and other monosaccharides, fatty acids, some amino acids, and glycerol enter the mitochondria and feed into a complex series of reactions called the *citric acid cycle,* or *Krebs cycle*. The citric acid cycle produces carbon dioxide and other molecules, such as NADH (not to be confused with NADPH) and ATP. This NADH and ATP then move through another set of reactions to produce more ATP and water.

The amount of energy released in catabolism depends on the amount of ATP that is made as the products of digestion are oxidized. The catabolism of 1 glucose molecule generally produces a total of 36 ATP molecules. This accounts for about 40% of the energy released by the complete oxidation of glucose. Most of the energy not converted to ATP is lost by the body as energy in the form of heat. **Figure 3.5** shows how much ATP is needed for some daily activities.

APPROXIMATE "COST" OF DAILY ACTIVITIES

Activity	Energy required (kJ)	ATP required (mol)
running	1120	56
swimming	840	42
bicycling	1400	70
walking	560	28

▶ MAIN IDEA
Smaller compounds get converted to larger ones during anabolism.

Cells use the simple molecules that result from the breakdown of food to make larger, more complex molecules. Energy released during catabolism powers the synthesis of new molecules as well as the active transport of ions and molecules across cell membranes. *Anabolic* processes are the energy-consuming pathways by which cells produce the molecules that they need for sustaining life and for growth and repair. The conversion of small biomolecules into larger ones is called **anabolism.**

In an anabolic pathway, small precursor molecules are converted into complex molecules, including lipids, polysaccharides, proteins, and nucleic acids. Energy from ATP and NADH is necessary for these biosynthesis reactions to occur. **Figure 3.4** illustrates that catabolism and anabolism occur simultaneously and that ATP and NADH serve as chemical "links" between the two processes.

One important anabolic pathway that is common to animals, plants, fungi, and microorganisms is *gluconeogenesis*. As the name implies, glucose is synthesized in this pathway from noncarbohydrate substances, including lactate, pyruvate, glycerol, and most of the amino acids. In mammals, glucose from the blood is the fuel source for the brain and nervous system as well as for the kidneys, red blood cells, and embryonic tissues.

✓ SECTION 3 FORMATIVE ASSESSMENT

▶ Reviewing Main Ideas

1. List four ways in which the body uses energy.

2. What is the total energy (in kilojoules) stored in the 36 ATP molecules that are made from the metabolism of 1 molecule of glucose in skeletal tissue?

3. The teeth break large pieces of food into smaller ones. However, this process is not considered part of digestion. Explain why.

4. How does the digestion of fat in a strip of ham differ from the digestion of starch in a piece of toast?

5. Why are diets that are severely restrictive in carbohydrate intake potentially dangerous to a person's health?

✓ Critical Thinking

6. **RELATING CONCEPTS** When a molecule of glucose is oxidized, only about 40% of the energy is captured in ATP molecules, and the rest is lost as energy in the form of heat. What do you think would happen if this energy remained in the body as heat?

▶ Nucleic acids are chains of nucleotides containing a sugar bonded to a phosphate and an organic base.

▶ RNA molecules synthesize proteins.

▶ Genetic engineers manipulate genetic material.

Nucleic Acids

Key Terms

nucleic acid   DNA replication   cloning

Nucleic acids contain all the genetic information of an organism. They are the means by which a living organism stores and conveys instructional information for all its activities. They are also the means by which an organism can reproduce. The two major nucleic acids found in organisms are *deoxyribonucleic acid (DNA)* and *ribonucleic acid (RNA)*.

▶ MAIN IDEA

Nucleic acids are chains of nucleotides containing a sugar bonded to a phosphate and an organic base.

A **nucleic acid** is an organic compound, either RNA or DNA, whose molecules carry genetic information and that is made up of one or two chains of monomer units called nucleotides. However, unlike the monomer units in polysaccharides and polypeptides, each nucleotide monomer can be further hydrolyzed into three different molecules. A nucleotide molecule is composed of a five-carbon sugar unit that is bonded to both a phosphate group and a cyclic, organic base that contains nitrogen.

The sugar unit in DNA is deoxyribose, and the sugar unit in RNA is ribose. The diagram below shows the sugar-phosphate arrangement in three nucleotides.

$$-\text{phosphate}-\text{sugar}-\text{phosphate}-\text{sugar}-\text{phosphate}-\text{sugar}-$$
$$\qquad\qquad\quad | \qquad\qquad\qquad | \qquad\qquad\qquad |$$
$$\qquad\qquad \text{base} \qquad\qquad\quad \text{base} \qquad\qquad\quad \text{base}$$

The five nitrogenous bases found in nucleic acids are shown in **Figure 4.1**. *Adenine* (A), *guanine* (G), and *cytosine* (C) are found in both DNA and RNA. *Thymine* (T) is found only in DNA, and *uracil* (U) is found only in RNA.

FIGURE 4.1

Bases in Nucleic Acid There are five common nitrogenous bases. Thymine (T), cytosine (C), and uracil (U) have a single six-member ring. Adenine (A) and guanine (G) have a six-member ring connected to a five-member ring.

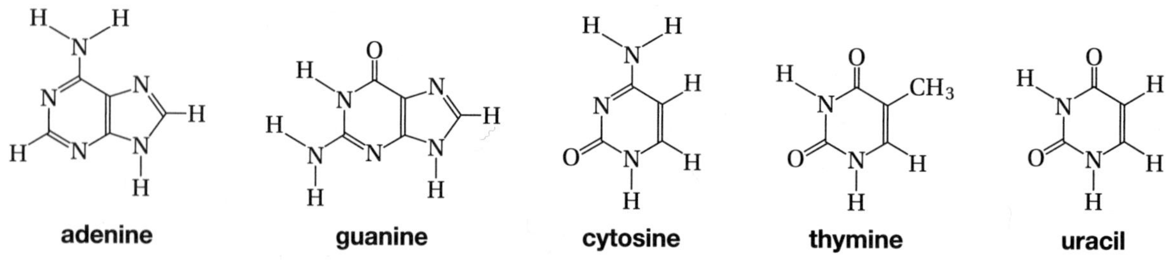

adenine   guanine   cytosine   thymine   uracil

DNA: Deoxyribonucleic Acid

Every single instruction for all the traits that you have inherited and all the life processes that occur in your cells is contained in your DNA. It is no wonder then that DNA molecules are the largest molecules found in cells. Living organisms vary widely in the size and number of DNA molecules in their cells. Some bacterial cells contain only 1 DNA molecule, while human cells contain 23 pairs of relatively large DNA molecules. Each human cell contains about 2 m of DNA, which is divided and packed into the cell's 46 *chromosomes*. An average cell is only about 6 μm in diameter and contains many organelles and structures. To fit in a cell, DNA must undergo extensive twisting, coiling, folding, and wrapping.

The Swedish scientist Friedrich Miescher first extracted DNA from cells in 1868, but its three-dimensional structure was not discovered until 1953. Using the x-ray data of Maurice Wilkins and Rosalind Franklin, James Watson of the United States and Francis Crick of England proposed that DNA was a double helix. In this structure, which has been confirmed by numerous methods, two strands of the sugar-phosphate backbone are wound around each other, and the nitrogenous bases point inward, as shown in **Figure 4.2**. The sequence of these nitrogenous bases along the phosphate-sugar backbone in DNA forms the code responsible for transferring genetic information. The three-dimensional DNA molecule is similar to a twisted ladder. The sides of the ladder are the sugar-phosphate backbone, and the rungs are base pairs of A—T (adenine–thymine) or G—C (guanine–cytosine) bases extending between the two backbones. Hydrogen bonding between these pairs of nitrogenous bases holds the rungs of the ladder together.

✔ **CHECK FOR UNDERSTANDING**

Identify How many DNA molecules does a human being have?

FIGURE 4.2

The DNA Double Helix Structure Hydrogen bonding between base pairs makes the three-dimensional structure of DNA stable. Base pairing occurs between adenine and thymine or guanine and cytosine, keeping the distance between the strands constant.

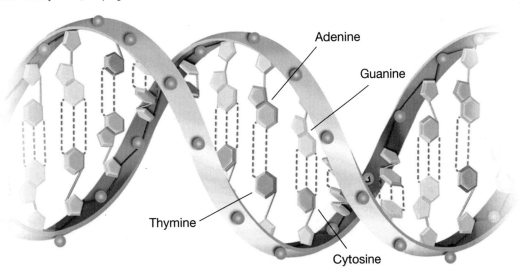

Adenine

Guanine

Thymine

Cytosine

FIGURE 4.3

STM Image of DNA Structure The double helix of DNA can be seen by using a scanning tunneling microscope (STM).

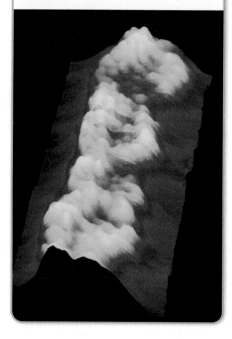

FIGURE 4.4

DNA Replication DNA replicates when its double helix unwinds and becomes single stranded. The single strands are used as a template for the formation of new complementary strands.

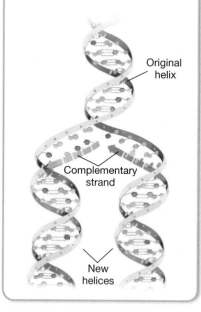

Original helix

Complementary strand

New helices

Nitrogenous Base Pairs

In the DNA double helix, base pairing exists only between A—T and between C—G, as you saw in **Figure 4.2.** The reason is that the pairing between one single-ringed base and one double-ringed base provides the correct orientation for the hydrogen bonds to form between the two sides of the DNA ladder. One thymine and one adenine form a link between the two strands of a DNA molecule that is exactly the same size as the link formed by one cytosine and one guanine.

The double-helix configuration of DNA, shown in **Figure 4.3,** can be seen by using a scanning tunneling microscope (STM). The discovery of the relative quantities of the nitrogenous bases A, T, G, and C present in DNA was the key to determining the three-dimensional molecular structure. Analysis of DNA from different organisms reveals that the amounts of A and T are the same and that the amounts of G and C are the same for all members of the same species. In humans, DNA is about 30% A, 30% T, 20% G, and 20% C.

The interaction between base pairs accounts for the ability of DNA to replicate, as you will learn below. Just as combinations of the 26 letters of the alphabet form words that tell a story in a novel, combinations of the four-letter alphabet of A, T, G, and C form the *genes* that define our heredity. Each gene is a section of DNA that contains a specific sequence of four bases (A, G, T, and C) and typically contains about 1000 to 2000 base pairs. As of 2004, researchers with the Human Genome Project had discovered that the human body contains about 20 000 to 25 000 genes.

DNA Replication

Like the two sides of a zipper, the two strands of the double helix of DNA are not identical. Instead, the two strands are complements of each other. Thus, a base on one strand is paired through hydrogen bonding to its complementary base on the other strand. For example, if one strand sequence is AGCTC, the complementary strand sequence will be TCGAG.

Each time a cell divides, an exact copy of the DNA of the parent cell is reproduced for the daughter cells. **The process by which an identical copy of the original DNA is formed is called DNA replication.** As replication begins, a portion of the two strands of the original DNA is uncoiled and "unzipped," as shown in **Figure 4.4,** by an enzyme called *helicase.* Each strand can then act as a template for the synthesis of a new, complementary strand. The result is two daughter DNA molecules, which have the same base-pair sequence as the original double helix.

✓ CRITICAL THINKING

Predict Hydrogen bonds hold DNA strands together. What would be the implication for life if DNA strands were held together by chemical bonds?

▶ MAIN IDEA
RNA molecules synthesize proteins.

Molecules of RNA make up about 5% to 10% of the mass of a cell. RNA molecules are responsible for the synthesis of proteins, which in turn control the operation and function of the cell. RNA differs from DNA in four basic ways: (1) the sugar unit in the backbone of RNA is ribose rather than deoxyribose, (2) RNA contains the base uracil, U, instead of thymine, which occurs in DNA, (3) RNA is a single-stranded molecule rather than a double-stranded helix like DNA, and (4) RNA molecules typically consist of 75 to a few thousand nucleotide units rather than the millions that exist in DNA. Even though RNA is much smaller than DNA, RNA can still twist, coil, bend, and fold back onto itself. In fact, it is not uncommon for up to 50% of an RNA molecule to have a double-helix structure. The reason is that the base sequences along the helical regions of the RNA strand are complementary, making hydrogen bonding possible.

Synthesis of RNA

RNA is synthesized in the nucleus of the cell, where DNA and protein molecules actually help synthesize specific RNA molecules. RNA can be seen by STM, as shown in **Figure 4.5.** As RNA is synthesized, information contained in the DNA is transferred to the RNA molecules. Like the genetic information of DNA, the genetic information of RNA is carried in its nucleotide sequence. One type of RNA molecule is called *messenger RNA* (mRNA) because it carries the instructions for making proteins out into the cytosol, where proteins are produced on ribosomes. A *ribosome* is a cell organelle composed of RNA and protein. Ribosomes are the main site of protein production in cells. The DNA template is also used to make two other types of RNA molecules: *ribosomal RNA* (rRNA) and *transfer RNA* (tRNA). Both of these types of RNA also leave the nucleus and come together in the ribosome, where they help synthesize proteins. Ribosomal RNA becomes part of the structure of the ribosome, and tRNA is used to transfer amino acids to the ribosome. Only mRNA carries the coded genetic information that is translated into proteins.

DNA supplies all the information necessary for RNA to make the proteins needed by the body. The portion of DNA that holds the genetic code for a single mRNA molecule is a gene. Each gene codes for a specific mRNA molecule, which produces a specific protein that has a specific function.

RNA and Protein Synthesis

RNA is made from DNA in a process that is similar to the way in which DNA replicates itself. A portion of DNA is uncoiled by helicase, and RNA is assembled along the unzipped strands of DNA, using the same complementary base pairs as DNA, except that uracil replaces the thymine. As in DNA replication, the RNA sequence that forms has the complementary base pairs of the DNA gene. The DNA sequence on the next page would form the complementary RNA sequence shown.

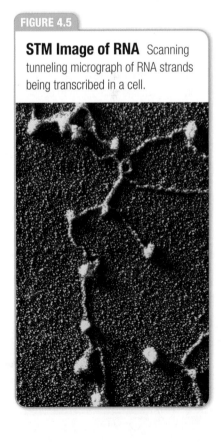

FIGURE 4.5

STM Image of RNA Scanning tunneling micrograph of RNA strands being transcribed in a cell.

✓ **CHECK FOR UNDERSTANDING**

Decode What do you think is significant about the three "stop" codes?

CAREERS IN CHEMISTRY

Forensic Chemist S.T.E.M.

A forensic chemist applies scientific methodology to physical evidence. Forensic chemists focus on analyzing evidence that has been collected at a crime scene. They then report any conclusions that they can draw from the analysis. Understanding evidence requires knowledge of biology, materials science, and genetics in addition to chemistry. Because forensic chemists are often asked to testify in court, they need to be comfortable speaking in public and be able to give clear and concise explanations to those who do not have a background in science.

FIGURE 4.6

DNA Autoradiograph A DNA autoradiograph shows the pattern of an organism's DNA fragments after they have been separated from each other by electrophoresis.

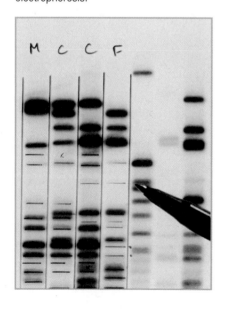

DNA strand: C C C C A C C C T A C G G T G
RNA strand: G G G G U G G G A U G C C A C

A sequence of three bases in mRNA, called *triplets*, or *codons*, code for specific amino acids. Thus, the sequence CAG codes for glutamic acid, and GUC codes for valine. There are 64 (4^3) unique combinations of three-base sequences made from four bases. Some amino acids have more than one code. For example, leucine is coded for by six different codons: UUA, UUG, CUU, CUC, CUA, and CUG. Methionine and tryptophan are the only amino acids that are coded by only one codon each. The same three-base sequence always codes for the same amino acid regardless of whether the organism is a bacterium or a human.

Once mRNA forms from DNA, it leaves the nucleus of the cell and attaches to a ribosome. tRNA molecules, each containing three *anti-codons* that complement the nitrogen-base sequences found in mRNA, bring amino acids from the cell's cytoplasm to the ribosome, where they are joined to form proteins. The process always begins with the "start" triplet AUG, which codes for methionine and signals the ribosome to begin making a protein. The process ends with the "stop" signals: UAG, UAA, or UGA.

Proteins are absolutely essential to the proper functioning of living organisms. Errors that occur during protein synthesis are known as *mutations*. There are a number of different ways that mutations can occur, such as the insertion or deletion of a nitrogen base or a triplet being reversed as it is inserted. Mutations caused by incorrect sequencing can lead to many types of genetic disorders and diseases, including cancer.

▶ **MAIN IDEA**

Genetic engineers manipulate genetic material.

Genetic engineers study how the manipulation of an organism's genetic material can modify the proteins that are produced and the changes that result in the organism. This provides new options for the production of food, medical diagnosis and treatments, and increased understanding of genetic disorders. Although selective breeding of organisms has been done for thousands of years, these scientists use recombinant DNA technology to adapt or clone existing life forms, which is controversial.

DNA Fingerprinting

One visible use of molecular technology is DNA fingerprinting. DNA is unique to an individual except for identical twins. This technology is used in forensic investigations, paternity testing, and victim identification. Often, there are only very small samples available, such as a single drop of blood or one strand of hair. A technique called *polymerase chain reaction* (PCR) may be used to copy a DNA sample to supply sufficient DNA for identification. Electrophoresis and autoradiography are processes used to compare DNA from a sample with the DNA of a known individual to confirm identification, as **Figure 4.6** shows.

Cloning

Cloning is the process of making an exact copy of an organism. One example of a natural occurrence of cloning is the formation of identical twins, which is the result of a chance splitting of the embryonic cells very early in development. Artificial cloning, mainly used with microbes, can produce identical replicas of the parent cells or, under specialized conditions, a complete organism that is identical to the original organism. The orchid shown in **Figure 4.7** is a clone of its parent plant. Cloning of plants may hold promise for increasing the yields of crops.

The first animal to be cloned, a sheep named Dolly, was born in 1997 in Scotland. The process of cloning higher organisms is so difficult that it took 200 tries to produce Dolly. Due to lung disease, Dolly was euthanized in 2003. She had also been diagnosed with arthritis. Both diseases are normally found in sheep older than Dolly was, so Dolly's early death may be related to the fact that she was cloned from cells obtained from a seven-year-old ewe. More recently, a number of vertebrates have been cloned, including dogs, cats, monkeys, and an endangered Asian oxen.

Therapeutic cloning of human tissues and organs may eventually provide significant advances in health care, but cloning an entire human remains science fiction.

FIGURE 4.7

Orchid Cloning Growers can produce many orchids by artificial cloning of the meristem tissue of a single orchid plant.

Recombinant DNA Technology

Recombinant DNA technology has been used to insert DNA from one organism into another. The technique splices a gene from one organism's DNA into a molecule of DNA from another organism. The genes in *Escherichia coli,* a bacterium found in human and animal intestinal tracts, are often used to obtain spliced segments of genetic material. When the spliced *E. coli* DNA is inserted into a cell, the cell is able to make the protein that is coded by the spliced gene.

One of the first applications of genetic engineering was the synthesis of human insulin. Previously, diabetics usually had to use either pig or cow insulin, which is not exactly the same as human insulin. Today, most insulin used is produced using *E. coli*. Human growth hormone is also commercially produced by using recombinant DNA technology.

✓ SECTION 4 FORMATIVE ASSESSMENT

▶ Reviewing Main Ideas

1. What sugar is present in DNA? What sugar is present in RNA?

2. Explain why the two strands of the DNA double helix are said to be complementary instead of identical.

3. Describe how DNA uses the genetic code to control the synthesis of proteins.

4. Why is a very small trace of blood enough for DNA fingerprinting?

✓ Critical Thinking

5. **INTERPRET AND APPLY** Is it possible to specify 20 amino acids by using only two base pairs instead of three for coding?

6. **DRAWING CONCLUSIONS** Why is the arrangement of base pairs that is found in DNA ideal for holding the double helix of DNA together?

In protein synthesis, the DNA sequence of bases is transcribed onto messenger RNA (mRNA). The mRNA base sequence is the complement of the DNA sequence, except that uracil takes the place of thymine as the complement of adenine.

Problem-Solving TIPS

- Find the first base of the mRNA triplet along the left side of the table.
- Follow that row to the right until you are beneath the second base of the triplet.
- Move up or down in the square that corresponds to the second base until you are even with the third base of the triplet on the right side of the chart.

The Genetic Code (mRNA)

First base	Second base				Third base
	U	**C**	**A**	**G**	
U	UUU UUC Phenylalanine; UUA UUG Leucine	UCU UCC UCA UCG Serine	UAU UAC Tyrosine; UAA UAG Stop	UGU UGC Cysteine; UGA—Stop; UGG—Tryptophan	U C A G
C	CUU CUC CUA CUG Leucine	CCU CCC CCA CCG Proline	CAU CAC Histidine; CAA CAG Glutamine	CGU CGC CGA CGG Arginine	U C A G
A	AUU AUC Isoleucine; AUA; AUG—Start	ACU ACC ACA ACG Threonine	AAU AAC Asparagine; AAA AAG Lysine	AGU AGC Serine; AGA AGG Arginine	U C A G
G	GUU GUC GUA GUG Valine	GCU GCC GCA GCG Alanine	GAU GAC Aspartic acid; GAA GAG Glutamic acid	GGU GGC GGA GGG Glycine	U C A G

Sample Problem

What sequence of amino acids will be incorporated into protein as a result of the mRNA sequence UUACCCGAGAAGUCC?

Divide the sequence into groups of three to clearly see the separate codons.

UUACCCGAGAAGUCC = UUA | CCC | GAG | AAG | UCC

Now, use the table to determine the match between codons and amino acids.

UUA	CCC	GAG	AAG	UCC
leucine	proline	glutamic acid	lysine	serine

Practice

1. What amino acid sequence will be added to a protein as a result of the mRNA sequence UUACACGACUAUAAUUGG?
2. What amino acid sequence will be added to a protein as a result of the mRNA sequence CUAACCGGGUGAGCUUCU?

> **BIG IDEA** The organic molecules in living things are classified into four major groups: carbohydrates, lipids, proteins, and nucleic acids.

SECTION 1 Carbohydrates and Lipids

- Carbohydrates are nutrients that are produced by plants and are made up of carbon, oxygen, and hydrogen.
- Monosaccharides are the simplest carbohydrates. Carbohydrates made of two monosaccharides are called *disaccharides*, and carbohydrates made of more than two monosaccharides are called *polysaccharides*.
- Carbohydrates undergo condensation reactions and hydrolysis reactions.
- Lipids are a varied group of biochemical molecules that have a high percentage of C and H atoms.

KEY TERMS

carbohydrate
monosaccharide
disaccharide
condensation reaction
hydrolysis
polysaccharide
lipid
fatty acid
saponification

SECTION 2 Amino Acids and Proteins

- Amino acid molecules are the basic building blocks of proteins.
- Proteins are biological polymers, each of which has a unique sequence of amino acid monomer molecules.
- The specific function of a protein is related to the shape of the protein.
- Side-chain interactions between amino acids result in secondary, tertiary, and quaternary protein structures.

KEY TERMS

amino acid
protein
enzyme
denaturation

SECTION 3 Metabolism

- ATP is a high-energy storage compound that the body uses to store and provide energy for life.
- The metabolic pathways involve both the conversion of ATP to ADP and the conversion of ADP to ATP.
- Metabolic pathways are classified as two types: catabolism and anabolism.
- Catabolism includes reactions in which large molecules are changed into simpler molecules. These reactions release energy.
- Anabolic processes are energy-consuming pathways by which cells produce the molecules needed for growth and repair.

KEY TERMS

metabolism
autotroph
adenosine triphosphate (ATP)
heterotroph
adenosine diphosphate (ADP)
catabolism
anabolism

SECTION 4 Nucleic Acids

- Deoxyribonucleic acid (DNA) and ribonucleic acid (RNA) are nucleic acids, the compounds by which living organisms can reproduce themselves.
- Nucleic acids are polymers of monomer units called *nucleotides*.
- The two strands of the double helix of DNA are complementary to each other, not identical. These strands are held together by hydrogen bonding of the base pairs.
- RNA is used to produce proteins in the cell.

KEY TERMS

nucleic acid
DNA replication
cloning

CHAPTER 23 **Review**

GO ONLINE

Interactive Review
HMHScience.com

Review Games
Concept Maps

SECTION 1
Carbohydrates and Lipids

▶ REVIEWING MAIN IDEAS

1. Describe the general chemical formula of carbohydrates.

2. Name two examples from each of the following classes of carbohydrates: monosaccharides, disaccharides, and polysaccharides.

3. What different roles do the polysaccharides starch and cellulose play in plant systems?

4. What word is used to describe fatty acids that contain at least one double bond?

5. Why are some triglycerides liquid, while others are solid?

6. What reagents are used to make soaps?

PRACTICE PROBLEMS

7. Draw the structural formula for glucose.

8. Using structural formulas, write the equation showing the formation of maltose, which is the disaccharide made of two glucose units.

9. Write the equation representing the formation of a soap molecule from stearic acid, $C_{17}H_{35}COOH$, and sodium hydroxide.

SECTION 2
Amino Acids and Proteins

▶ REVIEWING MAIN IDEAS

10. Describe the structure of an amino acid. Then, explain how amino acids become linked together to form a protein.

11. Circle and identify the carboxylic acid groups and the amino groups in the following molecule:

$$NH_2-CH-\overset{\overset{O}{\|}}{C}-\overset{H}{\underset{}{N}}-CH-\overset{\overset{O}{\|}}{C}-\overset{H}{\underset{}{N}}-CH-COOH$$

with side chains: CH_2 / $COOH$; $CH-OH$ / CH_3 ; CH_2 / $\overset{}{C}-NH_2$ with $\overset{\|}{O}$

12. Can two types of enzymes contain the same number and kinds of amino acids? Explain.

13. What happens when a protein is denatured?

14. Explain the cause of the genetic disease sickle-cell anemia.

15. Why is the water solubility of fibrous proteins so different from that of globular proteins?

PRACTICE PROBLEMS

16. Draw the structures of two dipeptides made up of glycine and valine.

17. How many different tripeptides can be formed from two molecules of glycine and one molecule of cysteine? Write all the structures by using the three-letter codes Gly and Cys.

SECTION 3
Metabolism

▶ REVIEWING MAIN IDEAS

18. What chemical gains the metabolic energy that is released as glucose is broken down in the body?

19. What does *ATP* stand for? What is the role of ATP in living organisms?

20. Describe the steps that occur in the digestion of fats.

21. Review the following diagram of catabolism.

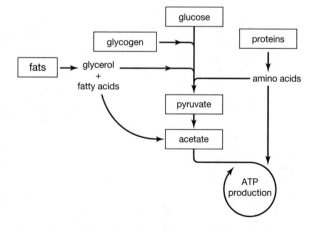

According to the diagram, what could happen in the cell when glucose and glycogen reserves are nearly gone?

PRACTICE PROBLEMS

22. Write the structural formula of ATP. Circle the bond that breaks when ADP forms.

SECTION 4

Nucleic Acids

▶ **REVIEWING MAIN IDEAS**

23. What are the three components of a nucleotide?

24. How are the two chains of DNA held together?

25. Describe in general terms the process of DNA replication.

26. What are the main differences between DNA and RNA?

27. Describe the similarities and differences between the three kinds of RNA molecules.

28. What is a ribosome? What is the function of a ribosome in a cell?

PRACTICE PROBLEMS

29. The following sequence of bases might be found on the gene that codes for oxytocin, the human pituitary hormone:

TACACAATGTAAGTTTTGACGGGGGACCCTATC

a. What is the base sequence of the complementary strand of DNA?

b. What is the base sequence that would occur on a strand of mRNA transcribed from the oxytocin DNA sequence?

Mixed Review

▶ **REVIEWING MAIN IDEAS**

30. Name the four main elements that make up compounds found in living organisms.

31. In each of the following groups, one of the items does not belong in the group. Identify the odd item in the group, and explain why it is different. Explain how the other items are related.

a. glycogen, starch, fructose, and cellulose

b. amino acids, dipeptides, polypeptides, and proteins

c. fats, oils, and fatty acids

d. cytosine, adenine, and uracil

32. What is the human body's *storage* form of each of the following?

a. glucose

b. lipids

c. protein

33. Is each of the following statements about proteins and triglycerides true or false?

a. Both contain the amide functional group.

b. Both are a part of a major class of biochemical molecules.

c. Both hydrolyze in order to enter the metabolic pathway in humans.

34. Circle the hydrophobic part in each of the figures shown below.

a.

$$H_3C \diagdown \qquad \diagup CH_3$$
$$CH$$
$$|$$
$$H_2N-C-COOH$$
$$|$$
$$H$$

b.

$$HO \diagdown \quad \diagup O$$
$$C$$
$$|$$
$$H-C-H$$
$$|$$
$$H-C-H$$
$$|$$
$$H-C-H$$
$$|$$
$$H-C-H$$
$$|$$
$$H-C-H$$
$$|$$
$$H-C-H$$
$$|$$
$$H-C-H$$
$$|$$
$$H-C$$
$$\|$$
$$H-C$$
$$|$$
$$H-C-H$$
$$|$$
$$H-C-H$$
$$|$$
$$H-C-H$$
$$|$$
$$H-C-H$$
$$|$$
$$H-C-H$$
$$|$$
$$H-C-H$$
$$|$$
$$H-C-H$$
$$|$$
$$H$$

35. Both celery and potato chips are composed of molecules that are polymers of glucose. Explain why celery is a good snack for people on a diet while potato chips are not.

36. Carbohydrates, fats, and proteins can produce energy for an organism.
   a. Which class of substances most rapidly provides energy?
   b. Which class can be used as a building material in the human body?
   c. Which is the most efficient as an energy storage system?

37. Describe the basic structure of the cell membrane. What is the cell membrane's main function?

CRITICAL THINKING

38. Interpreting Concepts A diet that consists primarily of corn can result in a protein-deficiency disease called *kwashiorkor*. What does this information indicate about the protein content of corn?

39. Inferring Relationships Explain how a similar reaction forms three kinds of biological polymers: polysaccharides, polypeptides, and nucleic acids.

40. Evaluating Ideas Some diets recommend severely restricting or eliminating the intake of carbohydrates. Why is it not a good idea to eliminate all carbohydrates from the diet?

41. Using Analogies Explain why the model of enzyme action is called the lock-and-key model.

RESEARCH AND WRITING

42. Conduct library research about how Olestra® decreases fat and caloric content of potato chips. What are the advantages and disadvantages of Olestra® in food products?

43. Write a summary discussing what you have learned about the four major classes of organic compounds found in living organisms—carbohydrates, lipids, proteins, and nucleic acids. Include a description of how these organic molecules are used by the body.

ALTERNATIVE ASSESSMENT

44. Amylase, the enzyme present in the mouth, catalyzes the digestion of starch. The pH of the mouth is almost neutral.
   a. Do you think that amylase is active in the stomach after you swallow the food? Why or why not?
   b. Design an experiment you could perform to test your answer to item a. Note: A common test for the presence of starch is the addition of tincture of iodine, which will produce a blue color if starch is present.

Standards-Based Assessment

Record your answers on a separate piece of paper.

MULTIPLE CHOICE

1 Some carbohydrates are produced by green plants through photosynthesis and become food. Photosynthesis is a process in green plants by which —

A light energy is stored as chemical energy

B water and oxygen are converted into chemical energy

C carbon dioxide and chlorophyll are converted into potential energy

D carbon dioxide and chemical energy are converted into kinetic energy

2 The catabolism of one glucose molecule produces about 36 ATP molecules. This accounts for only 40% of the energy released during the complete oxidation of glucose. What happens to the energy not converted to ATP?

A It is converted back into glucose.

B It is lost as heat.

C It is used to make molecules of ADP.

D It is stored in the body as fat.

3 Cellular respiration is a catabolic process that releases energy by breaking down carbohydrates into CO_2 and water. The chemical equation is shown below.

$$C_6H_{12}O_6 + \underline{?}\ O_2 \rightarrow 6CO_2 + 6H_2O$$

In order to balance this equation, what coefficient should you use for the oxygen molecule?

A 1

B 3

C 6

D 12

4 During the ATP hydrolysis, energy is released to power a cell's activities. Why is water important to this process?

A With the addition of water, ATP is converted into ADP and a phosphate group.

B With the removal of water, ATP is converted into ADP and a phosphate group.

C With the addition of water and a phosphate group, ATP is converted into ADP.

D With the removal of water and the addition of a phosphate group, ATP is converted into ADP.

5 Which of the following statements about fats is true?

A Fats serve as a reserve supply of energy.

B Fats are stored in the adipose tissue.

C Fats act as insulators.

D all of the above

6 What happens when carbohydrates are unavailable or unable to provide the body's energy needs?

A Glucose is converted to glycogen.

B Proteins or fats are used for energy.

C Amino acids form proteins.

D all of the above

7 Which of the following statements is true?

A RNA contains the base uracil rather than thymine, which occurs in DNA.

B Both RNA and DNA are double-stranded helices.

C The sugar ribose is in the backbone of DNA.

D DNA and RNA have different phosphate groups.

GRIDDED RESPONSE

8 How many levels of folding does a protein undergo before it reaches its biologically active three-dimensional structure?

Test Tip

If a question or an answer choice contains an unfamiliar term, try to break the word into parts to determine its meaning.

Reference Section

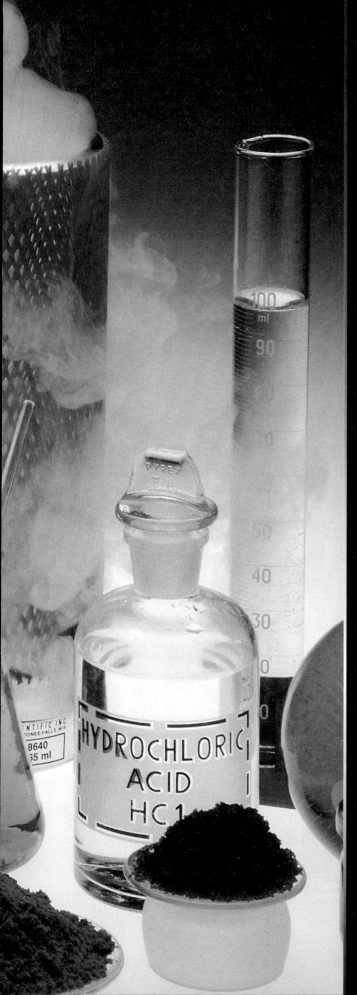

Contents

STUDY SKILLS HANDBOOK

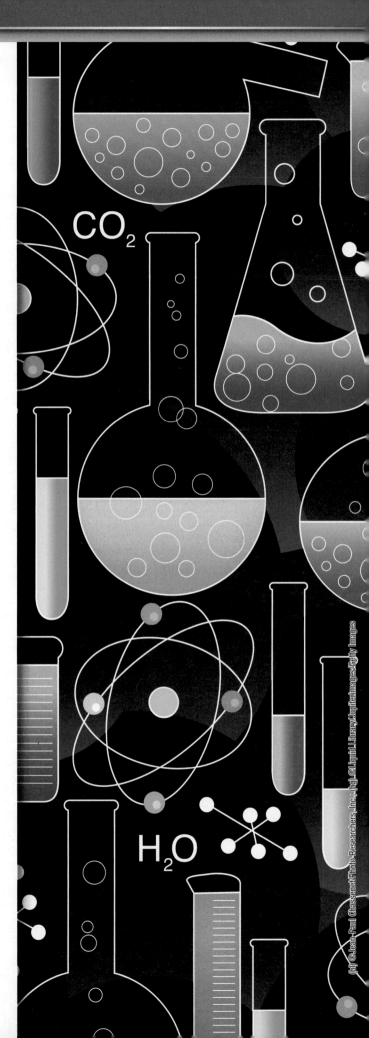

Secrets for Success in Chemistry

Some people are gifted scholars and naturally pick up the skills that enable them to be successful in their studies. Most of us, however, have to *learn* the study habits that will help us succeed. No two people learn in exactly the same way, so each of us has to find what works best for us.

You may have heard teachers use terms like *visual, auditory,* and *kinesthetic* when talking about learning styles. These terms are a fancy way of saying that a person learns best when *seeing* something, *hearing* something, or *doing* something hands-on. Most people actually learn in multiple styles, although they may favor one method over others.

The last thing you probably want to hear is that you have to study. You are not alone. Not many people actually *like* to study. What a surprise! You may have asked, "Why do I even need to take chemistry? I'm not going to be a scientist." The answer to that question is that you need chemistry because *everything* is chemistry. Every single thing around you, including you, is made up of atoms, molecules, and chemical compounds. Everything a person does has something to do with chemistry, from deciding what cleanser scrubs the bathtub best, to choosing what motor oil makes the car run smoothly in winter, or what toothpaste gives the whitest smile.

With all these decisions that depend on chemistry, wouldn't you like to know more about it?

Chemistry is a subject that builds on the knowledge that you start accumulating from the first day of class. Imagine what it would be like if you tried writing a novel before learning the entire alphabet. The further behind you fall at the beginning, the more likely you are to have trouble understanding things the rest of the course. So the best thing to do is to get it right the first time!

> **You may have asked, "Why do I even need to take chemistry? I'm not going to be a scientist." The answer to that question is that *everything* is chemistry.**

A textbook is one of the many tools you will use in order to be successful in class. This handbook will provide a number of additional useful tips, tricks, and skills— you might say study *secrets*—that can help you a lot in chemistry. However, they only help if you actually *use* them!

SECRET 1: READ THE BOOK.

No matter how useful your chemistry book may be for holding up the shelf in your locker, it is virtually impossible to pass the class if you don't take it out, open it up, and actually see what is inside. It was not meant to be just a heavy burden in your backpack. It was written to help you to learn chemistry. Here are some tips to put it to the best use:

1. Read the assigned pages *before* you come to class. That way, you'll have a better idea of what the lecture is about.

2. Keep some note cards with you when you read. When you have a question, write it down on one side of a card. When you find the answer or your teacher explains it to you, write the answer on the other side of the card. You may even add diagrams or sketches that help to explain things. There you have it! An instant flash card! Now you have a useful study tool to help you review a concept that you had a little trouble understanding.

3. Find a good place to study. Some people will tell you to find a quiet place, free from distractions, and that is what works best for them. If you're like many people, though, if a place is *too* quiet, you will *look* for distractions. Look at this realistically. If you study in front of the television, you *will* watch the television. If you study in a room where there are *video games*, and you happen to love video games, you will be distracted. However, there is nothing wrong with some quiet music while you study, if it helps you relax.

4. Use the Main Ideas in the section openers as a guide. These show you what is most important for you to focus on in each chapter. If you have looked at those carefully, you're one step ahead of the game.

SECRET 2: PAY ATTENTION IN CLASS.

The more actively you take part in things, the less bored and sleepy you will be. Sleep at night or on your vacation.

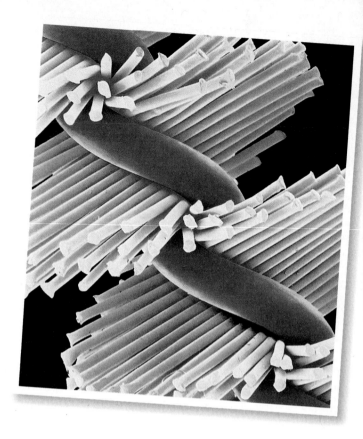

SECRET 3: WORK THE SAMPLE AND PRACTICE PROBLEMS.

For better or worse, problem solving is a big part of chemistry. Practicing problem-solving skills will be a major part of successfully passing the class.

1. The Sample Problems in the textbook will take you step-by-step through the process, teaching you how to solve them as you go.

2. The solutions to these problems are given in the book. Try covering them up and then using them to check your work when you finish.

3. The Practice Problems given right after the Sample Problems are there to reinforce what you just learned. The more you do something, the more it will stay in your memory. Practice is what helps you actually *learn* something, rather than just temporarily memorizing it for a test and then forgetting it when you need it later.

4. The problems in the Chapter Review are similar to the Sample Problems. If you can apply the things you learned in the Sample and Practice Problems to the ones in the Review, then you really know the concepts.

5. Plugging numbers into a calculator can be a great tool, but when something goes wrong, it's hard to see where you might have made a mistake. Use the four-step problem-solving format: *Analyze, Plan, Solve,* and *Check Your Work.* These will organize your work and help you to better understand the process of solving the problem.

6. If you work on a problem for 15 minutes or more and are still having trouble with it, make note of it so that you can ask your teacher or a friend who understands it for help. Then move on. Otherwise, you may just become frustrated and give up.

7. Always check your answer to see if it makes sense. Is the number realistic when you look back at what you were asked to find? Does your final answer have the correct unit of measurement? Were you supposed to convert something from one unit to another somewhere along the way? Taking a few moments to check these things will not only make you sure that you have the correct answer, it will also help you keep from making the same mistakes over and over again.

8. Write a problem on one side of a note card and the solution on the other. Use the problem cards to periodically practice solving that type of problem.

● SECRET 4: DO YOUR HOMEWORK.

You would be amazed at the difference it makes in your chemistry grade when you actually *do* your homework and turn it in on time. And it's important that you do *your own* homework. Friends may seem wonderful when they let you copy their homework in the morning, but they are not doing you any favors. If *they* did the work, *you* have not learned anything. Would you want to go to a doctor who copied someone else's work in school? Would you want to fly in an airplane designed by an engineer who had received all the answers from a friend? Think about it.

1. As soon as possible after class, review your notes and do your homework. This is the best time, when things are still fairly fresh in your mind. If you wait too long, what you learned in class will fade away. You also will be tired and thus more likely to become frustrated and give up. At this time in your life, one of the most important things you can do is to make the most of your education. It will definitely pay off in your future.

2. Define the key terms, even if they have not been assigned. Take your note cards, and put a term on one side and the definition on the other side. If the key term refers to a scientific equation, put the term on one side of the card and the equation on the other side.

● SECRET 5: TAKE NOTES IN CLASS.

Paying attention in class is great, but it is not enough! Very few people have perfect recall, and you can't expect to remember everything. If you don't take notes as you go along, you will forget things. Unless your teacher requires you to take notes in a specific way, there are a number of techniques you can try. Try several, and see which one works best for you.

1. Bring paper and pen or pencil. It's pretty hard to take notes without them, and your friends eventually will get tired of loaning them to you.

2. Bring your book, and follow along in the chapter as your teacher lectures. Add page numbers to your notes so that you can find things again later.

3. Use highlighting markers or colored pens to differentiate between different types of information. It will help keep your notes more organized, and it makes note taking a little more interesting.

4. Add diagrams or simple sketches to illustrate a concept. This will help you understand it better and also remember it later on, especially if you are mainly a visual learner.

5. It is impossible to write down every single thing a teacher says. If you try to do this, you'll just fall behind and aggravate the teacher and your peers by constantly asking them to wait or to repeat things. Focus on the main ideas, and add the details later.

6. Use abbreviations, and develop your own shorthand way of writing. Don't put in every *if, and, the,* or *but.*

7. Review your notes as soon as possible after class. Definitely do it within 24 to 48 hours; otherwise, it will fade from your mind. Use your note cards, and write down questions that arise as you review. Ask the teacher about them in the next class. Again, now you have a flash card!

8. Create a note-taking co-op with your classmates. Each person can make copies of their notes and share them. Others may have picked up on concepts that you missed, and you may have notes that others missed. Together, you can have it all.

9. With your teacher's permission, record the lecture. Listen to the recording later, and fill in any gaps in your class notes. Label recordings so that you know what subject each covers.

10. See the descriptions of simple outlines and Cornell notes in this handbook for additional note-taking suggestions.

▶ **SECRET 6:** START PREPARING FOR A TEST THE DAY YOU START A TOPIC.

Just because you may have been able to wait until the night before the test to study in the past, skim through the chapter quickly, and then pass the test, doesn't mean it will work for you forever. Each year there is more to learn, and the concepts are at a higher level of understanding. If you don't review and practice things as you go along, there will be too much material by the time of the test. You also will not have the time to get enough help.

1. Break it down! It is easier to do a big task in small pieces. Look through your notes for 10 to 15 minutes, and read a few pages of the chapter each night. By doing this, you will not have to learn new material the night before an exam.

2. Ask the teacher for specific things you need to memorize for the test. Don't try to memorize everything. If you have consistently reviewed the material, you will be more likely to remember it. If you haven't looked at it since the day you first saw it, you will have too much to relearn the night before the exam.

3. Use your flash cards. These address topics that you had questions about, and going over them will help you remember those questions. Again, don't think it's a waste of your time to make flash cards. Simply making the flash cards will help you better remember material, even if you don't look at them ever again.

4. Study with a friend, and test one another with the flash cards. You could try to set some goals to make things more interesting. For example, see which one of you could answer the questions or do the problems on ten flash cards in a row first. This could make studying more fun.

5. Do the review questions in the book, even if they weren't assigned. Test questions often come from the Section and Chapter Reviews. If you do them a few days in advance of the test, you can check with the teacher for the answers to see what you need to spend more time on.

6. Take online quizzes. They are often made up of questions in the test bank and may well reappear on the test. These can help you to pinpoint areas where you're having trouble so you can get help.

7. Some people, especially if they are in a note-taking co-op, find it beneficial to rewrite and reorganize their notes before a test, to make studying easier. In many cases, this can also refresh your memory and be a review in itself.

8. Get enough sleep. At your age, when you sleep is when your body is growing, building new bone and muscle, and doing general maintenance and repair. You actually require *more* than 8 hours of sleep a day while these things are going on. If you don't let your body and your brain rest, build, and repair, *things won't work right.*

9. Eat right. Your car won't run if it doesn't get the right fuel, and your body won't either. Save the junk food for a reward after the test. You'll certainly deserve it after all the hard work you've put into studying.

SECRET 7: BE PRACTICAL WHEN YOU TAKE A TEST.

There are skills that can help you be more successful when you take the test. Some of them are common-sense things that your parents probably told you a million times until you stopped listening. Pay close attention to the phrase *common sense.* Common means that a lot of people know about it (not just your parents) and it will benefit you to pay attention.

1. When test day comes, bring a pen and/or pencil to class. Teachers don't accept answers transmitted by telepathy.

2. Ask the teacher if you may use scratch paper to work problems out.

3. If it's permitted, bring a calculator to help speed up doing the math on problems. But don't let it take the place of a step-by-step approach, because you might miss an important step. Calculators are only as good as the data you put into them.

4. Dress comfortably. Although the school is unlikely to allow you to wear your pajamas in class, you're bound to have a favorite pair of jeans and shirt that don't scratch, pinch, ride up, or cause other discomfort.

5. Once you are given the test, look over the whole thing first, before you start.

6. Read the directions. Some teachers occasionally like to give tests that have directions like the following, just to see if you are paying attention: "Sign your name on your paper; wait two minutes; then turn it in. Grin at everyone as you walk back to your seat. Do this, and you'll get an A."

7. Start with the questions you're sure you know the answers to, and then go back and work on the harder ones. Doing the easier questions first may spark your memory and help you to answer the ones you skipped.

8. Remember your problem-solving skills, and check to make sure your answers make sense.

©Ed Bock/Corbis

Concept Maps

Making concept maps can help you decide what material in a chapter is important and how to efficiently learn that material. A concept map presents key ideas, meanings, and relationships for the concepts being studied. It can be thought of as a visual road map of the chapter. Learning happens efficiently when you use concept maps, because you work with only the key ideas and how they fit together.

The concept map shown as **Map A** was made from vocabulary terms in the chapter "Matter and Change." Vocabulary terms are generally labels for concepts, and concepts are generally nouns. In a concept map, linking words are used to form propositions that connect concepts and give them meaning in context. For example, on the map below, "matter is described by physical properties" is a proposition.

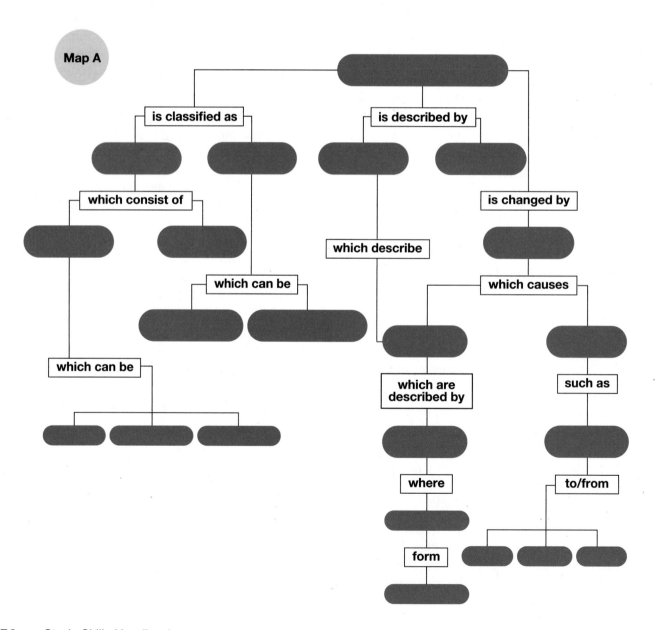

Studies show that people are better able to remember materials presented visually. In a concept map, you can see the relationships among many ideas.

The more concept maps you make, the better you will become at constructing them. Soon you may find that organizing them becomes second nature. You may even develop your own system of shapes, lines, and colors to emphasize different types of information contained in your concept maps. For example, you may decide to place all vocabulary terms in ovals, main ideas in squares, and clarifying examples in triangles. You could draw solid lines between concepts and terms that are very related and dotted lines between those that are only slightly related.

The great thing about concept maps is that they allow you the freedom to organize material in a way that makes sense to you.

To Make a Concept Map

1. **List all the important concepts.** We'll use some concepts from Section 2 of the chapter "Matter and Change."

matter	mixture
compound	pure substance
element	
homogeneous mixture	
heterogeneous mixture	

   From this list, group similar concepts together. For example, one way to group these concepts would be into two groups—one that is related to mixtures and one that is related to pure substances.

mixture	pure substance
heterogeneous mixture	compound
homogeneous mixture	element

2. **Select a main concept for the map.**
   We will use *matter* as the main concept for this map.

3. **Build the map by placing the concepts according to their importance under the main concept, *matter*.**
   One way of arranging the concepts is shown in **Map B.** (This map is continued on the next page.)

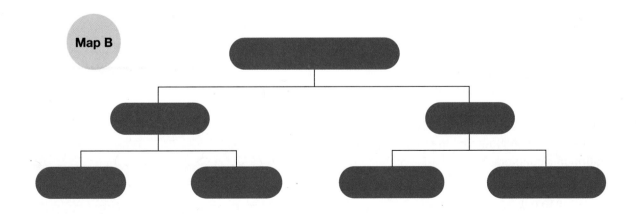

Map B

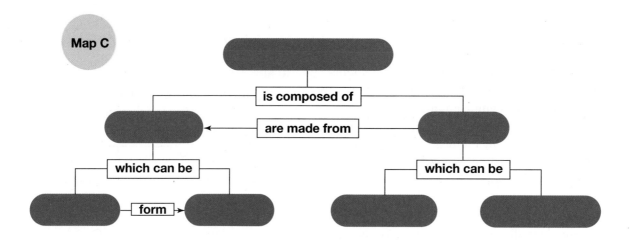

Map C

is composed of

are made from

which can be

form

which can be

4. Add linking words to give meaning to the arrangement of concepts.

When adding the links, be sure that each proposition makes sense. To distinguish concepts from links, place your concepts in circles, ovals, or rectangles, as shown in the maps. Then make cross-links. Cross-links are made of propositions and lines connecting concepts across the map. Links that apply in only one direction are indicated with an arrowhead.

Map C is a finished map covering the main ideas listed in Step 1. Making maps might seem difficult at first, but the process forces you to think about the meanings and relationships among the concepts. If you do not understand those relationships, you can get help early on.

Practice mapping by making concept maps about topics you know. For example, if you know a lot about a particular sport, such as basketball, or if you have a particular hobby, such as playing a musical instrument, you can use that topic to make a practice map. By perfecting your skills with information that you know very well, you will begin to feel more confident about making maps from the information in a chapter.

The time you devote to mapping will pay off when it is time to review for an exam.

PRACTICE

1. Classify each of the following as either a concept or linking word(s).

   a. classification _____

   b. is classified as _____

   c. forms _____

   d. is described by _____

   e. reaction _____

   f. reacts with _____

   g. metal _____

   h. defines _____

2. Write three propositions from the information in **Map A.**

   _____

   _____

   _____

3. List two cross-links shown on **Map C.**

   _____

   _____

   _____

Simple Outlines

Outlining is a skill that is useful in many different subject areas. An outline can help you quickly identify the major concepts of a topic, along with key supporting details or examples. Your textbook layout was designed to help you set up a simple outline. Each section has a title, main ideas, and examples that support the main ideas. Under each example are additional details that help to explain the concept more fully.

Here is a simple outline based on the sections in the chapter "Matter and Change:"

I.   **Chemistry Is a Physical Science**

II. **Matter and Its Properties**

III. **Elements**

Adding in the Main Ideas, subheadings, definitions, examples, and supporting information from the textbook can easily make this outline more detailed. A sample from the beginning of the section is shown below.

I.   **Chemistry Is a Physical Science (Section Title)**

    A. Chemistry is the study of matter and its processes. (Main Idea)

    B. There are several branches of chemistry. (Main Idea)

        1. organic chemistry

        2. inorganic chemistry

        3. physical chemistry

        4. analytical chemistry

        5. biochemistry

Cornell Notes

The Cornell note-taking system was developed in the 1950s by Walter Pauk, while he was teaching at Cornell University. The method is now widely recommended and is used by schools and colleges all over the world due to its effectiveness as a study tool. Make things easier by setting up or printing out a note-taking template in advance.

Here is a template that can be used for taking notes with the Cornell system:

Current Topic	Heading
	Unit Title

↕ 1"

Cues	Notes
Can Be:	• *Take notes with whatever method you are most comfortable.*
• *Main Ideas and Key Terms*	• *Add diagrams, concept maps, or simple sketches.*
• *Study questions about items in notes*	• *Review as soon as possible after class.*
• *Page numbers, section numbers, references, or other clues to finding more information*	• *When studying, cover this column up and use the cue questions or prompts to quiz yourself. Then, uncover this side to check your answers.*
Complete this column within 24 hours of taking notes.	*Complete this column during class.*

←— 2.5" —→ ←———— 6" ————→

Summary

2–3 sentences describing the topic

Complete this section within 24 hours of taking notes.

↕ 2"

K/W/L Strategy

The K/W/L strategy stands for "what I *Know*—what I *Want* to know—what I *Learned*." You start by brainstorming about the subject matter before reading the assigned material. Relating new ideas and concepts to those you have learned previously will help you better understand and apply the new knowledge you obtain. The main ideas throughout your textbook are ideal for using the K/W/L strategy.

1. **Read the main ideas.** You may also want to scan additional headings, highlighted terms, and equations before reading.

2. **Divide a sheet of paper into three columns, and label the columns "What I Know," "What I Want to Know," and "What I Learned."**

3. **Brainstorm what you know about the information in the objectives, and write these ideas in the first column.** Because this chart is designed primarily to help you integrate your own knowledge with new information, it is not necessary to write complete sentences.

4. **Think about what you want to know about the information in the objectives, and write these ideas in the second column.** Include information from both the section objectives and any other objectives your teacher has given you.

5. **While reading the section or afterwards, use the third column to write down the information you learned.** While reading, pay close attention to any information about the topics you wrote in the "What I Want to Know" column. If you do not find all of the answers you are looking for, you may need to reread the section or reference a second source. Be sure to ask your teacher if you still cannot find the information after reading the section a second time. It is also important to review your brainstormed ideas when you have completed reading the section. Compare your ideas in the first column with the information you wrote down in the third column.

If you find that some of your brainstormed ideas are incorrect, cross them out. It is extremely important to identify and correct any misconceptions you had prior to reading before you begin studying for your test.

The example below shows a K/W/L strategy a student may have written while studying about the different types of matter.

What I Know	What I Want to Know	What I Learned
• a gas has no definite shape or volume • a liquid has no definite shape but has definite volume • a solid has definite shape and volume • a mixture is a combination of substances • a pure substance has only one component	• how gas, liquid, and solid states depend on the movements of particles • how mixtures and pure substances are different at the particle level	• molecules in solid and liquid states are close together but are far apart in gas state • molecules in solid state have fixed positions, but molecules in liquid and gas states can flow • mixtures are combinations of pure substances • pure substances have fixed compositions and definite properties

Sequencing/Pattern Puzzles

You can use pattern puzzles to help you remember sequential information. Pattern puzzles are not just a tool for memorization. They also promote a greater understanding of a variety of chemical processes, from the steps in solving a mass-mass stoichiometry problem to the procedure for making a solution of specified molarity.

1. **Write down the steps of a process in your own words.** For an example, we will use the process for converting the amount of a substance in moles to mass in grams. (See Sample Problem B in the chapter "Atoms: The Building Blocks of Matter.") On a sheet of notebook paper, write down one step per line and do not number the steps. Also, do not copy the process straight from your textbook.
Writing the steps in your own words promotes a more thorough understanding of the process. You may want to divide longer steps into two or three shorter steps.

   • List the given and unknown information.

   • Look at the periodic table to determine the molar mass of the substance.

   • Write the correct conversion factor to convert moles to grams.

   • Multiply the amount of substance by the conversion factor.

   • Solve the equation and check your answer.

2. **Cut the sheet of paper into strips with only one step per strip of paper.** Shuffle the strips of paper so that they are out of sequence. Alternatively, you can write each step on a separate note card and then shuffle the note cards.

   • Look at the periodic table to determine the molar mass of the substance.

   • Solve the equation and check your answer.

   • List the given and unknown information.

   • Multiply the amount of substance by the conversion factor.

   • Write the correct conversion factor to convert moles to grams.

3. **Place the strips (or note cards) in their proper sequence.** Confirm the order of the process by checking your text or your class notes.

   • List the given and unknown information.

   • Look at the periodic table to determine the molar mass of the substance.

   • Write the correct conversion factor to convert moles to grams.

   • Multiply the amount of substance by the conversion factor.

   • Solve the equation and check your answer.

Pattern puzzles are especially helpful when you are studying for your chemistry tests. Before tests, use your puzzles to practice sequencing and to review the steps of chemistry processes. You and a classmate can also take turns creating your own pattern puzzles of different chemical processes and putting each other's puzzles in the correct sequence. Studying with a classmate in this manner will help make studying fun and will enable you to help each other.

Other Learning Strategies

▶ BRAINSTORMING

Brainstorming is a strategy that helps you recognize and evaluate the knowledge you already have before you start reading. It works well individually or in groups. When you brainstorm, you start with a central term or idea and then quickly list all the words, phrases, and other ideas that you think are related to it.

Because there are no "right" or "wrong" answers, you can use the list as a basis for classifying terms, developing a general explanation, or speculating about new relationships. For example, you might brainstorm a list of terms related to the word *element*. The list might include *gold*, *metals*, *chemicals*, *silver*, *carbon*, *oxygen*, and *water*. As you read the textbook, you might decide that some of the terms you listed are not elements. Later, you might use that information to help you distinguish between elements and compounds.

▶ BUILDING/INTERPRETING VOCABULARY

Using a dictionary to look up the meanings of prefixes and suffixes as well as word origins and meanings helps you build your vocabulary and interpret what you read. If you know the meaning of prefixes like *kilo-* (one thousand) and *milli-* (one thousandth), you have a good idea what kilograms, kilometers, milligrams, and millimeters are and how they are different.

Knowledge of prefixes, suffixes, and word origins can help you understand the meaning of new words. For example, if you know the suffix *-protic* comes from the same word as *proton*, it will help you understand what monoprotic and polyprotic acids are.

▶ READING HINTS

Reading hints help you identify and bookmark important charts, tables, and illustrations for easy reference. For example, you may want to use a self-adhesive note to bookmark the periodic table in your book so you can easily locate it and use it for reference as you study different aspects of chemistry and solve problems involving elements and compounds.

▶ INTERPRETING GRAPHIC SOURCES OF INFORMATION

Charts, tables, photographs, diagrams, and other illustrations are graphic, or visual, sources of information. The labels and captions, together with the illustrations, help you make connections between the words and the ideas presented in the text.

▶ READING-RESPONSE LOGS

Keeping a reading-response log helps you interpret what you read and gives you a chance to express your reactions and opinions about what you have read. Draw a vertical line down the center of a piece of paper. In the left-hand column, write down or make notes about passages you read to which you have reactions, thoughts, feelings, questions, or associations. In the right-hand column, write what those reactions, thoughts, feelings, questions, or associations are.

COMPARING AND CONTRASTING

Comparing and contrasting is a strategy that helps you note similarities and differences between two or more objects or events. When you determine similarities, you are comparing. When you determine differences, you are contrasting.

You can use comparing and contrasting to help you classify objects or properties, differentiate between similar concepts, and speculate about new relationships. For example, as you read the chapter "Matter and Change," you might begin to make a table in which you compare and contrast metals, nonmetals, and metalloids. As you continue to learn about these substances, you can add to your table, giving you a better understanding of the similarities and differences among elements.

IDENTIFYING CAUSE AND EFFECT

Identifying causes and effects as you read helps you understand the material and builds logical-reasoning skills. An effect is an event or the result of some action. A cause is the reason the event or action occurred. Signal words such as *because, so, since, therefore, as a result,* and *depends on* indicate a cause-and-effect relationship. You can use arrows to show cause and effect. For example, you might write this cause-and-effect relationship as you read the chapter on gases: At constant pressure, increase in temperature (cause) → increase in gas volume (effect).

MAKING A PREDICTION GUIDE

A prediction guide is a list of statements about which you express your opinions and then try to justify them based on your current knowledge. After reading the material, you re-evaluate your opinions in light of what you learned. Using prediction guides helps you assess your knowledge, identify assumptions you may have that could lead to mistaken conclusions, and form an idea of expected results. Here are some suggestions for how to make a prediction guide.

1. **Start with the statements your teacher writes on the board or you find listed in your textbook.** For example, look at the five statements from Dalton's atomic theory in your textbook, in the chapter "Atoms: The Building Blocks of Matter."

2. **Decide whether you think each statement is true or false.** Discuss the reasons that you think so, and write it all down. If someone disagrees with your conclusion, write down the reasons.

3. **After reading the section or listening to a lecture, re-evaluate your opinion of each statement.** Discuss why your opinion changed or remained the same. Find passages in the text that account for the change or reinforcement of your opinions. For example, you might have agreed with all five statements from Dalton's theory before reading the text. Then, after reading about atoms and sub-atomic particles, you might have changed your opinion about the first statement.

COOPERATIVE LEARNING TECHNIQUES

▶ READING WITH A PARTNER

Reading with a partner can help you understand what you read and point out where you need more study.

1. **First read the text silently by yourself, and take notes.** Use self-adhesive notes to mark those parts of the text that you do not understand. For example, you might have difficulty with some of the material about quantum numbers, while another student might not understand electron configurations.

2. **Work with a partner to discuss the passages each of you marked.** Take turns listening and trying to clarify the difficult passages for each other. Together, study the related tables and illustrations and explain how they relate to the text.

3. **Work together to formulate questions for class discussion or for your teacher to answer.** Make note of the complications you both encountered, and bring questions to your teacher.

▶ USING L.I.N.K.

The L.I.N.K. strategy stands for **L**ist, **I**nquire, **N**otes, **K**now. It is similar to the K/W/L strategy, but you work as a class or in groups.

1. **Brainstorm all the words, phrases, and ideas associated with a term your teacher provides.** Volunteers can keep track of contributions on the board or on a separate sheet of paper.

2. **Have your teacher direct you in a class or group discussion about the words and ideas listed.** Now is the time to ask your teacher and other students for clarification of the listed ideas.

3. **At the end of the discussion, make notes about everything you can remember.** Look over your notes to see if you have left anything out.

4. **See what you now know about the given concept based on the discussion.** Consider if what you now know is different from what you previously believed.

▶ SUMMARIZING/PAIRED SUMMARIZING

A summary is a brief statement of main ideas or important concepts. Making a summary of what you have read provides you with a way to review what you have learned, see what information needs further clarification, and make connections to material previously studied. Paired summarizing helps strengthen your ability to read, listen, and understand. It is especially useful when a section of text has several subdivisions, each dealing with different concepts.

1. **First read the material silently by yourself.**

2. **Then you and your partner take turns being the "listener" and the "speaker."** The speaker summarizes the material for the listener, who does not interrupt until the speaker has finished. If necessary, the speaker may consult the text, and the listener may ask for clarification. The listener then states any inaccuracies or omissions made by the speaker.

3. **Work together to refine the summary.** Make sure the summary states the important ideas in a clear and concise manner.

▶ DISCUSSING IDEAS

Discussing ideas with someone else before you read is a strategy that can help you broaden your knowledge base and decide what concepts to focus on. Discussing ideas after you have read a section or chapter can help you check your understanding, clarify difficult concepts, and speculate about new ideas.

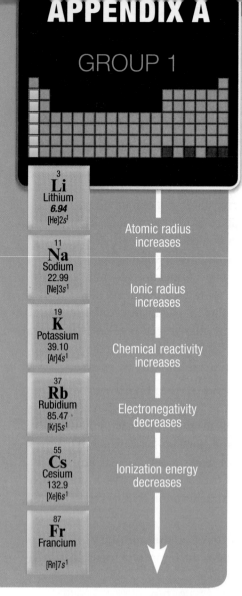

3 **Li** Lithium *6.94* [He]2s^1	
11 **Na** Sodium 22.99 [Ne]3s^1	Atomic radius increases
19 **K** Potassium 39.10 [Ar]4s^1	Ionic radius increases
37 **Rb** Rubidium 85.47 [Kr]5s^1	Chemical reactivity increases
55 **Cs** Cesium 132.9 [Xe]6s^1	Electronegativity decreases
87 **Fr** Francium [Rn]7s^1	Ionization energy decreases

Alkali Metals

Characteristics

▷ do not occur in nature as free elements

▷ are reactive metals and are obtained by reducing the 1+ ions in their natural compounds

▷ are stored under kerosene or other hydrocarbon solvent because they react with water vapor or oxygen in air

▷ consist of atoms with one electron in the outermost energy level

▷ form colorless ions in solution, each of which has a 1+ charge

▷ form ionic compounds

▷ form water-soluble bases

▷ are strong reducing agents

▷ consist of atoms that have low ionization energies

▷ are good heat and electrical conductors

▷ are ductile, malleable, and soft enough to be cut with a knife

▷ have a silvery luster, low density, and low melting point

▲
Lithium was discovered in 1817. It is found in most igneous rocks and is used in batteries as an anode because it has a very low reduction potential. Lithium is soft and is stored in oil or kerosene to prevent it from reacting with the air.

▲
Sodium derives its name from the word *soda*. It was first isolated in 1807 from the electrolysis of caustic soda, NaOH. Sodium is soft enough to be cut with a knife. It is shiny until it reacts with oxygen, which causes the surface to lose its luster.

▲
Potassium was first isolated in 1807 from the electrolysis of caustic potash, KOH.

Common Reactions

With Water to Form Bases and Hydrogen Gas
Example: $2Na(s) + 2H_2O(l) \longrightarrow 2NaOH(aq) + H_2(g)$

Li, K, Rb, and Cs also follow this pattern.

With Acids to Form Salts and Hydrogen Gas
Example: $2Na(s) + 2HCl(aq) \longrightarrow 2NaCl(aq) + H_2(g)$

Li, K, Rb, and Cs also follow this pattern.

With Halogens to Form Salts
Example: $2Na(s) + F_2(g) \longrightarrow 2NaF(s)$

Li, K, Rb, and Cs also follow this pattern in reacting with F_2, Cl_2, Br_2, and I_2.

With Oxygen to Form Oxides, Peroxides, or Superoxides
Lithium forms an oxide.

$4Li(s) + O_2(g) \longrightarrow 2Li_2O(s)$

Sodium also forms a peroxide.

$2Na(s) + O_2(g) \longrightarrow Na_2O_2(s)$

Alkali metals with higher molecular masses can also form superoxides.

$K(s) + O_2(g) \longrightarrow KO_2(s)$
Rb and Cs also follow this pattern.

Alkali-Metal Oxides with Water to Form Bases
Oxides of Na, K, Rb, and Cs can be prepared indirectly. These basic anhydrides form hydroxides in water.

Example: $K_2O(s) + H_2O(l) \longrightarrow 2KOH(aq)$
Li, Na, Rb, and Cs also follow this pattern.

Analytical Test

Alkali metals are easily detected by flame tests because each metal imparts a characteristic color to a flame.

When sodium and potassium are both present in a sample, the yellow color of the sodium masks the violet color of the potassium. The violet color can be seen only when the combined sodium-potassium flame is viewed through a cobalt-blue glass. The glass blocks the yellow flame of sodium and makes it possible to see the violet flame of potassium.

▲
A small piece of potassium dropped into water will react explosively, releasing H_2 to form a strongly basic hydroxide solution. The energy of the reaction ignites the hydrogen gas that is produced.

▲
Sodium reacts vigorously with chlorine to produce NaCl. Most salts of Group 1 metals are white crystalline compounds.

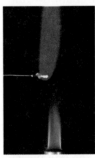

Lithium

Sodium

Potassium

Cesium

Properties

Quantity	Li	Na	K	Rb	Cs	Fr
GROUP 1 ELEMENTS						
Melting point (°C)	180.5	97.8	63.25	38.89	28.5	27
Boiling point (°C)	1342	882.9	760	691	668	677
Density (g/cm³)	0.534	0.971	0.862	1.53	1.87	—
Ionization energy (kJ/mol)	520	496	419	403	376	—
Atomic radius (pm)	152	186	227	248	265	270
Ionic radius (pm)	76	102	138	152	167	180
Common oxidation number in compounds	+1	+1	+1	+1	+1	—
Crystal structure	bcc*	bcc	bcc	bcc	bcc	—
Hardness (Mohs scale)	0.6	0.4	0.5	0.3	0.2	—

* body-centered cubic

S.T.E.M.
Application *Technology*

Sodium-Vapor Lighting

The flame test for sodium shows two bright lines at 589.0 and 589.6 nm, which is the yellow range of the emission spectrum. Sodium can be vaporized at high temperatures in a sealed tube and made to give off light using two electrodes connected to a power source. Sodium-vapor lighting is often used along highways and in parking lots because it provides good illumination while using less energy than other types of lighting.

Sodium-vapor lighting comes in both low-pressure and high-pressure bulbs. Low-pressure lamps reach an internal temperature of 270°C to vaporize the sodium under a pressure of about 1 Pa. High-pressure lamps contain mercury and xenon in addition to sodium. These substances reach an internal temperature of 1100°C under a pressure of about 100 000 Pa. The high-pressure lamp provides a higher light intensity. The design of both types of lamps must take into account the high reactivity of sodium, which increases at high temperatures. Because ordinary glass will react with sodium at 250°C, a special sodium-resistant glass is used for low-pressure lamps. High-pressure lamps use an aluminum-oxide material for the column containing the sodium, mercury, and xenon. Both types of lamps contain tungsten electrodes.

The light intensity per watt for sodium-vapor lamps far exceeds that of fluorescent lamps, high-pressure mercury-vapor lamps, tungsten-halogen lamps, and incandescent bulbs.

S.T.E.M.
Application *Health*

Electrolyte Balance in the Body

The elements of Group 1 are important to a person's diet and body maintenance because they form ionic compounds. These compounds are present in the body as solutions of the ions. All ions carry an electric charge, so they are electrolyte solutes. Two of the most important electrolyte solutes found in the body are K^+ and Na^+ ions. Both ions facilitate the transmission of nerve impulses and control the amount of water retained by cells.

▲ During situations where the body is losing water rapidly through intense sweating or diarrhea for a prolonged period (more than 5 hours), a sports drink can hydrate the body and restore electrolyte balance. However, using sports drinks regularly when not exercising can have a negative effect on electrolyte balance in the body. (See Table 1B.)

TABLE 1A

SODIUM-POTASSIUM CONCENTRATION IN BODY FLUIDS

Cation	Inside cells (mmol/L)	Outside cells or in plasma (mmol/L)
Na^+	12	145
K^+	140	4

The sodium- and potassium-ion concentrations in body fluids are shown in Table 1A. Sodium ions are found primarily in the fluid outside cells, while potassium ions are largely found in the fluid inside cells. Anions are present in the fluids to balance the electrical charge of the Na^+ and K^+ cations.

Abnormal electrolyte concentrations in blood serum can indicate the presence of disease. The ion concentrations that vary as a result of disease are Na^+, K^+, Cl^-, and HCO_3^-. Sodium-ion concentration is a good indicator of the water balance between blood and tissue cells. Unusual potassium-ion levels can indicate kidney or gastrointestinal problems. Chloride ion is the anion that balances the positive charge of the sodium ion in the fluid outside the cells. It also diffuses into a cell to maintain normal electrolyte balance when hydrogen-carbonate ions diffuse out of the cell into the blood. Table 1B shows medical conditions associated with electrolyte imbalances.

TABLE 1B

ELECTROLYTE IMBALANCES

Electrolyte	Normal Range (mmol/L)	Causes of Imbalance Excess	Deficiency
Sodium, Na^+	135–145	hypernatremia (increased urine excretion; excess water loss)	hyponatremia (dehydration; diabetes-related low blood pH; vomiting; diarrhea)
Potassium, K^+	3.5–5.0	hyperkalemia (renal failure; low blood pH)	hypokalemia (gastrointestinal conditions)
Hydrogen carbonate, HCO_3^-	24–30	hypercapnia (high blood pH; hypoventilation)	hypocapnia (low blood pH; hyperventilation; dehydration)
Chloride, Cl^-	100–106	hyperchloremia (anemia; heart conditions; dehydration)	hypochloremia (acute infection; burns; hypoventilation)

Sodium-Potassium Pump in the Cell Membrane

The process of active transport allows a cell to maintain its proper electrolyte balance. To keep the ion concentrations at the proper levels shown in Table 1B, a sodium-potassium pump embedded in the cell membrane shuttles sodium ions out of the cell across the cell membrane. A model for the action of the sodium-potassium pump is shown in the figure below.

Nerve Impulses and Ion Concentration

The difference in Na^+ and K^+ concentrations inside and outside nerve-cell membranes is essential for the operation of the nervous system.

This unequal concentration of ions creates a voltage across nerve-cell membranes. When a nerve cell is stimulated, sodium ions diffuse into the cell from the surrounding fluid, raising voltage across the nerve-cell membrane from -70 mV to nearly $+60$ mV. Potassium ions then diffuse out of the cell into the surrounding fluid, restoring the voltage across the nerve-cell membrane to -70 mV. This voltage fluctuation initiates the transmission of a nerve impulse. The amount of Na^+ inside the cell has increased slightly, and the amount of K^+ outside the cell has decreased. But the sodium-potassium pump will restore these ions to their proper concentrations.

Sodium-Potassium Pump

The sodium-potassium pump is a protein embedded within the cell membrane that allows the passage of Na^+ and K^+ into and out of the cell. Each figure depicts the action of a single protein.

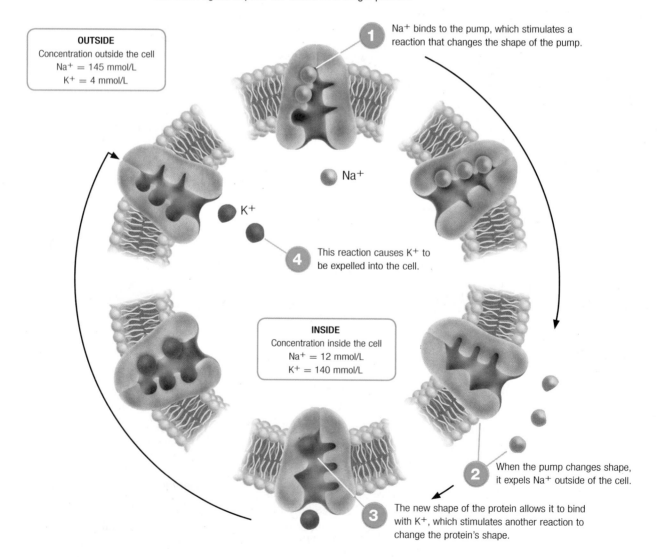

OUTSIDE
Concentration outside the cell
Na^+ = 145 mmol/L
K^+ = 4 mmol/L

INSIDE
Concentration inside the cell
Na^+ = 12 mmol/L
K^+ = 140 mmol/L

Na^+

K^+

1 Na^+ binds to the pump, which stimulates a reaction that changes the shape of the pump.

2 When the pump changes shape, it expels Na^+ outside of the cell.

3 The new shape of the protein allows it to bind with K^+, which stimulates another reaction to change the protein's shape.

4 This reaction causes K^+ to be expelled into the cell.

What's Your Sodium IQ?

Though sodium is an important mineral in your body, a diet that is high in sodium is one of several factors linked to high blood pressure, also known as hypertension. High Na^+ levels cause water retention, which results in increased blood pressure. Sodium is not the direct cause of all hypertension, but reducing sodium levels in the diet can affect individuals with a condition known as salt-sensitive hypertension. Therefore, the Dietary Guidelines for Americans recommend consuming salt and sodium in moderation. Test your knowledge about sodium in foods with the questions below.

1. Which of the following condiments has the lowest salt content?
   a. mustard   c. catsup   e. vinegar
   b. steak sauce   d. pickles

2. One-fourth of a teaspoon of salt contains about _____ of sodium.
   a. 10 mg   c. 500 mg   e. 1 kg
   b. 100 g   d. 500 g

3. According to FDA regulations for food product labels, a food labeled *salt-free* must contain less than _____ mg of sodium ion per serving.
   a. 100   c. 0.001   e. 0.00005
   b. 5   d. 0.005

4. The Nutrition Facts label for a particular food reads "Sodium 15 mg." This is the amount of sodium ions per _____.
   a. package   c. serving   e. RDA
   b. teaspoon   d. ounce

5. The recommended average daily intake of sodium ion for adults is 1500 mg. For a low-sodium diet the intake should be _____.
   a. 200 mg   c. 750 mg   e. 150 mg
   b. 2000 mg   d. 500 mg

6. Each of the following ingredients can be found in the ingredients lists for some common food products. Which ones indicate that the product contains sodium?
   a. trisodium phosphate   d. sodium sulfate
   b. sodium bicarbonate   e. MSG
   c. sodium benzoate   f. baking soda

7. Which of the following spices is NOT a salt substitute?
   a. caraway seeds   c. ginger
   b. dill   d. onion salt

8. Most salt in the average American diet comes from salting foods too heavily at the dinner table.
   a. true   b. false

9. Which of the following foods are high in sodium?
   a. potato chips   c. doughnuts   e. figs
   b. pizza   d. bananas

10. Your body requires about 200 mg of sodium ion, or 500 mg of salt, per day. Why do these numbers differ?

Answers 1. e; 2. c; 3. b; 4. c; 5. c; 6. all of them; 7. d; 8. b; processed foods can contain very high levels of sodium; 9. a, b, c; 10. Salt is not pure sodium.

(bl) ©Brian Hagiwara/Foodpix/Getty Images

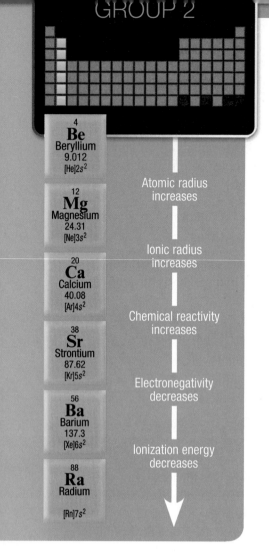

GROUP 2

4	**Be** Beryllium 9.012 [He]$2s^2$
12	**Mg** Magnesium 24.31 [Ne]$3s^2$
20	**Ca** Calcium 40.08 [Ar]$4s^2$
38	**Sr** Strontium 87.62 [Kr]$5s^2$
56	**Ba** Barium 137.3 [Xe]$6s^2$
88	**Ra** Radium [Rn]$7s^2$

Atomic radius increases

Ionic radius increases

Chemical reactivity increases

Electronegativity decreases

Ionization energy decreases

Alkaline-Earth Metals

Characteristics

▶ do not occur naturally as free elements

▶ occur most commonly as the carbonates, phosphates, silicates, and sulfates

▶ occur naturally as compounds that are either insoluble or only slightly soluble in water

▶ consist of atoms that contain two electrons in their outermost energy level

▶ consist of atoms that tend to lose two electrons per atom, forming ions with a 2+ charge

▶ are less reactive than alkali metals

▶ form ionic compounds primarily

▶ react with water to form bases and hydrogen gas

▶ are good heat and electrical conductors

▶ are ductile and malleable

▶ have a silvery luster

▶ include the naturally radioactive element radium

▶ Calcium carbonate is a major component of marble.

▶ Beryllium is found in the mineral compound beryl. Beryl crystals include the dark green emerald and the blue-green aquamarine. The colors of these gems come from other metal impurities.

▶ The mineral dolomite, $CaCO_3 \bullet MgCO_3$, is a natural source of both calcium and magnesium.

Common Reactions

With Water to Form Bases and Hydrogen Gas

Example: $Mg(s) + 2H_2O(l) \longrightarrow Mg(OH)_2(aq) + H_2(g)$
Ca, Sr, and Ba also follow this pattern.

With Acids to Form Salts and Hydrogen Gas

Example: $Mg(s) + 2HCl(aq) \longrightarrow MgCl_2(aq) + H_2(g)$
Be, Ca, Sr, and Ba also follow this pattern.

With Halogens to Form Salts

Example: $Mg(s) + F_2(g) \longrightarrow MgF_2(s)$
Ca, Sr, and Ba also follow this pattern in reacting
with F_2, Cl_2, Br_2, and I_2.

With Oxygen to Form Oxides or Peroxides

Magnesium forms an oxide.
$2Mg(s) + O_2(g) \longrightarrow 2MgO(s)$
Be and Ca also follow this pattern.

Strontium also forms a peroxide.
$Sr(s) + O_2(g) \longrightarrow SrO_2(s)$
Ba also reacts in this way.

With Hydrogen to Form Hydrides

Example: $Mg(s) + H_2(g) \longrightarrow MgH_2(s)$
Ca, Sr, and Ba also follow this pattern.

With Nitrogen to Form Nitrides

Example: $3Mg(s) + N_2(g) \longrightarrow Mg_3N_2(s)$
Be and Ca also follow this pattern.

▲
Calcium reacts with water to form
hydrogen gas.

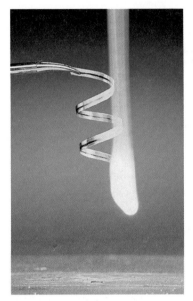

▲
Magnesium burns in air to form
MgO and Mg_3N_2.

▲
Magnesium reacts with HCl to
produce $H_2(g)$ and $MgCl_2(aq)$.

Analytical Test

Flame tests can be used to identify three of the alkaline-earth elements. The colors of both calcium and strontium can be masked by the
presence of barium, which produces a green flame.

Calcium

Strontium

Barium

Properties

GROUP 2 ELEMENTS						
Quantity	Be	Mg	Ca	Sr	Ba	Ra
Melting point (°C)	1278 ± 5	649	839 ± 2	769	725	700
Boiling point (°C)	2467	1090	1484	1384	1640	1140
Density (g/cm³)	1.85	1.74	1.54	2.6	3.51	5
Ionization energy (kJ/mol)	900	738	590	550	503	509
Atomic radius (pm)	112	160	197	215	222	220
Ionic radius (pm)	45	72	100	118	136	148
Common oxidation number in compounds	+2	+2	+2	+2	+2	+2
Crystal structure	hcp*	hcp	fcc**	fcc	bcc	bcc
Hardness (Mohs scale)	4.0	2.0	1.5	1.8	1.5	—

* hexagonal close-packed   ** face-centered cubic

S.T.E.M.
Application *Technology*

Fireworks

Fireworks are made from pyrotechnics—chemical substances that produce light and smoke when they are ignited. Pyrotechnics are also used in flares, smoke bombs, explosives, and matches. An aerial fireworks device is a rocket made of a cylinder, chemicals inside the cylinder, and fuses attached to the cylinder. The illustration on the right shows how the device works. The lift charge at the bottom of the cylinder consists of a small amount of black gunpowder. When the side fuse ignites the gunpowder, it explodes like a small bomb. The gunpowder consists of potassium nitrate, charcoal, and sulfur. When these three chemicals react with one another, they produce gases. In this case, the gases produced are carbon monoxide, carbon dioxide, sulfur dioxide, and nitrogen monoxide. These hot gases expand very rapidly, providing the thrust that lifts the rocket into the sky.

About the time the shell reaches its maximum altitude and minimum speed, the time fuse ignites the chemicals contained in the cylinder. The chemicals inside the cylinder determine the color of the burst.

Time-delay fuses activate the reactions in the other chambers

Ignition fuse activates the reaction in the bottom chamber

Red star bursts

Blue star bursts

Flash and sound mixture

Black powder propellant

▲
The cylinder of a multiple-burst rocket contains separate reaction chambers connected by fuses. A common fuse ignites the propellant and the time-delay fuse in the first reaction chamber.

©Mauritius/SuperStock

Chemical Composition and Color

One of the characteristics of fireworks that we enjoy most is their variety of rich colors. These colors are created in much the same way as the colors produced during a flame test. In a fireworks device, the chloride salt is heated to a high temperature, causing the excited atoms to give off a burst of light. The color of light produced depends on the metal used. The decomposition of barium chloride, $BaCl_2$, for example, produces a burst of green light, whereas strontium chloride, $SrCl_2$, releases red light.

People who design fireworks combine artistry with a technical knowledge of chemical properties. They have found ways to combine different colors within a single cylinder and to make parts of the cylinder explode at different times. Fireworks designers have a technical knowledge of projectile motion that is used to determine the height, direction, and angle at which a fireworks device will explode to produce a fan, fountain, flower, stream, comet, spider, star, or other shape.

Strontium and the Visible Spectrum

When heated, some metallic elements and their compounds emit light at specific wavelengths that are characteristic of the element or compound. Visible light includes wavelengths between about 400 and 700 nanometers. The figure below shows the emission spectrum for strontium. When heated, strontium gives off the maximum amount of visible light at about 700 nanometers, which falls in the red-light region of the visible spectrum.

Flares

Flares operate on a chemical principle that is different from that of fireworks. A typical flare consists of finely divided magnesium metal and an oxidizing agent. When the flare is ignited, the oxidizing agent reacts with the magnesium metal to produce magnesium oxide. This reaction releases so much energy that it produces a glow like that of the filaments in a light bulb. The brilliant white light produced by the flare is caused by billions of tiny particles of magnesium that glow when they react. If slightly larger particles of magnesium metal are used in the flare, the system glows for a longer period of time because the particles' reaction with the oxidizing agent is slower.

A colored flare can be thought of as a combination of a white flare and a chemical that produces colored light when burned. For example, a red flare can be made from magnesium metal, an oxidizing agent, and a compound of strontium. When the flare is ignited, the oxidizing agent and magnesium metal react, heating the magnesium to white-hot temperatures. The energy from this reaction causes the strontium compound to give off its characteristic red color.

▲ A flare is made up of reacting magnesium and strontium particles.

For safety reasons, some fireworks manufacturers store their products in metal sheds separated by sand banks. Also, people who work with fireworks are advised to wear cotton clothing because cotton is less likely than other fabrics to develop a static charge, which can cause a spark and accidentally ignite fireworks.

▶ The emission spectrum for strontium shows strong bands in the red region of the visible light spectrum.

| 4000 | 4500 | 5000 | 5500 | 6000 | 6500 | 7000 | 7500 |

Calcium: An Essential Mineral in the Diet

Calcium is the most abundant mineral in the body. It is the mineral that makes up a good portion of the teeth and the bone mass of the body. A small percentage of calcium in the body is used in the reactions by which cells communicate and in the regulation of certain body processes. Calcium is so important to normal body functioning that if the calcium level of the blood falls far below normal, hormones signal the release of calcium from bone and signal the gastrointestinal tract to absorb more calcium during the digestion process.

A prolonged diet that is low in calcium is linked to a disease characterized by a decrease in bone mass, a condition called osteoporosis. Reduced bone mass results in brittle bones that fracture easily. Osteoporosis generally occurs later in life and is more prevalent in females. However, because you achieve peak bone mass during the late teens or early twenties, it is critical that your diet meet the recommended requirements to increase your peak bone mass. The recommended dietary intake for calcium is 1000 mg per day. Maintaining that level in the diet along with regular exercise through adulthood are thought to reduce the rate of bone loss later in life. Excess calcium in the diet (consuming more than 2500 mg daily) can interfere with the absorption of other minerals.

▲
Dairy products are generally good sources of calcium.

Magnesium: An Essential Mineral in the Diet

Though magnesium has several functions in the body, one of the more important functions is its role in the absorption of calcium by cells. Magnesium, like sodium and potassium, is involved in the transmission of nerve impulses. Like calcium, magnesium is a component of bone.

A major source of magnesium in the diet is plants. Magnesium is the central atom in the green plant pigment chlorophyll. The structure of chlorophyll in plants is somewhat similar to the structure of heme—the oxygen-carrying molecule in animals.

TABLE 2A

GOOD SOURCES OF CALCIUM IN THE DIET		
Food	Serving size	Calcium present (mg)
Broccoli	6.3 oz	82
Cheddar cheese	1 oz	204
Cheese pizza, frozen	pizza for one	375
Milk, low-fat 1%	8 oz	300
Tofu, regular	4 oz	130
Vegetable pizza, frozen	pizza for one	500
Yogurt, low-fat	8 oz	415
Yogurt, plain whole milk	8 oz	274

The recommended dietary intake of magnesium is 400 mg per day for men and 315 mg per day for women. This is equivalent to just 4 oz of bran cereal. Because magnesium levels are easily maintained by a normal diet, it is unusual for anyone to have a magnesium deficiency. Most magnesium deficiencies are the result of factors that decrease magnesium absorption. People with gastrointestinal disorders, alcohol abusers, and the critically ill are most likely to have these types of absorption problems.

Excess magnesium in the diet is excreted by the kidneys, so there are no cumulative toxic effects.

Spinach is a good source of magnesium. Magnesium is the central atom in the green plant pigment chlorophyll. The chlorophyll structure is shown on the right.

Chlorophyll *a*

TABLE 2B		
GOOD SOURCES OF MAGNESIUM IN THE DIET		
Food	Serving size	Magnesium present (mg)
Barley, raw	1 cup	244
Beef, broiled sirloin	4 oz	36
Cabbage, raw	1 med. head	134
Cashews, dry-roasted	1 oz	74
Chicken, roasted breast	4 oz	31
Lima beans, boiled	1/2 cup	63
Oatmeal	1 oz	39
Potato, baked	7.1 oz	115
Prunes, dried	4 oz	51
Rice bran	8 oz	648
Salmon, canned	4 oz	39
Spinach, raw	10 oz	161

©Tony Craddock/Photo Researchers, Inc

Alkaline-Earth Metals **R29**

Elements Handbook

Transition Metals

Characteristics

▷ consist of metals in Groups 3 through 12

▷ contain one or two electrons in their outermost energy level

▷ are usually harder and more brittle than metals in Groups 1 and 2

▷ have higher melting and boiling points than metals in Groups 1 and 2

▷ are good heat and electrical conductors

▷ are malleable and ductile

▷ have a silvery luster, except copper and gold

▷ include radioactive elements with numbers 89 through 112

▷ include mercury, the only liquid metal at room temperature

▷ have chemical properties that differ from each other

▷ tend to have two or more common oxidation states

▷ often form colored compounds

▷ may form complex ions

▲
Iron ore is obtained from surface mines. Hematite, Fe_2O_3, is the most common iron ore.

▲
Gold, silver, platinum, palladium, iridium, rhodium, ruthenium, and osmium are sometimes referred to as the noble metals because they are not very reactive. These metals are found in coins, jewelry, and metal sculptures.

▲
Copper ores are also obtained from surface mines. Copper ore is shown here.

Common Reactions

Because this region of the periodic table is so large, you would expect great variety in the types of reaction characteristics of transition metals. For example, copper oxidizes in air to form the green patina you see on the Statue of Liberty. Copper reacts with concentrated HNO_3 but not with dilute HNO_3. Zinc, on the other hand, reacts readily with dilute HCl. Iron oxidizes in air to form rust, but chromium is generally unreactive in air. Some common reactions for transition elements are shown by the following:

May Form Two or More Different Ions

Example: $Fe(s) \longrightarrow Fe^{2+}(aq) + 2e^-$
Example: $Fe(s) \longrightarrow Fe^{3+}(aq) + 3e^-$

May React with Oxygen to Form Oxides

Example: $4Cr(s) + 3O_2(g) \longrightarrow 2Cr_2O_3(s)$
Example: $2Cu(s) + O_2(g) \longrightarrow 2CuO(s)$

May React with Halogens to Form Halides

Example: $Ni(s) + Cl_2(g) \longrightarrow NiCl_2(s)$

May Form Complex Ions

See examples in the lower right.

▲ Copper reacts with oxygen in air.

▲ Copper reacts with concentrated nitric acid.

▲ Zinc reacts with dilute hydrochloric acid.

▲ Soluble iron(III) salts form insoluble $Fe(OH)_3$ when they are reacted with a hydroxide base.

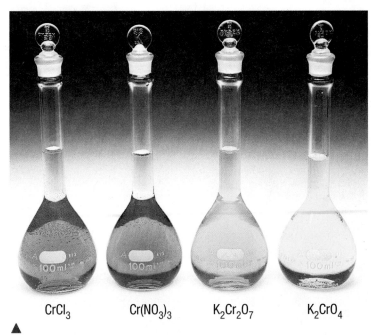

CrCl₃ Cr(NO₃)₃ K₂Cr₂O₇ K₂CrO₄

▲ Chromium has several common oxidation states, represented here by aqueous solutions of its compounds. The violet and green solutions contain chromium in the +3 state, and the orange and yellow solutions contain chromium in the +6 oxidation state.

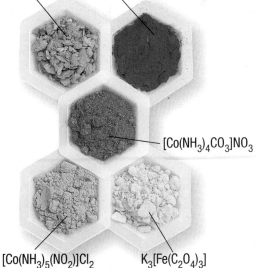

$Cu[(CH_3)_2SO]_2Cl_2$ $Cu(NH_3)_4SO_4 \bullet H_2O$

$[Co(NH_3)_4CO_3]NO_3$

$[Co(NH_3)_5(NO_2)]Cl_2$ $K_3[Fe(C_2O_4)_3]$

▲ Complex ions belong to a class of compounds called coordination compounds. Coordination compounds show great variety in colors. Several transition-metal coordination compounds are shown.

Analytical Test

Flame tests are not commonly used to identify transition metals. The presence of a certain transition-metal ion in a solution is sometimes obvious from the solution's color. Some transition-metal ions can be more accurately identified using a procedure called qualitative analysis. **Qualitative analysis** *is the identification of ions by their characteristic reactions.* The transition-metal ions most often identified through qualitative analysis include copper, nickel, zinc, chromium, iron, cobalt, cadmium, manganese, and tin. Most tests to identify the presence of an ion in a mixture involve causing the ion to precipitate out of solution. Some of the more dramatic precipitation reactions for transition metals are shown.

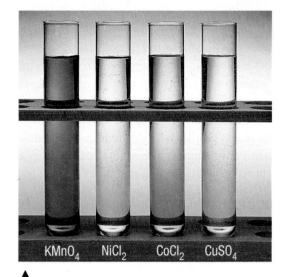

▲ Some transition metal ions can be identified by characteristic colors of their salt solutions.

▲ Copper (formation of $[Cu(NH_3)_4](OH)_2$)

▲ Cadmium (formation of CdS)

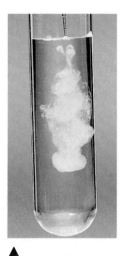

▲ Zinc (formation of ZnS)

▲ Chromium (formation of $PbCrO_4$)

▲ Iron (formation of $[Fe(SCN)]^{2+}$)

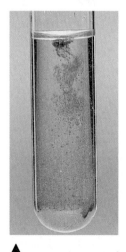

▲ Manganese (formation of MnO_4^-)

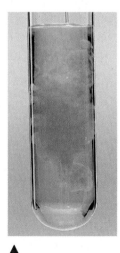

▲ Nickel (formation of a nickel dimethylglyoxime complex)

Properties

SELECTED TRANSITION METALS									
Quantity	Cr	Fe	Co	Ni	Cu	Zn	Ag	Au	Hg
Melting point (°C)	1857 ± 20	1535	1495	1455	1083	420	962	1064	−38.8
Boiling point (°C)	2672	2750	2870	2732	2567	907	2212	2808 ± 2	356.6
Density (g/cm³)	7.20	7.86	8.9	8.92	8.96	7.14	10.5	19.3	13.5
Ionization energy (kJ/mol)	653	762	760	737	746	906	731	890	1007
Atomic radius (pm)	128	126	125	124	128	134	144	144	151
Common oxidation numbers	+2, +3, +6	+2, +3	+2, +3	+2	+1, +2	+2	+1	+1, +3	+1, +2

S.T.E.M.
Application *Geology*

Gemstones and Color

A gemstone is a mineral that can be cut and polished to make gems for an ornament or piece of jewelry. At one time, all gemstones were naturally occurring minerals mined from Earth's crust. Today, however, chemists can duplicate natural processes to produce artificial gemstones. Amethyst, emerald, jade, opal, ruby, sapphire, and topaz occur naturally and can also be produced synthetically.

The color of a gemstone is determined by the presence of small amounts of one or more transition metals. For example, aluminum oxide, Al_2O_3, often occurs naturally as corundum—a clear, colorless mineral. However, if as few as 1 to 2% of the aluminum ions, Al^{3+}, are replaced by chromium ions, Cr^{3+}, the corundum takes on a reddish color and is known as the gemstone ruby.

If a small fraction of aluminum ions in corundum are replaced by Fe^{3+} and Ti^{3+}, the corundum has a greenish color and is known as emerald. In another variation, if vanadium ions, V^{3+}, replace a few Al^{3+} ions in corundum, the result is a gemstone known as alexandrite. This gemstone appears green in reflected natural light and red in transmitted or artificial light.

Table 3A on the next page lists transition metals that are responsible for the colors of various gemstones. The table provides only a general overview, however, as most naturally occurring gemstones occur in a range of hues, depending on the exact composition of the stone.

Artificial Gemstones

In 1902, the French chemist Auguste Verneuil found a way to melt a mixture of aluminum oxide and chromium salts and then cool the mixture very slowly to produce large crystals of reddish aluminum oxide—rubies.

Sapphire   Ruby   Peridot   Garnet

TRANSITION METALS AND GEMSTONE COLORS

Gemstone	Color	Element
Amethyst	purple	iron
Aquamarine	blue	iron
Emerald	green	iron/titanium
Garnet	red	iron
Peridot	yellow-green	iron
Ruby	red	chromium
Sapphire	blue	iron/titanium
Spinel	colorless to red to black	varies
Turquoise	blue	copper

Verneuil's method, although somewhat modified, is still widely used today for the manufacture of colored gemstones. When magnesium oxide is substituted for aluminum oxide, a colorless spinel-like product is formed. The addition of various transition metals then adds a tint to the spinel that results in the formation of synthetic emerald, aquamarine, tourmaline, or other gemstones. Synthetic gems look very much like their natural counterparts.

Synthetic sapphire

Synthetic ruby

S.T.E.M.
Application *Technology*

Alloys

An alloy is a mixture of a metal and one or more other elements. In most cases, the second component of the mixture is also a metal. Table 3B lists the composition and uses of some common alloys.

Alloys are desirable because mixtures of elements usually have properties different from and often superior to the properties of individual metals. For example, many alloys that contain iron are harder, stronger, and more resistant to oxidation than iron itself.

Amalgams are alloys that contain mercury. They are soft and pliable when first produced but later become solid and hard. Dental fillings are often made of an amalgam of mercury and silver. Concerns about the possible toxicity of mercury led to the development of other filling materials.

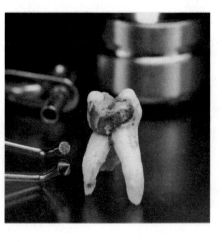

Cast Iron and Steel

The term *steel* applies to any alloy consisting of iron and less than 1.5% carbon, and often other elements. When iron ore is treated with carbon in the form of coke to extract pure iron metal, some of the carbon also reacts with the iron to produce a form of iron carbide known as cementite. The reaction can be represented by the following equation:

$$3Fe + C \longrightarrow Fe_3C$$

Cast iron is a mixture that consists of some pure iron, known as ferrite, some cementite, and some carbon atoms trapped within the crystalline structure of the iron and cementite. The rate at which cast iron is cooled changes the proportion of these three components. If the cast iron is cooled slowly, the ferrite and cementite tend to separate from each other, forming a banded product that is tough but not very hard.

However, if the cast iron is cooled quickly, the components of the original mixture cannot separate from each other, forming a product that is both tough and hard.

▲

Stainless steel, which is hard and resists corrosion, is made of iron and chromium (12–30%). The properties of stainless steel make it a suitable alloy for making cutlery and utensils.

TABLE 3B

COMPOSITION AND USES OF SOME ALLOYS

Name of alloy	Composition	Uses
Brass	copper with up to 50% zinc, some lead, and a small amount of tin	inexpensive jewelry; hose nozzles and couplings; piping; stamping dies
Bronze	copper with up to 12% tin	coins and medals; heavy gears; tools; electrical hardware
Coin metal	copper: 75% nickel: 25%	United States coins
Duralumin	aluminum: 95%; copper: 4%; magnesium: 0.5%; manganese: <1%	aircraft, boats, railroad cars, and machinery because of its high strength and resistance to corrosion
Nichrome	nickel: 80–85% chromium: 15–20%	heating elements in toasters, electric heaters, etc.
Phosphor bronze	bronze with a small amount of phosphorus	springs, electrical springs, boat propellers
Solder	lead: 50%; tin: 50% or tin: 98%; silver: 2%	joining two metals to each other; joining copper pipes
Sterling silver	silver: 92.5%; copper: 7.5%	jewelry, art objects, flatware
Type metal	lead: 75–95%; antimony: 2–18%; tin: trace	used to make type for printing because it expands as it cools

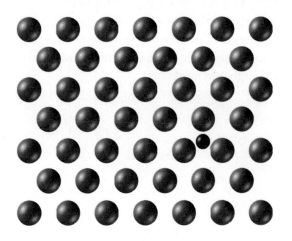

▲
Interstitial crystal A smaller atom or ion fits into a small space between particles in the array.

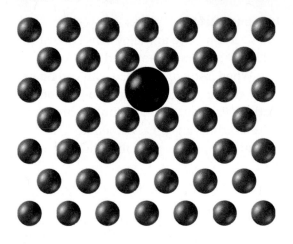

▲
Substitutional crystal A larger atom or ion is substituted for a particle in the array.

Structures and Preparation of Alloys

Alloys generally crystallize in one of two ways, depending on relative sizes of atoms. If the atoms of one of the metals present are small enough to fit into the spaces between the atoms of the second metal, they form an alloy with an interstitial structure (*inter* means "between," and *stitial* means "to stand"). If atoms of the two metals are of similar size or if one is larger, the atoms of one metal can substitute for the atoms of the second metal in its crystalline structure. Such alloys are substitutional alloys. Models for both types of crystals are shown above.

Techniques for making alloys depend on the metals used in the mixture. In some cases, the two metals can simply be melted together to form a mixture. The composition of the mixture often varies within a range, evidence that the final product is indeed a mixture and not a compound. In other cases, one metal may be melted first and the second dissolved in it. Brass is prepared in this way. If copper and zinc were heated together to a high temperature, zinc (bp 907°C) would evaporate before copper (mp 1084°C) melted. Therefore, the copper is melted first, and the zinc is added to it.

▲
Brass has a high luster and resembles gold when cleaned and polished. A brass object can be coated with a varnish to prevent reactions of the alloy with air and water.

▲
Sterling silver is more widely used than pure silver because it is stronger and more durable.

S.T.E.M.
Application *The Environment*

Mercury Poisoning

Mercury is the only metal that is liquid at room temperature. It has a very high density compared with most other common transition metals and has a very large surface tension and high vapor pressure. Mercury and many of its compounds must be handled with extreme care because they are highly toxic. Mercury spills are especially hazardous because the droplets scatter easily and are often undetected during cleanup. These droplets release toxic vapors into the air.

Overexposure to mercury vapor or its compounds can occur by absorption through the skin, respiratory tract, or digestive tract. Mercury is a cumulative poison, which means that its concentration in the body increases as exposure increases.

Mercury that enters the body damages the kidneys, heart, and brain. The action of mercury on the brain affects the nervous system. Symptoms of mercury poisoning include numbness, tunnel vision, garbled speech, bleeding and inflammation of the gums, muscle spasms, anemia, and emotional disorders, such as depression, irritability, and personality changes. The saying "mad as a hatter" probably came about because of mercury poisoning.

Mercury salts were once routinely used to process the felt used in hats. Hatters often displayed the nerve and mental impairments associated with overexposure to mercury.

Methylmercury in Freshwater Ecosystems

Mercury, Hg, can be found in our environment and in our food supply. Fortunately, the body has some protective mechanisms to deal with trace amounts of mercury. However, levels of mercury and of methylmercury, $(CH_3)Hg^+$, are increasing in the environment due to mercury mining operations and runoff from the application of pesticides and fungicides.

Mercury is easily converted to methylmercury by bacteria. Methylmercury is more readily absorbed by cells than mercury itself. As a result, methylmercury accumulates in the food chain as shown in the diagram below. A serious incident of methylmercury poisoning occurred in Japan in the 1950s. People living in Minamata, Japan, were exposed to high levels of methylmercury from eating shellfish.

In the United States, there is concern about mercury levels in fish from some freshwater lakes. Though environmental regulations have reduced the level of lake pollutants, it takes time to see a reduction in the concentration of an accumulated poison.

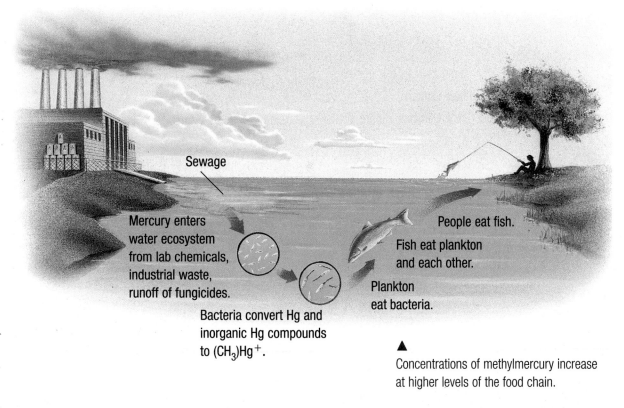

Sewage

Mercury enters water ecosystem from lab chemicals, industrial waste, runoff of fungicides.

Bacteria convert Hg and inorganic Hg compounds to $(CH_3)Hg^+$.

People eat fish.

Fish eat plankton and each other.

Plankton eat bacteria.

▲ Concentrations of methylmercury increase at higher levels of the food chain.

Elements in the Body

The four most abundant elements in the body (oxygen, carbon, hydrogen, and nitrogen) are the major components of organic biomolecules, such as carbohydrates, proteins, fats, and nucleic acids. Other elements compose a dietary category of compounds called minerals. Minerals are considered the inorganic elements of the body. Minerals fall into two categories—the major minerals and the trace minerals, or trace elements, as they are sometimes called. Notice in the periodic table below that most elements in the trace elements category of minerals are transition metals.

Trace elements are minerals with dietary daily requirements of 100 mg or less. They are found in foods derived from both plants and animals. Though these elements are present in very small quantities, they perform a variety of essential functions in the body, as shown in Table 3C on the next page.

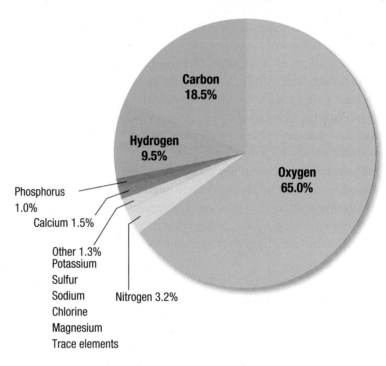

Abundance of Elements in the Body (by mass)

Carbon 18.5%

Hydrogen 9.5%

Oxygen 65.0%

Phosphorus 1.0%

Calcium 1.5%

Other 1.3%
Potassium
Sulfur
Sodium
Chlorine
Magnesium
Trace elements

Nitrogen 3.2%

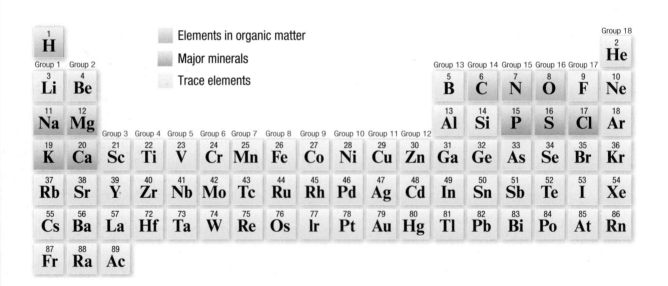

Elements in organic matter

Major minerals

Trace elements

TABLE 3C

TRANSITION METAL TRACE ELEMENTS

Transition metal	Function
Vanadium, Cadmium	function not fully determined, but linked to a reduced growth rate and impaired reproduction
Chromium	needed for glucose transport to cells
Manganese	used in the enzyme reactions that synthesize cholesterol and metabolize carbohydrates
Iron	central atom in the heme molecule—a component of hemoglobin, which binds oxygen in the blood for transport to cells
Cobalt	a component of vitamin B_{12}
Nickel	enzyme cofactor in the metabolism of fatty acids and amino acids
Copper	a major component of an enzyme that functions to protect cells from damage
Zinc	needed for tissue growth and repair and as an enzyme cofactor
Molybdenum	enzyme cofactor in the production of uric acid

Role of Iron

Most iron in the body is in hemoglobin. Fe^{3+} is the central ion in the heme molecule, which is a component of the proteins hemoglobin and myoglobin. Hemoglobin in red blood cells transports oxygen to cells and picks up carbon dioxide as waste. Myoglobin is a protein that stores oxygen to be used in muscle contraction. Iron is also in the proteins of the electron transport system and the immune system.

Mechanisms of the body control the rate of iron absorption from food in the diet. When iron reserves are low, chemical signals stimulate cells of the intestines to absorb more iron during digestion. If the diet is low in iron, causing a deficiency, hemoglobin production stops, and a condition called iron-deficiency anemia results. The blood cells produced during this state are stunted and unable to deliver adequate oxygen to cells. As a result, a person with iron-deficiency anemia feels tired and weak and has difficulty maintaining normal body temperature. The recommended daily intake of iron is 8 mg for men and 18 mg for women. The recommended level doubles for pregnant women. Iron supplements are for people who do not get enough iron in their daily diets. Table 3D lists some foods that are good sources of iron in the diet. Too much iron can be toxic, because the body stores iron once it is absorbed. Abusing iron supplements can cause severe liver and heart damage.

TABLE 3D

SOURCES OF IRON IN FOODS

Food	Serving size	Iron present (mg)
Beef roast (lean cut)	4 oz	3.55
Beef, T-bone steak (lean cut)	4 oz	3.40
Beef, ground (hamburger)	4 oz	2.78
Broccoli	6.3 oz	1.50
Chicken, breast	4 oz	1.35
Chicken, giblets	4 oz	7.30
Oatmeal, instant enriched	1 pkg	8.35
Pita bread, white enriched	6 1/2 in. diameter	1.40
Pork roast	4 oz	1.15
Prunes	4 oz	2.00
Raisins	4 oz	1.88

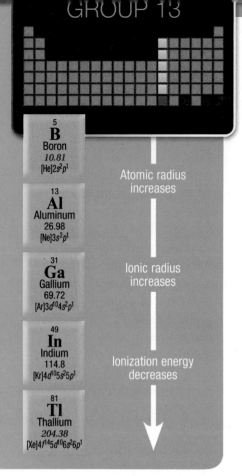

GROUP 13

5 **B** Boron *10.81* [He]$2s^2p^1$	Atomic radius increases
13 **Al** Aluminum *26.98* [Ne]$3s^2p^1$	
31 **Ga** Gallium *69.72* [Ar]$3d^{10}4s^2p^1$	Ionic radius increases
49 **In** Indium *114.8* [Kr]$4d^{10}5s^2p^1$	Ionization energy decreases
81 **Tl** Thallium *204.38* [Xe]$4f^{14}5d^{10}6s^2p^1$	

Boron Family

Characteristics

▷ do not occur in nature as free elements

▷ are scarce in nature (except aluminum, which is the most abundant metallic element)

▷ consist of atoms that have three electrons in their outer energy level

▷ are metallic solids (except boron, which is a solid metalloid)

▷ are soft and have low melting points (except boron, which is hard and has a high melting point)

▷ are chemically reactive at moderate temperatures (except boron)

▷ The discovery of the last member of the boron family has been reported but not confirmed.

▲ Boron is a covalent solid. Other members of the family are metallic solids.

▶ The warmth of a person's hand will melt gallium. Gallium metal has the lowest melting point (29.77°C) of any metal except mercury.

▲ Aluminum is the most abundant metal in Earth's crust. It exists in nature as an ore called bauxite.

Common Reactions

The reaction chemistry of boron differs greatly from that of the other members of this family. Pure boron is a covalent network solid, whereas the other members of the family are metallic crystals in pure form. Boron resembles silicon more closely than it resembles the other members of its family.

With Strong Bases to Form Hydrogen Gas and a Salt
Example: $2Al(s) + 2NaOH(aq) + 2H_2O(l) \longrightarrow 2NaAlO_2(aq) + 3H_2(g)$
Ga also follows this pattern.

With Dilute Acids to Form Hydrogen Gas and a Salt
Example: $2Al(s) + 6HCl(aq) \longrightarrow 2AlCl_3(aq) + 3H_2(g)$
Ga, In, and Tl follow this pattern in reacting with dilute HF, HCl, HBr, and HI.

With Halogens to Form Halides
Example: $2Al(s) + 3Cl_2(g) \longrightarrow 2AlCl_3(s)$
B, Al, Ga, In, and Tl also follow this pattern in reacting with F_2, Cl_2, Br_2, and I_2 (except BF_3).

With Oxygen to Form Oxides
Example: $4Al(s) + 3O_2(g) \longrightarrow 2Al_2O_3(s)$
Ga, In, and Tl also follow this pattern.

Analytical Test

Other than atomic absorption spectroscopy, there is no simple analytical test for all the members of the boron family.

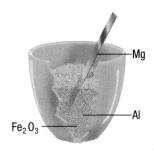
Mg
Al
Fe_2O_3

▶
A mixture of powdered aluminum and iron(III) oxide is called thermite. Al reacts with Fe_2O_3 using Mg ribbon as a fuse to provide activation energy. The energy produced by the thermite reaction is sufficient to produce molten iron (mp = 1535 C) as a product.

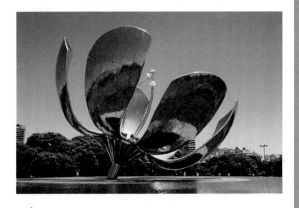

▲
Aluminum forms a thin layer of Al_2O_3 on its surface, which protects the metal from further oxidation and makes it suitable for outdoor use.

▶
The confirmatory test for the presence of aluminum in qualitative analysis is the red color formed by aluminum and the organic compound aluminon, $C_{22}H_{23}N_3O_9$.

Properties

GROUP 13 ELEMENTS					
	B	Al	Ga	In	Tl
Melting point (°C)	2300	660.37	29.77	156.61	303.5
Boiling point (°C)	2550	2467	2403	2080	1457
Density (g/cm^3)	2.34	2.702	5.904	7.31	11.85
Ionization energy (kJ/mol)	801	578	579	558	589
Atomic radius (pm)	85	143	135	167	170
Ionic radius (pm)	—	54	62	80	89
Common oxidation number in compounds	+3	+3	+1, +3	+1, +3	+1, +3
Crystal structure	monoclinic	fcc	orthorhombic	fcc	hcp
Hardness (Mohs scale)	9.3	2.75	1.5	1.2	1.2

S.T.E.M.
Application *Technology*

Aluminum

Chemically, aluminum is much more active than copper, and it belongs to the category of *self-protecting metals*. These metals are oxidized when exposed to oxygen in the air and form a hard, protective metal oxide on the surface. The oxidation of aluminum is shown by the following reaction:

$$4Al(s) + 3O_2(g) \longrightarrow 2Al_2O_3(s)$$

This oxide coating protects the underlying metal from further reaction with oxygen or other substances. Self-protecting metals are valuable in themselves or when used to coat iron and steel to keep them from corroding.

Aluminum is a very good conductor of electric current. Many years ago, most high-voltage electric power lines were made of copper. Although copper is a better conductor of electricity than aluminum, copper is heavier and more expensive. Today more than 90% of high-voltage transmission lines are made of relatively pure aluminum. The aluminum wire does not have to be self-supporting, because steel cable is incorporated to bear the weight of the wire in the long spans between towers.

In the 1960s, aluminum electric wiring was used in many houses and other buildings. Over time, however, the aluminum oxidized, and so the

▲
These high-voltage transmission lines are made of aluminum supported with steel cables.

electrical resistance increased where wires connected to outlets, switches, and other metals. As current flowed through the extra resistance, enough energy as heat was generated to cause a fire. Though some homes have been rewired, aluminum wiring is still prevalent in many homes.

Aluminum Alloys

Because aluminum has a low density and is inexpensive, it is used to construct aircraft, boats, sports equipment, and other lightweight, high-strength objects. The pure metal is not strong, so it is mixed with small quantities of other metals—usually manganese, copper, magnesium, zinc, or silicon—to produce strong low-density alloys. Typically, 80% of a modern aircraft frame consists of aluminum alloy.

Aluminum and its alloys are good heat conductors. An alloy of aluminum and manganese is used to make cookware. High-quality pots and pans made of stainless steel may have a plate of aluminum on the bottom to help conduct energy as heat quickly to the interior.

Automobile radiators made of aluminum conduct energy as heat as hot coolant from the engine enters the bottom of the radiator. The coolant is deflected into several channels. These channels are covered by thin vanes of aluminum, which conduct energy away from the coolant and transfer it to the cooler air rushing past. By the time the coolant reaches the top of the radiator, its temperature has dropped so that when it flows back into the engine it can absorb more energy as heat. To keep the process efficient, the outside of a radiator should be kept unobstructed and free of dirt buildup. Table 4A lists some aluminum alloying agents.

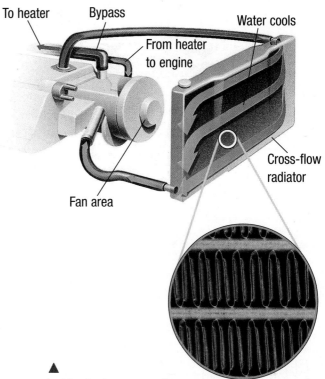

▲
In this aluminum car radiator, many thin vanes of aluminum conduct energy as heat, transferring it from the coolant to the air. Coolant is cycled from the hot engine through the radiator and back to the engine.

TABLE 4A

ALLOYS OF ALUMINUM AND THEIR USES		
Principal alloying element(s)*	Characteristics	Application examples
Manganese	moderately strong, easily worked	cookware, roofing, storage tanks, lawn furniture
Copper	strong, easily formed	aircraft structural parts; large, thin structural panels
Magnesium	strong, resists corrosion, easy to weld	parts for boats and ships, outdoor decorative objects, tall poles
Zinc and magnesium	very strong, resists corrosion	aircraft structural parts, vehicle parts, anything that needs high strength and low weight
Silicon	expands little on heating and cooling	aluminum castings
Magnesium and silicon	resists corrosion, easily formed	exposed parts of buildings, bridges

* All these alloys have small amounts of other elements.

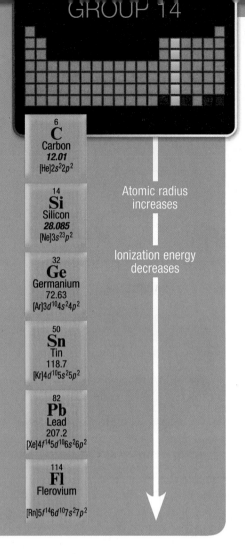

6 **C** Carbon *12.01* [He]$2s^2 2p^2$	
14 **Si** Silicon *28.085* [Ne]$3s^2 3p^2$	Atomic radius increases
32 **Ge** Germanium 72.63 [Ar]$3d^{10} 4s^2 4p^2$	Ionization energy decreases
50 **Sn** Tin 118.7 [Kr]$4d^{10} 5s^2 5p^2$	
82 **Pb** Lead 207.2 [Xe]$4f^{14} 5d^{10} 6s^2 6p^2$	
114 **Fl** Flerovium [Rn]$5f^{14} 6d^{10} 7s^2 7p^2$	

▲ Silicon has a luster but does not exhibit metallic properties. Most silicon in nature is silica, SiO_2, which occurs in sand and quartz, which is shown here.

GROUP 14

Carbon Family

Characteristics

▶ include a nonmetal (carbon), two metalloids (silicon and germanium), and two metals (tin and lead)

▶ vary greatly in both physical and chemical properties

▶ occur in nature in both combined and elemental forms

▶ consist of atoms that contain four electrons in the outermost energy level

▶ are relatively unreactive

▶ tend to form covalent compounds (tin and lead also form ionic compounds)

▶ The last member of the carbon family, flerovium, is a synthetic element that does not occur in nature.

▶
Lead has a low reactivity and is resistant to corrosion. It is very soft, highly ductile, and malleable. Lead is toxic, and like mercury, it is a cumulative poison.

▲ Tin, which is shown on the right, is a self-protecting metal like lead, but unlike lead, it has a high luster. Tin occurs in nature in cassiterite ore, which is shown above.

(bc) ©Dirk Wiersma/Science Source; ©J & L Weber/Peter Arnold, Inc

Common Reactions

With Oxygen to Form Oxides

Example: $Sn(s) + O_2(g) \rightarrow SnO_2(s)$
Pb follows this pattern, as do C, Si, and Ge at high temperatures.

With Acids to Form Salts and Hydrogen Gas

Only the metallic elements of this group react slowly with aqueous acids.
Example: $Sn(s) + 2HCl(aq) \rightarrow SnCl_2(aq) + H_2(g)$
Both Sn and Pb can also react to form tin(IV) and lead(IV) salts, respectively.

With Halogens to Form Halides

Example: $Sn(s) + 2Cl_2(g) \rightarrow SnCl_4(s)$
Si, Ge, and Pb follow this pattern, reacting with F_2, Cl_2, Br_2, and I_2.

Analytical Test

Ionic compounds of tin and lead can be identified in aqueous solutions by adding a solution containing sulfide ions. The formation of a yellow precipitate indicates the presence of Sn^{4+}, and the formation of a black precipitate indicates the presence of Pb^{2+}.

$$Sn^{4+}(aq) + 2S^{2-}(aq) \rightarrow SnS_2(s)$$
$$Pb^{2+}(aq) + S^{2-}(aq) \rightarrow PbS(s)$$

PbS | SnS$_2$

Properties

GROUP 14 ELEMENTS					
Quantity	C	Si	Ge	Sn	Pb
Melting point (°C)	3500/3652*	1410	937.4	231.88	327.502
Boiling point (°C)	4827	2355	2830	2260	1740
Density (g/cm³)	3.51/2.25*	2.33 ± 0.01	5.323	7.28	11.343
Ionization energy (kJ/mol)	1086	787	762	709	716
Atomic radius (pm)	77	118	122	140	175
Ionic radius (pm)	260 (C⁴⁻ ion)	—	—	118 (Sn²⁺ ion)	119 (Pb²⁺ ion)
Common oxidation number in compounds	+4, −4	+4	+2, +4	+2, +4	+2, +4
Crystal structure	cubic/hexagonal*	cubic	cubic	tetragonal	fcc
Hardness (Mohs scale)	10/0.5*	6.5	6.0	1.5	1.5

* The data are for two allotropic forms: diamond/graphite.

Carbon and the Reduction of Iron Ore

Some metals, especially iron, are separated from their ores through reduction reactions in a blast furnace. The blast furnace gets its name from the fact that air or pure oxygen is blown into the furnace, where it oxidizes carbon to form carbon monoxide, CO. Carbon and its compounds are important reactants in this process.

What happens inside the blast furnace to recover the iron from its ore? The actual chemical changes that occur are complex. A simplified explanation begins with the reaction of oxygen in hot air with coke, a form of carbon. Some of the coke burns to form carbon dioxide.

$$C(s) + O_2(g) \rightarrow CO_2(g)$$

As the concentration of oxygen is decreased, the carbon dioxide comes in contact with pieces of hot coke and is reduced to carbon monoxide.

$$CO_2(g) + C(s) \rightarrow 2CO(g)$$

The carbon monoxide now acts as a reducing agent to reduce the iron oxides in the ore to metallic iron.

$$Fe_2O_3(s) + 3CO(g) \rightarrow 2Fe(l) + 3CO_2(g)$$

The reduction is thought to occur in steps as the temperature in the furnace increases. The following are some of the possible steps.

$$Fe_2O_3 \rightarrow Fe_3O_4 \rightarrow FeO \rightarrow Fe$$

The white-hot liquid iron collects in the bottom of the furnace and is removed every four or five hours. The iron may be cast in molds or converted to steel in another process.

Limestone, present in the center of the furnace, decomposes to form calcium oxide and carbon dioxide.

$$CaCO_3(s) \rightarrow CaO(s) + CO_2(g)$$

The calcium oxide then combines with silica, a silicon compound, to form calcium silicate slag.

The relatively high carbon content of iron produced in a blast furnace makes the metal hard but brittle. It also has other impurities, like sulfur and phosphorus, that cause the recovered iron to be brittle. The conversion of iron to steel is essentially a purification process in which impurities are removed by oxidation. This purification process is carried out in another kind of furnace at very high temperatures. All steel contains 0.02 to 1.5% carbon. In fact, steels are graded by their carbon content. Low-carbon steels typically contain 0.02 to 0.3% carbon. Medium-carbon steels typically contain 0.03 to 0.7% carbon. High-carbon steels contain 0.7 to 1.5% carbon.

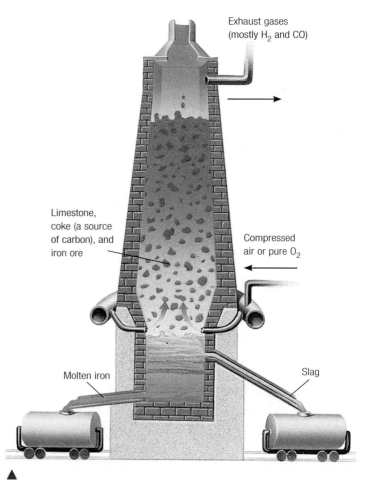

Exhaust gases (mostly H_2 and CO)

Limestone, coke (a source of carbon), and iron ore

Compressed air or pure O_2

Molten iron

Slag

▲ Molten iron flowing from the bottom of a blast furnace has been reduced from its ore through a series of reactions at high temperatures in different regions of the furnace.

Carbon Dioxide

Carbon dioxide is a colorless gas with a faint odor and a slightly sour taste. The sour taste is the result of the formation of carbonic acid when CO_2 dissolves in the water in saliva. It is a stable gas that does not burn or support combustion. At low temperatures, it exists in the solid state as "dry ice." The liquid state occurs only at pressures above atmospheric pressure. At normal atmospheric pressure, solid CO_2 (dry ice) sublimes at $-78.5°C$. The linear carbon dioxide molecule is nonpolar.

CO_2 is produced by the burning of organic fuels and from respiration processes in most living things. Most CO_2 released into the atmosphere is used by plants during photosynthesis, the process by which green plants and some forms of algae and bacteria make food. During photosynthesis, CO_2 reacts with H_2O, using the energy from sunlight. The relationships among the various processes on Earth that convert carbon to carbon dioxide are summarized in the diagram of the carbon cycle, which is pictured below.

Carbon Monoxide

Carbon monoxide is a poisonous gas produced naturally by decaying plants, certain types of algae, volcanic eruptions, and the oxidation of methane in the atmosphere.

Because CO is colorless, odorless, and tasteless, it is difficult to detect. It is slightly less dense than air and slightly soluble in water. Its main chemical uses are in the reduction of iron, described on page R46, and the production of organic compounds, such as methanol.

$$CO(g) + 2H_2(g) \rightarrow CH_3OH(l)$$

Carbon monoxide is also produced during the incomplete combustion of organic fuels. Incomplete combustion of methane occurs when the supply of oxygen is limited.

$$2CH_4(g) + 3O_2(g) \rightarrow 2CO(g) + 4H_2O(g)$$

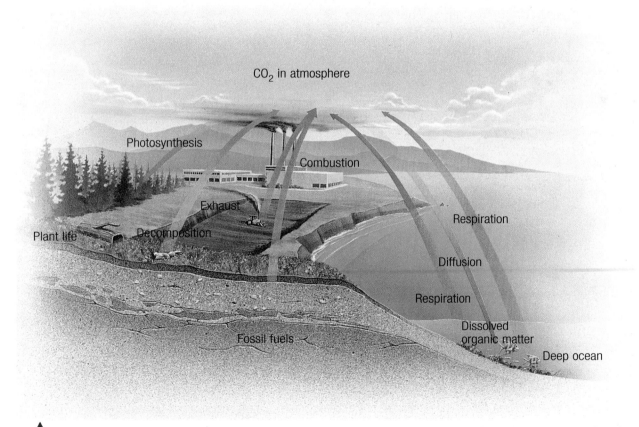

CO$_2$ in atmosphere

Photosynthesis

Combustion

Exhaust

Respiration

Plant life

Decomposition

Diffusion

Respiration

Fossil fuels

Dissolved organic matter

Deep ocean

▲
The processes that recycle CO_2 are collectively called the carbon cycle.

Application *Biochemistry*

Carbon Dioxide and Respiration

Many organisms, including humans, carry out cellular respiration. In this process, cells break down food molecules and release the energy used to build those molecules during photosynthesis. Glucose, $C_6H_{12}O_6$, is a common substance broken down in respiration. The following chemical equation expresses this process.

$$C_6H_{12}O_6 + 6O_2 \rightarrow 6CO_2 + 6H_2O + \text{energy}$$

In humans and most other vertebrate animals, the oxygen needed for this reaction is delivered to cells by hemoglobin found in red blood cells. Oxygen binds with hemoglobin as blood passes through capillaries in the lungs, as represented by the following reaction:

$$Hb + O_2 \rightarrow HbO_2$$

Hb represents the hemoglobin molecule, and HbO_2 represents oxyhemoglobin, which is hemoglobin with bound oxygen. When the red blood cells pass through capillaries near cells that have depleted their oxygen supply through respiration, the reaction reverses, and oxyhemoglobin gives up its oxygen.

$$HbO_2 \rightarrow Hb + O_2$$

Carbon dioxide produced during respiration is a waste product that must be expelled from an organism. Various things happen when CO_2 enters the blood; 7% dissolves in the plasma, about 23% binds loosely to hemoglobin, and the remaining 70% reacts reversibly with water in plasma to form hydrogen carbonate, HCO_3^- ions. To form HCO_3^- ions, CO_2 first combines with H_2O to form carbonic acid, H_2CO_3, in a reversible reaction.

$$CO_2(aq) + H_2O(l) \rightleftharpoons H_2CO_3(aq)$$

The dissolved carbonic acid ionizes to HCO_3^- ions and aqueous H^+ ions in the form of H_3O^+.

$$H_2CO_3(aq) + H_2O \rightleftharpoons H_3O^+(aq) + HCO_3^-(aq)$$

The combined equilibrium reaction follows:

$$CO_2(aq) + 2H_2O(l) \rightleftharpoons H_3O^+(aq) + HCO_3^-(aq)$$

When the blood reaches the lungs, the reaction reverses, and the blood releases CO_2, which is then exhaled to the surroundings.

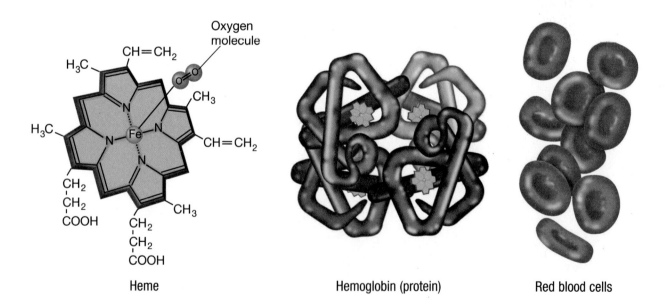

Heme   Hemoglobin (protein)   Red blood cells

▲ The oxygen carrier molecule, heme, is a component of the more-complex protein hemoglobin. Note that each hemoglobin molecule has four heme subunits. Hemoglobin is a component of red blood cells.

Exchange of CO₂ and O₂ in the Lungs

Why does CO_2 leave the blood as it passes through the lung's capillaries, and why does O_2 enter the blood? The exchange is caused by the difference in concentrations of CO_2 and O_2 in the blood and in the atmosphere. Oxygen is 21% of the atmosphere. Although the amount of CO_2 varies from place to place, it averages about 0.033% of the atmosphere. Thus, O_2 is about 640 times more concentrated in the atmosphere than is CO_2.

Substances tend to diffuse from regions of higher concentration toward regions of lower concentration. Thus, when blood reaches the capillaries of the lung, O_2 from the air diffuses into the blood, where its pressure is only 40 mm Hg, while CO_2 diffuses out of the blood, where its pressure is 45 mm Hg, and into the air. The diagram below summarizes the process.

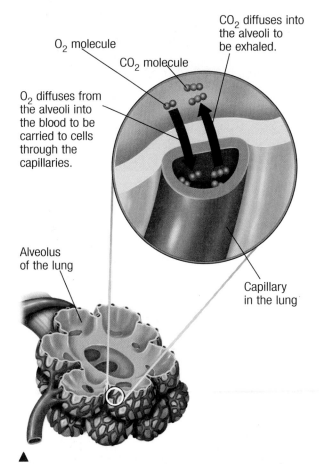

O₂ molecule

CO₂ molecule

CO₂ diffuses into the alveoli to be exhaled.

O₂ diffuses from the alveoli into the blood to be carried to cells through the capillaries.

Alveolus of the lung

Capillary in the lung

▲
The pressure of O_2 in the blood entering the lung is much lower than it is in the atmosphere. As a result, O_2 diffuses into the blood. The opposite situation exists for CO_2, so it diffuses from the blood into the air. Note that blood leaving the lung still contains a significant concentration of CO_2.

Acidosis and Alkalosis

In humans, blood is maintained between pH 7.3 and 7.5. The pH of blood is dependent on the concentration of CO_2 in the blood. Look again at this equilibrium system.

$$CO_2(aq) + 2H_2O(l) \rightleftharpoons H_3O^+(aq) + HCO_3^-(aq)$$

Notice that the right side of the equation contains the H_3O^+ ion, which determines the pH of the blood. If excess H_3O^+ enters the blood from tissues, the reverse reaction is favored. Excess H_3O^+ combines with HCO_3^- to produce more CO_2 and H_2O. If the H_3O^+ concentration begins to fall, the forward reaction is favored, producing additional H_3O^+ and HCO_3^-. To keep H_3O^+ in balance, adequate amounts of both CO_2 and HCO_3^- must be present. If something occurs that changes these conditions, a person can become very ill and can even die.

Hyperventilation occurs when a person breathes too rapidly for an extended time. Too much CO_2 is eliminated, causing the reverse reaction to be favored, and H_3O^+ and HCO_3^- are used up. As a result, the person develops a condition known as alkalosis because the pH of the blood rises to an abnormal alkaline level. The person begins to feel lightheaded and faint, and unless treatment is provided, he or she may fall into a coma. Alkalosis is treated by having the victim breathe air that is rich in CO_2. One way to accomplish this is to have the person breathe with a bag held tightly over the nose and mouth. Alkalosis is also caused by fever, infection, intoxication, hysteria, and prolonged vomiting.

The reverse of alkalosis is a condition known as acidosis. This condition is often caused by a depletion of HCO_3^- ions from the blood, which can occur as a result of kidney dysfunction. The kidney controls the excretion of HCO_3^- ions. If there are too few HCO_3^- ions in solution, the forward reaction is favored, and H_3O^+ ions accumulate, which lowers the blood's pH. Acidosis can also result from the body's inability to expel CO_2, which can occur during pneumonia, emphysema, and other respiratory disorders. Perhaps the single most common cause of acidosis is uncontrolled diabetes, in which acids normally excreted in the urinary system are instead retained by the body.

Application *The Environment*

Carbon-Monoxide Poisoning

Standing on a street corner in any major city exposes a person to above-normal concentrations of carbon monoxide from automobile exhaust. Carbon monoxide also reacts with hemoglobin. The following reaction takes place in the capillaries of the lung.

$$Hb + CO \rightarrow HbCO$$

Unlike CO_2 or O_2, CO binds strongly to hemoglobin. Carboxyhemoglobin, HbCO, is 200 times more stable than oxyhemoglobin, HbO_2. So as blood circulates, more and more CO molecules bind to hemoglobin, reducing the amount of O_2 binding sites available for transport. Eventually, CO occupies so many hemoglobin binding sites that cells die from lack of oxygen. Symptoms of carbon-monoxide poisoning include headache, mental confusion, dizziness, weakness, nausea, loss of muscular control, and decreased heart rate and respiratory rate. The victim loses consciousness and will die without treatment.

If the condition is caught in time, a victim of carbon-monoxide poisoning can be revived by breathing pure oxygen. This treatment causes carboxyhemoglobin to be converted slowly to oxyhemoglobin according to the following chemical equation.

$$O_2 + HbCO \rightarrow CO + HbO_2$$

Mild carbon-monoxide poisoning usually does not have long-term effects. In severe cases, cells are destroyed. Damage to brain cells is irreversible. The level of danger posed by carbon monoxide depends on two factors: the concentration of the gas in the air and the amount of time that a person is exposed to the gas. Table 5A shows the effects of increasing levels of carbon monoxide in the bloodstream. These effects vary considerably depending on a person's activity level and metabolic rate.

▲

Carbon-monoxide detectors are now available to reduce the risk of poisoning from defective home heating systems. The Consumer Products Safety Commission recommends that all homes have a CO detector with a UL label.

TABLE 5A

SYMPTOMS OF CO POISONING AT INCREASING LEVELS OF CO EXPOSURE AND CONCENTRATION		
Concentration of CO in air (ppm)*	Hemoglobin molecules as HbCO	Visible effects
100 for 1 hour or less	10% or less	no visible symptoms
500 for 1 hour or less	20%	mild to throbbing headache, some dizziness, impaired perception
500 for an extended period of time	30–50%	headache, confusion, nausea, dizziness, muscular weakness, fainting
1000 for 1 hour or less	50–80%	coma, convulsions, respiratory failure, death

* ppm is parts per million.

S.T.E.M.
Application *Biochemistry*

Macromolecules

Large organic polymers are called macromolecules (the prefix *macro* means "large"). Macromolecules play important roles in living systems. Most macromolecules essential to life belong to four main classes, three of which we know as nutrients in food:

1. **Proteins** Hair, tendons, ligaments, and silk are made of protein. Other proteins act as hormones, transport substances throughout the body, and fight infections. Enzymes are proteins that control the body's chemical reactions. Proteins provide energy, yielding 17 kJ/g.

2. **Carbohydrates** Sugars, starches, and cellulose are carbohydrates. Carbohydrates are sources of energy, yielding 17 kJ/g.

3. **Lipids** Fats, oils, waxes, and steroids are lipids, nonpolar substances that do not dissolve in water. Fats are sources of energy, yielding 38 kJ/g.

4. **Nucleic acids** DNA and RNA are nucleic acids. In most organisms, DNA is used to store hereditary information, and RNA helps to assemble proteins.

Proteins

Proteins are macromolecules formed by condensation reactions between amino acid monomers. Proteins contain carbon, oxygen, hydrogen, nitrogen, and usually some sulfur. Some of the amino acids that form proteins are shown below.

All amino acids have a carboxyl group, —COOH, and an amino group, —NH₂, attached to a central carbon atom, which is also attached to hydrogen, —H. Amino acids differ from one another at the fourth bond site of the central carbon, which is attached to a group of atoms (called an *R* group). *R* groups differ from one amino acid to another, as shown in the structures for several amino acids below. The proteins of all organisms contain a set of 20 common amino acids. Amino acids link together with condensation reactions.

There are 22 standard amino acids. Each protein has its own unique sequence of amino acids. A complex organism has at least several thousand different proteins, each with a special structure and function. There can be so many proteins because, just as the 26 letters of the English alphabet give us thousands of words, 22 amino acids arranged in different ways can create a similar number of proteins.

◄ Amino acids have the same general structure. These examples show some of the variations within this class of compounds.

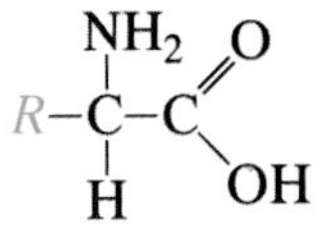

General structure

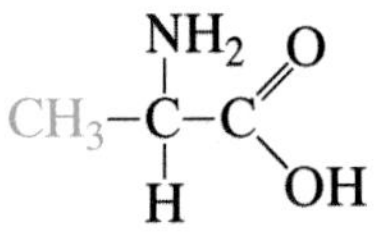

Alanine 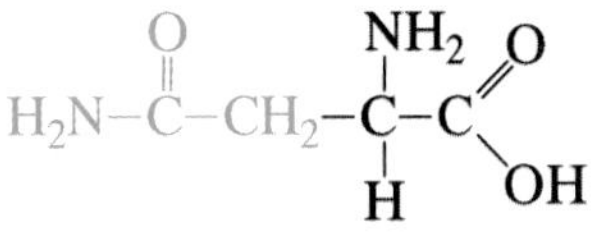 Asparagine 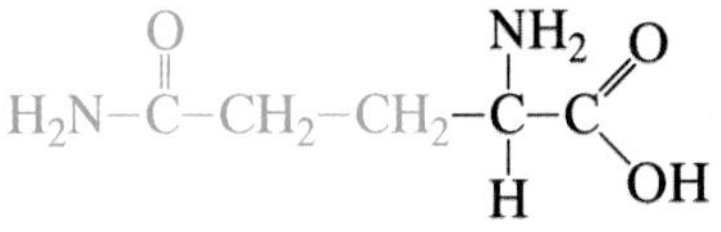 Glutamine

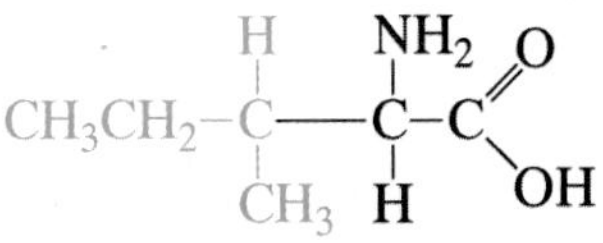

Isoleucine 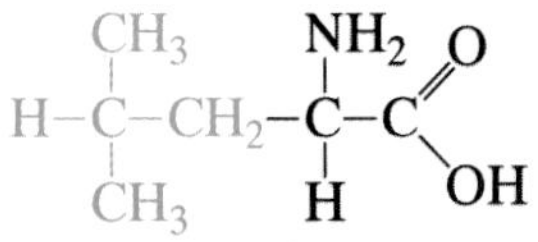 Leucine 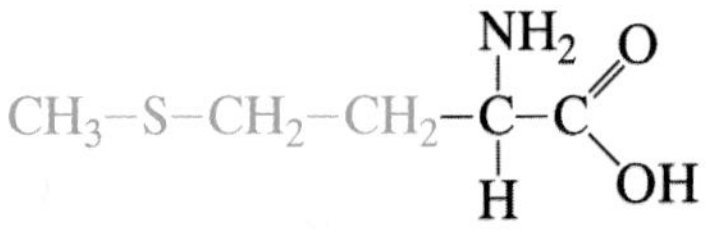 Methionine

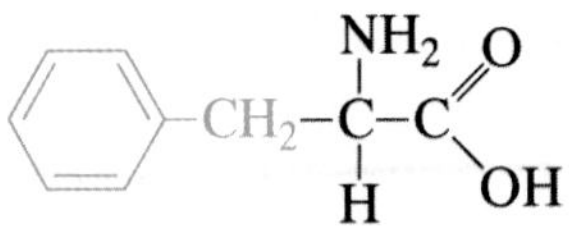

Phenylalanine 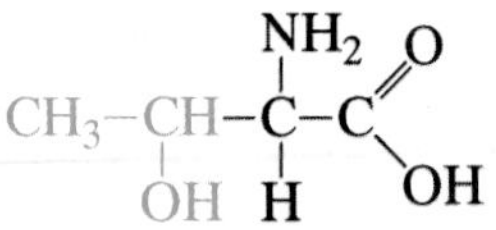 Threonine 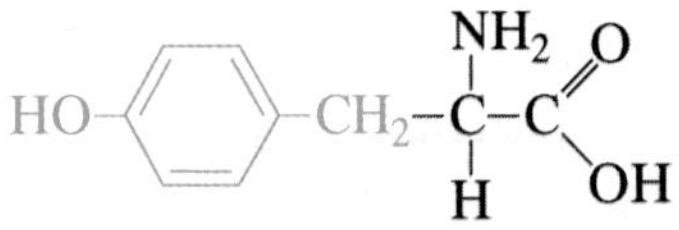 Tyrosine

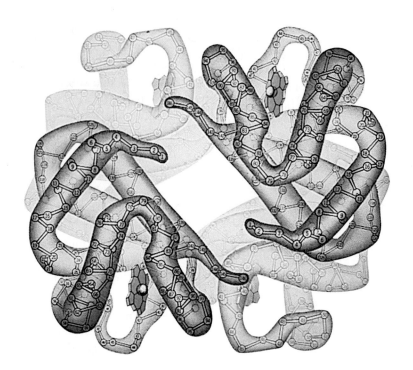

► Hemoglobin is a complex protein made of hundreds of amino acids. Its three-dimensional shape is called a tertiary structure. Tertiary structures break down when a protein is denatured.

For instance, *insulin*, a hormone that helps the body regulate the level of sugar in the blood, is made up of two linked chains. The chains are held together by S—S bonds between sulfur atoms in two cysteine amino acids. Insulin is one of the smaller proteins, containing only 51 amino acids. In contrast, hemoglobin, which carries oxygen in the blood, is a large protein consisting of four long chains with the complicated three-dimensional structures shown above. Proteins can lose their shape (become denatured) with increases in temperature or changes in the pH of their environment.

Changing even one amino acid can change a protein's structure and function. For example, the difference between normal hemoglobin and the hemoglobin that causes sickle-cell anemia is just one amino acid substituted for another.

Enzymes

Enzymes are catalysts that alter reaction rates in the body. Some enzymes cannot bind to their substrates without the help of additional molecules. These may be *minerals*, such as calcium or iron ions, or helper molecules called *coenzymes* that play accessory roles in enzyme-catalyzed reactions. Many vitamins are coenzymes or parts of coenzymes.

Vitamin C, $C_6H_8O_6$
Water-soluble

Vitamin A, $C_{20}H_{30}O$
Fat-soluble

Vitamins are organic molecules that we cannot manufacture and hence need to get from our diets. We need vitamins and minerals to enable our enzymes to work. We need only small amounts of them, however, because they are not destroyed in biochemical reactions. Like enzymes, coenzymes and minerals can be used over and over again.

Temperature and pH have the most significant effects on the rates of reactions catalyzed by enzymes. Most enzymes work best in a solution of approximately neutral pH. Most body cells have a pH of 7.4. However, some enzymes function only in acidic or basic environments.

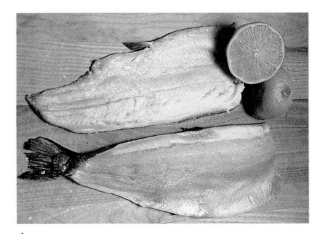

The protein in fish is denatured by the low pH of lime juice. Notice that the flesh shown with the limes has turned white compared with the flesh at normal pH.

For example, pepsin, the collective term for the digestive enzymes found in the human stomach, works best at a very acidic pH of about 1.5. Cells that line the stomach secrete hydrochloric acid to produce this low-pH environment. When food travels down the digestive tract, to the intestine, it carries these enzymes with it. In the intestine, stomach enzymes stop working, because sodium bicarbonate in the intestine raises the surroundings to a pH of 8. Intestinal enzymes are formed by the pancreas and work best at pH 8.

Most chemical reactions speed up with increases in temperature. However, high temperatures (above about 60°C) destroy, or denature, proteins by changing their three-dimensional structure. For example, the protein in an egg or a piece of meat denatures when the egg or meat is cooked. Heating can preserve food by denaturing the enzymes of organisms that cause decay. In milk pasteurization, the milk is heated to denature enzymes that would allow it to sour. Refrigeration and freezing also help preserve food by slowing the enzyme reactions that cause decay. The protein in the fish in the above photo has been denatured by the lime juice instead of cooking to be more tasty.

Carbohydrates

Carbohydrates are sugars, starches, and related compounds. The monomers of carbohydrates are monosaccharides, or simple sugars, such as fructose and glucose, shown at the top right. A monosaccharide contains carbon, hydrogen, and oxygen in about a 1:2:1 ratio, respectively.

Monosaccharides chain representation

Two monosaccharides may be joined together to form a disaccharide. Sucrose, shown below, is a disaccharide. A disaccharide can be hydrolyzed to produce the monosaccharides that formed it. By a series of condensation reactions, many monosaccharides can be joined to form a polymer called a polysaccharide (commonly known as a complex carbohydrate).

Lactose—made from glucose and galactose

Sucrose—made from glucose and fructose

Carbon Family   **R53**

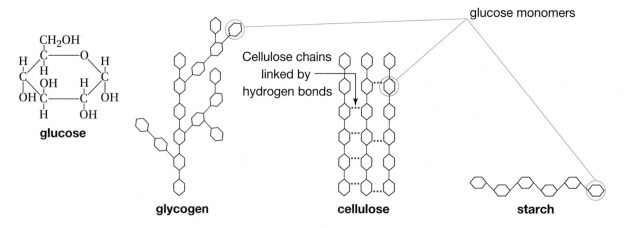

Glucose is the structural unit for glycogen, cellulose, and starch. Notice that these three polymers differ in the arrangement of glucose monomers.

Three important polysaccharides made of glucose monomers are glycogen, starch, and cellulose. The liver and muscles of animals remove glucose from the blood and condense it into glycogen, which can later be hydrolyzed back into glucose and used to supply energy as needed.

Starch consists of two kinds of glucose polymers. It is hydrolyzed in plants to form glucose for energy and for building material to produce more cells. The structural polysaccharide cellulose is probably the most common organic compound on Earth. Glucose monomers link cellulose chains together at the hydroxyl groups to form cellulose fibers. Cotton fibers consist almost entirely of cellulose.

Lipids

Lipids are a varied group of organic compounds that share one property: they are not very soluble in water. Lipids contain a high proportion of C—H bonds, and they dissolve in nonpolar organic solvents, such as ether, chloroform, and benzene.

Fatty acids, such as the ones shown below, are the simplest lipids. A fatty acid consists of an unbranched chain of carbon and hydrogen atoms with a carboxyl group at one end. Bonding within the carbon chain gives both saturated and unsaturated fatty acids, just as the simple hydrocarbons can be saturated or unsaturated.

The bonds in a carboxyl group are polar, and so the carboxyl end of a fatty acid attracts water molecules.

Palmitic acid — saturated

These examples of common fatty acids show the differences in saturation level.

Oleic acid — monounsaturated

Linoleic acid — polyunsaturated

This phospholipid molecule contains two fatty-acid chains.

The lipid bilayer is the framework of the cell membrane.

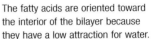

The fatty acids are oriented toward the interior of the bilayer because they have a low attraction for water.

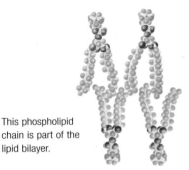

This phospholipid chain is part of the lipid bilayer.

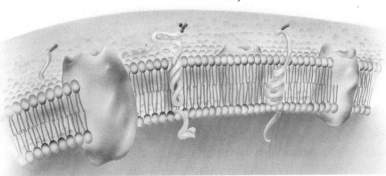

The carbon-hydrogen bonds of a lipid's hydrocarbon chain are nonpolar, however. The polar end will dissolve in water, and the other end will dissolve in nonpolar organic compounds. This behavior enables fatty acids to form membranes when they are dropped into water. It also gives soaps and detergents their cleaning power. The dual solubility of the lipids enables soapy water to "wash away" what it normally could not.

Lipids are the main compounds in biological membranes, such as the cell membrane. Because lipids are insoluble, the lipid bilayer of a cell membrane is adapted to keep the contents of the cell inside separated from the outer environment of the cell.

The structural component of a cell membrane is a phospholipid. The "head" of the phospholipid is polar, and the fatty-acid tails are nonpolar, as shown in the model above.

Most fatty acids found in foods and soaps belong to a class of compounds called triglycerides. The fat content shown on a nutrition label for packaged food represents a mixture of the triglycerides in the food. Triglycerides have the general structure shown below.

Fatty acids are usually combined with other molecules to form classes of biomolecules called glycolipids (made from a carbohydrate and a lipid) or lipoproteins (made from a lipid and a protein). These compounds are also parts of more-complex lipids found in the body.

▶ Triglycerides are made from three long-chain fatty acids bonded to a glycerol backbone.

Saturated fatty acids + Glycerol ⟶ Triglyceride

Nucleic Acids

Nucleic acids are macromolecules that transmit genetic information. Deoxyribonucleic acid (DNA) is the material that contains the genetic information that all organisms pass on to their offspring during reproduction. This information includes instructions for making proteins as well as for making the other nucleic acid, ribonucleic acid (RNA). RNA assists in protein synthesis by helping to coordinate protein assembly.

Nucleotides are the monomers of nucleic acids. A nucleotide has three parts: one or more phosphate groups, a sugar containing five carbon atoms, and a ring-shaped nitrogen base, as shown below. RNA nucleotides contain the simple sugar ribose. DNA nucleotides contain deoxyribose (ribose stripped of one oxygen atom). Structures for both of these sugars are shown on a previous page. Cells contain nucleotides with one, two, or three phosphate groups attached. Besides being the monomers of nucleic acids, several nucleotides play other roles.

ATP structure

For example, adenosine triphosphate (ATP) is the nucleotide that supplies the energy for many metabolic reactions. ATP is shown above.

The bases in nucleic acids attract each other in pairs, a phenomenon known as base-pairing. DNA is made of four different nucleotides—those containing the bases adenine (A), thymine (T), guanine (G), and cytosine (C). The attraction between base pairs is hydrogen bonding. Adenine forms hydrogen bonds with thymine. Similarly, cytosine bonds to guanine. This base-pairing holds strands of DNA together.

Adenine   Thymine   Cytosine   Guanine

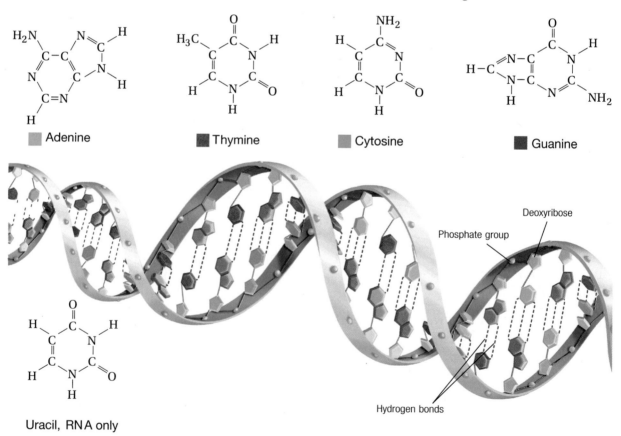

Deoxyribose

Phosphate group

Hydrogen bonds

Uracil, RNA only

S.T.E.M.
Application *Chemical Industry*

Silicon and Silicates

Silicon is as important in the mineral world as carbon is in living systems. Silicon dioxide and silicates make up about 87% of Earth's crust. Silicates are a class of compounds containing silicon, oxygen, one or more metals, and possibly hydrogen. Many mineral compounds are silicates. Sand is probably the most familiar silicate.

Glasses consist of 75% silicate. Borosilicate glass is the special heat-resistant glass used in making laboratory beakers and flasks. The addition of 5% boron oxide to the glass increases the softening temperature of the glass. Because boron and silicon atoms have roughly similar radii, these atoms can be substituted for one another to make borosilicate glass.

Asbestos is the name given to a class of fibrous magnesium silicate minerals. Asbestos is very strong and flexible, and it does not burn, so it was widely used as a heat-insulating material.

It is now known that asbestos is a carcinogen. When handled, asbestos releases dust particles that are easily inhaled and can cause lung cancer. Asbestos materials found in older homes and buildings should be removed by firms licensed by the Environmental Protection Agency (EPA).

Silicones

Silicones are a class of organic silicon polymers composed of silicon, carbon, oxygen, and hydrogen. The silicon chain is held together by bonding with the oxygen atoms. Each silicon atom is also bonded to different hydrocarbon groups to create a variety of silicone structures.

Silicones are widely used for their adhesive and protective properties. They have good electric insulating properties and are water-repellent. Some silicones have the character of oils or greases, so they are used as lubricants. Silicones are also used in automobile and furniture polishes as protective agents.

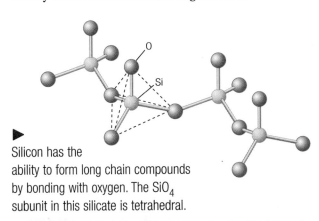

▶ Silicon has the ability to form long chain compounds by bonding with oxygen. The SiO_4 subunit in this silicate is tetrahedral.

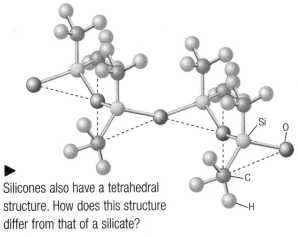

▶ Silicones also have a tetrahedral structure. How does this structure differ from that of a silicate?

▲ Silicates exist in a variety of mineral forms, including mica.

▲ Because of their protective properties, silicones are used in a number of consumer products, from cosmetics to caulkings.

S.T.E.M.
Application *Technology*

Semiconductors

When electrons can move freely through a material, the material is a conductor. The electrons in metals are loosely held and require little additional energy to move from one vacant orbital to the next. A set of overlapping orbitals is called a *conduction band*. Because electrons can easily jump to the conduction band, metals conduct electricity when only a very small voltage is applied.

Semiconductors conduct a current if the voltage applied is large enough to excite the outer-level electrons of their atoms into the higher energy levels. With semiconductors, more energy, and so a higher voltage, is required to cause conduction. By contrast, nonmetals are insulators because they do not conduct at ordinary voltages. The model below shows the energy required to excite electrons in metals, semiconductors, and insulators.

Semiconductor devices include transistors; diodes, including light-emitting diodes (LEDs); some lasers; and photovoltaic cells ("solar" cells). Though silicon is the basis of most semiconductor devices in the computer industry, pure silicon has little use as a semiconductor. Instead, small amounts of impurities are added to increase its conductive properties. Adding impurities to silicon is called *doping*, and the substances added are *dopants*. The dopant is usually incorporated into just the surface layer of a silicon chip. Typical dopants include the Group 15 elements phosphorus and arsenic and the Group 13 elements boron, aluminum, gallium, and indium.

A silicon atom has four electrons in its outer energy level. Group 13 atoms have three and Group 15 atoms have five. Adding boron to silicon creates a mix of atoms having four valence electrons and atoms having three valence electrons. Boron atoms form only three bonds with silicon, whereas silicon forms four bonds with other silicon atoms.

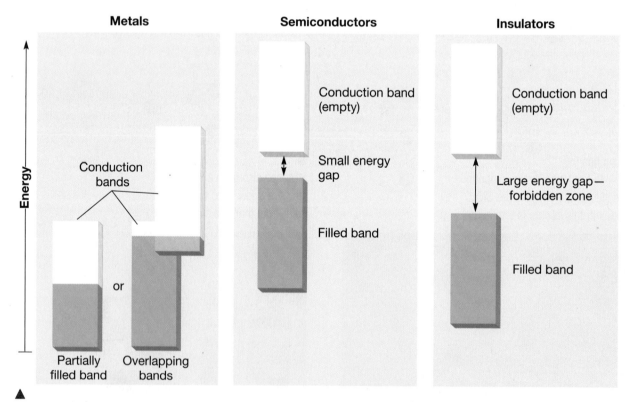

▲ This model shows the difference in the levels of energy required to excite electrons into the conduction band in metals, semiconductors, and insulators. The forbidden zone is too great an energy gap in insulators for these elements to function as conductors. The energy gap for semiconductors is small enough that it can be crossed under certain conditions.

																	Group 18
1 H																	2 He

Dopants

Semiconductor elements

Forms semiconductor compounds

Group 1 Group 2 — Group 13 Group 14 Group 15 Group 16 Group 17

3 Li, 4 Be, 5 B, 6 C, 7 N, 8 O, 9 F, 10 Ne

11 Na, 12 Mg, Group 3–Group 12, 13 Al, 14 Si, 15 P, 16 S, 17 Cl, 18 Ar

19 K, 20 Ca, 21 Sc, 22 Ti, 23 V, 24 Cr, 25 Mn, 26 Fe, 27 Co, 28 Ni, 29 Cu, 30 Zn, 31 Ga, 32 Ge, 33 As, 34 Se, 35 Br, 36 Kr

37 Rb, 38 Sr, 39 Y, 40 Zr, 41 Nb, 42 Mo, 43 Tc, 44 Ru, 45 Rh, 46 Pd, 47 Ag, 48 Cd, 49 In, 50 Sn, 51 Sb, 52 Te, 53 I, 54 Xe

55 Cs, 56 Ba, 57 La, 72 Hf, 73 Ta, 74 W, 75 Re, 76 Os, 77 Ir, 78 Pt, 79 Au, 80 Hg, 81 Tl, 82 Pb, 83 Bi, 84 Po, 85 At, 86 Rn

87 Fr, 88 Ra, 89 Ac

▲ Semiconductor elements and dopants fall in the metalloid region of the periodic table. Semiconductor compounds often contain metals.

The unbonded spot between a silicon atom and a boron atom is a hole that a free electron can occupy. Because this hole "attracts" an electron, it is viewed as if it were positively charged. Semiconductors that are doped with boron, aluminum, or gallium are *p-type semiconductors*, the *p* standing for "positive." P-type semiconductors conduct electricity better than pure silicon because they provide spaces that moving electrons can occupy as they flow through the material.

Doping silicon with phosphorus or arsenic produces the opposite effect. When phosphorus is added to silicon, it forms four bonds to silicon atoms and has a nonbonding electron left over. This extra electron is free to move through the material when a voltage is applied, thus increasing its conductivity compared with pure silicon. These extra electrons have a negative charge. Therefore, the material is an *n-type semiconductor*. The model below compares these two types of semiconductors.

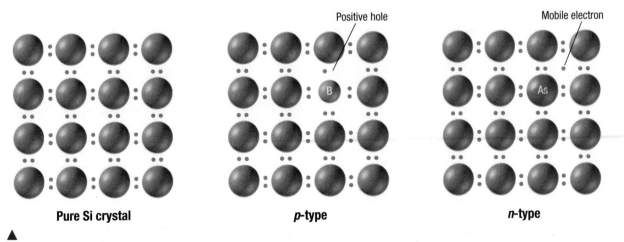

Pure Si crystal   *p*-type   *n*-type

▲ Each silicon atom in the pure crystal is surrounded by four pairs of electrons. The p-type semiconductor model contains an atom of boron with a hole that an electron can occupy. The n-type semiconductor model contains an atom of arsenic, which provides the extra electron that can move through the crystal.

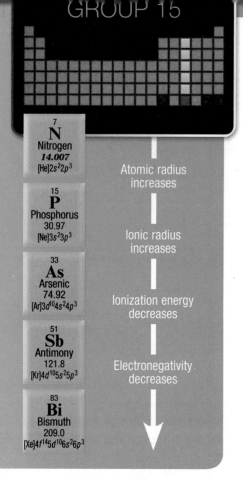

GROUP 15

7 **N** Nitrogen *14.007* [He]$2s^2 2p^3$	Atomic radius increases
15 **P** Phosphorus 30.97 [Ne]$3s^2 3p^3$	Ionic radius increases
33 **As** Arsenic 74.92 [Ar]$3d^{10}4s^2 4p^3$	Ionization energy decreases
51 **Sb** Antimony 121.8 [Kr]$4d^{10}5s^2 5p^3$	Electronegativity decreases
83 **Bi** Bismuth 209.0 [Xe]$4f^{14}5d^{10}6s^2 6p^3$	

Nitrogen Family

Characteristics

▷ consist of two nonmetals (nitrogen and phosphorus), two metalloids (arsenic and antimony), and one metal (bismuth)

▷ Nitrogen is most commonly found as atmospheric N_2; phosphorus as phosphate rock; and arsenic, antimony, and bismuth as sulfides or oxides. Antimony and bismuth are also found as free elements.

▷ range from very abundant elements (nitrogen and phosphorus) to relatively rare elements (arsenic, antimony, and bismuth)

▷ consist of atoms that contain five electrons in their outermost energy level

▷ tend to form covalent compounds, most commonly with oxidation numbers of +3 or +5

▷ exist in two or more allotropic forms, except nitrogen and bismuth

▷ are solids at room temperature, except nitrogen

▷ The discovery of the last member of the nitrogen family has been reported but not confirmed.

▲ You can see the contrast in physical properties among the elements of this family. Arsenic, antimony, and bismuth are shown.

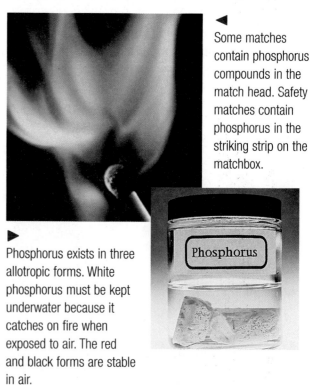

◀ Some matches contain phosphorus compounds in the match head. Safety matches contain phosphorus in the striking strip on the matchbox.

▶ Phosphorus exists in three allotropic forms. White phosphorus must be kept underwater because it catches on fire when exposed to air. The red and black forms are stable in air.

(bc) ©Myron Jay Dorf/Corbis

Common Reactions

With Oxygen to Form Oxides

Example: $P_4(s) + 5O_2(g) \longrightarrow P_4O_{10}(s)$

As, Sb, and Bi follow this reaction pattern but as monatomic elements. N reacts to form NO and NO_2. It also reacts as N_2 to form N_2O_3 and N_2O_5.

With Metals to Form Binary Compounds

Example: $3Mg(s) + N_2(g) \longrightarrow Mg_3N_2(s)$

Analytical Test

There are no simple analytical tests for the presence of nitrogen or phosphorus compounds in a sample. Antimony produces a pale green color in a flame test, and arsenic produces a light blue color. Arsenic, antimony, and bismuth are recognized in qualitative analyses by their characteristic sulfide colors.

Arsenic flame test   Antimony flame test

▲
Formation of sulfides is the confirmatory qualitative analysis test for the presence of bismuth, antimony, and arsenic.

Properties

GROUP 15 ELEMENTS					
Quantity	N	P*	As	Sb	Bi
Melting point (°C)	−209.86	44.1	817 (28 atm)	630.5	271.3
Boiling point (°C)	−195.8	280	613 (sublimes)	1750	1560 ± 5
Density (g/cm³)	1.25×10^{-3}	1.82	5.727	6.684	9.80
Ionization energy (kJ/mol)	1402	1012	947	834	703
Atomic radius (pm)	75	110	120	140	150
Ionic radius (pm)	146 (N^{3-})	212 (P^{3-})	—	76 (Sb^{3+})	103 (Bi^{3+})
Common oxidation number in compounds	−3, +3, +5	−3, +3, +5	+3, +5	+3, +5	+3
Crystal structure†	cubic (as a solid)	cubic	rhombohedral	hcp	rhombohedral
Hardness (Mohs scale)	none (gas)	—	3.5	3.0	2.25

* Data given apply to white phosphorus.
† Crystal structures are for the most common allotropes.

S.T.E.M.
Application *Biology*

Plants and Nitrogen

All organisms require certain elements to survive and grow. These elements include carbon, hydrogen, oxygen, nitrogen, phosphorus, potassium, sulfur, and several other elements needed in small amounts. An organism needs nitrogen to synthesize structural proteins, enzymes, and the nucleic acids DNA and RNA.

Carbon, hydrogen, and oxygen are available to plants from carbon dioxide in the air and from water in the air and the soil. Nitrogen is necessary for plants' survival. Nitrogen gas, N_2, makes up 78% of air, but most plants cannot take nitrogen out of the air and into their cells, because the triple covalent bond in N_2 is not easily broken. Plants need nitrogen in the form of a compound that they can take in and use. The process of using atmospheric N_2 to make NH_3 is called *nitrogen fixation*.

Several kinds of nitrogen-fixing bacteria live in the soil and in the root nodules of plants called legumes. Legumes obtain the nitrogen they need through a symbiotic relationship with nitrogen-fixing bacteria. Legumes include peas, beans, clover, alfalfa, and locust trees. The bacteria convert nitrogen into ammonia, NH_3, which is then absorbed by the host plants.

Because wheat, rice, corn, and potatoes cannot perform the same feat as legumes, these plants depend on nitrogen-fixing bacteria in the soil. Soil bacteria convert NH_3 into nitrate ions, NO_3^-, the form of nitrogen that can be absorbed and used by plants. These plants also often need nitrogen fertilizers to supplement the work of the bacteria. Besides supplying nitrogen, fertilizers are manufactured to contain phosphorus, potassium, and trace minerals.

▲ Nitrogen-fixing bacteria, *Rhizobium*, live in these small nodules that grow on the roots of soybeans.

▲ Soybeans are legumes that live in a symbiotic relationship with nitrogen-fixing bacteria.

(br) ©George Glod/SuperStock; (bl) ©Peter Beck/Corbis

S.T.E.M.
Application *Chemical Industry*

Fertilizers

Fertilizers can supply nitrogen to plants in the form of ammonium sulfate, ammonium nitrate, and urea, all of which are made from NH_3. Now you know why there is such a demand for ammonia. Though some soils contain sufficient concentrations of phosphorus and potassium, most soils need additional nitrogen for adequate plant growth. Ammonia, ammonium nitrate, or urea can fill that need.

Most fertilizers contain all three major plant nutrients N, P, and K and are called *complete fertilizers*. A typical complete fertilizer might contain ammonium nitrate or sodium nitrate to provide nitrogen. Calcium dihydrogen phosphate, $Ca(H_2PO_4)_2$, or the anhydrous form of phosphoric acid, P_4O_{10}, can provide phosphorus. Potassium chloride, KCl, or potassium oxide, K_2O, can provide potassium.

The proportion of each major nutrient in a fertilizer is indicated by a set of three numbers. These numbers are the N–P–K formula of the fertilizer and indicate the percentage of N, P, and K, respectively. A fertilizer graded as 6–12–6, for example, contains 6% nitrogen, 12% phosphorus, and 6% potassium by weight.

Nitrogen stimulates overall plant growth. Phosphorus promotes root growth and flowering. Potassium regulates the structures in leaves that allow CO_2 to enter the leaf and O_2 and H_2O to exit. Fertilizers are available in N–P–K formulas best suited for their intended use. For example, plants that produce large amounts of carbohydrates (sugars) need more potassium than most other types of plants. Grain crops need more phosphorus. Lawn fertilizers applied in the spring are generally high in nitrogen to stimulate shoot growth in grasses. Lawn fertilizers applied in the fall of the year should have a higher phosphorus content to stimulate root growth during the winter. Common fertilizer types are listed in Table 6A.

TABLE 6A

SOME COMMERCIAL FERTILIZERS AND USES	
Fertilizer composition (N–P–K)	Uses
1–2–1 ratio 10–20–10 15–30–15	early-spring application for trees and shrubs with flowers and fruit; general-purpose feedings of the following: cucumbers, peppers, tomatoes
3–1–2 ratio 12–4–8 15–5–10 21–7–4 16–4–8 20–5–10	lawns and general-purpose feedings of the following: trees, shrubs, most berries, apple trees, grapes, vines, walnut trees, broccoli, cabbage, carrots, onions
High nitrogen 33–0–0 21–0–0 40–4–4 36–6–6	pecan trees, lawns, early feedings of corn
Balanced 13–13–13	general-purpose feeding of the following: broccoli, cabbage, melons, potatoes
Special purpose: acid-loving flowering shrubs 12–10–4	azaleas, rhododendrons, camellias, gardenias
Special purpose 18–24–16	roses
Special purpose: flowering 12–55–6	flowering plants and shrubs (annuals and perennials)
Special purpose: root growth 5–20–10	starter fertilizer for transplants

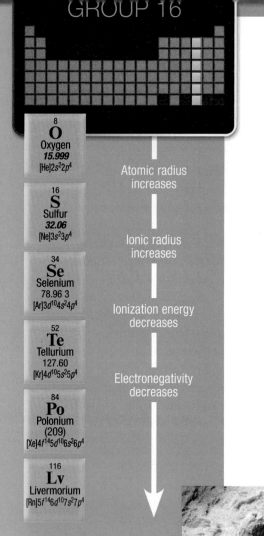

GROUP 16

Oxygen Family

8
O
Oxygen
15.999
[He]$2s^2 2p^4$

16
S
Sulfur
32.06
[Ne]$3s^2 3p^4$

34
Se
Selenium
78.96 3
[Ar]$3d^{10} 4s^2 4p^4$

52
Te
Tellurium
127.60
[Kr]$4d^{10} 5s^2 5p^4$

84
Po
Polonium
(209)
[Xe]$4f^{14} 5d^{10} 6s^2 6p^4$

116
Lv
Livermorium
[Rn]$5f^{14} 6d^{10} 7s^2 7p^4$

Atomic radius increases

Ionic radius increases

Ionization energy decreases

Electronegativity decreases

Characteristics

▷ occur naturally as free elements and in combined states

▷ consist of three nonmetals (oxygen, sulfur, and selenium), one metalloid (tellurium), and one metal (polonium)

▷ consist of atoms that have six electrons in their outermost energy level

▷ tend to form covalent compounds with other elements

▷ exist in several allotropic forms

▷ tend to exist as diatomic and polyatomic molecules, such as O_2, O_3, S_6, S_8, and Se_8

▷ commonly exist in compounds with the −2 oxidation state but often exhibit other oxidation states

▷ The last member of the oxygen family, livermorium, is a synthetic element not found in nature.

Orthorhombic

►
Sulfur is found naturally in underground deposits and in the steam vents near volcanoes.

►
Two allotropic forms of sulfur are orthorhombic and monoclinic. Each has a different crystal structure.

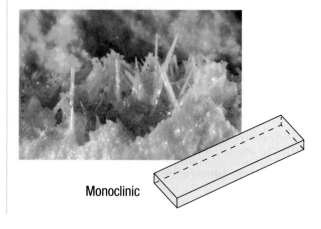
Monoclinic

▲
Sulfur exists in combined forms in many minerals. Iron pyrite, FeS_2, black galena, PbS, and yellow orpiment, As_2S_3, are shown.

(cr) ©Charles D. Winters/Photo Researchers, Inc; (br) ©sciencephotos/Alamy Images; (cl) ©Victor Englebert/Photo Researchers, Inc

Common Reactions

With Metals to Form Binary Compounds

Example: $8Mg(s) + S_8(l) \longrightarrow 8MgS(s)$

O_2, Se, and Te follow this pattern in reacting with Na, K, Ca, Mg, and Al.

With Oxygen to Form Oxides

Example: $Se(s) + O_2(g) \longrightarrow SeO_2(s)$

S, Te, and Po follow this pattern. S, Se, and Te can form SO_3, SeO_3, and TeO_3.

With Halogens to Form Binary Compounds

Example: $S_8(l) + 8Cl_2(g) \longrightarrow 8SCl_2(l)$

O, Se, Te, and Po follow this pattern in reacting with F_2, Cl_2, Br_2, and I_2.

With Hydrogen to Form Binary Compounds

$2H_2(g) + O_2(g) \longrightarrow 2H_2O(l)$

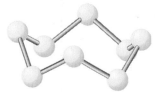

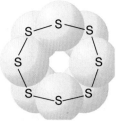

▲ Sulfur exists as S_8 molecules in which the atoms are bonded in a ring, as shown by the ball-and-stick and space-filling models.

Analytical Test

There is no simple analytical test to identify all elements of this family. Selenium and tellurium can be identified by flame tests. A light blue flame is characteristic of selenium, and a green flame is characteristic of tellurium. Oxygen can be identified by the splint test, in which a glowing splint bursts into flame when thrust into oxygen. Elemental sulfur is typically identified by its physical characteristics, especially its color and its properties when heated. It melts to form a viscous brown liquid and burns with a blue flame.

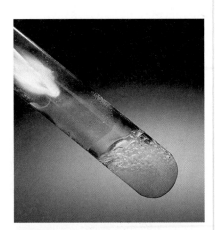

▲ A glowing splint thrust into oxygen bursts into a bright flame.

▲ Sulfur burns with a characteristically deep blue flame.

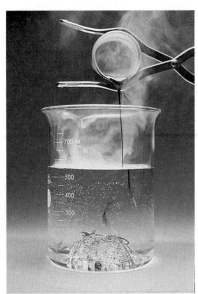

▲ Molten sulfur forms elastic strands with rapid cooling.

Properties

GROUP 16 ELEMENTS					
	O	S	Se	Te	Po
Melting point (°C)	−218.4	119.0	217	449.8	254
Boiling point (°C)	−182.962	444.674	685	989.9	962
Density (g/cm³)	1.429×10^{-3}	1.96	4.82	6.24	9.4
Ionization energy (kJ/mol)	1314	1000	941	869	812
Atomic radius (pm)	73	103	119	142	168
Ionic radius (pm)	140	184	198	221	–
Common oxidation number in compounds	−2	−2, +4, +6	−2, +2, +4, +6	−2, +2, +4, +6	−2, +2, +4, +6
Crystal structure*	orthorhombic, rhombohedral, cubic (when solid)	orthorhombic, monoclinic	hexagonal	hexagonal	cubic, rhombohedral
Hardness (Mohs scale)	none (gas)	2.0	2.0	2.3	–

* Most elements of this family can have more than one crystal structure.

S.T.E.M.

Application *Chemical Industry*

Oxides

Oxides of the reactive metals are ionic compounds. The oxide ion from any soluble oxide reacts immediately with water to form hydroxide ions as represented by the following equation:

$$O^{2-}(aq) + H_2O(l) \longrightarrow 2OH^-(aq)$$

The reactive metal oxides of Groups 1 and 2 react vigorously with water and release a large amount of energy as heat. The product of the reaction is a metal hydroxide. The following equation is an example of this reaction:

$$Na_2O(s) + H_2O(l) \longrightarrow 2NaOH(aq)$$

A basic oxide can be thought of as the dehydrated form of a hydroxide base. Oxides of the less reactive metals, such as magnesium, can be prepared by using thermal decomposition to drive off the water.

$$Mg(OH)_2(s) \xrightarrow{\text{heat}} MgO(s) + H_2O(g)$$

Hydroxides of the reactive metals of Group 1 are too stable to decompose in this manner.

If a hydroxide formed by a metal oxide is water-soluble, it dissolves to form a basic solution. An oxide that reacts with water to form a basic solution is called a basic oxide or a basic anhydride. Table 7A on the next page lists oxides that form basic solutions with water.

Molecular Oxides

Nonmetals, located on the right side of the periodic table, form molecular oxides. For example, sulfur forms two gaseous oxides: sulfur dioxide, SO_2, and sulfur trioxide, SO_3. In reactions typical of nonmetal oxides, each of the sulfur oxides reacts with water to form an oxyacid.

An oxide that reacts with water to form an acid is called an acidic oxide or an acid anhydride. As with the basic anhydrides, each acid anhydride can be thought of as the dehydrated form of the appropriate oxyacid. For example, when sulfuric acid decomposes, the loss of H_2O leaves the oxide SO_3, which is an anhydride.

$$H_2SO_4(aq) \xrightarrow{\text{heat}} H_2O(g) + SO_3(g)$$

Amphoteric Oxides

Table 7A lists some common oxides of main-group elements. You can see that the active metal oxides are basic and that the nonmetal oxides are acidic. Between these lies a group of oxides, the *amphoteric oxides*. The bonding in amphoteric oxides is intermediate between ionic and covalent bonding. As a result, oxides of this type show behavior intermediate between that of acidic oxides and basic oxides and react as both acids and bases.

Aluminum oxide, Al_2O_3, is a typical amphoteric oxide. With hydrochloric acid, aluminum oxide acts as a base. The reaction produces a salt and water.

$$Al_2O_3(s) + 6HCl(aq) \longrightarrow 2AlCl_3(aq) + 3H_2O(l)$$

With aqueous sodium hydroxide, aluminum oxide acts as an acid. The reaction forms a soluble ionic compound and water. That compound contains aluminate ions, AlO_2^-. (The AlO_2^- formula is used here rather than the more precise hydrated aluminate formula, $Al(OH)_4^-$.)

$$Al_2O_3(s) + 2NaOH(aq) \longrightarrow 2NaAlO_2(aq) + H_2O(l)$$

Reactions of Oxides

In the reaction between an acid and a metal oxide, the products are a salt and water—the same as the products in a neutralization reaction. For example, when magnesium oxide reacts with dilute sulfuric acid, magnesium sulfate and water are produced.

$$MgO(s) + H_2SO_4(dil.\ aq) \longrightarrow MgSO_4(aq) + H_2O(l)$$

The reaction between a basic metal oxide, such as MgO, and an acidic nonmetal oxide, such as CO_2, tends to produce an oxygen-containing salt. The dry oxides are mixed and heated without water. Salts such as metal carbonates, phosphates, and sulfates can be made by this synthesis reaction.

$$MgO(s) + CO_2(g) \longrightarrow MgCO_3(s)$$
$$6CaO(s) + P_4O_{10}(s) \longrightarrow 2Ca_3(PO_4)_2(s)$$
$$CaO(s) + SO_3(g) \longrightarrow CaSO_4(s)$$

Reactions of Hydroxides with Nonmetal Oxides

Nonmetal oxides tend to be acid anhydrides. The reaction of a hydroxide base with a nonmetal oxide is an acid-base reaction. The product is either a salt or a salt and water, depending on the identities and relative quantities of reactants. For example, 2 mol of the hydroxide base sodium hydroxide and 1 mol of the nonmetal oxide carbon dioxide form sodium carbonate, which is a salt, and water.

$$CO_2(g) + 2NaOH(aq) \longrightarrow Na_2CO_3(aq) + H_2O(l)$$

However, if sodium hydroxide is limited, only sodium hydrogen carbonate is produced.

$$CO_2(g) + NaOH(aq) \longrightarrow NaHCO_3(aq)$$

TABLE 7A

PERIODICITY OF ACIDIC AND BASIC OXIDES OF MAIN-GROUP ELEMENTS

Group Number						
1	2	13	14	15	16	17
Li_2O basic	BeO amphoteric	B_2O_3 acidic	CO_2 acidic	N_2O_5 acidic		
Na_2O basic	MgO basic	Al_2O_3 amphoteric	SiO_2 acidic	P_4O_{10} acidic	SO_3 acidic	Cl_2O acidic
K_2O basic	CaO basic	Ga_2O_3 amphoteric	GeO_2 amphoteric	As_4O_6 amphoteric	SeO_3 acidic	
Rb_2O basic	SrO basic	In_2O_3 basic	SnO_2 amphoteric	Sb_4O_6 amphoteric	TeO_3 acidic	I_2O_5 acidic
Cs_2O basic	BaO basic	Tl_2O_3 basic	PbO_2 amphoteric	Bi_2O_3 basic		

S.T.E.M.
Application *The Environment*

Ozone

Ozone, O_3, is an allotrope of oxygen that is important for life on Earth. Like O_2, O_3 is a gas at room temperature. However, unlike O_2, O_3 is a poisonous bluish gas with an irritating odor at high concentrations. The triatomic ozone molecule is angular (bent) with a bond angle of about 116.5°. The O—O bonds in ozone are shorter and stronger than a single bond but longer and weaker than a double bond. The ozone molecule is best represented by two resonance hybrid structures.

$$\overset{\cdot\cdot}{:}\overset{\overset{\cdot\cdot}{O}\cdot\cdot}{O}\overset{}{\underset{\overset{\cdot\cdot}{O}:}{}} \quad \longleftrightarrow \quad :\overset{\overset{\cdot\cdot}{O}\cdot\cdot}{O}\overset{}{\underset{\cdot\cdot}{O}}\overset{\cdot\cdot}{:}$$

Ozone forms naturally in Earth's atmosphere more than 24 km above the Earth's surface in a layer called the stratosphere. There, O_2 molecules absorb energy from ultraviolet light and split into free oxygen atoms.

$$O_2(g) \xrightarrow{\text{ultraviolet light}} 2O$$

A free oxygen atom has an unpaired electron and is highly reactive. A chemical species that has one or more unpaired or unshared electrons is referred to as a *free radical*. A free radical is a short-lived fragment of a molecule. The oxygen free radical can react with a molecule of O_2 to produce an ozone molecule.

$$O + O_2(g) \longrightarrow O_3(g)$$

A molecule of O_3 can then absorb ultraviolet light and split to produce O_2 and a free oxygen atom.

$$O_3(g) \xrightarrow{\text{ultraviolet light}} O_2(g) + O$$

The production and breakdown of ozone in the stratosphere are examples of *photochemical* processes, in which light causes a chemical reaction.

In this way, O_3 is constantly formed and destroyed in the stratosphere, and its concentration is determined by the balance among these reactions. The breakdown of ozone absorbs the sun's intense ultraviolet light in the range of wavelengths between 290 nm and 320 nm.

Light of these wavelengths damages and kills living cells, so if these wavelengths were to reach Earth's surface in large amounts, life would be impossible. Even now, the normal amount of ultraviolet light reaching Earth's surface is a major cause of skin cancer and the damage to DNA molecules that causes mutations. One life form that is very sensitive to ultraviolet radiation is the phytoplankton in the oceans. These organisms carry out photosynthesis and are the first level of oceanic food webs.

Ozone and Air Pollution

Ozone in the lower atmosphere is a harmful pollutant. Ozone is highly reactive and can oxidize organic compounds. The products of these reactions are harmful substances that, when mixed with air, water vapor, and dust, make up *photochemical smog*. This mixture is the smog typically found in cities.

Typically, ozone is produced in a complex series of reactions involving unburned hydrocarbons and nitrogen oxides given off from engines in the form of exhaust and from fuel-burning power plants. When fuel burns explosively in the cylinder of an internal-combustion engine, some of the nitrogen in the cylinder also combines with oxygen to form NO, a very reactive nitrogen oxide free radical.

$$N_2(g) + O_2(g) \longrightarrow 2NO$$

When the free radical reaches the air, it reacts with oxygen to produce NO_2 radicals, which react with water in the air to produce HNO_3.

$$2NO + O_2(g) \longrightarrow 2NO_2$$
$$3NO_2 + H_2O(l) \longrightarrow NO + 2HNO_3(aq)$$

In sunlight, nitrogen dioxide decomposes to give nitric oxide and an atom of oxygen. Note that the NO produced is free to undergo the previous reaction once more.

$$NO_2 \xrightarrow{\text{sunlight}} NO + O$$

Just as it is in the stratosphere, a free oxygen atom in the lower atmosphere is highly reactive and reacts with a molecule of diatomic oxygen to form ozone.

$$O + O_2(g) \longrightarrow O_3(g)$$

S.T.E.M.
Application *Chemical Industry*

Sulfuric Acid

Sulfuric acid is the so-called "king of chemicals" because it is produced in the largest volume in the United States. It is produced by the contact process. This process starts with the production of SO_2 by burning sulfur or roasting iron pyrite, FeS_2. The purified sulfur dioxide is mixed with air and passed through hot iron pipes containing a catalyst. The contact between the catalyst, SO_2, and O_2 produces sulfur trioxide, SO_3, and gives the contact process its name. SO_3 is dissolved in concentrated H_2SO_4 to produce pyrosulfuric acid, $H_2S_2O_7$.

$$SO_3(g) + H_2SO_4(aq) \longrightarrow H_2S_2O_7(aq)$$

The pyrosulfuric acid is then diluted with water to produce sulfuric acid.

$$H_2S_2O_7(aq) + H_2O(l) \longrightarrow 2H_2SO_4(aq)$$

Properties and Uses of Sulfuric Acid

Concentrated sulfuric acid is a good oxidizing agent. During the oxidation process, sulfur is reduced from +6 to +4 or −2. The change in oxidation state for a reaction depends on the concentration of the acid and on the nature of the reducing agent used in the reaction.

Sulfuric acid is also an important dehydrating agent. Gases that do not react with H_2SO_4 can be dried by being bubbled through concentrated sulfuric acid. Organic compounds, like sucrose, are dehydrated to leave carbon, as shown by the following reaction.

$$C_{12}H_{22}O_{11}(s) + 11H_2SO_4(aq) \longrightarrow$$
$$12C(s) + 11H_2SO_4 \longrightarrow H_2O(l)$$

The decomposition of sucrose proceeds rapidly and can be quite dramatic looking.

About 60% of the sulfuric acid produced in this country is used to make superphosphate, which is a mixture of phosphate compounds used in fertilizers.

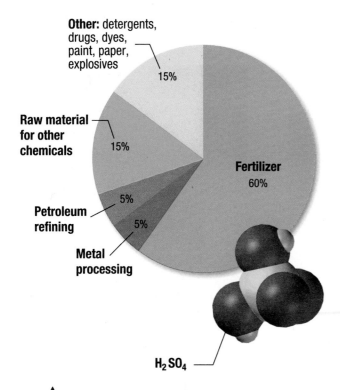

Other: detergents, drugs, dyes, paint, paper, explosives 15%

Raw material for other chemicals 15%

Petroleum refining 5%

Metal processing 5%

Fertilizer 60%

H_2SO_4

▲ Important uses of the U.S. supply of sulfuric acid

TABLE 7B

TOP TEN CHEMICALS PRODUCED IN THE UNITED STATES

Rank	Chemical	Physical state	Formula
1	sulfuric acid	*l*	H_2SO_4
2	nitrogen	*g*	N_2
3	oxygen	*g*	O_2
4	ethylene	*g*	C_2H_4
5	calcium oxide (lime)	*s*	CaO
6	ammonia	*g*	NH_3
7	phosphoric acid	*l*	H_3PO_4
8	sodium hydroxide	*s*	NaOH
9	propylene	*g*	C_3H_6
10	chlorine	*g*	Cl_2

9
F
Fluorine
19.00
[He]$2s^2p^5$

17
Cl
Chlorine
35.45
[Ne]$3s^2p^5$

35
Br
Bromine
79.90
[Ar]$3d^{10}4s^2p^5$

53
I
Iodine
126.9
[Kr]$4d^{10}5s^2 5p^5$

85
At
Astatine
[Xe]$4f^{14}5d^{10}6s^2 6p^5$

Atomic radius increases

Ionic radius increases

Ionization energy decreases

Electronegativity decreases

Halogen Family

Characteristics

▷ are all nonmetals and occur in combined form in nature, mainly as metal halides

▷ are found in the rocks of Earth's crust and dissolved in sea water

▷ range from fluorine, the 13th most abundant element, to astatine, which is one of the rarest elements

▷ exist at room temperature as diatomic molecules, a gas (F_2 and Cl_2), a liquid (Br_2), and a solid (I_2 and At)

▷ consist of atoms that have seven electrons in their outermost energy level

▷ tend to gain one electron to form a halide, X^- ion, but also share electrons and have positive oxidation states

▷ are reactive, with fluorine being the most reactive of all nonmetals

▷ The discovery of the final member of the halogen family has been reported but not confirmed.

▲ Halogens are the only family that contains elements representing all three states of matter at room temperature. Chlorine is a yellowish green gas; bromine is a reddish brown liquid; and iodine is a purple-black solid.

▲ Iodine sublimes to produce a violet vapor that recrystallizes on the bottom of the flask filled with ice.

Common Reactions*

With Metals to Form Halides

Example: $Mg(s) + Cl_2(g) \longrightarrow MgCl_2(s)$
Example: $Sn(s) + 2F_2(g) \longrightarrow SnF_4(s)$
The halide formula depends on the oxidation state of the metal.

With Hydrogen to Form Hydrogen Halides

Example: $H_2(g) + F_2(g) \longrightarrow 2HF(g)$
Cl_2, Br_2, and I_2 also follow this pattern.

With Nonmetals and Metalloids to Form Halides

Example: $Si(s) + 2Cl_2(g) \longrightarrow SiCl_4(s)$
Example: $N_2(g) + 3F_2(g) \longrightarrow 2NF_3(g)$
Example: $P_4(s) + 6Br_2(l) \longrightarrow 4PBr_3(s)$
The formula of the halide depends on the oxidation state of the metalloid or nonmetal.

With Other Halogens to Form Interhalogen Compounds

Example: $Br_2(l) + 3F_2(g) \longrightarrow 2BrF_3(l)$

* Chemists assume that astatine undergoes similar reactions, but few chemical tests have been made.

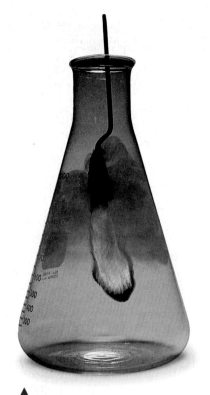

▲
Chlorine combines readily with iron wool, which ignites in chlorine gas to form $FeCl_3$.

▲
Hydrofluoric acid is used to etch patterns into glass.

▲
Shown here from left to right are precipitates of AgCl, AgBr, and AgI.

Analytical Test

As with most elements, the presence of each of the halogens can be determined by atomic absorption spectroscopy. Fluorides react with concentrated sulfuric acid, H_2SO_4, to release hydrogen fluoride gas. Three of the halide ions can be identified in solution by their reactions with silver nitrate.

$$Cl^-(aq) + Ag^+(aq) \longrightarrow AgCl(s)$$
$$Br^-(aq) + Ag^+(aq) \longrightarrow AgBr(s)$$
$$I^-(aq) + Ag^+(aq) \longrightarrow AgI(s)$$

Properties

GROUP 17 ELEMENTS					
	F	Cl	Br	I	At
Melting point (°C)	−219.62	−100.98	−7.2	113.5	302
Boiling point (°C)	−188.14	−34.6	58.78	184.35	337
Density (g/cm³)	1.69×10^{-3}	3.214×10^{-3}	3.119	4.93	not known
Ionization energy (kJ/mol)	1681	1251	1140	1008	–
Atomic radius (pm)	72	100	114	133	140
Ionic radius (pm)	133	181	196	220	–
Common oxidation number in compounds	−1	−1, +1, +3, +5, +7	−1, +1, +3, +5, +7	−1, +1, +3, +5, +7	−1, +5
Crystal structure	cubic	orthorhombic	orthorhombic	orthorhombic	not known

S.T.E.M.
Application *The Environment*

Chlorine in Water Treatment

For more than a century, communities have treated their water to prevent disease. A treatment process widely used in the United States is chlorination. All halogens kill bacteria and other microorganisms. Chlorine, however, is the only halogen acceptable for large-scale treatment of public water supplies.

When chlorine is added to water, the following reaction produces HCl and hypochlorous acid, HOCl:

$$Cl_2(g) + H_2O(l) \longrightarrow HCl(aq) + HOCl(aq)$$

Hypochlorous acid is a weak acid that ionizes to give hydrogen ions and hypochlorite ions, OCl^-.

$$HOCl(aq) + H_2O(l) \longrightarrow H_3O^+(aq) + OCl^-(aq)$$

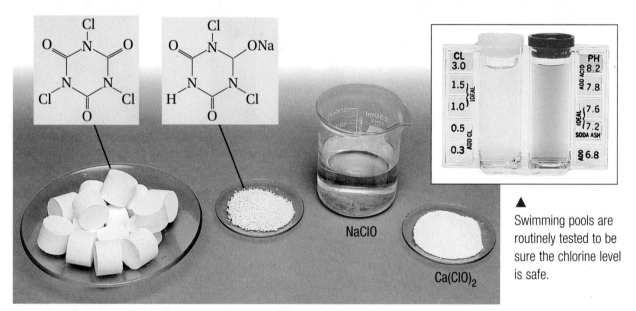

NaClO

$Ca(ClO)_2$

▲
Swimming pools are routinely tested to be sure the chlorine level is safe.

▲
The "chlorine" used in swimming pools is really one of these compounds and not pure chlorine.

The OCl$^-$ ions are strong oxidizing agents that can destroy microorganisms.

In some water-treatment plants, calcium hypochlorite, Ca(ClO)$_2$, a salt of hypochlorous acid, is added to water to provide OCl$^-$ ions. Similar treatments are used in swimming pools.

Nearly a hundred cities in the United States and thousands of communities in Europe use chlorine in the form of chlorine dioxide, ClO$_2$, as their primary means of disinfecting water. The main drawback to the use of ClO$_2$ is that it is unstable and cannot be stored. Instead, ClO$_2$ must be prepared on location by one of the following reactions involving sodium chlorite, NaClO$_2$.

$$10NaClO_2(aq) + 5H_2SO_4(aq) \longrightarrow$$
$$8ClO_2(g) + 5Na_2SO_4(aq) + 2HCl(aq) + 4H_2O(l)$$

$$2NaClO_2(aq) + Cl_2(g) \longrightarrow 2ClO_2(g) + 2NaCl(aq)$$

The expense of using ClO$_2$ makes it less desirable than Cl$_2$ in water-treatment systems unless there are other considerations. For example, the use of ClO$_2$ is likely to result in purified water with less of the aftertaste and odor associated with water purified by Cl$_2$.

Fluoride and Tooth Decay

In the 1940s, scientists noticed that people living in communities that have natural water supplies with high concentrations of fluoride ions, F$^-$, have significantly lower rates of dental caries (tooth decay) than most of the population.

In June 1944, a study on the effects of water fluoridation began in two Michigan cities, Muskegon and Grand Rapids, where the natural level of fluoride in drinking water was low (about 0.05 ppm). In Grand Rapids, sodium fluoride, NaF, was added to the drinking water to raise levels to 1.0 ppm. In Muskegon, no fluoride was added.

Also included in the study was Aurora, Illinois, a city that was similar to Grand Rapids and Muskegon, except that it had a natural F$^-$ concentration of 1.2 ppm in the water supply. After 10 years, the rate of tooth decay in Grand Rapids had dropped far below that in Muskegon and was about the same as it was in Aurora.

Tooth enamel is a strong, rocklike material consisting mostly of calcium hydroxyphosphate, Ca$_5$(PO$_4$)$_3$(OH), also known as apatite. Apatite is an insoluble and very hard compound—ideal for tooth enamel. Sometimes, however, saliva becomes more acidic, particularly after a person eats a high-sugar meal. Acids ionize to produce hydronium ions, which react with the hydroxide ion, OH$^-$, in the apatite to form water. The loss of OH$^-$ causes the apatite to dissolve.

$$Ca_5(PO_4)_3(OH)(s) + H_3O^+(aq) \longrightarrow$$
$$5Ca^{2+}(aq) + 3PO_4^{3-}(aq) + 2H_2O(l)$$

Saliva supplies more OH$^-$ ions, and new apatite is formed, but slowly.

If fluoride ions are present in saliva, some fluorapatite, Ca$_5$(PO$_4$)$_3$F, also forms.

$$5Ca^{2+}(aq) + 3PO_4^{3-}(aq) + F^-(aq) \longrightarrow$$
$$Ca_5(PO_4)_3F(s)$$

Fluorapatite resists attack by acids, so the tooth enamel resists decay better than enamel containing no fluoride.

When the beneficial effect of fluoride had been established, public-health authorities proposed that fluoride compounds be added to water supplies in low-fluoride communities. Fluoridation started in the 1950s, and by 1965, nearly every medical and dental association in the United States had endorsed fluoridation of water supplies. In the past decade, however, that trend slowed as opposition to fluoridation grew.

APPENDIX B

Reference Tables

SI MEASUREMENT

Metric Prefixes

Prefix	Symbol	Factor of Base Unit
giga	G	1 000 000 000
mega	M	1 000 000
kilo	k	1 000
hecto	h	100
deka	da	10
deci	d	0.1
centi	c	0.01
milli	m	0.001
micro	μ	0.000 001
nano	n	0.000 000 001
pico	p	0.000 000 000 001

Length

1 kilometer (km)	= 1 000 m
1 meter (m)	= SI base unit of length
1 centimeter (cm)	= 0.01 m
1 millimeter (mm)	= 0.001 m
1 micrometer (μm)	= 0.000 001 m
1 nanometer (nm)	= 0.000 000 001 m
1 picometer (pm)	= 0.000 000 000 001 m

Area

1 square kilometer (km^2)	= 100 hectares (ha)
1 hectare (ha)	= 10 000 square meters (m^2)
1 square meter (m^2)	= 10 000 square centimeters (cm^2)
1 square centimeter (cm^2)	= 100 square millimeters (mm^2)

Mass

1 kilogram (kg)	= SI base unit of mass
1 gram (g)	= 0.001 kg
1 milligram (mg)	= 0.000 001 kg
1 microgram (μg)	= 0.000 000 001 kg

Volume

1 liter (L)	= common unit for liquid volume (not SI)
1 cubic meter (m^3)	= 1000 L
1 kiloliter (kL)	= 1000 L
1 milliliter (mL)	= 0.001 L
1 milliliter (mL)	= 1 cubic centimeter (cm^3)

UNIT SYMBOLS

atm	= atmosphere (pressure, non-SI)		M	= molarity (concentration)
Bq	= becquerel (nuclear activity)		N	= newton (force)
°C	= degree Celsius (temperature)		Pa	= pascal (pressure)
J	= joule (energy)		s	= second (time)
K	= kelvin (temperature, thermodynamic)		u	= unified atomic mass unit (mass)
mol	= mole (quantity)		V	= volt (electric potential difference)

SYMBOLS

Symbol	Meaning	Symbol	Meaning
α	= helium nucleus (also $^{4}_{2}He$) emission from radioactive materials	ΔH^{0}	= standard enthalpy of reaction
		ΔH^{0}_{f}	= standard molar enthalpy of formation
β	= electron (also $^{0}_{-1}e$) emission from radioactive materials	K_{a}	= ionization constant (acid)
		K_{b}	= dissociation constant (base)
γ	= high-energy photon emission from radioactive materials	K_{eq}	= equilibrium constant
		K_{sp}	= solubility-product constant
Δ	= change in a given quantity (e.g., ΔH for change in enthalpy)	KE	= kinetic energy
		m	= mass
c	= speed of light in vacuum	N_{A}	= Avogadro's number
c_{p}	= specific heat capacity (at constant pressure)	n	= number of moles
D	= density	p	= pressure
E_{a}	= activation energy	pH	= measure of acidity $(-\log[H_3O^+])$
E^{0}	= standard electrode potential	R	= ideal gas law constant
E^{0} cell	= standard potential of an electrochemical cell	S	= entropy
G	= Gibbs free energy	S^{0}	= standard molar entropy
ΔG^{0}	= standard free energy of reaction	T	= temperature (thermodynamic, in kelvins)
ΔG^{0}_{f}	= standard molar free energy of formation	t	= temperature ($\pm$ degrees Celsius)
H	= enthalpy	V	= volume
		v	= velocity

PHYSICAL CONSTANTS

Quantity	Symbol	Value
unified atomic mass unit	u	$1.660\ 5402(10) \times 10^{-27}$ kg
Avogadro's number	N_A	$6.022\ 142 \times 10^{23}$/mol
electron rest mass	m_e	$9.109\ 3826 \times 10^{-31}$ kg; 5.4858×10^{-4} u
ideal gas law constant	R	8.314 L $\bullet$ kPa/(mol $\bullet$ K); 0.0821 L $\bullet$ atm/(mol $\bullet$ K)
molar volume of ideal gas at STP	V_M	22.414 10 L/mol
neutron rest mass	m_n	$1.674\ 9273 \times 10^{-27}$ kg; 1.008 665 u
normal boiling point of water	T_b	373.15 K = 100.0°C
normal freezing point of water	T_f	273.15 K = 0.00°C
Planck's constant	h	$6.626\ 069 \times 10^{-34}$ J $\bullet$ s
proton rest mass	m_p	$1.672\ 6217 \times 10^{-27}$ kg; 1.007 276 u
speed of light in a vacuum	c	$2.997\ 924\ 58 \times 10^{8}$ m/s
temperature of triple point of water	*(none)*	273.16 K = 0.01°C

ENTHALPY OF COMBUSTION

Substance	Formula	State	ΔH_c	Substance	Formula	State	ΔH_c
hydrogen	H_2	g	−285.8	benzene	C_6H_6	l	−3267.6
graphite	C	s	−393.5	toluene	C_7H_8	l	−3910.3
carbon monoxide	CO	g	−283.0	naphthalene	$C_{10}H_8$	s	−5156.3
methane	CH_4	g	−890.8	anthracene	$C_{14}H_{10}$	s	−7163.0
ethane	C_2H_6	g	−1560.7	methanol	CH_3OH	l	−726.1
propane	C_3H_8	g	−2219.2	ethanol	C_2H_5OH	l	−1366.8
butane	C_4H_{10}	g	−2877.6	ether	$(C_2H_5)_2O$	l	−2751.1
pentane	C_5H_{12}	g	−3535.6	formaldehyde	CH_2O	g	−570.7
hexane	C_6H_{14}	l	−4163.2	glucose	$C_6H_{12}O_6$	s	−2803.0
heptane	C_7H_{16}	l	−4817.0	sucrose	$C_{12}H_{22}O_{11}$	s	−5640.9
octane	C_8H_{18}	l	−5470.5				
ethene (ethylene)	C_2H_4	g	−1411.2				
propene (propylene)	C_3H_6	g	−2058.0				
ethyne (acetylene)	C_2H_2	g	−1301.1				

ΔH_c = enthalpy of combustion of the given substance. All values of ΔH_c are expressed as kJ/mol of substance oxidized to $H_2O(l)$ and/or $CO_2(g)$ at constant pressure and 25°C.

s = solid, l = liquid, g = gas

THE ELEMENTS: SYMBOLS, ATOMIC NUMBERS, AND ATOMIC MASSES

Name of element	Symbol	Atomic number	Atomic masses	Name of element	Symbol	Atomic number	Atomic masses
actinium	Ac	89	[227]	copper	Cu	29	63.546
aluminum	Al	13	26.981 5386	curium	Cm	96	[247]
americium	Am	95	[243]	darmstadtium	Ds	110	[271]
antimony	Sb	51	121.760	dubnium	Db	105	[262]
argon	Ar	18	39.948	dysprosium	Dy	66	162.500
arsenic	As	33	74.921 60	einsteinium	Es	99	[252]
astatine	At	85	[210]	erbium	Er	68	167.259
barium	Ba	56	137.327	europium	Eu	63	151.964
berkelium	Bk	97	[247]	fermium	Fm	100	[257]
beryllium	Be	4	9.012 182	flerovium	Fl	114	[289]
bismuth	Bi	83	208.980 40	fluorine	F	9	18.998 4032
bohrium	Bh	107	[264]	francium	Fr	87	[223]
boron	B	5	*10.81*	gadolinium	Gd	64	157.25
bromine	Br	35	79.904	gallium	Ga	31	69.723
cadmium	Cd	48	112.411	germanium	Ge	32	72.63
calcium	Ca	20	40.078	gold	Au	79	196.966 569
californium	Cf	98	[251]	hafnium	Hf	72	178.49
carbon	C	6	*12.01 1*	hassium	Hs	108	[277]
cerium	Ce	58	140.116	helium	He	2	4.002 60
cesium	Cs	55	132.905 4519	holmium	Ho	67	164.930 32
chlorine	Cl	17	*35.45*	hydrogen	H	1	*1.008*
chromium	Cr	24	51.9961	indium	In	49	114.818
cobalt	Co	27	58.933 195	iodine	I	53	126.904 47
copernicium	Cn	112	[285]	iridium	Ir	77	192.217

THE ELEMENTS — CONTINUED

Name of element	Symbol	Atomic number	Atomic masses	Name of element	Symbol	Atomic number	Atomic masses
iron	Fe	26	55.845	rhodium	Rh	45	102.905 50
krypton	Kr	36	83.798	roentgenium	Rg	111	[272]
lanthanum	La	57	138.905 47	rubidium	Rb	37	85.4678
lawrencium	Lr	103	[262]	ruthenium	Ru	44	101.07
lead	Pb	82	207.2	rutherfordium	Rf	104	[261]
lithium	Li	3	*6.94*	samarium	Sm	62	150.36
livermorium	Lv	116	[292]	scandium	Sc	21	44.955 912
lutetium	Lu	71	174.967	seaborgium	Sg	106	[266]
magnesium	Mg	12	24.3050	selenium	Se	34	78.96
manganese	Mn	25	54.938 045	silicon	Si	14	*28.085*
meitnerium	Mt	109	[268]	silver	Ag	47	107.8682
mendelevium	Md	101	[258]	sodium	Na	11	22.989 769 28
mercury	Hg	80	200.59	strontium	Sr	38	87.62
molybdenum	Mo	42	95.94	sulfur	S	16	*32.06*
neodymium	Nd	60	144.242	tantalum	Ta	73	180.947 88
neon	Ne	10	20.1797	technetium	Tc	43	[98]
neptunium	Np	93	[237]	tellurium	Te	52	127.60
nickel	Ni	28	58.6934	terbium	Tb	65	158.925 35
niobium	Nb	41	92.906 38	thallium	Tl	81	*204.38*
nitrogen	N	7	*14.007*	thorium	Th	90	232.038 06
nobelium	No	102	[259]	thulium	Tm	69	168.934 21
osmium	Os	76	190.23	tin	Sn	50	118.710
oxygen	O	8	*15.999*	titanium	Ti	22	47.867
palladium	Pd	46	106.42	tungsten	W	74	183.84
phosphorus	P	15	30.973 762	uranium	U	92	238.028 91
platinum	Pt	78	195.084	vanadium	V	23	50.9415
plutonium	Pu	94	[244]	xenon	Xe	54	131.293
polonium	Po	84	[209]	ytterbium	Yb	70	173.04
potassium	K	19	39.0983	yttrium	Y	39	88.905 85
praseodymium	Pr	59	140.907 65	zinc	Zn	30	65.409
promethium	Pm	61	[145]	zirconium	Zr	40	91.224
protactinium	Pa	91	231.035 88				
radium	Ra	88	[226]				
radon	Rn	86	[222]				
rhenium	Re	75	186.207				

The atomic weights of many elements vary due to variations in the abundances of their isotopes in natural terrestrial materials. Values in brackets denote the mass number of the most stable or common isotope. These atomic masses are believed to have an error no greater than ±1 in the last digit given. Atomic masses that are bold and italicized are considered representative of the range of masses found in nature for that element.

COMMON IONS

Cation	Symbol	Anion	Symbol
aluminum	Al^{3+}	acetate	CH_3COO^-
ammonium	NH_4^+	bromide	Br^-
arsenic(III)	As^{3+}	carbonate	CO_3^{2-}
barium	Ba^{2+}	chlorate	ClO_3^-
calcium	Ca^{2+}	chloride	Cl^-
chromium(II)	Cr^{2+}	chlorite	ClO_2^-
chromium(III)	Cr^{3+}	chromate	CrO_4^{2-}
cobalt(II)	Co^{2+}	cyanide	CN^-
cobalt(III)	Co^{3+}	dichromate	$Cr_2O_7^{2-}$
copper(I)	Cu^+	fluoride	F^-
copper(II)	Cu^{2+}	hexacyanoferrate(II)	$Fe(CN)_6^{4-}$
hydronium	H_3O^+	hexacyanoferrate(III)	$Fe(CN)_6^{3-}$
iron(II)	Fe^{2+}	hydride	H^-
iron(III)	Fe^{3+}	hydrogen carbonate	HCO_3^-
lead(II)	Pb^{2+}	hydrogen sulfate	HSO_4^-
magnesium	Mg^{2+}	hydroxide	OH^-
mercury(I)	Hg_2^{2+}	hypochlorite	ClO^-
mercury(II)	Hg^{2+}	iodide	I^-
nickel(II)	Ni^{2+}	nitrate	NO_3^-
potassium	K^+	nitrite	NO_2^-
silver	Ag^+	oxide	O^{2-}
sodium	Na^+	perchlorate	ClO_4^-
strontium	Sr^{2+}	permanganate	MnO_4^-
tin(II)	Sn^{2+}	peroxide	O_2^{2-}
tin(IV)	Sn^{4+}	phosphate	PO_4^{3-}
titanium(III)	Ti^{3+}	sulfate	SO_4^{2-}
titanium(IV)	Ti^{4+}	sulfide	S^{2-}
zinc	Zn^{2+}	sulfite	SO_3^{2-}

WATER-VAPOR PRESSURE

Temperature (°C)	Pressure (mm Hg)	Pressure (kPa)	Temperature (°C)	Pressure (mm Hg)	Pressure (kPa)
0.0	4.6	0.61	23.0	21.1	2.81
5.0	6.5	0.87	23.5	21.7	2.90
10.0	9.2	1.23	24.0	22.4	2.98
15.0	12.8	1.71	24.5	23.1	3.10
15.5	13.2	1.76	25.0	23.8	3.17
16.0	13.6	1.82	26.0	25.2	3.36
16.5	14.1	1.88	27.0	26.7	3.57
17.0	14.5	1.94	28.0	28.3	3.78
17.5	15.0	2.00	29.0	30.0	4.01
18.0	15.5	2.06	30.0	31.8	4.25
18.5	16.0	2.13	35.0	42.2	5.63
19.0	16.5	2.19	40.0	55.3	7.38
19.5	17.0	2.27	50.0	92.5	12.34
20.0	17.5	2.34	60.0	149.4	19.93
20.5	18.1	2.41	70.0	233.7	31.18
21.0	18.6	2.49	80.0	355.1	47.37
21.5	19.2	2.57	90.0	525.8	70.12
22.0	19.8	2.64	95.0	633.9	84.53
22.5	20.4	2.72	100.0	760.0	101.32

DENSITIES OF GASES AT STP

Gas	Density (g/L)
air, dry	1.293
ammonia	0.771
carbon dioxide	1.997
carbon monoxide	1.250
chlorine	3.214
dinitrogen monoxide	1.977
ethyne (acetylene)	1.165
helium	0.1785
hydrogen	0.0899
hydrogen chloride	1.639
hydrogen sulfide	1.539
methane	0.7168
nitrogen	1.2506
nitrogen monoxide (at 10°C)	1.340
oxygen	1.429
sulfur dioxide	2.927

DENSITY OF WATER

Temperature (°C)	Density (g/cm^3)
0	0.999 84
2	0.999 94
3.98 (maximum)	0.999 973
4	0.999 97
6	0.999 94
8	0.999 85
10	0.999 70
14	0.999 24
16	0.998 94
20	0.998 20
25	0.997 05
30	0.995 65
40	0.992 22
50	0.988 04
60	0.983 20
70	0.977 77
80	0.971 79
90	0.965 31
100	0.958 36

SOLUBILITIES OF GASES IN WATER

Volume of gas (in liters) at STP that can be dissolved in 1 L of water at the temperature (°C) indicated.

Gas	0°C	10°C	20°C	60°C
air	0.029 18	0.022 84	0.018 68	0.012 16
ammonia	1130	870	680	200
carbon dioxide	1.713	1.194	0.878	0.359
carbon monoxide	0.035 37	0.028 16	0.023 19	0.014 88
chlorine	—	3.148	2.299	1.023
hydrogen	0.021 48	0.019 55	0.018 19	0.016 00
hydrogen chloride	512	475	442	339
hydrogen sulfide	4.670	3.399	2.582	1.190
methane	0.055 63	0.041 77	0.033 08	0.019 54
nitrogen*	0.023 54	0.018 61	0.015 45	0.010 23
nitrogen monoxide	0.073 81	0.057 09	0.047 06	0.029 54
oxygen	0.048 89	0.038 02	0.031 02	0.019 46
sulfur dioxide	79.789	56.647	39.374	—

*Atmospheric nitrogen–98.815% N_2, 1.185% inert gases

SOLUBILITY CHART

	acetate	bromide	carbonate	chlorate	chloride	chromate	hydroxide	iodine	nitrate	oxide	phosphate	silicate	sulfate	sulfide
aluminum	S	S	—	S	S	—	A	S	S	a	A	I	S	d
ammonium	S	S	S	S	S	S	S	S	S	—	S	—	S	S
barium	S	S	P	S	S	A	S	S	S	S	A	S	a	d
calcium	S	S	P	S	S	S	S	S	S	P	P	P	S	S
copper(II)	S	S	—	S	S	—	A	—	S	A	A	A	S	A
hydrogen	S	S	—	S	S	—	—	S	S	S	S	I	S	S
iron(II)	—	S	P	S	S	—	A	S	S	A	A	—	S	A
iron(III)	—	S	—	S	S	A	A	S	S	A	P	—	P	d
lead(II)	S	S	A	S	S	A	P	P	S	P	A	A	P	A
magnesium	S	S	P	S	S	S	A	S	S	A	P	A	S	d
manganese(II)	S	S	P	S	S	—	A	S	S	A	P	I	S	A
mercury(I)	P	A	A	S	a	P	—	A	S	A	A	—	P	I
mercury(II)	S	S	—	S	S	P	A	P	S	P	A	—	d	I
potassium	S	S	S	S	S	S	S	S	S	S	S	S	S	S
silver	P	a	A	S	a	P	—	I	S	P	A	—	P	A
sodium	S	S	S	S	S	S	S	S	S	d	S	S	S	S
strontium	S	S	P	S	S	P	S	S	S	A	P	A	P	S
tin(II)	d	S	—	S	S	A	A	S	d	A	A	—	S	A
tin(IV)	S	S	—	—	S	S	P	d	—	A	—	—	S	A
zinc	S	S	P	S	S	P	A	S	S	P	A	A	S	A

S = soluble in water. A = soluble in acids, insoluble in water. P = partially soluble in water, soluble in dilute acids.
I = insoluble in dilute acids and in water. a = slightly soluble in acids, insoluble in water. d = decomposes in water.

SOLUBILITY OF COMPOUNDS

Solubilities are given in grams of solute that can be dissolved in 100 g of water at the temperature (°C) indicated.

Compound	Formula	0°C	20°C	60°C	100°C
aluminum sulfate	$Al_2(SO_4)_3$	31.2	36.4	59.2	89.0
ammonium chloride	NH_4Cl	29.4	37.2	55.3	77.3
ammonium nitrate	NH_4NO_3	118	192	421	871
ammonium sulfate	$(NH_4)_2SO_4$	70.6	75.4	88	103
barium carbonate	$BaCO_3$	—*	$0.0022^{18°}$	—*	0.0065
barium chloride dihydrate	$BaCl_2 \cdot 2H_2O$	31.2	35.8	46.2	59.4
barium hydroxide	$Ba(OH)_2$	1.67	3.89	20.94	$101.40^{80°}$
barium nitrate	$Ba(NO_3)_2$	4.95	9.02	20.4	34.4
barium sulfate	$BaSO_4$	—*	$0.000\ 246^{25°}$	—*	0.000 413
calcium carbonate	$CaCO_3$	—*	$0.0014^{25°}$	—*	$0.0018^{75°}$
calcium fluoride	CaF_2	$0.0016^{18°}$	$0.0017^{26°}$	—*	—*
calcium hydrogen carbonate	$Ca(HCO_3)_2$	16.15	16.60	17.50	18.40
calcium hydroxide	$Ca(OH)_2$	0.189	0.173	0.121	0.076
calcium sulfate	$CaSO_4$	—*	$0.209^{30°}$	—*	0.1619
copper(II) chloride	$CuCl_2$	68.6	73.0	96.5	120
copper(II) sulfate pentahydrate	$CuSO_4 \cdot 5H_2O$	23.1	32.0	61.8	114
lead(II) chloride	$PbCl_2$	0.67	1.00	1.94	3.20
lead(II) nitrate	$Pb(NO_3)_2$	37.5	54.3	91.6	133.
lithium chloride	$LiCl$	69.2	83.5	98.4	128.
lithium sulfate	Li_2SO_4	36.1	34.8	32.6	$30.9^{90°}$
magnesium hydroxide	$Mg(OH)_2$	—*	$0.0009^{18°}$	—*	0.004
magnesium sulfate	$MgSO_4$	22.0	33.7	54.6	68.3
mercury(I) chloride	Hg_2Cl_2	—*	$0.000\ 20^{25°}$	$0.001^{43°}$	—*
mercury(II) chloride	$HgCl_2$	3.63	6.57	16.3	61.3
potassium bromide	KBr	53.6	65.3	85.5	104
potassium chlorate	$KClO_3$	3.3	7.3	23.8	56.3
potassium chloride	KCl	28.0	34.2	45.8	56.3
potassium chromate	K_2CrO_4	56.3	63.7	70.1	$74.5^{90°}$
potassium iodide	KI	128	144	176	206
potassium nitrate	KNO_3	13.9	31.6	106	245
potassium permanganate	$KMnO_4$	2.83	6.34	22.1	—*
potassium sulfate	K_2SO_4	7.4	11.1	18.2	24.1
silver acetate	$AgC_2H_3O_2$	0.73	1.05	1.93	$2.59^{80°}$
silver chloride	$AgCl$	$0.000\ 089^{10°}$	—*	—*	0.0021
silver nitrate	$AgNO_3$	122	216	440	733
sodium acetate	$NaC_2H_3O_2$	36.2	46.4	139	170
sodium chlorate	$NaClO_3$	79.6	95.9	137.	204.
sodium chloride	$NaCl$	35.7	35.9	37.1	39.2
sodium nitrate	$NaNO_3$	73.0	87.6	122	180
sucrose	$C_{12}H_{22}O_{11}$	179.2	203.9	287.3	487.2

*Dashes indicate that values are not available.

ENTHALPY OF FORMATION

Substance	State	ΔH_f	Substance	State	ΔH_f
ammonia	g	–45.9	lead(IV) oxide	s	–274.5
ammonium chloride	s	–314.4	lead(II) nitrate	s	–451.9
ammonium sulfate	s	–1180.9	lead(II) sulfate	s	–919.94
barium chloride	s	–858.6	lithium chloride	s	–408.6
barium nitrate	s	–768.2	lithium nitrate	s	–483.1
barium sulfate	s	–1473.2	magnesium chloride	s	–641.5
benzene	g	+82.88	magnesium oxide	s	–601.6
benzene	l	+49.080	magnesium sulfate	s	–1261.79
calcium carbonate	s	–1207.6	manganese(IV) oxide	s	–520.0
calcium chloride	s	–795.4	manganese(II) sulfate	s	–1065.3
calcium hydroxide	s	–983.2	mercury(I) chloride	s	–264.2
calcium nitrate	s	–938.2	mercury(II) chloride	s	–230.0
calcium oxide	s	–634.9	mercury(II) oxide (red)	s	–90.8
calcium sulfate	s	–1434.5	methane	g	–74.9
carbon (diamond)	s	+1.9	nitrogen dioxide	g	+33.2
carbon (graphite)	s	0.00	nitrogen monoxide	g	+90.29
carbon dioxide	g	–393.5	dinitrogen monoxide	g	+82.1
carbon monoxide	g	–110.5	dinitrogen tetroxide	g	+9.2
copper(II) nitrate	s	–302.9	oxygen (O_2)	g	0.00
copper(II) oxide	s	–157.3	ozone (O_3)	g	+142.7
copper(II) sulfate	s	–771.4	tetraphosphorus decoxide	s	–3009.9
ethane	g	–83.8	potassium bromide	s	–393.8
ethyne (acetylene)	g	+228.2	potassium chloride	s	–436.49
hydrogen (H_2)	g	0.00	potassium hydroxide	s	–424.58
hydrogen bromide	g	–36.29	potassium nitrate	s	–494.6
hydrogen chloride	g	–92.3	potassium sulfate	s	–1437.8
hydrogen fluoride	g	–273.3	silicon dioxide (quartz)	s	–910.7
hydrogen iodide	g	+26.5	silver chloride	s	–127.01 ± 0.5
hydrogen oxide (water)	g	–241.8	silver nitrate	s	–120.5
hydrogen oxide (water)	l	–285.8	silver sulfide	s	–32.59
hydrogen peroxide	g	–136.3	sodium bromide	s	–361.8
hydrogen peroxide	l	–187.8	sodium chloride	s	–385.9
hydrogen sulfide	g	–20.6	sodium hydroxide	s	–425.9
iodine (I_2)	s	0.00	sodium nitrate	s	–467.9
iodine (I_2)	g	+62.4	sodium sulfate	l	–1387.1
iron(II) chloride	s	–399.4	sulfur dioxide	g	–296.8
iron(II) oxide	s	–272.0	sulfur trioxide	g	–395.7
iron(III) oxide	s	–824.2	tin(IV) chloride	l	–511.3
iron(II) sulfate	s	–928.4	zinc nitrate	s	–483.7
iron(II) sulfide	s	–100.0	zinc oxide	s	–350.5
lead(II) oxide	s	–217.3	zinc sulfate	s	–980.14

ΔH_f is enthalpy of formation of the given substance from its elements. All values of ΔH_f are expressed as kJ/mol at 25ºC. Negative values of ΔH_f indicate exothermic reactions. s = solid, l = liquid, g = gas

PROPERTIES OF COMMON ELEMENTS

Name	Form/color at room temperature	Density (g/cm³)†	Melting point (°C)	Boiling point (°C)	Common oxidation states
aluminum	silver metal	2.702	660.37	2467	3+
arsenic	gray metalloid	5.727[14]	817 (28 atm)	613 (sublimes)	3–, 3+, 5+
barium	bluish white metal	3.51	725	1640	2+
bromine	red-brown liquid	3.119	–7.2	58.78	1–, 1+, 3+, 5+, 7+
calcium	silver metal	1.54	839 ± 2	1484	2+
carbon	diamond	3.51	3500 (63.5 atm)	3930	2+, 4+
	graphite	2.25	3652 (sublimes)	—	
chlorine	green-yellow gas	3.214*	–100.98	–34.6	1–, 1+, 3+, 5+, 7+
chromium	gray metal	7.2028	1857 ± 20	2672	2+, 3+, 6+
cobalt	gray metal	8.9	1495	2870	2+, 3+
copper	red metal	8.92	1083.4 ± 0.2	2567	1+, 2+
fluorine	yellow gas	1.69‡	–219.62	–188.14	1–
germanium	gray metalloid	5.323[25]	937.4	2830	4+
gold	yellow metal	19.31	1064.43	2808 ± 2	1+, 3+
helium	colorless gas	0.1785*	–272.2 (26 atm)	–268.9	0
hydrogen	colorless gas	0.0899*	–259.14	–252.8	1–, 1+
iodine	blue-black solid	4.93	113.5	184.35	1–, 1+, 3+, 5+, 7+
iron	silver metal	7.86	1535	2750	2+, 3+
lead	bluish white metal	11.343716	327.502	1740	2+, 4+
lithium	silver metal	0.534	180.54	1342	1+
magnesium	silver metal	1.745	648.8	1107	2+
manganese	gray-white metal	7.20	1244 ± 3	1962	2+, 3+, 4+, 6+, 7+
mercury	silver liquid metal	13.5462	–38.87	356.58	1+, 2+
neon	colorless gas	0.9002*	+248.67	–245.9	0
nickel	silver metal	8.90	1455	2732	2+, 3+
nitrogen	colorless gas	1.2506*	–209.86	–195.8	3–, 3+, 5+
oxygen	colorless gas	1.429*	–218.4	–182.962	2–
phosphorus	yellow solid	1.82	44.1	280	3–, 3+, 5+
platinum	silver metal	21.45	1772	3827 ± 100	2+, 4+
potassium	silver metal	0.86	63.25	760	1+
silicon	gray metalloid	2.33 ± 0.01	1410	2355	2+, 4+
silver	white metal	10.5	961.93	2212	1+
sodium	silver metal	0.97	97.8	882.9	1+
strontium	silver metal	2.6	769	1384	2+
sulfur	yellow solid	1.96	119.0	444.674	2–, 4+, 6+
tin	white metal	7.28	231.88	2260	2+, 4+
titanium	white metal	4.5	1660 ± 10	3287	2+, 3+, 4+
uranium	silver metal	19.05 ± 0.02[25]	1132.3 ± 0.8	3818	3+, 4+, 6+
zinc	blue-white metal	7.14	419.58	907	2+

† Densities obtained at 20°C unless otherwise noted (superscript)

‡ Density of fluorine given in g/L at 1 atm and 15°C

* Densities of gases given in g/L at STP

Math Skills Handbook and Chemistry Equations

Scientific Notation

Positive exponents Many quantities that scientists deal with often have very large or very small values. For example, the speed of light is about 300 000 000 m/s, and the ink required to make the dot over an *i* in this textbook has a mass of about 0.000 000 001 kg. Obviously, it is cumbersome to work with numbers such as these. We avoid this problem by using a method based on powers of the number 10.

$$10^0 = 1$$
$$10^1 = 10$$
$$10^2 = 10 \times 10 = 100$$
$$10^3 = 10 \times 10 \times 10 = 1000$$
$$10^4 = 10 \times 10 \times 10 \times 10 = 10\ 000$$
$$10^5 = 10 \times 10 \times 10 \times 10 \times 10 = 100\ 000$$

The number of zeros determines the power to which 10 is raised, or the *exponent* of 10. For example, the speed of light, 300 000 000 m/s, can be expressed as 3×10^8 m/s. In this case, the exponent of 10 is 8.

Negative exponents For numbers less than one, we note the following:

$$10^{-1} = \frac{1}{10} = 0.1$$
$$10^{-2} = \frac{1}{10 \times 10} = 0.01$$
$$10^{-3} = \frac{1}{10 \times 10 \times 10} = 0.001$$
$$10^{-4} = \frac{1}{10 \times 10 \times 10 \times 10} = 0.0001$$
$$10^{-5} = \frac{1}{10 \times 10 \times 10 \times 10 \times 10} = 0.000\ 01$$

The value of the negative exponent equals the number of places the decimal point must be moved to be to the right of the first nonzero digit (in these cases, the digit 1). Numbers that are expressed as a number between 1 and 10 multiplied by a power of 10 are said to be in *scientific notation*. For example, 5 943 000 000 is 5.943×10^9 when expressed in scientific notation, and 0.000 083 2 is 8.32×10^{-5} when expressed in scientific notation.

Multiplication and division in scientific notation When numbers expressed in scientific notation are being multiplied, the following general rule is very useful:

$$10^n \times 10^m = 10^{(n+m)}$$

Note that n and m can be any numbers; they are not necessarily integers. For example, $10^2 \times 10^5 = 10^7$, and $10^{1/4} \times 10^{1/2} = 10^{3/4}$. The rule also applies to negative exponents. For example, $10^3 \times 10^{-8} = 10^{-5}$. When dividing numbers expressed in scientific notation, note the following:

$$\frac{10^n}{10^m} = 10^n \times 10^{-m} = 10^{(n-m)}$$

For example, $\dfrac{10^3}{10^2} = 10^{(3-2)} = 10^1$.

Fractions

The rules for multiplying, dividing, adding, and subtracting fractions are summarized in **Table C-1,** where a, b, c, and d are four numbers.

TABLE C-1

BASIC OPERATIONS FOR FRACTIONS

Operation	Rule	Example
Multiplication	$\left(\dfrac{a}{b}\right)\left(\dfrac{c}{d}\right) = \dfrac{ac}{bd}$	$\left(\dfrac{2}{3}\right)\left(\dfrac{4}{5}\right) = \dfrac{(2)(4)}{(3)(5)} = \dfrac{8}{15}$
Division	$\dfrac{\left(\dfrac{a}{b}\right)}{\left(\dfrac{c}{d}\right)} = \dfrac{ad}{bc}$	$\dfrac{\left(\dfrac{2}{3}\right)}{\left(\dfrac{4}{5}\right)} = \dfrac{(2)(5)}{(3)(4)} = \dfrac{10}{12} = \dfrac{5}{6}$
Addition and Subtraction	$\dfrac{a}{b} \pm \dfrac{c}{d} = \dfrac{ad \pm bc}{bd}$	$\dfrac{2}{3} - \dfrac{4}{5} = \dfrac{(2)(5) - (3)(4)}{(3)(5)} = -\dfrac{2}{15}$

Powers

Rules of exponents When powers of a given quantity, x, are multiplied, the rule used for scientific notation applies:

$$(x^n)(x^m) = x^{(n+m)}$$

For example, $(x^2)(x^4) = x^{(2+4)} = x^6$.

When dividing the powers of a given quantity, note the following:

$$\frac{x^n}{x^m} = x^{(n-m)}$$

For example, $\dfrac{x^8}{x^2} = x^{(8-2)} = x^6$.

A power that is a fraction, such as $\frac{1}{3}$, corresponds to a root as follows:
$$x^{1/n} = \sqrt[n]{x}$$

For example, $4^{1/3} = \sqrt[3]{4} \approx 1.5874$. (A scientific calculator is useful for such calculations.)

Finally, any quantity x^n that is raised to the mth power is as follows:
$$(x^n)^m = x^{nm}$$

For example, $(x^2)^3 = x^{(2)(3)} = x^6$.

The basic rules of exponents are summarized in **Table C-2.**

TABLE C-2

RULES OF EXPONENTS		
$x^0 = 1$	$x^1 = x$	$(x^n)(x^m) = x^{(n+m)}$
$\dfrac{x^n}{x^m} = x^{(n-m)}$	$x^{(1/n)} = \sqrt[n]{x}$	$(x^n)^m = x^{(nm)}$

Algebra

Solving for unknowns When algebraic operations are performed, the laws of arithmetic apply. Symbols such as x, y, and z are usually used to represent quantities that are not specified. Such unspecified quantities are called *unknowns.*

First, consider the following equation:
$$8x = 32$$

If we wish to solve for x, we can divide each side of the equation by the same factor without disturbing the equality. In this case, if we divide both sides by 8, we have the following:
$$\frac{8x}{8} = \frac{32}{8}$$
$$x = 4$$

Next, consider the following equation:
$$x + 2 = 8$$

In this type of expression, we can add or subtract the same quantity from each side. If we subtract 2 from each side, we get the following:
$$x + 2 - 2 = 8 - 2$$
$$x = 6$$

In general, if $x + a = b$, then $x = b - a$.

Now, consider the following equation:

$$\frac{x}{5} = 9$$

If we multiply each side by 5, we are left with x isolated on the left and a value of 45 on the right.

$$(5)\left(\frac{x}{5}\right) = (9)(5)$$

$$x = 45$$

In all cases, *whatever operation is performed on the left side of the equation must also be performed on the right side.*

Factoring

Some useful formulas for factoring an equation are given in **Table C-3.** As an example of a common factor, consider the equation $5x + 5y + 5z = 0$. This equation can be expressed as $5(x + y + z) = 0$. The expression $a^2 + 2ab + b^2$, which is an example of a perfect square, is equivalent to the expression $(a + b)^2$. For example, if $a = 2$ and $b = 3$, then $2^2 + (2)(2)(3) + 3^2 = (2 + 3)^2$, or $(4 + 12 + 9) = 5^2 = 25$. Finally, for an example of the difference of two squares, let $a = 6$ and $b = 3$. In this case, $(6^2 - 3^2) = (6 + 3)(6 - 3)$, or $(36 - 9) = (9)(3) = 27$.

TABLE C-3	
FACTORING EQUATIONS	
$ax + ay + az = a(x + y + z)$	common factor
$a^2 + 2ab + b^2 = (a + b)^2$	perfect square
$a^2 - b^2 = (a + b)(a - b)$	difference of two squares

Quadratic Equations

The general form of a quadratic equation is as follows:

$$ax^2 + bx + c = 0$$

In this equation, x is the unknown quantity, and a, b, and c are numerical factors known as *coefficients.* This equation has two roots, given by the following:

$$x = \frac{-b \pm \sqrt{b^2 - 4ac}}{2a}$$

If $b^2 \geq 4ac$, the value inside the square-root symbol will be positive or zero, and the roots will be real. If $b^2 < 4ac$, the value inside the square-root symbol will be negative, and the roots will be imaginary numbers. In chemistry, equilibrium calculations may result in a quadratic equation that needs to be solved.

Example

Find the solutions for the equation $x^2 + 5x + 4 = 0$.

SOLUTION

The given equation can be expressed as $(1)x^2 + (5)x + (4) = 0$. In other words, $a = 1$, $b = 5$, and $c = 4$. The two roots of this equation can be found by substituting these values into the quadratic equation, as follows:

$$x = \frac{-b \pm \sqrt{b^2 - 4ac}}{2a} = \frac{-5 \pm \sqrt{5^2 - (4)(1)(4)}}{(2)(1)} = \frac{-5 \pm \sqrt{9}}{2} = \frac{-5 \pm 3}{2}$$

The two roots are $x = \dfrac{-5 + 3}{2} = -1$ and $x = \dfrac{-5 - 3}{2} = -4$.

$$\boxed{x = -1 \text{ and } x = -4}$$

We can evaluate these answers by substituting them into the given equation and verifying that the result is zero.

$$x^2 + 5x + 4 = 0$$

For $x = -1$, $(-1)^2 + 5(-1) + 4 = 1 - 5 + 4 = 0$.

For $x = -4$, $(-4)^2 + 5(-4) + 4 = 16 - 20 + 4 = 0$.

Example

Factor the equation $2x^2 - 3x - 4 = 0$.

SOLUTION

The given equation can be expressed as $(2)x^2 + (-3)x + (-4) = 0$. Thus, $a = 2$, $b = -3$, and $c = -4$. Substitute these values into the quadratic equation to factor the given equation.

$$x = \frac{-b \pm \sqrt{b^2 - 4ac}}{2a} = \frac{3 \pm \sqrt{(-3)^2 - (4)(2)(-4)}}{(2)(2)} = \frac{3 \pm \sqrt{41}}{(2)(2)} \approx \frac{3 \pm 6.403}{(2)(2)}$$

The two roots are $x \approx \dfrac{3 + 6.403}{4} = 2.351$ and $x \approx \dfrac{3 - 6.403}{4} = -0.851$.

$$\boxed{x \approx 2.351 \text{ and } x \approx -0.851}$$

Again, evaluate these answers by substituting them into the given equation.

$$2x^2 - 5x - 4 = 0$$

For $x = 2.351$, $2(2.351)^2 - 3(2.351) - 4 = 11.054 - 7.053 - 4 \approx 0$.

For $x = -0.851$, $2(-0.851)^2 - 3(-0.851) - 4 = 1.448 + 2.553 - 4 \approx 0$.

Linear Equations

A linear equation has the following general form:

$$y = ax + b$$

In this equation, a and b are constants. This equation is called linear because the graph of y versus x is a straight line, as shown in **Figure 1.** The constant b, called the *intercept*, represents the value of y where the straight line intersects the y-axis. The constant a is equal to the *slope* of the straight line and is also equal to the tangent of the angle that the line makes with the x-axis (θ). If any two points on the straight line are specified by the coordinates (x_1, y_1) and (x_2, y_2), as in **Figure 1,** then the slope of the straight line can be expressed as follows:

$$\text{slope} = \frac{y_2 - y_1}{x_2 - x_1} = \frac{\Delta y}{\Delta x}$$

For example, if the two points shown in **Figure 1** are (2, 4) and (6, 9), then the slope of the line is as follows:

$$\text{slope} = \frac{(9-4)}{(6-2)} = \frac{5}{4}$$

Note that a and b can have either positive or negative values. If $a > 0$, the straight line has a *positive* slope, as in **Figure 1.** If $a < 0$, the straight line has a *negative* slope. Furthermore, if $b > 0$, the y-intercept is positive (above the x-axis), while if $b < 0$, the y-intercept is negative (below the x-axis). **Figure 2** gives an example of each of these four possible cases, which are summarized in **Table C-4.**

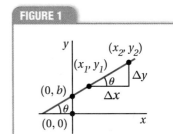

FIGURE 1

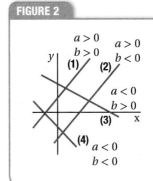

FIGURE 2

TABLE C-4

LINEAR EQUATIONS

Constants	Slope	y-intercept
$a > 0, b > 0$	positive slope	positive y-intercept
$a > 0, b < 0$	positive slope	negative y-intercept
$a < 0, b > 0$	negative slope	positive y-intercept
$a < 0, b < 0$	negative slope	negative y-intercept

Solving Simultaneous Linear Equations

Consider the following equations:

$$3x + 5y = 15$$

This equation has two unknowns, x and y. Such an equation does not have a unique solution. That is, $(x = 0, y = 3)$, $(x = 5, y = 0)$, and $(x = 2, y = \frac{9}{5})$ are all solutions to this equation.

If a problem has two unknowns, a unique solution is possible only if there are two independent equations. In general, if a problem has n unknowns, its solution requires n independent equations. There are three basic methods that can be used to solve simultaneous equations. Each of these methods is discussed below, and an example is given for each.

First method: substitution One way to solve two simultaneous equations involving two unknowns, x and y, is to solve one of the equations for one of the unknown values in terms of the other unknown value. In other words, either solve one equation for x in terms of y, or solve one equation for y in terms of x. Once you have an expression for either x or y, substitute this expression into the other original equation. At this point, the equation has only one unknown quantity. This unknown can be found through algebraic manipulations and then can be used to determine the other unknown.

Example

Solve the following two simultaneous equations:

1. $5x + y = -8$
2. $2x - 2y = 4$

SOLUTION

First solve for either x or y in one of the equations. We'll begin by solving equation 2 for x.

2. $2x - 2y = 4$

$2x = 4 + 2y$

$x = \dfrac{4 + 2y}{2} = 2 + y$

Next, we substitute this equation for x into equation 1 and solve for y.

1. $5x + y = -8$

$5(2 + y) + y = -8$

$10 + 5y + y = -8$

$6y = -18$

$\boxed{y = -3}$

To find x, substitute this value for y into the equation for x derived from equation 2.

$x = 2 + y = 2 - 3$

$\boxed{x = -1}$

There is always more than one way to solve simultaneous equations by substitution. In this example, we first solved equation 2 for x. However, we could have begun by solving equation 2 for y or equation 1 for x or y. Any of these processes would result in the same answer.

Second method: canceling one term Simultaneous equations can also be solved by multiplying both sides of one of the equations by a value that will make either the x-value or the y-value in that equation equal to and opposite the corresponding value in the second equation. When the two equations are added together, that unknown value drops out, and only one of the unknown values remains. This unknown can be found through algebraic manipulations and then can be used to determine the other unknown.

Example

Solve the following two simultaneous equations:

1. $3x + y = -6$
2. $-4x - 2y = 6$

SOLUTION

First, multiply each term of one of the equations by a factor that will make either the x- or the y-values cancel when the equations are added together. In this case, we can multiply each term in equation 1 by the factor 2. The positive $2y$ in equation 1 will then cancel the negative $2y$ in equation 2.

1. $3x + y = -6$
   $2(3x) + (2)(y) = -(2)(6)$
   $6x + 2y = -12$

Next, add the two equations together and solve for x.

2. $-4x - 2y = 6$

1. $6x + 2y = -12$
   $2x = -6$

   $\boxed{x = -3}$

Then, substitute this value of x into either equation to find y.

1. $3x + y = -6$
   $y = -6 - 3x = -6 - (3)(-3) = -6 + 9$

   $\boxed{y = 3}$

In this example, we multiplied both sides of equation 1 by 2 so that the y-terms would cancel when the two equations were added together. As with substitution, this is only one of many possible ways to solve the equations. For example, we could have multiplied both sides of equation 2 by $\frac{3}{4}$ so that the x-terms would cancel when the two equations were added together.

Third method: graphing the equations Two linear equations with two unknowns can also be solved by a graphical method. If the straight lines corresponding to the two equations are plotted in a conventional coordinate system, the intersection of the two lines represents the solution.

Example

Solve the following two simultaneous equations:

1. $x - y = 2$
2. $x - 2y = -1$

SOLUTION

These two equations are plotted in **Figure 3**. To plot an equation, rewrite the equation in the form $y = ax + b$, where a is the slope and b is the y intercept. In this example, the equations can be rewritten as follows:

$$y = x - 2$$

$$y = \frac{1}{2}x + \frac{1}{2}$$

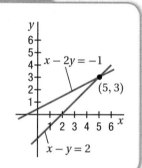

FIGURE 3

Once one point of a line is known, any other point on that line can be found with the slope of the line. For example, the slope of the first line is 1, and we know that $(0, -2)$ is a point on this line. If we choose the point $x = 2$, we have $(2, y_2)$. The coordinate y_2 can be found as follows:

$$\text{slope} = \frac{y_2 - y_1}{x_2 - x_1} = \frac{y_2 - (-2)}{2 - 0} = 1$$

$$y_2 = 0$$

Connecting the two known coordinates, $(0, -2)$ and $(2, 0)$, results in a graph of the line. The second line can be plotted with the same method.

As shown in **Figure 3**, the intersection of the two lines has the coordinates $x = 5$, $y = 3$. This intersection represents the solution to the equations. You should check this solution using either of the analytical techniques discussed above.

Logarithms

Suppose that a quantity, x, is expressed as a power of another quantity, a.

$$x = a^y$$

The number a is called the base. The logarithm of x with respect to the base, a, is equal to the exponent to which a must be raised in order to satisfy the expression $x = a^y$.

$$y = \log_a x$$

Conversely, the *antilogarithm* of y is the number x.

$$x = \text{antilog}_a y$$

In chemistry, pH is calculated using a logarithm.

Common and natural bases In practice, the two bases most often used are base 10, called the *common* logarithm base, and base $e = 2.718...$, called the *natural* logarithm base. When common logarithms are used, y and x are related as follows:

$$y = \log_{10} x, \text{ or } x = 10^y$$

When natural logarithms are used, the symbol ln is used to signify that the logarithm has a base of e; in other words, $\log_e x = \ln x$.

$$y = \ln x, \text{ or } x = e^y$$

For example, $\log_{10} 52 \approx 1.716$, so $\text{antilog}_{10} 1.716 = 10^{1.716} \approx 52$. Likewise, $\ln 52 \approx 3.951$, so $\text{antiln } 3.951 = e^{3.951} \approx 52$.

Note that you can convert between base 10 and base e with the equality

$$\ln x = (2.302\ 585)\log_{10} x.$$

Some useful properties of logarithms are summarized in **Table C-5.**

TABLE C-5

PROPERTIES OF LOGARITHMS	
$\log (ab) = \log a + \log b$	$\log (2)(5) = \log 2 + \log 5$
$\log \left(\dfrac{a}{b}\right) = \log a - \log b$	$\log \dfrac{3}{4} = \log 3 - \log 4$
$\log (a^n) = n \log a$	$\log 7^3 = 3 \log 7$
$\ln e = 1$	
$\ln e^a = a$	$\ln e^5 = 5$
$\ln \left(\dfrac{1}{a}\right) = -\ln a$	$\ln \dfrac{1}{8} = -\ln 8$

Calculating Mean

The **mean** of a data set is the average: the sum of the values divided by the number of values. In chemistry, average atomic masses are calculated in a similar way to mean.

EXAMPLE

To find the mean of the data set {14, 6, 10, 8, 4, 11, 6, 3, 5, 13}, add the values and then divide the sum by the number of values.

$$\textbf{ANSWER} \quad \frac{14 + 6 + 10 + 8 + 4 + 11 + 6 + 3 + 5 + 13}{10} = \frac{80}{10} = 8$$

Calculating Median

The **median** of a data set is the middle value when the values are ranked in numerical order. Half of the values fall above the median value, half below. If a data set has an even number of values, the median is the mean of the two middle values.

EXAMPLE

To find the median value of the data set {582, 133, 207, 87, 164, 290, 98, 155, 196, 278}, arrange the values in order from least to greatest. The median is the middle value.

87, 98, 133, 155, 164, 196, 207, 278, 290, 582

ANSWER The median is the mean of the two middle values, $\frac{164 + 196}{2} = 180$.

Finding Mode

The **mode** of a data set is the value that occurs most often. A data set can have more than one mode if two or more values are repeated the same number of times. A data set can have no mode if no values are repeated.

EXAMPLE

To find the mode of the data set {6, 7, 6, 4, 4, 4, 3, 6, 4, 6}, arrange the values in order from least to greatest and determine the value that occurs most often:

3, 4, 4, 4, 4, 6, 6, 6, 6, 7

ANSWER There are two modes, 4 and 6.

Constructing Graphs

After finishing an experiment, scientists often illustrate experimental data in graphs. There are three main types of graphs: line graphs, bar graphs, and pie graphs. Organizing data visually helps us identify relationships between variables—factors that change.

The data table on the next page shows data collected by a researcher who has hypothesized that increased salt intake will cause an increase in blood pressure. In this experiment, the independent variable was daily salt intake. Recall that the **independent variable** is the one that is changed by the researcher. You can see in the data table that the researcher varied daily salt intake between 0 and 30 g.

Recall that the **dependent variable** is the one that is observed to determine if it is affected by changes in the independent variable. The dependent variable in this experiment was systolic pressure. You can see that in this case, an increase in salt intake corresponds to an increase in systolic pressure. These data support the hypothesis that increases in salt intake cause a rise in blood pressure.

DATA TABLE	
Systolic pressure (mm Hg)	Daily salt intake (g)
110	0
120	10
140	20
165	30

The dependent variable is graphed on the vertical (y) axis.

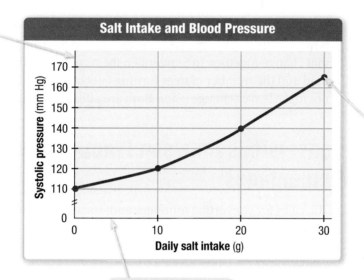

Salt Intake and Blood Pressure

This last data pair is plotted here on the graph.

The independent variable is graphed on the horizontal (x) axis.

Line Graphs

Line graphs, such as the one shown above, are most often used to compare or relate one or more sets of data that show continuous change. Each set of data—the independent variable and its corresponding dependent variables— is called a *data pair*.

To make a line graph, draw the horizontal (x) and vertical (y) axes of your graph. Label the x-axis with the independent variable and the y-axis with the dependent variable. (Refer to your data table to determine the scale and appropriate units for each axis). Plot each data pair, and then connect the data points to make a line or curve. Finally, give the graph a title that clearly indicates the relationship between the data shown by the graph.

Sometimes, line graphs can be more complex than the one shown. When a line graph has more than one line, each extra line illustrates another dependent variable. A key must accompany the graph so that the data plotted on the two or more lines are clear. Line graphs can also have data presented on two y-axes, which may have different units. In these graphs, the effect of the independent variable can be observed on two dependent variables.

Using Graphs to Make Predictions

Graphs show trends in data that allow us to make predictions. For example, how might taking in 40 g of salt per day affect blood pressure? Referring to the graph of blood pressure and salt intake, you might estimate that systolic pressure could be 190 mm Hg or more. Using a trend in a range of data to estimate values beyond that range is called **extrapolation.**

Likewise, we can use graphs to estimate values that are untested but that lie *within* the range of our data. How might taking in 15 g of salt per day affect blood pressure? You might use the graph to estimate that blood pressure would be about 130 mm Hg. Using a trend in a range of data to estimate values missing from that range is called **interpolation.**

Some data, such as the values for salt intake and blood pressure, interact in an expected way and seem to indicate a causal relationship. But beware of hastily drawing conclusions based on a graph of two variables that change together. In September, the number of school buses on the road and the number of trees turning fall colors rise. But school buses do not make leaves change color! Both are affected by the time of year.

Conversions Between Fractions, Decimals, and Percentages

The rules for converting numbers from fractions to decimals and percentages and from percentages to decimals are summarized in **Table C-6.**

TABLE C-6

CONVERSIONS		
Conversions	Rule	Example
Fraction to Decimal	divide numerator by denominator	$\frac{31}{45} \approx 0.69$
Fraction to Percentage	convert to decimal, then multiply by 100%	$\frac{31}{45} \approx (0.69)(100\%)$ $\approx 69\%$
Percentage to Decimal	move decimal point two decimal places to the left, and remove the percent sign	$69\% = 0.69$

Equations

Chapter 2 Measurements and Calculations

DENSITY

$$\text{density} = \frac{\text{mass}}{\text{volume}} \text{ or } D = \frac{m}{V}$$

PERCENTAGE ERROR

$$\% \text{ error} = \frac{\text{accepted value} - \text{experimental value}}{\text{accepted value}} \times 100$$

Chapter 3 Atoms: The Building Blocks of Matter

ATOMIC MASS NUMBER

$$\text{mass number} = \# \text{ of protons} + \# \text{ of neutrons}$$

Chapter 7 Chemical Formulas and Chemical Compounds

PERCENTAGE COMPOSITION BY MASS

$$\% \text{ of element in compound} = \frac{\text{mass of element in the sample}}{\text{mass of the whole sample}}$$

Chapter 9 Stoichiometry

PERCENTAGE YIELD

$$\% \text{ yield} = \frac{\text{actual yield}}{\text{theoretical yield}} \times 100$$

Chapter 10 States of Matter

KINETIC ENERGY

$$\text{kinetic energy} = \frac{1}{2} \text{ mass} \times \text{velocity}^2 \text{ or } KE = \frac{1}{2}(mv^2)$$

Chapter 11 Gases

PARTIAL PRESSURE

total pressure of a gas mixture = the sum of the partial pressures of the component gases

$$P_T = P_1 + P_2 + P_3 + \ldots$$

BOYLE'S LAW

The volume of a fixed mass of gas varies inversely with the pressure at constant temperature.

$$P_1V_1 = P_2V_2$$

CHARLES'S LAW

The pressure of a fixed mass of gas at constant volume varies directly with the Kelvin temperature.

$$\frac{P_1}{T_1} = \frac{P_2}{T_2}$$

COMBINED GAS LAW

This law expresses the relationship between pressure, volume, and the temperature of a fixed amount of gas.

$$\frac{P_1V_1}{T_1} = \frac{P_2V_2}{T_2} \ \text{ or } \ \frac{P_1V_1}{n_1T_1} = \frac{P_2V_2}{n_2T_2}$$

AVOGADRO'S LAW

This law states that equal volumes of gases at the same temperature and pressure contain equal numbers of particles.

$$V = kn$$

IDEAL GAS LAW

This law expresses the mathematical relationship among pressure, volume, temperature, and the number of moles of a gas.

$$PV = nRT$$

GRAHAM'S LAW OF EFFUSION

The rates of effusion of gases at the same temperature and pressure are inversely proportional to the square roots of their molar masses.

$$\frac{\text{rate of effusion of } A}{\text{rate of effusion of } B} = \frac{\sqrt{M_B}}{\sqrt{M_A}}$$

Chapter 12 Solutions

MOLARITY

A measure of concentration, relates the number of moles to the volume of solution.

$$\text{molarity} = \frac{\text{moles of solute}}{\text{liter of solution}}$$

MOLALITY

A measure of concentration, relates the number of moles to the mass of the solvent.

$$\text{molality} = \frac{\text{moles of solute}}{\text{mass of solvent (kg)}}$$

Chapter 13 Ions in Aqueous Solutions and Colligative Properties

FREEZING-POINT DEPRESSION

The difference between the freezing points of the pure solvent and the solution of a nonelectrolyte.

$$\Delta t_f = K_f m$$

BOILING-POINT ELEVATION

The difference between the boiling points of the pure solvent and the solution of a nonelectrolyte.

$$\Delta t_b = K_b m$$

Chapter 15 Acid-Base Titration and pH

pH

$$\text{pH} = -\log[\text{H}_3\text{O}^+]$$

pOH

$$\text{pOH} = -\log[\text{OH}^-]$$

Chapter 16 Reaction Energy

HEAT GAIN OR LOSS

$$Q = mc_p\Delta t$$

CHANGE IN ENTHALPY

$$\Delta H = H_{\text{products}} - H_{\text{reactants}}$$

FREE-ENERGY CHANGE

$$\Delta G^0 = \Delta H^0 - T\Delta S^0$$

Chapter 18 Chemical Equilibrium

CHEMICAL EQUILIBRIUM

$$K = \frac{[\text{C}]^x[\text{D}]^y}{[\text{A}]^n[\text{B}]^m}$$

Chapter 20 Electrochemistry

ELECTRODE POTENTIAL

$$E^0_{\text{cell}} = E^0_{\text{cathode}} - E^0_{\text{anode}}$$

Chapter 21 Nuclear Chemistry

ENERGY-MASS EQUIVALENCE

$$\text{energy} = \text{mass} \times [\text{speed of light}]^2$$
$$E = mc^2$$

Problem Bank

Conversions: Chap. 2, Sec. 2

CONVERTING SIMPLE SI UNITS

1. State the following measured quantities in the units indicated.
   a. 5.2 cm of magnesium ribbon in millimeters
   b. 0.049 kg of sulfur in grams
   c. 1.60 mL of ethanol in microliters
   d. 0.0025 g of vitamin A in micrograms
   e. 0.020 kg of tin in milligrams
   f. 3 kL of saline solution in liters

2. State the following measured quantities in the units indicated.
   a. 150 mg of aspirin in grams
   b. 2500 mL of hydrochloric acid in liters
   c. 0.5 g of sodium in kilograms
   d. 55 L of carbon dioxide gas in kiloliters
   e. 35 mm in centimeters
   f. 8740 m in kilometers
   g. 209 nm in millimeters
   h. 500 000 μg in kilograms

3. The greatest distance between Earth and the sun during Earth's revolution is 152 million kilometers. What is this distance in megameters?

4. How many milliliters of water will it take to fill a 2.00 L bottle that already contains 1.87 L of water?

5. A piece of copper wire is 150 cm long. How long is the wire in millimeters? How many 50 mm segments of wire can be cut from the length?

6. The ladle at an iron foundry can hold 8500 kg of molten iron; 646 metric tons of iron are needed to make rails. How many ladles full of iron will it take to make 646 metric tons of iron? (1 metric ton = 1000 kg)

CONVERTING DERIVED SI UNITS

7. State the following measured quantities in the units indicated.
   a. 310 000 cm^3 of concrete in cubic meters
   b. 6.5 m^2 of steel sheet in square centimeters
   c. 0.035 m^3 of chlorine gas in cubic centimeters
   d. 0.49 cm^2 of copper in square millimeters
   e. 1200 dm^3 of acetic-acid solution in cubic meters
   f. 87.5 mm^3 of actinium in cubic centimeters
   g. 250 000 cm^2 of polyethylene sheet in square meters

8. How many palisade cells from plant leaves would fit in a volume of 1.0 cm^3 of cells if the average volume of a palisade cell is 0.0147 mm^3?

MIXED REVIEW

9. Convert each of the following quantities to the required unit.
   a. 12.75 Mm to kilometers
   b. 277 cm to meters
   c. 30 560 m^2 to hectares (1 ha = 10 000 m^2)
   d. 81.9 cm^2 to square meters
   e. 300 000 km to megameters

10. Convert each of the following quantities to the required unit.
    a. 0.62 km to meters
    b. 3857 g to milligrams
    c. 0.0036 mL to microliters
    d. 0.342 metric tons to kg (1 metric ton = 1000 kg)
    e. 68.71 kL to liters

11. Convert each of the following quantities to the required unit.
    a. 856 mg to kilograms
    b. 1 210 000 μg to kilograms
    c. 6598 μL to cubic centimeters (1 mL = 1 cm^3)
    d. 80 600 nm to millimeters
    e. 10.74 cm^3 to liters

12. Convert each of the following quantities to the required unit.
    a. 7.93 L to cubic centimeters
    b. 0.0059 km to centimeters
    c. 4.19 L to cubic decimeters
    d. 7.48 m^2 to square centimeters
    e. 0.197 m^3 to liters

13. An automobile uses 0.05 mL of oil for each kilometer it is driven. How much oil in liters is consumed if the automobile is driven 20 000 km?

14. How many microliters are there in a volume of 370 mm^3 of cobra venom?

15. A baker uses 1.5 tsp of vanilla extract in each cake. How much vanilla extract in liters should the baker order to make 800 cakes? (1 tsp = 5 mL)

16. A person drinks eight glasses of water each day, and each glass contains 300 mL. How many liters of water will that person consume in a year? What is the mass of this volume of water in kilograms? (Assume one year has 365 days and the density of water is 1.00 kg/L.)

17. At the equator, Earth rotates with a velocity of about 465 m/s.
    a. What is this velocity in kilometers per hour?
    b. What is this velocity in kilometers per day?

18. A chemistry teacher needs to determine what quantity of sodium hydroxide to order. If each student will use 130 g and there are 60 students, how many kilograms of sodium hydroxide should the teacher order?

19. The teacher in item 18 also needs to order plastic tubing. If each of the 60 students needs 750 mm of tubing, what length of tubing in meters should the teacher order?

20. Convert the following to the required units.
   a. 550 µL/h to milliliters per day
   b. 9.00 metric tons/h to kilograms per minute
   c. 3.72 L/h to cubic centimeters per minute
   d. 6.12 km/h to meters per second

21. Express the following in the units indicated.
   a. 2.97 kg/L as grams per cubic centimeter
   b. 4128 g/dm^2 as kilograms per square centimeter
   c. 5.27 g/cm^3 as kilograms per cubic decimeter
   d. 6.91 kg/m^3 as milligrams per cubic millimeter

22. A gas has a density of 5.56 g/L.
   a. What volume in milliliters would 4.17 g of this gas occupy?
   b. What would be the mass in kilograms of 1 m^3 of this gas?

23. The average density of living matter on Earth's land areas is 0.10 g/cm^2. What mass of living matter in kilograms would occupy an area of 0.125 ha?

24. A textbook measures 250 mm long, 224 mm wide, and 50.0 mm thick. It has a mass of 2.94 kg.
   a. What is the volume of the book in cubic meters?
   b. What is the density of the book in grams per cubic centimeter?
   c. What is the area of one cover in square meters?

25. A glass dropper delivers liquid so that 25 drops equal 1.00 mL.
   a. What is the volume of one drop in milliliters?
   b. How many milliliters are in 37 drops?
   c. How many drops would be required to get 0.68 L?

26. Express each of the following in kilograms and grams.
   a. 504 700 mg   **c.** 122 mg
   b. 9 200 000 µg   **d.** 7195 cg

27. Express each of the following in liters and milliliters.
   a. 582 cm^3 **c.** 1.18 dm^3
   b. 0.0025 m^3 **d.** 32 900 µL

28. Express each of the following in grams per liter and kilograms per cubic meter.
   a. 1.37 g/cm^3 **d.** 38 000 g/m^3
   b. 0.692 kg/dm^3 **e.** 5.79 mg/mm^3
   c. 5.2 kg/L   **f.** 1.1 µg/mL

29. An industrial chemical reaction is run for 30.0 h and produces 648.0 kg of product. What is the average rate of product production in the stated units?
   a. grams per minute
   b. kilograms per day
   c. milligrams per millisecond

30. What is the speed of a car in meters per second when it is moving at 100 km/h?

31. A heater gives off energy as heat at a rate of 330 kJ/min. What is the rate of energy output in kilocalories per hour? (1 cal = 4.184 J)

32. The instructions on a package of fertilizer tell you to apply it at the rate of 62 g/m^2. How much fertilizer in kilograms would you need to apply to 1.0 ha? (1 ha = 10 000 m^2)

33. A water tank leaks water at the rate of 3.9 mL/h. If the tank is not repaired, what volume of water in liters will it leak in a year? Show your setup for solving this. Hint: Use one conversion factor to convert hours to days and another to convert days to years, and assume that one year has 365 days.

34. A nurse plans to give flu injections of 50 µL each from a bottle containing 2.0 mL of vaccine. How many doses are in the bottle?

Significant Figures: Chap. 2, Sec. 2

35. Determine the number of significant figures in the following measurements.
   a. 640 cm^3 **f.** 20.900 cm
   b. 200.0 mL   **g.** 0.000 000 56 g/L
   c. 0.5200 g   **h.** 0.040 02 kg/m^3
   d. 1.005 kg   **i.** 790 001 cm^2
   e. 10 000 L   **j.** 665.000 kg•m/s^2

36. Perform the following calculations, and express the results in the correct units and number of significant figures.
   a. 47.0 m ÷ 2.2 s
   b. 140 cm × 35 cm
   c. 5.88 kg ÷ 200 m^3
   d. 0.00 50 m^2 × 0.042 m
   e. 300.3 L ÷ 180 s
   f. 33.00 cm^2 × 2.70 cm
   g. 35 000 kJ ÷ 0.250 min

37. Perform the following calculations, and express the results in the correct units and number of significant figures.
   a. 22.0 m + 5.28 m + 15.5 m
   b. 0.042 kg + 1.229 kg + 0.502 kg
   c. 170 cm^2 + 3.5 cm^2 − 28 cm^2
   d. 0.003 L + 0.0048 L + 0.100 L
   e. 24.50 dL + 4.30 dL + 10.2 dL
   f. 3200 mg + 325 mg − 688 mg
   g. 14 000 kg + 8000 kg + 590 kg

MIXED REVIEW

38. Determine the number of significant figures in the following measurements.
   a. 0.0120 m   **f.** 1000 kg
   b. 100.5 mL   **g.** 180. mm
   c. 101 g   **h.** 0.4936 L
   d. 350 cm^2 **i.** 0.020 700 s
   e. 0.97 km

39. Round the following quantities to the specified number of significant figures.
    a. 5 487 129 m to three significant figures
    b. 0.013 479 265 mL to six significant figures
    c. 31 947.972 cm^2 to four significant figures
    d. 192.6739 m^2 to five significant figures
    e. 786.9164 cm to two significant figures
    f. 389 277 600 J to six significant figures
    g. 225 834.762 cm^3 to seven significant figures

40. Perform the following calculations, and express the answers in the correct units and number of significant figures.
    a. 651 cm × 75 cm
    b. 7.835 kg ÷ 2.5 L
    c. 14.75 L ÷ 1.20 s
    d. 360 cm × 51 cm × 9.07 cm
    e. 5.18 m × 0.77 m × 10.22 m
    f. 34.95 g ÷ 11.169 cm^3

41. Perform the following calculations, and express the answers in the correct units and number of significant figures.
    a. 7.945 J + 82.3 J − 0.02 J
    b. 0.0012 m − 0.000 45 m − 0.000 11 m
    c. 500 g + 432 g + 2 g
    d. 31.2 kPa + 0.0035 kPa − 0.147 kPa
    e. 312 dL − 31.2 dL − 3.12 dL
    f. 1701 kg + 50 kg + 43 kg

42. A rectangle measures 87.59 cm by 35.1 mm. Express its area with the proper number of significant figures in the specified unit.
    a. in cm^2 c. in m^2
    b. in mm^2

43. A box measures 900 mm by 31.5 mm by 6.3 cm. State its volume with the proper number of significant figures in the specified unit.
    a. in cm^3 c. in mm^3
    b. in m^3

44. A 125 mL sample of liquid has a mass of 0.16 kg. What is the density of the liquid in the following measurements?
    a. kg/m^3 c. kg/dm^3
    b. g/mL

45. Perform the following calculations, and express the results in the correct units and with the proper number of significant figures.
    a. 13.75 mm × 10.1 mm × 0.91 mm
    b. 89.4 cm^2 × 4.8 cm
    c. 14.9 m^3 ÷ 3.0 m^2
    d. 6.975 m × 30 m × 21.5 m

46. What is the volume of a region of space that measures 752 m × 319 m × 110 m? Give your answer in the correct unit and with the proper number of significant figures.

47. Perform the following calculations, and express the results in the correct units and with the proper number of significant figures.
    a. 7.382 g + 1.21 g + 4.7923 g
    b. 51.3 mg + 83 mg − 34.2 mg
    c. 0.007 L − 0.0037 L + 0.012 L
    d. 253.05 cm^2 + 33.9 cm^2 + 28 cm^2
    e. 14.77 kg + 0.086 kg − 0.391 kg
    f. 319 mL + 13.75 mL + 20. mL

48. A container measures 30.5 mm × 202 mm × 153 mm. When it is full of a liquid, it has a mass of 1.33 kg. When it is empty, it has a mass of 0.30 kg. What is the density of the liquid in kilograms per liter?

49. If 7.76 km of wire has a mass of 3.3 kg, what is the mass of the wire in g/m? What length in meters would have a mass of 1.0 g?

50. A container of plant food recommends an application rate of 52 kg/ha. If the container holds 10 kg of plant food, how many square meters will it cover? (1 ha = 10 000 m^2)

51. A chemical process produces 974 550 kJ of energy as heat in 37.0 min. What is the rate in kilojoules per minute? What is the rate in kilojoules per second?

52. A water pipe fills a container that measures 189 cm × 307 cm × 272 cm in 97 s.
    a. What is the volume of the container in cubic meters?
    b. What is the rate of flow in the pipe in liters per minute?
    c. What is the rate of flow in cubic meters per hour?

53. Perform the following calculations, and express the results in the correct units and with the proper number of significant figures. Note that in problems with multiple steps, it is better to perform the entire calculation and then round to significant figures.
    a. (0.054 kg + 1.33 kg) × 5.4 m^2
    b. 67.35 cm^2 ÷ (1.401 cm − 0.399 cm)
    c. 4.198 kg × (1019 m^2 − 40 m^2) ÷ (54.2 s × 31.3 s)
    d. 3.14159 m × (4.17 m + 2.150 m)
    e. 690 000 m ÷ (5.022 h − 4.31 h)
    f. (6.23 cm + 3.111 cm − 0.05 cm) × 14.99 cm

Scientific Notation: Chap. 2, Sec. 3

CONVERTING QUANTITIES TO SCIENTIFIC NOTATION

54. Express the following quantities in scientific notation.
    a. 8 800 000 000 m
    b. 0.0015 kg
    c. 0.000 000 000 06 kg/m^3
    d. 8 002 000 Hz
    e. 0.009 003 A
    f. 70 000 000 000 000 000 km
    g. 6028 L
    h. 0.2105 g
    i. 600 005 000 kJ/h
    j. 33.8 m^2

CALCULATING WITH QUANTITIES IN SCIENTIFIC NOTATION

55. Carry out the following calculations. Express the results in scientific notation and with the correct number of significant figures.
   a. 4.74×10^4 km $+ 7.71 \times 10^3$ km $+ 1.05 \times 10^3$ km
   b. 2.75×10^{-4} m $+ 8.03 \times 10^{-5}$ m $+ 2.122 \times 10^{-3}$ m
   c. 4.0×10^{-5} m^3 $+ 6.85 \times 10^{-6}$ m^3 $- 1.05 \times 10^{-5}$ m^3
   d. 3.15×10^2 mg $+ 3.15 \times 10^3$ mg $+ 3.15 \times 10^4$ mg
   e. 3.01×10^{22} atoms $+ 1.19 \times 10^{23}$ atoms $+ 9.80 \times 10^{21}$ atoms
   f. 6.85×10^7 nm $+ 4.0229 \times 10^8$ nm $- 8.38 \times 10^6$ nm

56. Carry out the following computations, and express the results in scientific notation.
   a. 7.20×10^3 cm $\times 8.08 \times 10^3$ cm
   b. 3.7×10^4 mm $\times 6.6 \times 10^4$ mm $\times 9.89 \times 10^3$ mm
   c. 8.27×10^2 m $\times 2.5 \times 10^{-3}$ m $\times 3.00 \times 10^{-4}$ m
   d. 4.44×10^{-35} m $\times 5.55 \times 10^{19}$ m $\times 7.69 \times 10^{-12}$ kg
   e. 6.55×10^4 dm $\times 7.89 \times 10^9$ dm $\times 4.01893 \times 10^5$ dm

57. Carry out the following computations, and express the results in scientific notation.
   a. 2.290×10^7 cm $\div 4.33 \times 10^3$ s
   b. 1.788×10^{-5} L $\div 7.111 \times 10^{-3}$ m^2
   c. 5.515×10^4 L $\div 6.04 \times 10^3$ km
   d. 3.29×10^{-4} km $\div 1.48 \times 10^{-2}$ min
   e. 4.73×10^{-4} g $\div (2.08 \times 10^{-3}$ km $\times 5.60 \times 10^{-4}$ km$)$

MIXED REVIEW

58. Express the following quantities in scientific notation.
   a. 158 000 km
   b. 0.000 009 782 L
   c. 837 100 000 cm^3
   d. 6 500 000 000 mm^2
   e. 0.005 93 g
   f. 0.000 000 006 13 m
   g. 12 552 000 J
   h. 0.000 008 004 g/L
   i. 0.010 995 kg
   j. 1 050 000 000 Hz

59. Perform the following calculations, and express the results in scientific notation with the correct number of significant figures.
   a. 2.48×10^2 kg $+ 9.17 \times 10^3$ kg $+ 7.2 \times 10^1$ kg
   b. 4.07×10^{-5} mg $+ 3.966 \times 10^{-4}$ mg $+ 7.1 \times 10^{-2}$ mg
   c. 1.39×10^4 m^3 $+ 6.52 \times 10^2$ m^3 $- 4.8 \times 10^3$ m^3
   d. 7.70×10^{-9} m $- 3.95 \times 10^{-8}$ m $+ 1.88 \times 10^{-7}$ m
   e. 1.111×10^5 J $+ 5.82 \times 10^4$ J $+ 3.01 \times 10^6$ J
   f. 9.81×10^{27} molecules $+ 3.18 \times 10^{25}$ molecules $- 2.09 \times 10^{26}$ molecules
   g. 1.36×10^7 cm $+ 3.456 \times 10^6$ cm $- 1.01 \times 10^7$ cm $+ 5.122 \times 10^5$ cm

60. Perform the following computations, and express the results in scientific notation with the correct number of significant figures.
   a. 1.54×10^{-1} L $\div 2.36 \times 10^{-4}$ s
   b. 3.890×10^4 mm $\times 4.71 \times 10^2$ mm^2

   c. 9.571×10^3 kg $\div 3.82 \times 10^{-1}$ m^2
   d. 8.33×10^3 km $\div 1.97 \times 10^2$ s
   e. 9.36×10^2 m $\times 3.82 \times 10^3$ m $\times 9.01 \times 10^{-1}$ m
   f. 6.377×10^4 J $\div 7.35 \times 10^{-3}$ s

61. Your electric company charges you for the electric energy you use, measured in kilowatt-hours (kWh). One kWh is equivalent to 3 600 000 J. Express this quantity in scientific notation.

62. The pressure in the deepest part of the ocean is 11 200 000 Pa. Express this pressure in scientific notation.

63. Convert 1.5 km to millimeters, and express the result in scientific notation.

64. Light travels at a speed of about 300 000 km/s.
   a. Express this value in scientific notation.
   b. Convert this value to meters per hour.
   c. What distance in centimeters does light travel in 1 μs?

65. There are 7.11×10^{24} molecules in 100.0 cm^3 of a certain substance.
   a. What is the number of molecules in 1.09 cm^3 of the substance?
   b. What would be the number of molecules in 2.24×10^4 cm^3 of the substance?
   c. What number of molecules are in 9.01×10^{-6} cm^3 of the substance?

66. The number of transistors on a particular integrated circuit is 3 578 000, and the integrated circuit measures 9.5 mm $\times$ 8.2 mm.
   a. What is the area occupied by each transistor?
   b. Using your answer from (a), how many transistors could be formed on a silicon sheet that measures 353 mm $\times$ 265 mm?

67. A solution has 0.0501 g of a substance in 1.00 L. Express this concentration in grams per microliter.

68. Cesium atoms are the largest of the naturally occurring elements. They have a diameter of 5.30×10^{-10} m. Calculate the number of cesium atoms that would have to be lined up to give a row of cesium atoms 2.54 cm (1 in.) long.

69. The neutron has a volume of approximately 1.4×10^{-44} m^3 and a mass of 1.675×10^{-24} g. Calculate the density of the neutron in g/m^3. What is the mass of 1.0 cm^3 of neutrons in kilograms?

70. The pits in a compact disc are some of the smallest things ever mass-produced mechanically by humans. These pits represent the 1s and 0s of digital information on a compact disc. These pits are only 1.6×10^{-8} m deep (1/4 the wavelength of red laser light). How many of these pits would have to be stacked on top of each other to make a hole 0.305 m deep?

71. 22 400 mL of oxygen gas contains 6.022×10^{23} oxygen molecules at 0°C and standard atmospheric pressure.
   a. How many oxygen molecules are in 0.100 mL of gas?
   b. How many oxygen molecules are in 1.00 L of gas?
   c. What is the average space in milliliters occupied by one oxygen molecule?

72. The mass of the atmosphere is calculated to be 5.136×10^{18} kg, and there are 6 500 000 000 people living on Earth. Calculate the following values.

 a. The mass of atmosphere in kilograms per person.

 b. The mass of atmosphere in metric tons per person.

 c. If the number of people increases to 9 500 000 000, what is the mass in kilograms per person?

73. The mass of the sun is 1.989×10^{30} kg, and the mass of Earth is 5.974×10^{24} kilograms. How many Earths would be needed to equal the mass of the sun?

74. A new landfill has dimensions of 2.3 km $\times$ 1.4 km $\times$ 0.15 km.

 a. What is the volume in cubic kilometers?

 b. What is the volume in cubic meters?

 c. If 250 000 000 objects averaging 0.060 m^3 each are placed into the landfill each year, how many years will it take to fill the landfill?

75. A dietary calorie (C) is exactly equal to 1000 cal. If your daily intake of food gives you 2400 C, what is your intake in joules per day? (1 cal = 4.184 J)

Four Steps for Solving Quantitative Problems: Chap. 2, Sec. 3

76. Gasoline has a density of 0.73 g/cm^3. How many liters of gasoline would be required to increase the mass of an automobile from 1271 kg to 1305 kg?

77. A swimming pool measures 9.0 m long by 3.5 m wide by 1.75 m deep. What mass of water in metric tons (1 metric ton = 1000 kg) does the pool contain when filled? The density of the water in the pool is 0.997 g/cm^3.

78. A tightly packed box of crackers contains 250 g of crackers and measures 7.0 cm $\times$ 17.0 cm $\times$ 19.0 cm. What is the average density in kilograms per liter of the crackers in the package? Assume that the unused volume is negligible.

MIXED REVIEW

Solve these problems by using the Four Steps for Solving Quantitative Problems.

79. The aluminum foil on a certain roll has a total area of 18.5 m^2 and a mass of 1275 g. Using a density of 2.7 g per cubic centimeter for aluminum, determine the thickness in millimeters of the aluminum foil.

80. If a liquid has a density of 1.17 g/cm^3, how many liters of the liquid have a mass of 3.75 kg?

81. A stack of 500 sheets of paper measuring 28 cm $\times$ 21 cm is 44.5 mm high and has a mass of 2090 g. What is the density of the paper in grams per cubic centimeter?

82. A triangular-shaped piece of a metal has a mass of 6.58 g. The triangle is 0.560 mm thick and measures 36.4 mm on the base and 30.1 mm in height. What is the density of the metal in grams per cubic centimeter?

83. A packing crate measures 0.40 m $\times$ 3 0.40 m $\times$ 3 0.25 m. You must fill the crate with boxes of cookies that each measure 22.0 cm $\times$ 12.0 cm $\times$ 5.0 cm. How many boxes of cookies can fit into the crate?

84. Calculate the unknown quantities in the following table. Use the following relationships for volumes of the various shapes.

 Volume of a cube = $\ell \times \ell \times \ell$
 Volume of a rectangle = $\ell \times w \times h$
 Volume of a sphere = $4/3\pi r^3$
 Volume of a cylinder = $\pi r^2 \times h$

	D	m	V	Shape	Dimensions
a.	2.27 g/cm^3	3.93 kg	? L	cube	? m $\times$? m $\times$? m
b.	1.85 g/cm^3	? g	? cm^3	rectangle	33 mm $\times$ 21 mm $\times$ 7.2 mm
c.	3.21 g/L	? kg	? dm^3	sphere	3.30 m diameter
d.	? g/cm^3	497 g	? m^3	cylinder	7.5 cm diameter $\times$ 12 cm
e.	0.92 g/cm^3	? kg	? cm^3	rectangle	3.5 m $\times$ 1.2 m $\times$ 6.5 m

85. When a sample of a metal alloy that has a mass of 9.65 g is placed into a graduated cylinder containing water, the volume reading in the cylinder increases from 16.0 mL to 19.5 mL. What is the density of the alloy sample in grams per cubic centimeter?

86. Pure gold can be made into extremely thin sheets called gold leaf. Suppose that 50. kg of gold is made into gold leaf having an area of 3620 m^2. The density of gold is 19.3 g/cm^3.

 a. How thick in micrometers is the gold leaf?

 b. A gold atom has a radius of 1.44×10^{-10} m. How many atoms thick is the gold leaf?

87. A chemical plant process requires that a cylindrical reaction tank be filled with a certain liquid in 238 s. The tank is 1.2 m in diameter and 4.6 m high. What flow rate in liters per minute is required to fill the reaction tank in the specified time?

88. The radioactive decay of 2.8 g of plutonium-238 generates 1.0 joule of energy as heat every second. Plutonium has a density of 19.86 g/cm^3. How many calories (1 cal = 4.184 J) of energy as heat will a rectangular piece of plutonium that is 4.5 cm $\times$ 3.05 cm $\times$ 15 cm generate per hour?

89. The mass of Earth is 5.974×10^{24} kg. Assume that Earth is a sphere of diameter 1.28×10^4 km, and calculate the average density of Earth in g/cm^3.

90. What volume of magnesium in cubic centimeters would have the same mass as 1.82 dm^3 of platinum? The density of magnesium is 1.74 g/cm^3, and the density of platinum is 21.45 g/cm^3.

91. A roll of transparent tape has 66 m of tape on it. If an average of 5.0 cm of tape is needed each time the tape is used, how many uses can you get from a case of tape containing 24 rolls?

92. An automobile can travel 38 km on 4.0 L of gasoline. If the automobile is driven 75% of the days in a year and the average distance traveled each day is 86 km, how many liters of gasoline will be consumed in one year (assume the year has 365 days)?

93. A hose delivers water to a swimming pool that measures 9.0 m long by 3.5 m wide by 1.75 m deep. It requires 97 h to fill the pool. At what rate in liters per minute will the hose fill the pool?

94. Automobile batteries are filled with a solution of sulfuric acid, which has a density of 1.285 g/cm^3. The solution used to fill the battery is 38% (by mass) sulfuric acid. How many grams of sulfuric acid are present in 500 mL of battery acid?

Mole Concept: Chap. 3, Sec. 3; Chap. 7, Sec. 3

PROBLEMS INVOLVING ATOMS AND ELEMENTS

95. Calculate the number of moles in each of the following masses.
    a. 64.1 g of aluminum
    b. 28.1 g of silicon
    c. 0.255 g of sulfur
    d. 850.5 g of zinc

96. Calculate the mass of each of the following amounts.
    a. 1.22 mol sodium
    b. 14.5 mol copper
    c. 0.275 mol mercury
    d. 9.37×10^{-3} mol magnesium

97. Calculate the amount in moles in each of the following quantities.
    a. 3.01×10^{23} atoms of rubidium
    b. 8.08×10^{22} atoms of krypton
    c. 5 700 000 000 atoms of lead
    d. 2.997×10^{25} atoms of vanadium

98. Calculate the number of atoms in each of the following amounts.
    a. 1.004 mol bismuth
    b. 2.5 mol manganese
    c. 0.000 0002 mol helium
    d. 32.6 mol strontium

99. Calculate the number of atoms in each of the following masses.
    a. 54.0 g of aluminum
    b. 69.45 g of lanthanum
    c. 0.697 g of gallium
    d. 0.000 000 020 g beryllium

100. Calculate the mass of the following numbers of atoms.
    a. 6.022×10^{24} atoms of tantalum
    b. 3.01×10^{21} atoms of cobalt
    c. 1.506×10^{24} atoms of argon
    d. 1.20×10^{25} atoms of helium

PROBLEMS INVOLVING MOLECULES, FORMULA UNITS, AND IONS

101. Calculate the number of moles in each of the following masses.
    a. 3.00 g of boron tribromide, BBr_3
    b. 0.472 g of sodium fluoride, NaF
    c. 7.50×10^2 g of methanol, CH_3OH
    d. 50.0 g of calcium chlorate, $Ca(ClO_3)_2$

102. Determine the mass of each of the following amounts.
    a. 1.366 mol of NH_3
    b. 0.120 mol of glucose, $C_6H_{12}O_6$
    c. 6.94 mol barium chloride, $BaCl_2$
    d. 0.005 mol of propane, C_3H_8

103. Calculate the number of molecules in each of the following amounts.
    a. 4.99 mol of methane, CH_4
    b. 0.005 20 mol of nitrogen gas, N_2
    c. 1.05 mol of phosphorus trichloride, PCl_3
    d. 3.5×10^{-5} mol of vitamin C, ascorbic acid, $C_6H_8O_6$

104. Calculate the number of formula units in the following amounts.
    a. 1.25 mol of potassium bromide, KBr
    b. 5.00 mol of magnesium chloride, $MgCl_2$
    c. 0.025 mol of sodium carbonate, Na_2CO_3
    d. 6.82×10^{-6} mol of lead(II) nitrate, $Pb(NO_3)_2$

105. Calculate the amount in moles of the following numbers of molecules or formula units.
    a. 3.34×10^{34} formula units of $Cu(OH)_2$
    b. 1.17×10^{16} molecules of H_2S
    c. 5.47×10^{21} formula units of nickel(II) sulfate, $NiSO_4$
    d. 7.66×10^{19} molecules of hydrogen peroxide, H_2O_2

106. Calculate the mass of each of the following quantities.
    a. 2.41×10^{24} molecules of hydrogen, H_2
    b. 5.00×10^{21} formula units of aluminum hydroxide, $Al(OH)_3$
    c. 8.25×10^{22} molecules of bromine pentafluoride, BrF_5
    d. 1.20×10^{23} formula units of sodium oxalate, $Na_2C_2O_4$

107. Calculate the number of molecules or formula units in each of the following masses.
    a. 22.9 g of sodium sulfide, Na_2S
    b. 0.272 g of nickel(II) nitrate, $Ni(NO_3)_2$
    c. 260 mg of acrylonitrile, CH_2CHCN

MIXED REVIEW

108. Calculate the number of moles in each of the following masses.
    a. 0.039 g of palladium
    b. 8200 g of iron
    c. 0.0073 kg of tantalum
    d. 0.006 55 g of antimony
    e. 5.64 kg of barium

109. Calculate the mass in grams of each of the following amounts.
   a. 1.002 mol of chromium
   b. 550 mol of aluminum
   c. 4.08×10^{-8} mol of neon
   d. 7 mol of titanium
   e. 0.0086 mol of xenon
   f. 3.29×10^4 mol of lithium

110. Calculate the number of atoms in each of the following amounts.
   a. 17.0 mol of germanium
   b. 0.6144 mol of copper
   c. 3.02 mol of tin
   d. 2.0×10^6 mol of carbon
   e. 0.0019 mol of zirconium
   f. 3.227×10^{-10} mol of potassium

111. Calculate the number of moles in each of the following quantities.
   a. 6.022×10^{24} atoms of cobalt
   b. 1.06×10^{23} atoms of tungsten
   c. 3.008×10^{19} atoms of silver
   d. 950 000 000 atoms of plutonium
   e. 4.61×10^{17} atoms of radon
   f. 8 trillion atoms of cerium

112. Calculate the number of atoms in each of the following masses.
   a. 0.0082 g of gold
   b. 812 g of molybdenum
   c. 2.00×10^2 mg of americium
   d. 10.09 kg of neon
   e. 0.705 mg of bismuth
   f. 37 μg of uranium

113. Calculate the mass of each of the following.
   a. 8.22×10^{23} atoms of rubidium
   b. 4.05 Avogadro's constants of manganese atoms
   c. 9.96×10^{26} atoms of tellurium
   d. 0.000 025 Avogadro's constants of rhodium atoms
   e. 88 300 000 000 000 atoms of radium
   f. 2.94×10^{17} atoms of hafnium

114. Calculate the number of moles in each of the following masses.
   a. 45.0 g of acetic acid, CH_3COOH
   b. 7.04 g of lead(II) nitrate, $Pb(NO_3)_2$
   c. 5000 kg of iron(III) oxide, Fe_2O_3
   d. 12.0 mg of ethylamine, $C_2H_5NH_2$
   e. 0.003 22 g of stearic acid, $C_{17}H_{35}COOH$
   f. 50.0 kg of ammonium sulfate, $(NH_4)_2SO_4$

115. Calculate the mass of each of the following amounts.
   a. 3.00 mol of selenium oxybromide, $SeOBr_2$
   b. 488 mol of calcium carbonate, $CaCO_3$
   c. 0.0091 mol of retinoic acid, $C_{20}H_{28}O_2$
   d. 6.00×10^{-8} mol of nicotine, $C_{10}H_{14}N_2$
   e. 2.50 mol of strontium nitrate, $Sr(NO_3)_2$
   f. 3.50×10^{-6} mol of uranium hexafluoride, UF_6

116. Calculate the number of molecules or formula units in each of the following amounts.
   a. 4.27 mol of tungsten(VI) oxide, WO_3
   b. 0.003 00 mol of strontium nitrate, $Sr(NO_3)_2$
   c. 72.5 mol of toluene, $C_6H_5CH_3$
   d. 5.11×10^{-7} mol of α-tocopherol (vitamin E), $C_{29}H_{50}O_2$
   e. 1500 mol of hydrazine, N_2H_4
   f. 0.989 mol of nitrobenzene $C_6H_5NO_2$

117. Calculate the number of molecules or formula units in each of the following masses.
   a. 285 g of iron(III) phosphate, $FePO_4$
   b. 0.0084 g of C_5H_5N
   c. 85 mg of 2-methyl-1-propanol, $(CH_3)_2CHCH_2OH$
   d. 4.6×10^{-4} g of mercury(II) acetate, $Hg(C_2H_3O_2)_2$
   e. 0.0067 g of lithium carbonate, Li_2CO_3

118. Calculate the mass of each of the following quantities.
   a. 8.39×10^{23} molecules of fluorine, F_2
   b. 6.82×10^{24} formula units of beryllium sulfate, $BeSO_4$
   c. 7.004×10^{26} molecules of chloroform, $CHCl_3$
   d. 31 billion formula units of chromium(III) formate, $Cr(CHO_2)_3$
   e. 6.3×10^{18} molecules of nitric acid, HNO_3
   f. 8.37×10^{25} molecules of Freon 114, $C_2Cl_2F_4$

119. Precious metals are commonly measured in troy ounces. A troy ounce is equivalent to 31.1 g. How many moles are in a troy ounce of gold? How many moles are in a troy ounce of platinum? of silver?

120. A chemist needs 22.0 g of phenol, C_6H_5OH, for an experiment. How many moles of phenol is this?

121. A student needs 0.015 mol of iodine crystals, I_2, for an experiment. What mass of iodine crystals should the student obtain?

122. The weight of a diamond is given in carats. One carat is equivalent to 200. mg. A pure diamond is made up entirely of carbon atoms. How many carbon atoms make up a 1.00 carat diamond?

123. 8.00 g of calcium chloride, $CaCl_2$, is dissolved in 1.000 kg of water.
   a. How many moles of $CaCl_2$ are in solution? How many moles of water are present?
   b. Assume that the ionic compound, $CaCl_2$, separates completely into Ca^{2+} and Cl^- ions when it dissolves in water. How many moles of each ion are present in the solution?

124. How many moles are in each of the following masses?
   a. 453.6 g (1.000 pound) of sucrose (table sugar), $C_{12}H_{22}O_{11}$
   b. 1.000 pound of table salt, NaCl

125. When the ionic compound NH_4Cl dissolves in water, it breaks into one ammonium ion, NH_4^+, and one chloride ion, Cl^-. If you dissolved 10.7 g of NH_4Cl in water, how many moles of ions would be in solution?

126. What is the total amount in moles of atoms in a jar that contains 2.41×10^{24} atoms of chromium, 1.51×10^{23} atoms of nickel, and 3.01×10^{23} atoms of copper?

127. The density of liquid water is 0.997 g/mL at 25°C.
    a. Calculate the mass of 250.0 mL (about a cupful) of water.
    b. How many moles of water are in 250.0 mL of water? Hint: Use the result of (a).
    c. Calculate the volume that would be occupied by 2.000 mol of water at 25°C.
    d. What mass of water is 2.000 mol of water?

128. An Avogadro's constant (1 mol) of sugar molecules has a mass of 342 g, but an Avogadro's constant (1 mol) of water molecules has a mass of only 18 g. Explain why there is such a difference between the mass of 1 mol of sugar and the mass of 1 mol of water.

129. Calculate the mass of aluminum that would have the same number of atoms as 6.35 g of cadmium.

130. A chemist weighs a steel cylinder of compressed oxygen, O_2, and finds that it has a mass of 1027.8 g. After some of the oxygen is used in an experiment, the cylinder has a mass of 1023.2 g. How many moles of oxygen gas are used in the experiment?

131. Suppose that you could decompose 0.250 mol of Ag_2S into its elements.
    a. How many moles of silver would you have? How many moles of sulfur would you have?
    b. How many moles of Ag_2S are there in 38.8 g of Ag_2S? How many moles of silver and sulfur would be produced from this amount of Ag_2S?
    c. Calculate the masses of silver and sulfur produced in (b).

Percentage Composition: Chap. 7, Sec. 3

132. Determine the percentage composition of each of the following compounds.
    a. sodium oxalate, $Na_2C_2O_4$
    b. ethanol, C_2H_5OH
    c. aluminum oxide, Al_2O_3
    d. potassium sulfate, K_2SO_4

133. Suppose that a laboratory analysis of white powder showed 42.59% Na, 12.02% C, and 44.99% O. Would you report that the compound is sodium oxalate or sodium carbonate? (Use 43.38% Na, 11.33% C, and 45.29% O for sodium carbonate, and 34.31% Na, 17.93% C, and 47.76% O for sodium oxalate.)

134. Calculate the mass of the given element in each of the following compounds.
    a. bromine in 50.0 g potassium bromide, KBr
    b. chromium in 1.00 kg sodium dichromate, $Na_2Cr_2O_7$
    c. nitrogen in 85.0 mg of the amino acid lysine, $C_6H_{14}N_2O_2$
    d. cobalt in 2.84 g cobalt(II) acetate, $Co(C_2H_3O_2)_2$

HYDRATES

135. Calculate the percentage of water in each of the following hydrates.
    a. sodium carbonate decahydrate, $Na_2CO_3 \bullet 10H_2O$
    b. nickel(II) iodide hexahydrate, $NiI_2 \bullet 6H_2O$
    c. ammonium hexacyanoferrate(III) trihydrate (commonly called ammonium ferricyanide), $(NH_4)_2Fe(CN)_6 \bullet 3H_2O$
    d. aluminum bromide hexahydrate, $AlBr_3 \bullet 6H_2O$

MIXED REVIEW

136. Write formulas for the following compounds, and determine the percentage composition of each.
    a. nitric acid
    b. ammonia
    c. mercury(II) sulfate
    d. antimony(V) fluoride

137. Calculate the percentage composition of the following compounds.
    a. lithium bromide, LiBr
    b. anthracene, $C_{14}H_{10}$
    c. ammonium nitrate, NH_4NO_3
    d. nitrous acid, HNO_2
    e. silver sulfide, Ag_2S
    f. iron(II) thiocyanate, $Fe(SCN)_2$
    g. lithium acetate
    h. nickel(II) formate

138. Calculate the percentage of the given element in each of the following compounds.
    a. nitrogen in urea, NH_2CONH_2
    b. sulfur in sulfuryl chloride, SO_2Cl_2
    c. thallium in thallium(III) oxide, Tl_2O_3
    d. oxygen in potassium chlorate, $KClO_3$
    e. bromine in calcium bromide, $CaBr_2$
    f. tin in tin(IV) oxide, SnO_2

139. Calculate the mass of the given element in each of the following quantities.
    a. oxygen in 4.00 g of manganese dioxide, MnO_2
    b. aluminum in 50.0 metric tons of aluminum oxide, Al_2O_3
    c. silver in 325 g silver cyanide, AgCN
    d. gold in 0.780 g of gold(III) selenide, Au_2Se_3
    e. selenium in 683 g sodium selenite, Na_2SeO_3
    f. chlorine in 5.0×10^4 g of 1,1-dichloropropane, $CHCl_2CH_2CH_3$

140. Calculate the percentage of water in each of the following hydrates.
    a. strontium chloride hexahydrate, $SrCl_2 \bullet 6H_2O$
    b. zinc sulfate heptahydrate, $ZnSO_4 \bullet 7H_2O$
    c. calcium fluorophosphate dihydrate, $CaFPO_3 \bullet 2H_2O$
    d. beryllium nitrate trihydrate, $Be(NO_3)_2 \bullet 3H_2O$

141. Calculate the percentage of the given element in each of the following hydrates. You must first determine the formulas of the hydrates.
   a. nickel in nickel(II) acetate tetrahydrate
   b. chromium in sodium chromate tetrahydrate
   c. cerium in cerium(IV) sulfate tetrahydrate

142. Cinnabar is a mineral that is mined in order to produce mercury. Cinnabar is mercury(II) sulfide, HgS. What mass of mercury can be obtained from 50.0 kg of cinnabar?

143. The minerals malachite, $Cu_2(OH)_2CO_3$, and chalcopyrite, $CuFeS_2$, can be mined to obtain copper metal. How much copper could be obtained from 1.00×10^3 kg of each? Which of the two has the greater copper content?

144. Calculate the percentage of the given element in each of the following hydrates.
   a. vanadium in vanadium oxysulfate dihydrate, $VOSO_4 \bullet 2H_2O$
   b. tin in potassium stannate trihydrate, $K_2SnO_3 \bullet 3H_2O$
   c. chlorine in calcium chlorate dihydrate, $CaClO_3 \bullet 2H_2O$

145. Heating copper sulfate pentahydrate will evaporate the water from the crystals, leaving anhydrous copper sulfate, a white powder. *Anhydrous* means "without water." What mass of anhydrous $CuSO_4$ would be produced by heating 500.0 g of $CuSO_4 \bullet 5H_2O$?

146. Silver metal may be precipitated from a solution of silver nitrate by placing a copper strip into the solution. What mass of $AgNO_3$ would you dissolve in water in order to get 1.00 g of silver?

147. A sample of Ag_2S has a mass of 62.4 g. What mass of each element could be obtained by decomposing this sample?

148. A quantity of epsom salts, magnesium sulfate heptahydrate, $MgSO_4 \bullet 7H_2O$, is heated until all the water is driven off. The sample loses 11.8 g in the process. What was the mass of the original sample?

149. The process of manufacturing sulfuric acid begins with the burning of sulfur. What mass of sulfur would have to be burned in order to produce 1.00 kg of H_2SO_4? Assume that all of the sulfur ends up in the sulfuric acid.

Empirical Formulas: Chap. 7, Sec. 4

150. Determine the empirical formula for compounds that have the following analyses.
   a. 28.4% copper, 71.6% bromine
   b. 39.0% potassium, 12.0% carbon, 1.01% hydrogen, and 47.9% oxygen
   c. 77.3% silver, 7.4% phosphorus, 15.3% oxygen
   d. 0.57% hydrogen, 72.1% iodine, 27.3% oxygen

151. Determine the simplest formula for compounds that have the following analyses. The data may not be exact.
   a. 36.2% aluminum and 63.8% sulfur
   b. 93.5% niobium and 6.50% oxygen
   c. 57.6% strontium, 13.8% phosphorus, and 28.6% oxygen
   d. 28.5% iron, 48.6% oxygen, and 22.9% sulfur

152. Determine the molecular formula of each of the following unknown substances.
   a. empirical formula CH_2
      experimental molar mass 28 g/mol
   b. empirical formula B_2H_5
      experimental molar mass 54 g/mol
   c. empirical formula C_2HCl
      experimental molar mass 179 g/mol
   d. empirical formula C_6H_8O
      experimental molar mass 290 g/mol
   e. empirical formula C_3H_2O
      experimental molar mass 216 g/mol

MIXED REVIEW

153. Determine the empirical formula for compounds that have the following analyses.
   a. 66.0% barium and 34.0% chlorine
   b. 80.38% bismuth, 18.46% oxygen, and 1.16% hydrogen
   c. 12.67% aluminum, 19.73% nitrogen, and 67.60% oxygen
   d. 35.64% zinc, 26.18% carbon, 34.88% oxygen, and 3.30% hydrogen
   e. 2.8% hydrogen, 9.8% nitrogen, 20.5% nickel, 44.5% oxygen, and 22.4% sulfur
   f. 8.09% carbon, 0.34% hydrogen, 10.78% oxygen, and 80.78% bromine

154. Sometimes, instead of percentage composition, you will have the composition of a sample by mass. Using the actual mass of the sample, determine the empirical formula for compounds that have the following analyses.
   a. a 0.858 g sample of an unknown substance is composed of 0.537 g of copper and 0.321 g of fluorine
   b. a 13.07 g sample of an unknown substance is composed of 9.48 g of barium, 1.66 g of carbon, and 1.93 g of nitrogen
   c. a 0.025 g sample of an unknown substance is composed of 0.0091 g manganese, 0.0106 g oxygen, and 0.0053 g sulfur

155. Determine the empirical formula for compounds that have the following analyses.
   a. a 0.0082 g sample contains 0.0015 g of nickel and 0.0067 g of iodine
   b. a 0.470 g sample contains 0.144 g of manganese, 0.074 g of nitrogen, and 0.252 g of oxygen
   c. a 3.880 g sample contains 0.691 g of magnesium, 1.824 g of sulfur, and 1.365 g of oxygen
   d. a 46.25 g sample contains 14.77 g of potassium, 9.06 g of oxygen, and 22.42 g of tin

156. Determine the empirical formula for compounds that have the following analyses:
   a. 60.9% As and 39.1% S
   b. 76.89% Re and 23.12% O
   c. 5.04% H, 35.00% N, and 59.96% O
   d. 24.3% Fe, 33.9% Cr, and 41.8% O
   e. 54.03% C, 37.81% N, and 8.16% H
   f. 55.81% C, 3.90% H, 29.43% F, and 10.85% N

157. Determine the molecular formulas for compounds having the following empirical formulas and molar masses.
  a. C_2H_4S; experimental molar mass 179
  b. C_2H_4O; experimental molar mass 176
  c. $C_2H_3O_2$; experimental molar mass 119
  d. C_2H_2O; experimental molar mass 254

158. Use the experimental molar mass to determine the molecular formula for compounds having the following analyses.
  a. 41.39% carbon, 3.47% hydrogen, and 55.14% oxygen; experimental molar mass 116.07
  b. 54.53% carbon, 9.15% hydrogen, and 36.32% oxygen; experimental molar mass 88
  c. 64.27% carbon, 7.19% hydrogen, and 28.54% oxygen; experimental molar mass 168.19

159. A 0.400 g sample of a white powder contains 0.141 g of potassium, 0.115 g of sulfur, and 0.144 g of oxygen. What is the empirical formula for the compound?

160. A 10.64 g sample of a lead compound is analyzed and found to be made up of 9.65 g of lead and 0.99 g of oxygen. Determine the empirical formula for this compound.

161. A 2.65 g sample of a salmon-colored powder contains 0.70 g of chromium, 0.65 g of sulfur, and 1.30 g of oxygen. The molar mass is 392.2. What is the formula of the compound?

162. Ninhydrin is a compound that reacts with amino acids and proteins to produce a dark-colored complex. It is used by forensic chemists and detectives to see fingerprints that might otherwise be invisible. Ninhydrin's composition is 60.68% carbon, 3.40% hydrogen, and 35.92% oxygen. What is the empirical formula for ninhydrin?

163. Histamine is a substance that is released by cells in response to injury, infection, stings, and materials that cause allergic responses, such as pollen. Histamine causes dilation of blood vessels and swelling due to accumulation of fluid in the tissues. People sometimes take *anti*histamine drugs to counteract the effects of histamine. A sample of histamine having a mass of 385 mg is composed of 208 mg of carbon, 31 mg of hydrogen, and 146 mg of nitrogen. The molar mass of histamine is 111 g/mol. What is the molecular formula for histamine?

164. You analyze two substances in the laboratory and discover that each has the empirical formula CH_2O. You can easily see that they are different substances because one is a liquid with a sharp, biting odor and the other is an odorless, crystalline solid. How can you account for the fact that both have the same empirical formula?

Stoichiometry: Chap. 9, Sec. 1–2

165. How many moles of sodium will react with water to produce 4.0 mol of hydrogen in the following reaction?
$$2Na(s) + 2H_2O(l) \longrightarrow 2NaOH(aq) + H_2(g)$$

166. How many moles of lithium chloride will be formed by the reaction of chlorine with 0.046 mol of lithium bromide in the following reaction?
$$2LiBr(aq) + Cl_2(g) \longrightarrow 2LiCl(aq) + Br_2(l)$$

167. Aluminum will react with sulfuric acid in the following reaction.
$$2Al(s) + 3H_2SO_4(l) \longrightarrow Al_2(SO_4)_3(aq) + 3H_2(g)$$
  a. How many moles of H_2SO_4 will react with 18 mol Al?
  b. How many moles of each product will be produced?

168. Propane burns in excess oxygen according to the following reaction.
$$C_3H_8 + 5O_2 \longrightarrow 3CO_2 + 4H_2O$$
  a. How many moles each of CO_2 and H_2O are formed from 3.85 mol of propane?
  b. If 0.647 mol of oxygen is used in the burning of propane, how many moles each of CO_2 and H_2O are produced? How many moles of C_3H_8 are consumed?

169. Phosphorus burns in air to produce a phosphorus oxide in the following reaction:
$$4P(s) + 5O_2(g) \longrightarrow P_4O_{10}(s)$$
  a. What mass of phosphorus will be needed to produce 3.25 mol of P_4O_{10}?
  b. If 0.489 mol of phosphorus burns, what mass of oxygen is used? What mass of P_4O_{10} is produced?

170. Hydrogen peroxide breaks down, releasing oxygen, in the following reaction.
$$2H_2O_2(aq) \longrightarrow 2H_2O(l) + O_2(g)$$
  a. What mass of oxygen is produced when 1.840 mol of H_2O_2 decompose?
  b. What mass of water is produced when 5.0 mol O_2 is produced by this reaction?

171. Sodium carbonate reacts with nitric acid according to the following equation:
$$Na_2CO_3(s) + 2HNO_3 \longrightarrow 2NaNO_3 + CO_2 + H_2O$$
  a. How many moles of Na_2CO_3 are required to produce 100.0 g of $NaNO_3$?
  b. If 7.50 g of Na_2CO_3 reacts, how many moles of CO_2 are produced?

172. Hydrogen is generated by passing hot steam over iron, which oxidizes to form Fe_3O_4, in the following equation:
$$3Fe(s) + 4H_2O(g) \longrightarrow 4H_2(g) + Fe_3O_4(s)$$
  a. If 625 g of Fe_3O_4 is produced in the reaction, how many moles of hydrogen are produced at the same time?
  b. How many moles of iron would be needed to generate 27 g of hydrogen?

173. Calculate the mass of silver bromide produced from 22.5 g of silver nitrate in the following reaction:
$$2AgNO_3(aq) + MgBr_2(aq) \longrightarrow$$
$$2AgBr(s) + Mg(NO_3)_2(aq)$$

174. What mass of acetylene, C_2H_2, will be produced from the reaction of 90. g of calcium carbide, CaC_2, with water in the following reaction?
$$CaC_2(s) + 2H_2O(l) \longrightarrow C_2H_2(g) + Ca(OH)_2(s)$$

175. Chlorine gas can be produced in the laboratory by adding concentrated hydrochloric acid to manganese(IV) oxide in the following reaction:

$$MnO_2(s) + 4HCl(aq) \longrightarrow$$
$$MnCl_2(aq) + 2H_2O(l) + Cl_2(g)$$

  a. Calculate the mass of MnO_2 needed to produce 25.0 g of Cl_2.

  b. What mass of $MnCl_2$ is produced when 0.091 g of Cl_2 is generated?

MIXED REVIEW

176. How many moles of ammonium sulfate can be made from the reaction of 30.0 mol of NH_3 with H_2SO_4 according to the following equation:

$$2NH_3 + H_2SO_4 \longrightarrow (NH_4)_2SO_4$$

177. In a very violent reaction called a thermite reaction, aluminum metal reacts with iron(III) oxide to form iron metal and aluminum oxide according to the following equation:

$$Fe_2O_3 + 2Al \longrightarrow 2Fe + Al_2O_3$$

  a. What mass of Al will react with 150 g of Fe_2O_3?

  b. If 0.905 mol Al_2O_3 is produced in the reaction, what mass of Fe is produced?

  c. How many moles of Fe_2O_3 will react with 99.0 g of Al?

178. The reaction $N_2(g) + 3H_2(g) \longrightarrow 2NH_3(g)$ is used to produce ammonia commercially. If 1.40 g of N_2 are used in the reaction, how many grams of H_2 will be needed?

179. What mass of sulfuric acid, H_2SO_4, is required to react with 1.27 g of potassium hydroxide, KOH? The products of this reaction are potassium sulfate and water.

180. Ammonium hydrogen phosphate, $(NH_4)_2HPO_4$, a common fertilizer, is made from reacting phosphoric acid, H_3PO_4, with ammonia.

  a. Write the equation for this reaction.

  b. If 10.00 g of ammonia react, how many moles of fertilizer will be produced?

  c. What mass of ammonia will react with 2800 kg of H_3PO_4?

181. The following reaction shows the synthesis of zinc citrate, an ingredient in toothpaste, from zinc carbonate and citric acid:

$$3ZnCO_3(s) + 2C_6H_8O_7(aq) \longrightarrow$$
$$Zn_3(C_6H_5O_7)_2(aq) + 3H_2O(l) + 3CO_2(g)$$

  a. How many moles of $ZnCO_3$ and $C_6H_8O_7$ are required to produce 30.0 mol of $Zn_3(C_6H_5O_7)_2$?

  b. What quantities, in kilograms, of H_2O and CO_2 are produced by the reaction of 500. mol of citric acid?

182. Methyl butanoate, an oily substance with a strong fruity fragrance, can be made by reacting butanoic acid with methanol according to the following equation:

$$C_3H_7COOH + CH_3OH \longrightarrow C_3H_7COOCH_3 + H_2O$$

  a. What mass of methyl butanoate is produced from the reaction of 52.5 g of butanoic acid?

  b. In order to purify methyl butanoate, water must be removed. What mass of water is produced from the reaction of 5800. g of methanol?

183. Ammonium nitrate decomposes to yield nitrogen gas, water, and oxygen gas in the following reaction:

$$2NH_4NO_3 \longrightarrow 2N_2 + O_2 + 4H_2O$$

  a. How many moles of nitrogen gas are produced when 36.0 g of NH_4NO_3 react?

  b. If 7.35 mol of H_2O are produced in this reaction, what mass of NH_4NO_3 reacted?

184. Lead(II) nitrate reacts with potassium iodide to produce lead(II) iodide and potassium nitrate. If 1.23 mg of lead nitrate are consumed, what is the mass of the potassium nitrate produced?

185. A car battery produces electrical energy with the following chemical reaction:

$$Pb(s) + PbO_2(s) + 2H_2SO_4(aq) \longrightarrow$$
$$2PbSO_4(s) + 2H_2O(l)$$

If the battery loses 0.34 kg of lead in this reaction, how many moles of lead(II) sulfate are produced?

186. In a space shuttle, the CO_2 that the crew exhales is removed from the air by a reaction within canisters of lithium hydroxide. On average, each astronaut exhales about 20.0 mol of CO_2 daily. What mass of water will be produced when this amount reacts with LiOH? The other product of the reaction is Li_2CO_3.

187. Water is sometimes removed from the products of a reaction by placing them in a closed container with excess P_4O_{10}. Water is absorbed by the following reaction:

$$P_4O_{10} + 6H_2O \longrightarrow 4H_3PO_4$$

  a. What mass of water can be absorbed by 1.00×10^2 g of P_4O_{10}?

  b. If the P_4O_{10} in the container absorbs 0.614 mol of water, what mass of H_3PO_4 is produced?

  c. If the mass of the container of P_4O_{10} increases from 56.64 g to 63.70 g, how many moles of water are absorbed?

188. Ethanol, C_2H_5OH, is considered a clean fuel because it burns in oxygen to produce carbon dioxide and water with few trace pollutants. If 95.0 g of H_2O are produced during the combustion of ethanol, how many grams of ethanol were present at the beginning of the reaction?

189. Sulfur dioxide is one of the major contributors to acid rain. Sulfur dioxide can react with oxygen and water in the atmosphere to form sulfuric acid, as shown in the following equation:

$$2H_2O(l) + O_2(g) + 2SO_2(g) \longrightarrow 2H_2SO_4(aq)$$

If 50.0 g of sulfur dioxide from pollutants react with water and oxygen found in the air, how many grams of sulfuric acid can be produced? How many grams of oxygen are used in the process?

190. When heated, sodium bicarbonate, $NaHCO_3$, decomposes into sodium carbonate, Na_2CO_3, water, and carbon dioxide. If 5.00 g of $NaHCO_3$ decomposes, what is the mass of the carbon dioxide produced?

191. A reaction between hydrazine, N_2H_4, and dinitrogen tetroxide, N_2O_4, has been used to launch rockets into space. The reaction produces nitrogen gas and water vapor.
  a. Write a balanced chemical equation for this reaction.
  b. What is the mole ratio of N_2O_4 to N_2?
  c. How many moles of N_2 will be produced if 20 000 mol of N_2H_4 are used by a rocket?
  d. How many grams of H_2O are made when 450. kg of N_2O_4 are consumed?

192. Joseph Priestley is credited with the discovery of oxygen. He produced O_2 by heating mercury(II) oxide, HgO, to decompose it into its elements. How many moles of oxygen could Priestley have produced if he had decomposed 517.84 g of mercury oxide?

193. Iron(III) chloride, $FeCl_3$, can be made by the reaction of iron with chlorine gas. How much iron, in grams, will be needed to completely react with 58.0 g of Cl_2?

194. Sodium sulfide and cadmium nitrate undergo a double-displacement reaction as shown by the following equation:
$$Na_2S + Cd(NO_3)_2 \longrightarrow 2NaNO_3 + CdS$$
What is the mass, in milligrams, of cadmium sulfide that can be made from 5.00 mg of sodium sulfide?

195. Potassium permanganate and glycerin react explosively according to the following equation:
$$14KMnO_4 + 4C_3H_5(OH)_3 \longrightarrow$$
$$7K_2CO_3 + 7Mn_2O_3 + 5CO_2 + 16H_2O$$
  a. How many moles of carbon dioxide can be produced from 4.44 mol of $KMnO_4$?
  b. If 5.21 g of H_2O are produced, how many moles of glycerin, $C_3H_5(OH)_3$, were used?
  c. If 3.39 mol of potassium carbonate are made, how many grams of manganese(III) oxide are also made?
  d. How many grams of glycerin will be needed to react with 50.0 g of $KMnO_4$? How many grams of CO_2 will be produced in the same reaction?

196. Calcium carbonate found in limestone and marble reacts with hydrochloric acid to form calcium chloride, carbon dioxide, and water according to the following equation:
$$CaCO_3(s) + 2HCl(aq) \longrightarrow$$
$$CaCl_2(aq) + CO_2(g) + H_2O(l)$$
  a. What mass of HCl will be needed to produce 5.00×10^3 kg of $CaCl_2$?
  b. What mass of CO_2 could be produced from the reaction of 750 g of $CaCO_3$?

197. The fuel used to power the booster rockets on the space shuttle is a mixture of aluminum metal and ammonium perchlorate. The following balanced equation represents the reaction of these two ingredients:
$$3Al(s) + 3NH_4ClO_4(s) \longrightarrow$$
$$Al_2O_3(s) + AlCl_3(g) + 3NO(g) + 6H_2O(g)$$
  a. If 1.50×10^5 g of Al react, what mass of NH_4ClO_4, in grams, is required?
  b. If aluminum reacts with 620 kg of NH_4ClO_4, what mass of nitrogen monoxide is produced?

198. Phosphoric acid is typically produced by the action of sulfuric acid on rock that has a high content of calcium phosphate according to the following equation:
$$3H_2SO_4 + Ca_3(PO_4)_2 + 6H_2O \longrightarrow$$
$$3[CaSO_4 \bullet 2H_2O] + 2H_3PO_4$$
  a. If 2.50×10^5 kg of H_2SO_4 react, how many moles of H_3PO_4 can be made?
  b. What mass of calcium sulfate dihydrate is produced by the reaction of 400. kg of calcium phosphate?
  c. If the rock being used contains 78.8% $Ca_3(PO_4)_2$, how many metric tons of H_3PO_4 can be produced from 68 metric tons of rock?

199. Rusting of iron occurs in the presence of moisture according to the following equation:
$$4Fe(s) + 3O_2(g) \longrightarrow 2Fe_2O_3(s)$$
Suppose that 3.19% of a heap of steel scrap with a mass of 1650 kg rusts in a year. What mass will the heap have after one year of rusting?

Limiting Reactants: Chap. 9, Sec. 3

200. Aluminum oxidizes according to the following equation:
$$4Al + 3O_2 \longrightarrow 2Al_2O_3$$
Powdered Al (0.048 mol) is placed into a container containing 0.030 mol O_2. What is the limiting reactant?

201. A process by which zirconium metal can be produced from the mineral zirconium(IV) orthosilicate, $ZrSiO_4$, starts by reacting it with chlorine gas to form zirconium(IV) chloride:
$$ZrSiO_4 + 2Cl_2 \longrightarrow ZrCl_4 + SiO_2 + O_2$$
What mass of $ZrCl_4$ can be produced if 862 g of $ZrSiO_4$ and 950. g of Cl_2 are available? You must first determine the limiting reactant.

MIXED REVIEW

202. Heating zinc sulfide in the presence of oxygen yields the following:
$$ZnS + O_2 \longrightarrow ZnO + SO_2$$
If 1.72 mol of ZnS is heated in the presence of 3.04 mol of O_2, which reactant will be used up? Balance the equation first.

203. Use the following equation for the oxidation of aluminum in the following problems:
$$4Al + 3O_2 \longrightarrow 2Al_2O_3$$
  a. Which reactant is limiting if 0.32 mol Al and 0.26 mol O_2 are available?
  b. How many moles of Al_2O_3 are formed from the reaction of 6.38×10^{-3} mol of O_2 and 9.15×10^{-3} mol of Al?
  c. If 3.17 g of Al and 2.55 g of O_2 are available, which reactant is limiting?

204. In the production of copper from ore containing copper(II) sulfide, the ore is first roasted to change it to the oxide according to the following equation:

$$2CuS + 3O_2 \longrightarrow 2CuO + 2SO_2$$

  a. If 100 g of CuS and 56 g of O_2 are available, which reactant is limiting?

  b. What mass of CuO can be formed from the reaction of 18.7 g of CuS and 12.0 g of O_2?

205. A reaction such as the one shown here is often used to demonstrate a single-displacement reaction:

$$3CuSO_4(aq) + 2Fe(s) \longrightarrow 3Cu(s) + Fe_2(SO_4)_3(aq)$$

If you place 0.092 mol of iron filings in a solution containing 0.158 mol of $CuSO_4$, what is the limiting reactant? How many moles of Cu will be formed?

206. In the reaction $BaCO_3 + 2HNO_3 \longrightarrow Ba(NO_3)_2 + CO_2 + H_2O$, what mass of $Ba(NO_3)_2$ can be formed by combining 55 g $BaCO_3$ and 26 g HNO_3?

207. Bromine replaces iodine in magnesium iodide by the following process:

$$MgI_2 + Br_2 \longrightarrow MgBr_2 + I_2$$

  a. Which is the excess reactant when 560 g of MgI_2 and 360 g of Br_2 react, and what mass remains?

  b. What mass of I_2 is formed in the same process?

208. Nickel replaces silver from silver nitrate in solution according to the following equation:

$$2AgNO_3 + Ni \longrightarrow 2Ag + Ni(NO_3)_2$$

  a. If you have 22.9 g of Ni and 112 g of $AgNO_3$, which reactant is in excess?

  b. What mass of nickel(II) nitrate would be produced given the quantities above?

209. Carbon disulfide, CS_2, is an important industrial substance. Its fumes can burn explosively in air to form sulfur dioxide and carbon dioxide:

$$CS_2(g) + O_2(g) \longrightarrow SO_2(g) + CO_2(g)$$

If 1.60 mol of CS_2 burn with 5.60 mol of O_2, how many moles of the excess reactant will still be present when the reaction is over?

210. Although poisonous, mercury compounds were once used to kill bacteria in wounds and on the skin. One was called "ammoniated mercury" and is made from mercury(II) chloride according to the following equation:

$$HgCl_2(aq) + 2NH_3(aq) \longrightarrow$$
$$Hg(NH_2)Cl(s) + NH_4Cl(aq)$$

  a. What mass of $Hg(NH_2)Cl$ could be produced from 0.91 g of $HgCl_2$ assuming plenty of ammonia is available?

  b. What mass of $Hg(NH_2)Cl$ could be produced from 0.91 g of $HgCl_2$ and 0.15 g of NH_3 in solution?

211. Aluminum chips are sometimes added to sodium hydroxide–based drain cleaners because they react to generate hydrogen gas, which bubbles and helps loosen material in the drain. The equation follows:

$$Al(s) + NaOH(aq) + H_2O(l) \longrightarrow NaAlO_2(aq) + H_2(g)$$

  a. Balance the equation.

  b. How many moles of H_2 can be generated from 0.57 mol Al and 0.37 mol NaOH in excess water?

  c. Which reactant should be limiting in order for the mixture to be most effective as a drain cleaner? Explain your choice.

212. Copper is changed to copper(II) ions by nitric acid according to the following equation:

$$4HNO_3 + Cu \longrightarrow Cu(NO_3)_2 + 2NO_2 + 2H_2O$$

  a. How many moles each of HNO_3 and Cu must react in order to produce 0.0845 mol of NO_2?

  b. If 5.94 g of Cu and 23.23 g of HNO_3 are combined, which reactant is in excess?

213. One industrial process for producing nitric acid begins with the following reaction:

$$4NH_3 + 5O_2 \longrightarrow 4NO + 6H_2O$$

  a. If 2.90 mol NH_3 and 3.75 mol O_2 are available, how many moles of each product are formed?

  b. Which reactant is limiting if 4.20×10^4 g of NH_3 and 1.31×10^5 g of O_2 are available?

  c. What mass of NO is formed in the reaction of 869 kg of NH_3 and 2480 kg O_2?

214. Acetaldehyde, CH_3CHO, is manufactured by the reaction of ethanol with copper(II) oxide according to the following equation:

$$CH_3CH_2OH + CuO \longrightarrow CH_3CHO + H_2O + Cu$$

What mass of acetaldehyde can be produced by the reaction between 620 g of ethanol and 1020 g of CuO? What mass of which reactant will be left over?

215. Hydrogen bromide can be produced by a reaction among bromine, sulfur dioxide, and water as follows:

$$SO_2 + Br_2 + H_2O \longrightarrow 2HBr + H_2SO_4$$

If 250 g of SO_2 and 650 g of Br_2 react in the presence of excess water, what mass of HBr will be formed?

216. Sulfur dioxide can be produced in the laboratory by the reaction of hydrochloric acid and a sulfite salt such as sodium sulfite:

$$Na_2SO_3 + 2HCl \longrightarrow 2NaCl + SO_2 + H_2O$$

What mass of SO_2 can be made from 25.0 g of Na_2SO_3 and 22.0 g of HCl?

217. The rare-earth metal terbium is produced from terbium(III) fluoride and calcium metal by the following single-displacement reaction:

$$2TbF_3 + 3Ca \longrightarrow 3CaF_2 + 2Tb$$

  a. Given 27.5 g of TbF_3 and 6.96 g of Ca, how many grams of terbium could be produced?

  b. How many grams of the excess reactant are left over?

Percentage Yield: Chap. 9, Sec. 3

218. Calculate the percentage yield in each of the following cases.

   a. theoretical yield is 50.0 g of product; actual yield is 41.9 g

   b. theoretical yield is 290 kg of product; actual yield is 270 kg

   c. theoretical yield is 6.05×10^4 kg of product; actual yield is 4.18×10^4 kg

   d. theoretical yield is 0.001 92 g of product; actual yield is 0.000 89 g

219. In the commercial production of the element arsenic, arsenic(III) oxide is heated with carbon, which reduces the oxide to the metal according to the following equation:
$$2As_2O_3 + 3C \longrightarrow 3CO_2 + 4As$$

   a. If 8.87 g of As_2O_3 is used in the reaction and 5.33 g of As is produced, what is the percentage yield?

   b. If 67 g of carbon is used up in a different reaction and 425 g of As is produced, calculate the percentage yield of this reaction.

MIXED REVIEW

220. Ethyl acetate is a sweet-smelling solvent used in varnishes and fingernail-polish remover. It is produced industrially by heating acetic acid and ethanol together in the presence of sulfuric acid, which is added to speed up the reaction. The ethyl acetate is distilled off as it is formed. The equation for the process is as follows:

$$\overset{acetic\ acid}{CH_3COOH} + \overset{ethanol}{CH_3CH_2OH} \xrightarrow{\ H_2SO_4\ }$$
$$\underset{ethyl\ acetate}{CH_3COOCH_2CH_3} + H_2O$$

Determine the percentage yield in the following cases.

   a. 68.3 g of ethyl acetate should be produced, but only 43.9 g is recovered.

   b. 0.0419 mol of ethyl acetate is produced, but 0.0722 mol is expected. (Hint: Percentage yield can also be calculated by dividing the actual yield in moles by the theoretical yield in moles.)

   c. 4.29 mol of ethanol is reacted with excess acetic acid, but only 2.98 mol of ethyl acetate is produced.

   d. A mixture of 0.58 mol ethanol and 0.82 mol acetic acid is reacted, and 0.46 mol ethyl acetate is produced. (Hint: What is the limiting reactant?)

221. Assume the following hypothetical reaction takes place:
$$2A + 7B \longrightarrow 4C + 3D$$

Calculate the percentage yield in each of the following cases.

   a. The reaction of 0.0251 mol of A gives 0.0349 mol of C.

   b. The reaction of 1.19 mol of A produces 1.41 mol of D.

   c. The reaction of 189 mol of B produces 39 mol of D.

   d. The reaction of 3500 mol of B produces 1700 mol of C.

222. Elemental phosphorus can be produced by heating calcium phosphate from rocks with silica sand (SiO_2) and carbon in the form of coke (a fuel resulting from distilling coal). The following reaction takes place:
$$Ca_3(PO_4)_2 + 3SiO_2 + 5C \longrightarrow 3CaSiO_3 + 2P + 5CO$$

   a. If 57 mol of $Ca_3(PO_4)_2$ is used and 101 mol of $CaSiO_3$ is obtained, what is the percentage yield?

   b. Determine the percentage yield obtained if 1280 mol of carbon is consumed and 622 mol of $CaSiO_3$ is produced.

   c. The engineer in charge of this process expects a yield of 81.5%. If 1.4×10^5 mol of $Ca_3(PO_4)_2$ is used, how many moles of phosphorus will be produced?

223. Tungsten (W) can be produced from its oxide by reacting the oxide with hydrogen at a high temperature according to the following equation:
$$WO_3 + 3H_2 \longrightarrow W + 3H_2O$$

   a. What is the percentage yield if 56.9 g of WO_3 yields 41.4 g of tungsten?

   b. How many moles of tungsten will be produced from 3.72 g of WO_3 if the yield is 92.0%?

   c. A chemist carries out this reaction and obtains 11.4 g of tungsten. If the percentage yield is 89.4%, what mass of WO_3 was used?

224. Carbon tetrachloride, CCl_4, is a solvent that was once used in large quantities in dry cleaning. Because it is a dense liquid that does not burn, it was also used in fire extinguishers. Unfortunately, its use was discontinued because it was found to be a carcinogen. It was manufactured by the following reaction:
$$CS_2 + 3Cl_2 \longrightarrow CCl_4 + S_2Cl_2$$

The reaction was economical because the byproduct disulfur dichloride, S_2Cl_2, could be used by industry in the manufacture of rubber products and other materials.

   a. What is the percentage yield of CCl_4 if 719 kg is produced from the reaction of 410. kg of CS_2?

   b. If 67.5 g of Cl_2 is used in the reaction and 39.5 g of S_2Cl_2 is produced, what is the percentage yield?

   c. If the percentage yield of the industrial process is 83.3%, how many kilograms of CS_2 should be reacted to obtain 5.00×10^4 kg of CCl_4? How many kilograms of S_2Cl_2 will be produced, assuming the same yield for that product?

225. Nitrogen dioxide, NO_2, can be converted to dinitrogen pentoxide, N_2O_5, by reacting it with ozone, O_3. The reaction of NO_2 takes place according to the following equation:
$$2NO_2(g) + O_3(g) \longrightarrow N_2O_5(s\ or\ g) + O_2(g)$$

   a. Calculate the percentage yield for a reaction in which 0.38 g of NO_2 reacts and 0.36 g of N_2O_5 is recovered.

   b. What mass of N_2O_5 will result from the reaction of 6.0 mol of NO_2 if there is a 61.1% yield in the reaction?

226. In the past, hydrogen chloride, HCl, was made using the *salt-cake* method as shown in the following equation:
$$2NaCl(s) + H_2SO_4(aq) \longrightarrow Na_2SO_4(s) + 2HCl(g)$$

If 30.0 g of NaCl and 0.250 mol of H_2SO_4 are available and 14.6 g of HCl is made, what is the percentage yield?

227. Cyanide compounds such as sodium cyanide, NaCN, are especially useful in gold refining because they will react with gold to form a stable compound that can then be separated and broken down to retrieve the gold. Ore containing only small quantities of gold can be used in this form of "chemical mining." The equation for the reaction follows:

$$4Au + 8NaCN + 2H_2O + O_2 \longrightarrow$$
$$4NaAu(CN)_2 + 4NaOH$$

  a. What percentage yield is obtained if 410 g of gold produces 540 g of $NaAu(CN)_2$?

  b. Assuming a 79.6% yield in the conversion of gold to $NaAu(CN)_2$, what mass of gold would produce 1.00 kg of $NaAu(CN)_2$?

  c. Given the conditions in (b), what mass of gold ore that is 0.001% gold would be needed to produce 1.00 kg of $NaAu(CN)_2$?

228. Diiodine pentoxide is useful in devices such as respirators because it reacts with the dangerous gas carbon monoxide, CO, to produce relatively harmless CO_2 according to the following equation:

$$I_2O_5 + 5CO \longrightarrow I_2 + 5CO_2$$

  a. In testing a respirator, 2.00 g of carbon monoxide gas is passed through diiodine pentoxide. Upon analyzing the results, it is found that 3.17 g of I_2 was produced. Calculate the percentage yield of the reaction.

  b. Assuming that the yield in (a) resulted because some of the CO did not react, calculate the mass of CO that passed through.

229. Sodium hypochlorite, NaClO, the main ingredient in household bleach, is produced by bubbling chlorine gas through a strong lye (sodium hydroxide, NaOH) solution. The following equation shows the reaction that occurs:

$$2NaOH(aq) + Cl_2(g) \longrightarrow$$
$$NaCl(aq) + NaClO(aq) + H_2O(l)$$

  a. What is the percentage yield of the reaction if 1.2 kg of Cl_2 reacts to form 0.90 kg of NaClO?

  b. If a plant operator wants to make 25 metric tons of NaClO per day at a yield of 91.8%, how many metric tons of chlorine gas must be on hand each day?

  c. What mass of NaCl is formed per mole of chlorine gas at a yield of 81.8%?

  d. At what rate in kg per hour must NaOH be replenished if the reaction produces 370 kg/h of NaClO at a yield of 79.5%? Assume that all of the NaOH reacts to produce this yield.

230. Magnesium burns in oxygen to form magnesium oxide. However, when magnesium burns in air, which is only about one-fifth oxygen, side reactions form other products, such as magnesium nitride, Mg_3N_2.

  a. Write a balanced equation for the burning of magnesium in oxygen.

  b. If enough magnesium burns in air to produce 2.04 g of magnesium oxide but only 1.79 g is obtained, what is the percentage yield?

  c. Magnesium will react with pure nitrogen to form the nitride Mg_3N_2. Write a balanced equation for this reaction.

  d. If 0.097 mol of Mg reacts with nitrogen and 0.027 mol of Mg_3N_2 is produced, what is the percentage yield of the reaction?

231. Some alcohols can be converted to organic acids by using sodium dichromate and sulfuric acid. The following equation shows the reaction of 1-propanol to propanoic acid:

$$3CH_3CH_2CH_2OH + 2Na_2Cr_2O_7 + 8H_2SO_4 \longrightarrow$$
$$3CH_3CH_2COOH + 2Cr_2(SO_4)_3 + 2Na_2SO_4 + 11H_2O$$

  a. If 0.89 g of 1-propanol reacts and 0.88 g of propanoic acid is produced, what is the percentage yield?

  b. A chemist uses this reaction to obtain 1.50 mol of propanoic acid. The reaction consumes 136 g of propanol. Calculate the percentage yield.

  c. Some 1-propanol of uncertain purity is used in the reaction. If 116 g of $Na_2Cr_2O_7$ is consumed in the reaction and 28.1 g of propanoic acid is produced, what is the percentage yield?

232. Acrylonitrile, $C_3H_3N(g)$, is an important ingredient in the production of various fibers and plastics. Acrylonitrile is produced from the following reaction:

$$C_3H_6(g) + NH_3(g) + O_2(g) \longrightarrow C_3H_3N(g) + H_2O(g)$$

If 850. g of C_3H_6 is mixed with 300. g of NH_3 and unlimited O_2 to produce 850. g of acrylonitrile, what is the percentage yield? You must first balance the equation.

233. Methanol, CH_3OH, is frequently used in race cars as fuel. It is produced as the sole product of the combination of carbon monoxide gas and hydrogen gas.

  a. If 430. kg of hydrogen reacts, what mass of methanol could be produced?

  b. If 3.12×10^3 kg of methanol is actually produced, what is the percentage yield?

234. The compound, $C_6H_{16}N_2$, is one of the starting materials in the production of nylon. It can be prepared from the following reaction involving adipic acid, $C_6H_{10}O_4$:

$$C_6H_{10}O_4(l) + 2NH_3(g) + 4H_2(g) \longrightarrow$$
$$C_6H_{16}N_2(l) + 4H_2O$$

What is the percentage yield if 750. g of adipic acid results in the production of 578 g of $C_6H_{16}N_2$?

235. Plants convert carbon dioxide to oxygen during photosynthesis according to the following equation:

$$CO_2 + H_2O \longrightarrow C_6H_{12}O_6 + O_2$$

Balance this equation, and calculate how much oxygen would be produced if 1.37×10^4 g of carbon dioxide reacts with a percentage yield of 63.4%.

236. Lime, CaO, is frequently added to streams and lakes that have been polluted by acid rain. The calcium oxide reacts with the water to form a base that can neutralize the acid as shown in the following reaction:

$$CaO(s) + H_2O(l) \longrightarrow Ca(OH)_2(s)$$

If 2.67×10^2 mol of base is needed to neutralize the acid in a lake and the above reaction has a percentage yield of 54.3%, what is the mass, in kilograms, of lime that must be added to the lake?

Gas Laws: Chap. 11, Sec. 2

BOYLE'S LAW

In each of the following problems, assume that the temperature and molar quantity of gas do not change.

237. Calculate the unknown quantity in each of the following measurements of gases.

	P_1	V_1	P_2	V_2
a.	3.0 atm	25 mL	6.0 atm	? mL
b.	99.97 kPa	550. mL	? kPa	275 mL
c.	0.89 atm	? L	3.56 atm	20.0 L
d.	? kPa	800. mL	500. kPa	160. mL
e.	0.040 atm	? L	250 atm	1.0×10^{-2} L

238. A sample of neon gas occupies a volume of 2.8 L at 1.8 atm. What will its volume be at 1.2 atm?

239. To what pressure would you have to compress 48.0 L of oxygen gas at 99.3 kPa in order to reduce its volume to 16.0 L?

240. A chemist collects 59.0 mL of sulfur dioxide gas on a day when the atmospheric pressure is 0.989 atm. On the next day, the pressure has changed to 0.967 atm. What will the volume of the SO_2 gas be on the second day?

241. 2.2 L of hydrogen at 6.5 atm pressure is used to fill a balloon at a final pressure of 1.15 atm. What is its final volume?

CHARLES'S LAW

In each of the following problems, assume that the pressure and molar quantity of gas do not change.

242. Calculate the unknown quantity in each of the following measurements of gases:

	V_1	T_1	V_2	T_2
a.	40.0 mL	280. K	? mL	350. K
b.	0.606 L	300. K	0.404 L	? K
c.	? mL	292 K	250. mL	365 K
d.	100. mL	? K	125 mL	305 K
e.	0.0024 L	22°C	? L	−14°C

243. A balloon full of air has a volume of 2.75 L at a temperature of 18°C. What is the balloon's volume at 45°C?

244. A sample of argon has a volume of 0.43 mL at 24°C. At what temperature in degrees Celsius will it have a volume of 0.57 mL?

GAY-LUSSAC'S LAW

In each of the following problems, assume that the volume and molar quantity of gas do not change.

245. Calculate the unknown quantity in each of the following measurements of gases.

	P_1	T_1	P_2	T_2
a.	1.50 atm	273 K	? atm	410 K
b.	0.208 atm	300. K	0.156 atm	? K
c.	? kPa	52°C	99.7 kPa	77°C
d.	5.20 atm	?°C	4.16 atm	−13°C
e.	8.33×10^{-4} atm	−84°C	3.92×10^{-3} atm	?°C

246. A cylinder of compressed gas has a pressure of 4.882 atm on one day. The next day, the same cylinder of gas has a pressure of 4.690 atm, and its temperature is 8°C. What was the temperature on the previous day in °C?

247. A mylar balloon is filled with helium gas to a pressure of 107 kPa when the temperature is 22°C. If the temperature changes to 45°C, what will be the pressure of the helium in the balloon?

THE COMBINED GAS LAW

In each of the following problems, it is assumed that the molar quantity of gas does not change.

248. Calculate the unknown quantity in each of the following measurements of gases.

	P_1	V_1	T_1	P_2	V_2	T_2
a.	99.3 kPa	225 mL	15°C	102.8 kPa	? mL	24°C
b.	0.959 atm	3.50 L	45°C	? atm	3.70 L	37°C
c.	0.0036 atm	62 mL	373 K	0.0029 atm	64 mL	? K
d.	100. kPa	43.2 mL	19°C	101.3 kPa	? mL	0°C

249. A student collects 450. mL of HCl(g) hydrogen chloride gas at a pressure of 100. kPa and a temperature of 17°C. What is the volume of the HCl at 0°C and 101.3 kPa?

DALTON'S LAW OF PARTIAL PRESSURES

250. A chemist collects a sample of $H_2S(g)$ over water at a temperature of 27°C. The total pressure of the gas that has displaced a volume of 15 mL of water is 207.33 kPa. What is the pressure of the H_2S gas collected?

In each of the following problems, assume that the molar quantity of gas does not change.

251. Some hydrogen is collected over water at 10°C and 105.5 kPa pressure. The total volume of the sample was 1.93 L. Calculate the volume of the hydrogen corrected to STP.

252. One student carries out a reaction that gives off methane gas and obtains a total volume by water displacement of 338 mL at a temperature of 19°C and a pressure of 0.9566 atm. Another student does the identical experiment on another day at a temperature of 26°C and a pressure of 0.989 atm. Which student collected more CH_4?

MIXED REVIEW

In each of the following problems, assume that the molar quantity of gas does not change.

253. Calculate the unknown quantity in each of the following measurements of gases.

	P_1	V_1	P_2	V_2
a.	127.3 kPa	796 cm^3	? kPa	965 cm^3
b.	7.1×10^2 atm	? mL	9.6×10^{-1} atm	3.7×10^3 mL
c.	? kPa	1.77 L	30.79 kPa	2.44 L
d.	114 kPa	2.93 dm^3	4.93×10^4 kPa	? dm^3
e.	1.00 atm	120. mL	? atm	97.0 mL
f.	0.77 atm	3.6 m^3	1.90 atm	? m^3

254. A gas cylinder contains 0.722 m^3 of hydrogen gas at a pressure of 10.6 atm. If the gas is used to fill a balloon at a pressure of 0.96 atm, what is the volume in m^3 of the filled balloon?

255. A weather balloon has a maximum volume of 7.50×10^3 L. The balloon contains 195 L of helium gas at a pressure of 0.993 atm. What will be the pressure when the balloon is at maximum volume?

256. A rubber ball contains 5.70×10^{-1} dm^3 of gas at a pressure of 1.05 atm. What volume will the gas occupy at 7.47 atm?

257. Calculate the unknown quantity in each of the following measurements of gases.

	V_1	T_1	V_2	T_2
a.	26.5 mL	? K	32.9 mL	290. K
b.	? dm^3	100.°C	0.83 dm^3	29°C
c.	7.44×10^4 mm^3	870.°C	2.59×10^2 mm^3	? °C
d.	5.63×10^{-2} L	132 K	? L	190. K
e.	? cm^3	243 K	819 cm^3	409 K
f.	679 m^3	−3°C	? m^3	−246°C

258. A bubble of carbon dioxide gas in some unbaked bread dough has a volume of 1.15 cm^3 at a temperature of 22°C. What volume will the bubble have when the bread is baked and the bubble reaches a temperature of 99°C?

259. A perfectly elastic balloon contains 6.75 dm^3 of air at a temperature of 40.°C. What is the temperature if the balloon has a volume of 5.03 dm^3?

260. Calculate the unknown quantity in each of the following measurements of gases.

	P_1	T_1	P_2	T_2
a.	0.777 atm	?°C	5.6 atm	192°C
b.	152 kPa	302 K	? kPa	11 K
c.	? atm	−76°C	3.97 atm	27°C
d.	395 atm	46°C	706 atm	?°C
e.	? atm	−37°C	350. atm	2050°C
f.	0.39 atm	263 K	0.058 atm	? K

261. A 2 L bottle containing only air is sealed at a temperature of 22°C and a pressure of 0.982 atm. The bottle is placed in a freezer and allowed to cool to −3°C. What is the pressure in the bottle?

262. The pressure in a car tire is 2.50 atm at a temperature of 33°C . What would the pressure be if the tire were allowed to cool to 0°C? Assume that the tire does not change volume.

263. A container filled with helium gas has a pressure of 127.5 kPa at a temperature of 290. K. What is the temperature when the pressure is 3.51 kPa?

264. Calculate the unknown quantity in each of the following measurements of gases.

	P_1	V_1	T_1	P_2	V_2	T_2
a.	1.03 atm	1.65 L	19°C	0.920 atm	? L	46°C
b.	107.0 kPa	3.79 dm^3	73°C	? kPa	7.58 dm^3	217°C
c.	0.029 atm	249 mL	? K	0.098 atm	197 mL	293 K
d.	113 kPa	? mm^3	12°C	149 kPa	3.18×10^3 mm^3	−18°C
e.	1.15 atm	0.93 m^3	−22°C	1.01 atm	0.85 m^3	?°C
f.	? atm	156 cm^3	195 K	2.25 atm	468 cm^3	585 K

265. A scientist has a sample of gas that was collected several days earlier. The sample has a volume of 392 cm^3 at a pressure of 0.987 atm and a temperature of 21°C. On the day the gas was collected, the temperature was 13°C, and the pressure was 0.992 atm. What volume did the gas have on the day it was collected?

266. Hydrogen gas is collected by water displacement. Total volume collected is 0.461 L at a temperature of 17°C and a pressure of 0.989 atm. What is the pressure of dry hydrogen gas collected?

267. One container with a volume of 1.00 L contains argon at a pressure of 1.77 atm, and a second container of 1.50 L volume contains argon at a pressure of 0.487 atm. They are then connected to each other so that the pressure can become equal in both containers. What is the equalized pressure? Hint: Each sample of gas now occupies the total space. Dalton's law of partial pressures applies here.

268. Oxygen gas is collected over water at a temperature of 10.°C and a pressure of 1.02 atm. The volume of gas plus water vapor collected is 293 mL. What volume of oxygen at STP was collected?

269. A 500 mL bottle is partially filled with water so that the total volume of gases (water vapor and air) remaining in the bottle is 325 cm^3, measured at 20.°C and 101.3 kPa. The bottle is sealed and taken to a mountaintop where the pressure is 76.24 kPa and the temperature is 10°C. If the bottle is upside down and the seal leaks, how much water will leak out? The key to this problem is to determine the pressure in the 325 cm^3 space when the bottle is at the top of the mountain.

270. An air thermometer can be constructed by using a glass bubble attached to a piece of small-diameter glass tubing. The tubing contains a small amount of colored water that rises when the temperature increases and the trapped air expands. You want a 0.20 cm³ change in volume to equal a 1°C change in temperature. What total volume of air at 20.°C should be trapped in the apparatus below the liquid?

271. A sample of nitrogen gas is collected over water, yielding a total volume of 62.25 mL at a temperature of 22°C and a total pressure of 97.7 kPa. At what pressure will the nitrogen alone occupy a volume of 50.00 mL at the same temperature?

272. The theoretical yield of a reaction that gives off nitrogen trifluoride gas is 844 mL at STP. What total volume of NF_3 plus water vapor will be collected over water at 25°C and a total pressure of 1.017 atm?

273. A weather balloon is inflated with 2.94 kL of helium at a location where the pressure is 1.06 atm and the temperature is 32°C. What will be the volume of the balloon at an altitude where the pressure is 0.092 atm and the temperature is 235°C?

274. The safety limit for a certain can of aerosol spray is 95°C. If the pressure of the gas in the can is 2.96 atm when it is 17°C, what will the pressure be at the safety limit?

275. A chemistry student collects a sample of ammonia gas at a temperature of 39°C. Later, the student measures the volume of the ammonia as 108 mL, but its temperature is now 21°C. What was the volume of the ammonia when it was collected?

276. A quantity of CO_2 gas occupies a volume of 624 L at a pressure of 1.40 atm. If this CO_2 is pumped into a gas cylinder that has a volume of 80.0 L, what pressure will the CO_2 exert on the cylinder?

The Ideal Gas Law: Chap. 11, Sec. 3

277. Use the ideal-gas-law equation to calculate the unknown quantity in each of the following sets of measurements. You will need to convert Celsius temperatures to Kelvin temperatures and volume units to liters.

	P	V	n	T
a.	1.09 atm	? L	0.0881 mol	302 K
b.	94.9 kPa	0.0350 L	? mol	55°C
c.	? kPa	15.7 L	0.815 mol	−20.°C
d.	0.500 atm	629 mL	0.0337 mol	? K
e.	0.950 atm	? L	0.0818 mol	19°C
f.	107 kPa	39.0 mL	? mol	27°C

278. A student collects 425 mL of oxygen at a temperature of 24°C and a pressure of 0.899 atm. How many moles of oxygen did the student collect?

APPLICATIONS OF THE IDEAL GAS LAW

279. A sample of an unknown gas has a mass of 0.116 g. It occupies a volume of 25.0 mL at a temperature of 127°C and has a pressure of 155.3 kPa. Calculate the molar mass of the gas.

280. Determine the mass of CO_2 gas that has a volume of 7.10 L at a pressure of 1.11 atm and a temperature of 31°C. Hint: Solve the equation for m, and calculate the molar mass using the chemical formula and the periodic table.

281. What is the density of silicon tetrafluoride gas at 72°C and a pressure of 144.5 kPa?

282. At what temperature will nitrogen gas have a density of 1.13 g/L at a pressure of 1.09 atm?

MIXED REVIEW

283. Use the ideal-gas-law equation to calculate the unknown quantity in each of the following sets of measurements.

	P	V	n	t
a.	0.0477 atm	15 200 L	? mol	−15°C
b.	? kPa	0.119 mL	0.000 350 mol	0°C
c.	500.0 kPa	250. mL	0.120 mol	?°C
d.	19.5 atm	?	4.7×10^4 mol	300.°C

284. Use the ideal-gas-law equation to calculate the unknown quantity in each of the following sets of measurements.

	P	V	m	M	t
a.	0.955 atm	3.77 L	8.23 g	? g/mol	25°C
b.	105.0 kPa	50.0 mL	? g	48.02 g/mol	0°C
c.	0.782 atm	? L	3.20×10^{-3} g	2.02 g/mol	−5°C
d.	? atm	2.00 L	7.19 g	159.8 g/mol	185°C
e.	107.2 kPa	26.1 mL	0.414 g	? g/mol	45°C

285. Determine the volume of one mole of an ideal gas at 25°C and 0.915 kPa.

286. Calculate the unknown quantity in each of the following sets of measurements.

	P	Molar mass	Density	t
a.	1.12 atm	? g/mol	2.40 g/L	2°C
b.	7.50 atm	30.07 g/mol	? g/L	20.°C
c.	97.4 kPa	104.09 g/mol	4.37 g/L	?°C
d.	? atm	77.95 g/mol	6.27 g/L	66°C

287. What pressure in atmospheres will 1.36 kg of N_2O gas exert when it is compressed in a 25.0 L cylinder and is stored in an outdoor shed where the temperature can reach 59°C during the summer?

288. Aluminum chloride sublimes at high temperatures. What density will the vapor have at 225°C and 0.939 atm pressure?

289. An unknown gas has a density of 0.0262 g/mL at a pressure of 0.918 atm and a temperature of 10.°C. What is the molar mass of the gas?

290. A large balloon contains 11.7 g of helium. What volume will the helium occupy at an altitude of 10 000 m, where the atmospheric pressure is 0.262 atm and the temperature is −50.°C?

291. A student collects ethane by water displacement at a temperature of 15°C (vapor pressure of water is 1.5988 kPa) and a total pressure of 100.0 kPa. The volume of the collection bottle is 245 mL. How many moles of ethane are in the bottle?

292. A reaction yields 3.75 L of nitrogen monoxide. The volume is measured at 19°C and at a pressure of 1.10 atm. What mass of NO was produced by the reaction?

293. A reaction has a theoretical yield of 8.83 g of ammonia. The reaction gives off 10.24 L of ammonia measured at 52°C and 105.3 kPa. What was the percent yield of the reaction?

294. An unknown gas has a density of 0.405 g/L at a pressure of 0.889 atm and a temperature of 7°C. Calculate its molar mass.

295. A paper label has been lost from an old tank of compressed gas. To help identify the unknown gas, you must calculate its molar mass. It is known that the tank has a capacity of 90.0 L and weighs 39.2 kg when empty. You find its current mass to be 50.5 kg. The gauge shows a pressure of 1780 kPa when the temperature is 18°C. What is the molar mass of the gas in the cylinder?

296. What is the pressure inside a tank that has a volume of 1.20×10^3 L and contains 12.0 kg of HCl gas at a temperature of 18°C?

297. What pressure in kPa is exerted at a temperature of 20.°C by compressed neon gas that has a density of 2.70 g/L?

298. A tank with a volume of 658 mL contains 1.50 g of neon gas. The maximum safe pressure that the tank can withstand is 4.50×10^2 kPa. At what temperature will the tank have that pressure?

299. The atmospheric pressure on Mars is about 6.75 millibars (1 bar = 100 kPa = 0.9869 atm), and the nighttime temperature can be about −75°C on the same day that the daytime temperature goes up to −8°C. What volume would a bag containing 1.00 g of H_2 gas have at both the daytime and nighttime temperatures?

300. What is the pressure in kPa of 3.95 mol of Cl_2 gas if it is compressed in a cylinder with a volume of 850. mL at a temperature of 15°C?

301. What volume in mL will 0.006 60 mol of hydrogen gas occupy at a pressure of 0.907 atm and a temperature of 9°C?

302. What volume will 8.47 kg of sulfur dioxide gas occupy at a pressure of 89.4 kPa and a temperature of 40.°C?

303. A cylinder contains 908 g of compressed helium. It is to be used to inflate a balloon to a final pressure of 128.3 kPa at a temperature of 2°C. What will the volume of the balloon be under these conditions?

304. The density of dry air at 27°C and 100.0 kPa is 1.162 g/L. Use this information to calculate the molar mass of air (calculate as if air were a pure substance).

Stoichiometry of Gases: Chap. 11, Sec. 3

305. In one method of manufacturing nitric acid, ammonia is oxidized to nitrogen monoxide and water:
$$4NH_3(g) + 5O_2(g) \longrightarrow 4NO(g) + 6H_2O(l)$$
What volume of oxygen will be used in a reaction of 2800 L of NH_3? What volume of NO will be produced? All volumes are measured under the same conditions.

306. Fluorine gas reacts violently with water to produce hydrogen fluoride and ozone according to the following equation:
$$3F_2(g) + 3H_2O(l) \longrightarrow 6HF(g) + O_3(g)$$
What volumes of O_3 and HF gas would be produced by the complete reaction of 3.60×10^4 mL of fluorine gas? All gases are measured under the same conditions.

307. A sample of ethanol burns in O_2 to form CO_2 and H_2O according to the following equation:
$$C_2H_5OH + 3O_2 \longrightarrow 2CO_2 + 3H_2O$$
If the combustion uses 55.8 mL of oxygen measured at 2.26 atm and 40.°C, what volume of CO_2 is produced when measured at STP?

308. Dinitrogen pentoxide decomposes into nitrogen dioxide and oxygen. If 5.00 L of N_2O_5 reacts at STP, what volume of NO_2 is produced when measured at 64.5°C and 1.76 atm?

309. Complete the table below using the following equation, which represents a reaction that produces aluminum chloride:
$$2Al(s) + 3Cl_2(g) \longrightarrow 2AlCl_3(s)$$

	Mass Al	Volume Cl_2	Conditions	Mass $AlCl_3$
a.	excess	? L	STP	7.15 g
b.	19.4 g	? L	STP	NA
c.	1.559 kg	? L	20.°C and 0.945 atm	NA
d.	excess	920. L	STP	? g
e.	? g	1.049 mL	37°C and 5.00 atm	NA
f.	500.00 kg	? m^3	15°C and 83.0 kPa	NA

MIXED REVIEW

310. The industrial production of ammonia proceeds according to the following equation:
$$N_2(g) + 3H_2(g) \longrightarrow 2NH_3(g)$$

  a. What volume of nitrogen at STP is needed to react with 57.0 mL of hydrogen measured at STP?

  b. What volume of NH_3 at STP can be produced from the complete reaction of 6.39×10^4 L of hydrogen?

  c. If 20.0 mol of nitrogen is available, what volume of NH_3 at STP can be produced?

  d. What volume of H_2 at STP will be needed to produce 800. L of ammonia, measured at 55°C and 0.900 atm?

311. Propane burns according to the following equation:
$$C_3H_8(g) + 5O_2(g) \longrightarrow 3CO_2(g) + 4H_2O(g)$$

  a. What volume of water vapor measured at 250.°C and 1.00 atm is produced when 3.0 L of propane at STP is burned?

  b. What volume of oxygen at 20.°C and 102.6 kPa is used if 640. L of CO_2 is produced? The CO_2 is also measured at 20.°C and 102.6 kPa.

  c. If 465 mL of oxygen at STP is used in the reaction, what volume of CO_2, measured at 37°C and 0.973 atm, is produced?

  d. When 2.50 L of C_3H_8 at STP burns, what total volume of gaseous products is formed? The volume of the products is measured at 175°C and 1.14 atm.

312. Carbon monoxide will burn in air to produce CO_2 according to the following equation:
$$2CO(g) + O_2(g) \longrightarrow 2CO_2(g)$$

What volume of oxygen at STP will be needed to react with 3500. L of CO measured at 20.°C and a pressure of 0.953 atm?

313. Silicon tetrafluoride gas can be produced by the action of HF on silica according to the following equation:
$$SiO_2(s) + 4HF(g) \longrightarrow SiF_4(g) + 2H_2O(l)$$

1.00 L of HF gas under pressure at 3.48 atm and a temperature of 25°C reacts completely with SiO_2 to form SiF_4. What volume of SiF_4, measured at 15°C and 0.940 atm, is produced by this reaction?

314. One method used in the eighteenth century to generate hydrogen was to pass steam through red-hot steel tubes. The following reaction takes place:
$$3Fe(s) + 4H_2O(g) \longrightarrow Fe_3O_4(s) + 4H_2(g)$$

  a. What volume of hydrogen at STP can be produced by the reaction of 6.28 g of iron?

  b. What mass of iron will react with 500. L of steam at 250.°C and 1.00 atm pressure?

  c. If 285 g of Fe_3O_4 are formed, what volume of hydrogen, measured at 20.°C and 1.06 atm, is produced?

315. Sodium reacts vigorously with water to produce hydrogen and sodium hydroxide according to the following equation:
$$2Na(s) + 2H_2O(l) \longrightarrow 2NaOH(aq) + H_2(g)$$

If 0.027 g of sodium reacts with excess water, what volume of hydrogen at STP is formed?

316. Diethyl ether burns in air according to the following equation:
$$C_4H_{10}O(l) + 6O_2(g) \longrightarrow 4CO_2(g) + 5H_2O(l)$$

If 7.15 L of CO_2 is produced at a temperature of 125°C and a pressure of 1.02 atm, what volume of oxygen, measured at STP, was consumed and what mass of diethyl ether was burned?

317. When nitroglycerin detonates, it produces large volumes of hot gases almost instantly according to the following equation:
$$4C_3H_5N_3O_9(l) \longrightarrow 6N_2(g) + 12CO_2(g) + 10H_2O(g) + O_2(g)$$

  a. When 0.100 mol of nitroglycerin explodes, what volume of each gas measured at STP is produced?

  b. What total volume of gases is produced at 300.°C and 1.00 atm when 10.0 g of nitroglycerin explodes?

318. Dinitrogen monoxide can be prepared by heating ammonium nitrate, which decomposes according to the following equation:
$$NH_4NO_3(s) \longrightarrow N_2O(g) + 2H_2O(l)$$

What mass of ammonium nitrate should be decomposed in order to produce 250. mL of N_2O, measured at STP?

319. Phosphine, PH_3, is the phosphorus analogue to ammonia, NH_3. It can be produced by the reaction between calcium phosphide and water according to the following equation:
$$Ca_3P_2(s) + 6H_2O(l) \longrightarrow 3Ca(OH)_2(s \text{ and } aq) + 2PH_3(g)$$

What volume of phosphine, measured at 18°C and 102.4 kPa, is produced by the reaction of 8.46 g of Ca_3P_2?

320. In one method of producing aluminum chloride, HCl gas is passed over aluminum, and the following reaction takes place:
$$2Al(s) + 6HCl(g) \longrightarrow 2AlCl_3(g) + 3H_2(g)$$

What mass of Al should be on hand in order to produce 6.0×10^3 kg of $AlCl_3$? What volume of compressed HCl at 4.71 atm and a temperature of 43°C should be on hand at the same time?

321. Urea, $(NH_2)_2CO$, is an important fertilizer that is manufactured by the following reaction:
$$2NH_3(g) + CO_2(g) \longrightarrow (NH_2)_2CO(s) + H_2O(g)$$

What volume of NH_3 at STP will be needed to produce 8.50×10^4 kg of urea if there is an 89.5% yield in the process?

322. An obsolete method of generating oxygen in the laboratory involves the decomposition of barium peroxide by the following equation:
$$2BaO_2(s) \longrightarrow 2BaO(s) + O_2(g)$$

What mass of BaO_2 reacted if 265 mL of O_2 is collected by water displacement at 0.975 atm and 10.°C?

323. It is possible to generate chlorine gas by dripping concentrated HCl solution onto solid potassium permanganate according to the following equation:

$$2KMnO_4(aq) + 16HCl(aq) \longrightarrow$$
$$2KCl(aq) + 2MnCl_2(aq) + 8H_2O(l) + 5Cl_2(g)$$

If excess HCl is dripped onto 15.0 g of $KMnO_4$, what volume of Cl_2 will be produced? The Cl_2 is measured at 15°C and 0.959 atm.

324. Ammonia can be oxidized in the presence of a platinum catalyst according to the following equation:

$$4NH_3(g) + 5O_2(g) \longrightarrow 4NO(g) + 6H_2O(l)$$

The NO that is produced reacts almost immediately with additional oxygen according to the following equation:

$$2NO(g) + O_2(g) \longrightarrow 2NO_2(g)$$

If 35.0 kL of oxygen at STP reacts in the first reaction, what volume of NH_3 at STP reacts with it? What volume of NO_2 at STP will be formed in the second reaction, assuming there is excess oxygen that was not used up in the first reaction?

325. Oxygen can be generated in the laboratory by heating potassium chlorate. The reaction is represented by the following equation:

$$2KClO_3(s) \longrightarrow 2KCl(s) + 3O_2(g)$$

What mass of $KClO_3$ must be used in order to generate 5.00 L of O_2, measured at STP?

326. One of the reactions in the Solvay process is used to make sodium hydrogen carbonate. It occurs when carbon dioxide and ammonia are passed through concentrated salt brine. The following equation represents the reaction:

$$NaCl(aq) + H_2O(l) + CO_2(g) + NH_3(g) \longrightarrow$$
$$NaHCO_3(s) + NH_4Cl(aq)$$

a. What volume of NH_3 at 25°C and 1.00 atm pressure will be required if 38 000 L of CO_2, measured under the same conditions, reacts to form $NaHCO_3$?

b. What mass of $NaHCO_3$ can be formed when the gases in (a) react with NaCl?

c. If this reaction forms 46.0 kg of $NaHCO_3$, what volume of NH_3, measured at STP, reacted?

d. What volume of CO_2, compressed in a tank at 5.50 atm and a temperature of 42°C, will be needed to produce 100.00 kg of $NaHCO_3$?

327. The combustion of butane is represented in the following equation:

$$2C_4H_{10}(g) + 13O_2(g) \longrightarrow 8CO_2(g) + 10H_2O(l)$$

a. If 4.74 g of butane reacts with excess oxygen, what volume of CO_2, measured at 150.°C and 1.14 atm, will be formed?

b. What volume of oxygen, measured at 0.980 atm and 75°C, will be consumed by the complete combustion of 0.500 g of butane?

c. A butane-fueled torch has a mass of 876.2 g. After burning for some time, the torch has a mass of 859.3 g. What volume of CO_2, at STP, was formed while the torch burned?

d. What mass of H_2O is produced when butane burns and produces 3720 L of CO_2, measured at 35°C and 0.993 atm pressure?

Concentration of Solutions: Chap. 12, Sec. 3

PERCENTAGE CONCENTRATION

328. What is the percentage concentration of 75.0 g of ethanol dissolved in 500.0 g of water?

329. A chemist dissolves 3.50 g of potassium iodate and 6.23 g of potassium hydroxide in 805.05 g of water. What is the percentage concentration of each solute in the solution?

330. A student wants to make a 5.00% solution of rubidium chloride using 0.377 g of the substance. What mass of water will be needed to make the solution?

331. What mass of lithium nitrate would have to be dissolved in 30.0 g of water in order to make an 18.0% solution?

MOLARITY

332. Determine the molarity of a solution prepared by dissolving 141.6 g of citric acid, $C_3H_5O(COOH)_3$, in water and then diluting the resulting solution to 3500.0 mL.

333. What is the molarity of a salt solution made by dissolving 280.0 mg of NaCl in 2.00 mL of water? Assume the final volume is the same as the volume of the water.

334. What is the molarity of a solution that contains 390.0 g of acetic acid, CH_3COOH, dissolved in enough acetone to make 1000.0 mL of solution?

335. What mass of glucose, $C_6H_{12}O_6$, would be required to prepare 5.000×10^3 L of a 0.215 M solution?

336. What mass of magnesium bromide would be required to prepare 720. mL of a 0.0939 M aqueous solution?

337. What mass of ammonium chloride is dissolved in 300. mL of a 0.875 M solution?

MOLALITY

338. Determine the molality of a solution of 560 g of acetone, CH_3COCH_3, in 620 g of water.

339. What is the molality of a solution of 12.9 g of fructose, $C_6H_{12}O_6$, in 31.0 g of water?

340. How many moles of 2-butanol, $CH_3CHOHCH_2CH_3$, must be dissolved in 125 g of ethanol in order to produce a 12.0 m 2-butanol solution? What mass of 2-butanol is this?

MIXED REVIEW

341. Complete the table below by determining the missing quantity in each example. All solutions are aqueous. Any quantity that is not applicable to a given solution is marked NA.

Solution made	Mass of solute used	Quantity of solution made	Quantity of solvent used
a. 12.0% $KMnO_4$	? g $KMnO_4$	500.0 g	? g H_2O
b. 0.60 M $BaCl_2$	? g $BaCl_2$	1.750 L	NA
c. 6.20 m glycerol, $HOCH_2CHOHCH_2OH$	? g glycerol	NA	800.0 g H_2O
d. ? M $K_2Cr_2O_7$	12.27 g $K_2Cr_2O_7$	650. mL	NA
e. ? m $CaCl_2$	288 g $CaCl_2$	NA	2.04 kg H_2O
f. 0.160 M NaCl	? g NaCl	25.0 mL	NA
g. 2.00 m glucose, $C_6H_{12}O_6$	? g glucose	? g solution	1.50 kg H_2O

342. How many moles of H_2SO_4 are in 2.50 L of a 4.25 M aqueous solution?

343. Determine the molal concentration of 71.5 g of linoleic acid, $C_{18}H_{32}O_2$, in 525 g of hexane, C_6H_{14}.

344. You have a solution that is 16.2% sodium thiosulfate, $Na_2S_2O_3$, by mass.
   a. What mass of sodium thiosulfate is in 80.0 g of solution?
   b. How many moles of sodium thiosulfate are in 80.0 g of solution?
   c. If 80.0 g of the sodium thiosulfate solution is diluted to 250.0 mL with water, what is the molarity of the resulting solution?

345. What mass of anhydrous cobalt(II) chloride would be needed in order to make 650.00 mL of a 4.00 M cobalt(II) chloride solution?

346. A student wants to make a 0.150 M aqueous solution of silver nitrate, $AgNO_3$, and has a bottle containing 11.27 g of silver nitrate. What should be the final volume of the solution?

347. What mass of urea, NH_2CONH_2, must be dissolved in 2250 g of water in order to prepare a 1.50 m solution?

348. What mass of barium nitrate is dissolved in 21.29 mL of a 3.38 M solution?

349. Describe what you would do to prepare 100.0 g of a 3.5% solution of ammonium sulfate in water.

350. What mass of anhydrous calcium chloride should be dissolved in 590.0 g of water in order to produce a 0.82 m solution?

351. How many moles of ammonia are in 0.250 L of a 5.00 M aqueous ammonia solution? If this solution were diluted to 1.000 L, what would be the molarity of the resulting solution?

352. What is the molar mass of a solute if 62.0 g of the solute in 125 g of water produce a 5.3 m solution?

353. A saline solution is 0.9% NaCl. What masses of NaCl and water would be required to prepare 50. L of this saline solution? Assume that the density of water is 1.000 g/mL and that the NaCl does not add to the volume of the solution.

354. A student weighs an empty beaker on a balance and finds its mass to be 68.60 g. The student weighs the beaker again after adding water and finds the new mass to be 115.12 g. A mass of 4.08 g of glucose is then dissolved in the water. What is the percentage concentration of glucose in the solution?

355. The density of ethyl acetate at 20°C is 0.902 g/mL. What volume of ethyl acetate at 20°C would be required to prepare a 2.0% solution of cellulose nitrate using 25 g of cellulose nitrate?

356. Aqueous cadmium chloride reacts with sodium sulfide to produce bright-yellow cadmium sulfide. Write the balanced equation for this reaction, and answer the following questions.
   a. How many moles of $CdCl_2$ are in 50.00 mL of a 3.91 M solution?
   b. If the solution in (a) reacted with excess sodium sulfide, how many moles of CdS would be formed?
   c. What mass of CdS would be formed?

357. What mass of H_2SO_4 is contained in 60.00 mL of a 5.85 M solution of sulfuric acid?

358. A truck carrying 22.5 kL of 6.83 M aqueous hydrochloric acid used to clean brick and masonry has overturned. The authorities plan to neutralize the acid with sodium carbonate. How many moles of HCl will have to be neutralized?

359. A chemist wants to produce 12.00 g of barium sulfate by reacting a 0.600 M $BaCl_2$ solution with excess H_2SO_4, as shown in the reaction below. What volume of the $BaCl_2$ solution should be used?
$$BaCl_2 + H_2SO_4 \rightarrow BaSO_4 + 2HCl$$

360. Many substances are hydrates. Whenever you make a solution, it is important to know whether or not the solute you are using is a hydrate and, if it is a hydrate, how many molecules of water are present per formula unit of the substance. This water must be taken into account when weighing out the solute. Something else to remember when making aqueous solutions from hydrates is that once the hydrate is dissolved, the water of hydration is considered to be part of the solvent. A common hydrate used in the chemistry laboratory is copper sulfate pentahydrate, $CuSO_4 \cdot 5H_2O$. Describe how you would make each of the following solutions using $CuSO_4 \cdot 5H_2O$. Specify masses and volumes as needed.
   a. 100. g of a 6.00% solution of $CuSO_4$
   b. 1.00 L of a 0.800 M solution of $CuSO_4$
   c. a 3.5 m solution of $CuSO_4$ in 1.0 kg of water

361. What mass of calcium chloride hexahydrate is required in order to make 700.0 mL of a 2.50 M solution?

362. What mass of the amino acid arginine, $C_6H_{14}N_4O_2$, would be required to make 1.250 L of a 0.002 05 M solution?

363. How much water would you have to add to 2.402 kg of nickel(II) sulfate hexahydrate in order to prepare a 25.00% solution?

364. What mass of potassium aluminum sulfate dodecahydrate, $KAl(SO_4)_2 \cdot 12H_2O$, would be needed to prepare 35.00 g of a 15.00% $KAl(SO_4)_2$ solution? What mass of water would be added to make this solution?

Dilutions: Chap. 12, Sec. 3

365. Complete the table below by calculating the missing value in each row.

Molarity of stock solution	Volume of stock solution	Molarity of dilute solution	Volume of dilute solution
a. 0.500 M KBr	20.00 mL	? M KBr	100.00 mL
b. 1.00 M LiOH	? mL	0.075 M LiOH	500.00 mL
c. ? M HI	5.00 mL	0.0493 M HI	100.00 mL
d. 12.0 M HCl	0.250 L	1.8 M HCl	? L
e. 7.44 M NH₃	? mL	0.093 M NH₃	4.00 L

366. What volume of water would be added to 16.5 mL of a 0.0813 M solution of sodium borate in order to get a 0.0200 M solution?

MIXED REVIEW

367. What is the molarity of a solution of ammonium chloride prepared by diluting 50.00 mL of a 3.79 M NH_4Cl solution to 2.00 L?

368. A student takes a sample of KOH solution and dilutes it with 100.00 mL of water. The student determines that the diluted solution is 0.046 M KOH but has forgotten to record the volume of the original sample. The concentration of the original solution is 2.09 M. What was the volume of the original sample?

369. A chemist wants to prepare a stock solution of H_2SO_4 so that samples of 20.00 mL will produce a solution with a concentration of 0.50 M when added to 100.0 mL of water.
  a. What should the molarity of the stock solution be?
  b. If the chemist wants to prepare 5.00 L of the stock solution from concentrated H_2SO_4, which is 18.0 M, what volume of concentrated acid should be used?
  c. The density of 18.0 M H_2SO_4 is 1.84 g/mL. What mass of concentrated H_2SO_4 should be used to make the stock solution in (b)?

370. To what volume should 1.19 mL of an 8.00 M acetic acid solution be diluted in order to obtain a final solution that is 1.50 M?

371. What volume of a 5.75 M formic acid solution should be used to prepare 2.00 L of a 1.00 M formic acid solution?

372. A 25.00 mL sample of ammonium nitrate solution produces a 0.186 M solution when diluted with 50.00 mL of water. What is the molarity of the stock solution?

373. Given a solution of known percentage concentration by mass, a laboratory worker can often measure out a calculated mass of the solution in order to obtain a certain mass of solute. Sometimes, though, it is impractical to use the mass of a solution, especially with fuming solutions, such as concentrated HCl and concentrated HNO_3. Measuring these solutions by volume is much more practical. In order to determine the volume that should be measured, a worker would need to know the density of the solution. This information usually appears on the label of the solution bottle.
  a. Concentrated hydrochloric acid is 36% HCl by mass and has a density of 1.18 g/mL. What is the volume of 1.0 kg of this HCl solution? What volume contains 1.0 g of HCl? What volume contains 1.0 mol of HCl?
  b. The density of concentrated nitric acid is 1.42 g/mL, and its concentration is 71% HNO_3 by mass. What volume of concentrated HNO_3 would be needed to prepare 10.0 L of a 2.00 M solution of HNO_3?
  c. What volume of concentrated HCl solution would be needed to prepare 4.50 L of 3.0 M HCl? See (a) for data.

374. A 3.8 M solution of $FeSO_4$ solution is diluted to eight times its original volume. What is the molarity of the diluted solution?

375. A chemist prepares 480. mL of a 2.50 M solution of $K_2Cr_2O_7$ in water. A week later, the chemist wants to use the solution, but the stopper has been left off the flask and 39 mL of water has evaporated. What is the new molarity of the solution?

376. You must write out procedures for a group of lab technicians. One test they will perform requires 25.00 mL of a 1.22 M solution of acetic acid. You decide to use a 6.45 M acetic acid solution that you have on hand. What procedure should the technicians use in order to get the solution they need?

377. A chemical test has determined the concentration of a solution of an unknown substance to be 2.41 M. A 100.0 mL volume of the solution is evaporated to dryness, leaving 9.56 g of crystals of the unknown solute. Calculate the molar mass of the unknown substance.

378. Tincture of iodine can be prepared by dissolving 34 g of I_2 and 25 g of KI in 25 mL of distilled water and diluting the solution to 500. mL with ethanol. What is the molarity of I_2 in the solution?

379. Phosphoric acid is commonly supplied as an 85% solution. What mass of this solution would be required to prepare 600.0 mL of a 2.80 M phosphoric acid solution?

380. Commercially available concentrated sulfuric acid is 18.0 M H_2SO_4. What volume of concentrated H_2SO_4 would you use in order to make 3.00 L of a 4.0 M stock solution?

381. Describe how to prepare 1.00 L of a 0.495 M solution of urea, NH_2CONH_2, starting with a 3.07 M stock solution.

382. Honey is a solution consisting almost entirely of a mixture of the hexose sugars fructose and glucose; both sugars have the formula $C_6H_{12}O_6$, but they differ in molecular structure.

   a. A sample of honey is found to be 76.2% $C_6H_{12}O_6$ by mass. What is the molality of the hexose sugars in honey? Consider the sugars to be equivalent.

   b. The density of the honey sample is 1.42 g/mL. What mass of hexose sugars are in 1.00 L of honey? What is the molarity of the mixed hexose sugars in honey?

383. Industrial chemicals used in manufacturing are almost never pure, and the content of the material may vary from one batch to the next. For these reasons, a sample is taken from each shipment and sent to a laboratory, where its makeup is determined. This procedure is called assaying. Once the content of a material is known, engineers adjust the manufacturing process to account for the degree of purity of the starting chemicals.

   Suppose you have just received a shipment of sodium carbonate, Na_2CO_3. You weigh out 50.00 g of the material, dissolve it in water, and dilute the solution to 1.000 L. You remove 10.00 mL from the solution and dilute it to 50.00 mL. By measuring the amount of a second substance that reacts with Na_2CO_3, you determine that the concentration of sodium carbonate in the diluted solution is 0.0890 M. Calculate the percentage of Na_2CO_3 in the original batch of material. The molar mass of Na_2CO_3 is 105.99 g. (Hint: Determine the number of moles in the original solution, and convert to mass of Na_2CO_3.)

384. A student wants to prepare 0.600 L of a stock solution of copper(II) chloride so that 20.0 mL of the stock solution diluted by adding 130.0 mL of water will yield a 0.250 M solution. What mass of $CuCl_2$ should be used to make the stock solution?

385. You have a bottle containing a 2.15 M $BaCl_2$ solution. You must tell other students how to dilute this solution to get various volumes of a 0.65 M $BaCl_2$ solution. By what factor will you tell them to dilute the stock solution? In other words, when a student removes any volume, V, of the stock solution, how many times V of water should be added to dilute to 0.65 M?

386. You have a bottle containing an 18.2% solution of strontium nitrate (density = 1.02 g/mL).

   a. What mass of strontium nitrate is dissolved in 80.0 mL of this solution?

   b. How many moles of strontium nitrate are dissolved in 80.0 mL of the solution?

   c. If 80.0 mL of this solution is diluted with 420.0 mL of water, what is the molarity of the solution?

Colligative Properties: Chap. 13, Sec. 2

387. Determine the freezing point of a solution of 60.0 g of glucose, $C_6H_{12}O_6$, dissolved in 80.0 g of water.

388. What is the freezing point of a solution of 645 g of urea, H_2NCONH_2, dissolved in 980. g of water?

389. What is the expected boiling point of a brine solution containing 30.00 g of KBr dissolved in 100.00 g of water?

390. What is the expected boiling point of a $CaCl_2$ solution containing 385 g of $CaCl_2$ dissolved in 1.230×10^3 g of water?

391. A solution of 0.827 g of an unknown nonelectrolyte compound in 2.500 g of water has a freezing point of $-10.18°C$. Calculate the molar mass of the compound.

392. A 0.171 g sample of an unknown organic compound is dissolved in ether. The solution has a total mass of 2.470 g. The boiling point of the solution is found to be 36.43°C. What is the molar mass of the organic compound?

MIXED REVIEW

In each of the following problems, assume that the solute is a nonelectrolyte unless otherwise stated.

393. Calculate the freezing point and boiling point of a solution of 383 g of glucose dissolved in 400. g of water.

394. Determine the boiling point of a solution of 72.4 g of glycerol dissolved in 122.5 g of water.

395. What is the boiling point of a solution of 30.20 g of ethylene glycol, $HOCH_2CH_2OH$, in 88.40 g of phenol?

396. What mass of ethanol, CH_3CH_2OH, should be dissolved in 450. g of water to obtain a freezing point of $-4.5°C$?

397. Calculate the molar mass of a nonelectrolyte that lowers the freezing point of 25.00 g of water to 23.9°C when 4.27 g of the substance is dissolved in the water.

398. What is the freezing point of a solution of 1.17 g of 1-naphthol, $C_{10}H_8O$, dissolved in 2.00 mL of benzene at 20°C? The density of benzene at 20°C is 0.876 g/mL. K_f for benzene is 25.12°C/m, and benzene's normal freezing point is 5.53°C.

399. The boiling point of a solution containing 10.44 g of an unknown nonelectrolyte in 50.00 g of acetic acid is 159.2°C. What is the molar mass of the solute?

400. A 0.0355 g sample of an unknown molecular compound is dissolved in 1.000 g of liquid camphor at 200.0°C. Upon cooling, the camphor freezes at 157.7°C. Calculate the molar mass of the unknown compound.

401. Determine the boiling point of a solution of 22.5 g of fructose, $C_6H_{12}O_6$, in 294 g of phenol.

402. Ethylene glycol, $HOCH_2CH_2OH$, is effective as an antifreeze, but it also raises the boiling temperature of automobile coolant, which helps prevent loss of coolant when the weather is hot.
  a. What is the freezing point of a 50.0% solution of ethylene glycol in water?
  b. What is the boiling point of the same 50.0% solution?

403. The value of K_f for cyclohexane is $-20.0°C/m$, and its normal freezing point is 6.6°C. A mass of 1.604 g of a waxy solid dissolved in 10.000 g of cyclohexane results in a freezing point of $-4.4°C$. Calculate the molar mass of the solid.

404. What is the expected freezing point of an aqueous solution of 2.62 kg of nitric acid, HNO_3, in a solution with a total mass of 5.91 kg? Assume that the nitric acid is completely ionized.

405. An unknown organic compound is mixed with 0.5190 g of naphthalene crystals to give a mixture having a total mass of 0.5959 g. The mixture is heated until the naphthalene melts and the unknown substance dissolves. Upon cooling, the solution freezes at a temperature of 74.8°C. What is the molar mass of the unknown compound?

406. What is the boiling point of a solution of 8.69 g of the electrolyte sodium acetate, $NaCH_3COO$, dissolved in 15.00 g of water?

407. What is the expected freezing point of a solution of 110.5 g of H_2SO_4 in 225 g of water? Assume sulfuric acid completely dissociates in water.

408. A compound called pyrene has the empirical formula C_8H_5. When 4.04 g of pyrene is dissolved in 10.00 g of benzene, the boiling point of the solution is 85.1°C. Calculate the molar mass of pyrene, and determine its molecular formula. The molal boiling-point constant for benzene is $2.53°C/m$. Its normal boiling point is 80.1°C.

409. What mass of $CaCl_2$ (which is ionic), when dissolved in 100.00 g of water, gives a freezing point of $-5.0°C$? What mass of glucose would give the same result?

410. A compound has the empirical formula CH_2O. When 0.0866 g is dissolved in 1.000 g of ether, the solution's boiling point is 36.5°C. Determine the molecular formula of this substance.

411. What is the freezing point of a 28.6% (by mass) aqueous solution of HCl? Assume the HCl is 100% ionized.

412. What mass of ethylene glycol, $HOCH_2CH_2OH$, must be dissolved in 4.510 kg of water to result in a freezing point of $-18.0°C$? What is the boiling point of the same solution?

413. A water solution containing 2.00 g of an unknown molecular substance dissolved in 10.00 g of water has a freezing point of $-4.0°C$.
  a. Calculate the molality of the solution.
  b. When 2.00 g of the substance is dissolved in acetone instead of in water, the boiling point of the solution is 58.9°C. The normal boiling point of acetone is 56.00°C, and its K_b is $1.71°C/m$. Calculate the molality of the solution from this data.

414. A chemist wants to prepare a solution with a freezing point of $-22.0°C$ and has 100.00 g of glycerol on hand. What mass of water should the chemist mix with the glycerol?

415. An unknown carbohydrate compound has the empirical formula CH_2O. A solution consisting of 0.515 g of the carbohydrate dissolved in 1.717 g of acetic acid freezes at 8.8°C. What is the molar mass of the carbohydrate? What is its molecular formula?

416. An unknown organic compound has the empirical formula C_2H_2O. A solution of 3.775 g of the unknown compound dissolved in 12.00 g of water is cooled until it freezes at a temperature of $-4.72°C$. Determine the molar mass and the molecular formula of the compound.

pH: Chap. 15, Sec. 1

417. The hydroxide ion concentration of an aqueous solution is 6.4×10^{-5} M. What is the hydronium ion concentration?

418. Calculate the H_3O^+ and OH^- concentrations in a 7.50×10^{-4} M solution of HNO_3, a strong acid.

419. Determine the pH of a 0.001 18 M solution of HBr.

420. a. What is the pH of a solution that has a hydronium ion concentration of 1.0 M?
  b. What is the pH of a 2.0 M solution of HCl, assuming the acid remains 100% ionized?
  c. What is the theoretical pH of a 10. M solution of HCl?

421. What is the pH of a solution with the following hydroxide ion concentrations?
  a. 1×10^{-5} M
  b. 5×10^{-8} M
  c. 2.90×10^{-11} M

422. What are the pOH and hydroxide ion concentrations of a solution with a pH of 8.92?

423. What are the pOH values of solutions with the following hydronium ion concentrations?
  a. 2.51×10^{-13} M
  b. 4.3×10^{-3} M
  c. 9.1×10^{-6} M
  d. 0.070 M

424. A solution is prepared by dissolving 3.50 g of sodium hydroxide in water and adding water until the total volume of the solution is 2.50 L. What are the OH^- and H_3O^+ concentrations?

425. If 1.00 L of a potassium hydroxide solution with a pH of 12.90 is diluted to 2.00 L, what is the pH of the resulting solution?

MIXED REVIEW

426. Calculate the H_3O^+ and OH^- concentrations in the following solutions. Each is either a strong acid or a strong base.
  a. 0.05 M sodium hydroxide
  b. 0.0025 M sulfuric acid
  c. 0.013 M lithium hydroxide
  d. 0.150 M nitric acid

e. 0.0200 M calcium hydroxide

f. 0.390 M perchloric acid

427. What is the pH of each solution in item 426?

428. Calculate $[H_3O^+]$ and $[OH^-]$ in a 0.160 M solution of potassium hydroxide. Assume that the solute is 100% dissociated at this concentration.

429. The pH of an aqueous solution of NaOH is 12.9. What is the molarity of the solution?

430. What is the pH of a 0.001 25 M HBr solution? If 175 mL of this solution is diluted to a total volume of 3.00 L, what is the pH of the diluted solution?

431. What is the pH of a 0.0001 M solution of NaOH? What is the pH of a 0.0005 M solution of NaOH?

432. A solution is prepared using 15.0 mL of 1.0 M HCl and 20.0 mL of 0.50 M HNO_3. The final volume of the solution is 1.25 L. Answer the following questions:

a. What are the $[H_3O^+]$ and $[OH^-]$ in the final solution?

b. What is the pH of the final solution?

433. A container is labeled 500.0 mL of 0.001 57 M nitric acid solution. A chemist finds that the container was not sealed and that some evaporation has taken place. The volume of solution is now 447.0 mL.

a. What was the original pH of the solution?

b. What is the pH of the solution now?

434. Calculate the hydroxide ion concentration in an aqueous solution that has a 0.000 35 M hydronium ion concentration.

435. A solution of sodium hydroxide has a pH of 12.14. If 50.00 mL of the solution is diluted to 2.000 L with water, what is the pH of the diluted solution?

436. An acetic acid solution has a pH of 4.0. What are the $[H_3O^+]$ and $[OH^-]$ in this solution?

437. What is the pH of a 0.000 460 M solution of $Ca(OH)_2$?

438. A solution of strontium hydroxide with a pH of 11.4 is to be prepared. What mass of strontium hydroxide would be required to make 1.00 L of this solution?

439. A solution of NH_3 has a pH of 11.00. What are the concentrations of hydronium and hydroxide ions in this solution?

440. Acetic acid does not completely ionize in solution. Percent ionization of a substance dissolved in water is equal to the moles of ions produced as a percentage of the moles of ions that would be produced if the substance were completely ionized. Calculate the percent ionization of acetic acid in the following solutions.

a. 1.0 M acetic acid solution with a pH of 2.40

b. 0.10 M acetic acid solution with a pH of 2.90

c. 0.010 M acetic acid solution with a pH of 3.40

441. Calculate the pH of a solution that contains 5.00 g of HNO_3 in 2.00 L of solution.

442. A solution of HCl has a pH of 1.50. Determine the pH of the solutions made in each of the following ways.

a. 1.00 mL of the solution is diluted to 1000. mL with water.

b. 25.00 mL is diluted to 200. mL with distilled water.

c. 18.83 mL of the solution is diluted to 4.000 L with distilled water.

d. 1.50 L is diluted to 20.0 kL with distilled water.

443. An aqueous solution contains 10 000 times more hydronium ions than hydroxide ions. What is the concentration of each ion?

444. A potassium hydroxide solution has a pH of 12.90. Enough acid is added to react with half of the OH^- ions present. What is the pH of the resulting solution? Assume that the products of the neutralization have no effect on pH and that the amount of additional water produced is negligible.

445. A hydrochloric acid solution has a pH of 1.70. What is the $[H_3O^+]$ in this solution? Considering that HCl is a strong acid, what is the HCl concentration of the solution?

446. What is the molarity of a solution of the strong base $Ca(OH)_2$ in a solution that has a pH of 10.80?

447. You have a 1.00 M solution of the strong acid, HCl. What is the pH of this solution? You need a solution of pH 4.00. To what volume would you dilute 1.00 L of the HCl solution to get this pH? To what volume would you dilute 1.00 L of the pH 4.00 solution to get a solution of pH 6.00? To what volume would you dilute 1.00 L of the pH 4.00 solution to get a solution of pH 8.00?

448. A solution of chloric acid, $HClO_3$, a strong acid, has a pH of 1.28. How many moles of NaOH would be required to react completely with the $HClO_3$ in 1.00 L of the solution? What mass of NaOH is required?

449. A solution of the weak base NH_3 has a pH of 11.90. How many moles of HCl would have to be added to 1.00 L of the ammonia to react with all of the OH^- ions present at pH 11.90?

450. The pH of a citric acid solution is 3.15. What are the $[H_3O^+]$ and $[OH^-]$ in this solution?

Titrations: Chap. 15, Sec. 2

In each of the following problems, the acids and bases react in a mole ratio of 1 mol base : 1 mol acid.

451. A student titrates a 20.00 mL sample of a solution of HBr with unknown molarity. The titration requires 20.05 mL of a 0.1819 M solution of NaOH. What is the molarity of the HBr solution?

452. Vinegar can be assayed to determine its acetic-acid content. Determine the molarity of acetic acid in a 15.00 mL sample of vinegar that requires 22.70 mL of a 0.550 M solution of NaOH to reach the equivalence point.

453. A 20.00 mL sample of a solution of $Sr(OH)_2$ is titrated to the equivalence point with 43.03 mL of 0.1159 M HCl. What is the molarity of the $Sr(OH)_2$ solution?

454. A 35.00 mL sample of ammonia solution is titrated to the equivalence point with 54.95 mL of a 0.400 M sulfuric acid solution. What is the molarity of the ammonia solution?

In the problems below, assume that impurities are not acidic or basic and that they do not react in an acid-base titration.

455. A supply of glacial acetic acid has absorbed water from the air. It must be assayed to determine the actual percentage of acetic acid. 2.000 g of the acid is diluted to 100.00 mL, and 20.00 mL is titrated with a solution of sodium hydroxide. The base solution has a concentration of 0.218 M, and 28.25 mL is used in the titration. Calculate the percentage of acetic acid in the original sample. Write the titration equation to get the mole ratio.

456. A shipment of crude sodium carbonate must be assayed for its Na_2CO_3 content. You receive a small jar containing a sample from the shipment and weigh out 9.709 g into a flask, where it is dissolved in water and diluted to 1.0000 L with distilled water. A 10.00 mL sample is taken from the flask and titrated to the equivalence point with 16.90 mL of a 0.1022 M HCl solution. Determine the percentage of Na_2CO_3 in the sample. Write the titration equation to get the mole ratio.

MIXED REVIEW

457. A 50.00 mL sample of a potassium hydroxide is titrated with a 0.8186 M HCl solution. The titration requires 27.87 mL of the HCl solution to reach the equivalence point. What is the molarity of the KOH solution?

458. A 15.00 mL sample of acetic acid is titrated with 34.13 mL of 0.9940 M NaOH. Determine the molarity of the acetic acid.

459. A 12.00 mL sample of an ammonia solution is titrated with 1.499 M HNO_3 solution. A total of 19.48 mL of acid is required to reach the equivalence point. What is the molarity of the ammonia solution?

460. A certain acid and base react in a 1:1 ratio.

   a. If the acid and base solutions are of equal concentration, what volume of acid will titrate a 20.00 mL sample of the base?

   b. If the acid is twice as concentrated as the base, what volume of acid will be required to titrate 20.00 mL of the base?

   c. How much acid will be required if the base is four times as concentrated as the acid, and 20.00 mL of base is used?

461. A 10.00 mL sample of a solution of hydrofluoric acid, HF, is diluted to 500.00 mL. A 20.00 mL sample of the diluted solution requires 13.51 mL of a 0.1500 M NaOH solution to be titrated to the equivalence point. What is the molarity of the original HF solution?

462. A solution of oxalic acid, a diprotic acid, is used to titrate a 16.22 mL sample of a 0.5030 M KOH solution. If the titration requires 18.41 mL of the oxalic acid solution, what is its molarity?

463. A H_2SO_4 solution of unknown molarity is titrated with a 1.209 M NaOH solution. The titration requires 42.27 mL of the NaOH solution to reach the equivalence point with 25.00 mL of the H_2SO_4 solution. What is the molarity of the acid solution?

464. Potassium hydrogen phthalate, $KHC_8H_4O_4$, is a solid acidic substance that reacts in a 1:1 mole ratio with bases that have one hydroxide ion. Suppose that 0.7025 g of potassium hydrogen phthalate is titrated to the equivalence point by 20.18 mL of a KOH solution. What is the molarity of the KOH solution?

465. A solution of citric acid, a triprotic acid, is titrated with a sodium hydroxide solution. A 20.00 mL sample of the citric acid solution requires 17.03 mL of a 2.025 M solution of NaOH to reach the equivalence point. What is the molarity of the acid solution?

466. A flask contains 41.04 mL of a solution of potassium hydroxide. The solution is titrated and reaches an equivalence point when 21.65 mL of a 0.6515 M solution of HNO_3 is added. Calculate the molarity of the base solution.

467. A bottle is labeled 2.00 M H_2SO_4. You decide to titrate a 20.00 mL sample with a 1.85 M NaOH solution. What volume of NaOH solution would you expect to use if the label is correct?

468. What volume of a 0.5200 M solution of H_2SO_4 would be needed to titrate 100.00 mL of a 0.1225 M solution of $Sr(OH)_2$?

469. A sample of a crude grade of KOH is sent to the lab to be tested for KOH content. A 4.005 g sample is dissolved and diluted to 200.00 mL with water. A 25.00 mL sample of the solution is titrated with a 0.4388 M HCl solution and requires 19.93 mL to reach the equivalence point. How many moles of KOH were in the 4.005 g sample? What mass of KOH is this? What is the percent of KOH in the crude material?

470. What mass of magnesium hydroxide would be required for the magnesium hydroxide to react to the equivalence point with 558 mL of 3.18 M hydrochloric acid?

471. An ammonia solution of unknown concentration is titrated with a solution of hydrochloric acid. The HCl solution is 1.25 M, and 5.19 mL is required to titrate 12.61 mL of the ammonia solution. What is the molarity of the ammonia solution?

472. What volume of 2.811 M oxalic acid solution is needed to react to the equivalence point with a 5.090 g sample of material that is 92.10% NaOH? Oxalic acid is a diprotic acid.

473. Standard solutions of accurately known concentration are available in most laboratories. These solutions are used to titrate other solutions to determine their concentrations. Once the concentration of the other solutions are accurately known, they may be used to titrate solutions of unknowns.

The molarity of a solution of HCl is determined by titrating the solution with an accurately known solution of $Ba(OH)_2$, which has a molar concentration of 0.1529 M. A volume of 43.09 mL of the $Ba(OH)_2$ solution titrates 26.06 mL of the acid solution. The acid solution is then used to titrate 15.00 mL of a solution of rubidium hydroxide. The titration requires 27.05 mL of the acid.
   a. What is the molarity of the HCl solution?
   b. What is the molarity of the RbOH solution?

474. A truck containing 2800 kg of a 6.0 M hydrochloric acid has been in an accident and is in danger of spilling its load. What mass of $Ca(OH)_2$ should be sent to the scene in order to neutralize all of the acid in case the tank bursts? The density of the 6.0 M HCl solution is 1.10 g/mL.

475. A 1.00 mL sample of a fairly concentrated nitric acid solution is diluted to 200.00 mL. A 10.00 mL sample of the diluted solution requires 23.94 mL of a 0.0177 M solution of $Ba(OH)_2$ to be titrated to the equivalence point. Determine the molarity of the original nitric acid solution.

476. What volume of 4.494 M H_2SO_4 solution would be required to react to the equivalence point with 7.2280 g of $LiOH(s)$?

Thermochemistry: Chap. 16, Sec. 1

477. Calculate the reaction enthalpy for the following reaction:
$$5CO_2(g) + Si_3N_4(s) \longrightarrow 3SiO(s) + 2N_2O(g) + 5CO(g)$$
Use the following equations and data:
(1) $CO(g) + SiO_2(s) \longrightarrow SiO(g) + CO_2(g)$
(2) $8CO_2(g) + Si_3N_4(s) \longrightarrow 3SiO_2(s) + 2N_2O(g) + 8CO(g)$
$\Delta H_{reaction\ 1} = +520.9$ kJ
$\Delta H_{reaction\ 2} = +461.05$ kJ
Determine ΔH for each of the following three reactions.

478. The following reaction is used to make CaO from limestone:
$$CaCO_3(s) \longrightarrow CaO(s) + CO_2(g)$$

479. The following reaction represents the oxidation of FeO to Fe_2O_3:
$$2FeO(s) + O2(g) \longrightarrow Fe_2O_3(s)$$

480. The following reaction of ammonia and hydrogen fluoride produces ammonium fluoride:
$$NH_3(g) + HF(g) \longrightarrow NH_4F(s)$$

481. Calculate the free-energy change, ΔG, for the combustion of hydrogen sulfide according to the following chemical equation. Assume reactants and products are at 25°C:
$$H_2S(g) + O_2(g) \longrightarrow H_2O(l) + SO_2(g)$$
$\Delta H_{reaction} = -562.1$ kJ/mol
$\Delta S_{reaction} = -0.092\ 78$ kJ/mol•K

482. Calculate the free-energy change for the decomposition of sodium chlorate. Assume reactants and products are at 25°C:
$$NaClO_3(s) \longrightarrow NaCl(s) + O_2(g)$$
$\Delta H_{reaction} = -19.1$ kJ/mol
$\Delta S_{reaction} = -0.1768$ kJ/mol•K

483. Calculate the free-energy change for the combustion of 1 mol of ethane. Assume reactants and products are at 25°C:
$$C_2H_6(g) + O_2(g) \longrightarrow 2CO_2(g) + 3H_2O(l)$$
$\Delta H_{reaction} = -1561$ kJ/mol
$\Delta S_{reaction} = -0.4084$ kJ/mol•K

MIXED REVIEW

484. Calculate ΔH for the reaction of fluorine with water:
$$F_2(g) + H_2O(l) \longrightarrow 2HF(g) + O_2(g)$$

485. Calculate ΔH for the reaction of calcium oxide and sulfur trioxide:
$$CaO(s) + SO_3(g) \longrightarrow CaSO_4(s)$$
Use the following equations and data:
$$H_2O(l) + SO_3(g) \longrightarrow H_2SO_4(l)$$
$\Delta H = -132.5$ kJ/mol
$$H_2SO_4(l) + Ca(s) \longrightarrow CaSO_4(s) + H_2(g)$$
$\Delta H = -602.5$ kJ/mol
$$Ca(s) + O_2(g) \longrightarrow CaO(s)$$
$\Delta H = -634.9$ kJ/mol
$$H_2(g) + O_2(g) \longrightarrow H_2O(l)$$
$\Delta H = -285.8$ kJ/mol

486. Calculate ΔH for the reaction of sodium oxide with sulfur dioxide:
$$Na_2O(s) + SO_2(g) \longrightarrow Na_2SO_3(s)$$

487. Use enthalpies of combustion to calculate ΔH for the oxidation of 1-butanol to make butanoic acid:
$$C_4H_9OH(l) + O_2(g) \longrightarrow C_3H_7COOH(l) + H_2O(l)$$
Combustion of butanol:
$$C_4H_9OH(l) + 6O_2(g) \longrightarrow 4CO_2(g) + 5H_2O(l)$$
$\Delta H_c = -2675.9$ kJ/mol
Combustion of butanoic acid:
$$C_3H_7COOH(l) + 5O_2(g) \longrightarrow 4CO_2(g) + 4H_2O(l)$$
$\Delta H_c = -2183.6$ kJ/mol

488. Determine the free-energy change for the reduction of CuO with hydrogen. Products and reactants are at 25°C.
$$CuO(s) + H_2(g) \longrightarrow Cu(s) + H_2O(l)$$
$\Delta H = -128.5$ kJ/mol
$\Delta S = -70.1$ J/mol•K

489. Calculate the enthalpy change at 25°C for the reaction of sodium iodide and chlorine. Use only the data given.
$$NaI(s) + Cl_2(g) \longrightarrow NaCl(s) + I_2(l)$$
$\Delta S = -79.9$ J/mol•K
$\Delta G = -98.0$ kJ/mol

490. The element bromine can be produced by the reaction of hydrogen bromide and manganese(IV) oxide: $4HBr(g) + MnO_2(s) \longrightarrow MnBr_2(s) + 2H_2O(l) + Br_2(l)$. ΔH for the reaction is -291.3 kJ/mol at 25°C. Use this value and the following values of ΔH_f^0 to calculate ΔH_f^0 of $MnBr_2(s)$.

$\Delta H_{fHBr}^0 = -36.29$ kJ/mol

$\Delta H_{fMnO_2}^0 = -520.0$ kJ/mol

$\Delta H_{fH_2O}^0 = -285.8$ kJ/mol

$\Delta H_{fBr_2}^0 = 0.00$ kJ/mol

491. Calculate the change in entropy, ΔS, at 25°C for the reaction of calcium carbide with water to produce acetylene gas:

$$CaC_2(s) + 2H_2O(l) \longrightarrow C_2H_2(g) + Ca(OH)_2(s)$$

$\Delta G = -147.7$ kJ/mol

$\Delta H = -125.6$ kJ/mol

492. Calculate the free-energy change for the explosive decomposition of ammonium nitrate at 25°C. Note that H_2O is a gas in this reaction:

$$NH_4NO_3(s) \longrightarrow N_2O(g) + 2H_2O(g)$$

$\Delta S = 446.4$ J/mol•K

493. In locations where natural gas, which is mostly methane, is not available, many people burn propane, which is delivered by truck and stored in a tank under pressure.
  a. Write the chemical equations for the complete combustion of 1 mol of methane, CH_4, and 1 mol of propane, C_3H_8.
  b. Calculate the enthalpy change for each reaction to determine the amount of energy as heat evolved by burning 1 mol of each fuel.
  c. Using the molar enthalpies of combustion you calculated, determine the energy output per kilogram of each fuel. Which fuel yields more energy per unit mass?

494. The hydration of acetylene to form acetaldehyde is shown in the following equation:

$$C_2H_2(g) + H_2O(l) \longrightarrow CH_3CHO(l)$$

Use enthalpies of combustion for C_2H_2 and CH_3CHO to compute the enthalpy of the above reaction.

$$C_2H_2(g) + 2O_2(g) \longrightarrow 2CO_2(g) + H_2O(l)$$

$\Delta H = -1299.6$ kJ/mol

$$CH_3CHO(l) + 2O_2(g) \longrightarrow 2CO_2(g) + 2H_2O(l)$$

$\Delta H = -1166.9$ kJ/mol

495. Calculate the enthalpy for the combustion of decane. ΔH_f^0 for liquid decane is -300.9 kJ/mol.

$$C_{10}H_{22}(l) + 15O_2(g) \longrightarrow 10CO_2(g) + 11H_2O(l)$$

496. Find the enthalpy of the reaction of magnesium oxide with hydrogen chloride:

$$MgO(s) + 2HCl(g) \longrightarrow MgCl_2(s) + H_2O(l)$$

Use the following equations and data.

$$Mg(s) + 2HCl(g) \longrightarrow MgCl_2(s) + H_2(g)$$

$\Delta H = -456.9$ kJ/mol

$$Mg(s) + O_2(g) \longrightarrow MgO(s)$$

$\Delta H = -601.6$ kJ/mol

$$H_2O(l) \longrightarrow H_2(g) + O_2(g)$$

$\Delta H = +285.8$ kJ/mol

497. What is the free-energy change for the following reaction at 25°C?

$$2NaOH(s) + 2Na(s) \xrightarrow{\Delta} 2Na_2O(s) + H_2(g)$$

$\Delta S = 10.6$ J/mol•K $\Delta H_{fNaOH}^0 = -425.9$ kJ/mol

498. The following equation represents the reaction between gaseous HCl and gaseous ammonia to form solid ammonium chloride:

$$NH_3(g) + HCl(g) \longrightarrow NH_4Cl(s)$$

Calculate the entropy change in J/mol•K for the reaction of hydrogen chloride and ammonia at 25°C using the following data and the table following item 499.

$\Delta G = -91.2$ kJ/mol

499. The production of steel from iron involves the removal of many impurities in the iron ore. The following equations show some of the purifying reactions. Calculate the enthalpy for each reaction. Use the table and the data given below.
  a. $3C(s) + Fe_2O_3(s) \longrightarrow 3CO(g) + 2Fe(s)$
     $\Delta H_{fCO(g)}^0 = -110.53$ kJ/mol
  b. $3Mn(s) + Fe_2O_3(s) \longrightarrow 3MnO(s) + 2Fe(s)$
     $\Delta H_{fMnO(s)}^0 = -384.9$ kJ/mol
  c. $12P(s) + 10Fe_2O_3(s) \longrightarrow 3P_4O_{10}(s) + 20Fe(s)$
     $\Delta H_{fP_4O_{10}(s)}^0 = -3009.9$ kJ/mol
  d. $3Si(s) + 2Fe_2O_3(s) \longrightarrow 3SiO_2(s) + 4Fe(s)$
     $\Delta H_{fSiO_2(s)}^0 = -910.9$ kJ/mol
  e. $3S(s) + 2Fe_2O_3(s) \longrightarrow 3SO_2(g) + 4Fe(s)$

For problems 498–499

Substance	ΔH_f^0 (kJ/mol)	Substance	ΔH_f^0 (kJ/mol)
$NH_3(g)$	−45.9	$HF(g)$	−273.3
$NH_4Cl(s)$	−314.4	$H_2O(g)$	−241.82
$NH_4F(s)$	−125	$H_2O(l)$	−285.8
$NH_4NO_3(s)$	−365.56	$H_2O_2(l)$	−187.8
$Br_2(l)$	0.00	$H_2SO_4(l)$	−813.989
$CaCO_3(s)$	−1207.6	$FeO(s)$	−825.5
$CaO(s)$	−634.9	$Fe_2O_3(s)$	−1118.4
$CH_4(g)$	−74.9	$MnO_2(s)$	−520.0
$C_3H_8(g)$	−104.7	$N_2O(g)$	+82.1
$CO_2(g)$	−393.5	$O_2(g)$	0.00
$F_2(g)$	0.00	$Na_2O(s)$	−414.2
$H_2(g)$	0.00	$Na_2SO_3(s)$	−1101
$HBr(g)$	−36.29	$SO_2(g)$	−296.8
$HCl(g)$	−92.3	$SO_3(g)$	−395.7

Equilibrium: Chap. 18, Sec. 1

500. Calculate the equilibrium constants for the following hypothetical reactions. Assume that all components of the reactions are gaseous.
  a. $A \rightleftharpoons C + D$
     At equilibrium, the concentration of A is 2.24×10^{-2} M, and the concentrations of both C and D are 6.41×10^{-3} M.

b. $A + B \rightleftarrows C + D$

At equilibrium, the concentrations of both A and B are 3.23×10^{-5} M, and the concentrations of both C and D are 1.27×10^{-2} M.

c. $A + B \rightleftarrows 2C$

At equilibrium, the concentrations of both A and B are 7.02×10^{-3} M, and the concentration of C is 2.16×10^{-2} M.

d. $2A \rightleftarrows 2C + D$

At equilibrium, the concentration of A is 6.59×10^{-4} M. The concentration of C is 4.06×10^{-3} M, and the concentration of D is 2.03×10^{-3} M.

e. $A + B \rightleftarrows C + D + E$

At equilibrium, the concentrations of both A and B are 3.73×10^{-4} M, and the concentrations of C, D, and E are 9.35×10^{-4} M.

f. $2A + B \rightleftarrows 2C$

At equilibrium, the concentration of A is 5.50×10^{-3} M, the concentration of B is 2.25×10^{-3} M, and the concentration of C is 1.02×10^{-2} M.

501. Calculate the concentration of product D in the following hypothetical reaction:

$$2A(g) \rightleftarrows 2C(g) + D(g)$$

At equilibrium, the concentration of A is 1.88×10^{-1} M, the concentration of C is 6.56 M, and the equilibrium constant is 2.403×10^2.

502. At a temperature of 700 K, the equilibrium constant is 3.164×10^3 for the following reaction system for the hydrogenation of ethene, C_2H_4, to ethane, C_2H_6:

$$C_2H_4(g) + H_2(g) \rightleftarrows C_2H_6(g)$$

What will be the equilibrium concentration of ethene if the concentration of H_2 is 0.0619 M and the concentration of C_2H_6 is 1.055 M?

MIXED REVIEW

503. Using the reaction $A + 2B \rightleftarrows C + 2D$, determine the equilibrium constant if the following equilibrium concentrations are found. All components are gases.

[A] = 0.0567 M

[B] = 0.1171 M

[C] = 0.000 3378 M

[D] = 0.000 6756 M

504. In the reaction $2A \rightleftarrows 2C + 2D$, determine the equilibrium constant when the following equilibrium concentrations are found. All components are gases.

[A] = 0.1077 M

[C] = 0.000 4104 M

[D] = 0.000 4104 M

505. Calculate the equilibrium constant for the following reaction. Note the phases of the components.

$$2A(g) + B(s) \rightleftarrows C(g) + D(g)$$

The equilibrium concentrations of the components are

[A] = 0.0922 M

[C] = 4.11×10^{-4} M

[D] = 8.22×10^{-4} M

506. The equilibrium constant of the following reaction for the decomposition of phosgene at 25°C is 4.282×10^{-2}.

$$COCl_2(g) \rightleftarrows CO(g) + Cl_2(g)$$

a. What is the concentration of $COCl_2$ when the concentrations of both CO and Cl_2 are 5.90×10^{-3} M?

b. When the equilibrium concentration of $COCl_2$ is 0.003 70 M, what are the concentrations of CO and Cl_2? Assume the concentrations are equal.

507. Consider the following hypothetical reaction.

$$A(g) + B(s) \rightleftarrows C(g) + D(s)$$

a. If $K = 1$ for this reaction at 500 K, what can you say about the concentrations of A and C at equilibrium?

b. If raising the temperature of the reaction results in an equilibrium with a higher concentration of C than A, how will the value of K change?

508. The following reaction occurs when steam is passed over hot carbon. The mixture of gases it generates is called *water gas* and is useful as an industrial fuel and as a source of hydrogen for the production of ammonia.

$$C(s) + H_2O(g) \rightleftarrows CO(g) + H_2(g)$$

The equilibrium constant for this reaction is 4.251×10^{-2} at 800 K. If the equilibrium concentration of $H_2O(g)$ is 0.1990 M, what concentrations of CO and H_2 would you expect to find?

509. When nitrogen monoxide gas comes in contact with air, it oxidizes to the brown gas nitrogen dioxide according to the following equation:

$$2NO(g) + O_2(g) \rightleftarrows 2NO_2(g)$$

a. The equilibrium constant for this reaction at 500 K is 1.671×10^4. What concentration of NO_2 is present at equilibrium if [NO] = 6.200×10^{-2} M and [O_2] = 8.305×10^{-3} M?

b. At 1000 K, the equilibrium constant, K, for the same reaction is 1.315×10^{-2}. What will be the concentration of NO_2 at 1000 K given the same concentrations of NO and O_2 as were in (a)?

510. Consider the following hypothetical reaction, for which $K = 1$ at 300 K:

$$A(g) + B(g) \rightleftarrows 2C(g)$$

a. If the reaction begins with equal concentrations of A and B and a zero concentration of C, what can you say about the relative concentrations of the components at equilibrium?

b. Additional C is introduced at equilibrium, and the temperature remains constant. When equilibrium is restored, how will the concentrations of all components have changed? How will K have changed?

511. The equilibrium constant for the following reaction of hydrogen gas and bromine gas at 25°C is 5.628×10^{18}:

$$H_2(g) + Br_2(g) \rightleftharpoons 2HBr(g)$$

  a. Write the equilibrium expression for this reaction.

  b. Assume that equimolar amounts of H_2 and Br_2 were present at the beginning. Calculate the equilibrium concentration of H_2 if the concentration of HBr is 0.500 M.

  c. If equal amounts of H_2 and Br_2 react, which reaction component will be present in the greatest concentration at equilibrium? Explain your reasoning.

512. The following reaction reaches an equilibrium state:

$$N_2F_4(g) \rightleftharpoons 2NF_2(g)$$

At equilibrium at 25°C, the concentration of N_2F_4 is 0.9989 M, and the concentration of NF_2 is 1.131×10^{-3} M. Calculate the equilibrium constant of the reaction.

513. The equilibrium between dinitrogen tetroxide and nitrogen dioxide is represented by the following equation:

$$N_2O_4(g) \rightleftharpoons 2NO_2(g)$$

A student places a mixture of the two gases into a closed gas tube and allows the reaction to reach equilibrium at 25°C. At equilibrium, the concentration of N_2O_4 is found to be 5.95×10^{-1} M, and the concentration of NO_2 is found to be 5.24×10^{-2} M. What is the equilibrium constant of the reaction?

514. Consider the following equilibrium system:

$$NaCN(s) + HCl(g) \rightleftharpoons HCN(g) + NaCl(s)$$

  a. Write a complete expression for the equilibrium constant of this system.

  b. The equilibrium constant for this reaction is 2.405×10^6. What is the concentration of HCl remaining when the concentration of HCN is 0.8959 M?

515. The following reaction is used in the industrial production of hydrogen gas:

$$CH_4(g) + H_2O(g) \rightleftharpoons CO(g) + 3H_2(g)$$

The equilibrium constant of this reaction at 298 K (25°C) is 3.896×10^{-27}, but at 1100 K the constant is 3.112×10^2.

  a. What do these equilibrium constants tell you about the progress of the reaction at the two temperatures?

  b. Suppose the reaction mixture is sampled at 1100 K and found to contain 1.56 M of hydrogen, 3.70×10^{-2} M of methane, and 8.27×10^{-1} M of gaseous H_2O. What concentration of carbon monoxide would you expect to find?

516. Dinitrogen tetroxide, N_2O_4, is soluble in cyclohexane, a common nonpolar solvent. While in solution, N_2O_4 can break down into NO_2 according to the following equation:

$$N_2O_4(cyclohexane) \rightleftharpoons NO_2(cyclohexane)$$

At 20°C, the following concentrations were observed for this equilibrium reaction:

$$[N_2O_4] = 2.55 \times 10^{-3} \text{ M}$$
$$[NO_2] = 10.4 \times 10^{-3} \text{ M}$$

What is the value of the equilibrium constant for this reaction? Note: the chemical equation must be balanced first.

517. The reaction given in item 516 also occurs when the dinitrogen tetroxide and nitrogen dioxide are dissolved in carbon tetrachloride, CCl_4, another nonpolar solvent.

$$N_2O_4(CCl_4) \rightleftharpoons NO_2(CCl_4)$$

The following experimental data were obtained at 20°C:

$$[N_2O_4] = 2.67 \times 10^{-3} \text{ M}$$
$$[NO_2] = 10.2 \times 10^{-3} \text{ M}$$

Calculate the value of the equilibrium constant for this reaction occurring in carbon tetrachloride.

Equilibrium of Acids and Bases K_a and K_b: Chap. 18, Sec. 3

518. At 25°C, a 0.025 M solution of formic acid, HCOOH, is found to have a hydronium ion concentration of 2.03×10^{-3} M. Calculate the ionization constant of formic acid.

519. The pH of a 0.400 M solution of iodic acid, HIO_3, is 0.726 at 25°C. What is the K_a at this temperature?

520. The pH of a 0.150 M solution of hypochlorous acid, HClO, is found to be 4.55 at 25°C. Calculate the K_a for HClO at this temperature.

521. The compound propylamine, $CH_3CH_2CH_2NH_2$, is a weak base. At equilibrium, a 0.039 M solution of propylamine has an OH^- concentration of 3.74×10^{-3} M. Calculate the pH of this solution and K_b for propylamine.

522. The K_a of nitrous acid is 4.6×10^{-4} at 25°C. Calculate the $[H_3O^+]$ of a 0.0450 M nitrous acid solution.

MIXED REVIEW

523. Hydrazoic acid, HN_3, is a weak acid. The $[H_3O^-]$ of a 0.102 M solution of hydrazoic acid is 1.39×10^{-3} M. Determine the pH of this solution, and calculate K_a at 25°C for HN_3.

524. Bromoacetic acid, $BrCH_2COOH$, is a moderately weak acid. A 0.200 M solution of bromoacetic acid has a H_3O^+ concentration of 0.0192 M. Determine the pH of this solution and the K_a of bromoacetic acid at 25°C.

525. A base, B, dissociates in water according to the following equation:

$$B + H_2O \rightleftharpoons BH^+ + OH^-$$

Complete the following table for base solutions with the characteristics given.

Initial [B]	[B] at equilibrium	[OH−]	K_b	[H₃O+]	pH
a. 0.400 M	NA	2.70×10^{-4} M	?	? M	?
b. 0.005 50 M	? M	8.45×10^{-4} M	?	NA	?
c. 0.0350 M	? M	? M	?	? M	11.29
d. ? M	0.006 28 M	0.000 92 M	?	NA	?

526. The solubility of benzoic acid, C_6H_5COOH, in water at 25°C is 2.9 g/L. The pH of this saturated solution is 2.92. Determine K_a at 25°C for benzoic acid. (Hint: First calculate the initial concentration of benzoic acid.)

527. A 0.006 50 M solution of ethanolamine, $H_2NCH_2CH_2OH$, has a pH of 10.64 at 25°C. Calculate the K_b of ethanolamine. What concentration of undissociated ethanolamine remains at equilibrium?

528. The weak acid hydrogen selenide, H_2Se, has two hydrogen atoms that can form hydronium ions. The second ionization is so small that the concentration of the resulting H_3O^+ is insignificant. If the $[H_3O^+]$ of a 0.060 M solution of H_2Se is 2.72×10^{-3} M at 25°C, what is the K_a of the first ionization?

529. Pyridine, C_5H_5N, is a very weak base. Its K_b at 25°C is 1.78×10^{-9}. Calculate the $[OH^-]$ and pH of a 0.140 M solution. Assume that the concentration of pyridine at equilibrium is equal to its initial concentration because so little pyridine is dissociated.

530. A solution of a monoprotic acid, HA, at equilibrium is found to have a 0.0208 M concentration of nonionized acid. The pH of the acid solution is 2.17. Calculate the initial acid concentration and K_a for this acid.

531. Pyruvic acid, $CH_3COCOOH$, is an important intermediate in the metabolism of carbohydrates in the cells of the body. A solution made by dissolving 438 mg of pyruvic acid in 10.00 mL of water is found to have a pH of 1.34 at 25°C. Calculate K_a for pyruvic acid.

532. The $[H_3O^+]$ of a solution of acetoacetic acid, CH_3COCH_2COOH, is 4.38×10^{-3} M at 25°C. The concentration of nonionized acid is 0.0731 M at equilibrium. Calculate K_a for acetoacetic acid at 25°C.

533. The K_a of 2-chloropropanoic acid, $CH_3CHClCOOH$, is 1.48×10^{-3}. Calculate the $[H_3O^+]$ and the pH of a 0.116 M solution of 2-chloropropionic acid. Let $x = [H_3O^+]$. The degree of ionization of the acid is too large to ignore. If your setup is correct, you will have a quadratic equation to solve.

534. Sulfuric acid ionizes in two steps in water solution. For the first ionization shown in the following equation, the K_a is so large that in moderately dilute solution the ionization can be considered 100%.

$$H_2SO_4 + H_2O \longrightarrow H_3O^+ + HSO_4^-$$

The second ionization is fairly strong, and $K_a = 1.3 \times 10^{-2}$:

$$HSO_4^- + H_2O \rightleftarrows H_3O^+ + SO_4^{2-}$$

Calculate the total $[H_3O^+]$ and pH of a 0.0788 M H_2SO_4 solution. Hint: If the first ionization is 100%, what will $[HSO_4^-]$ and $[H_3O^+]$ be? Remember to account for the already existing concentration of H_3O^+ in the second ionization. Let $x = [+ SO_4^{2-}]$.

535. The hydronium ion concentration of a 0.100 M solution of cyanic acid, HOCN, is found to be 5.74×10^{-3} M at 25°C. Calculate the ionization constant of cyanic acid. What is the pH of this solution?

536. A solution of hydrogen cyanide, HCN, has a 0.025 M concentration. The cyanide ion concentration is found to be 3.16×10^{-6} M.
   a. What is the hydronium ion concentration of this solution?
   b. What is the pH of this solution?
   c. What is the concentration of nonionized HCN in the solution? Be sure to use the correct number of significant figures.
   d. Calculate the ionization constant of HCN.
   e. How would you characterize the strength of HCN as an acid?
   f. Determine the $[H_3O^+]$ for a 0.085 M solution of HCN.

537. A 1.20 M solution of dichloroacetic acid, CCl_2HCOOH, at 25°C has a hydronium ion concentration of 0.182 M.
   a. What is the pH of this solution?
   b. What is the K_a of dichloroacetic acid at 25°C?
   c. What is the concentration of nonionized dichloroacetic acid in this solution?
   d. What can you say about the strength of dichloroacetic acid?

538. Phenol, C_6H_5OH, is a very weak acid. The pH of a 0.215 M solution of phenol at 25°C is found to be 5.61. Calculate the K_a for phenol.

539. A solution of the simplest amino acid, glycine (NH_2CH_2COOH), is prepared by dissolving 3.75 g in 250.0 mL of water at 25°C. The pH of this solution is found to be 0.890.
   a. Calculate the molarity of the glycine solution.
   b. Calculate the K_a for glycine.

540. Trimethylamine, $(CH_3)_3N$, dissociates in water the same way that NH_3 does—by accepting a proton from a water molecule. The $[OH^-]$ of a 0.0750 M solution of trimethylamine at 25°C is 2.32×10^{-3} M. Calculate the pH of this solution and the K_b of trimethylamine.

541. Dimethylamine, $(CH_3)_2NH$, is a weak base similar to the trimethylamine in item 540. A 5.00×10^{-3} M solution of dimethylamine has a pH of 11.20 at 25°C. Calculate the K_b of dimethylamine. Compare this K_b with the K_b for trimethylamine that you calculated in item 540. Which substance is the stronger base?

542. Hydrazine dissociates in water solution according to the following equations:

$$H_2NNH_2 + H_2O(l) \rightleftharpoons H_2NNH_3^+(aq) + OH^-(aq)$$
$$H_2NNH_3^+(aq) + H_2O(l) \rightleftharpoons H_3NNH_3^{2+}(aq) + OH^-(aq)$$

The K_b of this second dissociation is 8.9×10^{-16}, so it contributes almost no hydroxide ions in solution and can be ignored here.

    a. The pH of a 0.120 M solution of hydrazine at 25°C is 10.50. Calculate K_b for the first ionization of hydrazine. Assume that the original concentration of H_2NNH_2 does not change.

    b. Make the same assumption as you did in (a), and calculate the $[OH^-]$ of a 0.020 M solution.

    c. Calculate the pH of the solution in (b).

Equilibrium of Salts, K_{sp}: Chap. 18, Sec. 4

543. Silver bromate, $AgBrO_3$, is slightly soluble in water. A saturated solution is found to contain 0.276 g $AgBrO_3$ dissolved in 150.0 mL of water. Calculate K_{sp} for silver bromate.

544. 2.50 L of a saturated solution of calcium fluoride leaves a residue of 0.0427 g of CaF_2 when evaporated to dryness. Calculate the K_{sp} of CaF_2.

545. The K_{sp} of calcium sulfate, $CaSO_4$, is 9.1×10^{-6}. What is the molar concentration of $CaSO_4$ in a saturated solution?

546. A salt has the formula X_2Y, and its K_{sp} is 4.25×10^{-7}.

    a. What is the molarity of a saturated solution of the salt?

    b. What is the molarity of a solution of AZ if its K_{sp} is the same value?

In each of the following problems, include the calculated ion product with your answer.

547. Will a precipitate of $Ca(OH)_2$ form when 320. mL of a 0.046 M solution of NaOH mixes with 400. mL of a 0.085 M $CaCl_2$ solution? K_{sp} of $Ca(OH)_2$ is 5.5×10^{-6}.

548. 20.00 mL of a 0.077 M solution of silver nitrate, $AgNO_3$, is mixed with 30.00 mL of a 0.043 M solution of sodium acetate, $NaC_2H_3O_2$. Does a precipitate form? The K_{sp} of $AgC_2H_3O_2$ is 2.5×10^{-3}.

549. If you mix 100. mL of 0.036 M $Pb(C_2H_3O_2)_2$ with 50. mL of 0.074 M NaCl, will a precipitate of $PbCl_2$ form? The K_{sp} of $PbCl_2$ is 1.9×10^{-4}.

550. If 20.00 mL of a 0.0090 M solution of $(NH_4)_2S$ is mixed with 120.00 mL of a 0.0082 M solution of $Al(NO_3)_3$, does a precipitate form? The K_{sp} of Al_2S_3 is 2.00×10^{-7}.

MIXED REVIEW

551. The molar concentration of a saturated calcium chromate, $CaCrO_4$, solution is 0.010 M at 25°C. What is the K_{sp} of calcium chromate?

552. A 10.00 mL sample of a saturated lead selenate solution is found to contain 0.00136 g of dissolved $PbSeO_4$ at 25°C. Determine the K_{sp} of lead selenate.

553. A 22.50 mL sample of a saturated copper(I) thiocyanate, CuSCN, solution at 25°C is found to have a 4.0×10^{-6} M concentration.

    a. Determine the K_{sp} of CuSCN.

    b. What mass of CuSCN would be dissolved in 1.0×10^3 L of solution?

554. A saturated solution of silver dichromate, $Ag_2Cr_2O_7$, has a concentration of 3.684×10^{-3} M. Calculate the K_{sp} of silver dichromate.

555. The K_{sp} of barium sulfite, $BaSO_3$, at 25°C is 8.0×10^{-7}.

    a. What is the molar concentration of a saturated solution of $BaSO_3$?

    b. What mass of $BaSO_3$ would dissolve in 500. mL of water?

556. The K_{sp} of lead(II) chloride at 25°C is 1.9×10^{-4}. What is the molar concentration of a saturated solution at 25°C?

557. The K_{sp} of barium carbonate at 25°C is 1.2×10^{-8}.

    a. What is the molar concentration of a saturated solution of $BaCO_3$ at 25°C?

    b. What volume of water would be needed to dissolve 0.10 g of barium carbonate?

558. The K_{sp} of $SrSO_4$ is 3.2×10^{-7} at 25°C.

    a. What is the molar concentration of a saturated $SrSO_4$ solution?

    b. If 20.0 L of a saturated solution of $SrSO_4$ were evaporated to dryness, what mass of $SrSO_4$ would remain?

559. The K_{sp} of strontium sulfite, $SrSO_3$, is 4.0×10^{-8} at 25°C. If 1.0000 g of $SrSO_3$ is stirred in 5.0 L of water until the solution is saturated and then filtered, what mass of $SrSO_3$ would remain?

560. The K_{sp} of manganese(II) arsenate is 1.9×10^{-11} at 25°C. What is the molar concentration of $Mn_3(AsO_4)_2$ in a saturated solution? Note that five ions are produced from the dissociation of $Mn_3(AsO_4)_2$.

561. Suppose that 30.0 mL of a 0.0050 M solution of $Sr(NO_3)_2$ is mixed with 20.0 mL of a 0.010 M solution of K_2SO_4 at 25°C. The K_{sp} of $SrSO_4$ is 3.2×10^{-7}.

    a. What is the ion product of the ions that can potentially form a precipitate?

    b. Does a precipitate form?

562. Lead(II) bromide, $PbBr_2$, is slightly soluble in water. Its K_{sp} is 6.3×10^{-6} at 25°C. Suppose that 120. mL of a 0.0035 M solution of $MgBr_2$ is mixed with 180. mL of a 0.0024 M $Pb(C_2H_3O_2)_2$ solution at 25°C.

    a. What is the ion product of Br_2 and Pb^{2+} in the mixed solution?

    b. Does a precipitate form?

563. The K_{sp} of $Mg(OH)_2$ at 25°C is 1.5×10^{-11}.
   a. Write the equilibrium equation for the dissociation of $Mg(OH)_2$.
   b. What volume of water would be required to dissolve 0.10 g of $Mg(OH)_3$?
   c. Considering that magnesium hydroxide is essentially insoluble, why is it possible to titrate a suspension of $Mg(OH)_2$ to an equivalence point with a strong acid such as HCl?

564. Lithium carbonate is somewhat soluble in water; its K_{sp} at 25°C is 2.51×10^{-2}.
   a. What is the molar concentration of a saturated Li_2CO_3 solution?
   b. What mass of Li_2CO_3 would you dissolve in order to make 3440 mL of saturated solution?

565. A 50.00 mL sample of a saturated solution of barium hydroxide, $Ba(OH)_2$, is titrated to the equivalence point by 31.61 mL of a 0.3417 M solution of HCl. Determine the K_{sp} of $Ba(OH)_2$.

566. Calculate the K_{sp} for salts represented by QR that dissociate into two ions, Q^+ and R^-, in each of the following solutions:
   a. saturated solution of QR is 1.0 M
   b. saturated solution of QR is 0.50 M
   c. saturated solution of QR is 0.1 M
   d. saturated solution of QR is 0.001 M

567. Suppose that salts QR, X_2Y, KL_2, A_3Z, and D_2E_3 form saturated solutions that are 0.02 M in concentration. Calculate K_{sp} for each of these salts.

568. The K_{sp} at 25°C of silver bromide is 5.0×10^{-13}. What is the molar concentration of a saturated AgBr solution? What mass of silver bromide would dissolve in 10.0 L of saturated solution at 25°C?

569. The K_{sp} at 25°C for calcium hydroxide is 5.5×10^{-6}.
   a. Calculate the molarity of a saturated $Ca(OH)_2$ solution.
   b. What is the OH^- concentration of this solution?
   c. What is the pH of the saturated solution?

570. The K_{sp} of magnesium carbonate is 3.5×10^{-8} at 25°C. What mass of $MgCO_3$ would dissolve in 4.00 L of water at 25°C?

Redox Equations: Chap. 19, Sec. 2

REACTIONS IN ACIDIC SOLUTION

Balance the following redox equations. Assume that all reactions take place in an acid environment where H^+ and H_2O are readily available.

571. $Fe + SnCl_4 \longrightarrow FeCl_3 + SnCl_2$

572. $H_2O_2 + FeSO_4 + H_2SO_4 \longrightarrow Fe_2(SO_4)_3 + H_2O$

573. $CuS + HNO_3 \longrightarrow Cu(NO_3)_2 + NO + S + H_2O$

574. $K_2Cr_2O_7 + HI \longrightarrow CrI_3 + KI + I_2 + H_2O$

REACTIONS IN BASIC SOLUTION

Balance the following redox equations. Assume that all reactions take place in a basic environment where OH^- and H_2O are readily available.

575. $CO_2 + NH_2OH \longrightarrow CO + N_2 + H_2O$

576. $Bi(OH)_3 + K_2SnO_2 \longrightarrow Bi + K_2SnO_3$

(Both of the potassium-tin-oxygen compounds dissociate into potassium ions and tin-oxygen ions.)

MIXED REVIEW

Balance each of the following redox equations. Unless stated otherwise, assume that the reaction occurs in acidic solution.

577. $Mg + N_2 \longrightarrow Mg_3N_2$

578. $SO_2 + Br_2 + H_2O \longrightarrow HBr + H_2SO_4$

579. $H_2S + Cl_2 \longrightarrow S + HCl$

580. $PbO_2 + HBr \longrightarrow PbBr_2 + Br_2 + H_2O$

581. $S + HNO_3 \longrightarrow NO_2 + H_2SO_4 + H_2O$

582. $NaIO_3 + N_2H_4 + HCl \longrightarrow N_2 + NaICl_2 + H_2O$ (N_2H_4 is hydrazine; do not separate it into ions.)

583. $MnO_2 + H_2O_2 + HCl \longrightarrow MnCl_2 + O_2 + H_2O$

584. $AsH_3 + NaClO_3 \longrightarrow H_3AsO_4 + NaCl$ (AsH_3 is arsine, the arsenic analogue of ammonia, NH_3.)

585. $K_2Cr_2O_7 + H_2C_2O_4 + HCl \longrightarrow CrCl_3 + CO_2 + KCl + H_2O$ ($H_2C_2O_4$ is oxalic acid; it can be treated as $2H^+ + C_2O_4^{2-}$.)

586. $Hg(NO_3)_2 \xrightarrow{heat} HgO + NO_2 + O_2$ (The reaction is not in solution.)

587. $HAuCl_4 + N_2H_4 \longrightarrow Au + N_2 + HCl$ ($HAuCl_4$ can be considered as $H^+ + AuCl_4^-$.)

588. $Sb_2(SO_4)_3 + KMnO_4 + H_2O \longrightarrow$ $H_3SbO_4 + K_2SO_4 + MnSO_4 + H_2SO_4$

589. $Mn(NO_3)_2 + NaBiO_3 + HNO_3 \longrightarrow$ $Bi(NO_3)_2 + HMnO_4 + NaNO_3 + H_2O$

590. $H_3AsO_4 + Zn + HCl \longrightarrow AsH_3 + ZnCl_2 + H_2O$

591. $KClO_3 + HCl \longrightarrow Cl_2 + H_2O + KCl$

592. The same reactants as in item 591 can combine in the following way when more $KClO_3$ is present. Balance the equation.
   $KClO_3 + HCl \longrightarrow Cl_2 + ClO_2 + H_2O + KCl$

593. $MnCl_3 + H_2O \longrightarrow MnCl_2 + MnO_2 + HCl$

594. $NaOH + H_2O + Al \longrightarrow NaAl(OH)_4 + H_2$ in basic solution

595. $Br_2 + Ca(OH)_2 \longrightarrow CaBr_2 + Ca(BrO_3)_2 + H_2O$ in basic solution

596. $N_2O + NaClO + NaOH \longrightarrow NaCl + NaNO_2 + H_2O$ in basic solution

597. Balance the following reaction, which can be used to prepare bromine in the laboratory:
   $HBr + MnO_2 \longrightarrow MnBr_2 + H_2O + Br_2$

598. The following reaction occurs when gold is dissolved in *aqua regia*. Balance the equation.
   $Au + HCl + HNO_3 \longrightarrow HAuCl_4 + NO + H_2O$

Electrochemistry: Chap. 20, Sec. 2

Use the reduction potentials in the table below to determine whether the following reactions are spontaneous as written. Report the E^0_{cell} for the reactions.

599. $Cu^{2+} + Fe \longrightarrow Fe^{2+} + Cu$

600. $Pb^{2+} + Fe^{2+} \longrightarrow Fe^{3+} + Pb$

601. $Mn^{2+} + 4H_2O + Sn^{2+} \longrightarrow MnO_4^- + 8H^+ + Sn$

602. $MnO_4^{2-} + Cl_2 \longrightarrow MnO_4^- + 2Cl^-$

603. $Hg_2^{2+} + 2MnO_4^{2-} \longrightarrow 2Hg + 2MnO_4^-$

604. $2Li^+ + Pb \longrightarrow 2Li + Pb^{2+}$

605. $Br_2 + 2Cl^- \longrightarrow 2Br^- + Cl_2$

606. $S + 2I^- \longrightarrow S^{2-} + I_2$

For Problems 599–606

Reduction half-reaction	Standard electrode potential, E^0 (in volts)	Reduction half-reaction	Standard electrode potential, E^0 (in volts)
$MnO_4^- + 8H^+ + 5e^- \rightleftarrows Mn^{2+} + 4H_2O$	+1.50	$Fe^{3+} + 3e^- \rightleftarrows Fe$	−0.04
$Au^{3+} + 3e^- \rightleftarrows Au$	+1.50	$Pb^{2+} + 2e^- \rightleftarrows Pb$	−0.13
$Cl_2 + 2e^- \rightleftarrows 2Cl^-$	+1.36	$Sn^{2+} + 2e^- \rightleftarrows Sn$	−0.14
$Cr_2O_7^{2-} + 14H^+ + 6e^- \rightleftarrows 2Cr^{3+} + 7H_2O$	+1.23	$Ni^{2+} + 2e^- \rightleftarrows Ni$	−0.26
$MnO_2 + 4H^+ + 2e^- \rightleftarrows Mn^{2+} + 2H_2O$	+1.22	$Cd^{2+} + 2e^- \rightleftarrows Cd$	−0.40
$Br_2 + 2e^- \rightleftarrows 2Br^-$	+1.07	$Fe^{2+} + 2e^- \rightleftarrows Fe$	−0.45
$Hg^{2+} + 2e^- \rightleftarrows Hg$	+0.85	$S + 2e^- \rightleftarrows S^{2-}$	−0.48
$Ag^+ + e^- \rightleftarrows Ag$	+0.80	$Zn^{2+} + 2e^- \rightleftarrows Zn$	−0.76
$Hg_2^{2+} + 2e^- \rightleftarrows 2Hg$	+0.80	$Al^{3+} + 3e^- \rightleftarrows Al$	−1.66
$Fe^{3+} + e^- \rightleftarrows Fe^{2+}$	+0.77	$Mg^{2+} + 2e^- \rightleftarrows Mg$	−2.37
$MnO_4^- + e^- \overset{\leftarrow}{\rightarrow} MnO_4^{2-}$	+0.56	$Na^+ + e^- \rightleftarrows Na$	−2.71
$I_2 + 2e^- \rightleftarrows 2I^-$	+0.54	$Ca^{2+} + 2e^- \rightleftarrows Ca$	−2.87
$Cu^{2+} + 2e^- \rightleftarrows Cu$	+0.34	$Ba^{2+} + 2e^- \rightleftarrows Ba$	−2.91
$S + 2H^+(aq) + 2e^- \rightleftarrows H_2S(aq)$	+0.14	$K^+ + e^- \rightleftarrows K$	−2.93
$2H^+(aq) + 2e^- \rightleftarrows H_2$	0.00	$Li^+ + e^- \rightleftarrows Li$	−3.04

If a cell is constructed in which the following pairs of reactions are possible, what would be the cathode reaction, the anode reaction, and the overall cell voltage?

607. $Ca^{2+} + 2e^- \rightleftarrows Ca$
$Fe^{3+} + 3e^- \rightleftarrows Fe$

608. $Ag^+ + e^- \rightleftarrows Ag$
$S + 2H^+ + 2e^- \rightleftarrows H_2S$

609. $Fe^{3+} + e^- \rightleftarrows Fe^{2+}$
$Sn^{2+} + 2e^- \rightleftarrows Sn$

610. $Cu^{2+} + 2e^- \rightleftarrows Cu$
$Au^{3+} + 3e^- \rightleftarrows Au$

MIXED REVIEW

Use reduction potentials to determine whether the reactions in the following 10 problems are spontaneous.

611. $Ba + Sn^{2+} \longrightarrow Ba^{2+} + Sn$

612. $Ni + Hg^{2+} \longrightarrow Ni^{2+} + Hg$

613. $2Cr^{3+} + 7H_2O + 6Fe^{3+} \longrightarrow Cr_2O_7^{2-} + 14H^+ + 6Fe^{2+}$

614. $Cl_2 + Sn \longrightarrow 2Cl^- + Sn^{2+}$

615. $Al + 3Ag^+ \longrightarrow Al^{3+} + 3Ag$

616. $Hg_2^{2+} + S^{2-} \longrightarrow 2Hg + S$

617. $Ba + 2Ag^+ \longrightarrow Ba^{2+} + 2Ag$

618. $2I^- + Ca^{2+} \longrightarrow I_2 + Ca$

619. $Zn + 2MnO_4^- \longrightarrow Zn^{2+} + 2MnO_4^{2-}$

620. $2Cr^{3+} + 3Mg^{2+} + 7H_2O \longrightarrow Cr_2O_7^{2-} + 14H^+ + 3Mg$

In the following problems, you are given a pair of reduction half-reactions. If a cell were constructed in which the pairs of half-reactions were possible, what would be the balanced equation for the overall cell reaction that would occur? Write the half-reactions that occur at the cathode and anode, and calculate the cell voltage.

621. $Cl_2 + 2e^- \rightleftarrows 2Cl^-$
$Ni^{2+} + 2e^- \rightleftarrows Ni$

622. $Fe^{3+} + 3e^- \rightleftarrows Fe$
$Hg^{2+} + 2e^- \rightleftarrows Hg$

623. $MnO_4^- + e^- \rightleftarrows MnO_4^{2-}$
$Al^{3+} + 3e^- \rightleftarrows Al$

624. $MnO_4^- + 8H^+ + 5e^- \rightleftarrows Mn^{2+} + 4H_2O$
$S + 2H^+ + 2e^- \rightleftarrows H_2S$

625. $Ca^{2+} + 2e^- \rightleftarrows Ca$
$Li^+ + e^- \rightleftarrows Li$

626. $Br_2 + 2e^- \rightleftarrows 2Br^-$
$MnO_4^- + 8H^+ + 5e^- \rightleftarrows Mn^{2+} + 4H_2O$

627. $Sn^{2+} + 2e^- \rightleftarrows Sn$
$Fe^{3+} + e^- \rightleftarrows Fe^{2+}$

628. $Zn^{2+} + 2e^- \rightleftarrows Zn$
$Cr_2O_7^{2-} + 14H^+ + 6e^- \rightleftarrows 2Cr^{3+} + 7H_2O$

629. $Ba^{2+} + 2e^- \rightleftarrows Ba$
$Ca^{2+} + 2e^- \rightleftarrows Ca$

630. $Hg_2^{2+} + 2e^- \rightleftarrows 2Hg$
$Cd^{2+} + 2e^- \rightleftarrows Cd$

Selected Answers

CHAPTER 1
Matter and Change

MATH TUTOR PRACTICE, p. 25

1. **a.** 5 significant features
   b. 4 significant features
2. **a.** 4.21 g/cm^3
   b. 16.5 g

CHAPTER 2
Measurements and Calculations

PRACTICE PROBLEMS A, p. 43

1. 10.1 g/cm^3
2. 23.5 g
3. 5.60 mL

PRACTICE PROBLEMS B, p. 45

1. 1645 cm, 0.01645 km
2. 0.000 014 g

PRACTICE PROBLEMS C, p. 49

1. −17%
2. 2.7%

PRACTICE PROBLEMS D, p. 51

1. **a.** 2
   b. 4
   c. 4
   d. 4
   e. 1
   f. 5
2. **a.** 7000 cm
   b. 7000. cm
   c. 7000.00 cm

PRACTICE PROBLEMS E, p. 54

1. 1.151 μm
2. 45.9 mL
3. 1.00 μm^2
4. 440 g

PRACTICE PROBLEMS F, p. 58

1. 9.69 mL
2. 1.67 g/cm^3
3. 5.12 × 10^{11} mm
4. 5.2 × 10^3 s

MATH TUTOR PRACTICE, p. 62

1. **a.** 7.45 × 10^{-5} g
   b. 5.984 102 × 10^6 nm
2. **a.** −9.11 × 10^3
   b. 8.25 × 10^{-2}

CHAPTER 3
Atoms: The Building Blocks of Matter

PRACTICE PROBLEMS A, p. 81

1. 35 protons; 35 electrons; 45 neutrons
2. $^{50}_{24}$Cr
3. nickel-60

PRACTICE PROBLEMS B, p. 86

1. 126 g Fe
2. 14.7 g K
3. 0.310 g Na
4. 957 g Ni

PRACTICE PROBLEMS C, p. 87

1. 0.125 mol Ca
2. 1.83 × 10^{-7} mol Au
3. 8.18 × 10^{-3}

PRACTICE PROBLEMS D, p. 88

1. 2.49 × 10^{-12} mol Pb
2. 4.2 × 10^{-21} mol Sn
3. 1.66 × 10^{24} atoms Al

PRACTICE PROBLEMS E, p. 88

1. 7.3 × 10^{-7} g Ni
2. 1.61 × 10^{22} atoms Cd
3. 66 g Au

MATH TUTOR PRACTICE, p. 90

1. **a.** 2.25 g
   b. 59 300 L
2. **a.** 7.2 × 10^1 μg
   b. 3.98 × 10^3 km

CHAPTER 4
Arrangement of Electrons in Atoms

PRACTICE PROBLEMS A, p. 113

1. 7; 7; ↑↓ ↑↓ ↑ ↑ ↑
        1s 2s   2p
2. 9; 2

PRACTICE PROBLEMS B, p. 120

1. **a.** 1s^{2}2s^{2}2p^{6}3s^{2}3p^{6}3d^{10}4s^{2}4p^{6}4d^{10}5s^{2}5p^5; [Kr]4d^{10}5s^{2}5p^5; 46
   b. 27; 26; 1
2. **a.** [Kr]4d^{10}5s^{2}5p^2; 2
   b. 10; germanium

3. a. $1s^2 2s^2 2p^6 3s^2 3p^6 3d^5 4s^2$
   b. manganese
4. a. 9; $1s^2 2s^2 2p^6 3s^2 3p^6$
   b. argon

PRACTICE PROBLEMS C, p. 122

1. a. $1s^2 2s^2 2p^6 3s^2 3p^6 3d^{10} 4s^2$
      $4p^6 4d^{10} 5s^2 5p^6 6s^2$; [Xe]$6s^2$
   b. Be; Mg; Ca; Sr
2. a. [Kr]$4d^{10} 5s^2 5p^3$
   b. In, Sb, I

MATH TUTOR PRACTICE, p. 123

1. 85.47 u
2. 28.1 u

CHAPTER 5
The Periodic Law

PRACTICE PROBLEMS A, p. 141

1. Group 1; fifth period; s block
2. a. ns^2
   b. $1s^2 2s^2 2p^6 3s^2 3p^6 4s^2$
   c. Ca; [Ar]$4s^2$

PRACTICE PROBLEMS B, p. 144

1. sixth period, d-block, Group 7
2. $4d^{10} 5s^2$

PRACTICE PROBLEMS C, p. 146

1. a. $4d^{10} 5s^2 5p^2$
   b. tin, metal
2. a. fourth period; p block;
      Group 15
   b. arsenic; metalloid

PRACTICE PROBLEMS D, p. 146

1. a. p block; second period;
      Group 17; halogens;
      fluorine; nonmetal; high
      reactivity
   b. d block; fourth period;
      Group 11; transition
      elements; copper; metal;
      low reactivity

PRACTICE PROBLEMS E, p. 150

1. Li; F
2. All of the elements are in
   Group 2. Of the four, barium
   has the highest atomic
   number and is farthest down
   the group. Therefore, barium
   has the largest atomic radius
   because atomic radii increase
   down a group.
3. All of the elements are in
   Period 3. Of the four, silicon
   has the largest atomic number
   and therefore is the farthest to
   the right on the periodic table.
   Therefore, silicon has the
   smallest atomic radius
   because atomic radii decrease
   from *left to right* across a
   period.

PRACTICE PROBLEMS F, p. 154

1. a. Q is in the p block, R is in
      the s block, T is in the p
      block, and X is in the p
      block.
   b. Q and R are in the same
      period, and X and T are in
      the same period. There are
      none in the same group.
   c. Q would have the highest
      ionization energy, and R
      would have the lowest.
   d. R
   e. R

PRACTICE PROBLEMS G, p. 160

1. a. All are in the p block. E, J,
      and M are in the same
      period, and E, G, and L are
      in the same group.
   b. E should have the highest
      electron affinity; E, G, and L
      are most likely to form
      1– ions; E should have the
      highest electronegativity.
   c. The ionic radius would be
      larger.
   d. E, G, and L

MATH TUTOR PRACTICE, p. 163

1. a. $1s^2 2s^2 2p^6 3s^2 3p^1$
   b. $1s^2 2s^2 2p^6$
   c. $1s^2 2s^2 2p^6 3s^2 3p^6 3d^{10} 4s^2 4p^6$
      $4d^{10} 5s^2 5p^2$
   d. $1s^2 2s^2 2p^6 3s^2 3p^6 4s^1$
2. a. [Ne]$3s^2 3p^2$
   b. [Kr]$5s^1$
   c. [Kr]$4d^{10} 5s^2 5p^3$
   d. [Ar]$3d^{10} 4s^2 4p^3$

CHAPTER 6
Chemical Bonding

PRACTICE PROBLEMS A, p. 173

See table below.

PRACTICE PROBLEMS C, p. 181

1. H:N̈:H or H−N̈−H
       Ḧ |
                      H

2. H:S̈:H or H−S̈−H

BONDING BETWEEN OXYGEN AND	ELECTRONEGATIVITY DIFFERENCE	BOND TYPE	MORE-NEGATIVE ATOM
potassium	$3.5 - 0.8 = 2.7$	ionic	oxygen
phosphorus	$3.5 - 2.1 = 1.4$	polar-covalent	oxygen
fluorine	$4.0 - 3.5 = 0.2$	polar-covalent	fluorine

3. $H:\ddot{S}i:H$ or $H-Si-H$ (with H above and below Si)

4. $:\ddot{F}:\ddot{P}:\ddot{F}:$ or $:\ddot{F}-\ddot{P}-\ddot{F}:$ (with :F: below)

PRACTICE PROBLEMS D, p. 184

1. $\ddot{O}=C=\ddot{O}$
2. $H-C\equiv\ddot{N}:$

PRACTICE PROBLEMS E, p. 194

1. a. linear
   b. tetrahedral
   c. tetrahedral

PRACTICE PROBLEMS F, p. 197

1. a. tetrahedral
   b. trigonal-pyramidal

MATH TUTOR PRACTICE, p. 210

1. a. $\cdot\ddot{S}i\cdot$
   b. $\dot{S}r\cdot$
2. a. $H:\ddot{S}i:$ (with H above)

   $:\ddot{O}:$
   b. $H:\ddot{C}:\ddot{O}:H$

CHAPTER 7

Chemical Formulas and Chemical Compounds

PRACTICE PROBLEMS A, p. 217

1. a. KI
   b. $MgCl_2$
   c. Na_2S
   d. Al_2S_3
   e. AlN

2. a. silver chloride
   b. zinc oxide
   c. calcium bromide
   d. strontium fluoride
   e. barium oxide
   f. calcium chloride

PRACTICE PROBLEMS B, p. 219

1. a. $CuBr_2$; copper(II) bromide
   b. FeO; iron(II) oxide
   c. $PbCl_2$; lead(II) chloride
   d. HgS; mercury(II) sulfide
   e. SnF_2; tin(II) fluoride
   f. Fe_2O_3; iron(III) oxide
2. a. cobalt(II) iodide
   b. iron(II) sulfide
   c. copper(I) selenide
   d. lead(IV) oxide

PRACTICE PROBLEMS C, p. 221

1. a. NaI   **e.** $CuSO_4$
   b. $CaCl_2$ **f.** Na_2CO_3
   c. K_2S **g.** $Ca(NO_2)_2$
   d. $LiNO_3$ **h.** $KClO_4$
2. a. silver oxide
   b. calcium hydroxide
   c. potassium chlorate
   d. ammonium hydroxide
   e. iron(III) chromate
   f. potassium hypochlorite

PRACTICE PROBLEMS D, p. 223

1. a. sulfur trioxide
   b. iodine trichloride
   c. phosphorus pentabromide
2. a. CI_4
   b. PCl_3
   c. N_2O_3

PRACTICE PROBLEM E, p. 227

   a. +3, −2   **f.** +2, +7, −2
   b. +1, +5, −2 **g.** +1, +6, −2
   c. 0   **h.** +5, −2
   d. +1, −1   **i.** +4, −2
   e. +1, −2   **j.** −3, +1, −2

PRACTICE PROBLEM F, p. 232

   a. 98.09 u
   b. 164.10 u
   c. 94.97 u
   d. 95.21 u

PRACTICE PROBLEMS G, p. 233

1. a. 2 mol Al; 3 mol S
   b. 1 mol Na; 1 mol N; 3 mol O
   c. 1 mol Ba; 2 mol O; 2 mol H
2. a. 150.17 g/mol
   b. 85.00 g/mol
   c. 171.35 g/mol

PRACTICE PROBLEMS I, p. 235

1. a. 0.0499 mol
   b. 61 mol
2. a. 1.53×10^{23} molecules
   b. 2.20×10^{23} molecules
3. 1170 g

PRACTICE PROBLEMS K, p. 237

1. a. 81.7% C; 18.3% H
   b. 19.15% Na, 0.840% H, 26.71% S, 53.30% O
2. 43.85% H_2O
3. 96.0 g O; 6.00 mol O

PRACTICE PROBLEMS M, p. 242

1. HO
2. $K_2Cr_2O_7$
3. $CaBr_2$

PRACTICE PROBLEMS N, p. 243

1. C_6H_6
2. H_2O_2

MATH TUTOR PRACTICE, p. 244

1. 43.38% Na; 11.33% C; 45.29% O
2. 61.13% I

CHAPTER 8

Chemical Equations and Reactions

PRACTICE PROBLEMS B, p. 260

1. **a.** calcium + sulfur ⟶ calcium sulfide; $8Ca(s) + S_8(s) \longrightarrow 8CaS(s)$
    b. hydrogen + fluorine ⟶ hydrogen fluoride; $H_2(g) + F_2(g) \longrightarrow 2HF(g)$
    c. aluminum + zinc chloride ⟶ zinc + aluminum chloride; $2Al(s) + 3ZnCl_2(aq) \longrightarrow 3Zn(s) + 2AlCl_3(aq)$
2. **a.** Aqueous solutions of potassium hydroxide and phosphoric acid react to produce potassium phosphate in aqueous solution and water.
    b. Solid iron(II) sulfide and aqueous solution of hydrochloric acid react to produce solid iron(II) chloride and gaseous hydrogen sulfide.
3. $N_2H_4(l) + O_2(g) \longrightarrow N_2(g) + 2H_2O(l)$

PRACTICE PROBLEMS C, p. 264

1. **a.** Word: magnesium + hydrochloric acid ⟶ magnesium chloride + hydrogen
    Formula: $Mg(s) + HCl(aq) \longrightarrow MgCl_2(aq) + H_2(g)$
    Balanced: $Mg(s) + 2HCl(aq) \longrightarrow MgCl_2(aq) + H_2(g)$
    b. Word: nitric acid + magnesium hydroxide ⟶ magnesium nitrate + water
    Formula: $HNO_3(aq) + Mg(OH)_2(s) \longrightarrow Mg(NO_3)_2(aq) + H_2O(l)$
    Balanced: $2HNO_3(aq) + Mg(OH)_2(s) \longrightarrow Mg(NO_3)_2(aq) + 2H_2O(l)$
2. $Ca(s) + 2H_2O(l) \longrightarrow Ca(OH)_2(aq) + H_2(g)$

PRACTICE PROBLEMS E, p. 265

1. **a.** $Ca(s) + 2H_2O(l) \longrightarrow Ca(OH)_2(aq) + H_2(g)$
    b. $Cu(s) + 2AgNO_3(aq) \longrightarrow Cu(NO_3)_2(aq) + 2Ag(s)$
    c. $Fe_2O_3(s) + 3CO(g) \longrightarrow 2Fe(s) + 3CO_2(g)$

PRACTICE PROBLEMS F, p. 278

1. **a.** no
    b. no
    c. yes; $Cd(s) + 2HBr(aq) \longrightarrow CdBr_2(aq) + H_2(g)$
    d. yes; $Mg(s) + 2H_2O(g) \longrightarrow Mg(OH)_2(aq) + H_2(g)$
2. Pb
3. Mn

MATH TUTOR PRACTICE, p. 281

1. $C_3H_8 + 5O_2 \longrightarrow 3CO_2 + 4H_2O$
2. **a.** $2KI(aq) + Cl_2(g) \longrightarrow 2KCl(aq) + I_2(s)$
    b. $2Al(s) + 3H_2SO_4(aq) \longrightarrow Al_2(SO_4)_3(aq) + 3H_2(g)$

CHAPTER 9

Stoichiometry

PRACTICE PROBLEMS A, p. 295

1. 4 mol NH_3
2. 10. mol $KClO_3$

PRACTICE PROBLEMS C, p. 297

1. 80.6 g MgO
2. 300 g $C_6H_{12}O_6$

PRACTICE PROBLEMS D, p. 299

1. 7.81 mol HgO
2. 7.81 mol Hg

PRACTICE PROBLEMS E, p. 300

1. **a.** 60.0 g NH_4NO_3
    b. 27.0 g H_2O
2. 339 g Ag
3. 2.6 kg Al

PRACTICE PROBLEMS F, p. 303

1. **a.** Al is limiting
    b. O_2 is limiting
    c. 4.25×10^{-3} mol Al_2O_3

PRACTICE PROBLEMS G, p. 304

1. **a.** Zn
    b. 0.75 mol S_8 remains
    c. 2.00 mol ZnS
2. **a.** carbon
    b. 2.40 mol H_2 and 2.40 mol CO
    c. 4.85 g H_2 and 67.2 g CO

PRACTICE PROBLEMS H, p. 307

1. 92%
2. 3.70 g Cu

MATH TUTOR PRACTICE, p. 309

1. 24.48 mol SO_3
2. 30.75 g O_2

CHAPTER 10

States of Matter

PRACTICE PROBLEMS A, p. 339

1. 169 kJ
2. 2.19×10^5 g

MATH TUTOR PRACTICE, p. 342

1. 11.65 kJ/mol
2. 74.7 kJ

CHAPTER 11
Gases

CHAPTER 12
Solutions

CHAPTER 13
Ions in Aqueous Solutions and Colligative Properties

CHAPTER 14
Acids and Bases

MATH TUTOR PRACTICE, p. 472

1. Formula equation:
$$CuSO_4(aq) + Na_2S(aq) \longrightarrow$$
$$Na_2SO_4(aq) + CuS(s)$$
Full ionic equation:
$$Cu^{2+}(aq) + SO_4^{2-}(aq) +$$
$$2Na^+(aq) + S^{2-}(aq) \longrightarrow$$
$$2Na^+(aq) + SO_4^{2-}(aq) +$$
$$CuS(s)$$
Net ionic equation:
$$Cu^{2+}(aq) + S^{2-}(aq) \longrightarrow$$
$$CuS(s)$$

2. Full ionic equation:
$$Cd^{2+}(aq) + 2Cl^-(aq) +$$
$$2Na^+(aq) + CO_3^{2-}(aq) \longrightarrow$$
$$2Na^+(aq) + 2Cl^-(aq) +$$
$$CdCO_3(s)$$
Net ionic equation:
$$Cd^{2+}(aq) + CO_3^{2-}(aq) \longrightarrow$$
$$CdCO_3(s)$$

CHAPTER 15
Acid-Base Titration and pH

PRACTICE PROBLEMS A, p. 482

1. $[H_3O^+] = 1 \times 10^{-4}$ M;
$[OH^-] = 1 \times 10^{-10}$ M
2. $[H_3O^+] = 1.0 \times 10^{-3}$ M;
$[OH^-] = 1.0 \times 10^{-11}$ M
3. $[H_3O^+] = 3.3 \times 10^{-13}$ M;
$[OH^-] = 3.0 \times 10^{-2}$ M
4. $[H_3O^+] = 5.0 \times 10^{-11}$ M;
$[OH^-] = 2.0 \times 10^{-4}$ M

PRACTICE PROBLEMS B, p. 485

1. a. pH = 6.0
   b. pH = 5.00
   c. pH = 3.00
   d. pH = 12.00

PRACTICE PROBLEMS C, p. 486

1. pH = 3.17
2. pH = 1.60
3. pH = 5.60
4. pH = 12.60

PRACTICE PROBLEMS E, p. 488

1. $[H_3O^+] = 1 \times 10^{-5}$ M
2. $[H_3O^+] = 1 \times 10^{-11}$ M
3. $[H_3O^+] = 2.50 \times 10^{-3}$ M;
   $[OH^-] = 0.4 \times 10^{-11}$ M
4. $[H_3O^+] = 2.1 \times 10^{-4}$ M

PRACTICE PROBLEMS F, p. 500

1. 0.157 M CH_3COOH
2. 0.0128 M H_2SO_4

MATH TUTOR PRACTICE, p. 502

1. pH = 3.07
2. 8.9×10^{-5} M OH^-

CHAPTER 16
Reaction Energy

PRACTICE PROBLEMS A, p. 511

1. 0.14 J/(g•K)
2. 329 K

PRACTICE PROBLEMS B, p. 519

1. −260.8 kJ
2. 2 kJ

PRACTICE PROBLEMS C, p. 522

1. −125.4 kJ
2. −7171.4 kJ/mol
3. −296.1 kJ

PRACTICE PROBLEMS D, p. 528

1. above 333 K

MATH TUTOR PRACTICE, p. 529

1. $\Delta H^0 = -396.0$ kJ
2. $\Delta H^0 = -441.8$ kJ

CHAPTER 17
Reaction Kinetics

PRACTICE PROBLEMS A, p. 542

1. a. See figure below.
   $\Delta E_{forward} = -150$ kJ/mol
   $\Delta E_{reverse} = +150$ kJ/mol
   $E_a = 100$ kJ/mol
   $E_a' = 250$ kJ/mol

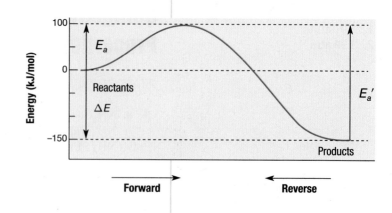

b. exothermic, because the energy of the reactants is greater than the energy of the products

2. a.

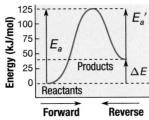

b. $\Delta E_{forward} = 39$ kJ/mol
$\Delta E_{reverse} = -39$ kJ/mol

c. Endothermic; the energy of the products is greater than the energy of the products.

3. a.

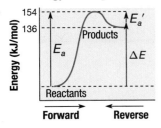

b. E_a (reverse) $= 18$ kJ/mol

PRACTICE PROBLEMS B, p. 550

1. rate $= k[A]^2$
2. 27

PRACTICE PROBLEMS E, p. 553

1. $R = k[L][M]^2$
2. $R = k[NO_2]^2$

MATH TUTOR PRACTICE, p. 556

1. $R = k[O_2][NO]_2$
2. $R = k[H_2]$; Students should observe that changing the concentration of C_2H_2 has no effect on the rate. The rate depends on only the concentration of hydrogen.

CHAPTER 18
Chemical Equilibrium

PRACTICE PROBLEMS A, p. 568

1. 0.286
2. 4.9×10^{-3}
3. 4.36

PRACTICE PROBLEMS B, p. 590

1. 1.9×10^{-4}
2. 1.6×10^{-5}

PRACTICE PROBLEMS C, p. 591

1. 2.8×10^{-8} mol/L
2. 5.7×10^{-4} mol/L

PRACTICE PROBLEMS D, p. 593

1. AgBr precipitates.
2. $PbCl_2$ does *not* precipitate.

MATH TUTOR PRACTICE, p. 595

1. a. $K = \dfrac{[AB_2]}{[A][B]^2}$

b. $K = \dfrac{[D_2][E_2]^2}{[DE_2]^2}$

2. $K = 2.6 \times 10^{-9}$

CHAPTER 19
Oxidation-Reduction Reactions

PRACTICE PROBLEMS A, p. 611

1. $Cu + 2H_2SO_4 \longrightarrow$
$CuSO_4 + SO_2 + 2H_2O$
2. $8HNO_3 + 6KI \longrightarrow$
$6KNO_3 + 3I_2 + 2NO + 4H_2O$

MATH TUTOR PRACTICE, p. 618

1. $2MnO_2 + NaClO_3 + 2NaOH$
$\longrightarrow 2NaMnO_4 + NaCl + H_2O$
2. $N_2O + 2KClO + 2KOH \longrightarrow$
$2KCl + 2KNO_2 + H_2O$

CHAPTER 20
Electrochemistry

PRACTICE PROBLEMS A, p. 635

1. a. $Cr_2O_7^{2-} + 14H^+ + 3Ni \longrightarrow$
$2Cr^{3+} + 3Ni^{2+} + 7H_2O$;
$E^0 = 1.33 - (-0.23) = 1.56$ V
b. $2Fe^{3+} + H_2 \longrightarrow$
$2Fe^{2+} + 2H^+$;
$E^0 = 0.77 - 0.0 = 0.77$ V

MATH TUTOR PRACTICE, p. 642

1. $E^0 = 1.82$ V
2. $E^0 = 1.20$ V

CHAPTER 21
Nuclear Chemistry

PRACTICE PROBLEMS A, p. 654

1. $^{253}_{99}Es + ^{4}_{2}He \longrightarrow ^{1}_{0}n + ^{256}_{101}Md$

2. $^{142}_{61}Pm + ^{0}_{-1}e \longrightarrow ^{142}_{60}Nd$

PRACTICE PROBLEMS B, p. 658

1. 0.25 mg
2. 6396 years
3. 7.648 days
4. 0.009 77 mg
5. 4.46×10^9 years

MATH TUTOR PRACTICE, p. 670

1. 1.4×10^{-6} g chromium-51
2. 8 half-lives or 420 000 years (expressed with 2 significant figures)

CHAPTER 22
Organic Chemistry

PRACTICE PROBLEMS A, p. 687

1. methylbutane
2. 3-ethyl-4-methylhexane

PRACTICE PROBLEMS B, p. 692

1. 2-hexene
2. 2-methyl-2-butene *or* methyl-2-butene
3. 2-methyl-3-hexene
4. 2,5-dimethyl-2,5-heptadiene

MATH TUTOR PRACTICE, p. 706

1. CH_4N_2O
2. C_3H_5Br
3. CH_2O

CHAPTER 23

Biological Chemistry

MATH TUTOR PRACTICE, p. 740

1. leucine–histidine–aspartic acid–tyrosine–asparagine–tryptophan
2. Leucine–threonine–glycine; the codon UGA is a stop codon, so no more amino acids will be added.

absolute zero the temperature at which all molecular motion stops (0 K on the Kelvin scale or −273.16°C on the Celsius scale)
cero absoluto temperatura a la que se detiene todo movimiento molecular (0 K en la escala de Kelvin o −273.16 °C en la escala de Celsius)

accuracy a description of how close a measurement is to the true value of the quantity measured
exactitud término que describe qué tanto se aproxima una medida al valor verdadero de la cantidad medida

acid-base indicator a substance that changes in color depending on the pH of the solution that the substance is in
indicador ácido-base sustancia que cambia de color dependiendo del pH de la solución en la que se encuentra

acid ionization constant an equilibrium constant for the dissociation of an acid at a specific temperature; denoted by the term K_a
constante de ionización ácida constante de equilibrio en la separación de un ácido a una temperatura específica; se indica con el término K_a

actinide any of the elements of the actinide series, which have atomic numbers from 89 (actinium, Ac) through 103 (lawrencium, Lr)
actínido cualquiera de los elementos del grupo de los actínidos, cuyo número atómico está comprendido entre el 89 (actinio, Ac) y el 103 (lawrencio, Lr)

activated complex a molecule in an unstable state intermediate to the reactants and the products in the chemical reaction
complejo activado molécula que está en un estado inestable, intermedio entre los reactivos y los productos de la reacción química

activation energy the minimum amount of energy required to start a chemical reaction
energía de activación cantidad mínima de energía que se requiere para iniciar una reacción química

activity series a series of elements that have similar properties and that are arranged in descending order of chemical activity; examples of activity series include metals and halogens
serie de actividad serie de elementos que tienen propiedades similares y que están ordenados en orden descendiente respecto a su actividad química; algunos ejemplos de series de actividad incluyen a los metales y los halógenos

actual yield the measured amount of a product of a reaction
rendimiento real cantidad medida del producto de una reacción

addition reaction a reaction in which an atom or molecule is added to an unsaturated molecule
reacción de adición reacción en la que se añade un átomo o una molécula a una molécula insaturada

adenosine diphosphate (ADP) an organic molecule that is involved in energy metabolism; composed of a nitrogenous base, a sugar, and two phosphate groups
adenosín difosfato (ADP) molécula orgánica que participa en el metabolismo de energía; formada por una base nitrogenada, un azúcar y dos grupos fosfato

adenosine triphosphate (ATP) an organic molecule that acts as the main energy source for cell processes; composed of a nitrogenous base, a sugar, and three phosphate groups
adenosín trifosfato (ATP) molécula orgánica que funciona como la fuente principal de energía para los procesos celulares; formada por una base nitrogenada, un azúcar y tres grupos fosfato

alcohol an organic compound that contains one or more hydroxyl groups attached to carbon atoms
alcohol compuesto orgánico que contiene uno o más grupos hidroxilo unidos a los átomos de carbono

aldehyde an organic compound that contains the carbonyl group, —CHO
aldehído compuesto orgánico que contiene el grupo carbonilo —CHO

alkali metal one of the elements of Group 1 of the periodic table (lithium, sodium, potassium, rubidium, cesium, and francium)
metal alcalino uno de los elementos del Grupo 1 de la tabla periódica (litio, sodio, potasio, rubidio, cesio y francio)

alkaline-earth metal one of the elements of Group 2 of the periodic table (beryllium, magnesium, calcium, strontium, barium, and radium)
metal alcalinotérreo uno de los elementos del Grupo 2 de la tabla periódica (berilio, magnesio, calcio, estroncio, bario y radio)

alkane a hydrocarbon characterized by a straight or branched carbon chain that contains only single bonds
alcano hidrocarburo formado por una cadena simple o ramificada de carbonos que únicamente contiene enlaces simples

alkene a hydrocarbon that contains one or more double bonds
alqueno hidrocarburo que contiene uno o más enlaces dobles

alkyl group a group of atoms that forms when one hydrogen atom is removed from an alkane molecule
grupo alquilo grupo de átomos que se forma cuando se elimina un átomo de hidrógeno de la molécula de un alcano

alkyl halide a compound formed from an alkyl group and a halogen (fluorine, chlorine, bromine, or iodine)
halogenuro de alquilo compuesto formado por un grupo alquilo y un halógeno (flúor, cloro, bromo o yodo)

alkyne a hydrocarbon that contains one or more triple bonds
alquino hidrocarburo que contiene uno o más enlaces triples

alpha particle a positively charged atom that is released in the disintegration of radioactive elements and that consists of two protons and two neutrons
partícula alfa átomo con carga positiva que se emite durante la desintegración de elementos radiactivos y que consiste en dos protones y dos neutrones

amine an organic compound that can be considered to be a derivative of ammonia
amina un compuesto orgánico que se puede considerar como un derivado del amoniaco

amino acid any one of 20 different organic molecules that contain a carboxyl and an amino group and that combine to form proteins
aminoácido una de las 20 moléculas orgánicas diferentes que contienen un grupo carboxilo y un grupo amino y que al combinarse forman proteínas

amorphous solid a solid in which the particles are not arranged with periodicity or order
sólido amorfo un sólido en el que las partículas no están dispuestas periódicamente ni en orden

amphoteric describes a substance, such as water, that has the properties of an acid and the properties of a base
anfotérico término que describe una sustancia, como el agua, que tiene propiedades tanto de ácido como de base

anabolism the metabolic synthesis of proteins, fats, and other large biomolecules from smaller molecules; requires energy in the form of ATP
anabolismo la síntesis metabólica de proteínas, grasas y otras biomoléculas grandes a partir de moléculas más pequeñas; requiere de energía en forma de ATP

angular momentum quantum number the quantum number that indicates the shape of an orbital
número cuántico del momento angular el número cuántico que indica la forma de un orbital

anion an ion that has a negative charge
anión un ion que tiene carga negativa

anode the electrode on whose surface oxidation takes place; anions migrate toward the anode, and electrons leave the system from the anode
ánodo el electrodo en cuya superficie ocurre la oxidación; los aniones migran hacia el ánodo y los electrones se alejan del sistema por el ánodo

aromatic hydrocarbon a member of the class of hydrocarbons (of which benzene is the first member) that consists of assemblages of cyclic conjugated carbon atoms and that is characterized by large resonance energies
hidrocarburo aromático un miembro de la clase de hidrocarburos (de la cual el primer miembro es el benceno) que consiste en conjuntos de átomos de carbono cíclicos conjugados y se caracteriza por grandes energías de resonancia

Arrhenius acid a substance that increases the concentration of hydronium ions in aqueous solution
ácido de Arrhenius una sustancia que aumenta la concentración de iones hidrógeno en solución acuosa

Arrhenius base a substance that increases the concentration of hydroxide ions in aqueous solution
base de Arrhenius una sustancia que aumenta la concentración de iones hidroxilo en solución acuosa

artificial transmutation the transformation of atoms of one element into atoms of another element as a result of a nuclear reaction, such as bombardment with neutrons
transmutación artificial la transformación de los átomos de un elemento en los átomos de otro elemento como resultado de una reacción nuclear, tal como el bombardeo con neutrones

atmosphere of pressure the pressure of Earth's atmosphere at sea level; exactly equivalent to 760 mm Hg
atmósfera de presión la presión de la atmósfera de la Tierra al nivel del mar, que equivale exactamente a 760 mm de Hg

atom the smallest unit of an element that maintains the chemical properties of that element
átomo la unidad más pequeña de un elemento que conserva las propiedades químicas de ese elemento

atomic number the number of protons in the nucleus of an atom; the atomic number is the same for all atoms of an element
número atómico el número de protones presentes en el núcleo de un átomo; el número atómico es el mismo para todos los átomos de un elemento

atomic radius one-half of the distance between the center of identical atoms that are not bonded together
radio atómico la mitad de la distancia entre el centro de dos átomos idénticos que no están enlazados

Aufbau principle the principle that states that the structure of each successive element is obtained by adding one proton to the nucleus of the atom and one electron to the lowest-energy orbital that is available
principio de Aufbau el principio que establece que la estructura de cada elemento sucesivo se obtiene añadiendo un protón al núcleo del átomo y un electrón al orbital de menor energía que se encuentre disponible

autotroph an organism that produces its own nutrients from inorganic substances or from the environment instead of consuming other organisms
autótrofo un organismo que produce sus propios nutrientes a partir de sustancias inorgánicas o del ambiente, en lugar de consumir otros organismos

average atomic mass the weighted average of the masses of all naturally occurring isotopes of an element
masa atómica promedio el promedio ponderado de las masas de todos los isótopos de un elemento que se encuentran en la naturaleza

Avogadro's law the law that states that equal volumes of gases at the same temperature and pressure contain equal numbers of molecules
ley de Avogadro la ley que establece que volúmenes iguales de gases a la misma temperatura y presión contienen el mismo número de moléculas

Avogadro's number 6.02×10^{23}, the number of atoms or molecules in 1 mol
número de Avogadro 6.02×10^{23}, el número de átomos o moléculas que hay en 1 mol

barometer an instrument that measures atmospheric pressure
barómetro instrumento que mide la presión atmosférica

benzene the simplest aromatic hydrocarbon
benceno el hidrocarburo aromático más sencillo

beta particle a charged electron emitted during certain types of radioactive decay, such as beta decay
partícula beta electrón con carga que se emite durante ciertos tipos de desintegración radiactiva, tal como la desintegración beta

binary acid an acid that contains only two different elements: hydrogen and one of the more-electronegative elements
ácido binario ácido que contiene solo dos elementos: hidrógeno y uno de los elementos más electronegativos

binary compound a compound composed of two different elements
compuesto binario compuesto formado por dos elementos diferentes

boiling the conversion of a liquid to a vapor within the liquid as well as at the surface of the liquid at a specific temperature and pressure; occurs when the vapor pressure of the liquid equals the atmospheric pressure
ebullición conversión de un líquido a vapor, tanto dentro del líquido como en la superficie del líquido a una presión y temperatura determinadas; ocurre cuando la presión de vapor del líquido es igual a la presión atmosférica

boiling point the temperature and pressure at which a liquid and a gas are in equilibrium
punto de ebullición temperatura y presión a las que un líquido y un gas están en equilibrio

boiling-point elevation the difference between the boiling point of a liquid in pure state and the boiling point of the liquid in solution; the increase depends on the number of solute particles present
elevación del punto de ebullición diferencia entre el punto de ebullición de un líquido en estado puro y el punto de ebullición del líquido en solución; el aumento depende de la cantidad de partículas de soluto presentes

bond energy the energy required to break a chemical bond and form neutral isolated atoms
energía de enlace energía requerida para romper un enlace químico y formar átomos neutros aislados

Boyle's law the law that states that for a fixed amount of gas at a constant temperature, the volume of the gas increases as the pressure of the gas decreases and the volume of the gas decreases as the pressure of the gas increases
ley de Boyle ley que establece que para una cantidad fija de un gas que está a una temperatura constante, el volumen del gas aumenta a medida que la presión del gas disminuye y el volumen del gas disminuye a medida que la presión del gas aumenta

Brønsted-Lowry acid a substance that donates a proton to another substance
ácido de Brønsted-Lowry sustancia que le dona un protón a otra sustancia

Brønsted-Lowry acid-base reaction the transfer of protons from one reactant (the acid) to another (the base)
reacción ácido-base de Brønsted-Lowry transferencia de protones de un reactivo (el ácido) a otro (la base)

Brønsted-Lowry base a substance that accepts a proton
base de Brønsted-Lowry sustancia que acepta un protón

buffered solution a solution that can resist changes in pH when an acid or a base is added to it; a buffer
solución amortiguadora solución que resiste los cambios en el pH cuando se le añade un ácido o una base; búfer o tampón químico

calorimeter a device used to measure the energy as heat absorbed or released in a chemical or physical change
calorímetro aparato que se usa para medir la cantidad de energía en forma de calor absorbido o liberado en un cambio físico o químico

capillary action the attraction of the surface of a liquid to the surface of a solid, which causes the liquid to rise or fall
acción capilar atracción entre la superficie de un líquido y la superficie de un sólido que hace que el líquido se eleve o descienda

carbohydrate any organic compound that is made of carbon, hydrogen, and oxygen and that provides nutrients to the cells of living things
carbohidrato cualquier compuesto orgánico que esté formado por carbono, hidrógeno y oxígeno y que proporcione nutrientes a las células de los seres vivos

carboxylic acid an organic acid that contains the carboxyl functional group
ácido carboxílico ácido orgánico que contiene el grupo funcional carboxilo

catabolism the chemical decomposition of complex biological substances, such as carbohydrates, proteins, and glycogen, accompanied by the release of energy
catabolismo descomposición química de sustancias biológicas complejas, tales como los carbohidratos, las proteínas y el glucógeno, acompañada por la liberación de energía

catalysis the acceleration of a chemical reaction by a catalyst
catálisis aceleración de una reacción química mediante un catalizador

catalyst a substance that changes the rate of a chemical reaction without being consumed or changed significantly
catalizador sustancia que cambia la tasa de una reacción química sin ser consumida ni cambiar significativamente

catenation the binding of an element to itself to form chains or rings
catenación enlace de un elemento consigo mismo para formar cadenas o anillos

cathode the electrode on whose surface reduction takes place
cátodo electrodo en cuya superficie ocurre la reducción

cation an ion that has a positive charge
catión ion que tiene carga positiva

chain reaction a continuous series of nuclear fission reactions
reacción en cadena serie continua de reacciones de fisión nuclear

change of state the change of a substance from one physical state to another
cambio de estado cambio de una sustancia de un estado físico a otro

Charles's law the law that states that for a fixed amount of gas at a constant pressure, the volume of the gas increases as the temperature of the gas increases and the volume of the gas decreases as the temperature of the gas decreases
ley de Charles ley que establece que para una cantidad fija de un gas que está a una presión constante, el volumen del gas aumenta a medida que la temperatura del gas aumenta y el volumen del gas disminuye a medida que la temperatura del gas disminuye

chemical any substance that has a defined composition
sustancia química cualquier sustancia que tiene una composición definida

chemical bond the attractive force that holds atoms or ions together
enlace químico fuerza de atracción que mantiene unidos a los átomos o iones

chemical change a change that occurs when one or more substances change into entirely new substances with different properties
cambio químico cambio que ocurre cuando una o más sustancias se transforman en sustancias totalmente nuevas con propiedades diferentes

chemical equation a representation of a chemical reaction that uses symbols to show the relationship between the reactants and the products
ecuación química representación de una reacción química que usa símbolos para mostrar la relación entre los reactivos y los productos

chemical equilibrium a state of balance in which the rate of a forward reaction equals the rate of the reverse reaction and the concentrations of products and reactants remain unchanged
equilibrio químico estado de equilibrio en el que la tasa de la reacción directa es igual a la tasa de la reacción inversa y las concentraciones de los productos y reactivos no sufren cambios

chemical equilibrium expression the equation for the equilibrium constant, K_{eq}
expresión de equilibrio químico ecuación para la constante de equilibrio, K_{eq}

chemical formula a combination of chemical symbols and numbers to represent a substance
fórmula química combinación de símbolos químicos y números que se usan para representar una sustancia

chemical kinetics the area of chemistry that is the study of reaction rates and reaction mechanisms
cinética química área de la química que se ocupa del estudio de las tasas de reacción y de los mecanismos de reacción

chemical property a property of matter that describes a substance's ability to participate in chemical reactions
propiedad química propiedad de la materia que describe la capacidad de una sustancia de participar en reacciones químicas

chemical reaction the process by which one or more substances change to produce one or more different substances
reacción química proceso por medio del cual una o más sustancias cambian para producir una o más sustancias distintas

chemistry the scientific study of the composition, structure, and properties of matter and the changes that matter undergoes
química estudio científico de la composición, estructura y propiedades de la materia y los cambios por los que pasa la materia

cloning the process of producing a genetically identical copy of an organism
clonación proceso mediante el cual se produce una copia genéticamente idéntica de un organismo

coefficient a small whole number that appears as a factor in front of a formula in a chemical equation
coeficiente número entero pequeño que aparece como un factor frente a una fórmula en una ecuación química

colligative property a property that is determined by the number of particles present in a system but that is independent of the properties of the particles themselves
propiedad coligativa propiedad que se determina por el número de partículas presentes en un sistema, pero que es independiente de las propiedades de las partículas mismas

collision theory the theory that states that in order for a chemical reaction to occur, collisions between particles must have sufficient energy and correct orientation
teoría de colisión teoría que establece que, para que ocurra una reacción química, las colisiones entre las partículas deben tener suficiente energía y la orientación correcta

colloid a mixture consisting of tiny particles that are intermediate in size between those in solutions and those in suspensions and that are suspended in a liquid, solid, or gas
coloide mezcla formada por partículas diminutas que son de tamaño intermedio entre las partículas de las soluciones y las de las suspensiones y que se encuentran suspendidas en un líquido, un sólido o un gas

combined gas law the relationship between the pressure, volume, and temperature of a fixed amount of gas
ley combinada de los gases relación entre la presión, el volumen y la temperatura de una cantidad fija de gas

combustion reaction the oxidation reaction of an element or compound, in which energy as heat is released
reacción de combustión reacción de oxidación de un elemento o compuesto durante la cual se libera energía en forma de calor

common-ion effect the phenomenon in which the addition of an ion common to two solutes brings about precipitation or reduces ionization
efecto del ion común fenómeno en el que la adición de un ion común a dos solutos produce precipitación o reduce la ionización

composition stoichiometry calculations involving the mass relationships of elements in compounds
estequiometría de composición cálculos que involucran las relaciones entre las masas de los elementos presentes en los compuestos

compound a substance made up of atoms of two or more different elements joined by chemical bonds
compuesto sustancia formada por átomos de dos o más elementos diferentes unidos por enlaces químicos

concentration the amount of a particular substance in a given quantity of a mixture, solution, or ore
concentración cantidad de una cierta sustancia en una cantidad determinada de mezcla, solución o mena

condensation the change of state from a gas to a liquid
condensación cambio de estado de gas a líquido

condensation reaction a chemical reaction in which two or more molecules combine to produce water or another simple molecule
reacción de condensación reacción química en la que dos o más moléculas se combinan para producir agua u otra molécula simple

conjugate acid an acid that forms when a base gains a proton
ácido conjugado ácido que se forma cuando una base gana un protón

conjugate base a base that forms when an acid loses a proton
base conjugada base que se forma cuando un ácido pierde un protón

continuous spectrum an unbroken sequence of frequencies or wavelengths of electromagnetic radiation, often emitted by an incandescent source
espectro continuo secuencia ininterrumpida de frecuencias o longitudes de onda de una radiación electromagnética, por lo general emitidas por una fuente incandescente

control rod a neutron-absorbing rod that helps control a nuclear reaction by limiting the number of free neutrons
barra de control barra que absorbe neutrones y que ayuda a controlar las reacciones nucleares al limitar el número de neutrones libres

conversion factor a ratio that is derived from the equality of two different units and that can be used to convert from one unit to the other
factor de conversión razón que se deriva de la igualdad entre dos unidades diferentes y que se puede usar para convertir una unidad en otra

copolymer a polymer made from two different monomers
copolímero polímero formado por dos monómeros distintos

covalent bond a bond formed when atoms share one or more pairs of electrons
enlace covalente enlace formado cuando los átomos comparten uno o más pares de electrones

critical mass the minimum mass of a fissionable isotope that provides the number of neutrons needed to sustain a chain reaction
masa crítica cantidad mínima de masa de un isótopo fisionable que proporciona el número de neutrones que se requieren para sostener una reacción en cadena

critical point the temperature and pressure at which the gas and liquid states of a substance become identical and form one phase
punto crítico temperatura y presión a la que los estados líquido y gaseoso de una sustancia se vuelven idénticos y forman una fase

critical pressure the lowest pressure at which a substance can exist as a liquid at the critical temperature
presión crítica presión más baja a la que una sustancia puede existir en estado líquido a la temperatura crítica

critical temperature the temperature above which a substance cannot exist in the liquid state
temperatura crítica temperatura por encima de la cual una sustancia no puede existir en estado líquido

crystal a solid whose atoms, ions, or molecules are arranged in a definite pattern
cristal sólido cuyos átomos, iones o moléculas están ordenados en un patrón definido

crystal structure the arrangement of atoms, ions, or molecules in a regular way to form a crystal
estructura cristalina ordenamiento de átomos, iones o moléculas en un patrón regular para formar un cristal

crystalline solid a solid that consists of crystals
sólido cristalino sólido formado por cristales

cycloalkane a saturated carbon chain that forms a loop or a ring
cicloalcano cadena saturada de carbonos que forma un circuito o anillo

Dalton's law of partial pressures the law that states that the total pressure of a mixture of gases is equal to the sum of the partial pressures of the component gases
ley de Dalton de las presiones parciales ley que establece que la presión total de una mezcla de gases es igual a la suma de las presiones parciales de los gases que la componen

daughter nuclide a nuclide produced by the radioactive decay of another nuclide
nucleido hijo nucleido producido por la desintegración radiactiva de otro nucleido

decay series a series of radioactive nuclides produced by successive radioactive decay until a stable nuclide is reached
serie de desintegración serie de nucleidos radiactivos producidos por un proceso de desintegración radiactiva sucesiva hasta que se obtiene un nucleido estable

decomposition reaction a reaction in which a single compound breaks down to form two or more simpler substances
reacción de descomposición reacción en la que un solo compuesto se descompone y forma dos o más sustancias más simples

denature to change irreversibly the structure or shape—and thus the solubility and other properties—of a protein by heating, shaking, or treating the protein with acid, alkali, or other species
desnaturalizar cambiar de forma irreversible la estructura o forma (y, por lo tanto, la solubilidad y otras propiedades) de una proteína mediante calentamiento, agitación o haciendo reaccionar a la proteína con ácidos, bases u otros compuestos

density the ratio of the mass of a substance to the volume of the substance; often expressed as grams per cubic centimeter for solids and liquids and as grams per liter for gases
densidad relación entre la masa de una sustancia y su volumen; frecuentemente se expresa en gramos por centímetro cúbico para los sólidos y líquidos, y como gramos por litro para los gases

deposition the change of state from a gas directly to a solid
deposición cambio de estado directo de gas a sólido

derived unit a unit of measure that is a combination of other measurements
unidad derivada unidad de medida que es una combinación de otras medidas

diffusion the movement of particles from regions of higher density to regions of lower density
difusión movimiento de partículas de regiones de mayor densidad a regiones de menor densidad

dimensional analysis a mathematical technique that allows one to use units to solve problems involving measurements
análisis dimensional técnica matemática que permite usar unidades para resolver problemas que incluyen unidades

dipole a molecule or a part of a molecule that contains both positively and negatively charged regions
dipolo molécula o parte de una molécula que contiene regiones con cargas tanto positivas como negativas

diprotic acid an acid that has two ionizable hydrogen atoms in each molecule, such as sulfuric acid
ácido diprótico ácido que tiene dos átomos de hidrógeno ionizables en cada molécula, como el ácido sulfúrico

direct proportion the relationship between two variables whose ratio is a constant value
proporción directa relación entre dos variables cuya razón es un valor constante

disaccharide a sugar formed from two monosaccharides
disacárido azúcar formado a partir de dos monosacáridos

disproportionation the process by which a substance is transformed into two or more dissimilar substances, usually by simultaneous oxidation and reduction
dismutación proceso mediante el cual una sustancia se transforma en dos o más sustancias distintas, usualmente mediante oxidación y reducción simultáneas

dissociation the separating of a molecule into simpler molecules, atoms, radicals, or ions
disociación separación de una molécula en moléculas más simples, átomos, radicales o iones

DNA replication the process of making a copy of DNA
replicación del ADN proceso de hacer una copia del ADN

double-displacement reaction a reaction in which the ions of two compounds exchange places in an aqueous solution to form two new compounds
reacción de doble desplazamiento reacción en la dos iones de dos compuestos intercambian lugares en una solución acuosa y forman dos compuestos nuevos

ductility the ability of a substance to be hammered thin or drawn out into a wire
ductilidad capacidad de una sustancia de formar láminas delgadas o alambres

effervescence a bubbling of a liquid caused by the rapid escape of a gas rather than by boiling
efervescencia burbujeo de un líquido producido por el escape rápido de gas en lugar de por ebullición

effusion the passage of a gas under pressure through a tiny opening
efusión paso de un gas bajo presión a través de una abertura diminuta

elastic collision a collision between ideally elastic bodies in which the final and initial kinetic energies are the same
colisión elástica colisión entre cuerpos elásticos ideales, en la que las energías cinéticas inicial y final son iguales

electrochemistry the branch of chemistry that is the study of the relationship between electric forces and chemical reactions
electroquímica rama de la química que se ocupa del estudio de la relación entre las fuerzas eléctricas y las reacciones químicas

electrode a conductor used to establish electrical contact with a nonmetallic part of a circuit, such as an electrolyte
electrodo conductor que se usa para establecer contacto eléctrico con una parte no metálica de un circuito, tal como un electrolito

electrode potential the difference in potential between an electrode and its solution
potencial del electrodo diferencia de potencial entre un electrodo y su solución

electrolysis the process in which an electric current is used to produce a chemical reaction, such as the decomposition of water
electrólisis proceso por medio del cual se utiliza una corriente eléctrica para producir una reacción química, como por ejemplo, la descomposición del agua

electrolyte a substance that dissolves in water to give a solution that conducts an electric current
electrolito sustancia que se disuelve en agua y crea una solución que conduce la corriente eléctrica

electrolytic cell an electrochemical device in which electrolysis takes place when an electric current is in the device
celda electrolítica aparato electroquímico en el que se da lugar la electrólisis cuando hay una corriente eléctrica en el aparato

electromagnetic radiation the radiation associated with an electric and magnetic field; it varies periodically and travels at the speed of light
radiación electromagnética radiación asociada con un campo eléctrico y magnético; varía periódicamente y se desplaza a la velocidad de la luz

electromagnetic spectrum all of the frequencies or wavelengths of electromagnetic radiation
espectro electromagnético todas las frecuencias o longitudes de onda de la radiación electromagnética

electron affinity the energy change that occurs when an electron is acquired by a neutral atom
afinidad electrónica cambio de energía que ocurre cuando un átomo neutro adquiere un electrón

electron capture the process in which an inner-orbital electron is captured by the nucleus of the atom that contains the electron
captura electrónica proceso por medio del cual un electrón del orbital interno es capturado por el núcleo del átomo que contiene el electrón

electron configuration the arrangement of electrons in an atom
configuración electrónica ordenamiento de los electrones en un átomo

electron-dot notation an electron-configuration notation in which only the valence electrons of an atom of a particular element are shown, indicated by dots placed around the element's symbol
notación electrónica de punto notación de la configuración electrónica en la cual solamente se muestran los electrones de valencia de un átomo de un elemento en particular, indicados por puntos ubicados alrededor del símbolo del elemento

electronegativity a measure of the ability of an atom in a chemical compound to attract electrons
electronegatividad medida de la capacidad de un átomo de un compuesto químico de atraer electrones

electroplating the electrolytic process of plating or coating an object with a metal
electrochapado proceso electrolítico de recubrir o aplicar una capa de un metal a un objeto

element a substance that cannot be separated or broken down into simpler substances by chemical means; all atoms of an element have the same atomic number
elemento sustancia que no se puede separar o descomponer en sustancias más simples por medio de métodos químicos; todos los átomos de un elemento tienen el mismo número atómico

elimination reaction a reaction in which a simple molecule, such as water or ammonia, is removed and a new compound is produced
reacción de eliminación reacción en la que se quita una molécula simple, como el agua o el amoniaco, y se produce un nuevo compuesto

emission-line spectrum a series of specific wavelengths of electromagnetic radiation emitted by electrons as they move from higher to lower energy states
espectro de la línea de emisión serie de longitudes de onda específicas de radiación electromagnética emitida por electrones a medida que se desplazan de estados de energía superiores a inferiores

empirical formula a chemical formula that shows the composition of a compound in terms of the relative numbers and kinds of atoms in the simplest ratio
fórmula empírica fórmula química que muestra la composición de un compuesto en función del número relativo y el tipo de átomos que hay en la proporción más simple

end point the point in a titration at which a marked color change takes place
punto final punto en una titulación en el que ocurre un cambio marcado de color

enthalpy change the amount of energy released or absorbed as heat by a system during a process at constant pressure
cambio de entalpía cantidad de energía que un sistema libera o absorbe en forma de calor durante un proceso a presión constante

enthalpy of combustion the energy released as heat by the complete combustion of a specific amount of a substance at constant pressure or constant volume
entalpía de combustión energía que libera en forma de calor la combustión completa de una cantidad determinada de una sustancia, a presión constante o con un volumen constante

enthalpy of reaction the amount of energy released or absorbed as heat during a chemical reaction
entalpia de reacción cantidad de energía que se libera o se absorbe en forma de calor durante una reacción química

enthalpy of solution the amount of energy released or absorbed as heat when a specific amount of solute dissolves in a solvent
entalpía de solución cantidad de energía que se libera o se absorbe en forma de calor cuando una cantidad determinada de soluto se disuelve en un solvente

entropy a measure of the randomness or disorder of a system
entropía medida del grado de aleatoriedad o desorden de un sistema

enzyme a type of protein that acts as a catalyst and speeds up metabolic reactions in plants and animals without being permanently changed or destroyed
enzima tipo de proteína que actúa como catalizador y acelera las reacciones metabólicas en plantas y animales sin cambiar permanentemente ni resultar destruida

equilibrium in chemistry, the state in which a chemical reaction and the reverse chemical reaction occur at the same rate such that the concentrations of reactants and products do not change
equilibrio en química, estado en el que una reacción química y la reacción química inversa ocurren a la misma tasa de modo que las concentraciones de los reactivos y los productos no cambian

equilibrium constant a number that relates the concentrations of starting materials and products of a reversible chemical reaction to one another at a given temperature
constante de equilibrio número que relaciona las concentraciones de los materiales de inicio y los productos de una reacción química reversible a una temperatura dada

equilibrium vapor pressure the vapor pressure of a system at equilibrium
presión de vapor en equilibrio presión de vapor en un sistema cuando éste está en equilibrio

equivalence point the point at which the two solutions used in a titration are present in chemically equivalent amounts
punto de equivalencia punto en el que dos soluciones usadas en una titulación están presentes en cantidades químicas equivalentes

ester an organic compound formed by combining an organic acid with an alcohol such that water is eliminated
éster compuesto orgánico que se forma al combinar un ácido orgánico con un alcohol de modo que se elimine agua

ether an organic compound in which two carbon atoms bond to the same oxygen atom
éter compuesto orgánico en el que dos átomos de carbono se unen al mismo átomo de oxígeno

evaporation the change of a substance from a liquid to a gas
evaporación cambio de estado de una sustancia de líquido a gas

excess reactant the substance that is not used up completely in a reaction
reactivo en exceso sustancia que no se usa por completo en una reacción

excited state a state in which an atom has more energy than it does at its ground state
estado de excitación estado en el que un átomo tiene más energía que en su estado fundamental

extensive property a property that depends on the extent or size of a system
propiedad extensiva propiedad de un sistema que depende de la extensión o tamaño del sistema

family a vertical column of the periodic table
familia columna vertical de la tabla periódica

fatty acid an organic acid that is contained in lipids, such as fats or oils
ácido graso ácido orgánico contenido en lípidos como las grasas o los aceites

film badge a device that measures the approximate amount of radiation received in a given period of time by people who work with radiation
lector de película aparato que mide la cantidad aproximada de radiación que las personas que trabajan con radiación reciben en un período de tiempo determinado

fluid a nonsolid state of matter in which the atoms or molecules are free to move past each other, as in a gas or liquid
fluido estado no sólido de la materia en el que los átomos o las moléculas tienen libertad de movimiento, como en el caso de un gas o un líquido

formula equation a representation of the reactants and products of a chemical reaction by their symbols or formulas
ecuación de una fórmula representación de los reactivos y los productos de una reacción química por medio de sus símbolos o fórmulas

formula mass the sum of the average atomic masses of all atoms represented in the formula of any molecule, formula unit, or ion
masa de la fórmula suma de las masas atómicas promedio de todos los átomos representados en la fórmula de una molécula, unidad de la fórmula o ion

formula unit the simplest collection of atoms from which an ionic compound's formula can be written
unidad de la fórmula el conjunto más simple de átomos a partir del cual puede escribirse la fórmula de un compuesto iónico

free energy the energy in a system that is available for work; a system's capacity to do useful work
energía libre energía de un sistema disponible para realizar un trabajo; capacidad de un sistema para realizar un trabajo útil

free-energy change the difference between the change in enthalpy, ΔH, and the product of the Kelvin temperature and the entropy change, which is defined as $T\Delta S$, at a constant pressure and temperature
cambio de energía libre diferencia entre el cambio de entalpía, ΔH, y el producto de la temperatura en Kelvin por el cambio de entropía, que se define como $T\Delta S$, a presión y temperatura constantes

freezing the change of state in which a liquid becomes a solid as energy as heat is removed
congelación cambio de estado en el cual un líquido se convierte en sólido al eliminar energía en forma de calor

freezing point the temperature at which a solid and liquid are in equilibrium at 1 atm pressure; the temperature at which a liquid substance freezes
punto de congelación temperatura a la que un sólido y un líquido están en equilibrio a 1 atm de presión; temperatura a la que una sustancia en estado líquido se congela

freezing-point depression the difference between the freezing points of a pure solvent and a solution, which is directly proportional to the amount of solute present
depresión del punto de congelación diferencia entre los puntos de congelación de un solvente puro y una solución, que es directamente proporcional a la cantidad de soluto presente

frequency the number of cycles or vibrations per unit of time; also the number of waves produced in a given amount of time
frecuencia número de ciclos o vibraciones por unidad de tiempo; también, número de ondas producidas en una cantidad de tiempo determinada

functional group the portion of a molecule that is active in a chemical reaction and that determines the properties of many organic compounds
grupo funcional la porción de una molécula que está involucrada en una reacción química y que determina las propiedades de muchos compuestos orgánicos

gamma ray the high-energy photon emitted by a nucleus during fission and radioactive decay
rayo gamma el fotón de alta energía emitido por un núcleo durante la fisión y la desintegración radiactiva

gas a form of matter that does not have a definite volume or shape
gas un estado de la materia que no tiene volumen ni forma definidos

Gay-Lussac's law the law that states that the volume occupied by a gas at a constant pressure is directly proportional to the absolute temperature
ley de Gay-Lussac la ley que establece que el volumen ocupado por un gas a presión constante es directamente proporcional a la temperatura absoluta

Gay-Lussac's law of combining volumes of gases the law that states that the volumes of gases involved in a chemical change can be represented by a ratio of small whole numbers
ley de combinación de los volúmenes de los gases de Gay-Lussac la ley que establece que los volúmenes de los gases que participan en un cambio químico se pueden representar mediante una razón de números enteros pequeños

Geiger-Müller counter an instrument that detects and measures the intensity of radiation by counting the number of electric pulses that pass between the anode and the cathode in a tube filled with gas
contador de Geiger-Müller un instrumento que detecta y mide la intensidad de la radiación contando el número de pulsos eléctricos que pasan entre el ánodo y el cátodo en un tubo lleno de gas

geometric isomer a compound that exists in two or more geometrically different configurations
isómero geométrico un compuesto que existe en dos o más configuraciones geométricamente diferentes

Graham's law of effusion the law that states that the rate of effusion of a gas is inversely proportional to the square root of the gas's density
ley de efusión de Graham la ley que establece que la tasa de efusión de un gas es inversamente proporcional a la raíz cuadrada de su densidad

ground state the lowest energy state of a quantized system
estado fundamental el estado de energía más bajo de un sistema cuantizado

group a vertical column of elements in the periodic table; elements in a group share chemical properties
grupo una columna vertical de elementos de la tabla periódica; los elementos de un grupo comparten propiedades químicas

half-cell a single electrode immersed in a solution of its ions
media celda un solo electrodo sumergido en una solución de sus iones

half-life the time required for half of a sample of a radioactive substance to disintegrate by radioactive decay or by natural processes
vida media el tiempo que se requiere para que la mitad de una muestra de una sustancia radiactiva se descomponga por desintegración radiactiva o por procesos naturales

half-reaction the part of a reaction that involves only oxidation or reduction
media reacción la parte de una reacción que solo involucra oxidación o reducción

halogen one of the elements of Group 17 (fluorine, chlorine, bromine, iodine, and astatine); halogens combine with most metals to form salts
halógeno uno de los elementos del Grupo 17 (flúor, cloro, bromo, yodo y ástato); los halógenos se combinan con la mayoría de los metales para formar sales

heat the energy transferred between objects that are at different temperatures; energy is always transferred from higher-temperature objects to lower-temperature objects until thermal equilibrium is reached
calor la energía que se transfiere entre objetos que están a temperaturas diferentes; la energía siempre se transfiere de los objetos que están a la temperatura más alta a los objetos que están a una temperatura más baja, hasta que se llega a un equilibrio térmico

Heisenberg uncertainty principle the principle that states that determining both the position and velocity of an electron or any other particle simultaneously is impossible
principio de incertidumbre de Heisenberg el principio que establece que es imposible determinar simultáneamente la posición y la velocidad de un electrón o cualquier otra partícula

Henry's law the law that states that at constant temperature, the solubility of a gas in a liquid is directly proportional to the partial pressure of the gas on the surface of the liquid
ley de Henry la ley que establece que a una temperatura constante, la solubilidad de un gas en un líquido es directamente proporcional a la presión parcial del gas en la superficie del líquido

Hess's law the overall enthalpy change in a reaction is equal to the sum of the enthalpy changes for the individual steps in the process
ley de Hess el cambio total de entalpía en una reacción es igual a la suma de los cambios de entalpía ocurridos en los pasos individuales del proceso

heterogeneous composed of dissimilar components
heterogéneo compuesto de componentes que no son iguales

heterogeneous catalyst a catalyst that is in a different phase from the phase of the reactants
catalizador heterogéneo un catalizador que está en una fase distinta de la fase de los reactivos

heterogeneous reaction a reaction in which the reactants are in two different phases
reacción heterogénea una reacción en la que los reactivos están en dos fases diferentes

heterotroph an organism that obtains organic food molecules by other organisms or their byproducts and that cannot synthesize organic compounds from inorganic materials
heterótrofo organismo que obtiene moléculas orgánicas de alimento a través de otros organismos o sus productos secundarios y que no puede sintetizar compuestos orgánicos a partir de materiales inorgánicos

homogeneous describes something that has a uniform structure or composition throughout
homogéneo término que describe algo que tiene una estructura o composición global uniforme

homogeneous catalyst a catalyst that is in the same phase as the reactants are
catalizador homogéneo catalizador que está en la misma fase que los reactivos

homogeneous reaction a reaction in which all of the reactants and products are in the same phase
reacción homogénea reacción en la que todos los reactivos y los productos están en la misma fase

Hund's rule the rule that states that for an atom in the ground state, the number of unpaired electrons is the maximum possible and these unpaired electrons have the same spin
regla de Hund regla que establece que para un átomo en estado fundamental, el número de electrones no apareados es el máximo posible y que estos electrones no apareados tienen el mismo espín

hybrid orbitals orbitals of equal energy produced by the combination of two or more orbitals on the same atom
orbitales híbridos orbitales con la misma energía producidos por la combinación de dos o más orbitales del mimo átomo

hybridization the mixing of two or more atomic orbitals of the same atom to produce new orbitals; hybridization represents the mixing of higher- and lower-energy orbitals to form orbitals of intermediate energy
hibridación mezcla de dos o más orbitales atómicos del mismo átomo para producir orbitales nuevos; esta hibridación representa la mezcla de orbitales de energía superior e inferior para formar orbitales de energía intermedia

hydration the strong affinity of water molecules for particles of dissolved or suspended substances that causes electrolytic dissociation
hidratación fuerte afinidad de las moléculas del agua para con las partículas de sustancias disueltas o suspendidas que causan disociación electrolítica

hydrocarbon an organic compound composed only of carbon and hydrogen
hidrocarburo compuesto orgánico compuesto únicamente por carbono e hidrógeno

hydrogen bond the intermolecular force occurring when a hydrogen atom that is bonded to a highly electronegative atom of one molecule is attracted to two unshared electrons of another molecule
enlace de hidrógeno fuerza intermolecular que se produce cuando un átomo de hidrógeno que está unido a un átomo muy electro-negativo de una molécula se ve atraído por dos electrones no compartidos de otra molécula

hydrolysis a chemical reaction between water and another substance to form two or more new substances; a reaction between water and a salt to create an acid or a base
hidrólisis reacción química entre el agua y otras sustancias para formar dos o más sustancias nuevas; reacción entre el agua y una sal para crear un ácido o una base

hydronium ion an ion consisting of a proton combined with a molecule of water; H_3O^+
ion hidronio ion formado por un protón combinado con una molécula de agua; H_3O^+

hypothesis an explanation that is based on prior scientific research or observations and that can be tested
hipótesis explicación que está basada en investigaciones u observaciones científicas previas y que puede ponerse a prueba

ideal gas an imaginary gas whose particles are infinitely small and do not interact with each other
gas ideal gas imaginario con partículas que son infinitamente pequeñas y que no interactúan unas con otras

ideal gas constant the proportionality constant that appears in the equation of state for 1 mol of an ideal gas; $R = 0.082\ 057\ 84$ L • atm/mol • K
constante de los gases ideales constante de proporcionalidad que aparece en la ecuación de estado para 1 mol de un gas ideal; $R = 0.082\ 057\ 84$ L • atm/mol • K

ideal gas law the law that states the mathematical relationship of pressure (P), volume (V), temperature (T), the gas constant (R), and the number of moles of a gas (n); $PV = nRT$
ley de los gases ideales ley que establece la relación matemática entre la presión (P), el volumen (V), la temperatura (T), la constante de los gases (R) y el número de moles de un gas (n); $PV = nRT$

immiscible describes two or more liquids that do not mix with each other
inmiscible término que describe dos o más líquidos que no se mezclan uno con otro

intensive property a property that does not depend on the amount of matter present, such as pressure, temperature, or density
propiedad intensiva propiedad que no depende de la cantidad de materia presente, como por ejemplo, la presión, la temperatura o la densidad

intermediate a substance that forms in a middle stage of a chemical reaction and is considered a stepping stone between the parent substance and the final product
intermediario sustancia que se forma en un estado medio de una reacción química y que se considera un paso importante entre la sustancia original y el producto final

inverse proportion the relationship between two variables whose product is constant
proporción inversa relación entre dos variables cuyo producto es constante

ion an atom, radical, or molecule that has gained or lost one or more electrons and has a negative or positive charge
ion átomo, radical o molécula que ha ganado o perdido uno o más electrones y que tiene una carga negativa o positiva

ionic bond a force that attracts electrons from one atom to another, which transforms a neutral atom into an ion
enlace iónico fuerza que atrae electrones de un átomo a otro, lo cual transforma un átomo neutro en un ion

ionic compound a compound composed of ions bound together by electrostatic attraction
compuesto iónico compuesto formado por iones unidos por atracción electrostática

ionization the process of adding or removing electrons from an atom or molecule, which gives the atom or molecule a net charge
ionización proceso de añadir o quitar electrones de un átomo o molécula, lo cual da al átomo o molécula una carga neta

ionization energy the energy required to remove an electron from an atom or ion (abbreviation, IE)
energía de ionización energía que se requiere para quitar un electrón de un átomo o ion (abreviatura: EI)

isomer one of two or more compounds that have the same chemical composition but different structures
isómero uno de dos o más compuestos que tienen la misma composición química pero diferentes estructuras

isotope an atom that has the same number of protons (or the same atomic number) as other atoms of the same element but that has a different number of neutrons (and thus a different atomic mass)
isótopo átomo que tiene el mismo número de protones (o el mismo número atómico) que otros átomos del mismo elemento, pero tiene un número diferente de neutrones (y, por lo tanto, una masa atómica diferente)

joule the unit used to express energy; equivalent to the amount of work done by a force of 1 N acting through a distance of 1 m in the direction of the force (abbreviation, J)
joule unidad que se usa para expresar energía; equivale a la cantidad de trabajo realizado por una fuerza de 1 N que actúa a través de una distancia de 1 m en la dirección de la fuerza (abreviatura: J)

ketone an organic compound in which a carbonyl group is attached to two alkyl groups; obtained by the oxidation of secondary alcohols
cetona compuesto orgánico en el que el grupo carbonilo está unido a dos grupos alquilo; se obtiene por medio de la oxidación de alcoholes secundarios

kinetic-molecular theory a theory that explains that the behavior of physical systems depends on the combined actions of the molecules constituting the system
teoría cinética molecular teoría que explica que el comportamiento de los sistemas físicos depende de las acciones combinadas de las moléculas que constituyen el sistema

lanthanide a member of the rare-earth series of elements, whose atomic numbers range from 58 (cerium) to 71 (lutetium)
lantánido miembro de la serie de elementos de tierras raras, cuyos números atómicos van del 58 (cerio) al 71 (lutecio)

lattice energy the energy released when one mole of an ionic crystalline compound is formed from gaseous ions
energía de la red cristalina energía liberada cuando se forma un mol de un compuesto iónico cristalino a partir de iones gaseosos

law of conservation of mass the law that states that mass cannot be created or destroyed in ordinary chemical and physical changes
ley de la conservación de la masa ley que establece que la masa no se crea ni se destruye por cambios químicos o físicos comunes

law of definite proportions the law that states that a chemical compound always contains the same elements in exactly the same proportions by weight or mass
ley de las proporciones definidas ley que establece que un compuesto químico siempre contiene los mismos elementos en exactamente las mismas proporciones de peso o masa

law of multiple proportions the law that states that when two elements combine to form two or more compounds, the mass of one element that combines with a given mass of the other is in the ratio of small whole numbers
ley de las proporciones múltiples ley que establece que cuando dos elementos se combinan para formar dos o más compuestos, la masa de un elemento que se combina con una cantidad determinada de masa de otro elemento es en la proporción de número enteros pequeños

Lewis acid an atom, ion, or molecule that accepts a pair of electrons
ácido de Lewis átomo, ion o molécula que acepta un par de electrones

Lewis acid-base reaction the formation of one or more covalent bonds between an electron-pair donor and an electron-pair acceptor
reacción ácido-base de Lewis formación de uno o más enlaces covalentes entre un donante de un par de electrones y un receptor de un par de electrones

Lewis base an atom, ion, or molecule that donates a pair of electrons
base de Lewis átomo, ion o molécula que dona un par de electrones

Lewis structure a structural formula in which electrons are represented by dots; dot pairs or dashes between two atomic symbols represent pairs in covalent bonds
estructura de Lewis fórmula estructural en la que los electrones se representan por medio de puntos; pares de puntos o líneas entre dos símbolos atómicos representan pares en los enlaces covalentes

limiting reactant the substance that controls the quantity of product that can form in a chemical reaction
reactivo limitante sustancia que controla la cantidad de producto que se puede formar en una reacción química

lipid a type of biochemical that does not dissolve in water, including fats and steroids; lipids store energy and make up cell membranes
lípido tipo de bioquímico que no se disuelve en agua, como las grasas y los esteroides; los lípidos almacenan energía y forman membranas celulares

liquid the state of matter that has a definite volume but not a definite shape
líquido estado de la materia que tiene un volumen definido, pero no una forma definida

London dispersion force the intermolecular attraction resulting from the uneven distribution of electrons and the creation of temporary dipoles
fuerza de dispersión de London atracción intermolecular que se produce como resultado de la distribución desigual de los electrones y la creación de dipolos temporales

magic numbers the numbers (2, 8, 20, 28, 50, 82, and 126) that represent the number of particles in an extra-stable atomic nucleus that has completed shells of protons and neutrons
números mágicos números (2, 8, 20, 28, 50, 82 y 126) que representan el número de partículas que existen en un núcleo atómico extraestable que tiene los orbitales de protones y neutrones completos

magnetic quantum number the quantum number that indicates the orientation of an orbital around the nucleus; symbolized by *m*
número cuántico magnético número cuántico que indica la orientación de un orbital alrededor del núcleo; su símbolo es *m*

main-group element an element in the *s*-block or *p*-block of the periodic table
elemento de grupo principal elemento que está en el bloque *s* o *p* de la tabla periódica

malleability the ability of a substance to be hammered or beaten into a sheet
maleabilidad capacidad de una sustancia de formar láminas al ser martillada o golpeada

mass a measure of the amount of matter in an object
masa medida de la cantidad de materia que tiene un objeto

mass defect the difference between the mass of an atom and the sum of the masses of the atom's protons, neutrons, and electrons
defecto de masa diferencia entre la masa de un átomo y la suma de la masa de los protones, neutrones y electrones del átomo

mass number the sum of the numbers of protons and neutrons that make up the nucleus of an atom
número de masa suma de los números de protones y neutrones que componen el núcleo de un átomo

matter anything that has mass and takes up space
materia cualquier cosa que tiene masa y ocupa un lugar en el espacio

melting the change of state in which a solid becomes a liquid by adding energy as heat or changing pressure
fusión cambio de estado en el que un sólido se convierte en líquido al añadir calor o al cambiar la presión

melting point the temperature and pressure at which a solid becomes a liquid
punto de fusión temperatura y presión a la cual un sólido se convierte en líquido

metabolism the sum of all chemical processes that occur in an organism
metabolismo suma de todos los procesos químicos que ocurren en un organismo

metal an element that is shiny and that conducts heat and electricity well
metal elemento que es brillante y conduce bien el calor y la electricidad

metallic bond a bond formed by the attraction between positively charged metal ions and the electrons around them
enlace metálico enlace formado por la atracción entre iones metálicos con carga positiva y los electrones que los rodean

metalloid an element that has properties of both metals and nonmetals; sometimes referred to as a semiconductor
metaloide elemento que tiene propiedades tanto de metal como de no metal; a veces se denomina semiconductor

millimeters of mercury a unit of pressure
milímetros de mercurio unidad de presión

miscible describes two or more liquids that can dissolve into each other in various proportions
miscible término que describe a dos o más líquidos que son capaces de disolverse uno en el otro en varias proporciones

mixture a combination of two or more substances that are not chemically combined
mezcla combinación de dos o más sustancias que no están combinadas químicamente

model a pattern, plan, representation, or description designed to show the structure or workings of an object, system, or concept
modelo diseño, plan, representación o descripción cuyo objetivo es mostrar la estructura o funcionamiento de un objeto, sistema o concepto

moderator a material that slows the velocity of neutrons so that they may be absorbed by the nuclei
moderador material que disminuye la velocidad de los neutrones de modo que estos puedan ser absorbidos por los núcleos

molal boiling-point constant a quantity calculated to represent the boiling-point elevation of a 1-molal solution of a nonvolatile, nonelectrolyte solution
constante molal del punto de ebullición cantidad que se calcula para representar la elevación en el punto de ebullición de una solución 1 molal de un soluto no-volátil, no-electrolito

molal freezing-point constant a quantity calculated to represent the freezing-point depression of a 1-molal solution of a nonvolatile, nonelectrolyte solute
constante molal del punto de congelación cantidad que se calcula para representar la disminución en el punto de congelación de una solución 1 molal de una solución no volátil, no-electrolito

molality the concentration of a solution expressed in moles of solute per kilogram of solvent
molalidad concentración de una solución expresada en moles de soluto por kilogramo de solvente

molar enthalpy of formation the amount of energy as heat resulting from the formation of 1 mol of a substance at constant pressure
entalpía molar de formación cantidad de energía en forma de calor que resulta debido a la formación de 1 mol de una sustancia a presión constante

molar enthalpy of fusion the amount of energy as heat required to change 1 mol of a substance from solid to liquid at constant temperature and pressure
entalpía molar de fusión cantidad de energía en forma de calor que se requiere para que 1 mol de una sustancia pase de sólido a líquido a una temperatura y presión constantes

molar enthalpy of vaporization the amount of energy as heat required to evaporate 1 mol of a liquid at constant pressure and temperature
entalpía molar de vaporización cantidad de energía en forma de calor que se requiere para que 1 mol de un líquido se evapore a una temperatura y presión constantes

molar mass the mass in grams of 1 mol of a substance
masa molar masa en gramos de 1 mol de una sustancia

molarity a concentration unit of a solution expressed as moles of solute dissolved per liter of solution
molaridad unidad de concentración de una solución, expresada en moles de soluto disuelto por litro de solución

mole the SI base unit used to measure the amount of a substance whose number of particles is the same as the number of atoms of carbon in exactly 12 g of carbon-12
mol unidad fundamental del Sistema Internacional de Unidades que se usa para medir la cantidad de una sustancia cuyo número de partículas es el mismo que el número de átomos de carbono en exactamente 12 g de carbono-12

mole ratio a conversion factor that relates the amounts in moles of any two substances involved in a chemical reaction
razón molar factor de conversión que relaciona las cantidades en moles de dos sustancias cualesquiera que participen en una reacción química

molecular compound a chemical compound whose simplest units are molecules
compuesto molecular compuesto químico cuyas unidades más simples son moléculas

molecular formula a chemical formula that shows the number and kinds of atoms in a molecule but not the arrangement of the atoms
fórmula molecular fórmula química que muestra el número y los tipos de átomos que hay en una molécula, pero que no muestra cómo están distribuidos los átomos

molecule a neutral group of atoms that are held together by covalent bonds
molécula grupo de átomos neutros que se unen mediante enlaces covalentes

monatomic ion an ion formed from a single atom
ion monoatómico ion que se formó a partir de un solo átomo

monomer a simple molecule that can combine with other like or unlike molecules to make a polymer
monómero molécula simple que se puede combinar con otras moléculas parecidas o diferentes y formar un polímero

monoprotic acid an acid that can donate only one proton to a base
ácido monoprótico ácido que solamente puede donar un protón a una base

monosaccharide a simple sugar that is the basic subunit of a carbohydrate
monosacárido azúcar simple que es la subunidad fundamental de un carbohidrato

multiple bond a bond in which the atoms share more than one pair of electrons, such as a double bond or a triple bond
enlace múltiple enlace en el que los átomos comparten más de un par de electrones, como un doble enlace o un triple enlace

natural gas a mixture of gaseous hydrocarbons located under the surface of Earth, often near petroleum deposits; used as a fuel
gas natural mezcla de hidrocarburos gaseosos que se encuentran debajo de la superficie de la Tierra, normalmente cerca de los depósitos de petróleo; se usa como combustible

net ionic equation an equation that includes only those compounds and ions that undergo a chemical change in a reaction in an aqueous solution
ecuación iónica neta ecuación que incluye solamente aquellos compuestos y iones que experimentan un cambio químico durante una reacción en una solución acuosa

neutralization the reaction of the ions that characterize acids (hydronium ions) and the ions that characterize bases (hydroxide ions) to form water molecules and a salt
neutralización reacción de los iones que caracterizan a los ácidos (iones hidronio) y de los iones que caracterizan a las bases (iones hidróxido) al formar moléculas de agua y una sal

newton the SI unit for force; the force that will increase the speed of a 1 kg mass by 1 m/s each second that the force is applied (abbreviation, N)
newton unidad de fuerza del Sistema Internacional de Unidades; la fuerza que aumentará la rapidez de un 1 kg de masa en 1 m/s cada segundo que se aplique la fuerza (abreviatura: N)

noble gas one of the elements of Group 18 of the periodic table (helium, neon, argon, krypton, xenon, and radon); noble gases are unreactive
gas noble uno de los elementos del Grupo 18 de la tabla periódica (helio, neón, argón, criptón, xenón y radón); los gases nobles son no reactivos

noble-gas configuration an outer main energy level fully occupied, in most cases, by eight electrons
configuración de gas noble nivel de energía principal externo totalmente ocupado, en la mayoría de los casos, por ocho electrones

nomenclature a naming system
nomenclatura sistema para nombrar algo

nonelectrolyte a substance that dissolves in water to give a solution that does not conduct an electric current
no-electrolito sustancia que se disuelve en agua y da una solución que no conduce corriente eléctrica

nonmetal an element that conducts heat and electricity poorly and that does not form positive ions in an electrolytic solution
no metal elemento que es mal conductor del calor y la electricidad y que no forma iones positivos en una solución de electrolitos

nonpolar covalent bond a covalent bond in which the bonding electrons are equally attracted to both bonded atoms
enlace covalente no polar enlace covalente en el que los electrones de enlace tienen la misma atracción por los dos átomos enlazados

nonvolatile substance a substance that has little tendency to become a gas under existing conditions
sustancia no volátil sustancia que tiene poca tendencia a convertirse en un gas bajo las condiciones existentes

nuclear binding energy the energy released when a nucleus is formed from nucleons
energía de enlace nuclear energía que se libera cuando se forma un núcleo a partir de nucleones

nuclear fission the splitting of the nucleus of a large atom into two or more fragments; releases additional neutrons and energy
fisión nuclear división del núcleo de un átomo grande en dos o más fragmentos; libera neutrones y energía adicionales

nuclear forces the interaction that binds protons and neutrons, protons and protons, and neutrons and neutrons together in a nucleus
fuerzas nucleares interacción que mantiene unidos a protones y neutrones, protones y protones, y neutrones y neutrones en un núcleo

nuclear fusion the combination of the nuclei of small atoms to form a larger nucleus; releases energy
fusión nuclear combinación de los núcleos de átomos pequeños para formar un núcleo más grande; libera energía

nuclear power plant a facility that uses heat from nuclear reactors to produce electrical energy
central nuclear instalación que usa el calor de los reactores nucleares para producir energía eléctrica

nuclear radiation the particles that are released from the nucleus during radioactive decay, such as neutrons, electrons, and photons
radiación nuclear partículas que el núcleo libera durante la desintegración radiactiva, tales como neutrones, electrones y fotones

nuclear reaction a reaction that affects the nucleus of an atom
reacción nuclear reacción que afecta al núcleo de un átomo

nuclear reactor a device that uses controlled nuclear reactions to produce energy or nuclides
reactor nuclear aparato que usa reacciones nucleares controladas para producir energía o nucleidos

nuclear shell model a model that represents nucleons as existing in different energy levels, or shells, in the nucleus
modelo de orbital nuclear modelo que representa los nucleones presentes en los diferentes niveles de energía, u orbitales, del núcleo

nuclear waste waste that contains radioisotopes
desechos nucleares desechos que contienen radioisótopos

nucleic acid an organic compound, either RNA or DNA, whose molecules are made up of one or two chains of nucleotides and carry genetic information
ácido nucleico compuesto orgánico, ya sea ARN o ADN, cuyas moléculas están formadas por una o dos cadenas de nucleótidos y que contiene información genética

nucleon a proton or neutron
nucleón protón o neutrón

nuclide an atom that is identified by the number of protons and neutrons in its nucleus
nucleido átomo que se identifica por el número de protones y neutrones que hay en su núcleo

orbital a region in an atom where there is a high probability of finding electrons
orbital región de un átomo donde hay una alta probabilidad de encontrar electrones

order in chemistry, a classification of chemical reactions that depends on the number of molecules that appear to enter into the reaction
orden en química, clasificación de reacciones químicas que depende del número de moléculas que parecen entrar en la reacción

organic compound a covalently bonded compound that contains carbon, excluding carbonates and oxides
compuesto orgánico compuesto enlazado de manera covalente que contiene carbono, excluyendo a los carbonatos y óxidos

osmosis the diffusion of water or another solvent from a more dilute solution (of a solute) to a more concentrated solution (of the solute) through a membrane that is permeable to the solvent
ósmosis difusión de agua u otro solvente de una solución más diluida (de un soluto) a una solución más concentrada (del soluto) a través de una membrana que es permeable al solvente

osmotic pressure the external pressure that must be applied to stop osmosis
presión osmótica presión externa que se debe ejercer para detener la ósmosis

oxidation a reaction that removes one or more electrons from a substance such that the substance's valence or oxidation state increases
oxidación reacción en la que se quitan uno o más electrones de una sustancia de tal manera que aumenta la valencia o el estado de oxidación de la sustancia

oxidation number the number of electrons that must be added to or removed from an atom in a combined state to convert the atom into the elemental form
número de oxidación número de electrones que se deben añadir o remover de un átomo en estado de combinación para convertirlo a su forma elemental

oxidation state the condition of an atom expressed by the number of electrons that the atom needs to reach its elemental form
estado de oxidación estado de un átomo expresado por el número de electrones que necesita para llegar a su forma elemental

oxidation-reduction reaction any chemical change in which one species is oxidized (loses electrons) and another species is reduced (gains electrons); also called redox reaction
reacción de óxido-reducción cualquier cambio químico en el que una especie se oxida (pierde electrones) y otra especie se reduce (gana electrones); también se denomina reacción redox

oxidized describes an element that has lost electrons and that has increased its oxidation number
oxidado término que describe a un elemento que ha perdido electrones y que ha aumentado su número de oxidación

oxidizing agent the substance that gains electrons in an oxidation-reduction reaction and that is reduced
agente oxidante sustancia que gana electrones en una reacción de óxido-reducción y que es reducida

oxyacid an acid that is a compound of hydrogen, oxygen, and a third element, usually a nonmetal
oxácido ácido que es un compuesto de hidrógeno, oxígeno y un tercer elemento, usualmente un no metal

oxyanion a polyatomic ion that contains oxygen
oxoanión ion poliatómico que contiene oxígeno

parent nuclide a radionuclide that yields a specific daughter nuclide as a later member of a radioactive series
nucleido padre radionucleido que produce un nucleido hijo específico en forma de un miembro posterior de una serie radiactiva

partial pressure the pressure of each gas in a mixture
presión parcial presión de cada gas en una mezcla

pascal the SI unit of pressure; equal to the force of 1 N exerted over an area of 1 m^2 (abbreviation, Pa)
pascal unidad de presión del Sistema Internacional de Unidades; es igual a la fuerza de 1 N ejercida sobre un área de 1 m^2 (abreviatura: Pa)

Pauli exclusion principle the principle that states that two particles of a certain class cannot be in exactly the same energy state
principio de exclusión de Pauli principio que establece que dos partículas de una cierta clase no pueden estar en exactamente el mismo estado de energía

percentage composition the percentage by mass of each element in a compound
composición porcentual porcentaje en masa de cada elemento que forma un compuesto

percentage error a qualitative comparison of the average experimental value to the correct or accepted value; it is calculated by subtracting the accepted value from the experimental value, dividing the difference by the accepted value, and then multiplying by 100
error porcentual comparación cualitativa del promedio del valor experimental con el valor correcto o aceptado; se calcula restando el valor aceptado del valor experimental, dividiendo la diferencia entre el valor aceptado y luego multiplicando por 100

percentage yield the ratio of the actual yield to the theoretical yield, multiplied by 100
rendimiento porcentual razón del rendimiento real al rendimiento teórico, multiplicado por 100

period in chemistry, a horizontal row of elements in the periodic table
período en química, hilera horizontal de elementos en la tabla periódica

periodic law the law that states that the repeating chemical and physical properties of elements change periodically with the atomic numbers of the elements
ley periódica ley que establece que las propiedades químicas y físicas repetitivas de los elementos cambian periódicamente en función del número atómico de los elementos

periodic table an arrangement of the elements in order of their atomic numbers such that elements with similar properties fall in the same column, or group
tabla periódica arreglo de los elementos ordenados en función de su número atómico de modo que los elementos que tienen propiedades similares se encuentran en la misma columna, o grupo

petroleum a liquid mixture of complex hydrocarbon compounds; used widely as a fuel source
petróleo mezcla líquida de compuestos de hidrocarburos complejos; se usa ampliamente como una fuente de combustible

pH a value that is used to express the acidity or alkalinity (basicity) of a system; each whole number on the scale indicates a tenfold change in acidity; a pH of 7 is neutral, a pH of less than 7 is acidic, and a pH of greater than 7 is basic
pH valor que expresa la acidez o la alcalinidad (basicidad) de un sistema; cada número entero de la escala indica un cambio de 10 veces en la acidez; un pH de 7 es neutro, un pH de menos de 7 es ácido y un pH de más de 7 es básico

pH meter a device used to determine the pH of a solution by measuring the voltage between the two electrodes that are placed in the solution
pH-metro aparato que se usa para determinar el pH de una solución al medir el voltaje entre los dos electrodos que están inmersos en la solución

phase in chemistry, one of the four states or conditions in which a substance can exist: solid, liquid, gas, or plasma; a part of matter that is uniform
fase en química, uno de los cuatro estados o condiciones en los que puede existir una sustancia: sólido, líquido, gas o plasma; parte de la materia que es uniforme

phase diagram a graph of the relationship between the physical state of a substance and the temperature and pressure of the substance
diagrama de fases gráfica de la relación entre el estado físico de una sustancia y la temperatura y presión de la sustancia

photoelectric effect the emission of electrons from a material when light of certain frequencies shines on the surface of the material
efecto fotoeléctrico la emisión de electrones de un material cuando luz de ciertas frecuencias se refleja en la superficie del material

photon a unit or quantum of light; a particle of electromagnetic radiation that has zero rest mass and carries a quantum of energy
fotón una unidad o quantum de luz; una partícula de radiación electro-magnética que tiene una masa de reposo de cero y que lleva un quantum de energía

physical change a change of matter from one form to another without a change in chemical properties
cambio físico un cambio de materia de una forma a otra sin que ocurra un cambio en sus propiedades químicas

physical property a characteristic of a substance that does not involve a chemical change, such as density, color, or hardness
propiedad física una característica de una sustancia que no implica un cambio químico, tal como la densidad, el color o la dureza

plasma in physical science, a state of matter that starts as a gas and then becomes ionized; it consists of free-moving ions and electrons, it takes on an electric charge, and its properties differ from those of a solid, liquid, or gas
plasma en ciencias físicas, un estado de la materia que comienza como un gas y luego se ioniza; consiste en iones y electrones que se mueven libre-mente, tiene una carga eléctrica y sus propiedades son distintas de las propiedades de un sólido, de un líquido o de un gas

pOH the negative of the common logarithm of the hydroxide ion concentration of a solution
pOH el logaritmo común negativo de la concentración de iones hidroxilo de una solución

polar describes a molecule in which the positive and negative charges are separated
polar término que describe una molécula en la que las cargas positivas y negativas están separadas

polar covalent bond a covalent bond in which a pair of electrons shared by two atoms is held more closely by one atom
enlace covalente polar un enlace covalente en el que un par de electrones que es compartido por dos átomos se mantiene más unido a uno de los átomos

polyatomic ion an ion made of two or more atoms
ion poliatómico un ion formado por dos o más átomos

polymer a large molecule that is formed by more than five monomers, or small units
polímero una molécula grande que está formada por más de cinco monómeros, o unidades pequeñas

polyprotic acid an acid that can donate more than one proton per molecule
ácido poliprótico un ácido que puede donar más de un protón por molécula

polysaccharide one of the carbohy-drates made up of long chains of simple sugars; polysaccharides include starch, cellulose, and glycogen
polisacárido uno de los carbohidra-tos formados por cadenas largas de azúcares simples; algunos ejemplos de polisacáridos incluyen al almidón, celulosa y glucógeno

positron a particle that has the same mass and spin as an electron but that has a positive charge
positrón una partícula que tiene la misma masa y el mismo espín que un electrón, pero que tiene carga positiva

precipitate a solid that is produced as a result of a chemical reaction in solution
precipitado un sólido que se produce como resultado de una reacción química en una solución

precision the exactness of a measurement
precisión la exactitud de una medición

pressure the amount of force exerted per unit area of a surface
presión la cantidad de fuerza ejercida en una superficie por unidad de área

primary standard a highly purified solid compound used to check the concentration of a known solution in a titration
patrón primario un compuesto sólido altamente purificado que se utiliza para comprobar la concentración de una solución conocida durante una titulación

principal quantum number the quantum number that indicates the energy and orbital of an electron in an atom
número cuántico principal el número cuántico que indica la energía y el orbital de un electrón en un átomo

product a substance that forms in a chemical reaction
producto una sustancia que se forma en una reacción química

protein an organic compound that is made of one or more chains of amino acids and that is a principal compo-nent of all cells
proteína un compuesto orgánico que está hecho de una o más cadenas de aminoácidos y que es el principal componente de todas las células

pure substance a sample of matter, either a single element or a single compound, that has definite chemical and physical properties
sustancia pura una muestra de materia, ya sea un solo elemento o un solo compuesto, que tiene propiedades químicas y físicas definidas

quantity something that has magni-tude, size, or amount
cantidad algo que tiene magnitud o tamaño

quantum the basic unit of electromag-netic energy; it characterizes the wave properties of electrons
quantum la unidad fundamental de la energía electromagnética; carac-teriza las propiedades de onda de los electrones

quantum number a number that specifies certain properties of electrons
número cuántico un número que especifica ciertas propiedades de los electrones

quantum theory the study of the structure and behavior of the atom and of subatomic particles from the view that all energy comes in tiny, indivisible bundles
teoría cuántica estudio de la estructura y comportamiento del átomo y de las partículas subatómicas desde el punto de vista de que toda la energía existe en paquetes diminutos e indivisibles

radioactive dating the process by which the approximate age of an object is determined based on the amount of certain radioactive nuclides present
datación radiactiva proceso por el cual se determina la edad aproximada de un objeto sobre la base de la cantidad presente de ciertos nucleidos radiactivos

radioactive decay the disintegration of an unstable atomic nucleus into one or more different nuclides, accompanied by the emission of radiation, the nuclear capture or ejection of electrons, or fission
desintegración radiactiva desintegración de un núcleo atómico inestable para formar uno o más nucleidos diferentes, lo cual va acompañado de emisión de radiación, captura o expulsión nuclear de electrones o fisión

radioactive nuclide a nuclide that contains isotopes that decay and that emit radiation
nucleido radiactivo nucleido que contiene isótopos que se desintegran y emiten radiación

radioactive tracer a radioactive material that is added to a substance so that its distribution can be detected later
trazador radiactivo material radiactivo que se añade a una sustancia de modo que su distribución pueda ser detectada posteriormente

rate law an equation that relates reaction rate and concentrations of reactants for a particular reaction
ley de la tasa ecuación que relaciona la tasa de reacción y las concentraciones de reactivos en una reacción en particular

rate-determining step in a multistep chemical reaction, the step that has the lowest velocity, which determines the rate of the overall reaction
paso determinante de la tasa en una reacción química de varios pasos, paso que tiene la velocidad más baja, la cual determina la tasa global de la reacción

reactant a substance or molecule that participates in a chemical reaction
reactivo sustancia o molécula que participa en una reacción química

reaction mechanism the way in which a chemical reaction takes place; expressed in a series of chemical equations
mecanismo de reacción manera en la que ocurre una reacción química; se expresa por medio de una serie de ecuaciones químicas

reaction rate the rate at which a chemical reaction takes place; measured by the rate of formation of the product or the rate of disappearance of the reactants
tasa de reacción tasa a la que ocurre una reacción química; se mide por la tasa de formación del producto o por la tasa de desaparición de los reactivos

reaction stoichiometry calculations involving the mass relationships between reactants and products in a chemical reaction
estequiometría de la reacción cálculos referidos a las relaciones cuantitativas entre los reactivos y los productos durante una reacción química

real gas a gas that does not behave completely like a hypothetical ideal gas, because of the interactions between the gas molecules
gas real gas que no se comporta totalmente como un gas ideal hipotético debido a las interacciones entre las moléculas del gas

redox reaction [see *oxidation-reduction reaction*]
reacción redox [ver *reacción de óxido-reducción*]

reduced describes a substance that has gained electrons, lost an oxygen atom, or gained a hydrogen atom
reducido término que describe a una sustancia que ha ganado electrones, perdido un átomo de oxígeno o ganado un átomo de hidrógeno

reducing agent a substance that has the potential to reduce another substance
agente reductor sustancia que tiene el potencial de reducir otra sustancia

reduction a chemical change in which electrons are gained, either by the removal of oxygen, the addition of hydrogen, or the addition of electrons
reducción cambio químico en el que se ganan electrones, ya sea por la remoción de oxígeno, la adición de hidrógeno o la adición de electrones

reduction potential the decrease in voltage that takes place when a positive ion becomes less positive or neutral or when a neutral atom becomes a negative ion
potencial de reducción disminución de voltaje que tiene lugar cuando un ion positivo se vuelve menos positivo o neutro o cuando un átomo neutro se convierte en un ion negativo

rem the quantity of ionizing radiation that does as much damage to human tissue as 1 roentgen of high-voltage x-rays does
rem cantidad de radiación ionizante que produce el mismo daño a los tejidos humanos que 1 roentgen de rayos X de alto voltaje

resonance the bonding in molecules or ions that cannot be correctly represented by a single Lewis structure
resonancia enlace de moléculas o iones que no se puede representar correctamente mediante una única estructura de Lewis

reversible reaction a chemical reaction in which the products re-form the original reactants
reacción inversa reacción química en la que los productos vuelven a formar los reactivos originales

roentgen a unit of radiation dose of x-rays or gamma rays that is equal to the amount of radiation that will produce 2.58×10^{-4} of ions per kilogram of air at atmospheric pressure
roentgen unidad de dosis de radiación de rayos X o de rayos gamma que es igual a la cantidad de radiación que producirán 2.58×10^{-4} iones por kilogramo de aire a presión atmosférica

salt an ionic compound that forms when a metal atom or a positive radical replaces the hydrogen of an acid
sal un compuesto iónico que se forma cuando el átomo de un metal o un radical positivo reemplaza el hidrógeno de un ácido

saponification a chemical reaction in which esters of fatty acids react with a strong base to produce glycerol and a fatty acid salt; the process that is used to make soap
saponificación una reacción química en la cual los ésteres de ácidos grasos reaccionan con una base fuerte para producir glicerol y una sal del ácido graso; el proceso que se utiliza para fabricar jabón

saturated hydrocarbon an organic compound formed only by carbon and hydrogen linked by single bonds
hidrocarburo saturado un compuesto orgánico formado solamente por carbono e hidrógeno unidos por enlaces simples

saturated solution a solution that cannot dissolve any more solute under the given conditions
solución saturada una solución que no puede disolver más soluto bajo las condiciones dadas

scientific method a series of steps followed to solve problems, including collecting data, formulating a hypothesis, testing the hypothesis, and stating conclusions
método científico una serie de pasos que se siguen para resolver problemas y que incluyen reunir datos, formular una hipótesis, poner a prueba la hipótesis y plantear conclusiones

scientific notation a method of expressing a quantity as a number multiplied by 10 to the appropriate power
notación científica un método para expresar una cantidad en forma de un número multiplicado por 10 a la potencia adecuada

scintillation counter an instrument that converts scintillating light into an electrical signal for detecting and measuring radiation
contador de centelleo un instrumento que convierte la luz de centelleo en una señal eléctrica para detectar y medir la radiación

self-ionization of water a process in which two water molecules produce a hydronium ion and a hydroxide ion by transfer of a proton
auto-ionización del agua un proceso por el cual dos moléculas de agua producen un ion hidronio y un ion hidroxilo al transferir un protón

semipermeable membrane a membrane that permits the passage of only certain molecules
membrana semipermeable una membrana que únicamente permite el paso de ciertas moléculas

shielding a radiation-absorbing material that is used to decrease radiation leakage from nuclear reactors
pantalla un material que absorbe la radiación, usado para disminuir las fugas de radiación de los reactores nucleares

SI Le Système International d'Unités, or the International System of Units, which is the measurement system that is accepted worldwide
SI Le Système International d'Unités, o el Sistema Internacional de Unidades, que es el sistema de medición que se acepta en todo el mundo

significant figure a prescribed decimal place that determines the amount of rounding off to be done based on the precision of the measurement
cifra significativa un lugar decimal prescrito que determina la cantidad de redondeo que se hará con base en la precisión de la medición

single bond a covalent bond in which two atoms share one pair of electrons
enlace simple un enlace covalente en el que dos átomos comparten un par de electrones

single-displacement reaction a reaction in which one element or radical takes the place of another element or radical in a compound
reacción de sustitución simple una reacción en la que un elemento o radical toma el lugar de otro elemento o radical en un compuesto

solid the state of matter in which the volume and shape of a substance are fixed
sólido el estado de la materia en el cual el volumen y la forma de una sustancia están fijos

solubility the ability of one substance to dissolve in another at a given temperature and pressure; expressed in terms of the amount of solute that will dissolve in a given amount of solvent to produce a saturated solution
solubilidad la capacidad de una sustancia de disolverse en otra a una temperatura y presión dadas; se expresa en términos de la cantidad de soluto que se disolverá en una cantidad determinada de solvente para producir una solución saturada

solubility product constant the equilibrium constant for a solid that is in equilibrium with the solid's dissolved ions
constante del producto de solubilidad la constante de equilibrio de un sólido que está en equilibrio con los iones disueltos del sólido

soluble capable of dissolving in a particular solvent
soluble capaz de disolverse en un solvente determinado

solute in a solution, the substance that dissolves in the solvent
soluto en una solución, la sustancia que se disuelve en el solvente

solution a homogeneous mixture of two or more substances uniformly dispersed throughout a single phase
solución una mezcla homogénea de dos o más sustancias que se dispersan de manera uniforme en una sola fase

solution equilibrium the physical state in which the opposing processes of dissolution and crystallization of a solute occur at equal rates
equilibrio de la solución la condición física en la cual los procesos opuestos de disolución y cristalización de un soluto ocurren a la misma tasa

solvated describes a solute molecule that is surrounded by solvent molecules
solvatado término que describe a una molécula de soluto que está rodeada por moléculas de solvente

solvent in a solution, the substance in which the solute dissolves
solvente en una solución, la sustancia en la que se disuelve el soluto

specific heat the quantity of heat required to raise a unit mass of homogeneous material 1 K or 1°C in a specified way given constant pressure and volume
calor específico la cantidad de calor que se requiere para aumentar una unidad de masa de un material homogéneo 1 K ó 1 °C de una manera especificada, dados un volumen y una presión constantes

spectator ions ions that are present in a solution in which a reaction is taking place but that do not participate in the reaction
iones espectadores iones que están presentes en una solución en la que está ocurriendo una reacción, pero que no participan en la reacción

spin quantum number the quantum number that describes the intrinsic angular momentum of a particle
número cuántico de espín el número cuántico que describe el ímpetu angular intrínseco de una partícula

standard electrode potential the potential developed by a metal or other material immersed in an electrolyte solution relative to the potential of the hydrogen electrode, which is set at zero
potencial estándar del electrodo el potencial que desarrolla un metal u otro material que se encuentre sumergido en una solución de electrolitos respecto al potencial del electrodo de hidrógeno, al cual se le da un valor de cero

standard solution a solution of known concentration, expressed in terms of the amount of solute in a given amount of solvent or solution
solución estándar una solución de concentración conocida, expresada en términos de la cantidad de soluto que se encuentra en una cantidad determinada de solvente o solución

standard temperature and pressure for a gas, the temperature of 0°C and the pressure 1.00 atm
temperatura y presión estándar para un gas, la temperatura de 0 °C y la presión de 1.00 atm

strong acid an acid that ionizes completely in a solvent
ácido fuerte un ácido que se ioniza completamente en un solvente

strong electrolyte a compound that completely or largely dissociates in an aqueous solution, such as soluble mineral salts
electrolito fuerte un compuesto que se disocia completamente o en gran medida en una solución acuosa, como las sales minerales solubles

structural formula a formula that indicates the location of the atoms, groups, or ions relative to one another in a molecule and that indicates the number and location of chemical bonds
fórmula estructural una fórmula que indica la ubicación de los átomos, grupos o iones, unos respecto a otros en una molécula, y que indica el número y la ubicación de los enlaces químicos

structural isomers two or more compounds that have the same number and kinds of atoms and the same molecular weight but that differ in the order in which the atoms are attached to one another
isómeros estructurales dos o más compuestos que tienen el mismo número y tipos de átomos y el mismo peso molecular, pero que se diferencian en el orden en el que los átomos están unidos unos a otros

sublimation the process in which a solid changes directly into a gas (the term is sometimes also used for the reverse process)
sublimación el proceso por medio del cual un sólido se transforma directamente en un gas (en ocasiones, este término también se usa para describir el proceso inverso)

substitution reaction a reaction in which one or more atoms replace another atom or group of atoms in a molecule
reacción de sustitución una reacción en la cual uno o más átomos reemplazan otro átomo o grupo de átomos en una molécula

supercooled liquid a liquid that is cooled below its normal freezing point without solidifying
líquido superenfriado un líquido que se enfría por debajo de su punto normal de congelación sin que se solidifique

supersaturated solution a solution that holds more dissolved solute than is required to reach equilibrium at a given temperature
solución sobresaturada una solución que contiene más soluto disuelto que el que se requiere para llegar al equilibro a una temperatura dada

surface tension the force that acts on the surface of a liquid and that tends to minimize the area of the surface
tensión superficial la fuerza que actúa en la superficie de un líquido y que tiende a minimizar el área de la superficie

suspension a mixture in which particles of a material are more or less evenly dispersed throughout a liquid or gas
suspensión una mezcla en la que las partículas de un material se encuentran dispersas de manera más o menos uniforme a través de un líquido o de un gas

synthesis reaction a reaction in which two or more substances combine to form a new compound
reacción de síntesis una reacción en la que dos o más sustancias se combinan para formar un compuesto nuevo

system a set of particles or interacting components considered to be a distinct physical entity for the purpose of study
sistema un conjunto de partículas o componentes que interactúan unos con otros, el cual se considera una entidad física independiente para fines de estudio

temperature a measure of how hot (or cold) something is; specifically, a measure of the average kinetic energy of the particles in an object
temperatura una medida de qué tan caliente (o frío) está algo; específicamente, una medida de la energía cinética promedio de las partículas de un objeto

theoretical yield the maximum amount of product that can be produced from a given amount of reactant
rendimiento teórico la cantidad máxima de producto que se puede producir con una cantidad dada de reactivo

theory an explanation for some phenomenon that is based on observation, experimentation, and reasoning
teoría una explicación de algunos fenómenos que está basada en la observación, la experimentación y el razonamiento

thermochemical equation an equation that includes the quantity of energy as heat released or absorbed during the reaction as written
ecuación termoquímica una ecuación que incluye la cantidad de energía en forma de calor que se libera o absorbe durante la reacción como se expresa

thermochemistry the branch of chemistry that is the study of the energy changes that accompany chemical reactions and changes of state
termoquímica la rama de la química que se ocupa del estudio de los cambios de energía que acompañan las reacciones químicas y los cambios de estado

titration a method to determine the concentration of a substance in solution by adding a solution of known volume and concentration until the reaction is completed, which is usually indicated by a change in color
titulación un método para determinar la concentración de una sustancia en una solución al añadir una solución de volumen y concentración conocidos hasta que se completa la reacción, lo cual normalmente es indicado por un cambio de color

transition element one of the metals that can use the inner shell before using the outer shell to bond
elemento de transición uno de los metales que tienen la capacidad de usar su orbital interno antes de usar su orbital externo para formar un enlace

transition interval the range in concentration over which a variation in a chemical indicator can be observed
intervalo de transición el rango de concentración en el cual se puede observar una variación en un indicador químico

transmutation the transformation of atoms of one element into atoms of a different element as a result of a nuclear reaction
transmutación la transformación de los átomos de un elemento en átomos de un elemento diferente como resultado de una reacción nuclear

transuranium element a synthetic element whose atomic number is greater than that of uranium (atomic number 92)
elemento transuranio un elemento sintético cuyo número atómico es mayor que el del uranio (número atómico 92)

triple point the temperature and pressure conditions at which the solid, liquid, and gaseous phases of a substance coexist at equilibrium
punto triple las condiciones de temperatura y presión en las que las fases sólida, líquida y gaseosa de una sustancia coexisten en equilibrio

triprotic acid an acid that has three ionizable protons per molecule, such as phosphoric acid
ácido triprótico un ácido que tiene tres protones ionizables por molécula, como por ejemplo, el ácido fosfórico

unified atomic mass unit a unit of mass that describes the mass of an atom or molecule; it is exactly 1/12 of the mass of a carbon atom with mass number 12 (abbreviation, u)
unidad de masa atómica unificada una unidad de masa que describe la masa de un átomo o molécula; es exactamente 1/12 de la masa de un átomo de carbono con un número de masa de 12 (abreviatura: u)

unit cell the smallest portion of a crystal lattice that shows the three-dimensional pattern of the entire lattice
celda unitaria la porción más pequeña de una red cristalina, la que muestra el patrón tridimensional de la red completa

unsaturated hydrocarbon a hydrocarbon that has available valence bonds, usually from double or triple bonds with carbon
hidrocarburo no saturado un hidrocarburo que tiene enlaces de valencia disponibles, normalmente de enlaces dobles o triples con carbono

unsaturated solution a solution that contains less solute than a saturated solution does and that is able to dissolve additional solute
solución no saturada una solución que contiene menos soluto que una solución saturada, y que tiene la capacidad de disolver más soluto

valence electron an electron that is found in the outermost shell of an atom and that determines the atom's chemical properties
electrón de valencia un electrón que se encuentra en el orbital más externo de un átomo y que determina las propiedades químicas del átomo

vaporization the process by which a liquid or solid changes to a gas
vaporización el proceso por el cual un líquido o un sólido se transforma en un gas

volatile liquid a liquid that evaporates readily or at a low temperature
líquido volátil un líquido que se evapora rápidamente o a una baja temperatura

voltaic cell a primary cell that consists of two electrodes made of different metals immersed in an electrolyte; used to generate voltage
pila voltaica una celda primaria formada por dos electrodos hechos de diferentes metales sumergidos en un electrolito; se usa para generar voltaje

volume a measure of the size of a body or region in three-dimensional space
volumen una medida del tamaño de un cuerpo o región en un espacio de tres dimensiones

VSEPR theory a theory that predicts some molecular shapes based on the idea that pairs of valence electrons surrounding an atom repel each other
teoría VSEPR una teoría que predice algunas formas moleculares con base en la idea de que los pares de electrones de valencia que rodean un átomo se repelen unos a otros

wavelength the distance from any point on a wave to an identical point on the next wave
longitud de onda la distancia entre cualquier punto de una onda y un punto idéntico ubicado en la onda siguiente

weak acid an acid that releases few hydrogen ions in aqueous solution
ácido débil un ácido que libera pocos iones de hidrógeno en una solución acuosa

weak electrolyte a compound that dissociates only to a small extent in aqueous solution
electrolito débil un compuesto que se disocia solamente en una pequeña medida en solución acuosa

weight a measure of the gravitational force exerted on an object; its value can change with the location of the object in the universe
peso una medida de la fuerza gravitacional ejercida sobre un objeto; su valor puede cambiar en función de la ubicación del objeto en el universo

word equation an equation in which the reactants and products in a chemical reaction are represented by words
ecuación verbal una ecuación en la cual los reactivos y los productos de una reacción química están representados con palabras

semiconductors, 143, 145, 329, R58-R59
semipermeable membranes, 436, *436f*
shielding, 666
sickle-cell anemia, 725, *725f*
significant figures, 50-54, *51f, 52f,* 485-486
silicon, *118f,* R44-R45, R57-R59
silver
   electron configuration, *120f*
   in electroplating, 638, *638f*
   ionization of, 162
   in photochromic lenses, 606
   properties, R33, R35-R36, R43
single bonds, 181
single-displacement reactions, 274-275, *274f*
SI units, 37-42
   base units, *38f*
   conversion factors, 25, 44-46
   derived, 40-43, *40f*
   prefixes, *25f,* 38-40, *39f*
soap, 718
sodium
   in the body, R21-R22, R23
   crystal structure, *191f*
   electron configuration, 117, *118f*
   industrial production of, 641
   oxidation of, 604, R19
   properties of, R18, R20
sodium chloride
   crystal structure, 186, *186f, 187f, 188f, 326f*
   dissociation of, 419-420, *419f*
   from neutralization reaction, 495
   percentage composition of, *70f*
   synthesis of, 604
sodium hydroxide, 449
sodium-potassium pump, R22
sodium-vapor lighting, R20
solids, 12, 325-329, *325f, 326f, 327f, 328f, 329f*
solid solutions, 388
solubility
   calculating, 591
   dissociation, 419-420, *419f,* 427
   of gases, 396, *396f,* 399-401, *399f, 400f*
   guidelines on, *421f*
   polarity and, 396, 397, *397f*
   precipitation reactions and, 592-594, *592f*
   pressure and, 399, *399f*
   saturation and, 394-395, *394f, 395f*
   solubility products, 587-594, *589f, 592f*

temperature and, 396, *396f,* 400-401, *400f*
   water and, 341
solubility product constants, 587-594, *589f, 592f*
soluble substances, 387
solutes. *See also* colligative properties
   dissolution rate, 393-394, *393f*
   electrolytes, 391-392, *392f,* 437-441
   hydration of, 397, *397f*
   liquid, 398, *398f*
   solubility of, 396, *396f*
   solute-solvent interactions, 396-397, *397f*
   types of, 388, *388f*
   vapor pressure and, 430-431, *430f, 431f*
solution equilibrium, 394-395, *394f*
solutions, 387-411. *See also* aqueous solutions
   buffered, 580-581, *580f,* 583, *584f,* 585, *585f*
   components of, 388, *388f*
   definition, 16, 387
   dissociation in, 419-420, *419f*
   dissolution rate, 393-394, *393f*
   electrolytes in, 391-392, *392f,* 437-441
   enthalpies of, 401-402, *401f, 402f*
   entropy in, 525-526, *526f*
   equilibrium in, 394-395, *394f*
   in Henry's law, 356, 399, *399f*
   as homogeneous mixtures, 387, *387f*
   liquid solutes and solvents, 398, *398f*
   molality, 408-410, *408f*
   molarity, 404-407, *405f,* 411, 500-501
   nonelectrolytes in, 391, *392f*
   observing, 391
   properties of, *390f*
   saturated vs. unsaturated, 395, *395f*
   solubility, 396-397, *396f, 397f*
   standard, 497, 500-501
   supersaturated, 395
   types of, 388
solvated particles, 401
solvents, 388, *388f,* 397
specific heat, 510-512, *511f*
specific rate constant, 548-549
spectator ions, 423
speed of light, 97
spin quantum number, 110, 112
squalane, 682
standard electrode potentials, 633-634, *634f*

standard hydrogen electrode (SHE), 633, *633f*
standard molar entropy, 525
standard molar volume of a gas, 368
standard reduction potentials, 633-634, *634f*
standard solutions, 497, 500-501
standard states, 516
standard temperature and pressure (STP), 352
starch, 717, *717f,* R54
states of matter, 12-13, 317-342
   changes of state, 330-336, *330f, 331f, 332f, 333f, 335f, 336f*
   gas properties, 13, 317-320, *318f, 319f, 320f*
   liquid properties, 13, 321-324, *321f, 322f, 323f, 324f*
   phase diagrams, 335-336, *335f, 336f*
   plasma properties, 13
   solid properties, 12, 325-329, *325f, 326f, 327f, 328f, 329f*
steel, R35, R46
steroids, 719
Stock system of naming, 215, 218-219, *218f,* 229
stoichiometry, 289-310
   composition vs. reaction, 289
   gas, 369-370
   limiting reactants, 302-305, *302f*
   mass-mass calculations, 290, 300, *300f*
   molar mass and, 298, *298f,* 300, *300f*
   mole-mass conversions, 289-290, 296-298, *297f, 298f*
   mole-mole conversions, 294, *294f*
   mole ratios, 239-240, 290-291, 295-297, 300-301, 309
   percentage yield, 307-308
strategies, study, R8, R11-R15. *See also* Study Skills Handbook.
Strategies for English Language Learners, xxiv-xxvii
strong acids, 456, *456f*
strong bases, 457, *457f*
strong electrolytes, 426-427, *426f*
strontium, *120f,* R25, R26-R27
structural formulas, 181, 678-679, *679f*
structural isomers, 679, *679f*
Study Skills Handbook, R2-R17
   Concept Maps, R8

Cooperative Learning Techniques, R17
Cornell Notes, R12
K/W/L Strategy, R13
Other Learning Strategies, R15
Secrets for Success in Chemistry, R3
Sequencing/Pattern Puzzles, R14
Simple Outlines, R11
subatomic particles, 74-78, *78f,* 650. *See also specific subatomic particles*
sublevels, orbital, 108, *108f, 110f*
sublimation, 334-335
substitution reactions, 701
sucrose, 17, *17f,* 716-717, *716f,* R53
suffixes
   hydrocarbons, 684, 685-688, 691
   molecular compounds, 222
   oxyanions, 219-220
sugars, 715-716, *715f, 716f*
sulfur
   chemical bonding, 173
   electron configuration, *118f*
   oxidation states, *229f*
   properties, R64, R66, R69
   reactions with, 269-270, *270f,* 272, R65
sulfuric acid
   in acid rain, 471
   in car batteries, 639, *639f*
   decomposition of, 273
   industrial use of, 452
   structure of, 462
superconductors, 22, *268f*
supercooled liquids, 326
supercorrosion, 523
supersaturated solutions, 395
surface area, 544-545
surface melting, 334
surface tension, 322-323, *323f*
suspensions, 389, *390f,* 391
symbols
   for elements, 20, *20f*
   in equations, 14, 255, 258-259, *258f*
   safety, xxxi
synthesis reactions, 269-272, *270f, 271f*
systems, 31

T

technetium, 83, *120f,* 663
tellurium, *120f,* 132, 133, R65-R66
temperature, 509
   absolute zero, 359
   Charles's law and, 359-360, *359f, 360f*
   chemical equilibrium and, 574-575, *575f*
   combined gas law, 362-363, 377, *377f*

Periodic Table of the Elements

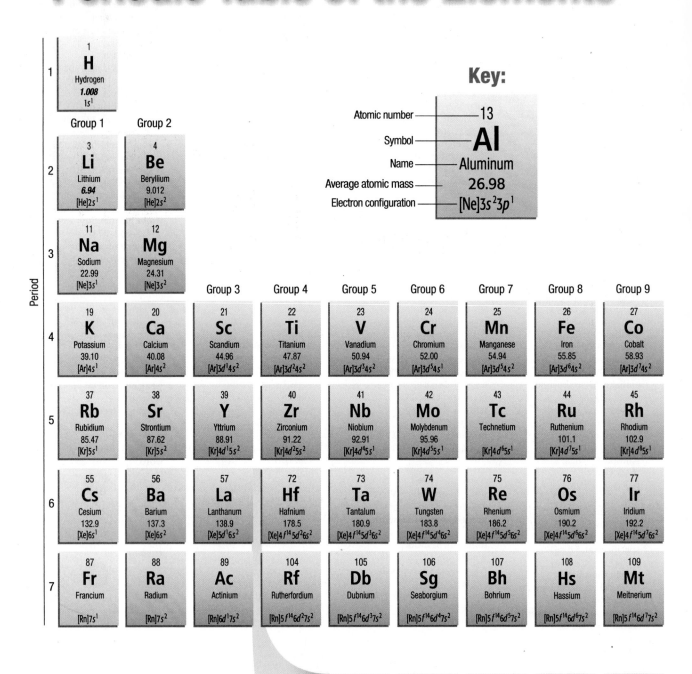

Key:

Atomic number —— 13

Symbol —— **Al**

Name —— Aluminum

Average atomic mass —— 26.98

Electron configuration —— $[Ne]3s^2 3p^1$

Period	Group 1	Group 2

1

1 **H** Hydrogen *1.008* $1s^1$

2

Group 1: 3 **Li** Lithium *6.94* $[He]2s^1$

Group 2: 4 **Be** Beryllium 9.012 $[He]2s^2$

3

11 **Na** Sodium 22.99 $[Ne]3s^1$

12 **Mg** Magnesium 24.31 $[Ne]3s^2$

Group 3	Group 4	Group 5	Group 6	Group 7	Group 8	Group 9

4

| 19 **K** Potassium 39.10 $[Ar]4s^1$ | 20 **Ca** Calcium 40.08 $[Ar]4s^2$ | 21 **Sc** Scandium 44.96 $[Ar]3d^1 4s^2$ | 22 **Ti** Titanium 47.87 $[Ar]3d^2 4s^2$ | 23 **V** Vanadium 50.94 $[Ar]3d^3 4s^2$ | 24 **Cr** Chromium 52.00 $[Ar]3d^5 4s^1$ | 25 **Mn** Manganese 54.94 $[Ar]3d^5 4s^2$ | 26 **Fe** Iron 55.85 $[Ar]3d^6 4s^2$ | 27 **Co** Cobalt 58.93 $[Ar]3d^7 4s^2$ |

5

| 37 **Rb** Rubidium 85.47 $[Kr]5s^1$ | 38 **Sr** Strontium 87.62 $[Kr]5s^2$ | 39 **Y** Yttrium 88.91 $[Kr]4d^1 5s^2$ | 40 **Zr** Zirconium 91.22 $[Kr]4d^2 5s^2$ | 41 **Nb** Niobium 92.91 $[Kr]4d^4 5s^1$ | 42 **Mo** Molybdenum 95.96 $[Kr]4d^5 5s^1$ | 43 **Tc** Technetium $[Kr]4d^6 5s^1$ | 44 **Ru** Ruthenium 101.1 $[Kr]4d^7 5s^1$ | 45 **Rh** Rhodium 102.9 $[Kr]4d^8 5s^1$ |

6

| 55 **Cs** Cesium 132.9 $[Xe]6s^1$ | 56 **Ba** Barium 137.3 $[Xe]6s^2$ | 57 **La** Lanthanum 138.9 $[Xe]5d^1 6s^2$ | 72 **Hf** Hafnium 178.5 $[Xe]4f^{14} 5d^2 6s^2$ | 73 **Ta** Tantalum 180.9 $[Xe]4f^{14} 5d^3 6s^2$ | 74 **W** Tungsten 183.8 $[Xe]4f^{14} 5d^4 6s^2$ | 75 **Re** Rhenium 186.2 $[Xe]4f^{14} 5d^5 6s^2$ | 76 **Os** Osmium 190.2 $[Xe]4f^{14} 5d^6 6s^2$ | 77 **Ir** Iridium 192.2 $[Xe]4f^{14} 5d^7 6s^2$ |

7

| 87 **Fr** Francium $[Rn]7s^1$ | 88 **Ra** Radium $[Rn]7s^2$ | 89 **Ac** Actinium $[Rn]6d^1 7s^2$ | 104 **Rf** Rutherfordium $[Rn]5f^{14} 6d^2 7s^2$ | 105 **Db** Dubnium $[Rn]5f^{14} 6d^3 7s^2$ | 106 **Sg** Seaborgium $[Rn]5f^{14} 6d^4 7s^2$ | 107 **Bh** Bohrium $[Rn]5f^{14} 6d^5 7s^2$ | 108 **Hs** Hassium $[Rn]5f^{14} 6d^6 7s^2$ | 109 **Mt** Meitnerium $[Rn]5f^{14} 6d^7 7s^2$ |

Atomic masses are averages based upon the naturally occurring composition of isotopes on Earth. For elements that have slightly different isotopic composition depending on the source, IUPAC now reports a range of values for atomic masses. These atomic masses are shown here in bold italics. The atomic masses in this table have been rounded to values sufficiently accurate for everyday calculations. Per IUPAC convention, no values are listed for elements whose isotopes lack a characteristic abundance in natural samples.

58 **Ce** Cerium 140.1 $[Xe]4f^1 5d^1 6s^2$	59 **Pr** Praseodymium 140.9 $[Xe]4f^3 6s^2$	60 **Nd** Neodymium 144.2 $[Xe]4f^4 6s^2$	61 **Pm** Promethium $[Xe]4f^5 6s^2$	62 **Sm** Samarium 150.4 $[Xe]4f^6 6s^2$
90 **Th** Thorium 232.0 $[Rn]6d^2 7s^2$	91 **Pa** Protactinium 231.0 $[Rn]5f^2 6d^1 7s^2$	92 **U** Uranium 238.0 $[Rn]5f^3 6d^1 7s^2$	93 **Np** Neptunium $[Rn]5f^4 6d^1 7s^2$	94 **Pu** Plutonium $[Rn]5f^6 7s^2$

Hydrogen
Semiconductors (also known as metalloids)

Metals
Alkali metals
Alkaline-earth metals
Transition metals
Other metals

Nonmetals
Halogens
Noble gases
Other nonmetals

Group 18

2 **He** Helium 4.003 $1s^2$

Group 13	**Group 14**	**Group 15**	**Group 16**	**Group 17**
5 **B** Boron 10.81 $[\text{He}]2s^22p^1$	6 **C** Carbon 12.01 $[\text{He}]2s^22p^2$	7 **N** Nitrogen 14.007 $[\text{He}]2s^22p^3$	8 **O** Oxygen 15.999 $[\text{He}]2s^22p^4$	9 **F** Fluorine 19.00 $[\text{He}]2s^22p^5$
13 **Al** Aluminum 26.98 $[\text{Ne}]3s^23p^1$	14 **Si** Silicon 28.085 $[\text{Ne}]3s^23p^2$	15 **P** Phosphorus 30.97 $[\text{Ne}]3s^23p^3$	16 **S** Sulfur 32.06 $[\text{Ne}]3s^23p^4$	17 **Cl** Chlorine 35.45 $[\text{Ne}]3s^23p^5$

(Group 17 continued: 10 **Ne** Neon 20.18 $[\text{He}]2s^22p^6$; 18 **Ar** Argon 39.95 $[\text{Ne}]3s^23p^6$ — Group 18 column)

Group 10	**Group 11**	**Group 12**
28 **Ni** Nickel 58.69 $[\text{Ar}]3d^84s^2$	29 **Cu** Copper 63.55 $[\text{Ar}]3d^{10}4s^1$	30 **Zn** Zinc 65.38 $[\text{Ar}]3d^{10}4s^2$
46 **Pd** Palladium 106.4 $[\text{Kr}]4d^{10}$	47 **Ag** Silver 107.9 $[\text{Kr}]4d^{10}5s^1$	48 **Cd** Cadmium 112.4 $[\text{Kr}]4d^{10}5s^2$
78 **Pt** Platinum 195.1 $[\text{Xe}]4f^{14}5d^96s^1$	79 **Au** Gold 197.0 $[\text{Xe}]4f^{14}5d^{10}6s^1$	80 **Hg** Mercury 200.6 $[\text{Xe}]4f^{14}5d^{10}6s^2$
110 **Ds** Darmstadtium $[\text{Rn}]5f^{14}6d^97s^1$	111 **Rg** Roentgenium $[\text{Rn}]5f^{14}6d^{10}7s^1$	112 **Cn** Copernicium $[\text{Rn}]5f^{14}6d^{10}7s^2$

Group 13	Group 14	Group 15	Group 16	Group 17	Group 18
31 **Ga** Gallium 69.72 $[\text{Ar}]3d^{10}4s^24p^1$	32 **Ge** Germanium 72.63 $[\text{Ar}]3d^{10}4s^24p^2$	33 **As** Arsenic 74.92 $[\text{Ar}]3d^{10}4s^24p^3$	34 **Se** Selenium 78.96 $[\text{Ar}]3d^{10}4s^24p^4$	35 **Br** Bromine 79.90 $[\text{Ar}]3d^{10}4s^24p^5$	36 **Kr** Krypton 83.80 $[\text{Ar}]3d^{10}4s^24p^6$
49 **In** Indium 114.8 $[\text{Kr}]4d^{10}5s^25p^1$	50 **Sn** Tin 118.7 $[\text{Kr}]4d^{10}5s^25p^2$	51 **Sb** Antimony 121.8 $[\text{Kr}]4d^{10}5s^25p^3$	52 **Te** Tellurium 127.6 $[\text{Kr}]4d^{10}5s^25p^4$	53 **I** Iodine 126.9 $[\text{Kr}]4d^{10}5s^25p^5$	54 **Xe** Xenon 131.3 $[\text{Kr}]4d^{10}5s^25p^6$
81 **Tl** Thallium 204.38 $[\text{Xe}]4f^{14}5d^{10}6s^26p^1$	82 **Pb** Lead 207.2 $[\text{Xe}]4f^{14}5d^{10}6s^26p^2$	83 **Bi** Bismuth 209.0 $[\text{Xe}]4f^{14}5d^{10}6s^26p^3$	84 **Po** Polonium $[\text{Xe}]4f^{14}5d^{10}6s^26p^4$	85 **At** Astatine $[\text{Xe}]4f^{14}5d^{10}6s^26p^5$	86 **Rn** Radon $[\text{Xe}]4f^{14}5d^{10}6s^26p^6$
113 **Nh** Nihonium $[\text{Rn}]5f^{14}6d^{10}7s^27p^1$	114 **Fl** Flerovium $[\text{Rn}]5f^{14}6d^{10}7s^27p^2$	115 **Mc** Moscovium $[\text{Rn}]5f^{14}6d^{10}7s^27p^3$	116 **Lv** Livermorium $[\text{Rn}]5f^{14}6d^{10}7s^27p^4$	117 **Ts** Tennessine $[\text{Rn}]5f^{14}6d^{10}7s^27p^5$	118 **Og** Oganesson $[\text{Rn}]5f^{14}6d^{10}7s^27p^6$

63 **Eu** Europium 152.0 $[\text{Xe}]4f^76s^2$	64 **Gd** Gadolinium 157.3 $[\text{Xe}]4f^75d^16s^2$	65 **Tb** Terbium 158.9 $[\text{Xe}]4f^96s^2$	66 **Dy** Dysprosium 162.5 $[\text{Xe}]4f^{10}6s^2$	67 **Ho** Holmium 164.9 $[\text{Xe}]4f^{11}6s^2$	68 **Er** Erbium 167.3 $[\text{Xe}]4f^{12}6s^2$	69 **Tm** Thulium 168.9 $[\text{Xe}]4f^{13}6s^2$	70 **Yb** Ytterbium 173.1 $[\text{Xe}]4f^{14}6s^2$	71 **Lu** Lutetium 175.0 $[\text{Xe}]4f^{14}5d^16s^2$
95 **Am** Americium $[\text{Rn}]5f^77s^2$	96 **Cm** Curium $[\text{Rn}]5f^76d^17s^2$	97 **Bk** Berkelium $[\text{Rn}]5f^97s^2$	98 **Cf** Californium $[\text{Rn}]5f^{10}7s^2$	99 **Es** Einsteinium $[\text{Rn}]5f^{11}7s^2$	100 **Fm** Fermium $[\text{Rn}]5f^{12}7s^2$	101 **Md** Mendelevium $[\text{Rn}]5f^{13}7s^2$	102 **No** Nobelium $[\text{Rn}]5f^{14}7s^2$	103 **Lr** Lawrencium $[\text{Rn}]5f^{14}6d^17s^2$